The Crossword Dictionary

The
Crossword
Dictionary

EDITED BY
Mike Grimshaw

First published in 1967 by Pan Books Ltd
Cavaye Place, London SW10 9PG

This edition produced for Parragon Books

ISBN 0-75250-020-1

Printed in Great Britain

FOREWORD

The 'Phrase' section of this book is unique in its method of presentation. Within its pages you will find: Films, Novels, Plays, Fictional and Historical Characters, Musical Works. Song Titles, Pop Groups, Animals, Birds, Insects, Fish, Television and Radio Programmes, Buildings, Streets, Locations, Geographical Names, Celebrities, Games, Hobbies, Foreign Terms, Things to Eat, Drink and Wear, and tens of thousands of everyday terms, phrases and expressions, plus many concerned with technology and the world of computers.

All the items are tabulated according to the number of letters which they contain, and are set out in strictly alphabetical order for quick and easy reference.

The section has been especially compiled as an aid to solvers of the more difficult 'Cryptic Crosswords published in *The Times*, *The Daily Telegraph*, the *Daily Express*, the *Evening News*, the *Evening Standard*, the *Sunday Times*, the *Sunday Telegraph*, the *Sunday Express*, and so on.

It frequently happens that a solver is held up by one particular clue, the answer to which is a phrase with one or two interlocking letters already inserted. Let us assume that the clue is: 'He might play one a single piece (8, 2, 5)', and that you have 'B' as the first letter. The second phrase under the heading 'B–15' at once gives you your answer: 'Bachelor of Music'. Naturally, when the first letter has not already been inserted, further research will be necessary.

In order to save space, most plurals and past participles have been omitted. Thus, when the 15-letter answer to a clue is obviously in the plural, it must, in most cases, be looked for under the '14' heading. A similar adjustment must be made when the answer is obviously a past participle. 'Backing down' and 'Holding over', for example, must be looked for under 'Back down' and 'Hold over'.

The 'Word' section will be extremely useful to solvers of the easier 'straightforward' crosswords as published in the *Evening Standard* and the *Daily Mirror*.

The compilation of this book has taken a little under five years. Here are some of the sources from which we culled our information: three standard dictionaries; one American dictionary; one 20-volume encyclopaedia; *Roget's Thesaurus*; *Brewer's Dictionary of Phrase and Fable*; *Who's Who in The Theatre*; *Pears Cyclopaedia*; *Whitaker's Almanack*; *Philip's Gazeteer*, and more than 20,000 published crosswords.

MIKE GRIMSHAW

CONTENTS

PHRASES

A – 8

A BAD TIME
A BIT MUCH
ABOVE ALL
ABOVE PAR
ACCEPT IT
ACES HIGH
ACES WILD
ACID BATH
ACID DROP
ACID RAIN
ACID TEST
ACT A PART
ACT BADLY
ACT OF GOD
ACT OF WAR
ACT THREE
ACUTE EAR
ADAM BEDE
ADAM'S ALE
ADAM'S RIB
ADDING UP
ADD WATER
ADMIT ONE
ADMIT TWO
A FAIR COP
A FAST ONE
AFTER ALL
AFTER TEA
AFTER YOU
AGE GROUP
A GOOD BUY
A GOOD FEW
A GOOD RUN
AIM A BLOW
AIR COVER
AIR FORCE
AIR LINER
AIR POWER
AIR RAIDS
AIR ROUTE
AIR SENSE
AIR SPACE
A LA CARTE
AL CAPONE
AL FRESCO
AL JOLSON
ALL ALIKE

ALL ALONE
ALL ALONG
ALL ASKEW
ALL AT SEA
ALL BLACK
ALL CLEAR
ALLEY CAT
ALL FARES
ALL FOUND
ALL FOURS
ALL HANDS
ALL HOURS
ALL IN ALL
ALL IN ONE
ALL KINDS
ALL MY EYE
ALL NIGHT
ALL QUIET
ALL READY
ALL RIGHT
ALL ROADS
ALL ROUND
ALL'S FAIR
ALL SIDES
ALL SORTS
ALL SOULS
ALL'S WELL
ALL THE GO
ALL THERE
ALL WRONG
ALPHA RAY
ALTER EGO
ANDY CAPP
A NEW LEAF
ANTS' NEST
ANZAC DAY
APPLE PIE
APPLE PIP
APTLY PUT
ARC LAMPS
ARC LIGHT
ARK ROYAL
ARMED MAN
ARM IN ARM
ARMS BEND
ARMS RACE
ARMY CAMP
ARMY LIFE
ARMY LIST

ARMY RANK
ARMY TYPE
ART CLASS
ART PAPER
ARTS CLUB
ARTY TYPE
ARUM LILY
AS A WHOLE
ASCOT HAT
AS GOOD AS
ASH GROVE
ASH TREES
AS IT WERE
ASK FOR IT
ASK LEAVE
ASK MERCY
AS STATED
ASWAN DAM
AS WELL AS
AT A GUESS
AT ANCHOR
AT A PARTY
AT A PINCH
AT A PRICE
AT BOTTOM
AT DINNER
AT HARROW
AT LENGTH
AT LOW EBB
AT NO TIME
ATOM BOMB
AT OXFORD
AT RANDOM
AT SCHOOL
AT SUNSET
AT THE BAR
AT THE END
AT THE OFF
AT THE TOP
AT THE ZOO
ATTIC WIT
AUDIT ALE
AU GRATIN
AU REVOIR
AUTO DA FE
AVE MARIA
AWAY GAME
AWAY TEAM
AWAY WINS

B – 8

BABE RUTH
BABY CARE
BABY CARS
BABY DOLL
BABY FACE
BABY FOOD
BABY GIRL
BABY LOVE
BABY MINE
BABY SHOW
BABY TALK
BABY WOOL
BACK AWAY
BACK AXLE
BACK DOOR
BACK DOWN
BACKED UP
BACK HAIR
BACK KICK
BACK PAGE
BACK RENT
BACK ROOM
BACK SEAT
BACKS OUT
BACK SPIN
BACK STUD
BACK VIEW
BACK YARD
BACON FAT
BAD ACTOR
BAD BLOOD
BAD BOOKS
BAD CAUSE
BAD COUGH
BAD DEBTS
BAD DREAM
BAD FAITH
BAD GRACE
BAD HABIT
BAD HEART
BAD IMAGE
BAD LANDS
BAD LAYER
BAD LIGHT
BAD LIVER
BAD LOGIC
BAD LOSER
BADLY OFF
BAD MARKS
BAD MIXER
BAD MONEY
BAD NIGHT
BAD ODOUR
BAD PATCH

BAD PENNY
BAD POINT
BAD PRESS
BAD SCORE
BAD SHAPE
BAD SHOTS
BAD SIGHT
BAD SMELL
BAD SPORT
BAD START
BAD STATE
BAD STORY
BAD TASTE
BAD TERMS
BAD THING
BAD TIMES
BAD TOOTH
BAD TRADE
BALD HEAD
BALD PATE
BALES OUT
BALL BOYS
BALL GAME
BALL GOWN
BANK DOWN
BANK LOAN
BANK NOTE
BANK ON IT
BANK RATE
BARE FEET
BARE HEAD
BARE IDEA
BARE LEGS
BARE NECK
BARE WORD
BASE COIN
BASS CLEF
BASS DRUM
BASS HORN
BASS NOTE
BATH BUNS
BATH CHAP
BATH CUBE
BATH ROBE
BATH SOAP
BATTLE ON
BAY HORSE
BAY TREES
BEACH HUT
BEADY EYE
BEAR ARMS
BEAR DOWN
BEAR LEFT
BEAR PAIN
BEARS OUT
BEAR WITH

BE A SPORT
BEAT BACK
BEAT DOWN
BEATEN UP
BEAT IT UP
BEAT TIME
BEAU NASH
BED LINEN
BEEF STEW
BEER HALL
BEE STING
BEG LEAVE
BE IN DEBT
BE IN LOVE
BELL TENT
BELOW PAR
BE MY LOVE
BEND DOWN
BEND OVER
BEN NEVIS
BE NO MORE
BENT BACK
BE ON CALL
BE ON EDGE
BE POLITE
BE SEATED
BE SILENT
BEST CUTS
BEST DAYS
BEST EVER
BEST FORM
BEST GIRL
BEST LOVE
BEST PART
BEST SUIT
BEST TEAM
BEST TIME
BEST TOGS
BEST WINE
BETEL NUT
BE UNKIND
BEVIN BOY
BID PRICE
BIG APPLE
BIG BREAK
BIG BUILD
BIG BULLY
BIG CHIEF
BIG CROWD
BIG DEALS
BIG DRINK
BIG FIGHT
BIG FILMS
BIG GIRLS
BIG HOUSE
BIG IDEAS

BIG MATCH	BLUE BOOK	BRAVE MAN
BIG MONEY	BLUE EYES	BREAD BIN
BIG MOUTH	BLUE FUNK	BREAK OFF
BIG NOISE	BLUE LAMP	BREAK OUT
BIG RACES	BLUE MOON	BREAKS IN
BIG SCORE	BLUE NILE	BREAKS UP
BIG SHOTS	BLUE ROOM	BREN GUNS
BIG STAND	BLUE RUIN	BRIAN RIX
BIG STICK	BLUE STAR	BRICK RED
BIG STORM	BLUE SUIT	BRIM OVER
BIG STUFF	BLUNT END	BRING OFF
BIG WHEEL	BLURT OUT	BRING OUT
BILLY BOY	BOARD OUT	BRINGS IN
BILLY CAN	BOAT CLUB	BRINGS ON
BIND OVER	BOAT RACE	BRINGS TO
BIRD CALL	BOBBY PIN	BRINGS UP
BIRD LIFE	BOB DYLAN	BROKEN IN
BIRD LORE	BODE EVIL	BROKEN UP
BIRD SEED	BODY BLOW	BROWN ALE
BIRD SONG	BODY HEAT	BROWN COW
BIT BY BIT	BOIL AWAY	BROWN EGG
BITE INTO	BOIL DOWN	BROWN OWL
BITER BIT	BOIL OVER	BROWN RAT
BIT OF FUN	BOLD DEED	BRUSH OFF
BLACK ART	BOLD FACE	BUBBLE UP
BLACK BAG	BOLD MOVE	BUCKLE ON
BLACK BAT	BOLD TYPE	BUCKLE TO
BLACK BOX	BOMB SITE	BUCKLE UP
BLACK CAP	BONA FIDE	BULL NECK
BLACK CAT	BONAR LAW	BULL'S EYE
BLACK DOG	BONE IDLE	BULLY OFF
BLACK EYE	BOOK CLUB	BUMP INTO
BLACK INK	BOOKED UP	BUMPS OFF
BLACK KEY	BOOK ENDS	BUN FIGHT
BLACK MAN	BOOK SHOP	BUNGED UP
BLACK OUT	BOOM TOWN	BUNNY HUG
BLACK RAT	BORN DEAD	BUOYED UP
BLACK ROD	BORN FOOL	BURN AWAY
BLACK SEA	BORN RICH	BURN DOWN
BLACK TEA	BOTH ENDS	BURNT OAK
BLACK TIE	BOTH WAYS	BURNT OUT
BLESS YOU	BOTTLE UP	BURST OUT
BLIND EYE	BOTTOM UP	BUS DEPOT
BLIND MAN	BOUGHT IN	BUS FARES
BLOCK OUT	BOUGHT UP	BUSH FIRE
BLOOD RED	BOUNCE IN	BUS QUEUE
BLOOD TIE	BOUNCE UP	BUS STOPS
BLOTS OUT	BOW BELLS	BUSY BEES
BLOW AWAY	BOWL OVER	BUSY LIFE
BLOW COLD	BOXER DOG	BUSY TIME
BLOW DOWN	BOYS' CLUB	BUSY TOWN
BLOW HARD	BOY SCOUT	BUTTED IN
BLOWN OUT	BRAIN BOX	BUTTER UP
BLOW OVER	BRAIN FAG	BUTTON UP
BLUE BABY	BRAND NEW	BUY BLIND
BLUE BIRD	BRASS HAT	BUY CHEAP

BUZZ BOMB
BY A FLUKE
BY CHANCE
BY CHEQUE
BY GEORGE
BY HALVES
BY INCHES
BY ITSELF
BY LETTER
BY MYSELF
BY MY WILL
BY NATURE
BY RETURN
BY RIGHTS
BY STAGES
BY THE ARM
BY THE SEA
BY THE WAY

C – 8

CABIN BOY
CABLE-CAR
CAB RANKS
CAFE NOIR
CALF LOVE
CALL A CAB
CALL AWAY
CALL BACK
CALL BOYS
CALL DOWN
CALLED IN
CALLED UP
CALL GIRL
CALL OVER
CALLS FOR
CALLS OFF
CALLS OUT
CALL TIME
CALL UPON
CALM DOWN
CAME DOWN
CAMP FIRE
CAMP SITE
CANON LAW
CAPE HORN
CAPE TOWN
CAP IT ALL
CAR CRASH
CARD GAME
CARD VOTE
CARE A LOT
CAR FERRY
CAR PARKS
CAR RALLY

CARRY OFF
CARRY OUT
CAR SMASH
CART AWAY
CARVE OUT
CASE BOOK
CASH BOOK
CASH DESK
CASH DOWN
CASHED IN
CASH SALE
CAST A FLY
CAST A NET
CAST AWAY
CAST DICE
CAST DOWN
CAST IRON
CAST LOTS
CASTS OFF
CASTS OUT
CATCH OUT
CAT LOVER
CATS' EYES
CATS' HOME
CAT SHOWS
CAT'S MEAT
CAUGHT ON
CAUGHT UP
CELL MATE
CHALK OUT
CHANCE IT
CHECK OFF
CHECK OUT
CHECKS IN
CHECKS UP
CHEERS UP
CHEESE IT
CHESS SET
CHEW OVER
CHEZ NOUS
CHINA CUP
CHINA EGG
CHINA SEA
CHINA TEA
CHIN CHIN
CHIP HEAD
CHIP SHOT
CHOIR BOY
CHOKE OFF
CHOP DOWN
CHOP SUEY
CHUCK KEY
CHURN OUT
CIDER CUP
CIGAR ASH
CIGAR BOX

CISCO KID
CITY DESK
CITY GENT
CITY HALL
CITY LIFE
CITY WALL
CIVIL LAW
CIVIL WAR
CLASS WAR
CLAY PIPE
CLEAN CUT
CLEAN OUT
CLEANS UP
CLEAR DAY
CLEAR OFF
CLEAR OUT
CLEAR SKY
CLEARS UP
CLEAR WIN
CLOCK OUT
CLOCKS IN
CLOSED IN
CLOSE FIT
CLOSE RUN
CLOSE SET
CLOSES UP
CLOSE TIE
CLOTH CAP
CLUB BORE
CLUB FEES
CLUB LIFE
COAL CART
COAL DUST
COAL FIRE
COAL MINE
COAL SEAM
COCA COLA
CODE NAME
CODE WORD
CODS' ROES
COKE FIRE
COLD BATH
COLD BEEF
COLD CURE
COLD DISH
COLD DUCK
COLD FEET
COLD FISH
COLD FOOD
COLD LAMB
COLD MEAL
COLD MEAT
COLD MILK
COLD PACK
COLD PORK
COLD ROOM

COLD SNAP	CROW OVER	DAVY LAMP
COLD WAVE	CRUDE OIL	DAY BOOKS
COLD WIND	CRUEL ACT	DAY BY DAY
COLOUR UP	CRUEL SEA	DAY DREAM
COME AWAY	CRY ALOUD	DAY NURSE
COME BACK	CRY 'HAVOC'	DAY OR TWO
COME DOWN	CRY OF JOY	DAY SHIFT
COME HERE	CRY QUITS	DAY'S WORK
COME HOME	CRY 'SHAME'	DEAD BALL
COME INTO	CUBE ROOT	DEAD BEAT
COME LAST	CUP FINAL	DEAD BODY
COME NEAR	CUP OF TEA	DEAD CALM
COME NEXT	CURLED UP	DEAD CERT
COME OVER	CUSHY JOB	DEAD DUCK
COMES OFF	CUT A DASH	DEAD EASY
COMES OUT	CUT GLASS	DEAD FLAT
COME TRUE	CUT GRASS	DEAD HAND
COME UPON	CUT IN TWO	DEAD HEAT
COME UP TO	CUT IT OFF	DEAD KEEN
COMING IN	CUT IT OUT	DEAD LEAF
COMING ON	CUT LOOSE	DEAD LOSS
COMING TO	CUT NO ICE	DEAD NUTS
CON AMORE	CUT PRICE	DEAD SHOT
COOL CARD	CUT RATES	DEAD SLOW
COOL DOWN	CUT ROUND	DEAD SPIT
COOL FISH	CUTS BACK	DEAD SURE
COOL HAND	CUTS DEAD	DEAD WOOD
COOL HEAD	CUTS DOWN	DEAF AIDS
COOPED UP	CUTS FINE	DEAF EARS
COPE WITH	CUT SHORT	DEAF MUTE
COPY DOWN		DEAL WITH
CORK TIPS		DEAR DEAR!
CORN CURE	**D – 8**	DEAR LIFE
CORN LAWS		DEAR SIRS
COSY CAFE	DAILY USE	DEATH BED
COSY CHAT	DAIRY COW	DEATH RAY
COTTON ON	DAMP DOWN	DEED POLL
COUGHS UP	DANNY BOY	DEEP BLUE
COUNT OUT	DARK AGES	DEEP COMA
COUNT TEN	DARK BLUE	DEEP DOWN
COUPLE UP	DARK DAYS	DEEP NOTE
COVERS UP	DARK DEED	DEEP SIGH
COW'S MILK	DARK GREY	DEEP SNOW
CRACKS UP	DARK HAIR	DEEP TONE
CREAM BUN	DARK LADY	DEER PARK
CREAM TEA	DARK ROOM	DEFY TIME
CREEP OFF	DARK SIDE	DE GAULLE
CREEP OUT	DARK SKIN	DE LA MARE
CREW CUTS	DARK SUIT	DENSE FOG
CRIED OUT	DART PAST	DERBY DAY
CRIES OFF	DASH AWAY	DEREK ROY
CROCKS UP	DASH DOWN	DESK WORK
CROSS NOW	DASH INTO	DE VALERA
CROSS OFF	DATE PALM	DEVON MAN
CROSS OUT	DAVE KING	DICE GAME
CROWN HIM	DAVID LOW	DID RIGHT
	DAVIS CUP	

DID WRONG	DRAWN OUT	EARL HAIG
DIED AWAY	DRAW REIN	EARLY AGE
DIED DOWN	DRAW WELL	EARLY MAN
DIED HARD	DREAM MAN	EARN FAME
DIE HAPPY	DRIED EGG	EARN LESS
DIG A HOLE	DRIED OUT	EARN MORE
DIG A MINE	DRILL BIT	EAR PLUGS
DIGS DEEP	DRINKS UP	EASED OFF
DIM LIGHT	DRIVE MAD	EASED OUT
DINED OUT	DRIVE OFF	EASE OVER
DINE LATE	DRIVE OUT	EAST SIDE
DIRTY DEN	DROP AWAY	EAST WIND
DIRTY DOG	DROP DEAD	EAST WING
DIRTY SKY	DROP DOWN	EASY BEAT
DISHED UP	DROPS OFF	EASY COME
DIVAN BED	DROPS OUT	EASY DROP
DO A TRICK	DRY BONES	EASY GAME
DO BATTLE	DRY BREAD	EASY LIFE
DO BETTER	DRY CELLS	EASY MIND
DOCTOR NO	DRY COUGH	EASY PACE
DOG FIGHT	DRY FACTS	EASY PREY
DOG LATIN	DRY FRUIT	EASY ROAD
DOG LOVER	DRY GOODS	EASY TASK
DOGS' HOME	DRYING UP	EASY TIME
DOG SHOWS	DRY PLATE	EASY WORD
DOG'S LIFE	DRY TOAST	EAT A MEAL
DOG'S NOSE	DR. WATSON	EATS AWAY
DOG'S TAIL	DUCK DOWN	EATS DIRT
DOG TEAMS	DUCK POND	EAU DE VIE
DOG TRACK	DUCK'S EGG	ECCE HOMO
DOG WATCH	DUCK SOUP	EDGE AWAY
DO HOMAGE	DUE NORTH	EGG FLIPS
DOLLED UP	DUE SOUTH	EGG PLANT
DONE DOWN	DULL ACHE	EGG SALAD
DO NO GOOD	DULL PAIN	EGG SAUCE
DO NO HARM	DULL THUD	EGG SPOON
DORIS DAY	DULL WORK	EGG TIMER
DO SCALES	DUMB SHOW	EIGHT MEN
DO THE LOT	DUMMY RUN	ELDER SON
DOUBLE UP	DUST BOWL	EL DORADO
DOVE GREY	DUST TRAP	ELM TREES
DO WISELY	DUTCH GIN	EMIT RAYS
DOWN BEAT	DUTCH HOE	EMPTY BOX
DOWN LINE	DUTY CALL	EMPTY CAN
DOWN TOWN	DUTY FREE	EMPTY TIN
DOWN WIND	DUTY LIST	END HOUSE
DRAG DOWN	DUTY PAID	END IT ALL
DRAG HUNT	DYED HAIR	END SEATS
DRAGS OUT	DYING BED	END TO END
DRAIN DRY	DYING DAY	ENEMY SPY
DRAW AWAY	DYING MAN	ENTRY FEE
DRAW BACK	DYING OUT	EPIC FILM
DRAW LOTS		EPIC POEM
DRAW NEAR		EPIC POET
DRAW NIGH	E – 8	EQUAL PAY
DRAWN OFF		ET CETERA
	EAGLE EYE	

ETON CROP
ETON SUIT
EVEN BEAT
EVEN DATE
EVEN KEEL
EVEN MORE
EVEN PACE
EVEN TIME
EVERY BIT
EVERY DAY
EVERY ONE
EVERY WAY
EVIL DAYS
EVIL DEED
EVIL HOUR
EVIL LIFE
EVIL OMEN
EVIL STAR
EXCUSE ME
EXTRA MAN
EXTRA PAY
EXTRA RUN
EYES LEFT
EYE TO EYE

F – 8

FACE CARD
FACE DOWN
FACE LIFT
FACE ODDS
FACE PACK
FACE RUIN
FACE UP TO
FADE AWAY
FADED OUT
FAIR COPY
FAIR DEAL
FAIR GAME
FAIR HAIR
FAIR HAND
FAIR ISLE
FAIR LADY
FAIR MAID
FAIR NAME
FAIR PLAY
FAIR SKIN
FAIR SWOP
FAIR WAGE
FAIR WIND
FALL AWAY
FALL BACK
FALL DOWN
FALL FLAT
FALL FOUL

FALL OPEN
FALL OVER
FALL SICK
FALLS ILL
FALLS OFF
FALLS OUT
FALL UPON
FALSE GOD
FALSE RIB
FAN CLUBS
FANCY BOX
FAN DANCE
FAR ABOVE
FAR AHEAD
FAR APART
FAR BELOW
FARM EGGS
FARM HAND
FARM LAND
FAR NORTH
FAR SIGHT
FAR SOUTH
FAST AWAY
FAST CARS
FAST DAYS
FAST LIFE
FAST RACE
FAST TIME
FAST WORK
FATAL DAY
FAT STOCK
FATTEN UP
FAT WOMAN
FAWN UPON
FEAST DAY
FEED WELL
FEEL BLUE
FEEL COLD
FEEL EASY
FEEL FINE
FEEL GOOD
FEEL HURT
FEEL LAZY
FEEL LIKE
FEEL PAIN
FEEL SAFE
FEEL SICK
FEELS ILL
FEEL SORE
FEEL SURE
FEEL WARM
FEEL WELL
FELL AN OX
FELL BACK
FELL DOWN
FELL FLAT

FELO DE SE
FELT HATS
FENCED IN
FETCH OUT
FEW WORDS
FIELD DAY
FIERY RED
FIFTH DAY
FIFTH ROW
FIFTH SET
FIFTH TEE
FIGHT FOR
FIGHT OFF
FIGHT SHY
FILE AWAY
FILE DOWN
FILE PAST
FILL A GAP
FILLED IN
FILM FANS
FILM PLAY
FILM SHOW
FILM STAR
FINAL BID
FINAL DAY
FIND A JOB
FIND A WAY
FIND BAIL
FIND ROOM
FINDS OUT
FIND TIME
FINE AIRS
FINE ARTS
FINE BIRD
FINE CHAP
FINE DAYS
FINE DOWN
FINE EDGE
FINE FARE
FINE GOLD
FINE LADY
FINE RAIN
FINE SHOW
FINE VIEW
FINISH UP
FIR CONES
FIRE AWAY
FIRE DAMP
FIRE RISK
FIRE UPON
FIRM DATE
FIRM GRIP
FIRM HAND
FIRM HOLD
FIRM HOPE
FIRST ACT

FIRST AID	FLIT PAST	FREE COPY
FIRST BID	FLOP DOWN	FREE FLOW
FIRST BUS	FLOUR BIN	FREE GIFT
FIRST DAY	FLOW BACK	FREE HAND
FIRST LAP	FLOW OVER	FREE KICK
FIRST MAN	FLUFF OUT	FREE LIFT
FIRST OUT	FLUSH OUT	FREE LIST
FIRST ROW	FLY ABOUT	FREE LOVE
FIRST SET	FLY A KITE	FREE MEAL
FIRST TEE	FLY APART	FREE MILK
FIR TREES	FOAM BATH	FREE PASS
FISH CAKE	FOG BOUND	FREE PLAY
FISH DISH	FOGGY DAY	FREE PORT
FISH FORK	FOIST OFF	FREE RIDE
FISH POND	FOLD ARMS	FREE SEAT
FISH SHOP	FOLD BACK	FREE TIME
FISH TANK	FOLD DOWN	FREE TO GO
FISH TEAS	FOLDED UP	FREE VOTE
FIT STATE	FOLD OVER	FREE WILL
FITS WELL	FOLK LORE	FRESH AIR
FITTED IN	FOLK SONG	FRESH EGG
FITTED UP	FOLK TALE	FRESH TEA
FIVE DAYS	FOLLOW ON	FRET AWAY
FIVE DEEP	FOLLOW UP	FRIED EGG
FIVE FEET	FOND HOPE	FROM AFAR
FIVE QUID	FOOD FISH	FRONT MAN
FIVE SETS	FOOL AWAY	FRONT ROW
FIX A DATE	FOR A JOKE	FROZEN UP
FIX A TIME	FOR A LARK	FRUIT PIE
FLAG DAYS	FOR A SONG	FUEL BILL
FLAG DOWN	FOR A TERM	FUEL TANK
FLARED UP	FOR A TIME	FULL BLUE
FLAT BEER	FORCE OUT	FULL CREW
FLAT FACE	FORGET IT	FULL FACE
FLAT FEET	FOR KEEPS	FULL LIFE
FLAT FISH	FOR KICKS	FULL LOAD
FLAT NOSE	FORKS OUT	FULL MEAL
FLAT PACK	FOR SHAME	FULL MOON
FLAT RACE	FORT KNOX	FULL OF GO
FLAT RATE	FORTY ALL	FULL PLAY
FLAT ROOF	FOUL BLOW	FULL SAIL
FLAT SPIN	FOUL DEED	FULL SIZE
FLAT TYRE	FOUL PLAY	FULL STOP
FLAT WASH	FOUND OUT	FULL TIDE
FLEA PITS	FOUR ACES	FULL TILT
FLEE FROM	FOUR DAYS	FULL TIME
FLEET ARM	FOUR DEEP	FULL TOSS
FLEW AWAY	FOUR FEET	FULL WELL
FLEW HIGH	FOUR LAPS	FUMED OAK
FLEW HOME	FOUR ONES	FUN FAIRS
FLEW SOLO	FOUR QUID	FUNNY HAT
FLICK OFF	FOUR TENS	FUNNY MAN
FLIES OFF	FOUR TWOS	FUR COATS
FLING OFF	FOWL PEST	FUR STOLE
FLING OUT	FREE BEER	FUR TRADE
FLIP SIDE	FREE CITY	FUR WRAPS

FUSE WIRE
FUSS OVER

G – 8

GAD ABOUT
GAG BOOKS
GAIN TIME
GAIN UPON
GAME BIRD
GAME LAWS
GAME PIES
GAMMA RAY
GAMMY LEG
GANG SHOW
GAOL BIRD
GAS BOARD
GAS FIRES
GAS METER
GAS PLANT
GAS POKER
GAS STOVE
GATHER IN
GATHER UP
GAVE A TUG
GAVE AWAY
GAVE BACK
GAY PARTY
GAY SMILE
GAY SPARK
GET ABOUT
GET A GOAL
GET AHEAD
GET A LIFT
GET ALONG
GET ANGRY
GET A RISE
GET BELOW
GET CLEAR
GET CROSS
GET DRUNK
GET FRESH
GET GOING
GET IDEAS
GET LEAVE
GET LOOSE
GET OLDER
GET RATTY
GET READY
GET RID OF
GET RIGHT
GET ROUGH
GET ROUND
GETS AWAY
GETS BACK
GETS EVEN

GETS OVER
GETS RICH
GETS WELL
GET THERE
GET TIRED
GET TOUGH
GET UPSET
GET WORSE
GIFT GOAL
GIFT SHOP
GIN AND IT
GINGER UP
GINNED UP
GIN RUMMY
GIN SLING
GIVE AWAY
GIVE BACK
GIVE HEED
GIVE HOPE
GIVE IN TO
GIVE IT UP
GIVEN OUT
GIVE ODDS
GIVE OVER
GIVE PAIN
GIVES EAR
GIVES WAY
GIVE VENT
GIVING UP
GLAD HAND
GLAD NEWS
GLAD RAGS
GLASS EYE
GLASS JAW
GLEE CLUB
GLUM FACE
GNAT BITE
GNAW AWAY
GO ABOARD
GO ABROAD
GO ABSENT
GO ACROSS
GO ADRIFT
GO ALL OUT
GO AND SEE
GO AROUND
GO ASHORE
GO ASTERN
GO ASTRAY
GOBBLE UP
GO BEHIND
GO BEYOND
GO BY BOAT
GO BY RAIL
GO BY ROAD
GO BY SHIP

GO BY TAXI
GO BY TRAM
GO BY TUBE
GOD BLESS
GO DIRECT
GOD OF WAR
GOD'S ACRE
GOD SPEED
GOD'S WILL
GOES AWAY
GOES BACK
GOES DOWN
GOES OVER
GOES SLOW
GOES WEST
GOES WITH
GO FOR HIM
GO HALVES
GO HUNGRY
GO IN FEAR
GOING MAD
GOING OFF
GOING OUT
GOINGS ON
GO IN RAGS
GO INSIDE
GOLD COIN
GOLD DUST
GOLD FOIL
GOLD LACE
GOLD LEAF
GOLD MINE
GOLD RING
GOLD REEF
GOLD RUSH
GOLD VASE
GOLD VEIN
GOLD WIRE
GOLF BALL
GOLF CLUB
GO MODERN
GO NATIVE
GONE AWAY
GONE DOWN
GONE WEST
GOOD BALL
GOOD BOOK
GOOD CASE
GOOD CAST
GOOD CHAP
GOOD COOK
GOOD COPY
GOOD CROP
GOOD DEAL
GOOD DEBT
GOOD DEED

GOOD DRAW
GOOD FACE
GOOD FARE
GOOD FEED
GOOD FIRE
GOOD FOLK
GOOD FOOD
GOOD FORM
GOOD GAME
GOOD GATE
GOOD GIRL
GOOD HAND
GOOD HAUL
GOOD HOPE
GOOD HOST
GOOD IDEA
GOOD KING
GOOD LADY
GOOD LAND
GOOD LIFE
GOOD LUCK
GOOD MEAL
GOOD MOOD
GOOD MOVE
GOOD NAME
GOOD NEWS
GOOD OMEN
GOOD PACE
GOOD PALS
GOOD PART
GOOD PLAN
GOOD SEAT
GOOD SHOT
GOOD SHOW
GOOD SIGN
GOOD SOIL
GOOD SORT
GOOD SOUL
GOOD TIME
GOOD TIPS
GOOD TRIM
GOOD TURN
GOOD TYPE
GOOD VIEW
GOOD WASH
GOOD WIFE
GOOD WILL
GOOD WINE
GOOD WORD
GOOD WORK
GOOD YEAR
GO ON DECK
GO ON FOOT
GOON SHOW
GO PLACES
GO PURPLE

GO RACING
GO SHARES
GO STEADY
GO SURETY
GO TO GAOL
GO TO HELL
GO TOO FAR
GO TO SEED
GO TO TOWN
GO TO WORK
GOUGE OUT
GRADE ONE
GRADE TWO
GRAF SPEE
GRAND AIR
GRAND SUM
GRAY'S INN
GREAT AGE
GREAT AUK
GREAT DAY
GREAT FUN
GREAT GUY
GREAT HIT
GREAT JOY
GREAT MAN
GREAT TOM
GREAT WAR
GREAT WIT
GREEK ART
GREEK GOD
GREEK URN
GREEN EYE
GREEN FEE
GREEN FLY
GREEN HAT
GREEN INK
GREEN MAN
GREEN TEA
GREY AREA
GREY COAT
GREY DAWN
GREY EYES
GREY HAIR
GREY MARE
GREY SUIT
GRIM FACE
GRIM JOKE
GRIM LOOK
GRIM TASK
GRIM VIEW
GRIP HARD
GROPE FOR
GROW COLD
GROW COOL
GROW DARK
GROW LESS

GROWN MAN
GROW PALE
GROW PEAS
GROW RICH
GROWS OLD
GROW UPON
GROW WEAK
GROW WILD
GUARD DOG
GUESS HOW
GUESS WHO
GUIDE DOG
GULP DOWN
GUN FIGHT
GUNGA DIN
GUN METAL
GYM DRESS
GYM SHOES
GYM SLIPS

H – 8

HAD WORDS
HAIL A BUS
HAIL A CAB
HAIL MARY
HAIRY APE
HALF A CUP
HALF A MAN
HALF A TON
HALF DEAD
HALF EACH
HALF FARE
HALF FULL
HALF MILE
HALF MOON
HALF OVER
HALF TIME
HALL MARK
HALT SIGN
HAM ACTOR
HAM HOUSE
HAMMER IN
HAM ROLLS
HAM SALAD
HAND BACK
HAND DOWN
HAND IT IN
HAND OVER
HAND PUMP
HANDS OFF
HANDS OUT
HANG BACK
HANG DOWN
HANG FIRE
HANG ON TO

HANG OVER	HEAT SPOT	HIND LEGS
HANGS OUT	HEAT WAVE	HIP FLASK
HAPPY BOY	HEAVED TO	HIRED BUS
HAPPY MAN	HEAVY DAY	HIRED CAR
HARD AT IT	HEAVY DEW	HIRED MAN
HARD BALL	HEAVY SEA	HIRED OUT
HARD BLOW	HEAVY TAX	HIRED VAN
HARD CASE	HEEL OVER	HIS GRACE
HARD CASH	HELD BACK	HIT IT OFF
HARD COAL	HELD OVER	HITS BACK
HARD CORE	HELP DOWN	HITS HARD
HARD FACT	HELP OVER	HIT TO LEG
HARD FATE	HELPS OUT	HOCK SHOP
HARD GAME	HEMMED IN	HOG'S BACK
HARD HEAD	HEN PARTY	HOLD BACK
HARD KICK	HEN'S EGGS	HOLD DEAR
HARD LIFE	HERE GOES	HOLD DOWN
HARD LOOK	HERE WE GO	HOLD FAST
HARD LUCK	HER GRACE	HOLD GOOD
HARD ROES	HERNE BAY	HOLD HARD
HARD SEAT	HIDE AWAY	HOLD ON TO
HARD TACK	HIGH AIMS	HOLD OVER
HARD TASK	HIGH BALL	HOLDS OFF
HARD TIME	HIGH CARD	HOLDS OUT
HARD TONE	HIGH COST	HOLD SWAY
HARD UPON	HIGH DIVE	HOLD WITH
HARD WEAR	HIGHER UP	HOLED OUT
HARD WORD	HIGH FEES	HOLY CITY
HARD WORK	HIGH GEAR	HOLY FEAR
HARK BACK	HIGH HAND	HOLY LAND
HARM'S WAY	HIGH HATS	HOLY LOCH
HARP UPON	HIGH HOPE	HOLY WARS
HAT TRICK	HIGH JUMP	HOLY WEEK
HAUL BACK	HIGH KICK	HOLY WRIT
HAUL DOWN	HIGH LAND	HOME FARM
HAULED IN	HIGH LIFE	HOME GAME
HAVE A BET	HIGH MASS	HOME HELP
HAVE A FAG	HIGH NECK	HOME LIFE
HAVE A FIT	HIGH NOON	HOME NEWS
HAVE A JOB	HIGH NOTE	HOME PARK
HAVE A NAP	HIGH RANK	HOME RULE
HAVE A PEW	HIGH RATE	HOME RUNS
HAVE A ROW	HIGH RENT	HOME SAFE
HAVE A RUN	HIGH ROAD	HOME TEAM
HAVE A TRY	HIGH SEAS	HOME TIES
HAVE DONE	HIGH SPOT	HOME TOWN
HAVE LIFE	HIGH TEAS	HOME WINS
HAVE PITY	HIGH TIDE	HONEY BEE
HAY FEVER	HIGH TIME	HONEY POT
HAZEL NUT	HIGH TONE	HONG KONG
HEAD BACK	HIGH WAGE	HOOKED IT
HEAD COOK	HIGH WALL	HOP ABOUT
HEAD GIRL	HIGH WIND	HOP ALONG
HEADS OFF	HILL FARM	HOP FIELD
HEAD WIND	HILL FOLK	HOT BATHS
HEAR HEAR!	HIND FOOT	HOT BLOOD

HOT CAKES
HOT COALS
HOT DRINK
HOT JOINT
HOT LUNCH
HOT MEALS
HOT MONEY
HOT MUSIC
HOT NIGHT
HOT PLATE
HOT PUNCH
HOT SCENT
HOT SPELL
HOT STOVE
HOT STUFF
HOTTED UP
HOT TODDY
HOT WATER
HOUR HAND
HOUSE BOY
HOUSE DOG
HOUSE FLY
HOWL DOWN
HOW'S THAT
HULL CITY
HULL DOWN
HUMAN CRY
HUM AND HA
HUNT BALL
HUNT DOWN
HURRY OFF
HURRY OUT
HURT LOOK
HUSHED UP
HYDE PARK
HYMN BOOK
HYMN TUNE

I – 8

IAN SMITH
ICE CREAM
ICE CUBES
ICED CAKE
ICY BLAST
ICY PATCH
ICY STARE
ICY WASTE
ICY WATER
IDEAL MAN
IDEAS MAN
IDÉE FIXE
IDLE JACK
IDLE RICH
IDLE TALK
ILEX TREE

ILL GRACE
ILL TASTE
ILL USAGE
IN ACCORD
IN A CROWD
IN A CRUSH
IN ACTION
IN A DREAM
IN A FAINT
IN A FEVER
IN A FIELD
IN A FLASH
IN A FRAME
IN AFRICA
IN A GROUP
IN A HURRY
IN A JIFFY
IN AMBUSH
IN AND OUT
IN A PADDY
IN A PANIC
IN ARABIC
IN ARMOUR
IN A SENSE
IN A SLING
IN A SNARE
IN A STATE
IN A SWEAT
IN A SWOON
IN A TRICE
IN AUGUST
IN AUTUMN
IN A WHIRL
IN CAMERA
IN CANADA
IN CHAINS
IN CHARGE
IN CHORUS
IN CHURCH
IN CLOVER
IN COLOUR
IN COLUMN
IN COMMON
IN CONVOY
IN CREDIT
IN DANGER
IN DEMAND
IN DETAIL
IN DUBLIN
IN EFFECT
IN EMBRYO
IN EUROPE
IN EXCESS
IN FAVOUR
IN FLAMES
IN FLIGHT

IN FLOWER
INFRA DIG
IN FRANCE
INFRA RED
IN FRENCH
IN GERMAN
IN GROUPS
IN HEAVEN
IN HIDING
IN HORROR
INK SPOTS
INK STAIN
IN LAYERS
IN LEAGUE
IN LONDON
IN LUXURY
IN MADRID
IN MEMORY
IN MID AIR
IN MOSCOW
IN MOTION
IN MY VIEW
INNER MAN
IN NORWAY
IN NO TIME
IN NO WISE
INN SIGNS
IN OFFICE
IN OFF RED
IN ONE WAY
IN ORDERS
IN PENCIL
IN PENURY
IN PERSON
IN PIECES
IN POCKET
IN POLAND
IN PRISON
IN PUBLIC
IN PURDAH
IN QUIRES
IN QUOTES
IN REASON
IN RECESS
IN RELIEF
IN REPAIR
IN REPOSE
IN REVOLT
IN RUSSIA
IN SAFETY
IN SEASON
IN SECRET
IN SERIES
IN SCHOOL
IN SHREDS
IN SPASMS

IN SPIRIT	J – 8	KEEP AWAY
IN SPRING		KEEP BACK
IN SUMMER	JACK CADE	KEEP CALM
IN SWEDEN	JACK PLUG	KEEP CAVE
IN TERROR	JAMMED IN	KEEP COOL
IN THE ACT	JAM PUFFS	KEEP DARK
IN THE AIR	JAM ROLLS	KEEP DOWN
IN THE ARK	JAM TARTS	KEEP FINE
IN THE BAG	JAM TIGHT	KEEP GOAL
IN THE BAR	JANE EYRE	KEEP HOLD
IN THE BOX	JAR OF JAM	KEEP IT UP
IN THE CUP	JAZZ BAND	KEEP LEFT
IN THE END	JAZZ CLUB	KEEP OPEN
IN THE GYM	JEST BOOK	KEEP PACE
IN THE NET	JET BLACK	KEEP SAFE
IN THEORY	JET PLANE	KEEPS FIT
IN THE PIT	JEW'S HARP	KEEP SHOP
IN THE RAW	JOE LOUIS	KEEPS MUM
IN THE RED	JOG ALONG	KEEPS OFF
IN THE SEA	JOHN ADAM	KEEPS OUT
IN THE SKY	JOHN BULL	KEEP STEP
IN THE SUN	JOHN DORY	KEEP TIME
IN THE VAN	JOHN KNOX	KEEP WARM
IN THE WAR	JOHN NASH	KEEP WELL
IN THE WAY	JOHN PEEL	KEMP TOWN
IN THE WET	JOINED IN	KEPT BACK
IN THE ZOO	JOKE BOOK	KEPT BUSY
IN TIGHTS	JUMP AT IT	KEW GREEN
IN UNISON	JUMP BACK	KEY ISSUE
IN VENICE	JUMP DOWN	KEY MONEY
IN VIENNA	JUMP INTO	KEY MOVES
IN WINTER	JUMP LEAD	KEY POINT
IRISH ELK	JUMP OVER	KEY POSTS
IRISH JIG	JUMP TO IT	KICK BACK
IRISH SEA	JUMP UPON	KICK OVER
IRON BAND	JUNK SHOP	KICKS OFF
IRON BARS	JURY LIST	KICKS OUT
IRON BOOT	JUST A BIT	KID STUFF
IRON DUKE	JUST A FEW	KILL PAIN
IRON FIST	JUST A SEC	KILLS OFF
IRON GATE	JUST GONE	KILL TIME
IRON GRIP	JUST LOSE	KIM NOVAK
IRON HAND	JUST MISS	KIND DEED
IRON HEEL	JUST THEN	KIND FACE
IRON LUNG		KIND HOST
IRON MASK		KIND LOOK
IRON MINE	K – 8	KIND SOUL
IRON RULE		KIND WORD
IRON SHOT	KARL MARX	KING COLE
IRON WILL	KEEL OVER	KING JOHN
IT'S A CERT	KEEN EDGE	KING KONG
IT'S A FACT	KEEN TYPE	KING LEAR
	KEEN WIND	KING'S CUP
	KEEP A CAT	KING SIZE
	KEEP A DOG	KISS AWAY
	KEEP A LOG	KNEE DEEP
	KEEP AT IT	

KNEE GRIP
KNOCK OFF
KNOCK OUT
KNOCKS UP
KNOW BEST
KNOW WELL

L – 8

LA BOHÈME
LADLE OUT
LADY HELP
LADY LUCK
LAID FLAT
LAKE COMO
LAKE ERIE
LAMB CHOP
LAME DOGS
LAME DUCK
LAND AHOY
LAND A JOB
LAND ARMY
LAND CRAB
LAND GIRL
LAND LINE
LAND'S END
LA PALOMA
LARGE EGG
LARGE GAP
LARGE GIN
LARGE RUM
LARGE SUM
LAST BALL
LAST BELL
LAST BOUT
LAST CALL
LAST CAST
LAST DAYS
LAST DROP
LAST GASP
LAST HEAT
LAST HOLE
LAST HOME
LAST HOPE
LAST HOUR
LAST JULY
LAST JUNE
LAST LEGS
LAST LINE
LAST LOOK
LAST LOVE
LAST MEAL
LAST MOVE
LAST NAME
LAST OVER
LAST PAGE

LAST PART
LAST POST
LAST RACE
LAST REST
LAST ROSE
LAST SEEN
LAST'S OUT
LAST TERM
LAST TEST
LAST TIME
LAST TO GO
LAST WEEK
LAST WILL
LAST WORD
LAST YEAR
LAS VEGAS
LATE BIRD
LATE CALL
LATE HOUR
LATE MEAL
LATE NEWS
LATE PASS
LATE POST
LATE SHOW
LATE WIFE
LATIN TAG
LAUGH OFF
LAW AGENT
LAW COURT
LAW SUITS
LAY ABOUT
LAY A FIRE
LAY AN EGG
LAY ASIDE
LAY A TRAP
LAYS BARE
LAYS DOWN
LAY SIEGE
LAYS OPEN
LAY WASTE
LEAD MINE
LEAD PIPE
LEAD SHOT
LEADS OFF
LEAD UP TO
LEAK AWAY
LEAKS OUT
LEAN BACK
LEAN DIET
LEAN MEAT
LEAN OVER
LEAP OVER
LEAP YEAR
LEAST BIT
LEAVE OFF
LEAVE OUT

LEEK SOUP
LEE SHORE
LEFT BACK
LEFT BANK
LEFT FACE
LEFT FLAT
LEFT FOOT
LEFT HALF
LEFT HAND
LEFT HOME
LEFT HOOK
LEFT OVER
LEFT SIDE
LEFT TURN
LEFT WING
LEGAL AGE
LEGAL AID
LEG BREAK
LEG DRIVE
LEG STUMP
LEMON TEA
LEMON PIE
LEND TONE
LENT TERM
LET ALONE
LET BLOOD
LET DRIVE
LET IT LIE
LET IT RIP
LET LOOSE
LET ME SEE
LETS DOWN
LETS FALL
LETS FREE
LET SLIDE
LETS PASS
LETS SLIP
LEVEL OFF
LEVEL OUT
LEVELS UP
LEWIS GUN
LIAR DICE
LIE ABOUT
LIE AWAKE
LIE CLOSE
LIE DOGGO
LIE HEAVY
LIE IN BED
LIES DOWN
LIES FLAT
LIE STILL
LIFE PEER
LIFE SPAN
LIFE WORK
LIGHT ALE
LIGHT CAR

LIGHT RAY	LONG LINE	LOOM OVER
LIGHTS UP	LONG LIST	LOOP LINE
LIGHT TEA	LONG LOST	LOOSE BOX
LIKE A MAN	LONG NOTE	LOOSE END
LIKE BEST	LONG ODDS	LOOSEN UP
LIKE FURY	LONG POEM	LORD AVON
LILY POND	LONG PULL	LORD'S DAY
LILY PONS	LONG PUTT	LOSE A LEG
LIMBER UP	LONG RACE	LOSE FACE
LINGER ON	LONG READ	LOSE HOPE
LINKED UP	LONG REST	LOSE TIME
LION CUBS	LONG RIDE	LOST BALL
LIONS DEN	LONG ROAD	LOST CITY
LIP SALVE	LONG ROOM	LOST GAME
LISTEN IN	LONG ROPE	LOST LOVE
LITA ROZA	LONG SHOT	LOST SOUL
LITTLE ME	LONG SLIP	LOST TIME
LITTLE MO	LONG STAY	LOT'S WIFE
LIVE A LIE	LONG STOP	LOUD BANG
LIVE BAIT	LONG SUIT	LOUD BOOM
LIVE COAL	LONG TAIL	LOUD PEAL
LIVED OUT	LONG TERM	LOUD RING
LIVE DOWN	LONG TIME	LOVED ONE
LIVE IT UP	LONG VIEW	LOVE GAME
LIVE RAIL	LONG WAIT	LOVE NEST
LIVE SHOW	LONG WALK	LOVE POEM
LIVE UP TO	LONG WAVE	LOVE SONG
LIVE WELL	LONG WORD	LOVE SUIT
LIVE WIRE	LOOK ARCH	LOW BIRTH
LIVING IN	LOOK AWAY	LOW CARDS
LOAN CLUB	LOOK BACK	LOW CLASS
LOCAL INN	LOOK BLUE	LOW DIVES
LOCAL LAD	LOOK COOL	LOW DUTCH
LOCAL PUB	LOOK DOWN	LOWER JAW
LOCAL RAG	LOOKED AT	LOWER LIP
LOCAL TAX	LOOKED IN	LOWER SET
LOCH NESS	LOOKED ON	LOW GRADE
LOCK AWAY	LOOKED UP	LOW HEELS
LOCKED IN	LOOK GLUM	LOW JOINT
LOCKED UP	LOOK GOOD	LOW LATIN
LOG CABIN	LOOK GRIM	LOW MARKS
LOG FIRES	LOOK HERE	LOW PITCH
LOIN CHOP	LOOK INTO	LOW POINT
LONE HAND	LOOK IT UP	LOW POWER
LONE WOLF	LOOK LEFT	LOW PRICE
LONG ACRE	LOOK LIKE	LOW RATES
LONG DROP	LOOK OVER	LOW RENTS
LONG FACE	LOOK PALE	LOW SCORE
LONG GONE	LOOKS BIG	LOW SOUND
LONG HAIR	LOOKS FOR	LOW SPEED
LONG HAUL	LOOK SICK	LOW TIDES
LONG JUMP	LOOKS OUT	LOW VOICE
LONG LANE	LOOK SPRY	LOW WAGES
LONG LEAD	LOOK TRUE	LOW WATER
LONG LEGS	LOOK UP TO	LUCKY BOY
LONG LIFE	LOOK WELL	LUCKY DAY

LUCKY DIP
LUCKY DOG
LUCKY HIT
LUCKY JIM
LUCKY MAN
LUCKY RUN
LUCKY WIN
LUG ABOUT
LUMP SUMS
LUNCH OUT
LUTON HOO
LYING LOW
LYNCH LAW
LYRE BIRD

M – 8
MADE EASY
MADE OVER
MAD PARTY
MAGIC BOX
MAGIC EYE
MAIL BOAT
MAIN BODY
MAIN CROP
MAIN DECK
MAIN DISH
MAIN FILM
MAIN HALL
MAIN IDEA
MAIN ITEM
MAIN LINE
MAIN MEAL
MAIN PART
MAIN ROAD
MAIN ROOM
MAINS HUM
MAJOR KEY
MAJOR WAR
MAKE A BED
MAKE A BET
MAKE A BID
MAKE A BOW
MAKE A HIT
MAKE A PUN
MAKE A ROW
MAKE A VOW
MAKE BOLD
MAKE EYES
MAKE FAST
MAKE FIRM
MAKE FREE
MAKE GOOD
MAKE IT UP
MAKE LAWS
MAKE LOVE
MAKE NEWS

MAKE OVER
MAKE PLAY
MAKE PORT
MAKE PUNS
MAKE REAL
MAKE ROOM
MAKE RUNS
MAKE SAFE
MAKE SAIL
MAKES HAY
MAKES OFF
MAKES OUT
MAKE SURE
MAKES WAY
MAKE TIME
MAKE UP TO
MAL DE MER
MALE HEIR
MAN ALIVE
MAN A SHIP
MAN OF GOD
MAN OF LAW
MAN POWER
MAN'S CLUB
MAN TO MAN
MANX CATS
MANY A ONE
MANY MORE
MARCH OFF
MARCH OUT
MARK DOWN
MARKS OFF
MARKS OUT
MARK TIME
MARK WELL
MARRY OFF
MARSH GAS
MARY RAND
MARY ROSE
MATA HARI
MAXIM GUN
MAY QUEEN
MEAN TIME
MEAN WELL
MEAT BALL
MEAT DISH
MEAT LOAF
MEAT PIES
MEAT SAFE
MELT AWAY
MELT DOWN
MEN OF OLD
MEN'S WEAR
MERE IDEA
MERE LUCK
MERRY MEN

MESS BILL
MESSED UP
MESS ROOM
METAL BOX
METAL CAP
MEWS FLAT
MILD BEER
MILE RACE
MILES OUT
MILK BARS
MILK BILL
MILK DIET
MILK JUGS
MILK LOAF
MILK MAID
MILK PAIL
MILKY WAY
MILL GIRL
MILL HILL
MILL POND
MIME SHOW
MIND'S EYE
MINE HOST
MING VASE
MINK COAT
MINK FARM
MINK WRAP
MINOR KEY
MINUS ONE
MINUS TWO
MISS OTIS
MIXED BAG
MIXED LOT
MOBY DICK
MODEL HAT
MONA LISA
MOOT CASE
MOPPED UP
MORAL LAW
MORE TIME
MORT SAHL
MOSS ROSE
MOTH BALL
MOT JUSTE
MOTOR OIL
MOURN FOR
MOVE AWAY
MOVE BACK
MOVED OFF
MOVED OUT
MOVE FAST
MOVE OVER
MOVIE FAN
MOVING UP
MOWN DOWN
MUCH LESS

MUCH MORE
MUCH ROOM
MUCH TIME
MUD BATHS
MUDDLE ON
MUFFLE UP
MUG'S GAME
MUSE UPON
MUSK ROSE
MUTE SWAN
MY CHOICE
MY FRIEND
MY OLD MAN
MY PUBLIC
MYRA HESS
MYRNA LOY

N – 8

NAG'S HEAD
NAIL A LIE
NAIL DOWN
NAIL FILE
NAKED EYE
NAKED MAN
NAME PART
NATAL DAY
NAVAL ARM
NAVAL GUN
NAVAL MAN
NAVY BLUE
NAVY LIST
NAVY WEEK
NEAP TIDE
NEAR BEER
NEAR EAST
NEAR HERE
NEAR HOME
NEAR MISS
NEAR ONES
NEAR SIDE
NEON LAMP
NEON SIGN
NEON TUBE
NEST EGGS
NET PRICE
NET SALES
NET VALUE
NEVER END
NEW ANGLE
NEW BALLS
NEW BIRTH
NEW BLOOD
NEW BRAND
NEW BREAD
NEW BREED

NEW BROOM
NEW CROSS
NEW DELHI
NEW DRESS
NEW FACES
NEW FLINT
NEW FRANC
NEW HEART
NEW HOUSE
NEW IDEAS
NEW ISSUE
NEW LAMPS
NEW LIGHT
NEW MODEL
NEW MONEY
NEW NOVEL
NEW ORDER
NEW OWNER
NEW PENNY
NEW PUPIL
NEW SHOES
NEW SHOOT
NEWS ITEM
NEWS ROOM
NEW STAGE
NEW STOCK
NEW STYLE
NEW SUITS
NEW TOWNS
NEW TRAIL
NEW TRIAL
NEW TRICK
NEW TYRES
NEW VISTA
NEW WOMAN
NEW WORLD
NEXT BEST
NEXT DOOR
NEXT MOVE
NEXT PAGE
NEXT RACE
NEXT STEP
NEXT TIME
NEXT WEEK
NEXT YEAR
NICE MESS
NICE TIME
NICE WORK
NIGHT AIR
NIGHT OFF
NIGHT OUT
NINE DAYS
NINE DEEP
NINE ELMS
NINE FEET
NINE QUID

NINTH DAY
NINTH ROW
NINTH TEE
NIP OF GIN
NO ACCENT
NOAH'S ARK
NO ANSWER
NO APPEAL
NO BETTER
NOBLE ART
NO BOTHER
NO CHANCE
NO CHANGE
NO CHARGE
NO CHOICE
NO COLOUR
NO DESIRE
NO EFFECT
NO EFFORT
NO ESCAPE
NO EXCUSE
NO FUTURE
NO LONGER
NO MATTER
NONE LEFT
NO NERVES
NO OBJECT
NO OPTION
NO QUORUM
NO REMEDY
NO RETURN
NORTH END
NORTH SEA
NO SECRET
NOSED OUT
NOTA BENE
NOT A SOUL
NOT AS YET
NOT AT ALL
NOT A WHIT
NOTE DOWN
NOTE WELL
NO THANKS
NOT LEAST
NOT OFTEN
NOT QUITE
NO TRUMPS
NOT SO BAD
NOT SO HOT
NOT TODAY
NOT VALID
NO WAY OUT
NOW FOR IT
NO WONDER
NUT BROWN
NUT CASES

O – 8

	OLD STOCK	ONE TRICK
	OLD STORY	ONE VERSE
OAK CHEST	OLD STYLE	ONE VOICE
OAK TREES	OLD SWEAT	ONE WHEEL
OCEAN BED	OLD THING	ON FRIDAY
ODD MONEY	OLD TIMER	ONLY A FEW
ODD SIGHT	OLD TIMES	ONLY HOPE
ODD TRICK	OLD TRICK	ONLY JUST
OF COURSE	OLD TUNES	ONLY ONCE
OFF AND ON	OLD WITCH	ON MONDAY
OFF BREAK	OLD WOMAN	ON MY LIFE
OFF DRINK	OLD WORLD	ON ONE LEG
OFF DRIVE	OLIVE OIL	ON PARADE
OFF GUARD	ON A BINGE	ON PAROLE
OFF PITCH	ON A CHAIR	ON PATROL
OFF SALES	ON A LEVEL	ON RECORD
OFF SHORE	ON AND OFF	ON REMAND
OFF STAGE	ON A PLATE	ON SAFARI
OFF STUMP	ON A SLOPE	ON SKATES
OFF TO BED	ON A TABLE	ON STILTS
OFF TO SEA	ON A VISIT	ON STRIKE
OIL DRUMS	ONCE A DAY	ON SUNDAY
OIL LAMPS	ONCE MORE	ON TARGET
OIL STOVE	ONCE ONLY	ON THE AIR
OIL WELLS	ONCE OVER	ON THE DOT
OLD BIRDS	ON COURSE	ON THE EBB
OLD BLUES	ON CREDIT	ON THE HOB
OLD BONES	ON DEMAND	ON THE HOP
OLD BOOTS	ONE BY ONE	ON THE JOB
OLD CHINA	ONE DOZEN	ON THE MAP
OLD CROCK	ONE ENTRY	ON THE MAT
OLD CRONY	ONE FIFTH	ON THE NOD
OLD DEBTS	ONE GROSS	ON THE RUN
OLD DRESS	ONE HEART	ON THE SEA
OLD DUTCH	ONE IN SIX	ON THE SET
OLD FACES	ONE IN TEN	ON THE SLY
OLD FLAME	ONE IN TWO	ON THE TOP
OLD FOGEY	ONE MATCH	ON THE WAY
OLD FOLKS	ONE MONTH	ON TIP-TOE
OLD FRUIT	ONE NINTH	ON VELVET
OLD GIRLS	ONE OR TWO	ON WHEELS
OLD GLORY	ONE OUNCE	OPEN ARMS
OLD GUARD	ONE PENNY	OPEN BOAT
OLD HABIT	ONE PIECE	OPEN BOOK
OLD HANDS	ONE POINT	OPEN CITY
OLD HARRY	ONE POUND	OPEN DOOR
OLD HAUNT	ONE QUART	OPENED UP
OLD HEADS	ONE ROUND	OPEN EYES
OLD MAIDS	ONE'S DUTY	OPEN FIRE
OLD MOORE	ONE'S HOST	OPEN GAME
OLD ORDER	ONE SIXTH	OPEN GATE
OLD ROGER	ONE SPADE	OPEN GOAL
OLD SALTS	ONE STONE	OPEN HAND
OLD SARUM	ONE'S WORD	OPEN LAND
OLD SCORE	ONE TENTH	OPEN MIND
OLD SCREW	ONE THIRD	OPEN NOTE

OPEN ROAD	PARDON ME	PET SHOPS
OPEN SHOP	PARK LANE	PHASE ONE
OPENS OUT	PART SONG	PHASE TWO
OPEN TART	PART TIME	PHONE BOX
OPEN TOWN	PART WITH	PHONE-INS
OPEN VOTE	PARTY MAN	PIANO KEY
OPEN WIDE	PAR VALUE	PICKED UP
OPEN WORK	PASS A LAW	PICK IT UP
OPERA HAT	PASS AWAY	PICKS OFF
OPIUM DEN	PASS BACK	PICKS OUT
OPTED OUT	PASS BOOK	PIG SWILL
ORB OF DAY	PASS DOWN	PILE ARMS
ORDER OFF	PASSED BY	PILE IT ON
ORDER OUT	PASSED ON	PINE AWAY
ORDER TEA	PASSED UP	PINE CONE
OUT AT SEA	PASS IT ON	PINE TREE
OUT FIRST	PASS OVER	PINK COAT
OUT OF BED	PAST CURE	PINK GINS
OUT OF GAS	PAST HELP	PINK GLOW
OUT OF OIL	PAST HOPE	PINK SPOT
OUT OF USE	PAST LIFE	PIN MONEY
OUT TO WIN	PAST TIME	PINNED IN
OVEN BIRD	PAST WORK	PINNED UP
OVEN DOOR	PAUL MUNI	PINS DOWN
OVERDO IT	PAY A CALL	PINT POTS
OVER HERE	PAY A FINE	PINT SIZE
OVER MUCH	PAY CLAIM	PIPE DOWN
OVER SEAS	PAY CORPS	PLACE BET
OVER WE GO	PAY COURT	PLAIN BOX
OWE MONEY	PAY EXTRA	PLAIN MAN
OX TONGUE	PAY FOR IT	PLANT OUT
	PAY PAUSE	PLAN WELL
P – 8	PAYS BACK	PLAY AWAY
PACK A GUN	PAYS CASH	PLAY BACK
PACKED UP	PAY SHEET	PLAY BALL
PACK IT IN	PAY WAGES	PLAY DICE
PACK IT UP	PEA GREEN	PLAY DOWN
PAGAN GOD	PEAK FORM	PLAYED ON
PAGE FIVE	PEAK HOUR	PLAY FAIR
PAGE FOUR	PEAR TREE	PLAY FLAT
PAGE NINE	PEAT FIRE	PLAY GOLF
PAID BACK	PEAT MOSS	PLAY HARD
PAID CASH	PEER GYNT	PLAY HIGH
PAID LESS	PEGGY LEE	PLAY HOST
PAID MORE	PEGS AWAY	PLAY POLO
PAINT OUT	PEN NAMES	PLAY SAFE
PAINT POT	PENNY BUN	PLAY SNAP
PAIRS OFF	PEP PILLS	PLAYS OFF
PALE BLUE	PEP TALKS	PLAY SOLO
PALE FACE	PER ANNUM	PLAY UP TO
PALE PINK	PERKED UP	PLAY WELL
PALL MALL	PETER MAY	PLAY WITH
PALM TREE	PETER OUT	PLEASE GO
PAPER BAG	PETER PAN	PLUG AWAY
PAPER HAT	PET HOBBY	PLUM CAKE
PAPER WAR	PET NAMES	PLUM DUFF

PLUNGE IN
PLUS SIGN
POINT OUT
POKED FUN
POLE JUMP
POLE STAR
POLISH UP
POLKA DOT
POLO NECK
POLO PONY
PONY CLUB
PONY RACE
POOL ROOM
POOLS WIN
POOR CAST
POOR CHAP
POOR CROP
POOR DEAL
POOR DEAR
POOR FISH
POOR FOLK
POOR GAME
POOR HAND
POOR JOHN
POOR LAND
POOR LAWS
POOR MAKE
POOR RATE
POOR RISK
POOR SHOT
POOR SHOW
POOR SIDE
POOR SOIL
POOR SOUL
POOR VIEW
POPE JOHN
POPE PAUL
POP MUSIC
POPPY DAY
POP SONGS
POP STARS
PORE OVER
PORK CHOP
PORK PIES
PORT ARMS
PORT BEAM
PORT ERIN
PORT SAID
PORT SIDE
PORT WINE
POST FREE
POT HERBS
POT OF JAM
POT OF TEA
POT ROAST
POT SHOTS

POURS OUT
POWER CUT
PRESS BOX
PREY UPON
PRICE CUT
PRICE WAR
PRIME CUT
PRIX FIXE
PRO FORMA
PROUD DAY
PROUD MAN
PUB CRAWL
PUB HOURS
PUFF AWAY
PUFFED UP
PULL AWAY
PULL BACK
PULL DOWN
PULLED IN
PULLED UP
PULL HARD
PULL OVER
PULLS OFF
PULLS OUT
PUMPED UP
PUNK ROCK
PUPPY FAT
PURE GOLD
PURE WOOL
PUSH AWAY
PUSH BACK
PUSH DOWN
PUSH HARD
PUSH OVER
PUSH PAST
PUSSY CAT
PUT ABOUT
PUT ASIDE
PUT FORTH
PUT ON TOP
PUT RIGHT
PUTS AWAY
PUTS BACK
PUTS DOWN
PUTS OVER
PUTS UPON
PUT TO BED
PUT TO SEA
PUT TO USE
PUT-UP JOB

Q – 8

QUART POT
QUEEN ANT
QUEEN BEE

QUEEN MAB
QUEUED UP
QUICK EAR
QUICK EYE
QUICK ONE
QUICK WIT
QUIET END
QUILL PEN
QUITE MAD
QUIT RENT
QUIZ GAME
QUIZ KIDS
QUIZ TEAM
QUO VADIS?

R – 8

RACE AWAY
RACE CARD
RADIO HAM
RADIO SET
RAG DOLLS
RAG TRADE
RAIN HARD
RAINY DAY
RAKE OVER
RAMS HOME
RANK HIGH
RARA AVIS
RARE BIRD
RARE GIFT
RAT'S TAIL
RATTLE ON
RAW DEALS
RAW EDGES
RAW STEAK
REACH OUT
READ OVER
READ WELL
READY CUT
READY FOR
READY PEN
READY WIT
REAL GOLD
REAL LIFE
REAL SELF
REAL SILK
REAL TEST
REAR RANK
REAR VIEW
RECKON ON
RECKON UP
RED ALERT
RED BERET
RED BERRY
RED BIDDY

RED BLOOD	RIGHT OUT	ROUND SIX
RED BRICK	RIGHT SET	ROUND SUM
RED CHINA	RIGHT WAY	ROUNDS UP
RED CROSS	RING ROAD	ROUND TEN
RED FACES	RINGS OFF	ROUND TIN
RED LABEL	RINGS OUT	ROUND TWO
RED LIGHT	RING TRUE	ROW A RACE
RED MAPLE	RINSE OUT	ROYAL BOX
RED OCHRE	RIPE CORN	ROYAL OAK
RED PAINT	RIPE LIPS	RUB ALONG
RED PERIL	RISE LATE	RUBBED IN
RED PIECE	RISEN SUN	RUB NOSES
RED QUEEN	RIVER CAM	RUBS DOWN
RED ROSES	RIVER DAM	RUBS IT IN
RED SAILS	RIVER DEE	RUBY LIPS
RED SHIRT	RIVER DON	RUBY PORT
RED SOCKS	RIVER EXE	RUDE WORD
RED SPOTS	RIVER GOD	RULED OUT
RED STAMP	RIVER TAY	RUM PUNCH
RED SUITS	RIVER USK	RUM START
REEF KNOT	RIVER WYE	RUN ABOUT
REELS OFF	ROAD FUND	RUN AFTER
REG DIXON	ROAD HOGS	RUN AHEAD
RELY UPON	ROAD MAPS	RUN ALONG
RENT ACTS	ROAD RACE	RUN A MILE
RENT BOOK	ROAD SHOW	RUN AMUCK
RENT FREE	ROAD SIGN	RUN A RACE
RENT ROLL	ROAD TEST	RUN A RISK
REST CAMP	ROAST PIG	RUN FOR IT
REST CURE	ROB A BANK	RUN RISKS
REST HOME	ROCK CAKE	RUN ROUND
RHUM BABA	ROD LAVER	RUNS AWAY
RICE CROP	ROLL BACK	RUNS BACK
RICE DISH	ROLL CALL	RUNS DOWN
RICH AUNT	ROLLED IN	RUNS HARD
RICH FARE	ROLLED UP	RUN SHORT
RICH FOLK	ROLL OVER	RUNS INTO
RICH FOOD	ROMAN GOD	RUNS OVER
RICH HAUL	ROMAN LAW	RUNS RIOT
RICH JOKE	ROMP HOME	RUNS WILD
RICH LAND	ROOM MATE	RUN THIRD
RICH MILK	ROOT CROP	RUN TO FAT
RICH SEAM	ROOTS OUT	RUSH AWAY
RICH SOIL	ROPED OFF	RUSH HOUR
RICH VEIN	ROPE'S END	RUSH INTO
RICH WIFE	ROSE BOWL	RUSH MATS
RIDE AWAY	ROSE BUSH	RYDER CUP
RIDE DOWN	ROSE PINK	RYE BREAD
RIDE HARD	ROSY GLOW	
RIDE OVER	ROUGH MAP	
RIGHT ARM	ROUGH OUT	S – 8
RIGHT EAR	ROUGH SEA	
RIGHT EYE	ROUND BOX	SABRE JET
RIGHT LEG	ROUND OFF	SACK RACE
RIGHT MAN	ROUND ONE	SADDLE UP
RIGHT OFF	ROUND PEG	SAD HEART

SAD SIGHT	SEE ABOUT	SEWER RAT
SAD SONGS	SEE AFTER	SHAKEN UP
SAD STORY	SEE AHEAD	SHAKE OFF
SAD TO SAY	SEED CAKE	SHAKE OUT
SAD WORLD	SEE IT ALL	SHARE OUT
SAFE SEAT	SEE IT OUT	SHARP EAR
SAFE SIDE	SEEKS OUT	SHARP END
SAIL AWAY	SEEM REAL	SHARP EYE
SAINT DAY	SEE NO ONE	SHARP WIT
SALAD OIL	SEES LIFE	SHEER OFF
SALE ROOM	SEE STARS	SHELL OUT
SALES TAX	SEIZED UP	SHIN BONE
SALT AWAY	SELF HELP	SHIP AHOY
SALT BEEF	SELL DEAR	SHIP OARS
SALT LAKE	SELLS OFF	SHIP'S LOG
SALT MINE	SELLS OUT	SHOE LANE
SALT PORK	SELL WELL	SHOE SHOP
SAME.DATE	SEND AWAY	SHOO AWAY
SAME KIND	SEND BACK	SHOOT LOW
SAME MIND	SEND DOWN	SHOOT OUT
SAME NAME	SEND HELP	SHOOTS UP
SAME TIME	SEND HOME	SHOP BELL
SAME VEIN	SEND WORD	SHOP GIRL
SAM·SMALL	SENNA POD	SHORT CUT
SAND DUNE	SENNA TEA	SHORT LEG
SANK DOWN	SERVE ILL	SHORT ONE
SAVE FACE	SERVE OUT	SHORT RUN
SAVE TIME	SET ABOUT	SHOT AWAY
SAVING UP	SET AFOOT	SHOT DEAD
SAXE BLUE	SET APART	SHOT DOWN
SAY GRACE	SET ASIDE	SHOT SILK
SCALED UP	SET A TRAP	SHOUT OUT
SCENE ONE	SET BOOKS	SHOVE OFF
SCENE TWO	SET FORTH	SHOW A LEG
SCENT OUT	SET GOING	SHOW BOAT
SCOOP OUT	SET IDEAS	SHOW CASE
SCORE OFF	SET LUNCH	SHOW DOWN
SCORE OUT	SET MEALS	SHOWED UP
SCOT FREE	SET PAPER	SHOW FEAR
SCOUT OUT	SET PIECE	SHOW GIRL
SCRAPE UP	SET PLANS	SHOWN OFF
SCRUB OUT	SET POINT	SHOWN OUT
SEA COAST	SET PRICE	SHOW OVER
SEA FEVER	SET RIGHT	SHOW PITY
SEA FLOOR	SET SCENE	SHOW ROOM
SEA GREEN	SETS DOWN	SHRUG OFF
SEALED UP	SETS FOOT	SHUT DOWN
SEA LORDS	SETS FREE	SHUTS OFF
SEA NYMPH	SET SMILE	SHUTS OUT
SEA POWER	SETS SAIL	SHY CHILD
SEA SCOUT	SET STARE	SHY SMILE
SEA SPRAY	SETS UPON	SHY THING
SEA STORY	SET TERMS	SHY WOMAN
SEAT BELT	SETTLE IN	SICK JOKE
SEA WATER	SETTLE UP	SICK LIST
SEA WINDS	SEVEN MEN	SICK ROOM

SIDE ARMS	SKIP OVER	SNEAKS UP
SIDE BETS	SKY PILOT	SNOWED IN
SIDE DISH	SLACK OFF	SNOWED UP
SIDE DOOR	SLAG HEAP	SNOW HILL
SIDE DRUM	SLAP DOWN	SNOW LINE
SIDE GATE	SLEEP OFF	SNUB NOSE
SIDE LINE	SLEEP OUT	SNUFF BOX
SIDE ROAD	SLEEPS IN	SNUFF OUT
SIDE SHOW	SLEEPS ON	SOBER MAN
SIDE VIEW	SLING OFF	SOB STORY
SIDE WIND	SLING OUT	SOB STUFF
SIDE WITH	SLINGS IN	SOFT BALL
SIEGE CAP	SLIP AWAY	SOFTEN UP
SIGN AWAY	SLIP BACK	SOFT EYES
SIGNED ON	SLIP INTO	SOFT HAIR
SIGN HERE	SLIP KNOT	SOFT ROES
SIGNS OFF	SLIP PAST	SOFT SEAT
SILK GOWN	SLIPS OFF	SOFT SKIN
SILLY ASS	SLIPS OUT	SOFT SOAP
SING HIGH	SLIT OPEN	SOFT SPOT
SING SING	SLOG AWAY	SOFT TOYS
SINGS OUT	SLOPE OFF	SOFT WORD
SINK BACK	SLOPES UP	SOHO FAIR
SINK DOWN	SLOP OVER	SOLD A PUP
SINN FEIN	SLOW BALL	SOLE HEIR
SIT ABOUT	SLOW BOAT	SOLO CALL
SIT ERECT	SLOW DOWN	SOME GOOD
SIT IT OUT	SLOWED UP	SOME MORE
SITS BACK	SLOW PACE	SONG BIRD
SITS DOWN	SLOW TIME	SONG HITS
SIT STILL	SLUM AREA	SONNY BOY
SIT TIGHT	SLY JOKES	SON OF GOD
SIT UNDER	SMALL ADS	SORE EYES
SITZ BATH	SMALL BOY	SORE FEET
SIX CLUBS	SMALL CAR	SORE HEAD
SIX DOZEN	SMALL EGG	SORE NEED
SIX GROSS	SMALL FRY	SORRY END
SIX HOLES	SMALL GIN	SORTS OUT
SIX HOURS	SMALL MAN	SO SIMPLE
SIX MILES	SMALL RUM	SOUND BET
SIX PARTS	SMALL SUM	SOUND BID
SIX PINTS	SMALL WAY	SOUND BOX
SIX SCORE	SMART LAD	SOUND MAN
SIXTH DAY	SMART MAN	SOUR LOOK
SIXTH ROW	SMART SET	SOUR MILK
SIXTH TEE	SMASH HIT	SOUTH SEA
SIX TIMES	SMELL OUT	SOYA BEAN
SIX TO ONE	SMOG MASK	SPACE AGE
SIX WEEKS	SMOKE OUT	SPACE MAN
SIX YEARS	SNACK BAR	SPACE OUT
SIZE FIVE	SNAKE PIT	SPARE BED
SIZE FOUR	SNAP VOTE	SPARE MAN
SIZE NINE	SNATCH UP	SPARE RIB
SKIM OVER	SNEAK OFF	SPARK OFF
SKIN DEEP	SNEAK OUT	SPEAK FOR
SKIN GAME	SNEAKS IN	SPEAK OUT

SPEAKS UP	STEEL BAR	SUMMON UP
SPEED COP	STEEL NIB	SUMS IT UP
SPELL OUT	STEN GUNS	SUM TOTAL
SPILT INK	STEP BACK	SUNNY DAY
SPIN A WEB	STEP DOWN	SUNNY JIM
SPINS OUT	STEP INTO	SUN SPOTS
SPLIT PIN	STEP IT UP	SUN'S RAYS
SPLITS UP	STEP ON IT	SURE CURE
SPONGE ON	STEP OVER	SURE GAIN
SPOON FED	STEPS OUT	SURE LOSS
SPORT AID	ST GEORGE	SURE SHOT
SPOT CASH	ST GILES'S	SWAN LAKE
SPRING UP	ST HELENA	SWAN SONG
SPRUCE UP	ST HELEN'S	SWAP NEWS
SPUN GOLD	ST HELIER	SWEAR OFF
SPUN SILK	STICK OUT	SWEARS IN
SPUN YARN	STICKS TO	SWEEP OUT
SQUAD CAR	STICKS UP	SWEEPS UP
SQUARE UP	STIFF LEG	SWEET AIR
STAFF CAR	ST JAMES'S	SWEET PEA
STAGE ONE	ST MORITZ	SWEET SUE
STAGE SET	STOCK CAR	SWEET TEA
STAG HUNT	STONE AGE	SWELL MOB
STAKE OUT	STOP AWAY	SWEEL OUT
ST ALBANS	STOP DEAD	SWELLS UP
STALE AIR	STOP HERE	SWIM SUIT
STALE BUN	STOP HOME	SWING LOW
STALL OFF	STOP OVER	SWITCH ON
STAMP ACT	STOP PLAY	SWOP OVER
STAMP OUT	STOPS OFF	
STAND FOR	STOPS OUT	**T – 8**
STAND OFF	STOP WORK	
STAND OUT	STOUT MAN	TABBY CAT
STAND PAT	STOW AWAY	TABLE BAY
ST ANDREW	ST PETER'S	TAG ALONG
STANDS BY	STRAW HAT	TAIL AWAY
STANDS IN	STRAY CAT	TAIL COAT
STANDS TO	STRAY DOG	TAIL WIND
STANDS UP	STREAK BY	TAJ MAHAL
STAR PART	STREAK IN	TAKE A BOW
START OFF	STREAM BY	TAKE A BUS
START OUT	STREAM IN	TAKE A CAB
STARTS UP	STRIKE UP	TAKE A NAP
STAR TURN	STRING UP	TAKE A NIP
STAR WARS	STRIP OFF	TAKE A PEW
STAVE OFF	STROLL BY	TAKE A TIP
STAY AWAY	STRUCK ON	TAKE A VOW
STAY DOWN	STRUNG UP	TAKE AWAY
STAYED IN	STUD BOOK	TAKE BACK
STAYED UP	STUD FARM	TAKE BETS
STAY HERE	STUDY ART	TAKE CARE
STAY OPEN	STUDY LAW	TAKE DOWN
STAYS PUT	STUMPS UP	TAKE FIRE
ST BRIDE'S	STUNT MAN	TAKE FOOD
ST DAVID'S	SUGAR RAY	TAKE HEED
STEAK PIE	SUMMED UP	TAKE HOLD
		TAKE IT IN

TAKE IT UP	TEARS OFF	THE CREED
TAKE LIFE	TEA SHOPS	THE CROWN
TAKEN ILL	TEDDY BOY	THE DALES
TAKEN OFF	TED HEATH	THE DERBY
TAKE NOTE	TEE SHOTS	THE DEVIL
TAKEN OUT	TELL A FIB	THE DOWNS
TAKE ODDS	TELL A LIE	THE DRAMA
TAKE OVER	TELL LIES	THE DUTCH
TAKE PART	TELLS OFF	THE EARTH
TAKE PITY	TEN CENTS	THE ELITE
TAKE ROOT	TEN DOZEN	THE ENEMY
TAKES AIM	TEN GROSS	THE FACTS
TAKE SILK	TEN HOURS	THE FATES
TAKES OFF	TEN MARKS	THE FIELD
TAKES OUT	TEN MILES	THE FILMS
TAKE THAT	TEN PARTS	THE FIRST
TAKE THIS	TEN SCORE	THE FLEET
TAKE TIME	TENSED UP	THE FLOOD
TAKE TOLL	TENTH DAY	THE GOODS
TAKE VOWS	TENTH MAN	THE GOONS
TAKE WINE	TENTH ROW	THE GRAVE
TAKE WING	TENTH TEE	THE GREAT
TAKING IN	TEN TIMES	THE GREYS
TALK A LOT	TEN TO ONE	THE GROOM
TALK BACK	TEN TO SIX	THE HAGUE
TALK BOSH	TEN TO TEN	THE HAVES
TALK DOWN	TEN TO TWO	THE HOUSE
TALK OVER	TEN WEEKS	THE IDEAL
TALKS BIG	TEN YEARS	THE IDIOT
TALK SHOP	TERM TIME	THE IRISH
TALL GIRL	TEST CASE	THE JOKER
TALL TALE	TEST TUBE	THE KORAN
TALL TALK	TEXAS TEA	THE LIMIT
TALL TREE	TEXT BOOK	THE LOCAL
TANK TRAP	THANK GOD	THE LORDS
TAP DANCE	THANK YOU	THE LOSER
TAPER OFF	THAT SIDE	THE MAFIA
TAP WATER	THE ANDES	THE MITRE
TAUT ROPE	THE ANGEL	THE MOORS
TAWNY OWL	THE ASHES	THE MUSES
TAXI FARE	THE BELLS	THE NORTH
TAXI RANK	THE BENCH	THE NOVEL
TEA BREAK	THE BIBLE	THE PANEL
TEA CADDY	THE BLIND	THE POINT
TEACH ART	THE BLITZ	THE POOLS
TEA DANCE	THE BLUES	THE PRESS
TEA IN BED	THE BRAVE	THE RAINS
TEAMED UP	THE BRIDE	THE RIGHT
TEAM GAME	THE BRINY	THE ROPES
TEAM MATE	THE BRONX	THE SHAKE
TEAM WORK	THE BUFFS	THE SHORE
TEA PARTY	THE CHAIR	THE SOMME
TEAR DOWN	THE CHASE	THE SOUTH
TEAR IT UP	THE CLOTH	THE SPURS
TEAR OPEN	THE CONGO	THE STAGE
TEA ROSES	THE COUNT	THE STAKE

THE STARS	TIED GAME	TOP LAYER
THE SUDAN	TIGER BAY	TOP MARKS
THE THING	TIGER CUB	TOP NOTCH
THE TIMES	TIGER RAG	TOP NOTES
THE TOWER	TIGHT FIT	TOPPED UP
THE TWINS	TILL THEN	TOP PLACE
THE TWIST	TILT OVER	TOP PRICE
THE URALS	TIME BASE	TOP PRIZE
THE USUAL	TIME BOMB	TOP RATES
THE VOLGA	TIME CARD	TOP SCORE
THE WAITS	TIME FUSE	TOP SPEED
THE WAY IN	TIME IS UP	TOP SPOTS
THE WEALD	TIME TEST	TOP STAIR
THE WELSH	TIME TO GO	TOP TABLE
THE WILDS	TIMOR SEA	TOP TO TOE
THE WOLDS	TIN LIZZY	TORY GAIN
THE WORLD	TIN MINES	TORY LOSS
THE WORKS	TINY HAND	TOSS AWAY
THE WORST	TINY MITE	TOSSED UP
THICK EAR	TINY TOTS	TOTAL SUM
THICK FOG	TIPPED UP	TOTAL WAR
THIN COAT	TIP TO TOE	TOTE A GUN
THIN DOWN	TIP TO WIN	TOTE ODDS
THIN EDGE	TIRED MAN	TO THE BAD
THIN HAIR	TIRED OUT	TO THE END
THINK BIG	TIRED TIM	TO THE TOP
THINK FIT	TO A FAULT	TOT OF RUM
THINK OUT	TO AND FRO	TOTTED UP
THINKS UP	TO BE SURE	TOTTER UP
THIN SKIN	TOBY JUGS	TOUCH OFF
THIN TIME	TODDLE IN	TOUGH GUY
THIN WIRE	TODDLE UP	TOUGH JOB
THIRD ACT	TOE TO TOE	TOUGH NUT
THIRD DAY	TOLL CALL	TOW ALONG
THIRD MAN	TOM BROWN	TOWN HALL
THIRD ROW	TOM JONES	TOWN LIFE
THIRD SET	TOMMY GUN	TOWN TALK
THIRD TEE	TOMMY ROT	TOY MAKER
THIS IS IT	TOM PINCH	TOY SHOPS
THIS SIDE	TOM THUMB	TOY TRAIN
THIS TIME	TOM WALLS	TRADE GAP
THIS WEEK	TO MY MIND	TRAIL OFF
THIS YEAR	TONE DEAF	TRAIN SET
THREE MEN	TONE DOWN	TRAM STOP
THROWN IN	TONE POEM	TRAP FIVE
THROW QFF	TON-UP BOY	TRAP FOUR
THROW OUT	TOO EAGER	TRIAL RUN
THUMBS UP	TOO EARLY	TRIED OUT
TICK OVER	TOO LARGE	TRIM AWAY
TICKS OFF	TOO QUICK	TRIP OVER
TIDE MARK	TOO SHARP	TROOP OFF
TIDE OVER	TOO SMALL	TROOP OUT
TIDIED UP	TOO STEEP	TROTS OFF
TIDY MIND	TOOTH OUT	TROTS OUT
TIE A KNOT	TOP BRASS	TRUE BILL
TIED DOWN	TOP FLOOR	TRUE BLUE

TRUE COPY
TRUE HEIR
TRUE LOVE
TRUE TIME
TRUE WORD
TRY AGAIN
TRY FOR IT
TRY IT OUT
TRY TO SAY
TUCK AWAY
TUCKED IN
TUCKED UP
TUCK SHOP
TUG ALONG
TUG OF WAR
TURN AWAY
TURN BACK
TURN BLUE
TURN COLD
TURN DOWN
TURNED IN
TURNED ON
TURNED UP
TURN GREY
TURN INTO
TURN IT IN
TURN IT ON
TURN IT UP
TURN LEFT
TURN OVER
TURN PALE
TURNS OFF
TURN SOFT
TURN SOUR
TURNS OUT
TURN TAIL
TURN UPON
TWICE ONE
TWICE SHY
TWICE SIX
TWICE TEN
TWICE TWO
TWIN BEDS
TWIN BOYS
TWO BRACE
TWO BY TWO
TWO CARDS
TWO CLUBS
TWO DOZEN
TWO GROSS
TWO HANDS
TWO HEADS
TWO HOLES
TWO HOURS
TWO IN ONE
TWO LUMPS

TWO MILES
TWO MINDS
TWO PAGES
TWO PAIRS
TWO PARTS
TWO PINTS
TWO PUTTS
TWO RANKS
TWO SCORE
TWO SIDES
TWO STARS
TWO TO ONE
TWO WEEKS
TWO WIVES
TWO WORDS
TWO YARDS
TWO YEARS
TYPE SIZE

U – 8

UGLY FACE
UGLY LOOK
UGLY MOOD
UGLY SCAR
UNCLE MAC
UNCLE SAM
UNCLE TOM
UNCUT GEM
UNDER AGE
UNDER PAR
UNDER WAY
UNTIL NOW
UPAS TREE
UP AT DAWN
UP IN ARMS
UP ON HIGH
UPON OATH
UPPER AIR
UPPER CUT
UPPER JAW
UPPER LIP
UPPER SET
UPPER TEN
UP STREAM
UP TO DATE
UP TO FORM
UP TO TIME
USED CARS
USED HALF
USED TO IT
USE FORCE
USHER OUT
USHERS IN
USUAL WAY
UTTER CAD

V – 8

VAIN HOPE
VAIN SHOW
VAST SIZE
VEER AWAY
VEER LEFT
VERA CRUZ
VERA LYNN
VERSED IN
VERY BEST
VERY COLD
VERY DEAR
VERY FAIR
VERY FULL
VERY GOOD
VERY HARD
VERY KEEN
VERY KIND
VERY LATE
VERY MANY
VERY MUCH
VERY NEAR
VERY NICE
VERY POOR
VERY RICH
VERY SLOW
VERY SOFT
VERY SOON
VERY TRUE
VERY WARM
VERY WELL
VINE LEAF
VIVA VOCE
VIVID RED
VOTE DOWN
VOTE TORY
VOUCH FOR

W – 8

WADE INTO
WAGE BILL
WAGED WAR
WAIT A BIT
WAITED ON
WAIT HERE
WAIT UPON
WALK AWAY
WALK BACK
WALK DOWN
WALK INTO
WALK OVER
WALK PAST
WALKS OFF
WALKS OUT

WALLED UP	WELL HELD	WIDE ROAD
WALL GAME	WELL MADE	WIDE VIEW
WALTZ OUT	WELL OVER	WILD BIRD
WANGLE IT	WELL PAID	WILD BLOW
WAN SMILE	WELL READ	WILD BOAR
WANT A LOT	WELL SAID	WILD DUCK
WANT MORE	WELL TO DO	WILD FOWL
WAR CRIME	WELL UP IN	WILD GOAT
WAR DANCE	WELL USED	WILD LIFE
WARDS OFF	WELL WELL!	WILD LOOK
WAR FEVER	WENT AWAY	WILD OATS
WAR HOUSE	WENT BACK	WILD ROSE
WAR LORDS	WENT DOWN	WILD TALK
WARMED UP	WENT EAST	WILD WEST
WARM OVEN	WENT FREE	WILD WIND
WARM WORK	WENT OVER	WILY BIRD
WAR PAINT	WENT WELL	WIN A GAME
WAR PARTY	WENT WEST	WIN A RACE
WAR POEMS	WEST DOOR	WIND SOCK
WAR POETS	WEST SIDE	WINDY DAY
WAR SCARE	WEST WIND	WINE BARS
WART HOGS	WEST WING	WINE GUMS
WAR YEARS	WET PAINT	WINE LIST
WASH AWAY	WET PLATE	WINE SHOP
WASH DOWN	WET SHEET	WING HALF
WASHED UP	WET SPELL	WIN GLORY
WATCH OUT!	WHALE OIL	WIN MONEY
WATER ICE	WHAT A FAG	WINS OVER
WATER JUG	WHAT IS IT	WIPE AWAY
WATER RAT	WHAT NEXT?	WIPED OUT
WAT TYLER	WHAT OF IT?	WIRE MESH
WAVE AWAY	WHAT'S NEW?	WIRE WOOL
WAVY HAIR	WHEEL OFF	WISE GUYS
WAVY LINE	WHEEL OUT	WISE HEAD
WAVY NAVY	WHICH WAY?	WISE MOVE
WAX MATCH	WHIP HAND	WITH CARE
WAX MERRY	WHISK OFF	WITH EASE
WAX MODEL	WHITE ANT	WITH LOVE
WAX VESTA	WHITE EGG	WITTY MAN
WAY AHEAD	WHITE HOT	WOLF CALL
WEAK CASE	WHITE KEY	WOLF CUBS
WEAK CHIN	WHITE LIE	WOOD FIRE
WEAK EYES	WHITE MAN	WOOD PULP
WEAK HEAD	WHITE SEA	WORD GAME
WEAK LINK	WHITE TIE	WORKED UP
WEAK SIDE	WHIT WEEK	WORK EVIL
WEAK SPOT	WHO DUN IT?	WORK HARD
WEAK WILL	WHOLE HOG	WORK LATE
WEAR AWAY	WHOLE LOT	WORK OVER
WEAR DOWN	WHO'S NEXT?	WORKS OFF
WEARS OFF	WHY WORRY?	WORKS OUT
WEARS OUT	WIDE BALL	WORLD WAR
WEAR WELL	WIDE BOYS	WORN DOWN
WEIGHS UP	WIDE FAME	WRAP IT UP
WELL AWAY	WIDE GULF	WRING DRY
WELL DONE	WIDE OPEN	WRING OUT

WRITE OFF	ACTING FOR	ALL ON DECK
WRITE OUT	ACT OF LOVE	ALL ON EDGE
WRITES UP	ACT WISELY	ALLOW BAIL
WRONG DAY	ACUTE PAIN	ALL SAINTS
WRONG MAN	ADAM SMITH	ALL SERENE
WRONG WAY	ADAM STYLE	ALL SQUARE
WRY SMILE	ADAM'S WINE	ALL THE DAY
WYCH ELMS	ADD A RIDER	ALL THE LOT
	ADD A TOUCH	ALL THE WAY
	ADD COLOUR	ALL THUMBS
X – 8	ADD FRILLS	ALL TIED UP
	ADDLED EGG	ALMA COGAN
X-RAY UNIT	AD NAUSEAM	ALMA MATER
	A DOG'S LIFE	ALMOND OIL
Y – 8	AD VALOREM	ALMOST ALL
	AEGEAN SEA	ALPHA PLUS
YALE LOCK	AER LINGUS	ALPHA RAYS
YEAR BOOK	AFTER DARK	AMPLE ROOM
YEARN FOR	AFTER TIME	AMPLE TIME
YEARS AGO	AGILE MIND	ANDY PANDY
YES AND NO	A GOOD DEAL	ANGEL CAKE
YET AGAIN	A GOOD MANY	ANGEL FACE
YOU AND ME	AGREE WITH	ANGEL FISH
YOUNG BOY	AHOY THERE	ANGORA CAT
YOUNG MAN	AIMED HIGH	ANGRY LOOK
YOUNG ONE	AIM HIGHER	ANIMAL CRY
YOUR CALL	AIM TO KILL	ANIMAL FAT
YOUR DEAL	AIR BATTLE	ANIMAL OIL
YOUR MOVE	AIR LETTER	ANITA LOOS
YOUR TURN	AIR LOSSES	ANKLE DEEP
YULE LOGS	AIR PIRACY	ANNUAL FEE
	AIR POCKET	ANY MOMENT
	AIR TRAVEL	ANY OFFERS?
Z – 8	ALARM BELL	ANY TO COME
	ALARM CALL	APPIAN WAY
ZANE GREY	ALEC WAUGH	APPLE A DAY
ZERO HOUR	ALERT MIND	APPLE CART
	ALICE BAND	APPLE TART
	ALIEN CORN	APPLE TREE
A – 9	ALIEN RACE	APRIL FOOL
	ALL ABOARD	ARAB HORSE
AARON'S ROD	ALL ACTION	ARAB STEED
A BIT FISHY	ALL ADRIFT	ARCH ENEMY
A BIT STEEP	ALL AGREED	ARCH KNAVE
A BIT STIFF	ALL AROUND	ARCH ROGUE
A BIT THICK	ALL ASHORE	ARCH SMILE
ABLE TO FLY	ALL AT ONCE	AREA STEPS
ABLE TO PAY	ALL BEHIND	ARID WASTE
ABOUT FACE	ALL BLACKS	ARMED BAND
ABOUT TIME	ALL BUT ONE	ARMS DEPOT
ABOUT TURN	ALL CHANGE	ARMS LOWER
ABOVE ZERO	ALL COMERS	ARMS RAISE
ACID REPLY	ALL FOR ONE	ARMY BOOTS
ACKER BILK	ALL IN VAIN	ARMY CADET
ACT AS HOST	ALL IS LOST	ARMY CORPS
ACTED WELL	ALL IS WELL	ARMY GROUP
ACT FAIRLY		

ARMY ISSUE	AT THE SIDE	BAD SECOND
ARNOLD BAX	AT THE TIME	BAD SPIRIT
ART CRITIC	ATTIC SALT	BAD TEMPER
ART DEALER	AUGUR WELL	BAD TIMING
ART EDITOR	AU NATUREL	BAG OF GOLD
ARTIE SHAW	AUNT SALLY	BAG O' NAILS
ART MASTER	AWAY MATCH	BAG THE LOT
ART MUSEUM	AZURE BLUE	BAKE A CAKE
ART SCHOOL		BAKE A LOAF
ART STUDIO		BAKE BREAD
AS A RESULT	B – 9	BALANCE UP
ASCOT MILE		BALD FACTS
ASCOT WEEK	BABY GRAND	BALD PATCH
ASH BLONDE	BABY LINEN	BALD TRUTH
ASIA MINOR	BACK AGAIN	BALLET FAN
AS IT COMES	BACK ALLEY	BALLOT BOX
ASK ADVICE	BACK BACON	BALSA WOOD
ASK A PRICE	BACKED OUT	BALTIC SEA
ASK NICELY	BACK OUT OF	BAND WAGON
ASK PARDON	BACK PEDAL	BANDY LEGS
ASK THE WAY	BACK SLANG	BANK CLERK
AS ORDERED	BACK STAGE	BANK PAPER
ASPEN LEAF	BACK TEETH	BAR CODING
AS PER PLAN	BACK TOOTH	BARE FACTS
AS PLANNED	BACK WATER	BARE FISTS
AS THEY SAY	BACK WHEEL	BARE KNEES
AT A CANTER	BACON RIND	BARE TRUTH
AT A GALLOP	BAD ADVICE	BARE WALLS
AT A GLANCE	BAD ATTACK	BARE WORDS
AT A LOW EBB	BAD CREDIT	BARGE INTO
AT AN ANGLE	BAD CUSTOM	BARLEY MOW
AT ANY RATE	BAD DRIVER	BAR MAGNET
AT ANY TIME	BAD ENOUGH	BARN DANCE
AT A PROFIT	BAD EXCUSE	BAR OF IRON
AT LEISURE	BAD FIGURE	BAR OF SOAP
AT LIBERTY	BAD FOR ONE	BAR PRINTER
AT LOW TIDE	BAD FRIEND	BARROW BOY
ATOMIC AGE	BAD HABITS	BAR THE WAY
ATOMIC WAR	BAD HEALTH	BASE METAL
AT ONE BLOW	BAD HUMOUR	BASIC NEED
AT ONE TIME	BAD INTENT	BASIC PLAN
AT PRESENT	BADLY DONE	BASIC WAGE
AT THE BACK	BADLY DOWN	BAS RELIEF
AT THE BANK	BADLY HURT	BASS NOTES
AT THE BEST	BAD MARKET	BASS VOICE
AT THE DOOR	BAD MEMORY	BATH BRICK
AT THE FAIR	BAD PLAYER	BATH NIGHT
AT THE HEAD	BAD POINTS	BATH SALTS
AT THE HELM	BAD POLICY	BATH TOWEL
AT THE MAIN	BAD RECORD	BATH WATER
AT THE MOST	BAD REPORT	BATTLE BUS
AT THE NETS	BAD REPUTE	BATTLE CRY
AT THE OVAL	BAD RESULT	BAY LEAVES
AT THE PEAK	BAD REVIEW	BAY WINDOW
AT THE POST	BAD SAILOR	BEACH SUIT
AT THE REAR	BAD SCRAPE	BEACH WEAR
	BAD SEAMAN	

BE ADVISED	BEST GRADE	BLACK KING
BE A MARTYR	BEST OF ALL	BLACK LACE
BE AN ANGEL	BEST SCORE	BLACK LEAD
BEAR FRUIT	BEST TASTE	BLACK LION
BEARING UP	BEST THING	BLACK LIST
BEAR RIGHT	BEST VALUE	BLACK LOOK
BE AT A LOSS	BE SWEET ON	BLACK MARK
BE AT FAULT	BÊTE NOIRE	BLACK MASS
BEAT MUSIC	BE THE BEST	BLACK MONK
BEAU GESTE	BETTER MAN	BLACK MOOD
BEAU IDEAL ·	BETTER OFF	BLACK NOTE
BEAU MONDE	BETTER 'OLE	BLACK OPAL
BE A YES-MAN	BETWEEN US	BLACK PAWN
BE CAREFUL	BEVIN BOYS	BLACK ROOK
BE CERTAIN	BEYOND ONE	BLACK RUIN
BECOME DUE	BIG BERTHA	BLACK SPOT
BECOME ONE	BIG CHANCE	BLACK SUIT
BEDDED OUT	BIG CHEESE	BLACK SWAN
BED OF PAIN	BIG DEMAND	BLANK FILE
BED SHEETS	BIG DIPPER	BLANK LOOK
BEECH TREE	BIG EFFORT	BLANK MIND
BEEF CURRY	BIG FREEZE	BLANK PAGE
BEER MONEY	BIG HEADED	BLANK WALL
BEER ON TAP	BIG MARGIN	BLAZE AWAY
BEER STAIN	BIG PROFIT	BLIND DATE
BEET SUGAR	BIG TALKER	BLIND ROAD
BEFORE ALL	BILL SIKES	BLIND SIDE
BEFORE NOW	BILLY FURY	BLIND SPOT
BEFORE TEA	BILLY GOAT	BLOCK PERM
BE FRIENDS	BILLY LIAR	BLOCK VOTE
BEGGED OFF	BINGO CLUB	BLOND HAIR
BEG IN VAIN	BINGO HALL	BLOOD BANK
BEGIN WELL	BIRCH TREE	BLOOD BATH
BEGIN WORK	BIRD BRAIN	BLOOD CLOT
BEG PARDON	BIRD'S NEST	BLOOD FEUD
BEL ESPRIT	BIRTH MARK	BLOOD HEAT
BELL METAL	BIRTH RATE	BLOOD TEST
BELL TOWER	BITE TO EAT	BLOOD TYPE
BELOW COST	BITING WIT	BLOW A FUSE
BELOW ZERO	BIT OF A JOB	BLOW ALONG
BELT ALONG	BIT OF A LAD	BLOWING UP
BEN JONSON	BIT OF LUCK	BLUE ANGEL
BEN LOMOND	BITTER CUP	BLUE BLOOD
BENNY HILL	BITTER END	BLUE CHIPS
BE ONE'S AGE	BLACK ARTS	BLUE GRASS
BE ONESELF	BLACK BALL	BLUE JEANS
BE ON GUARD	BLACK BEAR	BLUE LIGHT
BE PRESENT	BLACK BELT	BLUE MOVIE
BE PRUDENT	BLACK BESS	BLUE PAINT
BERTA RUCK	BLACK BOOK	BLUE PETER
BERYL GREY	BLACK FLAG	BLUE PRINT
BERYL REID	BLACK GOLD	BLUE RINSE
BE SERIOUS	BLACK HAIR	BLUE SKIES
BEST CHINA	BLACK HAND	BLUE SOCKS
BEST DRESS	BLACK HOLE	BLUE STAMP
BEST ENTRY	BLACK JACK	BLUE STEEL

BLUE STORY	BOWLER HAT	BROAD BACK
BLUE WATER	BOW STREET	BROAD BEAM
BLUE WHALE	BOW TO FATE	BROAD BEAN
BLUNT EDGE	BOW WINDOW	BROAD GRIN
BOARD A BUS	BOX AND COX	BROAD HINT
BOARDED UP	BOX CAMERA	BROAD JOKE
BOARD GAME	BOX CLEVER	BROAD MIND
BOARD ROOM	BOXING DAY	BROAD VIEW
BOAR'S HEAD	BOX NUMBER	BROKEN ARM
BOAT DRILL	BOX OFFICE	BROKEN LEG
BOAT TRAIN	BOX OF FIGS	BROKEN MAN
BOB SAWYER	BOY FRIEND	BROKEN RIB
BODY OF MEN	BOY GEORGE	BROKEN SET
BOIL AN EGG	BOYLE'S LAW	BROKE OPEN
BOILED EGG	BRAIN WAVE	BRONZE AGE
BOILED HAM	BRAKE DRUM	BROOD MARE
BOLD FRONT	BRANCH OFF	BROODY HEN
BOLD LINES	BRANCH OUT	BROUGHT UP
BOLD PRINT	BRASS BALL	BROWN BEAR
BOLSTER UP	BRASS BAND	BROWN BESS
BONA FIDES	BRASS RING	BROWN COAL
BON CHANCE	BRASS TACK	BROWN EYES
BONE CHINA	BRAVE DEED	BROWN HAIR
BON MARCHÉ	BRAVE FACE	BROWN LOAF
BON VIVANT	BRAZEN OUT	BROWN STEW
BON VIVEUR	BRAZIL NUT	BROWN SUIT
BON VOYAGE	BREAD LINE	BRUSH AWAY
BOOK A ROOM	BREAD ROLL	BRUSHED UP
BOOK A SEAT	BREAK A LEG	BRUSH DOWN
BOOK LOVER	BREAK AWAY	BRUSH OVER
BOOK OF JOB	BREAK BACK	BRUSH PAST
BOOK SEATS	BREAK BAIL	BUBBLE CAR
BOOK STORE	BREAK CAMP	BUBBLE GUM
BOOK TITLE	BREAK DOWN	BUCK TEETH
BOOK TOKEN	BREAK EVEN	BUDGET DAY
BORE A HOLE	BREAK IT UP	BUGLE CALL
BORN ACTOR	BREAK JAIL	BULLY BEEF
BORN AGAIN	BREAK OPEN	BUMBLE BEE
BORN ALIVE	BREAK STEP	BUMPED OFF
BORN MIMIC	BREATHE IN	BUNNY GIRL
BORN MIXER	BRENDA LEE	BURKE'S LAW
BORN SLAVE	BRET HARTE	BURMA ROAD
BOTANY BAY	BRIAR PIPE	BURMA STAR
BOTH HANDS	BRICK WALL	BURN A HOLE
BOTH SIDES	BRIDAL BED	BURN ALIVE
BOTTOM DOG	BRIDE TO BE	BURNT COKE
BOTTOMS UP	BRIGHT BOY	BURNT DOWN
BOUGHT OFF	BRIGHT LAD	BURST OPEN
BOUGHT OUT	BRIGHT RED	BURST PIPE
BOUNCE OUT	BRING BACK	BURST TYRE
BOUND BOOK	BRING DOWN	BUS DRIVER
BOUND OVER	BRING HOME	BUSH HOUSE
BOWED DOWN	BRING OVER	BUSH SKIRT
BOWED HEAD	BRING WORD	BUS STRIKE
BOWL ALONG	BRISK WALK	BUS TICKET
BOWLED OUT	BRISTLE UP	BUSY PLACE

BUY A HOUSE
BUY A ROUND
BUY ON TICK
BUY SHARES
BUZZ ABOUT
BUZZ ALONG
BY ACCLAIM
BY AIR MAIL
BY AUCTION
BY COMMAND
BY CONSENT
BY DEFAULT
BY DEGREES
BY HERSELF
BY HIMSELF
BY NO MEANS
BY NUMBERS
BY ONESELF
BY REQUEST
BY STEALTH
BY THE ACRE
BY THE BOOK
BY THE HOUR
BY THE NOSE
BY THE YARD
BY THUNDER

C – 9

CAB DRIVER
CADDIE CAR
CAFÉ ROYAL
CALF'S HEAD
CALL AGAIN
CALL A HALT
CALL A TAXI
CALLED FOR
CALLED OFF
CALLED OUT
CALL FORTH
CALL HEADS
CALL IT OFF
CALL TAILS
CALM CHEEK
CAME APART
CAME LOOSE
CAMERA SHY
CAMP DAVID
CAMPED OUT
CANAL BANK
CANAL TURN
CANAL ZONE
CANCEL OUT
CANE CHAIR
CANE SUGAR
CANNY SCOT

CAN OF BEER
CAPE DUTCH
CAPE WRATH
CAP IN HAND
CARD INDEX
CARD PARTY
CARD SENSE
CARD TABLE
CARD TRICK
CARGO SHIP
CAROL REED
CARPET BAG
CARRIED ON
CARRY AWAY
CARRY OVER
CARRY SAIL
CAR TRIALS
CAR WINDOW
CARY GRANT
CASHEW NUT
CASH PRICE
CASH PRIZE
CASH TERMS
CAST ABOUT
CAST A LOOK
CAST AN EYE
CAST A SHOE
CAST A SHOW
CAST ASIDE
CAST A SLUR
CAST A VOTE
CAST DOUBT
CAST FORTH
CAST LOOSE
CASTOR OIL
CAT AND DOG
CATCH A BUS
CATCH COLD
CATCH FIRE
CATCH FISH
CAT FAMILY
CATTLE PEN
CAUGHT OUT
CAUSE LIST
CAUSE PAIN
CEASE FIRE
CEASE TO BE
CEASE WORK
CEDAR TREE
CEYLON TEA
CHA CHA CHA
CHAIN DOWN
CHAIN GANG
CHAIN MAIL
CHALKED UP
CHALK FARM

CHALK IT UP
CHANCE HIT
CHASE AWAY
CHEAP FARE
CHEAP GIFT
CHEAP JACK
CHEAP LINE
CHEAP MILK
CHEAP RATE
CHEAP TRIP
CHEAP WINE
CHECK MATE
CHECK OVER
CHEERED UP
CHERRY PIE
CHESS CLUB
CHIEF COOK
CHIEF HOPE
CHIEF MEAL
CHIEF PART
CHIEF PORT
CHIEF WHIP
CHILD CARE
CHILD STAR
CHILD WIFE
CHINA CLAY
CHINA DOLL
CHINA ROSE
CHINA SHOP
CHIPPED IN
CHOICE BIT
CHOKE BACK
CHOKE DAMP
CHOKE DOWN
CHOP HOUSE
CHOPPY SEA
CHOSEN FEW
CHUMP CHOP
CIRCUS ACT
CITY GATES
CITY STATE
CIVIC DUTY
CIVIL CASE
CIVIL CODE
CIVIL LIFE
CIVIL LIST
CIVIL SUIT
CLAIM BACK
CLAMP DOWN
CLAP HANDS
CLARA BUTT
CLARET CUP
CLASH WITH
CLEAN BILL
CLEAN BLOW
CLEAN DOWN

CLEANED UP	COLD DRINK	CORNY JOKE
CLEAN LIFE	COLD FRAME	COSMIC RAY
CLEAR AWAY	COLD FRONT	COST PRICE
CLEAR CASE	COLD HANDS	COUGHED UP
CLEARED UP	COLD HEART	COUNT DOWN
CLEAR HEAD	COLD JOINT	COUNT UPON
CLEAR LEAD	COLD NIGHT	COUP D'ÉTAT
CLEAR MIND	COLD PLATE	COURT CARD
CLEAR NOTE	COLD SCENT	COURT CASE
CLEAR ROAD	COLD SNACK	COVERED UP
CLEAR SOUP	COLD SOBER	COVER GIRL
CLEAR VIEW	COLD SPELL	COVER OVER
CLEVER DOG	COLD STEEL	COWES WEEK
CLEVER MAN	COLD SWEAT	CRAB SALAD
CLIMB DOWN	COLD WATER	CRACK A NUT
CLIMB OVER	COLLIE DOG	CRACKED UP
CLIP JOINT	COLOUR BAR	CRACK OPEN
CLOCHE HAT	COLWYN BAY	CRACK SHOT
CLOCKED IN	COME ABOUT	CRASH DOWN
CLOCK GOLF	COME AFTER	CRAZY GANG
CLOG DANCE	COME ALIVE	CREAM CAKE
CLOSE CALL	COME ALONG	CREAM PUFF
CLOSE COPY	COME AND GO	CREEP AWAY
CLOSE CROP	COME APART	CRESTA RUN
CLOSED CAR	COME CLEAN	CRIED DOWN
CLOSE DOWN	COME CLOSE	CRIED WOLF
CLOSE GAME	COME EARLY	CRIME WAVE
CLOSE LOOK	COME FIRST	CROPPED UP
CLOSE RACE	COME FORTH	CROSS FIRE
CLOSE UPON	COME LOOSE	CROSS KEYS
CLOSING IN	COME OF AGE	CROSS OVER
CLOTH EARS	COME OFF IT	CROSS WIND
CLOTH FAIR	COME RIGHT	CROUCH END
CLOUD OVER	COME ROUND	CROUCH LOW
CLOUDY SKY	COME THIRD	CROWD WORK
CLUB MONEY	COME UNDER	CROWN CORK
CLUB NIGHT	COMIC CUTS	CROWN LAND
COACH TOUR	COMIC MASK	CROW'S FEET
COACH TRIP	COMIC MUSE	CROW'S NEST
COAL BLACK	COMIC SONG	CRUDE JOKE
COAL BOARD	COMING MAN	CRUDE SALT
COAL FIELD	COMING OUT	CRUEL BLOW
COAL TRUCK	COMMON END	CRUEL FATE
COAST ROAD	COMMON LAW	CRUMPLE UP
COCKED HAT	COMMON LOT	CRUSH DOWN
COCK ROBIN	COMMON MAN	CRY FOR JOY
COCOA BEAN	CONGER EEL	CUBAN HEEL
CODE OF LAW	CONJURE UP	CUBE SUGAR
COFFEE BAR	COOL CHEEK	CUBIC FOOT
COFFEE CUP	COOL DRINK	CUBIC INCH
COFFEE POT	COOLED OFF	CUBIC YARD
COIN A WORD	COOL WATER	CUB MASTER
COIN MONEY	COPIED OUT	CUFF LINKS
COLD AS ICE	COPPER AGE	CUPID'S BOW
COLD BLOOD	CORAL REEF	CUP OF MILK
COLD CREAM	CORDON OFF	CURIO SHOP

CURTAIN UP
CURTIS CUP
CURLY HAIR
CURLY KALE
CUT A CAPER
CUT ACROSS
CUT ADRIFT
CUT AND RUN
CUT A TOOTH
CUT CAPERS
CUT IN HALF
CUT IT FINE
CUTTING IN
CUTTY SARK
CUT UP WELL
CYCLE TOUR

D – 9

DAILY HELP
DAILY MAIL
DAILY WORK
DAIRY FARM
DAIRY HERD
DAIRY MAID
DAISY BELL
DALAI LAMA
DAMP PATCH
DAMP SQUIB
DAMSON JAM
DANCE A JIG
DANCE AWAY
DANCE BAND
DANCE HALL
DANCE STEP
DANCE TUNE
DANDY DICK
DANNY KAYE
DARK BLUES
DARK BROWN
DARK CLOUD
DARK DEEDS
DARK DRESS
DARK GREEN
DARK HORSE
DARK NIGHT
DARTED OUT
DARTS TEAM
DASHED OFF
DASHED OUT
DATE STAMP
DATUM LINE
DAVY JONES
DAWN OF DAY
DAY BEFORE
DAY IS DONE
DAY OF DOOM

DAY OF REST
DAY SCHOOL
DAYS OF OLD
DEAD AHEAD
DEAD DRUNK
DEAD FAINT
DEAD LUCKY
DEADLY SIN
DEAD MARCH
DEAD QUIET
DEAD RIGHT
DEAD SLEEP
DEAD SOBER
DEAD TIRED
DEAD WATER
DEAD WRONG
DEAL A BLOW
DEAL TABLE
DEAN SWIFT
DEAR ENEMY
DEAR HEART
DEAR MADAM
DEATH BLOW
DEATH CELL
DEATH MASK
DEATH RATE
DEATH ROLL
DEATH TRAP
DEATH WISH
DEBIT SIDE
DECK GAMES
DECOY DUCK
DEEP GRIEF
DEEP RIVER
DEEP SLEEP
DEEP SOUTH
DEEP VOICE
DEEP WATER
DEMON KING
DEN OF VICE
DEPOT ONLY
DEPOT SHIP
DE QUINCEY
DEREK BOND
DEREK HART
DE RIGUEUR
DESERT AIR
DESERT RAT
DEVIL'S OWN
DIANA DORS
DIESEL OIL
DIET SHEET
DIG DEEPLY
DIME NOVEL
DIM MEMORY
DINING CAR

DINING OUT
DINNER SET
DIRECT HIT
DIRECT TAX
DIRT CHEAP
DIRT TRACK
DIRTY DICK
DIRTY LOOK
DIRTY PLAY
DIRTY WORD
DIRTY WORK
DISH CLOUT
DISHED OUT
DISH OF TEA
DISK DRIVE
DIXIE LAND
DO A BAD JOB
DO A FAVOUR
DO AS ASKED
DOCK BRIEF
DOCK GREEN
DOCTOR WHO
DODGE CITY
DOG COLLAR
DOG EAT DOG
DOG KENNEL
DOG RACING
DOGS OF WAR
DOG'S TOOTH
DOING FINE
DOING GOOD
DOING TIME
DOING WELL
DO IT AGAIN
DO JUSTICE
DOLLAR GAP
DOLL'S PRAM
DOLLY BIRD
DONE BROWN
DONE THING
DO NOTHING
DON'T WORRY
DO ONE DOWN
DO ONE'S BIT
DOPE FIEND
DO PENANCE
DORA BRYAN
DO REPAIRS
DORSAL FIN
DO THE DEED
DO THE TOWN
DO TO DEATH
DOUBLE ACT
DOUBLE BED
DOUBLED UP
DOUBLE GIN

DOUBLE ONE	DRIVE A BUS	DYING TO GO
DOUBLE ROW	DRIVE A CAR	DYING WISH
DOUBLE RUM	DRIVE AWAY	DYING YEAR
DOUBLE SIX	DRIVE BACK	
DOUBLE TEN	DRIVE HARD	
DOUBLE TOP	DRIVE HOME	E – 9
DOUBLE TWO	DRIVEN MAD	
DOVER ROAD	DRIVE PAST	EACH OF TWO
DOVER SOLE	DR JOHNSON	EACH OTHER
DO WITHOUT	DR KILDARE	EARLY BIRD
DOWN BELOW	DROP A BOMB	EARLY CALL
DOWN GRADE	DROP A HINT	EARLY DAYS
DOWN IN ONE	DROP A LINE	EARLY DOOR
DOWN IN TWO	DROP A NOTE	EARLY HOUR
DOWN QUILT	DROP OF GIN	EARLY LIFE
DOWN RIVER	DROP OF TEA	EARLY PART
DOWN SOUTH	DROPPED IN	EARLY WORM
DOWN STAGE	DROP SHORT	EARN A NAME
DOWN THERE	DRUG FIEND	EARN MONEY
DOWN TOOLS	DRUG HABIT	EAR OF CORN
DOWN TRAIN	DRUG STORE	EASILY LED
DOWN UNDER	DRUM MAJOR	EAST COAST
DO YOU MIND?	DRURY LANE	EASTER DAY
DRAIN AWAY	DRY AS DUST	EASTER EGG
DRAW A BEAD	DRY GINGER	EASTER EVE
DRAW A LINE	DRY HUMOUR	EAST INDIA
DRAW APART	DRY REMARK	EAST LYNNE
DRAW A VEIL	DRY SEASON	EAST SHEEN
DRAW BLANK	DRY SHERRY	EASY AS PIE
DRAW BLOOD	DRY SUMMER	EASY CATCH
DRAW FORTH	DRY WICKET	EASY DEATH
DRAW LEVEL	DUBLIN BAY	EASY FIRST
DRAW MONEY	DUD CHEQUE	EASY GOING
DRAWN FACE	DUDE RANCH	EASY MONEY
DRAWN GAME	DUE NOTICE	EASY PITCH
DRAW TEARS	DUE REWARD	EASY TERMS
DRAW TIGHT	DULL LIGHT	EASY THING
DRAW WATER	DULL SOUND	EASY TIMES
DRAY HORSE	DU MAURIER	EASY TO RUN
DREAM BOAT	DUNCE'S CAP	EASY TO SEE
DREAM GIRL	DUST STORM	EATEN AWAY
DREAM LAND	DUSTY ROAD	EATING OUT
DRESS COAT	DUTCH BARN	EAT NO MEAT
DRESS DOWN	DUTCH DOLL	EDGED TOOL
DRESSED UP	DUTCH OVEN	EDGE ROUND
DRESS RING	DUTCH WIFE	EDGE TOOLS
DRESS SHOW	DUTY BOUND	EIGHT DAYS
DRESS SUIT	DUTY CALLS	EIGHT DEEP
DRESS WELL	DUTY FIRST	EIGHT FEET
DRIED EGGS	DUTY NURSE	EIGHTH DAY
DRIED FIGS	DWARF BEAN	EIGHTH MAN
DRIED MILK	DWELL UPON	EIGHTH ROW
DRIED PEAS	DYING DOWN	EIGHTH TEE
DRIFT AWAY	DYING DUCK	EIGHT QUID
DRILL HALL	DYING RACE	EITHER WAY
DRINK DEEP	DYING SWAN	EL ALAMEIN
		ELBOW ROOM

ELDER WINE
ELDEST SON
ELEVEN MEN
ELMER RICE
EMBER DAYS
EMILE ZOLA
EMIT WAVES
EMPIRE DAY
EMPTY LIFE
EMPTY ROOM
EMPTY SEAT
EMPTY SHOW
EMPTY TALK
EMPTY TANK
END IN GAOL
END IN VIEW
END OF PLAY
END OF TERM
END OF TIME
ENEMY FIRE
ENERGY GAP
EN FAMILLE
ENJOY LIFE
EN PASSANT
EN PENSION
EN RAPPORT
ENTER INTO
ENTRE NOUS
ENTRY CARD
ENTRY FORM
EPIC VERSE
EQUAL RANK
ERASE HEAD
ERIC SYKES
ERRAND BOY
ESKIMO DOG
ESTATE CAR
ET TU BRUTE
EVA BARTOK
EVEN MONEY
EVEN SCORE
EVEN TENOR
EVER AFTER
EVER SINCE
EVERY HOUR
EVERY INCH
EVERY SIDE
EVERY TIME
EVERY WEEK
EVERY WORD
EVERY YEAR
EXACT COPY
EXACT FARE
EXACT TIME
EXIT OMNES
EX OFFICIO

EXTRA COPY
EXTRA FOOD
EXTRA GOOD
EXTRA HELP
EXTRA ROOM
EXTRA SEAT
EXTRA TIME
EXTRA WORK
EYE APPEAL
EYE LOTION
EYE MAKE-UP
EYES FRONT
EYES RIGHT
EYE STRAIN
EZRA POUND

F– 9

FACE ABOUT
FACE CREAM
FACE DEATH
FACE FACTS
FACE IT OUT
FACE NORTH
FACE SOUTH
FACE TOWEL
FACE VALUE
FADING OUT
FAGGED OUT
FAIL TO ACT
FAIL TO SEE
FAIL TO WIN
FAINT HOPE
FAINT LINE
FAIR BREAK
FAIR FIELD
FAIR FIGHT
FAIR JUDGE
FAIRLY NEW
FAIR OFFER
FAIR PRICE
FAIR'S FAIR
FAIR SHARE
FAIR START
FAIR TRADE
FAIR TRIAL
FAIR VALUE
FAIR WORDS
FAIRY CAKE
FAIRY DOLL
FAIRY FOLK
FAIRY KING
FAIRY RING
FAIRY TALE
FAIRY WAND
FAITH CURE

FAKE ALIBI
FALL AMONG
FALL APART
FALLEN OUT
FALL FOR IT
FALL OF MAN
FALL SHORT
FALL UNDER
FALSE CARD
FALSE CASE
FALSE COIN
FALSE GODS
FALSE HAIR
FALSE IDEA
FALSE MOVE
FALSE NAME
FALSE NOSE
FALSE NOTE
FALSE OATH
FALSE PLEA
FALSE STEP
FAMILY CAR
FAMILY MAN
FAMILY PEW
FAMILY ROW
FAMOUS MAN
FANCY CAKE
FANCY FREE
FANCY WORK
FAN DANCER
FANNED OUT
FANNY HILL
FAR AFIELD
FAR BEHIND
FAR BETTER
FAR BEYOND
FAR CORNER
FAR ENOUGH
FARE STAGE
FAR FROM IT
FARMED OUT
FARM HORSE
FARTHER UP
FAR TOO FEW
FAST TRAIN
FAST WOMAN
FATAL BLOW
FATAL DOSE
FATAL HOUR
FATAL MOVE
FATAL URGE
FAT CATTLE
FAT CHANCE
FAT PROFIT
FEED A COLD
FEEL A NEED

FEEL ANGRY	FINALS DAY	FIRST LOVE
FEEL CHEAP	FINAL STEP	FIRST MATE
FEEL FAINT	FINAL TEST	FIRST MEAL
FEEL FRESH	FIND A CLUE	FIRST MOVE
FEEL FUNNY	FIND A FLAT	FIRST NAME
FEEL GIDDY	FIND A HOME	FIRST PAGE
FEEL GREAT	FIND A WIFE	FIRST PART
FEEL HAPPY	FIND FAULT	FIRST POST
FEEL QUEER	FIND MEANS	FIRST RACE
FEEL RIGHT	FIND PEACE	FIRST RATE
FEEL SEEDY	FIND WORDS	FIRST SHOT
FEEL SHAME	FINE BIRDS	FIRST SIGN
FEEL SMALL	FINE BLADE	FIRST SLIP
FEEL SORRY	FINE GRAIN	FIRST STEP
FEE SIMPLE	FINE LINEN	FIRST TEAM
FEET APART	FINE POINT	FIRST TERM
FEET FIRST	FINE SPORT	FIRST TEST
FELL APART	FINE SPRAY	FIRST TIME
FELT A FOOL	FINE TIMES	FIRST TO GO
FELT SILLY	FINE TOUCH	FIRST TURN
FEMALE SEX	FINE VOICE	FIRST WORD
FEMME SOLE	FINE WOMAN	FIRST YEAR
FENCED OUT	FINISH OFF	FISHED OUT
FERRET OUT	FIRE ALARM	FISH KNIFE
FERRY OVER	FIRE A SHOT	FISH PASTE
FEUDAL LAW	FIRE AT SEA	FISH SLICE
FEUDAL TAX	FIRE DRILL	FISH STEAK
FEVER HEAT	FIRE POWER	FISHY EYED
FIELD ARMY	FIRM BASIS	FISHY LOOK
FIELD GREY	FIRM FAITH	FISHY TALE
FIELD TEST	FIRM GOING	FIT FOR USE
FIFTH FORM	FIRM OFFER	FIT OF RAGE
FIFTH HOLE	FIRM PRICE	FIT PERSON
FIFTH PART	FIRM STAND	FITTED OUT
FIFTH RACE	FIRST ARMY	FIT TO BUST
FIFTH TEST	FIRST BALL	FIT TO DROP
FIFTH TIME	FIRST BASE	FIVE CARDS
FIFTY QUID	FIRST BELL	FIVE CLUBS
FIGHT BACK	FIRST BLOW	FIVE DOZEN
FIGHT FAIR	FIRST COAT	FIVE GROSS
FIGHT WITH	FIRST COME	FIVE HOLES
FIG LEAVES	FIRST COPY	FIVE HOURS
FIGURE ONE	FIRST COST	FIVE LUMPS
FIGURE OUT	FIRST CROP	FIVE MILES
FIGURE TEN	FIRST FOOT	FIVE OR SIX
FIGURE TWO	FIRST FORM	FIVE PARTS
FILE A SUIT	FIRST GEAR	FIVE PINTS
FILM ACTOR	FIRST HALF	FIVE SCORE
FILM EXTRA	FIRST HAND	FIVE TIMES
FILM STILL	FIRST HEAT	FIVE TO ONE
FILM STUNT	FIRST HOLE	FIVE TO TEN
FILTER TIP	FIRST HOME	FIVE TO TWO
FINAL BOUT	FIRST LADY	FIVE TOWNS
FINAL HEAT	FIRST LEAD	FIVE WEEKS
FINAL HOPE	FIRST LINE	FIVE YEARS
FINAL MOVE	FIRST LORD	FIX A PRICE

FIXED GAZE	FORM FOURS	FREE OFFER
FIXED IDEA	FOR MY PART	FREE OF TAX
FIXED LOOK	FORTY DAYS	FREE PLACE
FIXED ODDS	FORTY LOVE	FREE PRESS
FIXED STAR	FOR VALOUR	FREE RANGE
FIXED TIME	FOSTER SON	FREE SCOPE
FIXED TYPE	FOUL CRIME	FREE SPACE
FIXED WAYS	FOUL FIEND	FREE STATE
FIZZLE OUT	FOUL SMELL	FREE STYLE
FLAKED OUT	FOUL THROW	FREE TRADE
FLARE PATH	FOUR AWAYS	FREE UNION
FLASH BULB	FOUR BY TWO	FREE VERSE
FLAT BROKE	FOUR CARDS	FREE WHEEL
FLAT TO LET	FOUR CLUBS	FREE WORLD
FLAY ALIVE	FOUR DOZEN	FREEZE OUT
FLESH PINK	FOUR FIVES	FRESH BAIT
FLESH TINT	FOUR FOURS	FRESH EGGS
FLICK AWAY	FOUR GROSS	FRESHEN UP
FLING AWAY	FOUR HOLES	FRESH FACE
FLING DOWN	FOUR HOURS	FRESH FISH
FLING OPEN	FOUR IN ONE	FRESH FOOD
FLIRT WITH	FOUR JACKS	FRESH LOAF
FLIT ABOUT	FOUR KINGS	FRESH MEAT
FLOAT DOWN	FOUR LUMPS	FRESH MILK
FLOOD TIDE	FOUR MILES	FRESH NEWS
FLOOR PLAN	FOUR NINES	FRESH PEAS
FLOOR SHOW	FOUR PAIRS	FRESH ROLL
FLOUR MILL	FOUR PARTS	FRESH WIND
FLOW OF WIT	FOUR PINTS	FRIAR TUCK
FLY AT ZERO	FOUR SCORE	FRIED FISH
FLYING FOX	FOUR SIDES	FRIED FOOD
FLYING LOW	FOUR SIXES	FRIED RICE
FLYING MAN	FOURTH DAY	FRIGID BOW
FLY TO ARMS	FOURTH ROW	FROCK COAT
FOBBED OFF	FOURTH SET	FROM BELOW
FOG SIGNAL	FOURTH TEE	FROM BIRTH
FOLK DANCE	FOUR TIMES	FROM NOW ON
FOLK MUSIC	FOUR TO ONE	FRONT DOOR
FOLLOW OUT	FOUR WEEKS	FRONT LINE
FOOD STORE	FOUR WINDS	FRONT PAGE
FOOD VALUE	FOUR YEARS	FRONT RANK
FOOL ABOUT	FRANK MUIR	FRONT ROOM
FOOL'S MATE	FRANS HALS	FRONT SEAT
FOOT FAULT	FRED EMNEY	FRONT STEP
FORAGE CAP	FRED KARNO	FRONT STUD
FOR A START	FRED PERRY	FRONT VIEW
FOR A WHILE	FREE AGENT	FROWN DOWN
FORCE OPEN	FREE AS AIR	FROWN UPON
FOR EFFECT	FREE BOARD	FROZEN SEA
FOREST LAW	FREE CHINA	FRUIT BOWL
FOR EXPORT	FREE DRINK	FRUIT CAKE
FORKED OUT	FREE ENTRY	FRUIT TART
FORK LUNCH	FREE FIELD	FRUIT TREE
FORM A CORE	FREE FIGHT	FULL BLAST
FORMAL BOW	FREE HOUSE	FULL BLOOM
FORM A RING	FREE LUNCH	FULL BOARD

FULL COVER	GAMMA RAYS	GIVE BIRTH
FULL DRESS	GANG AGLEY	GIVE CHASE
FULL GLASS	GARDEN BED	GIVE EAR TO
FULL GROWN	GAS ATTACK	GIVE FORTH
FULL HEART	GAS COOKER	GIVEN NAME
FULL HOUSE	GAS ENGINE	GIVEN TIME
FULL MARKS	GAS ESCAPE	GIVE PAUSE
FULL OF FUN	GAS HEATER	GIVE PLACE
FULL OF JOY	GAS MANTLE	GIVE TERMS
FULL OF PEP	GATE HOUSE	GIVE VOICE
FULL OF WOE	GATE MONEY	GIVING OUT
FULL PITCH	GATHER WAY	GIVING WAY
FULL PURSE	GAVE CHASE	GLANCE OFF
FULL QUOTA	GAY REVELS	GLASS CASE
FULL SCOPE	GENE AUTRY	GLASS TUBE
FULL SCORE	GENOA CAKE	GLASS VASE
FULL SKIRT	GENTLE SEX	GLIDE AWAY
FULL SPEED	GEORGE FOX	GLOAT OVER
FULL STEAM	GET A CHILL	GLOBAL WAR
FULL STORY	GET ACROSS	GLOOMY DAY
FULL SWING	GET AROUND	GLORY HOLE
FULL TABLE	GET A START	GLOSS OVER
FULL TITLE	GET BEHIND	GNAW IN TWO
FULL VALUE	GET BETTER	GO AGAINST
FULLY CLAD	GET CREDIT	GO A-MAYING
FULLY PAID	GET KILLED	GO AND LOOK
FULLY RIPE	GET MOVING	GOAT'S HAIR
FUND OF WIT	GET THE PIP	GOAT'S MILK
FUNNY BONE	GETTING ON	GO BEGGING
FUNNY FACE	GETTING UP	GO BERSERK
FUNNY FILM	GET TO HEAR	GO BETWEEN
FUNNY HA-HA	GET TO KNOW	GO BOATING
FUNNY IDEA	GET UP LATE	GO BY COACH
FUNNY JOKE	GET WIND OF	GO BY PLANE
FUNNY LIFE	GET WITH IT	GO BY TRAIN
FUNNY TIME	GHOST TOWN	GO BY WATER
FUN PALACE	GIDDY GOAT	GO DANCING
FUR COLLAR	GIFTED MAN	GOD FORBID
FUR GLOVES	GIFT HORSE	GOD OF FIRE
FUR LINING	GIFT TOKEN	GOD OF LOVE
FUR MARKET	GIN AND PEP	GOD OF WINE
FURTHER ON	GIN BOTTLE	GOD'S IMAGE
FURTHER UP	GINGER ALE	GOD'S TRUTH
FUR TRADER	GINGER CAT	GOES ABOUT
	GINGER POP	GOES AFTER
G – 9	GINGER TOM	GOES AHEAD
GAG WRITER	GIN PALACE	GOES BELOW
GAIN POWER	GIPSY LOVE	GOES IN FOR
GALA DRESS	GIPSY MOTH	GOES ROUND
GALA NIGHT	GIRL GUIDE	GOES TO BED
GALE FORCE	GIRLS' HOME	GOES TO POT
GALLOP OFF	GIVE A HAND	GOES TO SEA
GALWAY BAY	GIVE A HINT	GOES TO SEE
GAME CHIPS	GIVE A LEAD	GOES UNDER
GAMES ROOM	GIVE A LIFT	GOES WRONG
GAMING ACT	GIVE A TALK	GO FISHING

GO FLAT OUT	GOOD EATER	GOOD THING
GO FOR A CAB	GOOD FAIRY	GOOD TIMES
GO FOR A DIP	GOOD FAITH	GOOD TO EAT
GO FOR A RUN	GOOD FAULT	GOOD TONIC
GO FOR HELP	GOOD FIELD	GOOD TO SEE
GO FORWARD	GOOD FIGHT	GOOD TRADE
GO HALF-WAY	GOOD GOING	GOOD USAGE
GO HAYWIRE	GOOD GRACE	GOOD VALUE
GO HUNTING	GOOD GRIEF	GOOD VOICE
GO INDOORS	GOOD GUESS	GOOD WAGES
GO IN FRONT	GOOD GUIDE	GOOD WOMAN
GOING AWAY	GOOD HABIT	GOOD WORKS
GOING BACK	GOOD HANDS	GOOD YIELD
GOING BALD	GOOD HEART	GO OFF DUTY
GOING DOWN	GOOD HOTEL	GO ON A DIET
GOING GREY	GOOD HOURS	GO ON AND ON
GOING HOME	GOOD HOUSE	GO ON BOARD
GOING OVER	GOOD IMAGE	GO ONE'S WAY
GOING SLOW	GOOD JUDGE	GO ON LEAVE
GOING WELL	GOOD LAYER	GOOSE FAIR
GOING WEST	GOOD LIGHT	GO OUTSIDE
GO IN ORBIT	GOOD LINES	GO QUIETLY
GO IT ALONE	GOOD LIVER	GO SAILING
GOLD BRAID	GOOD LOOKS	GO SKATING
GOLD BRICK	GOOD LOSER	GO THE PACE
GOLD CHAIN	GOOD LUNCH	GO THROUGH
GOLD COAST	GOOD LUNGS	GO TO EARTH
GOLDEN AGE	GOOD MARKS	GO TO GLORY
GOLDEN BOY	GOOD MATCH	GO TO GRASS
GOLDEN EGG	GOOD MIXER	GO TO HADES
GOLDEN KEY	GOOD MONEY	GO TO PRESS
GOLDEN ROD	GOOD MUSIC	GO TO SLEEP
GOLD FEVER	GOOD NIGHT	GO TOWARDS
GOLD INGOT	GOOD ODOUR	GO TO WASTE
GOLD MEDAL	GOOD OFFER	GO WITHOUT
GOLD MINER	GOOD ORDER	GRACE NOTE
GOLD PAINT	GOOD PATCH	GRAND DUKE
GOLD PLATE	GOOD POINT	GRAND JURY
GOLD TOOTH	GOOD PRICE	GRAND LAMA
GOLD WATCH	GOOD REPLY	GRAND PRIX
GOLF LINKS	GOOD SCORE	GRAND SLAM
GOLF MATCH	GOOD SENSE	GRAND TIME
GOLF WIDOW	GOOD SHAPE	GRAND TOUR
GONE TO BED	GOOD SHAVE	GRAND VIEW
GONE TO POT	GOOD SIGHT	GRASS PLOT
GONE UNDER	GOODS LIFT	GRAVEL PIT
GOOD ACTOR	GOOD SPEED	GRAVE NEWS
GOOD ALIBI	GOOD SPORT	GRAVE NOTE
GOOD ANGEL	GOOD START	GREAT AUNT
GOOD BOOKS	GOOD STATE	GREAT BEAR
GOOD CATCH	GOOD STOCK	GREAT BLOW
GOOD CAUSE	GOOD STORY	GREAT CARE
GOOD CHEER	GOOD STUFF	GREAT DANE
GOOD CLASS	GOOD TABLE	GREAT DEAL
GOOD DEBTS	GOOD TASTE	GREAT DEED
GOOD DODGE	GOOD TERMS	GREAT DRAW

GREAT FAME	GROW STALE	HANGING ON
GREAT FEAT	GROW TIRED	HANG IT ALL
GREAT FIRE	GROW WEARY	HANG ROUND
GREAT FOLK	GUARD DUTY	HANSOM CAB
GREAT GAIN	GUARD ROOM	HAPPY DAYS
GREAT GUNS	GUARDS' TIE	HAPPY GIRL
GREAT HALL	GUARD'S VAN	HAPPY HOME
GREAT HELP	GUESS WHEN	HAPPY IDEA
GREAT IDEA	GUEST ROOM	HAPPY LIFE
GREAT LIFE	GUEST STAR	HAPPY MEAN
GREAT LOSS·	GUIDE BOOK	HAPPY OMEN
GREAT MANY	GUILTY ACT	HAPPY PAIR
GREAT MIND	GUILTY MAN	HAPPY TRIO
GREAT NAME	GUINEA HEN	HARD APORT
GREAT NEWS	GUM ARABIC	HARD CATCH
GREAT PAIN	GUN BATTLE	HARD CLIMB
GREAT PITY	GUN TURRET	HARD COURT
GREAT SCOT	GUY FAWKES	HARD FACTS
GREAT SEAL	GYPSY BAND	HARD FIGHT
GREAT SHIP		HARD FRANC
GREAT TIME	**H – 9**	HARD FROST
GREEDY PIG		HARD FRUIT
GREEK CITY	HAIL A TAXI	HARD GOING
GREEK FIRE	HAIR CREAM	HARD GRIND
GREEK FLAG	HAIR SHIRT	HARD HEART
GREEK GIFT	HAIR STYLE	HARD KNOCK
GREEK MYTH	HAIR TONIC	HARD LINES
GREEK PLAY	HALF A LOAF	HARDLY ANY
GREEK BELT	HALF AN EYE	HARD MONEY
GREEN EYES	HALF A PINT	HARD STEEL
GREEN FEES	HALF A QUID	HARD STUFF
GREEN FIGS	HALF A TICK	HARD TIMES
GREEN FLAG	HALF AWAKE	HARD TO GET
GREEN HILL	HALF A YARD	HARD TO SAY
GREEN LINE	HALF CROWN	HARD TO SEE
GREEN PARK	HALF DRUNK	HARD USAGE
GREEN PEAS	HALF HITCH	HARD VOICE
GREEN ROOM	HALF LIGHT	HARD WATER
GREY CLOUD	HALF PRICE	HARD WORDS
GREY GOOSE	HALF SHARE	HARE'S FOOT
GREY HAIRS	HALF SPEED	HARRY LIME
GREY HORSE	HALF TRUTH	HARRY TATE
GREY SKIES	HALF WAY UP	HARSH NOTE
GRILL ROOM	HALL TABLE	HARSH TONE
GRIM DEATH	HAM AND EGG	HARSH WORD
GRIM SMILE	HAM COMMON	HAVE A BALL
GRIM TRUTH	HAMMER OUT	HAVE A BASH
GRIND DOWN	HAND BASIN	HAVE A BATH
GRIP TIGHT	HAND IT OUT	HAVE A BITE
GROUND NUT	HAND OF GOD	HAVE A CARE
GROW ANGRY	HAND ROUND	HAVE A CASE
GROW APART	HANDS DOWN	HAVE A CHAT
GROW FRUIT	HAND'S TURN	HAVE A COLD
GROWING UP	HAND TOWEL	HAVE A DATE
GROW OLDER	HANDY ANDY	HAVE A GAME
GROW PEARS	HANG ABOUT	HAVE A HOPE
	HANG HEAVY	

HAVE A LARK	HERE BELOW	HOLD AT BAY
HAVE A LOOK	HERNE HILL	HOLD CHEAP
HAVE A MEAL	HEROIC AGE	HOLD COURT
HAVE AN EGG	HEY PRESTO	HOLD FORTH
HAVE A PLAN	HIGH ABOVE	HOLD HANDS
HAVE A REST	HIGH ALTAR	HOLDING ON
HAVE A SEAT	HIGH BIRTH	HOLD STILL
HAVE A SHOT	HIGH BOOTS	HOLD TIGHT
HAVE A STAB	HIGH CHAIR	HOLD UNDER
HAVE A TRIM	HIGH COURT	HOLD WATER
HAVE A WISH	HIGH DUTCH	HOLE IN ONE
HAVE FAITH	HIGHER PAY	HOLLOW OUT
HAVE IT OUT	HIGH FEVER	HOLLY BUSH
HAVE LUNCH	HIGH GRADE	HOLY BIBLE
HAVE MERCY	HIGH HEELS	HOLY GHOST
HAVE ROOTS	HIGH HOPES	HOLY GRAIL
HAVE SENSE	HIGH HORSE	HOLY MOSES
HAVE TASTE	HIGH JINKS	HOLY PLACE
HAVE VIEWS	HIGH LEVEL	HOLY SMOKE
HAVE WORDS	HIGH MARKS	HOLY WATER
HAVING FUN	HIGH PITCH	HOME AGAIN
HAZEL EYES	HIGH PLANE	HOME FIRES
HEAD FIRST	HIGH PRICE	HOME FLEET
HEADS I WIN	HIGH SCORE	HOME FRONT
HEAD TO TOE	HIGH SPEED	HOME GROWN
HEAP ABUSE	HIGH SPOTS	HOME GUARD
HEAVE AWAY	HIGH STOOL	HOME JAMES
HEAVE COAL	HIGH TABLE	HOME LOVER
HEAVY BLOW	HIGH TOWER	HOMELY WIT
HEAVY COLD	HIGH VALUE	HOME MATCH
HEAVY COST	HIGH VOICE	HOME OF MAN
HEAVY FALL	HIGH WAGES	HOME TRADE
HEAVY FINE	HIGH WATER	HOME TRUTH
HEAVY GUNS	HIGH WORDS	HONEST MAN
HEAVY HAND	HILL TRIBE	HOOT OF JOY
HEAVY LIDS	HIRE A MAID	HOPE CHEST
HEAVY LOAD	HIRED HAND	HOP GARDEN
HEAVY LOSS	HIRED HELP	HOP PICKER
HEAVY MEAL	HIRED THUG	HORSE FAIR
HEAVY MIST	HIS HONOUR	HORSE RACE
HEAVY ODDS	HIT AND RUN	HORSE SHOW
HEAVY POLL	HITCH HIKE	HOT AIR GUN
HEAVY POST	HIT FOR SIX	HOT AS HELL
HEAVY RAIN	HIT NUMBER	HOTEL BILL
HEAVY SEAS	HIT OR MISS	HOTEL ROOM
HEAVY SNOW	HIT PARADE	HOT NUMBER
HEAVY TASK	HIT SINGLE	HOT POTATO
HEAVY TYPE	HIT THE HAY	HOT SHOWER
HEAVY WIND	HIT WICKET	HOT SPRING
HEAVY WORK	HIT WILDLY	HOT SUMMER
HELL TO PAY	HOG THE LOT	HOT TEMPER
HELP ALONG	HOI POLLOI	HOUND DOWN
HELPED OUT	HOIST SAIL	HOUSE BOAT
HEM STITCH	HOLD ALOFT	HOUSE FULL
HENRY FORD	HOLD ALOOF	HOUSE NAME
HENRY HALL	HOLD A SALE	HOUSE RENT

HOUSE ROOM
HOW ABSURD!
HOW AND WHY
HOW ARE YOU?
HOW GOES IT?
HUDSON BAY
HUE AND CRY
HUM AND HAW
HUMAN LIFE
HUMAN RACE
HUMAN SOUL
HUMBLE PIE
HUNGRY MAN
HUNTED AIR
HURL ABUSE
HURRIED UP
HURRY AWAY
HURRY BACK
HURRY DOWN
HURRY HOME
HURRY OVER
HURST PARK
HURT PRIDE
HUSH MONEY

I – 9

ICE CORNET
ICED DRINK
ICED WATER
ICE HOCKEY
ICY MANNER
ICY REMARK
IDA LUPINO
IDEAL GIFT
IDEAL HOME
IDEAL TIME
IDEAL TYPE
IDEAL WIFE
IDLE BOAST
IDLE FANCY
IDLE HANDS
IDLE HOURS
IDLE STORY
IDLE TEARS
ILL AT EASE
ILL CHANCE
ILL EFFECT
ILL FAVOUR
ILL HEALTH
ILL HUMOUR
ILL REPORT
ILL REPUTE
IN A BAD WAY
IN A BIG WAY
IN A BUNKER
IN A CANTER

IN A CLINCH
IN A CORNER
IN A CRISIS
IN ADVANCE
IN A FRENZY
IN A GROOVE
IN A HUDDLE
IN A MINUTE
IN A MOMENT
IN A MUDDLE
IN ANY CASE
IN A PICKLE
IN ARREARS
IN A SCRAPE
IN A SECOND
IN A STUPOR
IN A TANGLE
IN A TEMPER
IN A TRANCE
IN AUSTRIA
IN A VACUUM
IN BAD FORM
IN BAD PART
IN BELGIUM
IN BETWEEN
IN BILLETS
IN BLOSSOM
IN BORSTAL
IN CARDIFF
IN CIRCLES
IN CIVVIES
INCOME TAX
IN COMFORT
IN COMMAND
IN COMPANY
IN CONCERT
IN CONTACT
IN CONTROL
IN COPPERS
IN COSTUME
IN COUNCIL
IN CUSTODY
IN DEFAULT
IN DEFENCE
IN DENMARK
IN DESPAIR
IN DIALECT
INDIAN INK
INDIAN TEA
IN DISGUST
IN DISPUTE
IN DRY DOCK
IN DUE TIME
IN EARNEST
IN ECHELON
IN ENGLAND

IN ENGLISH
INERT MASS
IN FASHION
IN FETTERS
IN FRONT OF
IN FULL CRY
IN GENERAL
IN GERMANY
IN GLASGOW
INGLE NOOK
IN HARBOUR
IN HARMONY
IN HARNESS
IN HOLLAND
IN HUNGARY
IN INFANCY
IN IRELAND
IN ITALIAN
IN ITALICS
IN JANUARY
INK BOTTLE
IN KEEPING
INK ERASER
INLAND SEA
INNER CITY
INNER EDGE
INNER ROOM
INNER SELF
INNER TUBE
IN NEUTRAL
IN NEW YORK
IN NO DOUBT
IN OCTOBER
IN ONE MOVE
IN ONE WORD
IN OUTLINE
IN PASSING
IN POVERTY
IN PRIVATE
IN PROFILE
IN PROTEST
IN PURSUIT
IN REALITY
IN RESERVE
IN RESPECT
IN RETREAT
IN REVERSE
IN RUMANIA
IN RUSSIAN
IN SERVICE
IN SESSION
INSIDE JOB
INSIDE OUT
IN SILENCE
IN SLAVERY
IN SOCIETY

IN SOME WAY	IN THE ROAD	JADE GREEN
IN SPANISH	IN THE SAFE	JAMES BOND
IN SUPPORT	IN THE SNOW	JAMES DEAN
IN TATTERS	IN THE SOUP	JAMES WATT
INTER ALIA	IN THE SWIM	JAM SPONGE
IN THE ALPS	IN THE TEAM	JANE WYMAN
IN THE AREA	IN THE TILL	JAY WALKER
IN THE ARMY	IN THE TOWN	JELLY BABY
IN THE BAND	IN THE VEIN	JENNY LIND
IN THE BANK	IN THE WAKE	JENNY WREN
IN THE BATH	IN THE WARS	JERSEY COW
IN THE BUSH	IN THE WASH	JET ENGINE
IN THE CART	IN THE WEST	JET FLIGHT
IN THE CITY	IN THE WIND	JEWEL CASE
IN THE COLD	INTO FOCUS	JOAN OF ARC
IN THE DARK	IN TOP FORM	JOAN REGAN
IN THE DOCK	IN TOP GEAR	JOB CENTRE
IN THE DUSK	IN TORMENT	JOB OF WORK
IN THE EAST	INTO TOUCH	JOE MILLER
IN THE FACE	IN TRAFFIC	JO GRIMOND
IN THE FALL	IN TRANSIT	JOHN ADAMS
IN THE FILE	IN TRIUMPH	JOHN BLUNT
IN THE FIRE	IN TROUBLE	JOHN BROWN
IN THE FOLD	IN UNIFORM	JOHN CABOT
IN THE FRAY	INVOKE AID	JOHN KEATS
IN THE GODS	IN WAITING	JOHN MILLS
IN THE HOLD	IN WRITING	JOHN SMITH
IN THE HOME	IONIAN SEA	JOHN WAYNE
IN THE KNOW	IPSO FACTO	JOIN HANDS
IN THE LAKE	IRISH BULL	JOIN ISSUE
IN THE LEAD	IRISH EYES	JOINT HEIR
IN THE LIFT	IRISH FLAG	JOINT WILL
IN THE LOFT	IRISH PEER	JOLLY GOOD
IN THE MAIL	IRISH STEW	JOLLY TIME
IN THE MAIN	IRON CROSS	JOLLY WELL
IN THE MASS	IRONED OUT	JOT IT DOWN
IN THE MIND	IRON FRAME	JUDAS KISS
IN THE MINE	IRON GUARD	JUDAS TREE
IN THE MODE	IRON HORSE	JUDGE'S CAP
IN THE MOOD	IRON NERVE	JUDGE WELL
IN THE MOON	IRON TONIC	JUG OF MILK
IN THE NAVY	IRON WORKS	JUMP ABOUT
IN THE NECK	ILSE OF ELY	JUMP AHEAD
IN THE NEST	ISLE OF MAN	JUMP CLEAR
IN THE NEWS	IT'S A CINCH	JUNE BRIDE
IN THE NUDE	IVORY GATE	JUNGLE LAW
IN THE OPEN		JUST A DROP
IN THE OVEN	**J – 9**	JUST CAUSE
IN THE PACK	JACK BENNY	JUST CLAIM
IN THE PARK	JACK FROST	JUST FANCY
IN THE PAST	JACK HOBBS	JUST PRICE
IN THE PINK	JACK JONES	JUST RIGHT
IN THE POST	JACK KETCH	JUST THINK
IN THE RAIN	JACK PAYNE	
IN THE REAR	JACK SPRAT	**K – 9**
IN THE RING	JACK TRAIN	KEEN FIGHT

KEEN FROST
KEEN MATCH
KEEN PRICE
KEEN SIGHT
KEEP A DATE
KEEP AHEAD
KEEP ALIVE
KEEP APART
KEEP ASIDE
KEEP AT BAY
KEEP CLEAR'
KEEP CLOSE
KEEP COUNT
KEEP FAITH
KEEP FRESH
KEEP GOING
KEEP GUARD
KEEP HOUSE
KEEP ON ICE
KEEP ORDER
KEEP QUIET
KEEP SCORE
KEEP SHORT
KEEP SOBER
KEEP STILL
KEEP STOCK
KEEP UNDER
KEEP VIGIL
KEEP WATCH
KEG BITTER
KELLY'S EYE
KEPT AT BAY
KEPT ON ICE
KEPT WOMAN
KERRY BLUE
KEW BRIDGE
KEW PALACE
KEY MOMENT
KEY WORKER
KICKED OFF
KICKED OUT
KID GLOVES
KIEL CANAL
KIND HEART
KINDLY ACT
KIND WORDS
KING CAROL
KING COBRA
KING DAVID
KING HENRY
KING MIDAS
KING PRIAM
KING'S HEAD
KING'S LYNN
KING'S PAWN
KING'S ROAD

KING'S ROOK
KING STORK
KIRBY GRIP
KISS HANDS
KNEEL DOWN
KNEES BEND
KNOCK COLD
KNOCK DOWN
KNOCKED UP
KNOCK HARD
KNOCK ONCE
KNOCK OVER
KNOW AGAIN
KNOW NO LAW
KOREAN WAR
KUBLA KHAN

L – 9

LABOUR DAY
LACK DRIVE
LADIES' BAR
LADIES' DAY
LADIES' MAN
LADY'S MAID
LAG BEHIND
LAGER BEER
LA GUARDIA
LAID WASTE
LAKE HURON
LAKE POETS
LAMB'S WOOL
LAMP SHADE
LAND A BLOW
LAND AGENT
LAND AHEAD
LAND FORCE
LAND OF NOD
LAND ROVER
LAND SPEED
LAP RECORD
LARGE AREA
LARGE ARMY
LARGE BEER
LARGE BILL
LARGE CAST
LARGE CITY
LARGE FLAT
LARGE HEAD
LARGE LOAF
LARGE PORT
LARGE ROOM
LARGE SIZE
LARGE TOWN
LARGE TYPE
LARK ABOUT
LASER BEAM

LASER SHOW
LASHED OUT
LAS PALMAS
LAST APRIL
LAST CRUMB
LAST DANCE
LAST DITCH
LAST DREGS
LAST DRINK
LAST EVENT
LAST FLING
LAST HOURS
LAST LAUGH
LAST NIGHT
LAST MAN IN
LAST MARCH
LAST MATCH
LAST MONTH
LAST NIGHT
LAST OF ALL
LAST OFFER
LAST OF SIX
LAST OF TEN
LAST ORDER
LAST PENNY
LAST PLACE
LAST RITES
LAST ROUND
LAST SCENE
LAST SHIFT
LAST STAGE
LAST STAND
LAST STRAW
LAST TANGO
LAST THING
LAST THROW
LAST TRAIN
LAST TRUMP
LAST VERSE
LAST VISIT
LAST WALTZ
LAST WORDS
LATE CROPS
LATE ENTRY
LATE EXTRA
LATE FROST
LATE HOURS
LATE NIGHT
LATER DATE
LATE RISER
LATE SHIFT
LATE STAGE
LATE START
LATIN CRIB
LATIN RACE
LATTER END

LAUGH AWAY	LESSON TEN	LIME GROVE
LAUGH DOWN	LESSON TWO	LIME JUICE
LAUGH LINE	LESS SPEED	LION'S CAGE
LAUGH OVER	LET HER RIP	LION'S MANE
LAUNCH OUT	LE TOUQUET	LION'S SKIN
LAVA BREAD	LETTER BOX	LION'S TAIL
LAWFUL ACT	LETTING UP	LION TAMER
LAWFUL AGE	LET US PRAY	LIP READER
LAWN MOWER	LEVEL BEST	LIQUID AIR
LAW OFFICE	LEYDEN JAR	LIQUOR LAW
LAW REFORM	LIBEL CASE	LIST PRICE
LAW REPORT	LIBEL SUIT	LITTER BIN
LAW SCHOOL	LIE ASLEEP	LITTER BUG
LAZY BONES	LIE AT REST	LITTLE BIT
LEAD OXIDE	LIE DIRECT	LITTLE BOY
LEAF MOULD	LIE FALLOW	LITTLE DOG
LEAN YEARS	LIE HIDDEN	LITTLE MAN
LEASE LEND	LIE IN WAIT	LITTLE ONE
LEAST SAID	LIFE CLASS	LITTLE TOE
LEAVE A GAP	LIFE CYCLE	LITTLE WAY
LEAVE A TIP	LIFE FORCE	LIVE AGAIN
LEAVE HOME	LIFE STORY	LIVE ALONE
LEAVE OPEN	LIFE STUDY	LIVE ISSUE
LEAVE OVER	LIFE'S WORK	LIVE ON AIR
LEAVE ROOM	LIFT A HAND	LIVE OR DIE
LEAVE WORD	LIGHT BLUE	LIVE ROUGH
LEAVE WORK	LIGHT BULB	LIVING LIE
LE BOURGET	LIGHT DIET	LOADED GUN
LED ASTRAY	LIGHT MEAL	LOAD OF HAY
LEFT ALONE	LIGHT RAIN	LOAF SUGAR
LEFT FLANK	LIGHT SIDE	LOATH TO GO
LEFT TO DIE	LIGHTS OUT	LOCAL CALL
LEFT TO ROT	LIGHT SUIT	LOCAL NAME
LEFT WHEEL	LIGHT TANK	LOCAL NEWS
LEGAL CODE	LIGHT UPON	LOCAL TIME
LEGAL FARE	LIGHT WAVE	LOCAL VETO
LEGAL HEIR	LIGHT WINE	LOCKED OUT
LEGAL MIND	LIGHT WORK	LOFTY AIMS
LEGAL TERM	LIGHT YEAR	LOG OF WOOD
LEGER LINE	LIKE A BIRD	LONDON BUS
LEG GLANCE	LIKE A BOMB	LONDON ZOO
LEG OF LAMB	LIKE A CORK	LONG AFTER
LEG OF PORK	LIKE A DUCK	LONG BEACH
LEGS APART	LIKE A FOOL	LONG BEARD
LEG THEORY	LIKE A LAMB	LONG CHALK
LEIGH HUNT	LIKE A LION	LONG DELAY
LEMON CURD	LIKE A MULE	LONG DOZEN
LEMON PEEL	LIKE A SHOT	LONG DRESS
LEMON SOLE	LIKELY LAD	LONG DRINK
LENA HORNE	LIKE MAGIC	LONG DRIVE
LEND A HAND	LIKE MUSIC	LONG GRASS
LEND AN EAR	LIKE SMOKE	LONG HOURS
LEND MONEY	LIKE WATER	LONG LEASE
LEN HUTTON	LILAC TIME	LONG MARCH
LESSON ONE	LILAC TREE	LONG NIGHT
LESSON SIX	LIME GREEN	LONG PANTS

LONG PURSE
LONG QUEUE
LONG RANGE
LONG REACH
LONG REIGN
LONG SIEGE
LONG SIGHT
LONG SINCE
LONG SKIRT
LONG SLEEP
LONG SPELL
LONG STAGE
LONG STORY
LONG TRAIN
LONG TRIAL
LONG VISIT
LONG VOWEL
LONG WAVES
LONG·WHIST
LOOK A FOOL
LOOK AFTER
LOOK AHEAD
LOOK ALIVE
LOOK A MESS
LOOK BLACK
LOOK BLANK
LOOKED FOR
LOOK FRESH
LOOK GRAVE
LOOKING UP
LOOK NIPPY
LOOK RIGHT
LOOK ROUND
LOOK SEEDY
LOOK SHARP
LOOK SILLY
LOOK SMALL
LOOK SMART
LOOK THERE
LOOM LARGE
LOONY LEFT
LOOSE BALL
LOOSE CASH
LOOSE TALK
LOOSE TILE
LORD BYRON
LORD DERBY
LORD MAYOR
LOSE A LIMB
LOSE AN EYE
LOSE COUNT
LOSE FAITH
LOSE HEART
LOSE MONEY
LOSER PAYS
LOSE TOUCH

LOSE TRACK
LOSING BET
LOSING RUN
LOST AT SEA
LOST CAUSE
LOST CHORD
LOST COUNT
LOST HABIT
LOST SCENT
LOST SHEEP
LOST SKILL
LOT OF GOOD
LOTS OF FUN
LOUD KNOCK
LOUD LAUGH
LOUD MUSIC
LOUD NOISE
LOUD PEDAL
LOUD SOUND
LOUD VOICE
LOUNGE BAR
LOVE APPLE
LOVE CHILD
LOVED ONES
LOVE FORTY
LOVELY DAY
LOVE LYRIC
LOVE MATCH
LOVE MY DOG
LOVE OF WAR
LOVE STORY
LOVE TOKEN
LOVING CUP
LOW BRIDGE
LOW CHURCH
LOW COMEDY
LOW DEGREE
LOWER CASE
LOWER DECK
LOWER DOWN
LOWER FORM
LOWER LIFE
LOWER LIMB
LOWER PART
LOW FELLOW
LOW GERMAN
LOW GROUND
LOW INCOME
LOW IN TONE
LOW NUMBER
LOW PERSON
LOW RELIEF
LOW RESORT
LOW RETURN
LOW SALARY
LOW STAKES

LOW STATUS
LUCID MIND
LUCKY DRAW
LUCKY FIND
LUCKY GIRL
LUCKY MOVE
LUCKY OMEN
LUCKY SHOT
LUCKY STAR
LUMP SUGAR
LUNACY ACT
LUNAR YEAR
LUNCH DATE
LUNCH HOUR
LUNCH TIME
LURID PAST
LYING DOWN
LYME REGIS
LYRIC POEM
LYRIC POET

M – 9

MADE OF TIN
MADE READY
MAD HATTER
MAD SCHEME
MAGGIE MAY
MAGIC LAMP
MAGIC RING
MAGIC SIGN
MAGIC WAND
MAGIC WORD
MAIDA VALE
MAIL ORDER
MAIL PLANE
MAIL TRAIN
MAIN FORCE
MAIN ISSUE
MAIN POINT
MAIN THEME
MAIN THING
MAJOR DOMO
MAJOR PART
MAJOR POET
MAJOR ROAD
MAJOR SNAG
MAJOR SUIT
MAJOR WORK
MAKE A BACK
MAKE A BOOK
MAKE A CAKE
MAKE A CALL
MAKE A COPY
MAKE A DATE
MAKE A DEAL
MAKE A FACE

MAKE A FIRE	MAN OF NOTE	METAL RING
MAKE A FUSS	MAN OF RANK	METAL TUBE
MAKE A HOLE	MANOR FARM	METRIC TON
MAKE A JOKE	MANOR PARK	MID-DAY SUN
MAKE A KILL	MANY A SLIP	MIDDLE AGE
MAKE A LIST	MANY A TIME	MIDDLE WAY
MAKE A LOSS	MANY HANDS	MIGHTY FEW
MAKE A MESS	MANY TIMES	MIGHTY MAN
MAKE A MOVE	MANY WORDS	MILD STEEL
MAKE A NOTE	MANY YEARS	MILES AWAY
MAKE A PASS	MAPLE LEAF	MILK CHURN
MAKE A PILE	MAPLE TREE	MILK DRINK
MAKE A PLAN	MAP OF ROME	MILK FLOAT
MAKE A RING	MAPPED OUT	MILK PUNCH
MAKE A SHOW	MARCH AWAY	MILK ROUND
MAKE A SIGN	MARCH HARE	MILK SHAKE
MAKE A SLIP	MARCH PAST	MILK STOUT
MAKE A STIR	MARCH WIND	MILK TEETH
MAKE A TART	MARCO POLO	MILL ABOUT
MAKE A WILL	MARDI GRAS	MILLS BOMB
MAKE A WISH	MARE'S NEST	MINE SHAFT
MAKE CLEAR	MARIA MONK	MINI SKIRT
MAKE FACES	MARKED MAN	MINK STOLE
MAKE FUN OF	MARKET DAY	MINOR PART
MAKE HASTE	MARK TWAIN	MINOR POET
MAKE IT BIG	MARRY WELL	MINOR ROAD
MAKE KNOWN	MASKED MAN	MINOR ROLE
MAKE LEGAL	MASS MEDIA	MINOR SUIT
MAKE MERRY	MASTER KEY	MINT JULEP
MAKE MONEY	MASTER SPY	MINT SAUCE
MAKE MUSIC	MATCH PLAY	MINUS SIGN
MAKE NOTES	MATE IN ONE	MINUTE MAN
MAKE OR MAR	MATE IN TWO	MISSED OUT
MAKE PEACE	MATT MONRO	MISS WORLD
MAKE PLAIN	MAX ADRIAN	MIX A DRINK
MAKE PLANS	MAX MILLER	MIXED NUTS
MAKE READY	MEANS TEST	MOCK TRIAL
MAKE SENSE	MEAN TO SAY	MODEL FARM
MAKE TERMS	MEANT WELL	MODEL GIRL
MAKE TIGHT	MEASLY LOT	MODERN ART
MAKE-UP MAN	MEAT JELLY	MONEY DOWN
MAKE-UP SET	MEAT PASTE	MONIED MAN
MAKE VALID	MEDAL PLAY	MONKEY NUT
MAKE WHOLE	MEDIUM DRY	MONT BLANC
MAKE WORSE	MEIN KAMPF	MOON ABOUT
MAKING HAY	MEL FERRER	MOON RIVER
MALE CHOIR	MEN AT WORK	MOOT POINT
MALE MODEL	MEND A FUSE	MORAL CODE
MALE NURSE	MENTAL AGE	MORAL EVIL
MALE SCREW	MERCY SEAT	MORAL TONE
MALE VOICE	MERE TRUTH	MORE HASTE
MAN AND BOY	MERE WORDS	MORE LIGHT
MAN FRIDAY	MERRY QUIP	MORE MONEY
MAN OF IRON	MERRY TUNE	MORE SCOPE
MAN OF KENT	MESS ABOUT	MORSE CODE
MAN OF MARK	METAL DISC	MORTAL SIN

MOSAIC LAW	NAVAL RANK	NEXT OF KIN
MOSS GREEN	NAVAL TYPE	NEXT STAGE
MOST NOBLE	NAZI PARTY	NEXT TRAIN
MOST OF ALL	NEARLY ALL	NEXT WORLD
MOTHER WIT	NEAR SIGHT	NICE POINT
MOTOR RACE	NEAR THING	NICE SLEEP
MOTOR ROAD	NEAT DRINK	NICE TASTE
MOTOR SHOW	NEAT TRICK	NICE TO SEE
MOTOR TOUR	NEEDS MUST	NIGHT BELL
MOUNTED UP	NEON LIGHT	NIGHT CLUB
MOUNT ETNA	NET AMOUNT	NIGHT DUTY
MOUTH WASH	NET LOSSES	NIGHT LIFE
MOVE ABOUT	NET PROFIT	NIGHT SPOT
MOVE ALONG	NET RESULT	NIGHT WORK
MOVE APART	NET RETURN	NILE DELTA
MOVE HOUSE	NEVER A ONE	NILE GREEN
MOVE ROUND	NEVER FEAR	NINE CARAT
MOVIE STAR	NEVER MIND	NINE DOZEN
MOWED DOWN	NEVER MORE	NINE GROSS
MRS BEATON	NEVER REST	NINE HOLES
MRS GRUNDY	NEVER SEEN	NINE HOURS
MR SPEAKER	NEVER STOP	NINE LIVES
MUCH ALIKE	NEVER VARY	NINE MILES
MUCH LATER	NEW BARNET	NINE MUSES
MUCH MOVED	NEW BONNET	NINE OR TEN
MUCH NOISE	NEW CUSTOM	NINE PARTS
MUCH SPACE	NEW DEALER	NINE SCORE
MUCH WORSE	NEW ENERGY	NINE TIMES
MUFFIN MAN	NEW FOREST	NINE TO ONE
MUFFLED UP	NEW FRIEND	NINE WEEKS
MUG OF BEER	NEW GROUND	NINE YEARS
MUM AND DAD	NEW GUINEA	NINTH HOLE
MUSIC CASE	NEW JERSEY	NINTH PART
MUSIC HALL	NEW MASTER	NINTH TIME
MUSIC ROOM	NEW MEMBER	NISSEN HUT
MUTINY ACT	NEW METHOD	NOBLE LADY
MUTTON FAT	NEW MEXICO	NOBLE LINE
MUTUAL AID	NEW PLANET	NOBLE LORD
MUTUAL AIM	NEW POLICY	NOBLE PART
MY DARLING	NEW POTATO	NOBLE PILE
MY DEAR SIR	NEW READER	NO CHICKEN
MY HUSBAND	NEW RECORD	NO COMMENT
MY OPINION	NEW REGIME	NOD ASSENT
	NEW ROMNEY	NO DEFENCE
	NEW SCHOOL	NO EFFECTS
N – 9	NEW SERIES	NO FISHING
	NEWS FLASH	NO FLOWERS
NAKED CITY	NEWS SHEET	NO FOOLING
NAKED LADY	NEW STREET	NO FURTHER
NANNY GOAT	NEWS VALUE	NO GROUNDS
NARROW WIN	NEW YORKER	NO HAWKERS
NASTY BLOW	NEXT APRIL	NO INKLING
NASTY MESS	NEXT ISSUE	NOISES OFF
NASTY TYPE	NEXT MAN IN	NO KIDDING
NASTY WORD	NEXT MARCH	NO MANNERS
NATIVE WIT	NEXT MONTH	NO MEANING
NAVAL BASE		

NO MISTAKE	ODD PERSON	ON A STRING
NO MODESTY	OFF CENTRE	ON A TANDEM
NO ONE ELSE	OFF CHANCE	ON AVERAGE
NO PARKING	OFF COLOUR	ON BALANCE
NO QUARTER	OFF COURSE	ONCE AGAIN
NO REGRETS	OFFICE BOY	ONCE A WEEK
NORTH CAPE	OFFICE CAT	ONCE A YEAR
NORTH POLE	OFF MOMENT	ONCE ROUND
NORTH SIDE	OFF SEASON	ON DEPOSIT
NORTH STAR	OFF TARGET	ON DISPLAY
NORTH WIND	OFF THE AIR	ON DRAUGHT
NORTH ZONE	OFF THE MAP	ON DRY LAND
NOSMO KING	OFF THE PEG	ONE ACROSS
NO SMOKING	OFF THE SET	ONE AND ALL
NO SPIRITS	OF NO AVAIL	ONE BETTER
NO STRINGS	OF NO WORTH	ONE DEGREE
NOT AT HOME	OF ONE MIND	ONE DOLLAR
NOT FAR OFF	OF THAT ILK	ONE EIGHTH
NOT GUILTY	OIL COOKER	ONE FOR ALL
NOTHING ON	OILED SILK	ONE FOURTH
NOT HUNGRY	OIL HEATER	ONE GALLON
NOT IN TIME	OIL TANKER	ONE GUINEA
NOT LATELY	OIL TYCOON	ONE IN FIVE
NOT LIKELY	OLD AND NEW	ONE IN FOUR
NOT PROVEN	OLD AS ADAM	ONE IN NINE
NOTRE DAME	OLD AS TIME	ONE LENGTH
NO TROUBLE	OLD BAILEY	ONE-MAN DOG
NOT SO GOOD	OLD BRANDY	ONE MINUTE
NOT STRONG	OLD BUFFER	ONE MOMENT
NOT TOO BAD	OLD CODGER	ONE NATION
NOT UP TO IT	OLD COUPLE	ONE O'CLOCK
NOT WANTED	OLD CROCKS	ONE OCTAVE
NOVEL ITEM	OLD CUSTOM	ONE OF MANY
NO WAITING	OLD EMPIRE	ONE SECOND
NO WARNING	OLDEN DAYS	ONE'S EQUAL
NUMBER ONE	OLD FAMILY	ONE STRIPE
NUMBER SIX	OLD FELLOW	ONE STROKE
NUMBER TEN	OLD FOSSIL	ONE TO COME
NUMBER TWO	OLD FRIEND	ONE TOO FEW
NUTS IN MAY	OLD MASTER	ONE WICKET
	OLD METHOD	ON HALF PAY
	OLD PEOPLE	ON HOLIDAY
O – 9	OLD RECORD	ON IMPULSE
	OLD REEKIE	ONION SKIN
OAST HOUSE	OLD RÉGIME	ONION SOUP
OBJET D'ART	OLD ROWLEY	ONLY CHILD
OCEAN LANE	OLD SAYING	ONLY HUMAN
OCEAN WAVE	OLD SCHOOL	ON MY RIGHT
OCTANE GAS	OLD SCORES	ON ONE SIDE
ODD CHOICE	OLD STAGER	ON ONE'S OWN
ODD CORNER	OLD STREET	ON ONE'S WAY
ODD COUPLE	OLIVE TREE	ON PURPOSE
ODD JOB MAN	ON ACCOUNT	ON RATIONS
ODD MAN OUT	ON A CHARGE	ON RUNNERS
ODD MOMENT	ON A PICNIC	ON SUNDAYS
ODD NUMBER	ON ARRIVAL	ON THE BALL
ODD OR EVEN		

ON THE BEAM
ON THE BEAT
ON THE BOIL
ON THE BONE
ON THE CHIN
ON THE DOLE
ON THE EDGE
ON THE FARM
ON THE FIRE
ON THE FLAT
ON THE HEAD
ON THE HOOF
ON THE HOUR
ON THE HUNT
ON THE JURY
ON THE LAKE
ON THE LAND
ON THE LEAD
ON THE LEFT
ON THE LINE
ON THE LIST
ON THE MAKE
ON THE MARK
ON THE MEND
ON THE MENU
ON THE MOON
ON THE MOVE
ON THE NAIL
ON THE NOSE
ON THE PIER
ON THE RACK
ON THE RISE
ON THE ROAD
ON THE ROOF
ON THE SIDE
ON THE SPOT
ON THE TOTE
ON THE TOWN
ON THE TROT
ON THE TURF
ON THE TURN
ON THE WALL
ON THE WANE
ON THE WING
ON THIN ICE
ON TUESDAY
OPEN A SHOP
OPEN COURT
OPEN DRAIN
OPEN EVENT
OPEN FIELD
OPEN GRATE
OPEN GRAVE
OPEN HEART
OPEN HOUSE
OPEN MATCH

OPEN MOUTH
OPEN ORDER
OPEN PORES
OPEN PURSE
OPEN SHIRT
OPEN SKIES
OPEN SPACE
OPEN TO ALL
OPEN WOUND
ORANGE GIN
ORANGE PIP
ORDER ARMS
ORDER BOOK
ORDER FORM
ORGAN LOFT
ORGAN STOP
ORLOP DECK
ORRIS ROOT
OTHER DAYS
OTHER HALF
OTHER SELF
OTHER SIDE
OUR CHOICE
OUR FATHER
OUT AND OUT
OUT AT HEEL
OUTER EDGE
OUTER SKIN
OUTER TUBE
OUT FOR TEA
OUT OF A JOB
OUT OF BOND
OUT OF DATE
OUT OF DEBT
OUT OF FORM
OUT OF GEAR
OUT OF HAND
OUT OF LINE
OUT OF LOVE
OUT OF LUCK
OUT OF MIND
OUT OF PAIN
OUT OF PITY
OUT OF PLAY
OUT OF STEP
OUT OF TIME
OUT OF TOWN
OUT OF TRIM
OUT OF TRUE
OUT OF TUNE
OUT OF TURN
OUT OF WORK
OUT ON BAIL
OUT WITH IT
OUT YONDER
OVER AGAIN

OVER FORTY
OVER PROOF
OVER THERE
OVER TO YOU
OWEN NARES
OWEN TUDOR
OWN A HOUSE
OXFORD DON
OYSTER BAR
OYSTER BED

P – 9

PACKED OUT
PADDED OUT
PAGE EIGHT
PAGE PROOF
PAGE SEVEN
PAGE THREE
PAINT OVER
PAIRED OFF
PALE BROWN
PALE GREEN
PALE HANDS
PALM BEACH
PALMY DAYS
PANAMA HAT
PANEL GAME
PANT AFTER
PAPAL BULL
PAPER BACK
PAPER BILL
PAPER CLIP
PAPER DOLL
PAPER GAME
PAPER MILL
PAPER OVER
PAPER RACK
PAPER WORK
PARCEL OUT
PARIAH DOG
PARI PASSU
PARIS GOWN
PARK BENCH
PARKED CAR
PARK ROYAL
PARTY GAME
PARTY LINE
PARTY MOOD
PARTY RULE
PARTY WALL
PARTY WHIP
PAS DE DEUX
PAS DU TOUT
PASS ALONG
PASSED OFF
PASSED OUT

PASSING BY	PHONEY WAR	PLAY A FISH
PASSING ON	PIANO DUET	PLAY A JOKE
PASS ROUND	PIANO LEGS	PLAY AN ACE
PAST GLORY	PIANO SOLO	PLAY A NOTE
PAST SHAME	PICK A LOCK	PLAY A PART
PAST TENSE	PICK A TEAM	PLAY BINGO
PATCHED UP	PICKED MAN	PLAY BOWLS
PATCH IT UP	PICKED OFF	PLAY BY EAR
PATNA RICE	PICKED OUT	PLAY CARDS
PATROL CAR	PICK FRUIT	PLAY CHESS
PAVED ROAD	PICK HOLES	PLAY DARTS
PAVED WALK	PICKING UP	PLAYED OUT
PAWN'S MOVE	PICK OAKUM	PLAY FALSE
PAY A VISIT	PIECE RATE	PLAY GAMES
PAY DOUBLE	PIED PIPER	PLAY HAVOC
PAY HOMAGE	PIER GLASS	PLAY POKER
PAY IN FULL	PIGEON PIE	PLAY ROUGH
PAYING OUT	PIGGY BANK	PLAY SHARP
PAY IN KIND	PIG MARKET	PLAY TO WIN
PAY OFFICE	PILAU RICE	PLAY WHIST
PAY ON CALL	PILLAR BOX	PLEASE SIR
PAY ONE OUT	PILOT FISH	PLOD ALONG
PAY PACKET	PINE AFTER	PLUGGED IN
PAY RANSOM	PINK ICING	PLUMP DOWN
PEACE PACT	PINK PEARL	PLUS FOURS
PEACH TREE	PIN-UP GIRL	PLY A TRADE
PEAKED CAP	PIOUS DUTY	POETIC ART
PEARL BUCK	PIOUS HOPE	POINT DUTY
PEAR MELBA	PIPE DREAM	POISON GAS
PEGGED OUT	PIPE MAJOR	POISON IVY
PENAL CODE	PIPE MUSIC	POISON PEN
PENAL LAWS	PIPING HOT	POKE FUN AT
PENAL WORK	PISTON ROD	POKER DICE
PEN AND INK	PITCH DARK	POKER FACE
PEN FRIEND	PITCHED IN	POKER HAND
PENNY BANK	PITCH INTO	POLA NEGRI
PENNY POST	PITCH UPON	POLAR BEAR
PENNY WISE	PIT PONIES	POLE VAULT
PEPPER POT	PIT STALLS	POLICE BOX
PEP UP PILL	PIT WORKER	POLICE CAR
PER CAPITA	PIXIE RING	POLICE DOG
PER CENTUM	PLACE A BET	POLISH OFF
PER CONTRA	PLACE KICK	POLITE ACT
PERRY COMO	PLACE NAME	POLO MATCH
PETAL SOFT	PLAIN CAKE	POODLE CUT
PETER COOK	PLAIN COOK	POOK'S HILL
PETER WEST	PLAIN FACT	POOR CATCH
PETIT FOUR	PLAIN FOOD	POOR CHILD
PET NOTION	PLAIN JANE	POOR CLASS
PETROL CAN	PLAIN WORK	POOR DEVIL
PETROL TAX	PLAN AHEAD	POOR GRADE
PET THEORY	PLANE TREE	POOR GUIDE
PETTY CASH	PLANT LIFE	POOR HOUSE
PETTY JURY	PLATE RACK	POOR JUDGE
PEWTER POT	PLAY ABOUT	POOR LIGHT
PHONE CALL	PLAY A CARD	POOR MARKS

POOR MATCH	PRO PATRIA	Q – 9
POOR SCORE	PROPER DAY	
POOR SPORT	PROPER MAN	QUEEN ANNE
POOR START	PROPER WAY	QUEEN BESS
POOR STUFF	PROPPED UP	QUEEN MARY
POOR TABLE	PROSE POEM	QUEEN BIRD
POOR TASTE	PROUD STEP	QUEEN CARD
POOR THING	PROVE TRUE	QUEER COVE
POOR THROW	PRUNE AWAY	QUEER FISH
POOR VALUE	PUBLIC EYE	QUEUE HERE
POOR VOICE	PUFFED OUT	QUICK FIRE
POOR WOMAN	PULL A FACE	QUICK SALE
POOR YIELD	PULL AHEAD	QUICK STEP
POP NUMBER	PULL APART	QUICK TIME
POPPED OFF	PULL ASIDE	QUICK WITS
POP RECORD	PULLED OFF	QUICK WORK
POP SINGER	PULLED OUT	QUIET LIFE
PORT LIGHT	PULL FACES	QUIET READ
POST EARLY	PULL IT OFF	QUIET TIME
POT THE RED	PULL IT OUT	QUIET TONE
POUND AWAY	PULL ROUND	QUITE A FEW
POUND COIN	PULL TIGHT	QUITE FULL
POUND NOTE	PULL WIRES	QUITE GOOD
POUR FORTH	PUNCH BOWL	QUITE NEAR
POWDER KEG	PUNCH LINE	QUITE NICE
POWER DIVE	PUNIC WARS	QUITE SURE
POWER PACK	PUPPY LOVE	QUITE WELL
POWER UNIT	PURE SPITE	
PRAY ALOUD	PURE WATER	R – 9
PRESS BACK	PURE WHITE	
PRESS CLUB	PURE WOMAN	RABBIT PIE
PRESS DATE	PUSH ASIDE	RACE AHEAD
PRESS DOWN	PUSHED OFF	RACE RIOTS
PRESSED ON	PUSHED OUT	RACE TRACK
PRESS GANG	PUT ACROSS	RACING CAR
PRESS HARD	PUT AT EASE	RACING MAN
PRESS HOME	PUT IN GAOL	RACING SET
PRESS LAWS	PUT IN GEAR	RACING TIP
PRESS ROOM	PUT IN HAND	RACY STYLE
PRESS SEAT	PUT IN JAIL	RADIO MAST
PRESS SHOW	PUT IN MIND	RADIO PLAY
PRETTY BAD	PUT IN QUOD	RADIO STAR
PRETTY BIG	PUT IT DOWN	RADIO WAVE
PRICE LIST	PUT IT OVER	RAIN BLOWS
PRICE RING	PUT ON AIRS	RAIN CLOUD
PRIME BEEF	PUT ON OATH	RAIN GAUGE
PRIME COST	PUT ON SALE	RAIN WATER
PRISON VAN	PUT ON SHOW	RAISE CAIN
PRIVY SEAL	PUT ON SIDE	RAISE HELL
PRIZE BULL	PUT ON TAPE	RALPH LYNN
PRIZE CREW	PUT PAID TO	RAPID FIRE
PRIZE DRAW	PUT TO ROUT	RAPID RATE
PRIZE LIST	PUT TO WORK	RAREE SHOW
PRIZE POEM	PUT UP BAIL	RARE EVENT
PRIZE RING	PUT UP WITH	RARE STAMP
PROOF COPY	PUZZLE OUT	RARE STEAK
		RARE TREAT

RATE OF PAY	REELED OFF	RIO GRANDE
RAT POISON	REFUSE BIN	RIOT SQUAD
RATTLE OFF	RELAY RACE	RIPE FRUIT
RAVEN HAIR	RELIEF BUS	RISE ABOVE
RAVING MAD	RELIEF MAP	RISE EARLY
RAW CARROT	RENT A FLAT	RISING AIR
RAW COTTON	REPAIR JOB	RISING MAN
RAW SPIRIT	REPLY PAID	RISING SUN
RAW TOMATO	REP PLAYER	RITUAL ACT
RAY OF HOPE	RESCUE BID	RIVAL FIRM
REACH HOME	RHINE WINE	RIVER AVON
REACH LAND	RIB OF BEEF	RIVER BANK
READ A BOOK	RICE PAPER	RIVER BOAT
READ ALOUD	RICH UNCLE	RIVER FISH
READ IN BED	RICH WIDOW	RIVER NILE
READ MORSE	RICH WOMAN	RIVER STYX
READ MUSIC	RIDE IT OUT	RIVER TEST
READ VERSE	RIDE ROUGH	RIVER TRIP
READY CASH	RIDING CAP	ROAD AGENT
READY TO GO	RIDING KIT	ROAD BLOCK
REAL CREAM	RIFLE FIRE	ROAD DRILL
REAL DOUBT	RIFLE SHOT	ROAD METAL
REAL SPORT	RIGHT AWAY	ROAD SENSE
REAL THING	RIGHT BACK	ROAD TO RIO
REAL TONIC	RIGHT BANK	ROAD WORKS
REAL TRUTH	RIGHT CARD	ROAST BEEF
REAL WORLD	RIGHT DOWN	ROAST DUCK
REAR LIGHT	RIGHT FACE!	ROAST LAMB
REAR WHEEL	RIGHT FOOT	ROAST MEAT
REASON WHY	RIGHT FORM	ROAST PORK
REBEL ARMY	RIGHT HALF	ROAST VEAL
RECORD BID	RIGHT HAND	ROBIN HOOD
RECORD RUN	RIGHT HOOK	ROCK 'N' ROLL
RECORD SUM	RIGHT IDEA	ROCK PLANT
RED CARPET	RIGHT LINE	ROD OF IRON
RED CHEEKS	RIGHT MOOD	ROLL ALONG
RED CHEESE	RIGHT MOVE	ROLLING UP
RED CIRCLE	RIGHT NAME	ROLL OF FAT
RED COTTON	RIGHT NOTE	ROMAN BATH
RED DRAGON	RIGHT ROAD	ROMAN CAMP
RED DUSTER	RIGHT RULE	ROMAN NOSE
RED ENSIGN	RIGHT SIDE	ROMAN ORGY
RED GROUSE	RIGHT SIZE	ROMAN POET
RED INDIAN	RIGHT TIME	ROMAN ROAD
RED LETTER	RIGHT TURN	ROMAN TYPE
RED MENACE	RIGHT VIEW	ROMAN WALL
RED MULLET	RIGHT WING	ROMANY RYE
RED PENCIL	RIGHT WORD	ROOK RIFLE
RED PEPPER	RING A BELL	ROOK'S MOVE
RED PLANET	RING AGAIN	ROOK'S NEST
RED RIBAND	RING A PEAL	ROOK'S PAWN
RED RIBBON	RING CRAFT	ROOM TO LET
RED SETTER	RING FALSE	ROOT CAUSE
RED SQUARE	RING FENCE	ROOTED OUT
RED SPIDER	RING ROUND	ROPE ONE IN
REED ORGAN	RIN TIN TIN	ROPE TRICK

ROSE MARIE	RUGBY TEAM	SALT WATER
ROSE PETAL	RUINED MAN	SAM BROWNE
ROSE WATER	RULE OF LAW	SAME AGAIN
ROSS ON WYE	RUM AND PEP	SAME STAMP
ROTTEN EGG	RUM BOTTLE	SAME TO YOU
ROTTEN ROW	RUMP STEAK	SAM WELLER
ROUGH CAST	RUM RATION	SANDY SOIL
ROUGH COAT	RUM RUNNER	SAN MARINO
ROUGH COPY	RUN ACROSS	SANS SOUCI
ROUGH EDGE	RUN A HORSE	SANTA CRUZ
ROUGHED IT	RUN AROUND	SARAH GAMP
ROUGH GAME	RUN ASHORE	SAVAGE DOG
ROUGH IDEA	RUN IT FINE	SAVE MONEY
ROUGH LUCK	RUNNING IN	SAVE SPACE
ROUGH PLAN	RUNNING ON	SAVILE ROW
ROUGH PLAY	RUN OF LUCK	SAW THE AIR
ROUGH ROAD	RUN SECOND	SAX ROHMER
ROUGH SKIN	RUN TOO FAR	SAY CHEESE
ROUGH TIME	RUN TO SEED	SAY LITTLE
ROUGH TYPE	RURAL DEAN	SAY NO MORE
ROUGH WORK	RUSH ABOUT	SAY PLEASE
ROUND FACE	RUSH ORDER	SCALE DOWN
ROUND GAME	RUS IN URBE	SCAPA FLOW
ROUND HAND	RYE WHISKY	SCENT GAME
ROUND HEAD		SCHOOL AGE
ROUND HOLE	**S – 9**	SCHOOL CAP
ROUND OATH	SABLE COAT	SCHOOL TIE
ROUND POND	SACRED COW	SCORE A TRY
ROUND SHOT	SAD ENDING	SCORE CARD
ROUND TOUR	SAD PLIGHT	SCORE DRAW
ROUND TRIP	SAFE CATCH	SCOTCH EGG
ROUTED OUT	SAFE HANDS	SCOTCH FIR
ROVING EYE	SAFE PLACE	SCOTS PINE
ROWAN TREE	SAFEST WAY	SCRAPE OFF
ROWING MAN	SAFETY NET	SCRAP IRON
ROYAL ARMS	SAGE GREEN	SCREAM OUT
ROYAL BLUE	SAIL NORTH	SCREW DOWN
ROYAL DUKE	SAIL FORTH	SCRUM HALF
ROYAL LINE	SAILOR BOY	SEA BATTLE
ROYAL MAIL	SAILOR HAT	SEA BOTTOM
ROYAL MILE	SAIL ROUND	SEA BREEZE
ROYAL MINT	SAINT IVES	SEALED OFF
ROYAL NAVY	SAINT JOAN	SEAMY SIDE
ROYAL PARK	SAINT JOHN	SEARCH FEE
ROYAL ROAD	SAINT PAUL	SEARCH FOR
ROYAL ROBE	SAINT'S DAY	SEARCH OUT
ROYAL SCOT	SALAD BOWL	SEA SHANTY
ROYAL SEAT	SALAD DAYS	SEA TRAVEL
ROYAL TOUR	SALE PRICE	SEA URCHIN
ROY CASTLE	SALES TALK	SEA VOYAGE
ROY ROGERS	SALLY LUNN	SECOND ACT
RUBBED OUT	SALOON BAR	SECOND CUP
RUB GENTLY	SALOON CAR	SECOND DAY
RUDE WORDS	SALT FLATS	SECOND ROW
RUE THE DAY	SALT SPOON	SECOND SET
RUGBY BALL	SALT TALKS	SECOND TEE

SECOND TRY	SEVEN QUID	SHORT POEM
SECRET ART	SEVEN SEAS	SHORT PUTT
SECURE JOB	SEX APPEAL	SHORT READ
SEE A GHOST	SEX SYMBOL	SHORT REST
SEE DOUBLE	SHADY DEAL	SHORT SLIP
SEED PEARL	SHADY NOOK	SHORT SPAN
SEEING RED	SHADY SIDE	SHORT STAY
SEEK A CLUE	SHADY TREE	SHORT STEP
SEEK AFTER	SHAGGY DOG	SHORT TAIL
SEEK PEACE	SHAKE A LEG	SHORT TERM
SEEK SCOPE	SHAKE DOWN	SHORT TIME
SEE NO EVIL	SHAKY HAND	SHORT VIEW
SEE REASON	SHAM FIGHT	SHORT WALK
SEE THINGS	SHAM SLEEP	SHORT WAVE
SEIZE UPON	SHANGRI LA	SHORT WORD
SELECT FEW	SHAPE WELL	SHORT WORK
SELL BADLY	SHARP BEND	SHOUT DOWN
SELL SHORT	SHARP BLOW	SHOVEL HAT
SELL SPACE	SHARP EDGE	SHOVE PAST
SEND A CHIT	SHARP EYES	SHOW CAUSE
SEND A WIRE	SHARP FALL	SHOWED OFF
SEND FORTH	SHARP NOTE	SHOWED OUT
SENIOR BOY	SHARP PAIN	SHOW FIGHT
SENIOR MAN	SHARP RISE	SHOW MERCY
SENNA PODS	SHARP TURN	SHOW ONE IN
SERGE SUIT	SHARP WITS	SHOW PIECE
SERVE TIME	SHARP WORK	SHOW PLACE
SERVE WELL	SHED A TEAR	SHOW ROUND
SET ADRIFT	SHED BLOOD	SHOW SIGNS
SET ALIGHT	SHED LIGHT	SHOW STYLE
SET AT EASE	SHEEP FARM	SHRIEK OUT
SET AT ODDS	SHEER DROP	SHRILL CRY
SET AT REST	SHEER FUNK	SHRIVEL UP
SET A WATCH	SHEER LUCK	SHUT TIGHT
SET COURSE	SHEER SILK	SICK LEAVE
SET EYES ON	SHEET IRON	SICKLY HUE
SET FIRE TO	SHELF LIFE	SIDE ISSUE
SET IN HAND	SHELL PEAS	SIGHT GAME
SET MOVING	SHIP'S BELL	SIGHT LAND
SET ON EDGE	SHIP'S BOAT	SIGNAL BOX
SET ON FIRE	SHIP'S GUNS	SIGN A PACT
SET ON FOOT	SHOCK WAVE	SIGN BELOW
SET PHRASE	SHOE BRUSH	SIGNED OFF
SET SPEECH	SHOOT DOWN	SILK PURSE
SET SQUARE	SHOP FLOOR	SILK SCARF
SET THEM UP	SHOP FRONT	SILK SOCKS
SETTING IN	SHOP HOURS	SILLY FOOL
SETTING UP	SHOP TO LET	SILLY TALK
SETTLED IN	SHORN LAMB	SILVER CUP
SETTLED UP	SHORT HAIR	SILVER FIR
SET TO WORK	SHORT HEAD	SILVER FOX
SET UP SHOP	SHORT HOLE	SILVER SEA
SEVEN AGES	SHORT LIFE	SILVER URN
SEVEN DAYS	SHORT LIST	SIMON PURE
SEVEN DEEP	SHORT NOTE	SIMPLE SUM
SEVEN FEET	SHORT ODDS	SIMPLY FAB

SING A SONG	SLOUCH HAT	SMOOTH SEA
SINGLE BED	SLOW DEATH	SMUGGLE IN
SINGLE MAN	SLOW MARCH	SNAIL PACE
SINGLE OUT	SLOW MATCH	SNAKE BITE
SING SMALL	SLOW MUSIC	SNAPPED UP
SINK A PUTT	SLOW PULSE	SNEAK AWAY
SINK A WELL	SLOW START	SNEAK PAST
SIREN SONG	SLOW TEMPO	SNOB VALUE
SIREN SUIT	SLOW TRAIN	SNOW QUEEN
SIT AT HOME	SLOW WALTZ	SNOW SCENE
SITTING UP	SLY AS A FOX	SNOW STORM
SIT UP LATE	SLY CORNER	SNOW WHITE
SIX HEARTS	SLY HUMOUR	SNUGGLE UP
SIX MONTHS	SMALL ARMS	SOAP OPERA
SIX O'CLOCK	SMALL BEER	SOAR ABOVE
SIX OUNCES	SMALL BORE	SOBER DOWN
SIX POINTS	SMALL COAL	SOBER FACT
SIX POUNDS	SMALL COIN	SOB SISTER
SIX SPADES	SMALL DEBT	SOCIAL WAR
SIXTH FORM	SMALL DOOR	SODA WATER
SIXTH HOLE	SMALL FEET	SOFT DRINK
SIXTH PART	SMALL FLAT	SOFT FRUIT
SIXTH RACE	SMALL GAME	SOFT GOING
SIXTH TIME	SMALL HEAD	SOFT GOODS
SIX TO FOUR	SMALL HOLE	SOFT HEART
SIX TRICKS	SMALL ITEM	SOFT LIGHT
SIX WHEELS	SMALL LOAF	SOFT MUSIC
SIZE EIGHT	SMALL LOAN	SOFT PEDAL
SIZE SEVEN	SMALL MIND	SOFT THING
SIZE THREE	SMALL PART	SOFT TOUCH
SKATE OVER	SMALL PORT	SOFT VOICE
SKETCH MAP	SMALL RISK	SOFT WATER
SKETCH OUT	SMALL ROOM	SOFT WORDS
SKIM ALONG	SMALL SIZE	SO IT SEEMS
SKIN DIVER	SMALL SLAM	SOLAR TIME
SKIP A MEAL	SMALL SPOT	SOLAR YEAR
SLACK ROPE	SMALL TALK	SOLDIER ON
SLACK TIME	SMALL TOWN	SOLE AGENT
SLANG WORD	SMALL TWIG	SOLEMN VOW
SLATE CLUB	SMALL TYPE	SOLE OWNER
SLAVE AWAY	SMART ALEC	SO LET IT BE
SLAVE CAMP	SMARTEN UP	SOLE TRUST
SLEEP ON IT	SMART GIRL	SOLID BALL
SLEEP WELL	SMART PACE	SOLID BODY
SLEEPY AIR	SMART SUIT	SOLID FOOD
SLIDE BACK	SMART WALK	SOLID FUEL
SLIDE DOWN	SMELL A RAT	SOLID GOLD
SLIM WAIST	SMOKE A LOT	SOLID MASS
SLINK PAST	SMOKE BOMB	SOLID MEAL
SLIPPED IN	SMOKED EEL	SOLID TYRE
SLIPPED UP	SMOKED HAM	SOLID VOTE
SLIT SKIRT	SMOKE RING	SOLO DANCE
SLOP BASIN	SMOKY CITY	SOLO WHIST
SLOPE ARMS	SMOKY FIRE	SOME HOPES
SLOPE DOWN	SMOKY ROOM	SONG CYCLE
SLOPPY JOE	SMOOTH OUT	SONG TITLE

SON OF A GUN	SPOT DANCE	STATE FARM
SOON AFTER	SPOT OF INK	STATUS QUO
SORE PLACE	SPOT PRIZE	STAY ALIVE
SORE POINT	SPOT TO EAT	STAY AWAKE
SORE TRIAL	SPREAD OUT	STAYED OUT
SO TO SPEAK	SPRING OUT	STAYED PUT
SOTTO VOCE	SPUN GLASS	STAY IN BED
SOUL OF WIT	SQUARE JAW	STAY STILL
SOUND BODY	SQUARE LEG	ST BERNARD
SOUND MIND	SQUARE OFF	STEAL AWAY
SOUND TYPE	SQUARE ONE	STEAL PAST
SOUND WAVE	SQUARE PEG	STEAL UP ON
SOUP LADLE	SQUAT DOWN	STEAM BATH
SOUP PLATE	SQUEEZE IN	STEAM IRON
SOUP SPOON	STABLE BOY	STEAM OPEN
SOUR CREAM	STAFF FUND	STEEL BAND
SOUR TASTE	STAFF ROOM	STEEL BILL
SOUTH BANK	STAFF WORK	STEEL MILL
SOUTH POLE	STAGE DOOR	STEEL TAPE
SOUTH SEAS	STAGE NAME	STEEP HILL
SOUTH WIND	STAGE PLAY	STEP ASIDE
SOUTH ZONE	STAGE SHOW	STEP DANCE
SPACE RACE	STAGGER IN	STEP SHORT
SPACE SHIP	STAG PARTY	STEVE CRAM
SPACE SUIT	STALE CAKE	STICK AT IT
SPARE CASH	STALE JOKE	STICK 'EM UP
SPARE COPY	STALE LOAF	STICK FAST
SPARE PART	STALE NEWS	STICK IT ON
SPARE ROOM	STAMP DOWN	STICK TO IT
SPARE TIME	STAMP DUTY	STICKY END
SPARE TYRE	STAND AWAY	STIFF GALE
SPARKS FLY	STAND BACK	STIFF NECK
SPEAK WELL	STAND BAIL	STIFF TEST
SPEECH DAY	STAND DOWN	STILL LIFE
SPEEDED UP	STAND EASY	STILL MORE
SPEED IT UP	STAND FAST	STILL OPEN
SPEED KING	STAND FIRM	STILL ROOM
SPEND TIME	STAND HIGH	STILL WINE
SPILL OVER	STAND IDLE	STINK BOMB
SPILL SALT	STAND OVER	STIRRED UP
SPILT MILK	ST ANDREWS	ST MATTHEW
SPIN A COIN	STAND UP TO	ST MICHAEL
SPIN A DISC	STAR ACTOR	STOCK FARM
SPIN A YARN	STARE DOWN	STOCK LIST
SPIN DRIER	STAR PUPIL	STOCK PART
SPIN ROUND	STARRY SKY	STOCK PILE
SPIT IT OUT	STAR SHELL	STOCK SIZE
SPLIT OPEN	START A ROW	STOKE CITY
SPLIT PEAS	START A WAR	STOLE AWAY
SPLIT VOTE	START BACK	STONE COLD
SPONGE BAG	STARTED UP	STONE DEAD
SPONGE OUT	START TO GO	STONE DEAF
SPORTS CAR	START WITH	STONE WALL
SPORTS DAY	START WORK	STOOP DOWN
SPORTS FAN	STARVE OUT	STOP A BLOW
SPOT CHECK	STATE FAIR	STOP A LEAK

STOP AND GO	SUNK FENCE	TAKE A MEAL
STOP IN BED	SUN LOUNGE	TAKE AMISS
STOPPED UP	SUNNY SIDE	TAKE AN ELL
STOP PRESS	SUN VALLEY	TAKE A NOTE
STOP SHORT	SUN YAT-SEN	TAKE APART
STOP THIEF!	SUPPOSE SO	TAKE A PEEP
STOP VALVE	SURE THING	TAKE A PILL
STORE AWAY	SURE TO WIN	TAKE A REST
STORM CONE	SURVEY MAP	TAKE A RISK
STORMY SEA	SUSAN SHAW	TAKE A SEAT
ST PANCRAS	SWAGGER IN	TAKE A SNAP
ST PATRICK	SWALLOW UP	TAKE A TAXI
STRAP DOWN	SWARM OVER	TAKE A TEST
STRAW POLL	SWEAR BY IT	TAKE A TOSS
STRAW VOTE	SWEAR WORD	TAKE A TRAM
STRAY AWAY	SWEEP AWAY	TAKE A TRIP
STREAK OUT	SWEEP DOWN	TAKE A TURN
STREAM OUT	SWEEP PAST	TAKE A VIEW
STREET MAP	SWEET CORN	TAKE A VOTE
STRETCH UP	SWEET DISH	TAKE A WALK
STRIDE OFF	SWEET NELL	TAKE A WIFE
STRIDE OUT	SWEET PEAS	TAKE COVER
STRIKE OFF	SWEET SHOP	TAKE DRUGS
STRIKE OIL	SWEET SONG	TAKE HEART
STRIKE OUT	SWEET WINE	TAKE IN TOW
STRIKE PAY	SWELL IDEA	TAKE ISSUE
STRING BAG	SWELL TIME	TAKE LEAVE
STRING OUT	SWEPT AWAY	TAKE LUNCH
STRIP BARE	SWING BACK	TAKE MY TIP
STRIP CLUB	SWING HIGH	TAKEN DOWN
STRONG ALE	SWISS ALPS	TAKE NOTES
STRONG ARM	SWISS CITY	TAKE ON OIL
STRONG BOX	SWISS NAVY	TAKE PAINS
STRONG MAN	SWISS ROLL	TAKE PLACE
STRONG TEA	SWITCH OFF	TAKE PRIDE
STRUCK OFF	SWOOP DOWN	TAKE RISKS
STRUCK OUT		TAKE ROOMS
STRUNG OUT	T – 9	TAKE SHAPE
STUD HORSE	TAB HUNTER	TAKE SIDES
STUDIO ONE	TABLE BIRD	TAKE SNUFF
STUD POKER	TABLE FISH	TAKE STEPS
STUDY FORM	TABLE SALT	TAKE STOCK
STUDY HARD	TABLE TALK	TAKE TURNS
SUB JUDICE	TABLE WINE	TAKE UP ART
SUDDEN END	TAKE ABACK	TAKING OFF
SUDDEN FIT	TAKE A BATH	TAKING OUT
SUEZ CANAL	TAKE A CARD	TALE OF WOE
SUGAR BEET	TAKE A CASE	TALK ABOUT
SUGAR CANE	TAKE A COPY	TALKED BIG
SUGAR PLUM	TAKE A CURE	TALKED OUT
SUIT AT LAW	TAKE A DROP	TALK ROUND
SULTRY AIR	TAKE A FALL	TALK SENSE
SUMMING UP	TAKE AFTER	TALK TRIPE
SUN BONNET	TAKE A HAND	TALL ORDER
SUNDAY TEA	TAKE A HINT	TALL STORY
SUN HELMET	TAKE A LOOK	TALL WOMAN

TANK CORPS	THE BALTIC	THE OLD WAY
TAR BARREL	THE BIG TOP	THE ORIENT
TAROT CARD	THE BOARDS	THE PAPERS
TASK FORCE	THE BOTTOM	THE PEOPLE
TASMAN SEA	THE BOUNTY	THE PLAGUE
TAWNY PORT	THE BOURSE	THE PLOUGH
TAX DEMAND	THE BOWERY	THE POLICE
TAX FIDDLE	THE BROADS	THE PUBLIC
TAX REBATE	THE BUDGET	THE QUEENS
TAX RELIEF	THE CINEMA	THE RABBLE
TAY BRIDGE ·	THE CLERGY	THE RED SEA
TEA FOR TWO	THE COLBYS	THE RINGER
TEA GARDEN	THE CREEPS	THE RIVALS
TEA KETTLE	THE CRIMEA	THE ROCKET
TEA LEAVES	THE DALEKS	THE RUBBER
TEAR ABOUT	THE DANUBE	THE SCOTCH
TEAR ALONG	THE DELUGE	THE SCRIPT
TEAR APART	THE DESERT	THESE DAYS
TEA RATION	THE EMPIRE	THE SENATE
TEAR IN TWO	THE FALLEN	THE SEVERN
TEDDY BEAR	THE FINISH	THE SHAKES
TEDDY GIRL	THE FLICKS	THE SHIRES
TELL NO LIE	THE FLOODS	THE SIGHTS
TELL NO ONE	THE FRENCH	THE SOLENT
TELL TALES	THE FÜHRER	THE SPHINX
TEMPLE BAR	THE FUTURE	THE SPLITS
TEMPT FATE	THE GANGES	THE SPOILS
TENDER AGE	THE GENTRY	THE SPRING
TEN MONTHS	THE GOSPEL	THE SQUIRE
TENNIS ACE	THE GRACES	THE STATES
TENNIS NET	THE GUARDS	THE STITCH
TEN O'CLOCK	THE HILTON	THE STOCKS
TENOR CLEF	THE ICE AGE	THE STONES
TENOR DRUM	THE JET AGE	THE STRAND
TENOR OBOE	THE JUNGLE	THE SUMMER
TEN OUNCES	THE KAISER	THE TATLER
TEN POINTS	THE LANCET	THE TEMPLE
TEN POUNDS	THE LATEST	THE THAMES
TEN ROUNDS	THE LATTER	THE TICKET
TENTH HOLE	THE LEVANT	THE TIVOLI
TENTH PART	THE LIVING	THE UMPIRE
TENTH TIME	THE LIZARD	THE UNSEEN
TEST MATCH	THE LOSERS	THE WAY OUT
TEST PAPER	THE LOUVRE	THE WINNER
TEST PIECE	THE MAQUIS	THE WINTER
TEST PILOT	THE MASSES	·THEY'RE OFF!
TEXAS CITY	THE MASTER	THICK HAIR
THAT'S LIFE	THE MEDWAY	THICK HEAD
THAT'S THAT	THEME SONG	THICK MIST
THE ALBANY	THE METHOD	THICK SKIN
THE ALBION	THE MIKADO	THICK SNOW
THE ALLIES	THE MINUET	THICK SOUP
THE AMAZON	THE MORGUE	THICK WIRE
THE ARMADA	THE MOVIES	THIN BLOOD
THE AUTUMN	THE OCCULT	THINK BACK
THE AZORES	THE OLD VIC	THINK BEST

THINK FAST	TIED HOUSE	TOOL CHEST
THING HARD	TIE IN A BOW	TOO LITTLE
THINK LONG	TIGER HUNT	TO ONE SIDE
THINK OVER	TIGER LILY	TOO STRONG
THIN ON TOP	TIGER MOTH	TOP DRAWER
THIN SHELL	TIGHTEN UP	TOP PEOPLE
THIN SLICE	TIGHT GRIP	TOP SECRET
THIN TWINE	TIGHT HAND	TOP STOREY
THIRD FORM	TIGHT REIN	TOP TO TAIL
THIRD GEAR	TIGHT SPOT	TOP TWENTY
THIRD HAND	TIME BEING	TOP WEIGHT
THIRD HEAT	TIME CHECK	TORCH SONG
THIRD HOLE	TIME FLIES	TORY PARTY
THIRD JUMP	TIME LIMIT	TOSS ABOUT
THIRD LINE	TIME OF DAY	TOSS A COIN
THIRD PART	TIME OF WAR	TOSS ASIDE
THIRD RACE	TIME STUDY	TOSS FOR IT
THIRD RATE	TIME TAKEN	TOSSING UP
THIRD TEAM	TIME TO EAT	TOTAL COST
THIRD TERM	TIME TO PAY	TOTAL LOSS
THIRD TEST	TINDER BOX	TOTEM POLE
THIRD TIME	TIN HELMET	TOTE PRICE
THIRD WEEK	TIN LIZZIE	TO THE BONE
THIRD YEAR	TIN OF SOUP	TO THE BRIM
THIRST FOR	TIN OPENER	TO THE EAST
THIRTY ALL	TIP AND RUN	TO THE FORE
THIS EARTH	TIPPED OFF	TO THE FULL
THIS MONTH	TIPSY CAKE	TO THE GOOD
THIS WAY IN	TIP-UP SEAT	TO THE HILT
THIS WAY UP	TIRED EYES	TO THE LAST
THORPE BAY	TIRING JOB	TO THE LEFT
THRASH OUT	TIT FOR TAT	TO THE LIFE
THREE ACES	TITHE BARN	TO THE MOON
THREE ACTS	TITIAN RED	TO THE WEST
THREE DAYS	TITLE DEED	TO THIS DAY
THREE DEEP	TITLE PAGE	TOUCH DOWN
THREE EGGS	TITLE ROLE	TOUCHED UP
THREE FEET	TITO GOBBI	TOUCH UPON
THREE LAPS	TO A DEGREE	TOUCH WOOD
THREE PIPS	TOAST RACK	TOUGHEN UP
THREE QUID	TO BE BRIEF	TOUGH LUCK
THREE SETS	TODAY WEEK	TOUGH MEAT
THREE STAR	TODDLE OFF	TOUGH SKIN
THREE TENS	TOGGED OUT	TOUGH SPOT
THROW A FIT	TOILET SET	TOWER HILL
THROW AWAY	TOKEN VOTE	TOWER OVER
THROW BACK	TO LEEWARD	TOWN CLERK
THROW DOWN	TOMMY FARR	TOWN CRIER
THROWN OUT	TOM PEARSE	TOWN HOUSE
THROW OPEN	TOM SAWYER	TOWN MOUSE
THROW OVER	TON OF COAL	TOY POODLE
TICKED OFF	TON OF COKE	TRACE BACK
TIC-TAC MAN	TON OF LEAD	TRACK DOWN
TIDAL FLOW	TON OF SALT	TRACK SUIT
TIDAL RACE	TON WEIGHT	TRADE BOOM
TIDAL WAVE	TOOK PLACE	TRADE FAIR

TRADE MARK	TUN OF BEER	TWO WHEELS
TRADE NAME	TUN OF WINE	
TRADE WIND	TURFED OUT	U – 9
TRAIL ARMS	TURK'S HEAD	UGLY AS SIN
TRAIL BOSS	TURN ABOUT	UGLY CROWD
TRAIN FARE	TURN AGAIN	UNCLE TOBY
TRAIN LOAD	TURN A HAIR	UNDER A BAN
TRAM DEPOT	TURN ASIDE	UNDER ARMS
TRAMPLE ON	TURNED OFF	UNDER FIRE
TRAP THREE	TURNED OUT	UNDER OATH
TREAD DOWN·	TURN GREEN	UNDER SAIL
TREE HOUSE	TURNING IN	UNDER SEAL
TREE STUMP	TURNING UP	UNHEARD OF
TRIAL GAME	TURN IT OFF	UNHOLY JOY
TRIAL JURY	TURN LOOSE	UNHOLY ROW
TRIAL SPIN	TURN NASTY	UNION CARD
TRIAL TRIP	TURN RIGHT	UNION FLAG
TRIBAL LAW	TURN ROUND	UNION JACK
TRIBAL WAR	TURN TO ICE	UNIT TRUST
TRICKY BIT	TURN WHITE	UP AGAINST
TRICKY JOB	TWEED SUIT	UP AND AT 'EM
TRIED HARD	TWELVE MEN	UP AND AWAY
TRIED IT ON	TWICE A DAY	UP AND DOWN
TRILBY HAT	TWICE FIVE	UP AND OVER
TRIM WAIST	TWICE FOUR	UP COUNTRY
TRIPPED UP	TWICE NINE	UP FOR SALE
TROJAN WAR	TWICE OVER	UPPER CASE
TROT ALONG	TWICE TOLD	UPPER DECK
TROT IT OUT	TWIGGED IT	UPPER FORM
TRUDGE OFF	TWIN GIRLS	UPPER HAND
TRUE VALUE	TWIN SCREW	UPPER LIMB
TRUE WORTH	TWIN SOULS	UPPER PART
TRUMP CARD	TWO A PENNY	UP THE HILL
TRUNK CALL	TWO COPIES	UP THE LINE
TRUNK LINE	TWO FIFTHS	UP THE POLE
TRUNK ROAD	TWO FOR ONE	UP THE WALL
TRUSSED UP	TWO FOR TEA	UP TO SNUFF
TRUST DEED	TWO HALVES	URCHIN CUT
TRUST FUND	TWO HEARTS	URIAH HEEP
TRUTH DRUG	TWO LOAVES	URSA MAJOR
TRUTH GAME	TWO MONTHS	URSA MINOR
TRY HARDER	TWO NINTHS	USE AS A PEG
TRY IN VAIN	TWO O'CLOCK	USUAL TEXT
TRY TO STOP	TWO OUNCES	UTTER LOSS
TSETSE FLY	TWO POINTS	UTTER RUIN
TUBAL CAIN	TWO POUNDS	
TUBE TRAIN	TWO QUARTS	V – 9
TUCK ONE IN	TWO ROUNDS	VACANT LOT
TUCK ONE UP	TWO SPADES	VADE MECUM
TUDOR ROSE	TWO STOOLS	VAGUE HOPE
TULIP TREE	TWO STRAWS	VAGUE IDEA
TULSE HILL	TWO THIRDS	VAIN ABUSE
TUMBLE OFF	TWO TO COME	VAIN BOAST
TUMBLE OUT	TWO TRICKS	VAIN GLORY
TUMMY ACHE	TWO VERSES	VANITY BAG
TUNNY FISH	TWO VOICES	VAST FRAME

VAULT OVER
VEER RIGHT
VEER ROUND
VENIAL SIN
VERSE FORM
VERS LIBRE
VERY IMAGE
VERY LGHT
VERY OFTEN
VERY QUICK
VERY STEEP
VERY SWEET
VEX A SAINT
VICE SQUAD
VICE VERSA
VICKI BAUM
VIC OLIVER
VIDEO DISC
VIDEO TAPE
VILLA PARK
VIN DU PAYS
VINGT ET UN
VIOLIN BOW
VISUAL AID
VITAL PART
VITAL ROLE
VIVE LE ROI
VIVID BLUE
VOID SPACE
VOLTE FACE
VOLUME ONE
VOLUME SIX
VOLUME TEN
VOLUME TWO
VOTING AGE
VOTING DAY
VOX HUMANA
VOX POPULI

W – 9

WAGE CLAIM
WAGE PAUSE
WAGES BILL
WAGE SCALE
WAGE SLAVE
WAIST HIGH
WAIT ABOUT
WAIT FOR IT!
WAIT FOR ME!
WAIT TABLE
WAIT THERE
WAKE EARLY
WAKES WEEK
WALK ABOUT
WALKED OFF
WALKED OUT

WALKER CUP
WALK ON AIR
WALK OUT ON
WALTZ HOME
WALTZ KING
WALTZ TIME
WALTZ TUNE
WANDER OFF
WANDER OUT
WANTED MAN
WAR DAMAGE
WAR EFFORT
WAR GRAVES
WAR HEROES
WAR LEADER
WARM HEART
WARM NIGHT
WARM PLACE
WARM SPELL
WAR MUSEUM
WARM WATER
WARNED OFF
WAR OFFICE
WAR ON WANT
WAR POLICY
WAR RECORD
WAR VICTIM
WAR WORKER
WASH CLEAN
WASHED OUT
WASPS' NEST
WASP STING
WASP WAIST
WASTE AWAY
WASTE FOOD
WASTE LAND
WASTE TIME
WATCH OVER
WATER BABY
WATER DOWN
WATER FOWL
WATER HOLE
WATER JUMP
WATER LILY
WATER MAIN
WATER POLO
WATER RATE
WATER TANK
WAVE ASIDE
WAVE A WAND
WAX CANDLE
WAX EFFIGY
WAX FIGURE
WAX STRONG
WAY BEHIND
WAY OF LIFE

WEAK CHEST
WEAKER SEX
WEAK HEART
WEAK POINT
WEAK STATE
WEAK STYLE
WEAK THING
WEAK VOICE
WEAK WOMAN
WEALTH TAX
WEAR A HALO
WEAR A MASK
WEAR BLACK
WEAVE A WEB
WEB OF LIES
WEEDED OUT
WEIGH DOWN
WEIGHED IN
WELCOME IN
WELL AGAIN
WELL AHEAD
WELL AIRED
WELL BEGUN
WELL BELOW
WELL OILED
WELL SET UP
WELL SPENT
WELL TAPED
WELSH BARD
WELSH HARP
WENT AHEAD
WENT BELOW
WENT FORTH
WENT ROUND
WENT TO BED
WENT TO POT
WENT TO SEA
WENT TO WAR
WENT UNDER
WENT WRONG
WEST COAST
WEST FRONT
WEST POINT
WEST WALES
WET SEASON
WET SPONGE
WET WICKET
WHALE MEAT
WHAT A LARK!
WHAT A LIFE!
WHAT A PITY!
WHAT'S WHAT
WHEAT GERM
WHEEL AWAY
WHERE IS IT?
WHIP ROUND

WHISK AWAY	WIN A PRIZE	WRENCH OUT
WHITE BEAR	WIND GAUGE	WRITE BACK
WHITE CITY	WINDING UP	WRITE DOWN
WHITE FISH	WIND SCALE	WRITE HOME
WHITE FLAG	WINDY SIDE	WRITE WELL
WHITE GOLD	WIN EASILY	WRONG DATE
WHITE HAIR	WINE GLASS	WRONG DOOR
WHITE HEAT	WINE PARTY	WRONG IDEA
WHITE HOPE	WIN FAVOUR	WRONG MOVE
WHITE KING	WINGED ANT	WRONG NAME
WHITE LADY	WINKLE OUT	WRONG RATE
WHITE LEAD	WIN OR LOSE	WRONG ROAD
WHITE LINE	WIN RENOWN	WRONG SIDE
WHITE LOAF	WIN THE CUP	WRONG STEP
WHITE MARK	WIN THE DAY	WRONG TIME
WHITE MEAT	WIPE CLEAN	WRONG TURN
WHITE MICE	WIRE BRUSH	WRONG VIEW
WHITE NILE	WIRE FENCE	WRONG WORD
WHITE NOTE	WISE WOMAN	WROUGHT UP
WHITE PAWN	WITCH HUNT	WYATT EARP
WHITE PINE	WITH A BANG	WYE VALLEY
WHITE PORT	WITH A WILL	
WHITE RACE	WITH SKILL	Y – 9
WHITE ROOK	WITH SUGAR	YACHT CLUB
WHITE ROSE	WOMAN'S MAN	YACHT RACE
WHITE SALE	WOMEN ONLY	YARD OF ALE
WHITE SPOT	WOMEN'S LIB	YEA AND NAY
WHITE STAR	WONDER WHY	YELLOW DOG
WHITE WINE	WOODEN BOX	YELLOW SEA
WHOLE SKIN	WOODEN LEG	YES PLEASE
WICKED LIE	WOOD GREEN	YET TO COME
WICKED ONE	WOOD NYMPH	YORKED OUT
WIDE APART	WORD MAGIC	YOUNG BIRD
WIDE AWAKE	WORK BENCH	YOUNG GIRL
WIDE BERTH	WORKED OUT	YOUNG FOLK
WIDE FIELD	WORKER BEE	YOUNG IDEA
WIDE GUESS	WORK IT OUT	YOUNG LOVE
WIDE RANGE	WORK LOOSE	YOUNG THUG
WIDE SCOPE	WORK OF ART	YOUR FAULT
WIDE SWEEP	WORK PARTY	YOUR GRACE
WIDE WORLD	WORKS BAND	YOUR SHARE
WIGAN PIER	WORK STUDY	YOUTH CLUB
WILD BEAST	WORKS WELL	
WILD GOOSE	WORK TABLE	Z – 9
WILD GRASS	WORLD BANK	ZOO INMATE
WILD GUESS	WORLD FAIR	ZUYDER ZEE
WILD HORSE	WORLD'S END	
WILD NIGHT	WORLD TOUR	
WILD PARTY	WORSE LUCK	A – 10
WILD STATE	WORST PART	ABE LINCOLN
WILD THYME	WORST TEAM	A BIT PAST IT
WILL POWER	WORTH A LOT	ABJECT FEAR
WILL TO WIN	WORTH A TRY	ABLE FELLOW
WIN A FIGHT	WORTHY AIM	ABLE SEAMAN
WIN A MATCH	WRAPPED UP	ABLE TO COPE
WIN A POINT	WRAP ROUND	ABOARD SHIP

ABOVE BOARD
ABOVE IT ALL
ABOVE PRICE
ABOVE WATER
ABRUPT EXIT
ACCESS TIME
ACE OF CLUBS
ACE SERVICE
ACETIC ACID
ACHING FEET
ACHING VOID
ACID REMARK
ACID TONGUE
ACT AS AGENT
ACT AS COACH
ACT AS GUIDE
ACTIVE LIFE
ACTIVE LIST
ACTIVE MIND
ACTIVE PART
ACT OF FAITH
ACT OF FOLLY
ACT OF GRACE
ACT OF MERCY
ACT OF PIETY
ACT OF UNION
ACT THE FOOL
ACT THE GOAT
ACT THE HERO
ACT THE HOST
ACT THE PART
ACUTE ANGLE
ADAM AND EVE
ADAM'S APPLE
ADD A CLAUSE
ADDIS ABABA
ADELE LEIGH
ADOPTED SON
ADVICE NOTE
ADVISE WELL
AERIAL VIEW
AFRICA STAR
AFTER A TIME
AFTER DEATH
AFTER HOURS
AFTER LUNCH
AFTER TODAY
A GREAT DEAL
A GREAT MANY
AID AND ABET
AIM TOO HIGH
AIR CUSHION
AIR DEFENCE
AIR DISPLAY
AIR FREIGHT
AIR HOSTESS

AIR MARSHAL
AIR SERVICE
AIR WARFARE
ALARM CLOCK
ALBERT HALL
ALF'S BUTTON
ALL BUT A FEW
ALL COLOURS
ALL CORRECT
ALL DAY LONG
ALL FORLORN
ALL FOR LOVE
ALL HALLOWS
ALL HAYWIRE
ALL IN A HEAP
ALL IN ORDER
ALL KEYED UP
ALL MIXED UP
ALL MOD CONS
ALL OF A GLOW
ALL OF A HEAP
ALL OF A KIND
ALL PARTIES
ALL PRESENT
ALL SET TO GO
ALL THE BEST
ALL THE LUCK
ALL THE MORE
ALL THE RAGE
ALL THE REST
ALL THE SAME
ALL THE TIME
ALL THE YEAR
ALL THROUGH
ALL-TIME LOW
ALL TOO SOON
ALL TOO WELL
ALMOND CAKE
ALMOND TREE
ALMOST DEAD
ALMOST FULL
ALMOST OVER
ALPACA COAT
ALPINE CLUB
ALPINE RACE
ALTAR CLOTH
AMBER LIGHT
AMBLE ALONG
AMEN CORNER
AMPLE CAUSE
AMPLE MEANS
AMPLE SCOPE
AMY JOHNSON
AND ALL THAT
AND SO FORTH
AND SO TO BED

AND THE LIKE
AND THE REST
ANGEL CHILD
ANGLED SHOT
ANGORA GOAT
ANGORA WOOL
ANGRY SCENE
ANGRY WORDS
ANILINE DYE
ANIMAL FARM
ANIMAL FOOD
ANIMAL GRAB
ANIMAL LIFE
ANKLE SOCKS
ANNABEL LEE
ANNE BOLEYN
ANNO DOMINI
ANNUAL RENT
ANOTHER DAY
ANOTHER WAY
ANSWER BACK
ANY OLD IRON
ANY OLD TIME
APPLE GREEN
APPLE SAUCE
APPLIED ART
APRICOT JAM
APRON STAGE
APT ANALOGY
APT SCHOLAR
AQUA FORTIS
ARABIAN SEA
ARAB LEAGUE
ARABLE FARM
ARAB LEGION
ARABLE LAND
ARAB STATES
ARCHED BACK
ARENA STAGE
ARMED FORCE
ARMED GUARD
ARMED TRUCE
ARMS AKIMBO
ARM'S LENGTH
ARMY DOCTOR
ARMY ORDERS
ARRIVE LATE
ART GALLERY
ARTHUR RANK
ART STUDENT
ART SUBJECT
ART THEATRE
AS ARRANGED
ASCOT HEATH
ASCOT RACES
AS INTENDED

ASK A FAVOUR
ASK FOR HELP
ASK FOR MORE
ASK FOR TIME
ASK TOO MUCH
AS MAN TO MAN
AS PER USUAL
AS PROMISED
ASTON VILLA
ASTRAL BODY
AT ALL COSTS
AT ALL HOURS
AT ALL TIMES
AT ANY PRICE
AT A PREMIUM
AT A STRETCH
AT A TANGENT
AT A VENTURE
AT DAYBREAK
AT DAYLIGHT
AT FULL TIDE
AT GUN-POINT
AT HALF-MAST
AT ITS WORST
AT LONG LAST
ATOMIC BOMB
ATOMIC PILE
AT ONE'S BEST
AT ONE'S SCOOP
AT ONE'S DOOR
AT ONE'S EASE
AT ONE'S FEET
AT ONE'S POST
AT ONE'S SIDE
AT SEA LEVEL
ATTEND MASS
AT THE ALTAR
AT THE DERBY
AT THE FRONT
AT THE LOCAL
AT THE OPERA
AT THE READY
AT THE SLOPE
AT THE WHEEL
AT THE WORST
AT VARIANCE
AT WHAT TIME?
AUBURN HAIR
AULD REEKIE
AU PAIR GIRL
AUTO-REPEAT
AUTUMN WIND
AVA GARDNER
AVANT GARDE
AVERAGE AGE
AVERAGE MAN

AVERAGE OUT
AVID DESIRE
AWFUL SIGHT
AWKWARD AGE
AXE TO GRIND
AXLE GREASE

B – 10

BABE IN ARMS
BABE UNBORN
BABY FARMER
BABY'S DUMMY
BABY SITTER
BACK A HORSE
BACK A LOSER
BACK GARDEN
BACK IN TIME
BACK MARKER
BACK NUMBER
BACK RASHER
BACK STAIRS
BACK STITCH
BACK STREET
BACK STROKE
BACK TO BACK
BACK TO BASE
BACK TO WORK
BACON CURER
BAD ACCOUNT
BAD ACTRESS
BAD BARGAIN
BAD CLIMATE
BAD COMPANY
BAD CONDUCT
BAD DICTION
BAD EXAMPLE
BAD FORTUNE
BAD GRAMMAR
BAD HARVEST
BAD HUSBAND
BAD LEARNER
BAD LOOKOUT
BAD MANAGER
BAD MANNERS
BAD MISTAKE
BAD OUTLOOK
BAD QUALITY
BAD SERVANT
BAD SERVICE
BAD SOCIETY
BAD TACTICS
BAD THEATRE
BAD WEATHER
BAD WRITING
BAG OF BONES
BAG OF FLOUR

BAG OF NAILS
BAGS OF TIME
BAITED TRAP
BAKED APPLE
BAKED BEANS
BAKER'S SHOP
BALANCE DUE
BALLET SHOE
BALL OF FIRE
BALL OF WOOL
BALTIC PORT
BANANA BOAT
BANANA SKIN
BAND LEADER
BAND OF HOPE
BAND OF IRON
BANDY WORDS
BANK RAIDER
BANK ROBBER
BANK TO BANK
BANK VAULTS
BANNED BOOK
BANTAM COCK
BAN THE BOMB
BARBARY APE
BARBED WIRE
BARD OF AVON
BARE BOARDS
BARE CHANCE
BARELY PASS
BARLEY WINE
BAR PARLOUR
BARREN LAND
BASE MOTIVE
BASIC TRUTH
BASIL BRUSH
BAT AND BALL
BATH OLIVER
BATTEN DOWN
BATTER DOWN
BATTERY HEN
BAWDY HOUSE
BEACH GAMES
BEACHY HEAD
BEACON FIRE
BEAK STREET
BEARER BOND
BEAR GARDEN
BEAR IN MIND
BEAR MALICE
BEAR WITH ME
BEAT HOLLOW
BEAT THE AIR
BEAUTY SHOP
BEAUTY SPOT
BE CHAIRMAN

BECKY SHARP
BECOME LESS
BECOME SANE
BEDDED DOWN
BED OF NAILS
BED OF ROSES
BEEF CATTLE
BEER BARREL
BEER BOTTLE
BEER CELLAR
BEER GARDEN
BEFORE DAWN
BEFORE DUSK
BEFORE LONG
BEFORE NOON
BEFORE TIME
BEG A FAVOUR
BEG FOR MORE
BEG FOR TIME
BEGGAR MAID
BEGIN AGAIN
BEHAVE WELL
BEHIND BARS
BEHIND TIME
BE INFERIOR
BELL THE CAT
BELOW DECKS
BELTED EARL
BELT SANDER
BE MERCIFUL
BE MISTAKEN
BENDED KNEE
BENEATH ONE
BENT DOUBLE
BEN TRAVERS
BE PREPARED
BERLIN WALL
BE SENSIBLE
BE SOCIABLE
BEST BITTER
BEST CHANCE
BEST EFFORT
BEST FRIEND
BEST OF FIVE
BEST OF PALS
BEST PEOPLE
BEST POLICY
BEST SELLER
BEST SILVER
BEST WAY OUT
BEST WISHES
BE SUPERIOR
BE TOO SMART
BETTE DAVIS
BETTER DAYS
BETTER DEAD

BETTER HALF
BETTER HOLE
BETTER IDEA
BETTER SELF
BETTER SORT
BETTING ACT
BETTING MAN
BEYOND HOPE
BE YOURSELF
BIBLE CLASS
BID AGAINST
BIG BAD WOLF
BIG BROTHER
BIGGER SIZE
BIGGIN HILL
BIG HELPING
BIG SUCCESS
BIG SWINDLE
BIJOU VILLA
BILL AND COO
BILL BENBOW
BILL OF FARE
BILL OF SALE
BINARY CODE
BING CROSBY
BINGO NIGHT
BIRD IN HAND
BIRD OF PREY
BISCUIT BOX
BISCUIT TIN
BISHOP'S HAT
BITE THE LIP
BITING WIND
BIT OF A MESS
BIT OF FLUFF
BIT PATTERN
BITTER BEER
BITTER BLOW
BITTER PILL
BITTER RICE
BLACK ANGUS
BLACK ARROW
BLACK AS INK
BLACK AS JET
BLACK BEARD
BLACK BEAST
BLACK BOOKS
BLACK BOOTS
BLACK BREAD
BLACK CLOUD
BLACK DEATH
BLACK DRESS
BLACKED OUT
BLACK FRIAR
BLACK HEART
BLACK HORSE

BLACK LACES
BLACK LOOKS
BLACK MAGIC
BLACK MARIA
BLACK PAINT
BLACK PAPER
BLACK PATCH
BLACK PIECE
BLACK QUEEN
BLACK SHEEP
BLACK SHIRT
BLACK SHOES
BLACK SOCKS
BLACK WATCH
BLACK WIDOW
BLANK PAPER
BLANK SHEET
BLANK SPACE
BLANK STARE
BLANK VERSE
BLASTED OAK
BLAZE A PATH
BLAZING SUN
BLEAK HOUSE
BLEED WHITE
BLEW THE LOT
BLIND ALLEY
BLIND DRUNK
BLIND FAITH
BLIND GUESS
BLITZ KRIEG
BLOCK OF ICE
BLONDE HAIR
BLOOD COUNT
BLOOD DONOR
BLOOD GROUP
BLOOD HORSE
BLOOD MONEY
BLOOD ROYAL
BLOOD SERUM
BLOOD SPORT
BLOODY MARY
BLOTTED OUT
BLOW BY BLOW
BLOW ME DOWN
BLUE AND RED
BLUE CHEESE
BLUE DANUBE
BLUE DEVILS
BLUE ENSIGN
BLUE GROTTO
BLUE LAGOON
BLUE MONDAY
BLUE MURDER
BLUE PENCIL
BLUE RIBAND

BLUE RIBBON	BOX BARRAGE	BRING ROUND
BLUE STREAK	BOXING RING	BRING TO BAY
BLUNT WORDS	BOX OF DATES	BRISK TRADE
BOAT PEOPLE	BOX OF PILLS	BROAD ACRES
BOAT RACING	BOY AND GIRL	BROAD ARROW
BOBBED HAIR	BOYS IN BLUE	BROAD BEANS
BOBBY HOWES	BRACING AIR	BROAD GAUGE
BODILY HARM	BRAIN CHILD	BROKEN BACK
BODILY PAIN	BRAIN DRAIN	BROKEN BONE
BODY SWERVE	BRAIN FEVER	BROKEN DOWN
BOGGED DOWN	BRAIN STORM	BROKEN HOME
BOILED BEEF	BRANCH LINE	BROKEN LINE
BOILED FISH	BRASS PLATE	BROKEN NECK
BOILED RICE	BRASS TACKS	BROKEN NOSE
BOILER ROOM	BRAVE FRONT	BROKEN REED
BOILER SUIT	BRAVE IT OUT	BROKEN WORD
BOILING HOT	BREAD FRUIT	BROKER'S MAN
BOILING OIL	BREAD ROUND	BROUGHT LOW
BOLD DESIGN	BREAD SAUCE	BROWN BOOTS
BOLD RELIEF	BREAK A BONE	BROWN BREAD
BOLD STROKE	BREAK A DATE	BROWNED OFF
BOMBAY DUCK	BREAK A FALL	BROWN LACES
BOMB CRATER	BREAK AN ARM	BROWN PAINT
BOMB DAMAGE	BREAK BREAD	BROWN PAPER
BONDED DEBT	BREAK COVER	BROWN SHIRT
BOND STREET	BREAK FAITH	BROWN SHOES
BONE TO PICK	BREAK FORTH	BROWN STONE
BONUS ISSUE	BREAK IN TWO	BROWN STUDY
BOOBY PRIZE	BREAK IT OFF	BROWN SUGAR
BOOK A TABLE	BREAK LOOSE	BRUSH ASIDE
BOOK CRITIC	BREAK OF DAY	BRUTE FORCE
BOOKING FEE	BREAK RANKS	BUBBLE BATH
BOOK OF FATE	BREAK SHORT	BUBBLE OVER
BOOK REVIEW	BREATHE OUT	BUCKET SEAT
BOOK RIGHTS	BRER RABBIT	BUCKET SHOP
BOOT POLISH	BRETT YOUNG	BUCK RABBIT
BORED STIFF	BRIDAL GOWN	BULK BUYING
BORING WORK	BRIDAL VEIL	BULLET HEAD
BORN LEADER	BRIDGE A GAP	BULLET HOLE
BORN TO RULE	BRIDGE CLUB	BULL MARKET
BORSTAL BOY	BRIDGE HAND	BUMPER CROP
BOSTON REEL	BRIDGE OVER	BUMPING CAR
BO TO A GOOSE	BRIDGE ROLL	BUMP SUPPER
BOTTLED ALE	BRIDLE PATH	BURNE JONES
BOTTOM GEAR	BRIDLE REIN	BURNT AMBER
BOTTOM RUNG	BRIEF VISIT	BURNT BLACK
BOUGHT OVER	BRIGHT BLUE	BURNT TOAST
BOULDER DAM	BRIGHT EYES	BURST FORTH
BOUNCE BACK	BRIGHT IDEA	BUSHEY PARK
BOUND TO WIN	BRIGHT SIDE	BUS SHELTER
BOWIE KNIFE	BRIGHT SPOT	BUS STATION
BOWL A BREAK	BRIGHT STAR	BUSY AS A BEE
BOWLED OVER	BRING ABOUT	BUSY PERSON
BOWL OF RICE	BRING A CASE	BUSY STREET
BOWL OF SOUP	BRING A SUIT	BUSY WORKER
BOW THE KNEE	BRING FORTH	BUTTER DISH

BUTTONED UP
BUY AND SELL
BUY BRITISH
BY ACCIDENT
BY ALL MEANS
BY AND LARGE
BY ANY MEANS
BY CONTRAST
BY DAYLIGHT
BY GASLIGHT
BYGONE DAYS
BY INSTINCT
BY SNATCHES
BY SURPRISE
BY THE CLOCK
BY THE DOZEN
BY THE RIVER
BY TRANSFER
BY YOURSELF

C – 10

CABIN TRUNK
CADET CORPS
CADET FORCE
CADGE A LIFT
CAFÉ AU LAIT
CAKE OF SOAP
CALL A TRUCE
CALL BY NAME
CALLED AWAY
CALL IT A DAY
CALL OF DUTY
CALL SPADES
CALL TO ARMS
CALL TO MIND
CALL TRUMPS
CAMDEN TOWN
CAME IN LAST
CAME IN VIEW
CAMEL CORPS
CAMEL'S HUMP
CAMEL'S MILK
CAMEL TRAIN
CAMPING OUT
CANDY FLOSS
CANNED BEER
CANNED FOOD
CANNEL COAL
CANNON BALL
CAP AND GOWN
CAPE COLONY
CAPER SAUCE
CARBON COPY
CARD PLAYER
CAREER GIRL
CARGO SPACE

CAR LICENCE
CAROLE CARR
CARRIED OFF
CARRIER BAG
CARRY COALS
CARRY IT OFF
CARSON CITY
CART GREASE
CASE A JOINT
CASE OF WINE
CASE RECORD
CASHEW NUTS
CASH IN HAND
CASK OF WINE
CASPIAN SEA
CAST A CLOUT
CAST ANCHOR
CAST A SPELL
CASTING OFF
CASUAL WARD
CASUS BELLI
CAT BURGLAR
CATCH A BALL
CATCH A COLD
CATCH A CRAB
CATCH A TRAM
CATCHY TUNE
CATHODE RAY
CATO STREET
CAT'S CRADLE
CATTLE FARM
CATTLE FOOD
CATTLE SHOW
CAUGHT COLD
CAUGHT FIRE
CAUSE ALARM
CAUSE A RIOT
CAUSE A STIR
CAUSTIC WIT
CAXTON HALL
CELERY SALT
CENTRE HALF
CERTAIN DAY
CHAIN SMOKE
CHAIN STORE
CHAIR COVER
CHANCE SHOT
CHANGE ENDS
CHANGE GEAR
CHANGE OVER
CHANGE STEP
CHAPEL FOLK
CHAPTER ONE
CHAPTER SIX
CHAPTER TWO
CHARGE CARD

CHARGE HAND
CHEAP MONEY
CHEAP PAPER
CHEAP SKATE
CHEAT DEATH
CHECK POINT
CHEESE DISH
CHEESED OFF
CHEESE RIND
CHEESE ROLL
CHELSEA BUN
CHELSEA SET
CHEQUE BOOK
CHERRY LIPS
CHERRY RIPE
CHERRY TART
CHERRY TREE
CHESS BOARD
CHESS MATCH
CHESS PIECE
CHEST OF TEA
CHEVY CHASE
CHEWING GUM
CHEW THE CUD
CHEW THE FAT
CHEW THE RAG
CHEYNE WALK
CHICKEN RUN
CHIEF CLERK
CHIEF POINT
CHIEF SCOUT
CHILD BRIDE
CHILD'S PLAY
CHILLY ROOM
CHIMNEY TOP
CHINA PLATE
CHINESE BOX
CHIPPING IN
CHORUS GIRL
CHOSEN RACE
CHURCH ARMY
CHURCH DOOR
CHURN IT OUT
CIDER APPLE
CIGAR SMOKE
CIGAR STORE
CILLA BLACK
CINQUE PORT
CIRCUS RING
CITRIC ACID
CITY CENTRE
CITY EDITOR
CITY FATHER
CITY LIGHTS
CITY LIMITS
CITY OF BATH

CITY OFFICE	CLOSE OF DAY	COME NEARER
CITY POLICE	CLOSE ORDER	COME SECOND
CITY STREET	CLOSE SHAVE	COME TO BITS
CITY TEMPLE	CLOSE STUDY	COME TO HAND
CITY WORKER	CLOSE THING	COME TO HARM
CIVIC CROWN	CLOSE WATCH	COME TO HEEL
CIVIC PRIDE	CLOSING BID	COME TO KNOW
CIVIL COURT	CLOVE HITCH	COME TO LIFE
CIVIL STATE	CLOVEN FOOT	COME TO PASS
CIVIL WRONG	CLOVEN HOOF	COME TO REST
CLAP EYES ON	CLOVER LEAF	COME TO STAY
CLAP HOLD OF	CLUB MEMBER	COME UNDONE
CLAP ON SAIL	CLUMSY HAND	COMIC OPERA
CLARK GABLE	COACH PARTY	COMIC PAPER
CLASP HANDS	COAL CELLAR	COMIC STRIP
CLASSY DAME	COARSE FISH	COMIC VERSE
CLAY PIGEON	COARSE JOKE	COMMON BOND
CLEAN BREAK	COARSE MIND	COMMON COLD
CLEANED OUT	COAST ALONG	COMMON FORM
CLEAN FIGHT	COAT OF ARMS	COMMON FUND
CLEAN HABIT	COAT OF MAIL	COMMON GOOD
CLEAN HANDS	COAT POCKET	COMMON HERD
CLEAN LINEN	COBALT BLUE	COMMON JEST
CLEAN LIVER	COBALT BOMB	COMMON LAND
CLEAN SHAVE	COCK A SNOOK	COMMON NAME
CLEAN SHEET	COCONUT OIL	COMMON NOUN
CLEAN SLATE	COCONUT SHY	COMMON ROOM
CLEAN SWEEP	CODDLED EGG	COMMON SALT
CLEAN TOWEL	COFFEE BEAN	COMMON SEAL
CLEAN WATER	COFFEE ROOM	COMMON SORT
CLEAR AS DAY	COFFIN NAIL	COMMON TALK
CLEAR AS MUD	COIL MAGNET	COMMON TASK
CLEAR FIELD	COLD BUFFET	COMMON TIME
CLEAR IMAGE	COLD REASON	COMMON TYPE
CLEAR LIGHT	COLD REGION	COMPANY LAW
CLEAR PRINT	COLD SEASON	COMPANY TAX
CLEAR ROUND	COLD SHOWER	CONAN DOYLE
CLEAR SPACE	COLD TONGUE	CONTACT MAN
CLEAR STYLE	COLD TURKEY	CONTOUR MAP
CLEAR VOICE	COLD WINTER	COOKED MEAT
CLEAR WATER	COLE PORTER	COPPER BELT
CLEFT STICK	COLLEGE BOY	COPPER COIN
CLEVER DICK	COLLEGE RAG	COPPER MINE
CLEVER IDEA	COLOUR FILM	COPPER WIRE
CLEVER MOVE	COLOUR TONE	COPYING INK
CLEVER SAVE	COME ACROSS	COPY TYPIST
CLIMB A HILL	COME ADRIFT	COR ANGLAIS
CLIMB A TREE	COME AND SEE	CORDON BLEU
CLIVE JAMES	COME AROUND	CORK JACKET
CLOCK TOWER	COME ASHORE	CORNED BEEF
CLOSED BOOK	COME AT ONCE	CORNER FLAG
CLOSED DOOR	COME CLOSER	CORNER KICK
CLOSED MIND	COMEDY HOUR	CORNER POST
CLOSED SHOP	COME HITHER	CORNER SEAT
CLOSE GRIPS	COME IN LAST	CORNER SHOP
CLOSE MATCH	COME INSIDE	CORNER SITE

CORNET SOLO	CROWN AGENT	DAILY DOZEN
COS LETTUCE	CROWN DERBY	DAILY EVENT
COSMIC RAYS	CROWN GLASS	DAILY GRIND
COSTA BRAVA	CROWN LEASE	DAILY HABIT
COSY CORNER	CROWN PIECE	DAILY PAPER
COTTAGE PIE	CRUDE FACTS	DAILY PRESS
COTTON MILL	CRUDE FORCE	DAILY ROUND
COTTON REEL	CRUDE METAL	DAINTY DISH
COTTON YARN	CRUEL SHAME	DAIRY CREAM
COUNTED OUT	CRUSTY LOAF	DAIRY FRESH
COUNT HANDS	CRUSTY PORT	DAISY CHAIN
COUNT HEADS	CRY FOR HELP	DAMASK ROSE
COUNT ME OUT	CRYING FOUL	DAMP COURSE
COUNTRY INN	CRY OF AGONY	DANCE MUSIC
COUNTRY PUB	CRY OUT LOUD	DANCING MAN
COUNT SHEEP	CRYSTAL SET	DANGER LINE
COUNTY CORK	CRY TOO SOON	DANGER LIST
COUNTY DOWN	CUCKOO PINT	DANISH BLUE
COUNTY HALL	CUNARD LINE	DARK CLOUDS
COUNTY MAYO	CUP AND BALL	DARK COLOUR
COUNTY TOWN	CUPID'S DART	DARK CORNER
COUP DE MAIN	CUP OF COCOA	DARK PURPLE
COURT DRESS	CUP OF WATER	DARK SECRET
COURT OF LAW	CUP WINNERS	DARTS BOARD
COURT ORDER	CURATE'S EGG	DARTS MATCH
COURT SCENE	CURED BACON	DASH OF SODA
COURT USHER	CURL THE LIP	DAS KAPITAL
COVER DRIVE	CURRANT BUN	DATA SOURCE
COVERED WAY	CURRENT HIT	DATIVE CASE
COVER POINT	CURTAIN OFF	DAVID FROST
COWBOY SUIT	CURTAIN ROD	DAVID NIVEN
COW PARSLEY	CURT ANSWER	DAVID NIXON
COX'S ORANGE	CURVED LINE	DAWN ATTACK
CRACK A CRIB	CURZON LINE	DAWN CHORUS
CRACK A JOKE	CUSTARD PIE	DAWN OF HOPE
CRACKED EGG	CUT A FIGURE	DAWN OF LIFE
CRADLE SONG	CUT ASUNDER	DAWN OF LOVE
CRAWL ABOUT	CUT A TUNNEL	DAWN PATROL
CREDIT CARD	CUT CORNERS	DAY DREAMER
CREDIT NOTE	CUT FLOWERS	DAY NURSERY
CREDIT SIDE	CUT FOR DEAL	DAY OF GRACE
CRÊPE PAPER	CUT IT SHORT	DAYS GONE BY
CRÊPE SOLES	CUT THE CAKE	DAYS OF YORE
CRICKET BAT	CUT THE COST	DAYS TO COME
CRICKET CAP	CUT THE KNOT	DAY TRIPPER
CRIMEAN WAR	CUT THE TAPE	DEAD CENTRE
CRIME STORY	CUT THROUGH	DEADEN PAIN
CROOKED MAN	CUTTING OUT	DEAD GROUND
CROSS IT OFF	CUTTLE FISH	DEAD LETTER
CROSS IT OUT	CUT UP ROUGH	DEADLY BLOW
CROSS PATHS	CYCLE RALLY	DEADLY DULL
CROSS WORDS		DEAD MATTER
CROUCH DOWN		DEAD ON TIME
CROWDED OUT	D – 10	DEAD SEASON
CROWD ROUND		DEAD SECRET
CROWD SCENE	DAB OF PAINT	DEAD WEIGHT
	DAILY BREAD	

DEAL GENTLY	DIESEL FUEL	DONE BY HAND
DEALT A BLOW	DIG A TRENCH	DONEGAL BAY
DEAN MARTIN	DIG FOR GOLD	DONKEY WORK
DEAR BRUTUS	DILLY DALLY	DO NOT TOUCH!
DEAR FRIEND	DINAH SHORE	DON QUIXOTE
DEAR READER	DINE AT HOME	DON'T BE RUDE!
DEATH HOUSE	DINING CLUB	DO ONE PROUD
DEATH KNELL	DINING HALL	DO ONE'S BEST
DEATH SCENE	DINING ROOM	DO ONE'S DUTY
DEATH'S DOOR	DINNER BELL	DO ONE'S HAIR
DEATH'S HEAD	DINNER GONG	DOOR HANDLE
DEBIT ENTRY	DINNER HOUR	DOOR TO DOOR
DEBT CRISIS	DINNER SUIT	DO OVERTIME
DECENT TYPE	DINNER TIME	DOPE ADDICT
DECK QUOITS	DIP THE FLAG	DOPE PEDLAR
DECK TENNIS	DIRECT LINE	DORIAN GRAY
DECLARE OFF	DIRTY HABIT	DOROTHY BAG
DECLARE WAR	DIRTY LINEN	DO THE HALLS
DECREE NISI	DIRTY MONEY	DO THE TANGO
DEEP BREATH	DIRTY STORY	DO THE TRICK
DEEPEST DYE	DIRTY TRICK	DO THE TWIST
DEEP FREEZE	DIRTY WATER	DOTTED LINE
DEEP IN DEBT	DISC JOCKEY	DOTTED NOTE
DEEP LITTER	DISC BRAKES	DOUBLE BACK
DEEPLY HURT	DISH AERIAL	DOUBLE BASS
DEEP PURPLE	DISPEL FEAR	DOUBLE BLUE
DEEP REGRET	DIVINE KING	DOUBLE CHIN
DEEP SECRET	DIVING BIRD	DOUBLE DATE
DEEP SORROW	DIZZY ROUND	DOUBLE FIVE
DEEP WATERS	DIZZY SPELL	DOUBLE FOUR
DEEP YELLOW	DIZZY WHIRL	DOUBLE LIFE
DEER FOREST	DO A BAD TURN	DOUBLE LOCK
DELFT CHINA	DO A STRETCH	DOUBLE NINE
DEL CHANNON	DO AWAY WITH	DOUBLE ROOM
DEMAND NOTE	DO BUSINESS	DOUBLE STAR
DEMON RUMMY	DOCK LABOUR	DOUBLE TAKE
DEN OF LIONS	DOCK MASTER	DOUBLE TALK
DENSE CROWD	DOCTOR FELL	DOUBLE TIME
DENY ACCESS	DOCTOR'S FEE	DOUBLING UP
DEODAR TREE	DOG BISCUIT	DOUBLY SURE
DEPTH GUIDE	DOG EATS DOG	DOUGLAS FIR
DERBY CHINA	DOGGER BANK	DO VIOLENCE
DERBY HORSE	DOG LICENCE	DOWER HOUSE
DERBY SWEEP	DOG'S CHANCE	DOWN AND OUT
DERNIER CRI	DOG'S DINNER	DOWN AT HEEL
DESERT SONG	DOG TRAINER	DOWN THE PIT
DEUCES WILD	DOING RIGHT	D'OYLE CARTE
DEVIL'S DYKE	DOING WRONG	DRAKE'S DRUM
DEVIL'S LUCK	DO IN THE EYE	DRAUGHT ALE
DEVIL TO PAY	DO IT AT ONCE	DRAW A BLANK
DICK BARTON	DO LIKEWISE	DRAW A PRIZE
DICK TURPIN	DOLLAR AREA	DRAW BREATH
DIE FOR LOVE	DOLLAR BILL	DRAWING INK
DIE OF GRIEF	DOLL'S HOUSE	DRAW IT FINE
DIE OF SHOCK	DONALD DUCK	DRAW IT MILD
DIEPPE RAID	DON BRADMAN	DRAWN MATCH

DRAWN SWORD
DRAW ONE OUT
DRAW STUMPS
DRAW SWORDS
DR BARNARDO
DREAM HOUSE
DREAM WORLD
DREAMY EYES
DREAMY LOOK
DRESS SENSE
DRESS SHIRT
DRIED FRUIT
DRIFT ALONG
DRIFT APART
DRINK MONEY
DRINK VODKA
DRINK WATER
DRIVEN SNOW
DROP A BRICK
DROP A CATCH
DROP ANCHOR
DROP ASTERN
DROP BEHIND
DROP BY DROP
DROP OF RAIN
DROPPED OFF
DROPPED OUT
DROP THE HEM
DROWNED OUT
DROWNED RAT
DRUG ADDICT
DRUG DEALER
DRUG PUSHER
DRUMMED OUT
DRUMMER BOY
DRY AS A BONE
DRY BATTERY
DRY CANTEEN
DRY CLIMATE
DRY MARTINI
DRY MEASURE
DRY ONESELF
DRY SHAMPOO
DRY THE EYES
DRY WEATHER
DUEL OF WITS
DUE RESPECT
DUFFEL COAT
DUKE OF KENT
DUKE OF YORK
DULCE DOMUM
DULL COLOUR
DULL MOMENT
DUMB ANIMAL
DUMB BLONDE
DUMB CRAMBO

DUMB WAITER
DUMMY WHIST
DUNDEE CAKE
DUSKY BRIDE
DUSTBIN LID
DUST JACKET
DUST TO DUST
DUTCH BULBS
DUTCH PARTY
DUTCH TREAT
DUTCH UNCLE
DUTY ROSTER
DWARF BEANS
DWARF PLANT
DYING CAUSE
DYING WORDS

E – 10

EACH AND ALL
EACH TO EACH
EACH-WAY BET
EAGLE'S NEST
EARL'S COURT
EARLY DOORS
EARLY HOURS
EARLY LUNCH
EARLY NIGHT
EARLY RISER
EARLY STAGE
EARLY START
EARLY TO BED
EARLY TRAIN
EARLY TUDOR
EARLY VISIT
EARLY WORKS
EARTHA KITT
EAR TRUMPET
EASILY DONE
EAST AFRICA
EAST ANGLIA
EAST BERLIN
EASTER TERM
EASTER TIME
EASTER WEEK
EAST INDIAN
EAST INDIES
EAST IS EAST
EAST LONDON
EAST OF SUEZ
EAST RIDING
EAST TO WEST
EASY ACCESS
EASY DOES IT
EASY GALLOP
EASY IN MIND
EASY MANNER

EASY MARKET
EASY STAGES
EASY STREET
EASY TARGET
EASY TO COPY
EASY VIRTUE
EASY WAY OUT
EASY WICKET
EASY WINNER
EAT ONE'S HAT
EBB AND FLOW
ECCLES CAKE
EDAM CHEESE
EDISON BELL
EDMUNDO ROS
EDWARD LEAR
EDWIN DROOD
EFFECTS MAN
EGG CUSTARD
EGG ON CHIPS
EGG ON TOAST
EGG SHAMPOO
EIGHT BELLS
EIGHT DOZEN
EIGHT DRAWS
EIGHT GROSS
EIGHTH ARMY
EIGHTH HOLE
EIGHT HOURS
EIGHTH PART
EIGHTH RACE
EIGHTH TIME
EIGHT MILES
EIGHT PARTS
EIGHT PINTS
EIGHT SCORE
EIGHTS WEEK
EIGHT TIMES
EIGHT TO ONE
EIGHT WEEKS
EIGHTY DAYS
EIGHT YEARS
ELEVEN DAYS
ELEVEN FEET
ELEVEN PLUS
ELEVEN QUID
ELINOR GLYN
ELLEN TERRY
EMERY CLOTH
EMERY PAPER
EMPIRE GOWN
EMPTY BOAST
EMPTY CHAIR
EMPTY CURSE
EMPTY GLASS
EMPTY HOUSE

EMPTY PURSE
EMPTY SHELL
EMPTY SOUND
EMPTY SPACE
EMPTY TRUCK
EMPTY WORDS
END IN SMOKE
END PRODUCT
ENEMY AGENT
ENEMY ALIEN
ENEMY FLEET
ENEMY LINES
ENGAGE A CAB
ENGINE ROOM
ENJOY PEACE
ENOCH ARDEN
ENOUGH ROOM
ENOUGH SAID
ENOUGH TIME
ENOUGH TO DO
ENTICE AWAY
ENTRY MONEY
EPIC POETRY
EPSOM DOWNS
EPSOM RACES
EPSOM SALTS
EQUAL PARTS
EQUAL SHARE
EQUALS SIGN
EQUAL TERMS
EQUAL VALUE
ERIC AMBLER
ERIC BARKER
ERIC COATES
ERRING WIFE
ERROL FLYNN
ESCORT DUTY
ESTATE DUTY
ETHEL M. DELL
ETON COLLAR
ETON JACKET
EUSTON ROAD
EVE BOSWELL
EVELYN LAYE
EVEN CHANCE
EVEN HIGHER
EVEN NUMBER
EVEN TEMPER
EVER SO MANY
EVER SO MUCH
EVERY MONTH
EVERY OTHER
EVERY WOMAN
EVIL GENIUS
EVIL INTENT
EVIL SPIRIT

EVIL TEMPER
EXACT IMAGE
EXACT SENSE
EXCESS FARE
EXCISE BILL
EXCISE DUTY
EX DIVIDEND
EXETER CITY
EXIT PERMIT
EXPERT SHOT
EXPORT ONLY
EXPRESS FEE
EXTRA COVER
EXTRA MONEY
EXTRA POWER
EYES OF BLUE
EYE WITNESS

F – 10

FACE DANGER
FACE DEFEAT
FACE POWDER
FACE TO FACE
FACE UP TO IT
FACTORY ACT
FADED YOUTH
FAIL TO COME
FAIL TO MEET
FAIL TO MOVE
FAIL TO OBEY
FAINT HEART
FAINT LIGHT
FAINT SOUND
FAIR AMOUNT
FAIR CHANCE
FAIR ENOUGH
FAIR EXCUSE
FAIR INCOME
FAIRLY GOOD
FAIRLY WARM
FAIRLY WELL
FAIR OF FACE
FAIR REPORT
FAIR SAMPLE
FAIR SHARES
FAIR TACKLE
FAIRY QUEEN
FAIRY STORY
FAIRY WORLD
FALL ASLEEP
FALL ASTERN
FALL BEHIND
FALLEN IDOL
FALL FOUL OF
FALLING OFF
FALL IN LINE

FALL IN LOVE
FALL IN WITH
FALL OF SNOW
FALL OF TROY
FALLOW DEER
FALLOW LAND
FALL SILENT
FALL TO BITS
FALSE ALARM
FALSE ALIBI
FALSE BEARD
FALSE CLAIM
FALSE CREED
FALSE FRONT
FALSE HOPES
FALSE IMAGE
FALSE LIGHT
FALSE LOGIC
FALSE PRIDE
FALSE SCENT
FALSE SHAME
FALSE START
FALSE TEETH
FAMILY FEUD
FAMILY FIRM
FAMILY LIFE
FAMILY NAME
FAMILY SEAT
FAMILY TIES
FAMILY TREE
FAMOUS DEED
FAMOUS NAME
FAMOUS WORK
FANCY DRESS
FANCY GOODS
FANCY PRICE
FANCY SOCKS
FANNY ADAMS
FAN THE FIRE
FAR AND AWAY
FAR AND NEAR
FAR AND WIDE
FAR BETWEEN
FAR COUNTRY
FARM ANIMAL
FARM BUTTER
FARMER'S BOY
FARM WORKER
FAR-OFF LAND
FAR THE BEST
FAR TOO MANY
FAR TOO MUCH
FAST ASLEEP
FAST BOWLER
FAST COLOUR
FAST READER

FAST WICKET	FIFTY TIMES	FIRE ESCAPE
FAST WORKER	FIFTY TO ONE	FIRE POLICY
FATAL CAUSE	FIFTY YEARS	FIRE SCREEN
FATAL CRASH	FIGHT A DUEL	FIRING LINE
FATAL ERROR	FIGHT FOR IT	FIRM ADVICE
FATAL WOUND	FIGHT IT OUT	FIRM BELIEF
FAT AND LEAN	FIGHT SHY OF	FIRM DEMAND
FATHER'S DAY	FILE A CLAIM	FIRM DENIAL
FATHER TIME	FILIAL DUTY	FIRM FRIEND
FATS WALLER	FILL IN TIME	FIRM GROUND
FATTED CALF	FILL THE AIR	FIRST BATCH
FAY COMPTON	FILL THE GAP	FIRST BLOOD
FEARFUL DIN	FILM ADDICT	FIRST BLUSH
FEATHER BED	FILM CENSOR	FIRST CAUSE
FEATHER BOA	FILM COLONY	FIRST CHILD
FEAT OF ARMS	FILM CRITIC	FIRST CLAIM
FEEBLE JOKE	FILM OF DUST	FIRST DANCE
FEEBLE MIND	FILM REVIEW	FIRST DRAFT
FEED THE CAT	FILM RIGHTS	FIRST ENTRY
FEED THE DOG	FILM STUDIO	FIRST EVENT
FEEL AT EASE	FILTHY TALK	FIRST FLOOR
FEEL AT HOME	FINAL CAUSE	FIRST FLUSH
FEEL BETTER	FINAL CLAIM	FIRST GREEN
FEEL CHILLY	FINAL COUNT	FIRST HOUSE
FEEL DEEPLY	FINAL EVENT	FIRST ISSUE
FEEL GROGGY	FINAL FLING	FIRST LIGHT
FEEL HUNGRY	FINAL ISSUE	FIRST MAN IN
FEELING ILL	FINAL OFFER	FIRST MATCH
FEELING SAD	FINAL POINT	FIRST NIGHT
FEEL NO PITY	FINAL PROOF	FIRST NOVEL
FEEL RELIEF	FINAL SCENE	FIRST OF ALL
FEEL SECURE	FINAL SCORE	FIRST OF MAY
FEEL SLEEPY	FINAL STAGE	FIRST PLACE
FEEL UNWELL	FINAL TERMS	FIRST PRIZE
FEEL UP TO IT	FINAL TOUCH	FIRST PROOF
FEET OF CLAY	FINANCE ACT	FIRST ROUND
FELL INTENT	FIND A BASIS	FIRST SHIFT
FENCE ROUND	FIND A PLACE	FIRST SIGHT
FEN COUNTRY	FIND FAVOUR	FIRST STAGE
FETTER LANE	FIND GUILTY	FIRST STEPS
FEUDAL LORD	FIND RELIEF	FIRST TEETH
FEVER PITCH	FIND THE WAY	FIRST THING
FIBRE GLASS	FINE CHANCE	FIRST THROW
FIELD EVENT	FINE FELLOW	FIRST TO ACT
FIELD SPORT	FINE FETTLE	FIRST VERSE
FIERY CROSS	FINE FIGURE	FIRST WATCH
FIERY STEED	FINE PERSON	FIRST WATER
FIESTA TIME	FINE SHOWER	FIRST WOMAN
FIFTEEN ALL	FINEST HOUR	FIRTH OF TAY
FIFTEEN MEN	FINE VELLUM	FISH COURSE
FIFTH FLOOR	FINE WRITER	FISH DINNER
FIFTH GREEN	FINGER WAVE	FISH FINGER
FIFTH OF MAY	FINISH LAST	FISHING NET
FIFTH PLACE	FINITE VERB	FISH KETTLE
FIFTH ROUND	FIRE A SALVO	FISH MARKET
FIFTY MILES	FIRE BUCKET	FISH SUPPER

FISHY STORY	FLOAT ON AIR	FORGED NOTE
FIT AND WELL	FLOODED OUT	FORK SUPPER
FIT OF ANGER	FLOOD GATES	FORMAL CALL
FIT OF BLUES	FLOOD LEVEL	FORM A QUEUE
FIT THE BILL	FLOOD WATER	FORMER DAYS
FIT TO BURST	FLOOR SPACE	FORMER LAND
FIT TO PLEAD	FLOPPY DISK	FORM MASTER
FIVE AND ONE	FLOUNCE OUT	FOR NOTHING
FIVE AND SIX	FLOWER SHOW	FOR THE BEST
FIVE AND TEN	FLOWER VASE	FOR TWO PINS
FIVE AND TWO	FLUID OUNCE	FORTY MILES
FIVE A PENNY	FLY FOR HELP	FORTY TIMES
FIVE FIFTHS	FLYING BOAT	FORTY WINKS
FIVE HEARTS	FLYING BOMB	FORTY YEARS
FIVE MONTHS	FLYING CLUB	FOSTER HOPE
FIVE NINTHS	FLYING FISH	FOUL MANNER
FIVE O'CLOCK	FLYING HIGH	FOUL MOTIVE
FIVE OUNCES	FLYING JUMP	FOUL STROKE
FIVE POINTS	FLYING KICK	FOUL TEMPER
FIVE POUNDS	FLYING LEAP	FOUR-ALE BAR
FIVE QUARTS	FLYING SHOT	FOUR AND SIX
FIVE ROUNDS	FLY THE FLAG	FOUR AND TEN
FIVES COURT	FOAM RUBBER	FOUR AND TWO
FIVE SENSES	FOCAL POINT	FOUR A PENNY
FIVE SIXTHS	FOGGY NIGHT	FOUR BY FOUR
FIVE SPADES	FOG WARNING	FOUR EIGHTS
FIVE STONES	FOLDED ARMS	FOUR FIFTHS
FIVE TO FOUR	FOLK DANCER	FOUR HEARTS
FIVE TRICKS	FOLK SINGER	FOUR IN HAND
FIXED ABODE	FOLLOW SUIT	FOUR KNAVES
FIXED IDEAS	FOND BELIEF	FOUR MONTHS
FIXED POINT	FOND PARENT	FOUR NINTHS
FIXED PRICE	FOOD PARCEL	FOUR O'CLOCK
FIXED SMILE	FOOD SUPPLY	FOUR OR FIVE
FIXED STARS	FOOD TABLET	FOUR OUNCES
FIX THE DATE	FOOL AROUND	FOUR POINTS
FIX THE TIME	FOOT BY FOOT	FOUR POUNDS
FLAG WAVING	FOR A CHANGE	FOUR QUARTS
FLAMING RED	FOR ALL THAT	FOUR QUEENS
FLASH POINT	FOR ALL TIME	FOUR SEVENS
FLAT DENIAL	FOR A SEASON	FOUR SPADES
FLAT GROUND	FORCE A DRAW	FOURTH FORM
FLAT IN TOWN	FORCE APART	FOURTH HAND
FLAT RACING	FORCED LOAN	FOURTH HOLE
FLAT SCREEN	FORCED SALE	FOURTH PART
FLAT SEASON	FORCE OF LAW	FOURTH RACE
FLATTEN OUT	FOR CERTAIN	FOUR THREES
FLAXEN HAIR	FOR CHARITY	FOURTH TEST
FLEA CIRCUS	FORE AND AFT	FOURTH TIME
FLESH WOUND	FOREIGN LAW	FOUR TRICKS
FLIGHT DECK	FOREST FIRE	FOUR WHEELS
FLING ABOUT	FOREST HILL	FOX HUNTING
FLING ASIDE	FOREST LAND	FOX TERRIER
FLINT GLASS	FOREST TREE	FRANZ KAFKA
FLOAT ABOUT	FOR EXAMPLE	FRANZ LEHAR
FLOAT A LOAN	FORGE AHEAD	FRANZ LISZT

FRAYED EDGE
FREE ACCESS
FREE ACTION
FREE ADVICE
FREE CHOICE
FREE CHURCH
FREE DRINKS
FREE FOR ALL
FREE FRENCH
FREE LABOUR
FREE LIVING
FREE MARKET
FREE OF COST
FREE OF DEBT
FREE OF DUTY
FREE ON RAIL
FREE PARDON
FREE SAMPLE
FREE SPEECH
FREE TICKET
FREEZE HARD
FREEZE ON TO
FREEZE OVER
FRENCH ALPS
FRENCH BEAN
FRENCH BRED
FRENCH HORN
FRENCH LOAF
FRENCH PORT
FRENCH ROLL
FRENCH WINE
FRESH BLOOD
FRESH BREAD
FRESH CREAM
FRESH FRUIT
FRESH HOPES
FRESH LIGHT
FRESH PAINT
FRESH SLANT
FRESH SPURT
FRESH START
FRESH WATER
FRESH WOUND
FRIED BACON
FRIED BREAD
FRIGID TONE
FRIGID ZONE
FROM ABROAD
FROM BEHIND
FROM MEMORY
FROM THE AIR
FROM THE TOP
FRONT BENCH
FRONT COVER
FRONT TEETH
FRONT TOOTH

FRONT WHEEL
FROZEN FISH
FROZEN FOOD
FROZEN OVER
FROZEN PEAS
FROZEN SNOW
FRUGAL DIET
FRUGAL MEAL
FRUIT DRINK
FRUIT JELLY
FRUIT JUICE
FRUIT LOLLY
FRUIT SALAD
FUEL CRISIS
FULL BELIEF
FULL BOTTLE
FULL CHORUS
FULL CIRCLE
FULL EXTENT
FULL FIGURE
FULL GALLOP
FULL GROWTH
FULL IMPORT
FULL LENGTH
FULL OF HATE
FULL OF HOPE
FULL OF LIFE
FULL OF LOVE
FULL OF NEWS
FULL OF ZEAL
FULL OF ZEST
FULL PARDON
FULL REPORT
FULL SISTER
FULL TRAVEL
FULL VOLUME
FULLY ARMED
FULLY AWARE
FULLY WOUND
FUNDED DEBT
FUNNY STORY
FUNNY THING
FUSSY STYLE

G – 10

GAIETY GIRL
GAIN ACCESS
GAIN CREDIT
GAIN FAVOUR
GAIN GROUND
GAIN HEIGHT
GAIN THE DAY
GAIN WEIGHT
GALLANT ACT
GALLUP POLL
GAMBLE AWAY

GAME AND SET
GAME OF DICE
GAME WARDEN
GAMING LAWS
GARAGE HAND
GARBAGE MAN
GARDEN CITY
GARDEN FETE
GARDEN FLAT
GARDEN GATE
GARDEN HOSE
GARDEN PATH
GARDEN PEAS
GARDEN PEST
GARDEN SEAT
GARDEN WALL
GARLIC SALT
GARY COOPER
GAS CHAMBER
GAS COMPANY
GAS COUNCIL
GAS LIGHTER
GAS ONESELF
GAS TURBINE
GAS WARFARE
GATHER FOOD
GATHER WOOL
GATLING GUN
GAVE GROUND
GAVE NOTICE
GAVE VENT TO
GAY COLOURS
GAY GORDONS
GEISHA GIRL
GENE PITNEY
GENERAL LEE
GENERAL RUN
GENE TUNNEY
GENIAL HOST
GENTLE BLOW
GENTLE HEAT
GENTLE PUSH
GEORGE SAND
GERMAN BAND
GERMAN MARK
GET A LIVING
GET A LOOK IN
GET A MOVE ON
GET A WICKET
GET DRESSED
GET ELECTED
GET ENGAGED
GET EXCITED
GET HITCHED
GET IN A MESS
GET IN TOUCH

GET MARRIED	GIVE THE CUE	GOLDEN RULE
GET NOWHERE	GIVE TONGUE	GOLD NUGGET
GET RATTLED	GIVE UP HOPE	GOLD SHARES
GET SPLICED	GIVE UP WORK	GOLD STRIKE
GET STARTED	GLANCE BACK	GOLD THREAD
GET THE BIRD	GLANCE DOWN	GOLF COURSE
GET THE BOOT	GLANCE OVER	GOLF STROKE
GET THE FEEL	GLASS BEADS	GONE TO SEED
GET THE HUMP	GLASS COACH	GOOD ACCORD
GET THE PUSH	GLASS OF ALE	GOOD ADVICE
GET THE SACK	GLASS PRISM	GOOD AND ILL
GET THROUGH	GLASSY LOOK	GOOD AND BAD
GETTING HOT	GLAZED EYES	GOOD AS GOLD
GETTING OFF	GLAZED LOOK	GOOD BRAINS
GETTING OLD	GLEE SINGER	GOOD CARVER
GETTING OUT	GLIB TONGUE	GOOD CELLAR
GET TO GRIPS	GLOVE MONEY	GOOD CHANCE
GET UP EARLY	GO ALL FUNNY	GOOD CINEMA
GET UP STEAM	GO A LONG WAY	GOOD DINNER
GET WEAVING	GO BACKWARD	GOOD DRIVER
GHOST STORY	GO BANKRUPT	GOOD EATING
GHOST TRAIN	GOBI DESERT	GOOD EFFECT
GIANT CRANE	GO CRACKERS	GOOD EFFORT
GIANT PANDA	GOD OF MERCY	GOOD ENDING
GIDDY LIMIT	GO DOWNHILL	GOOD ENOUGH
GIDDY SPELL	GO DOWN WELL	GOOD EXCUSE
GIFT COUPON	GOD WILLING	GOOD FAMILY
GIFT OF LIFE	GO FOR A BLOW	GOOD FARMER
GIFT PARCEL	GO FOR A RIDE	GOOD FELLOW
GILDED CAGE	GO FOR A SAIL	GOOD FIGURE
GIN AND LIME	GO FOR A SPIN	GOOD FOR ONE
GINGER BEER	GO FOR A SWIM	GOOD FOR YOU
GINGER WINE	GO FOR A TRIP	GOOD FRIDAY
GIPSY DANCE	GO FOR A WALK	GOOD FRIEND
GIPSY QUEEN	GO GINGERLY	GOOD GRACES
GIRL FRIEND	GO IN AND OUT	GOOD GROUND
GIVE A CATCH	GO IN AND WIN	GOOD HABITS
GIVE ADVICE	GO IN EASILY	GOOD HEALTH
GIVE A LEG UP	GOING BADLY	GOOD HIDING
GIVE AN INCH	GOING CHEAP	GOOD HUMOUR
GIVE A PARTY	GOING FORTH	GOOD INCOME
GIVE A SHOUT	GOING ROUND	GOOD INTENT
GIVE BATTLE	GOING SOUTH	GOOD JUMPER
GIVE BY WILL	GOING UNDER	GOOD LENGTH
GIVE COLOUR	GOLDEN CALF	GOOD LIVING
GIVE CREDIT	GOLDEN DAYS	GOOD MARGIN
GIVE FREELY	GOLDEN DISC	GOOD MARKET
GIVE GROUND	GOLDEN GATE	GOOD MEMORY
GIVE IT A TRY	GOLDEN GIRL	GOOD MORALS
GIVEN A LIFT	GOLDEN HAIR	GOOD MORROW
GIVEN LEAVE	GOLDEN HIND	GOOD NATURE
GIVE NOTICE	GOLDEN HORN	GOOD NOTICE
GIVE ORDERS	GOLDEN HOUR	GOOD NUMBER
GIVE PRAISE	GOLDEN MEAN	GOOD PEOPLE
GIVE RISE TO	GOLDEN MILE	GOOD PLAYER
GIVE THANKS	GOLDEN RAIN	GOOD POLICY

GOOD REASON	GRAND CANAL	GREEN CLOTH
GOOD RECORD	GRAND CROSS	GREEN FIELD
GOOD REPORT	GRAND DUCHY	GREEN FLASH
GOOD REPUTE	GRAND HOTEL	GREEN GRASS
GOOD RESULT	GRAND LODGE	GREEN LIGHT
GOOD RETURN	GRAND MARCH	GREEN PAINT
GOOD SAILOR	GRAND OPERA	GREEN SALAD
GOOD SEAMAN	GRAND PIANO	GREEN STAMP
GOOD SECOND	GRAND SCALE	GREEN STUFF
GOOD SELLER	GRAND STAND	GREEN TABLE
GOOD SERMON	GRAND STYLE	GRETA GARBO
GOOD SPEECH	GRAND TOTAL	GREY FRIARS
GOOD STAYER	GRANNY KNOT	GREY FUTURE
GOOD STRAIN	GRANT A LOAN	GREY MATTER
GOODS TRAIN	GRANT A WISH	GREY STREAK
GOOD STROKE	GRAPE JUICE	GREY TOPPER
GOOD SUPPLY	GRAPHIC ART	GRID SYSTEM
GOODS WAGON	GRASS COURT	GRILLED HAM
GOOD TEMPER	GRASS SKIRT	GRIP OF IRON
GOOD TENANT	GRASS SNAKE	GROSS ERROR
GOOD TIMING	GRASS VERGE	GROSS VALUE
GOOD TIPPER	GRASS WIDOW	GROUND ARMS
GOOD TO HEAR	GRASSY BANK	GROUND BAIT
GOOD TO KNOW	GRAVE DOUBT	GROUND CORN
GOOD WICKET	GRAVE FEARS	GROUND CREW
GOOD WISHES	GRAVEL PATH	GROUND DOWN
GOOD WORKER	GRAVELY ILL	GROUND PLAN
GO ON A BLIND	GRAVE WORDS	GROUND RENT
GO ON A SPREE	GRAY'S ELEGY	GROUND RICE
GO ON TIPTOE	GREASY POLE	GROUP OF SIX
GO ON WHEELS	GREASY ROAD	GROUP OF TEN
GO OVERSEAS	GREAT ASSET	GROUSE MOOR
GO SCOT-FREE	GREAT CATCH	GROW A BEARD
GO SHOOTING	GREAT GROSS	GROW APPLES
GO SHOPPING	GREAT HEART	GROW BETTER
GO SLUMMING	GREAT HOPES	GROW BIGGER
GO STRAIGHT	GREAT JUDGE	GROWING BOY
GO SWIMMING	GREAT LAKES	GROWING OLD
GO THE LIMIT	GREAT MERIT	GROW LARGER
GOTHIC ARCH	GREAT MINDS	GROW LONGER
GO TO BLAZES!	GREAT MOGUL	GROWN WOMAN
GO TO CHURCH	GREAT NIECE	GROW TALLER
GO TOGETHER	GREAT POWER	GRUB STREET
GO TO GROUND	GREAT SAINT	GRUFF VOICE
GO TO HEAVEN	GREAT SHOCK	GUESS AGAIN
GO TO MARKET	GREAT SPEED	GUESS RIGHT
GO TO PIECES	GREAT TREAT	GUESS WRONG
GO TO PRISON	GREAT UNCLE	GUEST HOUSE
GO TO SCHOOL	GREAT VALUE	GUEST NIGHT
GO TO THE BAD	GREAT WHEEL	GUEST TOWEL
GO TO THE BAR	GREAT WOMAN	GUILTY LOOK
GO TO THE TOP	GRECIAN URN	GUILTY MIND
GO TO THE ZOO	GREEK CROSS	GUINEA FOWL
GOT THE SACK	GREEK DRAMA	GUITAR SOLO
GO UPSTAIRS	GREEK VERSE	GULF OF ADEN
GRACE KELLY	GREEN BAIZE	GULF OF SUEZ

GULF STREAM
GUN LICENCE
GUST OF WIND

H – 10
HACKNEY CAB
HACK WRITER
HAIR LOTION
HALF A CROWN
HALF A DOZEN
HALF A GLASS
HALF A GROSS
HALF A JIFFY
HALF AN ACRE
HALF AN HOUR
HALF AN INCH
HALF A POUND
HALF A SCORE
HALF A SHAKE
HALF ASLEEP
HALF AS MUCH
HALF BOTTLE
HALF DOLLAR
HALF LENGTH
HALF OF MILD
HALF SHARES
HALF STEWED
HALF VOLLEY
HALF YEARLY
HALL OF FAME
HALL PORTER
HAM AND EGGS
HAMMER AWAY
HAMMER DOWN
HAMMER HOME
HAMMER TOES
HAND IN HAND
HAND IT OVER
HAND LOTION
HAND OF TIME
HAND SIGNAL
HAND TO HAND
HANG AROUND
HANG BEHIND
HAPPY BREED
HAPPY CHILD
HAPPY EVENT
HAPPY KNACK
HAPPY WOMAN
HARBOUR BAR
HARD AS IRON
HARD AS TEAK
HARD ASTERN
HARD AT WORK
HARD CENTRE
HARD CHEESE

HARD GROUND
HARD HITTER
HARD KERNEL
HARD KNOCKS
HARD LABOUR
HARD LESSON
HARD LIQUOR
HARDLY EVER
HARD MASTER
HARD NATURE
HARD PENCIL
HARD RIDING
HARD SCHOOL
HARD TO BEAR
HARD TO HOLD
HARD TO TAKE
HARD WINTER
HARD WORKER
HARPOON GUN
HARRY WORTH
HARSH SOUND
HARSH VOICE
HASTY WORDS
HATCH AN EGG
HATCH A PLOT
HAVE A CHAIR
HAVE A CRACK
HAVE A DRINK
HAVE A FIGHT
HAVE A FLING
HAVE A GUESS
HAVE A HEART
HAVE A HUNCH
HAVE AN IDEA
HAVE A PARTY
HAVE A SMOKE
HAVE A SNACK
HAVE BRAINS
HAVE DINNER
HAVE DOUBTS
HAVE EFFECT
HAVE FAULTS
HAVE IN HAND
HAVE IN MIND
HAVE IN VIEW
HAVE NO FEAR
HAVE NO HOPE
HAVE NO VOTE
HAVE QUALMS
HEAD HUNTER
HEAD KEEPER
HEAD OFFICE
HEAD OF HAIR
HEAD TO FOOT
HEAD TO TAIL
HEAD WAITER

HEAD WARDER
HEADY DRINK
HEALING ART
HEALTH,CURE
HEAP OF WORK
HEARING AID
HEAR NO EVIL
HEART OF OAK
HEART'S EASE
HEARTY MEAL
HEAR VOICES
HEAT STROKE
HEAVE A SIGH
HEAVY CHILL
HEAVY CLOUD
HEAVY GOING
HEAVY HEART
HEAVY METAL
HEAVY NIGHT
HEAVY SLEEP
HEAVY STORM
HEAVY STUFF
HEAVY STYLE
HEAVY SWELL
HEAVY TOUCH
HEAVY TREAD
HEAVY WATER
HECTIC TIME
HEDY LAMARR
HEEL AND TOE
HELEN WILLS
HELLO DOLLY
HELL'S BELLS
HENNA RINSE
HENRY FONDA
HENRY JAMES
HENRY MOORE
HENRY TUDOR
HERB GARDEN
HERD OF DEER
HERE AND NOW
HERE YOU ARE
HER MAJESTY
HERMIT CRAB
HEROIC DEED
HEROIC POEM
HERR HITLER
HIDDEN HAND
HIGH AND DRY
HIGH AND LOW
HIGH CASTLE
HIGH CHURCH
HIGH COLLAR
HIGH COLOUR
HIGH COMEDY
HIGH DEGREE

HIGHER RANK	HOME CIRCLE	HUMAN ERROR
HIGH ESTEEM	HOME COUNTY	HUMAN FRAME
HIGH FAVOUR	HOME FORCES	HUMAN SKILL
HIGH FIGURE	HOME FOR TEA	HUMAN VOICE
HIGH FLYING	HOME GROUND	HUMBLE FARE
HIGH GERMAN	HOME MARKET	HUMBLE FOLK
HIGH GROUND	HOME OFFICE	HUMBLE HOME
HIGH IDEALS	HOME TRUTHS	HUMMING TOP
HIGH INCOME	HOME WATERS	HUNDRED MEN
HIGH LIVING	HONEST FACE	HUNGRY LOOK
HIGHLY PAID	HONEST FOLK	HUNTING DOG
HIGH MORALE	HONEST JOHN	HUNTING KIT
HIGH NUMBER	HONEST LOOK	HUNT THE FOX
HIGH OCTANE	HONEST TOIL	HURDLE RACE
HIGH OFFICE	HONEST WORK	HURRY ALONG
HIGH PLACES	HONOURS MAN	HUSKY VOICE
HIGH POLISH	HOOK AND EYE	HYBRID RACE
HIGH PRAISE	HOOKED NOSE	HYMN OF HATE
HIGH PRIEST	HOPPING MAD	
HIGH REGARD	HORNED MOON	I – 10
HIGH RELIEF	HORNED TOAD	ICED COFFEE
HIGH REPUTE	HORROR FILM	ICE SKATING
HIGH SALARY	HORSE LAUGH	ICING SUGAR
HIGH SCHOOL	HORSE OPERA	ICY COLD DAY
HIGH STAKES	HORSE SENSE	ICY SURFACE
HIGH STATUS	HORSE THIEF	IDEAL PLACE
HIGH STREET	HOSTILE ACT	IDEAL WOMAN
HIGH SUMMER	HOT AND COLD	IDLE GOSSIP
HILARY TERM	HOT AS HADES	IDLE MOMENT
HINDER PART	HOT CLIMATE	IDLE RUMOUR
HIS AND HERS	HOT COCKLES	IDLE THREAT
HIS MAJESTY	HOTEL STAFF	IF POSSIBLE
HIS WORSHIP	HOTEL SUITE	ILKLEY MOOR
HIT AND MISS	HOT PURSUIT	ILL CONTENT
HIT THE MARK	HOT WEATHER	ILLEGAL ACT
HIT THE POST	HOUR BY HOUR	ILL FEELING
HOBBY HORSE	HOUR OF DOOM	ILL FORTUNE
HOCKEY BALL	HOUR OF NEED	ILL MANNERS
HOCKEY CLUB	HOURS ON END	IMPORT DUTY
HOCKEY TEAM	HOUSE AGENT	IMPOSE A BAN
HOCUS POCUS	HOUSE GUEST	IMPOSE UPON
HOLD A PARTY	HOUSE OF GOD	IN A BAD MOOD
HOLD NO HOPE	HOUSE ORGAN	IN ABEYANCE
HOLD OFFICE	HOUSE PARTY	IN ADDITION
HOLD THE KEY	HOUSE RULES	IN A DECLINE
HOLIDAY PAY	HOUSE TO LET	IN A DILEMMA
HOLLOW TREE	HOUSING ACT	IN A DRAUGHT
HOLY FATHER	HOVER ABOUT	IN A FAIR WAY
HOLY GROUND	HOW DARE YOU!	IN A FASHION
HOLY ISLAND	HOW DO YOU DO?	IN A FERMENT
HOLY OFFICE	HOW ON EARTH	IN A FLUTTER
HOLY ORDERS	HUGE PROFIT	IN A GOOD WAY
HOLY SPIRIT	HUG ONESELF	IN ALLIANCE
HOLY TEMPLE	HUG THE LAND	IN AN ASYLUM
HOLY TERROR	HUMAN BEING	IN AN UPROAR
HOME AND DRY	HUMAN CHAIN	IN ANY EVENT

IN A PASSION	INLAND PORT	IN THE DRINK
IN A TANTRUM	INLAND TOWN	IN THE DUMPS
IN AT THE END	INLET VALVE	IN THE EVENT
IN A TURMOIL	IN LONGHAND	IN THE FIELD
IN A WHISPER	IN LOW WATER	IN THE FILES
IN BAD ODOUR	IN MANY WAYS	IN THE FINAL
IN BAD SHAPE	IN MEMORIAM	IN THE FLESH
IN BAD TASTE	IN MOURNING	IN THE FRONT
IN BARRACKS	IN NAME ONLY	IN THE GRAVE
IN BOOK FORM	INNER HOUSE	IN THE HOUSE
IN BRACKETS	INNER LIGHT	IN THE INDEX
IN BUSINESS	INNER VOICE	IN THE KITTY
IN CHAMBERS	IN NOVEMBER	IN THE LIGHT
IN CHANCERY	IN OFF WHITE	IN THE LOCAL
INCH BY INCH	IN ONE PIECE	IN THE LURCH
IN CONFLICT	IN ONE'S CUPS	IN THE MONEY
IN CONTEMPT	IN ONE SENSE	IN THE NIGHT
IN CONTRAST	IN ONE'S HEAD	IN THE NORTH
IN DARKNESS	IN ONE'S MIND	IN THE OCEAN
IN DARTMOOR	IN ONE'S ROOM	IN THE PAPER
IN DAYLIGHT	IN PAKISTAN	IN THE PRESS
IN DECEMBER	IN PARADISE	IN THE QUEUE
IN DEFIANCE	IN PARALLEL	IN THE RANKS
INDEX TABLE	IN POLITICS	IN THE RIGHT
INDIAN ARMY	IN PORTUGAL	IN THE RIVER
INDIAN CLUB	IN POSITION	IN THE ROUGH
INDIAN CORN	IN PRACTICE	IN THE ROUND
INDIAN FILE	IN PROGRESS	IN THE SCRUM
INDIAN HEMP	IN PROSPECT	IN THE SHADE
INDIAN MEAL	IN QUESTION	IN THE SLIPS
INDIA PAPER	IN REAL LIFE	IN THE SLUMS
INDIGO BLUE	IN RESPONSE	IN THE SOUTH
IN DISARRAY	IN ROTATION	IN THE STAND
IN DISGRACE	INS AND OUTS	IN THE STARS
IN DISGUISE	INSANE IDEA	IN THE STUDY
IN DISORDER	IN SCOTLAND	IN THE SWING
IN DISTRESS	IN SEQUENCE	IN THE TOWER
INDOOR GAME	INSIDE EDGE	IN THE TRADE
IN EVERY WAY	INSIDE LEFT	IN THE TRAIN
IN EVIDENCE	INSIDE SEAT	IN THE VOGUE
IN EXCHANGE	IN SLOW TIME	IN THE WATER
IN EXTREMIS	IN SOMERSET	IN THE WILDS
IN FAVOUR OF	IN SOME WAYS	IN THE WINGS
IN FEBRUARY	IN STERLING	IN THE WOODS
IN FULL SAIL	IN STITCHES	IN THE WORLD
IN FULL VIEW	IN SUSPENSE	IN THE WRONG
IN GOOD FORM	IN SYMPATHY	INTO BATTLE
IN GOOD PART	INTENT LOOK	IN TRAINING
IN GOOD TIME	IN THE ATTIC	IN TWO MINDS
IN GOOD TRIM	IN THE BLOOD	IN TWO TICKS
IN HOSPITAL	IN THE CHAIR	INVALID OUT
IN HOT BLOOD	IN THE CHOIR	IN WHISPERS
IN HOT WATER	IN THE CLEAR	IRISH LINEN
INIGO JONES	IN THE DERBY	IRISH SWEEP
IN JEOPARDY	IN THE DITCH	IRISH TWEED
INJURY TIME	IN THE DOUGH	IRON RATION

ISLAND RACE
ISLE OF BUTE
ISLE OF DOGS
ISLE OF ELBA
ISLE OF MULL
ISLE OF SARK
ISLE OF SKYE
ISSUE A WRIT
ISSUE FORTH
ISSUE PRICE
ITALIAN CUT
ITALIC TYPE
IT'S A WANGLE
IVORY BLACK
IVORY COAST
IVORY PAINT
IVORY TOWER

J – 10

JACK ARCHER
JACK HORNER
JACK HYLTON
JACK LONDON
JACK SOCKET
JACK SPRATT
JAGGED EDGE
JAMAICA INN
JAMAICA RUM
JAMES AGATE
JAMES JOYCE
JAMES MASON
JAM SESSION
JANE AUSTEN
JAR OF HONEY
JIMMY YOUNG
JOCKEY CLUB
JOCKEY'S CAP
JOE BECKETT
JOHN ARLOTT
JOHN BRIGHT
JOHN BUCHAN
JOHN BUNYAN
JOHN CALVIN
JOHN CLEESE
JOHN DRYDEN
JOHN GILPIN
JOHN LENNON
JOHN MILTON
JOHN O'GAUNT
JOHN RUSKIN
JOHN WESLEY
JOIN BATTLE
JOIN FORCES
JOINT STOCK
JOLLY ROGER
JOSE FERRER

JO STAFFORD
JOYS OF LIFE
JUDO EXPERT
JUDO LESSON
JUGGED HARE
JULES VERNE
JUMBLE SALE
JUMP A CLAIM
JUMP FOR JOY
JUMP THE GUN
JUNGLE BOOK
JUNIOR MISS
JURY SYSTEM
JUST AN IDEA
JUST AS WELL
JUST BEFORE
JUST ENOUGH
JUST FOR FUN
JUST FOR NOW
JUST IN CASE
JUST IN TIME
JUST REWARD

K – 10

KANSAS CITY
KATHY KIRBY
KAY HAMMOND
KAY KENDALL
KEEN GLANCE
KEEN MEMBER
KEEP A DIARY
KEEP AFLOAT
KEEPING FIT
KEEP IN HAND
KEEP IN MIND
KEEP IN PAWN
KEEP IN PLAY
KEEP IN STEP
KEEP IN TUNE
KEEP IN VIEW
KEEP IT DARK
KEEP MOVING
KEEP POSTED
KEEP SECRET
KEEP SILENT
KEEP STEADY
KEEP TABS ON
KEEP TRYING
KEEP WICKET
KEIR HARDY
KENNEL CLUB
KENNEL MAID
KENNY BAKER
KENNY LYNCH
KENTISH COB
KENTISH MAN

KETTLE DRUM
KEW GARDENS
KEY WITNESS
KICK UP A ROW
KID BROTHER
KIDNEY BEAN
KID ONESELF
KILL OR CURE
KIND HEARTS
KIND PERSON
KING ALFRED
KING ARTHUR
KING CANUTE
KING EDWARD
KING GEORGE
KING HAROLD
KING OF ARMS
KING'S BENCH
KING'S COURT
KING'S CROSS
KING'S PRIZE
KING'S SCOUT
KING WILLOW
KISS CANNON
KISS ME KATE
KISS OF LIFE
KISS THE ROD
KITCHEN BOY
KITH AND KIN
KNIFE WOUND
KNOCK ABOUT
KNOCKED OUT
KNOT OF HAIR
KNOW BETTER
KNOW THE LAW
KNOW THE WAY
KU KLUX KLAN

L – 10

LABOUR CAMP
LABOUR CLUB
LABOUR POOL
LABOUR VOTE
LACE STITCH
LACK BRAINS
LACK FINISH
LACK OF FOOD
LACK OF FORM
LACK OF NEWS
LACK OF TIME
LACK OF ZEAL
LACK SPIRIT
LADIES' MAID
LADY BE GOOD
LADY DOCKER
LADY DOCTOR

LADY GODIVA
LA GIOCONDA
LAID TO REST
LAKE GENEVA
LAKE LUGANO
LAKE SCHOOL
LAMB CUTLET
LAMB'S TALES
LAME EXCUSE
LAND AGENCY
LAND AND SEA
LAND FORCES
LAND IN GAOL
LAND OF SONG
LAND REFORM
LAND TENURE
LAND TRAVEL
LARA'S THEME
LARCENY ACT
LARGE CROWD
LARGE DRINK
LARGE FLEET
LARGE HOUSE
LARGE ORDER
LARGE PARTY
LARGE PIECE
LARGE POWER
LARGE PRINT
LARGE SCALE
LARGE SPACE
LARGE STAFF
LARGE STOCK
LARGE STONE
LARGE VODKA
LARGE WAIST
LARRY ADLER
LAST AUTUMN
LAST BREATH
LAST BUT ONE
LAST BUT TWO
LAST CHANCE
LAST COURSE
LAST DEMAND
LAST EASTER
LAST FRIDAY
LAST GLANCE
LAST IN LINE
LAST LESSON
LAST LETTER
LAST MAN OUT
LAST MINUTE
LAST MOMENT
LAST MONDAY
LAST OF FIVE
LAST OF FOUR
LAST OF NINE

LAST ORDERS
LAST PERSON
LAST REFUGE
LAST RESORT
LAST RUBBER
LAST SEASON
LAST SERIES
LAST SPRING
LAST STROKE
LAST SUMMER
LAST SUNDAY
LAST SUPPER
LAST TO COME
LAST VOLUME
LAST WINTER
LATE AUTUMN
LATE DINNER
LATE FOR TEA
LATE GOTHIC
LATE IN LIFE
LATENT HEAT
LATE SPRING
LATEST NEWS
LATEST WORD
LATE SUMMER
LATE SUPPER
LATIN PROSE
LATIN VERSE
LA TRAVIATA
LATTER HALF
LAUGH IT OFF
LAVISH CARE
LAWFUL WIFE
LAWN TENNIS
LAW OFFICER
LAW OF LIBEL
LAW SOCIETY
LAW STUDENT
LAWYER'S FEE
LAY A COURSE
LAY BROTHER
LAY CLAIM TO
LAY HANDS ON
LAY IN DRINK
LAY IN RUINS
LAY IN STOCK
LAY SIEGE TO
LAY THE DUST
LAY THE FIRE
LAY THE ODDS
LAZY PERSON
LEAD A PARTY
LEAD ASTRAY
LEAD A TRUMP
LEADED TYPE
LEADEN FEET

LEADER PAGE
LEADING MAN
LEAD PENCIL
LEAD THE WAY
LEAD TRUMPS
LEAD WEIGHT
LEAP FOR JOY
LEARNED MAN
LEARN MUSIC
LEARN TO FLY
LEAST OF ALL
LEATHER BAG
LEAVE ALONE
LEAVE A MARK
LEAVE A NOTE
LEAVE A WILL
LEAVE EARLY
LED TO AGREE
LEFT BEHIND
LEFT INSIDE
LEFT WINGER
LEGAL CLAIM
LEGAL COSTS
LEGAL FORCE
LEGAL ISSUE
LEGAL LIGHT
LEGAL OWNER
LEGAL RIGHT
LEGAL TITLE
LEGAL TRIAL
LEGS ELEVEN
LEMON DRINK
LEMON JUICE
LEND COLOUR
LEND WEIGHT
LENIN'S TOMB
LENTIL SOUP
LESSER EVIL
LESSON FIVE
LESSON FOUR
LESSON NINE
LETHAL DOSE
LET IT SLIDE
LET IT STAND
LET ONE KNOW
LET'S FACE IT
LETTER BOMB
LETTER CARD
LETTER CASE
LETTER FILE
LETTER POST
LETTER RATE
LETTING OFF
LETTING OUT
LEVEL SCORE
LIE DORMANT

LIE IN STATE
LIE IN STATE
LIFE MEMBER
LIFE OF EASE
LIFE POLICY
LIFE'S BLOOD
LIFE TO COME
LIGHT A FIRE
LIGHT A PIPE
LIGHT AS AIR
LIGHT AS DAY
LIGHT BLUES
LIGHT BROWN
LIGHT GREEN
LIGHT HEART
LIGHT LUNCH
LIGHT MUSIC
LIGHT OF DAY
LIGHT OPERA
LIGHT SLEEP
LIGHT SNACK
LIGHT TOUCH
LIGHT TREAD
LIGHT VERSE
LIKE A CHARM
LIKE A FLASH
LIKE A THIEF
LIKELY SPOT
LIKELY TALE
LIME STREET
LIMPET MINE
LINDEN TREE
LINEN CHEST
LINE OF DUTY
LINE OF FIRE
LINE OF LIFE
LINE OF TYPE
LINSEED OIL
LIONEL BART
LION'S MOUTH
LION'S SHARE
LIP READING
LIP SERVICE
LIQUID DIET
LIQUID FIRE
LIQUID FOOD
LIQUID FUEL
LIQUID MEAL
LIQUOR LAWS
LITTER LOUT
LITTLE BEAR
LITTLE BIRD
LITTLE DROP
LITTLE FISH
LITTLE FOLK
LITTLE GAIN

LITTLE GIRL
LITTLE GOOD
LITTLE HOPE
LITTLE JOHN
LITTLE LAMB
LITTLE LESS
LITTLE MARY
LITTLE MORE
LITTLE NELL
LITTLE ROCK
LITTLE ROOM
LITTLE SHIP
LITTLE SLAM
LITTLE TIME
LITTLE USED
LIVE ABROAD
LIVE AFLOAT
LIVE AT EASE
LIVE IN DIGS
LIVE IN FEAR
LIVE IN HOPE
LIVE IN WANT
LIVE IT DOWN
LIVELY MIND
LIVELY TUNE
LIVE UP TO IT
LIVING ROOM
LIVING SOUL
LIVING WAGE
LLOYDS BANK
LLOYDS LIST
LOADED DICE
LOADING BAY
LOAD OF COAL
LOAD OF COKE
LOBSTER POT
LOCAL BOARD
LOCAL IDIOM
LOCAL PAPER
LOCAL RATES
LOCAL TRAIN
LOCAL VICAR
LOCH LOMOND
LOCK AND KEY
LOCKED DOOR
LOCK OF HAIR
LOCK-UP SHOP
LONDON AREA
LONDON TOWN
LONDON WALL
LONELY LIFE
LONE RANGER
LONG CAREER
LONG CREDIT
LONG CRUISE
LONG ENOUGH

LONGER ODDS
LONGEST DAY
LONGEST WAY
LONG FIGHT
LONG ISLAND
LONG LADDER
LONG LETTER
LONG MEMORY
LONG PERIOD
LONG PLAYER
LONG SPEECH
LONG TUNNEL
LONG VISION
LONG VOYAGE
LONG WINTER
LOOK AGHAST
LOOK AROUND
LOOK AT LIFE
LOOK A TREAT
LOOK A WRECK
LOOK DOWN ON
LOOK GUILTY
LOOK INSIDE
LOOK INTO IT
LOOK IN VAIN
LOOK LIVELY
LOOK-OUT MAN
LOOK SLIPPY
LOOK YONDER
LOOSE COVER
LOOSE LIVER
LOOSE STATE
LOOSE TOOTH
LOOSE WOMAN
LORD ATTLEE
LORD CURZON
LORD HAW-HAW
LORD HELP US!
LORD LISTER
LORD NELSON
LORD'S TABLE
LORD WARDEN
LORNA DOONE
LOS ANGELES
LOSE A TRICK
LOSE COLOUR
LOSE CREDIT
LOSE FAVOUR
LOSE GROUND
LOSE HEIGHT
LOSE NO TIME
LOSE THE DAY
LOSE THE WAY
LOSE WEIGHT
LOSING GAME
LOSING HAND

LOSING SIDE
LOSING TEAM
LOSING TOSS
LOSS OF FACE
LOSS OF HOPE
LOSS OF LIFE
LOSS OF TIME
LOST BATTLE
LOST CHANCE
LOST LABOUR
LOST LEADER
LOST TO VIEW
LOST TRIBES
LOTS OF LUCK
LOTS OF ROOM
LOTS OF TIME
LOUD CHEERS
LOUD COLOUR
LOUD OUTCRY
LOUD PRAISE
LOUD REPORT
LOUIS SEIZE
LOUNGE SUIT
LOVE AFFAIR
LOVE DEARLY
LOVE EMBLEM
LOVE LETTER
LOVELY GRUB
LOVELY TIME
LOVE OF LIFE
LOVE POTION
LOVERS' KNOT
LOVERS' LANE
LOVERS' LEAP
LOVERS' TIFF
LOVERS' VOWS
LOVE THIRTY
LOVING CARE
LOW CEILING
LOW COMPANY
LOW CONTENT
LOW CUNNING
LOW DENSITY
LOWER A FLAG
LOWER CLASS
LOWER FARES
LOWER HOUSE
LOWER LIMIT
LOWER PITCH
LOWER RANKS
LOWER SIXTH
LOWER WAGES
LOWER WORLD
LOW IN PRICE
LOW OPINION
LOW QUALITY

LOW SPIRITS
LOW STATION
LOW STATURE
LOW TENSION
LUCID STYLE
LUCKY BREAK
LUCKY CHARM
LUCKY GUESS
LUCKY PATCH
LUCKY PENNY
LUCKY STARS
LUCKY START
LUGGAGE VAN
LUMP OF CLAY
LUMP OF LEAD
LUNAR MONTH
LUNCH BREAK
LUNCH SCORE
LUPINO LANE
LURID LIGHT
LURID STYLE
LUTINE BELL
LUXURY FLAT
LYING KNAVE
LYRIC DRAMA
LYRIC VERSE

M – 10

MACHINE AGE
MADE BY HAND
MADE FAMOUS
MADE TO LAST
MADE-UP DISH
MADE USEFUL
MAD WITH JOY
MAGIC FLUTE
MAGIC POWER
MAGIC RITES
MAGIC SPELL
MAGIC SWORD
MAGIC TOUCH
MAGIC TRICK
MAGIC WORDS
MAGIC WORLD
MAGNA CARTA
MAGNUM OPUS
MAIDEN AUNT
MAIDEN LANE
MAIDEN NAME
MAIDEN OVER
MAID MARIAN
MAILED FIST
MAIL PACKET
MAIN ARTERY
MAIN CHANCE
MAIN CHARGE

MAIN CLAUSE
MAIN COURSE
MAIN OFFICE
MAIN REASON
MAIN SOURCE
MAIN STREAM
MAIN STREET
MAIN SWITCH
MAJOR CHORD
MAJOR ISSUE
MAJOR SCALE
MAJOR THIRD
MAKE A BREAK
MAKE A CATCH
MAKE A CLAIM
MAKE A GUESS
MAKE A JOINT
MAKE A MATCH
MAKE AMENDS
MAKE AN EXIT
MAKE A NOISE
MAKE A POINT
MAKE A SCENE
MAKE A STAND
MAKE A START
MAKE BETTER
MAKE EYES AT
MAKE GAME OF
MAKE IT A DAY
MAKE NO SIGN
MAKE PASSES
MAKE PUBLIC
MAKE SPARKS
MAKE THE BED
MAKE THE TEA
MAKE TRACKS
MAKE-UP ROOM
MAKE UP TIME
MALE CHORUS
MALE DANCER
MALTED MILK
MALT LIQUOR
MAN AND WIFE
MAN OF DEEDS
MAN OF IDEAS
MAN OF MONEY
MAN OF MOODS
MAN OF PARTS
MAN OF PEACE
MAN OF STEEL
MAN OF STRAW
MAN OF TASTE
MAN ON TRIAL
MANOR HOUSE
MAN OR MOUSE?
MAN'S ESTATE

MAN THE GUNS
MAN TO WATCH
MANUAL WORK
MANY THANKS
MAO-TSE TUNG
MAPLE SUGAR
MAPLE SYRUP
MAP OF SPAIN
MAP READING
MARBLE ARCH
MARCEL WAVE
MARCH FORTH
MARCH TO WAR
MARCH WINDS
MARIA BUENO
MARIE CURIE
MARIE LLOYD
MARIO LANZA
MARK ANTONY
MARKET HALL
MARKET TOWN
MARKING INK
MARK OF CAIN
MARK WYNTER
MARRIED MAN
MARRY YOUNG
MARTIAL ART
MARTIAL LAW
MARY MARTIN
MARY STUART
MASKED BALL
MASONRY BIT
MASS APPEAL
MASS ATTACK
MASS MARKET
MASS MURDER
MASTER MIND
MASTER PLAN
MASTER RACE
MATCH POINT
MATCH TRICK
MATINÉE HAT
MATING CALL
MATT DILLON
MATTED HAIR
MATURE MIND
MAXIM GORKY
MAY BLOSSOM
MAY FLOWERS
MAY MORNING
MEADOW LAND
MEAGRE DIET
MEAL TICKET
MEAN NO HARM
MEAN STREAK
MEASURE OUT

MEAT COURSE
MEAT MARKET
MEAT RATION
MEDICAL ART
MEDICAL MAN
MEDIUM DONE
MEDIUM RARE
MEDIUM SIZE
MEDIUM WAVE
MEET THE BUS
MEET THE EYE
MELBA TOAST
MELTING POT
MELT THE ICE
MEMORY LANE
MEMORY TEST
MENIAL WORK
MENTAL CASE
MENTAL HOME
MENTAL PAIN
MENTAL TEST
MENTAL WARD
MERE NOTION
MERE NOVICE
MERINO WOOL
MERRY DANCE
MERRY HEART
MERRY MONTH
MERRY PRANK
MERRY WIDOW
MERRY WIVES
MERSEY BEAT
MESS JACKET
METAL PLATE
MEXICO CITY
MIAMI BEACH
MICE AND MEN
MICKEY FINN
MICK JAGGER
MIDAS TOUCH
MIDDAY MEAL
MIDDLE AGES
MIDDLE DECK
MIDDLE EAST
MIDDLE LIFE
MIDDLE PART
MIDDLE ROAD
MIDDLE TERM
MIDDLE WEST
MIGHTY ATOM
MIGHTY DEEP
MIGHTY FINE
MILD ANSWER
MILD AS MILK
MILD REBUKE
MILD SPOKEN

MILD WINTER
MILES APART
MILK BOTTLE
MILL AROUND
MILLED EDGE
MINCED MEAT
MINCED OATH
MINCE WORDS
MINERAL OIL
MINER'S LAMP
MINOR CANON
MINOR CHORD
MINOR POINT
MINOR SCALE
MINOR THIRD
MINUS THREE
MINUTE BOOK
MINUTE HAND
MIRACLE MAN
MISERLY PAY
MISS A CATCH
MISS A TRICK
MISS MUFFET
MISS POINTS
MISS THE BUS
MIXED BLOOD
MIXED BREED
MIXED BUNCH
MIXED DRINK
MIXED GRILL
MIXED HERBS
MIXED PARTY
MIXED TRAIN
MIXED-UP KID
MOBILE UNIT
MOCK TURTLE
MODEL DRESS
MODEL PLANE
MODEL TRAIN
MODEL YACHT
MODE OF LIFE
MODERN GIRL
MODERN MISS
MOIST SUGAR
MONEYED MAN
MONEY ORDER
MONEY PRIZE
MONEY TALKS
MONKEY SUIT
MONK'S HABIT
MONTE CARLO
MONTEGO BAY
MONTE VIDEO
MOON AROUND
MOORING FEE
MORAL BLAME

MORAL FIBRE
MORAL ISSUE
MORAL LAPSE
MORAL POWER
MORAL RIGHT
MORAL SENSE
MORAY FIRTH
MORBID FEAR
MORDANT WIT
MORE OR LESS
MORE TO COME
MORNING SUN
MORNING TEA
MORTAL BLOW
MORTAL COIL
MORTAL FEAR
MORTAL SPAN
MOSAIC WORK
MOSS STITCH
MOST LIKELY
MOST PEOPLE
MOTHER LOVE
MOTHER'S BOY
MOTHER'S DAY
MOTHER SHIP
MOTOR COACH
MOTOR RALLY
MOUNT GUARD
MOUNT KENYA
MOUNT SINAI
MOUTH ORGAN
MOVE ACROSS
MOVE IN A RUT
MOVE SLOWLY
MOVE TROOPS
MOVING BELT
MOVING PART
MOW THE LAWN
MR MICAWBER
MRS SQUEERS
MR UNIVERSE
MUCH BETTER
MUCH SORROW
MUDDY BOOTS
MUDDY WATER
MUFFIN BELL
MULLED WINE
MUMBO JUMBO
MURDER CASE
MUSICAL BOX
MUSICAL EAR
MUSIC LOVER
MUSIC STAND
MUSIC STOOL
MUSKET FIRE
MUSTARD GAS

MUSTARD POT
MUTE APPEAL
MUTTON CHOP
MUTUAL LOVE
MY CUP OF TEA
MY DEAR CHAP
MY FAIR LADY
MY GOODNESS!
MY HEARTIES
MY OLD DUTCH
MY OLD WOMAN
MYSTERY MAN

N – 10

NAIL POLISH
NAKED FACTS
NAKED FLAME
NAKED LIGHT
NAKED STEEL
NAKED SWORD
NAKED TRUTH
NAME THE DAY
NARROW DOWN
NARROW MIND
NARROW MISS
NARROW PATH
NARROW ROAD
NARROW VIEW
NASAL ORGAN
NASAL TWANG
NASTY HABIT
NASTY KNOCK
NASTY SHOCK
NASTY SPILL
NASTY TASTE
NASTY TRICK
NATIVE LAND
NATIVE RACE
NATIVE SOIL
NATURAL GAS
NATURAL KEY
NATURAL LAW
NATURAL WIT
NATURE CURE
NAUGHTY BOY
NAUTCH GIRL
NAVAL CADET
NAVAL CRAFT
NAVAL POWER
NAVAL STORE
NAVY LEAGUE
NAZI RÉGIME
NEAR AND FAR
NEAR AT HAND
NEAR ENOUGH
NEAR FRIEND

NEAR FUTURE
NEARLY OVER
NEAR THE END
NEAR THE SEA
NEAR THE TOP
NEAT AS A PIN
NEAT FIGURE
NEAT SCOTCH
NEAT STROKE
NEAT WHISKY
NECK OF LAMB
NECK OF LAND
NEEDLE'S EYE
NEGRO MUSIC
NELSON EDDY
NERVE TONIC
NERVOUS TIC
NESTLE DOWN
NEVER AGAIN
NEVER LEARN
NEVER NEVER
NEVER WAVER
NEVER WORRY
NEVER WRONG
NEVIL SHUTE
NEW ADDRESS
NEW ARRIVAL
NEW CHAPTER
NEW CLOTHES
NEW COINAGE
NEW COLLEGE
NEW CONVERT
NEW EDITION
NEW ENGLAND
NEW FASHION
NEW HORIZON
NEW-LAID EGG
NEW-MOWN HAY
NEW ORLEANS
NEW PROCESS
NEW RECRUIT
NEW RESOLVE
NEWS AGENCY
NEWS CINEMA
NEWS EDITOR
NEWS LETTER
NEW SPEAKER
NEWS REPORT
NEW UNIFORM
NEW VERSION
NEW ZEALAND
NEXT AUTUMN
NEXT BUT ONE
NEXT BUT TWO
NEXT DOOR TO
NEXT FRIDAY

NEXT IN LINE	NO MEAN CITY	NUTTY SLACK
NEXT MONDAY	NOMINAL FEE	
NEXT PERSON	NOMINAL SUM	O – 10
NEXT PLEASE	NONE OF THAT!	
NEXT SEASON	NO NONSENSE	OBEY ORDERS
NEXT SPRING	NON-STOP RUN	OCEAN LINER
NEXT SUMMER	NOODLE SOUP	OCEAN WAVES
NEXT SUNDAY	NOONDAY SUN	ODD AND EVEN
NEXT TO COME	NO PATIENCE	OEDIPUS REX
NEXT VICTIM	NO RESPONSE	OF A PATTERN
NEXT WINTER	NORMAL LIFE	OFF BALANCE
NICE ENOUGH	NORMAL LOAD	OFFER TO PAY
NICE PEOPLE	NORMAL PACE	OFFICE DESK
NICE TO KNOW	NORTH COAST	OFFICE GIRL
NICKEL COIN	NORTH DEVON	OFFICE SAFE
NICK OF TIME	NORTH DOWNS	OFFICE WORK
NIGHT FROST	NORTH WALES	OFF LICENCE
NIGHT NURSE	NOSE TO TAIL	OFF ONE'S NUT
NIGHT SHIFT	NO SHORTAGE	OFFSIDE LAW
NIGHT SIGHT	NO SOLUTION	OFF THE BEAM
NIGHT TRAIN	NO STANDING	OFF THE CUFF
NIGHT WATCH	NO STRANGER	OFF THE CUSH
NINE AND ONE	NO SUCH LUCK	OFF THE HOOK
NINE AND SIX	NOSY PARKER	OFF THE LAND
NINE AND TEN	NOT A CHANCE	OFF THE MARK
NINE AND TWO	NOT CRICKET	OFF THE MENU
NINE MONTHS	NOTE OF HAND	OFF THE REEL
NINE O'CLOCK	NOT FAR AWAY	OIL COMPANY
NINE OUNCES	NOT FOR SALE	OLD AND MILD
NINE POINTS	NO THANK YOU	OLD AND TRUE
NINE POUNDS	NOTHING NEW	OLD BRIGADE
NINE TENTHS	NOT JUST NOW	OLD CLOTHES
NINTH GREEN	NOT LONG AGO	OLD COUNTRY
NINTH OF MAY	NOT ONE OF US	OLD EDITION
NINTH PLACE	NOT PRESENT	OLD ENGLAND
NINTH ROUND	NOT SO DUSTY	OLD ENGLISH
NIP ON AHEAD	NOT THE SAME	OLDEN TIMES
NITRIC ACID	NOT THE TYPE	OLD ETONIAN
NO APPETITE	NOT TO WORRY	OLD OAK TREE
NOBEL PRIZE	NOT VISIBLE	OLD PALS ACT
NOBLE BIRTH	NOT WORKING	OLD ROUTINE
NOBLE BLOOD	NOT WORTH IT	OLD SO-AND-SO
NOBLE HOUSE	NOVA SCOTIA	OLD SOLDIER
NOBODY ELSE	NOVEL TITLE	OLD VERSION
NO DECISION	NOW AND THEN	OLD VETERAN
NO DISTANCE	NO WEAKNESS	OLD WARRIOR
NOD THE HEAD	NOW OR NEVER	OLD WINDBAG
NOEL COWARD	NUCLEAR WAR	OLD YEAR OUT
NO ENTRANCE	NUDE FIGURE	OLIVE GREEN
NO FRICTION	NUDIST CAMP	OLIVE GROVE
NO HARM DONE	NUDIST CLUB	OL' MAN RIVER
NO INTEREST	NUMBER FIVE	ON A CRUSADE
NO LEFT TURN	NUMBER FOUR	ON ALL FOURS
NO LOVE LOST	NUMBER NINE	ON ALL HANDS
NO MAN'S LAND	NUT AND BOLT	ON ALL SIDES
NOM DE PLUME	NUTS AND MAY	ON APPROVAL
		ON BAD TERMS

ON BUSINESS	ON THE BRAIN	OPEN ARREST
ONCE A MONTH	ON THE BRINK	OPEN BREACH
ONCE BITTEN	ON THE CARDS	OPEN CHEQUE
ONCE IN A WAY	ON THE CHEAP	OPEN CREDIT
ON CRUTCHES	ON THE CLOCK	OPEN DRAWER
ON DELIVERY	ON THE CLYDE	OPEN GROUND
ON EACH SIDE	ON THE COAST	OPEN HEARTH
ONE-ACT PLAY	ON THE CREST	OPENING BID
ONE AND FIVE	ON THE CROSS	OPENING DAY
ONE AND FOUR	ON THE FENCE	OPEN LETTER
ONE AND NINE	ON THE FILES	OPEN MARKET
ONE AND ONLY	ON THE FLANK	OPEN PRISON
ONE ANOTHER	ON THE FLOOR	OPEN REVOLT
ONE AT A TIME	ON THE GREEN	OPEN SEASON
ONE BILLION	ON THE HALLS	OPEN SECRET
ONE DIAMOND	ON THE HOUSE	OPEN SESAME
ONE FINE DAY	ON THE LATCH	OPEN TO VIEW
ONE FURLONG	ON THE LEVEL	OPEN WINDOW
ONE HUNDRED	ON THE LINKS	OPERA GLASS
ONE IN EIGHT	ON THE LOOSE	OPERA HOUSE
ONE IN SEVEN	ON THE MARCH	OPERA MUSIC
ONE IN THREE	ON THE PANEL	OPIUM EATER
ONE-MAN BAND	ON THE PHONE	OPIUM HABBIT
ONE MILLION	ON THE PROWL	OPIUM POPPY
ONE NO-TRUMP	ON THE QUIET	OPTIC NERVE
ONE PER CENT	ON THE RADIO	ORANGE PEEL
ONE QUARTER	ON THE RAILS	ORANGE TREE
ONE SEVENTH	ON THE RHINE	ORANGE WINE
ONE'S OWN WAY	ON THE RIGHT	ORDER A MEAL
ONE SQUARED	ON THE RIVER	ORDER PAPER
ONE SWALLOW	ON THE ROCKS	ORGAN MUSIC
ONE TOO MANY	ON THE SANDS	ORIENT LINE
ONE TWELFTH	ON THE SCENT	ORION'S BELT
ONE WAY ONLY	ON THE SHELF	OSCAR AWARD
ON FURLOUGH	ON THE SLANT	OSCAR WILDE
ONION SAUCE	ON THE SLATE	OSTRICH EGG
ON LOCATION	ON THE SOMME	OTHER RANKS
ONLY CHANCE	ON THE SPREE	OTHER WORLD
ONLY CHOICE	ON THE STAFF	OUIJA BOARD
ON MORTGAGE	ON THE STAGE	OUR BETTERS
ON MY HONOUR	ON THE STAND	OUR VERSION
ON OCCASION	ON THE TABLE	OUT AND HOME
ON ONE'S BACK	ON THE TELLY	OUT AT ELBOW
ON ONE'S FEET	ON THE TILES	OUTER COVER
ON ONE'S LEGS	ON THE TRACK	OUTER SPACE
ON ONE'S TOES	ON THE TRAIL	OUTER WORLD
ON SATURDAY	ON THE VERGE	OUT IN FORCE
ON SCHEDULE	ON THE WAGON	OUT IN FRONT
ON SENTRY-GO	ON THE WATCH	OUT OF COURT
ON THE ALERT	ON THE WATER	OUT OF DOORS
ON THE BEACH	ON THE WAY IN	OUT OF FOCUS
ON THE BENCH	ON THE WAY UP	OUT OF FUNDS
ON THE BIBLE	ON THE WHOLE	OUT OF HOURS
ON THE BOARD	ON THIS SIDE	OUT OF JOINT
ON THE BOOKS	ON THURSDAY	OUT OF MONEY
ON THE BOOZE	ON VACATION	OUT OF MY WAY

OUT OF ORBIT	PAPER MONEY	PEARL DIVER
OUT OF ORDER	PAPER ROUND	PEARLY KING
OUT OF PLACE	PARCEL POST	PEAS IN A POD
OUT OF PRINT	PAR CONTEST	PEA-SOUP FOG
OUT OF RANGE	PARENT BIRD	PECKHAM RYE
OUT OF REACH	PARENTS' DAY	PECK OF DIRT
OUT OF SCALE	PARENT SHIP	PEDDLE DOPE
OUT OF SHAPE	PARENT TREE	PEEPING TOM
OUT OF SIGHT	PARI MUTUEL	PEGGED DOWN
OUT OF SORTS	PARISH PUMP	PEGGY MOUNT
OUT OF SPITE	PARK AVENUE	PENALTY BOX
OUT OF STOCK	PARKING BAY	PENCIL CASE
OUT OF TOUCH	PARKING FEE	PENNY BLACK
OUT OF WATER	PARKING LOT	PENNY PIECE
OUT ON A LIMB	PART BY PART	PENNY PLAIN
OUT PATIENT	PARTED LIPS	PENNY STAMP
OUTWARD EYE	PARTY DRESS	PENSION OFF
OVAL OFFICE	PARTY FROCK	PEPPER MILL
OVER AND OUT	PARTY FUNDS	PEPYS' DIARY
OVER EXPOSE	PARTY PIECE	PERFECT FIT
OVER POLITE	PARTY TRICK	PERIOD PLAY
OVER THE AIR	PASS FRIEND	PERRY MASON
OVER THE BAR	PASSING FAD	PERSIAN CAT
OVER THE SEA	PASS MUSTER	PERSIAN MAT
OVER THE TOP	PASS ORDERS	PERSIAN RUG
OVER THE WAY	PASS THE CAN	PETE MURRAY
OWE LOYALTY	PASS THE HAT	PETER FINCH
OWNER'S RISK	PAST BELIEF	PETER PIPER
OX-EYE DAISY	PAST CARING	PETER SCOTT
OXFORD BAGS	PAST MASTER	PETIT POINT
OXFORD BLUE	PAST RECORD	PETITS POIS
OXTAIL SOUP	PASTRY CHEF	PETROL DUMP
OXYGEN MASK	PASTRY COOK	PETROL PUMP
OXYGEN TENT	PATH OF DUTY	PETROL TANK
	PATROL DUTY	PETTY CRIME
P – 10	PAUL DOMBEY	PETTY THEFT
	PAUL REVERE	PETTY THIEF
PACK ANIMAL	PAUL TEMPLE	PHIL ARCHER
PACK A PUNCH	PAVE THE WAY	PHIL HARRIS
PACK OF LIES	PAWN TICKET	PHRASE BOOK
PADDED CELL	PAY A REWARD	PIANO STOOL
PADDY FIELD	PAY AS YOU GO	PIANO TUNER
PAGE ELEVEN	PAY CORKAGE	PICK A FIGHT
PAGE TWELVE	PAY DAMAGES	PICKET LINE
PAID A VISIT	PAYING GAME	PICK FAULTS
PAIL OF MILK	PAY-OFF LINE	PICK STRAWS
PAINED LOOK	PAY ONE'S WAY	PICK UP NEWS
PAIR OF ACES	PAY ON SIGHT	PICTURE HAT
PAIR OF OARS	PAY THE BILL	PIED-À-TERRE
PAIR OF TENS	PAY THE RENT	PIER MASTER
PAIR OF TWOS	PAY TRIBUTE	PIGEON POST
PALE AND WAN	PEACE OFFER	PIG IN A POKE
PALE YELLOW	PEACE PARTY	PILOT LIGHT
PALM SUNDAY	PEACE TERMS	PINA COLADA
PANCAKE DAY	PEACH MELBA	PINE FOREST
PAPAL COURT	PEAK PERIOD	PINK RIBBON
PAPER CHAIN		

PINNED DOWN	PLAY THE WAG	PORT TALBOT
PINT OF BEER	PLAY TRICKS	POSTAL RATE
PINT OF MILD	PLAY TRUANT	POST MORTEM
PINT OF MILK	PLAY TRUMPS	POST OFFICE
PIOUS HOPES	PLENTY MORE	POTATO PEEL
PIOUS TRUTH	PLENTY TO DO	POT HUNTING
PIPED MUSIC	PLOT OF LAND	POT OF HONEY
PIPES OF PAN	PLOUGH BACK	POT OF MONEY
PIRATE FLAG	PLOVER'S EGG	POT OF PAINT
PIRATE SHIP	PLUCKY CHAP	POTTED MEAT
PISTOL SHOT	PLUMB CRAZY	POTTER'S BAR
PITCH A TENT	PLY FOR HIRE	POT THE BLUE
PITCH A YARN	POACHED EGG	POT THE PINK
PITCH BLACK	POCKET COMB	POUNCE UPON
PITH HELMET	POETIC VEIN	POUND OF TEA
PLACED LAST	POINT BLANK	POULTRY RUN
PLACE MONEY	POINT OF LAW	POURING WET
PLACE ON END	POKER PARTY	POWDER BLUE
PLAGUE SPOT	POLES APART	POWDER BOWL
PLAIN FACTS	POLE TO POLE	POWDER PUFF
PLAIN FOLLY	POLICE BALL	POWDER ROOM
PLAIN PAPER	POLICE RAID	POWER HOUSE
PLAIN SKIRT	POLICE TRAP	POWER PLANT
PLAIN SOCKS	POLLING DAY	POWER POINT
PLAIN TERMS	POLO GROUND	POWER PRESS
PLAIN TO SEE	POLO PLAYER	PRAIRIE DOG
PLAIN TRUTH	POMPOUS ASS	PRAWN CURRY
PLAIN WORDS	PONDER'S END	PRAWN SALAD
PLANE CRASH	POOR BEGGAR	PRAYER BOOK
PLANT A TREE	POOR CHANCE	PREP. SCHOOL
PLASTIC ART	POOR CHOICE	PRESENT DAY
PLASTIC BAG	POOR EXCUSE	PRESS AGENT
PLASTIC MAC	POOR FELLOW	PRESS AHEAD
PLASTIC TOY	POOR GROUND	PRESS BARON
PLAT DU JOUR	POOR HEALTH	PRETTY FACE
PLATE GLASS	POOR PEOPLE	PRETTY FAIR
PLAY A CHORD	POOR PLAYER	PRETTY GIRL
PLAY A SCALE	POOR RELIEF	PRETTY GOOD
PLAY AT HOME	POOR RESULT	PRETTY MESS
PLAY A TRICK	POOR RETURN	PRETTY PASS
PLAY A WALTZ	POOR SAILOR	PRETTY POLL
PLAY BO-PEEP	POOR SECOND	PRETTY SURE
PLAY BRIDGE	POOR SERMON	PRETTY TUNE
PLAY HAMLET	POOR STAYER	PRETTY WELL
PLAY HOCKEY	POOR WRETCH	PRICE INDEX
PLAY HOOKEY	POOR YORICK	PRICE LABEL
PLAY IT COOL	POPLAR TREE	PRICE LEVEL
PLAY POSSUM	POPULAR AIR	PRIMA DONNA
PLAY PRANKS	PORK FILLET	PRIMA FACIE
PLAY RUGGER	PORK-PIE HAT	PRIME CAUSE
PLAY SCALES	PORT ARTHUR	PRIME MOVER
PLAY SOCCER	PORT DARWIN	PRINCE IGOR
PLAY SQUASH	PORT ENGINE	PRINT DRESS
PLAY STREET	PORTION OUT	PRIOR CLAIM
PLAY TENNIS	PORT NELSON	PRISON BARS
PLAY THE MAN	PORT OF CALL	PRISON CAMP

PRISON CELL
PRISON DIET
PRISON FARE
PRISON GATE
PRISON YARD
PRIVATE BAR
PRIVATE BUS
PRIVATE CAR
PRIVATE EYE
PRIVATE LAW
PRIVATE WAR
PRIVATE WAY
PRIVY PURSE
PRIZE COURT
PRIZE ENTRY
PRIZE ESSAY
PRIZE FIGHT
PRIZE IDIOT
PRIZE MONEY
PROFITS TAX
PROMPT BOOK
PROPER CARE
PROPER MIND
PROPER NAME
PROPER NOUN
PROPER TIME
PROSE WORKS
PRO TEMPORE
PROUD BOAST
PROUD FLESH
PROUD HEART
PROUD SIGHT
PROVEN FACT
PROWL ABOUT
PRYING EYES
PSYCHIC BID
PUBLIC GOOD
PUBLIC LIFE
PUBLIC PARK
PUBLIC PATH
PUBLIC ROAD
PUBLIC ROOM
PUBLIC SALE
PUBLIC WEAL
PUERTO RICO
PUFF OF WIND
PUFF PASTRY
PULLMAN CAR
PUNCH DRUNK
PUPPET SHOW
PURE ACCENT
PURE CHANCE
PURE COLOUR
PURE REASON
PURE SILVER
PURSED LIPS

PUSH AROUND
PUSH TOO FAR
PUT AND TAKE
PUT AN END TO
PUT A STOP TO
PUT ASUNDER
PUT FORWARD
PUT IN A BOOK
PUT IN A CELL
PUT IN A WORD
PUT IN FRONT
PUT IN IRONS
PUT IN ORDER
PUT IN POWER
PUT IN RHYME
PUT IN VERSE
PUT IN WORDS
PUT ON AN ACT
PUT ON A SHOW
PUT ON BLACK
PUT ON BOARD
PUT ONE OVER
PUT ONE WISE
PUT ON FLESH
PUT ON SPEED
PUT ON TRIAL
PUT THE SHOT
PUT THROUGH
PUTTING OFF
PUTTING OUT
PUT TO DEATH
PUT TO MUSIC
PUT TO SHAME
PUT TO SLEEP
PUTTY MEDAL
PUT UP A SHOW
PUT UP A SIGN
PUZZLED AIR
PUZZLE OVER

Q – 10

QUACK, QUACK
QUAI D'ORSAY
QUAINT IDEA
QUAKER GIRL
QUARTER DAY
QUEEN'S HALL
QUEEN'S HEAD
QUEEN'S PAWN
QUEEN'S ROOK
QUEER SOUND
QUICK LUNCH
QUICK MARCH
QUICK TEMPO
QUICK TRICK
QUID PRO QUO

QUIET START
QUITE CLEAR
QUITE CLOSE
QUITE EMPTY
QUITE HAPPY
QUITE RIGHT
QUITE STILL
QUITE WRONG
QUIT OFFICE
QUIZ MASTER

R – 10

RABBIT SKIN
RACE HATRED
RACING CARD
RACING FORM
RACING NEWS
RACING TOUT
RADIATE JOY
RADIO DRAMA
RADIO TIMES
RADIUM BOMB
RAGGED EDGE
RAILWAY ACT
RAISE A DUST
RAISE A HAND
RAISE A LOAN
RAISE ALOFT
RAISE MONEY
RAISE STEAM
RAISE TAXES
RALLY ROUND
RANCH HOUSE
RANDOM SHOT
RAPID PULSE
RARE CHANCE
RARING TO GO
RASH BELIEF
RATHER COOL
RATHER FLAT
RATHER GOOD
RATHER LATE
RATION BOOK
RATION CARD
RATTLE AWAY
RAW RECRUIT
RAY CHARLES
RAYNES PARK
RAY OF LIGHT
RAZOR BLADE
RAZOR'S EDGE
RAZOR SHARP
RAZOR STROP
READ A STORY
READ DEEPLY

READY FOR IT	REST CENTRE	RIVER BASIN
READY MONEY	REST PERIOD	RIVER CLYDE
READY REPLY	RETAIL SHOP	RIVER CRAFT
READY TO CRY	RETIRED PAY	RIVER LEVEL
READY TO DIE	RETIRE HURT	RIVER MOUTH
READY TO EAT	RETURN FARE	RIVER PLATE
REAL DANGER	RETURN GAME	RIVER RHINE
REAL ESTATE	RETURN HALF	RIVER RHONE
REAL FRIEND	RETURN HOME	RIVER TRENT
REALLY MEAN	REVIEW COPY	RIVER TROUT
REAL MADRID	RICHARD ROE	RIVER TWEED
REAL OBJECT	RICH PEOPLE	ROAD SAFETY
REAL PERSON	RICH REWARD	ROAD TO FAME
REAL SCHOOL	RICH SOURCE	ROAD TO HELL
REAL TENNIS	RICH SUPPLY	ROAD TO RUIN
REAR WINDOW	RIDING COAT	ROAD-UP SIGN
RECENT DATE	RIDING CROP	ROAST ALIVE
RECENT PAST	RIDING HIGH	ROBBER BAND
RECIPE BOOK	RIDING SEAT	ROBERT ADAM
RECORD CROP	RIDING WHIP	ROBERT PEEL
RECORD GATE	RIFLE CORPS	ROBIN ADAIR
RECORD ROOM	RIFLE RANGE	ROB THE TILL
RECORD SALE	RIGHT ABOUT	ROCK BOTTOM
RECORD SHOP	RIGHT AHEAD	ROCKET BASE
RECORD TIME	RIGHT ANGLE	ROCKET SITE
RED ADMIRAL	RIGHT DRESS	ROCK GARDEN
RED AS A ROSE	RIGHT FLANK	ROCK HUDSON
RED BALLOON	RIGHT LINES	ROCK OF AGES
RED BIRETTA	RIGHT OF WAY	ROCKS AHEAD
RED CABBAGE	RIGHT ON TOP	ROCK SALMON
RED CURRANT	RIGHT PLACE	ROCKY COAST
RED FLANNEL	RIGHT ROUND	ROD AND LINE
RED HERRING	RIGHT ROYAL	ROGER BACON
RED PIGMENT	RIGHT THING	ROGER MOORE
RED, RED ROSE	RIGHT TO BUY	ROLLED GOLD
REFINED OIL	RIGHT TOTAL	ROLLED OATS
REFORM BILL	RIGHT TRACK	ROLLS OF FAT
REFORM CLUB	RIGHT TRAIL	ROMAN EAGLE
REFUSE BAIL	RIGHT WAY UP	ROMAN FORUM
REFUSE DUMP	RIGHT WHEEL	ROMAN RUINS
REFUSE TO GO	RIGHT WOMAN	ROMAN TUNIC
RELIEF FUND	RING FINGER	ROMAN VILLA
REMAIN CALM	RING MASTER	ROMPER SUIT
REMAIN DUMB	RINGO STARR	ROOF GARDEN
REMAND HOME	RIOT POLICE	ROOM NUMBER
REMOTE AGES	RIOT SHIELD	ROOM TO MOVE
REMOVAL VAN	RIPEN EARLY	ROOM TO TURN
RENEW A BOOK	RIPE OLD AGE	ROPE A STEER
RENT A HOUSE	RIPE TOMATO	ROPE LADDER
REPAY A LOAN	RISE HIGHER	ROSE COLOUR
REPORT BACK	RISE IN ARMS	ROSE GARDEN
REPORT SICK	RISING COST	ROSY CHEEKS
RESCUE SHIP	RISING TIDE	ROTARY CLUB
RESCUE TEAM	RIVAL CAMPS	ROTTEN HAND
RESCUE WORK	RIVAL CAUSE	ROTTEN IDEA
REST AWHILE	RIVAL CLAIM	ROTTEN LUCK

ROUGH CIDER
ROUGH DRAFT
ROUGH GOING
ROUGH GUESS
ROUGH GUIDE
ROUGH HANDS
ROUGH HOUSE
ROUGH NIGHT
ROUGH STATE
ROUGH STONE
ROUGH STUFF
ROUGH TRACK
ROUGH USAGE
ROUGH WATER
ROUGH WORDS
ROUND ABOUT
ROUND DANCE
ROUND DOZEN
ROUND GUESS
ROUND ROBIN
ROUND SCORE
ROUND TABLE
ROUND TERMS
ROUND TOWER
ROUTE MARCH
ROWING BLUE
ROWING BOAT
ROWING CLUB
ROW OF BEANS
ROW OF TREES
ROW UPON ROW
ROYAL ASCOT
ROYAL BARGE
ROYAL BIRTH
ROYAL BLOOD
ROYAL FLUSH
ROYAL HOUSE
ROYAL LODGE
ROYAL SCOTS
ROYAL SUITE
ROYAL TRAIN
ROYAL VISIT
ROYAL YACHT
ROY EMERSON
ROY ORBISON
RUB AGAINST
RUBBER BALL
RUBBER BAND
RUBBER HOSE
RUBBER SOLE
RUBBER TUBE
RUBBER TYRE
RUBIKS CUBE
RUBY MURRAY
RUDE ANSWER
RUDE HEALTH

RUDE PERSON
RUDE REMARK
RUDOLF HESS
RUGBY FIELD
RUGBY MATCH
RUGBY PITCH
RUGBY SCRUM
RUGBY TRIAL
RUGBY UNION
RUGGER BLUE
RUM AND LIME
RUN ABREAST
RUN AGAINST
RUN AGROUND
RUN A MINUTE
RUN AT A LOSS
RUN ERRANDS
RUN FOR HELP
RUN FOR PORT
RUN IN PAIRS
RUN LIKE MAD
RUNNER BEAN
RUNNING OUT
RUN THE RISK
RUN THE SHOW
RUN THROUGH
RUN TO EARTH
RUN TO WASTE
RUN UP A BILL
RURAL SCENE
RUSS CONWAY
RUSSIAN EGG
RUSSIAN TEA
RUSTIC ARCH
RUSTIC SEAT
RUSTIC WORK

S – 10

SABBATH DAY
SABLE STOLE
SACK OF COAL
SACK OF COKE
SACK OF CORN
SACK THE LOT
SACRED BOOK
SACRED RITE
SACRED WRIT
SAD OUTLOOK
SAD TIDINGS
SAFE IN PORT
SAFE METHOD
SAFE POLICY
SAFE REFUGE
SAFETY BELT
SAFETY LAMP
SAIL A YACHT

SAILING AID
SAILOR SUIT
SAINT LOUIS
SAINT PETER
SALAD CREAM
SALE OF WORK
SALES STAFF
SALLY FORTH
SALMON PINK
SALT CELLAR
SALTED AWAY
SALTED BEEF
SALT OF LIFE
SALT TREATY
SAM GOLDWYN
SAMPLE BOOK
SAND CASTLE
SANDIE SHAW
SANDS OF DEE
SANDY BEACH
SANE ENOUGH
SANTA CLAUS
SANTA LUCIA
SARAH MILES
SARDINE TIN
SATIN DRESS
SAUCER EYES
SAVAGE BLOW
SAVAGE CLUB
SAVAGE RACE
SAVE A TRICK
SAVE LABOUR
SAVE THE DAY
SAVING GAME
SAVOY HOTEL
SAY A PRAYER
SAY GOOD-BYE
SAY NOTHING
SAY THE WORD
SCALDED CAT
SCALE MODEL
SCAMPER OFF
SCARLET HAT
SCARS OF WAR
SCENE THREE
SCENT SPRAY
SCHOOL BELL
SCHOOL BOOK
SCHOOL DAYS
SCHOOL FEES
SCHOOL SONG
SCHOOL TERM
SCHOOL YEAR
SCORE A BULL
SCORE A DUCK
SCORE A GOAL

SCOTCH KALE	SECOND WEEK	SET OF CHESS
SCOTCH MIST	SECOND WIFE	SET OF CLUBS
SCOTCH PINE	SECOND WIND	SET OF DARTS
SCOTCH REEL	SECOND YEAR	SET OF EIGHT
SCOTS GREYS	SECRET CODE	SET OF RULES
SCOUT ROUND	SECRET DOOR	SET OF SEVEN
SCRAPE AWAY	SECRET FILE	SET OF STUDS
SCRAPE HOME	SECRET PACT	SET OF TEETH
SCRAP METAL	SECRET SIGN	SET OF THREE
SCRAP PAPER	SECRET VICE	SET OF TOOLS
SCRATCH MAN	SECRET VOTE	SET PROBLEM
SCRATCH OUT	SEDAN CHAIR	SET PURPOSE
SCREECH OWL	SEE ABOUT IT	SET STORE BY
SCREEN IDOL	SEE A DOCTOR	SET THE PACE
SCREEN TEST	SEE A LAWYER	SETTING OFF
SCREW LOOSE	SEE CLEARLY	SETTING OUT
SCRIP ISSUE	SEEING LIFE	SETTING SUN
SCUTTLE OFF	SEEK ACCORD	SETTLE DOWN
SEA ANEMONE	SEEK ADVICE	SET TO MUSIC
SEA BATHING	SEEK OFFICE	SET UP HOUSE
SEA CAPTAIN	SEEK REFUGE	SEVEN A SIDE
SEALED BOOK	SEEK SAFETY	SEVEN CLUBS
SEALED LIPS	SEE NOTHING	SEVEN DIALS
SEA MONSTER	SEE ONE'S WAY	SEVEN DOZEN
SEAN O'CASEY	SEE SERVICE	SEVEN GROSS
SEA OF FACES	SEE THE JOKE	SEVEN HOURS
SEA PASSAGE	SEE THROUGH	SEVEN KINGS
SEA SERPENT	SEE VISIONS	SEVEN MILES
SECOND BELL	SEIZE POWER	SEVEN PARTS
SECOND BEST	SELECT CLUB	SEVEN PINTS
SECOND COAT	SELL AN IDEA	SEVEN SCORE
SECOND COPY	SELL IN BULK	SEVEN STARS
SECOND CROP	SELL SHARES	SEVENTH DAY
SECOND FORM	SELSEY BILL	SEVENTH ROW
SECOND GEAR	SEND A CABLE	SEVENTH TEE
SECOND HALF	SEND BY HAND	SEVEN TIMES
SECOND HAND	SEND BY POST	SEVEN TO ONE
SECOND HEAT	SEND FLYING	SEVEN VEILS
SECOND HOLE	SENIOR GIRL:	SEVEN WEEKS
SECOND HOME	SENSE ORGAN	SEVEN YEARS
SECOND JUMP	SENT FLYING	SEVERE BLOW
SECOND LEAD	SENTRY DUTY	SEVERE LOOK
SECOND LINE	SERENE LOOK	SEVERE LOSS
SECOND MATE	SERIOUS AIR	SEVERE PAIN
SECOND NAME	SERVE A MEAL	SEVERE TEST
SECOND PART	SERVE AN ACE	SEVERN BORE
SECOND POST	SERVE A WRIT	SEWAGE FARM
SECOND RACE	SERVE BADLY	SHABBY DEAL
SECOND RANK	SERVING MAN	SHADY PLACE
SECOND SELF	SET A COURSE	SHADY TRICK
SECOND SLIP	SET AGAINST	SHAKE HANDS
SECONDS OUT	SET AT LARGE	SHAKE IT OFF
SECOND TEAM	SET FORMULA	SHALLOW END
SECOND TERM	SET IN ORDER	SHANK'S PONY
SECOND TEST	SET IN PLACE	SHANTY TOWN
SECOND TIME	SET OF BELLS	SHAPE BADLY

SHARE A FLAT	SHOW FAVOUR	SILVER BAND
SHARE A TAXI	SHOW NO PITY	SILVER COIN
SHARE ISSUE	SHOW NO SIGN	SILVER DISC
SHARP FROST	SHOW SPIRIT	SILVER FOIL
SHARP KNIFE	SHOW TALENT	SILVER HAIR
SHARP POINT	SHOW THE WAY	SILVER MINE
SHARP TASTE	SHOW UP WELL	SILVER RING
SHARP TWIST	SHOW VALOUR	SILVER STAR
SHARP VOICE	SHREWD BLOW	SILVER TRAY
SHARP WORDS	SHREWD FACE	SILVER WIRE
SHED A LIGHT	SHREWD IDEA	SIMMER DOWN
SHEEP'S EYES	SHREWD MOVE	SIMNEL CAKE
SHEER FLUKE	SHREWD TURN	SIMON PETER
SHEER FOLLY	SHRILL NOTE	SIMPLE DIET
SHEER FORCE	SHRILL TONE	SIMPLE FARE
SHEER WASTE	SHRINK AWAY	SIMPLE IDEA
SHEET GLASS	SHRINK BACK	SIMPLE LIFE
SHEET METAL	SHUFFLE OFF	SIMPLE MIND
SHEET MUSIC	SHUFFLE OUT	SIMPLE PAST
SHEET OF ICE	SHUTTING UP	SIMPLE SOUL
SHIFT ABOUT	SHUT UP SHOP	SINE QUA NON
SHINE FORTH	SIAMESE CAT	SING A DIRGE
SHIN OF BEEF	SICK AS A DOG	SING FOR JOY
SHIP'S CARGO	SICK HUMOUR	SING IN TUNE
SHIRE HORSE	SICKLY LOOK	SINGLE BLOW
SHOE A HORSE	SICK OF WORK	SINGLE FARE
SHOE POLISH	SICK PARADE	SINGLE FILE
SHOOT AHEAD	SICK PERSON	SINGLE LIFE
SHOOT A LINE	SIDE BY SIDE	SINGLE LINE
SHOOT FORTH	SIDE EFFECT	SINGLE MIND
SHOOT IT OUT	SIDE OF BEEF	SINGLE NOTE
SHOP WINDOW	SIDE POCKET	SINGLE ROOM
SHORE LEAVE	SIDE STAKES	SINGLE VOTE
SHORT BURST	SIDE STREET	SINK A SHAFT
SHORT DRINK	SIDE TO SIDE	SINK OR SWIM
SHORT DRIVE	SIDE WINDOW	SIRE AND DAM
SHORT HAIRS	SIDLE ALONG	SIR GALAHAD
SHORT HOURS	SIGH DEEPLY	SIR OR MADAM
SHORT LEASE	SIGH NO MORE	SISTER SHIP
SHORT LEAVE	SIGNAL LAMP	SIT AND FUME
SHORT PANTS	SIGNED COPY	SITTING OUT
SHORT PRICE	SIGNET RING	SIX BILLION
SHORT QUEUE	SIGN MANUAL	SIX COURSES
SHORT RANGE	SIGN OF LIFE	SIX DEGREES
SHORT SIGHT	SILENT FILM	SIX DOLLARS
SHORT SKIRT	SILKEN HAIR	SIX FATHOMS
SHORT SLEEP	SILKEN HOSE	SIX GALLONS
SHORT SOCKS	SILK FABRIC	SIX HUNDRED
SHORT SPELL	SILK GLOVES	SIX MINUTES
SHORT STAGE	SILK SQUARES	SIX OCTAVES
SHORT STORY	SILLY BILLY	SIX OF CLUBS
SHORT VISIT	SILLY DEVIL	SIX OR SEVEN
SHOT AT DAWN	SILLY GOOSE	SIX PER CENT
SHOVE ASIDE	SILLY IDIOT	SIX SHOOTER
SHOW A LIGHT	SILLY MID-ON	SIX SQUARED
SHOWER BATH	SILLY POINT	SIX STROKES

SIXTH FLOOR	SMALL PRINT	SOFT PALATE
SIXTH GREEN	SMALL SCALE	SOFT PENCIL
SIXTH OF MAY	SMALL THING	SOFT TONGUE
SIXTH PLACE	SMALL VOICE	SOFT WICKET
SIXTH ROUND	SMALL WAIST	SOHO SQUARE
SIXTH SENSE	SMALL WOMAN	SOLAR MONTH
SIXTY MILES	SMALL WORLD	SOLEMN FACE
SIXTY TIMES	SMART HOUSE	SOLEMN LOOK
SIXTY YEARS	SMART WOMAN	SOLEMN OATH
SIX WICKETS	SMILE AGAIN	SOLE RIGHTS
SIZE ELEVEN	SMOKE A PIPE	SOLE TRADER
SIZE OF TYPE	SMOKED FISH	SOLID BUILD
SIZE TWELVE	SMOKING CAP	SOLID FACTS
SKETCH BOOK	SMOKING HOT	SOLID IVORY
SKIPPED OFF	SMOOTH AWAY	SOLID SENSE
SKIPPED OUT	SMOOTH CHIN	SOLID WATER
SKIRT ROUND	SMOOTH DOWN	SOLO EFFORT
SKITTLE OUT	SMOOTH FACE	SOLO FLIGHT
SLACKEN OFF	SMOOTH HAIR	SON AND HEIR
SLACK WATER	SMOOTH OVER	SONG OF LOVE
SLAP-UP MEAL	SMOOTH SKIN	SONG WRITER
SLATE LOOSE	SMUGGLE OUT	SONJA HENIE
SLAVE DANCE	SNAIL'S PACE	SONNIE HALE
SLAVE STATE	SNAP ANSWER	SOON ENOUGH
SLAVE TRADE	SNAP INTO IT	SOOTH TO SAY
SLEEP IT OFF	SNATCH AWAY	SORDID GAIN
SLEEP ROUGH	SNEAK ABOUT	SORE THROAT
SLEEP TIGHT	SNEAK ROUND	SORRY SIGHT
SLEIGH RIDE	SNEAK THIEF	SORRY STATE
SLICED LOAF	SNOW AND ICE	SORRY TO SAY
SLICK CHICK	SNOW MAIDEN	SOUND BASIS
SLIDE VALVE	SNOWY WHITE	SOUND RADIO
SLIGHT BLOW	SOAKING WET	SOUND SENSE
SLIGHT COLD	SOAP BUBBLE	SOUND SLEEP
SLIM CHANCE	SOAP FLAKES	SOUND TRACK
SLIM FIGURE	SOAP POWDER	SOUND VIEWS
SLIM VOLUME	SOAP RATION	SOUND WAVES
SLIP OF A BOY	SOAPY WATER	SOUP COURSE
SLIPPED OFF	SOBER TRUTH	SOUP TICKET
SLIPPED OUT	SOCCER TEAM	SOUR GRAPES
SLOW BOWLER	SOCIAL CLUB	SOUR NATURE
SLOW GROWTH	SOCIAL EVIL	SOUTH COAST
SLOW MOTION	SOCIAL ILLS	SOUTH DEVON
SLOW POISON	SOCIAL LIFE	SOUTH DOWNS
SLOW WICKET	SOCIAL RANK	SOUTH WALES
SMALL BLAME	SOCIAL RUIN	SOW THE SEED
SMALL BUILD	SOCIAL WORK	SPACE PROBE
SMALL CHILD	SODIUM LAMP	SPANISH FLY
SMALL CRAFT	SOFT ANSWER	SPAN OF LIFE
SMALL CROWD	SOFT AS SILK	SPARE FRAME
SMALL HOPES	SOFT AS SOAP	SPARE WHEEL
SMALL HOURS	SOFT CENTRE	SPEAK ALOUD
SMALL HOUSE	SOFT COLLAR	SPEAK DUTCH
SMALL MEANS	SOFT COLOUR	SPEAK WELSH
SMALL ORDER	SOFT GROUND	SPECIAL BUS
SMALL PIECE	SOFT NUMBER	SPECIAL DAY

SPEED FIEND	STAFF NURSE	STEADY RAIN
SPEED GAUGE	STAG BEETLE	STEADY SALE
SPEED LIMIT	STAGE FEVER	STEADY WIND
SPEED TRIAL	STAGGER OFF	STEAK HOUSE
SPELL IT OUT	STAGGER OUT	STEAL A KISS
SPEND MONEY	STAKE MONEY	STEAL ALONG
SPENT FORCE	STALE BREAD	STEALING BY
SPICED WINE	STAMP ALBUM	STEALING UP
SPICY STORY	STAND ABOUT	STEAM NAVVY
SPIDER'S WEB	STAND ALONE	STEAM ORGAN
SPIKE JONES	STAND ALOOF	STEAM POWER
SPILL BLOOD	STAND APART	STEAM RADIO
SPINAL CORD	STAND ASIDE	STEAM TRAIN
SPIN BOWLER	STAND AT BAY	STEAM YACHT
SPIRAL DOWN	STAND CLEAR	STEEL WORKS
SPIRIT AWAY	STAND ERECT	STEELY LOOK
SPIRIT LAMP	STAND FOR IT	STEEP CLIMB
SPLIT HAIRS	STAND GUARD	STEEP PRICE
SPLIT IN TWO	STAND IN AWE	STEER CLEAR
SPODE CHINA	STANDING BY	STEP ASHORE
SPOKEN WORD	STANDING UP	STEP BY STEP
SPONGE CAKE	STAND ON END	STEP INSIDE
SPONGE DOWN	STAND READY	STEP LIVELY
SPORTS CLUB	STAND STILL	STEPPED OUT
SPORTS COAT	STAND TO WIN	STERN CHASE
SPORTS PAGE	STAND TREAT	STERN TRUTH
SPOTTED DOG	STAND TRIAL	STERN WORDS
SPREAD FEAR	STAND UP FOR	STEWED BEEF
SPREAD SAIL	STAPLE DIET	STEWED EELS
SPRING AWAY	STARK NAKED	STEWED LAMB
SPRING BACK	STARLIT SKY	STEWED MEAT
SPRING DOWN	STAR OF HOPE	STICK IT OUT
SPRING OPEN	STAR PLAYER	STICK TIGHT
SPRING OVER	START A FIRE	STICK UP FOR
SPRING SALE	START AGAIN	STICKY BOMB
SPRING SONG	START A RIOT	STICKY MESS
SPRING TIDE	START YOUNG	STIFF CLIMB
SPUN SILVER	STATE A CASE	STIFF DRINK
SQUAD DRILL	STATE COACH	STIFF FENCE
SQUARE CHIN	STATED TIME	STIFF PRICE
SQUARE DEAL	STATE GRANT	STILL OWING
SQUARE FOOT	STATE NURSE	STILL THERE
SQUARE GAME	STATE OF WAR	STILL WATER
SQUARE HOLE	STATE TRIAL	STIRRUP CUP
SQUARE INCH	STATE VISIT	STIR THE POT
SQUARE MEAL	STATUTE LAW	STITCHED UP
SQUARE MILE	STAY AT HOME	ST LAWRENCE
SQUARE ROOT	STAY BEHIND	ST LUKE'S DAY
SQUARE SAIL	STAY IN A RUT	STOCK REPLY
SQUARE UP TO	STAY INSIDE	STOCK STILL:
SQUARE YARD	STAY UP LATE	STODGY FOOD
SQUEEZE DRY	ST DUNSTAN'S	STOKE POGES
SQUEEZE OUT	STEADY BEAM	STOLE A KISS
STABLE DOOR	STEADY FLOW	STONE STEPS
STABLE MATE	STEADY HAND	STONE WALLS
STACK OF HAY	STEADY PACE	STONY BROKE

STONY HEART
STONY STARE
STOOD TRIAL
STOP AT HOME
STOP A TOOTH
STOP AT WILL
STOP CRYING
STOP FOR TEA
STOP IN TIME
STOPPED ONE
STOPPED OUT
STOP THE BUS
STOP THE GAP
STOP THE ROT
STORE OF WIT
STORK'S NEST
STORMY LIFE
STOUT HEART
STOUT WOMAN
STRAIGHT BY
STRAIGHT IN
STRAIGHT ON
STRAIGHT UP
STRANGE MAN
STREAK AWAY
STREAK PAST
STREET ARAB
STREET DOOR
STREET LAMP
STRETCH OUT
STRICT DIET
STRICT TIME
STRIKE BACK
STRIKE CAMP
STRIKE DOWN
STRIKE DUMB
STRIKE GOLD
STRIKE HARD
STRIKE HOME
STRIKE SAIL
STRING BAND
STRING TRIO
STRING VEST
STRIP POKER
STRIP TEASE
STROKE PLAY
STRONG BREW
STRONG CASE
STRONG GRIP
STRONG HAND
STRONG HEAD
STRONG LINE
STRONG MEAT
STRONG MIND
STRONG PULL
STRONG ROOM

STRONG SIDE
STRONG SUIT
STRONG WILL
STRONG WIND
STRUCK DOWN
STRUCK DUMB
STRUGGLE BY
STRUGGLE ON
ST STEPHEN'S
STUDIO FLAT
STUDY MUSIC
STUFFED OWL
STUFFY ROOM
STUMP ALONG
STUMPED OUT
STUMPY TAIL
STURDY LEGS
SUCH IS LIFE
SUCKING PIG
SUDDEN BANG
SUDDEN BLOW
SUDDEN FEAR
SUDDEN HUSH
SUDDEN STOP
SUEDE SHOES
SUFFER LOSS
SUFFER PAIN
SUGAR CANDY
SUGAR DADDY
SUMMER CAMP
SUMMER HEAT
SUMMER RAIN
SUMMER SALE
SUMMER TERM
SUMMER TIME
SUM OF MONEY
SUN AND MOON
SUNDAY BEST
SUNDAY SUIT
SUN GLASSES
SUNKEN REEF
SUNNY SMILE
SUNNY SOUTH
SUN-RAY LAMP
SUNSET GLOW
SUPERB VIEW
SUPPER TIME
SUPPLY BASE
SUPPLY SHIP
SURE AS FATE
SURE ENOUGH
SURE GROUND
SURGE AHEAD
SURPLUS FAT
SWAGGER OUT
SWAN OF AVON

SWEARING IN
SWEAT BLOOD
SWEAT IT OUT
SWEEP ALONG
SWEEP ASIDE
SWEEP CLEAN
SWEET DRINK
SWEET HERBS
SWEET MUSIC
SWEET SLEEP
SWEET SMELL
SWEET SMILE
SWEET SOUND
SWEET SYRUP
SWEET TOOTH
SWEET VOICE
SWEET WORDS
SWERVE PAST
SWIM ACROSS
SWINE FEVER
SWING ALONG
SWING FOR IT
SWING MUSIC
SWING ROUND
SWISS GUARD
SWISS WATCH
SWITCH BACK
SWITCH OVER
SWORD DANCE
SWORN ENEMY

T – 10

TABLE D'HÔTE
TABLE KNIFE
TABLE LINEN
TABLE MONEY
TABLE WATER
TAKE A BRIEF
TAKE A CHAIR
TAKE ACTION
TAKE A DEKKO
TAKE ADVICE
TAKE AN OATH
TAKE A PHOTO
TAKE A PUNCH
TAKE A SHARE
TAKE A SNACK
TAKE AS READ
TAKE A STAND
TAKE A TiTLE
TAKE A TRAIN
TAKE CHARGE
TAKE CREDIT
TAKE EFFECT
TAKE FLIGHT

TAKE FRIGHT	TEA CLIPPER	THEATRE FAN
TAKE IN HAND	TEA DRINKER	THE BACKING
TAKE IN SAIL	TEAM OF FOUR	THE BAHAMAS
TAKE IN VAIN	TEAM SPIRIT	THE BALKANS
TAKE IT BACK	TEA PLANTER	THE BEATLES
TAKE IT EASY	TEAR IN HALF	THE BEST MAN
TAKE IT HARD	TEAR TO BITS	THE BIG FIVE
TAKE KINDLY	TEA SERVICE	THE BOER WAR
TAKE MY HAND	TEENY WEENY	THE BRAVEST
TAKE MY WORD	TELL A STORY	THE BRONTËS
TAKEN ABACK	TELLING OFF	THE CABINET
TAKE NO PART	TEN BILLION	THE CAPITAL
TAKE NOTICE	TEN DEGREES	THE CHANNEL
TAKE OFFICE	TENDER CARE	THE COLD WAR
TAKE ON A JOB	TENDER LOVE	THE COMMONS
TAKE ORDERS	TENDER MEAT	THE CRITICS
TAKE PITY ON	TENDER SPOT	THE CURRAGH
TAKE POISON	TEN DOLLARS	THE CUSTOMS
TAKE REFUGE	TEN FATHOMS	THE DANSANT
TAKE THE AIR	TEN GALLONS	THE DEAD SEA
TAKE THE CUP	TEN GUINEAS	THE DEEP END
TAKE THE RAP	TEN MILLION	THE DYNASTS
TAKE TO ARMS	TEN MINUTES	THE EAST END
TAKE TO TASK	TENNIS BALL	THE ENGLISH
TAKE UP ARMS	TENNIS CLUB	THE ETERNAL
TAKE UP TIME	TENNIS STAR	THE EVIL EYE
TAKING WAYS	TEN OF CLUBS	THE EVIL ONE
TALENT SHOW	TENOR VOICE	THE EXPERTS
TALE OF A TUB	TEN PAST ONE	THE FAIR SEX
TALK AWHILE	TEN PAST SIX	THE FAR EAST
TALK IT OVER	TEN PAST TWO	THE FIDGETS
TALK TURKEY	TEN PER CENT	THE FIFTIES
TALLEST BOY	TEN SECONDS	THE FORTIES
TALLEST MAN	TEN SQUARED	THE GALLERY
TAME AFFAIR	TENTH GREEN	THE GALLOWS
TAME ANIMAL	TENTH OF MAY	THE GESTAPO
TANGLED WEB	TENTH PLACE	THE GIGGLES
TAP LIGHTLY	TENTH ROUND	THE GLAD EYE
TAP THE LINE	TEN TO EIGHT	THE GORBALS
TAP THE WIRE	TEN TO SEVEN	THE GUNNERS
TARGET AREA	TEN TO THREE	THE HARD WAY
TARGET DATE	TEN WICKETS	THE HEIRESS
TARGET SHIP	TEPID WATER	THE HERMITS
TARIFF WALL	TERRA COTTA	THE HOLLIES
TARTAN KILT	TERRA FIRMA	THE HORRORS
TART ANSWER	TERRY WOGAN	THE JACKPOT
TASK IN HAND	TEST FLIGHT	THE JONESES
TASTE BLOOD	TEST OF TIME	THE KNOW-HOW
TASTY SNACK	TEST RESULT	THE KREMLIN
TATTOO MARK	TEST WICKET	THE LANCERS
TAUT NERVES	THE ACCUSED	THE LAST BUS
TAX EVASION	THE AMAZONS	THE LAST LAP
TAXI DRIVER	THE ANIMALS	THE LINCOLN
T-BONE STEAK	THE ARCHERS	THE LOW-DOWN
TEACH CLASS	THE ARSENAL	THE MAESTRO
TEACH MUSIC	THEATRE BAR	THE MARINES

THE MAZURKA	THE WEST END	THREE FOURS
THEME MUSIC	THE WILLIES	THREE GROSS
THE MENDIPS	THICK SKULL	THREE HOLES
THE MESSIAH	THICK SLICE	THREE HOURS
THE MILITIA	THICK TWINE	THREE IN ONE
THE MIXTURE	THIN EXCUSE	THREE JACKS
THE NEEDFUL	THING OR TWO	THREE KINGS
THE NEEDLES	THINK ABOUT	THREE LUMPS
THE NEW LOOK	THINK AGAIN	THREE MILES
THE ODYSSEY	THINK AHEAD	THREE NINES
THE OLD ADAM	THINK ALIKE	THREE PAIRS
THE OLD FIRM	THINK ALOUD	THREE PARTS
THE ORKNEYS	THINK IT OUT	THREE PINTS
THE PEERAGE	THINK TWICE	THREE PUTTS
THE PLANETS	THINNED OUT	THREE SCORE
THE PRELUDE	THIN STRING	THREE SIDES
THE PREMIER	THIRD CHILD	THREE SIXES
THE QUAKERS	THIRD CLASS	THREE STARS
THE QUALITY	THIRD FLOOR	THREE TIMES
THE RED ARMY	THIRD GREEN	THREE TO ONE
THE RED FLAG	THIRD MONTH	THREE WEEKS
THE REGENCY	THIRD OF MAY	THREE YEARS
THE RENT ACT	THIRD PARTY	THRIFT CLUB
THERE THERE!	THIRD PLACE	THROW ABOUT
THE REVENGE	THIRD POWER	THROW A KISS
THE RIOT ACT	THIRD PRIZE	THROW ASIDE
THE RIVIERA	THIRD REICH	THRUST DOWN
THE ROCKERS	THIRD ROUND	THRUST HOME
THE ROCKIES	THIRD STAGE	THRUST OPEN
THE SABBATH	THIRD VERSE	THRUST PAST
THE SAME KEY	THIRD WORLD	THUMB A LIFT
THE SAPPERS	THIRTY DAYS	THUMB A RIDE
THE SEASONS	THIRTY LOVE	THUMB INDEX
THE SEEKERS	THIS FRIDAY	THUMBS DOWN
THE SHADOWS	THIS MONDAY	TIDAL BASIN
THE SHIVERS	THIS OR THAT	TIDAL RIVER
THE SIXTIES	THIS SEASON	TIDY INCOME
THE SPEAKER	THIS SIDE UP	TIE IN KNOTS
THE STARTER	THIS SPRING	TIE-ON LABEL
THE STEPPES	THIS SUMMER	TIES OF RACE
THE ST LEGER	THIS SUNDAY	TIE THE KNOT
THE SUBURBS	THIS WAY OUT	TIGHT DRESS
THE TAIL-END	THIS WINTER	TIGHT GRASP
THE TEMPEST	THOMAS GRAY	TIGHT PLACE
THE THEATRE	THOMAS HOOD	TIGHT SKIRT
THE THINKER	THORNY PATH	TILLER GIRL
THE THIN MAN	THREE BALLS	TIMBER TREE
THE TITANIC	THREE BEARS	TIME A PUNCH
THE TROPICS	THREE BRACE	TIME ENOUGH
THE TWELFTH	THREE CARDS	TIME FACTOR
THE UNITIES	THREE CLUBS	TIME FOR BED
THE UNKNOWN	THREE DARTS	TIME FOR TEA
THE VATICAN	THREE DOZEN	TIME IN HAND
THE VICTORY	THREE DRAWS	TIMELY EXIT
THE VIKINGS	THREE FATES	TIMELY WORD
THE WEATHER	THREE FIVES	TIME OF LIFE

TIME OF YEAR
TIME, PLEASE
TIME SIGNAL
TIME SWITCH
TIME TO COME
TIME TO KILL
TIME TO LOSE
TIME TO STOP
TINKER BELL
TINKER WITH
TINNED CRAB
TINNED FISH
TINNED FOOD
TINNED MEAT
TINNED MILK
TINNED SOUP
TINNY NOISE
TINNY SOUND
TIN OF BEANS
TIN OF COCOA
TIN OF FRUIT
TIN OF PAINT
TIN SOLDIER
TIN WHISTLE
TIP A WINNER
TIP THE WINK
TITIAN HAIR
TITLED RANK
TITLE FIGHT
TITUS OATES
TOBACCO ROW
TODAY'S DATE
TOE THE LINE
TOE THE MARK
TOILET SOAP
TOKEN MONEY
TOLL BRIDGE
TOMATO SOUP
TOM BOWLING
TONIC SOLFA
TONIC WATER
TONS OF LOVE
TONS OF TIME
TONY CURTIS
TONY WELLER
TOO FAR GONE
TOOL SETTER
TO ONE'S FACE
TOOTING BEC
TOP AND TAIL
TOP BILLING
TOP HONOURS
TOPPLE DOWN
TOPPLE OVER
TOP QUALITY
TOP THE BILL

TORRID ZONE
TORY LEADER
TOTAL BLANK
TOTAL WRECK
TO THE ALTAR
TO THE NORTH
TO THE POINT
TO THE RIGHT
TO THE SOUTH
TOUCH AND GO
TOUCH JUDGE
TOUCH LUCKY
TOUGH BREAK
TOUGH FIGHT
TOUR AROUND
TOURING CAR
TOUR OF DUTY
TO WINDWARD
TOWN CENTRE
TOWN SQUARE
TOY SOLDIER
TOY SPANIEL
TOY TERRIER
TRACKER DOG
TRACK EVENT
TRADE CYCLE
TRADE PAPER
TRADE PRICE
TRADER HORN
TRADE ROUTE
TRADE TERMS
TRADE UNION
TRADE WINDS
TRAFFIC COP
TRAFFIC JAM
TRAGIC MASK
TRAGIC MUSE
TRAGIC NEWS
TRAGIC TALE
TRAIN CRASH
TRAINED EYE
TRAINED MAN
TRAIN FERRY
TRAIN SMASH
TRAM DRIVER
TRAMPLED ON
TRAM TICKET
TRAPEZE ACT
TRAVEL BOOK
TREAD ON AIR
TREAD WATER
TREAT BADLY
TREATY PORT
TREBLE CLEF
TREE DOCTOR
TREE OF LIFE

TRENCH COAT
TRENCH FEET
TRIAL MATCH
TRIAL SCENE
TRICK OR TWO
TRIFLE WITH
TRIGGER OFF
TRIM ANKLES
TRIM FIGURE
TRIP ABROAD
TRIPLE STAR
TRIPLE TIME
TRIP TO TOWN
TROLLEY BUS
TROOP TRAIN
TROTTED OFF
TROTTED OUT
TROY WEIGHT
TRUDGE PAST
TRUE CHARGE
TRUE FRIEND
TRUE REPORT
TRUE SAMPLE
TRUE TO FORM
TRUE TO LIFE
TRUE TO TYPE
TRULY RURAL
TRUSS OF HAY
TRUSTEE ACT
TRUST HOUSE
TRY A NEW WAY
TRYING TIME
TUDOR HOUSE
TUDOR KINGS
TUDOR STYLE
TUFT OF HAIR
TUMBLE DOWN
TUMBLE OVER
TUNING FORK
TUNNEL INTO
TURKEY TROT
TURN ADRIFT
TURN AROUND
TURN COLOUR
TURN IT DOWN
TURN OF DUTY
TURN THE KEY
TURN TO DUST
TURN TO GOLD
TURN TURTLE
TURN YELLOW
TURTLE DOVE
TURTLE SOUP
TWELFTH DAY
TWELFTH MAN
TWELFTH ROW

TWELVE DAYS
TWELVE FEET
TWELVE QUID
TWENTY QUID
TWICE A WEEK
TWICE A YEAR
TWICE DAILY
TWICE EIGHT
TWICE ROUND
TWICE SEVEN
TWICE THREE
TWINE ROUND
TWIN SISTER
TWIRL ROUND
TWIST ABOUT
TWIST DRILL
TWIST MY ARM
TWIST ROUND
TWO AND FIVE
TWO AND FOUR
TWO AND NINE
TWO AT A TIME
TWO BILLION
TWO COLOURS
TWO COURSES
TWO DEGREES
TWO DOLLARS
TWO FATHOMS
TWO GALLONS
TWO GUINEAS
TWO HUNDRED
TWO LENGTHS
TWO MASTERS
TWO MILLION
TWO MINUTES
TWO NATIONS
TWO OCTAVES
TWO OF A KIND
TWO OF CLUBS
TWO OR THREE
TWO PER CENT
TWO RASHERS
TWO SECONDS
TWO SQUARED
TWO STRIPES
TWO STROKES
TWO WICKETS
TYBURN TREE
TYPING POOL

U – 10

UGLY RUMOUR
UGLY SISTER
UGLY THREAT

ULTRA VIRES
UNCLE REMUS
UNCUT PAGES
UNCUT STONE
UNDER A TREE
UNDER COVER
UNDER GLASS
UNDER PROOF
UNDER STEAM
UNDER TRIAL
UNDER WATER
UNDUE HASTE
UNION BOARD
UNION CHIEF
UNION RULES
UNIQUE CASE
UNIT OF HEAT
UNIT OF TIME
UNIT OF WORK
UNKIND DEED
UNKIND WORD
UNPAID BILL
UNSOLD BOOK
UNTIDY MIND
UNTIE A KNOT
UP A GUM TREE
UP ALL NIGHT
UP AND ABOUT
UP AND DOING
UP AT OXFORD
UP FOR TRIAL
UPHILL TASK
UPHILL WALK
UPHILL WORK
UP IN A PLANE
UP IN THE AIR
UP IN THE SKY
UPON MY SOUL
UPON MY WORD
UPPER BERTH
UPPER CLASS
UPPER CRUST
UPPER HOUSE
UPPER LIMIT
UPPER SIXTH
UPPER STORY
UPRIGHT MAN
UPSIDE DOWN
UP THE AISLE
UP THE CREEK
UP THE RIVER
UP THE SPOUT
UP TO A POINT
UP TO NO GOOD
UP TO SAMPLE
UP TO THE HUB

USE FINESSE
USEFUL HINT
USE THE POST
USUAL THING
UTTERLY BAD
UTTER TRIPE

V – 10

VACANT LOOK
VACANT POST
VACUUM PUMP
VAIN EFFORT
VAIN PERSON
VAIN REGRET
VALE AND LEA
VALID POINT
VAL PARNELL
VAMPIRE BAT
VANESSA LEE
VANILLA ICE
VANITY CASE
VANITY FAIR
VANTAGE OUT
VAPOUR BATH
VARIETY ACT
VAST EXTENT
VAST PLAINS
VEAL AND HAM
VEAL CUTLET
VENTURE OUT
VERY HUNGRY
VERY LIKELY
VERY LITTLE
VERY NEARLY
VERY SELDOM
VETERAN CAR
VICHY WATER
VICIOUS LIE
VICTOR HUGO
VICTORY DAY
VIDEO NASTY
VILE BODIES
VILLAGE INN
VINE GROWER
VINTAGE CAR
VIOLENT END
VIOLIN CASE
VIOLIN SOLO
VIRGIN CLAY
VIRGIN LAND
VIRGIN MARY
VIRGIN SOIL
VITAL ERROR
VITAL FLAME
VITAL FORCE

VITAL POINT
VITAL POWER
VITAL SPARK
VITAL WOUND
VIVID GREEN
VOCAL CORDS
VOCAL GROUP
VOCAL MUSIC
VOCAL ORGAN
VOLLEY BALL
VOTE LABOUR
VOTING LIST
VOUCH FOR IT
VOWEL SOUND
VULGAR HERD

W – 10

WADE ACROSS
WADING BIRD
WAD OF MONEY
WAD OF NOTES
WAGE FREEZE
WAGE PACKET
WAGES CLERK
WAGES OF SIN
WAGON TRAIN
WAG THE HEAD
WAIT AND SEE
WAIT AROUND
WAIT AWHILE
WALK ACROSS
WALK AROUND
WALK BEHIND
WALK IN FEAR
WALK OF LIFE
WALK SLOWLY
WALK SOFTLY
WALL OF FIRE
WALL STREET
WALNUT TREE
WALT DISNEY
WALTZ MUSIC
WALTZ ROUND
WANDER AWAY
WANING MOON
WANT OF CARE
WANT OF LOVE
WANT OF ZEAL
WARD SISTER
WAR FOOTING
WAR MEMOIRS
WARM FRIEND
WARMING PAN
WARNING CRY
WAR OF WORDS

WARPED MIND
WAR SAVINGS
WASH AND DRY
WASHING DAY
WASP'S STING
WASTE MONEY
WASTE PAPER
WASTE WORDS
WATCH CHAIN
WATCHED POT
WATCH FOR IT
WATER BOARD
WATER LEVEL
WATER MELON
WATER MUSIC
WATER NYMPH
WATER ON TAP
WATER POWER
WATER'S EDGE
WATER TOWER
WAVE LENGTH
WAX AND WANE
WAXED PAPER
WAXING MOON
WAY IN FRONT
WAY OFF BEAM
WAYSIDE INN
WAY THROUGH
WEAK EXCUSE
WEAK STROKE
WEAK WILLED
WEALTHY MAN
WEARY WORLD
WEATHER EYE
WEATHER MAP
WEBBED FEET
WEDDED PAIR
WEDDED WIFE
WEDDING DAY
WEED KILLER
WEEK BY WEEK
WEEKLY RENT
WEEKLY WAGE
WEEP FOR JOY
WEEP NO MORE
WEIGH HEAVY
WEIGHING IN
WELCOME END
WELL BEATEN
WELL BEHIND
WELL CAUGHT
WELL ENOUGH
WELL I NEVER!
WELL IN HAND
WELL OF LIFE
WELL PLACED

WELL PLAYED
WELLS FARGO
WELL VERSED
WELSH CORGI
WELSH WALES
WENT AROUND
WENT DIRECT
WENT TO TOWN
WEST AFRICA
WEST BERLIN
WEST INDIAN
WEST INDIES
WEST IS WEST
WEST LONDON
WEST RIDING
WESTWARD HO!
WET BATTERY
WET BLANKET
WET CANTEEN
WET CLOTHES
WET SHAMPOO
WET THROUGH
WET WEATHER
WHAT AM I BID?
WHAT A NERVE!
WHAT A SHAME!
WHAT GOES ON?
WHAT'S YOURS?
WHEAT FIELD
WHEEL ABOUT
WHEEL ROUND
WHELK STALL
WHIFF OF AIR
WHIPPED OFF
WHIRL ROUND
WHIST DRIVE
WHISTLE FOR
WHITE BREAD
WHITE CARGO
WHITE CHALK
WHITE FRIAR
WHITE FROST
WHITE HORSE
WHITE HOUSE
WHITE LIGHT
WHITE MAGIC
WHITE METAL
WHITE MOUSE
WHITE NOISE
WHITE PAINT
WHITE PAPER
WHITE PIECE
WHITE QUEEN
WHITE SAUCE
WHITE SHEET
WHITE SHIRT

WHITE SLAVE
WHITE SUGAR
WHITE TRASH
WHIT MONDAY
WHIT SUNDAY
WHOLE TRUTH
WHOLE WORLD
WICKED DEED
WICKED WAYS
WIDE APPEAL
WIDE CHOICE
WIDE CIRCLE
WIDELY HELD
WIDE MARGIN
WIDE SCREEN
WIDE VISION
WIDOW'S MITE
WIDOW'S PEAK
WIDOW WOMAN
WIELD POWER
WIFE BEATER
WIG AND GOWN
WILD ANIMAL
WILD CHEERS
WILD CHERRY
WILD FLOWER
WILD HORSES
WILD SCHEME
WILL OF IRON
WILLOW TREE
WILL TO LIVE
WILLY NILLY
WILY PERSON
WIN A RUBBER
WIN BY A GOAL
WIN BY A HEAD
WIN BY A NECK
WINDOW PANE
WINE BIBBER
WINE CELLAR
WINE TASTER
WINE TAVERN
WINE WAITER
WIN FREEDOM
WIN HONOURS
WINNING BET
WINNING HIT
WINNING RUN
WINNING TRY
WIN ON MERIT
WINTER COAT
WINTER FEED
WINTER SALE
WINTER TIME
WINTER WEAR
WIN THE GAME

WIN THE RACE
WIN THE TOSS
WIN THROUGH
WIRE BASKET
WIRE PUZZLE
WISE CHOICE
WISE OLD OWL
WISH IN VAIN
WISH UNDONE
WITCH HAZEL
WITH A SMILE
WITHER AWAY
WITHIN CALL
WITHIN HAIL
WITHOUT END
WITH REGRET
WITNESS BOX
WIZARD OF OZ
WOMAN HATER
WOMAN'S HOUR
WOMAN'S WORK
WOMEN'S ARMY
WOMEN'S PAGE
WOMEN'S WEAR
WON BY A HEAD
WON BY A NECK
WONDER DRUG
WOODEN CLUB
WOODEN SEAT
WOODEN SHOE
WOOD STREET
WOODY ALLEN
WOOLLY HAIR
WORD MAKING
WORD OF A LIE
WORD PUZZLE
WORD SQUARE
WORKING DAY
WORKING MAN
WORKING OUT
WORK IN HAND
WORK IN VAIN
WORK ON HAND
WORK PERMIT
WORK TO RULE
WORK UNDONE
WORLD ATLAS
WORLD CLASS
WORLD COURT
WORLD POWER
WORLD TITLE
WORLD TRADE
WORRIED MAN
WORST OF ALL
WORST TASTE
WORTH WHILE

WOUNDED MAN
WREAK HAVOC
WRIGGLE OUT
WRITE A BOOK
WRITE ABOUT
WRITE AGAIN
WRITE A NOTE
WRITE A POEM
WRITE A SONG
WRITE BADLY
WRITE BOOKS
WRITE IN INK
WRITE IT OFF
WRITE MUSIC
WRITE NOTES
WRITE PLAYS
WRITE VERSE
WRITING INK
WRITTEN LAW
WRONG LINES
WRONG PLACE
WRONG TOTAL
WRONG TRACK
WRONG WOMAN

X – 10

X-RAY CAMERA

Y – 10

YARD BY YARD
YEAR BY YEAR
YEARLY RENT
YEAR TO YEAR
YELLOW BOOK
YELLOW CARD
YELLOW FLAG
YELLOW JACK
YELLOW RACE
YELLOW ROSE
YELLOW STAR
YIELD CROPS
YIELD FRUIT
YOUNG BLOOD
YOUNG CHILD
YOUNG FOGEY
YOUNGER SON
YOUNG IDEAS
YOUNG WOMAN
YOUR CHOICE
YOUR HONOUR
YOURS TRULY
YOU'VE HAD IT
YUL BRYNNER

Z – 10

ZIG-ZAG LINE
ZOO ANIMALS

A – 11

AARON'S BEARD
ABANDON HOPE
ABANDON SHIP
ABIDE WITH ME
ABLE TO SPEAK
ABODE OF LOVE
ABOVE GROUND
ABOVE NORMAL
ABOVE RUBIES
ABOVE THE LAW
ABSTRACT ART
ACCENT GRAVE
ACCOUNT BOOK
ACCOUNT PAID
ACE OF HEARTS
ACE OF SPADES
ACE OF TRUMPS
ACHING HEART
ACHING TOOTH
ACT AS A'BRAKE
ACT IN UNISON
ACTIVE VOICE
ACT OF HOMAGE
ACT ON ADVICE
ACT TOGETHER
ACUTE ACCENT
ACUTE ATTACK
ADD A CODICIL
ADDRESS BOOK
ADDRESS CARD
ADEQUATE SUM
AD INFINITUM
ADMIT BEARER
ADMIT DEFEAT
ADOLF HITLER
ADOPTION ACT
ADRIATIC SEA
ADVANCE BASE
ADVANCE COPY
ADVANCED AGE
ADVANCE DATE
ADVANCE FATE
AEOLIAN HARP
AFFECTED AIR
AFGHAN HOUND
AFRICA HOUSE
AFTER A WHILE
AFTER CHURCH
AFTER DINNER

AFTER SCHOOL
AFTER SUNSET
AFTER SUPPER
AFTER THE WAR
AGAINST TIME
AGE OF WISDOM
AGES AND AGES
AGONY COLUMN
AHEAD OF TIME
AID TO BEAUTY
AID TO MEMORY
AIM STRAIGHT
AIM TO PLEASE
AIR MINISTER
AIR MINISTRY
AIR TERMINAL
AIR TERMINUS
AL A MODE BEEF
ALARM SIGNAL
ALDGATE PUMP
ALFRED MARKS
ALFRED NOYES
ALASTAIR SIM
ALIVE OR DEAD
ALL COCK-EYED
ALL CREATION
ALL FALL DOWN
ALL FOOL'S DAY
ALL FOR MONEY
ALL GOES WELL
ALL HOPE GONE
ALL IN FAVOUR
ALL OF A PIECE
ALL OF A SHAKE
ALL ONE CAN DO
ALLOT SHARES
ALL-OUT DRIVE
ALLOW CREDIT
ALL QUARTERS
ALL SOULS' DAY
ALL STANDING
ALL-STAR CAST
ALL STRAIGHT
ALL THAT JAZZ
ALL THE SIGNS
ALL THE VOGUE
ALL THE WHILE
ALL THE WORLD
ALL TOGETHER
ALL TOGGED UP
ALL TO PIECES
ALL VERY FINE
ALL VERY WELL
ALL WASHED-UP
ALL WEEK LONG
ALMIGHTY GOD

ALMOND PASTE
ALMOST THERE
ALONE I DID IT
ALPINE GUIDE
ALSATIAN DOG
ALTER COURSE
AMATEUR SIDE
AMATEUR TEAM
AMERICAN BAR
AMERICAN WAR
AMERICA'S CUP
AMOS AND ANDY
AMOUR PROPRE
AN APPLE A DAY
ANCIENT CITY
ANCIENT ROME
ANDY STEWART
ANGELIC HOST
ANGELIC LOOK
ANGLING CLUB
ANIMAL TAMER
ANIMAL WORLD
ANISEED BALL
ANITA EKBERG
ANNA LUCASTA
ANNA PAVLOVA
ANNE SHELTON
ANN HATHAWAY
ANNIE BESANT
ANNIE LAURIE
ANNIE OAKLEY
ANN SHERIDAN
ANNUAL EVENT
ANNUAL LEAVE
ANNUAL TREAT
ANN VERONICA
ANOTHER TIME
ANTHONY EDEN
ANTHONY HOPE
ANTIQUE SHOP
ANTI-TANK GUN
ANVIL CHORUS
ANXIOUS TIME
APACHE DANCE
APPEAL COURT
APPEAL JUDGE
APPLE-PIE BED
APRIL SHOWER
ARCTIC OCEAN
ARE YOU READY?
ARMED ATTACK
ARMED BANDIT
ARMED COMBAT
ARMED ESCORT
ARMED FORCES
ARM OF THE LAW

ARM OF THE SEA
ARMOURED CAR
ARMOUR PLATE
ARMS AND LEGS
ARMS COUNCIL
ARMS STRETCH
ARMS TRAFFIC
ARMY BLANKET
ARMY CANTEEN
ARMY OFFICER
ARMY RESERVE
ARMY SURPLUS
AROMATIC GUM
ARRIVE EARLY
ARSENE LUPIN
ART DIRECTOR
ARTEMUS WARD
ARTFUL DODGE
ARTHUR ASKEY
ARTHUR'S SEAT
ARTS COUNCIL
ARTS THEATRE
ASCOT STAKES
AS DRY AS DUST
AS EASY AS PIE
AS GOOD AS NEW
ASK FOR A RISE
ASK FOR MERCY
ASK FOR TERMS
ASK THE PRICE
AS MUCH AGAIN
AS NICE AS PIE
ASSUME A RÔLE
ASSUMED NAME
A STAR IS BORN
ASTRAL PLANE
AS UGLY AS SIN
AS YOU LIKE IT
AT A DISCOUNT
AT A DISTANCE
AT ALL EVENTS
AT ALL POINTS
AT A LOOSE END
AT ATTENTION
AT CAMBRIDGE
AT FIRST HAND
AT FULL SPEED
AT GREAT RISK
AT HALF PRICE
A THING OR TWO
ATHOLE BROSE
AT INTERVALS
ATOMIC CLOCK
ATOMIC POWER
AT ONE'S ELBOW
AT ONE'S HEEL

AT ONE'S PERIL
AT ONE'S WORST
ATTACHÉ CASE
AT THE BOTTOM
AT THE CINEMA
AT THE CIRCUS
AT THE DOUBLE
AT THE FINISH
AT THE MOMENT
AT THE SUMMIT
AT THE TILLER
AT THE WICKET
AT THE ZENITH
AT WHAT PLACE?
AT WHICH TIME?
AUCTION ROOM
AUCTION SALE
AUTHOR'S NOTE
AUTUMN TINTS
AVERAGE HAND
AVERAGE TYPE
AVERAGE WAGE
AVERTED EYES
AVOCADO PEAR
AVOID DEFEAT
AWAY WITH YOU!
AWKWARD TIME
AYES AND NOES

B – 11

BABY BUNTING
BABY CLOTHES
BACK A WINNER
BACK HEAVILY
BACK PAYMENT
BACK-ROOM BOY
BACK TO FRONT
BACKWARD BOY
BACON AND EGG
BACON SLICER
BAD BUSINESS
BADEN POWELL
BAD EYESIGHT
BAD FEELINGS
BAD FOR TRADE
BADGE OF RANK
BAD JUDGEMENT
BAD LANGUAGE
BAD LIKENESS
BADLY PLACED
BADLY SHAKEN
BADLY WANTED
BAD PRACTICE
BAD TEACHING
BAG OF CRISPS

BAG OF NERVES
BAG OF SWEETS
BAG OF TRICKS
BAGS OF MONEY
BAIT THE TRAP
BAKED POTATO
BAKER'S DOZEN
BAKER STREET
BALCONY SEAT
BALD AS A COOT
BALLOT PAPER
BANANA SKIN
BANBURY CAKE
BANG THE DOOR
BANK ACCOUNT
BANK BALANCE
BANK CHARGES
BANK DEPOSIT
BANK HOLIDAY
BANK MANAGER
BANK THE FIRE
BARBED ARROW
BARBED SHAFT
BARBED WORDS
BARBER'S POLE
BARBER'S SHOP
BARE MIDRIFF
BARE MINIMUM
BARGAIN SALE
BARKING DOGS
BARLEY SUGAR
BARLEY WATER
BARNARD'S INN
BARON OF BEEF
BARON'S COURT
BARRACK ROOM
BARREL ORGAN
BARREN HEATH
BARREN WASTE
BARRIER REEF
BAR SINISTER
BASIC RIGHTS
BASKET CHAIR
BAT AN EYELID
BATED BREATH
BATHING POOL
BATTING SIDE
BATTLE ABBEY
BATTLE ARRAY
BATTLE DRESS
BATTLE ORDER
BATTLE ROYAL
BATTLE SCENE
BAY OF BENGAL
BAY OF BISCAY
BAY OF NAPLES

BEAM OF LIGHT	BERNARD SHAW	BLACK CASTLE
BEAR A GRUDGE	BERNESE ALPS	BLACK COFFEE
BEAR BAITING	BEST CIRCLES	BLACK COTTON
BEARDED LADY	BEST CLOTHES	BLACK FRIARS
BEARER BONDS	BEST EDITION	BLACK FRIDAY
BEAR ILL-WILL	BEST OF TASTE	BLACK FOREST
BEARING REIN	BEST OF TERMS	BLACK GRAPES
BEARSKIN RUG	BEST OF THREE	BLACK KNIGHT
BEAR THE COST	BEST QUALITY	BLACK LETTER
BEAR THE NAME	BEST REGARDS	BLACK MARKET
BEAR WITNESS	BETTER BY FAR	BLACK MONDAY
BEAST OF PREY	BETTER TERMS	BLACK PEPPER
BEAT A TATTOO	BETTER TIMES	BLACK PRINCE
BEATEN TRACK	BETTER VALUE	BLACK SQUARE
BEAT THE BAND	BETTER WAGES	BLACK TO MOVE
BEAT THE BANK	BETTING SHOP	BLACK TO PLAY
BEAT THE BOOK	BETTING SLIP	BLACK VELVET
BEAT THE DRUM	BETTY GRABLE	BLANK CHEQUE
BEAU BRUMMEL	BETTY HUTTON	BLANKET BATH
BEAU SABREUR	BETTY MARTIN	BLAZE A TRAIL
BEAUTY QUEEN	BETWEEN MAID	BLAZING FIRE
BEAUTY SALON	BEYOND A JOKE	BLESS MY SOUL!
BEAUTY SLEEP	BEYOND DOUBT	BLESS THE DAY
BEBE DANIELS	BEYOND PRICE	BLIND AS A BAT
BECK AND CALL	BICYCLE BELL	BLIND CHANCE
BECOME AWARE	BID DEFIANCE	BLIND CORNER
BECOME SOLID	BID FAREWELL	BLIND FLYING
BED AND BOARD	BIG BUSINESS	BLOCK LETTER
BE DIFFERENT	BIG TURNOVER	BLOCK OF WOOD
BED OF THE SEA	BILLIARD CUE	BLOCK THE WAY
BED OF THORNS	BILL OF COSTS	BLOOD ORANGE
BEDSIDE LAMP	BILLY BUNTER	BLOOD STREAM
BEEF EXTRACT	BILLY COTTON	BLOOD VESSEL
BEER SHAMPOO	BILLY THE KID	BLOODY TOWER
BEER TANKARD	BILLY WALKER	BLOSSOM TIME
BEES' WEDDING	BIRD FANCIER	BLOW BUBBLES
BEFORE LUNCH	BIRD WATCHER	BLOW FOR BLOW
BEG FOR MERCY	BISHOP'S MOVE	BLOW ME TIGHT!
BEGGING BOWL	BISHOP'S PAWN	BLOW ONE'S TOP
BEGIN TO PALL	BITE ONE'S LIP	BLOW SKY-HIGH
BEG TO DIFFER	BITE THE DUST	BLOW THE FIRE
BEHAVE BADLY	BITTER ALOES	BLOW THE GAFF
BELGIAN PORT	BITTER ENEMY	BLUE-COAT BOY
BELGIAN TOWN	BITTER GRIEF	BLUE-EYED BOY
BELINDA FAIR	BITTER LEMON	BLUE FOR A BOY
BELLY DANCER	BITTER SWEET	BLUE HORIZON
BELOW GROUND	BITTER TASTE	BLUNT REMARK
BELOW STAIRS	BITTER TEARS	BLUSH UNSEEN
BELT OF TREES	BITTER WORDS	BOARD SCHOOL
BEND FORWARD	BLACK AND TAN	BOATING SONG
BEND THE KNEE	BLACK AS COAL	BOB CRATCHIT
BEND THE MIND	BLACK AS SOOT	BODY AND SOUL
BENGAL LIGHT	BLACK BEAUTY	BODY POLITIC
BENGAL TIGER	BLACK BEETLE	BOGNOR REGIS
BE OF SERVICE	BLACK BISHOP	BOILED BACON
BE REALISTIC	BLACK BOTTOM	BOILED SHIRT

BOILED SWEET
BOLD AS A LION
BOLD AS BRASS
BOLD ATTEMPT
BOLD OUTLINE
BOLT THE DOOR
BOLT UPRIGHT
BOMBER PILOT
BOMB SHELTER
BOND OF UNION
BONNE BOUCHE
BONNY DUNDEE
BOOKING HALL
BOOK OF VERSE
BOOK OF WORDS
BOOK VOUCHER
BORACIC ACID
BORIS BECKER
BORN ACTRESS
BORN AND BRED
BORROW A BOOK
BORROW MONEY
BOSOM FRIEND
BOSS THE SHOW
BOSTON BEANS
BOTTLED BEER
BOTTLE GREEN
BOTTLE OF GIN
BOTTLE OF INK
BOTTLE OF RUM
BOTTLE PARTY
BOTTOM LAYER
BOTTOM MARKS
BOTTOM TEETH
BOUND TO LOSE
BOW AND ARROW
BOWL A YORKER
BOWL OF FRUIT
BOWL OF PUNCH
BOXER SHORTS
BOXING BOOTH
BOXING GLOVE
BOXING MATCH
BOX OF BRICKS
BOX OF CIGARS
BOX OF PAINTS
BOX OF TRICKS
BOY NEXT DOOR
BOYS' BRIGADE
BRACE AND BIT
BRACING WIND
BRAIN DAMAGE
BRAIN INJURY
BRAINS TRUST
BRAISED BEEF
BRANDY GLASS

BRASS MONKEY
BRASSY VOICE
BRAVE EFFORT
BRAVE PERSON
BRAZEN IT OUT
BREAD AND JAM
BREAD OF LIFE
BREAD RATION
BREAD STREET
BREAD WINNER
BREAK A HABIT
BREAK BOUNDS
BREAK FOR TEA
BREAK GROUND
BREAK STONES
BREAK THE ICE
BREAK THE LAW
BREATHE FIRE
BREATHE HARD
BREATH OF AIR
BREEZE BLOCK
BRENNER PASS
BREWER'S DRAY
BRIAN INGLIS
BRIDAL MARCH
BRIDAL PARTY
BRIDAL SUITE
BRIDAL TRAIN
BRIDGE DRIVE
BRIDGE FIEND
BRIDGE PARTY
BRIDGE TABLE
BRIDLE STRAP
BRIEF MOMENT
BRIEF SKETCH
BRIGHT CHILD
BRIGHT GREEN
BRIGHT LIGHT
BRIGHT PUPIL
BRIGHT SPARK
BRING TO BEAR
BRING TO BOOK
BRING TO HEEL
BRING TO LIFE
BRING TO MIND
BRING TO PASS
BRING TO REST
BRING TO RUIN
BRISTOL CITY
BRISTOL MILK
BRITISH ARMY
BRITISH CAMP
BRITISH FLAG
BRITISH LION
BRITISH MADE
BRITISH NAVY

BRITISH RAIL
BRITISH RULE
BRITISH SOIL
BRITISH WARM
BRITISH ZONE
BROAD ACCENT
BROAD COMEDY
BROAD SCOTCH
BROADSIDE ON
BROAD STREET
BROGUE SHOES
BROKE GROUND
BROKEN ANKLE
BROKEN BONES
BROKEN GLASS
BROKEN HEART
BRONZED SKIN
BRONZE MEDAL
BROTHER LOVE
BROUGHT HOME
BROWN BOMBER
BROWN RIBBON
BROWN SHERRY
BRUNO WALTER
BUDDING POET
BUD FLANAGAN
BUENOS AIRES
BUFFALO BILL
BUFFER STATE
BUILD A HOUSE
BUILT ON SAND
BUILT TO LAST
BUILT-UP AREA
BULGING EYES
BULL AND BUSH
BULL AT A GATE
BULL BAITING
BULLET WOUND
BULL TERRIER
BULLY FOR YOU!
BUMPING RACE
BUNCH OF KEYS
BUNDLE OF FUN
BUNNY RABBIT
BURGLAR BILL
BURIAL AT SEA
BURIAL PLACE
BURIED ALIVE
BURIED AT SEA
BURNING BUSH
BURNT ALMOND
BURNT EFFIGY
BURN TO ASHES
BURNT SIENNA
BURST OF FIRE
BURY ONESELF

BUSHEY HEATH
BUSINESS END
BUSINESS MAN
BUS TERMINUS
BUTTER BEANS
BUYING PRICE
BUYING SPREE
BUY ON CREDIT
BUY OUTRIGHT
BY AUTHORITY
BY FAIR MEANS
BYGONE TIMES
BY LAMPLIGHT
BY MAIN FORCE
BY MESSENGER
BY MISCHANCE
BY MOONLIGHT
BY THAT MEANS
BY THIS TOKEN
BY TRADITION
BY YOUR LEAVE

C – 11

CABARET STAR
CABBAGE LEAF
CABBAGE MOTH
CABBAGE ROSE
CABINET SIZE
CABIN WINDOW
CABLE STITCH
CAESAR'S WIFE
CAFÉ DE PARIS
CAFÉ SOCIETY
CAGED ANIMAL
CAIN AND ABEL
CAKE MIXTURE
CAKES AND ALE
CALCUTTA CUP
CALL FOR HELP
CALLING CARD
CALL IT QUITS
CALL ME MADAM
CALLOW YOUTH
CALL THE ROLL
CALL THE TIME
CALL THE TUNE
CALL TO A HALT
CALL TO ORDER
CALM WEATHER
CALYPSO BAND
CAME FORWARD
CAMOMILE TEA
CAMPING SITE
CANADA HOUSE
CANCEL LEAVE

CANDIED PEEL
CANDY KISSES
CANDY STRIPE
CANINE TOOTH
CANNED BEANS
CANNED FRUIT
CANNED GOODS
CANNED MUSIC
CANNING TOWN
CAN OF PETROL
CAP AND BELLS
CAPITAL CITY
CAPITAL FUND
CAPITAL GAIN
CAPITAL IDEA
CAPITAL LEVY
CAPITAL SHIP
CAPTAIN AHAB
CAPTAIN COOK
CAPTAIN HOOK
CAPTAIN KIDD
CAPTAIN WEBB
CARAVAN SITE
CARAWAY SEED
CARBON PAPER
CARDIGAN BAY
CARDINAL RED
CARDINAL SIN
CAREER WOMAN
CARGO VESSEL
CAR INDUSTRY
CARLTON CLUB
CARMEN JONES
CAROL SINGER
CARRION CROW
CARRY ACROSS
CARRY A TORCH
CARRY THE CAN
CARRY THE DAY
CARRY TOO FAR
CARRY WEIGHT
CASE HISTORY
CASE IN POINT
CASH ACCOUNT
CASH A CHEQUE
CASH BETTING
CASH CHEMIST
CASH PAYMENT
CASSIUS CLAY
CAST A GLANCE
CAST AN EYE ON
CAST A SHADOW
CASTILE SOAP
CASTING VOTE
CASTOR SUGAR
CASUAL VISIT

CAT AND MOUSE
CATCH A CHILL
CATCH ALIGHT
CATCH A PLANE
CATCH A THIEF
CATCH A TRAIN
CATCH PHRASE
CATCH THE EYE
CATHODE RAYS
CATS AND DOGS
CATS' CONCERT
CAT'S WHISKER
CATTLE RANCH
CATTLE THIEF
CATTY REMARK
CAUSE DAMAGE
CAUSTIC SODA
CAVALRY UNIT
CAVE DRAWING
CAVE DWELLER
CEASE TO LIVE
CECIL BEATON
CECIL RHODES
CELLAR STEPS
CELLO PLAYER
CELTIC CROSS
CEMENT MIXER
CENTRAL ASIA
CENTRAL HALL
CENTRAL IDEA
CENTRAL LINE
CENTRAL PARK
CENTRE COURT
CENTRE PARTY
CEREAL PLANT
CERTAIN CURE
CERTAIN HOPE
CHAFING DISH
CHAIN LETTER
CHAIN SMOKER
CHAIN STITCH
CHALK CLIFFS
CHALK GARDEN
CHANCERY INN
CHANGE A NOTE
CHANGE BUSES
CHANGE HANDS
CHANGE OF AIR
CHANGE ROUND
CHANGE SEATS
CHANGE SIDES
CHANNEL FOUR
CHAPEL ROYAL
CHAPTER FIVE
CHAPTER FOUR
CHARGE EXTRA

CHARGE SHEET	CIRCUS RIDER	CLOTHES LINE
CHARIOT RACE	CITIZEN KANE	CLOTH OF GOLD
CHARITY BALL	CITRUS FRUIT	CLOT OF BLOOD
CHARLES LAMB	CITY COMPANY	CLOUD OF DUST
CHARMED LIFE	CITY COUNCIL	CLUB COLOURS
CHARM SCHOOL	CITY FATHERS	CLUB STEWARD
CHEAP AS DIRT	CIVIC CENTRE	CLUB TO DEATH
CHEAP LABOUR	CIVIC RIGHTS	CLUMSY STYLE
CHEAP REMARK	CIVIL ACTION	COACHING INN
CHEAP RETURN	CIVIL ANSWER	COAL SCUTTLE
CHEAP THRILL	CIVIL RIGHTS	COALS OF FIRE
CHEAP TICKET	CIVIL TONGUE	COARSE CLOTH
CHEEK BY JOWL	CIVVY STREET	COARSE GRAIN
CHEEKY DEVIL	CLAIM TO FAME	COARSE GRASS
CHEER LEADER	CLAIM TO KNOW	COARSE VOICE
CHEESE SALAD	CLAIRE BLOOM	COASTAL ROAD
CHEESE STRAW	CLAM CHOWDER	COAT OF PAINT
CHEMIN DE FER	CLAP IN IRONS	COAT THE PILL
CHERRY STONE	CLARET GLASS	COAXING WAYS
CHESHIRE CAT	CLARION CALL	COCK AND BULL
CHESS PLAYER	CLASH OF ARMS	COCK ONE'S EYE
CHEVAL GLASS	CLASS HATRED	COCK SPARROW
CHICKEN COOP	CLASSIC RACE	COCKTAIL BAR
CHICKEN FARM	CLASS SYMBOL	COCOA BUTTER
CHICKEN FEED	CLAUDE DUVAL	COCOANUT OIL
CHICKEN SOUP	CLEAN BOWLED	COCONUT PALM
CHIEF PRIEST	CLEAN BREAST	CODE MESSAGE
CHIEF STOKER	CLEAN COLLAR	COD-LIVER OIL
CHILD LABOUR	CLEAN FORGOT	COFFEE BEANS
CHILLED BEEF	CLEAN RECORD	COFFEE BREAK
CHINA ORANGE	CLEAR A HEDGE	COFFEE CREAM
CHINESE FOOD	CLEARLY SEEN	COFFEE HOUSE
CHINESE JUNK	CLEAR OF DEBT	COFFEE SPOON
CHINESE MEAL	CLEAR PROFIT	COFFEE STALL
CHIT OF A GIRL	CLEAR THE AIR	COFFEE TABLE
CHOICE OF TWO	CLEAR THE WAY	COIN A PHRASE
CHOIR MASTER	CLEFT PALATE	COLD AS DEATH
CHOOSE A WIFE	CLEVER DODGE	COLD CLIMATE
CHOOSE SIDES	CLEVER STUFF	COLD COMFORT
CHU CHIN CHOW	CLEVER TRICK	COLD DRAUGHT
CHURCH BELLS	CLINCH A DEAL	COLD SHIVERS
CHURCH CHOIR	CLOSE ARREST	COLD STORAGE
CHURCH HOUSE	CLOSE AT HAND	COLD WEATHER
CHURCH LANDS	CLOSE BEHIND	COLD WELCOME
CHURCH MOUSE	CLOSE COMBAT	COLLECT DUST
CHURCH MUSIC	CLOSED DOORS	COLLEGE GIRL
CHURCH ORGAN	CLOSED PURSE	COLNEY HATCH
CHURCH SPIRE	CLOSE FINISH	COLOMBO PLAN
CHURCH TOWER	CLOSE FRIEND	COLONIAL WAR
CINDER TRACK	CLOSE OF PLAY	COLOUR BLIND
CINEMA QUEUE	CLOSE SEASON	COLOUR CHART
CINEMA USHER	CLOSE SECOND	COLOURED MAN
CINEMA WORLD	CLOSE SECRET	COLOUR PHOTO
CINQUE PORTS	CLOSE THE GAP	COLOUR PLATE
CIRCLE ROUND	CLOSING DATE	COME BETWEEN
CIRCULAR SAW	CLOSING TIME	COME FORWARD

COME IN FIRST	COOL HUNDRED	CREATE A STIR
COME IN FRONT	COPPER BEACH	CREATE HAVOC
COME IN HANDY	COPPER'S NARK	CREDIT ENTRY
COMELY WENCH	CORAL ISLAND	CREDIT TERMS
COME OFF BEST	CORDON ROUGE	CREDIT TITLE
COME OFF WELL	CORFE CASTLE	CRÊPE RUBBER
COME OUT BEST	CORNERED RAT	CRICKET BALL
COME OUTSIDE	CORNER TABLE	CRICKET CLUB
COME THIS WAY	CORN IN EGYPT	CRICKET TEAM
COME THROUGH	CORN PLASTER	CRIMINAL LAW
COME TO A HALT	CORPS D'ÉLITE	CRIMSON LAKE
COME TO A HEAD	CORRECT TIME	CRITICAL AGE
COME TO AN END	COSTUME BALL	CROCK OF GOLD
COME TO A STOP	COSTUME PLAY	CROOKED DEAL
COME TO BLOWS	COTTAGE LOAF	CROOKED PATH
COME TO EARTH	COTTON CLOTH	CROP FAILURE
COME TO GRIEF	COTTON DRESS	CROPPED HAIR
COME TO GRIPS	COTTON FIELD	CROQUET BALL
COME TO LIGHT	COTTON FROCK	CROQUET CLUB
COME TO ORDER	COTTON GOODS	CROQUET HOOP
COME TO POWER	COTTON PLANT	CROQUET LAWN
COME TO TERMS	COTTON SOCKS	CROSSBOW MAN
COME UNSTUCK	COTTON WASTE	CROSS STITCH
COME WHAT MAY	COUNCIL FLAT	CROSS SWORDS
COMIC RELIEF	COUNTER HAND	CROSS THE BAR
COMME IL FAUT	COUNTRY CLUB	CROSS THE SEA
COMMON CAUSE	COUNTRY CODE	CROWDED HOUR
COMMON CHORD	COUNTRY FOLK	CROWDED ROOM
COMMON ENEMY	COUNTRY LANE	CROWN A TOOTH
COMMON FAULT	COUNTRY LIFE	CROWN COLONY
COMMON FRONT	COUNTRY SEAT	CROWNED HEAD
COMMON PLEAS	COUNTRY TOWN	CROWN JEWELS
COMMON PURSE	COUNTRY WALK	CROWN OFFICE
COMMON SENSE	COUNTY CLARE	CROWN PRINCE
COMMON STOCK	COUNTY COURT	CRUCIAL TEST
COMMON THIEF	COUNTY MATCH	CRUEL TYRANT
COMMON TO ALL	COUP DE GRÂCE	CRUMBLE AWAY
COMMON TOUCH	COURT DEFEAT	CRY FOR MERCY
COMMON USAGE	COURT JESTER	CRYING SHAME
COMPACT DISC	COVER A STORY	CRYPTIC CLUE
COMPLETE ASS	COVER CHARGE	CRYSTAL BALL
COMPLETE SET	COVER GROUND	CUB REPORTER
COMPOST HEAP	COWSLIP WINE	CUCKOO CLOCK
COMPUTER AGE	CRACK OF DAWN	CULINARY ART
CONCERT HALL	CRACK OF DOOM	CUPID'S ARROW
CONEY ISLAND	CRACK PLAYER	CUP OF COFFEE
CONSTANT USE	CRACK TROOPS	CUP OF POISON
CONTACT LENS	CRANE DRIVER	CUP OF SORROW
CONTACT MINE	CRASH COURSE	CUPPED HANDS
CONTOUR LINE	CRASH HELMET	CURDLED MILK
CONTRACT OUT	CRAZY NOTION	CURE OF SOULS
CONTROL ROOM	CRAZY PAVING	CURLING CLUB
CONVERT A TRY	CREAM CHEESE	CURLING IRON
COOKERY BOOK	CREAMED RICE	CURL OF SMOKE
COOK GENERAL	CREATE A NEED	CURL ONE'S LIP
COOL AND CALM	CREATE A RÔLE	CURRANT CAKE

CURRANT LOAF
CURRENT DATE
CURRENT NEWS
CURRENT WEEK
CURRENT YEAR
CURRY FAVOUR
CURRY POWDER
CURSE OF CAIN
CURTAIN CALL
CUSTARD TART
CUSTOM HOUSE
CUSTOMS DUTY
CUT A LECTURE
CUT AND DRIED
CUT-AWAY COAT
CUT BOTH WAYS
CUT IN SALARY
CUT OFF SHORT
CUT OF HIS JIB
CUT ONE'S HAIR
CUT THE CARDS
CUT THE GRASS
CUT THE SCENE
CUTTING EDGE
CUTTING WIND
CUT TO PIECES
CYCLE TO WORK
CYCLING CLUB

D – 11

DAILY MARKET
DAILY MIRROR
DAILY RECORD
DAILY REPORT
DAILY SKETCH
DAILY WORKER
DAIRY CATTLE
DAME FORTUNE
DAMON RUNYON
DANA ANDREWS
DANCE A TANGO
DANCE A WALTZ
DANCE FOR JOY
DANCING BEAR
DANCING GIRL
DANGER MONEY
DANGER POINT
DANIEL DEFOE
DANISH BACON
DARK CLOTHES
DARKEST HOUR
DARK GLASSES
DARK LANTERN
DART FORWARD
DARTING PAIN

DARTS PLAYER
DASHED HOPES
DASH FORWARD
DASH THROUGH
DATE OF BIRTH
DATE OF DEATH
DAVID JACOBS
DAWN GODDESS
DAY AFTER DAY
DAY AND NIGHT
DAY IN, DAY OUT
DAY LABOURER
DAY OF ACTION
DAY OF PRAYER
DAYS AND DAYS
DAY'S JOURNEY
DAYS OF GRACE
DAZZLING WIT
DEAD AGAINST
DEAD AND GONE
DEAD AS A DODO
DEAD CERTAIN
DEAD EARNEST
DEADEN SOUND
DEAD FAILURE
DEAD FLOWERS
DEADLY CRIME
DEADLY ENEMY
DEADLY PERIL
DEADLY RIVAL
DEAD OF NIGHT
DEAD OR ALIVE
DEAD SILENCE
DEAD TO SHAME
DEAF AND DUMB
DEAF AS A POST
DEAF TO MUSIC
DEAR BELOVED
DEAR OCTOPUS
DEAR OLD PALS
DEATH COLUMN
DEATHLY HUSH
DEATHLY PALE
DEATH NOTICE
DEATH RATTLE
DEBORAH KERR
DEB'S DELIGHT
DECK OF CARDS
DEED OF MERCY
DEEP BLUE SEA
DEEP CONCERN
DEEP FEELING
DEEP IN A BOOK
DEEP INSIGHT
DEEP MYSTERY
DEEP REMORSE

DEEP THINKER
DEEP THOUGHT
DEFENCE WORK
DEFERRED PAY
DEFY THE WHIP
DELIVERY MAN
DELLA ROBBIA
DE-LUXE MODEL
DEMON BARBER
DEMON BOWLER
DENIS NORDEN
DENMARK HILL
DENNIS NOBLE
DENSE FOREST
DENTAL CHAIR
DE PROFUNDIS
DEPTH CHARGE
DERBY COUNTY
DERBY STAKES
DERBY WINNER
DESERT SANDS
DESERT WASTE
DESERVE WELL
DEVIL OF A JOB
DEVIL'S ELBOW
DEVOTED WIFE
DIAMOND MINE
DIAMOND RING
DICK BENTLEY
DICK VAN DYKE
DO THE TWIST
DIE BY INCHES
DIE FIGHTING
DIE LIKE A DOG
DIE OF FRIGHT
DIE OF HUNGER
DIESEL TRAIN
DIET OF WORMS
DIG AND DELVE
DINNER DANCE
DINNER PARTY
DINNER WAGON
DIRECT ROUTE
DIRECT STYLE
DIRE STRAITS
DIRK BOGARDE
DISMAL JIMMY
DISPATCH BOX
DISPLAY CARD
DISTAFF SIDE
DISTANT PAST
DISTANT VIEW
DISUSED WELL
DIVIDE BY SIX
DIVIDE BY TEN
DIVIDE BY TWO

DIVINE BEING
DIVINE GRACE
DIVINE RIGHT
DIVINING ROD
DIVISION ONE
DIVISION SUM
DIVISION TWO
DIVORCE CASE
DIVORCE LAWS
DIVORCE SUIT
DIZZY HEIGHT
DO A GOOD TURN
DO ALL ONE CAN
DO A MISCHIEF
DO A WAR-DANCE
DOCTOR OF LAW
DOFF ONE'S HAT
DOING NICELY
DO IT IN STYLE
DOLEFUL LOOK
DOLEFUL TALE
DOLLY VARDEN
DO ME A FAVOUR
DOMESTIC PET
DONALD PEERS
DONE TO A TURN
DONE TO DEATH
DOOMED TO DIE
DO ONE'S WORST?
DO REVERENCE
DORIC COLUMN
DORIS ARCHER
DOT AND CARRY
DO THE ROUNDS
DO THE SPLITS
DOUBLE BLANK
DOUBLE CROSS
DOUBLE DOORS
DOUBLE DUMMY
DOUBLE DUTCH
DOUBLE EAGLE
DOUBLE EIGHT
DOUBLE ENTRY
DOUBLE EVENT
DOUBLE FAULT
DOUBLE FIRST
DOUBLE MARCH
DOUBLE SEVEN
DOUBLE SHARE
DOUBLE SHIFT
DOUBLE THREE
DOUBLE TRACK
DOVE OF PEACE
DOVER CASTLE
DOVER PATROL
DOWN AT HEART

DOWN IN PRICE
DOWN PAYMENT
DOWN THE AGES
DOWN THE HILL
DOWN THE LINE
DOWN THE MINE
DOWN THE ROAD
DOWN THE SINK
DOWN THE WELL
DOWN TO EARTH
DOWN YOUR WAY
DRAMA CRITIC
DRAMA SCHOOL
DRAMATIC ART
DRAUGHT BEER
DRAW A CIRCLE
DRAW A SALARY
DRAWING ROOM
DRAW RATIONS
DRAW THE CORK
DRAW THE LINE
DRAW TO AN END
DRAW TO SCALE
DRAW UP A PLAN
DREAM DREAMS
DREAMY MUSIC
DRESS CIRCLE
DRESSED CRAB
DRESS TO KILL
DREYFUS CASE
DRINK ADDICT
DRINK A PINTA
DRINK A TOAST
DRINKING DEN
DRIPPING WET
DRIVE AROUND
DRIVE INSANE
DRIVE ONE MAD
DRIVE SLOWLY
DRIVING RAIN
DRIVING TEST
DROP A CURTSY
DROP A LETTER
DROP AN AITCH
DROP A REMARK
DROP A SITTER
DROP A STITCH
DROP IN PRICE
DROP ME A LINE
DROP OF BLOOD
DROP OF WATER
DROPPED GOAL
DROP THE MASK
DROP TOO MUCH
DROWNING MAN
DRUG PEDDLER

DRUG TRAFFIC
DRUNKEN ORGY
DRY AS A STICK
DRY CLEANERS
DRY CLEANING
DRY ONE'S EYES
DUAL CONTROL
DUAL PURPOSE
DUCHESSE SET
DUCK-EGG BLUE
DULCET TONES
DULL READING
DULL SCHOLAR
DULL WEATHER
DUMB CHARADE
DUMB DESPAIR
DUMB FRIENDS
DURANCE VILE
DUSTY MILLER
DUTCH CHEESE
DUTCH SCHOOL
DUTCH TULIPS
DUTY OFFICER
DWINDLE AWAY
DYE ONE'S HAIR
DYING BREATH
DYING EMBERS
DYING TO KNOW
DYLAN THOMAS

E – 11

EAGER BEAVER
EAR FOR MUSIC
EARL MARSHAL
EARL OF ARRAN
EARLY AUTUMN
EARLY CHURCH
EARLY GOTHIC
EARLY IN LIFE
EARLY RISING
EARLY SPRING
EARLY SUMMER
EARLY TO RISE
EARN A LIVING
EARTH'S CRUST
EARTH TREMOR
EASE THE PAIN
EASILY MOVED
EAST AND WEST
EAST GERMANY
EAST LOTHIAN
EASY PROBLEM
EASY TO GRASP
EASY VICTORY
EAT AND DRINK

EAT AND SLEEP	ELEVEN PARTS	ESTATE AGENT
EATING HOUSE	ELEVEN SCORE	ETERNAL CITY
EAT LIKE A PIG	ELEVENTH DAY	ETERNAL HOME
EAT ONE'S FILL	ELEVENTH ROW	ETERNAL LIFE
ECONOMIC AID	ELEVEN TIMES	ETERNAL REST
ECONOMY SIZE	ELEVEN WEEKS	ETHEL MERMAN
EDDIE FISHER	ELLIS ISLAND	ETON COLLEGE
EDGE ONE'S WAY	EMERALD ISLE	EVADE THE LAW
EDGEWARE ROAD	EMERALD RING	EVELYN WAUGH
EDIBLE FUNGI	EMPIRE STYLE	EVENING MEAL
EDITH CAVELL	EMPIRE TRADE	EVENING NEWS
EDMUND BURKE	EMPTY BOTTLE	EVENING STAR
EDUCATED MAN	EMPTY LARDER	EVER AND A DAY
EDWARD HEATH	EMPTY POCKET	EVER AND ANON
EDWARD MY SON	EMPTY STREET	EVER AND EVER
EGG AND BACON	EMPTY THE BAG	EVERY EXCUSE
EGG AND CHIPS	EMPTY THREAT	EVERY MINUTE
EGG SANDWICH	EMPTY WALLET	EVERY VIRTUE
EIFFEL TOWER	EN CASSEROLE	EVIL CONDUCT
EIGHTH FLOOR	ENDLESS BAND	EVIL THOUGHT
EIGHTH GREEN	ENDLESS BELT	EXACT AMOUNT
EIGHTH MONTH	ENDLESS TIME	EXALTED RANK
EIGHTH OF MAY	END OF THE DAY	EXEUNT OMNES
EIGHTH PLACE	END OF THE WAR	EXHAUST PIPE
EIGHTH ROUND	END ONE'S DAYS	EXPLAIN AWAY
EIGHT MONTHS	END ONE'S LIFE	EXPORT DRIVE
EIGHT NINTHS	ENEMY ACTION	EXPORT ORDER
EIGHT O'CLOCK	ENEMY PATROL	EXPORT TRADE
EIGHT OR NINE	ENEMY TROOPS	EXPRESS LIFT
EIGHT OUNCES	ENEMY VESSEL	EXPRESS POST
EIGHT POINTS	ENGAGED TONE	EXTRA CHARGE
EIGHT POUNDS	ENGINE HOUSE	EXTRA STRONG
EIGHT ROUNDS	ENGINE POWER	EXTREME CASE
EIGHTY MILES	ENGLISH HORN	EXTREME EDGE
EIGHTY TIMES	ENGLISH POET	EXTREME PAIN
EIGHTY YEARS	ENGLISH PORT	EYE FOR AN EYE
EILEEN JOYCE	ENGLISH ROSE	EYES AND EARS
ELASTIC BAND	ENLARGE UPON	
ELBOW GREASE	ENLISTED MAN	
ELDERS FIRST	ENOCH POWELL	F – 11
ELDER SISTER	ENTER A PHASE	
ELDEST CHILD	ENTER A STAGE	FACE MASSAGE
ELECTION DAY	ENTRANCE FEE	FACE REALITY
ELECTRIC EEL	EQUAL CHANCE	FACE THE ODDS
ELECTRIC EYE	EQUAL HEIGHT	FACE UPWARDS
ELECTRIC FAN	EQUAL RIGHTS	FACTORY ACTS
ELECTRIC RAY	EQUAL SHARES	FACTORY BAND
ELECTRIC VAN	EQUAL WEIGHT	FACTORY HAND
ELECTRON GUN	ERECT FIGURE	FACTS OF LIFE
ELEPHANT BOY	ERIC PORTMAN	FADED BEAUTY
ELEPHANT GUN	ERMINE STOLE	FADING HOPES
ELEVEN A SIDE	ERNEST BEVIN	FADING LIGHT
ELEVEN DOZEN	ESCAPE DEATH	FAIL THE TEST
ELEVEN GROSS	ESCAPE HATCH	FAIL TO AGREE
ELEVEN HOURS	ESCAPE ROUTE	FAIL TO REPLY
ELEVEN MILES	ESCAPING GAS	FAIL TO SCORE
		FAINT EFFORT

FAINTING FIT	FAST FRIENDS	FIFTEEN LOVE
FAINT PRAISE	FATAL ATTACK	FIFTH AVENUE
FAIR COMMENT	FATAL INJURY	FIFTH COLUMN
FAIR FORTUNE	FATA MORGANA	FIFTH LETTER
FAIR HEARING	FAT AS BUTTER	FIFTH OF JULY
FAIRLY CLOSE	FATHER BROWN	FIFTH OF JUNE
FAIR WARNING	FATHER IMAGE	FIFTH STOREY
FAIR WEATHER	FATHERLY EYE	FIFTH VOLUME
FAIRY CIRCLE	FATIGUE DUTY	FIGHT FOR AIR
FAIRY LIGHTS	FATTY TISSUE	FIGHTING FIT
FAITH HEALER	FEARFUL BORE	FIGHTING MAD
FALL ASUNDER	FEARFUL ODDS	FIGHTING MAN
FALLEN ANGEL	FEAR OF DEATH	FIGURE EIGHT
FALL IN DROPS	FEAR TO TREAD	FIGURE IT OUT
FALLING STAR	FEATURE FILM	FIGURE OF FUN
FALL IN PLACE	FEEBLE BRAIN	FIJI ISLANDS
FALL IN PRICE	FEEBLE GRASP	FILING CLERK
FALL IN RUINS	FEEDING TIME	FILL AN ORDER
FALL IN VALUE	FEEL CERTAIN	FILLET STEAK
FALL THROUGH	FEEL NO SHAME	FILL THE BILL
FALL TO EARTH	FEEL NOTHING	FILL THE TILL
FALSE BOTTOM	FEEL ONE'S WAY	FILM ACTRESS
FALSE CHARGE	FEEL PECKISH	FILM COMPANY
FALSE COLOUR	FEEL REMORSE	FILTHY LUCRE
FALSE FRIEND	FEEL STRANGE	FINAL ANSWER
FALSE REPORT	FEEL THE COLD	FINAL CHOICE
FALSE RUMOUR	FEEL THE HEAT	FINAL CLAUSE
FALSE VALUES	FEEL THE URGE	FINAL DEFEAT
FALSE VANITY	FEEL THE WIND	FINAL DEMAND
FAMILY ALBUM	FELIX AYLMER	FINAL NOTICE
FAMILY BIBLE	FELIX THE CAT	FINAL REPORT
FAMILY CARES	FELL THROUGH	FINAL RESULT
FAMILY CREST	FEMALE SCREW	FINAL SPEECH
FAMILY HOTEL	FEMALE VOICE	FINAL STROKE
FAMILY MOTTO	FEMME FATALE	FINANCE BILL
FAMILY PARTY	FEN DISTRICT	FIND A REFUGE
FAMILY PRIDE	FERTILE LAND	FIND A REMEDY
FAMILY TREAT	FERTILE MIND	FIND A WAY OUT
FAMILY VAULT	FERTILE SOIL	FIND FREEDOM
FAMINE PRICE	FERVENT HOPE	FIND ONESELF
FAMOUS WOMEN	FESTIVE MOOD	FIND ONE'S WAY
FAN THE FLAME	FEVERED BROW	FIND SHELTER
FAR-AWAY LOOK	FIBRE OPTICS	FIND THE LADY
FAR DISTANCE	FIDDLE ABOUT	FIND THE TIME
FARES PLEASE	FIDEL CASTRO	FINE FLAVOUR
FAR FROM HERE	FIELD EVENTS	FINE RAIMENT
FAR FROM HOME	FIELD OF CORN	FINE SOLDIER
FARMER GILES	FIELD OF PLAY	FINE TEXTURE
FARMER'S WIFE	FIELD OF VIEW	FINE WEATHER
FARMING TYPE	FIELD SPORTS	FINE WRITING
FARM MANAGER	FIERCE GLARE	FINGAL'S CAVE
FARM PRODUCE	FIERY DRAGON	FINISH EARLY
FASHION SHOW	FIERY ORDEAL	FINISH FIRST
FAST BOWLING	FIERY SPEECH	FINNISH BATH
FAST BREEDER	FIERY SPIRIT	FIRE AND FURY
FAST COLOURS	FIERY TEMPER	FIRE A SALUTE

FIRE A VOLLEY	FIT OF NERVES	FLIMSY PAPER
FIRE BRIGADE	FIT OF TEMPER	FLOATING RIB
FIRE CURTAIN	FIT OF TERROR	FLOOD DAMAGE
FIRE SERVICE	FITTING ROOM	FLOOR POLISH
FIRE STATION	FITTING SHOP	FLORAL DANCE
FIRING PARTY	FITTING TIME	FLORA ROBSON
FIRING SQUAD	FIT TO BE SEEN	FLORID STYLE
FIRM AS A ROCK	FIVE AT A TIME	FLOWING BOWL
FIRM BACKING	FIVE-BAR GATE	FLOWING HAND
FIRM CONTROL	FIVE COURSES	FLOWING TIDE
FIRM FRIENDS	FIVE-DAY WEEK	FLOW OF WORDS
FIRM PROMISE	FIVE DOLLARS	FLOW THROUGH
FIRM RESOLVE	FIVE EIGHTHS	FLOW TOWARDS
FIRST CHARGE	FIVE FATHOMS	FLUID INTAKE
FIRST CHOICE	FIVE FINGERS	FLUSH OF DAWN
FIRST COURSE	FIVE GALLONS	FLUSH OF HOPE
FIRST COUSIN	FIVE GUINEAS	FLUTTER DOWN
FIRST DEGREE	FIVE HUNDRED	FLY AWAY PAUL
FIRST ELEVEN	FIVE MINUTES	FLYING CORPS
FIRST FIDDLE	FIVE OCTAVES	FLYING FIELD
FIRST FINGER	FIVE OF CLUBS	FLYING SPEED
FIRST FLIGHT	FIVE PER CENT	FLYING SQUAD
FIRST FRUITS	FIVE SQUARED	FLYING START
FIRST GLANCE	FIVE STROKES	FLYING VISIT
FIRST IN LINE	FIVE WICKETS	FOLDED HANDS
FIRST LEADER	FIX BAYONETS	FOLK DANCING
FIRST LEAGUE	FIXED AMOUNT	FOLLOW AFTER
FIRST LESSON	FIXED ASSETS	FOLLOW A PLAN
FIRST LETTER	FIXED BELIEF	FOND EMBRACE
FIRST MAN OUT	FIXED CHARGE	FONDEST LOVE
FIRST OF JULY	FIXED INCOME	FOND OF A DRAM
FIRST OF JUNE	FIXED SALARY	FOND REGARDS
FIRST PERSON	FIX THE PRICE	FOOD COUNTER
FIRST REMOVE	FIX THE TERMS	FOOD SUBSIDY
FIRST RUBBER	FIXTURE LIST	FOOLISH IDEA
FIRST SEASON	FLAG CAPTAIN	FOOLISH TALK
FIRST SERIES	FLAG OFFICER	FOOL'S ERRAND
FIRST SERVED	FLAG OF TRUCE	FOOLS RUSH IN
FIRST SINGLE	FLAKY PASTRY	FOOTBALL FAN
FIRST SKETCH	FLAME COLOUR	FOOT THE BILL
FIRST STOREY	FLAMING JUNE	FOR ALL TO SEE
FIRST STRING	FLANK ATTACK	FOR A PURPOSE
FIRST STROKE	FLASH A SMILE	FORCE A WAY IN
FIRST TO COME	FLASK OF WINE	FORCED ENTRY
FIRST TO LAND	FLAT FOR SALE	FORCED LAUGH
FIRST TO LAST	FLAT HUNTING	FORCED MARCH
FIRST VIOLIN	FLAT REFUSAL	FORCED SMILE
FIRST VOLUME	FLAT SURFACE	FORCE OF ARMS
FIRST WICKET	FLEET AIR-ARM	FOR DEAR LIFE
FISHER OF MEN	FLEET OF CABS	FOREIGN BODY
FISH FINGERS	FLEET OF CARS	FOREIGN COIN
FISHING BIRD	FLEET OF FOOT	FOREIGN FILM
FISHING BOAT	FLEET PRISON	FOREIGN LAND
FISHING LINE	FLEET STREET	FOREIGN NAME
FIT FOR A KING	FLESH COLOUR	FOREIGN NEWS
FIT OF ENERGY	FLESH TIGHTS	FOREIGN RULE

FOREIGN SOIL
FOREIGN TOUR
FOR INSTANCE
FORLORN HOPE
FORMAL DRESS
FORMAL OFFER
FORMAL VISIT
FORM AN IMAGE
FORMER PUPIL
FORMER TIMES
FOR PLEASURE
FOR SOME TIME
FORSYTE SAGA
FORTH BRIDGE
FOR THE NONCE
FOR THE WORSE
FORT WILLIAM
FORTY NIGHTS
FORTY THIRTY
FORWARD LINE
FORWARD MOVE
FORWARD PLAY
FOSTER CHILD
FOUL JOURNEY
FOUL THE LINE
FOUL WEATHER
FOUND A PARTY
FOUNDERS' DAY
FOUND GUILTY
FOUNTAIN PEN
FOUR AT A TIME
FOUR CORNERS
FOUR COURSES
FOUR-DAY WEEK
FOUR DEGREES
FOUR DOLLARS
FOUR FATHOMS
FOUR FIGURES
FOUR GALLONS
FOUR GUINEAS
FOUR HUNDRED
FOUR JUST MEN
FOUR MINUTES
FOUR OCTAVES
FOUR OF CLUBS
FOUR PER CENT
FOUR SEASONS
FOUR SQUARED
FOUR STROKES
FOURTH FLOOR
FOURTH GREEN
FOURTH OF MAY
FOURTH PLACE
FOURTH ROUND
FOUR WICKETS
FOX AND GEESE

FRAME OF MIND
FRANK AVOWAL
FRANTIC PACE
FRANTIC RUSH
FRED ASTAIRE
FREE AND EASY
FREE AS A BIRD
FREE CITIZEN
FREE COUNTRY
FREE ECONOMY
FREE LIBRARY
FREE ON BOARD
FREE ONESELF
FREE PARKING
FREE PASSAGE
FREE SERVICE
FREE SPENDER
FREE THINKER
FREE THOUGHT
FREE TO SPEAK
FREE TRIBUTE
FRENCH BEANS
FRENCH BREAD
FRENCH CHALK
FRENCH COAST
FRENCH FARCE
FRENCH FRANC
FRENCH FRIED
FRENCH LEAVE
FRENCH MONEY
FRENCH NOVEL
FRENCH SALON
FRESH BREEZE
FRESH BUTTER
FRESH FIELDS
FRESH GROUND
FRESH SALMON
FRESH TROOPS
FRET AND FUME
FRIDAY NIGHT
FRIED ONIONS
FRIENDLY ACT
FRIENDLY TIP
FRIEND OF MAN
FRIEND OR FOE
FRIGHTEN OFF
FRITTER AWAY
FROM SCRATCH
FROM THE EAST
FROM THE WEST
FROM THE WOOD
FROM WITHOUT
FRONT GARDEN
FRONT LIGHTS
FRONT WINDOW
FROSTED LENS

FROSTY SMILE
FROZEN NORTH
FROZEN PIPES
FROZEN SOLID
FROZEN STIFF
FROZEN WATER
FRUIT MARKET
FRUITY VOICE
FULL ACCOUNT
FULL ADDRESS
FULL APOLOGY
FULL AS AN EGG
FULL BROTHER
FULL CONSENT
FULL DETAILS
FULL ENQUIRY
FULL FLAVOUR
FULL GENERAL
FULL MEASURE
FULL OF BEANS
FULL OF FIGHT
FULL OF GRACE
FULL OF HOLES
FULL OF IDEAS
FULL OF MIRTH
FULL OF PRIDE
FULL REGALIA
FULL SERVICE
FULL SUPPORT
FULL-TIME JOB
FULLY BOOKED
FULLY RIGGED
FUN AND GAMES
FUNERAL HYMN
FUNERAL PACE
FUNERAL PILE
FUNERAL PYRE
FUNERAL SONG
FUNNY AFFAIR
FUNNY PERSON
FURIOUS PACE
FUTURE HOPES
FUTURE PLANS
FUTURE STATE
FUTURE TENSE

G – 11

GAIN CONTROL
GAIN IN VALUE
GAIN THE LEAD
GALA EVENING
GALE WARNING
GALLERY SEAT
GALLEY PROOF
GALLEY SLAVE

GALLON OF OIL	GET EVEN WITH	GLANCE TO LEG
GAMBLING DEN	GET IN THE WAY	GLASS HOUSES
GAME CHICKEN	GET INTO A ROW	GLASS OF BEER
GAME LICENCE	GET INTO A RUT	GLASS OF MILK
GAME OF BOWLS	GET INTO DEBT	GLASS OF PORT
GAME OF CARDS	GET ONE'S GOAT	GLASS OF WINE
GAME OF CHESS	GET ONE'S WISH	GLASS VESSEL
GAME OF SKILL	GET ON WITH IT	GLASSY STARE
GAME OF WHIST	GET OUT OF BED	GLEAM OF HOPE
GAME RESERVE	GET SUNBURNT	GLEEFUL MOOD
GAMES MASTER	GET THE FACTS	GLEEFUL NEWS
GAMING HOUSE	GET THE KNACK	GLEE SINGERS
GAMING TABLE	GET THE POINT	GLIB SPEAKER
GAMMON STEAK	GET THE TASTE	GLIDER PILOT
GANG ROBBERY	GETTING WARM	GLYNIS JOHNS
GANG WARFARE	GETTING WELL	GLORIOUS DAY
GARDEN CHAIR	GET TOGETHER	GLORIOUS FUN
GARDEN FENCE	GET TO THE TOP	GLORIOUS ROW
GARDEN PARTY	GET UNDER WAY	GLOSSY PAINT
GARDEN TOOLS	GET WELL SOON	GNAWING PAIN
GARRICK CLUB	GET WISE TO IT	GO-AHEAD SIGN
GATHER ROSES	GHASTLY MESS	GO ALL THE WAY
GATHER ROUND	GHASTLY PALE	GO BACKWARDS
GATHER SPEED	GHOST WRITER	GO BY DEFAULT
GAY BACHELOR	GIANT KILLER	GO BY THE BOOK
GAY DECEIVER	GIANT OF A MAN	GODFREY WINN
GAY LOTHARIO	GIFT OF MONEY	GOD OF THE SEA
GAY NINETIES	GIFT VOUCHER	GOG AND MAGOG
GENERAL IDEA	GILDED YOUTH	GO GREAT GUNS
GENERAL LEVY	GILD THE LILY	GOING STEADY
GENERAL POST	GILD THE PILL	GOING STRONG
GENERAL RATE	GIN AND LEMON	GO IN PURSUIT
GENERAL VIEW	GIN AND TONIC	GO INTO EXILE
GENERIC NAME	GINGER GROUP	GO INTO ORBIT
GENEROUS ACT	GIRLS' SCHOOL	GOLD BULLION
GENEVA CROSS	GIRL STUDENT	GOLD COINAGE
GENTLE BIRTH	GIVE AND TAKE	GOLD DEPOSIT
GENTLE SLOPE	GIVE AN ORDER	GOLDEN APPLE
GENTLE TOUCH	GIVE A REASON	GOLDEN ARROW
GENTLE VOICE	GIVE A RULING	GOLDEN BOUGH
GENUINE CASE	GIVE IT A MISS	GOLDEN BROWN
GEORGE BROWN	GIVE IT A NAME	GOLDEN DREAM
GEORGE CROSS	GIVE IT A REST	GOLDEN EAGLE
GEORGE ELIOT	GIVE LESSONS	GOLDEN GATES
GEORGE MEDAL	GIVEN PERIOD	GOLDEN GOOSE
GEORGE ROBEY	GIVEN THE TIP	GOLDEN SANDS
GERMAN MONEY	GIVE OFFENCE	GOLDEN SYRUP
GERM CARRIER	GIVE QUARTER	GOLDEN TOUCH
GERM WARFARE	GIVE SUPPORT	GOLD FILLING
GET A BAD NAME	GIVE THE SACK	GOLD RESERVE
GET A DIVORCE	GIVE THE WORD	GO LIKE A BOMB
GET A MENTION	GIVE TROUBLE	GONE FOR EVER
GET AN ENCORE	GIVE WARNING	GONE FOR GOOD
GET A RECEIPT	GLAD TIDINGS	GONE TO EARTH
GET CRACKING	GLAMOUR GIRL	GONE TO GLORY
GET DOWN TO IT	GLANCE ASIDE	GONE TO LUNCH

GONE TO WASTE
GOOD ACCOUNT
GOOD ACTRESS
GOOD ADDRESS
GOOD AND EVIL
GOOD AS A PLAY
GOOD AT HEART
GOOD BARGAIN
GOOD BEARING
GOOD BEATING
GOOD CITIZEN
GOOD COMPANY
GOOD CONDUCT
GOOD COUNSEL
GOOD DEFENCE
GOOD DICTION
GOOD EVENING
GOOD EXAMPLE
GOOD FEEDING
GOOD FEELING
GOOD FICTION
GOOD FORTUNE
GOOD FRIENDS
GOOD GRAMMAR
GOOD GROUNDS
GOOD HARMONY
GOOD HARVEST
GOOD HEARING
GOOD HEAVENS
GOOD HUNTING
GOOD HUSBAND
GOOD INNINGS
GOOD IN PARTS
GOOD MANAGER
GOOD MANNERS
GOOD MEASURE
GOOD MORNING
GOOD OFFICES
GOOD OLD DAYS
GOOD OLD TIME
GOOD OPENING
GOOD OPINION
GOOD QUALITY
GOOD READING
GOOD SCHOLAR
GOOD SEND OFF
GOOD SERVANT
GOOD SERVICE
GOOD SOCIETY
GOOD SOLDIER
GOOD SPENDER
GOOD SPIRITS
GOOD SWIMMER
GOOD TEMPLAR
GOOD THEATRE
GOOD TIDINGS

GOOD WEATHER
GOOD WORKMAN
GOOD WRITE-UP
GO ON A PICNIC
GO ONE BETTER
GO ON FOR EVER
GO ON HOLIDAY
GO ON THE DOLE
GO OUT TO WORK
GO OVER THERE
GORDIAN KNOT
GORDON RIOTS
GORGON'S HEAD
GOSPEL TRUTH
GO THE ROUNDS
GOTHIC STYLE
GO THROUGH IT
GO TO BED LATE
GO TO HALIFAX
GO TO JERICHO
GO TO PARTIES
GO TO THE DOGS
GO TO THE FAIR
GO TO THE MOON
GO TO THE WALL
GO TO THE WARS
GOT UP TO KILL
GO UP IN SMOKE
GRAIN OF GOLD
GRAIN OF SALT
GRAIN OF SAND
GRAND CANYON
GRAND CIRCLE
GRAND FELLOW
GRAND FINALE
GRAND MANNER
GRAND MASTER
GRAND OLD MAN
GRAND REVIEW
GRAND VIZIER
GRANITE CITY
GRANT ACCESS
GRANT ASYLUM
GRANT A TRUCE
GRAPHIC ARTS
GRAVE ACCENT
GRAVE AFFAIR
GRAVE CHARGE
GRAVE CRISIS
GRAVE DOUBTS
GRAVE MATTER
GRAVEN IMAGE
GRAVE SPEECH
GREASE PAINT
GREAT AMOUNT
GREAT BEAUTY

GREAT BURDEN
GREAT CAESAR
GREAT CHANCE
GREAT CHANGE
GREAT CIRCLE
GREAT DAMAGE
GREAT DANCER
GREAT DANGER
GREAT DARING
GREAT DETAIL
GREAT DIVIDE
GREAT DOINGS
GREAT EFFORT
GREATER GOOD
GREATER PART
GREAT FAVOUR
GREAT FRIEND
GREAT HEALER
GREAT HEIGHT
GREAT HONOUR
GREAT IMPORT
GREAT NEPHEW
GREAT NUMBER
GREAT PLAGUE
GREAT PLAYER
GREAT REGRET
GREAT RELIEF
GREAT SNAKES
GREAT SORROW
GREAT STRAIN
GREAT STRESS
GREAT TALKER
GREAT THINGS
GREAT UNPAID
GREAT WEALTH
GREAT WEIGHT
GRECIAN BEND
GRECIAN KNOT
GRECIAN NOSE
GREEK CHURCH
GREEK COMEDY
GREEK LEGEND
GREEK STATUE
GREEN BOTTLE
GREEN CHEESE
GREEN FIELDS
GREEN GABLES
GREEN GINGER
GREEN PEPPER
GREEN RIBBON
GREER GARSON
GREGORY PECK
GRESHAM'S LAW
GRETNA GREEN
GRILLED CHOP
GRILLED FISH

GRILLED SOLE	HALF AND HALF	HARRY LAUDER
GRIM COURAGE	HALF AN OUNCE	HARRY TRUMAN
GRIM OUTLOOK	HALF A SECOND	HARVEST HOME
GRIM PASTIME	HALF BROTHER	HARVEST MOON
GRIND TO BITS	HALF HOLIDAY	HARVEST TIME
GRIP OF STEEL	HALF THE TIME	HASTY GLANCE
GRIZZLY BEAR	HALTING GAIT	HASTY TEMPER
GROCER'S SHOP	HAMMER DRILL	HATCHET FACE
GROSS AMOUNT	HAMMER IT OUT	HATEFUL TASK
GROSS INCOME	HAMMER THROW	HAUNT OF VICE
GROSS PROFIT	HAM OMELETTE	HAVANA CIGAR
GROSS RETURN	HAMPTON WICK	HAVE A CHOICE
GROSS WEIGHT	HAM SANDWICH	HAVE A FRIGHT
GROUND FLOOR	HAND AND FOOT	HAVE A HAIR-DO
GROUND FROST	HAND GRENADE	HAVE A LIKING
GROUND GLASS	HAND IN GLOVE	HAVE AND HOLD
GROUND LEVEL	HAND OF CARDS	HAVE AN EYE ON
GROUND SPEED	HAND OF DEATH	HAVE AN EYE TO
GROUND STAFF	HANDSOME BOY	HAVE ANOTHER
GROUND SWELL	HANDSOME MAN	HAVE A PICNIC
GROUND TO AIR	HANDSOME SUM	HAVE A POLICY
GROUP OF FIVE	HANDSOME TIP	HAVE A SECRET
GROUP OF FOUR	HANDS ON HIPS	HAVE A SHOWER
GROUP OF NINE	HAND TO MOUTH	HAVE A SNOOZE
GROUSE MOORS	HANG-DOG LOOK	HAVE A SQUINT
GROWING GIRL	HANGING BILL	HAVE A STROKE
GROW SHORTER	HANG ONESELF	HAVE A THEORY
GROW SMALLER	HANG THE HEAD	HAVE A THIRST
GROW UPWARDS	HANG UP TO DRY	HAVE COMPANY
GROW YOUNGER	HANKER AFTER	HAVE COURAGE
GUAVA CHEESE	HAPPY CHANCE	HAVE IN STORE
GUERILLA WAR	HAPPY COUPLE	HAVE NO DOUBT
GUEST ARTIST	HAPPY DREAMS	HAVEN OF REST
GUIDING HAND	HAPPY ENDING	HAVE NO MERCY
GUIDING STAR	HAPPY FAMILY	HAVE NO VOICE
GUILTY PARTY	HAPPY MEDIUM	HAVE ONE'S DAY
GUILTY WOMAN	HAPPY VALLEY	HAVE ONE'S SAY
GULF OF GENOA	HARBOUR A SPY	HAVE ONE'S WAY
GUMMED LABEL	HARBOUR DUES	HAVE REGRETS
GUSTAV HOLST	HARD AND FAST	HAVE THE URGE
GUTTER PRESS	HARD AS NAILS	HAVE THE VOTE
	HARD AS STEEL	HAVE TROUBLE
	HARD BARGAIN	HAYLEY MILLS
H – 11	HARD CONTEST	HEAD AND TAIL
	HARD DRINKER	HEAD TEACHER
HACKNEY WICK	HARD DRIVING	HEAD THE LIST
HAGGARD LOOK	HARD MEASURE	HEALING GIFT
HAIRPIN BEND	HARD PRESSED	HEAL THE SICK
HALCYON DAYS	HARD PUT TO IT	HEALTHY FEAR
HALF A BOTTLE	HARD SURFACE	HEALTHY MIND
HALF A DOLLAR	HARD TO CATCH	HEAPED PLATE
HALF A GALLON	HARD TO GRASP	HEAPS OF TIME
HALF A GUINEA	HARDY ANNUAL	HEAR NOTHING
HALF A LEAGUE	HARICOT BEAN	HEART ATTACK
HALF A LENGTH	HAROLD LLOYD	HEAR THE CALL
HALF A MINUTE	HARRIS TWEED	HEART OF GOLD
HALF A MOMENT		

HEART'S BLOOD
HEARTS OF OAK
HEARTY CHEER
HEARTY EATER
HEARTY LAUGH
HEARTY SMACK
HEAT BARRIER
HEATED WORDS
HEAVE A BRICK
HEAVY AS LEAD
HEAVY BOMBER
HEAVY BURDEN
HEAVY EATING
HEAVY FATHER
HEAVY HUMOUR
HEAVY OBJECT
HEAVY SHOWER
HEAVY SMOKER
HEAVY WEIGHT
HECTIC FLUSH
HEDDA GABLER
HELD CAPTIVE
HELD HOSTAGE
HELD IN CHECK
HELD IN TRUST
HELEN JACOBS
HELEN OF TROY
HELL ON EARTH
HELPING HAND
HENRIK IBSEN
HENRY COOPER
HENRY COTTON
HENRY ESMOND
HENRY IRVING
HERALDIC ART
HERD OF GOATS
HER HIGHNESS
HER LADYSHIP
HEROIC VERSE
HERO WORSHIP
HERRING GULL
HERRING POND
HIDDEN FIRES
HIDDEN MERIT
HIDDEN PANEL
HIDE AND SEEK
HIDING PLACE
HIGH ACCOUNT
HIGH CALLING
HIGH CEILING
HIGH CIRCLES
HIGH COMMAND
HIGH CONTENT
HIGH COURAGE
HIGH DENSITY
HIGH DUDGEON

HIGHER CLASS
HIGHER FARES
HIGHER LEVEL
HIGHER POWER
HIGHER WAGES
HIGH FEATHER
HIGH FINANCE
HIGH HOLBORN
HIGH MOTIVES
HIGH OLD TIME
HIGH OPINION
HIGH QUALITY
HIGH RESOLVE
HIGH SHERIFF
HIGH SOCIETY
HIGH SPIRITS
HIGH STATION
HIGH TENSION
HIGH TRAGEDY
HIGH TREASON
HIGH VOLTAGE
HIGHWAY CODE
HIGH-WIRE ACT
HIGH WYCOMBE
HILL AND DALE
HILL COUNTRY
HILTON HOTEL
HINDLE WAKES
HIP AND THIGH
HIP AND HAWS
HIS EMINENCE
HIS HIGHNESS
HIS LORDSHIP
HISTORY BOOK
HITHER GREEN
HITLER YOUTH
HIT THE TRAIL
H.M.S. PINAFORE
HOARD WEALTH
HOARSE COUGH
HOARSE LAUGH
HOARSE VOICE
HOBBLE SKIRT
HOCKEY MATCH
HOCKEY STICK
HOLD CLASSES
HOLD IN CHECK
HOLD IN LEASH
HOLD IN TRUST
HOLD ONE'S JAW
HOLD ONE'S OWN
HOLD ON TIGHT
HOLD OUT HOPE
HOLD THE BABY
HOLD THE FORT
HOLD THE LEAD

HOLD THE LINE
HOLD THE ROAD
HOLD TO SCORN
HOLIDAY CAMP
HOLIDAY HOME
HOLIDAY MOOD
HOLIDAY SNAP
HOLIDAY TASK
HOLIDAY TIME
HOLIDAY WEAR
HOLLAND PARK
HOLLAND'S GIN
HOLLOW LAUGH
HOLLOW SOUND
HOLLOW TOOTH
HOLLOW TRUCE
HOLLOW TRUTH
HOLLOW VOICE
HOLY TRINITY
HOLY UNCTION
HOLY WEDLOCK
HOME AFFAIRS
HOME AND AWAY
HOME CIRCUIT
HOME COOKING
HOME COUNTRY
HOME FOR GOOD
HOME-MADE JAM
HOME ON LEAVE
HOME SERVICE
HOME STRETCH
HOMO SAPIENS
HONEST DOUBT
HONEST INJUN
HONEST MONEY
HONEST PENNY
HONEST TRUTH
HONEST WOMAN
HONITON LACE
HONOUR A BILL
HONOUR BOUND
HONOURED SIR
HONOURS EASY
HONOURS EVEN
HONOURS LIST
HOPE AND PRAY
HOPE DIAMOND
HOPEFUL SIGN
HORNED VIPER
HORNETS' NEST
HORROR COMIC
HORS D'OEUVRE
HORSE DEALER
HORSE DOCTOR
HORSE GUARDS
HORSE MARINE

HORSE PISTOL
HORSE RACING
HORSE'S MOUTH
HOSPITAL BED
HOSTILE ARMY
HOSTILE VOTE
HOT AS PEPPER
HOT CHESTNUT
HOT-CROSS BUN
HOT-DOG STAND
HOTEL ANNEXE
HOTEL KEEPER
HOTEL LOUNGE
HOTEL PORTER
HOT-WATER TAP
HOUND'S TOOTH
HOURLY VIGIL
HOUR OF TRIAL
HOURS OF WORK
HOUSE ARREST
HOUSE HUNTER
HOUSE MARTIN
HOUSE MASTER
HOUSE MOTHER
HOUSE NUMBER
HOUSE OF CALL
HOUSE OF KEYS
HOUSE OF REST
HOUSE OF YORK
HOUSE ON FIRE
HOVER AROUND
HOWLING WIND
HUDSON RIVER
HUGE EXPENSE
HUGE SUCCESS
HUGHIE GREEN
HUG THE COAST
HUG THE SHORE
HUMAN DYNAMO
HUMAN EFFORT
HUMAN FAMILY
HUMAN NATURE
HUMAN RIGHTS
HUMBLE BIRTH
HUMBLE HEART
HUMBLE STOCK
HUMMING BIRD
HUMS AND HAWS
HUNDRED DAYS
HUNGER MARCH
HUNK OF BREAD
HUNT BIG GAME
HUNTER'S MOON
HUNT FOR A JOB
HUNTING CROP
HUNTING HORN

HUNTING PACK
HUNTING PINK
HUNTING SONG
HUNT IN PAIRS
HUNT THE HARE
HURRIED MEAL
HUSBAND TO BE
HUSHED TONES
HUSH-HUSH JOB

I – 11

IAIN MACLEOD
IDEAL SCHEME
IDES OF MARCH
IDLE DISPLAY
IDLE THOUGHT
IF YOU PLEASE
IGNEOUS ROCK
IGNITION KEY
IGNORANT MAN
ILE DE FRANCE
I'LL BE HANGED!
ILLICIT LOVE
IL PENSEROSO
IL TROVATORE
IMPOSE A DUTY
IMPROPER USE
IN A BAD STATE
IN A FEW WORDS
IN A FLAT SPIN
IN A GOOD MOOD
IN AGREEMENT
IN A HAYSTACK
IN ALL EVENTS
IN A LOW VOICE
IN A MINORITY
IN AND AROUND
INANE REMARK
IN AN INSTANT
IN A NUTSHELL
IN A QUANDARY
IN A REAL MESS
IN A SMALL WAY
IN AT THE KILL
IN AUSTRALIA
IN AUTHORITY
IN BAD REPAIR
IN CAPTIVITY
IN CHARACTER
IN COLD BLOOD
IN COLLISION
IN COLLUSION
IN COMMITTEE
IN CONDITION

IN CONFUSION
INCUR LOSSES
IN DAYS OF OLD
IN DEEP WATER
IN DETENTION
INDEX FINGER
INDEX NUMBER
INDIAN BRAVE
INDIAN CHIEF
INDIAN CURRY
INDIAN OCEAN
INDIAN SQUAW
INDIAN TRIBE
INDIA OFFICE
INDIA RUBBER
INDIRECT TAX
INDOOR GAMES
IN DREAMLAND
IN DUE COURSE
IN DUE SEASON
IN DUPLICATE
IN DUTY BOUND
IN ECSTASIES
IN EDINBURGH
IN EVERY PORT
IN EXISTENCE
IN FACSIMILE
IN FINE STYLE
IN FOR A PENNY
IN FOR A POUND
IN FOR A STORM
IN FORMATION
INFRA-RED RAY
IN FULL BLAST
IN FULL BLOOM
IN FULL SPATE
IN FULL SWING
IN GOOD FAITH
IN GOOD HANDS
IN GOOD HEART
IN GOOD ODOUR
IN GOOD SHAPE
IN GOOD TASTE
IN GOOD VOICE
IN GRATITUDE
IN GREAT FORM
IN HYSTERICS
IN IGNORANCE
INITIAL MOVE
INJURED BACK
INJURED LOOK
IN LOW RELIEF
IN MINIATURE
INMOST BEING
IN MY OPINION
INNER CIRCLE

INNER MARGIN
INNER TEMPLE
INNOCENT MAN
IN NO RESPECT
INNS OF COURT
IN ONE'S HEART
IN ONE'S POWER
IN ONE'S PRIME
IN ONE'S SHELL
IN ONE'S SLEEP
IN ONE'S TEENS
IN OPEN COURT
IN OPERATION
IN PANTOMIME
IN PRINCIPLE
IN PROFUSION
IN PURGATORY
IN READINESS
IN REBELLION
IN REPERTORY
IN RESIDENCE
IN SAFE HANDS
IN SECLUSION
INSECT WORLD
IN SEPTEMBER
IN SHORTHAND
INSIDE RIGHT
INSIDE STORY
INSIDE TRACK
INSTANT CURE
INTENSE COLD
INTENSE HEAT
IN THAT PLACE
IN THE CELLAR
IN THE CENTRE
IN THE CHARTS
IN THE CHORUS
IN THE CHURCH
IN THE CINEMA
IN THE CIRCLE
IN THE CLOUDS
IN THE CORNER
IN THE CRADLE
IN THE DEPTHS
IN THE DESERT
IN THE FAMILY
IN THE FIELDS
IN THE FINISH
IN THE FOREST
IN THE FRIDGE
IN THE FUTURE
IN THE GARAGE
IN THE GARDEN
IN THE GROOVE
IN THE GROUND
IN THE GUARDS

IN THE GUTTER
IN THE JUNGLE
IN THE LOCK-UP
IN THE MAKING
IN THE MARGIN
IN THE MARKET
IN THE MIDDLE
IN THE MIRROR
IN THE MORGUE
IN THE NAME OF
IN THE OFFICE
IN THE OFFING
IN THE PAPERS
IN THE PLURAL
IN THE PULPIT
IN THE PURPLE
IN THE SADDLE
IN THE SEASON
IN THE SECRET
IN THE SPRING
IN THE STALLS
IN THE STOCKS
IN THE STREET
IN THE STUDIO
IN THE THROES
IN THE VALLEY
IN THE WAKE OF
IN THE WINDOW
IN THE WINTER
IN THE ZENITH
IN THIS PLACE
INTO THE BLUE
INTO THE WIND
INTO THIN AIR
IN TWO SHAKES
INVALID DIET
INVERT SUGAR
IN WHICH CASE
IONIC COLUMN
IRISH BROGUE
IRISH GUARDS
IRISH SETTER
IRMA LA DOUCE
IRON CURTAIN
IRON FILINGS
IRON FOUNDRY
IRON PYRITES
IRON RATIONS
IRONY OF FATE
ISAAC NEWTON
ISAAC PITMAN
ISLE OF ARRAN
ISLE OF CAPRI
ISLE OF WIGHT
ISSUE SHARES
ITALIA CONTI

ITALIAN ALPS
ITALIAN WINE
ITCHING PALM
IT'S A FAIR COP
IT STRIKES ME
IVOR NOVELLO
IVORY CASTLE
IZAAK WALTON

J – 11

JACK AND JILL
JACK DEMPSEY
JACK HAWKINS
JACK HULBERT
JACK JACKSON
JACK JOHNSON
JACK OF CLUBS
JAFFA ORANGE
JAMES BRIDIE
JAMES CAGNEY
JAMESON RAID
JAM SANDWICH
JAM TOMORROW
JANE SEYMOUR
JAPANESE ART
JARRING NOTE
JAUNTING CAR
JAWS OF DEATH
JAZZ SESSION
JEALOUS WIFE
JEAN BOROTRA
JEAN COCTEAU
JEAN SIMMONS
JELLIED EELS
JEREMY IRONS
JET AIRCRAFT
JINGLE BELLS
JOAN COLLINS
JOAN HAMMOND
JOHN GIELGUD
JOHN GREGSON
JOHN HALIFAX
JOHN OF GAUNT
JOHN O' GROATS
JOHN O' LONDON
JOHN OSBORNE
JOIE DE VIVRE
JOINT ACTION
JOINT APPEAL
JOINT EFFORT
JOIN THE ARMY
JOIN THE NAVY
JOINT OF BEEF
JOINT OF LAMB

JOINT OF PORK
JOINT OF VEAL
JOINT TENANT
JOKING APART
JOLLY HUNGRY
JOSEPH'S COAT
JOURNEY'S END
JUBILEE YEAR
JUDGMENT DAY
JUDY GARLAND
JUGULAR VEIN
JUKE-BOX JURY
JUMPING BEAN
JUMPING JACK
JUNE WEDDING
JUNGLE FEVER
JUNGLE GREEN
JUNGLE JUICE
JUNIPER TREE
JURY SERVICE
JUST A CHANCE
JUST A LITTLE
JUST A MINUTE
JUST A MOMENT
JUST A SECOND
JUST DESERTS
JUST FOR ONCE
JUST IMAGINE
JUST MARRIED
JUST PERFECT
JUST THE SAME
JUST THE TIME
JUST VISIBLE
JUST WILLIAM

K – 11

KEEN BARGAIN
KEEN CONTEST
KEEN HEARING
KEEN STUDENT
KEEP ABREAST
KEEP AN EYE ON
KEEP A RECORD
KEEP A SECRET
KEEP COMPANY
KEEP COUNSEL
KEEP IN CHECK
KEEP IN SIGHT
KEEP IN STOCK
KEEP IN STORE
KEEP IN TOUCH
KEEP IT GOING
KEEP ONE'S JOB
KEEP OUT OF IT
KEEP RIGHT ON

KEEP SMILING
KEEP THE CASH
KEEP TRACK OF
KEEP WAITING
KELLOGG PACT
KEMPTON PARK
KENNETH MORE
KENSAL GREEN
KENTISH TOWN
KEY INDUSTRY
KEY POSITION
KEY QUESTION
KHAKI SHORTS
KICK AGAINST
KICK UP A DUST
KICK UP A FUSS
KIDNEY BEANS
KILKENNY CAT
KILLER WHALE
KILLING PACE
KILL ONESELF
KIND FRIENDS
KIND GESTURE
KINDRED SOUL
KIND REGARDS
KIND THOUGHT
KIND WELCOME
KING CHARLES
KINGDOM COME
KING EMPEROR
KING OF BIRDS
KING OF CLUBS
KING OF KINGS
KING PENGUIN
KING RICHARD
KING'S BISHOP
KING'S BOUNTY
KING'S COLOUR
KING'S FLIGHT
KING'S KNIGHT
KING SOLOMON
KING'S RANSOM
KING WILLIAM
KIRK DOUGLAS
KISSING GAME
KISSING GATE
KISS ME, HARDY
KISS OF JUDAS
KISS OF PEACE
KISS THE BOOK
KISS THE DUST
KITCHEN FIRE
KITCHEN HAND
KITCHEN MAID
KITCHEN SINK
KITCHEN UNIT

KNIGHT'S MOVE
KNIGHT'S PAWN
KNIT THE BROW
KNITTING BEE
KNOCK AROUND
KNOCK IT BACK
KNOCK ON WOOD
KNOTTY POINT
KNOW A LITTLE
KNOW BY HEART
KNOW BY SIGHT
KNOWING LOOK
KNOW ONE'S JOB
KNOW ONE'S WAY
KNOW THE FORM
KNOW THYSELF
KNOW TOO MUCH
KNUCKLE DOWN
KUALA LUMPUR

L – 11

LABOUR FORCE
LABOUR PARTY
LABRADOR DOG
LACK COURAGE
LACK OF DRIVE
LACK OF FAITH
LACK OF FLAIR
LACK OF MONEY
LACK OF POWER
LACK OF SCOPE
LACK OF SENSE
LACK OF SHAPE
LACK OF SLEEP
LACK OF TASTE
LACK SPARKLE
LADIES FIRST
LADIES' NIGHT
LA DOLCE VITA
LADY ALMONER
LADY BARNETT
LADY MACBETH
LADY MACDUFF
LADY'S FINGER
LADY TEACHER
LAKE LUCERNE
LAKE ONTARIO
LAKE SUCCESS
LAMBETH WALK
LANDING GEAR
LAND MEASURE
LAND OF ROSES
LANKY FIGURE
LANTERN JAWS
LAPIS LAZULI

LAP OF LUXURY	LATEST THING	LEAVE SCHOOL
LAPSE OF TIME	LATIN CHURCH	LEAVE UNDONE
LARGE AMOUNT	LATIN LESSON	LEAVE UNSAID
LARGE AS LIFE	LATIN MASTER	LECTURE HALL
LARGE BRANDY	LATIN PRIMER	LECTURE TOUR
LARGE CIRCLE	LAUGHING GAS	LEDGER CLERK
LARGE FAMILY	LAUNDRY BILL	LEFT HANGING
LARGE INCOME	LAUNDRY MAID	LEFT LUGGAGE
LARGE NUMBER	LAUREL CROWN	LEFT OUTSIDE
LARGE PROFIT	LAW AND ORDER	LEGAL ACTION
LARGE SALARY	LAWFUL ORDER	LEGAL ADVICE
LARGE SCOTCH	LAW MERCHANT	LEGAL BATTLE
LARGE SCREEN	LAW OF NATURE	LEGAL ENTITY
LARGE SHERRY	LAW OF THE SEA	LEGAL JARGON
LARGE SUPPLY	LAY ABOUT ONE	LEGAL REMEDY
LARGE VESSEL	LAY IN AMBUSH	LEGAL RULING
LARGE VOLUME	LAY IN A STOCK	LEGAL TENDER
LARGE WHISKY	LAY OUT MONEY	LEG OF MUTTON
LASH OF A WHIP	LAY PREACHER	LEISURE TIME
LAST ADDRESS	LAY THE CLOTH	LEMON BARLEY
LAST ARRIVAL	LAY THE GHOST	LEMON SQUASH
LAST ATTEMPT	LAY THE TABLE	LEMON YELLOW
LAST BASTION	LAZY HOLIDAY	LEND SUPPORT
LAST CENTURY	LEADEN HOURS	LEON TROTSKY
LAST CHAPTER	LEADING CASE	LESLIE CARON
LAST EDITION	LEADING EDGE	LESS AND LESS
LAST EVENING	LEADING LADY	LESSER BREED
LAST FOR EVER	LEADING NOTE	LESSON EIGHT
LAST HONOURS	LEADING PART	LESSON SEVEN
LAST INNINGS	LEADING RÔLE	LESSON THREE
LAST JANUARY	LEADING WREN	LESS TROUBLE
LAST JOURNEY	LEAGUE MATCH	LET A MAN DOWN
LAST OF EIGHT	LEAN AGAINST	LET IN THE SUN
LAST OF SEVEN	LEAN AS A RAKE	LET OFF STEAM
LAST OF THREE	LEAN FORWARD	LEVEL FLIGHT
LAST OUTPOST	LEAN TOWARDS	LEVEL TEMPER
LAST QUARTER	LEARN A HABIT	LIBEL ACTION
LAST TO LEAVE	LEARN A TRADE	LIBERAL ARTS
LAST TRIBUTE	LEARN TO HATE	LIBERAL VIEW
LAST TUESDAY	LEARN TO LOVE	LIBERTY BOAT
LAST VESTIGE	LEARN TO PLAY	LIBERTY HALL
LATE ARRIVAL	LEARN TO READ	LIBERTY SHIP
LATE AT NIGHT	LEARN TO RIDE	LIBRARY BOOK
LATE BOOKING	LEARN TO WALK	LIBRARY LIST
LATE EDITION	LEARN WISDOM	LICK OF PAINT
LATE EVENING	LEATHER BELT	LICK THE DUST
LATE FOR WORK	LEATHER COAT	LIE AT ANCHOR
LATE HARVEST	LEATHER LANE	LIE DETECTOR
LATE HUSBAND	LEATHER SOLE	LIE END TO END
LATE STARTER	LEAVE A SPACE	LIE IN AMBUSH
LATEST CRAZE	LEAVE A TRAIL	LIE IN PRISON
LATEST ISSUE	LEAVE BEHIND	LIE ON VELVET
LATEST MODEL	LEAVE FALLOW	LIE PARALLEL
LATEST SCORE	LEAVE IT OPEN	LIFE CHANCES
LATEST SHADE	LEAVE IT TO ME	LIFE HISTORY
LATEST STYLE	LEAVE NO HOPE	LIFE OF BLISS

LIFE OF CRIME	LITTLE DEVIL	LONG SERVICE
LIFE OR DEATH	LITTLE KNOWN	LONG SESSION
LIFE PARTNER	LITTLE SPACE	LONG STRETCH
LIFE PEERAGE	LITTLE THING	LONG STRIDES
LIFE SAVINGS	LITTLE TO SAY	LONG TIME AGO
LIFT A FINGER	LITTLE WHILE	LONG WEEK-END
LIFT THE ROOF	LITTLE WOMAN	LOOK A FRIGHT
LIFT THE VEIL	LITTLE WOMEN	LOOK ASKANCE
LIGHT A MATCH	LITTLE VALUE	LOOK DAGGERS
LIGHT BOMBER	LIVE FOR EVER	LOOK FOOLISH
LIGHT BREEZE	LIVE IN DREAD	LOOK FOR DIGS
LIGHT COLOUR	LIVE IN PEACE	LOOK FORWARD
LIGHT COMEDY	LIVE IN STYLE	LOOK FOR WORK
LIGHT DUTIES	LIVELONG DAY	LOOK GHASTLY
LIGHTER FUEL	LIVELY DANCE	LOOK LIKE NEW
LIGHTER VEIN	LIVELY PARTY	LOOK-OUT POST
LIGHT OF FOOT	LIVELY PITCH	LOOK OUTSIDE
LIGHT RELIEF	LIVE ON BOARD	LOOK PLEASED
LIGHT REMARK	LIVE THEATRE	LOOK THE PART
LIGHT THE GAS	LIVE THROUGH	LOOK THROUGH
LIGHT THE WAY	LIVING BEING	LOOK VOLUMES
LIGHT VESSEL	LIVING DEATH	LOOP THE LOOP
LIGHT WEIGHT	LIVING IMAGE	LOOSE CHANGE
LIGHT YELLOW	LIVING PROOF	LOOSE COVERS
LIKE A MASTER	LIVING SPACE	LOOSE LIVING
LIKE AN ARROW	LIVING THING	LOOSE MORALS
LIKE AN IDIOT	LIZARD POINT	LOOSE THREAD
LIKE A PARROT	LLOYD GEORGE	LORD BALDWIN
LIKE A STATUE	LOAD OF STRAW	LORD BOOTHBY
LIKE A STREAK	LOAD OF TRIPE	LORD PROVOST
LIKE A TROJAN	LOAF OF BREAD	LORD RUSSELL
LIKE FOR LIKE	LO AND BEHOLD	LORDS' DEBATE
LIKE IT OR NOT	LOAN OF MONEY	LORD'S PRAYER
LIKELY STORY	LOCAL BRANCH	LORD'S SUPPER
LIKE THE IDEA	LOCAL COLOUR	LORRY DRIVER
LIKE THE WIND	LOCAL CUSTOM	LOSE A CHANCE
LILAC DOMINO	LOCAL GOSSIP	LOSE CONTROL
LILLI PALMER	LOCAL OPTION	LOSE COURAGE
LILY LANGTRY	LOCAL TALENT	LOSE FRIENDS
LILI MARLENE	LOCK THE DOOR	LOSE ONE'S ALL
LIMITED TIME	LOCUM TENENS	LOSE ONESELF
LIMPID STYLE	LOGICAL MIND	LOSE ONE'S WAY
LINCOLN CITY	LOGICAL STEP	LOSE SIGHT OF
LINCOLN'S INN	LONDON CRIES	LOSE THE GAME
LINE DRAWING	LONDON DOCKS	LOSE THE LEAD
LINEN DRAPER	LONDON PRIDE	LOSE THE RACE
LINE OF MARCH	LONDON STAGE	LOSE THE TOSS
LINE OF SIGHT	LONDON STONE	LOSE THE VOTE
LION RAMPANT	LONG ACCOUNT	LOSS OF BLOOD
LISLE THREAD	LONG CLOTHES	LOSS OF FAITH
LIST OF ITEMS	LONG DROUGHT	LOSS OF MONEY
LIST OF NAMES	LONG HOLIDAY	LOSS OF NERVE
LITERARY MAN	LONG INNINGS	LOSS OF SIGHT
LITERARY SET	LONG JOURNEY	LOSS OF SOUND
LITMUS PAPER	LONG, LONG AGO	LOSS OF SMELL
LITTLE ANGEL	LONG MEASURE	LOSS OF TOUCH

LOSS OF VALUE
LOSS OF VOICE
LOST HORIZON
LOST TO SHAME
LOST TO SIGHT
LOST WEEK-END
LOTS AND LOTS
LOTS OF MONEY
LOUD AND LONG
LOUD PROTEST
LOUD SPEAKER
LOUIS QUINZE
LOUIS TREIZE
LOUNGE ABOUT
LOVE AND HATE
LOVE FIFTEEN
LOVE IS BLIND
LOVELY MONEY
LOVELY NIGHT
LOVELY SIGHT
LOVE OF MONEY
LOVE OF ORDER
LOVE OF TRUTH
LOVE OR MONEY
LOVE PHILTRE
LOVING WORDS
LOW ALTITUDE
LOW COMEDIAN
LOWER ANIMAL
LOWER SCHOOL
LOW ESTIMATE
LOW FOREHEAD
LOW LATITUDE
LOW POSITION
LOW PRESSURE
LOW RAINFALL
LOW STANDARD
LOYAL FRIEND
L-SHAPED ROOM
LUCID MOMENT
LUCILLE BALL
LUCKY BEGGAR
LUCKY CHANCE
LUCKY ESCAPE
LUCKY FELLOW
LUCKY MASCOT
LUCKY MOMENT
LUCKY NUMBER
LUCKY RASCAL
LUCKY STREAK
LUCKY STRIKE
LUCKY STROKE
LUCKY WINNER
LUDGATE HILL
LUGGAGE RACK
LULL TO SLEEP

LUMP OF SUGAR
LUNCHEON CAR
LUNDY ISLAND
LUXURY FOODS
LUXURY GOODS
LUXURY HOTEL
LUXURY PRICE
LYRIC POETRY

M – 11

MACASSAR OIL
MACHINE CODE
MACHINE HAND
MACHINE SHOP
MACHINE TOOL
MACKEREL SKY
MADE A KNIGHT
MADE A MEMBER
MADE IN ITALY
MADE IN JAPAN
MADE IN SPAIN
MADEIRA CAKE
MADEIRA WINE
MADE OF MONEY
MADE OF STRAW
MADE TO ORDER
MADE WELCOME
MADONNA LILY
MADRAS CURRY
MAD SCRAMBLE
MAD WITH RAGE
MAGIC CARPET
MAGIC CIRCLE
MAGIC MIRROR
MAGIC MOMENT
MAGIC POTION
MAGIC RECIPE
MAGIC REMEDY
MAGIC SQUARE
MAGINOT LINE
MAGNUM BONUM
MAILING LIST
MAIL SERVICE
MAIN ELEMENT
MAIN FEATURE
MAIN MEANING
MAIN PROBLEM
MAIN PURPOSE
MAIN STATION
MAJOR CRISIS
MAJOR PLANET
MAKE A CHANGE
MAKE A CHOICE
MAKE A CORNER
MAKE A DETOUR
MAKE A FOOL OF

MAKE A LIVING
MAKE AND MEND
MAKE AN ENTRY
MAKE AN ERROR
MAKE AN OFFER
MAKE A PACKET
MAKE A PROFIT
MAKE A RECORD
MAKE A REMARK
MAKE A REPORT
MAKE A SEARCH
MAKE A SIGNAL
MAKE A SPEECH
MAKE A SPLASH
MAKE BELIEVE
MAKE CERTAIN
MAKE CHANGES
MAKE CONTACT
MAKE DEMANDS
MAKE ENEMIES
MAKE EXCUSES
MAKE FRIENDS
MAKE HEADWAY
MAKE HISTORY
MAKE INROADS
MAKE IT CLEAR
MAKE IT PLAIN
MAKE IT STICK
MAKE LIGHTER
MAKE LIGHT OF
MAKE MUCH ADO
MAKE NO NOISE
MAKE NO SOUND
MAKE OBVIOUS
MAKE ONE'S BED
MAKE ONE'S BOW
MAKE ONE'S WAY
MAKE OR BREAK
MAKE SMALLER
MAKES NO ODDS
MAKE SPORT OF
MAKE THE FIRE
MAKE THE PACE
MAKE TROUBLE
MAKE WELCOME
MAKE WHOOPEE
MALACCA CANE
MALAY STATES
MALE DESCENT
MALMSEY WINE
MALT VINEGAR
MAN AND WOMAN
MAN AT THE TOP
MAN BITES DOG
MANFRED MANN
MAN FROM MARS

MANICURE SET	MASSIVE ROCK	MERVYN JOHNS
MAN IN CHARGE	MASS MEETING	METAL POLISH
MAN IN OFFICE	MATE IN THREE	METHOD ACTOR
MANLY FIGURE	MATERIAL AID	MEWS COTTAGE
MANLY SPIRIT	MATINÉE IDOL	MICKEY MOUSE
MAN OF ACTION	MATT SURFACE	MIDDLE CLASS
MAN OF GENIUS	MATURE YEARS	MIDDLE POINT
MAN OF HONOUR	MAUNDY MONEY	MIDDLE STUMP
MAN OF METTLE	MAX BEERBOHM	MIDDLE WATCH
MAN OF MUSCLE	MAX BYGRAVES	MIDLAND BANK
MAN OF PRAYER	MAY THE FIFTH	MIDLAND TOWN
MAN OF RENOWN	MAY THE FIRST	MIDNIGHT OIL
MAN OF REPUTE	MAY THE NINTH	MIDNIGHT SUN
MAN ON THE JOB	MAY THE SIXTH	MIGHT AS WELL
MAN PROPOSES	MAY THE TENTH	MILD CLIMATE
MANSARD ROOF	ME AND MY GIRL	MILD FLUTTER
MAN THE PUMPS	MEANING LOOK	MILD REPROOF
MAN THE WALLS	MEAN NOTHING	MILD WEATHER
MAP OF EUROPE	MEASURE TIME	MILE A MINUTE
MAP OF FRANCE	MEAT EXTRACT	MILE END ROAD
MAP OF GREECE	MEDAL RIBBON	MILITARY AID
MAP OF LONDON	MEDICAL BOOK	MILITARY LAW
MAP OF NORWAY	MEDICAL CARE	MILITARY MAN
MAP OF SWEDEN	MEDICAL CASE	MILKING TIME
MARBLE HALLS	MEDICAL TEST	MILK PUDDING
MARCH IN STEP	MEDICAL WARD	MINCING LANE
MARCH OF TIME	MEDICINE HAT	MIND THE BABY
MARIA CALLAS	MEDICINE MAN	MIND THE STEP
MARIE STOPES	MEDIUM BUILD	MINERAL VEIN
MARINE CORPS	MEEK AND MILD	MINIMUM WAGE
MARINE STORE	MEET HALFWAY	MINOR DETAIL
MARITIME LAW	MEET ONE'S END	MINOR INJURY
MARKED CARDS	MEET THE BILL	MINOR MATTER
MARKET OVERT	MEGATON BOMB	MINOR PLANET
MARKET PLACE	MELODY MAKER	MINSTREL BOY
MARKET PRICE	MELTING MOOD	MINT FLAVOUR
MARKET RASEN	MELT IN TEARS	MINT OF MONEY
MARKET TREND	MEMBERS ONLY	MINUTE STEAK
MARKET VALUE	MEMORIAL DAY	MINUTE WALTZ
MARKET WOMAN	MENAI STRAIT	MIRACLE DRUG
MARK MY WORDS	MEN AND WOMEN	MIRACLE PLAY
MARK THE SPOT	MENDIP HILLS	MISS A CHANCE
MARRIAGE TIE	MENTAL ERROR	MISS A SITTER
MARRIED LIFE	MENTAL GRASP	MISSED CATCH
MARRIED NAME	MENTAL IMAGE	MISS ENGLAND
MARRON GLACÉ	MENTAL LAPSE	MISSING HEIR
MARRYING MAN	MENTALLY ILL	MISSING LINK
MARSHAL FOCH	MENTAL POWER	MISS NOTHING
MARSHAL TITO	MENTAL SHOCK	MISS ONE'S WAY
MARSTON MOOR	MENTAL STATE	MISS THE BOAT
MARTIAL ARTS	MERE FEELING	MISS THE MARK
MARTIAL RACE	MERE NOTHING	MISS THE POST
MARTIN'S BANK	MERLE OBERON	MISTER RIGHT
MASONIC HALL	MERRY ANDREW	MIXED SCHOOL
MASSED BANDS	MERSEY DOCKS	MOB HYSTERIA
MASS EMOTION	MERSEY SOUND	MOB VIOLENCE

MOCKING BIRD
MOCK MODESTY
MODERN BLOCK
MODERN DANCE
MODERN DRESS
MODERN HOUSE
MODERN IDEAS
MODERN IDIOM
MODERN LATIN
MODERN MUSIC
MODERN NOVEL
MODERN STYLE
MODERN TIMES
MODERN TREND
MODERN USAGE
MODERN YOUTH
MODEST HOPES
MODEST MEANS
MOIRA LISTER
MOLLY MALONE
MONDAY NIGHT
MONEY FOR JAM
MONEY MARKET
MONEY MATTER
MONEY SPIDER
MONEY'S WORTH
MONEY TO BURN
MONKEY ABOUT
MONTE CRISTO
MONTHLY RENT
MONTH'S LEAVE
MOON GODDESS
MOON LANDING
MOP ONE'S BROW
MORAL APATHY
MORAL DEFECT
MORAL EFFECT
MORAL IMPACT
MORE AND MORE
MORE THAN ONE
MORNING CALL
MORNING COAT
MORNING POST
MORNING STAR
MORRIS DANCE
MORTAL AGONY
MORTAL ENEMY
MORTALLY ILL
MORTAL PERIL
MORTAL WOUND
MORTISE LOCK
MOSAIC FLOOR
MOSELLE WINE
MOSQUITO NET
MOTHER CAREY
MOTHER EARTH

MOTHER GOOSE
MOTHER'S HELP
MOTHER'S MILK
MOTHER'S RUIN
MOTION STUDY
MOTIVE FORCE
MOTIVE POWER
MOTLEY CROWD
MOTOR LAUNCH
MOTOR RACING
MOTOR TRIALS
MOULIN ROUGE
MOUNT A HORSE
MOUNTAIN AIR
MOUNTAIN ASH
MOUNTAIN DEW
MOUNTAIN TOP
MOUNT ARARAT
MOUNT VERNON
MOUTH HONOUR
MOVABLE TYPE
MOVE FORWARD
MOVE QUICKLY
MOVE TO ANGER
MOVE TO TEARS
MOVE TOWARDS
MOVING FORCE
MOVING SCENE
MOVING STORY
MOVING WORDS
MOW THE GRASS
MRS MALAPROP
MRS THATCHER
MUCH MARRIED
MUCH OBLIGED
MUCH THE SAME
MUCH TROUBLE
MUCH WENLOCK
MUFFLED DRUM
MUM'S THE WORD
MURDER TRIAL
MURKY DEPTHS
MUSCOVY DUCK
MUSEUM PIECE
MUSICAL NOTE
MUSICAL SHOW
MUSICAL TRIO
MUSICAL WORK
MUSIC CRITIC
MUSIC LESSON
MUSIC MASTER
MUSTARD BATH
MUSTARD SEED
MUSWELL HILL
MUTTON CURRY
MUTUAL TERMS

MYSTERY BOAT
MYSTERY PLAY
MYSTERY SHIP
MYSTERY TOUR
MYSTERY TRIP
MYSTIC RITES

N – 11

NAGGING PAIN
NAGGING WIFE
NAIL VARNISH
NAME NO NAMES
NAOMI JACOBS
NARROW GAUGE
NARROW SHAVE
NARROW TRAIL
NASAL ACCENT
NASTY PEOPLE
NASTY TEMPER
NASTY TUMBLE
NATIVE CHIEF
NATIVE DRESS
NATIVE HEATH
NATIVE STATE
NATIVE TRIBE
NAT KING COLE
NATURAL BENT
NATURAL GIFT
NATURAL LIFE
NATURE LOVER
NATURE STUDY
NAUGHTY GIRL
NAUGHTY WORD
NAVAL BATTLE
NAVAL RATING
NAVAL STORES
NAVEL ORANGE
NAZI GERMANY
NEAR AND DEAR
NEAR FAILURE
NEARLY READY
NEARLY THERE
NEAR ONE'S END
NEAR PERFECT
NEAR THE BONE
NEAR THE EDGE
NEAR THE MARK
NEAR THE WIND
NEAT AND TIDY
NEAT AND TRIM
NECK AND CROP
NECK AND NECK
NEEDLE MATCH
NEEDLE POINT
NEGRO MELODY

NELSON TOUCH
NE PLUS ULTRA
NERVE CENTRE
NETBALL TEAM
NET CURTAINS
NETHER LIMBS
NETHER WORLD
NET PRACTICE
NET RECEIPTS
NEUTRAL TINT
NEUTRAL ZONE
NEVER BEFORE
NEVER ENDING
NEVER FORGET
NEVER ON TIME
NEVER SAY DIE
NEW APPROACH
NEW ATLANTIS
NEW-BORN BABE
NEW-BORN BABY
NEW BRIGHTON
NEWGATE GAOL
NEW HEBRIDES
NEW POTATOES
NEW PROSPECT
NEWS CAPTION
NEWS IN BRIEF
NEWS SUMMARY
NEWTON ABBOT
NEW TO THE JOB
NEW YEAR'S DAY
NEW YEAR'S EVE
NEW YORK CITY
NEXT CENTURY
NEXT CHAPTER
NEXT IN ORDER
NEXT JANUARY
NEXT OCTOBER
NEXT STATION
NEXT TUESDAY
NICE AND EVEN
NICE MANNERS
NICE PICTURE
NIGHT AND DAY
NIGHT ATTIRE
NIGHT CURFEW
NIGHT EDITOR
NIGHT FLIGHT
NIGHT FLYING
NIGHT PATROL
NIGHT PORTER
NIGHT SCHOOL
NIGHT SISTER
NIGHT WORKER
NINE DEGREES
NINE DOLLARS

NINE FATHOMS
NINE GALLONS
NINE GUINEAS
NINE HUNDRED
NINE MINUTES
NINE OF CLUBS
NINE PER CENT
NINE SQUARED
NINETY MILES
NINETY TIMES
NINETY YEARS
NINE WICKETS
NINTH LETTER
NINTH OF JULY
NINTH OF JUNE
NINTH STOREY
NINTH VOLUME
NIP IN THE AIR
NIP IN THE BUD
NIP OF BRANDY
NIP OF WHISKY
NO ADDITIVES
NO ADMISSION
NO AUTHORITY
NOBBY CLARKE
NOBLE EFFORT
NOBLE FAMILY
NOBLE FIGURE
NOBLE NATURE
NOBLE SAVAGE
NOBLE STRAIN
NOBODY'S FOOL
NO CIRCULARS
NOD ONE'S HEAD
NO EXCEPTION
NO GENTLEMAN
NOGGIN OF ALE
NO GREAT LOSS
NO HOPE AT ALL
NO ILLUSIONS
NOISE ABROAD
NOMADIC RACE
NOM DE GUERRE
NOMINAL HEAD
NOMINAL LIST
NOMINAL RATE
NOMINAL RENT
NONE SO BLIND
NONE THE LESS
NONE TOO WARM
NO, NO, NANETTE
NON-STOP SHOW
NO OBJECTION
NO QUESTIONS
NORFOLK SUIT
NO RIGHT TURN

NORMAL SIGHT
NORMAL STATE
NORMAN STYLE
NORTH AFRICA
NORTH BORNEO
NORTH DAKOTA
NORTH ISLAND
NORTH LONDON
NORTH RIDING
NORTH SEA OIL
NO SCORE DRAW
NOSE FOR NEWS
NOSEY PARKER
NOT A BIT OF IT
NOT ALL THERE
NOT A RED CENT
NOT FAR WRONG
NOTHING LEFT
NOTHING LIKE
NOTHING MUCH
NOTHING TO DO
NOTHING TO IT
NOTICE BOARD
NOT MUCH GOOD
NOT-OUT SCORE
NO-TRUMP HAND
NOT SPEAKING
NOT THE THING
NOTTING HILL
NOTTS COUNTY
NOTTS FOREST
NOT UP-TO-DATE
NOT UP TO MUCH
NOT VERY MANY
NOT VERY MUCH
NOT VERY WELL
NOT YOUR TYPE
NO VACANCIES
NOW AND AGAIN
NOWHERE NEAR
NOWHERE TO GO
NUCLEAR BOMB
NULL AND VOID
NUMBER EIGHT
NUMBER PLATE
NUMBER SEVEN
NUMBER THREE
NUPTIAL VOWS
NURSE CAVELL
NURSERY GAME
NURSERY MAID
NURSERY TALE
NURSING HOME

O – 11

	OLD WAR-HORSE	ON THE GROUND
	OLIVE BRANCH	ON THE INSIDE
OAK-APPLE DAY	OLIVER LODGE	ON THE MARKET
OBITER DICTA	OLIVER TWIST	ON THE MORROW
OBLIQUE LINE	OMAR KHAYYAM	ON THE PARISH
OBTUSE ANGLE	OMNIBUS BOOK	ON THE RAZZLE
OCEAN TRAVEL	ON ALL POINTS	ON THE RECORD
ODDLY ENOUGH	ON AN AVERAGE	ON THE SCALES
ODDS AGAINST	ON A PEDESTAL	ON THE SCREEN
ODDS AND ENDS	ON A PITTANCE	ON THE SQUARE
OFFER ADVICE	ON AUTHORITY	ON THE STAIRS
OFFER A PRICE	ON BOARD SHIP	ON THE STOCKS
OFFER NO HOPE	ON BOTH SIDES	ON THE SWINGS
OFFICE BLOCK	ONCE OR TWICE	ON THE TARGET
OFFICE CLOCK	ONCE REMOVED	ON THE THAMES
OFFICE HOURS	ONE AND A HALF	ON THE THRONE
OFFICE PARTY	ON EASY TERMS	ON THE WAGGON
OFFICE STAFF	ONE ELEVENTH	ON THE WAY OUT
OFFICE STOOL	ONE GOOD TURN	ON TWO WHEELS
OFFICE SWEEP	ONE IN THE EYE	ONUS OF PROOF
OFF ONE'S BEAT	ONE IN TWELVE	ONWARD MARCH
OFF ONE'S FEED	ONE-MAN REVUE	ON WEDNESDAY
OFF ONE'S FOOD	ONE MAN'S MEAT	OPAQUE GLASS
OFF ONE'S HEAD	ONE MEAT BALL	OPEN ACCOUNT
OFF-SIDE RULE	ONE'S BETTERS	OPEN-AIR LIFE
OFF THE BOOZE	ONE'S HOSTESS	OPEN-AIR TYPE
OFF THE COAST	ONE SPOONFUL	OPEN AND SHUT
OFF THE GREEN	ONE'S VERY OWN	OPEN CIRCUIT
OFF THE LEASH	ONE SYLLABLE	OPEN COUNTRY
OFF THE POINT	ONE THOUSAND	OPENING MOVE
OFF THE RAILS	ON EVERY SIDE	OPENING TIME
OFF THE SCENT	ON GOOD TERMS	OPEN MEETING
OFF THE STAGE	ON HORSEBACK	OPEN OUTWARD
OFF THE TRACK	ONION SELLER	OPEN QUARREL
OF GOOD STOCK	ONLY THE BEST	OPEN RUPTURE
OF ILL REPUTE	ON NO ACCOUNT	OPEN SCANDAL
OFF LATE YEARS	ON ONE'S GUARD	OPEN THE BALL
OF NO ACCOUNT	ON ONE'S HANDS	OPEN THE CASE
OIL AND WATER	ON ONE'S KNEES	OPEN THE DOOR
OIL OF CLOVES	ON ONE'S PLATE	OPEN THE EYES
OIL PAINTING	ON ONE'S RIGHT	OPEN THE GATE
OIL REFINERY	ON POINT DUTY	OPEN THE SAFE
OLD AND TRIED	ON PRINCIPLE	OPEN THIS END
OLD CUSTOMER	ON PROBATION	OPEN TO DOUBT
OLDER SISTER	ON THE AGENDA	OPEN TO ERROR
OLD FAITHFUL	ON THE ATTACK	OPEN TO OFFER
OLD GREY MARE	ON THE BOARDS	OPEN VERDICT
OLD KENT ROAD	ON THE BOTTLE	OPEN WARFARE
OLD KING COLE	ON THE BRIDGE	OPERA BOUFFE
OLD MAN RIVER	ON THE CARPET	OPERA SINGER
OLD MEMORIES	ON THE COMMON	OPINION POLL
OLD OAK CHEST	ON THE CORNER	OPIUM ADDICT
OLD OFFENDER	ON THE COURSE	OPIUM SMOKER
OLD OLD STORY	ON THE DANUBE	OPPOSITE SEX
OLD POTATOES	ON THE FIDDLE	OPPOSITE WAY
OLD TRAFFORD	ON THE FRINGE	ORANGE DRINK

ORANGE GROVE
ORANGE JUICE
ORCHID HOUSE
ORDER DINNER
ORDERLY DUTY
ORDERLY ROOM
ORDER TO VIEW
ORDINARY MAN
ORDNANCE MAP
ORGANIC LIFE
ORIEL WINDOW
ORIENTAL ART
ORIGINAL SIN
ORNATE STYLE
ORPHAN CHILD
ORSON WELLES
ORTHODOX JEW
OSTRICH FARM
OTHER PEOPLE
OUT AND ABOUT
OUT COURTING
OUTDOOR GAME
OUTDOOR LIFE
OUTER CIRCLE
OUTER OFFICE
OUTER TEMPLE
OUT FOR A DUCK
OUT FOR BLOOD
OUT FOR KICKS
OUT OF ACTION
OUT OF BOUNDS
OUT OF BREATH
OUT OF DANGER
OUT OF FAVOUR
OUT OF HUMOUR
OUT OF OFFICE
OUT OF PETROL
OUT OF POCKET
OUT OF REPAIR
OUT OF SCHOOL
OUT OF SEASON
OUT OF THE ARK
OUT OF THE BAG
OUT OF THE CUP
OUT OF THE SKY
OUT OF THE SUN
OUT OF THE WAY
OUT ON STRIKE
OUTRIGHT WIN
OUTSIDE EDGE
OUTSIDE HELP
OUTSIDE LEFT
OUTSIDE WORK
OUTWARD SELF
OUTWARD SHOW
OVER AGAINST

OVER AND OVER
OVER ANXIOUS
OVERCAST SKY
OVER SHE GOES
OVER THE EDGE
OVER THE HILL
OVER THE LINE
OVER THE MARK
OVER THE MOON
OVER THE ODDS
OVER THE ROAD
OVER THE SIDE
OVER THE WALL
OVERTIME PAY
OWNER DRIVER
OWN FREE WILL
OXFORD COACH
OXFORD GROUP
OXFORD SHOES
OXFORD UNION
OYSTER SHELL

P – 11

PABLO CASALS
PACE THE DECK
PACKAGE DEAL
PACKED HOUSE
PACKED LUNCH
PACKET OF TEN
PACK OF CARDS
PACK OF FOOLS
PACK UP AND GO
PAGAN PEOPLE
PAGE HEADING
PAID SERVANT
PAID TRIBUTE
PAIL OF WATER
PAINFUL TASK
PAINTED LADY
PAINTED SHIP
PAINTED VEIL
PAINT IN OILS
PAIR OF BOOTS
PAIR OF CLOGS
PAIR OF CUFFS
PAIR OF DUCKS
PAIR OF FIVES
PAIR OF FOURS
PAIR OF HANDS
PAIR OF HORNS
PAIR OF JACKS
PAIR OF KINGS
PAIR OF LACES
PAIR OF NINES
PAIR OF PANTS

PAIR OF PUMPS
PAIR OF SHOES
PAIR OF SIXES
PAIR OF SOCKS
PAIR OF SPATS
PAIR OF SPURS
PAIR OF STAYS
PAIR OF STEPS
PAIR OF TONGS
PALACE GUARD
PALAIS GLIDE
PALE AS DEATH
PAMPAS GRASS
PANAMA CANAL
PANCAKE RACE
PANDIT NEHRU
PANDORA'S BOX
PANEL DOCTOR
PANE OF GLASS
PAPER PROFIT
PAPIER MÂCHÉ
PARAFFIN OIL
PARISH CLERK
PARISH VICAR
PARLOUR GAME
PARLOUR MAID
PARSNIP WINE
PARSON'S NOSE
PART COMPANY
PART FRIENDS
PARTING GIFT
PARTING SHOT
PART PAYMENT
PART-TIME JOB
PARTY LEADER
PARTY MEMBER
PARTY SLOGAN
PARTY SPIRIT
PARTY SYSTEM
PAS DE CALAIS
PASS A REMARK
PASSING RICH
PASSING SHOW
PASSING WHIM
PASSING WORD
PASSING PLAY
PASSION WEEK
PASSIVE ROLE
PASS THE BALL
PASS THE BUCK
PASS THE PORT
PASS THE SALT
PASS THE TEST
PASS THE TIME
PASS THIS WAY
PASS THROUGH

PAST AND GONE	PENSION FUND	PILTDOWN MAN
PASTEL SHADE	PENSIVE MOOD	PINCH OF SALT
PAST HISTORY	PERFECT CASE	PINT MEASURE
PAST THE POST	PERFECT CURE	PINT OF CIDER
PATH TO GLORY	PERFECT FOOL	PINT OF STOUT
PAT OF BUTTER	PERFECT LADY	PINT TANKARD
PATROL PLANE	PERFECT TRIM	PIPE CLEANER
PATRON OF ART	PERIOD DRESS	PIPE OF PEACE
PATRON SAINT	PERIOD HOUSE	PIPE ON BOARD
PATTERN SHOP	PERIOD PIECE	PIPE TOBACCO
PAUL ROBESON	PERSIAN GULF	PIRATE RADIO
PAX VOBISCUM	PERSIAN LAMB	PITHY REMARK
PAY A FORFEIT	PERSONAL LAW	PITHY SAYING
PAY AND A HALF	PET AVERSION	PLACE OF CALL
PAY A PENALTY	PETER DAWSON	PLACE OF REST
PAY A PREMIUM	PETER GRIMES	PLAIN ANSWER
PAY BY CHEQUE	PETER O'TOOLE	PLAIN FIGURE
PAY CASH DOWN	PETER'S PENCE	PLAIN LIVING
PAY INCREASE	PETER WIMSEY	PLAIN PEOPLE
PAYING GUEST	PETROL FUMES	PLAIN SPEECH
PAY INTEREST	PETTY TYRANT	PLAIN STUPID
PAY ON DEMAND	PETULA CLARK	PLASTER CAST
PAY ON THE DOT	PEWTER PLATE	PLASTIC BOMB
PAY THE COSTS	PHANTOM SHIP	PLATE ARMOUR
PAY THE DEVIL	PHOENIX PARK	PLAY AGAINST
PAY THE PIPER	PHONE NUMBER	PLAY-BOY TYPE
PAY THE PRICE	PHOTO FINISH	PLAY COWBOYS
PAY THE SCORE	PIANO LESSON	PLAY CRICKET
PAY THE TABLE	PIANO PLAYER	PLAYER PIANO
PAY UP OR ELSE!	PICK A WINNER	PLAY FOR LOVE
PEACEFUL END	PICKET FENCE	PLAY FOR TIME
PEACE OF MIND	PICK FLOWERS	PLAY FORWARD
PEACE PLEDGE	PICK HOLES IN	PLAYING CARD
PEACE SPEECH	PICK ONE'S WAY	PLAY MARBLES
PEACE TREATY	PICK POCKETS	PLAY ON WORDS
PEACH BRANDY	PICK THE BEST	PLAY PONTOON
PEACOCK BLUE	PICK THE LOCK	PLAY THE BALL
PEAL OF BELLS	PICK UP SPEED	PLAY THE FOOL
PEARL BAILEY	PICNIC PARTY	PLAY THE GAME
PEARL BARLEY	PICTURE BOOK	PLAY THE HARP
PEARL BUTTON	PIECE OF CAKE	PLAY THE HERO
PEARLY GATES	PIECE OF LAND	PLAY THE HOST
PEARLY QUEEN	PIECE OF LUCK	PLAY THE LEAD
PEBBLE BEACH	PIECE OF NEWS	PLEAD GUILTY
PEBBLY BEACH	PIE IN THE SKY	PLEASANT DAY
PELTING RAIN	PIERCED EARS	PLEASURE MAD
PENAL COLONY	PIGEON'S MILK	PLENTY TO EAT
PENAL REFORM	PILE OF CHIPS	PLOT A COURSE
PENAL SYSTEM	PILE OF MONEY	PLUMB WICKET
PENALTY AREA	PILLION RIDE	PLUM PUDDING
PENALTY GOAL	PILLION SEAT	PLUS OR MINUS
PENALTY KICK	PILLOW FIGHT	PLYMOUTH HOE
PENALTY LINE	PILOT ENGINE	POCKET GUIDE
PENALTY SPOT	PILOT SCHEME	POCKET MONEY
PEN AND PAPER	PILOT VESSEL	POCKET VENUS
PENNY POINTS	PILSEN LAGER	POETIC STYLE

POETS' CORNER	POTTED PLANT	PRISON HOUSE
POINT A MORAL	POTTER ABOUT	PRISON WALLS
POINTED CLUE	POTTER'S CLAY	PRIVATE BANK
POINT OF SALE	POT THE BLACK	PRIVATE BILL
POINT OF TIME	POTTING SHED	PRIVATE HELL
POINT OF VIEW	POULTRY FARM	PRIVATE LIFE
POINT THE WAY	POURING RAIN	PRIVATE LINE
POKER PLAYER	POWER OF GOOD	PRIVATE MASS
POKER SCHOOL	POWER SUPPLY	PRIVATE PATH
POKE THE FIRE	PRACTICE RUN	PRIVATE ROAD
POLAR CIRCLE	PRACTISE LAW	PRIVATE ROOM
POLAR LIGHTS	PRAED STREET	PRIVATE SALE
POLAR REGION	PRAIRIE FIRE	PRIVATE TALK
POLE VAULTER	PRAIRIE WOLF	PRIVATE VIEW
POLICE COURT	PRANCE ABOUT	PRIVATE WARD
POLICE FORCE	PRAY FOR RAIN	PRIVET HEDGE
POLICE STATE	PRECISE TIME	PRIZE CATTLE
POLO SWEATER	PREMIUM BOND	PROBATE DUTY
PONY AND TRAP	PRESENT ARMS	PROBE DEEPLY
PONY EXPRESS	PRESENT TIME	PROBLEM PLAY
POOLS COUPON	PRESS A CLAIM	PRODIGAL SON
POOR CALIBRE	PRESSED BEEF	PROM CONCERT
POOR COMPANY	PRESS NOTICE	PROMISE WELL
POOR HARVEST	PRESS OFFICE	PROMPT REPLY
POOR LOOK-OUT	PRESS ONWARD	PROOF READER
POOR OLD SOUL	PRESS TICKET	PROOF SPIRIT
POOR OPINION	PRETTY AWFUL	PROPER PLACE
POOR OUTLOOK	PRETTY DANCE	PROPER PRIDE
POOR QUALITY	PRETTY PENNY	PROPER SENSE
POOR SOLDIER	PRETTY POLLY	PROPERTY TAX
POOR SWIMMER	PRETTY SCENE	PROS AND CONS
POOR VINTAGE	PRETTY SMART	PROSE POETRY
POPULAR HERO	PRE-WAR PRICE	PROTEIN DIET
POPULAR NAME	PREY TO FEARS	PROUD FATHER
POPULAR PLAY	PRICE OF FAME	PROVE GUILTY
POPULAR SONG	PRICE TICKET	PRUSSIC ACID
POPULAR TUNE	PRICKLY HEAT	PUBLIC ALARM
POPULAR WILL	PRICKLY PEAR	PUBLIC BATHS
PORK BUTCHER	PRIDE AND JOY	PUBLIC ENEMY
PORTLAND BAY	PRIDE OF RANK	PUBLIC FUNDS
PORT OF ENTRY	PRIEST'S HOLE	PUBLIC HOUSE
PORT OF SPAIN	PRIME FACTOR	PUBLIC IMAGE
PORT STANLEY	PRIME NUMBER	PUBLIC MONEY
PORT THE HELM	PRIME OF LIFE	PUBLIC PURSE
POSTAGE FREE	PRIMROSE DAY	PUBLIC TASTE
POSTAGE PAID	PRIMUS STOVE	PUBLIC WORKS
POST A LETTER	PRINCE HARRY	PUBLIC WRONG
POSTAL ORDER	PRINCESS IDA	PUDDING FACE
POSTAL UNION	PRINTED PAGE	PUDDING LANE
POSTERN GATE	PRINTED WORD	PUFF AND BLOW
POTATO CHIPS	PRINTER'S INK	PUFF OF SMOKE
POTATO CRISP	PRINTER'S PIE	PULL ASUNDER
POTATO SALAD	PRINTING INK	PULL ONE'S LEG
POT OF COFFEE	PRISON BREAK	PULL STRINGS
POTS AND PANS	PRISON GATES	PULL THROUGH
POTS OF MONEY	PRISON GUARD	PULL UP SHORT

PUMICE STONE	QUART BOTTLE	RAILWAY ARCH
PUPPET STATE	QUARTER DECK	RAILWAY LINE
PURCHASE TAX	QUARTER LEFT	RAINBOW'S END
PURE ALCOHOL	QUARTER MILE	RAIN OF BLOWS
PURE ENGLISH	QUART OF BEER	RAIN OR SHINE
PURE FICTION	QUARTO PAPER	RAINY SEASON
PURE IN HEART	QUEEN MOTHER	RAISE A CHEER
PURE MOTIVES	QUEEN SALOTE	RAISE A LAUGH
PURE SCIENCE	QUEEN'S BENCH	RAISE A STORM
PURL OR PLAIN	QUEEN'S COURT	RAISED VOICE
PURPLE HEART	QUEER PERSON	RAISE MORALE
PURPLE PATCH	QUEER STREET	RAISE ON HIGH
PURSE OF GOLD	QUICK ANSWER	RAISE PRICES
PUSH AND PULL	QUICK FREEZE	RAISE THE BID
PUSH FORWARD	QUICK GLANCE	RAISE THE HEM
PUSH THROUGH	QUICK GROWTH	RAISON D'ÊTRE
PUSS IN BOOTS	QUICK PROFIT	RALLY AROUND
PUT A SPOKE IN	QUICK RETURN	RALLYING CRY
PUT IN A CLAIM	QUICK TEMPER	RAMBLER ROSE
PUT IN CHARGE	QUICK TONGUE	RANGING SHOT
PUT IN DANGER	QUICK WORKER	RANK AND FILE
PUT IN LIGHTS	QUIET DREAMS	RANSOM MONEY
PUT IN MOTION	QUIETEN DOWN	RANT AND RAVE
PUT IN OFFICE	QUIET PLEASE!	RAPID CHANGE
PUT IN PRISON	QUITE AT HOME	RAPID EFFECT
PUT IN THE WAY	QUITE ENOUGH	RAPID GLANCE
PUT INTO CODE	QUITE LIKELY	RAPID GROWTH
PUT INTO TYPE	QUIT THE RING	RAPID MOTION
PUT IT MILDLY	QUOTED PRICE	RAPID SPEECH
PUT ON A SPURT		RARE EXAMPLE
PUT ON A STUNT		RARE QUALITY
PUT ONE'S CASE	R – 11	RASH PROMISE
PUT ON PAROLE		RATTLE ALONG
PUT ON RECORD	RABBIT PUNCH	RAW MATERIAL
PUT ON THE MAP	RABBIT'S FOOT	REACH BOTTOM
PUT ON WEIGHT	RACE HISTORY	REACH SAFETY
PUT OUT TO SEA	RACE MEETING	REACH THE END
PUT STRAIGHT	RACE PROBLEM	REACH THE TOP
PUT THE LID ON	RACIAL PRIDE	READ A SPEECH
PUT TO FLIGHT	RACING EIGHT	READING DESK
PUT TOGETHER	RACING MODEL	READING GAOL
PUT TO RANSOM	RACING SLANG	READING LAMP
PUT TO RIGHTS	RACING WORLD	READING LIST
PUTT THE SHOT	RACING YACHT	READING ROOM
PUT UP A BLACK	RACK AND RUIN	READ THE WILL
PUT UP A BLUFF	RACY FLAVOUR	READ THROUGH
PUT-UP AFFAIR	RADAR SCREEN	READY ACCESS
PUT UP A FIGHT	RADIANT HEAT	READY ANSWER
PUT WISE TO IT	RADIATE LOVE	READY ENOUGH
PUZZLE IT OUT	RADICAL CURE	READY FOR BED
PYJAMA PARTY	RADICAL IDEA	READY FOR USE
	RADICAL SIGN	READY RETORT
	RADIO BEACON	READY TO DROP
Q – 11	RADIO SIGNAL	READY TO HAND
	RAGGED ROBIN	READY TONGUE
QUACK DOCTOR	RAGTIME ARMY	READY TO WEAR
QUACK REMEDY	RAGTIME BAND	

READY WORKER
REAM OF PAPER
REAP A PROFIT
REAPING HOOK
REAR ADMIRAL
REBECCA WEST
REBEL ATTACK
REBEL LEADER
RECEIPT BOOK
RECEIVE NEWS
RECENT ISSUE
RECENT TIMES
RECORD ALBUM
RECORD CROWD
RECORD ENTRY
RECORD SCORE
RECORD TOKEN
RED AND BLACK
RED AND GREEN
RED AND WHITE
RED BURGUNDY
RED-HOT COALS
RED-HOT POKER
RED MAHOGANY
RED, RED ROBIN
RED SQUIRREL
RED TRIANGLE
REDUCED FARE
REDUCED RATE
REDUCE SPEED
REFINED GOLD
REFLEX LIGHT
REFUGEE CAMP
REFUSE A GIFT
REFUSE TO ACT
REFUSE TO MIX
REFUSE TO PAY
REGATTA WEEK
REGENCY BUCK
REGENT'S PARK
REGULAR ARMY
REGULAR HERO
REGULAR LIFE
REGULAR VERB
REGULAR WORK
RELEASE DATE
RELIEF FORCE
RELIEF PARTY
REMAIN ALOOF
REMAIN AWAKE
REMNANT SALE
REMOTE CAUSE
RENEW A LEASE
RENEWED HOPE
RENTAL VALUE
RENT ASUNDER

RENT CONTROL
REPORT STAGE
REQUEST ITEM
REQUEST NOTE
REQUEST STOP
REQUIEM MASS
RESCUE FORCE
RESCUE PARTY
RESCUE SQUAD
RESERVE FUND
RESERVE TEAM
REST ASSURED
REST CONTENT
REST IN PEACE
RETAIL PRICE
RETAIL TRADE
RETIRED LIFE
RETIRED LIST
RETIRE TO BED
RETIRING AGE
RETURN A BLOW
RETURN FIGHT
RETURN MATCH
RETURN VISIT
REVERSE GEAR
REVERSE SIDE
REVISED COPY
REX HARRISON
RHODE ISLAND
RHUBARB TART
RHYMED VERSE
RICE PUDDING
RICH HARVEST
RICH HUSBAND
RICH IN IDEAS
RIDE A TANDEM
RIDING BOOTS
RIDING HABIT
RIGGED TRIAL
RIGHT AMOUNT
RIGHT ANSWER
RIGHT AS RAIN
RIGHT A WRONG
RIGHT INSIDE
RIGHT MOMENT
RIGHT NUMBER
RIGHT PEOPLE
RIGHT SIDE UP
RIGHTS OF MAN
RIGHT TO VOTE
RIGHT WINGER
RIGHT YOU ARE
RIGOR MORTIS
RINGING TONE
RING OF ROSES
RING OF TRUTH

RING THE BELL
RIOT OF SOUND
RISE AGAINST
RISE AND FALL
RISE IN PRICE
RISE TO A PEAK
RISE TO POWER
RISE TO SPEAK
RISING COSTS
RISING SALES
RITUAL DANCE
RIVER DANUBE
RIVER GANGES
RIVER JORDAN
RIVER LAUNCH
RIVER MEDWAY
RIVER MERSEY
RIVER OF LAVA
RIVER PATROL
RIVER POLICE
RIVER SEVERN
RIVER THAMES
RIVER TRAVEL
ROAD HAULAGE
ROAD REPAIRS
ROADSIDE INN
ROAD SURFACE
ROAD SWEEPER
ROAD TRAFFIC
ROARING FIRE
ROAR OF ANGER
ROASTING HOT
ROAST MUTTON
ROAST POTATO
ROAST TURKEY
ROBBER BARON
ROBE OF STATE
ROBERT BRUCE
ROBERT BURNS
ROBERT CLIVE
ROBERT DONAT
ROCK AND ROLL
ROCK CONCERT
ROCKET RANGE
ROCK THE BOAT
ROCK TO SLEEP
ROD IN PICKLE
ROES ON TOAST
ROLLER BLIND
ROLLER TOWEL
ROLLING GAIT
ROLLING HOME
ROLLING ROAD
ROLL INTO ONE
ROLL OF DRUMS
ROLL OF PAPER

ROLL THE LAWN
ROLL-TOP DESK
ROMAN CANDLE
ROMAN CHURCH
ROMAN EMPIRE
ROMANTIC ART
ROMNEY MARSH
ROOKERY NOOK
ROOM SERVICE
ROSES ARE RED
ROSY OUTLOOK
ROSY PICTURE
ROTARY PRESS
ROTARY VALVE
ROTTEN APPLE
ROUGE ET NOIR
ROUGH GROUND
ROUGH MANNER
ROUGH SCHEME
ROUGH SKETCH
ROUGH TONGUE
ROUND CHEEKS
ROUND FIGURE
ROUND LETTER
ROUND NUMBER
ROUND OBJECT
ROUND OF BEEF
ROUND OF FIRE
ROUND OF GOLF
ROUSING SONG
ROW OF HOUSES
ROW OF MEDALS
ROWS AND ROWS
ROWTON HOUSE
ROYAL ASSENT
ROYAL CIRCLE
ROYAL FAMILY
ROYAL MARINE
ROYAL OCTAVO
ROYAL PALACE
ROYAL PARDON
ROYAL PURPLE
ROYAL SALUTE
RUBBER GLOVE
RUBBER HEELS
RUBBER PLANT
RUBBER SOLES
RUBBER STAMP
RUBBISH DUMP
RUBBISH HEAP
RUB TOGETHER
RUBY WEDDING
RUDDY CHEEKS
RUDE GESTURE
RUGBY LEAGUE
RUGBY SCHOOL

RUGBY TACKLE
RUGGER FIELD
RUGGER MATCH
RUGGER PITCH
RUGGER SCRUM
RUINED HOUSE
RUIN ONESELF
RULE OF FORCE
RULE OF MIGHT
RULE OF THREE
RULE OF THUMB
RULING CLASS
RULING PARTY
RULING POWER
RULING PRICE
RUM CUSTOMER
RUMMAGE SALE
RUMOUR HAS IT
RUN A MAN DOWN
RUN AN ERRAND
RUN FOR COVER
RUN FOR MAYOR
RUN INTO DEBT
RUN INTO FORM
RUN INTO PORT
RUN MESSAGES
RUNNER BEANS
RUNNING AMOK
RUNNING COLD
RUNNING COST
RUNNING DOWN
RUNNING FIRE
RUNNING JUMP
RUNNING KNOT
RUNNING OVER
RUNNING RIOT
RUNNING WILD
RUN PARALLEL
RUN SMOOTHLY
RUN STRAIGHT
RUN TOGETHER
RUN UP A SCORE
RUSH FORWARD
RUSH THROUGH
RUSSIAN BATH
RUSSIAN EGGS

S – 11

SABRINA FAIR
SACK OF FLOUR
SACRED HEART
SACRED MUSIC
SACRED TRUST
SAD FAREWELL
SADLY MISSED

SAD TO RELATE
SAFE AND SURE
SAFE AND WELL
SAFE BREAKER
SAFE COMPANY
SAFE CONDUCT
SAFE CUSTODY
SAFE DEPOSIT
SAFE JOURNEY
SAFE KEEPING
SAFE LANDING
SAFE RETREAT
SAFETY CATCH
SAFETY FIRST
SAFETY MATCH
SAFETY RAZOR
SAFETY STRAP
SAFETY VALVE
SAFFRON CAKE
SAGO PUDDING
SAILING BOAT
SAILING CLUB
SAILING DATE
SAILING SHIP
SAILING TIME
SAILOR'S HOME
SAILOR'S KNOT
SAINT GEORGE
SAINT HELENA
SAINT HELIER
SALMON STEAK
SALMON TROUT
SAL VOLATILE
SAME FOOTING
SAME MEANING
SAME OLD GAME
SAME PATTERN
SAMUEL PEPYS
SANCHO PANZA
SANDOWN PARK
SANDS OF TIME
SANDWICH BAR
SAPPHIRE SEA
SATANIC HOST
SATIN FINISH
SATIN STITCH
SAUCEPAN LID
SAUDI ARABIA
SAUSAGE MEAT
SAUSAGE ROLL
SAVAGE BEAST
SAVAGE BRUTE
SAVAGE SCENE
SAVAGE TRIBE
SAVE NOTHING
SAVE ONESELF

SAVE THE MARK	SECOND SHIFT	SERIOUS PLAY
SAVING GRACE	SECOND SIGHT	SERIOUS STEP
SAVINGS BANK	SECONDS LATE	SERIOUS TALK
SAVOIR FAIRE	SECOND STAGE	SERIOUS VEIN
SAVOURY DISH	SECOND TEETH	SERIOUS VIEW
SCALDED MILK	SECOND VERSE	SERVANT GIRL
SCARED STIFF	SECOND YOUTH	SERVE A FAULT
SCENT BOTTLE	SECRET AGENT	SERVE NOTICE
SCENT DANGER	SECRET ENEMY	SERVICE FLAT
SCENTED SOAP	SECRET HAUNT	SERVICE ROAD
SCILLY ISLES	SECRET PLACE	SERVICE ROOM
SCHOOL BADGE	SECURED LOAN	SERVING TIME
SCHOOL BOARD	SECURE GRASP	SET AN AMBUSH
SCHOOL HOURS	SEE A DENTIST	SET AND MATCH
SCHOOL HOUSE	SEE DAYLIGHT	SET A PROBLEM
SCHOOL OF ART	SEED OF DOUBT	SET AT NAUGHT
SCHOOL TREAT	SEE EYE TO EYE	SET IN MOTION
SCORE A POINT	SEE FAIR PLAY	SET MOVEMENT
SCORE FREELY	SEEK A WAY OUT	SET OF CHAIRS
SCORE SLOWLY	SEE NEXT WEEK	SET OF STAMPS
SCOTCH BROTH	SEE STRAIGHT	SET ONE RIGHT
SCOTS ACCENT	SEE THE LIGHT	SET QUESTION
SCOTS GUARDS	SEE THE POINT	SET STANDARD
SCOUT AROUND	SEE THE TRUTH	SET STRAIGHT
SCOUT MASTER	SEE THE WORLD	SET THE ALARM
SCRAP DEALER	SEETHING MOB	SET THE FIELD
SCRAPE ALONG	SELF CONTROL	SET THE SCENE
SCRAPPY MEAL	SELF-MADE MAN	SETTING FREE
SCRATCH CREW	SELL AT A LOSS	SETTLING DAY
SCRATCH RACE	SELLING LINE	SET TO RIGHTS
SCRATCH SIDE	SELLING RACE	SET UP A CLAIM
SCRATCH TEAM	SELL THE PASS	SET UP IN TYPE
SCRATCHY PEN	SELL TICKETS	SEVEN AND ONE
SEA ELEPHANT	SENATE HOUSE	SEVEN AND SIX
SEA FRONTAGE	SEND A LETTER	SEVEN AND TEN
SEAM BOWLING	SEND AN ORDER	SEVEN AND TWO
SEARCH PARTY	SEND A SIGNAL	SEVEN DWARFS
SEASIDE TOWN	SEND FOR A CAB	SEVEN HEARTS
SEAT OF KINGS	SEND FOR HELP	SEVEN MONTHS
SEAT OF POWER	SEND PACKING	SEVEN NINTHS
SEAT ONESELF	SEND TO SLEEP	SEVEN O'CLOCK
SECOND CHILD	SENILE DECAY	SEVEN OUNCES
SECOND CLASS	SENIOR PUPIL	SEVEN POINTS
SECOND EVENT	SENSE OF DUTY	SEVEN POUNDS
SECOND FLOOR	SENSE OF LOSS	SEVEN SPADES
SECOND FRONT	SENSE OF PAIN	SEVEN TENTHS
SECOND GRADE	SENSIBLE BOY	SEVENTH HOLE
SECOND GREEN	SENSIBLE MAN	SEVENTH PART
SECOND HOUSE	SENT HAYWIRE	SEVENTH RACE
SECOND JOINT	SENT PACKING	SEVENTH TIME
SECOND MONTH	SERIAL STORY	SEVEN TO FOUR
SECOND OF MAY	SERIOUS BOOK	SEVERE FROST
SECOND PARTY	SERIOUS LOOK	SEVERE SHOCK
SECOND PLACE	SERIOUS LOSS	SEVERE STYLE
SECOND PRIZE	SERIOUS MIND	SEWING CLASS
SECOND ROUND	SERIOUS MOOD	SEXTON BLAKE

SHABBY TRICK	SHORT LETTER	SILENT NIGHT
SHAGGY BEARD	SHORT MEMORY	SILICON CHIP
SHALLOW DISH	SHORT NOTICE	SILLY ANSWER
SHALLOW MIND	SHORT OF CASH	SILLY DONKEY
SHAM ILLNESS	SHORT OF FOOD	SILLY DUFFER
SHANKS'S PONY	SHORT OF TIME	SILLY PERSON
SHARP ANSWER	SHORT OF WORK	SILLY REMARK
SHARP ATTACK	SHORT PERIOD	SILLY SEASON
SHARP CORNER	SHORT SHRIFT	SILVER BIRCH
SHARP LESSON	SHORT SPEECH	SILVER MEDAL
SHARP REBUFF	SHORT STROLL	SILVER MONEY
SHARP TEMPER	SHORT SUPPLY	SILVER PAPER
SHARP TONGUE	SHORT TEMPER	SILVER PLATE
SHARP TWINGE	SHORT VOYAGE	SILVER SPOON
SHAVEN CROWN	SHORT WAY OFF	SILVERY MOON
SHAVING SOAP	SHORT WEIGHT	SILVERY TONE
SHEAF OF CORN	SHOT THROUGH	SIMNEL BREAD
SHED THE LOAD	SHOUT FOR JOY	SIMPLE HEART
SHEEP FARMER	SHOUT HURRAH	SIMPLE SIMON
SHEER LUNACY	SHOW A PROFIT	SIMPLE SOUND
SHEER MURDER	SHOW COURAGE	SIMPLE STYLE
SHEET ANCHOR	SHOW FEELING	SIMPLE TASTE
SHEET COPPER	SHOW NO FIGHT	SIMPLE TRUTH
SHERRY GLASS	SHOW NO MERCY	SIMPLON PASS
SHERRY PARTY	SHOW OF FORCE	SIMPLY AWFUL
SHIFT WORKER	SHOW OF HANDS	SINEWS OF WAR
SHINING HOUR	SHOW ONE'S AGE	SINGING BIRD
SHIP OF STATE	SHOW ONESELF	SINGING FOOL
SHIP'S COURSE	SHOW PROMISE	SINGLE BERTH
SHIP'S DOCTOR	SHOW PROWESS	SINGLE ENTRY
SHIP'S MASTER	SHOW RESPECT	SINGLE HEART
SHIP'S PAPERS	SHOW RESULTS	SINGLE PIECE
SHIP'S PURSER	SHOW THE FLAG	SINGLE STATE
SHIP'S STOKER	SHOW UP AGAIN	SINGLE TRACK
SHOAL OF FISH	SHOW WILLING	SINGLE VOICE
SHOCK OF HAIR	SHREWD GUESS	SINGLE WOMAN
SHOCK TROOPS	SHRILL SOUND	SINKING FAST
SHODDY GOODS	SHRILL VOICE	SINKING FUND
SHOE LEATHER	SHUN COMPANY	SINKING SHIP
SHOOTING BOX	SHUT THE DOOR	SINK THE BOAT
SHOOTING WAR	SHUT THE GATE	SIP OF BRANDY
SHOOT TO KILL	SIAMESE TWIN	SIR JOHN HUNT
SHOP COUNTER	SICK AT HEART	SIR LANCELOT
SHOP DOORWAY	SICK BENEFIT	SISTER SHIPS
SHOP FOR SALE	SICKLY SMILE	SISTER SUSIE
SHOPPING BAG	SICK TO DEATH	SIT-DOWN MEAL
SHOP STEWARD	SIDE AGAINST	SITTING BULL
SHORT AND FAT	SIDE OF BACON	SITTING DOWN
SHORT ANSWER	SIDE TURNING	SITTING DUCK
SHORTEN SAIL	SIEGE OF TROY	SITTING ROOM
SHORTEST BOY	SIERRA LEONE	SITTING SHOT
SHORTEST DAY	SIGNAL CORPS	SIX AND A HALF
SHORTEST MAN	SIGNAL LIGHT	SIX DIAMONDS
SHORTEST WAY	SIGNS OF WEAR	SIX FEET TALL
SHORT JACKET	SILAS MARNER	SIX FURLONGS
SHORT LESSON	SILENT MIRTH	SIX NO-TRUMPS

SIX OF HEARTS	SLOPPY SMILE	SOBER PERSON
SIX OF SPADES	SLOT MACHINE	SOCCER MATCH
SIX OF TRUMPS	SLOUCH ALONG	SOCIAL CLASS
SIXPENNY TIP	SLOW AND SURE	SOCIAL GROUP
SIX SEVENTHS	SLOW BOWLING	SOCIAL PARTY
SIXTH LETTER	SLOW BUT SURE	SOCIAL ROUND
SIXTH OF JULY	SLOW DECLINE	SOCIAL SCALE
SIXTH OF JUNE	SLOW DEGREES	SOCIAL WHIRL
SIX THOUSAND	SLOW FOXTROT	SOCIETY LADY
SIXTH STOREY	SLOW PROCESS	SOCIETY NEWS
SIXTH VOLUME	SLOW STARTER	SOCIETY PAGE
SKATING RINK	SLOW TO ANGER	SODA AND MILK
SKEIN OF WOOL	SLOW TO LEARN	SO FAR, SO GOOD
SKELETON KEY	SLUM DWELLER	SOFT AND RIPE
SKETCHY MEAL	SMALL AMOUNT	SOFT OUTLINE
SKILLED WORK	SMALL BITTER	SOILED GOODS
SKIMMED MILK	SMALL CHANCE	SOILED LINEN
SKIM THROUGH	SMALL CHANGE	SOIL EROSION
SKIN AND BONE	SMALL CHARGE	SOLAR PLEXUS
SKIN DISEASE	SMALL CIRCLE	SOLAR SYSTEM
SKIN MASSAGE	SMALL FAMILY	SOLD FOR A PUP
SKYE TERRIER	SMALL FARMER	SOLDIER KING
SLAB OF STONE	SMALL INCOME	SOLDIER'S KIT
SLACK MARKET	SMALL LETTER	SOLDIER'S PAY
SLACK SEASON	SMALL MATTER	SOLE AND HEEL
SLADE SCHOOL	SMALL NUMBER	SOLE COMFORT
SLAM THE DOOR	SMALL PROFIT	SOLEMN MUSIC
SLATE PENCIL	SMALL SALARY	SOLEMN TRUTH
SLAVE LABOUR	SMALL SCOTCH	SOLE SUPPORT
SLAVE MARKET	SMALL SHERRY	SOLID FIGURE
SLAVE TO DUTY	SMALL VESSEL	SOLID GROUND
SLEEP DOUBLE	SMALL WHISKY	SOLID MATTER
SLEEPING BAG	SMART DEVICE	SOLID SILVER
SLEEPING CAR	SMART PEOPLE	SOLITARY MAN
SLEEPING DOG	SMART PERSON	SOLWAY FIRTH
SLEIGH BELLS	SMART RETORT	SOMEONE ELSE
SLENDER HOPE	SMART SAYING	SOME TIME AGO
SLICED BREAD	SMART TALKER	SONG CONTEST
SLICE OF CAKE	SMELL DANGER	SONG OF SONGS
SLICE OF LUCK	SMILE PLEASE	SONG RECITAL
SLICE OF MEAT	SMOKE A CIGAR	SONNY LISTON
SLIDING DOOR	SMOKED GLASS	SOPHIA LOREN
SLIDING ROOF	SMOKED TROUT	SORDID STORY
SLIDING SEAT	SMOKE SCREEN	SORELY TRIED
SLIGHT DOUBT	SMOKE SIGNAL	SORE PRESSED
SLIGHT PAUSE	SMOKING ROOM	SORE SUBJECT
SLIPPED DISC	SMOOTH AS ICE	SORRY FIGURE
SLIPPER BATH	SMOOTH WATER	SORRY PLIGHT
SLIP OF A GIRL	SNAKE POISON	SOUND ADVICE
SLIP OF PAPER	SNAKES ALIVE!	SOUND ASLEEP
SLIP THROUGH	SNAP OUT OF IT	SOUND CREDIT
SLOPING DESK	SNATCH A KISS	SOUND IN MIND
SLOPING EDGE	SNOWED UNDER	SOUND PLAYER
SLOPING FACE	SNOW LEOPARD	SOUND POLICY
SLOPING ROOF	SOB BITTERLY	SOUND REASON
SLOPING TYPE	SOBER COLOUR	SOUP KITCHEN

SOUTH AFRICA	SPOIL THE FUN	STAR STUDDED
SOUTH BY EAST	SPORTING DOG	START A FIGHT
SOUTH BY WEST	SPORTING GUN	START AFRESH
SOUTH DAKOTA	SPORTING MAN	STARTER'S GUN
SOUTH EALING	SPORTS ARENA	START SAVING
SOUTH HARROW	SPORTS MODEL	STATE A CLAIM
SOUTH LONDON	SPORTS SHIRT	STATED TERMS
SOUTH MOLTON	SPOTTED DICK	STATELY HOME
SOUTH RIDING	SPOT THE BALL	STATE OF FLUX
SOVIET UNION	SPREAD GLOOM	STATE OF MIND
SPACE FLIGHT	SPRING A LEAK	STATE PRISON
SPACE OF TIME	SPRING APART	STATE SCHOOL
SPACE TRAVEL	SPRING A TRAP	STATE SECRET
SPADE GUINEA	SPRING FEVER	STATUTE BOOK
SPANISH GOLD	SPRING ONION	STATUTE MILE
SPANISH MAIN	SPRING VALVE	ST AUGUSTINE
SPANISH TOWN	SPRING WATER	STAY INDOORS
SPANISH WINE	SPROUT WINGS	STAY IN SIGHT
SPARE A PENNY	SQUARE DANCE	STAY NEUTRAL
SPARE THE ROD	SQUARE WORLD	STAY OUTSIDE
SPARK OF LIFE	SQUASH COURT	STAY THE PACE
SPARTAN FARE	SQUEEZE PLAY	STAY TOO LONG
SPARTAN LIFE	SQUIRE'S LADY	ST DAVID'S DAY
SPATE OF NEWS	STACK OF COAL	STEADY FLAME
SPEAK FIRMLY	STACK OF WORK	STEADY LIGHT
SPEAK FREELY	STAFF OF LIFE	STEADY PULSE
SPEAK FRENCH	STAGE EFFECT	STEADY TREND
SPEAK GERMAN	STAGE FRIGHT	STEAL A MARCH
SPEAK NO EVIL	STAGE MAKE-UP	STEAMED FISH
SPEAK OPENLY	STAGE PLAYER	STEAM ENGINE
SPEAK POLISH	STAGE STRUCK	STEAMING HOT
SPEAK SLOWLY	STAIR CARPET	STEAM LAUNCH
SPEAK SOFTLY	STAKE A CLAIM	STEEL GIRDER
SPECIAL CASE	STALK ABROAD	STEEL HELMET
SPECIAL DIET	STALKY AND CO.	ST ELMO'S FIRE
SPECIAL DUTY	STAMP DEALER	STEM THE TIDE
SPECIAL GIFT	STAND A DRINK	STEM TO STERN
SPECIAL JURY	STAND AGHAST	STEP FORWARD
SPECIAL LINE	STANDARD ONE	STEP OUTSIDE
SPECIAL NOTE	STAND A ROUND	STEP THIS WAY
SPECK OF DUST	STAND AROUND	STERILE LAND
SPEED MANIAC	STAND AT EASE	STERN REBUKE
SPEED RECORD	STAND IN FEAR	STEWED FRUIT
SPEED TRIALS	STAND IN LINE	STEWED PEARS
SPELL DANGER	STAND IN NEED	STICK IN A RUT
SPELLING BEE	STAND OR FALL	STICK OF ROCK
SPELL OF DUTY	STAND SQUARE	STICKY LABEL
SPELL OF WORK	STAND TO GAIN	STICKY PAPER
SPEND FREELY	STAND TO LOSE	STICKY STUFF
SPICE OF LIFE	STAR CHAMBER	STIFF BREEZE
SPIKED SHOES	STARCHY FOOD	STIFF COLOUR
SPINNING TOP	STAR CLUSTER	STIFLE A YAWN
SPIRIT LEVEL	STAR OF DAVID	STILL HOPING
SPLIT SECOND	STAR OF INDIA	STILL TO COME
SPOILS OF WAR	STAR QUALITY	STILL TONGUE
SPOILT CHILD	STARRY NIGHT	STILL WATERS

STILL WITH IT
STIR A FINGER
STIR ONE'S TEA
STIRRUP PUMP
STIR THE FIRE
ST JOHN'S WOOD
ST MARGARET'S
STOCK ANSWER
STOCK EXCUSE
STOCK IN HAND
STOCK LETTER
STOCK MARKET
STOCK PHRASE
STOLE A MARCH
STOLEN FRUIT
STOLEN GOODS
STONE QUARRY
STONE'S THROW
STONY GROUND
STOP A BULLET
STOP BURNING
STOP OUTSIDE
STOP PAYMENT
STOP SMOKING
STOP TALKING
STOP TEASING
STOP THE FLOW
STOP TO THINK
STOP WORKING
STORE OF NUTS
STORM CENTRE
STORM CLOUDS
STORM SIGNAL
STORM TROOPS
STORMY NIGHT
STORMY SCENE
STORY WRITER
STOUT CORTEZ
STOUT EFFORT
STOUT FELLOW
STRAIGHT BAT
STRAIGHT HIT
STRAIGHT MAN
STRAIGHT OFF
STRAIGHT OUT
STRAIGHT RUN
STRAIGHT SET
STRAIGHT TIP
STRAIGHT WIN
STRANGE LAND
STRAY BULLET
STRAY REMARK
STREAM FORTH
STREET CRIES
STREET LEVEL
STREET OF INK

STREET SCENE
STRICT ORDER
STRICT TEMPO
STRICT TRUTH
STRIDE ALONG
STRIKE A BLOW
STRIKE A NOTE
STRIKE A POSE
STRIKE BLIND
STRIKE LUCKY
STRING ALONG
STRING BEANS
STRING MUSIC
STRIP OF LAND
STRIVE AFTER
STRONG DRINK
STRONG FAITH
STRONG LIGHT
STRONG POINT
STRONG PULSE
STRONG SMELL
STRONG TASTE
STRONG VIEWS
STRONG VOICE
STRONG WORDS
STUB ONE'S TOE
STUDENT BODY
STUDENT DAYS
STUDENTS' RAG
STUDIO COUCH
STUFFED BIRD
STUFFED FOWL
STUFF IT AWAY
STUMBLE OVER
STUMBLE UPON
STUMP ORATOR
STUNT FLYING
STURDY FRAME
STURDY LIMBS
ST VALENTINE
SUAVE MANNER
SUBLIME LIFE
SUCH AND SUCH
SUDDEN BREAK
SUDDEN DEATH
SUDDEN SHOCK
SUE FOR LIBEL
SUE FOR PEACE
SUET PUDDING
SUFFER A BLOW
SUFFER A LOSS
SUICIDE CLUB
SUICIDE NOTE
SUICIDE PACT
SUIT OF CARDS
SUMMER DRESS

SUMMIT LEVEL
SUMMIT TALKS
SUM OF THINGS
SUNDAY HOURS
SUNDAY JOINT
SUNDAY LUNCH
SUNDAY NIGHT
SUNDAY PAPER
SUNDAY TIMES
SUNDRY ITEMS
SUNK IN GLOOM
SUNNY SIDE UP
SUNSET STRIP
SUPERIOR AIR
SUPPER PARTY
SUPPER TABLE
SUPPORT LIFE
SUPPLY DEPOT
SUPREME GOOD
SURE FOOTING
SURFACE AREA
SURFACE MAIL
SURPLUS CASH
SURREY HILLS
SUSSEX DOWNS
SWALLOW DIVE
SWANEE RIVER
SWANSEA TOWN
SWARM OF ANTS
SWARM OF BEES
SWEAR AN OATH
SWEAR ON OATH
SWEDISH BATH
SWEENEY TODD
SWEET AND LOW
SWEET AS A NUT
SWEET DREAMS
SWEET NATURE
SWEET PICKLE
SWEET POTATO
SWEET SHERRY
SWEET TEMPER
SWEET THINGS
SWELLED HEAD
SWIFT GLANCE
SWIFT OF FOOT
SWISS CANTON
SWISS CHALET
SWISS CHEESE
SWISS GUARDS
SWISS RESORT
SWIVEL CHAIR
SWOLLEN HEAD
SWORD IN HAND
SWORD THRUST
SYDNEY SMITH

SYRUP OF FIGS

T – 11

TABLE FOR TWO
TABLE TENNIS
TACTICAL WAR
TAINTED GOLD
TAKE A CENSUS
TAKE A CHANCE
TAKE A CORNER
TAKE A COURSE
TAKE A CRUISE
TAKE A DEGREE
TAKE A GANDER
TAKE A HEADER
TAKE A LETTER
TAKE AN OFFER
TAKE A NUMBER
TAKE A PLEDGE
TAKE A POWDER
TAKE A STROLL
TAKE A TICKET
TAKE A TUMBLE
TAKE A WICKET
TAKE BY FORCE
TAKE BY STORM
TAKE CAPTIVE
TAKE CHANCES
TAKE COMFORT
TAKE COMMAND
TAKE COUNSEL
TAKE COURAGE
TAKE LESSONS
TAKE LIGHTLY
TAKE NO RISKS
TAKE OFFENCE
TAKE ON BOARD
TAKE ONE'S CUE
TAKE ON TRUST
TAKE ON WATER
TAKE-OVER BID
TAKE POT-LUCK
TAKE SHELTER
TAKE STOCK OF
TAKE THE BAIT
TAKE THE CAKE
TAKE THE HELM
TAKE THE HINT
TAKE THE LEAD
TAKE THE LIFT
TAKE THE OATH
TAKE THE VEIL
TAKE THOUGHT
TAKE TIME OFF
TAKE TO COURT

TAKE TO DRINK
TAKE TO HEART
TAKE TOO MUCH
TAKE TROUBLE
TAKE UMBRAGE
TAKE UP A CASE
TAKE WARNING
TALENT MONEY
TALENT SCOUT
TALKING BIRD
TALKING DOLL
TALKING SHOP
TALK OUT TIME
TALK RUBBISH
TALK TOO MUCH
TALK TREASON
TALK TWADDLE
TALL AND SLIM
TALLEST GIRL
TAMMANY HALL
TAM O'SHANTER
TANK WARFARE
TAPE MACHINE
TAP ONE'S FEET
TAP ONE'S FOOT
TAP THE WIRES
TARRY AWHILE
TARTAN PLAID
TARTAN SHIRT
TARTAN SKIRT
TARTAN SOCKS
TASTY MORSEL
TATE GALLERY
TAX INCREASE
TEA AND CAKES
TEA AND TOAST
TEA CANISTER
TEACHER'S PET
TEACH SCHOOL
TEACH TO READ
TEACH TO RIDE
TEACH TO SWIM
TEA FOR THREE
TEA INTERVAL
TEAM CAPTAIN
TEA MERCHANT
TEAM OF MULES
TEAM SUPPORT
TEAR ASUNDER
TEARS OF PITY
TEARS OF RAGE
TEA STRAINER
TEA WITH MILK
TEDIOUS TASK
TEDIOUS WORK
TEEMING RAIN

TEEN-AGE CLUB
TEETH ON EDGE
TELEGRAM BOY
TELL AGAINST
TELL NO TALES
TELL THE TALE
TELL THE TIME
TEMPLE BELLS
TEMPUS FUGIT
TEN AND A HALF
TENDER HEART
TENDER MERCY
TENDER STEAK
TENDER YEARS
TEND THE SICK
TENNIS COURT
TENNIS DRESS
TENNIS ELBOW
TENNIS MATCH
TEN OF HEARTS
TEN OF SPADES
TEN OF TRUMPS
TEN OR ELEVEN
TENSE MOMENT
TENTH LETTER
TENTH OF JULY
TENTH OF JUNE
TEN THOUSAND
TENTH STOREY
TENTH VOLUME
TERM OF ABUSE
TERM OF YEARS
TERSE SPEECH
TEST CRICKET
TESTING TIME
TEST OF SKILL
THAMES BASIN
THANK HEAVEN!
THAT IS TO SAY
THAT'S THE WAY
THAT'S TORN IT
THE ALMIGHTY
THE ALPHABET
THE ATLANTIC
THEATRE BILL
THEATRE CLUB
THEATRE LAND
THEATRE SEAT
THEATRE SHOW
THE AVENGERS
THE BARBICAN
THE BASTILLE
THE BEREAVED
THE BEST PART
THE BIG HOUSE
THE BISMARCK

THE BITER BIT	THE MINORITY	THINK IT OVER
THE BLUE LAMP	THE MOHICANS	THINK MUCH OF
THE BOAT RACE	THE MONUMENT	THINK WELL OF
THE CANARIES	THE MOUNTIES	THIN RED LINE
THE CENOTAPH	THE NAKED EYE	THIRD CHOICE
THE CHAMPION	THE NEAR EAST	THIRD COURSE
THE CHEVIOTS	THE NEW WORLD	THIRD DEGREE
THE CLASSICS	THE NINETIES	THIRD ESTATE
THE COLONIES	THE OBSERVER	THIRD FINGER
THE CONQUEST	THE OCCIDENT	THIRD LEAGUE
THE CREATION	THE OLD FOLKS	THIRD LESSON
THE CRUEL SEA	THE OLD GUARD	THIRD LETTER
THE CRUSADES	THE OLD WORLD	THIRD OF JULY
THE DAY AFTER	THE ONCE-OVER	THIRD OF JUNE
THE EIGHTIES	THE OPEN ROAD	THIRD PERSON
THE ELEMENTS	THE OTHER DAY	THIRD SEASON
THE FAITHFUL	THE OTHER MAN	THIRD STOREY
THE FINE ARTS	THE OTHER ONE	THIRD STROKE
THE FIRST TWO	THE OTHER WAY	THIRD VOLUME
THE FUGITIVE	THE PANTHEON	THIRST AFTER
THE GAME IS UP	THE PENNINES	THIRSTY WORK
THE GREATEST	THE PENTAGON	THIRTY FORTY
THE GREAT WAR	THE PROPHETS	THIRTY MILES
THE GREEN MAN	THE PYRAMIDS	THIRTY TIMES
THE GOLD RUSH	THE PYRENEES	THIRTY YEARS
THE GOOD BOOK	THE REVEREND	THIS AND THAT
THE HAVE-NOTS	THERMAL UNIT	THIS CENTURY
THE HEBRIDES	THE SERVICES	THIS DAY WEEK
THE HIGH SEAS	THE SKIN GAME	THIS ENGLAND
THE HOLY CITY	THE SORBONNE	THIS INSTANT
THE HOLY LAND	THESPIAN ART	THIS MORNING
THE HUNT IS UP	THE SQUEAKER	THIS TUESDAY
THE HUSTINGS	THE SUPREMES	THOMAS HARDY
THE INFINITE	THE TAJ MAHAL	THRASH IT OUT
THE INKSPOTS	THE TALISMAN	THREAD BEADS
THE INNER MAN	THE THIRD MAN	THREAT OF WAR
THE INNOCENT	THE THIRTIES	THREE A PENNY
THE INTERIOR	THE TWENTIES	THREE CHEERS
THE JUNGFRAU	THE TREASURY	THREE COPIES
THE KATTEGAT	THE UNIVERSE	THREE DECKER
THE KING AND I	THE VERY FACT	THREE EIGHTS
THE LAST GASP	THE VERY SAME	THREE FIFTHS
THE LAST PAGE	THE VERY SPOT	THREE GRACES
THE LAST POST	THE WALL GAME	THREE HEARTS
THE LAST WORD	THE WAXWORKS	THREE KNAVES
THE LIBERALS	THE WELL-TO-DO	THREE MONTHS
THE LISTENER	THE WHOLE HOG	THREE O'CLOCK
THE LOVED ONE	THE WHOLE LOT	THREE OR FOUR
THE LOWLANDS	THE WILD DUCK	THREE OUNCES
THE LUDDITES	THE WOOLSACK	THREE POINTS
THE MAJORITY	THICK SPEECH	THREE POUNDS
THE MARATHON	THICK STRING	THREE QUARTS
THE MIDLANDS	THIEF OF TIME	THREE QUEENS
THE MILKY WAY	THIN AS A LATH	THREE SEVENS
THE MIND'S EYE	THIN AS A RAKE	THREE SPADES
THE MINISTRY	THINKING CAP	THREE TENTHS

THREE THREES	TOBOGGAN RUN	TRADE SECRET
THREE TRICKS	TODDLE ALONG	TRADING POST
THREE WHEELS	TOFFEE APPLE	TRAFFIC LANE
THREE WISHES	TOILET WATER	TRAGIC EVENT
THREE VERSES	TOKEN OF LOVE	TRAGIC IRONY
THRESH ABOUT	TOLL THE BELL	TRAGIC SCENE
THROUGH ROAD	TOMATO JUICE	TRAIL BEHIND
THROUGH TRIP	TOMATO SAUCE	TRAIL BLAZER
THROW A LIGHT	TOMMY ATKINS	TRAIL DRIVER
THROW A PARTY	TOMMY COOPER	TRAIL OF DUST
THROW A PUNCH	TOMMY DORSEY	TRAIL OF SAND
THROW STONES	TOMMY STEELE	TRAINED BAND
THRUST ASIDE	TOMMY TUCKER	TRAMPLE DOWN
THUMPING LIE	TONE CONTROL	TRANSFER FEE
TICKLED PINK	TONE OF VOICE	TRAVEL ABOUT
TICKLE TROUT	TON OF BRICKS	TRAVEL AGENT
TICKLISH JOB	TO NO PURPOSE	TRAVEL ALONG
TIDAL WATERS	TONS AND TONS	TRAVEL LIGHT
TIDE ONE OVER	TONS OF MONEY	TREACLE TART
TIED COTTAGE	TONY HANCOCK	TREAD SOFTLY
TIED IN A KNOT	TOO FAMILIAR	TREAD WARILY
TIES OF BLOOD	TOO MUCH ROOM	TREE DWELLER
TIGHT CORNER	TOP-BACK ROOM	TREE SURGERY
TILL THE SOIL	TOPICAL NEWS	TRENCH FEVER
TIMBER TRADE	TOP SERGEANT	TRENT BRIDGE
TIME AND TIDE	TOP TO BOTTOM	TRIAL BY JURY
TIME ELEMENT	TORCH SINGER	TRIAL FLIGHT
TIME IS MONEY	TORPEDO BOAT	TRIAL PERIOD
TIME MACHINE	TORPEDO TUBE	TRIAL STAKES
TIME OF NIGHT	TOSS AND TURN	TRICK RIDING
TIMES CHANGE	TOTAL AMOUNT	TRIED BY JURY
TIMES SQUARE	TOTAL CHANGE	TRIM THE HAIR
TIME TO GET UP	TOTAL DEFEAT	TRIM THE LAMP
TIME TO LEAVE	TOTAL NUMBER	TRIM THE WICK
TIME TO SPARE	TOTAL OUTPUT	TRINITY HALL
TIME TO START	TO THE BOTTOM	TRINITY TERM
TIME TO THINK	TO THE LETTER	TRIPLE CROWN
TIME TO WASTE	TO THE MINUTE	TRIPLE EVENT
TINKER'S CUSS	TO THE RESCUE	TRIP LIGHTLY
TINKER'S DAMN	TO THE TUNE OF	TRITE REMARK
TINNED BEANS	TO THE UTMOST	TRIUMPH OVER
TINNED FRUIT	TOTTER ABOUT	TRIVIAL LOSS
TINNED GOODS	TOUCH BOTTOM	TROJAN HORSE
TINNED MUSIC	TOUCH GROUND	TROPICAL KIT
TINNED PEARS	TOUCH TYPING	TROPICAL SEA
TIN OF POLISH	TOUCH TYPIST	TROPICAL SUN
TIN OF SALMON	TOUGH AS TEAK	TROUBLE FREE
TIN PAN ALLEY	TOUR DE FORCE	TROUBLE SPOT
TIN SOLDIERS	TOUSLED HAIR	TROUT STREAM
TIP THE SCALE	TOUT DE SUITE	TRUCK DRIVER
TIRED OF LIFE	TOUT LE MONDE	TRUDGE ALONG
TISSUE PAPER	TOWER BRIDGE	TRUE ACCOUNT
TITLE HOLDER	TOWER OF PISA	TRUE COLOURS
TOAST MASTER	TOWN AND GOWN	TRUE EQUINOX
TOBACCO DUTY	TOWN COUNCIL	TRUE PICTURE
TOBACCO ROAD	TOWN DWELLER	TRUE READING

TRUE TO SCALE
TRULY SPOKEN
TRUMPET CALL
TRUNDLE DOWN
TRUST TO LUCK
TRUSTY STEED
TRUSTY SWORD
TRUTH TO TELL
TRYING TIMES
TRY ONE'S BEST
TRY ONE'S HAND
TRY ONE'S LUCK
TRY TO BE FAIR
TRY TO PLEASE
TRY, TRY AGAIN
TUBE STATION
TUDOR PERIOD
TUESDAY WEEK
TUFT OF GRASS
TUITION FEES
TURKISH BATH
TURN AGAINST
TURN CRIMSON
TURN HOSTILE
TURN OF SPEED
TURN OUT WELL
TURN THE PAGE
TURN THE TIDE
TURN TO ASHES
TURN TO STONE
TURN TRAITOR
TURN UPWARDS
TWEED JACKET
TWELFTH HOLE
TWELFTH HOUR
TWELFTH PART
TWELVE DOZEN
TWELVE GROSS
TWELVE HOURS
TWELVE MILES
TWELVE PARTS
TWELVE SCORE
TWELVE TIMES
TWELVE WEEKS
TWELVE YEARS
TWENTY MILES
TWENTY TIMES
TWENTY TO ONE
TWENTY WEEKS
TWICE A MONTH
TWICE AS MUCH
TWICE AS NICE
TWICE ELEVEN
TWICE THE MAN
TWICE TWELVE
TWICE WEEKLY

TWICE YEARLY
TWIN BROTHER
TWIN SISTERS
TWIST AROUND
TWIST THE ARM
TWO AND A HALF
TWO DIAMONDS
TWO EXTREMES
TWO-FEET TALL
TWO-FOOT RULE
TWO FURLONGS
TWO HUSBANDS
TWO NO-TRUMPS
TWO OF A TRADE
TWO OF SPADES
TWO OF TRUMPS
TWO'S COMPANY
TWO SEVENTHS
TWO THOUSAND
TYPE A LETTER
TYPICAL CASE
TYPING ERROR
TYPING SPEED
TYPISTS' POOL
TYROLEAN HAT

U – 11

UGLY RUFFIAN
UGLY SISTERS
UGLY THOUGHT
UGLY WEATHER
ULTIMATE END
ULTIMA THULE
ULTRA VIOLET
UMBRELLA MAN
UNABLE TO PAY
UNBROKEN RUN
UNCALLED FOR
UNDER A CLOUD
UNDER A CURSE
UNDER ARREST
UNDER A SPELL
UNDER CANVAS
UNDER DURESS
UNDER NOTICE
UNDER ORDERS
UNDER PAROLE
UNDER REPAIR
UNDER REVIEW
UNDER STRAIN
UNDER STRESS
UNDER THE MAT
UNDER THE SEA
UNDER THE SUN
UNDER WEIGHT

UNDYING LOVE
UNEASY TRUCE
UNFAIR MEANS
UNFAIR PRICE
UNFIT FOR USE
UNFOLD A TALE
UNHOLY NOISE
UNIFORM HEAT
UNIFORM SIZE
UNION LEADER
UNITED FRONT
UNITED PRESS
UNIT OF SOUND
UNLAWFUL ACT
UNLICKED CUB
UNLUCKY STAR
UNSHED TEARS
UNSOUND MIND
UNTIMELY END
UNUSUAL NAME
UP AGAINST IT
UP AND COMING
UP FOR THE CUP
UP FOR THE DAY
UPHILL CLIMB
UPHILL FIGHT
UP ON A CHARGE
UPPER CIRCLE
UPPER SCHOOL
UPPER STOREY
UPRIGHT POST
UPS AND DOWNS
UP THE REBELS!
UP THE STAIRS
UP THE STREET
UP THE THAMES
UP TO SCRATCH
UP TO THE EARS
UP TO THE EYES
UP TO THE HILT
UP TO THE MARK
UP TO THE NECK
UPWARD TREND
URSULA BLOOM
USELESS WORD
USE ONE'S EARS
USE ONE'S HEAD
USE ONE'S LOAF
USE ONE'S WITS
USE THE KNIFE
USE THE 'PHONE
USE THE PRESS
USE VIOLENCE
USUAL CUSTOM
UTMOST SPEED
UTTER BUNKUM

UTTER COWARD
UTTER DEFEAT
UTTER MISERY

V – 11

VACANT HOUSE
VACANT STARE
VACUUM BRAKE
VACUUM FLASK
VAGRANCY ACT
VAIN ATTEMPT
VAL DOONICAN
VALE OF TEARS
VALID REASON
VALLEY FORGE
VANITY TABLE
VAPOUR TRAIL
VARIETY SHOW
VAST ACREAGE
VAST EXPANSE
VAST EXPENSE
VATICAN CITY
VAULTED ROOF
VELVET GLOVE
VELVET TREAD
VENETIAN RED
VENUS DI MILO
VERY PLEASED
VERY SPECIAL
VERY STRANGE
VERY WELL OFF
VERY WORRIED
VESTA TILLEY
V FOR VICTORY
VICAR OF BRAY
VICTORIA DAY
VICTORY ROLL
VICTORY SIGN
VIDEO CAMERA
VIDEO SIGNAL
VIENNA WOODS
VILLAGE FÉTE
VILLAGE HALL
VILLAGE LIFE
VILLAGE POND
VILLAGE PUMP
VILLAGE SHOP
VILLAGE TALK
VILLAGE TEAM
VINTAGE PORT
VINTAGE WINE
VINTAGE YEAR
VIOLENT BLOW
VIOLENT RAGE
VIRGIN BIRTH

VIRGIN QUEEN
VIRILE STYLE
VISITING DAY
VITAL ENERGY
VITAMIN PILL
VIVID COLOUR
VIVID YELLOW
VIVIEN LEIGH
VOCAL CHORDS
VOCAL EFFORT
VOCAL NUMBER
VOCAL ORGANS
VOCAL TALENT
VOICE OF DOOM
VOID OF SENSE
VOLATILE OIL
VOLATILE WIT
VOLCANIC ASH
VOLUME THREE
VOTE AGAINST
VOTE BY PROXY
VOTE LIBERAL
VOTE TO ORDER
VOTING PAPER

W – 11

WADDLE ALONG
WADE THROUGH
WAG ONE'S HEAD
WAGON WHEELS
WAILING WALL
WAIT A MINUTE
WAIT A MOMENT
WAIT A SECOND
WAIT AT TABLE
WAITING GAME
WAITING LIST
WAITING ROOM
WAKE THE DEAD
WAKE UP EARLY
WAKING DREAM
WAKING HOURS
WALK IN FRONT
WALKING PACE
WALKING RACE
WALKING TOUR
WALK OFF WITH
WALK OUT WITH
WALK QUICKLY
WALK TOWARDS
WALK UPRIGHT
WALL OF DEATH
WALL OF FLAME
WALLOW IN MUD
WALTER MITTY

WALTER SCOTT
WALT WHITMAN
WANDER ABOUT
WANDER ALONG
WANING LIGHT
WANT OF FAITH
WAR AND PEACE
WAR CRIMINAL
WARD OF COURT
WARD ORDERLY
WARM AS TOAST
WARM CLIMATE
WARM CLOTHES
WARM COUNTRY
WAR MEASURES
WAR MEMORIAL
WAR MINISTER
WARM WEATHER
WARM WELCOME
WAR NEUROSES
WARNING LOOK
WARNING NOTE
WARNING SHOT
WARNING SIGN
WAR OF NERVES
WARP AND WEFT
WARP AND WOOF
WASHING SOAP
WASHING SODA
WASTE GROUND
WASTE NO TIME
WASTE OF TIME
WATCHFUL EYE
WATCH POCKET
WATCH POINTS
WATER BABIES
WATER COLOUR
WATERED SILK
WATERLOO CUP
WATER OF LIFE
WATER PISTOL
WATER SKIING
WATER SPORTS
WATER SUPPLY
WATER TRAVEL
WATER VAPOUR
WATERY GRAVE
WAVE GOODBYE
WEAK AS WATER
WEAKEST LINK
WEAK LOOKING
WEAK SERVICE
WEAK STOMACH
WEALD OF KENT
WEAR AND TEAR
WEARY WILLIE

WEATHER SHIP	WHISTLE STOP	WINE HARVEST
WEATHER SIDE	WHITE AS MILK	WINE VINEGAR
WEAVE A SPELL	WHITE AS SNOW	WINGED HORSE
WEAVE SPELLS	WHITE BISHOP	WINGED WORDS
WEB OF DECEIT	WHITE CASTLE	WING FORWARD
WEDDED BLISS	WHITE CIRCLE	WING ONE'S WAY
WEDDING CAKE	WHITE CLIFFS	WINK OF SLEEP
WEDDING CARD	WHITE COFFEE	WINNING CARD
WEDDING HYMN	WHITE COLLAR	WINNING GAME
WEDDING RING	WHITE COTTON	WINNING GOAL
WEDDING VOWS	WHITE ENSIGN	WINNING HAND
WEEKLY PAPER	WHITE FRIARS	WINNING LEAD
WEEK'S NOTICE	WHITE HORSES	WINNING LINE
WEIGH ANCHOR	WHITE KNIGHT	WINNING MOVE
WEIRD SISTER	WHITE PEPPER	WINNING POST
WELCOME GIFT	WHITE POWDER	WINNING SHOT
WELCOME HOME	WHITE RABBIT	WINNING SIDE
WELCOME SIGN	WHITE RIBBON	WINNING TEAM
WELFARE WORK	WHITE RUSSIA	WINNING TOSS
WELL AND GOOD	WHITE SQUARE	WINNING WAYS
WELL CONTENT	WHITE TO MOVE	WIN ON POINTS
WELL GROOMED	WHITE TO PLAY	WIN OUTRIGHT
WELL IN FRONT	WHITSUN WEEK	WINSOME WAYS
WELL MATCHED	WHITTLE AWAY	WINSON GREEN
WELL OUT OF IT	WHITTLE DOWN	WINTER SLEEP
WELL-READ MAN	WHO GOES HOME?	WINTER WHEAT
WELL-TO-DO MAN	WHOLE NUMBER	WIN THE FIGHT
WELL WORTH IT	WICKED FAIRY	WIN THE MATCH
WELL WRITTEN	WICKED UNCLE	WIN THE POOLS
WELSH ACCENT	WICKED WITCH	WIN THE TITLE
WELSH BORDER	WICKED WORLD	WIN THE TRICK
WELSH COLLIE	WICKER CHAIR	WINTRY SMILE
WELSH GUARDS	WIDEN THE GAP	WIPE THE EYES
WELSH LEGEND	WIDE READING	WIRELESS SET
WELSH RABBIT	WIDE VARIETY	WISDOM TOOTH
WELSH WIZARD	WIDOW'S CRUSE	WISE AS AN OWL
WEND ONE'S WAY	WIDOW'S WEEDS	WISE AS SOLON
WENT FLAT OUT	WIELD THE BAT	WISE COUNSEL
WEST AFRICAN	WIGHTMAN CUP	WISE OLD BIRD
WEST BY NORTH	WILD COUNTRY	WISHING WELL
WEST BY SOUTH	WILD DELIGHT	WITCH DOCTOR
WEST CENTRAL	WILD FLOWERS	WITCHES' BREW
WEST COUNTRY	WILFUL WASTE	WITCH'S SPELL
WESTERN ROLE	WILLIAM PEAR	WITH ABANDON
WESTERN ROLL	WILLIAM PENN	WITH HONOURS
WEST GERMANY	WILLIAM PITT	WITHIN AN ACE
WET ONE'S LIPS	WILLIAM TELL	WITHIN DOORS
WHACKING LIE	WILLING HAND	WITHIN RANGE
WHAT A RELIEF!	WILLING HELP	WITHIN REACH
WHAT HAVE YOU	WILL OF ALLAH	WITHIN SIGHT
WHAT'S MY LINE?	WILL SCARLET	WITH KNOBS ON
WHAT YOU WILL	WIN A FORTUNE	WITH MEANING
WHEEL OF LIFE	WINDING ROAD	WITHOUT BIAS
WHEN PIGS FLY	WIND ONE'S WAY	WITHOUT FAIL
WHIPPING BOY	WINDY CORNER	WITHOUT HOPE
WHISTLE AWAY	WINE AND DINE	WITHOUT LOSS

WITHOUT PEER
WITHOUT PITY
WITH RESERVE
WITH RESPECT
WITH THE TIDE
WITH THE WIND
WITTY REMARK
WITTY RETORT
WITTY SPEECH
WIZARD PRANG
WOBURN ABBEY
WOLF WHISTLE
WOMAN DOCTOR
WOMAN DRIVER
WOMAN'S WORLD
WOMEN POLICE
WOMEN'S GUILD
WOOD ALCOHOL
WOODEN FRAME
WOODEN HORSE
WOODEN SPOON
WOOL SHEARER
WORD FOR WORD
WORD OF MOUTH
WORD PERFECT
WORD PICTURE
WORDS FAIL ME!
WORK AGAINST
WORK AND PLAY
WORK AS A TEAM
WORKING LIFE
WORKING WEEK
WORKS OUTING
WORK TO DEATH
WORK WONDERS
WORLD BEATER
WORLD CRUISE
WORLD EVENTS
WORLDLY WISE
WORLD RECORD
WORLDS APART
WORLD TO COME
WORLD-WAR ONE
WORLD-WAR TWO
WORM ONE'S WAY
WORRIED LOOK
WORSE TO COME
WORTH SEEING
WORTHY CAUSE
WRAPPED LOAF
WRESTLE WITH
WRETCHED MAN
WRINGING WET
WRITE A LYRIC
WRITE A NOVEL
WRITE A STORY

WRITE IT DOWN
WRITE POETRY
WRITING DESK
WRITING ROOM
WRITTEN WORD
WRONG ANSWER
WRONG CHANGE
WRONG COURSE
WRONG MOMENT
WRONG NUMBER
WRONG PERSON
WRONG TICKET
WROUGHT IRON

Y – 11

YACHTING CAP
YACHT RACING
YARD MEASURE
YEAR AND A DAY
YEAR OF GRACE
YEARS GONE BY
YEARS TO COME
YELLOW FEVER
YELLOW METAL
YELLOW OCHRE
YELLOW PAINT
YELLOW PERIL
YELLOW PRESS
YELLOW RIVER
YELLOW SANDS
YELLOW SPOTS
YIELD A POINT
YOLK OF AN EGG
YORK MINSTER
YOU AND YOURS
YOUNG AND OLD
YOUNGEST BOY
YOUNGEST SON
YOUNG MONKEY
YOUNG PEOPLE
YOUNG PERSON
YOUNG RASCAL
YOUR MAJESTY
YOUR OPINION
YOURS ALWAYS
YOUR VERSION
YOUR VERY OWN
YOUR WORSHIP
YOUTH CENTRE
YOUTH HOSTEL
YOUTH LEADER

A – 12

ABBEY THEATRE

ABILITY TO MIX
ABJECT SPIRIT
ABLATIVE CASE
ABOUT AVERAGE
ABOVE AVERAGE
ABOVE THE LINE
ABRUPT MANNER
ABSOLUTE COLD
ABSOLUTE FACT
ABSOLUTE FOOL
ABSOLUTE RULE
ABSOLUTE ZERO
ABSTRACT IDEA
ABSTRACT NOUN
ABSTRACT TERM
ABSURD MANNER
ABUSE THE MIND
ACADEMY AWARD
ACCEPT ADVICE
ACCEPT DEFEAT
ACCEPT IN TOTO
ACCEPT OFFICE
ACCIDENT SPOT
ACE IN THE HOLE
ACHILLES' HEEL
ACROSS THE SKY
ACROSS THE WAY
ACT FOOLISHLY
ACT IN CONCERT
ACTION SCHOOL
ACTIVE MEMBER
ACT LIKE A FOOL
ACT LIKE MAGIC
ACT OF CHARITY
ACT OF COURAGE
ACT OF TREASON
ACT OF WORSHIP
ACT OF IMPULSE
ACTOR MANAGER
ADAGIO DANCER
ADD A FEW WORDS
ADDER'S TONGUE
ADDITION SIGN
ADD TO THE LIST
ADELINA PATTI
ADHESIVE TAPE
ADJUTANT BIRD
ADMIT NOTHING
ADMIT ONE'S AGE
ADMITTED FACT
ADMITTED FREE
ADOPTED CHILD
ADVANCED IDEA
ADVANCE GUARD
ADVANCE PARTY
AERATED WATER

AERIAL SURVEY	ALL OR NOTHING	ANYTHING GOES
AESOP'S FABLES	ALLOTTED SPAN	APOSTLE SPOON
AFFECTED AIRS	ALLOTTED TASK	APPEAL TO ARMS
A FINE ROMANCE	ALLOW TO STAND	APPLE BLOSSOM
AFRICAN QUEEN	ALL SAINTS' DAY	APPLE FRITTER
AFTERNOON NAP	ALL STEAMED UP	APPLE HARVEST
AFTERNOON TEA	ALL THE BETTER	APPLE OF SODOM
AFTER SUNDOWN	ALL THE FAMILY	APPLE ORCHARD
AFTER THE BALL	ALL THE OTHERS	APPLY FOR A JOB
AFTER THE FACT	ALL TO PLAY FOR	APPLY FOR BAIL
AFTER THE RAIN	ALL TO THE GOOD	APPLY ONESELF
AGE OF CONSENT	ALMOND TOFFEE	APPLY THE MIND
AGREED RESULT	A LONG TIME AGO	APPROACH ROAD
AGREE TO TERMS	ALPACA JACKET	APPROACH SHOT
AIM AT THE MOON	ALPHA TO OMEGA	APPROVED LIST
AIR COMMODORE	ALPINE FLOWER	APRIL IN PARIS
AIR-FORCE BLUE	ALPINE GARDEN	APRIL SHOWERS
AIR OF MYSTERY	ALTER THE CASE	APRON STRINGS
AIR OF TRIUMPH	AMATEUR ACTOR	APTITUDE TEST
AIR ONE'S VIEWS	AMATEUR BOXER	APT QUOTATION
AIR PASSENGER	AMATEUR STAGE	AQUATIC PLANT
AIR PERSONNEL	AMERICAN FILM	AQUATIC SPORT
AIR-SEA RESCUE	AMERICAN FLAG	AQUILINE NOSE
AIR TRANSPORT	AMERICAN NAVY	ARCH CRIMINAL
AIR TRAVELLER	A MILE A MINUTE	ARCH OF HEAVEN
ALADDIN'S CAVE	AMONG FRIENDS	ARCH ONE'S BACK
ALADDIN'S LAMP	AMOROUS DITTY	ARCTIC CIRCLE
ALAN MELVILLE	AMUSE ONESELF	ARCTIC REGION
ALAS AND ALACK!	ANCHOVY PASTE	ARCTIC WINTER
ALBERT BRIDGE	ANCHOVY SAUCE	ARDENT SPIRIT
ALBERT FINNEY	ANCIENT HOUSE	ARGUE THE CASE
ALDOUS HUXLEY	ANCIENT ROMAN	ARGUE THE TOSS
ALEC GUINNESS	ANCIENT RUINS	ARMED ROBBERY
ALEXANDRA DAY	ANCIENT TIMES	ARMISTICE DAY
ALFRESCO MEAL	ANCIENT WORLD	ARMY CHAPLAIN
ALGERIAN WINE	ANEURIN BEVAN	ARMY EXERCISE
ALICE SPRINGS	ANGELIC SMILE	ARMY GRATUITY
ALIEN ELEMENT	ANGEL OF DEATH	ARMY PAY CORPS
ALIGN ONESELF	ANGEL OF MERCY	ARMY QUARTERS
ALL AND SUNDRY	ANGELS OF MONS	ARNOLD WESKER
ALL ATTENTION	ANGORA RABBIT	ARRANGE A DATE
ALL BY ONESELF	ANGRY SILENCE	ARRESTER GEAR
ALLIED FORCES	ANIMAL DOCTOR	ARRIVE ON TIME
ALLIED TROOPS	ANNA KARENINA	ART CRITICISM
ALL IN THE GAME	ANNE HATHAWAY	ARTERIAL ROAD
ALL IN THE MIND	ANNE OF CLEVES	ARTESIAN WELL
ALL IS NOT LOST	ANNUAL AFFAIR	ARTFUL DODGER
ALL MOONSHINE	ANNUAL BUDGET	ARTHUR MILLER
ALL MY OWN WORK	ANNUAL DINNER	ARTISTIC WORK
ALL NIGHT LONG	ANNUAL OUTING	ARTIST'S MODEL
ALL OF A DITHER	ANNUAL REPORT	ARTIST'S PROOF
ALL OF A QUIVER	ANNUAL RETURN	ART OF DEFENCE
ALL OF A SUDDEN	ANOTHER GUESS	ART OF HEALING
ALL OF THE TIME	ANOTHER STORY	ART TREASURES
ALL ON ONE SIDE	ANOTHER THING	ASBESTOS SUIT
ALL ON ONE'S OWN	ANY QUESTIONS	AS BLACK AS INK

AS BUSY AS A BEE	AVERAGE SPEED	BALKAN STATES
ASCENSION DAY	AVERAGE WOMAN	BALLAD SINGER
AS CLEAR AS DAY	AWAIT PAYMENT	BALL AND CHAIN
AS CLEAR AS MUD	AWAKE THE DEAD	BALL BEARINGS
ASCOT GOLD CUP	AWAY DULL CARE!	BALLET DANCER
AS GOOD AS DEAD	AWAY FROM HOME	BALLET MASTER
AS GOOD AS EVER	AWFUL SILENCE	BALLET SCHOOL
AS GOOD AS GOLD	AWKWARD SQUAD	BALL OF STRING
ASHES TO ASHES		BALL OF THREAD
ASH WEDNESDAY		BALL-POINT PEN
ASK A QUESTION	B – 12	BALM OF GILEAD
ASK FOR ADVICE		BALTIC STATES
ASK FOR CREDIT	BABY CARRIAGE	BAMBOO SHOOTS
ASK ME ANOTHER	BABY SNATCHER	BANBURY CROSS
ASK NO FAVOURS	BACHELOR FLAT	BAND OF HEROES
ASK QUESTIONS	BACHELOR GIRL	BAND TOGETHER
AS LIGHT AS AIR	BACK AND FORTH	BANG IN THE EYE
AS MUCH AS EVER	BACK AND FRONT	BANG ONE'S HEAD
ASSEMBLY HALL	BACK ENTRANCE	BANKER'S DRAFT
ASSEMBLY LINE	BACKING STORE	BANKER'S ORDER
ASSEMBLY ROOM	BACK OF BEYOND	BANKING HOURS
ASSUMED TITLE	BACK-ROOM BOYS	BANK INTEREST
AS SURE AS EGGS	BACK THE FIELD	BARBARY COAST
AS SURE AS FATE	BACK TO MOTHER	BARBARY SHEEP
AS SWEET AS PIE	BACK TO NATURE	BARBER'S CHAIR
AS UNDERSTOOD	BACK TO NORMAL	BARCLAYS BANK
AT A LATER DATE	BACKWARD STEP	BARE CUPBOARD
AT ALL HAZARDS	BACON AND EGGS	BAREFACED LIE
AT ARM'S LENGTH	BAD BEGINNING	BARE MAJORITY
AT CLOSE GRIPS	BAD BEHAVIOUR	BARE ONE'S HEAD
AT DEATH'S DOOR	BAD CHARACTER	BARGAIN PRICE
AT FIRST SIGHT	BAD CONDUCTOR	BARKING CREEK
AT FULL GALLOP	BAD DIGESTION	BARNABY RUDGE
AT FULL LENGTH	BAD ELOCUTION	BARNACLE BILL
ATHLETE'S FOOT	BADGE OF MERIT	BARNES BRIDGE
ATLANTIC CITY	BAD HALFPENNY	BARNES COMMON
ATOMIC ENERGY	BAD HOUSEWIFE	BARNYARD FOWL
ATOMIC NUMBER	BAD INFLUENCE	BAROQUE STYLE
ATOMIC THEORY	BADLY BEHAVED	BARRED WINDOW
ATOMIC WEIGHT	BADLY DAMAGED	BARREL OF BEER
AT SECOND-HAND	BADLY WOUNDED	BARS AND BOLTS
AT SOME LENGTH	BAD NEIGHBOUR	BASEBALL TEAM
ATTAR OF ROSES	BAD OF ITS KIND	BASEMENT FLAT
ATTEND CHURCH	BAD QUALITIES	BASIC ENGLISH
AT THE LAUNDRY	BAD REPORTING	BASK IN THE SUN
AT THE SEASIDE	BAD TREATMENT	BASS CLARINET
AT THE STATION	BAG OF TOFFEES	BATCH OF BREAD
AT THE THEATRE	BAILEY BRIDGE	BATHING BEACH
AT THE WEIGH-IN	BAKED CUSTARD	BATTERING RAM
AT WHICH PLACE	BAKEWELL TART	BATTING ORDER
AUCTION ROOMS	BAKING POWDER	BATTLE OF LIFE
AULD LANG SYNE	BALANCED DIET	BATTLE OF WITS
AUSTIN FRIARS	BALANCED MIND	BAY AT THE MOON
AUSTIN CROCUS	BALANCE SHEET	BAYONET DRILL
AUTUMN CROCUS	BALANCE WHEEL	BEACH PYJAMAS
AUTUMN LEAVES	BALANCING ACT	BEAMING SMILE
AVERAGE CHILD	BALCONY SCENE	

BEANS ON TOAST
BEARDED WOMAN
BEAR DOWN UPON
BEARD THE LION
BEARER CHEQUE
BEAR THE BLAME
BEAR THE BRUNT
BEAT A RETREAT
BEATEN HOLLOW
BEATING HEART
BEAT THE CLOCK
BEAT THE COUNT
BEAUTY OF MIND
BECHER'S BROOK
BECOME PUBLIC
BECOME SILENT
BED OF NETTLES
BED-TIME STORY
BEEF SANDWICH
BEEF SAUSAGES
BEFORE CHRIST
BEFORE DINNER
BEFORE SUPPER
BEFORE THE WAR
BEG FOR CRUMBS
BEGGAR'S OPERA
BEHIND THE BAR
BELGIAN CONGO
BELOVED ENEMY
BELOW AVERAGE
BELOW THE BELT
BELOW THE KNEE
BELOW THE LINE
BELOW THE MARK
BENARES BRASS
BEND BACKWARD
BEND SINISTER
BEND THE ELBOW
BEND THE RULES
BENEFIT MATCH
BENEFIT NIGHT
BENIGN MANNER
BENNY GOODMAN
BE OFF WITH YOU!
BEREFT OF LIFE
BERING STRAIT
BERTRAM MILLS
BESETTING SIN
BESIDE THE SEA
BEST OF THE LOT
BEST ONE CAN DO
BETHNAL GREEN
BET ON THE SIDE
BETRAY A TRUST
BETTER CHOICE
BETTER THINGS

BETTING HOUSE
BETWEEN MEALS
BETWEEN TIMES
BEVERLY HILLS
BEXHILL ON SEA
BEYOND A DOUBT
BEYOND BELIEF
BEYOND BOUNDS
BEYOND REASON
BEYOND RECALL
BEYOND REPAIR
BEYOND THE LAW
BIB AND TUCKER
BIBLE SOCIETY
BIBLE THUMPER
BICYCLE CHAIN
BICYCLE THIEF
BIDE ONE'S TIME
BIG AND LITTLE
BIG HINDRANCE
BIG OFFENSIVE
BILLIARD BALL
BILLIARD HALL
BILLIARD REST
BILLIARD ROOM
BILL OF HEALTH
BILL OF LADING
BILL OF RIGHTS
BILLYCOCK HAT
BINARY NUMBER
BIRDCAGE WALK
BIRD'S-EYE VIEW
BIRD WATCHING
BIRTH CONTROL
BIRTHDAY CAKE
BIRTHDAY CARD
BIRTHDAY GIFT
BIRTHDAY SUIT
BISHOP'S APRON
BISHOP'S MITRE
BITE ONE'S LIPS
BITE THE THUMB
BIT OF AN UPSET
BIT OF SCANDAL
BIT OF TROUBLE
BITTERLY COLD
BITTER MEMORY
BITTER ORANGE
BITTER STRIFE
BITTER TONGUE
BLACK AND BLUE
BLACK AND TANS
BLACK AS NIGHT
BLACK AS PITCH
BLACK CLOTHES
BLACK COUNTRY

BLACK DESPAIR
BLACK LOOK-OUT
BLACK OR WHITE
BLACK OUTLOOK
BLACK PUDDING
BLADE OF GRASS
BLARNEY STONE
BLASTED HEATH
BLAST FURNACE
BLAZE OF GLORY
BLAZE OF LIGHT
BLEACHED HAIR
BLEAK OUTLOOK
BLEED TO DEATH
BLESSED STATE
BLIND BARGAIN
BLIND IMPULSE
BLITHE SPIRIT
BLOATER PASTE
BLOCK LETTERS
BLOCK OF FLATS
BLOCK OF STONE
BLONDE HAIRED
BLOOD AND IRON
BLOOD AND SAND
BLOOD BROTHER
BLOOD DISEASE
BLOOM OF YOUTH
BLOSSOM FORTH
BLOW A WHISTLE
BLOWN SKY-HIGH
BLOW OFF STEAM
BLOW TO PIECES
BLUE AS THE SKY
BLUE-BLACK INK
BLUE STOCKING
BLUE WITH COLD
BLUFF KING HAL
BOARD MEETING
BOARD OF TRADE
BOB MONKHOUSE
BOB UP AND DOWN
BODY OF TROOPS
BODY SNATCHER
BOHEMIAN GIRL
BOILED SWEETS
BOILING POINT
BOILING WATER
BOIL WITH RAGE
BOLT ONE'S FOOD
BOMB DISPOSAL
BONFIRE NIGHT
BONNY WEE LASS
BOOK A PASSAGE
BOOK A SLEEPER
BOOKING CLERK

BOOK LEARNING
BOOK OF PSALMS
BOOK OF STAMPS
BOOK OF WISDOM
BORDER BALLAD
BORED TO DEATH
BORED TO TEARS
BORIS KARLOFF
BORN IN A TRUNK
BORN OPTIMIST
BORROW A FIVER
BORROW A POUND
BORROWED TIME
BOSOM FRIENDS
BOTH ENDS MEET
BOTH TOGETHER
BOTTLED CIDER
BOTTLED FRUIT
BOTTLE OF BEER
BOTTLE OF HOCK
BOTTLE OF MILK
BOTTLE OF PORT
BOTTLE OF WINE
BOTTLE OPENER
BOTTOM DOLLAR
BOTTOM DRAWER
BOTTOM WEIGHT
BOULTER'S LOCK
BOUNCING BABY
BOUNDARY LINE
BOUND EDITION
BOW AND SCRAPE
BOWLING ALLEY
BOWLING GREEN
BOXING GLOVES
BOX OF MATCHES
BOX ON THE EARS
BOY ARTIFICER
BOY MEETS GIRL
BRACE OF BIRDS
BRACE ONESELF
BRAIN SURGEON
BRAIN SURGERY
BRAIN WASHING
BRAISED STEAK
BRAMBLE JELLY
BRANCH MEMBER
BRANCH OFFICE
BRANDED GOODS
BRANDING IRON
BRANDY BOTTLE
BRANDY BUTTER
BRASS SECTION
BRAVE AS A LION
BRAVE ATTEMPT
BRAVE WARRIOR

BREAD AND MILK
BREAD AND WINE
BREAD PUDDING
BREAK A RECORD
BREAK CONTACT
BREAKFAST CUP
BREAK NO BONES
BREAK RECORDS
BREAK SURFACE
BREAK THE BANK
BREAK THE NEWS
BREAK THE RULE
BREAK THE SEAL
BREAK THROUGH
BREAST POCKET
BREAST STROKE
BREATHE AGAIN
BREATH OF LIFE
BREECHES BUOY
BREEZY MANNER
BRICK BY BRICK
BRIDGE LESSON
BRIDGE PLAYER
BRIDGE THE GAP
BRIEF OUTLINE
BRIEF SUMMARY
BRIGADE MAJOR
BRIGHT COLOUR
BRIGHT LIGHTS
BRIGHTON ROCK
BRIGHT PERIOD
BRIGHT PURPLE
BRIGHT YELLOW
BRILLIANT WIT
BRING A CHARGE
BRING COMFORT
BRING FORWARD
BRING THROUGH
BRING TO A HEAD
BRING TO AN END
BRING TO LIGHT
BRING TO TERMS
BRING TO TRIAL
BRISTOL BOARD
BRISTOL CREAM
BRITISH ISLES
BROAD OUTLINE
BROAD OUTLOOK
BROKEN ACCENT
BROKEN GROUND
BROKEN THREAD
BROKEN VOYAGE
BROKEN WINDOW
BROOK NO DELAY
BROUGHT FORTH
BROWN AND MILD

BROWN WINDSOR
BRUCE FORSYTH
BRUIN THE BEAR
BRUSH AGAINST
BRUSH AND COMB
BRUSSELS LACE
BUCKING HORSE
BUDDHIST MONK
BUDDING ACTOR
BUDDING YOUTH
BUDGET SPEECH
BUGLE-CALL RAG
BUILD A BRIDGE
BUILDER'S MATE
BUILDING LAND
BUILDING PLOT
BUILDING SITE
BUILT OF STONE
BUILT ON A ROCK
BULBOUS PLANT
BULLDOG BREED
BULL ELEPHANT
BUNCH OF ROSES
BUNDLE OF RAGS
BUNSEN BURNER
BURGLAR ALARM
BURIAL GROUND
BURMA CHEROOT
BURNHAM SCALE
BURNING FEVER
BURNING GLASS
BURNING SHAME
BURNING TORCH
BURNT ALMONDS
BURNT FINGERS
BURNT TO ASHES
BURN WITH LOVE
BURST OF ANGER
BURST OF SOUND
BURST OF SPEED
BURY ONE'S HEAD
BUS CONDUCTOR
BUSINESS DEAL
BUSINESS LIFE
BUSINESS TRIP
BUSTER KEATON
BUTCHER'S SHOP
BUTTERED ROLL
BUTTERFLY NET
BUYER'S MARKET
BY A LONG CHALK
BY COMPARISON
BY EASY STAGES
BY FAR THE BEST
BY PERSUASION
BY THE SEASIDE

BY THE WAYSIDE
BY WAY OF A JOKE

C – 12

CABBAGE PATCH
CABIN CRUISER
CABINET MAKER
CABIN STEWARD
CABLE RAILWAY
CABLE'S LENGTH
CAFÉ CHANTANT
CAIRN TERRIER
CAKED WITH MUD
CALABASH PIPE
CALAMITY JANE
CALENDAR YEAR
CALL A MEETING
CALL FOR ORDER
CALL INTO PLAY
CALL IT SQUARE
CALL OF THE SEA
CALL THE BANNS
CALL TO PRAYER
CALL TO THE BAR
CALYPSO MUSIC
CAMP FOLLOWER
CANARY YELLOW
CANDID CAMERA
CANDID CRITIC
CANDID FRIEND
CANDLE GREASE
CANNON FODDER
CANNON STREET
CANON COLLINS
CANVEY ISLAND
CAPABLE HANDS
CAPE PROVINCE
CAPITAL ASSET
CAPITAL CRIME
CAPITAL GAINS
CAPITAL GOODS
CAPTAIN BLOOD
CAPTAIN SCOTT
CARAFE OF WINE
CARAWAY SEEDS
CARBOLIC ACID
CARBOLIC SOAP
CARDBOARD BOX
CARDINAL'S HAT
CAREFREE MIND
CAREFUL STUDY
CARELESS TALK
CARIBBEAN SEA
CARNEGIE HALL
CARNIVAL TIME

CARNIVAL WEEK
CARPET KNIGHT
CARRIAGE PAID
CARRY A REPORT
CARRY FORWARD
CARRY ONE'S BAT
CARRY THROUGH
CARTE BLANCHE
CARVING KNIFE
CASE OF MURDER
CASE OF SCOTCH
CASE OF WHISKY
CASE THE JOINT
CASE TO ANSWER
CASH AND CARRY
CASH CUSTOMER
CASH ON DEMAND
CASH REGISTER
CAST AWAY FEAR
CAST-IRON CASE
CAST ONE'S VOTE
CAST THE BLAME
CASUAL GLANCE
CASUAL LABOUR
CASUAL MANNER
CASUAL REMARK
CASUALTY LIST
CASUALTY WARD
CASUAL WORKER
CAT AND FIDDLE
CATCH A TARTAR
CATCH BENDING
CATCH NAPPING
CATCH SIGHT OF
CATCH THE POST
CATCH THE TUBE
CAT'S WHISKERS
CATTLE DEALER
CATTLE MARKET
CAUSE CÉLÈBRE
CAUSE OF DELAY
CAUSE OFFENCE
CAUSE TROUBLE
CAUTION MONEY
CAUTIOUS MOVE
CAUTIOUS TYPE
CAVALRY HORSE
CAVALRY TWILL
CAVEAT EMPTOR
CEASE TO EXIST
CEILING PRICE
CEMENT A UNION
CENTURIES OLD
CERTAIN DEATH
CERTAIN ISSUE
CERTAINLY NOT

CERTAIN PLACE
C'EST LA GUERRE
CHAISE LONGUE
CHALLENGE CUP
CHAMBER MUSIC
CHAMPAGNE CUP
CHANCE REMARK
CHANCERY LANE
CHANGE COLOUR
CHANGE COURSE
CHANGE HORSES
CHANGE OF DIET
CHANGE OF FACE
CHANGE OF LUCK
CHANGE OF MIND
CHANGE OF MOOD
CHANGE PLACES
CHANGE TRAINS
CHANGING ROOM
CHAOTIC STATE
CHAPTER HOUSE
CHAPTER THREE
CHARING CROSS
CHARITY MATCH
CHARLES BOYER
CHARLES PEACE
CHARLES READE
CHARLES'S WAIN
CHARLEY'S AUNT
CHARLIE DRAKE
CHARNEL HOUSE
CHARTER PARTY
CHARTER PLANE
CHASE SHADOWS
CHEAP-DAY FARE
CHEAP EDITION
CHEAP SUCCESS
CHEAP TWISTER
CHEAT AT CARDS
CHECK THE TILL
CHEDDAR GORGE
CHEEK TO CHEEK
CHEEKY MONKEY
CHEERFUL FIRE
CHEERFUL MOOD
CHEERY MANNER
CHEESE STRAWS
CHELSEA CHINA
CHEMICAL FUEL
CHEMICAL TEST
CHEMISTRY SET
CHEMIST'S SHOP
CHERISH HOPES
CHERRY BRANDY
CHESS OPENING
CHESS PROBLEM

CHESTNUT TREE
CHEVIOT HILLS
CHICKEN CURRY
CHICKEN LIVER
CHIEF CASHIER
CHIEF JUSTICE
CHIEF MOURNER
CHIEF OFFICER
CHIEF OF STAFF
CHIEF SKIPPER
CHIEF STEWARD
CHIEF SUSPECT
CHIEF WITNESS
CHILDE HAROLD
CHILDISH WAYS
CHILD PRODIGY
CHILDREN'S TOY
CHILD WELFARE
CHILLI PEPPER
CHILLY MANNER
CHIMNEY SWEEP
CHINA CABINET
CHINESE WHITE
CHOCOLATE BAR
CHOCOLATE BOX
CHOCOLATE EGG
CHOICE MORSEL
CHOOSE FREELY
CHOP AND CHIPS
CHOSEN CAREER
CHOSEN PEOPLE
CHRISTIAN ERA
CHRISTMAS BOX
CHRISTMAS DAY
CHRISTMAS EVE
CHROME YELLOW
CHUBBY CHEEKS
CHURCH BAZAAR
CHURCH LIVING
CHURCH MEMBER
CHURCH OF ROME
CHURCH PARADE
CHURCH SCHOOL
CIGARETTE ASH
CIGARETTE END
CIGARETTE TIN
CINEMA SCREEN
CINEMA STUDIO
CIRCLE AROUND
CIRCUIT COURT
CIRCUIT JUDGE
CIRCULAR TOUR
CITY ALDERMAN
CITY BOUNDARY
CITY MERCHANT
CITY OF LONDON

CIVIC WELCOME
CIVIL DEFENCE
CIVILIAN LIFE
CIVILIZED MAN
CIVIL LIBERTY
CIVIL SERVANT
CIVIL SERVICE
CLAIM A REWARD
CLAIM DAMAGES
CLAP THE HANDS
CLASH OF STEEL
CLASH OF VIEWS
CLASPED HANDS
CLASSICAL AGE
CLASSICAL ART
CLASSIC STYLE
CLASS WARFARE
CLEAN LICENCE
CLEAR AS A BELL
CLEAR OUTLINE
CLEAR PASSAGE
CLEAR THE PATH
CLEAR THE ROAD
CLEAR THE ROOM
CLEAR THOUGHT
CLEAR WARNING
CLEAR WEATHER
CLENCHED FIST
CLERICAL GARB
CLERICAL GREY
CLERICAL WORK
CLERK OF WORKS
CLEVER MANNER
CLEVER SPEECH
CLEVER STROKE
CLIFFORD'S INN
CLIFF RAILWAY
CLIFF RICHARD
CLIMB TO POWER
CLINGING VINE
CLING LIKE IVY
CLINK GLASSES
CLIPPED HEDGE
CLIP THE WINGS
CLIVE OF INDIA
CLOCK WATCHER
CLOCKWORK TOY
CLOSE BARGAIN
CLOSE CONTACT
CLOSE CONTEST
CLOSED CIRCLE
CLOSED DRAWER
CLOSE HARMONY
CLOSE TEXTURE
CLOSE THE DOOR
CLOSE THE EYES

CLOSE THE GATE
CLOSE TO DEATH
CLOSING PRICE
CLOSING WORDS
CLOTHES BRUSH
CLOTHES HORSE
CLOTHES SENSE
CLOTHING CLUB
CLOTTED CREAM
CLOUD EFFECTS
CLOUDLESS SKY
CLOUD OF SMOKE
CLOUD OF STEAM
CLUB OFFICIAL
CLUB SANDWICH
CLUB TOGETHER
CLUMP OF TREES
CLUTCH OF EGGS
COACH AND FOUR
COACH AND PAIR
COACHING DAYS
COACH STATION
COAL INDUSTRY
COAL MERCHANT
COAL SHORTAGE
COARSE FABRIC
COARSE MANNER
COASTAL TRADE
COAST TO COAST
COAT AND SKIRT
CODE NAPOLEON
CODE OF HONOUR
COILED SPRING
COLD AS MARBLE
COLD COMPRESS
COLD SHOULDER
COLD-WATER TAP
COLIN COWDREY
COLLAR AND TIE
COLLECT TAXES
COLOGNE WATER
COLONEL BLIMP
COLONEL BOGEY
COLONIAL LIFE
COLOURED BIRD
COLOUR SCHEME
COMBAT TROOPS
COMB ONE'S HAIR
COME A CROPPER
COME AND GET IT
COME DOWN A PEG
COME IN SECOND
COME IN TO LAND
COME INTO LINE
COME INTO PLAY
COME INTO VIEW

COME IN USEFUL
COME IT STRONG
COME OUT ON TOP
COME OVER HERE
COME TO A CLOSE
COME TO A POINT
COME TOGETHER
COME TO NAUGHT
COME TO NO GOOD
COME TO NO HARM
COME TO PIECES
COME TO THE END
COME UP FOR AIR
COME UPSTAIRS
COME UP TRUMPS
COMIC SECTION
COMING EVENTS
COMMANDO RAID
COMMANDO UNIT
COMMIT A CRIME
COMMIT BIGAMY
COMMIT MURDER
COMMITTEE MAN
COMMON ACCENT
COMMON AS DIRT
COMMON CENTRE
COMMON FACTOR
COMMON FRIEND
COMMON GENDER
COMMON GOSSIP
COMMON GROUND
COMMON HATRED
COMMON LAWYER
COMMON MARKET
COMMON ORIGIN
COMMON PEOPLE
COMMON PERSON
COMMON PRAYER
COMMON PRISON
COMMON SAYING
COMMON SPEECH
COMMUNAL FARM
COMPANIES ACT
COMPANION WAY
COMPARE NOTES
COMPASS POINT
COMPLETE LIST
COMPOSE MUSIC
COMPOS MENTIS
COMPOUND TIME
CONCEITED PUP
CONCERT GRAND
CONCERT PARTY
CONCERT PITCH
CONCRETE FACT
CONCRETE PATH

CONCRETE POST
CONDEMNED MAN
CONFUSED MIND
CONIC SECTION
CONSOLE TABLE
CONTENTED MAN
CONTOUR LINES
CONTROL LINES
CONTROL PANEL
CONTROL TOWER
CONVEX MIRROR
CONVEYOR BELT
CONVICTED MAN
COOKERY CLASS
COOKING APPLE
COOK THE BOOKS
COOK UP A STORY
COOL CUSTOMER
COOLING AGENT
COOLING PLANT
COOL JUDGMENT
COOL THOUSAND
COPIOUS NOTES
COPPER KETTLE
COPYRIGHT ACT
CORDIAL SMILE
CORNET PLAYER
CORN EXCHANGE
CORN IN ISRAEL
CORNISH CREAM
CORNISH PASTY
CORN MERCHANT
CORN ON THE COB
CORONER'S JURY
CORRECT DRESS
CORRECT STYLE
CORRECT THING
COSSACK DANCE
COST ACCOUNTS
COST OF LIVING
COST OF UPKEEP
COST THE EARTH
COSTUME PIECE
COTTAGE PIANO
COTTON GLOVES
COTTON THREAD
COUGH MIXTURE
COULD BE WORSE
COUNCIL HOUSE
COUNCIL OF WAR
COUNT DRACULA
COUNTER CLAIM
COUNTRY DANCE
COUNTRY HOUSE
COUNTRY MOUSE
COUNT THE COST

COUNT THE DAYS
COUNT THE RISK
COUNT UP TO TEN
COUNTY ANTRIM
COUNTY FAMILY
COUNTY SCHOOL
COUPE JACQUES
COURSE OF DUTY
COURSE OF LIFE
COURSE OF LOVE
COURSE OF TIME
COURSE OF WORK
COURSE RECORD
COURTEOUS ACT
COURTESY CALL
COURT MARTIAL
COURT OFFICER
COURT PLASTER
COURT SUMMONS
COUSIN GERMAN
COVENT GARDEN
COVENTRY CITY
COVERED COURT
COVERED DRAIN
COVERED WAGON
COVER THE COST
COVER THE LOSS
CRACK A BOTTLE
CRACKED VOICE
CRACKING PACE
CRACKING SHOW
CRACK-POT IDEA
CRACK THE WHIP
CRAFTY FELLOW
CRAIG DOUGLAS
CRAMPED STYLE
CRASHING BORE
CRASH LANDING
CRAVEN SPIRIT
CREAM CRACKER
CREAM SHAMPOO
CREATE A SCENE
CREATIVE MIND
CREATIVE MOOD
CREATIVE URGE
CREATIVE WORK
CREDIT TITLES
CRÊPE DE CHINE
CRÊPE SUZETTE
CRESCENT MOON
CRICKET EXTRA
CRICKET MATCH
CRICKET PITCH
CRICKET SCORE
CRICKET STUMP
CRIMINAL CASE

CRIMINAL CODE
CRIMINAL SUIT
CRIMINAL TYPE
CRIPPLING TAX
CRITICAL TIME
CROMWELL ROAD
CROSSED LINES
CROSSED WIRES
CROSS OF DAVID
CROSS SECTION
CROSS THE LINE
CROSS THE ROAD
CROSSWORD FAN
CROWD CONTROL
CROWNED HEADS
CROWN WITNESS
CRUDE MANNERS
CRUDE METHODS
CRUISE AROUND
CRUSHING BLOW
CRUST OF BREAD
CRY LIKE A BABY
CRY OF DESPAIR
CRY ONE'S WARES
CRYPTIC SMILE
CRYSTAL CLEAR
CRYSTAL GLASS
CUBIC CONTENT
CULINARY HERB
CULLODEN MOOR
CUP AND SAUCER
CUPBOARD LOVE
CUP FINALISTS
CURDS AND WHEY
CURIOUS SIGHT
CURIOUS SOUND
CURIOUS THING
CURL OF THE LIP
CURL UP AND DIE
CURRANT BREAD
CURRENCY NOTE
CURRENT CRAZE
CURRENT ISSUE
CURRENT MONTH
CURRENT OF AIR
CURRENT PRICE
CURRENT TIMES
CURRENT TREND
CURRENT YIELD
CURRY AND RICE
CURTIS REPORT
CURVE INWARDS
CUSHION COVER
CUSHION OF AIR
CUSTOM DUTIES
CUSTOMS UNION

CUT AND THRUST
CUT FOR TRUMPS
CUT OFF THE GAS
CUT OF ONE'S JIB
CUT ONE'S NAILS
CUT ONE'S TEETH
CUT THE CACKLE
CUTTING TEETH
CUTTING WORDS
CUT TO RIBBONS
CUT TO THE BONE
CYNICAL SMILE
CZAR OF RUSSIA

D – 12

DAGGERS DRAWN
DAILY EXPRESS
DAILY ROUTINE
DAILY SERVICE
DAINTY HABITS
DAINTY PALATE
DAIRY FARMING
DAIRY PRODUCE
DALAMATIAN DOG
DAMAGED GOODS
DAME MYRA HESS
DANCE HOSTESS
DANCE OF DEATH
DANCE ROUTINE
DANCE SESSION
DANDY DINMONT
DANGEROUS JOB
DANGEROUS MAN
DANGER SIGNAL
DANISH BUTTER
DANISH PASTRY
DANSE MACABRE
DARBY AND JOAN
DARKENED MIND
DARK THOUGHTS
DASH TO PIECES
DAVID GARRICK
DAVID KOSSOFF
DAYLIGHT RAID
DAY OF LEISURE
DAY OF WORSHIP
DEAD AS MUTTON
DEAD LANGUAGE
DEADLY COMBAT
DEADLY POISON
DEADLY SECRET
DEADLY WEAPON
DEAD MAN'S HAND
DEAD-SEA FRUIT
DEAD STRAIGHT
DEAFENING ROW

DEAF TO REASON
DEAL THE CARDS
DEAR DEPARTED
DEAREST HEART
DEAR OLD THING
DEARTH OF FOOD
DEATH CHAMBER
DEATH PENALTY
DEATH WARRANT
DEBATING HALL
DEBIT BALANCE
DEBT OF HONOUR
DECIDING VOTE
DECIMAL POINT
DEEP FEELINGS
DEEP INTEREST
DEEP-LAID PLOT
DEEP MOURNING
DEEP-SEA DIVER
DEEP THOUGHTS
DEFENCE BONDS
DEFENCE MEDAL
DEFINITE TIME
DEJECTED LOOK
DELICATE HINT
DELIVERY DATE
DELIVERY NOTE
DEMAND RANSOM
DEMON FOR WORK
DENIS COMPTON
DEN OF THIEVES
DEPUTY LEADER
DESCENT OF MAN
DESERT ISLAND
DESERVE A RISE
DESIGN CENTRE
DESK CALENDAR
DESPATCH CASE
DESPERATE BID
DESPERATE DAN
DESPERATE MAN
DESSERT KNIFE
DESSERT SPOON
DETACHED MIND
DETACHED VIEW
DETAILED PLAN
DEVIL MAY CARE
DEVIL OF A MESS
DEVIL OF A TIME
DEVIL'S ISLAND
DEVIL'S TATTOO
DEVIL WORSHIP
DEVIOUS MEANS
DEVIOUS PATHS
DEVOID OF FEAR
DEVON VIOLETS

DIAGONAL LINE
DIALLING TONE
DIAMOND CLASP
DIAMOND TIARA
DIANA'S TEMPLE
DICTATE TERMS
DIE IN HARNESS
DIE IN ONE'S BED
DIESEL ENGINE
DIFFICULT JOB
DIFFICULT SUM
DIFFUSED HEAT
DIG IN THE RIBS
DIGITAL WATCH
DIG ONESELF IN
DIG ONE'S GRAVE
DIG UP THE PAST
DINING SALOON
DIN IN THE EARS
DIRECT ACCESS
DIRECT ACTION
DIRECT COURSE
DIRECT METHOD
DIRECT OBJECT
DIRECT SPEECH
DIRE DISTRESS
DIRTY WEATHER
DISASTER AREA
DISCOVERY BAY
DISHONEST ACT
DISPATCH CASE
DISPENSE WITH
DISTRICT BANK
DISTRICT LINE
DIVE FOR COVER
DIVIDE BY FIVE
DIVIDE BY FOUR
DIVIDE BY NINE
DIVIDED SKIRT
DIVIDING LINE
DIVIDING WALL
DIVINE COMEDY
DIVINE NATURE
DIVINE RIGHTS
DIVISION BELL
DIVISION SIGN
DIVORCE COURT
DIZZY FEELING
DIZZY HEIGHTS
DO A HAND'S TURN
DO AS ONE'S TOLD
DO AS OTHERS DO
DO AS ROME DOES
DOCK LABOURER
DOCTOR FOSTER
DOCTOR JEKYLL

DOCTOR WATSON
DOG IN A MANGER
DO IT YOURSELF
DOMBEY AND SON
DOMESDAY BOOK
DOMESTIC HELP
DOMINANT FACT
DONALD WOLFIT
DONEGAL TWEED
DONKEY ENGINE
DONKEY'S YEARS
DO NO MAN WRONG
DO NOT DISTURB
DO ONE A FAVOUR
DO ONE'S UTMOST
DORMER WINDOW
DOROTHY TUTIN
DORSET SQUARE
DOSE OF PHYSIC
DO THE HONOURS
DO THE NEEDFUL
DO THE WASHING
DOUBLE BARREL
DOUBLE BRANDY
DOUBLE ELEVEN
DOUBLE FLOWER
DOUBLE SCOTCH
DOUBLES MATCH
DOUBLE THE BID
DOUBLE TWELVE
DOUBLE TWENTY
DOUBLE VISION
DOUBLE WHISKY
DOUGHTY DEEDS
DOWN PLATFORM
DOWNRIGHT LIE
DOWN THE AISLE
DOWN THE DRAIN
DOWN THE FIELD
DOWN THE HATCH
DOWN THE RIVER
DOWN THE SPOUT
DOWN THE YEARS
DOWNWARD BEND
DOWNWARD PATH
DOZEN OYSTERS
DRAGGING FEET
DRAG ONE'S FEET
DRAGON'S BLOOD
DRAGON'S TEETH
DRAMATIC FORM
DRAMATIC POEM
DRAMATIC POET
DRAPERY STORE
DRAUGHT CIDER
DRAUGHT HORSE

DRAUGHT STOUT
DRAW A MEANING
DRAW A PENSION
DRAW A PICTURE
DRAWING PAPER
DRAW INTEREST
DRAWN TO SCALE
DRAW THE BLIND
DRAW THE MORAL
DRAW THE SWORD
DRAW THE TEETH
DRAW TO A CLOSE
DRAW TOGETHER
DREADFUL BORE
DREADFUL PAIN
DREAD SUMMONS
DREAM OF YOUTH
DRESDEN CHINA
DRESS CLOTHES
DRESSED IN RED
DRESSING CASE
DRESSING DOWN
DRESSING GOWN
DRESSING ROOM
DRESS THE PART
DRESS UNIFORM
DRINK HEAVILY
DRINKING BOUT
DRINKING CLUB
DRINKING ORGY
DRINKING SONG
DRINKING TIME
DRINK OF WATER
DRIVE FORWARD
DRIVE THROUGH
DRIVE TO DRINK
DRIVING FORCE
DROP A CLANGER
DROP A CURTSEY
DROP A BRANDY
DROP OF SCOTCH
DROP OF WHISKY
DROPPED CATCH
DROP THE PILOT
DROWN ONESELF
DRUNK AS A LORD
DRUNKEN BRAWL
DUCKING STOOL
DUCK ONE'S HEAD
DUCK'S DISEASE
DUE DEFERENCE
DULL MONOTONY
DUMB CHARADES
DUMB CREATURE
DUM-DUM BULLET
DUNMOW FLITCH

DUPLICATE KEY
DURING THE DAY
DURING THE WAR
DUST AND ASHES
DUTCH AUCTION
DUTCH COMFORT
DUTCH COURAGE
DUTCH GUILDER
DYERS' COMPANY
DYNAMIC FORCE

E – 12

EALING COMMON
EAR AND THROAT
EARLY CLOSING
EARLY EDITION
EARLY ENGLISH
EARLY MORNING
EARLY WARNING
EARNED INCOME
EARNEST MONEY
EARN ONE'S KEEP
EASE ONE'S MIND
EASILY SOLVED
EAST CHINA SEA
EASTER BONNET
EASTER ISLAND
EASTERLY GALE
EASTER MONDAY
EASTER PARADE
EASTER RISING
EASTER SUNDAY
EASY ON THE EYE
EASY PAYMENTS
EASY SOLUTION
EASY TO PLEASE
EAT HUMBLE-PIE
EATING HABITS
EAT ONE'S WORDS
EAT SPARINGLY
EAU DE COLOGNE
ECONOMY DRIVE
EDGAR WALLACE
EDGE OF BEYOND
EDIBLE FUNGUS
EDITH SITWELL
EDWARD GIBBON
EEL-PIE ISLAND
EFFORT OF WILL
EGGS AND BACON
EGYPTIAN GODS
EIGHT DEGREES
EIGHT DOLLARS
EIGHT FATHOMS

EIGHT GALLONS
EIGHT GUINEAS
EIGHTH LETTER
EIGHTH OF JULY
EIGHTH OF JUNE
EIGHTH STOREY
EIGHT HUNDRED
EIGHTH VOLUME
EIGHT MINUTES
EIGHT OF CLUBS
EIGHT PER CENT
EIGHT SQUARED
EIGHT WICKETS
ELBOW ONE'S WAY
ELDER BROTHER
ELDEST SISTER
ELECTION DATE
ELECTION YEAR
ELECTRIC BELL
ELECTRIC BLUE
ELECTRIC BULB
ELECTRIC FIRE
ELECTRIC HARE
ELECTRIC HORN
ELECTRIC IRON
ELECTRIC LAMP
ELECTRIC OVEN
ELECTRIC PLUG
ELECTRIC WIRE
ELEGANT LINES
ELEVEN MONTHS
ELEVEN O'CLOCK
ELEVEN OUNCES
ELEVEN POINTS
ELEVENTH HOLE
ELEVENTH HOUR
ELGIN MARBLES
ELIXIR OF LIFE
ELVIS PRESLEY
ELY CATHEDRAL
EMERALD GREEN
EMPEROR WALTZ
EMPTY FEELING
EMPTY STOMACH
EMPTY VESSELS
END IN FAILURE
ENDLESS CHAIN
ENDLESS WORRY
END OF CHAPTER
END OF THE LINE
END OF THE ROAD
END OF THE WEEK
END OF THE YEAR
ENDURING FAME
ENDURING LOVE
ENFIELD RIFLE

ENGAGED IN WAR
ENGINE DRIVER
ENGLISH MONEY
ENGLISH VERSE
ENJOY ONESELF
ENORMOUS MEAL
ENQUIRE AFTER
ENQUIRY AGENT
ENRICO CARUSO
ENTERIC FEVER
ENTRANCE FREE
ENTRANCE HALL
EPPING FOREST
EQUAL CONTEST
EQUAL THE BEST
ERIC ROBINSON
ERMINE COLLAR
ERUDITE STYLE
ESCAPE CLAUSE
ESCAPE NOTICE
ESCORT VESSEL
ESSAYS OF ELIA
ESSENTIAL OIL
ESTEEM HIGHLY
ETERNAL YOUTH
ETERNITY RING
ETON WALL-GAME
EUGENE O'NEILL
EUROPEAN CITY
EVENING CLASS
EVENING DRESS
EVENING PAPER
EVEN TEMPERED
EVE OF THE POLL
EVER AND AGAIN
EVER-OPEN DOOR
EVER SO LITTLE
EVERY FEW DAYS
EVERY MAN JACK
EVERY MORNING
EVERY QUARTER
EVERY SO OFTEN
EVERY TUESDAY
EVIL SPEAKING
EVIL THOUGHTS
EVOKE THE PAST
EXACT ACCOUNT
EXACTLY RIGHT
EXACT MEANING
EXACT SCIENCE
EXALTED STYLE
EXCEL ONESELF
EXCESS PROFIT
EXCESS WEIGHT
EXCHANGE RATE
EXCITING BOOK

EXCITING NEWS
EXCITING PLAY
EXERCISE BOOK
EXERT ONESELF
EXHAUST VALVE
EXPANSE OF SEA
EXPANSE OF SKY
EXPERT ADVICE
EXPLODED IDEA
EXPORT MARKET
EXPOSED NERVE
EXPRESS GRIEF
EXPRESS SPEED
EXPRESS TRAIN
EX-SERVICE MAN
EXTEND CREDIT
EXTENDED PLAY
EXTERIOR WALL
EXTRA EDITION
EXTRA SPECIAL
EXTREMES MEET
EXTREME VIEWS
EXTREME YOUTH
EYE FOR BEAUTY
EYE FOR COLOUR
EYE OF A NEEDLE
EYES OF THE LAW
EYE ON THE BALL

F – 12

FABLED ANIMAL
FABULOUS SIZE
FACE BOTH WAYS
FACE DISGRACE
FACE THE ENEMY
FACE THE FACTS
FACE THE FRONT
FACE THE ISSUE
FACE THE MUSIC
FACE THE TRUTH
FACT AND FANCY
FAERIE QUEENE
FAILING LIGHT
FAILING SIGHT
FAIL IN HEALTH
FAIL TO APPEAR
FAIL TO FINISH
FAINT ATTEMPT
FAIR DECISION
FAIR EXCHANGE
FAIR PROSPECT
FAIR QUESTION
FAIR TO MEDIUM
FAIT ACCOMPLI
FAITHFUL COPY

FALL BACK UPON
FALL BY THE WAY
FALLEN ARCHES
FALL HEADLONG
FALL IN BATTLE
FALLING SALES
FALLING TEARS
FALL IN PRICE
FALL INTO LINE
FALL INTO RUIN
FALL OF FRANCE
FALL TO PIECES
FALSE ACCOUNT
FALSE ADDRESS
FALSE COLOURS
FALSE ECONOMY
FALSE HORIZON
FALSE MODESTY
FALSE PICTURE
FALSE PROPHET
FALSE VERDICT
FALSE WITNESS
FALSE WORSHIP
FAMILIAR FACE
FAMILIAR RING
FAMILY AFFAIR
FAMILY CIRCLE
FAMILY DOCTOR
FAMILY FRIEND
FAMILY JEWELS
FAMILY LAWYER
FAMILY MATTER
FAMINE RELIEF
FANCY ONESELF
FAN THE EMBERS
FAN THE FLAMES
FAR DIFFERENT
FARE THEE WELL
FAREWELL SONG
FARMHOUSE TEA
FARMING STOCK
FARM LABOURER
FAROE ISLANDS
FASCIST PARTY
FASHION HOUSE
FASHION MODEL
FASHION PLATE
FAST AND LOOSE
FAST THINKING
FATAL BLUNDER
FATAL DISEASE
FATAL MISTAKE
FATHER AND SON
FATHER FIGURE
FATHER THAMES
FATIGUE PARTY

FAT LOT OF GOOD
FAT OF THE LAND
FATUOUS SMILE
FAULTY SWITCH
FEAR EXPOSURE
FEAR THE WORST
FEAT OF MEMORY
FEATURE STORY
FEDERAL AGENT
FEDERAL COURT
FEDERAL STATE
FEDERAL UNION
FEEBLE ATTACK
FEEBLE EFFORT
FEEBLE EXCUSE
FEEBLE SPEECH
FEED THE BRUTE
FEEL DOUBTFUL
FEEL GRATEFUL
FEEL HELPLESS
FEEL HOMESICK
FEEL ONE'S FEET
FEEL STRONGLY
FEEL SUPERIOR
FEEL SYMPATHY
FEEL THE PANGS
FEEL THE PINCH
FEET FOREMOST
FELL HEADLONG
FELLOW MEMBER
FERTILE BRAIN
FESTIVAL HALL
FESTIVE BOARD
FEUDAL SYSTEM
FEUDAL TENURE
FEVERISH COLD
FIELDING SIDE
FIELD KITCHEN
FIELD MARSHAL
FIELD OFFICER
FIELD OF STUDY
FIELD OF WHEAT
FIERCE ATTACK
FIERCE HATRED
FIERCE TEMPER
FIERY FURNACE
FIFTEEN FORTY
FIFTEEN MILES
FIFTH CENTURY
FIFTH OF APRIL
FIFTH OF MARCH
FIFTY DOLLARS
FIFTY GUINEAS
FIFTY PER CENT
FIGHT AGAINST
FIGHTER PILOT

FIGHTER PLANE
FIGHTING COCK
FIGHTING TALK
FIGHTING TRIM
FIGHT ONE'S WAY
FIGURE SKATER
FILING SYSTEM
FILL A VACANCY
FILM DIRECTOR
FILM FESTIVAL
FILM INDUSTRY
FILM MAGAZINE
FILM PREMIERE
FILM PRODUCER
FINAL ACCOUNT
FINAL ATTEMPT
FINAL CURTAIN
FINAL EDITION
FINAL EPISODE
FINAL OPINION
FINAL OUTCOME
FINAL PAYMENT
FINAL PROCESS
FINAL VICTORY
FINAL WARNING
FINANCIAL AID
FIND A FORMULA
FIND A HUSBAND
FIND AN OUTLET
FIND NO FAVOUR
FIND ONE'S FEET
FIND ONE'S LEGS
FIND PLEASURE
FIND THE CAUSE
FIND THE MONEY
FIND THE PLACE
FINE AND DANDY
FINE AND LARGE
FINE FEATHERS
FINE FEATURES
FINE GOINGS-ON
FINE PROSPECT
FINER FEELING
FINE SPECIMEN
FINISHED WORK
FINISH SECOND
FINISH THE JOB
FINSBURY PARK
FIRE AND SWORD
FIRE AND WATER
FIRE AT RANDOM
FIREMAN'S LIFT
FIRE OF LONDON
FIRE PRACTICE
FIRESIDE CHAT
FIRESIDE TALK

FIRM DECISION
FIRM FOOTHOLD
FIRMLY ROOTED
FIRM MEASURES
FIRM PRESSURE
FIRM PROPOSAL
FIRST-AID POST
FIRST AND LAST
FIRST ARRIVAL
FIRST ATTEMPT
FIRST CENTURY
FIRST CHAPTER
FIRST EDITION
FIRST FOOTING
FIRST INNINGS
FIRST OF APRIL
FIRST OFFENCE
FIRST OFFICER
FIRST OF MARCH
FIRST PAYMENT
FIRST QUARTER
FIRST READING
FIRST REFUSAL
FIRST RESERVE
FIRST SEA-LORD
FIRST SERVICE
FIRST SESSION
FIRST THOUGHT
FIRST TIME OUT
FIRST TO LEAVE
FIRST TURNING
FIRST-YEAR MAN
FIRTH OF CLYDE
FIRTH OF FORTH
FISH AND CHIPS
FISH FOR TROUT
FISHING FLEET
FISHING SMACK
FISHING SPEAR
FIT AND PROPER
FIT AS A FIDDLE
FITFUL BREEZE
FIT OF MADNESS
FITTED CARPET
FIVE AND A HALF
FIVE AND EIGHT
FIVE AND SEVEN
FIVE AND THREE
FIVE-DAY MATCH
FIVE DIAMONDS
FIVE FEET TALL
FIVE FURLONGS
FIVE-LINE WHIP
FIVE NO-TRUMPS
FIVE OF HEARTS
FIVE OF SPADES

FIVE OF TRUMPS
FIVE SEVENTHS
FIVE THOUSAND
FIVE-YEAR PLAN
FIXED CAPITAL
FIXED PAYMENT
FIXED PURPOSE
FIXED ROUTINE
FLAGON OF WINE
FLAMING HEART
FLASHING EYES
FLASH OF LIGHT
FLEECY CLOUDS
FLEET OF SHIPS
FLEET OF TAXIS
FLIGHT NUMBER
FLIGHT OF TIME
FLIMSY EXCUSE
FLOATING DEBT
FLOATING DOCK
FLOATING FUND
FLOATING MINE
FLOATING VOTE
FLOCK OF BIRDS
FLOCK OF GEESE
FLOCK OF GOATS
FLOCK OF SHEEP
FLODDEN FIELD
FLOOD OF TEARS
FLOOD OF WATER
FLOOD OF WORDS
FLOOR SERVICE
FLOUNCE ABOUT
FLOWERED SILK
FLOWER GARDEN
FLOWER MARKET
FLOWER-POT MEN
FLOWER SELLER
FLOWERY STYLE
FLOWERY LOCKS
FLOWING WATER
FLUENT FRENCH
FLUID MEASURE
FLURRY OF SNOW
FLUSH OF YOUTH
FLUTED COLUMN
FLY AWAY PETER
FLYING BEETLE
FLYING CARPET
FLYING CIRCUS
FLYING COLUMN
FLYING DOCTOR
FLYING GROUND
FLYING SAUCER
FLYING TACKLE
FLY INTO A RAGE

FOAM MATTRESS	FOSTER FATHER	FRENCH ACCENT
FOGGY WEATHER	FOSTER MOTHER	FRENCH CUSTOM
FOLDING CHAIR	FOSTER PARENT	FRENCH GUINEA
FOLDING DOORS	FOSTER SISTER	FRENCH LESSON
FOLDING STOOL	FOUL LANGUAGE	FRENCH MASTER
FOLD ONE'S ARMS	FOUND MISSING	FRENCH PASTRY
FOLLOW ADVICE	FOUND WANTING	FRENCH POLISH
FOLLOW MY LEAD	FOUR AND A HALF	FRENCH POODLE
FOLLOW THE SEA	FOUR DIAMONDS	FRENCH WINDOW
FOND OF A GLASS	FOUR FEATHERS	FRENZIED RAGE
FOOD AND DRINK	FOUR FEET TALL	FRESH ADVANCE
FOOD SHORTAGE	FOUR FREEDOMS	FRESH AS PAINT
FOOD SUPPLIES	FOUR FURLONGS	FRESH CHAPTER
FOOT AND MOUTH	FOUR HORSEMEN	FRESH COURAGE
FOOTBALL CLUB	FOUR NO-TRUMPS	FRESH FLOWERS
FOOTBALL POOL	FOUR OF HEARTS	FRESH HERRING
FOOTBALL TEAM	FOUR OF SPADES	FRESH OUTLOOK
FOOTPLATE MAN	FOUR OF TRUMPS	FRIAR'S BALSAM
FOOT REGIMENT	FOURPENNY ONE	FRICTION FEED
FOR A LIFETIME	FOUR QUARTERS	FRIDAY'S CHILD
FOR AMUSEMENT	FOUR SEVENTHS	FRIEND INDEED
FOR A RAINY DAY	FOURTEEN DAYS	FRIEND IN NEED
FORCE AN ENTRY	FOURTH ESTATE	FRIENDLY CHAT
FORCE AN ISSUE	FOURTH FINGER	FRIENDLY FACE
FORCED GAIETY	FOURTH LEAGUE	FRIENDLY HAND
FORCED LABOUR	FOURTH LETTER	FRIENDLY WORD
FORCE MAJEURE	FOURTH OF JULY	FRIGHTEN AWAY
FORCE OF HABIT	FOURTH OF JUNE	FROM ALL SIDES
FORCE ONE'S WAY	FOUR THOUSAND	FROM DAY TO DAY
FORCE THE PACE	FOURTH SEASON	FROM END TO END
FOREIGN AGENT	FOURTH STOREY	FROM THE FIRST
FOREIGN LANDS	FOURTH VOLUME	FROM THE NORTH
FOREIGN MONEY	FOX AND HOUNDS	FROM THE SOUTH
FOREIGN PARTS	FRACTURED ARM	FROM THE START
FOREIGN STAMP	FRACTURED LEG	FROM TOP TO TOE
FOREIGN TRADE	FRAGRANT WEED	FRONT AND BACK
FOREST OF DEAN	FRANCIS BACON	FRONTIER ZONE
FOREST RANGER	FRANCIS DRAKE	FRONT PARLOUR
FOREVER AMBER	FRANK SINATRA	FROSTED GLASS
FOR GALLANTRY	FRANTIC HASTE	FROZEN ASSETS
FORGE A CHEQUE	FRAYED NERVES	FRUIT MACHINE
FORGE ONE'S WAY	FREE AS THE AIR	FUEL MERCHANT
FORK OUT MONEY	FREE DELIVERY	FULHAM PALACE
FORMAL GARDEN	FREE FROM CARE	FUEL CAPACITY
FORMAL SPEECH	FREE FROM DEBT	FULL COVERAGE
FORMER FRIEND	FREE FROM PAIN	FULL DAYLIGHT
FOR PITY'S SAKE	FREE FROM RAIN	FULLER'S EARTH
FOR THE BETTER	FREE FROM VICE	FULL MATURITY
FOR THE MOMENT	FREE FROM WANT	FULL OF ACTION
FOR THE RECORD	FREE MOVEMENT	FULL OF ENERGY
FORTY FIFTEEN	FREE OF CHARGE	FULL OF HORROR
FORTY PER CENT	FREE QUARTERS	FULL OF SORROW
FORTY THIEVES	FREE THINKING	FULL OF SPIRIT
FORWARD DRIVE	FREE TO CHOOSE	FULL PRESSURE
FORWARD MARCH	FREEZING COLD	FULLY DRESSED
FORWARD PUPIL	FREIGHT TRAIN	FULLY ENGAGED

FULLY SECURED
FUME WITH RAGE
FUND OF HUMOUR
FUNERAL MARCH
FUNERAL RITES
FUNNY FEELING
FUN OF THE FAIR
FUR-LINED COAT
FURNITURE VAN
FURNIVAL'S INN
FURTHER DELAY
FURTHER PLANS
FUTILE EFFORT
FUTURE EVENTS

G – 12

GAIN A FOOTING
GAIN A HEARING
GAIN A VICTORY
GAIN CURRENCY
GAIN ONE'S ENDS
GAIN PRESTIGE
GAIN STRENGTH
GALA OCCASION
GALLON OF BEER
GALLON OF MILK
GAMBLING DEBT
GAMBLING GAME
GAMBLING HELL
GAME AND MATCH
GAME OF CHANCE
GAME OF TENNIS
GAME PRESERVE
GAMING TABLES
GAMMA COUNTER
GAMMON RASHER
GARBLED STORY
GARDEN OF EDEN
GARDEN ROLLER
GARDEN SUBURB
GARDEN TROWEL
GARRISON TOWN
GARTER STITCH
GAS POISONING
GATE-LEG TABLE
GENERAL ALARM
GENERAL ALERT
GENERAL BOOTH
GENERAL GRANT
GENERAL ISSUE
GENERAL SMUTS
GENERAL STAFF
GENERAL STALL
GENERAL TERMS
GENERAL TREND

GENERAL USAGE
GENERAL VOICE
GENERAL WOLFE
GENITIVE CASE
GENTLE BREEZE
GENTLEMAN JIM
GENTLE NATURE
GENTLE READER
GENTLE REBUKE
GENTLY DOES IT!
GEORGE BORROW
GEORGE ORWELL
GEORGE ROMNEY
GERMAN LESSON
GERMAN SCHOOL
GERMAN SILVER
GERM OF AN IDEA
GET CLEAN AWAY
GET CLEAR AWAY
GET INTO A MESS
GET NO SUPPORT
GET ONE'S CARDS
GET ONE'S EYE IN
GET OUT OF HAND
GET PLASTERED
GET PROMOTION
GET TECHNICAL
GET THE CREDIT
GET THE NEEDLE
GET THE STITCH
GET THE WIND UP
GET WELL-OILED
GIANT DESPAIR
GIANT'S STRIDE
GIDDY FEELING
GIDDY HEIGHTS
GIFT OF THE GAB
GIN AND FRENCH
GIN AND ORANGE
GINGER BRANDY
GINGER ROGERS
GINGHAM FROCK
GIPSY CARAVAN
GIRLS AND BOYS
GIVE A CONCERT
GIVE A LECTURE
GIVE AN ENCORE
GIVE A PRESENT
GIVE A RECEIPT
GIVE A SUMMARY
GIVE AUDIENCE
GIVE EVIDENCE
GIVE FIRST-AID
GIVE HIM SOCKS
GIVE IN CHARGE
GIVE IT A TWIST

GIVE IT THE GUN
GIVE JUDGMENT
GIVEN A CHANCE
GIVEN A PARDON
GIVEN THE BIRD
GIVEN THE BOOT
GIVEN THE CANE
GIVEN THE PUSH
GIVEN THE SACK
GIVEN THE SLIP
GIVEN THE VOTE
GIVE ONE A LIFT
GIVE ONE'S BEST
GIVE ONE'S LIFE
GIVE ONE'S VOTE
GIVE ONE'S WORD
GIVE PLEASURE
GIVE SECURITY
GIVE THE ALARM
GIVE THE FACTS
GIVE THE ORDER
GIVE UP EATING
GIVE UP OFFICE
GIVE UP TRYING
GLADSTONE BAG
GLANCING BLOW
GLARING ERROR
GLASS FACTORY
GLASS OF STOUT
GLASS OF WATER
GLASS SLIPPER
GLASS STOPPER
GLASS TANKARD
GLASS TOO MUCH
GLASS TUMBLER
GLEAM OF LIGHT
GLOBE THEATRE
GLOOMY ASPECT
GLORIOUS MESS
GLORIOUS TIME
GLORIOUS VIEW
GLOWING TERMS
GO AND EAT COKE
GO BACK IN TIME
GO BACK TO WORK
GO BY THE BOARD
GOD BE WITH YOU
GO DOWNSTAIRS
GO FIFTY-FIFTY
GO FOR A BURTON
GO FOR A CRUISE
GO FOR A STROLL
GO FOR A VOYAGE
GO FOR NOTHING
GO HOT AND COLD
GOING BEGGING

GOING CONCERN	GOOD WATCH-DOG	GREAT COMFORT
GO INTO DETAIL	GOODWIN SANDS	GREAT COMPANY
GO INTO HIDING	GOODWOOD PARK	GREAT EASTERN
GOLD BRACELET	GO ON ALL FOURS	GREAT EXPENSE
GOLDEN FLEECE	GO ON AN ERRAND	GREAT FORTUNE
GOLDEN GLOVES	GO ON AS BEFORE	GREAT FRIENDS
GOLDEN NUMBER	GO ONE'S OWN WAY	GREAT MALVERN
GOLDEN REMEDY	GO ON THE SPREE	GREAT PAINTER
GOLDEN SQUARE	GO ON THE STAGE	GREAT RESPECT
GOLDEN SUNSET	GOOSE PIMPLES	GREAT SECRECY
GOLDERS GREEN	GO OVER THE TOP	GREAT SOLDIER
GOLDFISH BOWL	GORGEOUS TIME	GREAT SUCCESS
GOLDFISH POND	GO-SLOW POLICY	GREAT TRAGEDY
GOLD MERCHANT	GO-SLOW STRIKE	GREAT TRIUMPH
GOLD RESERVE	GOSSIP COLUMN	GREAT URGENCY
GOLD STANDARD	GOSSIP WRITER	GREAT VARIETY
GOLF CHAMPION	GO SWIMMINGLY	GREAT VICTORY
GONE IN A FLASH	GO THE SAME WAY	GRECIAN STYLE
GONE TO GROUND	GOTHIC SCRIPT	GREEK PROFILE
GOOD AND READY	GO TO A WEDDING	GREEK SCHOLAR
GOOD APPETITE	GO TO EXTREMES	GREEK THEATRE
GOOD ARGUMENT	GO TO HOSPITAL	GREEK TRAGEDY
GOOD BREEDING	GO TO ONE'S HEAD	GREEK VERSION
GOOD BUSINESS	GO TO THE DEVIL	GREEN FINGERS
GOOD CLEAN FUN	GO TO THE FRONT	GREEN HOWARDS
GOOD CROSSING	GO TO THE OPERA	GREEN IN MY EYE
GOOD DAY'S WORK	GO TO THE POLLS	GREEN WITH AGE
GOOD DELIVERY	GO TO THE RACES	GREY EMINENCE
GOOD EYESIGHT	GO UP IN FLAMES	GREY SQUIRREL
GOOD FEATURES	GO WITH A SWING	GRIEVOUS PAIN
GOOD FOR TRADE	GRACE DARLING	GRILLED BACON
GOOD GRACIOUS	GRACEFUL EXIT	GRILLED STEAK
GOOD JUDGMENT	GRACIE FIELDS	GRILLED TROUT
GOOD LIKENESS	GRACIOUS LADY	GRIM BUSINESS
GOOD LINGUIST	GRAHAME GREENE	GRIM LAUGHTER
GOOD LISTENER	GRAIN HARVEST	GRIND ONE'S AXE
GOOD MATERIAL	GRAIN OF SENSE	GRIPPING TALE
GOOD OLD TIMES	GRAIN OF TRUTH	GRIT THE TEETH
GOOD PHYSIQUE	GRAND CENTRAL	GROCERY CHAIN
GOOD POSITION	GRAND DUCHESS	GROCERY STORE
GOOD PRACTICE	GRAND FEELING	GROPE ONE'S WAY
GOOD PROGRESS	GRAND GUIGNOL	GROSS BLUNDER
GOOD QUARTERS	GRAND LARCENY	GROSS NEGLECT
GOOD QUESTION	GRAND MISTAKE	GROSS RETURNS
GOOD RECOVERY	GRAND OPENING	GROSS TONNAGE
GOOD RIDDANCE	GRAND SEND-OFF	GROUND GINGER
GOOD ROUND SUM	GRAPE HARVEST	GROUND TO DUST
GOOD SHEPHERD	GRASS WIDOWER	GROUP CAPTAIN
GOOD SHOOTING	GRATED CHEESE	GROUP OF EIGHT
GOOD SMACKING	GRATING LAUGH	GROUP OF SEVEN
GOOD SPANKING	GRATING VOICE	GROUP OF THREE
GOODS STATION	GRAVE MISTAKE	GROUP THERAPY
GOOD TEMPLARS	GRAVE OFFENCE	GROUSE SEASON
GOOD THINKING	GRAVE SCANDAL	GROW ANIMATED
GOOD THRILLER	GREAT BRAVERY	GROWING CHILD
GOOD-TIME GIRL	GREAT BRITAIN	GROWING PAINS

GROWING THING
GROW POTATOES
GROW RADISHES
GROW TOGETHER
GRUDGING HAND
GUARD AGAINST
GUARDED REPLY
GUERRILLA WAR
GUESSING GAME
GUIDING LIGHT
GUILT COMPLEX
GUILTY PERSON
GUILTY SECRET
GUITAR PLAYER
GUITAR STRING
GULF OF MEXICO
GUNSHOT WOUND
GUY MANNERING
GUYS AND DOLLS
GUY'S HOSPITAL

H – 12

HABEAS CORPUS
HABIT FORMING
HABITUAL LIAR
HACKING COUGH
HACK TO PIECES
HADRIAN'S WALL
HAIR MATTRESS
HAIR OF THE DOG
HAIR RESTORER
HAIR'S BREADTH
HALF DISTANCE
HALF MEASURES
HALF MOURNING
HALF OF BITTER
HALF-SEAS OVER
HALF-WAY HOUSE
HALLEY'S COMET
HALL OF MEMORY
HALTING PLACE
HAM AND TONGUE
HAMBURG STEAK
HAMPTON COURT
HANDEL'S LARGO
HANDFUL OF MEN
HANDICAP RACE
HAND OVER FIST
HAND OVER HAND
HANDS AND FEET
HAND'S BREADTH
HANGING JUDGE
HANGMAN'S ROPE
HANG ONE'S HEAD
HANG TOGETHER

HANS ANDERSEN
HAPPY AS A KING
HAPPY AS A LARK
HAPPY HOLIDAY
HAPPY LANDING
HAPPY NEW YEAR
HAPPY OUTCOME
HAPPY RELEASE
HAPPY RETURNS
HAPPY THOUGHT
HAPPY WARRIOR
HARBOUR LIGHT
HARD CURRENCY
HARD DRINKING
HARD FEELINGS
HARD MATTRESS
HARD MEASURES
HARD QUESTION
HARD SHOULDER
HARD STRUGGLE
HARD SWEARING
HARD THINKING
HARD THOUGHTS
HARD TO COME BY
HARD TO FATHOM
HARD TO HANDLE
HARD TO PLEASE
HARD TRAINING
HARE AND HOUND
HARICOT BEANS
HARLEY STREET
HARMLESS DRUG
HAROLD PINTER
HAROLD WILSON
HARRY CORBETT
HARRY SECOMBE
HARVEST MOUSE
HARVEST QUEEN
HASTY PUDDING
HASTY RETREAT
HATTON GARDEN
HAUNTED HOUSE
HAUTE COUTURE
HAVE A FLUTTER
HAVE A PURPOSE
HAVE A RELAPSE
HAVE A VACANCY
HAVE FEELINGS
HAVE NO ANSWER
HAVE NO CHOICE
HAVE NO DOUBTS
HAVE NO OPTION
HAVE ONE'S WILL
HAVE PATIENCE
HAVE PRIORITY
HAVE SCRUPLES

HAVE THE FACTS
HAVE THE FLOOR
HAVE THE KNACK
HAVE THE LAUGH
HAVE THE MEANS
HAVE THE POWER
HAZARD A GUESS
HEAD FOREMOST
HEAD GARDENER
HEAD IN THE AIR
HEADLINE NEWS
HEAD MISTRESS
HEAD OF CATTLE
HEAD OUT TO SEA
HEAD SHRINKER
HEADS OR TAILS
HEAD THE QUEUE
HEADY MIXTURE
HEADY PERFUME
HEALING CREAM
HEALING POWER
HEALING TOUCH
HEALTH CENTRE
HEALTH RESORT
HEALTHY STATE
HEAP OF STONES
HEAPS OF MONEY
HEAR A PIN DROP
HEAR IN CAMERA
HEART AND HAND
HEART AND SOUL
HEART DISEASE
HEART FAILURE
HEAR THE TRUTH
HEART OF FLINT
HEART OF STONE
HEART'S DESIRE
HEART SURGERY
HEART TO HEART
HEART TROUBLE
HEARTY ASSENT
HEATING AGENT
HEAT OF BATTLE
HEAT OF THE DAY
HEAT OF THE SUN
HEAVE IN SIGHT
HEAVEN FORBID!
HEAVENLY BODY
HEAVENLY CITY
HEAVENLY HOST
HEAVENS ABOVE!
HEAVY AT HEART
HEAVY BIDDING
HEAVY BRIGADE
HEAVY DRINKER
HEAVY PENALTY

HEAVY SLEEPER	HIGH RAINFALL	HONEYED WORDS
HEAVY TRAFFIC	HIGH STANDARD	HONORARY RANK
HEAVY VEHICLE	HIGH STANDING	HONOUR BRIGHT
HEAVY WEATHER	HIGH VELOCITY	HONOURED NAME
HEDGE SPARROW	HILLY COUNTRY	HONOURS OF WAR
HEIGHT OF FAME	HIP-HIP HURRAH!	HOODED TERROR
HEINOUS CRIME	HIRED SERVANT	HOOKS AND EYES
HEIR APPARENT	HIRE PURCHASE	HOPE DEFERRED
HELD IN COMMON	HIS REVERENCE	HOPELESS CASE
HELD TO RANSOM	HIT A BOUNDARY	HOPELESS LOSS
HELEN SHAPIRO	HITCHING POST	HOPELESS MESS
HELL LET LOOSE	HIT ON THE HEAD	HOPELESS TASK
HELL OF A NOISE	HIT THE BOTTLE	HORN OF PLENTY
HELP YOURSELF	HIT THE STUMPS	HORRIBLE BORE
HENRY PURCELL	HIT THE TARGET	HORS DE COMBAT
HERBAL REMEDY	HOARY WITH AGE	HORSE AND CART
HERD INSTINCT	HOCKEY PLAYER	HORSE AND TRAP
HERD OF CATTLE	HOIST THE FLAG	HORSE BLANKET
HERD TOGETHER	HOIST THE SAIL	HORSE DEALING
HERE AND THERE	HOLD A MEETING	HORSE MARINES
HEROIC POETRY	HOLD DOWN A JOB	HORSE SOLDIER
HERO OF THE DAY	HOLD IN COMMON	HORSE TRAINER
HERO'S WELCOME	HOLD IN ESTEEM	HOSPITAL CASE
HEWERS OF WOOD	HOLD IN HORROR	HOSPITAL SHIP
HIDDEN DANGER	HOLD IN PLEDGE	HOSPITAL WARD
HIDDEN DEPTHS	HOLD ONE'S LEAD	HOSTILE CROWD
HIDDEN MENACE	HOLD OUT A HAND	HOSTILE FORCE
HIDDEN TALENT	HOLD OUT HOPES	HOSTILE PRESS
HIDDEN WEALTH	HOLD THE CARDS	HOT AND STRONG
HIDE ONE'S FACE	HOLD THE FIELD	HOTBED OF VICE
HIDE ONE'S HEAD	HOLD THE REINS	HOT CHESTNUTS
HIDEOUS CRIME	HOLD THE STAGE	HOT CHOCOLATE
HIDEOUS NOISE	HOLD TOGETHER	HOT CROSS-BUNS
HIDE THE TRUTH	HOLD TO RANSOM	HOTEL OMNIBUS
HIGH ALTITUDE	HOLIDAY HAUNT	HOT FAVOURITE
HIGH BUILDING	HOLIDAY MONEY	HOT GOSPELLER
HIGH DIVIDEND	HOLLAND HOUSE	HOT-WATER PIPE
HIGHER DEGREE	HOLLOW CHEEKS	HOUND TO DEATH
HIGHER ORDERS	HOLLOW SPHERE	HOURLY CHIMES
HIGH ESTIMATE	HOLLOW SQUARE	HOUR OF DANGER
HIGHEST POINT	HOLLOW THREAT	HOUR OF THE DAY
HIGHEST SCORE	HOLLOW VESSEL	HOUSE AND HOME
HIGH FIDELITY	HOLY ALLIANCE	HOUSE BREAKER
HIGHGATE HILL	HOLY MACKEREL	HOUSE COLOURS
HIGH INTEREST	HOLY OF HOLIES	HOUSE FOR SALE
HIGH IN THE AIR	HOME COMFORTS	HOUSEHOLD GOD
HIGHLAND CLAN	HOME COUNTIES	HOUSE OF CARDS
HIGHLAND REEL	HOME FROM HOME	HOUSE OF LORDS
HIGH LATITUDE	HOME INDUSTRY	HOUSE OF PEERS
HIGHLY AMUSED	HOMELY PERSON	HOUSE OF TUDOR
HIGHLY STRUNG	HOME-MADE CAKE	HOUSE OF USHER
HIGHLY VALUED	HOME PRODUCTS	HOUSE PAINTER
HIGH MOUNTAIN	HOMING PIGEON	HOUSE SPARROW
HIGH OFFICIAL	HONEST FELLOW	HOUSE SURGEON
HIGH POSITION	HONEST LABOUR	HOUSE TO HOUSE
HIGH PRESSURE	HONEST LIVING	HOUSE WARMING

HOUSEY HOUSEY
HOW'S THE ENEMY?
HUMAN AFFAIRS
HUMANE KILLER
HUMAN ELEMENT
HUMAN FAILING
HUMAN FRAILTY
HUMAN REMAINS
HUMAN SPECIES
HUMBLE ORIGIN
HUMBLE PERSON
HUMMING SOUND
HUMOROUS VEIN
HUMPTY DUMPTY
HUNDRED A YEAR
HUNDRED LINES
HUNDRED MILES
HUNDRED TO ONE
HUNDRED YARDS
HUNDRED YEARS
HUNGER STRIKE
HUNK OF CHEESE
HUNTING FIELD
HUNTING LODGE
HUNTING SPEAR
HUNTSMAN'S CRY
HURL DEFIANCE
HURRIED VISIT
HURT FEELINGS
HYDRAULIC RAM
HYDROGEN BOMB
HYMN OF PRAISE

I – 12

ICE-CREAM SODA
ICY RECEPTION
IDEAL HUSBAND
IDENTITY CARD
IDENTITY DISC
IDLE THOUGHTS
IF THE CAP FITS
IGNEOUS ROCKS
ILLEGAL ENTRY
ILLICIT GAINS
ILLICIT MEANS
ILLICIT STILL
ILL-TIMED JEST
IMMORTAL FAME
IMMORTAL NAME
IMMORTAL POET
IMMORTAL SOUL
IMPERIAL PINT
IMPERIAL RULE
IMPLIED TRUTH
IMPROPER WORD

IN A BAD TEMPER
IN A COLD SWEAT
IN A DEAD FAINT
IN A GOOD LIGHT
IN ALL HONESTY
IN A LOUD VOICE
IN AN ACCIDENT
IN AN ARMCHAIR
IN APPEARANCE
IN A SHORT TIME
IN ATTENDANCE
IN AT THE DEATH
IN CASE OF NEED
INCHCAPE ROCK
INCHES TALLER
INCOMING TIDE
IN CONCLUSION
IN CONFERENCE
IN CONFIDENCE
INCREASED PAY
IN DEEP WATERS
INDELIBLE INK
INDIAN MILLET
INDIAN MUTINY
INDIAN SUMMER
IN DIFFICULTY
INDIRECT HINT
INDOOR AERIAL
INDOOR SPORTS
IN EMPLOYMENT
INFANT IN ARMS
INFANTRY UNIT
INFANT SCHOOL
INFERIOR RANK
IN FINE FETTLE
INFINITE TIME
INFRA-RED LAMP
INFRA-RED RAYS
IN FULL FLIGHT
IN GOOD HEALTH
IN GOOD REPAIR
IN GOOD SUPPLY
IN HIGH FAVOUR
IN HIGH RELIEF
IN HOLY ORDERS
IN HOT PURSUIT
INITIAL STAGE
INJURED PARTY
INJURED PRIDE
IN LEAGUE WITH
IN LIKE MANNER
IN LOVE AND WAR
IN LOW SPIRITS
IN MODERATION
IN NEED OF HELP
INNER CABINET

INNER SANCTUM
IN NO FIT STATE
IN OCCUPATION
IN ONE RESPECT
IN ONE'S FAVOUR
IN ONE'S HEYDAY
IN ONE'S OLD AGE
IN ONE'S SENSES
IN ONE'S STRIDE
IN OPPOSITION
IN OTHER WORDS
IN OUR OPINION
IN PARTICULAR
IN POOR HEALTH
IN POSSESSION
IN PROCESSION
IN PROPORTION
IN QUARANTINE
IN RECORD TIME
IN RETIREMENT
IN RETROSPECT
INSANE ASYLUM
INSECURE HOLD
IN SETTLEMENT
IN SILHOUETTE
IN SINGLE FILE
IN SLOW MOTION
IN SUBJECTION
IN SUCCESSION
INTEGRAL PART
INTEREST FREE
INTEREST RATE
INTERIOR WALL
IN TERMS OF LAW
IN THE BALANCE
IN THE BALCONY
IN THE BEDROOM
IN THE CABINET
IN THE CAPITAL
IN THE COUNTRY
IN THE CRYSTAL
IN THE DAYTIME
IN THE DEEP END
IN THE EVENING
IN THE EXTREME
IN THE FASHION
IN THE GALLERY
IN THE HONOURS
IN THE INTERIM
IN THE KITCHEN
IN THE LIBRARY
IN THE LONG RUN
IN THE MORNING
IN THE NURSERY
IN THE OLD DAYS
IN THE OPEN AIR

IN THE PADDOCK
IN THE PARLOUR
IN THE PEERAGE
IN THE PICTURE
IN THE PRESENT
IN THE RUNNING
IN THE SHADOWS
IN THE SUBURBS
IN THE THEATRE
IN THE TROPICS
IN THE VERY ACT
IN THE VILLAGE
IN THE YEAR ONE
IN TRIPLICATE
IN UNDERTONES
IN UTMOST NEED
INVALID CHAIR
INVERSE ORDER
INVERSE RATIO
INVERTED SNOB
INVERTED TURN
INVISIBLE INK
INVISIBLE MAN
INVOICE CLERK
IN YUGOSLAVIA
IRISH COLLEEN
IRISH TERRIER
IRISH WHISKEY
IRON AND STEEL
IRONING BOARD
IRVING BERLIN
ISLAND OF CUBA
ISLE OF CYPRUS
ISLE OF THANET
ISOLATED CASE
ISSUE A THREAT
ITALIAN MONEY
IT ALL DEPENDS
IT'S AN ILL WIND
IT'S A PLEASURE

J – 12

JACKET POTATO
JACKIE COOGAN
JACK IN OFFICE
JACK OF HEARTS
JACK OF SPADES
JACK OF TRUMPS
JACK ROBINSON
JACK SHEPPARD
JACOB'S LADDER
JADE NECKLACE
JAMES BOSWELL
JAMES STEWART
JAMES THURBER

JANETTE SCOTT
JANUARY SALES
JAUNDICED EYE
JAZZ FESTIVAL
JEAN METCALFE
JE NE SAIS QUOI
JERMYN STREET
JIG-SAW PUZZLE
JIMMY DURANTE
JIMMY EDWARDS
JIMMY WHEELER
JIM THE PENMAN
JOAN CRAWFORD
JOG THE MEMORY
JOHN CLEMENTS
JOHNNY MATHIS
JOHN TRAVOLTA
JOIN IN THE FUN
JOIN ONE'S SHIP
JOINT ACCOUNT
JOINT CONCERN
JOIN THE CHOIR
JOIN THE DANCE
JOIN THE ENEMY
JOIN THE PARTY
JOIN THE QUEUE
JOIN THE RANKS
JOINT HOLDING
JOIN TOGETHER
JOINT TENANCY
JOINT TRUSTEE
JOKING MATTER
JOLLY JACK TAR
JOLLY SWAGMAN
JONATHAN WILD
JORDAN ALMOND
JOSEPH CONRAD
JOSEPH COTTON
JOSEPH STALIN
JUDGE AND JURY
JUDGMENT SEAT
JULIAN HUXLEY
JULIE ANDREWS
JULIENNE SOUP
JULIE WALTERS
JULIUS CAESAR
JULY THE FIFTH
JULY THE FIRST
JULY THE NINTH
JULY THE SIXTH
JULY THE TENTH
JULY THE THIRD
JUMP THE QUEUE
JUMP THE RAILS
JUNE THE FIFTH
JUNE THE FIRST

JUNE THE NINTH
JUNE THE SIXTH
JUNE THE TENTH
JUNE THE THIRD
JUNIOR SCHOOL
JUNIOR TYPIST
JUST AS YOU SAY
JUST FOR SPITE
JUST THE THING
JUST THIS ONCE
JUVENILE LEAD

K – 12

KEEN APPETITE
KEEN AS A RAZOR
KEEN INTEREST
KEEN PLEASURE
KEEP ACCOUNTS
KEEP A LOOK-OUT
KEEP A PROMISE
KEEP CHEERFUL
KEEP-FIT CLASS
KEEP GOOD TIME
KEEP GUESSING
KEEP IN PRISON
KEEP IN PURDAH
KEEP IN REPAIR
KEEP ONE'S FEET
KEEP ONE'S HEAD
KEEP ONE'S SEAT
KEEP ONE'S WORD
KEEP ON TRYING
KEEP PRISONER
KEEP THE BOOKS
KEEP THE PEACE
KEEP THE SCORE
KEEP TOGETHER
KEEP UP-TO-DATE
KENNETH HORNE
KEPT ON A LEASH
KETTLE OF FISH
KEY OF THE DOOR
KEY SIGNATURE
KEYSTONE COPS
KEY TO THE SAFE
KHAKI UNIFORM
KILL BY INCHES
KILL OUTRIGHT
KINDLING WOOD
KING AND QUEEN
KING OF BEASTS
KING OF FRANCE
KING OF HEARTS
KING OF SPADES
KING OF TRUMPS

KING'S COLLEGE
KING'S COUNSEL
KING'S ENGLISH
KING'S HIGHWAY
KING'S PROCTOR
KITCHEN CHAIR
KITCHEN RANGE
KITCHEN STOVE
KITCHEN TABLE
KNACKER'S YARD
KNAVE OF CLUBS
KNEE BREECHES
KNIFE AND FORK
KNIFE GRINDER
KNIGHT ERRANT
KNIGHTLY DEED
KNIT A SWEATER
KNIT ONE'S BROW
KNIT THE BROWS
KNIT TOGETHER
KNOCK AGAINST
KNOCK OFF WORK
KNOCK-OUT BLOW
KNOW FOR A FACT
KNOW FULL WELL
KNOW NO BETTER
KNOW NO BOUNDS
KNOW ONE'S DUTY
KNOW THE DRILL
KNOW THE FACTS
KNOW THE ROPES
KNOW THE SCORE
KNOW THE TRUTH
KNOW THE WORST
KNOW WHAT TO DO
KNUCKLE UNDER
KNUR AND SPELL

L – 12

LABOURED JOKE
LABOUR IN VAIN
LABOUR LEADER
LABOUR MARKET
LABOUR OFFICE
LABOUR OF LOVE
LABOUR POLICY
LACE CURTAINS
LACKING MONEY
LACKING POINT
LACKING POISE
LACKING PROOF
LACKING SENSE
LACK INTEREST
LACK OF BRAINS
LACK OF FINISH

LACK OF POLISH
LACK OF PROFIT
LACK OF REASON
LACK OF SPIRIT
LACK OF WISDOM
LACROSSE TEAM
LADDER OF FAME
LADY HAMILTON
LADY JANE GREY
LADY MARGARET
LADY MAYORESS
LADY NICOTINE
LADY'S BICYCLE
LADY SUPERIOR
LAGER AND LIME
LAISSEZ FAIRE
LAKE DISTRICT
LAKE MAGGIORE
LAKE MICHIGAN
LAKE SUPERIOR
LAKE VICTORIA
LAKE WINNIPEG
LAMBENT LIGHT
LAMB SANDWICH
LANDED ESTATE
LANDED GENTRY
LANDING CRAFT
LANDING PARTY
LANDING PLACE
LANDING STRIP
LAND OF DREAMS
LAND OF PLENTY
LAND SURVEYOR
LAND TRANSFER
LANTERN SLIDE
LAP OF THE GODS
LARGE ACCOUNT
LARGE EXPANSE
LARGE HELPING
LARGE PORTION
LARGE SECTION
LARGE VARIETY
LASER PRINTER
LASH THE WAVES
LAST BUT THREE
LAST DELIVERY
LAST ELECTION
LAST FRONTIER
LASTING PEACE
LAST JUDGMENT
LAST RESOURCE
LAST SATURDAY
LAST SYLLABLE
LAST THURSDAY
LAST TO ARRIVE
LATE IN THE DAY

LATE LAMENTED
LATE MARRIAGE
LATENT ENERGY
LATENT TALENT
LATEST REPORT
LATIN AMERICA
LATIN GRAMMAR
LATIN QUARTER
LATIN TEACHER
LAUGH OUT LOUD
LAUGH TO SCORN
LAUNCHING PAD
LAUREL WREATH
LAVENDER HILL
LAVISH PRAISE
LAW OF ENGLAND
LAW OF GRAVITY
LAW OF THE LAND
LAWS OF MOTION
LAWYER'S BRIEF
LAY A FINGER ON
LAY DOWN A PLAN
LAYER ON LAYER
LAY IT ON THICK
LEAD A GAY LIFE
LEADER WRITER
LEADING ACTOR
LEADING LIGHT
LEAD IN PRAYER
LEAD THE DANCE
LEAD THE FIELD
LEANING TOWER
LEAP IN THE AIR
LEARN A LESSON
LEARN BY HEART
LEARNED JUDGE
LEARN TO DRIVE
LEARN TO RELAX
LEARN TO WRITE
LEATHER GOODS
LEATHER STRAP
LEAVE A LEGACY
LEAVE IT ALONE
LEAVE NO DOUBT
LEAVE NO TRACE
LEAVE NO WISER
LEAVE OFF WORK
LEAVE THE ARMY
LEAVE THE NAVY
LEAVE THE NEST
LEAVE THE ROOM
LED ONE A DANCE
LED TO BELIEVE
LEFT AND RIGHT
LEFT-HAND BEND
LEFT-HAND SIDE

LEFT-HAND TURN
LEFT IN THE AIR
LEFT NO CHOICE
LEFT SHOULDER
LEFT STANDING
LEFT TO CHANCE
LEGAL ADVISER
LEGAL CUSTODY
LEGAL DEFENCE
LEGAL FICTION
LEGAL JOURNAL
LEGAL OPINION
LEGAL PROCESS
LEGAL VERDICT
LEGS TOGETHER
LEG TO STAND ON
LEISURE HOURS
LEMON PUDDING
LENGTH OF TIME
LESSON ELEVEN
LESSON TWELVE
LESS THAN COST
LETHAL WEAPON
LET ONESELF GO
LET OUT ON HIRE
LETTER OPENER
LETTER WRITER
LET THINGS RIP
LET WELL ALONE
LEVEL PEGGING
LEVEL STRETCH
LEWIS CARROLL
LEYTON ORIENT
LIBERAL DONOR
LIBERAL PARTY
LIBERAL SHARE
LIBERTY HORSE
LIBYAN DESERT
LICENSING ACT
LICENSING LAW
LICK ONE'S LIPS
LIE OF THE LAND
LIE PROSTRATE
LIFE AND DEATH
LIFE IMMORTAL
LIFE INSTINCT
LIFE INTEREST
LIFE IN THE RAW
LIFE OF LUXURY
LIFE SENTENCE
LIFT ONE'S HAND
LIFT THE ELBOW
LIGHT A CANDLE
LIGHT AND AIRY
LIGHT AND DARK
LIGHT BRIGADE

LIGHT CAVALRY
LIGHT CRUISER
LIGHT DRAGOON
LIGHTED TORCH
LIGHT FINGERS
LIGHTNING ROD
LIGHT OF HEART
LIGHT RAILWAY
LIGHT READING
LIGHT SLEEPER
LIGHT THE LAMP
LIGHT TRAFFIC
LIGHT VEHICLE
LIKE HOT CAKES
LIKE OLD BOOTS
LIKE SARDINES
LIKE THE DEVIL
LIKE UNTO LIKE
LIKE WILDFIRE
LILY OF LAGUNA
LIMB FROM LIMB
LIMB OF THE LAW
LIMITED MEANS
LIMITED OVERS
LIMITED SCOPE
LIMITED SCORE
LIMITED SPACE
LINCOLN GREEN
LINE OF ACTION
LINE OF BATTLE
LINE OF FLIGHT
LINE REGIMENT
LINE UPON LINE
LINGUA FRANCA
LINK TOGETHER
LIQUEUR GLASS
LIQUID ASSETS
LIQUID MAKE-UP
LIST OF VOTERS
LITERAL ERROR
LITERAL TRUTH
LITERARY AIMS
LITERARY CLUB
LITERARY FAME
LITERARY HACK
LITERARY LION
LITERARY PAGE
LITERARY STAR
LITERARY WORK
LITTER BASKET
LITTLE CHANCE
LITTLE CHANGE
LITTLE DEMAND
LITTLE DORRIT
LITTLE ENOUGH
LITTLE FINGER

LITTLE HITLER
LITTLE MONKEY
LITTLE PEOPLE
LITTLE SISTER
LITTLE SQUIRT
LITTLE TERROR
LITTLE THANKS
LITTLE THINGS
LITTLE TIN GOD
LITTLE WONDER
LIVE AND LEARN
LIVE FOR KICKS
LIVE FOR TODAY
LIVE IN A DREAM
LIVE IN CLOVER
LIVE IN LUXURY
LIVELY DEBATE
LIVE ON CREDIT
LIVE ONE'S LIFE
LIVER SAUSAGE
LIVERY STABLE
LIVE TOGETHER
LIVING MATTER
LIVING MEMORY
LIVING TISSUE
LOAD SHEDDING
LOBSTER PATTY
LOBSTER SALAD
LOCAL AFFAIRS
LOCAL DIALECT
LOCAL FEELING
LOCALISED WAR
LOCK-UP GARAGE
LODGING HOUSE
LOGICAL ERROR
LOGICAL ORDER
LONDON BRIDGE
LONDON EDITOR
LONDON LIGHTS
LONDON SEASON
LONG ANCESTRY
LONG AND OFTEN
LONG CORRIDOR
LONG DISTANCE
LONG DIVISION
LONG DRAWN-OUT
LONGEST NIGHT
LONG EXPECTED
LONG FAREWELL
LONG-FELT WANT
LONG FOR PEACE
LONG SENTENCE
LONG STANDING
LONG-TERM LOAN
LONG-TERM VIEW
LONG TROUSERS

LONG VACATION
LONG WAY ROUND
LONSDALE BELT
LOOK BOTH WAYS
LOOK DOWNCAST
LOOK DOWN UPON
LOOK ONE'S BEST
LOOK PECULIAR
LOOK PLEASANT
LOOK SHEEPISH
LOOK SIDEWAYS
LOOK SUPERIOR
LOOSE CLOTHES
LOOSE CONDUCT
LOOSE GARMENT
LORD ADVOCATE
LORD ALMIGHTY
LORD LEIGHTON
LORD MACAULAY
LORD OF APPEAL
LORD TENNYSON
LORETTA YOUNG
LOSE BUSINESS
LOSE INTEREST
LOSE MOMENTUM
LOSE ONE'S FORM
LOSE ONE'S GRIP
LOSE ONE'S HAIR
LOSE ONE'S HEAD
LOSE ONE'S LIFE
LOSE ONE'S SEAT
LOSE ONE'S WIFE
LOSE ONE'S WITS
LOSE PATIENCE
LOSE PRESTIGE
LOSE STRENGTH
LOSE THE ASHES
LOSE THE MATCH
LOSE THE SCENT
LOSING BATTLE
LOSING HAZARD
LOSING TICKET
LOSS OF CUSTOM
LOSS OF ENERGY
LOSS OF HEALTH
LOSS OF HONOUR
LOSS OF MEMORY
LOSS OF MORALE
LOSS OF PROFIT
LOSS OF REASON
LOSS OF SPEECH
LOSS OF VISION
LOSS OF WEIGHT
LOST AND FOUND
LOST ELECTION
LOST FOR A WORD

LOST FOR WORDS
LOST IN WONDER
LOST PROPERTY
LOTUS BLOSSOM
LOUD AND CLEAR
LOUD APPLAUSE
LOUD LAUGHTER
LOUIS GOLDING
LOUIS PASTEUR
LOUNGE LIZARD
LOVE INTEREST
LOVELY FIGURE
LOVE OF NATURE
LOVING COUPLE
LOW CHURCHMAN
LOW CONDITION
LOW COUNTRIES
LOW-DOWN TRICK
LOWER ANIMALS
LOWER BRACKET
LOWER CHAMBER
LOWER CLASSES
LOWER ONESELF
LOWER REGIONS
LOWER THE FLAG
LOWEST BIDDER
LOWEST DEPTHS
LOW FREQUENCY
LOW VALUATION
LOW WATER MARK
LOYAL CITIZEN
LOYAL SUBJECT
LOYAL SUPPORT
LUCIFER MATCH
LUCKY AT CARDS
LUCKY VENTURE
LUGGAGE LABEL
LULWORTH COVE
LUMBER JACKET
LUMP TOGETHER
LUSH PASTURES
LUST FOR POWER
LUXURIOUS BED
LUXURY CRUISE
LYRIC THEATRE

M – 12

MACHINE TOOLS
MAD AS A HATTER
MADDING CROWD
MADE IN FRANCE
MADE IN HEAVEN
MAGIC FORMULA
MAGIC LANTERN
MAGNETIC FISH

MAGNETIC MINE
MAGNETIC POLE
MAGNETIC TAPE
MAIDEN FLIGHT
MAIDEN SPEECH
MAIDEN STAKES
MAIDEN VOYAGE
MAID OF HONOUR
MAIN BUSINESS
MAIN DRAINAGE
MAIN ENTRANCE
MAIN INDUSTRY
MAIN QUESTION
MAIN SEQUENCE
MAÎTRE D'HÔTEL
MAJOR BARBARA
MAJOR EDITION
MAJOR GENERAL
MAJORITY RULE
MAJORITY VOTE
MAJOR PREMISE
MAJOR PROPHET
MAJOR TRAGEDY
MAKE A BARGAIN
MAKE A BEE-LINE
MAKE A BEQUEST
MAKE A BONFIRE
MAKE ABSOLUTE
MAKE A CENTURY
MAKE A CIRCUIT
MAKE A CURTSEY
MAKE A DEAD SET
MAKE ADVANCES
MAKE A FAUX PAS
MAKE A FORTUNE
MAKE A GESTURE
MAKE A GET-AWAY
MAKE A HUNDRED
MAKE A LANDING
MAKE A LONG ARM
MAKE A MISTAKE
MAKE AN APPEAL
MAKE AN ARREST
MAKE AN EFFORT
MAKE AN ESCAPE
MAKE A NEW WILL
MAKE A PRESENT
MAKE A PROMISE
MAKE A PROTEST
MAKE A REQUEST
MAKE BAD BLOOD
MAKE BANKRUPT
MAKE ENDS MEET
MAKE IT SNAPPY
MAKE MISCHIEF
MAKE NO PROFIT

MAKE ONE'S EXIT	MARIE CORELLI	MAXIMUM BREAK
MAKE ONE SIT UP	MARIE TEMPEST	MAXIMUM PRICE
MAKE ONE'S MARK	MARIE THERESA	MAXIMUM SPEED
MAKE ONE'S PILE	MARINE ANIMAL	MAYPOLE DANCE
MAKE ONE'S WILL	MARINE ENGINE	MAY THE EIGHTH
MAKE OUT A CASE	MARINE GROWTH	MAY THE FOURTH
MAKE PROGRESS	MARINE PARADE	MAY THE SECOND
MAKE SPEECHES	MARINE STORES	MEAN BUSINESS
MAKE THE GRADE	MARITIME ALPS	MEAN MISCHIEF
MAKE-UP ARTIST	MARIUS GORING	MEANS TO AN END
MAKE UP LEEWAY	MARKED MANNER	MEASURED MILE
MALAY STRAITS	MARKET GARDEN	MEAT AND DRINK
MALE STRIPPER	MARKET SQUARE	MEAT SANDWICH
MALTESE CROSS	MARKET STREET	MEDICAL BOARD
MALVERN HILLS	MARKET TRENDS	MEDICAL CHECK
MAN ABOUT TOWN	MARK OF ESTEEM	MEDICAL STAFF
MAN AT THE HELM	MARK OF GENIUS	MEDICINE BALL
MANDARIN DUCK	MARK THE CARDS	MEDIUM HEIGHT
MANGO CHUTNEY	MARK THE SCORE	MEDIUM SHERRY
MANILLA PAPER	MARLEY'S GHOST	MEET BY CHANCE
MAN IN THE DOCK	MARLON BRANDO	MEETING HOUSE
MAN IN THE MOON	MARMALADE CAT	MEETING PLACE
MAN-MADE FIBRE	MARRIAGE KNOT	MEETING POINT
MAN OF DESTINY	MARRIAGE RATE	MEET IN SECRET
MAN OF FASHION	MARRIAGE TIES	MEET ONE'S FATE
MAN OF FORTUNE	MARRIAGE VOWS	MEET THE PLANE
MAN OF HIS WORD	MARRIED BLISS	MEET THE TRAIN
MAN OF LEISURE	MARRIED WOMAN	MELTED BUTTER
MAN OF LETTERS	MARRY BY PROXY	MELTED CHEESE
MAN OF MYSTERY	MARRY IN HASTE	MELTING POINT
MAN OF SCIENCE	MARSHALL PLAN	MELT THE HEART
MAN OF THE HOUR	MARTIAL MUSIC	MEMORIAL HALL
MAN ON THE MOON	MARTIN LUTHER	MEND ONE'S WAYS
MAN ON THE SPOT	MARX BROTHERS	MEN OF HARLECH
MAN OVERBOARD	MARY OF ARGYLL	MENTAL ASYLUM
MANSION HOUSE	MARY PICKFORD	MENTAL EFFORT
MAN THE BREACH	MASONIC LODGE	MENTAL ENERGY
MAN-TO-MAN TALK	MASSED CHOIRS	MENTAL HEALTH
MANUAL LABOUR	MASSES OF FOOD	MENTALLY SICK
MANUAL WORKER	MASS HYSTERIA	MENTAL STRAIN
MANY A LONG DAY	MASS MOVEMENT	MENTAL STRESS
MANY RESPECTS	MASS MURDERER	MERCHANT BANK
MANY YEARS AGO	MASS OF NERVES	MERCHANT NAVY
MAP OF AUSTRIA	MASTER AND MAN	MERCHANT SHIP
MAP OF BELGIUM	MASTER CUTLER	MERCY KILLING
MAP OF DENMARK	MASTER GUNNER	MERE FLEA-BITE
MAP OF ENGLAND	MASTER OF ARTS	MERE PITTANCE
MAP OF GERMANY	MASTER SPIRIT	MERRY MONARCH
MAP OF HOLLAND	MASTER STROKE	MERRY OLD SOUL
MAP OF IRELAND	MASTER TAILOR	MERSEY TUNNEL
MARATHON RACE	MATCHING PAIR	MESSENGER BOY
MARCHING SONG	MATERIAL GAIN	METAL FATIGUE
MARGINAL LAND	MATERNAL LOVE	METEOR SHOWER
MARGINAL NOTE	MATING SEASON	METHOD ACTING
MARGINAL SEAT	MATTER IN HAND	METRICAL UNIT
MARIE CELESTE	MATTER OF FACT	METRIC SYSTEM

MEZZO SOPRANO	MINOR SET-BACK	MORAL SUPPORT
MICHAEL ARLEN	MINOR TRAGEDY	MORAL VICTORY
MICHAEL ASPEL	MINSTREL SHOW	MORE'S THE PITY
MICHAEL CAINE	MISPLACED WIT	MORE THAN EVER
MICHAEL ROONEY	MISSED CHANCE	MORE THAN ONCE
MIDDLE AND LEG	MISSING PIECE	MORMON CHURCH
MIDDLE COURSE	MISS THE PLANE	MORNING AFTER
MIDDLE FINGER	MISS THE POINT	MORNING DRESS
MIDDLE TEMPLE	MISS THE TRAIN	MORNING GLORY
MIDDLE WICKET	MISS UNIVERSE	MORNING PAPER
MIDNIGHT BLUE	MISTAKEN IDEA	MORRIS DANCER
MIDNIGHT HOUR	MISTRESS FORD	MORTAL COMBAT
MIDNIGHT MASS	MIXED BATHING	MORTAL TERROR
MIDNIGHT SWIM	MIXED COMPANY	MORTE D'ARTHUR
MIDSUMMER DAY	MIXED DOUBLES	MORTGAGE DEED
MIGHT AND MAIN	MIXED FARMING	MOSQUITO BITE
MIGHT IS RIGHT	MIXED MOTIVES	MOST EXCITING
MIGHTY EFFORT	MIXED PICKLES	MOST GRACIOUS
MIGHTY HUNTER	MIX IN SOCIETY	MOST OF THE DAY
MILES PER HOUR	MOATED GRANGE	MOST REVEREND
MILE UPON MILE	MOBILE COLUMN	MOTE IN THE EYE
MILFORD HAVEN	MODEL HUSBAND	MOTHER AND SON
MILITARY BAND	MODEL PATIENT	MOTHER CHURCH
MILITARY BASE	MODEL RAILWAY	MOTHER GRUNDY
MILITARY BODY	MODE OF LIVING	MOTHERLY LOVE
MILITARY CAMP	MODERATE RENT	MOTHER NATURE
MILITARY DUTY	MODERN SCHOOL	MOTHER OF MINE
MILITARY LIFE	MODEST INCOME	MOTHERS' UNION
MILITARY PACE	MODEST PERSON	MOTHER TONGUE
MILITARY RANK	MODUS VIVENDI	MOTOR BICYCLE
MILITARY TYPE	MOIRA SHEARER	MOTOR CRUISER
MILITARY UNIT	MOLL FLANDERS	MOTORING CLUB
MILK AND A DASH	MOMENT OF TIME	MOTOR LICENCE
MILK AND HONEY	MONASTIC LIFE	MOTOR SCOOTER
MILK AND SUGAR	MONASTIC VOWS	MOTOR VEHICLE
MILK AND WATER	MONDAY'S CHILD	MOUNTAIN GOAT
MILKING STOOL	MONETARY HELP	MOUNTAIN LAKE
MILK SHORTAGE	MONETARY UNIT	MOUNTAIN PASS
MILLION YEARS	MONEYED CLASS	MOUNTAIN PEAK
MINCE MATTERS	MONEY MATTERS	MOUNTAIN TARN
MINCING STEPS	MONEY TO SPARE	MOUNT A LADDER
MIND HOW YOU GO!	MONKEY GLANDS	MOUNT EVEREST
MIND YOUR HEAD!	MONKEY JACKET	MOUNT OF VENUS
MIND YOUR STEP!	MONKEY PUZZLE	MOUNT OLYMPUS
MINERAL SALTS	MONKEY TRICKS	MOUNT PEGASUS
MINERAL WATER	MONTH BY MONTH	MOURA LYMPANY
MINERAL WORLD	MONTHLY VISIT	MOUSTACHE CUP
MINERS STRIKE	MONTH'S NOTICE	MOUTH TO MOUTH
MINIATURE DOG	MOOR OF VENICE	MOVABLE FEAST
MINING EXPERT	MOOT QUESTION	MOVED TO TEARS
MINING RIGHTS	MORAL CONDUCT	MOVE SIDEWAYS
MINOR AILMENT	MORAL COURAGE	MOVING APPEAL
MINORITY RULE	MORALITY PLAY	MOVING FINGER
MINORITY VOTE	MORALLY BOUND	MOVING SPEECH
MINOR PREMISE	MORAL SCIENCE	MOVING SPIRIT
MINOR PROPHET	MORAL STAMINA	MOVING TARGET

MUCH IMPROVED
MUCH IN DEMAND
MUCH MISTAKEN
MUD IN YOUR EYE
MUFFLED DRUMS
MUFFLED TONES
MUFFLED VOICE
MUGGY WEATHER
MULBERRY BUSH
MULBERRY TREE
MULTIPLE SHOP
MULTIPLE STAR
MUNICH CRISIS
MUNICIPAL LAW
MURDER CHARGE
MURDER VICTIM
MURDER WEAPON
MURIEL PAVLOW
MUSCATEL WINE
MUSHROOM SOUP
MUSICAL PIECE
MUSICAL SCALE
MUSICAL SCORE
MUSICAL SOUND
MUSICAL VOICE
MUSIC AT NIGHT
MUSIC LICENCE
MUSIC TEACHER
MUTED STRINGS
MUTTON CUTLET
MUTUAL FRIEND
MUTUAL HATRED
MUTUAL PROFIT
MUTUAL REGARD
MY BLUE HEAVEN
MY DEAR FELLOW
MY DEAR WATSON
MY GOOD FRIEND
MYSTERY STORY

N – 12

NAIL POLISHER
NAIL SCISSORS
NAKED REALITY
NAME IN LIGHTS
NARROW DEFEAT
NARROW ESCAPE
NARROW GROOVE
NARROW MARGIN
NARROW SQUEAK
NARROW STREET
NARROW THE GAP
NARROW TUNNEL
NATIONAL BANK
NATIONAL DEBT

NATIONAL DISH
NATIONAL FLAG
NATIONAL GAME
NATIONAL GRID
NATIONAL HERO
NATIONAL PARK
NATIONAL POLL
NATIONAL ROAD
NATIONAL STUD
NATION IN ARMS
NATIVE CUSTOM
NATIVE TONGUE
NATIVE TROOPS
NATIVITY PLAY
NATURAL BREAK
NATURAL CHARM
NATURAL CHILD
NATURAL COVER
NATURAL DEATH
NATURAL ENEMY
NATURAL FIBRE
NATURAL ORDER
NATURAL PRIDE
NATURAL SCALE
NATURAL STATE
NAUGHTY CHILD
NAUTICAL FLAG
NAUTICAL LIFE
NAUTICAL MILE
NAUTICAL ROLL
NAVAL ATTACHÉ
NAVAL BRIGADE
NAVAL COLLEGE
NAVAL COMMAND
NAVAL OFFICER
NAVAL RESERVE
NAVAL SERVICE
NAVAL STATION
NAVAL TACTICS
NAVAL UNIFORM
NAVAL WARFARE
NEAR DISTANCE
NEAR RELATION
NEAR RELATIVE
NEAR THE COAST
NEAR THE SHORE
NEAR THE TRUTH
NECKING PARTY
NECK OF MUTTON
NEEDLESS RISK
NEGATIVE POLE
NEGATIVE SIGN
NEGATIVE VOTE
NEON LIGHTING
NERVE ONESELF
NERVOUS STATE

NERVOUS WRECK
NEST OF TABLES
NEUTER GENDER
NEUTRAL POWER
NEUTRAL STATE
NEVER DESPAIR
NEVER GO WRONG
NEVER THE SAME
NEVER TOO LATE
NEVER YOU MIND!
NEW AMSTERDAM
NEW BRUNSWICK
NEW DEPARTURE
NEW ENGLANDER
NEW HAMPSHIRE
NEW INVENTION
NEW JERUSALEM
NEWLY MARRIED
NEW PARAGRAPH
NEWS BULLETIN
NEWS OF THE DAY
NEW STATESMAN
NEW TECHNIQUE
NEW TESTAMENT
NEW YORK STATE
NEW ZEALANDER
NEXT ELECTION
NEXT QUESTION
NEXT SATURDAY
NEXT THURSDAY
NIAGARA FALLS
NICE AND HANDY
NICE AND SWEET
NICE AND TIGHT
NICE BUSINESS
NICELY PLACED
NICE QUESTION
NICKEL SILVER
NIGEL PATRICK
NIGGLING PAIN
NIGHT CLASSES
NIGHT CLOTHES
NIGHT DRIVING
NIGHT FIGHTER
NIGHT NURSERY
NIGHT OF BLISS
NIGHT PROWLER
NINE AND A HALF
NINE AND EIGHT
NINE AND SEVEN
NINE AND THREE
NINE OF HEARTS
NINE OF SPADES
NINE OF TRUMPS
NINE OUT OF TEN
NINE THOUSAND

NINTH CENTURY
NINTH OF APRIL
NINTH OF MARCH
NITROUS OXIDE
NO ADMITTANCE
NO BED OF ROSES
NOBLE BEARING
NOBLE DESCENT
NOBLE EDIFICE
NOBLE GESTURE
NOBLE MANNERS
NOBODY'S CHILD
NOBODY'S FAULT
NO-CLAIM BONUS
NO COMPARISON
NO DIFFERENCE
NO DOUBT AT ALL
NO EARTHLY USE
NO END OF MONEY
NO FIXED ABODE
NO FLIES ON HIM
NO IMPORTANCE
NOLENS VOLENS
NOMINAL POWER
NOMINAL PRICE
NOMINAL RULER
NOMINAL VALUE
NONE THE WISER
NONE THE WORSE
NONE WHATEVER
NON-STOP REVUE
NON-STOP TRAIN
NO PREFERENCE
NORMAN WISDOM
NORTH AMERICA
NORTH BRITAIN
NORTH COUNTRY
NORTHERN LINE
NORTH GERMANY
NORTH SHIELDS
NORTH TO SOUTH
NOTABLE POINT
NOTARY PUBLIC
NOT A STITCH ON
NOTHING AMISS
NOTHING AT ALL
NOTHING DOING
NOTHING FOR IT
NOTHING KNOWN
NOTHING TO ADD
NOTHING TO EAT
NOTHING TO PAY
NOTHING TO SAY
NOTICE TO QUIT
NO TIME TO LOSE
NOT IN KEEPING

NOT IN THE MOOD
NOT WORTH A RAP
NOUVEAU RICHE
NOVEMBER DAYS
NUCLEAR POWER
NUDIST COLONY
NUMBER ELEVEN
NUMBER-ONE MAN
NUMBER, PLEASE
NUMBER TWELVE
NUMBER TWENTY
NUMB WITH COLD
NURSERY CLASS
NURSERY RHYME
NURSERY STORY
NURSING STAFF
NUT CHOCOLATE
NUTMEG GRATER
NUTS AND BOLTS

O – 12

OBITER DICTUM
OBJECT LESSON
OBJECT OF PITY
OBLIQUE ANGLE
OBSTACLE RACE
OCCULT POWERS
OCEANS OF TIME
OCEAN TRAFFIC
ODDS AND EVENS
ODD SENSATION
ODDS-ON CHANCE
OF EVIL REPUTE
OFFER A CHOICE
OFFER A REWARD
OFFER FOR SALE
OFFERTORY BOX
OFF HIS OWN BAT
OFF HIS ROCKER
OFFICER CADET
OFFICERS' MESS
OFFICIAL COPY
OFFICIAL DUTY
OFFICIAL FORM
OFFICIAL LIST
OFFICIAL VIEW
OFF LIKE A SHOT
OFF ONE'S CHUMP
OFF ONE'S GUARD
OFF ONE'S HANDS
OFF THE COURSE
OFF THE RECORD
OFF THE SCREEN
OF GREAT WORTH
OF MICE AND MEN

OIL OF JUNIPER
OIL OF VITRIOL
OIL THE WHEELS
OKLAHOMA CITY
OLD AS HISTORY
OLD BATTLE-AXE
OLDER BROTHER
OLD FAVOURITE
OLD FOLKS' HOME
OLD FOR HIS AGE
OLD GENTLEMAN
OLD HARROVIAN
OLD HUNDREDTH
OLD MAN'S BEARD
OLD MORTALITY
OLD PRETENDER
OLD SCHOOL TIE
OLD SHOULDERS
OLD TESTAMENT
OLD-TIME DANCE
OLD-TIME WALTZ
OLD WIVES' TALE
OLYMPIC GAMES
OLYMPIC MEDAL
OMINOUS CLOUD
OMISSION MARK
OMIT NO DETAIL
ON A GOOD THING
ON A LEVEL WITH
ON AN EVEN KEEL
ON A STRETCHER
ONCE AND AGAIN
ONCE IN A WHILE
ONCE TOO OFTEN
ON COMMISSION
ONE AND TWENTY
ONE-DAY STRIKE
ONE FELL SWOOP
ONE FOR HIS NOB
ONE FOR THE POT
ONE-HORSE SHOW
ONE-HORSE TOWN
ONE JUMP AHEAD
ONE-LEGGED MAN
ONE LONG DREAM
ONE MOVE AHEAD
ONE OF THE BEST
ONE OF THE GANG
ONE OF THE LADS
ON EQUAL TERMS
ONE'S FAIR NAME
ONE-SIDED VIEW
ONE-TRACK MIND
ONE-WAY STREET
ON FIRM GROUND
ON FOUR WHEELS

ONLY DAUGHTER
ON ONE'S HONOUR
ON ONE'S METTLE
ON ONE'S UPPERS
ON REFLECTION
ON SAFE GROUND
ON SENTRY DUTY
ON SUFFERANCE
ON TELEVISION
ON THE AVERAGE
ON THE CEILING
ON THE COUNCIL
ON THE COUNTER
ON THE DECLINE
ON THE DEFENCE
ON THE FAIRWAY
ON THE FAR SIDE
ON THE HORIZON
ON THE LEE-SIDE
ON THE LOOK-OUT
ON THE OFF-SIDE
ON THE ONE HAND
ON THE OUTSIDE
ON THE PAY-ROLL
ON THE QUI VIVE
ON THE RAMPAGE
ON THE REBOUND
ON THE RETREAT
ON THE SURFACE
ON THE TERRACE
ON THE TOP RUNG
ON THE TOW-PATH
ON THE UP-AND-UP
ON THE UPGRADE
ON THE WARPATH
ON THE WAY DOWN
ON WITH THE JOB
OPEN ALL NIGHT
OPEN CARRIAGE
OPEN CHAMPION
OPEN CONFLICT
OPENING NIGHT
OPENING SCENE
OPENING WORDS
OPEN ONE'S EYES
OPEN OUTWARDS
OPEN QUESTION
OPEN SANDWICH
OPEN TO ATTACK
OPEN TO CHANCE
OPEN TO CHOICE
OPERA COMIQUE
OPERA GLASSES
OPERATIC ARIA
OPERATIC STAR
OPIUM TRAFFIC

OPPOSING SIDE
OPPOSING TEAM
OPPOSITE CAMP
OPPOSITE ENDS
OPPOSITE SIDE
OPTICAL FIBRE
OPTICAL GLASS
ORANGE PIPPIN
ORANGE SQUASH
ORDEAL BY FIRE
ORDER IN COURT
ORDER OF MERIT
ORDINARY FARE
ORGAN BUILDER
ORGAN GRINDER
ORGAN OF SIGHT
ORGAN RECITAL
ORIEL COLLEGE
ORIGINAL COPY
ORIGINAL COST
ORIGINAL IDEA
ORIGINAL PLAN
OSBORNE HOUSE
OTHER EXTREME
OUNCE OF FLESH
OUNCE OF SENSE
OUNCE OF SNUFF
OUR ANCESTORS
OUTDATED WORD
OUTDOOR GAMES
OUTDOOR SPORT
OUTDOOR STAFF
OUTER GARMENT
OUT FIRST BALL
OUT FOR A SPREE
OUT FOR SCALPS
OUTGOING SHIP
OUTGOING TIDE
OUT IN THE COLD
OUT IN THE OPEN
OUT OF BALANCE
OUT OF COMPANY
OUT OF CONCEIT
OUT OF CONTEXT
OUT OF CONTROL
OUT OF EARSHOT
OUT OF FASHION
OUT OF HARMONY
OUT OF HARNESS
OUT OF HEARING
OUT OF KEEPING
OUT OF ONE'S WAY
OUT OF SERVICE
OUT OF SPIRITS
OUT OF THE BLUE
OUT OF THE RACE

OUT OF THE ROAD
OUT OF THE ROOM
OUT OF THE WIND
OUT OF THE WOOD
OUT OF TROUBLE
OUT OF UNIFORM
OUTRIGHT GIFT
OUTSIDE COURT
OUTSIDE PRICE
OUTSIDE RIGHT
OUTWARD BOUND
OUTWARD SIGNS
OVER AND ABOVE
OVERDO THINGS
OVERNIGHT BAG
OVER ONE'S HEAD
OVER THE COALS
OVER THE HILLS
OVER THE LIMIT
OVER THE VERGE
OVER THE WATER
OVER THE WAVES
OVER THE WORST
OVER THE YEARS
OWE OBEDIENCE
OXFORD ACCENT
OXFORD CIRCUS
OXFORD STREET

P – 12

PABLO PICASSO
PACIFIC OCEAN
PACKAGE COUNT
PACKET OF PINS
PACK OF HOUNDS
PACK OF WOLVES
PACK ONE'S BAGS
PADDLING POOL
PAGE OF HONOUR
PAID-UP MEMBER
PAINFUL SIGHT
PAINTED IMAGE
PAINTED OCEAN
PAINTED WOMAN
PAINTING BOOK
PAINT THE LILY
PAINT THE WALL
PAIR OF BRACES
PAIR OF EIGHTS
PAIR OF GLOVES
PAIR OF HORSES
PAIR OF KNAVES
PAIR OF PLIERS
PAIR OF QUEENS
PAIR OF SCALES

PAIR OF SEVENS	PASTORAL POEM	PERSONAL HI-FI
PAIR OF SHEARS	PATENT OFFICE	PERSONAL LOAN
PAIR OF SHORTS	PATENT REMEDY	PERSONAL NOTE
PAIR OF SKATES	PATENT RIGHTS	PERSON OF NOTE
PAIR OF SLACKS	PATERNAL LOVE	PETER CUSHING
PAIR OF THREES	PATERNAL ROOF	PETER SELLERS
PAIR OF TIGHTS	PATIENT AS JOB	PETER USTINOV
PAIR OF TRUNKS	PAT ON THE BACK	PET GRIEVANCE
PAISLEY SCARF	PAT ON THE HEAD	PETROL ENGINE
PAISLEY SHAWL	PATRICK MOORE	PETROL RATION
PALE AS A GHOST	PATROL LEADER	PETTING PARTY
PALETTE KNIFE	PATTERN MAKER	PETTY DETAILS
PALMERS GREEN	PAUPER'S GRAVE	PETTY LARCENY
PAPER PATTERN	PAW THE GROUND	PETTY OFFICER
PAPER THE ROOM	PAY A DIVIDEND	PETTY TREASON
PAPER THE WALL	PAY AS YOU EARN	PHARAOH'S TOMB
PAPER WEDDING	PAY AS YOU WEAR	PHONE CHARGES
PARADE GROUND	PAY ATTENTION	PHYSICAL PAIN
PARADISE LOST	PAY DIVIDENDS	PIANO RECITAL
PARAFFIN LAMP	PAY IN ADVANCE	PICK A QUARREL
PARALLEL BARS	PAYING-IN BOOK	PICKED TROOPS
PARISH CHURCH	PAYING-IN SLIP	PICKLED ONION
PARISH PRIEST	PAY ONE'S DEBTS	PICK OUT A TUNE
PARISH RELIEF	PAY ONE'S SHARE	PICK TO PIECES
PARISH SCHOOL	PAY ON THE NAIL	PICNIC BASKET
PARKING METER	PEACE ON EARTH	PICNIC HAMPER
PARKING PLACE	PEACH BLOSSOM	PICTORIAL ART
PARKING SPACE	PEACOCK'S TAIL	PICTURE FRAME
PARLOUR TRICK	PEAK DISTRICT	PICTURE HOUSE
PARLOUS STATE	PEANUT BUTTER	PICTURE PAPER
PARMA VIOLETS	PEARL FISHING	PICTURE STORY
PARQUET FLOOR	PEARL HARBOUR	PIECE BY PIECE
PARSLEY SAUCE	PEASE PUDDING	PIECE OF BREAD
PART EXCHANGE	PEDIGREE HERD	PIECE OF CHALK
PARTHIAN SHOT	PELT WITH RAIN	PIECE OF MUSIC
PARTIAL TRUTH	PEN AND PENCIL	PIECE OF PAPER
PARTING GUEST	PENCIL SKETCH	PIERCED HEART
PARTING WORDS	PENNY FOR THEM	PIERCING LOOK
PART OF SPEECH	PENNY WHISTLE	PIERCING NOTE
PART OF THE ACT	PEOPLE'S PARTY	PIG'S TROTTERS
PART OF THE WAY	PEPPER'S GHOST	PILE UP A SCORE
PART ONE'S HAIR	PERFECT FIFTH	PILLAR-BOX RED
PART-TIME WORK	PERFECT IMAGE	PILLAR OF SALT
PARTY IN POWER	PERFECT MATCH	PILLAR TO POST
PARTY MANNERS	PERFECT ORDER	PILLION RIDER
PASSAGE MONEY	PERFECT PEACE	PILOT OFFICER
PASSING FANCY	PERFECT SIGHT	PINCH OF SNUFF
PASSING PHASE	PERFECT STYLE	PING-PONG BALL
PASSION FRUIT	PERFECT TENSE	PINK AND WHITE
PASSIVE VOICE	PERFECT WRECK	PINK ELEPHANT
PASS JUDGMENT	PERMANENT JOB	PINK FOR A GIRL
PASS SENTENCE	PERMANENT WAY	PIN ONE'S FAITH
PASS THE CRUET	PERMIT TO LAND	PIN ONE'S HOPES
PASS THE SAUCE	PERSONA GRATA	PINT OF BITTER
PAST MIDNIGHT	PERSONAL CALL	PINT OF WALLOP
PAST ONE'S BEST	PERSONAL GAIN	PIONEER CORPS

PITCH AND TOSS
PLACE AN ORDER
PLACE BETTING
PLACE IN ORDER
PLACE OF BIRTH
PLACE OF EXILE
PLAIN AND PURL
PLAIN CLOTHES
PLAIN COOKING
PLAIN DEALING
PLAIN ENGLISH
PLAIN SAILING
PLAINTIVE CRY
PLAIN WRAPPER
PLANE SPOTTER
PLAN OF ACTION
PLAN OF ATTACK
PLANT ONESELF
PLASTER SAINT
PLATES OF MEAT
PLATINUM RING
PLATONIC LOVE
PLAY CHARADES
PLAY DOMINOES
PLAY DRAUGHTS
PLAY FOOTBALL
PLAY FOR A DRAW
PLAY FORFEITS
PLAY FOR MONEY
PLAYING CARDS
PLAYING FIELD
PLAY LEAP-FROG
PLAY OLD HARRY
PLAY ONE FALSE
PLAY ONE'S PART
PLAY OPPOSITE
PLAY ROULETTE
PLAY SKITTLES
PLAY THE BANJO
PLAY THE CLOWN
PLAY THE DEUCE
PLAY THE DEVIL
PLAY THE FIELD
PLAY THE HALLS
PLAY THE ORGAN
PLAY THE PIANO
PLAY WITH FIRE
PLEAD POVERTY
PLEA FOR MERCY
PLEA FOR PEACE
PLEA OF GUILTY
PLEASANT NEWS
PLEASANT TIME
PLEASANT TRIP
PLEASANT WEEK
PLEASURE BOAT

PLEASURE TRIP
PLEATED DRESS
PLEATED SKIRT
PLENTY IN HAND
PLENTY OF GUTS
PLENTY OF ROOM
PLENTY OF ROPE
PLENTY OF TIME
PLIGHTED WORD
PLIMSOLL LINE
PLIMSOLL MARK
PLOUGHED LAND
PLOUGH MONDAY
PLUCK A PIGEON
PLUMBER'S MATE
PLUS AND MINUS
PLYMOUTH ROCK
POETIC FRENZY
POET LAUREATE
POINT AT ISSUE
POINT BY POINT
POINT OF ISSUE
POINT OF ORDER
POINTS SYSTEM
POINT TO POINT
POISONED DART
POKE IN THE EYE
POKER SESSION
POLAR REGIONS
POLES ASUNDER
POLICE ACTION
POLICE CORDON
POLICE ESCORT
POLICE MATTER
POLICE PATROL
POLICE PERMIT
POLITE PHRASE
POLITICAL MAP
POLITICAL SET
POLLING BOOTH
POLYTHENE BAG
PONS ASINORUM
POOL OF LABOUR
POOL OF LONDON
POOR ARGUMENT
POOR CREATURE
POOR DELIVERY
POOR FEATURES
POOR IN SPIRIT
POOR LINGUIST
POOR PHYSIQUE
POOR PROSPECT
POOR RELATION
POOR RELATIVE
POOR SPECIMEN
POPULAR BRAND

POPULAR FANCY
POPULAR FRONT
POPULAR MUSIC
POPULAR NOVEL
POPULAR PRESS
POPULAR PRICE
POPULAR SPORT
PORGY AND BESS
PORK AND BEANS
PORK SAUSAGES
PORT ADELAIDE
PORT AND LEMON
PORTER'S LODGE
PORTLAND BILL
PORTLAND BOWL
PORTLAND VASE
PORTLY FIGURE
PORT OF LONDON
PORT SUNLIGHT
POSE A PROBLEM
POSITIVE POLE
POSITIVE SIGN
POSSIBLE NEED
POSTAGE STAMP
POSTED ABROAD
POST MERIDIAN
POST OF HONOUR
POST-WAR WORLD
POTATO CRISPS
POTATO FAMINE
POTTER'S WHEEL
POULTRY HOUSE
POUND FOOLISH
POUND OF FLESH
POUND OF SUGAR
POUND THE BEAT
POUR WITH RAIN
POUTER PIGEON
POWDER MONKEY
POWER OF SIGHT
POWER STATION
POWERS THAT BE
PRACTICE GAME
PRACTISED EYE
PRAY FOR MERCY
PRAY FOR PEACE
PRECIOUS BANE
PRECIOUS LAMB
PREEN ONESELF
PREMIUM BONDS
PREMIUM OFFER
PREPARE A CASE
PREPARE A MEAL
PREPARED TEXT
PRESENT TENSE
PRESS COUNCIL

PRESS CUTTING
PRESSED STEEL
PRESS FORWARD
PRESS GALLERY
PRESS HAND-OUT
PRESSING NEED
PRESS OFFICER
PRESS ONWARDS
PRESS THE BELL
PRESSURE PUMP
PRETTY ACTIVE
PRETTY PICKLE
PRETTY SPEECH
PRETTY USEFUL
PRICE CONTROL
PRICE OF MONEY
PRICKLY PLANT
PRIDE OF LIONS
PRIDE OF PLACE
PRIDE ONESELF
PRIMITIVE ART
PRIMITIVE MAN
PRIMO CARNERA
PRIMROSE HILL
PRIMROSE PATH
PRINCE ALBERT
PRINCE EDWARD
PRINCE GEORGE
PRINCE PHILIP
PRINCE REGENT
PRINCE RUPERT
PRINCESS ANNE
PRINCIPAL BOY
PRINTED SHEET
PRINTER'S COPY
PRISON RECORD
PRISON REFORM
PRISON WARDEN
PRISON WARDER
PRIVATE BEACH
PRIVATE CLASS
PRIVATE FIGHT
PRIVATE HOTEL
PRIVATE HOUSE
PRIVATE LIVES
PRIVATE MEANS
PRIVATE PARTY
PRIVATE TUTOR
PRIVATE VISIT
PRIVATE WORLD
PRIVATE WRONG
PRIVY COUNCIL
PRIZE EDITION
PROBATE COURT
PROBLEM CHILD
PROFIT MARGIN

PROFIT MOTIVE
PROMISED LAND
PROMISE TO PAY
PROMPT ACTION
PROMPT ANSWER
PROMPT CORNER
PROOF OF GUILT
PROPER COURSE
PROPER PERSON
PROPERTY DEAL
PROPHET OF WOE
PROTEST MARCH
PROTOTYPE CAR
PROUD AS PUNCH
PROUD PRESTON
PROVEN GUILTY
PROVE THE RULE
PROVIDE LUNCH
PRUNING KNIFE
PRUSSIAN BLUE
PSYCHIC FORCE
PUBLIC AFFAIR
PUBLIC APATHY
PUBLIC DEMAND
PUBLIC FIGURE
PUBLIC HEALTH
PUBLIC NOTICE
PUBLIC OFFICE
PUBLIC ORATOR
PUBLIC OUTCRY
PUBLIC POLICY
PUBLIC SCHOOL
PUBLIC SPEECH
PUBLIC SPIRIT
PUDDING BASIN
PUFFING BILLY
PUFFIN ISLAND
PULL A FAST ONE
PULLING POWER
PULL THE WIRES
PULL TOGETHER
PULL TO PIECES
PULP MAGAZINE
PUNCH AND JUDY
PUPIL TEACHER
PURE NONSENSE
PURL AND PLAIN
PURSE THE LIPS
PURSUE A THEME
PURSUIT PLANE
PUSH ONE'S LUCK
PUT AN END TO IT
PUT A QUESTION
PUT A SOCK IN IT
PUT A STOP TO IT
PUT IN ITALICS

PUT IN SPLINTS
PUT IN THE DOCK
PUT INTO FORCE
PUT INTO RHYME
PUT INTO SHAPE
PUT INTO WORDS
PUT IN WRITING
PUT IT BLUNTLY
PUTNEY BRIDGE
PUTNEY COMMON
PUT ONE ACROSS
PUT ONE'S OAR IN
PUT ON ONE SIDE
PUT ON THE LIST
PUT ON THE RACK
PUT OUT OF GEAR
PUT THE CAT OUT
PUT THE WIND UP
PUTTING GREEN
PUT TO AUCTION
PUT TO GOOD USE
PUT TO THE RACK
PUT TO THE TEST
PUT TO THE VOTE
PUT TO TORTURE
PUT UP FOR SALE

Q – 12

QUARTER FINAL
QUARTER RIGHT
QUARTER TO ONE
QUARTER TO SIX
QUARTER TO TEN
QUARTER TO TWO
QUART MEASURE
QUEEN CONSORT
QUEEN OF CLUBS
QUEEN OF SHEBA
QUEEN OF TONGA
QUEEN'S BISHOP
QUEEN'S BOUNTY
QUEEN'S COLOUR
QUEEN'S FLIGHT
QUEEN'S GAMBIT
QUEEN'S KNIGHT
QUEEN'S SPEECH
QUEEN TITANIA
QUEER FEELING
QUESTION MARK
QUESTION TIME
QUEUE JUMPING
QUICK JOURNEY
QUICK RETURNS
QUIET WEDDING
QUIET WEEK-END

QUITE CERTAIN
QUITE CORRECT
QUITE IN ORDER
QUIT ONE'S POST
QUIT THE SCENE
QUIT THE STAGE
QUOTE THE ODDS

R – 12

RABBIT WARREN
RACE OF GIANTS
RACIAL HATRED
RACING DRIVER
RACING JARGON
RACING SEASON
RACING STABLE
RADAR STATION
RADIANT SMILE
RADICAL ERROR
RADIO AMATEUR
RADIO LICENCE
RADIO MESSAGE
RADIO NETWORK
RADIO STATION
RAFFLE TICKET
RAGING TEMPER
RAGLAN SLEEVE
RAGS AND BONES
RAGS TO RICHES
RAIDING PARTY
RAILWAY HOTEL
RAILWAY LINES
RAILWAY TRAIN
RAILWAY TRUCK
RAINBOW TROUT
RAINY CLIMATE
RAINY WEATHER
RAISE A FAMILY
RAISED VOICES
RAISE ONE'S HAT
RAISE THE ANTE
RAISE THE DEAD
RAISE THE DUST
RAISE THE FARE
RAISE THE RENT
RAISE THE ROOF
RAISE THE WIND
RAKE TOGETHER
RAMBLING ROSE
RANDOM EFFORT
RANDOM SAMPLE
RANK OUTSIDER
RAPID DECLINE
RAPID SPEAKER
RAPID STRIDES

RAPID TRANSIT
RAPIER THRUST
RASPBERRY JAM
RASPING VOICE
RATABLE VALUE
RATHER LITTLE
RATHER POORLY
RAVEN TRESSES
RAY ELLINGTON
RAY OF COMFORT
REACH FORWARD
REACT AGAINST
REACT SHARPLY
READ AND WRITE
READING GLASS
READ ONE'S HAND
READ ONE'S PALM
READ THE CARDS
READ THE SIGNS
READ THE STARS
READY CONSENT
READY FOR WEAR
READY TO BURST
READY TO LEARN
READY TO LEAVE
READY TO START
REALM OF PLUTO
REAL PRESENCE
REAL PROPERTY
REAL SECURITY
REAR ENTRANCE
REAR ONE'S HEAD
RECALL TO LIFE
RECALL TO MIND
RECEIVING END
RECEIVING SET
RECENT EVENTS
RECITE POETRY
RECORD OFFICE
RECORD OUTPUT
RECORD PLAYER
RED AND YELLOW
RED CORPUSCLE
RED FOR DANGER
RED IN THE FACE
RED-LETTER DAY
RED STOCKINGS
REDUCED FARES
REDUCED PRICE
REDUCED SPEED
REDUCE IN RANK
REDUCE TO PULP
REDUCE TO SIZE
RED WITH ANGER
REEFER JACKET
REEL OF COTTON

REFINED SUGAR
REFINED TASTE
REFLEX ACTION
REFORM SCHOOL
REFUSE CREDIT
REFUSE OFFICE
REFUSE TO MEET
REFUSE TO MOVE
REFUSE TO PLAY
REFUSE TO SIGN
REFUSE TO VOTE
REFUSE TO WORK
REGAL BEARING
REGENCY HOUSE
REGENCY STYLE
REGENT'S CANAL
REGENT STREET
REGIONAL NEWS
REGULAR BRICK
REGULAR DEMON
REGULAR HABIT
REGULAR HOURS
REGULAR MEALS
REGULAR ORDER
REIGN SUPREME
REITH LECTURE
RELAY STATION
RELEVANT FACT
RELIEF WORKER
RELIGIOUS WAR
REMAIN AT HOME
REMAIN BEHIND
REMAIN SEATED
REMAIN SILENT
REMAIN SINGLE
REMOTE CHANCE
REMOTE FUTURE
REMOTE OBJECT
REMOVE BODILY
REMOVE ERRORS
RENDER THANKS
REND THE SKIES
RENÉE HOUSTON
RENT A CARAVAN
RENT A COTTAGE
RENT TRIBUNAL
REPAIR OUTFIT
REPEAT ACTION
REPORTED CASE
REPTILE HOUSE
REPUTED OWNER
RESCUE WORKER
RESEARCH TEAM
RESEARCH WORK
RESERVED LIST
RESERVED SEAT

RESERVE PRICE
RESERVE STOCK
RESIDE ABROAD
RESORT TO ARMS
RESPONSE TIME
RESTING ACTOR
RESTING PLACE
REST OF THE DAY
REST ONE'S CASE
REST ONE'S EYES
RESTORE ORDER
RETAIL DEALER
RETAINING FEE
RETURN A VISIT
RETURN OF POST
RETURN TICKET
RETURN TO BASE
RETURN TO PORT
RETURN VOYAGE
REVERSE ORDER
REVERT TO TYPE
REVOLVER SHOT
RHESUS MONKEY
RHYMING SLANG
RICHARD CONTE
RICHMOND HILL
RICHMOND PARK
RICH RELATION
RICH RELATIVE
RIDE AT ANCHOR
RIDE BARE-BACK
RIDE FOR A FALL
RIDE FULL TILT
RIDER HAGGARD
RIDE THE STORM
RIDE TO HOUNDS
RIDING LESSON
RIDING MASTER
RIDING SCHOOL
RIDING STABLE
RIFLE BRIGADE
RIGHT AND LEFT
RIGHTFUL HEIR
RIGHT-HAND MAN
RIGHT OF ENTRY
RIGHT OR WRONG
RIGHT OUTSIDE
RIGHT QUALITY
RIGHT THROUGH
RIG THE MARKET
RINGING LAUGH
RINGING SOUND
RINGING TONES
RING·IN THE NEW
RINGSIDE SEAT
RIO DE JANEIRO

RIOT OF COLOUR
RIPE TOMATOES
RIP VAN WINKLE
RISE AND SHINE
RISE IN REVOLT
RISE TO THE FLY
RISE TO THE TOP
RISING GROUND
RISING PRICES
RISK ONE'S LIFE
RISK ONE'S NECK
RIVAL COMPANY
RIVER OF BLOOD
RIVER SHANNON
RIVER STEAMER
RIVER TRAFFIC
ROAD ACCIDENT
ROAD JUNCTION
ROADSIDE CAFÉ
ROAR FOR MERCY
ROARING TRADE
ROAR WITH PAIN
ROAR WITH RAGE
ROAST CHICKEN
ROASTED ALIVE
ROBE OF HONOUR
ROBERT BEATTY
ROBERT GRAVES
ROBERT MORLEY
ROBERT NEWTON
ROBERT TAYLOR
ROBUST HEALTH
ROCKING HORSE
ROGATION DAYS
ROGATION WEEK
ROLLER SKATES
ROLLING STOCK
ROLLING STONE
ROLL OF HONOUR
ROLL ONE'S EYES
ROMAN EMPEROR
ROMAN FIGURES
ROMAN HISTORY
ROMAN HOLIDAY
ROMAN LETTERS
ROMAN NUMBERS
ROMAN REMAINS
ROMAN SOLDIER
ROMANTIC FOOL
ROMANTIC GIRL
ROMANTIC IDEA
RONALD COLMAN
RONALD REAGAN
RONALD SHINER
ROOM AT THE TOP
ROOM FOR DOUBT

ROOM THIRTEEN
ROOM TO EXPAND
ROPE OF ONIONS
ROPE OF PEARLS
ROSE AND CROWN
ROSE-HIP SYRUP
ROSE OF TRALEE
ROSE TO THE TOP
ROSETTA STONE
ROSY PROSPECT
ROTARY ACTION
ROTTEN BRANCH
ROUGH COUNTRY
ROUGH DIAMOND
ROUGH DRAWING
ROUGH JUSTICE
ROUGH MANNERS
ROUGH PASSAGE
ROUGH PICTURE
ROUGH SURFACE
ROUGH TEXTURE
ROUGH WEATHER
ROUND BY ROUND
ROUND FIGURES
ROUND OF CALLS
ROUND OF TOAST
ROUND THE BACK
ROUND THE BEND
ROUND THE CAPE
ROUND THE EDGE
ROUND THE FIRE
ROUND THE MOON
ROUND THE TOWN
ROUSE ONESELF
ROUSING CHEER
ROUTINE CHECK
· ROVING REPORT
ROW OF BUTTONS
ROYAL ACADEMY
ROYAL ARSENAL
ROYAL BANQUET
ROYAL CHARTER
ROYAL CIRCLES
ROYAL COMMAND
ROYAL CONSENT
ROYAL DYNASTY
ROYAL HUNT CAP
ROYAL MARINES
ROYAL SOCIETY
ROYAL WARRANT
ROYAL WEDDING
ROYAL WELCOME
RUBBER CHEQUE
RUBBER DINGHY
RUBBER GLOVES
RUB ONE'S HANDS

RUB SHOULDERS
RUDE REMINDER
RUGBY COLOURS
RUGGER GROUND
RUGGER PLAYER
RUINED CASTLE
RUINOUS FOLLY
RULE OF TERROR
RULE THE ROOST
RUMOURS OF WAR
RUN-AWAY HORSE
RUN-AWAY MATCH
RUN AWAY TO SEA
RUN-AWAY TRAIN
RUN FOR OFFICE
RUN FOR SAFETY
RUN LIKE A DEER
RUN LIKE A HARE
RUNNING COSTS
RUNNING FIGHT
RUNNING FLUSH
RUNNING TITLE
RUNNING TRACK
RUNNING WATER
RUN OF BAD LUCK
RUN OF THE MILL
RUN ON THE BANK
RUPERT BROOKE
RUSH HEADLONG
RUSHING WATER
RUSSIAN BOOTS
RUSSIAN DANCE
RUSSIAN NOVEL
RUSSIAN SALAD
RUSSIAN VODKA
RUSTIC BRIDGE

S – 12

SACRED NUMBER
SACRED PLEDGE
SADDLE OF LAMB
SADLER'S WELLS
SAD SPECTACLE
SAFE AND SOUND
SAFE AS HOUSES
SAFE CROSSING
SAFE DISTANCE
SAFETY DEVICE
SAFETY FACTOR
SAGE AND ONION
SAHARA DESERT
SAILING BARGE
SAINT BERNARD
SAINT PANCRAS
SAINT PATRICK

SAINT SWITHIN
SALE OR RETURN
SALES FIGURES
SALES MANAGER
SALIENT ANGLE
SALIENT POINT
SALOON PRICES
SALTED ALMOND
SALTED BUTTER
SALT LAKE CITY
SALUTING BASE
SALVADOR DALI
SALVAGE CORPS
SALVAGE MONEY
SAMPLE BOTTLE
SAMUEL BUTLER
SAN FRANCISCO
SAN SEBASTIAN
SAPPHIRE RING
SARACEN'S HEAD
SARDONIC GRIN
SATAN'S PALACE
SATURDAY CLUB
SAUCE TARTARE
SAVAGE ATTACK
SAVAGE TEMPER
SAVE ONE'S FACE
SAVE ONE'S LIFE
SAVE ONE'S NECK
SAVE ONE'S SKIN
SAVE OUR SOULS
SAVING CLAUSE
SAVING FACTOR
SAVINGS STAMP
SAVOY CABBAGE
SAY A FEW WORDS
SAY A GOOD WORD
SAY A MOUTHFUL
SAY ONE'S PIECE
SAY SOMETHING
SCALE DRAWING
SCALLOP SHELL
SCARLET FEVER
SCARLET WOMAN
SCENE OF CHAOS
SCENE STEALER
SCENTED PAPER
SCEPTRED ISLE
SCHOLAR GIPSY
SCHOOL BLAZER
SCHOOL FRIEND
SCHOOL MATRON
SCHOOL OUTING
SCHOOL REPORT
SCHOOL SPORTS
SCOOP THE POOL

SCORCHING HOT
SCORE A SINGLE
SCORE THROUGH
SCOTCH BONNET
SCOTCH HUMOUR
SCOTCH WHISKY
SCOTLAND YARD
SCOTTISH PEER
SCOTTISH REEL
SCOUT'S HONOUR
SCRAMBLED EGG
SCRAP OF PAPER
SCRIPT WRITER
SCROLL OF FAME
SCULLERY MAID
SEAFARING MAN
SEAL A BARGAIN
SEALED ORDERS
SEAL OF OFFICE
SEALSKIN COAT
SEA OF GALILEE
SEA OF MARMARA
SEA OF TROUBLE
SEARCH IN VAIN
SEASONAL WIND
SEASON TICKET
SEAT OF HONOUR
SEBASTIAN COE
SECLUDED SPOT
SECOND CHANCE
SECOND CHOICE
SECOND COURSE
SECOND COUSIN
SECOND DANIEL
SECOND DEGREE
SECOND ELEVEN
SECOND FIDDLE
SECOND FINGER
SECOND GLANCE
SECOND LEAGUE
SECOND LESSON
SECOND LETTER
SECOND NATURE
SECOND OF JULY
SECOND OF JUNE
SECOND PERSON
SECOND RUBBER
SECOND SEASON
SECOND SERIES
SECOND STOREY
SECOND STRING
SECOND TO NONE
SECOND VIOLIN
SECOND VOLUME
SECRET BALLOT
SECRET DRAWER

SECRET ERRAND
SECRET PAPERS
SECRET POLICE
SECRET TREATY
SECRET WEAPON
SECURE FUTURE
SECURE OLD AGE
SECURITY LEAK
SECURITY RISK
SEE AT A GLANCE
SEEDED PLAYER
SEED MERCHANT
SEEDS OF DECAY
SEEDS OF DOUBT
SEE IN THE DARK
SEE IT THROUGH
SEEK A FORMULA
SEEK A FORTUNE
SEEK AN EFFECT
SEEK A QUARREL
SEEK GUIDANCE
SEESAW MOTION
SEE THE SIGHTS
SEETHING MASS
SELL FOR A SONG
SELLING PLATE
SELLING PRICE
SELL ON CREDIT
SELL ONE'S SOUL
SELL THE DUMMY
SEND A MESSAGE
SEND TO PRISON
SENIOR BRANCH
SENIOR MASTER
SENIOR MEMBER
SENIOR PURSER
SENIOR SCHOOL
SENSE OF GUILT
SENSE OF SHAME
SENSE OF SIGHT
SENSE OF SMELL
SENSE OF TASTE
SENSE OF TOUCH
SENSE OF WRONG
SENSIBLE GIRL
SENSITIVE EAR
SENT TO BLAZES
SENT TO SCHOOL
SEPARATE WAYS
SERENE NATURE
SERENE TEMPER
SERIAL NUMBER
SERIAL RIGHTS
SERIOUSLY ILL
SERIOUS MUSIC
SERIOUS OFFER

SERIOUS RIVAL
SERIOUS WOUND
SERRIED RANKS
SERVANT CLASS
SERVANTS' HALL
SERVE AT TABLE
SERVE ITS TURN
SERVICE CHIEF
SERVICE DEPOT
SERVICE DRESS
SERVICE OF GOD
SERVICE RIFLE
SERVING HATCH
SET AN EXAMPLE
SET A STANDARD
SET AT LIBERTY
SET BY THE EARS
SET OF LANCERS
SET ONE AT EASE
SET ONE'S TEETH
SET PROGRAMME
SETTLE A SCORE
SETTLE IN TOWN
SETTLE THE DAY
SEVEN COURSES
SEVEN DEGREES
SEVEN DOLLARS
SEVEN EIGHTHS
SEVEN FATHOMS
SEVEN GALLONS
SEVEN GUINEAS
SEVEN HUNDRED
SEVEN LEAGUES
SEVEN MINUTES
SEVEN OCTAVES
SEVEN OF CLUBS
SEVEN OR EIGHT
SEVEN PER CENT
SEVEN SISTERS
SEVEN SQUARED
SEVENTH FLOOR
SEVENTH GREEN
SEVENTH OF MAY
SEVENTH PLACE
SEVENTH ROUND
SEVENTY MILES
SEVENTY TIMES
SEVENTY YEARS
SEVEN VIRTUES
SEVEN WICKETS
SEVEN WISE MEN
SEVEN WONDERS
SEVERAL TIMES
SEVERE ATTACK
SEVERE CRITIC
SEVERE MASTER

SEVERE STRAIN
SEVERE WINTER
SEVERN BRIDGE
SEVERN TUNNEL
SEWING CIRCLE
SEW ON A BUTTON
SHADE OF DOUBT
SHADOW BOXING
SHADY RETREAT
SHAFT OF LIGHT
SHAH OF PERSIA
SHAKE THE HEAD
SHALLOW GRAVE
SHALLOW WATER
SHAMELESS LIE
SHARE CAPITAL
SHARE THE LOAD
SHARE THE LOOT
SHARP LOOK-OUT
SHARP OUTLINE
SHARP REPROOF
SHAVING BRUSH
SHAVING STICK
SHEEPISH GRIN
SHEEPISH LOOK
SHEEP'S TONGUE
SHEER TORTURE
SHEET OF FLAME
SHEET OF GLASS
SHEET OF PAPER
SHEET OF WATER
SHEIK OF ARABY
SHELLING PEAS
SHEPHERD'S PIE
SHERRY TRIFLE
SHETLAND PONY
SHINING LIGHT
SHINING WHITE
SHIPPING LANE
SHIPPING LINE
SHIP'S BISCUIT
SHIP'S CAPTAIN
SHIP'S COMPANY
SHIP'S COMPASS
SHIP'S STEWARD
SHIRLEY EATON
SHIRT SLEEVES
SHIVERING FIT
SHOCKING COLD
SHOCKING PINK
SHOCK TACTICS
SHOCK THERAPY
SHOE REPAIRER
SHOE-SHINE BOY
SHOOTER'S HILL
SHOOTING PAIN

SHOOTING STAR	SIDNEY STREET	SIXTY MINUTES
SHOOT ONESELF	SIEGE OF PARIS	SIXTY PER CENT
SHOOT THE MOON	SIERRA NEVADA	SIXTY SECONDS
SHOPPING LIST	SIGH OF RELIEF	SKEIN OF GEESE
SHORE TO SHORE	SIGHTING SHOT	SKELETON CREW
SHORN OF GLORY	SIGMUND FREUD	SKIFFLE GROUP
SHORT ACCOUNT	SIGNAL DEFEAT	SKIN AND BONES
SHORT CIRCUIT	SIGNAL REWARD	SKIN GRAFTING
SHORT COMMONS	SIGN LANGUAGE	SKITTLE ALLEY
SHORTER HOURS	SIGN OF DANGER	SKYE BOAT-SONG
SHORTEST GIRL	SIGN ONE'S NAME	SLACKEN SPEED
SHORT EXTRACT	SILENT LETTER	SLAP IN THE EYE
SHORT JOURNEY	SILENT PRAYER	SLAVE TO DRINK
SHORTLY AFTER	SILK STOCKING	SLAVE TRAFFIC
SHORT MEASURE	SILLY SUFFOLK	SLEEPING DOGS
SHORT OF FUNDS	SILVER DOLLAR	SLEEPING LION
SHORT OF MONEY	SILVER LINING	SLEEPING PILL
SHORT OF SPACE	SILVER SALVER	SLEEP SOUNDLY
SHORT OF STAFF	SILVER SCREEN	SLEEP SWEETLY
SHORT OF WORDS	SILVER STREAK	SLENDER HOPES
SHORT PASSAGE	SILVER TEA-POT	SLENDER MEANS
SHORT ROMANCE	SILVER THREAD	SLENDER PURSE
SHORT SESSION	SIMON TEMPLAR	SLENDER WAIST
SHORT SUMMARY	SIMPLE ANSWER	SLICE OF BREAD
SHORT TENANCY	SIMPLE ATTIRE	SLICE OF LEMON
SHORT TIME AGO	SIMPLE BEAUTY	SLICE OF TOAST
SHORT VERSION	SIMPLE DEVICE	SLICE THE BALL
SHOT AND SHELL	SIMPLE EFFORT	SLIDING PANEL
SHOT IN THE ARM	SIMPLE MATTER	SLIDING SCALE
SHOT ONE'S BOLT	SIMPLE PERSON	SLIGHT CHANCE
SHOT TO PIECES	SIMPLE REMEDY	SLIGHT CHANGE
SHOULDER ARMS	SINGING VOICE	SLIGHT DAMAGE
SHOUT FOR HELP	SING IN UNISON	SLIGHT FIGURE
SHOUT THE ODDS	SINGLE COMBAT	SLIGHT INJURY
SHOVE HA'PENNY	SINGLE HANDED	SLIGHTLY DEAF
SHOW APTITUDE	SINGLE NUMBER	SLIMMING DIET
SHOW BUSINESS	SINGLE PERSON	SLIP AND SLIDE
SHOWER OF RAIN	SINGLE SCOTCH	SLIP OF A THING
SHOW INTEREST	SINGLES MATCH	SLIP OF THE PEN
SHOWN THE DOOR	SINGLE TICKET	SLIP THE CABLE
SHOW OF REASON	SINGLE WHISKY	SLIP UP ON A JOB
SHOW ONE ROUND	SINISTER MOVE	SLITHER ALONG
SHOW ONE'S FACE	SIR HENRY WOOD	SLOANE RANGER
SHOW ONE'S HAND	SIR JOHN MOORE	SLOANE SQUARE
SHOW PRUDENCE	SIR PETER HALL	SLOANE STREET
SHRIMPING NET	SIR TOBY BELCH	SLOPING SIDES
SHUFFLE ALONG	SIT AT THE BACK	SLOW MOVEMENT
SHUT OFF STEAM	SIT IN COUNCIL	SLOW OF SPEECH
SHUT ONE'S EYES	SIX FEET UNDER	SLOW PROGRESS
SHUT YOUR TRAP!	SIX OF THE BEST	SLOW PUNCTURE
SIAMESE TWINS	SIXPENCE EACH	SLUM PROPERTY
SICK AND TIRED	SIX SHILLINGS	SMALL ACCOUNT
SICK OF TRYING	SIXTEEN MILES	SMALL COMFORT
SIDE ENTRANCE	SIXTH CENTURY	SMALL FORTUNE
SIDE MOVEMENT	SIXTH OF APRIL	SMALL HELPING
SIDE OF MUTTON	SIXTH OF MARCH	SMALL HOLDING

SMALL LETTERS
SMALL MEASURE
SMALL MERCIES
SMALL PORTION
SMALL PURPOSE
SMALL SAVINGS
SMALL WRITING
SMART CLOTHES
SMART DEALING
SMART OFFICER
SMART SERVANT
SMART TURN-OUT
SMASH AND GRAB
SMASHING BLOW
SMELL SWEETLY
SMILE SWEETLY
SMOKE A LITTLE
SMOKED SALMON
SMOKED TONGUE
SMOKER'S COUGH
SMOKER'S HEART
SMOKE TOO MUCH
SMOOTH TEMPER
SMOOTH THE WAY
SMOOTH TONGUE
SNACK COUNTER
SNAKE CHARMER
SNAP AND SNARL
SNAP DECISION
SNAP JUDGMENT
SNOW CRYSTALS
SOAP AND WATER
SOBER THOUGHT
SOCIAL CENTRE
SOCIAL CIRCLE
SOCIAL CREDIT
SOCIAL MISFIT
SOCIAL SEASON
SOCIAL STATUS
SOCIAL SURVEY
SOCIAL UNREST
SOCIAL WORKER
SOCIETY WOMAN
SOCK IN THE EYE
SODA FOUNTAIN
SOFT AS BUTTER
SOFT AS VELVET
SOFT CURRENCY
SOFT HANDLING
SOFT NOTHINGS
SOLAR ECLIPSE
SOLDERING GUN
SOLEMN THREAT
SOLE SURVIVOR
SOLID CITIZEN
SOLITARY LIFE

SOLITARY WALK
SOLOMON'S SEAL
SOMETHING NEW
SOMETHING OLD
SOME TIME BACK
SON ET LUMIÈRE
SONG AND DANCE
SONG OF A SHIRT
SONG OF PRAISE
SONIC BARRIER
SON OF THE SOIL
SONS OF BELIAL
SOPRANO VOICE
SORE DISTRESS
SORRY OUTCOME
SOUL OF HONOUR
SOUND AND FURY
SOUND AS A BELL
SOUND BACKING
SOUND BARRIER
SOUND EFFECTS
SOUND OF MUSIC
SOUND SLEEPER
SOUND TACTICS
SOUP OF THE DAY
SOUTH AFRICAN
SOUTH AMERICA
SOUTHEND PIER
SOUTHERN AREA
SOUTH PACIFIC
SOUTH SHIELDS
SOVIET RUSSIA
SPACE FICTION
SPACE SHUTTLE
SPACE STATION
SPACE TO BUILD
SPADE AND FORK
SPANISH DANCE
SPANISH MONEY
SPANISH ONION
SPANISH TANGO
SPANKING PACE
SPARE A COPPER
SPARE BEDROOM
SPARE NO PAINS
SPARE-TIME JOB
SPARKING PLUG
SPARKLING WIT
SPARTAN BREED
SPATE OF WORDS
SPEAK CLEARLY
SPEAK ENGLISH
SPEAKING PART
SPEAKING TUBE
SPEAK ITALIAN
SPEAK PLAINLY

SPEAK RAPIDLY
SPEAK RUSSIAN
SPEAK SPANISH
SPEAK VOLUMES
SPECIAL AGENT
SPECIAL CHARM
SPECIAL ISSUE
SPECIAL NURSE
SPECIAL OFFER
SPECIAL POINT
SPECIAL PRICE
SPECIAL TERMS
SPECIAL TRAIN
SPECIAL TREAT
SPECIFIC HEAT
SPECIMEN COPY
SPECIMEN PAGE
SPEECH DEFECT
SPEED OF LIGHT
SPEED OF SOUND
SPEEDY ANSWER
SPELLING GAME
SPENCER TRACY
SPEND A PACKET
SPICK AND SPAN
SPIDER AND FLY
SPIKE THE GUNS
SPILL THE MILK
SPILL THE SALT
SPINAL COLUMN
SPIN LIKE A TOP
SPIN THE WHEEL
SPIRIT OF EVIL
SPLENDID TIME
SPLIT THE ATOM
SPLIT THE VOTE
SPOILED CHILD
SPORTING LIFE
SPORTING NEWS
SPORT OF KINGS
SPORT ONE'S OAK
SPORTS EDITOR
SPORTS GROUND
SPORTS JACKET
SPORTS MASTER
SPORTS REPORT
SPORTS TROPHY
SPOT AND PLAIN
SPOT OF BOTHER
SPOT OF WHISKY
SPREAD ABROAD
SPREAD CANVAS
SPRING BUDGET
SPRING GREENS
SPRING ONIONS
SPRING SEASON

SPRING TO MIND	START TOO LATE	STITCH IN TIME
SPURN AN OFFER	START TOO SOON	ST JAMES'S PARK
SQUARE NUMBER	STARVE A FEVER	ST LOUIS BLUES
STACK OF CHIPS	STATE CONTROL	ST MARYLEBONE
STACK OF STRAW	STATED PERIOD	STOCK COMPANY
STACK THE DECK	STATE FUNERAL	STOCK EXAMPLE
STAFF CAPTAIN	STATE LIBRARY	STOCKING FEET
STAFF COLLEGE	STATE LOTTERY	STOCK IN TRADE
STAFF OFFICER	STATE OF BLISS	STOKE THE FIRE
STAFF PROBLEM	STATE OF GRACE	STOLEN KISSES
STAGE A STRIKE	STATE OF PEACE	STONE OF SCONE
STAGE BY STAGE	STATE OF SIEGE	STONE TO DEATH
STAGE EFFECTS	STATE PENSION	STOOD THE TEST
STAGE MANAGER	STATE SCHOLAR	STOOGE AROUND
STAGE VILLAIN	STATE SUBSIDY	STOP AND START
STAGE WHISPER	STATION HOTEL	STOP DRINKING
STAINED GLASS	STATION WAGON	STOP FIGHTING
STALL FOR TIME	STATUE OF EROS	STOP-GO POLICY
STAMP AUCTION	STATUS SYMBOL	STOP LAUGHING
STAMP MACHINE	STAYING POWER	STOP ONE'S EARS
STAMP OF TRUTH	STAY ONE'S HAND	STOP THE CLOCK
STAND ABASHED	STAY THE NIGHT	STOP THE FIGHT
STAND ACCUSED	STAY TO DINNER	STOP THE NIGHT
STAND A CHANCE	STAY TO THE END	STOP WORRYING
STAND AGAINST	ST BERNARD DOG	STORAGE SPACE
STAND AND WAIT	STEADY DEMAND	STORM BREWING
STANDARD LAMP	STEADY INCOME	STORM OF ABUSE
STANDARD RATE	STEAK TARTARE	STORM TROOPER
STANDARD ROSE	STEAL THE SHOW	STORM WARNING
STANDARD SIZE	STEALTHY STEP	STORMY CAREER
STANDARD TIME	STEAM TURBINE	STORMY DEBATE
STANDARD WORK	STEAM WHISTLE	STORMY PETREL
STAND BETWEEN	STEERING GEAR	STORMY TEMPER
STAND IN FRONT	STEP BACKWARD	STOUT AND MILD
STANDING ARMY	STEP ON THE GAS	STOUT OF HEART
STANDING JOKE	STERLING AREA	STOVEPIPE HAT
STANDING ONLY	STERN REALITY	ST PETERSBURG
STANDING ROOM	STEWED APPLES	STRAIGHT AWAY
ST ANDREW'S DAY	STEWED PRUNES	STRAIGHT BACK
STAND THE PACE	ST GEORGE'S DAY	STRAIGHT DEAL
STAND THE TEST	STICK NO BILLS	STRAIGHT DOWN
STAND-UP FIGHT	STICK OF BOMBS	STRAIGHT DROP
STAND UPRIGHT	STICK OF CHALK	STRAIGHTEN UP
STAND WAITING	STICK OR TWIST	STRAIGHT FACE
STANLEY BLACK	STICK TO PROSE	STRAIGHT HAIR
ST ANNE'S ON SEA	STICKY TOFFEE	STRAIGHT HOME
STARK MADNESS	STICKY WICKET	STRAIGHT LEFT
STARK REALITY	STIFF PENALTY	STRAIGHT LINE
STARLIT NIGHT	STILETTO HEEL	STRAIGHT NOSE
STAR MATERIAL	STINGING BLOW	STRAIGHT PART
STARRING ROLE	STINGING PAIN	STRAIGHT PLAY
STARTING GATE	STIRRING GAME	STRAIGHT ROAD
STARTING POST	STIRRING NEWS	STRAIGHT SETS
START PACKING	STIRRING TALE	STRAIGHT SHOT
START TALKING	STIR THE BLOOD	STRAIGHT TALK
START TO CHEER	STIR UP STRIFE	STRAIN A POINT

STRAIT JACKET
STRAND OF HAIR
STRANGE FACES
STRANGE PLACE
STRANGE TO SAY
STRANGE WOMAN
STRAPPING LAD
STREAK OF LUCK
STREAKY BACON
STREAM OF CARS
STREET ARTIST
STREET CORNER
STREET MARKET
STREETS AHEAD
STREET SELLER
STREET SINGER
STREET TRADER
STREET URCHIN
STREET VENDOR
STRETCH NYLON
STRETCH TIGHT
STRICTLY TRUE
STRICT ORDERS
STRIFE AND WOE
STRIKE A CHORD
STRIKE ACTION
STRIKE A LIGHT
STRIKE A MATCH
STRIKE BOTTOM
STRIKE IT RICH
STRIKE ME DEAD!
STRIKE ME PINK!
STRIKE TERROR
STRIKE THE EYE
STRIKE WEAPON
STRING OF LIES
STRIP CARTOON
STRIP OF PAPER
STRIP OF WATER
STRIVE IN VAIN
STROKE OF LUCK
STROKE OF WORK
STROKE THE CAT
STROKE THE DOG
STRONG-ARM MAN
STRONG AS AN OX
STRONG COLOUR
STRONG DEMAND
STRONG DENIAL
STRONG DESIRE
STRONGLY MADE
STRONG NERVES
STRONG THIRST
STRONG WHISKY
STRUGGLE HARD
STUDENT OF LAW

STUDY CLOSELY
STUFFED HEART
STUFFED OLIVE
STUFFED SHIRT
STUFF ONESELF
STUMBLE ALONG
STUMP ORATORY
STUNNING BLOW
STUPID ANSWER
STUPID FELLOW
STYGIAN SHORE
SUBDUED LIGHT
SUBMARINE PEN
SUBTLE CHANGE
SUCCESS STORY
SUCK AN ORANGE
SUDDEN ATTACK
SUDDEN CHANGE
SUDDEN MOTION
SUDDEN STRAIN
SUDDEN TWITCH
SUFFER DEFEAT
SUFFOLK PUNCH
SUGAR CONTENT
SUGAR IS SWEET
SUGAR REFINER
SUGAR THE PILL
SUICIDAL IDEA
SUITE OF ROOMS
SUIT OF ARMOUR
SUIT YOURSELF
SULTAN'S HAREM
SULTAN'S WIVES
SUMMARY COURT
SUMMER MONTHS
SUMMER RESORT
SUMMER SCHOOL
SUMMER SEASON
SUNDAY DINNER
SUNDAY'S CHILD
SUNDAY SCHOOL
SUNKEN CHEEKS
SUNKEN GARDEN
SUNNY WEATHER
SUNSHINE ROOF
SUN-TAN LOTION
SUPERB FIGURE
SUPERB FINISH
SUPERIOR AIRS
SUPERIOR RANK
SUPERIOR TYPE
SUPPORT A WIFE
SUPREME BEING
SUPREME COURT
SUPREME ISSUE
SUPREME POWER

SURE TO PLEASE
SURGE FORWARD
SURGERY HOURS
SURGICAL CASE
SURGICAL WARD
SURPLUS FLESH
SURPLUS GOODS
SURPLUS STOCK
SURPRISE MOVE
SUSAN HAYWARD
SUSTAIN A LOSS
SWALLOW WHOLE
SWARM OF FLIES
SWARM OF GNATS
SWARM UP A ROPE
SWAY TO AND FRO
SWEAR FALSELY
SWEDISH DRILL
SWEEP THE DECK
SWEEP THROUGH
SWEET ADELINE
SWEET AND SOUR
SWEET AS HONEY
SWEET AS SUGAR
SWEET CONTENT
SWEET MARTINI
SWEET PICKLES
SWEET REVENGE
SWEET SIXTEEN
SWEET SUCCESS
SWEET THOUGHT
SWEET VIOLETS
SWEET WILLIAM
SWIFT CURRENT
SWIFT TO ANGER
SWIMMING BATH
SWIMMING CLUB
SWIMMING GALA
SWIMMING POOL
SWIM UP-STREAM
SWING THE LEAD
SWISS COTTAGE
SWOLLEN RIVER
SWORD OF STATE
SWORN ENEMIES
SYCAMORE TREE
SYDNEY BRIDGE
SYDNEY CARTON

T – 12

TABLE A MOTION
TABLE MANNERS
TABLET OF SOAP
TAIL OF THE EYE
TAILORED SUIT

TAILOR'S DUMMY	TALK NONSENSE	TERRACED ROOF
TAILOR'S GOOSE	TALK OF ANGELS	TERRIBLE TIME
TAILS YOU LOSE!	TALK POLITICS	TEST-TUBE BABY
TAINTED GOODS	TALK STRAIGHT	TEXAS RANGERS
TAINTED MONEY	TALK TO NOBODY	THAMES DITTON
TAKE A BEATING	TALLEST WOMAN	THAMES TUNNEL
TAKE A HOLIDAY	TALLOW CANDLE	THAMES VALLEY
TAKE A LIBERTY	TANGLED SKEIN	THATCHED ROOF
TAKE A LOOK-SEE	TANKARD OF ALE	THE ACROPOLIS
TAKE A PENALTY	TANK REGIMENT	THE ADMIRALTY
TAKE A POT-SHOT	TAP AT THE DOOR	THE ALCHEMIST
TAKE A PRIDE IN	TAPE RECORDER	THE ALL-BLACKS
TAKE A READING	TAP ON THE HEAD	THE ANTARCTIC
TAKE DELIVERY	TAP THE BARREL	THE ANTIPODES
TAKE DOWN A PEG	TARIFF REFORM	THE APPLE-CART
TAKE EXERCISE	TASTE OF HONEY	THE ARCADIANS
TAKE FOR A RIDE	TASTES DIFFER	THE ARGENTINE
TAKE GOOD CARE	TAX COLLECTOR	THE ARGONAUTS
TAKE IT FROM ME	TAX INSPECTOR	THEATRE OF WAR
TAKE MEASURES	TEACH SKATING	THEATRE QUEUE
TAKE MY ADVICE	TEAM OF HORSES	THEATRE ROYAL
TAKE NO DENIAL	TEARING HURRY	THEATRE USHER
TAKE NO NOTICE	TEAR ONE'S HAIR	THEATRE WORLD
TAKE ON A PILOT	TEARS OF GRIEF	THE BACHELORS
TAKE ONE'S EASE	TEAR TO PIECES	THE BIG DIPPER
TAKE ONE'S HOOK	TEAR TO SHREDS	THE BITTER END
TAKE ONE'S NAME	TEA WITH LEMON	THE BLUE ANGEL
TAKE ONE'S PICK	TEEM WITH RAIN	THE BOSPHORUS
TAKE ONE'S TIME	TEEN-AGE DREAM	THE BOY FRIEND
TAKE ONE'S TURN	TEEN-AGE YEARS	THE CATACOMBS
TAKE ONE'S WORD	TEENY-BOPPERS	THE CATECHISM
TAKE PLEASURE	TELEGRAPH BOY	THE CHILTERNS
TAKE PRISONER	TELEPHONE BOX	THE COMMON MAN
TAKE THE BLAME	TELL A WHOPPER	THE CONQUEROR
TAKE THE CHAIR	TELL EVERYONE	THE CONTINENT
TAKE THE COUNT	TELL FORTUNES	THE COTSWOLDS
TAKE THE FIELD	TELL ME A STORY	THE CRUSADERS
TAKE THE FLOOR	TELL-TALE SIGN	THE DARK BLUES
TAKE THE MICKY	TELL THE TRUTH	THE DAY BEFORE
TAKE THE POINT	TELL THE WORLD	THE DEEP SOUTH
TAKE THE PRIZE	TEMPLE OF FAME	THE DEFENDERS
TAKE THE REINS	TEMPORARY JOB	THE DEVIL'S OWN
TAKE THE STAGE	TEMPT FORTUNE	THE DIE IS CAST
TAKE THE STAND	TEMPTING BAIT	THE DOLOMITES
TAKE THE TRICK	TENANT FARMER	THE DONE THING
TAKE TO FLIGHT	TEN-GALLON HAT	THE DOVER ROAD
TAKE TO PIECES	TENNIS LESSON	THE FALKLANDS
TAKE TO THE AIR	TENNIS PLAYER	THE FALL OF MAN
TAKE UP A STAND	TENNIS RACKET	THE FAVOURITE
TAKE UP OFFICE	TEN-POUND NOTE	THE FIVE TOWNS
TALCUM POWDER	TEN SHILLINGS	THE FOLLOWING
TALE OF A SHIRT	TENTH CENTURY	THE FOUR WINDS
TALK AT LENGTH	TENTH OF APRIL	THE GENTLE SEX
TALK AT RANDOM	TENTH OF MARCH	THE GRAMPIANS
TALK BUSINESS	TERMINAL HOME	THE GUILDHALL
TALKING POINT	TERM OF OFFICE	THE HAPPY MEAN

THE HAYMARKET
THE HEREAFTER
THE HERMITAGE
THE HIGHLANDS
THE HIMALAYAS
THE IMMORTALS
THE IRONSIDES
THE IVY LEAGUE
THE LAST DITCH
THE LAST LAUGH
THE LAST STRAW
THE LAST TRUMP
THE LIMELIGHT
THE LISTENERS
THE LOST CHORD
THE MAD HATTER
THE MAYFLOWER
THE MORSE CODE
THE MOUSETRAP
THEN AND THERE
THE NEW FOREST
THE NORTH-EAST
THE NORTH-WEST
THE OLD BAILEY
THE OLD ONE-TWO
THE OLD SCHOOL
THE OTHER SIDE
THE OUTSKIRTS
THE PALLADIUM
THE PARTHENON
THE PIPER'S SON
THE POLONAISE
THE POTTERIES
THE PROVINCES
THE REAL THING
THERE AND BACK
THERE AND THEN
THE REICHSTAG
THE REMAINDER
THERE'S THE RUB
THERMOS FLASK
THE SAME THING
THE SEAMY SIDE
THE SEARCHERS
THE SEVEN SEAS
THE SEVENTIES
THE SOUTH-EAST
THE SOUTH-WEST
THE SPECTATOR
THE STORY GOES
THE THING TO DO
THE TRUTH GAME
THE UPPER HAND
THE VERY DEVIL
THE VERY IMAGE
THE VERY PLACE

THE VERY THING
THE WEAKER SEX
THE WHOLE TIME
THE WILL TO WIN
THE WOMENFOLK
THE WORM TURNS
THE WORST OF IT
THE YARDBIRDS
THE YOUNG IDEA
THICK AND FAST
THICK AND THIN
THICK GLASSES
THIEVES' SLANG
THIN AS A WAFER
THIN DISGUISE
THINGS CHANGE
THINGS TO COME
THINK ABOUT IT
THIN MATERIAL
THIRD CENTURY
THIRD CHANNEL
THIRD CHAPTER
THIRD EDITION
THIRD OF APRIL
THIRD OFFICER
THIRD OF MARCH
THIRD QUARTER
THIRD READING
THIRTEEN DAYS
THIS ABOVE ALL
THIS SATURDAY
THIS THURSDAY
THIS VERY ROOM
THOMAS ARNOLD
THOMAS EDISON
THOMAS WOLSEY
THOSE AGAINST
THREAD OF LIFE
THREAT OF RAIN
THREE-ACT PLAY
THREE AT A TIME
THREE BY THREE
THREE COLOURS
THREE COURSES
THREE-DAY WEEK
THREE DEGREES
THREE DOLLARS
THREE EIGHTHS
THREE FATHOMS
THREE FIGURES
THREE GALLONS
THREE GUESSES
THREE GUINEAS
THREE HUNDRED
THREE LENGTHS
THREE MILLION

THREE MINUTES
THREE OCTAVES
THREE OF A KIND
THREE OF CLUBS
THREE PER CENT
THREE-PLY WOOD
THREE-PLY WOOL
THREE RASHERS
THREE'S A CROWD
THREE SISTERS
THREE SQUARED
THREE STOOGES
THREE STRIPES
THREE STROKES
THREE UNITIES
THREE WICKETS
THREE WISE MEN
THREE WITCHES
THROATY LAUGH
THROTTLE DOWN
THROUGH COACH
THROUGH TRAIN
THROW A GLANCE
THROW A SWITCH
THYROID GLAND
TICKET HOLDER
TICKET OFFICE
TICKET POCKET
TIDE OF EVENTS
TIE ONE'S HANDS
TIGHT AS A LORD
TIGHT BANDAGE
TIGHT SQUEEZE
TILL ALL HOURS
TILL DOOMSDAY
TILL NEXT TIME
TILTING MATCH
TIMBERED ROOF
TIME AND AGAIN
TIME AND A HALF
TIME AND MONEY
TIME AND PLACE
TIME AND SPACE
TIME EXPOSURE
TIME FOR LUNCH
TIMELY ADVICE
TIME SCHEDULE
TIME TO FINISH
TIME TO GO HOME
TIME WILL TELL
TINKER'S CURSE
TINNED SALMON
TINTERN ABBEY
TIP THE SCALES
TIP THE WINNER
TIRED OF IT ALL

TIRED TO DEATH	TOUT ENSEMBLE	TRICK CYCLIST
TISSUE OF LIES	TOWERING RAGE	TRIED IN COURT
TITLED PEOPLE	TOWER OF BABEL	TRIFLING TALK
TITLED PERSON	TOWN PLANNING	TRIGGER HAPPY
TITTLE TATTLE	TOWN SURVEYOR	TRIM THE SAILS
TO ALL INTENTS	TRACER BULLET	TRINITY HOUSE
TOASTING FORK	TRACING PAPER	TRIPE DRESSER
TOBACCO JUICE	TRADE FIGURES	TRIVIAL ROUND
TOBACCO PLANT	TRADE JOURNAL	TROMBONE SOLO
TOBACCO POUCH	TRADE RETURNS	TROOP CARRIER
TOBACCO SMOKE	TRADE SURPLUS	TROPHY HUNTER
TOBACCO STAIN	TRADING HOUSE	TROPICAL BIRD
TO ERR IS HUMAN	TRADING STAMP	TROPICAL FISH
TOKEN GESTURE	TRAFFIC LIGHT	TROPICAL HEAT
TOKEN PAYMENT	TRAFFIC RULES	TROPICAL MOON
TOMATO CATSUP	TRAFFORD PARK	TROPICAL SUIT
TOM COURTENAY	TRAGIC ENDING	TROPICAL WIND
TOMMY HANDLEY	TRAGIC LOVERS	TROTTING PACE
TOMMY TRINDER	TRAILING EDGE	TROUBLE AHEAD
TONGUE OF LAND	TRAINED NURSE	TROUBLED MIND
TOO HOT TO HOLD	TRAINED VOICE	TROUSER PRESS
TOOK A DIM VIEW	TRAINING SHIP	TROUT FISHING
TOOLS OF TRADE	TRAIN JOURNEY	TRUE BELIEVER
TOO MANY COOKS	TRAIN OF IDEAS	TRUE FEELINGS
TO ONE'S CREDIT	TRAIN ROBBERY	TRUE TO NATURE
TOOTH AND CLAW	TRAIN SERVICE	TRUE TO THE END
TOOTH AND NAIL	TRAIN SPOTTER	TRUMPET BLAST
TOOT ONE'S HORN	TRAIN THE MIND	TRUNDLE ALONG
TOPLESS DRESS	TRAITOR'S GATE	TRUSS OF STRAW
TOP OF THE BILL	TRAMP STEAMER	TRUST COMPANY
TOP OF THE FORM	TRANQUIL MIND	TRUSTEE STOCK
TOP OF THE HILL	TRAPPIST MONK	TRUSTY FRIEND
TOP OF THE MILK	TRAVEL ABROAD	TRUTH WILL OUT
TOP OF THE POLL	TRAVEL AGENCY	TRYING PERSON
TOP OF THE POPS	TRAVEL AROUND	TRY ONE'S SKILL
TOP OF THE TREE	TRAVEL BUREAU	TSAR OF RUSSIA
TOREADOR SONG	TRAVEL BY LAND	TUBELESS TYRE
TORN TO SHREDS	TRAVEL BY TUBE	TUESDAY NIGHT
TORY MAJORITY	TREAD LIGHTLY	TUGBOAT ANNIE
TORY MINORITY	TREASURE HUNT	TUNES OF GLORY
TOSS A PANCAKE	TREASURY BILL	TUNNEL OF LOVE
TOSS FOR SIDES	TREASURY NOTE	TURKISH TOWEL
TOSS ONE'S HEAD	TREAT IN STORE	TURN A DEAF EAR
TOSS THE CABER	TREAT LIGHTLY	TURNED-UP NOSE
TOTAL ECLIPSE	TREAT ROUGHLY	TURNHAM GREEN
TO THE GALLOWS	TREATY OF ROME	TURNING POINT
TO THE LAST MAN	TREBLE CHANCE	TURN INTO CASH
TOTTER AROUND	TRENCHANT WIT	TURN OF EVENTS
TOUCH OF FROST	TRENCH MORTAR	TURN OF PHRASE
TOUCH ONE'S CAP	TRESPASS UPON	TURN OF SPEECH
TOUCHY PERSON	TRESTLE TABLE	TURN ONE'S BACK
TOUGH AS NAILS	TREVOR HOWARD	TURN ONE'S HEAD
TOUGH AS STEEL	TRIAL BALANCE	TURN ON THE GAS
TOUR DE FRANCE	TRIAL IN COURT	TURN ON THE TAP
TOURIST CLASS	TRIBAL CUSTOM	TURN THE PAGES
TOURIST TRADE	TRIBAL SYSTEM	TURN THE SCALE

TURN THE SCREW
TURN THE TAP ON
TURN UP TRUMPS
TWELFTH GREEN
TWELFTH NIGHT
TWELFTH OF MAY
TWELFTH PLACE
TWELFTH ROUND
TWELVE MONTHS
TWELVE O'CLOCK
TWELVE OUNCES
TWELVES POINTS
TWELVE POUNDS
TWELVE TRICKS
TWENTY POINTS
TWENTY POUNDS
TWICE AS HEAVY
TWICE AS QUICK
TWICE MONTHLY
TWICE NIGHTLY
TWICE REMOVED
TWICE THE SIZE
TWIN BROTHERS
TWIN CHILDREN
TWINGE OF PAIN
TWIST AND BUST
TWIST AND TURN
TWIST ONE'S ARM
TWO AND ELEVEN
TWO IN THE BUSH
TWO-SEATER CAR
TWO SHILLINGS
TWO SIXPENCES
TWO-SPEED GEAR
TWO SYLLABLES
TWO-WAY STREET
TYPHOID FEVER
TYPING LESSON
TYPIST'S ERROR
TYRE PRESSURE

U – 12

UGLY CUSTOMER
UGLY DUCKLING
UMBRELLA BIRD
UMPTEEN TIMES
UNABLE TO COPE
UNABLE TO HELP
UNABLE TO MOVE
UNBROKEN LINE
UNCERTAIN JOY
UNCUT DIAMOND
UNDER A BUSHEL
UNDER A LADDER
UNDER AND OVER

UNDER A STRAIN
UNDER CONTROL
UNDER ENQUIRY
UNDER HATCHES
UNDER LICENCE
UNDER ONE ROOF
UNDER ONE'S HAT
UNDER PROTEST
UNDER SHERIFF
UNDER TENSION
UNDER THE HEEL
UNDER THE LASH
UNDER THE ROSE
UNDER THE SKIN
UNDER THE WING
UNEVEN CHANCE
UNFAIR CHOICE
UNFIT FOR WORK
UNHAPPY TIMES
UNIFORM SPEED
UNION MEETING
UNITED ACTION
UNITED EFFORT
UNITED STATES
UNIT OF ENERGY
UNIT OF LENGTH
UNKINDEST CUT
UNKNOWN THING
UNLUCKY PATCH
UNMARRIED MAN
UNPAID LABOUR
UNPAID WORKER
UNTIE THE KNOT
UNTIMELY JEST
UNTOLD WEALTH
UNUSUAL TWIST
UNWORTHY PART
UNWRITTEN LAW
UP FOR AUCTION
UP IN A BALLOON
UP IN THE HILLS
UP ONE'S SLEEVE
UP ONE'S STREET
UPON MY HONOUR
UPPER CHAMBER
UPPER CIRCLES
UPPER CLASSES
UPPER REGIONS
UPRIGHT GRAND
UPRIGHT PIANO
UPSTAIRS ROOM
UP THE CHIMNEY
UP TO MISCHIEF
UP TO ONE'S EYES
UP TO ONE'S NECK
UP TO STANDARD

UP TO STRENGTH
UP TO THE NINES
UP TO THE WAIST
UPWARD GLANCE
UPWARD MOTION
UPWARD STROKE
UP WITH THE SUN
URGENT DEMAND
URGENT MATTER
USEFUL ADVICE
USE OF KITCHEN
USE ONE'S BRAIN
USE ONE'S HANDS
UTMOST EXTENT
UTTER FAILURE
UTTER POVERTY
UTTER RUBBISH
UTTER SILENCE
UTTER THREATS

V – 12

VACANT OFFICE
VALE OF SORROW
VALET SERVICE
VALIANT HEART
VALUED ADVICE
VALUED FRIEND
VANDYKE BEARD
VANTAGE POINT
VARIABLE GEAR
VARIETY HOUSE
VARIETY STAGE
VARIOUS TYPES
VARSITY MATCH
VAST QUANTITY
VEGETABLE DYE
VEGETABLE OIL
VEILED THREAT
VENETIAN LACE
VENI, VIDI, VICI
VENTURE FORTH
VENTURE TO SAY
VERBAL ATTACK
VERNAL SEASON
VERONICA LAKE
VERTICAL LINE
VERY REVEREND
VERY TOUCHING
VESTED RIGHTS
VIALS OF WRATH
VICE-LIKE GRIP
VICTIM OF FATE
VICTORIA LINE
VICTORIAN AGE
VICTORIAN ERA

VICTORIA PLUM
VICTORIA WOOD
VICTORY AT SEA
VICTORY BONDS
VICTORY MARCH
VICTORY MEDAL
VIDEO JUKEBOX
VILLAGE GREEN
VILLAGE IDIOT
VIM AND VIGOUR
VINCENT PRICE
VIN ORDINAIRE
VIOLENT DEATH
VIOLENT STORM
VIOLENT UPSET
VIOLIN PLAYER
VIOLIN STRING
VIRGIN FOREST
VIRGINIA MAYO
VIRGINIA REEL
VIRULENT TONE
VISIBLE MEANS
VISIT FRIENDS
VISITING CARD
VISITING TEAM
VISITING TIME
VISITORS' BOOK
VISIT THE SICK
VITAL CONCERN
VIVE LA FRANCE
VIVID PICTURE
VOCATIVE CASE
VODKA AND LIME
VOLCANIC ROCK
VOLGA BOATMAN
VOLUME OF FIRE
VOODOO DOCTOR
VOODOO PRIEST
VOTE IN FAVOUR
VOTE OF THANKS
VOW OF SILENCE
VULGAR TASTES

W – 12

WAGE INCREASE
WAG OF THE HEAD
WAG THE FINGER
WAITING WOMAN
WAIT ONE'S TURN
WALK GINGERLY
WALKING MATCH
WALK ON STILTS
WALK ON TIPTOE
WALK SIDEWAYS
WALK STRAIGHT

WALK THE EARTH
WALK THE PLANK
WALK TOGETHER
WALK WITH EASE
WALLED GARDEN
WANDERING JEW
WAND OF OFFICE
WANTED PERSON
WARLIKE TRIBE
WARM THE BLOOD
WARM THE HEART
WARNING LIGHT
WARNING SOUND
WARNING VOICE
WAR TO END WARS
WASH AND DRY UP
WASHED ASHORE
WASH ONE'S FACE
WASH ONE'S HAIR
WASTED EFFORT
WASTED LABOUR
WASTE NOTHING
WASTE NO WORDS
WASTE OF MONEY
WASTE PRODUCT
WATCH AND PRAY
WATCH AND WAIT
WATCH CLOSELY
WATCH REPAIRS
WATER BISCUIT
WATER COLOURS
WATER DIVINER
WATER HYDRANT
WATERING CART
WATER SPANIEL
WAVE FAREWELL
WAXWORKS SHOW
WAYS AND MEANS
WAYWARD CHILD
WEAK APPROACH
WEAK ARGUMENT
WEAKER VESSEL
WEAKEST POINT
WEAK SOLUTION
WEALTHY WIDOW
WEAPONS OF WAR
WEAR BLINKERS
WEAR MOURNING
WEAR THE CLOTH
WEAR THE CROWN
WEATHER CHART
WEATHER GAUGE
WEATHER GLASS
WEB OF CUNNING
WEDDED COUPLE
WEDDING BELLS

WEDDING DRESS
WEDDING FEAST
WEDDING GROUP
WEDDING GUEST
WEDDING MARCH
WEDDING RITES
WEDGWOOD BLUE
WEEK-END LEAVE
WEEK-END PARTY
WEEKLY COLUMN
WEEKLY MARKET
WEEKLY REPORT
WEEKLY SALARY
WEEP WITH RAGE
WEIGH HEAVILY
WEIGH ONESELF
WEIGHT FOR AGE
WEIRD SISTERS
WELCOME EVENT
WELCOME GUEST
WELCOME SIGHT
WELD TOGETHER
WELFARE STATE
WELL ADVANCED
WELL AND TRULY
WELL DESERVED
WELL DISPOSED
WELL IN POCKET
WELL-MADE SUIT
WELL REPORTED
WELL TAILORED
WELL-TIMED ACT
WELSH COSTUME
WELSH DRESSER
WELSH RAREBIT
WEST BROMWICH
WEST-END STAGE
WESTERLY WIND
WESTERN FRONT
WESTERN ISLES
WESTERN UNION
WESTERN WORLD
WEST VIRGINIA
WET TO THE SKIN
WHALE OF A TIME
WHAT'S COOKING?
WHAT'S THE GAME?
WHAT'S THE ODDS?
WHAT THE DEUCE?
WHEN AND WHERE?
WHERE AND WHEN?
WHETHER OR NOT
WHET THE KNIFE
WHICH IS WHICH?
WHIFF OF SMOKE
WHILE YOU WAIT

WHIPPED CREAM
WHIPPING POST
WHIP SCORPION
WHIPSNADE ZOO
WHISKY GALORE
WHISTLE FOR IT
WHITE CABBAGE
WHITE FEATHER
WHITE HEATHER
WHITE OF AN EGG
WHITE RUSSIAN
WHITE WEDDING
WHITHER BOUND?
WHO GOES THERE?
WICKED TYRANT
WICKER BASKET
WICKET KEEPER
WIDE CURRENCY
WIDELY SPACED
WIDOW TWANKEY
WILBUR WRIGHT
WILD APPLAUSE
WILD CREATURE
WILD HYACINTH
WILD LAUGHTER
WILD-WEST SHOW
WILFUL DAMAGE
WILFUL MURDER
WILLIAM BLAKE
WILLIAM BOOTH
WILLIAM RUFUS
WILLING HANDS
WILLING HEART
WILLING HORSE
WILLING PARTY
WILLING SLAVE
WILLING VOTER
WILL OF HEAVEN
WILL O' THE WISP
WILTON CARPET
WIN BY A LENGTH
WINDING TRAIL
WINDMILL GIRL
WIND OF CHANGE
WINDOW SCREEN
WINDSOR CHAIR
WIND THE CLOCK
WINDY WEATHER
WINE AND WOMEN
WINE IMPORTER
WINE MERCHANT
WINGED INSECT
WIN HANDS DOWN
WIN IN A CANTER
WINNING HORSE
WINNING SCORE

WINNING SMILE
WIN ONE'S SPURS
WINSOME SMILE
WINTER ABROAD
WINTER GARDEN
WINTER RESORT
WINTER SEASON
WINTER SPORTS
WIN THE BATTLE
WIN THE RUBBER
WIPE ONE'S EYES
WIPE ONE'S FEET
WIPE THE FLOOR
WISE DECISION
WIT AND WISDOM
WITCHING HOUR
WITCH OF ENDOR
WITH ALL HASTE
WITH ALL SPEED
WITH AN ACCENT
WITH A PURPOSE
WITH IMPUNITY
WITHIN BOUNDS
WITHIN LIMITS
WITHIN RADIUS
WITHIN REASON
WITH INTEREST
WITHIN THE LAW
WITH ONE VOICE
WITH OPEN ARMS
WITH OPEN EYES
WITHOUT A BEAN
WITHOUT A CARE
WITHOUT A CENT
WITHOUT A HOPE
WITHOUT A WORD
WITHOUT CAUSE
WITHOUT DELAY
WITHOUT DOUBT
WITHOUT FAULT
WITHOUT LIMIT
WITHOUT PRICE
WITHOUT STINT
WITHOUT SUGAR
WITH PLEASURE
WITH THIS RING
WOMAN IN WHITE
WOMAN'S HONOUR
WOMAN STUDENT
WOMAN TO WOMAN
WOMEN'S RIGHTS
WON BY A STREET
WON IN A CANTER
WOODEN BUCKET
WOOD SHAVINGS
WOOLLEN SOCKS

WOOL MERCHANT
WORD IN SEASON
WORD IN THE EAR
WORD OF ADVICE
WORD OF HONOUR
WORDS OF CHEER
WORDY WARFARE
WORKABLE PLAN
WORK FOR PEACE
WORKING CLASS
WORKING HOURS
WORKING MODEL
WORKING ORDER
WORKING PARTY
WORKING WIVES
WORKING WOMAN
WORK MIRACLES
WORK OFF STEAM
WORK ONE'S WILL
WORK OVERTIME
WORKS CANTEEN
WORKS COUNCIL
WORKS MANAGER
WORK TOGETHER
WORLDLY GOODS
WORLD OF SPORT
WORLD OF TODAY
WORM'S EYE VIEW
WORRIED FROWN
WORRYING TIME
WORRY TO DEATH
WORSE FOR WEAR
WORTH A PACKET
WORTH NOTHING
WORTHY OF NOTE
WOULD YOU MIND?
WOUNDED PRIDE
WRACK AND RUIN
WRETCHED DIGS
WRISTWATCH TV
WRITE A CHEQUE
WRITE A LETTER
WRITE AN ESSAY
WRITE A REPORT
WRITE A SONNET
WRITER'S CRAMP
WRITHE IN PAIN
WRITING PAPER
WRITING TABLE
WRITTEN MUSIC
WRITTEN ORDER
WRITTEN REPLY
WRITTEN TERMS
WRONG ADDRESS
WRONG MEANING
WRONG SIDE OUT

WRONG SOCIETY
WRONG TURNING
WRONG VERDICT

Y – 12

YACHTING CLUB
YANKEE DOODLE
YARD AND A HALF
YEARLY SALARY
YEARS OF STUDY
YELLOW BASKET

YELLOW COLOUR
YELLOW FLOWER
YELLOW RIBBON
YELLOW STREAK
YELL WITH PAIN
YOUNG AT HEART
YOUNG ENGLAND
YOUNGEST GIRL
YOUNG HOPEFUL
YOUNG IN HEART
YOUNG WOODLEY

YOUR EMINENCE
YOUR HIGHNESS
YOUR LADYSHIP
YOUR LORDSHIP
YOUR OWN FAULT
YOURS IN HASTE

Z – 12

ZACHARY SCOTT
ZIGZAG COURSE

A – 13

ABERDEEN ANGUS
ABIDE BY THE LAW
ABJECT APOLOGY
ABJECT POVERTY
ABJECT SLAVERY
ABOUT ONE'S EARS
ABOVE ONE'S HEAD
ABOVE REPROACH
ABOVE SEA-LEVEL
ABOVE STRENGTH
ABRAHAM'S BOSOM
ABRUPT DESCENT
ABSENCE OF MIND
ABSENT FRIENDS
ABSOLUTE POWER
ABSOLUTE PROOF
ABSOLUTE RULER
ABSOLUTE TRUST
ABSTRACT TERMS
ABUSIVE SPEECH
ABYSSINIAN CAT
ACADEMIC DRESS
ACADEMIC TITLE
ACCEPT AN OFFER
ACCEPTED TRUTH
ACCEPT PAYMENT
ACCIDENT PRONE
ACCORDION BAND
ACCOUNTS CLERK
ACCUSED PERSON
ACCUSE FALSELY
ACE OF DIAMONDS
ACHES AND PAINS
ACQUIRED SKILL
ACQUIRED TASTE
ACQUIT ONESELF
ACROSS AND DOWN
ACROSS COUNTRY
ACROSS THE ROAD
ACT AS CHAIRMAN
ACT FOR THE BEST
ACTING CAPTAIN
ACTING MANAGER
ACTION PAINTER
ACTION PICTURE
ACTIVE PARTNER
ACTIVE SERVICE
ACTIVE VOLCANO
ACT LIKE A CHARM
ACT LIKE A TONIC
ACT OF COURTESY
ACT OF HUMANITY
ACT OF KINDNESS
ACT OF VIOLENCE

ACUTE DISTRESS
ADAM FIREPLACE
ADDED PLEASURE
ADDED STRENGTH
ADDING MACHINE
ADEQUATE CAUSE
A DEUCE OF A MESS
ADIPOSE TISSUE
ADJUST THE TYPE
ADMIRAL NELSON
ADMIRALTY ARCH
ADMISSION CARD
ADMISSION FREE
ADMITTED GUILT
ADVANCED LEVEL
ADVANCED PUPIL
ADVANCE NOTICE
ADVENTURE GAME
ADVISE AGAINST
ADVISORY BOARD
AERIAL RAILWAY
AERIAL TORPEDO
AERIAL WARFARE
AFFECTED STYLE
AFFECTED VOICE
AFFORDING HOPE
AFRAID TO SPEAK
AFTER A FASHION
AFTER MIDNIGHT
AFTERNOON POST
AFTERNOON REST
AFTER THE EVENT
AFTER THE STORM
AGAIN AND AGAIN
AGAINST THE LAW
AGE OF CHIVALRY
AGREE TO DIFFER
AIR A GRIEVANCE
AIR FORCE CROSS
AIR OF APPROVAL
AIR ON A G STRING
AIR OPERATIONS
AIRPORT LOUNGE
AIR RAID WARDEN
AIRS AND GRACES
ALEXANDER POPE
ALEXANDRA PARK
ALFRED DREYFUS
ALICE BLUE GOWN
ALL CHANGE HERE
ALL-DAY SESSION
ALLEGED MOTIVE
ALLEGED REASON
ALL FOR NOTHING
ALL FOR THE BEST
ALL FOR THE GOOD

ALL HALLOWS' EVE	ANNOTATED TEXT
ALLIED ADVANCE	ANNUAL ECLIPSE
ALLIED LANDING	ANNUAL FIXTURE
ALLIGATOR PEAR	ANNUAL HOLIDAY
ALLIGATOR SKIN	ANNUAL MEETING
ALL IN A FLUSTER	ANNUAL PAYMENT
ALL IN GOOD TIME	ANNUAL PREMIUM
ALL IN ONE PIECE	ANOINT WITH OIL
ALL-IN WRESTLER	ANONYMOUS GIFT
ALL OF A TREMBLE	ANOTHER CHANCE
ALL OF A TWITTER	ANOTHER MATTER
ALL THE ANSWERS	ANOTHER PLEASE
ALL THE WINNERS	ANSWER THE BELL
ALL-TIME RECORD	ANSWER THE HELM
ALLUVIAL PLAIN	ANTHONY NEWLEY
ALMOND BLOSSOM	ANTHONY QUAYLE
ALONG THE COAST	ANTHROPOID APE
A LONG WAY AFTER	ANTIQUE DEALER
A LONG WAY AHEAD	ANTONY ADVERSE
ALPHA AND OMEGA	ANXIOUS MOMENT
ALPINE CLIMBER	ANYBODY'S GUESS
ALTER THE RULES	APPEAL FOR HELP
ALTOGETHER BAD	APPEALING LOOK
ALWAYS ON THE GO	APPEAR IN COURT
AMATEUR BOXING	APPLE DUMPLING
AMATEUR GOLFER	APPLE FRITTERS
AMATEUR PLAYER	APPLE OF THE EYE
AMATEUR SLEUTH	APPLE-PIE ORDER
AMATEUR STATUS	APPLE TURNOVER
AMATEUR TALENT	APPLY FOR A LOAN
AMERICAN CLOTH	APPLY FOR LEAVE
AMERICAN EAGLE	APPLY PRESSURE
AMERICAN NEGRO	APPLY THE BRAKE
AMERICAN ORGAN	APPLY THE MATCH
AMERICAN SLANG	APOLLO THEATRE
AMOROUS GLANCE	APOSTLES' CREED
AMUSEMENT PARK	APPOINTED TIME
ANATOLE FRANCE	APRICOT BRANDY
ANCESTRAL HALL	APRIL FOOL'S DAY
ANCESTRAL HOME	APRIL THE FIFTH
ANCIENT BRITON	APRIL THE FIRST
ANCIENT GREECE	APRIL THE NINTH
ANCIENT GRUDGE	APRIL THE SIXTH
ANCIENT LIGHTS	APRIL THE TENTH
ANCIENT WISDOM	APRIL THE THIRD
ANDREW JACKSON	ARABIAN DESERT
ANGELIC VOICES	ARABIAN NIGHTS
ANGEL PAVEMENT	ARC DE TRIOMPHE
ANGRY YOUNG MAN	ARCHIE ANDREWS
ANGUISH OF MIND	ARCTIC REGIONS
ANGULAR FIGURE	ARDENT ADMIRER
ANIMAL KINGDOM	ARDENT SPIRITS
ANIMAL RESERVE	ARGUE THE POINT
ANIMAL SPIRITS	ARMAMENTS RACE
ANIMAL TRAINER	ARMED CONFLICT
ANIMATED SMILE	ARMS AND THE MAN

ARMS PROGRAMME
ARMY COMMANDER
ARMY ESTIMATES
ARMY EXERCISES
ARMY PAY-OFFICE
ARNOLD BENNETT
AROUND THE TOWN
ARRANGE A MATCH
ARREARS OF WORK
ART COLLECTION
ART DEPARTMENT
ART EXHIBITION
ARTHUR ENGLISH
ARTICLED CLERK
ARTICLES OF WAR
ARTIFICIAL ARM
ARTIFICIAL FLY
ARTIFICIAL LEG
ARTILLERY FIRE
ARTISTIC VALUE
ARTISTS' COLONY
ARTISTS' RIFLES
ASTIST'S STUDIO
ART OF SPEAKING
ARTS AND CRAFTS
AS BLIND AS A BAT
AS BOLD AS BRASS
AS DARK AS NIGHT
AS DARK AS PITCH
AS FAR AS IT GOES
AS FULL AS AN EGG
AS GOOD AS A PLAY
AS HARD AS NAILS
ASHDOWN FOREST
AS HEAVY AS LEAD
ASK A POLICEMAN
ASK FOR NOTHING
ASK FOR TROUBLE
ASK PERMISSION
AS LARGE AS LIFE
AS LIKELY AS NOT
AS LONG AS MY ARM
AS PALE AS DEATH
ASPARAGUS TIPS
AS RIGHT AS RAIN
ASSEMBLY ROOMS
ASSERT ONESELF
ASSUME AN ALIAS
ASSUME COMMAND
AS SURE AS CAN BE
AS SWEET AS A NUT
AS THIN AS A LATH
A STITCH IN TIME
AS TRUE AS STEEL
AS WARM AS TOAST
AS WEAK AS WATER

ATALANTA'S RACE
AT AN ADVANTAGE
AT A STANDSTILL
AT FULL STRETCH
AT GREAT LENGTH
ATHLETE'S HEART
ATHLETIC COACH
ATLANTIC LINER
ATLANTIC OCEAN
AT LOGGERHEADS
ATOMIC FISSION
ATOMIC REACTOR
ATOMIC WARFARE
ATOMIC WARHEAD
AT ONE'S LEISURE
AT ONE'S OWN RISK
AT ONE'S WITS' END
AT RIGHT-ANGLES
AT SHORT NOTICE
ATTEND COLLEGE
AT THE CONTROLS
AT THE DENTIST'S
AT THE LAST GASP
AT THE RINGSIDE
AT THE SAME TIME
AT THE WAXWORKS
ATTORNEY AT LAW
ATTRACT NOTICE
AT YOUR SERVICE
AUCTION BRIDGE
AUDITORY NERVE
AUDREY HEPBURN
AUGEAN STABLES
AUTHENTIC WORK
AUTOMATIC LIFT
AUTOMATIC LOCK
AUTUMN COLOURS
AUXILIARY VERB
AVENGING ANGEL
AVENUE OF TREES
AVERAGE AMOUNT
AVERAGE FIGURE
AVERAGE HEIGHT
AVERAGE PERSON
AVERAGE WEIGHT
AVERT ONE'S EYES
AVOID THE ISSUE
AWAY FROM IT ALL
AWKWARD PERSON

B – 13

BABBLING BROOK
BACHELOR OF LAW
BACK-HAND DRIVE
BACK IN HARNESS

BACK IN THE FOLD
BACK OF THE HAND
BACK OF THE HEAD
BACK OF THE NECK
BACK ONE'S FANCY
BACK THE WINNER
BACK TO THE LAND
BACK TO THE WALL
BACKWARD CHILD
BACON SANDWICH
BAD COMPLEXION
BAD CONNECTION
BAD CONSCIENCE
BADGE OF OFFICE
BAD IMPRESSION
BADLY HAMMERED
BADLY REPORTED
BAD MANAGEMENT
BAD REPUTATION
BAD UPBRINGING
BAG AND BAGGAGE
BAGGY TROUSERS
BALANCE IN HAND
BALD ADMISSION
BALD STATEMENT
BALL AND SOCKET
BALLET DANCING
BALLOON ASCENT
BALLY NUISANCE
BAMBOO CURTAIN
BAND OF OUTLAWS
BAND OF ROBBERS
BANG ON THE HEAD
BANKER'S CREDIT
BANK MESSENGER
BANK OF ENGLAND
BANK OF IRELAND
BANK OVERDRAFT
BANKRUPT STOCK
BANKS AND BRAES
BANK STATEMENT
BAPTISMAL NAME
BAPTISM OF FIRE
BAPTIST CHURCH
BARBARA MULLEN
BARBECUE PARTY
BARBER SURGEON
BARCELONA NUTS
BARE-BACK RIDER
BARE EXISTENCE
BARE-FACED LIAR
BARE ONE'S TEETH
BARGAIN HUNTER
BARK AT THE MOON
BARK ONE'S SHINS
BAR OF THE HOUSE

BARRISTER'S WIG
BARTERED BRIDE
BASHFUL MANNER
BASIC INSTINCT
BASQUE COUNTRY.
BASSO PROFUNDO
BATHED IN TEARS
BATHING BEAUTY
BATHING TRUNKS
BATTER PUDDING
BATTERSEA PARK
BATTERY BACKUP
BATTERY OF GUNS
BATTLE CRUISER
BATTLE HONOURS
BATTLE OF WORDS
BAYONET CHARGE
BAYSWATER ROAD
BEANS AND BACON
BEAR THE BURDEN
BEAST OF BELSEN
BEAST OF BURDEN
BEAT ALL COMERS
BEATLES' RECORD
BEAT ONE HOLLOW
BEAT THE BOUNDS
BEAT THE RECORD
BEAUFORT SCALE
BEAUTIFUL FACE
BEAUTIFUL VIEW
BEAUTY CONTEST
BEAUTY CULTURE
BEAUTY PARLOUR
BECOME A MARTYR
BECOME A MEMBER
BECOME A NEW MAN
BECOME ENGAGED
BECOME EXTINCT
BECOMF FRIENDS
BE CONSPICUOUS
BEDSIDE MANNER
BEETLING BROWS
BEFORE THE DAWN
BEFORE THE FACT
BEFORE THE MAST
BEFORE THE WIND
BEG FOR FAVOURS
BEGGING LETTER
BEGINNER'S LUCK
BEGIN TO WEAKEN
BEG PERMISSION
BEHAVE ONESELF
BEHIND THE LINE
BEHIND THE VEIL
BE IN DISFAVOUR
BE IN THE SADDLE

BELATED EFFORT
BELISHA BEACON
BELLES LETTRES
BELONGING TO ME
BELONGING TO US
BELOVED OBJECT
BELOW FREEZING
BELOW SEA-LEVEL
BELOW STANDARD
BELOW STRENGTH
BE MY VALENTINE
BEND BACKWARDS
BEND IN THE ROAD
BENEATH NOTICE
BENEATH THE SUN
BE OF GOOD CHEER
BE OF GOOD HEART
BERNARD BRADEN
BESIDE ONESELF
BESIDE THE MARK
BESSEMER STEEL
BEST BEHAVIOUR
BEST END OF NECK
BESTIR ONESELF
BEST OF A BAD JOB
BEST OF FRIENDS
BEST OF ITS KIND
BEST OF MOTIVES
BEST THING TO DO
BETTER ONESELF
BETTER OR WORSE
BEYOND ALL HELP
BEYOND COMPARE
BEYOND CONTROL
BEYOND DISPUTE
BEYOND MEASURE
BEYOND ONE'S KEN
BEYOND THE PALE
BEYOND THE VEIL
BICYCLE RACING
BID FOR FREEDOM
BIG-GAME HUNTER
BIG WHITE CHIEF
BILLIARD TABLE
BIRD IN THE HAND
BIRD OF ILL OMEN
BIRD OF PASSAGE
BIRD ON THE WING
BIRD SANCTUARY
BIRD'S-NEST SOUP
BIRDS OF THE AIR
BIRTHDAY PARTY
BIRTHDAY TREAT
BISCUIT BARREL
BITE ONE'S NAILS
BITE ONE'S THUMB

BITING SARCASM
BIT OF A MYSTERY
BIT OF NONSENSE
BITS AND PIECES
BITTER DRAUGHT
BITTER FLAVOUR
BITTER QUARREL
BITTER REMORSE
BLACK AND WHITE
BLACK AS A SWEEP
BLACK DIAMONDS
BLACKPOOL ROCK
BLANKET FINISH
BLANKET OF SNOW
BLANKET STITCH
BLANKETY BLANK
BLAZE OF COLOUR
BLAZE THE TRAIL
BLAZING TEMPER
BLEEDING HEART
BLESS THE BRIDE
BLIGHTED HOPES
BLINDING LIGHT
BLINDING STORM
BLIND IN ONE EYE
BLINDMAN'S BUFF
BLISSFUL STATE
BLOCK CAPITALS
BLOOD BROTHERS
BLOOD PRESSURE
BLOOD RELATION
BLOODSHOT EYES
BLOODY ASSIZES
BLOTTING PAPER
BLOW GREAT GUNS
BLUE IN THE FACE
BLUNT QUESTION
BLUSH FOR SHAME
BLUSHING BRIDE
BOARDING HOUSE
BOARDING PARTY
BOB'S YOUR UNCLE
BODY CORPORATE
BODY OF OPINION
BOHEMIAN GLASS
BOLSHOI BALLET
BOMBER COMMAND
BONY STRUCTURE
BOOKING OFFICE
BOOK OF GENESIS
BOOK OF THE FILM
BOOK OF THE PLAY
BOOK OF THE YEAR
BOOK OF TICKETS
BOOK ONE'S BERTH
BOOMING MARKET

BOON COMPANION
BOOSTER ROCKET
BOOT AND SADDLE
BORDER BALLADS
BORDER COUNTRY
BORN IN WEDLOCK
BORN ORGANISER
BORN YESTERDAY
BORROWED MONEY
BORSTAL SYSTEM
BOSTON TERRIER
BOSTON TWO-STEP
BOTTLED SWEEETS
BOTTLE OF SCENT
BOTTLE OF STOUT
BOTTLE OF WATER
BOTTOMLESS PIT
BOUGHT AND SOLD
BOUNDARY FENCE
BOUNDARY STONE
BOUNDLESS DEEP
BOWLER'S WICKET
BOWLING CREASE
BOW TO THE STORM
BOX OF BISCUITS
BOX OF CRACKERS
BOX THE COMPASS
BRACE OF SHAKES
BRANCH LIBRARY
BRANCH MEETING
BRANCH OFFICE
BRANDY AND SODA
BRASS BEDSTEAD
BRASS FARTHING
BRAVE NEW WORLD
BREACH OF FAITH
BREACH OF TRUST
BREAD AND WATER
BREAD OF HEAVEN
BREAD POULTICE
BREAD SHORTAGE
BREADTH OF MIND
BREADTH OF VIEW
BREAK A JOURNEY
BREAK A PROMISE
BREAKDOWN GANG
BREAKERS AHEAD
BREAKFAST DISH
BREAKFAST FOOD
BREAKFAST TIME
BREAKING POINT
BREAK INTO A RUN
BREAK INTO SONG
BREAK IT GENTLY
BREAK OFF SHORT
BREAK ONE'S BACK

BREAK ONE'S DUCK
BREAK ONE'S FAST
BREAK ONE'S WORD
BREAK THE PEACE
BREAK THE RULES
BREAK THE SPELL
BREAK TO PIECES
BREAST THE TAPE
BREATHE FREELY
BREATHING ROOM
BREATHING TUBE
BRED IN THE BONE
BRIDE AND GROOM
BRIDGE BUILDER
BRIDGE OF BOATS
BRIDGE OF SIGHS
BRIDGE PROBLEM
BRIEF INTERVAL
BRIGHTON BEACH
BRIGHTON BELLE
BRIGHTON RACES
BRILLIANT IDEA
BRILLIANT MIND
BRING AN ACTION
BRING INTO LINE
BRING NTO PLAY
BRING TO A CLOSE
BRING TOGETHER
BRING UP TO DATE
BRISKET OF BEEF
BRISK MOVEMENT
BRISTOL ROVERS
BRITISH COLONY
BRITISH CONSUL
BRITISH EMPIRE
BRITISH GUIANA
BRITISH LEGION
BRITISH MUSEUM
BRITISH PUBLIC
BROAD DAYLIGHT
BROKEN ENGLISH
BROKEN PROMISE
BROKEN ROMANCE
BROKEN SILENCE
BROOK NO DENIAL
BROTHERLY LOVE
BROUGHT TO BOOK
BROWN AS A BERRY
BRUSH ONE'S HAIR
BRUSQUE MANNER
BRUTE STRENGTH
BUBONIC PLAGUE
BUCKET OF WATER
BUDDING AUTHOR
BUDDING GENIUS
BUDGET SURPLUS

BUFF ORPINGTON
BUILDING BLOCK
BULLS AND BEARS
BUMPER HARVEST
BUNCH OF GRAPES
BURDEN OF GUILT
BURDEN OF POWER
BURDEN OF PROOF
BURIAL CUSTOMS
BURIAL SERVICE
BURKE'S PEERAGE
BURLESQUE SHOW
BURNING DESIRE
BURNING THIRST
BURN ONE'S BOATS
BURN ONE'S MONEY
BURN TO A CINDER
BURNT OFFERING
BURN WITH ANGER
BURSTING POINT
BURST OF ENERGY
BURST THE BONDS
BURTON ON TRENT
BUSH TELEGRAPH
BUSINESS HOURS
BUSINESS HOUSE
BUSINESS LUNCH
BUSINESS TERMS
BUSINESS WOMAN
BUSINESS WORLD
BUTLER'S PANTRY
BUTTERED TOAST
BUTTERFLY KISS
BUTTON YOUR LIP
BY ALL ACCOUNTS
BY APPOINTMENT
BY ARRANGEMENT
BY CANDLELIGHT
BY INSTALMENTS
BY THE ROADSIDE
BY UNDERGROUND
BY WORD OF MOUTH

C – 13

CABINET MEMBER
CALCULATED LIE
CALENDAR MONTH
CALL FOR TRUMPS
CALL INTO BEING
CALL OF THE WILD
CLL ONE'S BLUFF
CALL THE POLICE
CALL TO ACCOUNT
CALL TO WITNESS
CAMBRIDGE BLUE

CAMEL-HAIR COAT
CAMERA OBSCURA
CAMPAIGN MEDAL
CAMPING GROUND
CANARY ISLANDS
CANDID OPINION
CANNIBAL TRIBE
CAPACITY CROWD
CAPACITY HOUSE
CAPE CANAVERAL
CAPITAL CHARGE
CAPITAL FELLOW
CAPITAL LETTER
CAPITAL MURDER
CAP OF DARKNESS
CAPTAIN CUTTLE
CAPTAIN KETTLE
CAPTAIN'S TABLE
CARAFE OF WATER
CARBON DIOXIDE
CARDINAL POINT
CAREER OF CRIME
CAREFUL DRIVER
CARNEGIE TRUST
CARNIVAL QUEEN
CARPET CLEANER
CARPET SWEEPER
CARRIER PIGEON
CARRY THE BLAME
CARRY THE TORCH
CARRY TO EXCESS
CARTRIDGE CASE
CARVE ONE'S NAME
CARVE THE JOINT
CASH DISPENSER
CASH IN ADVANCE
CASH IN THE BANK
CASHMERE SHAWL
CASH ON THE NAIL
CASSE NOISETTE
CAST IN ONE'S LOT
CAST-IRON ALIBI
CASTLE IN SPAIN
CASUAL CLOTHES
CASUAL MEETING
CASUAL VISITOR
CAT-AND-DOG LIFE
CATCH A GLIMPSE
CATCH AT STRAWS
CATCH UNAWARES
CATERING CORPS
CATHEDRAL CITY
CATHEDRAL TOWN
CATHERINE PARR
CATHOLIC FAITH
CAT O' NINE TAILS

CATTLE BREEDER
CATTLE FARMING
CAUGHT BENDING
CAUGHT IN A TRAP
CAUGHT NAPPING
CAUSE A FLUTTER
CAUSE FOR ALARM
CAUSE OF INJURY
CAUSTIC REMARK
CAVALRY CHARGE
CAVALRY SCHOOL
CAVALRY TROOPS
CAYENNE PEPPER
CELEBRATED MAN
CELESTIAL BODY
CELESTIAL CITY
CELESTIAL POLE
CEMENT MIXTURE
CENTRAL AFRICA
CENTRAL EUROPE
CENTRAL FIGURE
CENTRAL LONDON
CENTRAL OFFICE
CENTRE FORWARD
CENTRE OF TRADE
CERTAIN EXTENT
CERTAIN PERSON
CERTIFIED MILK
CHAIN OF EVENTS
CHAIN OF OFFICE
CHAIN REACTION
CHALLENGE FATE
CHAMP AT THE BIT
CHAMPION BOXER
CHANCE MEETING
CHANCE ONE'S ARM
CHANGE A CHEQUE
CHANGED PERSON
CHANGE OF FRONT
CHANGE OF HEART
CHANGE OF PLACE
CHANGE OF SCENE
CHANGE OF VENUE
CHANGING ROOMS
CHANGING VOICE
CHANNEL BRIDGE
CHANNEL TUNNEL
CHARACTER PART
CHARGE ACCOUNT
CHARGE TOO MUCH
CHARITY BAZAAR
CHARLES DARWIN
CHARLES WESLEY
CHARLOT'S REVUE
CHARM BRACELET
CHARMED CIRCLE

CHARM OF MANNER
CHARTER FLIGHT
CHASE ONE'S TAIL
CHEAP AND NASTY
CHECK THE SPEED
CHEDDAR CHEESE
CHEERFUL GIVER
CHEERFUL SIGHT
CHEESE AND WINE
CHEESE BISCUIT
CHEF DE CUISINE
CHELSEA BRIDGE
CHELTENHAM SPA
CHEMICAL AGENT
CHERISH AN IDEA
CHERRY BLOSSOM
CHERRY ORCHARD
CHESS CHAMPION
CHEST EXPANDER
CHESTNUT BROWN
CHESTNUT HORSE
CHICKEN FARMER
CHIEF ARMOURER
CHIEF ENGINEER
CHIEF OF POLICE
CHILDHOOD DAYS
CHILDISH PRANK
CHILD OF NATURE
CHILDREN'S BOOK
CHILDREN'S GAME
CHILDREN'S HOME
CHILDREN'S HOUR
CHILLY WELCOME
CHILTERN HILLS
CHIMNEY CORNER
CHIMNEY-POT HAT
CHINESE PUZZLE
CHOCOLATE DROP
CHOICE OF WORDS
CHOIR PRACTICE
CHOP AND CHANGE
CHOPPING BLOCK
CHORAL CONCERT
CHORAL SERVICE
CHORAL SOCIETY
CHORUS OF ABUSE
CHRIS CHATAWAY
CHRISTIAN NAME
CHRISTMAS CAKE
CHRISTMAS CARD
CHRISTMAS FAIR
CHRISTMAS GIFT
CHRISTMAS TREE
CHURCHILL TANK
CHURCH OFFICER
CHURCH SERVICE

CHURCH STEEPLE
CHURCH WEDDING
CIGARETTE CARD
CIGARETTE CASE
CIGARETTE GIRL
CIRCLE OF LIGHT
CIRCUS MANAGER
CITY OF THE DEAD
CIVIL AVIATION
CIVIL ENGINEER
CIVILIAN DRESS
CIVIL MARRIAGE
CIVIL QUESTION
CLAIM THE CROWN
CLAPHAM COMMON
CLAP OF THUNDER
CLAP ONE'S HANDS
CLAP ON THE BACK
CLARENCE HOUSE
CLASSIC REMARK
CLASS STRUGGLE
CLEAN THE SLATE
CLEARANCE SALE
CLEARING HOUSE
CLEAR SPEAKING
CLEAR THE COURT
CLEAR THE DECKS
CLEAR THE TABLE
CLEAR THINKING
CLEMENT ATTLEE
CLENCHED TEETH
CLERICAL BLACK
CLERICAL DRESS
CLERICAL ERROR
CLERICAL STAFF
CLIFFS OF DOVER
CLIMBING IRONS
CLIMBING PLANT
CLIMBING SHRUB
CLIMB LIKE A CAT
CLINCH THE DEAL
CLING TOGETHER
CLIP ONE'S WINGS
CLIP ONE'S WORDS
CLIPPED SPEECH
CLOSED CHAPTER
CLOSED CIRCUIT
CLOSE FIGHTING
CLOSELY ALLIED
CLOSE ONE'S EYES
CLOSE PRISONER
CLOSE QUARTERS
CLOSE RELATIVE
CLOSE SECURITY
CLOSE THE RANKS
CLOSE TOGETHER

CLOSE TO NATURE
CLOSING SEASON
CLOSING SPEECH
CLOSING STAGES
CLOTHES BASKET
CLOTHING TRADE
CLOUD THE ISSUE
COARSE FISHING
COASTAL RESORT
COASTAL WATERS
COAST DOWNHILL
COBBLED STREET
COCKER SPANIEL
COCKNEY ACCENT
COCK OF THE WALK
COCKTAIL DRESS
COCKTAIL PARTY
COCKTAIL STICK
CODE OF CONDUCT
COFFEE ESSENCE
COFFEE GROUNDS
COFFEE PLANTER
COLD AS CHARITY
COLD COLLATION
COLD IN THE HEAD
COLD RECEPTION
COLD-WATER CURE
COLLECTION BOX
COLLECT STAMPS
COLLEGE OF ARMS
COLONIAL HOUSE
COLONIAL STYLE
COLOURED CHALK
COLOURED SLIDE
COLOURED WATER
COLOUR PROBLEM
COLUMN OF ROUTE
COLUMN OF SMOKE
COMBINED FORCE
COMBINE FORCES
COME ALONGSIDE
COME AWAY EMPTY
COME BACK AGAIN
COME DOWN HEADS
COME DOWN TAILS
COMEDY ACTRESS
COMEDY THEATRE
COME IN CONTACT
COME INTO BEING
COME INTO FORCE
COME INTO MONEY
COME INTO SIGHT
COME OUT EASILY
COME OVER QUEER
COME TO A BAD END
COME TO A CLIMAX

COME TO A CRISIS
COME TO NOTHING
COME TO ONESELF
COME TO THE BALL
COME TO THE FAIR
COME TO THE FORE
COME UNDER FIRE
COME UNINVITED
COME UP FOR MORE
COME UP SMILING
COMING SHORTLY
COMMERCIAL ART
COMMERCIAL LAW
COMMIT A FELONY
COMMIT AN ERROR
COMMIT ONESELF
COMMIT PERJURY
COMMIT SUICIDE
COMMITTEE ROOM
COMMIT TO PAPER
COMMON ASSAULT
COMMON CARRIER
COMMON CONSENT
COMMON FEATURE
COMMON GROUNDS
COMMON HONESTY
COMMON MEASURE
COMMON MISTAKE
COMMON PATTERN
COMMON PURPOSE
COMMON SOLDIER
COMMUNION WINE
COMMUNISTIC BLOC
COMPACT CAMERA
COMPANY LAWYER
COMPANY MERGER
COMPANY REPORT
COMPASS NEEDLE
COMPLAINT BOOK
COMPLETE WORKS
COMPLEX SYSTEM
COMPONENT PART
COMPOSING ROOM
COMPRESSED AIR
COMRADE IN ARMS
CONCEDE A POINT
CONCERT ARTIST
CONCRETE MIXER
CONCRETE OFFER
CONDEMNED CELL
CONDEMNED FORM
CONDENSED MILK
CONDUCTED TOUR
CONFIDENCE MAN
CONFINED PLACE
CONFINED SPACE

CONFINED TO BED
CONFIRMED CASE
CONFIRMED LIAR
CONGRESS MEDAL
CONGRESS PARTY
CONISTON WATER
CONNECTING ROD
CONSCRIPT ARMY
CONSTANT LOSER
CONSTANT NYMPH
CONSUL GENERAL
CONSUMER GOODS
CONTACT LENSES
CONTENTED MIND
CONTENT TO REST
CONTINUITY MAN
CONTRITE HEART
CONTROL CENTRE
CONTROL PRICES
CONVENT SCHOOL
COOKERY LESSON
COOKING MEDIUM
COOKING SHERRY
COOK ONE'S GOOSE
COOLING BREEZE
COOL ONE'S HEELS
COOL RECEPTION
COPPER COINAGE
CORAL NECKLACE
CORONATION CUP
CORONER'S COURT
CORPORATE BODY
CORPS DE BALLET
CORPUS CHRISTI
CORPUS DELICTI
CORRECT ACCENT
CORRECT ANSWER
CORRECT SPEECH
CORRIDOR TRAIN
COSTLY FAILURE
COSTLY VENTURE
COTSWOLD HILLS
COTSWOLD STONE
COTTAGE CHEESE
COTTON PLANTER
COULD BE BETTER
COULEUR DE ROSE
COUNCIL ESTATE
COUNCIL SCHOOL
COUNTING HOUSE
COUNTRY COUSIN
COUNTRY CUSTOM
COUNTRY SQUIRE
COUNT THE HOURS
COUNTY BOROUGH
COUNTY COUNCIL

COUNTY CRICKET
COURSE BETTING
COURSE OF STUDY
COURT CIRCULAR
COURT DISASTER
COURTESY TITLE
COURT INTRIGUE
COURT OF APPEAL
COURT OF RECORD
COURT REPORTER
COVERED MARKET
COWARD AT HEART
CRABBED OLD AGE
CRACK REGIMENT
CRAFTSMAN'S JOB
CRAVEN COTTAGE
CRAZY PAVEMENT
CREAM OF TARTAR
CREATE A RUMPUS
CREATE A VACUUM
CREATE DISCORD
CREATE TROUBLE
CREDIT ACCOUNT
CREDIT BALANCE
CREDIT COMPANY
CREDIT SQUEEZE
CREEPING JENNY
CRÊME DE MENTHE
CRIBBAGE BOARD
CRICKET ELEVEN
CRICKET GROUND
CRICKET SEASON
CRICKET UMPIRE
CRICK ONE'S NECK
CRIME REPORTER
CRIMINAL CLASS
CRIMINAL COURT
CRIMINAL ERROR
CRIMINAL TRIAL
CRIMINAL WORLD
CRIPPLING BLOW
CRITICAL ANGLE
CRITICALLY ILL
CRITICAL POWER
CRITICAL STAGE
CROCHET NEEDLE
CROIX DE GUERRE
CROQUET MALLET
CROSSED CHEQUE
CROSSED IN LOVE
CROSS EXAMINED
CROSS ONE'S MIND
CROSS ONE'S PALM
CROSS ONE'S PATH
CROSS PURPOSES
CROSS THE FLOOR

CROSS THE OCEAN
CROWDED CANVAS
CROWDED STREET
CROWD OF PEOPLE
CROWD TOGETHER
CROWN COLONIES
CROWNING GLORY
CROWNING MERCY
CROWN OF THORNS
CROWN PRINCESS
CROWN PROPERTY
CRUCIAL MOMENT
CRUCIAL PERIOD
CRUDE ESTIMATE
CRUISE MISSILE
CRUISING SPEED
CRUSHING REPLY
CRUSH TO PIECES
CRY BLUE MURDER
CRY FOR NOTHING
CRY FOR THE MOON
CRY LIKE A CHILD
CRY OF DERISION
CRYPTIC REMARK
CRYSTAL GAZING
CRYSTAL PALACE
CUBIC CAPACITY
CUBIC CONTENTS
CUCUMBER FRAME
CUDDLE UP CLOSE
CULTIVATED MAN
CUNNING FELLOW
CUP THAT CHEERS
CURIOSITY SHOP
CURIOUS DESIGN
CURIOUS EFFECT
CURIOUS TO KNOW
CURRENT ASSETS
CURRENT BELIEF
CURRENT EVENTS
CURRENT NUMBER
CURRENT REPORT
CURRENT RUMOUR
CURRENT SERIES
CURSE AND SWEAR
CURSORY GLANCE
CURTAIN OF FIRE
CURTAIN RAISER
CUT DOWN TO SIZE
CUT OFF A CORNER
CUT ONE'S LOSSES
CUT ONE'S THROAT
CUT THE PAINTER
CUTTING REMARK
CUTTING RETORT
CUT TO THE QUICK

CYCLE OF EVENTS
CYCLE OF THE SUN
CYRIL FLETCHER

D – 13

DADDY AND MUMMY
DADDY-LONG-LEGS
DAILY DELIVERY
DAILY PRACTICE
DAILY PURSUITS
DAME CLARA BUTT
DAME COMMANDER
DAMP THE ARDOUR
DANCE THE POLKA
DANCE THE TANGO
DANCE WITH RAGE
DANCING LESSON
DANCING MASTER
DANCING SCHOOL
DANDELION WINE
DANDIE DINMONT
DANGEROUS BEND
DANGEROUS DRUG
DANGEROUS GAME
DANGEROUS LEAK
DANTE'S INFERNO
DARE-DEVIL TYPE
DARING ATTEMPT
DARK CONTINENT
DARKEST AFRICA
DARNING NEEDLE
DASH ONE'S HOPES
DATA RETRIEVAL
DAUGHTER OF EVE
DAUNTLESS HERO
DAWN OF A NEW ERA
DAY OF JUDGMENT
DAY OF MOURNING
DAYS AND NIGHTS
DAYS OF THE WEEK
DAY TO REMEMBER
DAZZLING SMILE
DEAD AND BURIED
DEAD AS THE DODO
DEAD CERTAINTY
DEADLY SILENCE
DEAD MAN'S CHEST
DEAD MAN'S SHOES
DEAD RECKONING
DEARLY BELOVED
DEATH AND GLORY
DEATH-BED SCENE
DEATH BY INCHES
DEATH REGISTER
DEATH SENTENCE

DEATH STRUGGLE
DEBATING POINT
DEBT COLLECTOR
DEBTORS' PRISON
DECIDE AGAINST
DECIDUOUS TREE
DECIMAL SYSTEM
DECLINE OF LIFE
DECORATIVE ART
DEDICATED LIFE
DEED OF RELEASE
DEEP ANTIPATHY
DEEP BREATHING
DEEP GRATITUDE
DEEP IN THOUGHT
DEEPLY TOUCHED
DEEP-SEA DIVING
DEFEND ONESELF
DEFINITE PROOF
DEFRAY THE COST
DEFY AUTHORITY
DEGREE OF SKILL
DEIGN TO NOTICE
DELAYED ACTION
DELIBERATE LIE
DELICATE CHILD
DELICATE POINT
DELICATE SHADE
DELICATE STAGE
DELICATE TOUCH
DELIGHT THE EAR
DELPHIC ORACLE
DELUDE ONESELF
DE LUXE EDITION
DEMAND JUSTICE
DEMAND PAYMENT
DEMERARA SUGAR
DEMON PATIENCE
DEN OF INIQUITY
DENTAL SURGEON
DENTAL SURGERY
DENTIST'S CHAIR
DENTIST'S DRILL
DENY THE CHARGE
DEPARTED GLORY
DEPRESSED AREA
DEPRIVE OF LIFE
DEPTH OF WINTER
DEPUTY PREMIER
DEPUTY SHERIFF
DESERT WARFARE
DESERVE NOTICE
DESERVING CASE
DESERVING POOR
DESIRED EFFECT
DESIRED OBJECT

DESOLATE SCENE
DESPATCH CLERK
DESPATCH RIDER
DESPERATE MOVE
DESPERATE RUSH
DETACHED HOUSE
DETECTIVE WORK
DEUCE OF HEARTS
DEVILISH FUNNY
DEVIL'S KITCHEN
DEVIL'S OWN LUCK
DEVIOUS MANNER
DEVOID OF SENSE
DEVOID OF TRUTH
DEVOUT ADMIRER
DIAGONAL LINES
DIAL THE POLICE
DIAMOND BROOCH
DIAMOND CUTTER
DIAMOND SCULLS
DIATONIC SCALE
DICE WITH DEATH
DIE AT ONE'S POST
DIE FLEDERMAUS
DIE OF EXPOSURE
DIE OF LAUGHING
DIFFERENT KIND
DIFFERENT TUNE
DIFFERENT VIEW
DIFFICULT CASE
DIFFICULT TASK
DIFFUSED LIGHT
DIGESTIVE PILL
DIG FOR VICTORY
DIG IN ONE'S TOES
DIGNIFIED EXIT
DIG ONE'S TOES IN
DING-DONG FIGHT
DINNER AT EIGHT
DINNER SERVICE
DIONNE WARWICK
DIPLOMATIC BAG
DIRECT CONTACT
DIRECT CURRENT
DIRECT DESCENT
DIRECTION POST
DIRE NECESSITY
DISCOUNT HOUSE
DISMAL FAILURE
DISOBEY ORDERS
DISPATCH RIDER
DISPUTED POINT
DISTANT COUSIN
DISTANT FUTURE
DISTANT OBJECT
DISTRICT COURT

DISTRICT NURSE
DISTURBED MIND
DIVIDE AND RULE
DIVIDE BY EIGHT
DIVIDE BY SEVEN
DIVIDE BY THREE
DIVIDED WE FALL
DIVINE JUSTICE
DIVINE SERVICE
DIVISION LOBBY
DIVISION THREE
DIVORCE DECREE
DO AS YOU PLEASE
DOCTOR FAUSTUS
DOCTOR JOHNSON
DOCTOR KILDARE
DOCTOR OF MUSIC
DOCTOR'S ORDERS
DOCTOR THE WINE
DODGE IN AND OUT
DODGE THE ISSUE
DOLL'S HOSPITAL
DOLPHIN SQUARE
DOME OF ST PAUL'S
DOMESTIC BLISS
DONE FOR EFFECT
DON'T BELIEVE IT
DON'T FENCE ME IN
DON'T MENTION IT
DO ONESELF WELL
DOOR TO SUCCESS
DORMITORY AREA
DORMITORY TOWN
DOROTHY LAMOUR
DOROTHY SAYERS
DOTING HUSBAND
DOTS AND DASHES
DOUBLE BASSOON
DOUBLE DEALING
DOUBLE FIFTEEN
DOUBLE FIGURES
DOUBLE HARNESS
DOUBLE HELPING
DOUBLE MEANING
DOUBLE OR QUITS
DOUBLE PORTION
DOUBLE SIXTEEN
DOUBLE TROUBLE
DOUBLE WEDDING
DOUBTFUL POINT
DOUBTFUL REPLY
DOWNING STREET
DOWN ON THE FARM
DOWNRIGHT LIAR
DOWN THE COURSE
DOWN THE STAIRS

DOWN THE STRAND
DOWN THE STREET
DOWN THE THAMES
DOWN TO BEDROCK
DOWNWARD CURVE
DOWNWARD SLOPE
DOWNWARD TREND
DRAB EXISTENCE
DRAGOON GUARDS
DRAINING BOARD
DRAIN THE DREGS
DRAMA FESTIVAL
DRAMATIC SCENE
DRASTIC REMEDY
DRAW A PARALLEL
DRAW ATTENTION
DRAW A VEIL OVER
DRAWING MASTER
DRAWN FROM LIFE
DRAW ONE'S SCREW
DRAW ONE'S SWORD
DRAW THE BLINDS
DREADED MOMENT
DREADFUL SIGHT
DREADFUL STORY
DREADFUL VOICE
DREAM SEQUENCE
DREARY OUTLOOK
DRENCHING RAIN
DRESS DESIGNER
DRESSED TO KILL
DRESSING TABLE
DRESS MATERIAL
DRESS OPTIONAL
DRIBS AND DRABS
DRILL SERGEANT
DRINKING GLASS
DRINKING PARTY
DRINKING STRAW
DRINKING WATER
DRINK ONE'S FILL
DRINK TO EXCESS
DRIVE A BARGAIN
DRIVE HEADLONG
DRIVE-IN CINEMA
DRIVEN TO DRINK
DRIVE WITH CARE
DRIVING LESSON
DRIVING MIRROR
DRIVING SCHOOL
DROP OF QUININE
DROP ONE'S GUARD
DROP ONE'S VOICE
DROPPED STITCH
DRUM-HEAD COURT
DRUNKEN SAILOR

DRUNKEN STUPOR
DRYING MACHINE
DUAL OWNERSHIP
DUBIOUS MANNER
DUCHESS OF KENT
DUELLING SWORD
DUE REFLECTION
DUKE ELLINGTON
DUKE OF BEDFORD
DUKE OF NORFOLK
DUKE OF WINDSOR
DULL AND DREARY
DULLING EFFECT
DUMB INSOLENCE
DUODENAL ULCER
DURING REPAIRS
DUSTING POWDER
DWELLING HOUSE
DYED IN THE WOOL
DYNAMIC ENERGY

E – 13

EACH-WAY DOUBLE
EACH-WAY TREBLE
EAGER TO PLEASE
EAMONN ANDREWS
EARL OF WARWICK
EARLY DECISION
EARN A DIVIDEND
EARNEST DESIRE
EARTHLY THINGS
EASE THE BURDEN
EASILY AROUSED
EASILY MANAGED
EASILY PLEASED
EASTERN BAZAAR
EASTERN CHURCH
EAST GRINSTEAD
EAT LIKE A HORSE
EAT WITH RELISH
ECLIPSE STAKES
ECONOMIC VALUE
EDGAR ALLAN POE
EDIFYING STORY
EDINBURGH ROCK
EDITION DE LUXE
EDITORIAL DESK
EDITOR IN CHIEF
EDMUND SPENSER
EDWARDIAN DAYS
EFFACE ONESELF
EGGSHELL CHINA
EGYPTIAN MUMMY
EIGHT AND A HALF

EIGHT-DAY CLOCK
EIGHTEEN CARAT
EIGHTEEN HOLES
EIGHTEEN MILES
EIGHT FURLONGS
EIGHTH CENTURY
EIGHTH OF APRIL
EIGHTH OF MARCH
EIGHT OF HEARTS
EIGHT OF SPADES
EIGHT OF TRUMPS
EIGHTSOME REEL
EIGHT THOUSAND
EIGHTY PER CENT
EJECTION ORDER
ELABORATE MEAL
ELECTION AGENT
ELECTION FEVER
ELECTION NIGHT
ELECTORAL ROLL
ELECTRIC CABLE
ELECTRIC CHAIR
ELECTRIC CLOCK
ELECTRIC DRILL
ELECTRIC FENCE
ELECTRIC LIGHT
ELECTRIC METER
ELECTRIC MIXER
ELECTRIC MOTOR
ELECTRIC ORGAN
ELECTRIC PIANO
ELECTRIC POWER
ELECTRIC RAZOR
ELECTRIC SHOCK
ELECTRIC STORM
ELECTRIC STOVE
ELECTRIC TORCH
ELECTRIC TRAIN
ELECTRONIC TOY
ELEMENT OF RISK
ELEPHANT'S TUSK
ELEVEN GUINEAS
ELEVEN MINUTES
ELEVEN PER CENT
ELEVENTH GREEN
ELEVENTH OF MAY
ELEVENTH PLACE
ELEVENTH ROUND
ELUSIVE PERSON
ELY CULBERTSON
ELYSIAN FIELDS
EMERGENCY CALL
EMERGENCY EXIT
EMERGENCY STOP
EMERGENCY WARD
EMINENTLY FAIR

EMOTIONAL LIFE
EMPIRE BUILDER
EMPTY PROMISES
EMULSION PAINT
END OF DISASTER
ENDLESS EFFORT
END OF THE MONTH
END OF THE STORY
END OF THE WORLD
END UP IN PRISON
ENDURANCE TEST
ENDURE FOR EVER
ENEMY AIRCRAFT
ENFORCE THE LAW
ENGAGED COUPLE
ENGAGED SIGNAL
ENGAGING SMILE
ENGINE FAILURE
ENGINE TROUBLE
ENGLISH GARDEN
ENGLISH LESSON
ENGLISH MASTER
ENGLISH SETTER
ENJOY IMMUNITY
ENJOY IMPUNITY
ENLARGED HEART
ENORMOUS SALES
ENOUGH'S ENOUGH
ENQUIRING MIND
ENTER A PROTEST
ENTER THE LISTS
ENTRANCE MONEY
EQUABLE TEMPER
EQUAL DIVISION
EQUAL QUANTITY
ERECT A BARRIER
ERIC LINKLATER
ERNEST MARPLES
ERRAND OF MERCY
ESCAPE ME NEVER
ESCORT CARRIER
ESPRIT DE CORPS
ESSENTIAL PART
ESTIMATED COST
ESTIMATED TIME
ETON AND HARROW
EUCALYPTUS OIL
EUSTON STATION
EVADE THE ISSUE
EVASION OF DUTY
EVASIVE ACTION
EVASIVE ANSWER
EVENING PRAYER
EVENING STROLL
EVEN THINGS OUT
EVERGREEN TREE

EVERY FEW HOURS
EVERY FEW YEARS
EVERY OTHER DAY
EVERY SATURDAY
EVERY THURSDAY
EVIL INFLUENCE
EXACT LIKENESS
EXALTED PERSON
EXCELLENT SHOT
EXCESS BAGGAGE
EXCESSIVE ZEAL
EXCESS LUGGAGE
EXCESS PROFITS
EXCHANGE BLOWS
EXCHANGE CARDS
EXCHANGE IDEAS
EXCHANGE SHOTS
EXCHANGE VALUE
EXCHANGE VIEWS
EXCHANGE WORDS
EXCHEQUER BOND
EXCISE OFFICER
EXCITING MATCH
EXCITING SCENE
EXCLUSIVE CLUB
EXCURSION RATE
EXCUSE-ME DANCE
EXCUSE ONESELF
EXECUTIVE BODY
EXEMPLI GRATIA
EXERCISE A PULL
EXERCISE POWER
EXERT PRESSURE
EXORBITANT FEE
EXPECTANT HEIR
EXPECTED THING
EXPECT TOO MUCH
EXPENSIVE ITEM
EXPENSIVE LINE
EXPERT OPINION
EXPERT TUITION
EXPERT WITNESS
EXPLOSION SHOT
EXPOSED TO VIEW
EXPRESS DESIRE
EXPRESS LETTER
EXPRESS REGRET
EXTENSIVE VIEW
EXTERIOR ANGLE
EXTINCT ANIMAL
EXTRACT A TOOTH
EXTRACT OF BEEF
EXTREME HATRED
EXTREMELY NICE
EXTREME OLD AGE
EYEBROW PENCIL

EYELASH CURLER
EYELESS IN GAZA
EYES LIKE A HAWK
EYES LIKE STARS
EYE TO BUSINESS

F – 13

FABIAN SOCIETY
FABULOUS BEAST
FABULOUS STORY
FACE DOWNWARDS
FACED WITH RUIN
FACE HEAVY ODDS
FACIAL MASSAGE
FACT OR FICTION
FACTORY HOOTER
FACULTY MEMBER
FACULTY OF ARTS
FAEROE ISLANDS
FAILING HEALTH
FAIL MISERABLY
FAIL TO CONNECT
FAINT WITH FEAR
FAIR AND SQUARE
FAIR APPRAISAL
FAIR CONDITION
FAIRLY CERTAIN
FAIRLY CONTENT
FAIRLY WELL OFF
FAIRLY WRITTEN
FAIR RECEPTION
FAIR TREATMENT
FAIRY PRINCESS
FAKE JEWELLERY
FALL FROM GRACE
FALLING LEAVES
FALLING PRICES
FALLING VALUES
FALL INTO A RAGE
FALL INTO A TRAP
FALL INTO ERROR
FALL INTO PLACE
FALL OF JERICHO
FALL OUT OF LOVE
FALL OVERBOARD
FALL PROSTRATE
FALSE CLAIMANT
FALSE EVIDENCE
FALSE OPTIMISM
FALSE POSITION
FALSE TEACHING
FALSETTO VOICE
FAMILIAR FACES
FAMILIAR SIGHT
FAMILIAR STYLE

FAMILIAR TERMS
FAMILIAR VOICE
FAMILY BUTCHER
FAMILY CONCERN
FAMILY FAILING
FAMILY MATTERS
FAMILY PRAYERS
FAMILY QUARREL
FAMILY REUNION
FAMILY WELFARE
FAR-AWAY PLACES
FAREWELL PARTY
FARM BUILDING
FARTHEST POINT
FASCIST REGIME
FASHION PARADE
FATAL ACCIDENT
FATAL CASUALTY
FATAL DECISION
FATHER NEPTUNE
FATHER WILLIAM
FAVOURITE TUNE
FAVOUR ONE SIDE
FEAR OF HEIGHTS
FEAR OF THE DARK
FEAST OF REASON
FEAST ONE'S EYES
FEATHER DUSTER
FEATHER PILLOW
FEATHER STITCH
FEATURE EDITOR
FED AND WATERED
FEDERAL STATES
FED TO THE TEETH
FEEBLE ATTEMPT
FEEBLE GESTURE
FEEDING BOTTLE
FEED THE FLAMES
FEEL EXHAUSTED
FEEL MORTIFIED
FEEL NO EMOTION
FEEL ONE'S PULSE
FEIGN SICKNESS
FELLOW CITIZEN
FELLOW FEELING
FELLOW SOLDIER
FEMALE WARRIOR
FEMININE CHARM
FEMININE LOGIC
FEMININE WILES
FENCING LESSON
FENCING MASTER
FENCING SCHOOL
FERTILE GROUND
FERTILE REGION
FERVENT DESIRE

FESTIVE SEASON
FESTIVE SPIRIT
FETCH AND CARRY
FEVER HOSPITAL
FEVERISH HASTE
FEVERISH STATE
FICTION WRITER
FIDDLERS THREE
FIELD DRESSING
FIELD HOSPITAL
FIELD OF ACTION
FIELD OF BATTLE
FIELD OF HONOUR
FIELD OF VISION
FIFTEEN ROUNDS
FIFTEEN THIRTY
FIFTEENTH HOLE
FIFTH DIVIDEND
FIFTH OF AUGUST
FIFTH SYMPHONY
FIFTY THOUSAND
FIGHTER PATROL
FIGHTING DRUNK
FIGHT PROMOTER
FIGURE OF EIGHT
FIGURE SKATING
FILING CABINET
FILLET OF STEAK
FILL ONE'S GLASS
FILM PROJECTOR
FILTER THROUGH
FINAL DECISION
FINAL DIVIDEND
FINAL ESTIMATE
FINAL JUDGMENT
FINAL MOVEMENT
FINANCIAL NEWS
FINANCIAL PAGE
FINANCIAL RUIN
FINANCIAL YEAR
FIND A FOOTHOLD
FIND A LOOP-HOLE
FIND A SOLUTION
FIND ONE'S LEVEL
FINE ONE'S MATCH
FIND SALVATION
FIND THE NEEDLE
FIND THE REMEDY
FINE CHARACTER
FINE GENTLEMAN
FINER FEELINGS
FINE SELECTION
FINE SITUATION
FINE TOOTH-COMB
FINGER OF SCORN
FINISHING POST

FINISH THE RACE
FINNAN HADDOCK
FINNEGAN'S WAKE
FIRE A QUESTION
FIRE INSURANCE
FIREWORK PARTY
FIRM FAVOURITE
FIRM HANDSHAKE
FIRM PRINCIPLE
FIRM TREATMENT
FIRST-AID CLASS
FIRST BIRTHDAY
FIRST DELIVERY
FIRST DIVIDEND
FIRST DIVISION
FIRST LANGUAGE
FIRST OF AUGUST
FIRST OFFENDER
FIRST OF THE FEW
FIRST QUESTION
FIRST SYMPHONY
FIRST THOUGHTS
FIRST TO ARRIVE
FIRST WORLD WAR
FISHING RIGHTS
FISHING SEASON
FISHING TACKLE
FISHY BUSINESS
FIT FOR NOTHING
FIT FOR THE GODS
FITFUL SLUMBER
FIT LIKE A GLOVE
FIT OF COUGHING
FIT OF LAUGHTER
FIT OF THE BLUES
FIT OF THE SULKS
FITS AND STARTS
FIVE-O'CLOCK TEA
FIVE-POUND NOTE
FIXED DOMICILE
FIXED INTERVAL
FLANDERS POPPY
FLANK MOVEMENT
FLASHING SMILE
FLASH IN THE PAN
FLASH OF GENIUS
FLAT OF THE HAND
FLEA IN ONE'S EAR
FLEMISH SCHOOL
FLESH AND BLOOD
FLICKER OF HOPE
FLIGHT OF FANCY
FLIGHT OF STEPS
FLITCH OF BACON
FLOAT A COMPANY
FLOATING VOTER

FLOCK TOGETHER
FLOODS OF TEARS
FLORA AND FAUNA
FLORAL PATTERN
FLORAL TRIBUTE
FLOUR AND WATER
FLOWERING TREE
FLOWER OF YOUTH
FLOWERY SPEECH
FLOW LIKE WATER
FLOW OF SPIRITS
FLOW.OF TRAFFIC
FLUSHED CHEEKS
FLYING COLOURS
FLYING MACHINE
FLYING OFFICER
FLYING TRAPEZE
FLY THE COUNTRY
FOLD ONE'S HANDS
FOLIES BERGÈRE
FOLLOWING WIND
FOLLOW ROUTINE
FOLLOW THE BAND
FOLLOW THE FLAG
FOLLOW THE HERD
FOLLOW THE HUNT
FOLLOW THE ROAD
FOLLOW THROUGH
FOND OF COMFORT
FOND OF DISPLAY
FOOD AND WARMTH
FOOD FOR FISHES
FOOD OF THE GODS
FOOD POISONING
FOOLISH ACTION
FOOLISH FELLOW
FOOLISH PERSON
FOOLISH VIRGIN
FOOLSCAP PAPER
FOOL'S PARADISE
FOOTBALL FIELD
FOOTBALL MATCH
FOOTBALL PITCH
FOOTBALL POOLS
FOR AND AGAINST
FORBIDDEN GAME
FORBIDDEN TREE
FORCE A PASSAGE
FORCED LANDING
FORCED SAVINGS
FORCE ONE'S HAND
FORCE THE ISSUE
FORCIBLE ENTRY
FOREHAND DRIVE
FOREIGN ACCENT
FOREIGN EDITOR

FOREIGN FIELDS
FOREIGN LEGION
FOREIGN MARKET
FOREIGN OFFICE
FOREIGN ORIGIN
FOREIGN POLICY
FOREIGN SHORES
FOREIGN TONGUE
FOREIGN TRAVEL
FOREST OF ARDEN
FOREST OF MASTS
FORGET ONESELF
FOR GOOD AND ALL
FORK LIGHTNING
FORMAL PROTEST
FORMAL REQUEST
FORM AN OPINION
FOR MERCY'S SAKE
FORMER STUDENT
FORM OF ADDRESS
FORM OF WORSHIP
FOR THE PRESENT
FORTIFIED POST
FORTIFIED TOWN
FORTIFIED WINE
FORTUNE HUNTER
FORTUNES OF WAR
FORTUNE'S WHEEL
FORTUNE TELLER
FORTY-HOUR WEEK
FORTY THOUSAND
FOSTER BROTHER
FOUNDED ON FACT
FOUNDER MEMBER
FOUNT OF HONOUR
FOUNT OF WISDOM
FOUR AND TWENTY
FOUR-POSTER BED
FOUR SYLLABLES
FOURTEEN MILES
FOURTH CENTURY
FOURTH OF APRIL
FOURTH OFFICER
FOURTH OF MARCH
FOWLS OF THE AIR
FRAGRANT SMELL
FRAME A PICTURE
FRANKIE HOWERD
FRANTIC APPEAL
FRATERNITY PIN
FREAK OF NATURE
FREE ADMISSION
FREE AS THE WIND
FREE FROM BLAME
FREE FROM ERROR
FREE FROM FAULT

FREE FROM GUILE
FREE FROM GUILT
FREEHOLD HOUSE
FREE-RANGE EGGS
FREE RENDERING
FREE TO CONFESS
FREE-TRADE AREA
FREEZE TO DEATH
FREEZING AGENT
FREEZING POINT
FREIGHT CHARGE
FRENCH ACADEMY
FRENCH CRICKET
FRENCH CUISINE
FRENCH GRAMMAR
FRENCH MUSTARD
FRENCH PERFUME
FRENCH TEACHER
FRENCH WINDOWS
FREQUENCY BAND
FRESH-AIR FIEND
FRESH APPROACH
FRESH AS A DAISY
FRESH EVIDENCE
FRESH OUTBREAK
FRICTION MATCH
FRIDAY EVENING
FRIDAY MORNING
FRIED POTATOES
FRIED TOMATOES
FRIEND AT COURT
FRIEND IN COURT
FRIENDLY MATCH
FRIENDLY TERMS
FRIENDLY TOUCH
FRIEND'S FRIEND
FRIGHTFUL TIME
FRINGE BENEFIT
FRITZ KREISLER
FROM A DISTANCE
FROM ONE'S HEART
FROM THE BOTTOM
FROM THE CRADLE
FROM THE OUTSET
FRONTAL ATTACK
FRONT ENTRANCE
FRONTIER GUARD
FRONT-PAGE NEWS
FRONT POSITION
FROSTY WEATHER
FROSTY WELCOME
FROZEN BALANCE
FROZEN TO DEATH
FRUIT AND CREAM
FRUITLESS TASK
FRUIT MERCHANT

FRYING TONIGHT
FULL ASSURANCE
FULL IN THE FACE
FULL OF COURAGE
FULL OF MEANING
FULL OF PROMISE
FULL OF REGRETS
FULL OF THE NEWS
FULL OWNERSHIP
FULL PROGRAMME
FULL TO THE BRIM
FULL TREATMENT
FULLY EQUIPPED
FULLY LICENSED
FULLY OCCUPIED
FULLY RESTORED
FUMBLE THE BALL
FUME WITH ANGER
FUNERAL SERMON
FUNNY BUSINESS
FUNNY PECULIAR
FUR AND FEATHER
FURIOUS TEMPER
FURNISHED FLAT
FURNISHED ROOM
FURTHER NOTICE
FURTHEST POINT
FUSS AND BOTHER
FUTILE ATTEMPT
FUTILE PURSUIT
FUTURE HUSBAND
FUTURE OUTLOOK
FUTURE PERFECT
FUTURES MARKET

G – 13

GADARENE SWINE
GAGGLE OF GEESE
GAIETY THEATRE
GAIN ADMISSION
GAIN SUPREMACY
GALE-FORCE WIND
GALLANT MEMBER
GAMES MISTRESS
GAME TO THE LAST
GANG OF THIEVES
GANGWAY PLEASE
GARBLED REPORT
GARDENING CLUB
GARDEN OF WEEDS
GARDEN PRODUCE
GARDEN SYRINGE
GARLIC SAUSAGE
GASP FOR BREATH
GATHER FLOWERS

GEIGER COUNTER
GENERAL CUSTER
GENERAL DEALER
GENERAL EXODUS
GENERAL FRANCO
GENERAL GORDON
GENERAL MARKET
GENERAL PARDON
GENERAL PUBLIC
GENERAL READER
GENERAL STORES
GENERAL STRIKE
GENERAL SURVEY
GENERATION GAP
GENEROUS GIVER
GENEROUS OFFER
GENEROUS SHARE
GENEROUS TERMS
GENIUS WILL OUT
GENTLE AS A LAMB
GENTLE BEARING
GENTLE MANNERS
GENTLE REPROOF
GENUINE REGARD
GEORGE GISSING
GEORGIAN HOUSE
GERMAN MEASLES
GERMAN SAUSAGE
GET AT THE FACTS
GET AT THE TRUTH
GET AWAY WITH IT
GET IN ON THE ACT
GET IT STRAIGHT
GET OFF LIGHTLY
GET ONE'S HAND IN
GET ONE'S OWN WAY
GET ON TOGETHER
GET OUT OF SIGHT
GET THE GIGGLES
GET THE MESSAGE
GET THERE FIRST
GETTING ON A BIT
GETTING STONED
GET TO ONE'S FEET
GET TO WINDWARD
GIACONDA SMILE
GIFT OF TONGUES
GIN AND BITTERS
GIN AND ITALIAN
GIPSY'S WARNING
GIRTON COLLEGE
GIUSEPPE VERDI
GIVE A DOG A BONE
GIVE A FIRM DATE
GIVE AN ACCOUNT
GIVE AN EXAMPLE

GIVE AN OPINION
GIVE-AWAY PRICE
GIVE COMMUNION
GIVE IT A CHANCE
GIVE A NEW LOOK
GIVEN IN CHARGE
GIVE NO QUARTER
GIVE NO TROUBLE
GIVEN THE STRAP
GIVEN THE WORKS
GIVEN TO EXCESS
GIVE ONESELF UP
GIVE ONE THE LIE
GIVE ONE THE PIP
GIVE THE SIGNAL
GIVE UP ALL HOPE
GIVE UP SMOKING
GIVE UP THE IDEA
GIVE UTTERANCE
GLACIAL PERIOD
GLAD OF A CHANCE
GLASS AND CHINA
GLASS MOUNTAIN
GLASS OF SHERRY
GLASS OF WHISKY
GLASS WITH CARE
GLASSY SURFACE
GLEAM OF HUMOUR
GLIMMER OF HOPE
GLOATING SMILE
GLOOMY OUTLOOK
GLOOMY PICTURE
GLORIA SWANSON
GLORIOUS DEVON
GLORIOUS MUSIC
GLORIOUS REIGN
GLORIOUS YEARS
GLOWING CHEEKS
GLOWING EMBERS
GLOWING REPORT
GLOW WITH PRIDE
GNASH THE TEETH
GO AS YOU PLEASE
GODDESS OF LOVE
GOD OF LAUGHTER
GO FOR A JOURNEY
GOING FOR A SONG
GOING STRAIGHT
GO INTO A TRANCE
GO INTO DETAILS
GOLD AND SILVER
GOLDEN HAMSTER
GOLDEN JUBILEE
GOLDEN TRESSES
GOLDEN WEDDING
GOLD MEDALLIST

GO LIKE THE WIND
GONE TO THE DOGS
GOOD ACOUSTICS
GOOD AFTERNOON
GOOD AND PROPER
GOOD AT FIGURES
GOOD BEGINNING
GOOD BEHAVIOUR
GOOD BREAKFAST
GOOD CHARACTER
GOOD CONDITION
GOOD CONDUCTOR
GOOD DIGESTION
GOOD FOR A LAUGH
GOOD GROUNDING
GOOD HOUSEWIFE
GOOD HUSBANDRY
GOOD INFLUENCE
GOOD NEIGHBOUR
GOOD PROSPECTS
GOOD QUEEN BESS
GOOD RECEPTION
GOOD SAMARITAN
GOOD SELECTION
GOOD SPORTSMAN
GOOD TALKING-TO
GOOD THRASHING
GOOD WALLOPING
GOODWOOD RACES
GOODY TWO-SHOES
GO OFF ONE'S HEAD
GO ON THE PARISH
GO THE WHOLE HOG
GO TO THE BOTTOM
GO TO THE CINEMA
GO TO THE CIRCUS
GO TO THE MOVIES
GO TO THE OFFICE
GO TO THE RESCUE
GO UNDERGROUND
GOVERNING BODY
GO WITH THE TIDE
GRADUAL CHANGE
GRAIN OF POWDER
GRAMMAR SCHOOL
GRAND ALLIANCE
GRAND ENTRANCE
GRAND FUNCTION
GRAND JUNCTION
GRAND NATIONAL
GRAND STRATEGY
GRANT A DIVORCE
GRANT A REQUEST
GRANT IMMUNITY
GRAPES OF WRATH
GRAPPLING IRON

GRASP AT A STRAW
GRASP OF DETAIL
GRATEFUL HEART
GRATE ON THE EAR
GRAVE DECISION
GRAVE THOUGHTS
GREASE THE PALM
GREAT DISTANCE
GREATER LONDON
GREAT IN NUMBER
GREAT INTEREST
GREAT KINDNESS
GREATLY MISSED
GREAT MAJORITY
GREAT OCCASION
GREAT PATIENCE
GREAT PLEASURE
GREAT QUANTITY
GREAT SALT LAKE
GREAT STRENGTH
GREAT THOUGHTS
GREAT UNWASHED
GREAT WEST ROAD
GREAT WHITE WAY
GREAT YARMOUTH
GREEK ALPHABET
GREEK LANGUAGE
GREEN FRACTURE
GREEN PASTURES
GREENWICH TIME
GREEN WITH ENVY
GREENWOOD TREE
GREETINGS CARD
GREYHOUND RACE
GRILLED CUTLET
GRIN AND BEAR IT
GRIND INTO DUST
GRIND THE TEETH
GRIND TO POWDER
GRIP LIKE A VICE
GRIPPING STORY
GRIT ONE'S TEETH
GROANING BOARD
GROAN INWARDLY
GROSS RECEIPTS
GROUP ACTIVITY
GROW BEAUTIFUL
GROW DESPERATE
GROW DOWNWARDS
GRUELLING HEAT
GRUELLING PACE
GRUELLING RACE
GRUELLING TIME
GRUYÈRE CHEESE
GUARDED REMARK
GUARDIAN ANGEL

GUARD OF HONOUR
GUARDS' OFFICER
GUERRILLA BAND
GUEST OF HONOUR
GUIDED MISSILE
GUILTY FEELING
GUNNERY SCHOOL
GUNPOWDER PLOT
GUSHING LETTER
GUTTERAL VOICE
GYPSY'S WARNING

H – 13

HACKING JACKET
HAILE SELASSIE
HAIL OF BULLETS
HAIR OF THE HEAD
HALE AND HEARTY
HALF THE BATTLE
HALF THE NUMBER
HALF-TIME SCORE
HALL OF JUSTICE
HALL OF MIRRORS
HALLOWED PLACE
HALTING SPEECH
HALVE THE MATCH
HAMILTON HOUSE
HANDLE ROUGHLY
HAND OF BANANAS
HAND OUT ADVICE
HANDSOME OFFER
HANDSOME STYLE
HANDSOME THING
HANG BY A THREAD
HANGING GARDEN
HANGING MATTER
HANG ONE'S HAT UP
HANG UP ONE'S HAT
HANNEN SWAFFER
HANOVER SQUARE
HAPPILY IN LOVE
HAPPY ACCIDENT
HAPPY BIRTHDAY
HAPPY FAMILIES
HAPPY MARRIAGE
HAPPY MEMORIES
HAPPY WANDERER
HARBOUR LIGHTS
HARBOUR MASTER
HARD-BOILED EGG
HARDEN ONESELF
HARD-LUCK STORY
HARD NECESSITY
HARD OF HEARING
HARD TO BELIEVE

HARD TO IMAGINE	HEAR BOTH SIDES
HARD TO SATISFY	HEARD IN CAMERA
HARD TO SWALLOW	HEARTH AND HOME
HARDWARE STORE	HEART OF HEARTS
HARE AND HOUNDS	HEART OF MARBLE
HARMONIC SCALE	HEART'S CONTENT
HARROWING TALE	HEARTY DISLIKE
HARROWING TIME	HEARTY WELCOME
HARRY THE HORSE	HEATED DISPUTE
HARSH CONTRAST	HEATED QUARREL
HARSH DECISION	HEATH ROBINSON
HARSH SENTENCE	HEAT TREATMENT
HARVEST SUNDAY	HEAVEN HELP HIM!
HARVEST SUPPER	HEAVENLY CHOIR
HASTEN ONE'S END	HEAVENLY TWINS
HASTY DECISION	HEAVEN ON EARTH
HATEFUL OBJECT	HEAVILY LOADED
HATFIELD HOUSE	HEAVY DOWNPOUR
HATTER'S CASTLE	HEAVY EXPENSES
HAVE A BAD NIGHT	HEAVY HYDROGEN
HAVE A BREATHER	HEAVY INDUSTRY
HAVE A GOOD MIND	HEAVY MATERIAL
HAVE A GOOD TALK	HEAVY SENTENCE
HAVE A GOOD TIME	HEIGHT OF FOLLY
HAVE A MANICURE	HELD FOR RANSOM
HAVE AN ADDRESS	HELL UPON EARTH
HAVE A TOOTH OUT	HELPFUL ADVICE
HAVE A WALK-OVER	HENLEY REGATTA
HAVE DELUSIONS	HENRY FIELDING
HAVE HALF A MIND	HENRY THE FIFTH
HAVE HYSTERICS	HENRY THE FIRST
HAVELOCK ELLIS	HENRY THE SIXTH
HAVEN OF REFUGE	HENRY THE THIRD
HAVE NO REGRETS	HERALDIC SWORD
HAVE NO SECRETS	HERCULEAN TASK
HAVE NO TROUBLE	HERCULE POIROT
HAVE ONE'S FLING	HER EXCELLENCY
HAVE ONE'S WHACK	HEROIC COUPLET
HAVE THE ANSWER	HEW OUT A CAREER
HAVE THE HONOUR	HIDDEN MEANING
HAVE THE OPTION	HIDDEN RESERVE
HAVE THE WIND UP	HIGH AND MIGHTY
HAYLING ISLAND	HIGH BIRTH-RATE
HAYWARDS HEATH	HIGH CHARACTER
HEADLONG SPEED	HIGH CHURCHMAN
HEAD OF THE FORM	HIGH COLOURING
HEAD OF THE POLL	HIGH ENDEAVOUR
HEAD OVER HEELS	HIGHER BRACKET
HEADS TOGETHER	HIGHEST BIDDER
HEALING SPIRIT	HIGH EXPLOSIVE
HEAL THE BREACH	HIGH FREQUENCY
HEALTH OFFICER	HIGHLAND CHIEF
HEALTH SERVICE	HIGHLAND DANCE
HEALTH VISITOR	HIGHLAND DRESS
HEALTHY COLOUR	HIGHLAND FLING
HEAPS OF PEOPLE	HIGHLAND GAMES

HIGHLY PLEASED
HIGH VALUATION
HIGH-WATER MARK
HIGHWAY PATROL
HIGHWAY ROBBER
HIKING HOLIDAY
HILAIRE BELLOC
HINDU RELIGION
HIRED ASSASSIN
HIS EXCELLENCY
HISTORIC SCENE
HISTORIC TENSE
HISTORY LESSON
HISTORY MASTER
HISTRIONIC ART
HIT THE JACKPOT
HIT THE UPRIGHT
HOBSON'S CHOICE
HOLD AN INQUEST
HOLD AN INQUIRY
HOLD AN OPINION
HOLD IN BONDAGE
HOLD IN RESPECT
HOLD ONE GUILTY
HOLD ONE'S PEACE
HOLD THAT TIGER!
HOLD THE RECORD
HOLD THE RUDDER
HOLD THE SCALES
HOLD THE STAKES
HOLE AND CORNER
HOLE IN THE ROAD
HOLIDAY CHALET
HOLIDAY COURSE
HOLIDAY RESORT
HOLIDAY SEASON
HOLIDAY SPIRIT
HOLLOW FEELING
HOLLOW MOCKERY
HOLLOW VICTORY
HOLLYWOOD BOWL
HOLY COMMUNION
HOLY INNOCENTS
HOLY MATRIMONY
HOME ECONOMICS
HOME FOR THE DAY
HOME INTERESTS
HOME-MADE BREAD
HOME PROGRAMME
HOMERIC BATTLE
HOME SECRETARY
HOME SWEET HOME
HOMEWARD BOUND
HONEST ATTEMPT
HONEST DEALING
HONEYDEW MELON

HONOR BLACKMAN
HONOURABLE MAN
HONOUR AND OBEY
HONOURED GUEST
HONOURS DEGREE
HOOK OF HOLLAND
HOPE AND BELIEF
HOPELESS STATE
HORACE WALPOLE
HORATIO NELSON
HORRIBLE NOISE
HORRIBLE CRIME
HORRIBLE SIGHT
HORSE AND GROOM
HORSE CHESTNUT
HORSESHOE BEND
HOSPITAL NURSE
HOSPITAL TRAIN
HOSTILE ATTACK
HOSTILE CRITIC
HOSTILE MANNER
HOST OF FRIENDS
HOT-HOUSE PLANT
HOT ON THE SCENT
HOT ON THE TRAIL
HOUR AFTER HOUR
HOURLY SERVICE
HOUR OF TRIUMPH
HOURS AND HOURS
HOUSEHOLD GODS
HOUSEHOLD HINT
HOUSEHOLD LOAF
HOUSEHOLD WORD
HOUSE MAGAZINE
HOUSE OF BRICKS
HOUSE OF ORANGE
HOUSE OF PRAYER
HOUSE OF REFUGE
HOUSE ON WHEELS
HOUSE PROPERTY
HOUSING ESTATE
HUB OF INDUSTRY
HUGH GAITSKELL
HUMAN ACTIVITY
HUMAN CREATURE
HUMAN DOCUMENT
HUMAN SOCIETY
HUMAN INTEREST
HUMAN PROGRESS
HUMAN TRIANGLE
HUMAN WEAKNESS
HUMBLE ADMIRER
HUMBLE APOLOGY
HUMBLE OPINION
HUMBLE REQUEST
HUMBLE SERVANT

HUMBLE STATION
HUMPBACK WHALE
HUNDRED AND ONE
HUNDRED POUNDS
HUNGER MARCHER
HUNGER STRIKER
HUNGRY FORTIES
HUNTING SEASON
HURRICANE LAMP
HURRIED GLANCE
HURRIED SPEECH
HURT ONE'S PRIDE
HYDRAULIC JACK
HYDRAULIC LIFT

I – 13

IAN CARMICHAEL
ICE-CREAM WAFER
IDEALLY SUITED
IDENTICAL TWIN
IF YOU DON'T MIND!
ILL MANAGEMENT
IMAGINARY LINE
IMITATION WARE
IMPENDING DOOM
IMPERIAL CROWN
IMPERIAL EAGLE
IMPERIAL GUARD
IMPERIAL TOKAY
IMPLICIT FAITH
IMPORTANT POST
IMPUDENT ROGUE
IN A CLEFT STICK
IN A GENERAL WAY
IN A GOOD TEMPER
IN ALL FAIRNESS
IN ALL RESPECTS
IN ALL WEATHERS
IN AN AMBULANCE
IN AN EMERGENCY
IN AN UNDERTONE
IN A SORRY STATE
IN A STILL VOICE
IN A STRANGE WAY
IN AT THE FINISH
INBORN ABILITY
INCENSE BURNER
IN CIRCULATION
INCLINED PLANE
IN COLD STORAGE
INCOME BRACKET
INCOMES POLICY
INCOME-TAX FORM
IN COMPETITION

IN CONFINEMENT
IN CONSEQUENCE
IN CONVULSIONS
INCREASED WAGE
INCREASE OF PAY
INCUR A PENALTY
IN DEAD EARNEST
INDECENT HASTE
IN DESPERATION
INDIAN CHUTNEY
INDIRECT ROUTE
IN DIRE TROUBLE
INDOOR SERVANT
IN EVERY DETAIL
INFANT BAPTISM
INFANT PRODIGY
INFERIOR GOODS
IN FINE FEATHER
INFINITE SPACE
INFLATED IDEAS
INFLATED PRICE
IN FOR A STRETCH
INFORM AGAINST
INFORMAL DRESS
INFORMAL PARTY
IN FORMER TIMES
IN FULL FEATHER
IN FULL MEASURE
IN FULL RETREAT
IN GREAT DEMAND
INGRID BERGMAN
IN HIGH FEATHER
IN HONOUR BOUND
IN IMAGINATION
INITIAL LETTER
INITIAL OUTLAY
INITIAL STAGES
INITIATION FEE
INK ERADICATOR
INLAND REVENUE
IN LIQUIDATION
IN MORTAL PERIL
INNATE ABILITY
INNER CONFLICT
INNER HEBRIDES
INNOCENT PARTY
IN ONE'S ELEMENT
IN ONE SENTENCE
IN ONE'S OWN NAME
IN PARTNERSHIP
IN PERSPECTIVE
IN POINT OF FACT
IN PREPARATION
IN QUEER STREET
INQUIRING MIND
INQUIRY OFFICE

IN SAFE KEEPING
IN SCANDINAVIA
IN SELF-DEFENCE
INSERT A NOTICE
IN SHORT SUPPLY
INSIDE FORWARD
IN SIGHT OF LAND
IN SO MANY WORDS
IN SOME MEASURE
INSPECTION PIT
INSPIRED GUESS
INSPIRED WORDS
INSTANT COFFEE
INSULAR HABITS
INSURANCE CARD
INSURANCE RISK
INSURED PERSON
IN SWITZERLAND
INTEREST RATES
INTERIM PERIOD
INTERIM REPORT
INTERVAL MUSIC
IN THE ABSTRACT
IN THE AIR FORCE
IN THE AUDIENCE
IN THE BASEMENT
IN THE BUSINESS
IN THE CORRIDOR
IN THE DARKNESS
IN THE DAYLIGHT
IN THE DISTANCE
IN THE DISTRICT
IN THE DOG-HOUSE
IN THE DOLDRUMS
IN THE FOUNTAIN
IN THE GLOAMING
IN THE INTERIOR
IN THE INTERVAL
IN THE LION'S DEN
IN THE MAJORITY
IN THE MEANTIME
IN THE MIND'S EYE
IN THE MINORITY
IN THE NEGATIVE
IN THE ORIGINAL
IN THE PAVILION
IN THE SAME BOAT
IN THE SAME CAMP
IN THE SERVICES
IN THE SINGULAR
IN THE STIRRUPS
IN THE STRAIGHT
IN THE SUNSHINE
IN THE TREASURY
IN THE TRENCHES
IN THE TWILIGHT

IN THE USUAL WAY
IN THE VANGUARD
IN THE VICINITY
IN THE WRONG BOX
INTIMATE REVUE
INTIMATE STYLE
INTIMATE TERMS
IN TIMES OF YORE
INTO THE BREACH
IN TOWN TONIGHT
IN TREPIDATION
IN VARIOUS WAYS
INVERNESS CAPE
INVERTED ORDER
INVERTED PLEAT
IN VINO VERITAS
INVITE TENDERS
INVOLVED STYLE
IRISH BAGPIPES
IRISH LANGUAGE
IRISH REGIMENT
IRREGULAR VERB
ISLE OF SHEPPEY
ISLES OF GREECE
ISOBEL BARNETT
ISOLATION WARD
ISSUE A COMMAND
ISSUE A SUMMONS
ISSUED CAPITAL
ITALIAN LESSON
IT'S NOT CRICKET
IVORY CHESSMAN

J – 13

JACK THE RIPPER
JACOBEAN STYLE
JAUNDICED VIEW
JEKYLL AND HYDE
JENNIFER JONES
JET PROPULSION
JEWELLER'S SHOP
JOAN GREENWOOD
JOB'S COMFORTER
JOG ONE'S MEMORY
JOHANN STRAUSS
JOHN CONSTABLE
JOHN MASEFIELD
JOIN THE ANGELS
JOIN THE FORCES
JOINT PARTNERS
JOLLY GOOD CHAP
JONATHAN SWIFT
JORDAN ALMONDS
JOSEPH ADDISON
JOYCE GRENFELL

JUDAS ISCARIOT
JUDGE ADVOCATE
JUDGE JEFFREYS
JUDICIAL COURT
JULIA LOCKWOOD
JULY THE EIGHTH
JULY THE FOURTH
JULY THE SECOND
JUMP AT AN OFFER
JUMPING SEASON
JUMP OVERBOARD
JUMP THE COURSE
JUNE THE EIGHTH
JUNE THE FOURTH
JUNE THE SECOND
JUNGLE WARFARE
JUNIOR COUNSEL
JUNIOR PARTNER
JUNIOR SERVICE
JUST A FEW LINES
JUST AS YOU LIKE
JUST PUBLISHED
JUST-SO STORIES
JUVENILE COURT

K – 13

KAISER WILHELM
KEEN AS MUSTARD
KEEP AN ACCOUNT
KEEP GOOD HOURS
KEEP IN CUSTODY
KEEP IN THE DARK
KEEP LATE HOURS
KEEP ONE'S END UP
KEEP ONE'S EYE IN
KEEP ONE'S HAT ON
KEEP ONE'S PLACE
KEEP ON THE BEAM
KEEP OPEN HOUSE
KEEP THE CHANGE
KEEP TO ONESELF
KEEP TO THE LEFT
KEEP UP THE PACE
KEEP YOUR SEATS
KENTUCKY DERBY
KEPT IN REVERSE
KEPT IN THE DARK
KEPT ON THE TROT
KEY TO A MYSTERY
KICK ONE'S HEELS
KICK THE BUCKET
KICK UP A SHINDY
KILL THE RUMOUR
KINDRED SPIRIT
KING OF DENMARK

KING OF ENGLAND
KING'S BIRTHDAY
KING'S CHAMPION
KING'S EVIDENCE
KING'S RHAPSODY
KISS AND CUDDLE
KISS AND MAKE UP
KISSING COUSIN
KISS IN THE RING
KISS THE GROUND
KITCHEN GARDEN
KIT INSPECTION
KNAVE OF HEARTS
KNAVE OF SPADES
KNAVE OF TRUMPS
KNAVISH TRICKS
KNEW IN ADVANCE
KNIT ONE'S BROWS
KNOCK-DOWN BLOW
KNOCK-OUT DROPS
KNOCK SIDEWAYS
KNOCK SPOTS OFF
KNOTTY PROBLEM
KNOW BACKWARDS
KNOWING FELLOW
KNOWING PERSON
KNOW ONE'S PLACE
KNOW WHAT'S WHAT

L – 13

LA BELLE FRANCE
LABOUR TROUBLE
LABOUR VICTORY
LABURNUM GROVE
LACE INSERTION
LACK OF CANDOUR
LACK OF CAUTION
LACK OF FEELING
LACK OF HARMONY
LACK OF MEANING
LACK OF RESPECT
LACK OF WARNING
LADIES' GALLERY
LADS AND LASSES
LADY BOUNTIFUL
LADY COMPANION
LADY IN WAITING
LADY OF LEISURE
LADY OF QUALITY
LADY OF SHALOTT
LADY OF THE LAKE
LADY OF THE LAMP
LADY PRINCIPAL
LAKE CONSTANCE
LAKE ULLSWATER

LAMBETH BRIDGE
LAMBETH PALACE
LAMBING SEASON
LANCE PERCIVAL
LANDING GROUND
LAND IN THE SOUP
LAND-LOCKED SEA
LAND OF PROMISE
LAND OF THE FREE
LAND OF THE MOON
LANE OF TRAFFIC
LAPSE OF MEMORY
LAPSUS LINGUAE
LARGE AND SMALL
LARGE AUDIENCE
LARGE MAJORITY
LARGE MINORITY
LARGE PRACTICE
LARGE QUANTITY
LARGE-SCALE MAP
LAST CHRISTMAS
LAST EXTREMITY
LAST HANDSHAKE
LAST OF THE LINE
LAST WEDNESDAY
LATE AFTERNOON
LATE BREAKFAST
LATE FOR DINNER
LATE FOR SCHOOL
LATE-NIGHT NEWS
LATENT ABILITY
LATEST FASHION
LATIN AMERICA
LATIN LANGUAGE
LATTICE WINDOW
LAUGH AT DANGER
LAUGHING HYENA
LAUGHING STOCK
LAUGHING WATER
LAUGH OUTRIGHT
LAUNCHING SITE
LAUNDRY BASKET
LAVENDER WATER
LAWFUL WEDLOCK
LAW OF AVERAGES
LAW OF CONTRACT
LAY BY THE HEELS
LAY DOWN THE LAW
LAY IN THE GRAVE
LEAD A DOG'S LIFE
LEAD BY THE HAND
LEAD BY THE NOSE
LEADING DANCER
LEADING SEAMAN
LEADING STOKER
LEAD ONE A DANCE

LEAD ONE STRAY
LEAD POISONING
LEAGUE CRICKET
LEAGUE OF PEACE
LEAMINGTON SPA
LEAN BACKWARDS
LEAP IN THE DARK
LEARNED FRIEND
LEARNER DRIVER
LEARN THE ROPES
LEARN THE TRUTH
LEATHER GLOVES
LEATHER JACKET
LEAVE A FORTUNE
LEAVE A MESSAGE
LEAVE HALF-DONE
LEAVE HOSPITAL
LEAVE IN THE AIR
LEAVE NO CHOICE
LEAVE NO OPTION
LEAVE ONE'S CARD
LEAVE STANDING
LEAVE THE STAGE
LEAVE TO APPEAL
LED TO THE ALTAR
LEFT AT THE POST
LEFT-HAND DRIVE
LEFT-HAND SCREW
LEFT TO ONESELF
LEGAL CURRENCY
LEGAL DOCUMENT
LEGAL EVIDENCE
LEGAL GUARDIAN
LEGAL LANGUAGE
LEGAL POSITION
LEGAL SENTENCE
LEMON MERINGUE
LEMON SQUEEZER
LEOPARD'S SPOTS
LES MISERABLES
LESTER PIGGOTT
LET GO THE REINS
LETHAL CHAMBER
LET IN DAYLIGHT
LET OUT A SECRET
LETTER PERFECT
LETTERS OF FIRE
LETTERS OF GOLD
LETTERS PATENT
LET THINGS SLIP
LEVEL CROSSING
LIABLE TO ERROR
LIBERAL LEADER
LIBERAL MINDED
LIBERAL POLICY
LIBRARY TICKET

LICENCE HOLDER
LICENCE TO KILL
LICENSED TRADE
LICENSING LAWS
LICK INTO SHAPE
LICK ONE'S CHOPS
LIE ON ONE'S BACK
LIFE ASSURANCE
LIFEBOAT DRILL
LIFE HEREAFTER
LIFE INSURANCE
LIFELONG ENEMY
LIFELONG HABIT
LIFE OF LEISURE
LIFETIME'S WORK
LIFT ATTENDANT
LIGHT AND SHADE
LIGHT AS A FAIRY
LIGHT COMEDIAN
LIGHT-FINGERED
LIGHT INDUSTRY
LIGHT INFANTRY
LIGHTNING MOVE
LIGHT OF MY EYES!
LIGHT OF MY LIFE!
LIGHT OF NATURE
LIGHT SENTENCE
LIGHT THE STOVE
LIGHT TRAINING
LIKE A BAD PENNY
LIKE CLOCKWORK
LIKE GRIM DEATH
LIKE LIGHTNING
LIKE MEETS LIKE
LIKE ONE O'CLOCK
LIMITED AMOUNT
LIMITED APPEAL
LIMITED CHOICE
LIMITED NUMBER
LIMITED PERIOD
LIMITED SEASON
LIMITED SUPPLY
LIMP HANDSHAKE
LINEAR MEASURE
LINE OF ADVANCE
LINE OF CONDUCT
LINE OF COUNTRY
LINE OF DEFENCE
LINE OF RETREAT
LINE OF THOUGHT
LINGERING LOOK
LINGERING NOTE
LIQUEUR BRANDY
LIQUEUR WHISKY
LIQUID MEASURE
LIQUID SHAMPOO

LISTENING POST
LIST OF RUNNERS
LITERARY AGENT
LITERARY STYLE
LITERARY THEFT
LITERARY WORKS
LITERARY WORLD
LITTLE AND GOOD
LITTLE BOY BLUE
LITTLE BUT GOOD
LITTLE COMFORT
LITTLE SIR ECHO
LITTLE THEATRE
LITTLE TO SPARE
LITTLE TROUBLE
LIVE BROADCAST
LIVE CARTRIDGE
LIVE FOR THE DAY
LIVE IN COMFORT
LIVE IN HARMONY
LIVE IN HISTORY
LIVE IN POVERTY
LIVE IN SQUALOR
LIVE IN THE PAST
LIVE LIKE A LORD
LIVEN THINGS UP
LIVE ON NOTHING
LIVE PROGRAMME
LIVER AND BACON
LIVE RECORDING
LIVERY COMPANY
LIVERY SERVANT
LIVID WITH RAGE
LIVING THEATRE
LOAD OF RUBBISH
LOAD OF TROUBLE
LOCAL CURRENCY
LOCAL LANDMARK
LOCAL PREACHER
LODGE AN APPEAL
LOFTY AMBITION
LOFTY CONTEMPT
LOFTY THOUGHTS
LOGICAL ACTION
LOGICAL RESULT
LOMBARD STREET
LONDON AIRPORT
LONDON GAZETTE
LONDON SPECIAL
LONE-STAR STATE
LONG PARAGRAPH
LONG TIME NO SEE!
LONG WAY BEHIND
LONG WAY TO FALL
LONNIE DONEGAN
LOOK DANGEROUS

LOOK DIFFERENT
LOOK IMPORTANT
LOOK IN THE FACE
LOOK OVER THERE
LOOK SURPRISED
LOOK UP AND DOWN
LOOSE THINKING
LORD AND MASTER
LORD KITCHENER
LORDLY GESTURE
LORD MAYOR'S DAY
LORD PRESIDENT
LORD PRIVY SEAL
LORD PROTECTOR
LORDS TEMPORAL
LOSE COHERENCE
LOSE HANDS DOWN
LOSE ONE'S FAITH
LOSE ONE'S HEART
LOSE ONE'S LOOKS
LOSE ONE'S MONEY
LOSE ONE'S NERVE
LOSE ONE'S PLACE
LOSE ONE'S SHIRT
LOSE ONE'S SIGHT
LOSE ONE'S STAKE
LOSE ONE'S VOICE
LOSE THE BATTLE
LOSE THE RUBBER
LOSE THE THREAD
LOSS OF BALANCE
LOSS OF CONTROL
LOSS OF FORTUNE
LOSS OF FREEDOM
LOST IN THOUGHT
LOST IN TRANSIT
LOTS OF FRIENDS
LOTTERY TICKET
LOUD EXPLOSION
LOUIS QUATORZE
LOVE AND KISSES
LOVE OF COUNTRY
LOVE OF THE GAME
LOVE ONE'S ENEMY
LOVE ON THE DOLE
LOVING GESTURE
LOWER AND LOWER
LOWER ONE'S FLAG
LOWER REGISTER
LOWER THE LIGHT
LOWER THE PRICE
LOWLAND SCOTCH
LOW VISIBILITY
LOYAL DEVOTION
LOYALIST CAUSE
LUCID ARGUMENT

LUCID INTERVAL
LUCK OF THE DRAW
LUCK OF THE GAME
LUCKY SIXPENCE
LUCKY TALISMAN
LUCRATIVE DEAL
LUDGATE CIRCUS
LUKEWARM WATER
LUMINOUS PAINT
LUNATIC ASYLUM
LUNATIC FRINGE
LUNCHEON PARTY
LUNCHEON TABLE
LUXURIOUS FOOD
LUXURY HOLIDAY
LYCEUM THEATRE
LYRICAL POETRY
LYRICAL PRAISE

M – 13

MACHINE MINDER
MADAME TUSSAUD
MADE IN ENGLAND
MADE IN GERMANY
MADE IN IRELAND
MAD ENTERPRISE
MADE THE WEIGHT
MADE TO MEASURE
MADISON SQUARE
MAGAZINE RIFLE
MAGAZINE STORY
MAGNETIC FIELD
MAGNETIC NORTH
MAGNETIC POLES
MAGNETIC STORM
MAIDEN CENTURY
MAID OF ALL WORK
MADE OF ORLEANS
MAIDS OF HONOUR
MAIMED FOR LIFE
MAIN CHARACTER
MAJOR DISASTER
MAJOR INCIDENT
MAJOR INTERVAL
MAKE A COMEBACK
MAKE A CONQUEST
MAKE A CROSSING
MAKE A DECISION
MAKE A GOOD WIFE
MAKE ALLOWANCE
MAKE A LONG NOSE
MAKE A MESS OF IT
MAKE AN ATTEMPT
MAKE AN OPENING
MAKE A PROPOSAL

MAKE DO AND MEND
MAKE ECONOMIES
MAKE INQUIRIES
MAKE MINCEMEAT
MAKE MINE MUSIC
MAKE NO DEMANDS
MAKE NO MISTAKE
MAKE OBEISANCE
MAKE ONE'S DEBUT
MAKE ONE'S PEACE
MAKE ONE'S POINT
MAKE OVERTURES
MAKE PROVISION
MAKE REDUNDANT
MAKE SHORT WORK
MAKE THE ASCENT
MAKE THE EFFORT
MAKE THE FUR FLY
MAKE THINGS HUM
MALADIE DU PAYS
MALTESE FALCON
MANAGING CLERK
MAN AT THE WHEEL
MAN OF BREEDING
MAN OF BUSINESS
MAN OF DECISION
MAN OF EMINENCE
MAN OF FEW WORDS
MAN OF LEARNING
MAN OF PROPERTY
MAN OF THE WORLD
MANSFIELD PARK
MAP OF SCOTLAND
MAP OF THE WORLD
MARCH OF EVENTS
MARCH THE FIFTH
MARCH THE FIRST
MARCH THE NINTH
MARCH THE SIXTH
MARCH THE TENTH
MARCH THE THIRD
MARGARET SMITH
MARGIN OF ERROR
MARGIN OF PROOF
MARGOT FONTEYN
MARILYN MONROE
MARINE COMPASS
MARINE OFFICER
MARITIME TRADE
MARKET DRAYTON
MARK OF RESPECT
MARRIAGE BANNS
MARRIAGE BELLS
MARRIAGE FEAST
MARRIAGE LINES
MARRIAGE RITES

MARRIED COUPLE
MARRY A FORTUNE
MARTELLO TOWER
MARTIAL SPIRIT
MARY MAGDALENE
MASS EXECUTION
MASS FORMATION
MASTER BUILDER
MASTER MARINER
MASTER'S TICKET
MATCH-BOX LABEL
MATCH ONE'S WITS
MATERIAL ISSUE
MATERIAL POINT
MATERIAL SENSE
MATERNITY WARD
MATINÉE JACKET
MATTHEW ARNOLD
MATURE THOUGHT
MAXIMUM AMOUNT
MAXIMUM CHARGE
MAXIMUM GROWTH
MAXIMUM POINTS
MAY THE SEVENTH
MAY THE TWELFTH
MEALS ON WHEELS
MEANS OF ACCESS
MEANS OF ASCENT
MEANS OF ESCAPE
MEANS OF SAFETY
MEASURED TREAD
MEASURE OF LAND
MEASURE SWORDS
MEASURING TAPE
MEAT AND TWO VEG
MECHANICAL AID
MECHANICAL MAN
MEDAL OF HONOUR
MEDICAL ADVICE
MEDICAL SCHOOL
MEDICINAL BATH
MEDICINE CHEST
MEDICINE GLASS
MEDIUM QUALITY
MEET ONE'S MAKER
MEET ONE'S MATCH
MELTON MOWBRAY
MEMORIAL STONE
MEND A PUNCTURE
MENTAL BALANCE
MENTAL CALIBRE
MENTAL CRUELTY
MENTAL DISEASE
MENTAL FATIGUE
MENTAL HYGIENE
MENTAL ILLNESS

MENTALLY ALERT
MENTALLY BLIND
MENTALLY SOUND
MENTAL PATIENT
MENTAL PICTURE
MENTAL PROCESS
MENTAL RESERVE
MENTAL THERAPY
MENTAL TORMENT
MENTAL TORTURE
MENTAL TROUBLE
MERCANTILE LAW
MERCENARY ARMY
MERCI BEAUCOUP
MERE BAGATELLE
MERE EXISTENCE
MERMAID TAVERN
MERRIE ENGLAND
MERTHYR TYDFIL
MERTON COLLEGE
MESS OF POTTAGE
MESSY BUSINESS
METALLIC SOUND
METAL MERCHANT
METRIC MEASURE
MICHAELMAS DAY
MICK THE MILLER
MICROWAVE OVEN
MIDDLE-AGED MAN
MIDDLE CLASSES
MIDDLE ENGLISH
MIDLAND ACCENT
MIDLAND COUNTY
MIDSUMMER'S DAY
MILD AND BITTER
MILD EXPLETIVE
MILE AFTER MILE
MILES AND MILES
MILITARY CLOAK
MILITARY CROSS
MILITARY DRESS
MILITARY FORCE
MILITARY MARCH
MILITARY MEDAL
MILITARY MUSIC
MILITARY STAFF
MILITARY STORE
MILK CHOCOLATE
MILLING THRONG
MIND OF ONE'S OWN
MINERAL SPRING
MINIMUM AMOUNT
MINIMUM CHARGE
MINISTER OF WAR
MINOR COUNTIES
MINOR INCIDENT

MINOR INTERVAL
MINT CONDITION
MINUS QUANTITY
MIRACLE WORKER
MISCHIEF AFOOT
MISSING PERSON
MISSPENT YOUTH
MISS PINKERTON
MISS THE TARGET
MIXED BLESSING
MIXED FEELINGS
MIXED FOURSOME
MIXED MARRIAGE
MIXED METAPHOR
MOBILE CANTEEN
MOBILE LIBRARY
MOBILE WARFARE
MODELLING CLAY
MODE OF ADDRESS
MODERATE MEANS
MODERATE PRICE
MODERATE SKILL
MODERATE SPEED
MODERN COSTUME
MODERN ENGLISH
MODERN FASHION
MODERN HISTORY
MODERN METHODS
MODERN OUTLOOK
MODERN PAINTER
MODERN SETTING
MODERN SOCIETY
MODERN WARFARE
MODEST DEMANDS
MODEST FORTUNE
MODEST REQUEST
MODUS OPERANDI
MOMENT OF TRUTH
MONASTIC ORDER
MONDAY EVENING
MONDAY MORNING
MONETARY VALUE
MONEY IN THE BAG
MONEY TROUBLES
MONOTONOUS JOB
MONTHLY REPORT
MONTHLY SALARY
MOONLESS NIGHT
MOONLIGHT FLIT
MORAL CONFLICT
MORAL PRESSURE
MORAL STRENGTH
MORAL TRAINING
MORAL WEAKNESS
MORBID CRAVING
MORE THAN A JOKE

MORNING COFFEE
MORNING PRAYER
MORTALITY RATE
MORTAL REMAINS
MOST DESIRABLE
MOST EXCELLENT
MOTH-BALL FLEET
MOTHER COUNTRY
MOTHER HUBBARD
MOTHER OF PEARL
MOTHER SHIPTON
MOTION PICTURE
MOTOR MECHANIC
MOUNTAIN CHAIN
MOUNTAIN RANGE
MOUNTAIN SHEEP
MOUNTAIN SLOPE
MOUNTAIN TRAIL
MOUNTED POLICE
MOUNTED TROOPS
MOUNTING ANGER
MOUNT OF OLIVES
MOUNT PLEASANT
MOVE IN SOCIETY
MOVE MOUNTAINS
MOVING ACCOUNT
MOVING PICTURE
MOWING MACHINE
MUCH REGRETTED
MUDDLE THROUGH
MULTIPLE STORE
MULTIPLY BY SIX
MULTIPLY BY TEN
MULTIPLY BY TWO
MULTUM IN PARVO
MUMMY AND DADDY
MUNICIPAL BANK
MUNICIPAL PARK
MURAL PAINTING
MURDER MYSTERY
MURDER WILL OUT
MUSE OF DANCING
MUSE OF HISTORY
MUSICAL CHAIRS
MUSICAL COMEDY
MUSICAL STRESS
MUSICAL FESTIVAL
MUSIC-HALL JOKE
MUSIC-HALL STAR
MUSIC-HALL TURN
MUSIC MISTRESS
MUSTARD PICKLE
MUSTARD YELLOW
MUTUAL BENEFIT
MUTUAL CONSENT
MUTUAL DISLIKE

MUTUAL FRIENDS
MUTUAL RESPECT
MYSTERY OF LIFE
MYSTERY WRITER
MYTHICAL BEING

N – 13

NAGGING TONGUE
NAME ONE'S PRICE
NARRATIVE POEM
NARROW OUTLOOK
NARROW PASSAGE
NARROW VICTORY
NASTY BUSINESS
NATIONAL DANCE
NATIONAL DRESS
NATIONAL DRINK
NATIONAL GUARD
NATIONAL PRIDE
NATIONAL SPORT
NATIONAL TRUST
NATIONAL UNITY
NATIVE COSTUME
NATIVE QUARTER
NATURAL BEAUTY
NATURAL CAUSES
NATURAL COLOUR
NATURAL COURSE
NATURAL HAZARD
NATURAL SYSTEM
NATURAL TALENT
NATURAL WEALTH
NATURE RESERVE
NATURE WORSHIP
NAVAL BARRACKS
NAVAL EXPLOITS
NAVAL HOSPITAL
NEAPOLITAN ICE
NEAR NEIGHBOUR
NEAR ONE'S HEART
NEAR THE GROUND
NEAR THE WICKET
NEAT AS A NEW PIN
NECESSARY EVIL
NECK OR NOTHING
NEEDLESS TO SAY
NEGATIVE REPLY
NELLIE WALLACE
NELSON'S COLUMN
NERVE HOSPITAL
NERVES OF STEEL
NERVOUS ENERGY
NERVOUS SYSTEM
NERVOUS TWITCH
NESTING SEASON

NEST OF HORNETS
NETHER REGIONS
NEUTRAL COLOUR
NEUTRAL CORNER
NEUTRAL GROUND
NEVER LOOK BACK
NEVER ON SUNDAY
NEW BOND STREET
NEW EXPERIMENT
NEW FOUNDATION
NEWGATE PRISON
NEW IMPRESSION
NEW REGULATION
NEW RESOLUTION
NEW SOUTH WALES
NEWSPAPER FILE
NEWSPAPER RACK
NEXT BEST THING
NEXT CHRISTMAS
NEXT GENTLEMAN
NEXT ON THE LIST
NEXT TO NOTHING
NEXT WEDNESDAY
NICE AND TENDER
NICKEL COINAGE
NIGHTLY VISITS
NIGHT MUST FALL
NIGHT OF TERROR
NIGHT WATCHMAN
NIMBLE FINGERS
NINETEEN MILES
NINETY PER CENT
NINTH OF AUGUST
NINTH SYMPHONY
NO ALTERNATIVE
NOBLE AMBITION
NOBODY ON EARTH
NO BONES BROKEN
NO EXPECTATION
NO EXTRA CHARGE
NO GREAT SHAKES
NO HIDING PLACE
NO HOLDS BARRED
NOMINAL CHARGE
NOMINATION DAY
NONSENSE RHYME
NONSENSE VERSE
NON-STOP TALKER
NO OIL PAINTING
NOOK AND CRANNY
NORFOLK BROADS
NORFOLK JACKET
NORMAL SERVICE
NORMAN ENGLISH
NORMAN VAUGHAN
NORTH AMERICAN

NORTH AND SOUTH
NORTH ATLANTIC
NORTH CAROLINA
NORTH-EAST WIND
NOTABLE SPEECH
NOTE OF CENSURE
NOTE OF TRIUMPH
NOTE OF WARNING
NOT GOOD ENOUGH
NOTHING LIKE IT
NOTHING TO COME
NOTHING TO GAIN
NOTHING TO GO ON
NOTHING TO LOSE
NOT IMPOSSIBLE
NOT IN LUCK'S WAY
NOT IN THE LEAST
NOT LONG TO WAIT
NOT MY CUP OF TEA
NOT NEGOTIABLE
NOT ON YOUR LIFE
NUCLEAR ENERGY
NUCLEAR WEAPON
NUISANCE VALUE
NUMBER ENGAGED
NUMERICAL LIST
NURSERY GARDEN
NURSERY SCHOOL
NURSERY SLOPES
NURSING SISTER

O – 13

OBEY AN IMPULSE
OBJECTIVE CASE
OBJECT OF MIRTH
OBJECT OF PRIDE
OBJECT OF SCORN
OBLIGE A FRIEND
OBSCURE MOTIVE
OBSERVER CORPS
OCCUPY THE MIND
OCEANS OF MONEY
OFF AT A TANGENT
OFFER AN EXCUSE
OFF-HAND MANNER
OFFICE CLEANER
OFFICE MANAGER
OFFICE OF WORKS
OFFICE ROUTINE
OFFICIAL REPLY
OFF ONE'S OWN BAT
OFF ONE'S ROCKER
OFF-SEASON RATE
OFF THE DEEP END
OFF THE FAIRWAY

OFF THE SUBJECT
OF LITTLE WORTH
OIL AND VINEGAR
OLD-AGE PENSION
OLD AS THE HILLS
OLD CAMPAIGNER
OLD-CLOTHES MAN
OLD CROCKS' RACE
OLDER AND WISER
OLDER THAN TIME
OLD FATHER TIME
OLD FOUNDATION
OLD IN THE TOOTH
OLD TRADITIONS
OLD WIVES' TALES
OLYMPIC RECORD
OMNIBUS VOLUME
ON A BROOMSTICK
ON A GRAND SCALE
ON A LARGE SCALE
ON A SHOE-STRING
ON A SMALL SCALE
ON BENDED KNEES
ONCE AND FOR ALL
ONCE UPON A TIME
ONE AND THE SAME
ONE DAY CRICKET
ONE FOR THE ROAD
ONE IN A HUNDRED
ONE IN A MILLION
ONE OF THE CROWD
ONE OR THE OTHER
ONE'S PROSPECTS
ONE'S RELATIVES
ONE-WAY TRAFFIC
ONE WICKET DOWN
ON HER BEAM ENDS
ON ITS LAST LEGS
ONLY EXCEPTION
ON ONE'S OWN FEET
ON PAIN OF DEATH
ON TENTER-HOOKS
ON THE CONTRARY
ON THE DOOR-STEP
ON THE FACE OF IT
ON THE FIRST LAP
ON THE FRONTIER
ON THE HIGH SEAS
ON THE INCREASE
ON THE LEFT SIDE
ON THE LONG SIDE
ON THE NEAR-SIDE
ON THE PAVEMENT
ON THE PLATFORM
ON THE PREMISES
ON THE ROOF-TOPS

ON THE SAFE SIDE
ON THE SCAFFOLD
ON THE SCROUNGE
ON THE SICK LIST
ON THE STRENGTH
ON THE WIRELESS
ON WINGS OF SONG
OPEN A CAMPAIGN
OPEN-AIR MARKET
OPEN AN ACCOUNT
OPEN CONSONANT
OPENED IN ERROR
OPEN HOSTILITY
OPENING GAMBIT
OPENING SPEECH
OPEN ONE'S HEART
OPEN ONE'S MOUTH
OPEN ONE'S PURSE
OPEN REBELLION
OPEN THE DEBATE
OPEN THE DRAWER
OPEN THE WINDOW
OPERATION ROOM
OPERATIVE WORD
OPPOSITE CAMPS
OPPOSITE POLES
OPPOSITE SIDES
OPPOSITE VIEWS
OPTICAL DEVICE
ORANGE BITTERS
ORANGE BLOSSOM
ORANGE FLAVOUR
ORB AND SCEPTRE
ORBITAL SANDER
ORDEAL BY WATER
ORDER A RETREAT
ORDERLY MANNER
ORDER OF BATTLE
ORDER OF THE DAY
ORDINAL NUMBER
ORDINARY SHARE
ORDINARY STOCK
ORDNANCE CORPS
ORGANIC CHANGE
ORGANIC MATTER
ORGAN OF SPEECH
ORGAN OF VISION
ORIGINAL MODEL
ORKNEY ISLANDS
OSBERT SITWELL
OTHER WAY ROUND
OTTOMAN EMPIRE
OUT AT THE ELBOW
OUTBOARD MOTOR
OUTBREAK OF WAR
OUTDOOR RELIEF

OUTDOOR SPORTS
OUTER DARKNESS
OUTER HEBRIDES
OUT FOR THRILLS
OUT-HEROD HEROD
OUT LIKE A LIGHT
OUT OF BUSINESS
OUT-OF-DATE IDEA
OUT OF HARM'S WAY
OUT OF INTEREST
OUT OF KINDNESS
OUT OF MISCHIEF
OUT OF MOURNING
OUT OF ONE'S HEAD
OUT OF ONE'S MIND
OUT OF PATIENCE
OUT OF POSITION
OUT OF PRACTICE
OUT OF SYMPATHY
OUT OF TRAINING
OUT ON ONE'S FEET
OUTSIDE CHANCE
OUTSIDE THE LAW
OVER-ALL LENGTH
OVERHEAD CABLE
OVERHEAD WIRES
OVERLAND ROUTE
OVERLAND TRAIN
OVERNIGHT CASE
OVERSEAS TRADE
OVER THE BORDER
OVER THE STICKS
OVER THE WICKET
OVER TWENTY-ONE
OWNER OCCUPIER
OXFORD COLLEGE
OXFORD ENGLISH

P – 13

PACE UP AND DOWN
PACIFIC ISLAND
PACKET OF SEEDS
PACK OF THIEVES
PAGAN FESTIVAL
PAGAN LOVE SONG
PAGE THREE GIRL
PAID BY THE HOUR
PAIN IN THE NECK
PAINT A PICTURE
PAINT ONE'S FACE
PAIR OF BELLOWS
PAIR OF GARTERS
PAIR OF GLASSES
PAIR OF KIPPERS
PAIR OF PINCERS

PAIR OF PYJAMAS
PAIR OF SANDALS
PALACE THEATRE
PALAIS DE DANSE
PALE AS A CORPSE
PALE IMITATION
PALE WITH ANGER
PAMELA FRANKAU
PANDA CROSSING
PANELLED WALLS
PANEL OF JUDGES
PANG OF REMORSE
PANGS OF HUNGER
PANIC MEASURES
PANTOMINE DAME
PAPER-BACK BOOK
PAPER CLIPPING
PAPER CURRENCY
PAPER SHORTAGE
PAPER THE WALLS
PARACHUTE JUMP
PARAFFIN STOVE
PARALLEL LINES
PAR EXCELLENCE
PARIS AND HELEN
PARIS CREATION
PARIS FASHIONS
PARISH COUNCIL
PARK ATTENDANT
PARKINSON'S LAW
PAR OF EXCHANGE
PARROT FASHION
PART AND PARCEL
PARTIAL CHANGE
PARTIAL EXCUSE
PARTLY COVERED
PART OF HISTORY
PART OF THE PLAN
PART OF THE TIME
PARTY OFFICIAL
PARTY POLITICS
PASSAGE OF ARMS
PASSAGE OF TIME
PASS AND REPASS
PASS AN OPINION
PASSENGER LIST
PASSENGER SHIP
PASSING GLANCE
PASSING REMARK
PASSION FLOWER
PASSION SUNDAY
PASS THE BUTTER
PASS THE PEPPER
PASS UNNOTICED
PAST BEHAVIOUR
PAST ENDURANCE

PAST ONE'S PRIME
PATENT LEATHER
PATENT PENDING
PATENT SWINDLE
PATHETIC SIGHT
PATIENCE OF JOB
PATRIOTIC SONG
PAUL McCARTNEY
PAVED WITH GOLD
PAWN IN THE GAME
PAX BRITANNICA
PAY BY THE PIECE
PAY LIP-SERVICE
PAYMENT IN KIND
PAYMENT IN LIEU
PAY THE PENALTY
PEACE AND QUIET
PEACE OFFERING
PEAK OF SUCCESS
PEAL OF THUNDER
PEARL NECKLACE
PEBBLE GLASSES
PECULIAR SMELL
PECUNIARY LOSS
PEGGY ASHCROFT
PENALTY CLAUSE
PENCIL DRAWING
PENDULUM CLOCK
PENINSULAR WAR
PENNY DREADFUL
PENNY FARTHING
PENSION SCHEME
PEOPLE AT LARGE
PEPPER AND SALT
PERCUSSION CAP
PERFECT CIRCLE
PERFECT FOURTH
PERFECT FRIGHT
PERFECT NUMBER
PERFECT RYHTHM
PERFECT SCREAM
PERFECT SQUARE
PERFECT TIMING
PERFECT WICKET
PERFORM A STUNT
PERIOD COSTUME
PERISHING COLD
PERKIN WARBECK
PERMANENT HOME
PERMANENT PASS
PERMANENT POST
PERMANENT WAVE
PERSIAN CARPET
PERSIAN GARDEN
PERSIAN MARKET
PERSONAL ABUSE

PERSONAL CHARM
PERSONAL CLAIM
PERSONAL GUEST
PERSONAL PRIDE
PERSONAL STYLE
PERSONAL TOUCH
PETER CAVANAGH
PETER THE GREAT
PETIT DÉJEUNER
PETROL LIGHTER
PETROL STATION
PETTICOAT LANE
PETTY OFFICIAL
PETTY SESSIONS
PEWTER TANKARD
PHANTOM FIGURE
PHYSICAL FORCE
PHYSICAL JERKS
PHYSICALLY FIT
PHYSICAL POWER
PHYSICAL WRECK
PHYSICS MASTER
PIANO CONCERTO
PIANO EXERCISE
PICK AND CHOOSE
PICK AND SHOVEL
PICKLED WALNUT
PICK OF THE POPS
PICK ONE'S WORDS
PICK THE WINNER
PICK UP A LIVING
PICTS AND SCOTS
PICTURE PALACE
PIDGIN ENGLISH
PIECE OF ADVICE
PIECE OF STRING
PIECES OF EIGHT
PIECE TOGETHER
PIG AND WHISTLE
PIGEON FANCIER
PILE OF RUBBISH
PILOT'S LICENCE
PILTDOWN SKULL
PING-PONG TABLE
PINK ELEPHANTS
PINKY AND PERKY
PIN-STRIPE SUIT
PIONEER SPIRIT
PIOUS THOUGHTS
PIPE OF TOBACCO
PISTACHIO NUTS
PISTOLS FOR TWO
PITCH DARKNESS
PITCHED BATTLE
PITCH ONE'S TENT
PITH AND MARROW

PLACE END TO END
PLACE IN THE SUN
PLACE OF HONOUR
PLACE OF REFUGE
PLACE ON RECORD
PLAIN ENVELOPE
PLAIN FEATURES
PLAIN LANGUAGE
PLAIN QUESTION
PLAIN SPEAKING
PLAUSIBLE TALE
PLAY A LONE HAND
PLAY FOR SAFETY
PLAY HARD TO GET
PLAYING TRICKS
PLAY ONE'S CARDS
PLAY THE DESPOT
PLAY THE FIDDLE
PLAY THE GUITAR
PLAY THE MARKET
PLAY THE MARTYR
PLAY THE TYRANT
PLAY THE VIOLIN
PLAY THE WANTON
PLAY UPON WORDS
PLEAD FOR MERCY
PLEAD INNOCENT
PLEAD THE CAUSE
PLEA OF ABSENCE
PLEASED TO COME
PLEASE ONESELF
PLEDGE ONESELF
PLENTIFUL FARE
PLENTY OF MONEY
PLENTY TO SPARE
PLOUGH A FURROW
PLOUGHED FIELD
PLOUGH THE LAND
PLUCKED PIGEON
PLUMB NONSENSE
PLYMOUTH SOUND
PNEUMATIC TYRE
POCKET BOROUGH
POCKET EDITION
POETICAL WORKS
POETIC JUSTICE
POETIC LICENCE
POETRY READING
POINTED REMARK
POINTED SAYING
POINT FOR POINT
POINT IN COMMON
POINT IN FAVOUR
POINT OF HONOUR
POINT OF THE JAW
POISONED ARROW

POISON THE MIND
POLAR EXPLORER
POLICEMAN'S LOT
POLICE MESSAGE
POLICE OFFICER
POLICE STATION
POLICE TACTICS
POLICE WHISTLE
POLISHED ACTOR
POLISHED STYLE
POLITE FICTION
POLITE FORMULA
POLITE REFUSAL
POLITE SOCIETY
POLITE WELCOME
POLITICAL BLOC
POLITICAL NEWS
POLITICAL UNIT
POLITICAL VIEW
POMERANIAN DOG
PONTIUS PILATE
PONTOON BRIDGE
POOL RESOURCES
POOR BUT HONEST
POOR CONDITION
POOR IN QUALITY
POORLY DRESSED
POOR PERFORMER
POOR PROSPECTS
POOR RECEPTION
POPPING CREASE
POPULAR BALLAD
POPULAR CHOICE
POPULAR DECREE
POPULAR DEMAND
POPULAR ESTEEM
POPULAR FIGURE
POPULAR PEOPLE
POPULAR PRICES
POPULAR RESORT
POPULAR SINGER
POPULATED AREA
PORTABLE RADIO
PORT ELIZABETH
PORTLAND STONE
POSE A QUESTION
POSITIVE PROOF
POSTAL ADDRESS
POSTAL SERVICE
POSTED MISSING
POSTER COLOURS
POSTE RESTANTE
POSTMAN'S KNOCK
POST-OFFICE RED
POST-WAR CREDIT
POTTED SHRIMPS

POULTRY FARMER	PRINCE OF WALES
POUND OF APPLES	PRINCESS DIANA
POUND OF BUTTER	PRINCESS DRESS
POUND STERLING	PRINCESS ROYAL
POUR OUT THE TEA	PRINCE'S STREET
POWDER AND SHOT	PRINCE WILLIAM
POWDER COMPACT	PRINCIPAL FOOD
POWDER SHAMPOO	PRINCIPAL PART
POWER AND GLORY	PRINCIPAL TOWN
POWERFUL VOICE	PRINTED LETTER
POWER OF SPEECH	PRINTED MATTER
POWER OF THE LAW	PRINTER'S DEVIL
POWER POLITICS	PRINTER'S ERROR
PRACTICAL JOKE	PRINTING PRESS
PRACTICAL MIND	PRINTING WORKS
PRACTICAL TEST	PRISONER OF WAR
PRACTICE MATCH	PRISONER'S BASE
PRACTICE ROUND	PRISON VISITOR
PRACTISED HAND	PRIVATE AFFAIR
PRACTISED LIAR	PRIVATE INCOME
PRAIRIE OYSTER	PRIVATE LESSON
PRAWN COCKTAIL	PRIVATE LETTER
PRAYER MEETING	PRIVATE MATTER
PRAYING MANTIS	PRIVATE MEMBER
PRECIOUS METAL	PRIVATE OFFICE
PRECIOUS STONE	PRIVATE PERSON
PRECIOUS WORDS	PRIVATE REASON
PRECISE MOMENT	PRIVATE SCHOOL
PRECISION TOOL	PRIVATE SOURCE
PREFER A CHARGE	PRIZE SPECIMEN
PREPARE A DRINK	PROBABLE ERROR
PREPARE FOR WAR	PROCESSED FOOD
PRESENT EVENTS	PROCESS OF TIME
PRESENT MOMENT	PRODUCER GOODS
PRESS CAMPAIGN	PROFANE PERSON
PRESS CUTTINGS	PROFIT AND LOSS
PRESSED FLOWER	PROFIT SHARING
PRESSED TONGUE	PROFOUND SLEEP
PRESS EXCHANGE	PROFUSE THANKS
PRESS FASTENER	PROGRESS CHART
PRESSING CLAIM	PROLONGED NOTE
PRESS ONE'S SUIT	PROMENADE DECK
PRESSURE GAUGE	PROMISING IDEA
PRESSURE GROUP	PROMPT PAYMENT
PRETTY PICTURE	PROMPT SERVICE
PREY ON THE MIND	PROOF POSITIVE
PRICE INCREASE	PROPER CHARLEY
PRIM AND PROPER	PROPERTY OWNER
PRIMARY COLOUR	PROPOSE A TOAST
PRIMARY SCHOOL	PROSAIC PERSON
PRIME MINISTER	PROSPEROUS MAN
PRIMEVAL CHAOS	PROVE ONE'S CASE
PRIMITIVE FORM	PROVIDE AN HEIR
PRINCE CHARLES	PROVING GROUND
PRINCE CONSORT	PUBLIC ADDRESS
PRINCE OF PEACE	PUBLIC AFFAIRS

PUBLIC ANALYST	PUT ON PRESSURE
PUBLIC COMMENT	PUT ON THE BRAKE
PUBLIC COMPANY	PUT ON THE LIGHT
PUBLIC GALLERY	PUT ON THE SCREW
PUBLIC HANGING	PUT ON THE STAGE
PUBLIC HIGHWAY	PUT OUT A FEELER
PUBLIC HOLIDAY	PUT OUT FEELERS
PUBLIC INQUIRY	PUT OUT OF COURT
PUBLIC LECTURE	PUT OUT OF JOINT
PUBLIC LIBRARY	PUT OUT OF SIGHT
PUBLIC MEETING	PUT OUT TO GRASS
PUBLIC OPINION	PUT PEN TO PAPER
PUBLIC OUTRAGE	PUT THE BRAKE ON
PUBLIC PROTEST	PUT THE CAP ON IT
PUBLIC RECORDS	PUT THE LID ON IT
PUBLIC SCANDAL	PUT TO THE BLUSH
PUBLIC SERVANT	PUT TO THE PROOF
PUBLIC SERVICE	PUT TO THE SWORD
PUBLIC SPEAKER	PUT UP THE BANNS
PUBLIC TRUSTEE	PUT UP THE MONEY
PUBLIC UTILITY	PUT UP THE PRICE
PUBLIC VEHICLE	
PUBLIC WARNING	
PUBLIC WORSHIP	**Q – 13**
PUBLISHED WORK	QUADRUPLE TIME
PULITZER PRIZE	QUALITY STREET
PULL A LONG FACE	QUANTUM THEORY
PULL INTO SHAPE	QUARTER BOTTLE
PULL NO PUNCHES	QUARTERLY RENT
PUNCTURED TYRE	QUARTER TO FIVE
PUNISHING WORK	QUARTER TO FOUR
PUPPET THEATRE	QUARTER TO NINE
PURCHASE MONEY	QUEEN CAROLINE
PURCHASE PRICE	QUEEN OF HEARTS
PURE AND SIMPLE	QUEEN OF SPADES
PURE IN THOUGHT	QUEEN OF THE MAY
PURE MISCHANCE	QUEEN OF TRUMPS
PURE PREJUDICE	QUEEN'S COLLEGE
PURPLE AND GOLD	QUEEN'S COUNSEL
PURPLE EMPEROR	QUEEN'S ENGLISH
PURPLE HEATHER	QUEEN'S HIGHWAY
PURPLE PASSAGE	QUEEN'S PROCTOR
PURSE ONE'S LIPS	QUEEN VICTORIA
PURSER'S OFFICE	QUEER CUSTOMER
PUSH-BUTTON WAR	QUEER GOINGS-ON
PUSHED FOR TIME	QUEER THE PITCH
PUSH TO THE WALL	QUICK AS A FLASH
PUT IN FOR A RISE	QUICK MOVEMENT
PUT IN JEOPARDY	QUICK RECOVERY
PUT IN THE KITTY	QUICK-SET HEDGE
PUT IN THE SHADE	QUICK THINKING
PUT IN THE WRONG	QUICK TURNOVER
PUT ONE'S BACK UP	QUIET AS A MOUSE
PUT ONESELF OUT	QUITE POSITIVE
PUT ONE'S FEET UP	QUITE POSSIBLE
PUT ONE'S HAIR UP	QUITE THE THING

QUIZ PROGRAMME
QUOTATION MARK

R – 13

RACE PREJUDICE
RACING CIRCUIT
RACING TIPSTER
RACING TRAINER
RACK ONE'S BRAIN
RADIANT ENERGY
RADIATION BELT
RADICAL CHANGE
RADICAL REFORM
RADIO OPERATOR
RADIO RECEIVER
RAG-AND-BONE MAN
RAGING TEMPEST
RAGING TORRENT
RAID THE LARDER
RAILWAY BRIDGE
RAILWAY ENGINE
RAILWAY SHARES
RAILWAY SIDING
RAILWAY SIGNAL
RAILWAY SYSTEM
RAILWAY TICKET
RAILWAY TUNNEL
RAISE A BARRIER
RAISE CHICKENS
RAISED GLASSES
RAISE ONE'S EYES
RAISE ONE'S HAND
RAISE THE ALARM
RAISE THE FUNDS
RAISE THE MONEY
RAISE THE PRICE
RAISE THE SIEGE
RAISE THE TEMPO
RAISE THE VOICE
RAKE'S PROGRESS
RAKE UP THE PAST
RALLYING POINT
RALPH WIGHTMAN
RANGE OF CHOICE
RANGE OF COLOUR
RAPE OF THE LOCK
RAPID PROGRESS
RAPID TURNOVER
RAPT ATTENTION
RASH BEHAVIOUR
RASHER OF BACON
RASH STATEMENT
RASPBERRY CANE
RATEABLE VALUE
RATE COLLECTOR

RATE FOR THE JOB
RATES AND TAXES
RATIONAL DRESS
RAVAGES OF TIME
RAVENOUS BEAST
RAVING LUNATIC
RAYMOND BAXTER
RAYMOND MASSEY
RAY OF SUNSHINE
REACH A NEW HIGH
REACH A VERDICT
REACH MATURITY
REACH ONE'S GOAL
REACH THE LIMIT
REACT IN FAVOUR
READER'S DIGEST
READ FOR THE BAR
READING MATTER
READING PUBLIC
READ THE FUTURE
READ THE LESSON
READY-MADE SUIT
READY RECKONER
READY RESPONSE
READY, STEADY, GO!
READY TO ATTACK
READY TO POUNCE
READY TO SPRING
REAL-LIFE STORY
REALMS OF FANCY
REAP THE FRUITS
REAP THE REWARD
RECEIPT IN FULL
RECEIVE NOTICE
RECEIVE ORDERS
RECENT ARRIVAL
RECEPTION DESK
RECEPTION ROOM
RECEPTIVE MIND
RECKLESS SPEED
RECKLESS YOUTH
RECLAIMED LAND
RECORD ATTEMPT
RECORD BREAKER
RECORD COUNTER
RECORDED MUSIC
RECORD ROUND-UP
RECORD SESSION
RED AS A LOBSTER
RED-CROSS NURSE
REDEEM A PLEDGE
RED RAG TO A BULL
RED RIDING HOOD
RED SEALING-WAX
RED SKY AT NIGHT
REDUCE TO ASHES

REDUCE TO SCALE
REDUCE TO TEARS
REDUCING AGENT
REDUCING PILLS
REFERENCE BOOK
REFER TO DRAWER
REFINED ACCENT
REFINED PALATE
REFUSE A CHANCE
REFUSE AN OFFER
REFUSE PAYMENT
REFUSE THE BAIT
REFUSE TO SPEAK
REGAIN COMMAND
REGAIN CONTROL
REGAIN THE LEAD
REGENCY STRIPE
REGRET THE LOSS
REGULAR FORCES
REGULAR HABITS
REGULAR INCOME
REGULAR PEOPLE
REGULAR READER
REGULAR SALARY
REGULAR STAGES
REGULAR TROOPS
REGULAR VISITS
REHEARSAL ROOM
REIGNING QUEEN
REIGN OF TERROR
REJECTION SLIP
RELATIVE MERIT
RELATIVE PROOF
RELATIVE VALUE
RELATIVE WORTH
RELAXED THROAT
RELEASE ON BAIL
REMAIN AT PEACE
REMAIN HOPEFUL
REMAIN NEUTRAL
REMAIN PASSIVE
REMAIN THE SAME
REMAIN UPRIGHT
REMAIN VISIBLE
REMARKABLE BOY
REMARKABLE MAN
REMITTANCE MAN
REMOTE CONTROL
REMOTE VILLAGE
REMOVE ONE'S HAT
RENEWED ENERGY
RENEW ONE'S VOWS
RENT COLLECTOR
RENT IN ADVANCE
REPEAT A SIGNAL
REPEAT ONESELF

REPEL AN ATTACK
REPETITIVE JOB
REPLY BY RETURN
REPORT FOR DUTY
REPUBLICAN ERA
RESERVED TABLE
RESERVE ELEVEN
RESIGN ONESELF
RESPECT THE LAW
RESTAURANT CAR
RESTIVE NATURE
RESTLESS NIGHT
REST ONE'S BONES
RESTORE TO LIFE
REST SATISFIED
RETAIL TRADING
RETAINING WALL
RETARDED BRAIN
RETARDED CHILD
RETIRED PEOPLE
RETROUSSÉ NOSE
RETURN A FAVOUR
RETURN A PROFIT
RETURN JOURNEY
RETURN SERVICE
RETURN TO EARTH
REVENUE CUTTER
REVERSE MOTION
REVOLT AGAINST
REVOLVING DOOR
REWARD OFFERED
REYNARD THE FOX
RHODES SCHOLAR
RHONDDA VALLEY
RHYMED COUPLET
RIBSTON PIPPIN
RICEYMAN STEPS
RICHARD BURTON
RICHARD HEARNE
RICHARD TAUBER
RICHARD WAGNER
RICH AS CROESUS
RICHMOND GREEN
RICH OFFERINGS
RIDE A TRICYCLE
RIDE POST-HASTE
RIDE ROUGH-SHOD
RIDE THE WINNER
RIFLE PRACTICE
RIFT IN THE LUTE
RIGHT AND WRONG
RIGHT APPROACH
RIGHT AT THE END
RIGHT DECISION
RIGHT-DOWN LIAR
RIGHTFUL OWNER

RIGHTFUL SHARE
RIGHT-HAND BEND
RIGHT-HAND SIDE
RIGHT-HAND TURN
RIGHT OF ACCESS
RIGHT OF APPEAL
RIGHT OF CHOICE
RIGHT OF SEARCH
RIGHT ON THE DOT
RIGHT OPPOSITE
RIGHT REVEREND
RIGHT SHOULDER
RIGHT TO STRIKE
RIGHT TO THE END
RIGHT TO THE TOP
RIGHT UP TO DATE
RING OUT THE OLD
RIOT OF EMOTION
RIOTOUS LIVING
RISE IN DISGUST
RISE OF THE TIDE
RISE TO THE BAIT
RISING SPIRITS
RISK ONE'S MONEY
RISKY BUSINESS
RITUAL KILLING
RIVAL BUSINESS
RIVER CROSSING
RIVERSIDE WALK
ROAD DIVERSION
ROAD TO SUCCESS
ROAD TRANSPORT
ROAST CHESTNUT
ROAST POTATOES
ROBBINS REPORT
ROBERT BRIDGES
ROBERT MITCHUM
ROBERTSON HARE
ROBERT SOUTHEY
ROCKET WARFARE
ROCK THE CRADLE
ROGUE ELEPHANT
ROGUES' GALLERY
ROLL AND BUTTER
ROLLED INTO ONE
ROLLER COASTER
ROLLING IN CASH
ROLLING STONES
ROLL IN THE DUST
ROMAN ALPHABET
ROMAN CATHOLIC
ROMAN NUMERALS
ROMANTIC NOVEL
ROMANTIC SCENE
ROMANTIC STORY
ROMNEY MARSHES

RONALD CHESNEY
ROOM TO BREATHE
ROOM WITH A VIEW
ROOT AND BRANCH
ROOTED DISLIKE
ROOT OF ALL EVIL
ROOT VEGETABLE
ROPE AND PULLEY
ROTATE THE CROP
ROTTEN BOROUGH
ROUGH AND READY
ROUGH CROSSING
ROUGH CUSTOMER
ROUGH ESTIMATE
ROUGH EXTERIOR
ROUGH HANDLING
ROUGH QUARTERS
ROULETTE TABLE
ROULETTE WHEEL
ROUND-ABOUT WAY
ROUND AND ABOUT
ROUND AND ROUND
ROUNDLY ABUSED
ROUND OF DRINKS
ROUND OF GAIETY
ROUND OF VISITS
ROUND THE BLOCK
ROUND THE CLOCK
ROUND THE EARTH
ROUND THE HOUSE
ROUND THE TABLE
ROUND THE WAIST
ROUND THE WORLD
ROUSING CHEERS
ROUSING CHORUS
ROUSING SERMON
ROUTINE DUTIES
ROUTINE MATTER
ROYAL AERO CLUB
ROYAL AIR FORCE
ROYAL EXCHANGE
ROYAL FUNCTION
ROYAL HIGHNESS
ROYAL HOSPITAL
ROYAL MARRIAGE
ROYAL OCCASION
ROYAL STANDARD
RUBBER PLANTER
RUB OF THE GREEN
RUDE AWAKENING
RUGBY FOOTBALL
RUGGED COUNTRY
RUINED FOR LIFE
RUINOUS CHARGE
RULE BRITANNIA
RULE OF THE ROAD

RULING CLASSES
RULING PASSION
RUN FOR SHELTER
RUN IN THE BLOOD
RUN INTO DANGER
RUN LIKE BLAZES
RUNNING BATTLE
RUNNING BUFFET
RUNNING STREAM
RUN OF THE GREEN
RUN OF THE HOUSE
RUN ON SMOOTHLY
RUN ON THE ROCKS
RUN OUT OF FUNDS
RUN OUT OF MONEY
RUN OUT OF STEAM
RUN OUT OF WORDS
RUN THINGS FINE
RURAL DISTRICT
RURAL INDUSTRY
RUSHING STREAM
RUSH INTO PRINT
RUSSELL SQUARE
RUSSIAN BALLET
RUSSIAN LESSON

S – 13

SACRED EDIFICE
SAFE ANCHORAGE
SAFETY CURTAIN
SAFETY GLASSES
SAFETY GOGGLES
SAFETY HARNESS
SAFETY MEASURE
SAFFRON WALDEN
SAGE AND ONIONS
SAILING MASTER
SAILING ORDERS
SAILING VESSEL
SAINT AUGUSTUS
SAINT LAWRENCE
SAINT NICHOLAS
SALAD DRESSING
SALARIED CLASS
SALE BY AUCTION
SALMON FISHING
SALT AND PEPPER
SALT-WATER FISH
SALUTE THE FLAG
SALVATION ARMY
SAMUEL JOHNSON
SAND IN THE EYES
SARATOGA TRUNK
SATELLITE DISH
SATELLITE TOWN
SATURDAY NIGHT

SAUCE PIQUANTE
SAUTÉ POTATOES
SAVE ONE'S BACON
SAY BO TO A GOOSE
SCALDING TEARS
SCARCITY VALUE
SCARED TO DEATH
SCARLET RUNNER
SCARLETT O'HARA
SCENE OF STRIFE
SCENIC RAILWAY
SCHOOL EDITION
SCHOOL HOLIDAY
SCHOOL OF MUSIC
SCHOOL PREFECT
SCHOOL UNIFORM
SCIENCE MASTER
SCIENCE MUSEUM
SCIENTIFIC AGE
SCILLY ISLANDS
SCORCHED EARTH
SCORE A CENTURY
SCORE A SUCCESS
SCORING STROKE
SCOTCH AND SODA
SCOTCH TERRIER
SCRAMBLED EGGS
SCRAPE A LIVING
SCRAPE THROUGH
SCRAP MERCHANT
SCRATCH PLAYER
SCRATCH RUNNER
SCREEN VERSION
SCRIBBLED NOTE
SCRIPT WRITING
SEALED VERDICT
SEAL OF SECRECY
SEA OF TROUBLES
SEA OPERATIONS
SEARCHING LOOK
SEARCH WARRANT
SEASIDE RESORT
SEAT OF JUSTICE
SECOND ATTEMPT
SECOND CENTURY
SECOND CHAMBER
SECOND CHAPTER
SECOND EDITION
SECOND FEATURE
SECOND-HAND CAR
SECOND HELPING
SECOND HUSBAND
SECOND INNINGS
SECOND OF APRIL
SECOND OFFENCE
SECOND OFFICER

SECOND OF MARCH
SECOND OPINION
SECOND QUARTER
SECOND READING
SECOND SERVICE
SECOND TURNING
SECRET ARRIVAL
SECRETARY BIRD
SECRET FORMULA
SECRET INQUIRY
SECRET MEETING
SECRET PASSAGE
SECRET PROCESS
SECRET SERVICE
SECRET SESSION
SECRET SOCIETY
SECRET THOUGHT
SECRET WRITING
SECURE FOOTING
SECURITY CHECK
SEDENTARY LIFE
SEE FOR ONESELF
SEE HOW THEY RUN
SEEK ADVENTURE
SEEK A SOLUTION
SEEMLY CONDUCT
SEE ONE THROUGH
SEE THINGS DONE
SEIZE THE CROWN
SELECT CIRCLES
SELECT COMPANY
SELECTION LIST
SELFISH MOTIVE
SELL AT A PROFIT
SELL BY AUCTION
SELLER'S MARKET
SEMPER FIDELIS
SEND A POSTCARD
SEND A REMINDER
SEND A TELEGRAM
SEND TO JERICHO
SENIOR PARTNER
SENIOR SERVICE
SENSELESS TALK
SENSE OF DANGER
SENSE OF HUMOUR
SENSE OF INJURY
SENSE OF RELIEF
SENSE OF TIMING
SENSE OF VALUES
SENSIBLE CHILD
SENSIBLE WOMAN
SEPARATE COVER
SEPARATE ROOMS
SEPTEMBER MORN
SEPTEMBER TIDE

SERGEANT MAJOR
SERGEANTS' MESS
SERIOUS CHARGE
SERIOUS DAMAGE
SERIOUS DANGER
SERIOUS DEFEAT
SERIOUS INJURY
SERIOUS MATTER
SERIOUS PERSON
SERPENT'S TOOTH
SERVE A PURPOSE
SERVE AS A MODEL
SERVE ONE RIGHT
SERVE ONE'S TIME
SERVE ONE'S TURN
SERVE THE DEVIL
SERVE UP DINNER
SERVICE CHARGE
SERVIETTE RING
SET A NEW RECORD
SET AT DEFIANCE
SET AT VARIANCE
SET ONE'S SIGHTS
SET THE FASHION
SETTING LOTION
SETTLEMENT DAY
SEVEN AND A HALF
SEVEN DIAMONDS
SEVEN FURLONGS
SEVEN NO-TRUMPS
SEVEN OF HEARTS
SEVEN OF SPADES
SEVEN OF TRUMPS
SEVEN SLEEPERS
SEVENTH HEAVEN
SEVENTH LETTER
SEVENTH OF JULY
SEVENTH OF JUNE
SEVEN THOUSAND
SEVENTH STOREY
SEVENTH VOLUME
SEVEN-YEAR ITCH
SEVEN YEARS OLD
SEVEN YEARS' WAR
SEVERE ILLNESS
SEVERE WEATHER
SEVILLE ORANGE
SEWING MACHINE
SHADES OF NIGHT
SHADOW CABINET
SHADOW FACTORY
SHADOW OF DEATH
SHADOW OF DOUBT
SHADY BUSINESS
SHAKE ONE'S FIST
SHAKE ONE'S HEAD

SHAKE WITH COLD
SHAKE WITH FEAR
SHALLOW STREAM
SHALLOW VESSEL
SHAME THE DEVIL
SHAMPOO AND SET
SHAPELY FIGURE
SHARE EXPENSES
SHARE THE BLAME
SHARP AS A KNIFE
SHARP AS A RAZOR
SHARP FEATURES
SHARP PRACTICE
SHARP'S THE WORD
SHAVING SALOON
SHED LIGHT UPON
SHEEP AND GOATS
SHEEPSKIN COAT
SHEER NONSENSE
SHELTERED LIFE
SHELTERED SIDE
SHELTERED SPOT
SHEPHERD'S BUSH
SHEPTON MALLET
SHERATON TABLE
SHERIFF'S POSSE
SHERRY COBBLER
SHETLAND ISLES
SHIFTING SANDS
SHIFTING SCENE
SHIFT THE BLAME
SHIFT THE SCENE
SHILLING PIECE
SHILLING STAMP
SHINING ARMOUR
SHINING KNIGHT
SHIP IN A BOTTLE
SHIP OF THE LINE
SHIPPING AGENT
SHIPPING CLERK
SHIPPING ORDER
SHIP'S CHANDLER
SHIP'S CORPORAL
SHIP'S REGISTER
SHIRLEY BASSEY
SHIRLEY TEMPLE
SHOCK ABSORBER
SHOCKING STATE
SHOOTING BRAKE
SHOOTING MATCH
SHOOTING PAINS
SHOOTING PARTY
SHOOTING RANGE
SHOOT STRAIGHT
SHOOT THE WORKS
SHOP ASSISTANT

SHOP DETECTIVE
SHOPPING SPREE
SHORT AND SWEET
SHORT DISTANCE
SHORTEST NIGHT
SHORTEST ROUTE
SHORTEST WOMAN
SHORTHAND NOTE
SHORTLY BEFORE
SHORT OF BREATH
SHORT OF CHANGE
SHORT OF SPEECH
SHORT OF TALENT
SHORT SENTENCE
SHORT SYNOPSIS
SHORT-TERM LOAN
SHORT TROUSERS
SHORT VACATION
SHOT IN THE BACK
SHOT IN THE DARK
SHOULDER STRAP
SHOUTING MATCH
SHOW ANIMOSITY
SHOW DEFERENCE
SHOW FORESIGHT
SHOW NO REMORSE
SHOW NO RESPECT
SHOW ONE'S CARDS
SHOW ONE'S PACES
SHOW ONE'S TEETH
SHOW RESTRAINT
SHREDDED WHEAT
SHROPSHIRE LAD
SHROVE TUESDAY
SHUT YOUR MOUTH
SICK AS A PARROT
SICK OF WAITING
SICK UNTO DEATH
SIDE ELEVATION
SIEGFRIED LINE
SIGNAL EXAMPLE
SIGNAL FAILURE
SIGNAL SUCCESS
SIGNAL VICTORY
SIGNATURE TUNE
SIGNED ARTICLE
SIGNIFY ASSENT
SIGNIFY LITTLE
SIGN OF EMOTION
SIGN OF FATIGUE
SIGN OF SUCCESS
SIGN THE PLEDGE
SILENT CONSENT
SILENT PARTNER
SILENT PROTEST
SILENT SERVICE

SILICON VALLEY
SILK STOCKINGS
SILLY QUESTION
SILLY SYMPHONY
SILVER AND GOLD
SILVER COINAGE
SILVER JUBILEE
SILVER PLATTER
SILVER TANKARD
SILVER THIMBLE
SILVER THREADS
SILVER WEDDING
SIMON STYLITES
SIMPLE PROBLEM
SIMPLE REQUEST
SIMPLY FURIOUS
SIMPLY KILLING
SINCERELY FELT
SINGING MASTER
SING IN HARMONY
SINGLE ARTICLE
SINGLE PURPOSE
SINGLE THOUGHT
SINGLETON LEAD
SING LIKE A BIRD
SING LIKE A LARK
SING ME TO SLEEP
SING-SONG VOICE
SING THE CHORUS
SIR DON BRADMAN
SIRLOIN OF BEEF
SIR ROBERT PEEL
SISTER OF MERCY
SISTINE CHAPEL
SIT-DOWN STRIKE
SIT IN CONCLAVE
SIT IN JUDGMENT
SIT IN THE FRONT
SIT ON ONE'S TAIL
SIT ON THE FENCE
SIT ON THE FLOOR
SITTING PRETTY
SITTING TARGET
SITTING TENANT
SIX O'CLOCK NEWS
SIX OF DIAMONDS
SIXTEEN OUNCES
SIXTEENTH HOLE
SIXTH OF AUGUST
SIXTH SYMPHONY
SIXTY THOUSAND
SKELETON STAFF
SKETCHES BY BOZ
SKIING HOLIDAY
SKILLED LABOUR
SKILLED WORKER

SKINFUL OF WINE
SKIN TREATMENT
SKITTLES MATCH
SLANDER ACTION
SLANGING MATCH
SLAP AND TICKLE
SLAP IN THE FACE
SLAP ON THE BACK
SLEEPING PILLS
SLEEP LIKE A LOG
SLEEP LIKE A TOP
SLEIGHT OF HAND
SLENDER CHANCE
SLENDER INCOME
SLICK OPERATOR
SLIGHTLY BUILT
SLIGHT QUARREL
SLING ONE'S HOOK
SLIP INTO PLACE
SLIPPERY SLOPE
SLIP THE COLLAR
SLOPING GROUND
SLOW AND STEADY
SLUM CLEARANCE
SMACK ONE'S LIPS
SMALL ADDITION
SMALL BUSINESS
SMALL CAPITALS
SMALL DIVIDEND
SMALL INVESTOR
SMALL MAJORITY
SMALL OFFERING
SMALL POTATOES
SMALL PRACTICE
SMALL QUANTITY
SMART TROUSERS
SMASH TO PIECES
SMEAR CAMPAIGN
SMELLING SALTS
SMOKED HADDOCK
SMOKED SAUSAGE
SMOKE-FREE ZONE
SMOKELESS FUEL
SMOKELESS ZONE
SMOKER'S THROAT
SMOKING JACKET
SMOOTH AS GLASS
SMOOTHING IRON
SMOOTH JOURNEY
SMOOTH MANNERS
SMOOTH PASSAGE
SMOOTH SAILING
SMOOTH SURFACE
SMOOTH TEXTURE
SMUGGLED GOODS
SNOOKER PLAYER

SNOWBALL FIGHT
SOAP-BOX ORATOR
SOARING PRICES
SOBER AS A JUDGE
SOBER ESTIMATE
SOBER THOUGHTS
SOCIAL CIRCLES
SOCIAL CLIMBER
SOCIAL DEMANDS
SOCIAL EVENING
SOCIAL MACHINE
SOCIAL OUTCAST
SOCIAL PROBLEM
SOCIAL REUNION
SOCIAL SCIENCE
SOCIAL SERVICE
SOCIAL SUCCESS
SOCIAL WELFARE
SOCIETY COLUMN
SOCIETY GOSSIP
SOCIETY PEOPLE
SOFTEN THE BLOW
SOFT IN THE HEAD
SOFTWARE HOUSE
SOIL ONE'S HANDS
SOLDERING IRON
SOLDIERS THREE
SOLDIER'S TUNIC
SOLEMN PROMISE
SOLEMN SILENCE
SOLEMN WARNING
SOLE OWNERSHIP
SOLICIT ORDERS
SOLITAIRE RING
SOLOMON GRUNDY
SOLVE A PROBLEM
SOME OF THE TIME
SOME OTHER TIME
SOMERSET HOUSE
SOMETHING DONE
SOMETHING ELSE
SOMETHING LIKE
SOMETHING NICE
SOMETHING OVER
SOMETHING TO DO
SOME TIME LATER
SOMEWHERE ELSE
SONG OF SOLOMON
SONG OF THE FLEA
SONG OF TRIUMPH
SON OF A SEA COOK
SONS AND LOVERS
SOONER OR LATER
SOONEST MENDED
SOON FORGOTTEN
SOOTHING MUSIC

SOOTHING SYRUP
SOOTHING TOUCH
SOOTHING WORDS
SOP TO CERBERUS
SORRY BUSINESS
SORTING OFFICE
SORT THINGS OUT
SOUND A FANFARE
SOUND ARGUMENT
SOUND CURRENCY
SOUND DETECTOR
SOUND DOCTRINE
SOUNDING BOARD
SOUNDING BRASS
SOUND JUDGMENT
SOUND MATERIAL
SOUND ONE'S HORN
SOUND THE ALARM
SOURCE OF LIGHT
SOURCE OF POWER
SOURCE OF PRIDE
SOUR SUBSTANCE
SOUSED HERRING
SOUTH CAROLINA
SOUTH CHINA SEA
SOUTH-EAST WIND
SOUTHERN CROSS
SOUTHERN STATE
SOUTH OF FRANCE
SPANISH ARMADA
SPANISH GUITAR
SPANISH LESSON
SPANISH ONIONS
SPARE A THOUGHT
SPARE NO EFFORT
SPARKLING WINE
SPARK OF GENIUS
SPARTAN REGIME
SPEAK AT LENGTH
SPEAKER'S NOTES
SPEAKING TERMS
SPEAKING VOICE
SPEAK ONE'S MIND
SPEAK THE TRUTH
SPECIAL BRANCH
SPECIAL FAVOUR
SPECIAL FRIEND
SPECIAL NUMBER
SPECIAL PRAYER
SPECIAL SCHOOL
SPECIFIED DOSE
SPECK OF COLOUR
SPECTACLE CASE
SPEECH THERAPY
SPEED MERCHANT
SPEEDWAY TRACK

SPELL DISASTER
SPEND A FORTUNE
SPENDING MONEY
SPENDING POWER
SPENDING SPREE
SPIKE MILLIGAN
SPIKE ONE'S GUNS
SPILL THE BEANS
SPINNING JENNY
SPINNING WHEEL
SPIN THE COIN
SPIRITED REPLY
SPIRIT OF YOUTH
SPIRITUAL LIFE
SPIRITUAL PEER
SPIRITUAL SELF
SPIRITUAL SONG
SPIRIT WRITING
SPIT AND POLISH
SPITEFUL WOMAN
SPITTING IMAGE
SPLINTER GROUP
SPLINTER PARTY
SPLIT DECISION
SPLITTING HEAD
SPOILT DARLING
SPOIL THE CHILD
SPORTING EVENT
SPORTING GOODS
SPORTING OFFER
SPORTING PRESS
SPORTING PRINT
SPORTING RIFLE
SPORTING WORLD
SPORTS EDITION
SPORTS STADIUM
SPOT OF TROUBLE
SPOT THE WINNER
SPRAINED ANKLE
SPREAD A RUMOUR
SPREAD THE LOAD
SPREAD THE NEWS
SPRING BALANCE
SPRING BLOSSOM
SPRING CHICKEN
SPRING FLOWERS
SPRING MADNESS
SPRING MEETING
SPRING THE TRAP
SPRING THROUGH
SPY OUT THE LAND
SQUARE BASHING
SQUARE MEASURE
SQUASH RACKETS
SQUIRE OF DAMES
STAB IN THE BACK

STACK THE CARDS
STAFF ENTRANCE
STAFF OF OFFICE
STAFF PROBLEMS
STAFF SERGEANT
STAGGERING SUM
STAKE ONE'S LIFE
STAMP OF GENIUS
STAND AND FIGHT
STAND AND STARE
STANDARD BREAD
STANDARD GAUGE
STANDARD MODEL
STANDARD PRICE
STANDARD USAGE
STANDING ORDER
STANDING START
STAND IN THE WAY
STAND ON TIPTOE
STAND OPPOSITE
STAND OUT A MILE
STAND PREPARED
STAND TOGETHER
STAND TO REASON
STANLEY LUPINO
STAR AND GARTER
STARBOARD BEAM
STARBOARD SIDE
STAR OF THE SHOW
STAR PERFORMER
START A QUARREL
STARTING POINT
STARTING PRICE
START LAUGHING
STARTLING NEWS
STAR TREATMENT
START THINKING
START TO FINISH
START TOGETHER
STATE BOUNDARY
STATE CARRIAGE
STATE CRIMINAL
STATE FUNCTION
STATE MONOPOLY
STATE OCCASION
STATE OF FRENZY
STATE OF NATURE
STATE OF REASON
STATE OF UNREST
STATE ONE'S CASE
STATE PRISONER
STATE RELIGION
STATIC WARFARE
STATION IN LIFE
STATION MASTER
STATUTORY MILE

STAY OVERNIGHT
STAY THE COURSE
STAY UNMARRIED
ST BARTHOLOMEW
ST BERNARD PASS
ST CRISPIN'S DAY
STEADY ADVANCE
STEADY AS A ROCK
STEAK AND CHIPS
STEAL A MARCH ON
STEEL INDUSTRY
STEERAGE CLASS
STEERING WHEEL
STEP OUT OF LINE
STEPTOE AND SON
STERLING WORTH
STERN MEASURES
STEVE DONOGHUE
STICKING POINT
STICK IN THE MUD
STICK LIKE GLUE
STICK OF CELERY
STICK OUT A MILE
STICK TOGETHER
STICKY PROBLEM
STIFF AND STARK
STIFF AS A BOARD
STIFF AS A POKER
STIFF SENTENCE
STIFF UPPER-LIP
STILETTO HEELS
STILL LEMONADE
STILTON CHEESE
STIR IN THE WIND
STIRRING MUSIC
STIRRING TIMES
STIR THE EMBERS
STIR UP TROUBLE
STOCK EXCHANGE
STOCK QUESTION
STOLEN ARTICLE
STOLE THE TARTS
STOMACH POWDER
STONE THE CROWS!
STOP AT NOTHING
STOP BREATHING
STOPPING PLACE
STOPPING TRAIN
STOP-PRESS NEWS
STORMY MEETING
STORMY PASSAGE
STORMY SESSION
STORMY WEATHER
ST PATRICK'S DAY
ST PAUL'S SCHOOL
STRAIGHT ACTOR

STRAIGHT AHEAD
STRAIGHT ANGLE
STRAIGHT DRAMA
STRAIGHT DRIVE
STRAIGHTEN OUT
STRAIGHT FIGHT
STRAIGHT FLUSH
STRAIGHT RIGHT
STRAIN AT A GNAT
STRAIN ONESELF
STRAIN THE EYES
STRAIT OF DOVER
STRANGE DEVICE
STRANGE GROUND
STRANGE MANNER
STRAPPING GIRL
STRAWBERRY BED
STRAWBERRY ICE
STRAWBERRY JAM
STRAWBERRY TEA
STRAW MATTRESS
STRAY CUSTOMER
STRAY FROM HOME
STREAK OF LIGHT
STREAMING COLD
STREAM OF BLOOD
STREAM OF LIGHT
STREAM OF TEARS
STREAM OF WATER
STREET BETTING
STREET CLOTHES
STRESS THE FACT
STRETCH A POINT
STRETCHER CASE
STRETCH OF LAND
STRETCH OF ROAD
STRICT INQUIRY
STRICTLY LEGAL
STRICT PARENTS
STRIKE IT LUCKY
STRIKE THE BALL
STRIKE THE FLAG
STRIKE THE HOUR
STRIKE UP A TUNE
STRIKING CLOCK
STRIKING FORCE
STRING OF BEADS
STRING OF NAMES
STRING OF OATHS
STRING QUARTET
STRIP LIGHTING
STRONG AS A LION
STRONG BACKING
STRONG CURRENT
STRONG DEFENCE
STRONG DISLIKE

STRONG EMOTION
STRONG FEELING
STRONG GROUNDS
STRONG PROTEST
STRONG REQUEST
STRONG STOMACH
STRONG SUPPORT
STRONG SWIMMER
STRUGGLE ALONG
ST SWITHIN'S DAY
STUDENT PRINCE
STUDY ALL SIDES
STUDY MEDICINE
STUDY THE FACTS
STUDY THE PLANS
STUDY THE STARS
STUFFED MARROW
STUFFED OLIVES
STUFFED TURKEY
STUMBLE ACROSS
STUNG TO ACTION
STUNTED GROWTH
ST VITUS'S DANCE
SUBJECT MATTER
SUBJECT TO DUTY
SUB-MACHINE GUN
SUBMARINE BASE
SUBMARINE CREW
SUBMIT A REPORT
SUBURBAN HOUSE
SUBURBAN VILLA
SUCCESSFUL MAN
SUCCESS SYMBOL
SUCK ONE'S THUMB
SUDDEN DISLIKE
SUDDEN IMPULSE
SUDDEN THOUGHT
SUE FOR DAMAGES
SUE FOR DIVORCE
SUFFER A STROKE
SUFFER DAMAGES
SUFFERING CATS!
SUFFER TORMENT
SUGAR AND SPICE
SUGARED ALMOND
SUGARLESS DIET
SUGAR REFINERY
SUGGESTION BOX
SUICIDAL MANIA
SUITABLE MATCH
SUIT OF CLOTHES
SULPHURIC ACID
SULTAN'S PALACE
SUMMER HOLIDAY
SUMMER MADNESS
SUMMER SESSION

SUMMER VISITOR
SUMMIT MEETING
SUNBURN LOTION
SUNDAY CLOSING
SUNDAY CLOTHES
SUNDAY EVENING
SUNDAY MORNING
SUNDAY SERVICE
SUN-DRIED BRICK
SUNK IN DESPAIR
SUPERIOR BEING
SUPERIOR COURT
SUPERIOR FORCE
SUPREME SOVIET
SURE OF ONESELF
SURE OF SUCCESS
SURFACE RAIDER
SURGEON'S KNIFE
SURGICAL KNIFE
SURPLUS ENERGY
SURPRISE PARTY
SURPRISE VISIT
SURTAX BRACKET
SUSPECT A TRICK
SUSPENDER BELT
SUSTAINED NOTE
SWANEE WHISTLE
SWAP AND CHANGE
SWAY IN THE WIND
SWEATED LABOUR
SWEEPING CLAIM
SWEEPING GAINS
SWEEP THE BOARD
SWEEP THE FLOOR
SWEET CHESTNUT
SWEET LAVENDER
SWEET NOTHING
SWEET SURPRISE
SWEET THOUGHTS
SWEET TO THE EAR
SWELLING SAILS
SWELL THE RANKS
SWELTERING SUN
SWIM LIKE A FISH
SWIMMING MATCH
SWING ONE'S ARMS
SWORN EVIDENCE
SYDNEY HARBOUR
SYMPHONIC POEM

T – 13

TABLEAU VIVANT
TABLE DELICACY
TABLE MOUNTAIN
TAKE A BACK SEAT

TAKE A BREATHER	TALK OF THE TOWN
TAKE ADVANTAGE	TALK OUT OF TURN
TAKE A FIRM HOLD	TALK PRIVATELY
TAKE A HIGH TONE	TALK TO ONESELF
TAKE A LONG TIME	TANGIBLE ASSET
TAKE AN AVERAGE	TANKARD OF BEER
TAKE A SHORT CUT	TANKARD OF MILD
TAKE A SNAPSHOT	TAN THE HIDE OFF
TAKE BY THE HAND	TAPE RECORDING
TAKE DICTATION	TAP ONE'S CLARET
TAKE EXCEPTION	TAR AND FEATHER
TAKE FOR GOSPEL	TASTE FOR MUSIC
TAKE GREAT CARE	TAUGHT A LESSON
TAKE IN BAD PART	TAURUS THE BULL
TAKE IN LODGERS	TAWNY COLOURED
TAKE IN WASHING	TAXABLE INCOME
TAKE IT IN TURNS	TAX CONCESSION
TAKE IT TO COURT	TAX ONE'S MEMORY
TAKE IT TO HEART	TEACHING STAFF
TAKE LIBERTIES	TEACH SWIMMING
TAKEN AT RANDOM	TEAM OF EXPERTS
TAKEN DOWN A PEG	TEA PLANTATION
TAKEN FOR A RIDE	TEAR OFF A STRIP
TAKE NO CHANCES	TEARS OF SORROW
TAKE NO REFUSAL	TEAR TO RIBBONS
TAKEN PRISONER	TEAR UP THE ROAD
TAKEN UNAWARES	TECHNICAL TERM
TAKE OFF WEIGHT	TELEGRAPH LINE
TAKE ONE'S FANCY	TELEGRAPH POLE
TAKE ONE'S LEAVE	TELEGRAPH POST
TAKE ONE'S PLACE	TELEGRAPH WIRE
TAKE ONE'S PULSE	TELEPHONE BILL
TAKE ONE'S STAND	TELEPHONE BOOK
TAKE OUT TRUMPS	TELEPHONE CALL
TAKE SANCTUARY	TELEPHONE LINE
TAKE SERIOUSLY	TELEPHOTO LENS
TAKE SHORTHAND	TELEVISION FAN
TAKE SOUNDINGS	TELEVISION SET
TAKE THE CREDIT	TELL A GOOD TALE
TAKE THE DAY OFF	TELL A GOOD YARN
TAKE THE MICKEY	TELL AN UNTRUTH
TAKE THE PLEDGE	TELL AT A GLANCE
TAKE THE PLUNGE	TELLING EFFECT
TAKE THE SALUTE	TELL ME ANOTHER
TAKE THE STRAIN	TELL ONE'S BEADS
TAKE THE TILLER	TEMPERATE ZONE
TAKE THE WATERS	TEMPER THE WIND
TAKE TO ONE'S BED	TEMPLE OF DIANA
TAKE TO THE ROAD	TEMPORAL POWER
TALENT CONTEST	TEMPORARY HOME
TALENT SPOTTER	TEMPORARY LEAD
TALK FOR EFFECT	TEMPORARY LOAN
TALK GIBBERISH	TEMPORARY RANK
TALKING PARROT	TEMPORARY STOP
TALK IN RIDDLES	TEMPTING OFFER
TALK LIKE A FOOL	TEMPT THE DEVIL

TENANT FOR LIFE
TEN CIGARETTES
TENDER FEELING
TENDER MERCIES
TENDER PASSION
TEN-DOLLAR BILL
TENEMENT HOUSE
TEN OF DIAMONDS
TENOR CLARINET
TENPIN BOWLING
TENTH OF AUGUST
TEPID RESPONSE
TERMINAL POINT
TERRIBLE CHILD
TERRIBLE HAVOC
TERRIBLE TWINS
TERRIFIC STORM
TERRORIST ARMY
TERRORIST BAND
TEST-BAN TREATY
TEST CRICKETER
THANE OF CAWDOR
THANK GOODNESS!
THANKLESS TASK
THE ABDICATION
THEATRE CRITIC
THEATRE SISTER
THEATRE TICKET
THE BARBARIANS
THE BEST OF LUCK
THE BEST PEOPLE
THE BIG BAD WOLF
THE BLUE DANUBE
THE CHALLENGER
THE CHARLESTON
THE COLLECTION
THE COMMON HERD
THE DEEPEST DYE
THE DEUCE TO PAY
THE DEVIL TO PAY
THE DIRECT ROAD
THE DOLL'S HOUSE
THE EISTEDDFOD
THE EMBANKMENT
THE FIRST TRAIN
THE FIRST WATER
THE FOOTLIGHTS
THE GIDDY LIMIT
THE GOLDEN RULE
THE GONDOLIERS
THE GOVERNMENT
THE GUILLOTINE
THE HONOURABLE
THE INS AND OUTS
THE ISRAELITES
THE JOY STRINGS

THE KERRY DANCE
THE LAST SUPPER
THE LAW IS AN ASS
THE LIBERATION
THE LIGHT BLUES
THE MAGIC FLUTE
THE MAIN CHANCE
THE MATTERHORN
THE MERRY WIDOW
THE METROPOLIS
THE MILLENNIUM
THE MOODY BLUES
THE NOES HAVE IT
THE NORTH DOWNS
THE OLD BRIGADE
THE OLD COUNTRY
THE OPPOSITION
THE OTHER WOMAN
THE OTHER WORLD
THE QUAKER GIRL
THE RESISTANCE
THE ROUNDHEADS
THE SAME ANSWER
THE SCOTS GREYS
THE SECOND-RATE
THE SERPENTINE
THE SHALLOW END
THE SIMPLE LIFE
THE SMALL HOURS
THE SNOW MAIDEN
THE SOUTH DOWNS
THE SPOKEN WORD
THE THREE BEARS
THE TIME IS RIPE
THE TWO RONNIES
THE UNDERWORLD
THE UNEMPLOYED
THE UNEXPECTED
THE UNFORESEEN
THE VANQUISHED
THE VIGILANTES
THE WATER-WAGON
THE WHITE HOUSE
THE WHOLE TRUTH
THE WHOLE WORLD
THE WILDERNESS
THE WILL TO LIVE
THE WINSLOW BOY
THE WIZARD OF OZ
THICK WITH DUST
THIEF OF BAGDAD
THING OF BEAUTY
THINK BETTER OF
THINK LITTLE OF
THINK STRAIGHT
THINK THE WORST

THIRD DIVIDEND
THIRD DIVISION
THIRD ENGINEER
THIRD OF AUGUST
THIRD SYMPHONY
THIRTEEN HOURS
THIRTEEN MILES
THIRTEEN TIMES
THIRTEEN WEEKS
THIRTEEN YEARS
THIRTY FIFTEEN
THIRTY GUINEAS
THIRTY MINUTES
THIRTY-ONE DAYS
THIRTY PER CENT
THIRTY SECONDS
THIS LITTLE PIG
THIS WEDNESDAY
THOMAS À BECKET
THOMAS BEECHAM
THOMAS CARLYLE
THORNY PROBLEM
THORNY SUBJECT
THOROUGH ROGUE
THOSE IN FAVOUR
THOUSAND MILES
THOUSAND YEARS
THREAD A NEEDLE
THREAD ONE'S WAY
THREE AND A HALF
THREE BAGS FULL
THREE-DAY MATCH
THREE DIAMONDS
THREE FEET TALL
THREE-FOOT RULE
THREE FURLONGS
THREE-LINE WHIP
THREE NO-TRUMPS
THREE OF HEARTS
THREE OF SPADES
THREE OF TRUMPS
THREE QUARTERS
THREE SEVENTHS
THREE THOUSAND
THRICE BLESSED
THROES OF AGONY
THROUGH A STRAW
THROW A LIGHT ON
THROW IN THE AIR
THUMB ONE'S NOSE
THUMP THE TABLE
THURSDAY NIGHT
TICHBORNE CASE
TICKET MACHINE
TICKET OF LEAVE
TICKETS PLEASE

TIDAL MOVEMENT
TIDE OF AFFAIRS
TIED UP IN KNOTS
TIE WITH STRING
TILT AT THE RING
TILT THE SCALES
TIME AFTER TIME
TIME AND MOTION
TIME FOR DINNER
TIME FOR SUPPER
TIMELY RETREAT
TIMELY WARNING
TIME MARCHES ON
TIME OF ARRIVAL
TIME OUT OF MIND
TIMES OF STRESS
TIME TO REFLECT
TIMID AS A MOUSE
TIMON OF ATHENS
TINNED PEACHES
TIN OF SARDINES
TIP-AND-RUN RAID
TIP ONE THE WINK
TIPPED THE WINK
TIRED OF LIVING
TIRESOME CHORE
TITLE OF HONOUR
TOAD IN THE HOLE
TO A HIGH DEGREE
TOASTED CHEESE
TO BE CONTINUED
TO BE OR NOT TO BE
TOGETHER AGAIN
TOKEN OF ESTEEM
TOLL OF THE ROAD
TOMATO KETCHUP
TOMORROW NIGHT
TOMORROW WE DIE
TONGUE IN CHEEK
TONGUE OF FLAME
TONGUE TWISTER
TONGUE WAGGING
TOO GOOD BY HALF
TOO GOOD TO LAST
TOO LITTLE ROOM
TOO MUCH PEPPER
TOOTING COMMON
TOO WEAK TO RISE
TOP OF THE CLASS
TOP OF THE SCALE
TOP OF THE TABLE
TOP-SECRET FILE
TORE OFF A STRIP
TORRENT OF RAIN
TO SOME PURPOSE
TOSTI'S 'GOODBYE'

TOTAL DARKNESS
TO THE BACKBONE
TOUCHING SCENE
TOUCH OF COLOUR
TOUCH OF GARLIC
TOUCH OF GENIUS
TOUCH OF NATURE
TOUCH OF THE SUN
TOUCH ONE'S TOES
TOUCH ON THE RAW
TOUCH THE HEART
TOUGH CUSTOMER
TOURIST AGENCY
TOURIST CENTRE
TOURIST SEASON
TOURIST TICKET
TOURIST TROPHY
TOUR OF BRITAIN
TOUT FOR CUSTOM
TOWER OF LONDON
TOWN AND AROUND
TOY WITH AN IDEA
TRACTOR DRIVER
TRADE DISCOUNT
TRADE ENTRANCE
TRADE MAGAZINE
TRADE UNIONIST
TRADING CENTRE
TRADING ESTATE
TRADING VESSEL
TRAFFIC ISLAND
TRAFFIC LIGHTS
TRAFFIC SIGNAL
TRAFFIC WARDEN
TRAIL ONE'S COAT
TRAINED SINGER
TRAIN OF CAMELS
TRAIN OF EVENTS
TRAIN SPOTTING
TRAIN TERMINUS
TRAITOR'S DEATH
TRAM CONDUCTOR
TRANQUIL SCENE
TRANSISTOR SET
TRANSPORT CAFÉ
TRAPEZE ARTIST
TRAVEL BY TRAIN
TRAVELLER'S JOY
TRAVEL LIGHTLY
TREACLE TOFFEE
TREAD THE STAGE
TREASURE CHEST
TREASURE HOUSE
TREASURE TRAIL
TREASURE TROVE
TREASURY BENCH

TREASURY BILLS
TREASURY BONDS
TREAT LIKE DIRT
TREAT WITH CARE
TREE OF LIBERTY
TREMENDOUS JOB
TRENCH WARFARE
TREND OF EVENTS
TRIAL AND ERROR
TRIAL MARRIAGE
TRIBAL WARFARE
TRICK QUESTION
TRICKY PROBLEM
TRIFLING ERROR
TRIGGER FINGER
TRILLING SOUND
TRINITY CHURCH
TRIUMPHAL ARCH
TRIVIAL MATTER
TROPICAL FRUIT
TROPICAL PLANT
TROPICAL STORM
TROTTING RACES
TROUSER BUTTON
TRUE CRITERION
TRUE STATEMENT
TRUE TO HIS SALT
TRUE TO ONESELF
TRUE TO THE LAST
TRUE UNTO DEATH
TRULY GRATEFUL
TRULY GREAT MAN
TRUMPET PLAYER
TRUST ACCOUNTS
TRUST TO CHANCE
TRUSTY SERVANT
TRYING JOURNEY
TRYSTING PLACE
TRYSTING POINT
TUBE OF MUSTARD
TUESDAY'S CHILD
TUNNEL THROUGH
TURKISH COFFEE
TURN A BLIND EYE
TURN CLOCKWISE
TURN DOWNWARDS
TURNED TO STONE
TURNING WICKET
TURN INSIDE OUT
TURN INTO MONEY
TURN OFF THE GAS
TURN OFF THE TAP
TURN OF THE CARD
TURN OF THE TIDE
TURN ON THE HEAT
TURN THE CORNER

TURN THE HEAT ON
TURN THE TABLES
TURN TO ACCOUNT
TURN TO THE LEFT
TURQUOISE BLUE
TWEED TROUSERS
TWELFTH LETTER
TWELFTH OF JULY
TWELFTH OF JUNE
TWELVE DOLLARS
TWELVE GOOD MEN
TWELVE GUINEAS
TWELVE MINUTES
TWELVE PER CENT
TWELVE SQUARED
TWENTY DOLLARS
TWENTY GUINEAS
TWENTY MINUTES
TWENTY-ONE DAYS
TWENTY PER CENT
TWICE-TOLD TALE
TWILIGHT SLEEP
TWINKLING EYES
TWINKLING FEET
TWINKLING STAR
TWIST AND SHAKE
TWIST AND TWIRL
TWISTED NATURE
TWIST THE WORDS
TWO-EDGED SWORD
TWO-LETTER WORD
TWO-MASTED SHIP
TWO OF DIAMONDS
TWOS AND THREES
TWO-TIERED CAKE
TWO-WAY STRETCH
TWO-WAY TRAFFIC

U – 13

UGLY SITUATION
ULTERIOR PLANS
ULTIMATE CAUSE
UMBILICAL CORD
UMBRELLA STAND
UNABLE TO PLEAD
UNANIMOUS VOTE
UNARMED COMBAT
UNATTACHED MAN
UNBOLT THE DOOR
UNBOUNDED LOVE
UNBROKEN FRONT
UNBROKEN HORSE
UNCROWNED KING
UNDATED CHEQUE
UNDECLARED WAR

UNDER CONTRACT
UNDER-COVER MAN
UNDER MILK WOOD
UNDER ONE'S NOSE
UNDER ONE'S SKIN
UNDER ONE'S WING
UNDER PRESSURE
UNDER SENTENCE
UNDER STRENGTH
UNDER THE KNIFE
UNDER THE TABLE
UNDER THE THUMB
UNDER TRAINING
UNDER TWO FLAGS
UNDUE PRESSURE
UNEASY FEELING
UNEVEN CONTEST
UNEVEN SURFACE
UNFAIR PICTURE
UNFAIR VERDICT
UNFRIENDLY ACT
UNFURL THE FLAG
UNGUARDED HOUR
UNHAPPY REMARK
UNIFORM WEIGHT
UNIONIST PARTY
UNION JACK CLUB
UNITED IN DEATH
UNITED KINGDOM
UNITED NATIONS
UNITED WE STAND
UNIT OF CURRENT
UNIVERSAL AUNT
UNIVERSAL BUTT
UNIVERSITY RAG
UNKIND THOUGHT
UNKNOWN ORIGIN
UNKNOWN PERSON
UNLAWFUL ENTRY
UNLOCK THE DOOR
UNLUCKY CHOICE
UNLUCKY COLOUR
UNLUCKY IN LOVE
UNLUCKY NUMBER
UNLUCKY PERSON
UNPAID SERVANT
UNSECURED DEBT
UNSECURED LOAN
UNSEEN DANGERS
UNSKILLED WORK
UNSOLVED CRIME
UNTIMELY DEATH
UNTOLD NUMBERS
UNVEIL A STATUE
UNWANTED CHILD
UNWORTHY CAUSE

UP AT CAMBRIDGE
UP BOYS AND AT 'EM
UP IN THE CLOUDS
UP IN THE SADDLE
UPPER REGISTER
UPRIGHT FELLOW
UPRIGHT FIGURE
UPRIGHT PERSON
UP THE MOUNTAIN
UP TO HIS TRICKS
UP TO SOMETHING
UP TO THE ELBOWS
UP TO THE MINUTE
UPTURNED GLASS
UP WITH THE DAWN
UP WITH THE LARK
URBAN DISTRICT
USEFUL PURPOSE
USEFUL STAND-BY
USE OF BATHROOM
USE ONE'S BRAINS
USUAL CHANNELS
USUAL QUESTION
UTTER CONTEMPT
UTTER DEVOTION
UTTER NONSENSE

V – 13

VACUUM CLEANER
VALENTINE CARD
VALENTINE'S DAY
VALE OF EVESHAM
VALIANT EFFORT
VALID ARGUMENT
VALID CONTRACT
VALLEY OF DEATH
VALUE FOR MONEY
VALUE ONE'S LIFE
VALUE RECEIVED
VANTAGE GROUND
VARIABLE WINDS
VARICOSE VEINS
VARIETY ARTIST
VARNISHING DAY
VAUDEVILLE ACT
VAULTING HORSE
VAULT OF HEAVEN
VEAL AND HAM PIE
VEER TO THE LEFT
VEGETABLE DIET
VEGETABLE DISH
VEGETABLE LIFE
VEGETABLE SOUP
VENERABLE BEDE
VENETIAN BLIND

VENETIAN GLASS
VENOMOUS SNAKE
VERBAL QUIBBLE
VERNAL EQUINOX
VERSATILE MIND
VERTICAL PLANE
VERY DIFFERENT
VESSEL OF WRATH
VETERAN TROOPS
VEXED IN SPIRIT
VEXED QUESTION
VICIOUS CIRCLE
VICIOUS GOSSIP
VICTOR HERBERT
VICTORIA CROSS
VICTORIA FALLS
VICTORIAN DAYS
VICTORY PARADE
VIDEO CASSETTE
VIDEO RECORDER
VIENNESE GLASS
VIENNESE WALTZ
VILLAGE BEAUTY
VILLAGE CHURCH
VILLAGE GOSSIP
VILLAGE SCHOOL
VILLAGE SMITHY
VILLAGE SQUIRE
VILLAGE STREET
VINEGARY SMILE
VIOLATE THE LAW
VIOLENT ATTACK
VIOLENT CHANGE
VIOLENT EFFORT
VIOLENT NATURE
VIOLENT SPEECH
VIOLENT TEMPER
VIOLIN RECITAL
VIRGINIA STOCK
VIRGINIA WATER
VIRGINIA WOOLF
VIRGIN ISLANDS
VIRULENT ABUSE
VISIBLE EFFECT
VISITING HOURS
VISITING TERMS
VISUAL DISPLAY
VITAL QUESTION
VITAMIN TABLET
VOICE OF REASON
VOICE TRAINING
VOID OF FEELING
VOLLEY OF ABUSE
VOLUME CONTROL
VOLUME OF SMOKE
VOLUNTARY ARMY

VOLUNTARY GIFT
VOLUNTARY WORK
VOLUNTEER ARMY
VOTED A FAILURE
VOTE OF CENSURE
VOTES FOR WOMEN
VULGAR DISPLAY

W – 13

WAG ONE'S FINGER
WAIT FOR ORDERS
WAIT PATIENTLY
WALK BACKWARDS
WALKING-ON PART
WALK INTO A TRAP
WALK THE BOARDS
WALK UP AND DOWN
WALLOW IN MONEY
WALLS HAVE EARS
WALTER PIDGEON
WALTER RALEIGH
WANDERING MIND
WANTED ON BOARD
WANT OF COURAGE
WANT OF THOUGHT
WAR DEPARTMENT
WARDOUR STREET
WARLIKE HABITS
WARLIKE MANNER
WARLIKE PEOPLE
WARM RECEPTION
WARNING NOTICE
WARNING SIGNAL
WAR TO THE DEATH
WAR TO THE KNIFE
WASHING POWDER
WASH ONE'S HANDS
WASH THE DISHES
WASPISH NATURE
WASTE OF BREATH
WATCH AND CHAIN
WATCH EXPENSES
WATCHING BRIEF
WATCH ONE'S STEP
WATCH THE BIRDY
WATCH THE CLOCK
WATERING PLACE
WATER SHORTAGE
WATER SOFTENER
WATLING STREET
WAVE OF FEELING
WAVE OF THE HAND
WAY OF ALL FLESH
WAY OF THE CROSS
WAY OF THE WORLD

WAY OF THINKING
WAYSIDE TAVERN
WAY TO THE STARS
WEAK AS A KITTEN
WEAK CHARACTER
WEAK IN THE HEAD
WEAK ON HIS PINS
WEATHER BUREAU
WEATHER EXPERT
WEATHER REPORT
WEB OF INTRIGUE
WEDGWOOD CHINA
WEDNESDAY WEEK
WEED THE GARDEN
WEEK AFTER NEXT
WEEK AFTER WEEK
WEEK IN, WEEK OUT
WEEKLY ACCOUNT
WEEKLY PAYMENT
WEEK OF SUNDAYS
WEEKS AND WEEKS
WEEPING WILLOW
WEIGH THINGS UP
WEIGHTY MATTER
WELCOME RELIEF
WELFARE CENTRE
WELFARE WORKER
WELL-AIMED SHOT
WELL BROUGHT UP
WELL-KNIT FRAME
WELL PRESERVED
WELL-SPENT LIFE
WELL THOUGHT OF
WELL TO THE FORE
WELL TURNED OUT
WELSH REGIMENT
WENT LIKE A BOMB
WENT TO THE DOGS
WESTERLY WINDS
WESTERN CHURCH
WESTERN DESERT
WESTERN EUROPE
WESTERN POWERS
WEST HAM UNITED
WEST OF ENGLAND
WEST SIDE STORY
WHAT DO YOU KNOW?
WHATEVER YOU DO
WHIRLING ROUND
WHISKY AND SODA
WHISPER SOFTLY
WHITE AS A GHOST
WHITE AS A SHEET
WHITE AS MARBLE
WHITE ELEPHANT
WHITE FLANNELS

WHITE HORSE INN
WHITE OF THE EYE
WHITE SAPPHIRE
WHOLE OF THE DAY
WHOLESOME FOOD
WHOOPING COUGH
WIDE INTERESTS
WIDE KNOWLEDGE
WIDE OF THE MARK
WIDE PUBLICITY
WIDOW'S PENSION
WIELD THE BATON
WILD AND WOOLLY
WILD-CAT STRIKE
WILDEST DREAMS
WILFUL SILENCE
WILLIAM CAXTON
WILLIAM COWPER
WILLIAM MORRIS
WILLIAM WALTON
WILLING HELPER
WILLING WORKER
WILL OF ONE'S OWN
WILLOW PATTERN
WILLOWY FIGURE
WIMPOLE STREET
WINDING COURSE
WINDING STAIRS
WINDOW CLEANER
WINDOW DRESSER
WINDOW SHOPPER
WINDSOR CASTLE
WINED AND DINED
WIN FIRST PRIZE
WING COMMANDER
WINGED MONSTER
WINGED VICTORY
WINNIE THE POOH
WINNING COUPON
WINNING DOUBLE
WINNING HAZARD
WINNING NUMBER
WINNING STREAK
WINNING STROKE
WINNING TICKET
WINNING TREBLE
WINTER GARDENS
WINTER HOLIDAY
WINTER SESSION
WINTER VISITOR
WINTER WEATHER
WIN THE JACKPOT
WINTRY WEATHER
WIPE OFF THE MAP
WIPE ONE'S HANDS
WIRED FOR SOUND

WIRELESS WAVES
WISE AS SOLOMON
WISH OTHERWISE
WITH A BAD GRACE
WITH A FLOURISH
WITH A HIGH HAND
WITH AUTHORITY
WITH BOTH HANDS
WITH CERTAINTY
WITHERING LOOK
WITHIN EARSHOT
WITHIN HEARING
WITHIN MEASURE
WITH ONE ACCORD
WITHOUT A DOUBT
WITHOUT A HITCH
WITHOUT A RIVAL
WITHOUT CHARGE
WITHOUT MALICE
WITHOUT NOTICE
WITHOUT NUMBER
WITHOUT REASON
WITHOUT REGARD
WITHOUT REMARK
WITHOUT WARMTH
WITHOUT WEIGHT
WITH RESTRAINT
WITH THE LID OFF
WITH THE STREAM
WOLF AT THE DOOR
WOLF IN THE FOLD
WONDERFUL NEWS
WOOD ENGRAVING
WOOLLEN GLOVES
WORD IN ONE'S EAR
WORD OF COMFORT
WORD OF COMMAND
WORD OF WARNING
WORDS AND MUSIC
WORDS OF WISDOM
WORD TO THE WISE
WORDY ARGUMENT
WORK LIKE MAGIC
WORKMEN'S TRAIN
WORK OF FICTION
WORK ONE'S WAY UP
WORK THE ORACLE
WORK UP A LATHER
WORK WITH A WILL
WORLD CHAMPION
WORLDLY WISDOM
WORLD OF NATURE
WORLD PREMIÈRE
WORLD-WIDE FAME
WORM ONE'S WAY IN
WORN TO A SHADOW

WORSE AND WORSE
WORSE THAN EVER
WORST POSSIBLE
WORTH A FORTUNE
WORTH A MILLION
WORTHLESS JUNK
WORTH MILLIONS
WORTH ONE'S SALT
WORTH VISITING
WOW AND FLUTTER
WRAPPING PAPER
WRITE AT LENGTH
WRITE IN PENCIL
WRITE ONE'S NAME
WRITHE IN AGONY
WRITTEN ANSWER
WRITTEN MATTER
WRITTEN PERMIT
WRITTEN SPEECH
WRONG APPROACH
WRONG DECISION
WRONG TENDENCY

X – 13

X-RAY APPARATUS

Y – 13

YARDS AND YARDS
YEAR AFTER YEAR
YEAR IN, YEAR OUT
YEHUDI MENUHIN
YELLOW BUNTING
YELLOW WAGTAIL
YELLOW WITH AGE
YEOMAN SERVICE
YORKSHIRE POST
YOUNG CHILDREN
YOUNGER SISTER
YOUNGEST CHILD
YOUNG HOOLIGAN
YOUR NUMBER'S UP
YOUTH MOVEMENT

Z – 13

ZEBRA CROSSING

A – 14

A BOOK AT BEDTIME
ABOVE CRITICISM
ABOVE SUSPICION
ABOVE THE GROUND
A BOW AT A VENTURE

ABRAHAM LINCOLN
ABRUPT ENTRANCE
ABSOLUTE DECREE
ABSOLUTE MASTER
ABSOLUTE PIFFLE
ABSTRACT DESIGN
ABSTRACT NUMBER
ABUSE ONE'S POWER
ACADEMIC DEGREE
ACADEMIC MANNER
ACCESSIBLE SPOT
ACCIDENT POLICY
ACCORDING TO LAW
ACCORDION PLEAT
ACCUSATIVE CASE
ACCUSING FINGER
ACHIEVE ONE'S AIM
ACHIEVE VICTORY
ACHILLES' TENDON
ACROSS THE OCEAN
ACROSS THE RIVER
ACT ACCORDINGLY
ACT AS A LANDMARK
ACT AS GUARANTOR
ACT IMMEDIATELY
ACT IN GOOD FAITH
ACTION FOR LIBEL
ACTION PAINTING
ACTION STATIONS
ACTIVE INTEREST
ACTIVE STRENGTH
ACT THE BUSYBODY
ADDRESS THE BALL
ADDRESS UNKNOWN
ADD TO ONE'S GRIEF
ADELPHI TERRACE
ADELPHI THEATRE
ADEQUATE AMOUNT
ADEQUATE INCOME
ADEQUATE REASON
ADJUST THE HANDS
ADMIRALTY CHART
ADMIRALTY HOUSE
ADMIT THE CHARGE
ADOPTION PAPERS
ADULT EDUCATION
ADVANCE BOOKING
ADVANCING YEARS
ADVENTURE STORY
ADVERSE BALANCE
AESTHETIC SENSE
AESTHETIC TASTE
AFFAIRE DE COEUR
AFFAIR OF HONOUR
AFFAIRS OF STATE
AFFECTED MANNER

AFFECTED SPEECH
AFFILIATED BODY
AFTER BREAKFAST
AFTER CHRISTMAS
AFTER-DINNER NAP
AFTER LIGHTS-OUT
AFTER THE DELUGE
AGAINST ALL ODDS
AGAINST THE ODDS
AGAINST THE TIDE
AGAINST THE WIND
AGATHA CHRISTIE
AGE OF IGNORANCE
AGE OF INNOCENCE
AGREE IN MEANING
AIM AT THE TARGET
AIRBORNE FORCES
AIRBORNE TROOPS
AIRING CUPBOARD
AIR OF GRIEVANCE
AIR ONE'S OPINION
AIR PHOTOGRAPHY
AIR RAID SHELTER
AIR RAID WARNING
AIR VICE-MARSHAL
ALBERT EINSTEIN
ALBERT MEMORIAL
ALCOCK AND BROWN
ALCOHOLIC DRINK
ALDWYCH THEATRE
ALEXANDER DUMAS
ALFRED TENNYSON
ALFRED THE GREAT
ALL GUNS BLAZING
ALL HANDS ON DECK
ALLIED LANDINGS
ALL IN A DAY'S WORK
ALL-IN WRESTLING
ALL KINDS OF WAYS
ALLOTTED SPHERE
ALL OVER THE SHOP
ALL-ROUND PLAYER
ALL THE KING'S MEN
ALL WELL AND GOOD
ALMIGHTY DOLLAR
ALPES MARITIMES
ALSACE LORRAINE
AMATEUR COMPANY
AMERICAN ACCENT
AMERICAN INDIAN
AMERICAN LEGION
AMERICAN PATROL
AMERICAN SCHOOL
AMERICAN TROOPS
AMMUNITION DUMP
AMONGST FRIENDS

ANCIENT BRITAIN
ANCIENT HISTORY
ANCIENT LINEAGE
ANCIENT MARINER
ANDAMAN ISLANDS
ANDREW CARNEGIE
ANGINA PECTORIS
ANGLICAN CHURCH
ANIMAL CRACKERS
ANNUAL TURNOVER
ANNUS MIRABILIS
ANONYMOUS DONOR
ANOTHER OPINION
ANOTHER VERSION
ANSWER ONE'S NAME
ANTARCTIC OCEAN
ANY SUGGESTIONS?
ANYTHING TO COME
APARTMENT HOUSE
APARTMENT TO LET
APPEAL FOR FUNDS
APPEAL FOR MERCY
APPEAL TO REASON
APPEAR IN PUBLIC
APPLE CHARLOTTE
APPLE OF DISCORD
APPLE OF ONE'S EYE
APPLES AND PEARS
APPLIED PHYSICS
APPLIED SCIENCE
APPLY THE BRAKES
APPROVED SCHOOL
APRIL THE EIGHTH
APRIL THE FOURTH
APRIL THE SECOND
ARABIC NUMERALS
ARBITER OF TASTE
ARMCHAIR CRITIC
ARMS OF MORPHEUS
ARMY CADET FORCE
ARMY MANOEUVRES
AROUND THE WORLD
ARRANT NONSENSE
ARROGANT MANNER
ART FOR ART'S SAKE
ARTFUL CUSTOMER
ARTICLE OF FAITH
ARTIFICIAL HAND
ARTIFICIAL LAKE
ARTIFICIAL LIMB
ARTIFICIAL POND
ARTIFICIAL SILK
ARTISTIC EFFECT
ARTISTIC EFFORT
ART OF REASONING
AS A GENERAL RULE

AS BLACK AS NIGHT
AS BRAVE AS A LION
ASCENDING ORDER
ASCENDING SCALE
AS DEAD AS MUTTON
AS DRUNK AS A LORD
AS FAST AS YOU CAN
AS FIT AS A FIDDLE
AS FRESH AS PAINT
AS GOOD AS A FEAST
AS GREEN AS GRASS
AS HARD AS A STONE
ASK FORGIVENESS
AS MAD AS A HATTER
AS PALE AS A GHOST
AS PLAIN AS PLAIN
AS SAFE AS HOUSES
ASSENTING PARTY
AS SMART AS PAINT
ASSOCIATION CUP
AS SOFT AS BUTTER
AS SOFT AS VELVET
AS SOUND AS A BELL
AS SWEET AS SUGAR
AS THE CASE MAY BE
AS THE CROW FLIES
AS TIGHT AS A DRUM
AT DAGGERS DRAWN
ATHLETIC GROUND
ATHLETIC SPORTS
ATLANTIC FLIGHT
ATLANTIC ROLLER
ATLAS MOUNTAINS
AT ONE FELL SWOOP
AT ONE'S DISPOSAL
A TOWN LIKE ALICE
ATTACKING FIELD
ATTACK OF NERVES
ATTEMPT TOO MUCH
AT THE RIGHT TIME
AT THE THRESHOLD
AT THIS JUNCTURE
ATTITUDE OF MIND
AUF WIEDERSEHEN
AUGUST THE FIFTH
AUGUST THE FIRST
AUGUST THE NINTH
AUGUST THE SIXTH
AUGUST THE TENTH
AUGUST THE THIRD
AUGUSTUS CAESAR
AURORA BOREALIS
AUSTRALIA HOUSE
AUSTRALIAN BUSH
AUTOGRAPH ALBUM
AUTOMATIC RIFLE

AUTOMOBILE CLUB
AVERAGE ABILITY
AVIATION SPIRIT
AVOID A DECISION
AVOID BLOODSHED
AWKWARD SILENCE

B – 14

BABES IN THE WOOD
BACHELOR OF ARTS
BACK-SEAT DRIVER
BACKS TO THE WALL
BACKWARD GLANCE
BACONIAN THEORY
BAD CIRCULATION
BAD FOR BUSINESS
BAD HANDWRITING
BAD HOUSEKEEPER
BADMINTON COURT
BAD VENTILATION
BAGATELLE TABLE
BALANCED BUDGET
BALANCE OF POWER
BALANCE OF TRADE
BALANCING TRICK
BALL AT ONE'S FEET
BALLET MISTRESS
BALLIOL COLLEGE
BALL OF THE THUMB
BALLOON BARRAGE
BALMORAL CASTLE
BALTIC EXCHANGE
BANANA FRITTERS
BANANA REPUBLIC
BANDED TOGETHER
BAND OF BROTHERS
BAND OF PILGRIMS
BANE OF ONE'S LIFE
BANGERS AND MASH
BANKING ACCOUNT
BANK OF SCOTLAND
BANNER HEADLINE
BANQUETING HALL
BARE-BACK RIDING
BARE ESSENTIALS
BARELY POSSIBLE
BARGAIN COUNTER
BARKIS IS WILLIN'
BAR OF CHOCOLATE
BARRAGE BALLOON
BAR THE ENTRANCE
BASIC SUBSTANCE
BASKET-BALL TEAM
BATHING COSTUME
BATHING MACHINE

BATHROOM SCALES
BATTING AVERAGE
BATTLE OF NASEBY
BATTLE STATIONS
BAYEUX TAPESTRY
BEACH INSPECTOR
BE-ALL AND END-ALL
BEAR ALLEGIANCE
BEAT GENERATION
BEAT ONE'S BRAINS
BEAT ONE'S BREAST
BEAT THE BIG DRUM
BEAT TO A FRAZZLE
BEAUTIFUL VOICE
BEAUTIFUL WOMAN
BECOME A CITIZEN
BECOME AIRBORNE
BECOME A PATIENT
BECOME CHAMPION
BEDROOM SLIPPER
BEDSIDE READING
BED-SITTING ROOM
BEFORE AND AFTER
BEFORE AND SINCE
BEFORE DAYLIGHT
BEFORE MIDNIGHT
BEFORE ONE'S EYES
BEFORE ONE'S TIME
BEFORE THE JUDGE
BEG FORGIVENESS
BEG THE QUESTION
BEHIND ONE'S BACK
BEHIND SCHEDULE
BEHIND THE CLOCK
BEHIND THE TIMES
BEHIND THE WHEEL
BELGRAVE SQUARE
BELIEVE IT OR NOT
BELLE OF NEW YORK
BELLE OF THE BALL
BELOW THE GROUND
BENCH OF BISHOPS
BENEATH ACCOUNT
BENEFIT SOCIETY
BENEVOLENT FUND
BEREFT OF REASON
BERKELEY SQUARE
BERLIN QUESTION
BESEECHING LOOK
BESIDE THE POINT
BEST DRESSED MAN
BEST INTENTIONS
BEST LEG FORWARD
BEST OF THE BUNCH
BETSEY TROTWOOD
BETTER FEELINGS

BETTER THAN EVER
BETTER THAN MOST
BETTER THOUGHTS
BETWEEN FRIENDS
BETWEEN THE EYES
BEWARE OF THE DOG
BEYOND ALL DOUBT
BEYOND HUMAN AID
BEYOND REPROACH
BEYOND THE GRAVE
BEYOND THE LIMIT
BID GOOD MORNING
BIFOCAL GLASSES
BIG-GAME HUNTING
BIGGEST PORTION
BIJOU RESIDENCE
BILLIARD MARKER
BILLIARD PLAYER
BILLIARD SALOON
BILL OF EXCHANGE
BIRD OF PARADISE
BIRTH OF A NATION
BISHOP AUCKLAND
BITE ONE'S TONGUE
BIT OF A COME-DOWN
BIT OF A NUISANCE
BITTER FEELINGS
BITTER MEMORIES
BITTER STRUGGLE
BITTER THOUGHTS
BITUMINOUS COAL
BLACK AS THUNDER
BLACK-EYED SUSIE
BLACK IN THE FACE
BLACKPOOL TOWER
BLACK STOCKINGS
BLACK CARTRIDGE
BLASTING POWDER
BLAZING INFERNO
BLEACHING AGENT
BLENHEIM ORANGE
BLENHEIM PALACE
BLESS THIS HOUSE
BLIND IGNORANCE
BLIND REASONING
BLOCK AND TACKLE
BLOCK OF OFFICES
BLOOD POISONING
BLOUSE AND SKIRT
BLOW EVERYTHING
BLOW HOT AND COLD
BLOWING BUBBLES
BLOW SMOKE-RINGS
BLOW THE EXPENSE
BLOW THE MAN DOWN
BLUE-COAT SCHOOL

BLUE SPECTACLES
BLUNT STATEMENT
BOA CONSTRICTOR
BOARDING SCHOOL
BOARD OF CONTROL
BOARD OF INQUIRY
BOARD RESIDENCE
BODILY MOVEMENT
BODILY STRENGTH
BODILY WEAKNESS
BODY OF SOLDIERS
BOILED POTATOES
BOLD EXPERIMENT
BONNIE SCOTLAND
BOOK DEPARTMENT
BOOK OF NONSENSE
BOOK OF PROVERBS
BOOK OF THE MONTH
BOOK PRODUCTION
BOOMING ECONOMY
BOON COMPANIONS
BORDERLINE CASE
BORDER MINSTREL
BORDER REGIMENT
BORDER SKIRMISH
BOROUGH COUNCIL
BORROWED PLUMES
BOSTON CRACKERS
BOSTON TEA PARTY
BOTTLE OF BRANDY
BOTTLE OF BUBBLY
BOTTLE OF CLARET
BOTTLE OF SCOTCH
BOTTLE OF SWEETS
BOTTLE OF WHISKY
BOTTOM OF THE BAG
BOTTOM OF THE SEA
BOUGHT FOR A SONG
BOUT OF SICKNESS
BOWLING AVERAGE
BOWL OF CHERRIES
BOXER REBELLION
BOYS WILL BE BOYS
BRACING CLIMATE
BRADSHAW'S GUIDE
BREACH OF ORDERS
BREAD AND BUTTER
BREAD AND CHEESE
BREAD AND SCRAPE
BREADFRUIT TREE
BREAKFAST IN BED
BREAKFAST TABLE
BREAKNECK SPEED
BREAK NEW GROUND
BREAK ONE'S HEART
BREAK THE CORDON

BREAK THE RECORD
BREAK THE THREAD
BREAST THE WAVES
BREATHE HEAVILY
BREATHE REVENGE
BREATHING SPACE
BREATH OF SEA AIR
BREATH OF SPRING
BREEDING GROUND
BREWERS' COMPANY
BRIEF ENCOUNTER
BRIEF INTERLUDE
BRIGHT AND EARLY
BRIGHT AS SILVER
BRIGHT PROSPECT
BRIGHT'S DISEASE
BRIGITTE BARDOT
BRIMFUL OF IDEAS
BRING GOOD CHEER
BRING IN A PROFIT
BRING INTO BEING
BRING INTO FOCUS
BRING TO ACCOUNT
BRING TO JUSTICE
BRING TO THE BOIL
BRING TO THE FORE
BRING UP THE REAR
BRISTOL CHANNEL
BRISTOL FASHION
BRITANNIA METAL
BRITISH BULLDOG
BRITISH COUNCIL
BRITISH EMBASSY
BRITISH SUBJECT
BRITTLE AS GLASS
BROAD IN THE BEAM
BROAD SHOULDERS
BROADWAY MELODY
BROKEN CONTRACT
BROKEN MARRIAGE
BROKE THE WICKET
BROKE TO THE WIDE
BRONCHIAL TUBES
BROOKLYN BRIDGE
BROOK NO REFUSAL
BROTHER OFFICER
BROTHERS IN ARMS
BROUGHT TO LIGHT
BRUSH ONE'S TEETH
BRUSSELS CARPET
BUBBLING STREAM
BUCKET AND SPADE
BUILDING BRICKS
BULLDOG COURAGE
BULLET-PROOF CAR
BUMP OF LOCALITY

BUNCH OF BANANAS
BUNCH OF FLOWERS
BUNDLE OF NERVES
BURIED TREASURE
BURN AT THE STAKE
BURNHAM BEECHES
BURNISHED BRASS
BURNT SACRIFICE
BURNT TO A CINDER
BURST INTO FLAME
BURST INTO TEARS
BURST ONE'S BONDS
BURST THE BUBBLE
BURY ONE'S TALENT
BURY THE HATCHET
BUS CONDUCTRESS
BUSINESS CAREER
BUSINESS LETTER
BUSINESS MATTER
BUSINESS ON HAND
BUSINESS TYCOON
BUSMAN'S HOLIDAY
BUTTONS AND BOWS
BUY A PIG IN A POKE
BY A LONG STRETCH
BY PRESCRIPTION
BY THE SAME TOKEN

C – 14

CABBAGE LETTUCE
CABINET MEETING
CABINET PUDDING
CAGE ME A PEACOCK
CALAMINE LOTION
CALCIUM CARBIDE
CALCULATED ODDS
CALCULATED RISK
CALF'S-FOOT JELLY
CALLED TO THE BAR
CALL FOR A REPORT
CALLING ALL CARS
CALL IN QUESTION
CALL OFF THE DOGS
CALM REFLECTION
CAMBRIDGE COACH
CAMP COMMANDANT
CAMPHORATED OIL
CAMPING HOLIDAY
CANADIAN POLICE
CANNING FACTORY
CANTERBURY BELL
CANTERBURY LAMB
CAPABLE OF PROOF
CAPE OF GOOD HOPE
CAPITAL OFFENCE

CAPITAL OF ITALY
CAPITAL OF SPAIN
CAPTAIN BOYCOTT
CAPTIVE BALLOON
CARAVAN HOLIDAY
CARBON MONOXIDE
CARDEW ROBINSON
CARDIAC DISEASE
CARDINAL NEWMAN
CARDINAL NUMBER
CARDINAL POINTS
CARDINAL VIRTUE
CARDINAL WOLSEY
CAREFUL THOUGHT
CARMELITE ORDER
CARPET SLIPPERS
CARRY ONE'S POINT
CARTRIDGE PAPER
CASEMENT WINDOW
CASH ON DELIVERY
CAST ASPERSIONS
CAST INTO PRISON
CAST-IRON EXCUSE
CASTLE IN THE AIR
CASTLES IN SPAIN
CAST SHEEP'S EYES
CASUAL LABOURER
CASUAL OBSERVER
CATCH ONE'S DEATH
CATCH RED-HANDED
CATCH THE BREATH
CATHEDRAL CLOSE
CATHERINE BOYLE
CATHERINE WHEEL
CATHODE-RAY TUBE
CAT ON HOT BRICKS
CAT OUT OF THE BAG
CAUGHT IN A STORM
CAUGHT IN THE ACT
CAUGHT ON THE HOP
CAUGHT STEALING
CAUGHT UNAWARES
CAULIFLOWER EAR
CAUSE AND EFFECT
CAUSE A STOPPAGE
CAUSE CONFUSION
CAUSE FOR REGRET
CAUTIONARY TALE
CAVALRY OFFICER
CELESTIAL BLISS
CELESTIAL GLOBE
CENTRAL AMERICA
CENTRAL HEATING
CENTRAL STATION
CERTAIN VICTORY
CHAINED TO A DESK

CHAIN OF COMMAND	CHILD ALLOWANCE
CHAIN OF THOUGHT	CHILD OF FORTUNE
CHAIR THE WINNER	CHILDREN'S NURSE
CHALK AND CHEESE	CHILDREN'S PARTY
CHALLENGE ROUND	CHILDREN'S STORY
CHAMPAGNE GLASS	CHINESE CRACKER
CHAMPAGNE LUNCH	CHINESE LANTERN
CHAMPION GOLFER	CHINESE LAUNDRY
CHAMPION JOCKEY	CHINESE TORTURE
CHANCERY OFFICE	CHIPPING BARNET
CHANGE OF BELIEF	CHIPPING NORTON
CHANGE OF COURSE	CHOCOLATE CREAM
CHANGE ONE'S LUCK	CHOCOLATE WAFER
CHANGE ONE'S MIND	CHOPPED PARSLEY
CHANGE ONE'S NAME	CHRISTMAS BONUS
CHANGE ONE'S TUNE	CHRISTMAS CAROL
CHANGE ONE'S WAYS	CHRISTMAS CHEER
CHANGE PARTNERS	CHRISTMAS DAISY
CHANGE THE ORDER	CHRISTMAS PARTY
CHANGE THE VENUE	CHRISTOPHER FRY
CHANNEL ISLANDS	CHROMATIC SCALE
CHANNEL STEAMER	CHRONIC INVALID
CHANNEL SWIMMER	CHUCK OVERBOARD
CHAPTER HEADING	CHUCK UP ONE'S JOB
CHARACTER ACTOR	CHURCH ASSEMBLY
CHARACTER STUDY	CHURCH DOCTRINE
CHARCOAL BURNER	CHURCH MILITANT
CHARGE THE EARTH	CHURCH PROPERTY
CHARITABLE DEED	CIGARETTE PAPER
CHARITABLE GIFT	CIRCLE THE EARTH
CHARITY MEETING	CIRCULAR COURSE
CHARLES CHAPLIN	CIRCULAR LETTER
CHARLES DICKENS	CIRCULAR TICKET
CHARLES GARVICE	CITY MAGISTRATE
CHARLIE CHESTER	CIVILIZED WORLD
CHARLOTTE RUSSE	CIVIL LIBERTIES
CHARMING FELLOW	CLAIM ATTENTION
CHARMING MANNER	CLAIM THE REWARD
CHARRED REMAINS	CLAP INTO PRISON
CHASE ME CHARLIE	CLARENDON PRESS
CHEAP EXCURSION	CLASH OF CYMBALS
CHECKING SYSTEM	CLASS CONSCIOUS
CHEER TO THE ECHO	CLASSICAL LATIN
CHEESE SANDWICH	CLASSICAL MUSIC
CHEMICAL CHANGE	CLASSICAL TASTE
CHEMICAL ENERGY	CLASSIC EXAMPLE
CHEMISTRY CLASS	CLASSIC QUALITY
CHESHIRE CHEESE	CLASSICS MASTER
CHESTNUT SUNDAE	CLASS PREJUDICE
CHEST OF DRAWERS	CLEAN AS A NEW PIN
CHEST PROTECTOR	CLEAN ONE'S TEETH
CHEWING TOBACCO	CLEANSING CREAM
CHICKEN IN ASPIC	CLEAN THE SILVER
CHIEF CONSTABLE	CLEAR AS CRYSTAL
CHIEF EXECUTIVE	CLEAR STATEMENT
CHIEF INSPECTOR	CLEAR THE GROUND

CLEAR THE THROAT
CLEMENT WEATHER
CLERICAL COLLAR
CLERICAL DUTIES
CLERICAL WORKER
CLICK ONE'S HEELS
CLIMB A MOUNTAIN
CLIMBING PRICES
CLOAK AND DAGGER
CLOCKWORK TRAIN
CLOISTERED LIFE
CLOSE AN ACCOUNT
CLOSE ATTENTION
CLOSELY GUARDED
CLOSE ONE'S MOUTH
CLOSE PROXIMITY
CLOSE THE WINDOW
CLOSE TO THE WIND
CLOTHING COUPON
CLOUD FORMATION
CLOUT ON THE HEAD
CLUB MEMBERSHIP
CLUBS ARE TRUMPS
CLUSTER OF STARS
CLUTCH AT STRAWS
COACH AND HORSES
COALING STATION
COARSE LANGUAGE
COASTAL BATTERY
COASTAL COMMAND
COASTAL EROSION
COCK OF THE NORTH
COCKTAIL SHAKER
COFFEE STRAINER
COHERENT MANNER
COIN OF THE REALM
COLLAR ATTACHED
COLLECTED POEMS
COLLECTIVE FARM
COLLECTIVE NOUN
COLLECT ONESELF
COLLECTOR'S ITEM
COLLEGE PUDDING
COLLEGE STUDENT
COLONIAL OFFICE
COLONIAL SYSTEM
COLORADO BEETLE
COLOUR QUESTION
COLOUR SERGEANT
COMBINED EFFORT
COME BACK TO ERIN
COME DOWNSTAIRS
COMEDY OF ERRORS
COME FACE TO FACE
COME FROM BEHIND
COME FULL CIRCLE

COME-HITHER LOOK
COME INTO FAVOUR
COME ON THE SCENE
COME ROUND AGAIN
COME SECOND BEST
COME TO A DEAD-END
COME TO THE FRONT
COME TO THE POINT
COMFORTABLY OFF
COMIC INTERLUDE
COMING OF ARTHUR
COMING-OUT PARTY
COMMANDING LEAD
COMMAND OF WORDS
COMMAND RESPECT
COMMAND SILENCE
COMMAND SUPPORT
COMMERCIAL ROOM
COMMIT A FAUX PAS
COMMIT FOR TRIAL
COMMIT HARA-KIRI
COMMITTEE STAGE
COMMIT TO MEMORY
COMMIT TO PRISON
COMMON ANCESTOR
COMMON COURTESY
COMMON CURRENCY
COMMON ENTRANCE
COMMON FRONTIER
COMMON HUMANITY
COMMON INFORMER
COMMON INTEREST
COMMON MULTIPLE
COMMON NUISANCE
COMMON OR GARDEN
COMMON PARLANCE
COMMON PRACTICE
COMMON PROPERTY
COMMON SERJEANT
COMMUNION BREAD
COMMUNION TABLE
COMMUNIST PARTY
COMMUNITY CHEST
COMPANION PIECE
COMPANY MANNERS
COMPANY MATTERS
COMPANY MEETING
COMPANY OFFICER
COMPASS BEARING
COMPASS READING
COMPLEAT ANGLER
COMPLETE ANSWER
COMPLETE CHANGE
COMPLETE FIASCO
COMPONENT PARTS
COMPOSED MANNER

COMPOSE ONESELF
COMPULSORY LOAN
COMRADES IN ARMS
CONCEALED DRIVE
CONCERT PIANIST
CONDEMN TO DEATH
CONDUCT A SEARCH
CONFER A BENEFIT
CONFERENCE ROOM
CONFIRMED ENEMY
CONFIRMED HABIT
CONIFEROUS TREE
CONJUGAL RIGHTS
CONJURING TRICK
CONQUERING HERO
CONSIGN TO EARTH
CONSTANT READER
CONSTANT STRAIN
CONSTANT SUPPLY
CONSULTING ROOM
CONSUMER DEMAND
CONTAIN ONESELF
CONTINUITY GIRL
CONTRACT BRIDGE
CONTRARY ADVICE
CONTROLLED RENT
CONTROL ONESELF
CONVERSION LOAN
CONVEY A MEANING
COOKING UTENSIL
COPPER SULPHATE
COPS AND ROBBERS
COPYHOLD ESTATE
CORDIAL WELCOME
CORNFLOWER BLUE
CORNISH RIVIERA
CORPORATION TAX
CORRUGATED IRON
COTTON EXCHANGE
COTTON INDUSTRY
COUNCIL CHAMBER
COUNCIL MEETING
COUNCIL OF STATE
COUNTLESS TIMES
COUNT ONE'S BEADS
COUNT ONE'S MONEY
COUNTRY BUMPKIN
COUNTRY COTTAGE
COUNTRY RETREAT
COUNTY PALATINE
COURSE OF ACTION
COURSE OF EVENTS
COURTING COUPLE
COURT OF INQUIRY
COURT OF JUSTICE
COURT PROCEDURE

COVERED WITH ICE
COVERING LETTER
CRACK OF THE WHIP
CRADLE SNATCHER ,
CRAMP ONE'S STYLE
CRANBERRY SAUCE
CRASH ONE'S GEARS
CRASS IGNORANCE
CRASS STUPIDITY
CREAM OF SOCIETY
CREATE AN EFFECT
CREATE AN UPROAR
CREATE A SCANDAL
CREATIVE ARTIST
CREATIVE GENIUS
CREATIVE WORKER
CREATIVE WRITER
CREDIT CUSTOMER
CREDIT TRANSFER
CRÈME DE LA CRÈME
CREST OF THE WAVE
CRICKET FIXTURE
CRICKET RESULTS
CRIME DETECTION
CRIME DOESN'T PAY
CRIME OF PASSION
CRIME PASSIONEL
CRIMINAL CHARGE
CRIMINAL LAWYER
CRIMINAL RECORD
CRINOLINE DRESS
CRITICAL MOMENT
CRITICAL PERIOD
CROCODILE TEARS
CROOK THE FINGER
CROSSED FINGERS
CROSS ONE'S HEART
CROSS REFERENCE
CROSS THE BORDER
CROSS THE BRIDGE
CROSS THE STREET
CROWN AND ANCHOR
CROWNING STROKE
CROWN OF THE HEAD
CROWN OF THE ROAD
CRUMBLING POWER
CRUMB OF COMFORT
CRUSHING DEFEAT
CRUSHING REMARK
CRUSHING RETORT
CRY ONE'S EYES OUT
CULTIVATED LAND
CULTIVATED MIND
CULTURAL CENTRE
CUP FINAL TICKET
CUP OF HAPPINESS

CURB ONE'S TEMPER
CURDLE THE BLOOD
CURIOUS MIXTURE
CURRANT PUDDING
CURRENT ACCOUNT
CURRENT AFFAIRS
CURRENT EDITION
CURRENT FASHION
CURRENT OPINION
CURRIED CHICKEN
CURTAIN LECTURE
CURTAIN OF SMOKE
CUSTOM AND USAGE
CUSTOMS BARRIER
CUSTOMS OFFICER
CUT A FINE FIGURE
CUT A POOR FIGURE
CUT FOR PARTNERS
CUTLERS' COMPANY
CUT OFF ONE'S NOSE
CUT OFF THE JOINT
CUT-THROAT PRICE
CUT-THROAT RAZOR

D – 14

DAILY ENDEAVOUR
DAILY HAPPENING
DAILY NEWSPAPER
DAILY TELEGRAPH
DAILY TRAVELLER
DAMAGING REPORT
DAME EDITH EVANS
DAME ELLEN TERRY
DANCE PROGRAMME
DANCING ACADEMY
DANCING DERVISH
DANCING LICENCE
DANCING PARTNER
DANGEROUSLY ILL
DARING YOUNG MAN
DARK COMPLEXION
DARKEN ONE'S DOOR
DAVID TOMLINSON
DAVID WHITFIELD
DAY IN AND DAY OUT
DAYLIGHT SAVING
DAY OF ATONEMENT
DAY OF RECKONING
DAZZLING BEAUTY
DEAD MAN'S HANDLE
DEAD TO THE WORLD
DEAL A DEATH BLOW
DEAN AND CHAPTER
DEAR AT THE PRICE
DEATH BY BURNING

DEATHLY SILENCE
DEBASED COINAGE
DEBATABLE POINT
DEBIT AND CREDIT
DECEIVE ONESELF
DECENT INTERVAL
DECENTLY HOUSED
DECIDING FACTOR
DECIMAL COINAGE
DECISIVE FACTOR
DECLINE AND FALL
DECLINE IN VALUE
DECLINE TO STAND
DECLINING YEARS
DECREE ABSOLUTE
DEEP DEPRESSION
DEEPLY AFFECTED
DEEPLY OFFENDED
DEEP REFLECTION
DEEP-SEA FISHING
DEFEAT THE ENEMY
DEFENCE COUNSEL
DEFENCE IN DEPTH
DEFENCE MEASURE
DEFENCE WITNESS
DEFERRED SHARES
DEFINITE FIGURE
DEFRAY EXPENSES
DEGREES OF FROST
DELAYING ACTION
DELICATE HEALTH
DELICIOUS TASTE
DELIVER A SERMON
DELIVER A SPEECH
DEMAND A HEARING
DEMAND A RE-COUNT
DEMAND ENTRANCE
DEMAND SECURITY
DENTAL PRACTICE
DEPARTED SPIRIT
DEPART FROM LIFE
DEPARTING GUEST
DEPOSIT ACCOUNT
DEPRESSED CLASS
DEPRESSING NEWS
DEPRIVED PERSON
DEPTH OF FEELING
DEPTHS OF MISERY
DEPUTY CHAIRMAN
DERBY FAVOURITE
DERELICT VESSEL
DEROGATORY TERM
DESERT ONE'S POST
DESIRABLE THING
DESPATCH BY MAIL
DESPERATE STATE

DETACHED MANNER
DETAILED REPORT
DETECTIVE NOVEL
DETECTIVE STORY
DETENTION ORDER
DEVELOP THE MIND
DEVIL INCARNATE
DEVIL OF A TEMPER .
DEVIL'S ADVOCATE
DEVIL'S DISCIPLE
DEVOTED ADMIRER
DEVOTED HUSBAND
DEVOTION TO DUTY
DIAMOND JUBILEE
DIAMOND WEDDING
DIARY OF A NOBODY
DICTATE A LETTER
DICTATION SPEED
DICTIONARY WORD
DIE IN ONE'S SHOES
DIEU ET MON DROIT
DIFFERENT ANGLE
DIFFICULT CATCH
DIFFICULT CLIMB
DIG IN ONE'S HEELS
DIGNIFIED STYLE
DIG ONE'S SPURS IN
DIMINUTIVE SIZE
DING-DONG BATTLE
DINNER AND DANCE
DINNER IS SERVED
DIPLOMATIC BODY
DIPLOMATIC MOVE
DIRECT APPROACH
DIRECT EVIDENCE
DIRECT OPPOSITE
DIRECT QUESTION
DIRECT TAXATION
DISABLED PERSON
DISCHARGED A DEBT
DISCORDANT NOTE
DISCOUNT BROKER
DISGUISED VOICE
DISORDERED MIND
DISTILLED WATER
DISTORTED IMAGE
DISTRESSED AREA
DISTRESS SIGNAL
DISTURBED NIGHT
DISTURBED SLEEP
DIVIDE BY ELEVEN
DIVIDE BY TWELVE
DIVIDED LOYALTY
DIVIDE THE HOUSE
DIVISION OF WORK
DIVORCED PERSON

DOCTOR BARNARDO
DOCTORS' COMMONS
DOCTOR'S DILEMMA
DOCTOR'S MANDATE
DODGE THE COLUMN
DOG IN THE MANGER
DOLL'S FURNITURE
DOMESTIC ANIMAL
DOMESTIC DRUDGE
DOMESTIC POLICY
DOMINION STATUS
DONALD CAMPBELL
DONKEY SERENADE
DO ONESELF PROUD
DOROTHY PERKINS
DOSE OF MEDICINE
DOT AND CARRY ONE
DOUBLE EIGHTEEN
DOUBLE ENTENDRE
DOUBLE EXPOSURE
DOUBLE FOURTEEN
DOUBLE NEGATIVE
DOUBLE NINETEEN
DOUBLE STANDARD
DOUBLE STOPPING
DOUBLET AND HOSE
DOUBLE THIRTEEN
DOUBTFUL FUTURE
DOUBTFUL ORIGIN
DOUBTFUL TEMPER
DOUBTING THOMAS
DOUGHTY WARRIOR
DOWAGER DUCHESS
DOWN IN THE DUMPS
DOWN IN THE MOUTH
DOWN IN THE WORLD
DOWN LAMBETH WAY
DOWN MEMORY LANE
DOWN ON ONE'S LUCK
DOWNSTAIRS ROOM
DOWN THE CHIMNEY
DOWNWARD MOTION
DOWNWARD STROKE
DOZENS OF PEOPLE
DRAIN ONE'S GLASS
DRAMATIC CRITIC
DRAMATIC EFFECT
DRAMATIC FINISH
DRAPERS' COMPANY
DRAWERS OF WATER
DRAW FIRST BLOOD
DRAW THE CURTAIN
DRAW THE LONG-BOW
DRAW THE RATIONS
DREAMING SPIRES
DREGS OF SOCIETY

DRESSED IN BLACK
DRESSED OVER ALL
DRESS FOR DINNER
DRESS REHEARSAL
DRINKING HABITS
DRINKING TROUGH
DRINKING VESSEL
DRINK LIKE A FISH
DRIVE CAREFULLY
DRIVE TO DESPAIR
DRIVE TO THE WALL
DRIVING LICENCE
DROP FROM THE SKY
DROP IN THE OCEAN
DROP OFF TO SLEEP
DROP THE SUBJECT
DROWNED IN TEARS
DUBIOUS COMPANY
DUBLIN BAY PRAWN
DUCKS AND DRAKES
DUELLING PISTOL
DUEL TO THE DEATH
DUKE OF BURGUNDY
DUKE OF CLARENCE
DUKE OF CORNWALL
DUPLICATE SHEET
DURATION OF LIFE
DURING THE NIGHT
DUTY-FREE DRINKS
DWELL ON THE PAST
DYING FOR A DRINK

E – 14

EACH FOR HIMSELF
EARL OF HAREWOOD
EARLY BREAKFAST
EARLY VICTORIAN
EARN ONE'S LIVING
EARTH SATELLITE
EAR TO THE GROUND
EASE OF HANDLING
EASTER HOLIDAYS
EASTER OFFERING
EASTER VACATION
EASY COME, EASY GO
EASY CONSCIENCE
EASY IN ONE'S MIND
EAT ONE'S HEAD OFF
ECONOMIC CRISIS
ECONOMY OF WORDS
EDITORIAL CHAIR
EDITORIAL STAFF
EDUCATE THE MIND
EDUCATIONAL TOY
EDWARDIAN HOUSE

EFFICIENCY TEST
EIGHTEEN AND SIX
EIGHTEENTH HOLE
EIGHTH OF AUGUST
EIGHTH SYMPHONY
EIGHTY THOUSAND
ELABORATE STYLE
ELDERBERRY WINE
ELDER STATESMAN
ELDEST DAUGHTER
ELECTION RESULT
ELECTRICAL UNIT
ELECTRIC CHARGE
ELECTRICAL COOKER
ELECTRIC GUITAR
ELECTRIC HEATER
ELECTRICITY CUT
ELECTRIC KETTLE
ELECTRIC SHAVER
ELECTRIC WASHER
ELEMENTARY RULE
ELEMENT OF DOUBT
ELEMENT OF TRUTH
ELEPHANT'S TRUNK
ELEVEN OR TWELVE
ELEVENTH LETTER
ELEVENTH OF JULY
ELEVENTH OF JUNE
ELEVEN THOUSAND
ELICIT THE TRUTH
ELIZABETHAN AGE
ELIZABETHAN ERA
ELIZA DOOLITTLE
ELLA FITZGERALD
ELOCUTION CLASS
ELOQUENT TONGUE
EMINENT SOLDIER
EMINENT SPEAKER
EMOTIONAL WRECK
EMPEROR OF JAPAN
EMPHATICAL DENIAL
EMPIRE LOYALIST
EMPTY OF MEANING
EMPTY PLEASURES
ENCLOSE A CHEQUE
ENDEARING SMILE
ENDLESS PROBLEM
ENDLESS TROUBLE
END OF ALL THINGS
END OF THE MATTER
END OF THE STREET
ENDS OF THE EARTH
ENDURE TO THE END
ENEMY OF FREEDOM
ENEMY OF MANKIND
ENEMY TERRITORY

ENFANT TERRIBLE
ENGAGED IN TRADE
ENGAGEMENT RING
ENGAGE THE ENEMY
ENGAGING MANNER
ENGLISH BY BIRTH
ENGLISH CHANNEL
ENGLISH GRAMMAR
ENGLISH HISTORY
ENGLISH MUSTARD
ENGLISH TEACHER
ENIGMATIC SMILE
ENJOY ILL HEALTH
ENLARGE THE MIND
ENLIGHTENED AGE
ENORMOUS NUMBER
ENTERTAIN A HOPE
ENTER THE CHURCH
ENTRECOTE STEAK
EQUABLE CLIMATE
EQUALLY DIVIDED
EQUAL THE RECORD
ERRATIC CONDUCT
ESCAPED CONVICT
ESPRESSO COFFEE
ETHEREAL BEAUTY
EUCALYPTUS TREE
EVADE DETECTION
EVAPORATED MILK
EVENING CLOTHES
EVENING SERVICE
EVERGREEN PLANT
EVERGREEN SHRUB
EVERY BIT AS MUCH
EVERY INCH A KING
EVERY SECOND DAY
EVERYTHING GOES
EVIDENCE ON OATH
EVIL REPUTATION
EXACTING MASTER
EXCEED THE LIMIT
EXCELLENT MARKS
EXCHANGE OF VOWS
EXCHANGE VISITS
EXCITABLE STATE
EXCURSION TRAIN
EXECUTION BLOCK
EXECUTIVE SUITE
EXERT AUTHORITY
EXHIBIT FEELING
EXPANSIVE SMILE
EXPENSE ACCOUNT
EXPLAIN ONESELF
EXPLODED BELIEF
EXPORT MERCHANT
EXPOSE TO DANGER

EXPRESS COMMAND
EXPRESS ONESELF
EXPRESS PURPOSE
EXPRESS REGRETS
EXPURGATED BOOK
EXQUISITE TASTE
EXTENDED CREDIT
EXTENSIVE FIELD
EXTENSIVE SALES
EXTINCT VOLCANO
EXTREME DISLIKE
EXTREME PENALTY
EXTREME POVERTY
EXTREME UNCTION
EYE FOR BUSINESS

F – 14

FABULOUS WEALTH
FABULOUS WRITER
FACE OF THE GLOBE
FACE UP TO THINGS
FACT AND FICTION
FACTORY CHIMNEY
FACTS OF THE CASE
FAIL IN ONE'S DUTY
FAIL TO INTEREST
FAIR COMPARISON
FAIR COMPLEXION
FAIR TO MIDDLING
FAIR TO MODERATE
FAIRY GODMOTHER
FAITHFUL FRIEND
FAITHFUL REPORT
FAITHFUL SPOUSE
FALL DOWNSTAIRS
FALL INTO DISUSE
FALL ON EVIL DAYS
FALL ON ONE'S FEET
FALSE COLOURING
FALSE EYELASHES
FALSELY ACCUSED
FALSE MOUSTACHE
FALSE PRETENCES
FALSE REASONING
FALSE STATEMENT
FALTERING STEPS
FALTERING VOICE
FAME AND FORTUNE
FAMILIAR MANNER
FAMILIAR SPIRIT
FAMILY BUSINESS
FAMILY HEIRLOOM
FAMILY LIKENESS
FAMILY PORTRAIT
FAMILY RETAINER

FAMILY SKELETON	FIND A PUBLISHER
FANCY-DRESS BALL	FINDERS, KEEPERS
FAREWELL SPEECH	FIND THE MEANING
FAREWELL TO ARMS	FINGER IN THE PIE
FAR-FLUNG EMPIRE	FINGERS AND TOES
FARMING SUBSIDY	FINGER'S BREADTH
FAST AND FURIOUS	FINIAN'S RAINBOW
FATALLY WOUNDED	FINISHING TOUCH
FATHER SUPERIOR	FINISH STRONGLY
FAT-STOCK PRICES	FINITE QUANTITY
FATUOUS ATTEMPT	FIRE A BROADSIDE
FAVOURABLE WIND	FIRE DEPARTMENT
FAVOURED PERSON	FIREMAN'S HELMET
FAVOURITE PIECE	FIREMAN'S LADDER
FEARLESS HITTER	FIRE PROTECTION
FEAST OF STEPHEN	FIRM CONVICTION
FEAT OF STRENGTH	FIRM FOUNDATION
FEATURE PICTURE	FIRM GOVERNMENT
FEATURES EDITOR	FIRM IMPRESSION
FEDERAL COUNCIL	FIRM MANAGEMENT
FEEL THE BENEFIT	FIRM OPPOSITION
FEEL THE DRAUGHT	FIRST AND SECOND
FELLOW COMMONER	FIRST-BORN CHILD
FELLOW CREATURE	FIRST CHRISTMAS
FEMININE APPEAL	FIRST-CLASS FARE
FEMININE GENDER	FIRST-CLASS IDEA
FEMME DE CHAMBRE	FIRST-CLASS SHOT
FEND FOR ONESELF	FIRST CONDITION
FEVERISH DESIRE	FIRST-FLOOR FLAT
FICTITIOUS NAME	FIRST INTENTION
FIELD AMBULANCE	FIRST MAGNITUDE
FIELD ARTILLERY	FIRST OF JANUARY
FIELD OF INQUIRY	FIRST OF OCTOBER
FIELD TELEGRAPH	FIRST ON THE LIST
FIFTEEN PER CENT	FIRST PRINCIPLE
FIFTEENTH GREEN	FIRST-RATE ACTOR
FIFTEENTH OF MAY	FIRST SECRETARY
FIFTEENTH ROUND	FIRST TIME LUCKY
FIFTH COLUMNIST	FIRST TIME ROUND
FIFTH OF JANUARY	FIRST VIOLINIST
FIFTH OF OCTOBER	FISHERMAN'S YARN
FIGHTER COMMAND	FISHING LICENCE
FIGHTING CHANCE	FISHING VILLAGE
FIGHTING SPIRIT	FISH OUT OF WATER
FIGHT TO A FINISH	FIT OF GIDDINESS
FIGURE OF SPEECH	FIT THE OCCASION
FILLETED PLAICE	FIVE-BARRED GATE
FILLING STATION	FIVE-DOLLAR BILL
FILL THE VACANCY	FIVE OF DIAMONDS
FILL UP THE RANKS	FIXED ALLOWANCE
FILL WITH DISMAY	FLAG LIEUTENANT
FILTHY LANGUAGE	FLAG OF DISTRESS
FINAL INTENTION	FLASHING STREAM
FINAL RECKONING	FLAT AS A PANCAKE
FINANCIAL TIMES	FLAT ON ONE'S BACK
FINANCIAL WORRY	FLAT ON ONE'S FACE

FLATTER ONESELF
FLEE THE COUNTRY
FLEETING GLANCE
FLIGHT OF STAIRS
FLIGHT SERGEANT
FLIPPANT SPEECH
FLOATING BRIDGE
FLOATING KIDNEY
FLOATING PALACE
FLOCK OF PIGEONS
FLOG A DEAD HORSE
FLOOD WITH LIGHT
FLOWERING PLANT
FLOWERING SHRUB
FLUSH OF TRIUMPH
FLUSH WITH ANGER
FLUSH WITH MONEY
FLY FOR ONE'S LIFE
FLYING BEDSTEAD
FLYING BUTTRESS
FLYING DUTCHMAN
FLYING FORTRESS
FLYING SCOTSMAN
FLYING SQUIRREL
FLY INTO A TEMPER
FLY TO THE RESCUE
FLY-WEIGHT TITLE
FOAM AT THE MOUTH
FOLD UP ONE'S TENT
FOLLOW A CALLING
FOLLOW A PATTERN
FOLLOW MY LEADER
FOLLOW ONE'S NOSE
FOLLOW THE CROWD
FOLLOW THE SCENT
FOLLOW THE TRAIL
FOOD CONTROLLER
FOOD FOR THE GODS
FOOD FOR THE MIND
FOOD FOR THOUGHT
FOOD PRODUCTION
FOOTBALL COUPON
FOOTBALL GROUND
FOOTBALL LEAGUE
FOOTBALL PLAYER
FOOTBALL SEASON
FOR ALL THE WORLD
FORBIDDEN FRUIT
FORBID THE BANNS
FORCED MARRIAGE
FORCE OF GRAVITY
FORCIBLE DEMAND
FOREIGN AFFAIRS
FOREIGN CAPITAL
FOREIGN COUNTRY
FOREIGN SERVICE

FOREIGN STATION
FOR EVER AND A DAY
FOR EVER AND EVER
FOR HEAVEN'S SAKE!
FOR LOVE OR MONEY
FORMAL APPROACH
FORMAL OCCASION
FORMAL SANCTION
FORM AN ESTIMATE
FORMATIVE YEARS
FORMIDABLE TASK
FOR THE DURATION
FOR THE LAST TIME
FOR THE LIFE OF ME
FOR THE MOST PART
FORTUNATE EVENT
FOR WANT OF A NAIL
FOSTER DAUGHTER
FOUNDER'S SHARES
FOUR-DOOR SALOON
FOUR-LEAF CLOVER
FOUR-LETTER WORD
FOUR-MASTED SHIP
FOUR-MILE RADIUS
FOUR-MINUTE MILE
FOUR OF DIAMONDS
FOURPENNY STAMP
FOURTEEN OUNCES
FOURTEEN POUNDS
FOURTEENTH HOLE
FOURTH DIVIDEND
FOURTH DIVISION
FOURTH OF AUGUST
FOURTH SYMPHONY
FRACTIONAL PART
FRAGRANT MEMORY
FRAIL STRUCTURE
FRANKIE VAUGHAN
FRANK STATEMENT
FREEDOM FROM WAR
FREE ENTERPRISE
FREE FROM DANGER
FREEMASONS' HALL
FREE OF INTEREST
FREEZING MANNER
FRENCH CANADIAN
FRENCH DRESSING
FRENCH LANGUAGE
FRENCH POLISHER
FRENCH VERMOUTH
FRESHWATER FISH
FREUDIAN SCHOOL
FRIENDLY ACTION
FRIENDLY CRITIC
FRIENDLY DEBATE
FRIENDLY NATION

FRIGHTFUL SIGHT
FROM BAD TO WORSE
FROM BANK TO BANK
FROM EAST TO WEST
FROM HAND TO HAND
FROM HEAD TO FOOT
FROM SIDE TO SIDE
FROM THE CONTEXT
FROM TIME TO TIME
FROM WALL TO WALL
FRONT ELEVATION
FRONT-PAGE STORY
FROTH AND BUBBLE
FROZEN SHOULDER
FULFIL A PROMISE
FULHAM BROADWAY
FULL COMPLEMENT
FULL DIRECTIONS
FULL EMPLOYMENT
FULL MEMBERSHIP
FULL OF INTEREST
FULL OF MISCHIEF
FULL OF NONSENSE
FULL OF VITALITY
FULL-SCALE MODEL
FULL SETTLEMENT
FULL SPEED AHEAD
FULL STEAM AHEAD
FULL TO CAPACITY
FULLY CONSCIOUS
FULLY DEVELOPED
FULLY FASHIONED
FULLY FURNISHED
FUNERAL ORATION
FUNERAL PARLOUR
FUNNY PROGRAMME
FUR-LINED GLOVES
FURNISHED HOUSE
FURNISH SUPPORT
FURNITURE STORE
FURTHER DETAILS
FURTHER OUTLOOK

G – 14

GAIN ADMITTANCE
GAIN CONFIDENCE
GAIN EXPERIENCE
GAIN POSSESSION
GAINS AND LOSSES
GAIN THE MASTERY
GAIN THE VICTORY
GALLANT COMPANY
GALLANT SOLDIER
GALLOPING MAJOR
GALVANIZED IRON

GAMBLING CHANCE
GAME OF DRAUGHTS
GAME OF SKITTLES
GARBLED VERSION
GARGANTUAN MEAL
GARLAND OF ROSES
GATHERING STORM
GATHER MOMENTUM
GATHER STRENGTH
GATHER TOGETHER
GATWICK AIRPORT
GENERAL AMNESTY
GENERAL BENEFIT
GENERAL CONSENT
GENERAL COUNCIL
GENERAL MANAGER
GENERAL MEETING
GENERAL OFFICER
GENERAL OUTLINE
GENERAL OUTLOOK
GENERAL POVERTY
GENERAL RELEASE
GENERAL ROUTINE
GENERAL SERVANT
GENERAL SERVICE
GENERAL SURGEON
GENERAL SURGERY
GENERAL WARRANT
GENEROUS AMOUNT
GENEROUS NATURE
GENEROUS PRAISE
GENEROUS SPIRIT
GENIE OF THE LAMP
GENTLE BREEDING
GENTLE HANDLING
GENTLEMAN CROOK
GENTLEMAN'S CODE
GENTLEMAN USHER
GENTLE REMINDER
GENUINE ARTICLE
GENUINE EXAMPLE
GENUINE RESPECT
GEORGE BRADSHAW
GEORGE GERSHWIN
GEORGE HARRISON
GEORGE MEREDITH
GEORGE MITCHELL
GEORGES SIMENON
GERMAN LANGUAGE
GET AN EXTENSION
GET INTO TROUBLE
GET IT IN THE NECK
GET OFF SCOT-FREE
GET ONE'S DESERTS
GET ONE'S FEET WET
GET ONE'S OWN BACK

GET OUT OF THE WAY
GET THE BEST OF IT
GET THE BETTER OF
GET THE BREEZE UP
GET THE HANG OF IT
GET THE WHIP-HAND
GHASTLY MISTAKE
GHOST OF A CHANCE
GIANT REFRESHED
GIANT'S CAUSEWAY
GIFTED COMPOSER
GILBERT HARDING
GIMCRACK STAKES
GINGERBREAD MAN
GIRD UP THE LOINS
GIRL IN A MILLION
GIVE A MAN HIS DUE
GIVE AN INSTANCE
GIVE ASSISTANCE
GIVE ASSURANCES
GIVE FULL CREDIT
GIVE GENEROUSLY
GIVE IN MARRIAGE
GIVE IT A THOUGHT
GIVEN A REPRIEVE
GIVE ONE A ROCKET
GIVE ONE HIS HEAD
GIVE ONE'S ASSENT
GIVE ONE THE BIRD
GIVE ONE THE PUSH
GIVE ONE THE SLIP
GIVE PERMISSION
GIVE THE GLAD EYE
GIVE TO THE WORLD
GIVE UP DRINKING
GIVE UP ONE'S SEAT
GIVE UP THE GHOST
GLAMOROUS NIGHT
GLARING MISTAKE
GLASGOW RANGERS
GLEAMING ARMOUR
GLOBE ARTICHOKE
GLOOMY FORECAST
GLOOMY PROSPECT
GLORIOUS MUDDLE
GLORIOUS SUNSET
GLOSSY MAGAZINE
GLOWING ACCOUNT
GLOWING COLOURS
GLOW WITH HEALTH
GLUTTON FOR FOOD
GLUTTON FOR WORK
GNASH ONE'S TEETH
GO DOWN FIGHTING
GOD SAVE THE KING!
GOD'S OWN COUNTRY

GOING! GOING! GONE!
GOING GREAT GUNS
GOING TO THE DOGS
GO INTO HOSPITAL
GO INTO MOURNING
GO INTO RAPTURES
GOLDEN PHEASANT
GOLDEN TREASURY
GOLSMITHS' HALL
GOLF TOURNAMENT
GO LIKE HOT CAKES
GONE BY THE BOARD
GONE FOR A BURTON
GOOD BACKGROUND
GOOD-BYE MR CHIPS
GOOD COMPANIONS
GOOD COMPLEXION
GOOD CONSCIENCE
GOOD DISCIPLINE
GOOD FELLOWSHIP
GOOD FOR NOTHING
GOOD FOR THE SOUL
GOOD FOUNDATION
GOOD IMPRESSION
GOOD INTENTIONS
GOOD INVESTMENT
GOOD LITERATURE
GOOD MANAGEMENT
GOOD NEIGHBOURS
GOOD REPUTATION
GOOD RESOLUTION
GOODS IN TRANSIT
GOOD TIME-KEEPER
GOOD UPBRINGING
GO OFF LIKE A BOMB
GO OFF THE HANDLE
GOOSEBERRY BUSH
GOOSEBERRY FOOL
GO OUT OF ONE'S WAY
GORDON RICHARDS
GO TO ANY LENGTHS
GO TO CONFESSION
GO TO THE COUNTRY
GO TO THE SEASIDE
GO TO THE THEATRE
GO UP IN THE WORLD
GOVERNMENT LOAN
GOVERNMENT POST
GOVERNMENT WHIP
GO WEST, YOUNG MAN
GO WITH THE TIMES
GRACE AND FAVOUR
GRACIOUS LIVING
GRADUAL DECLINE
GRADUATED SCALE
GRAIN OF COMFORT

GRAIN OF MUSTARD
GRAND COMMITTEE
GRAND CONDITION
GRANDSTAND VIEW
GRAPHIC ACCOUNT
GRAPHIC DRAWING
GRASP THE NETTLE
GRAVE ADMISSION
GRAVE SITUATION
GRAVE STATEMENT
GRAVE SUSPICION
GRAVEYARD COUGH
GREASE ONE'S PALM
GREAT BED OF WARE
GREAT IGNORANCE
GREAT INJUSTICE
GREAT IN STATURE
GREAT NORTH ROAD
GREAT RECEPTION
GREAT SACRIFICE
GREAT SCOUNDREL
GREAT STATESMAN
GREAT VARIATION
GRECIAN PROFILE
GREENHAM COMMON
GREEN LINE COACH
GREEN VEGETABLE
GRENADIER GUARD
GREYHOUND DERBY
GREYHOUND TRACK
GRIND ONE'S TEETH
GRIST TO THE MILL
GROCERS' COMPANY
GROPE IN THE DARK
GROSS INJUSTICE
GROSVENOR HOUSE
GROUND LANDLORD
GROUNDLESS FEAR
GROUSE SHOOTING
GROWING ANXIETY
GROW UP TOGETHER
GROW VEGETABLES
GRUB STREET HACK
GRUDGING PRAISE
GUERRILLA CHIEF
GUERRILLA FORCE
GUESS THE ANSWER
GUEST CELEBRITY
GUIDED BY REASON
GUILTY OF MURDER
GUN EMPLACEMENT
GURKHA REGIMENT
GUTTURAL ACCENT
GUTTURAL SPEECH

H – 14

HACKNEY MARSHES
HALF-DAY HOLIDAY
HALF-MOON STREET
HALF-SPOKEN WORD
HALLÉ ORCHESTRA
HALLOWEEN PARTY
HALT FOR A MOMENT
HAMMER AND TONGS
HAMPSTEAD HEATH
HAND EMBROIDERY
HANDLE TENDERLY
HANDLE WITH CARE
HAND ON THE TORCH
HANDSOME MARGIN
HANDSOME PROFIT
HANGING GARDENS
HANG OUT A SIGNAL
HANG THE EXPENSE
HAPPILY MARRIED
HAPPY CHILDHOOD
HAPPY CHRISTMAS
HARBOUR REVENGE
HARD DISCIPLINE
HARDENED SINNER
HARDLY ANYTHING
HARDLY CREDIBLE
HARD NUT TO CRACK
HARD TASKMASTER
HARD TO CONVINCE
HARD TO DESCRIBE
HARRY BELAFONTE
HARSH TREATMENT
HAUNTING MELODY
HAVE A GOOD NIGHT
HAVE A SUSPICION
HAVE COMPASSION
HAVE CONFIDENCE
HAVE IT BOTH WAYS
HAVE MISGIVINGS
HAVE NO SCRUPLES
HAVE ONE'S DOUBTS
HAVE ONE'S OWN WAY
HAVE THE COURAGE
HAVE THE KNOW-HOW
HEAD ABOVE WATER
HEADACHE POWDER
HEAD FOR FIGURES
HEAD FOR HEIGHTS
HEADLONG FLIGHT
HEAD OF THE HOUSE
HEAD OF THE RIVER
HEAD OF THE TABLE
HEALTHY OUTLOOK
HEALTHY RESPECT

HEART CONDITION
HEART OF ENGLAND
HEARTY APPETITE
HEARTY APPROVAL
HEARTY LAUGHTER
HEATED ARGUMENT
HEATHER MIXTURE
HEAVEN AND EARTH
HEAVIER THAN AIR
HEAVY ARTILLERY
HEAVY TRANSPORT
HEAVY WITH SLEEP
HEEL OF ACHILLES
HEIGHT OF GENIUS
HEIGHT OF SUMMER
HEIR TO A FORTUNE
HELD IN CONTEMPT
HELL-FIRE CORNER
HELL FOR LEATHER
HELL HATH NO FURY
HELPLESS VICTIM
HELP ONE ANOTHER
HEMEL HEMPSTEAD
HENLEY ON THAMES
HENRY KISSINGER
HENRY THE EIGHTH
HENRY THE FOURTH
HENRY THE SECOND
HERALDIC COLOUR
HERALDIC DEVICE
HERALDIC SHIELD
HERALD'S COLLEGE
HERBERT SPENCER
HEREFORD CASTLE
HERO AND LEANDER
HIDDEN TREASURE
HIGH AS A STEEPLE
HIGH CASUALTIES
HIGH CHANCELLOR
HIGH COMMISSION
HIGH COURT JUDGE
HIGH IN THE SCALE
HIGHLAND CATTLE
HIGH-LEVEL TALKS
HIGHLY EDUCATED
HIGHLY ESTEEMED
HIGHLY ORIGINAL
HIGHLY POLISHED
HIGHLY POSSIBLE
HIGHLY SEASONED
HIGH PERCENTAGE
HIGHWAY ROBBERY
HIP MEASUREMENT
HISTORICAL PLAY
HISTORICAL WORK
HISTORIC MOMENT

HISTORY TEACHER
HIT OVER THE HEAD
HIVE OF ACTIVITY
HIVE OF INDUSTRY
HOBNAILED BOOTS
HOLD AN ARGUMENT
HOLD AN ELECTION
HOLD EVERYTHING
HOLD IN ABEYANCE
HOLD IN CONTEMPT
HOLDING COMPANY
HOLDING QUALITY
HOLD IN SUSPENSE
HOLD ONE'S BREATH
HOLD ONE'S GROUND
HOLD ONE'S HEAD UP
HOLD ONE'S HORSES
HOLD ONE'S TONGUE
HOLD UP ONE'S HEAD
HOLIDAY TRAFFIC
HOLIDAY WITH PAY
HOLIER THAN THOU
HOLLOWAY PRISON
HOLLOW LAUGHTER
HOLLOW PRETENCE
HOME DEPARTMENT
HOMELESS PERSON
HOME ON THE RANGE
HOMES FOR HEROES
HONEYMOON HOTEL
HONORARY DEGREE
HONORARY FELLOW
HONORARY MEMBER
HONORARY STATUS
HONOUR AND GLORY
HOPE AND BELIEVE
HOPE FOR THE BEST
HOPELESS MISFIT
HOP, SKIP AND JUMP
HORIZONTAL BARS
HORIZONTAL LINE
HORSE AND HOUNDS
HORSE ARTILLERY
HORSE OF THE YEAR
HOSPITAL ANNEXE
HOSPITAL MATRON
HOSPITAL SUNDAY
HOSTILE COUNTRY
HOSTILE VERDICT
HOSTILE WITNESS
HOT-AIR MERCHANT
HOT AND BOTHERED
HOTEL DETECTIVE
HOTLY CONTESTED
HOT ON ONE'S HEELS
HOT ON ONE'S TRAIL

HOT-WATER BOTTLE
HOT-WATER SUPPLY
HOT-WATER SYSTEM
HOUSE DECORATOR
HOUSE DETECTIVE
HOUSEHOLD GOODS
HOUSEHOLD LINEN
HOUSEHOLD STAFF
HOUSEMAID'S KNEE
HOUSE OF COMMONS
HOUSE OF HANOVER
HOUSE OF ONE'S OWN
HOUSE OF THE LORD
HOUSE OF WINDSOR
HOUSE OF WORSHIP
HOUSE PHYSICIAN
HOUSING PROBLEM
HOUSING PROJECT
HOWLING DERVISH
HOWLING SUCCESS
HOW THE LAND LIES
HUMAN ENDEAVOUR
HUMAN RELATIONS
HUMAN SACRIFICE
HUMAN SUFFERING
HUMBLE DWELLING
HUMBLE PETITION
HUMPBACK BRIDGE
HUMPHREY BOGART
HUNDRED DOLLARS
HUNDRED GUINEAS
HUNDRED PER CENT
HUNG PARLIAMENT
HUNT HIGH AND LOW
HUNT THE SLIPPER
HUNT THE THIMBLE
HURT EXPRESSION
HUSBAND AND WIFE
HYDE PARK CORNER
HYDE PARK ORATOR
HYDRAULIC POWER
HYDRAULIC PRESS
HYPHENATED WORD
HYPNOTIC TRANCE

1 – 14

ICE-CREAM CORNET
ICE-CREAM SUNDAE
IDEAL COMPANION
IDENTICAL TWINS
IDENTITY PARADE
IGNOMINIOUS END
IGNORANT MASSES
IGNORANT PERSON
ILLEGAL TRAFFIC

ILL-GOTTEN GAINS
ILL-TIMED REMARK
IMAGINARY POINT
IMMEDIATE REPLY
IMMEMORIAL ELMS
IMMINENT DANGER
IMMORAL CONDUCT
IMMOVABLE FEAST
IMPART MOMENTUM
IMPENDING STORM
IMPERATIVE MOOD
IMPERFECT RHYME
IMPERFECT TENSE
IMPERIAL BALLET
IMPERIAL GALLEON
IMPERIAL PURPLE
IMPERIAL WEIGHT
IMPLACABLE MOOD
IMPLIED CONSENT
IMPORTANT EVENT
IMPOSING FIGURE
IMPOSSIBLE TASK
IMPROPER PERSON
IMPROVE MATTERS
IMPROVE ONESELF
IMPUDENT CHARGE
IMPUDENT SPEECH
IMPURE THOUGHTS
IN A LITTLE WHILE
IN ALL INNOCENCE
IN A MORTAL HURRY
IN ANCIENT TIMES
IN ANOTHER CLASS
IN ANTICIPATION
IN A STATE OF FLUX
INCENDIARY BOMB
IN CERTAIN CASES
INCLINE ONE'S EAR
INCLUSIVE TERMS
INCOMING TENANT
IN COURSE OF TIME
INCREASED FARES
INCREASED SPEED
IN DEEP MOURNING
INDEFINITE TIME
INDEPENDENT AIR
INDIAN ELEPHANT
INDICATIVE MOOD
IN DIFFICULTIES
INDIRECT EFFECT
INDIRECT METHOD
INDIRECT OBJECT
INDIRECT SPEECH
INDUSTRIAL AREA
INDUSTRIAL ARTS
IN EVERY QUARTER

IN EVERY RESPECT
INEXORABLE FATE
INFERIOR NATURE
INFERIOR STATUS
INFINITE NUMBER
INFORMAL SPEECH
INFRINGE THE LAW
INGRAINED HABIT
INITIAL ATTEMPT
INITIAL EXPENSE
INITIATIVE TEST
INJURED HUSBAND
INLAND WATERWAY
IN LOCO PARENTIS
INMOST THOUGHS
INNER CITY RIOTS
INNERMOST BEING
INNER SANCTUARY
INNINGS VICTORY
INNOCENT ABROAD
INNOCENT REMARK
INNOCENT VICTIM
INNS OF CHANCERY
IN ONE'S BORN DAYS
IN ONE'S MIND'S EYE
IN ONE'S OWN LIGHT
IN ONE'S OWN RIGHT
IN ORDER OF MERIT
IN RELATIONSHIP
IN ROUND NUMBERS
INSIDE POSITION
IN SOUTH AMERICA
INSPIRE RESPECT
INSTANT DISLIKE
INSULATED CABLE
INSULTING WORDS
INSULT TO INJURY
INSURANCE AGENT
INSURANCE CLAIM
INTENSE DISLIKE
INTENSE FEELING
INTENSE LONGING
INTENSIVE STUDY
INTERESTED LOOK
INTERNAL STRIFE
INTERNMENT CAMP
INTERVAL OF TIME
IN THE AFTERNOON
IN THE AGGREGATE
IN THE ASCENDANT
IN THE BEGINNING
IN THE FIRM'S TIME
IN THE FOREFRONT
IN THE HEADLINES
IN THE LIMELIGHT
IN THE MEANWHILE

IN THE MOONLIGHT
IN THE MOUNTAINS
IN THE NEWSPAPER
IN THE NEXT WORLD
IN THE ORCHESTRA
IN THE PROVINCES
IN THE PUBLIC EYE
IN THE SAME CLASS
IN THE THICK OF IT
INTIMATE CIRCLE
INTIMATE FRIEND
INTO A COCKED HAT
INTO THE BARGAIN
INTRINSIC VALUE
INTRINSIC WORTH
INTRODUCE A BILL
INVARIABLE RULE
INVENT AN EXCUSE
INVERTED COMMAS
INVETERATE LIAR
INVINCIBLE ARMY
INVITE A QUARREL
INVITE RIDICULE
IRISH FREE STATE
IRISH PEASANTRY
IRONS IN THE FIRE
IRREGULAR UNION
ISLAND IN THE SUN
ISLAND PARADISE
IT'S A SMALL WORLD

J – 14

JACK OF DIAMONDS
JACOBITE RISING
JAYNE MANSFIELD
JEALOUS HUSBAND
JESSIE MATTHEWS
JIMMINY CRICKET
JOAN SUTHERLAND
JOBS FOR THE BOYS
JOHN BARLEYCORN
JOHN BROWN'S BODY
JOHN DRINKWATER
JOHN GALSWORTHY
JOHN LOGIE BAIRD
JOHN THE BAPTIST
JOIN IN MARRIAGE
JOINT COMMITTEE
JOIN THE COLOURS
JOIN THE RAT-RACE
JOINT LIABILITY
JOINT OWNERSHIP
JOINT-STOCK BANK
JOSHUA REYNOLDS
JUDE THE OBSCURE

JUDICIAL MANNER
JUDICIAL MURDER
JUDICIAL NOTICE
JULIAN CALENDAR
JULY THE SEVENTH
JULY THE TWELFTH
JUMPING CRACKER
JUNE THE SEVENTH
JUNE THE TWELFTH
JUNIOR REPORTER
JUPITER PLUVIUS

K – 14

KEEP A GOOD TABLE
KEEP A TIGHT REIN
KEEP EARLY HOURS
KEEP IN SUSPENSE
KEEP IN THE SHADE
KEEP ONE'S CHIN UP
KEEP ONE'S FIGURE
KEEP ONE'S HAIR ON
KEEP ONE'S HAND IN
KEEP ONE'S SENSES
KEEP ONE'S TEMPER
KEEP OUT OF SIGHT
KEEP STRAIGHT ON
KEEP THE COLD OUT
KEEP THE RIGHT
KEEP TO THE RULES
KEEP UNDER COVER
KEEP WELL IN HAND
KENSINGTON GORE
KEPT IN HIS PLACE
KEYSTONE COMEDY
KIDNEY AND BACON
KIDNEY POTATOES
KILLED IN ACTION
KINDLY INTEREST
KING AND COUNTRY
KING ARTHUR'S MEN
KING OF DIAMONDS
KING'S MESSENGER
KITCHEN CABINET
KITCHEN DRESSER
KITCHEN UTENSIL
KNIGHT IN ARMOUR
KNIGHTS OF MALTA
KNITTING NEEDLE
KNIVES AND FORKS
KNOCK-ABOUT TURN
KNOCK AT THE DOOR
KNOCK-DOWN PRICE
KNOCK INTO SHAPE
KNOCK ON THE DOOR
KNOCK ON THE HEAD

KNOW A MOVE OR TWO
KNOW BY INSTINCT
KNOW FOR CERTAIN
KNOWLEDGE OF LAW
KNOWN CHARACTER
KNOW ONE'S ONIONS
KNOW WHEN TO STOP

L – 14

LABOUR EXCHANGE
LABOUR MAJORITY
LABOUR MINORITY
LABOUR MOVEMENT
LABOUR THE POINT
LACK OF EVIDENCE
LACK OF FRICTION
LACK OF INTEREST
LACK OF JUDGMENT
LACK OF PRACTICE
LACK OF STRENGTH
LACK OF SYMPATHY
LACK OF TRAINING
LACRIMA CHRISTI
LADY CHATTERLEY
LADY OF THE HOUSE
LADY OF THE MANOR
LADY WINDERMERE
LAID BY THE HEELS
LAID ON THE SHELF
LAKE WINDERMERE
LAME CONCLUSION
LANCASTER HOUSE
LAND COMMISSION
LANDED INTEREST
LANDED PROPERTY
LAND OF NO RETURN
LAND ON ONE'S FEET
LANGUAGE MASTER
LANTERN LECTURE
LARGE OVERDRAFT
LARGER THAN LIFE
LASSIES AND LADS
LAST APPEARANCE
LAST CONNECTION
LAST GENERATION
LASTING BENEFIT
LASTING QUALITY
LASTING SUCCESS
LAST INSTALMENT
LAST IN THE QUEUE
LATE NIGHT FINAL
LATEST BULLETIN
LATH AND PLASTER
LATTER-DAY SAINT

LAUGHING MATTER
LAUNCH AN ATTACK
LAUNCHING STAGE
LAUREL AND HARDY
LAURENCE HARVEY
LAURENCE STERNE
LAW ENFORCEMENT
LAWFUL OCCASION
LAW OF THE JUNGLE
LAY DOWN A CELLAR
LAY ON TRANSPORT
LEADING ACTRESS
LEADING ARTICLE
LEADING CITIZEN
LEADING COUNSEL
LEADING STRINGS
LEAD THE FASHION
LEAD TO THE ALTAR
LEAGUE FOOTBALL
LEAPS AND BOUNDS
LEARNED COUNSEL
LEARNED SOCIETY
LEASEHOLD HOUSE
LEAVE A LOOPHOLE
LEAVE DESTITUTE
LEAVE NO ADDRESS
LEAVE OF ABSENCE
LEAVE SENSELESS
LEAVE THE GROUND
LEAVE WELL ALONE
LEDA AND THE SWAN
LEEWARD ISLANDS
LEFT HIGH AND DRY
LEFT IN THE LURCH
LEFT SPEECHLESS
LEFT UNFINISHED
LEGAL AUTHORITY
LEGAL CHICANERY
LEGAL ETIQUETTE
LEGAL FORMALITY
LEGAL LIABILITY
LEGALLY BINDING
LEGAL OWNERSHIP
LEGAL PROCEDURE
LEGION OF HONOUR
LEMONADE POWDER
LEMONADE SHANDY
LENDING LIBRARY
LEND ME YOUR EARS
LESLIE MITCHELL
LET DOWN LIGHTLY
LET DOWN THE SIDE
LET OR HINDRANCE
LETTER OF ADVICE
LETTER OF CREDIT
LETTER OF THE LAW

LET THE SIDE DOWN
LET THINGS SLIDE
LETTRE DE CACHET
LIAISON OFFICER
LIBERAL HELPING
LIBRARY EDITION
LICK ONE'S WOUNDS
LICK THE PLATTER
LIFE EXPECTANCY
LIFELONG FRIEND
LIFE OF PLEASURE
LIFE WITH FATHER
LIFT UP ONE'S HEAD
LIGHT AND BITTER
LIGHT ARTILLERY
LIGHT BREAKFAST
LIGHTEN THE LOAD
LIGHTER THAN AIR
LIGHT FANTASTIC
LIGHTING-UP TIME
LIGHTNING FLASH
LIGHTNING SPEED
LIGHT PROGRAMME
LIGHTS OF LONDON
LIGHT TRANSPORT
LIKE A BOMBSHELL
LIKE A MILLSTONE
LILY-WHITE HANDS
LIMITED COMPANY
LIMITED EDITION
LIMITING FACTOR
LINE OF APPROACH
LINE OF BUSINESS
LINGERING DEATH
LINK IN THE CHAIN
LION OF THE NORTH
LISLE STOCKINGS
LISTEN TO REASON
LIST OF CONTENTS
LITERAL ACCOUNT
LITERAL MEANING
LITERARY CRITIC
LITERARY DIGEST
LITERARY EDITOR
LITERARY OUTPUT
LITTLE AND OFTEN
LITTLE BROWN JUG
LITTLE BY LITTLE
LITTLE CHILDREN
LITTLE CORPORAL
LITTLE DISTANCE
LITTLE IN COMMON
LITTLE INTEREST
LITTLE LEARNING
LITTLE PITCHERS
LITTLE PROGRESS

LITTLE RESPONSE
LITTLE STRANGER
LIVE A CLEAN LIFE
LIVE AMMUNITION
LIVE AND LET LIVE
LIVE ON ONE'S WITS
LIVER AND ONIONS
LIVE TO A HUNDRED
LIVING LANGUAGE
LIVING QUARTERS
LIVING REMINDER
LIVING STANDARD
LLOYD'S REGISTER
LOADED QUESTION
LOAD ON ONE'S MIND
LOAD WITH CHAINS
LOCAL AUTHORITY
LOCAL NEWSPAPER
LOFTY AMBITIONS
LOGICAL CONDUCT
LOGICAL PROCESS
LONDONDERRY AIR
LONDON HOSPITAL
LONDON MARATHON
LONDON REGIMENT
LONDON RHAPSODY
LONDON SCOTTISH
LONDON TERMINUS
LONG ENGAGEMENT
LONGHAND WRITER
LONG IN THE TOOTH
LONG JOHN SILVER
LONG-LOST FRIEND
LONG PARLIAMENT
LONG-TERM POLICY
LOOK FOR TROUBLE
LOOK IN THE GLASS
LOOK ON ALL SIDES
LOOK PROSPEROUS
LOOK TO THE FRONT
LOOSE BEHAVIOUR
LOOSE RENDERING
LORD CHANCELLOR
LORD LIEUTENANT
LORD MAYOR'S SHOW
LORD OF CREATION
LORD OF THE ISLES
LORD OF THE MANOR
LORD PALMERSTON
LORDS AND LADIES
LORDS SPIRITUAL
LORDS' TAVERNERS
LOSE CONFIDENCE
LOSE ONE'S MEMORY
LOSE ONE'S REASON
LOSE ONE'S TEMPER

LOSE ONE'S TICKET
LOSE ONE'S TONGUE
LOSS OF APPETITE
LOSS OF INTEREST
LOSS OF PRESTIGE
LOSS OF STRENGTH
LOST TO THE WORLD
LOT TO ANSWER FOR
LOUIS ARMSTRONG
LOVE IN A COTTAGE
LOVE IN IDLENESS
LOVELY TO LOOK AT
LOVE OF PLEASURE
LOVING KINDNESS
LOWER ONE'S VOICE
LOW TEMPERATURE
LOYAL SUPPORTER
LUBRICATING OIL
LUCK OF THE DEVIL
LUCK OF THE IRISH
LUCREZIA BORGIA
LUNATIC AT LARGE
LUNCHEON BASKET
LUNCH-TIME SCORE
LYON KING OF ARMS
LYTTON STRACHEY

M – 14

MACARONI CHEESE
MACHINE-GUN POST
MADAM BUTTERFLY
MADAM POMPADOUR
MADE FOR THE PART
MAGNETIC NEEDLE
MAGNOLIA STREET
MAIL VAN ROBBERY
MAIN ATTRACTION
MAIN INGREDIENT
MAINTENANCE MAN
MAJOR OPERATION
MAJOR ROAD AHEAD
MAKE A BEGINING
MAKE A BIG SPLASH
MAKE A BOLT FOR IT
MAKE A COMPLAINT
MAKE A DISCOVERY
MAKE A GOOD GUESS
MAKE A GOOD SCORE
MAKE A GOOD START
MAKE ALLOWANCES
MAKE AN ENTRANCE
MAKE AN ESTIMATE
MAKE A NIGHT OF IT
MAKE A REFERENCE
MAKE A STATEMENT

MAKE DELIVERIES
MAKE EXCEPTIONS
MAKE FEW DEMANDS
MAKE FOR THE DOOR
MAKE NO PROGRESS
MAKE PROVISIONS
MAKE REPARATION
MAKE RINGS ROUND
MAKE SACRIFICES
MAKE THE RUNNING
MAKE THINGS EASY
MAKE UP A QUARREL
MAKE UP ONE'S MIND
MALCOLM SARGENT
MALE VOICE CHOIR
MANAGING EDITOR
MAN AND SUPERMAN
MANCHESTER CITY
MANDARIN ORANGE
MAN-EATING SHARK
MAN IN THE STREET
MAN OF CHARACTER
MAN OF INFLUENCE
MAN OF MANY PARTS
MAN OF SUBSTANCE
MAN OF THE MOMENT
MAN OF THE PEOPLE
MAN ON HORSEBACK
MAN'S BEST FRIEND
MAN THE DEFENCES
MANUAL LABOURER
MAPPIN TERRACES
MARATHON RUNNER
MARCHING ORDERS
MARCH THE EIGHTH
MARCH THE FOURTH
MARCH THE SECOND
MARCUS ANTONIUS
MARCUS AURELIUS
MARGIN OF ERROR
MARGIN OF PROFIT
MARGIN OF SAFETY
MARINE ENGINEER
MARITIME NATION
MARKED TENDENCY
MARKET GARDENER
MARKETING BOARD
MARKET RESEARCH
MARK OF APPROVAL
MARK OF THE BEAST
MARK OUT A COURSE
MARRIAGE BROKER
MARRIAGE BUREAU
MARRIAGE MARKET
MARSUPIAL POUCH
MASHED POTATOES

MASS PRODUCTION
MASTERMAN READY
MASTER OF HOUNDS
MATCH FOR ANYONE,
MATERIAL WEALTH
MATRON OF HONOUR
MATTER OF CHOICE
MATTER OF COURSE
MATTER OF RECORD
MATTER OF REGRET
MATTERS OF STATE
MAUNDY THURSDAY
MAY THE ELEVENTH
MEANS OF SUPPORT
MECHANISED ARMY
MEDICAL ADVISER
MEDICAL COLLEGE
MEDICAL HISTORY
MEDICAL OFFICER
MEDICAL SCIENCE
MEDICAL STUDENT
MEDICINAL VALUE
MEDICINE BOTTLE
MEERSCHAUM PIPE
MELT IN THE MOUTH
MEMBER OF THE BAR
MEMBERSHIP CARD
MENDICANT ORDER
MENTAL ATTITUDE
MENTAL CAPACITY
MENTAL CONFLICT
MENTAL DISORDER
MENTAL EXERCISE
MENTAL HOSPITAL
MENTAL SICKNESS
MENTAL STIMULUS
MENTAL STRUGGLE
MENTAL WEAKNESS
MERCHANT BANKER
MERCHANT PRINCE
MERCHANT SEAMAN
MERCHANT TAILOR
MERCHANT VESSEL
MERMAID THEATRE
MERRY AND BRIGHT
MERRY CHRISTMAS
METEORIC SHOWER
MEZZANINE FLOR
MICHAEL BENTINE
MICHAEL FARADAY
MICHAEL JACKSON
MICHAELMAS TERM
MICHAEL WILDING
MIDDLE DISTANCE
MIDDLE OF THE DAY
MIDDLE REGISTER

MIDNIGHT REVELS
MIDSHIPMAN EASY
MIDSUMMER NIGHT
MILD PUNISHMENT
MILITARY ATTACK
MILITARY CAREER
MILITARY ESCORT
MILITARY GENIUS
MILITARY PARADE
MILITARY POLICE
MILITARY SCHOOL
MILITARY SPIRIT
MILITARY TATTOO
MILK OF MAGNESIA
MILLION DOLLARS
MILL ON THE FLOSS
MIND OVER MATTER
MINERAL DEPOSIT
MINERAL KINGDOM
MINESTRONE SOUP
MINING ENGINEER
MINISTRY OF FOOD
MINOR OPERATION
MISSIONARY WORK
MISTER MICAWBER
MISTLETOE BOUGH
MNEMONIC DEVICE
MOBILE FEATURES
MOCK TURTLE SOUP
MODEL AEROPLANE
MODEL BEHAVIOUR
MODEL HOUSEHOLD
MODERATE DEGREE
MODERATE HEALTH
MODERATE HEIGHT
MODERATE INCOME
MODERATE WEIGHT
MODERN BUILDING
MODERN LANGUAGE
MODS AND ROCKERS
MONEY IN THE BANK
MONKEY BUSINESS
MONOTONOUS LIFE
MONROE DOCTRINE
MONSTROUS CRIME
MONTHLY ACCOUNT
MONTHLY PAYMENT
MONTH OF SUNDAYS
MONUMENTAL WORK
MOONLIGHT NIGHT
MORAL BLACKMAIL
MORAL CERTAINTY
MORAL CHARACTER
MORAL COWARDICE
MORAL IGNORANCE
MORAL NECESSITY

MORAL PRINCIPLE
MORAL TURPITUDE
MORE THAN A MATCH
MORE THAN ENOUGH
MORE TO THE POINT
MORNING SERVICE
MOROCCO LEATHER
MOST HONOURABLE
MOST OF THE NIGHT
MOTHER AND CHILD
MOTHER'S DARLING
MOTHERS' MEETING
MOTHER SUPERIOR
MOTLEY ASSEMBLY
MOTOR AMBULANCE
MOTOR TRANSPORT
MOUNTAIN RESORT
MOUNTING DANGER
MOUNT THE THRONE
MOVE TO LAUGHTER
MOVING PAVEMENT
MUCH IN EVIDENCE
MUCH-MARRIED MAN
MULTIPLY BY FIVE
MULTIPLY BY FOUR
MULTIPLY BY NINE
MUNITIONS OF WAR
MURDER MOST FOUL
MUSCULAR ENERGY
MUSEUM SPECIMEN
MUSHROOM GROWTH
MUSHROOM SUBURB
MUSICAL ABILITY
MUSICAL EVENING
MUSICAL GLASSES
MUSICAL MOMENTS
MUSICAL PRODIGY
MUSICAL QUALITY
MUSIC PUBLISHER
MUSTARD PLASTER
MUTE ADMIRATION
MUTUAL GOODWILL
MUTUAL SYMPATHY
MUZZLE VELOCITY
MY LADY NICOTINE

N – 14

NAME AND ADDRESS
NAMELESS TERROR
NAME YOUR POISON
NAMING CEREMONY
NAPOLEON BRANDY
NAPOLEONIC CODE
NAPOLEONIC WARS
NARRATIVE VERSE

NARROW INTERVAL
NARROW MAJORITY
NASTY BIT OF WORK
NATIONAL ANTHEM
NATIONAL CREDIT
NATIONAL CRISIS
NATIONAL DEVICE
NATIONAL EMBLEM
NATIONAL FIGURE
NATIONAL HEALTH
NATIONAL INCOME
NATIONAL SPIRIT
NATIONAL STATUS
NATIONAL WEALTH
NATIONAL WINNER
NATION-WIDE HUNT
NATIVE COMPOUND
NATIVE LANGUAGE
NATIVE QUARTERS
NATURAL HARBOUR
NATURAL HISTORY
NATURAL IMPULSE
NATURAL PROCESS
NATURAL SCIENCE
NAVAL ARCHITECT
NAVAL EXERCISES
NAVAL OPERATION
NAVIGABLE RIVER
NEANDERTHAL MAN
NEAR NEIGHBOURS
NEAR THE KNUCKLE
NEAT AS A BANDBOX
NEEDLES AND PINS
NE'ER CAST A CLOUT
NEGATIVE ACTION
NEGATIVE ANSWER
NEGATIVE RESULT
NEGRO SPIRITUAL
NERVOUS TENSION
NETHER GARMENTS
NEUTRAL COUNTRY
NEVER-NEVER LAND
NEVER SATISFIED
NEW CONSIGNMENT
NEW-FANGLED IDEA
NEW LAMPS FOR OLD
NEW LEASE OF LIFE
NEWS OF THE WORLD
NEWSPAPER WORLD
NEXT BEST FRIEND
NEXT GENERATION
NICE DIFFERENCE
NICELY BALANCED
NICE PERCEPTION
NIGGER MINSTREL
NIGHT BLINDNESS

NIGHT-CLUB QUEEN
NIL DESPERANDUM
NINE DAYS' WONDER
NINE MEN'S MORRIS
NINE O'CLOCK NEWS
NINE OF DIAMONDS
NINETEENTH HOLE
NINETEEN TWENTY
NINETY THOUSANDS
NINTH OF JANUARY
NINTH OF OCTOBER
NIPPED IN THE BUD
NOBLESSE OBLIGE
NOBODY'S DARLING
NO END OF A FELLOW
NO FIXED ADDRESS
NO HALF MEASURES
NOISE ABATEMENT
NOISE REDUCTION
NO JOKING MATTER
NOMINAL CAPITAL
NOMINAL DAMAGES
NOMINATIVE CASE
NORMAL SOLUTION
NORMAN CONQUEST
NO ROOM AT THE INN
NO ROOM FOR DOUBT
NORTH AUSTRALIA
NORTHERN ACCENT
NORTHERN LIGHTS
NORTH OF ENGLAND
NORTH OF THE WASH
NORTHWARD BOUND
NOSE OUT OF JOINT
NO STOMACH FOR IT
NOTHING DAUNTED
NOTHING TO OFFER
NOTHING TO SPARE
NOTHING VENTURE
NO THOROUGHFARE
NO TROUBLE AT ALL
NOUN OF ASSEMBLY
NOVEL SITUATION
NO VISIBLE MEANS
NUCLEAR FALLOUT
NUCLEAR FISSION
NUCLEAR PHYSICS
NUCLEAR REACTOR
NUCLEAR WARFARE
NUMBER CRUNCHER
NUMBER THIRTEEN
NUMERICAL ORDER
NURSING SERVICE
NUTS AND RAISINS
NYLON STOCKINGS

O – 14

OBITUARY NOTICE
OBJECT OF TERROR
OBSCURE PROBLEM
OBSERVATION CAR
OCCASIONAL SHOT
OCCUPYING FORCE
OCEAN GREYHOUND
OCTAVIUS CAESAR
OEDIPUS COMPLEX
OFFER AN OPINION
OFFICE BUILDING
OFFICE OF PROFIT
OFFICER OF STATE
OFFICERS AND MEN
OFFICIAL CENSUS
OFFICIAL NOTICE
OFFICIAL REPORT
OFFICIAL SECRET
OFFICIAL SOURCE
OFFICIAL STRIKE
OFF LIKE A STREAK
OFFSET PRINTING
OFF THE PREMISES
OFF WITH THE HEAD
OF HUMAN BONDAGE
OLD BOYS' REUNION
OLD CLOTHES SHOP
OLD FOLKS AT HOME
OLD MAN OF THE SEA
OLD MOTHER RILEY
OLD PEOPLE'S HOME
OLD-TIME DANCING
OLD-WORLD GARDEN
OLIVER CROMWELL
OMNIBUS EDITION
ON A HEROIC SCALE
ON A HIGHER PLANE
ONE AND A QUARTER
ONE-ARMED BANDIT
ONE CLAIM TO FAME
ONE CROWDED HOUR
ONE FINE MORNING
ONE IN A THOUSAND
ONE-MAN BUSINESS
ONE NIGHT OF LOVE
ONE OF THE FAMILY
ONE OF THE PEOPLE
ONE OF THESE DAYS
ONE THAT GOT AWAY
ONLY TOO PLEASED
ON ONE CONDITION
ON ONE'S BEAM-ENDS
ON ONE'S DEATH-BED
ON ONE'S HIND LEGS

ON ONE'S LAST LEGS
ON ONE'S OWN TERMS
ON PLEASURE BENT
ON PUBLIC GROUND
ON SHORT RATIONS
ON SUBSCRIPTION
ON THE BAND-WAGON
ON THE CONTINENT
ON THE DEBIT SIDE
ON THE DEFENSIVE
ON THE DOWNGRADE
ON THE HOME FRONT
ON THE LARGE SIZE
ON THE OFF CHANCE
ON THE OFFENSIVE
ON THE OTHER HAND
ON THE OTHER SIDE
ON THE OUTSKIRTS
ON THE PROMENADE
ON THE RIGHT SIDE
ON THE SHADY SIDE
ON THE SHORT LIST
ON THE SHORT SIDE
ON THE SMALL SIDE
ON THE SUNNY SIDE
ON THE TELEPHONE
ON THE THRESHOLD
ON THE TIGHT SIDE
ON THE TOUCH-LINE
ON THE WRONG FOOT
ON THE WRONG SIDE
ON THE WRONG TRACK
ONTO A GOOD THING
ON WITH THE DANCE
OPEN-AIR CONCERT
OPEN-AIR SERVICE
OPEN-AIR SPEAKER
OPEN-AIR THEATRE
OPEN-CAST MINING
OPEN CONFESSION
OPEN DISCUSSION
OPEN-DOOR POLICY
OPENING BATSMAN
OPEN PARLIAMENT
OPEN THE BIDDING
OPEN THE INNINGS
OPEN THE SLUICES
OPEN TO ARGUMENT
OPEN TO QUESTION
OPEN TOURNAMENT
OPEN UNIVERSITY
OPERATING TABLE
OPERATIONS ROOM
OPPOSITE NUMBER
OPPOSITION WHIP
ORCHESTRA STALL

ORDER IN ADVANCE
ORDER IN COUNCIL
ORDERLY CONDUCT
ORDERLY OFFICER
ORDER OF THE BATH
ORDER OF THE BOOT
ORDINARY SEAMAN
ORDINARY SHARES
ORDNANCE SURVEY
ORGANIC DISEASE
ORGANIC FARMING
ORGANISED GAMES
ORNAMENTAL POND
ORNAMENTAL TREE
ORTHODOX CHURCH
OSTRICH FEATHER
OTHER FISH TO FRY
OUNCE OF TOBACCO
OUT-AND-OUT ROGUE
OUTDOOR MEETING
OUTDOOR SERVANT
OUT FOR THE COUNT
OUTGOING TENANT
OUT OF CHARACTER
OUT OF CONDITION
OUT OF CURIOSITY
OUT OF ONE'S DEPTH
OUT OF ONE'S SHELL
OUT OF THE COMMON
OUT OF THE GUTTER
OUT OF THIS WORLD
OUTSIDE ONE'S KEN
OUTSIDE OPINION
OVERCOME BY FEAR
OVERDUE ACCOUNT
OVER THE COUNTER
OVER THE RAINBOW
OXFORD MOVEMENT
OXYGEN CYLINDER

P – 14

PACKET OF CRISPS
PACKET OF TWENTY
PACKING STATION
PACK OF NONSENSE
PACK ONE'S TRUNKS
PAGES OF HISTORY
PAINT AND POWDER
PAINT A PORTRAIT
PAIR OF BREECHES
PAIR OF CALIPERS
PAIR OF CLIPPERS
PAIR OF CRUTCHES
PAIR OF SCISSORS
PAIR OF SLIPPERS

PAIR OF TROUSERS
PAIR OF TWEEZERS
PALM OF ONE'S HAND
PANCAKE LANDING
PANCAKE TUESDAY
PANGS OF REMORSE
PANTOMIME QUEEN
PANZER DIVISION
PARADISE FOR TWO
PARALLEL COURSE
PARCHMENT PAPER
PARISH MAGAZINE
PARISH REGISTER
PARKING PROBLEM
PARLIAMENT HILL
PARMESAN CHEESE
PAROXYSM OF RAGE
PARTIAL CONSENT
PARTIAL ECLIPSE
PARTIAL SUCCESS
PARTING PRESENT
PARTISAN SPIRIT
PARTNER IN CRIME
PARTY MACHINERY
PARTY PROGRAMME
PASS DOWN THE CAR
PASSENGER PLANE
PASSENGER TRAIN
PASSING THOUGHT
PASSIONATE PLEA
PASS THE MUSTARD
PAST AND PRESENT
PAST EXPERIENCE
PASTORAL LETTER
PAST PARTICIPLE
PAST REDEMPTION
PATCHWORK QUILT
PATÉ DE FOIS GRAS
PATENT MEDICINE
PATERNOSTER ROW
PAUSE FOR A WHILE
PAUSE FOR BREATH
PAVEMENT ARTIST
PAVING MATERIAL
PAYABLE AT SIGHT
PAY A COMPLIMENT
PAY NO ATTENTION
PEACE AND PLENTY
PEACEFUL ENDING
PEACE IN OUR TIME
PEAL OF LAUGHTER
PEARLS OF WISDOM
PECULIAR PEOPLE
PECULIAR PERSON
PEDIGREE CATTLE
PEER OF THE REALM

PEG-TOP TROUSERS
PENAL SERVITUDE
PENCIL AND PAPER
PENNY FOR THE GUY
PENNY IN THE SLOT
PENSIONABLE AGE
PEPPERCORN RENT
PERCUSSION BAND
PERFECT DARLING
PERFECT EXAMPLE
PERFECT SETTING
PERFECT SILENCE
PERFORMING BEAR
PERFORMING FLEA
PERFORMING SEAL
PERPETUAL BLISS
PERPETUAL WORRY
PERSONAL APPEAL
PERSONAL COLUMN
PERSONAL ESTATE
PERSONAL ESTEEM
PERSONAL FACTOR
PERSONAL FAVOUR
PERSONAL LETTER
PERSONAL MATTER
PERSONAL REMARK
PERSONAL STEREO
PERSON IN CHARGE
PERSON OF REPUTE
PERSONS UNKNOWN
PERSON TO PERSON
PERTINENT REPLY
PETER THE HERMIT
PETROLEUM JELLY
PETROL SHORTAGE
PETTY GRIEVANCE
PHOTOGRAPH WELL
PHRASE AND FABLE
PHYSICAL BEAUTY
PHYSICAL ENERGY
PICCADILLY LINE
PICKLED CABBAGE
PICKLED HERRING
PICK OF THE BUNCH
PICK UP A FEW TIPS
PICK UP STRENGTH
PICKWICK PAPERS
PICTURE GALLERY
PICTURE OF GLOOM
PICTURE WRITING
PIERCE THE HEART
PIERCING GLANCE
PIETRO ANNIGONI
PILE ON THE AGONY
PILGRIM FATHERS
PILLAR OF THE LAW

PILLAR OF WISDOM
PILOTLESS PLANE
PINCER MOVEMENT
PINCH AND SCRAPE
PINEAPPLE JUICE
PINNACLE OF FAME
PINS AND NEEDLES
PITCH OVERBOARD
PLACE IN HISTORY
PLACE OF ONE'S OWN
PLACE OF WORSHIP
PLAGUE OF LONDON
PLAICE AND CHIPS
PLAIN AND SIMPLE
PLAIN CHOCOLATE
PLAIN STATEMENT
PLANETARY ORBIT
PLANNED ECONOMY
PLANNING OFFICE
PLAN OF CAMPAIGN
PLANTATION SONG
PLASTER OF PARIS
PLASTIC SURGEON
PLASTIC SURGERY
PLATFORM ORATOR
PLATFORM TICKET
PLATINUM BLONDE
PLAUSIBLE ROGUE
PLAY AT SOLDIERS
PLAY FOR ENGLAND
PLAY GOOSEBERRY
PLAY THE TRAITOR
PLAY THE VILLAIN
PLAY TO THE CROWD
PLEAD IGNORANCE
PLEAD NOT GUILTY
PLEAD ONE'S CAUSE
PLEASANT DREAMS
PLEASANT MANNER
PLEASANT PEOPLE
PLEASED AS PUNCH
PLEASE TURN OVER
PLEASURE CRUISE
PLEASURE GROUND
PLEASURE LAUNCH
PLEASURE SEEKER
PLEDGE ONE'S WORD
PLOT ONE'S COURSE
PLOUGHING MATCH
PLOUGH THE WAVES
PLUCK UP COURAGE
PLUMB THE DEPTHS
PLUNGED IN GRIEF
PLUNGE INTO DEBT
PNEUMATIC BRAKE
PNEUMATIC DRILL

POCKET AN INSULT
POET AND PEASANT
POETRY IN MOTION
POINT OF CONTACT
POINT OUT THE WAY
POINT WELL TAKEN
POISED TO STRIKE
POISONOUS PLANT
POKE ONE'S NOSE IN
POLARIZED GLASS
POLICEMAN'S BEAT
POLICE SERGEANT
POLISH CORRIDOR
POLISH OFF A MEAL
POLITICAL AGENT
POLITICAL EXILE
POLITICAL PARTY
POLITICAL SPIRIT
POLLING STATION
PONTEFRACT CAKE
POOR MAN'S FRIEND
POOR MAN'S LAWYER
POOR VISIBILITY
POOR VOCABULARY
POPPA PICCOLINO
POP THE QUESTION
POPULAR CONCERT
POPULAR EDITION
POPULAR OPINION
POPULAR REQUEST
POPULAR SCIENCE
POPULAR VERDICT
PORTLAND CEMENT
PORTRAIT ARTIST
POSITIVE ACTION
POSITIVE CHARGE
POSITIVE COLOUR
POSITIVE DEGREE
POSITIVE MENACE
POSSESSIVE CASE
POSSESSIVE LOVE
POSTAL DELIVERY
POSTAL DISTRICT
POSTHUMOUS FAME
POST-WAR CREDITS
POWDER AND PAINT
POWDER MAGAZINE
POWERFUL SPEECH
PRACTICAL JOKER
PRACTISE DECEIT
PRECIOUS LITTLE
PRE-NATAL CLINIC
PREPARE A BUDGET
PREPARED SPEECH
PREPARE ONESELF
PRESCRIBED TEXT

PRESENCE OF MIND
PRESENT A CHEQUE
PRESENT ADDRESS
PRESENT COMPANY
PRESERVED FRUIT
PRESIDENT ELECT
PRESIDING JUDGE
PRESSED FOR TIME
PRESS FOR ACTION
PRESSING DANGER
PRESSING DUTIES
PRESS THE BUTTON
PRESSURE COOKER
PRESSURE OF WORK
PREVAILING WIND
PREY ON ONE'S MIND
PRICE OF SILENCE
PRICE REDUCTION
PRICKLY FEELING
PRIMA BALLERINA
PRIMARY MEANING
PRIME CONDITION
PRIMEVAL FOREST
PRIMITIVE TRIBE
PRIMROSE LEAGUE
PRIMROSE YELLOW
PRINCE CHARMING
PRINCE OF ORANGE
PRINCE OF ROGUES
PRISON CHAPLAIN
PRISON GOVERNOR
PRISON SENTENCE
PRIVATE ADDRESS
PRIVATE CITIZEN
PRIVATE COMPANY
PRIVATE HEARING
PRIVATE OPINION
PRIVATE SOCIETY
PRIVATE SOLDIER
PRIVATE TEACHER
PRIVATE TUITION
PRIZE-GIVING DAY
PROBABLE WINNER
PRO BONO PUBLICO
PRODUCE RESULTS
PRODUCTION LINE
PROFITABLE DEAL
PROFITLESS TASK
PROFOUND EFFECT
PROFOUND SECRET
PROGRAMME MUSIC
PROGRESS OF TIME
PROGRESS REPORT
PROHIBITION ERA
PROLIFIC WRITER
PROMISING PUPIL

PROMISING START
PROMISSORY NOTE
PROMPT DECISION
PROMPT DELIVERY
PROOF OF POSTING
PROPER FRACTION
PROPOSE A MOTION
PROPOSED ACTION
PROSCENIUM ARCH
PROSPEROUS YEAR
PROTECTED STATE
PROTEST AGAINST
PROTEST MEETING
PROTEST TOO MUCH
PROVE EXPENSIVE
PROVEN INNOCENT
PROVE ONE'S POINT
PROVIDE HEATING
PROVOST MARSHAL
PUBLIC APPLAUSE
PUBLIC DISGRACE
PUBLIC ENTRANCE
PUBLIC EXPOSURE
PUBLIC FOOTPATH
PUBLIC INTEREST
PUBLICITY AGENT
PUBLIC NUISANCE
PUBLIC PROPERTY
PUBLIC SPIRITED
PUBLISHER'S NOTE
PULL ONE'S WEIGHT
PULL THE STRINGS
PULL THE TRIGGER
PUMPING STATION
PUNCH ON THE HEAD
PUNCH ON THE NOSE
PUNITIVE ACTION
PURE CONJECTURE
PURSUIT OF POWER
PUSHED FOR MONEY
PUSH OUT THE BOAT
PUSH THE BOAT OUT
PUT IN A BAD LIGHT
PUT IN A GOOD WORD
PUT IN ONE'S PLACE
PUT IN THE MIDDLE
PUT IN THE STOCKS
PUT IT IN WRITING
PUT IT TO THE VOTE
PUT NEW LIFE INTO
PUT OFF THE SCENT
PUT ON A BOLD FACE
PUT ON A PEDESTAL
PUT ONE'S SPOKE IN
PUT ON THE AGENDA
PUT ON THE MARKET

PUT ON THE SCALES
PUT OUT OF ACTION
PUT OUT THE LIGHT
PUT THE CLOCKS ON
PUT THE HELM DOWN
PUT THE KETTLE ON
PUT THE KIBOSH ON
PUT THE QUESTION
PUT THINGS RIGHT
PUT UNDER ARREST
PUT UP A GOOD SHOW
PUT UP A STRUGGLE
PYRRHIC VICTORY

Q – 14

QUALITY OF MERCY
QUARTER OF A YARD
QUARTER PAST ONE
QUARTER PAST SIX
QUARTER PAST TEN
QUARTER PAST TWO
QUARTER TO EIGHT
QUARTER TO SEVEN
QUARTER TO THREE
QUEEN ANNE HOUSE
QUEEN ANNE'S GATE
QUEEN ANNE STYLE
QUEEN CHARLOTTE
QUEEN ELIZABETH
QUEEN OF ENGLAND
QUEEN'S BIRTHDAY
QUEEN'S EVIDENCE
QUEEN'S PLEASURE
QUEEN'S SHILLING
QUEEN'S SUBJECT
QUEER IN THE HEAD
QUEER ONE'S PITCH
QUEER SITUATION
QUESTION MASTER
QUESTION OF TIME
QUICK AS THOUGHT
QUICK-FIRING GUN
QUICK LOOK ROUND
QUICK ON THE DRAW
QUICK VENGEANCE
QUITE A STRANGER
QUITE DIFFERENT
QUIVER AND SHAKE
QUIVER WITH RAGE
QUOTATION MARKS
QWERTY KEYBOARD

R – 14

RACING CALENDAR

RACKED WITH PAIN
RADICAL OUTLOOK
RADIO ANNOUNCER
RADIO ASTRONOMY
RADIO FREQUENCY
RADIO PROGRAMME
RADIO TELEGRAPH
RADIO TELEPHONE
RADIO TELESCOPE
RADIO THERAPIST
RAGS AND TATTERS
RAILWAY COMPANY
RAILWAY CUTTING
RAILWAY JOURNEY
RAILWAY SLEEPER
RAILWAY STATION
RAILWAY VIADUCT
RAILWAY WARRANT
RAIN IN TORRENTS
RAISE A MEMORIAL
RAISE A QUESTION
RAISED EYEBROWS
RAISED PLATFORM
RAISE ONE'S GLASS
RAISE ONE'S HOPES
RAISE ONE'S VOICE
RAISE THE SIGHTS
RAKE IN THE MONEY
RAKE OUT THE FIRE
RANGE OF MEANING
RAPID PROMOTION
RAPT EXPRESSION
RARE ATMOSPHERE
RARE OCCURRENCE
RASH ASSUMPTION
RATE OF EXCHANGE
RATE OF INTEREST
RATE OF PROGRESS
RATTLE THE SABRE
RAVENOUS HUNGER
REACH A DECISION
REACH AGREEMENT
REACH FOR THE SKY
REACH THE DEPTHS
REACH THE ZENITH
READING GLASSES
READ MEN'S HEARTS
READ THE MINUTES
READ THE RIOT ACT
REALLY AND TRULY
REAPING MACHINE
REAP THE BENEFIT
REAP THE HARVEST
REAR-VIEW MIRROR
REAR-VIEW WINDOW
REASONABLE TIME

RECEIVE A LEGACY
RECEIVE A LETTER
RECEIVE QUARTER
RECEIVING ORDER
RECEPTION CLERK
RECKLESS DRIVER
RECKLESS GAMBLE
RECORDING ANGEL
RECORD TURNOVER
RECOVER ONESELF
RECREATION ROOM
REDUCE IN NUMBER
REDUCE TO POWDER
REED INSTRUMENT
REFECTORY TABLE
REFINED SOCIETY
REFLECTED GLORY
REFLECTED IMAGE
REFLECTIVE MOOD
REFORMED CHURCH
REFRESHMENT BAR
REFRESH ONESELF
REFUGEE PROBLEM
REFUSE A HEARING
REFUSE DISPOSAL
REGAL SPLENDOUR
REGIMENTAL BAND
REGISTERED MAIL
REGISTERED POST
REGISTER OFFICE
REGULAR BEDTIME
REGULAR SERVICE
REGULAR SOLDIER
REGULATION SIZE
REIGNING BEAUTY
REIGNING FAMILY
RELATIVE CLAUSE
RELATIVE VALUES
RELIC OF THE PAST
RELIEVING FORCE
RELIGIOUS FAITH
RELIGIOUS HOUSE
RELIGIOUS MANIA
RELIGIOUS ORDER
RELIGIOUS RITES
RELIGIOUS TRACT
REMAINS OF A MEAL
REMARKABLE GIRL
REMEMBRANCE DAY
REMOTE ANCESTOR
REMOVE FRICTION
RENDER A SERVICE
RENEW ONE'S YOUTH
RENEW THE ATTACK
REPAIRING LEASE
REPEATING RIFLE

REPEATING WATCH
REPORTED SPEECH
REPORT PROGRESS
REPRESS THE NEWS
REPUBLICAN VOTE
REPULSIVE FORCE
RESEARCH WORKER
RESERVE ACCOUNT
RESIDENT ABROAD
RESISTANCE COIL
RESISTANCE UNIT
RESPECT ONESELF
RESPONSIBLE MAN
RESTLESS NATURE
REST ON ONE'S OARS
RESTORE HARMONY
RESTORE TO POWER
RESTRICTED AREA
RETAILER OF NEWS
RETAINING FORCE
RETROGRADE STEP
RETURN A VERDICT
RETURN TO HEALTH
RETURN TO NORMAL
RETURN TO SENDER
REVENGE IS SWEET
REVENGE ONESELF
REVENUE OFFICER
REVERSIBLE COAT
REVERT TO NORMAL
REVISED EDITION
REVISED VERSION
REVOLVING DOORS
REVOLVING STAGE
RHAPSODY IN BLUE
RHEUMATIC FEVER
RHINOCEROS HIDE
RHODE ISLAND RED
RHYME NOR REASON
RHYMING COUPLET
RICHARD BRANSON
RICHARD MURDOCH
RICHARD STRAUSS
RICH IN VITAMINS
RICHMOND BRIDGE
RICH VOCABULARY
RIDE A COCK-HORSE
RIDE SIDE-SADDLE
RIDING BREECHES
RIGHT ABOUT FACE
RIGHT ABOUT TURN
RIGHT AND PROPER
RIGHT AS A TRIVET
RIGHT DIRECTION
RIGHT FIRST TIME
RIGHT FROM WRONG

RIGHT-HAND DRIVE
RING IN ONE'S EARS
RING THE CHANGES
RIPE EXPERIENCE
RISE IN THE WORLD
RISE TO ONE'S FEET
RISK EVERYTHING
RITUAL PRACTICE
ROAD TO THE ISLES
ROAD TRAFFIC ACT
ROARING FORTIES
ROARING SUCCESS
ROAR OF LAUGHTER
ROBERT BROWNING
ROBERT CUMMINGS
ROBERT HELPMANN
ROBERT THE BRUCE
ROBIN REDBREAST
ROBINSON CRUSOE
ROCKY MOUNTAINS
RODENT OPERATOR
ROD FOR ONE'S BACK
ROD, POLE OR PERCH
ROGER BANNISTER
ROLL A CIGARETTE
ROLLED UMBRELLA
ROLLING COUNTRY
ROLLING EXPANSE
ROLLING IN MONEY
ROMANTIC AFFAIR
ROMANTIC COMEDY
ROMEO AND JULIET
ROOF OF THE MOUTH
ROOF OF THE WORLD
ROOM FOR DISPUTE
ROSES ALL THE WAY
ROSES OF PICARDY
ROUGH AND TUMBLE
ROUGH TREATMENT
ROUND SHOULDERS
ROUND THE CORNER
ROUND THE HOUSES
ROUND THE WICKET
ROUSE CURIOSITY
ROUTE NATIONALE
ROVING REPORTER
ROW OVER NOTHING
ROYAL ARTILLERY
ROYAL AUTHORITY
ROYAL ENCLOSURE
ROYAL ENGINEERS
ROYAL FUSILIERS
ROYAL HOUSEHOLD
ROYAL RECEPTION
ROYAL RESIDENCE
ROYAL TANK CORPS

RUBBER OF BRIDGE
RUB THE WRONG WAY
RUDYARD KIPLING
RUGGED FEATURES
RUINOUS EXPENSE
RULE ABSOLUTELY
RULE OUT OF ORDER
RULES OF CRICKET
RULES OF THE GAME
RUMP PARLIAMENT
RUNAWAY VICTORY
RUN FOR DEAR LIFE
RUN FOR ONE'S LIFE
RUN INTO TROUBLE
RUN LIKE A RABBIT
RUN LIKE THE WIND
RUNNING ACCOUNT
RUNNING REMARKS
RUNNING REPAIRS
RUN OF THE MARKET
RUN OUT OF PETROL
RUN THE GAUNTLET
RUN UP AN ACCOUNT
RUN WITH THE HARE
RUN WITH THE PACK
RUSH-HOUR TRAVEL
RUSH INTO THINGS
RUSH ONE'S FENCES
RUSSIAN LEATHER
RUSTLE OF SPRING

S – 14

SACK OF POTATOES
SACRED PRECINCT
SACRED WRITINGS
SADDER AND WISER
SADDLE OF MUTTON
SAFETY MEASURES
SAGE REFLECTION
SALIENT FEATURE
SALINE SOLUTION
SALISBURY PLAIN
SALT OF THE EARTH
SALUTARY LESSON
SAMUEL PICKWICK
SAMUEL PLIMSOLL
SARAH BERNHARDT
SARTOR RESARTUS
SATANIC MAJESTY
SATELLITE STATE
SATURDAY'S CHILD
SAUSAGE AND MASH
SAVELOY SAUSAGE
SAVE ONE'S BREATH
SAVINGS ACCOUNT

SAY GOOD MORNING
SAYING AND DOING
SAY ONE'S PRAYERS
SCALE OF CHARGES
SCALP TREATMENT
SCATTER THE SEED
SCENARIO WRITER
SCHEME OF THINGS
SCHOLASTIC POST
SCHOOL BUILDING
SCHOOL GOVERNOR
SCHOOL HOLIDAYS
SCHOOL MAGAZINE
SCHOOL OF WHALES
SCIENCE FICTION
SCIENTIFIC GAME
SCOBIE BREASLEY
SCORE A BULL'S EYE
SCOTCH AND WATER
SCOTCH THE SNAKE
SCOTCH WOODCOCK
SCOTS FUSILIERS
SCOTTISH CHURCH
SCOTTISH LEAGUE
SCOTTISH OFFICE
SCRAPE TOGETHER
SCATCH A LIVING
SCREAMING FARCE
SCROLL OF HONOUR
SCRUBBING BRUSH
SCRUPULOUS CARE
SCUM OF THE EARTH
SEA-GOING VESSEL
SEALED ENVELOPE
SEAL OF APPROVAL
SEARCH FOR TRUTH
SEASIDE HOLIDAY
SEASONABLE GIFT
SEASONABLE TIME
SEASONED TIMBER
SEAT IN THE LORDS
SEAT OF LEARNING
SEAT ON THE BENCH
SEAT ON THE BOARD
SECLUDED CORNER
SECOND DIVIDEND
SECOND DIVISION
SECOND ENGINEER
SECOND-HAND BOOK
SECOND-HAND SHOP
SECOND INTERVAL
SECOND MARRIAGE
SECOND OF AUGUST
SECOND-RATE MIND
SECOND SYMPHONY
SECOND THOUGHTS

SECOND WORLD WAR
SECRET INTRIGUE
SECURE A VICTORY
SECURE FOOTHOLD
SECURE POSITION
SECURITY POLICE
SEE JUSTICE DONE
SEE WHAT HAPPENS
SEIDLITZ POWDER
SEIZE THE CHANCE
SELECTION BOARD
SELF-SERVICE BAR
SEMI-FINAL MATCH
SEMI-FINAL ROUND
SEND A MESSENGER
SEND IN ONE'S CARD
SEND ONE PACKING
SEND TO THE STAKE
SENIOR REGIMENT
SENIOR WRANGLER
SENSELESS ORDER
SENSE OF BALANCE
SENSE OF DECENCY
SENSE OF HEARING
SENSE OF LOYALTY
SENSE OF PURPOSE
SENSITIVE PAPER
SENSITIVE PLANT
SENTIMENTAL BOY
SENT TO COVENTRY
SEPARATE TABLES
SERENE HIGHNESS
SERIES OF EVENTS
SERIOUS ATTEMPT
SERIOUS ILLNESS
SERIOUS MISTAKE
SERIOUS OFFENCE
SERIOUS STUDENT
SERIOUS SUBJECT
SERIOUS THOUGHT
SERIOUS TROUBLE
SERVANT PROBLEM
SERVE A SENTENCE
SERVES ONE RIGHT
SERVICE STATION
SET A BAD EXAMPLE
SET ARRANGEMENT
SET OF GOLF-CLUBS
SET THINGS RIGHT
SETTLE ACCOUNTS
SETTLE A QUARREL
SETTLED PURPOSE
SETTLED WEATHER
SETTLE ONE'S HASH
SEVEN AGES OF MAN
SEVENTEEN MILES

SEVENTH CENTURY
SEVENTH OF APRIL
SEVENTH OF MARCH
SEVENTY PER CENT
SEVERE SENTENCE
SHADOW MINISTER
SHADOW OF A DOUBT
SHADY CHARACTER
SHAGGY-DOG STORY
SHAKE BEFORE USE
SHAKE LIKE A LEAF
SHAKE OF THE HEAD
SHAKE THE BOTTLE
SHAKE UP AND DOWN
SHALLOW PRETEXT
SHANNON AIRPORT
SHARE OWNERSHIP
SHARE THE SPOILS
SHARP AS A NEEDLE
SHARP ENCOUNTER
SHARPEN THE WITS
SHARP REJOINDER
SHARPS AND FLATS
SHATTERING BLOW
SHEEPDOG TRIALS
SHEEP'S CLOTHING
SHEET LIGHTNING
SHEFFIELD PLATE
SHEFFIELD STEEL
SHEPHERD MARKET
SHEPHERD'S CROOK
SHEPHERD'S PURSE
SHERLOCK HOLMES
SHERWOOD FOREST
SHILLING A POUND
SHINING EXAMPLE
SHIP IN DISTRESS
SHIPPING CENTRE
SHIPPING OFFICE
SHIP'S CARPENTER
SHIVER AND SHAKE
SHOCKED SILENCE
SHOCKING TEMPER
SHOCK TREATMENT
SHOOTING RIGHTS
SHOOTING SEASON
SHOOTING TROPHY
SHOOT THE RAPIDS
SHOPPING ARCADE
SHOPPING BASKET
SHOPPING CENTRE
SHORT AND STOCKY
SHORTHAND SPEED
SHORT OF CAPITAL
SHORT PARAGRAPH
SHORT STATEMENT

SHOT-GUN WEDDING
SHOULDER OF LAMB
SHOULDER OF VEAL
SHOW A BOLD FRONT
SHOW COMPASSION
SHOW MODERATION
SHOW OF STRENGTH
SHOW OF SYMPATHY
SHOW ONE'S TICKET
SHOW ONE THE DOOR
SHOW RELUCTANCE
SHOW REPENTANCE
SHREWD OBSERVER
SHRIMP COCKTAIL
SHUTTLE SERVICE
SICKENING SIGHT
SIEGE OF LUCKNOW
SIGH WITH RELIEF
SIGMUND ROMBERG
SIGNALS OFFICER
SIGN OF GOOD LUCK
SIGN OF STRENGTH
SIGN OF THE CROSS
SIGN OF THE TIMES
SIGN OF WEAKNESS
SILENCE IN COURT
SILENCE REIGNED
SILENT REPROACH
SILKS AND SATINS
SILVANA MANGANO
SILVER BRACELET
SILVER STANDARD
SIMPLE ADDITION
SIMPLE EQUATION
SIMPLE FRACTION
SIMPLE FRACTURE
SIMPLE INTEREST
SIMPLE SENTENCE
SIMPLE SOLUTION
SIMPLY FABULOUS
SIMPLY STARVING
SINCERE APOLOGY
SINGLE INSTANCE
SINGULAR NUMBER
SINKING FEELING
SINK LIKE A STONE
SINK OF INIQUITY
SINS OF OMISSION
SINS OF THE FLESH
SIR ADRIAN BOULT
SIR EDWARD ELGAR
SIR HENRY IRVING
SIR HUGH WALPOLE
SIR ISAAC NEWTON
SIR ISAAC PITMAN
SIR JAMES BARRIE

SIR JOHN GIELGUD
SIR WALTER SCOTT
SIT ON THE GROUND
SIT ON THE THRONE
SIXES AND SEVENS
SIX FEET OF EARTH
SIXTEEN PER CENT
SIXTEENTH GREEN
SIXTEENTH OF MAY
SIXTH OF JANUARY
SIXTH OF OCTOBER
SIX WICKETS DOWN
SKATE ON THIN ICE
SKILLED WORKMAN
SKITTLES PLAYER
SLASHING ATTACK
SLAVE OF FASHION
SLAVE OF THE LAMP
SLAVE TO FASHION
SLEEPING BEAUTY
SLEEPING TABLET
SLEEPLESS NIGHT
SLEEP LIKE A BABY
SLEEP OF THE JUST
SLEEPY SICKNESS
SLIP ONE'S MEMORY
SLOW-MOTION FILM
SLOW PROCESSION
SLUGS AND SNAILS
SLUM POPULATION
SMALL-BORE RIFLE
SMALL OF THE BACK
SMALL REDUCTION
SMALL-TIME CROOK
SMART INVENTION
SMASHING DEFEAT
SMELL OF BURNING
SMILING THROUGH
SMOKE-ROOM STORY
SMOKING CONCERT
SMOOTH AS MARBLE
SMOOTH AS VELVET
SMOOTH CROSSING
SMOOTH ONE'S PATH
SNATCH A VERDICT
SNIP OFF THE ENDS
SOBERLY DRESSED
SOCIAL ACTIVITY
SOCIAL CLIMBING
SOCIAL DEMOCRAT
SOCIAL INFERIOR
SOCIAL PLANNING
SOCIAL POSITION
SOCIAL REGISTER
SOCIAL SECURITY
SOCIAL STANDING

SOCIAL SUPERIOR
SOCIETY ISLANDS
SOCIETY WEDDING
SODIUM CHLORIDE
SOFT FURNISHING
SOFT-SHOE DANCER
SOLDIER'S CHORUS
SOLE BONNE FEMME
SOLED AND HEELED
SOLEMN ENTREATY
SOLEMNLY AFFIRM
SOLEMN OCCASION
SOLE POSSESSION
SOLE PROPRIETOR
SOLID SUBSTANCE
SOLOMON ISLANDS
SOLVE THE RIDDLE
SOME DAY OR OTHER
SOMETHING EXTRA
SOMETHING FISHY
SOMETHING TO SAY
SOMEHWERE ABOUT
SO MUCH THE WORSE
SONG OF THE SHIRT
SONGS OF SOLOMON
SORE AFFLICTION
SOUND CHARACTER
SOUND EDUCATION
SOUND PRINCIPLE
SOUND REASONING
SOUND RECORDING
SOUND THE CHARGE
SOURCE OF DANGER
SOUR EXPRESSION
SOUSED MACKEREL
SOUTH AUSTRALIA
SOUTHERN ACCENT
SOUTHERN ASPECT
SOUTHERN REGION
SOUTHERN STATES
SOUTH OF ENGLAND
SOUTH SEA BUBBLE
SOVEREIGN POWER
SOVEREIGN STATE
SPACE PROGRAMME
SPACE TRAVELLER
SPARE NO EXPENSE
SPARING OF WORDS
SPEAKERS' CORNER
SPEAK ESPERANTO
SPEAK IN EARNEST
SPEAK IN RIDDLES
SPEAK OUT OF TURN
SPEAK THE TONGUE
SPECIAL DAMAGES
SPECIAL EDITION

SPECIAL FEATURE
SPECIAL LICENCE
SPECIAL MENTION
SPECIAL MISSION
SPECIAL REQUEST
SPECIAL SERVICE
SPECIAL TROUBLE
SPECIAL VERDICT
SPECIFIC ANSWER
SPECIFIC OBJECT
SPECIFIC REMEDY
SPEECH TRAINING
SPEED OF THOUGHT
SPEED THE PLOUGH
SPEEDWAY RACING
SPEEDY RECOVERY
SPELLING LESSON
SPENT CARTRIDGE
SPINNING MOTION
SPIRITED ATTACK
SPIRIT OF THE AGE
SPIRIT OF THE LAW
SPIRITS OF SALTS
SPIRITUAL NEEDS
SPIRITUAL POWER
SPLENDID CHANCE
SPLIT ONE'S SIDES
SPOIL FOR A FIGHT
SPOIL THE EFFECT
SPOIL THE MARKET
SPOKEN LANGUAGE
SPOKEN LIKE A MAN
SPORTING CHANCE
SPORTING FINISH
SPORTS PAVILION
SPORTS REPORTER
SPRAY OF FLOWERS
SPREAD MISCHIEF
SPRIG OF HEATHER
SPRINGHEEL JACK
SPRING IN THE AIR
SPRING MATTRESS
SQUADRON LEADER
SQUARE ACCOUNTS
SQUARE BRACKETS
SQUASH RACKETS
STAGE A COMEBACK
STAGE CARPENTER
STAGE DIRECTION
STAGGERED HOURS
STAGGERING BLOW
STAINLESS STEEL
STAKE ONE'S CLAIM
STAMFORD BRIDGE
STAMP COLLECTOR
STAMPING GROUND

STANDARD WEIGHT
STAND CONDEMNED
STAND CONVICTED
STAND CORRECTED
STANDING CUSTOM
STANDING ORDERS
STAND IN THE DOCK
ST ANDREW'S CROSS
STANDS TO REASON
STAND THE RACKET
STAND THE STRAIN
STANLEY BALDWIN
STAPLE INDUSTRY
STAR ATTRACTION
STARBOARD WATCH
STARE IN THE FACE
STARTER'S ORDERS
STARTING HANDLE
STARTING PISTOL
START SOMETHING
START TO QUARREL
STARVATION DIET
STARVATION WAGE
STATE DOCUMENTS
STATE OF AFFAIRS
STATE OF DENMARK
STATE OWNERSHIP
STATIONERS' HALL
STAY-AT-HOME TYPE
STAY ON THE SHELF
ST CLEMENT DANES
STEADY INCREASE
STEADY PROGRESS
STEAK AND KIDNEY
STEAK AND ONIONS
STEEL ENGRAVING
STEEL ONE'S HEART
STEEPED IN CRIME
STEERING COLUMN
STEM THE CURRENT
STEPHEN LEACOCK
STEPHEN SPENDER
STEP ON THE JUICE
STEP UP THE SPEED
STERLING SILVER
STEWART GRANGER
ST GEORGE'S CROSS
STICK AT NOTHING
STICK OF RHUBARB
STICKS OUT A MILE
STICK UP A NOTICE
STIFF AS A RAMROD
STILL-LIFE STUDY
STINGING NETTLE
STING IN THE TAIL
STIRLING CASTLE

STIR ONE'S STUMPS
STIRRING SPEECH
ST JAMES'S PALACE
ST JAMES'S STREET
STOCK-CAR RACING
STOCK CHARACTER
STOCKINGED FEET
STOCKTON ON TEES
STOKE NEWINGTON
STOKE THE BOILER
STOLEN PROPERTY
STOMACH TROUBLE
STONE-COLD SOBER
STOOP TO CONQUER
STORAGE BATTERY
STORE DETECTIVE
STORM IN A TEA-CUP
STORMY EXCHANGE
STRADDLE A HORSE
STRAIGHT ANSWER
STRAIGHT AS A DIE
STRAIGHT COMEDY
STRAIN AT THE BIT
STRAINED MUSCLE
STRAIN ONE'S EYES
STRAIN THE TRUTH
STRAITS OF DOVER
STRAND OF COTTON
STRANGE BUT TRUE
STRANGE DESTINY
STRANGE FEELING
STRANGE REQUEST
STRATEGIC SKILL
STRAWBERRY FAIR
STRAWBERRY HILL
STRAWBERRY MARK
STRAWBERRY ROAN
STRAW IN THE WIND
STREAK OF HUMOUR
STREAMLINED CAR
STREET FIGHTING
STREET LIGHTING
STREET MUSICIAN
STRENGTH OF MIND
STRENGTH OF WILL
STRETCH OF WATER
STRICTLY HONEST
STRICT TRAINING
STRIKE A BALANCE
STRIKE A BARGAIN
STRIKE A NEW NOTE
STRIKE ONE'S FLAG
STRIKE WITH FEAR
STRIKING EFFECT
STRING OF HORSES
STRING OF ONIONS

STRING OF PEARLS
STRING TOGETHER
STRIP FOR ACTION
STIP-TEASE SHOW
STRIVE FOR GLORY
STROKE OF GENIUS
STROKE OF THE PEN
STRONG ARGUMENT
STRONG AS A HORSE
STRONG FEELINGS
STRONG IN THE ARM
STRONG LANGUAGE
STRONGLY WORDED
STRONG MEASURES
STRONG POSITION
STRONG RIGHT ARM
STRONG SOLUTION
STUBBORN FELLOW
STUDIO AUDIENCE
STUDIO PORTRAIT
STUMBLING BLOCK
STUPID QUESTION
STYLISH FASHION
SUBMERGED TENTH
SUBMIT TO DEFEAT
SUBSTANTIAL SUM
SUCCESSFUL PLAY
SUDDEN DOWNPOUR
SUDDEN MOVEMENT
SUDDEN PROGRESS
SUGAR-PLUM FAIRY
SUITABLE TENANT
SUMMARY JUSTICE
SUMMER HOLIDAYS
SUMMER VACATION
SUMPTUOUS FEAST
SUNK IN OBLIVION
SUPERIOR PERSON
SUPPORT A FAMILY
SUPPORTERS' CLUB
SUPPORTING CAST
SUPPORTING FILM
SUPPORTING PART
SUPPORTING ROLE
SUPREME COMMAND
SUPREME CONTROL
SUPREME COUNCIL
SURFACE TENSION
SURGICAL SPIRIT
SURPRISE ATTACK
SURPRISE PACKET
SURRENDER VALUE
SUSPEND PAYMENT
SUSPICIOUS MIND
SUZANNE LENGLEN
SWAGGER CLOTHES

SWALLOW THE BAIT
SWALLOW THE PILL
SWARM OF INSECTS
SWARTHY SKINNED
SWEAR TO SECRECY
SWEEPING ACTION
SWEEPING GLANCE
SWEEPING REMARK
SWEEP THE BOARDS
SWEET AND TWENTY
SWEET SEVENTEEN
SWEETS OF OFFICE
SWEET SUBSTANCE
SWEET SURRENDER
SWELL WITH PRIDE
SWELTERING HEAT
SWIFT AS AN ARROW
SWIMMING LESSON
SWIMMING TRUNKS
SWIM THE CHANNEL
SWORD SWALLOWER
SWORN STATEMENT
SWORN TO SECRECY
SYBIL THORNDIKE

T – 14

TABLE OF WEIGHTS
TACTICAL VOTING
TACTICAL WEAPON
TAILOR-MADE SUIT
TAKE AN INTEREST
TAKE A RISE OUT OF
TAKE BY SURPRISE
TAKE FIRST PRIZE
TAKE FOR GRANTED
TAKE IN GOOD PART
TAKE IN MARRIAGE
TAKE IT FROM HERE
TAKE NO INTEREST
TAKE ONE'S CHANCE
TAKE ONE'S CHOICE
TAKE ONESELF OFF
TAKE ONE'S FENCES
TAKE ONE'S HAT OFF
TAKE OUT A PATENT
TAKE OUT A POLICY
TAKE POSSESSION
TAKE PRECEDENCE
TAKE THE BISCUIT
TAKE THE EDGE OFF
TAKE THE GILT OFF
TAKE THE LIBERTY
TAKE THE TROUBLE
TAKE THINGS EASY
TAKE TO THE BOATS

TAKE TO THE HILLS
TAKE TO THE WATER
TAKE TO THE WOODS
TAKE UP AN OPTION
TAKE UP THE SLACK
TALK IN A WHISPER
TALKING PICTURE
TALK OF THE DEVIL
TANGIBLE OBJECT
TANGLED THREADS
TANNED BY THE SUN
TAPIOCA PUDDING
TAP OUT A MESSAGE
TARGET PRACTICE
TARPAULIN SHEET
TARTAN TROUSERS
TASTE OF THE WHIP
TAXED TO THE HILT
TEA AND BISCUITS
TEA AND SYMPATHY
TEAR OFF THE MASK
TECHNICAL HITCH
TECHNICAL SKILL
TEETH OF THE WIND
TELEGRAPH WIRES
TELEPHONE KIOSK
TELEPHONE WIRES
TELESCOPIC LENS
TELESCOPIC VIEW
TELEVISION MAST
TELEVISION PLAY
TELEVISION STAR
TELL A TALL STORY
TELL EVERYTHING
TEMPLE OF APOLLO
TEMPORARY ABODE
TEMPORARY LEASE
TEMPORARY VISIT
TEN AND A QUARTER
TEN AND SIXPENCE
TEN AND TENPENCE
TEN AND TWOPENCE
TENDER FEELINGS
TEN-MINUTE ALIBI
TENSE SITUATION
TENTH OF JANUARY
TENTH OF OCTOBER
TERM OF CONTEMPT
TERMS OF THE WILL
TERRIBLE ORDEAL
TERRIBLE WRENCH
TESTIFY AGAINST
TEST OF STRENGTH
THANKLESS CHILD
THANKS A MILLION
THANKS VERY MUCH

THAT CERTAIN AGE
THAT'S THE TICKET
THE ARMED FORCES
THEATRICAL STAR
THE AUTHORITIES
THE BEE'S WEDDING
THE BEST CIRCLES
THE BLACK FOREST
THE BLACK PRINCE
THE CESAREWITCH
THE COMMON TOUCH
THE CORINTHIANS
THE CRUCIFIXION
THE DARDENELLES
THE END OF THE DAY
THE ETERNAL CITY
THE EXACT AMOUNT
THE EXTREMITIES
THE FIRST CUCKOO
THE FIRST PERSON
THE FLINTSTONES
THE FORSYTE SAGA
THE FOUR JUST MEN
THE GOLDEN BOUGH
THE GOOD OLD DAYS
THE GRAND MANNER
THE GRAND OLD MAN
THE GREAT DIVIDE
THE HIGHWAY CODE
THE INQUISITION
THEIR MAJESTIES
THE JUNGLE BOOKS
THE LILAC DOMINO
THE LORD'S PRAYER
THE LOTUS-EATERS
THE MINSTREL BOY
THE NELSON TOUCH
THE NETHERLANDS
THE OLD GREY MARE
THE OLD OAK CHEST
THE PHILLIPINES
THE PLANEMAKERS
THE PLANETARIUM
THE POLICE FORCE
THE POLYTECHNIC
THE QUEEN MOTHER
THE REFORMATION
THE RENAISSANCE
THE RESTORATION
THE SEVEN DWARFS
THE SHINING HOUR
THE SINGING FOOL
THE STAR CHAMBER
THE TIME MACHINE
THE UNCONSCIOUS
THE UNDERGROUND

THE UNDERSIGNED
THE VICAR OF BRAY
THE WATER BABIES
THE WHEREWITHAL
THE WINTER'S TALE
THE WORST IS OVER
THICK AS THIEVES
THICK OF THE FRAY
THIEVES' KITCHEN
THIEVING MAGPIE
THINK CAREFULLY
THINK OF ANOTHER
THINK OF A NUMBER
THINK OF THE PAST
THINK THINGS OUT
THIRD DIMENSION
THIRD-FLOOR BACK
THIRD OF JANUARY
THIRD OF OCTOBER
THIRD-PARTY RISK
THIRD PROGRAMME
THIRD TIME LUCKY
THIRST FOR BLOOD
THIRTEEN MONTHS
THIRTEEN OUNCES
THIRTEENTH HOLE
THIRTEEN TRICKS
THIRTIETH OF MAY
THIRTY THOUSAND
THIRTY YEARS' WAR
THIS HAPPY BREED
THIS IS YOUR LIFE
THOMAS SHERATON
THORN IN THE SIDE
THOROUGH SEARCH
THOUGHTFUL MOOD
THOUSAND AND ONE
THOUSAND POUNDS
THREADING BEADS
THREAD TOGETHER
THREATEN DANGER
THREE BLIND MICE
THREE-BOTTLE MAN
THREE-CARD TRICK
THREE MEN IN A TUB
THREE-MILE LIMIT
THREE-PIECE SUIT
THREE SHILLINGS
THREE-SPEED GEAR
THREE SYLLABLES
THRILLER WRITER
THROAT PASTILLE
THROATY CHUCKLE
THROUGH THE AGES
THROUGH THE MILL
THROUGH THE NOSE

THROUGH THE POST
THROUGH THE TOWN
THROW IN ONE'S LOT
THROW LIGHT UPON
THROW OF THE DICE
THROW OVERBOARD
THROW THE HAMMER
THROW TO THE DOGS
THURSDAY ISLAND
THURSDAY'S CHILD
TICKLED TO DEATH
TICKLISH MATTER
TIMBER MERCHANT
TIME FOR THOUGHT
TIME IMMEMORIAL
TIMELY REMINDER
TIME OF ONE'S LIFE
TIME WITHOUT END
TIN OF PILCHARDS
TIP OF THE TONGUE
TIRELESS WORKER
TOAD OF TOAD HALL
TO A GREAT EXTENT
TO A LARGE DEGREE
TO A LARGE EXTENT
TOASTED TEA-CAKE
TOAST OF THE TOWN
TOBACCO AUCTION
TOBACCO LICENCE
TOBACCO PLANTER
TOIL AND TROUBLE
TOKEN OF RESPECT
TOOTH FOR A TOOTH
TOP-HAT AND TAILS
TOPICAL SUBJECT
TOP OF ONE'S VOICE
TOP OF THE CHARTS
TOP OF THE LADDER
TOP OF THE LEAGUE
TORRENTIAL RAIN
TORRENT OF ABUSE
TORTURE CHAMBER
TORTURED BY FEAR
TORVILL AND DEAN
TOTAL ABSTAINER
TOTAL IGNORANCE
TOTAL IMMERSION
TO THE BITTER END
TO THE END OF TIME
TOUCH A SOFT SPOT
TOUGH AS LEATHER
TOURING COMPANY
TOURING THE COUNTRY
TOWN AND COUNTRY
TOWN COUNCILLOR
TRACKED VEHICLE

TRACTION ENGINE
TRADE REFERENCE
TRADING STATION
TRAFFIC CONTROL
TRAFFIC DENSITY
TRAFFIC PROBLEM
TRAINED SOLDIER
TRAINING GROUND
TRAINING SCHOOL
TRAIN OF THOUGHT
TRANSFER BY DEED
TRANSITIVE VERB
TRANSPORT HOUSE
TRANSPORT PLANE
TRAVEL BROCHURE
TRAVELLER'S REST
TRAVELLER'S TALE
TRAVELLING TIME
TRAVEL THE WORLD
TREACLE PUDDING
TREAD THE BOARDS
TREAD UNDERFOOT
TREASURE ISLAND
TREMBLE TO THINK
TREMBLING HANDS
TREMBLING VOICE
TRIANGULAR DUEL
TRICKLE OF BLOOD
TRICKLE OF WATER
TRICK OF FORTUNE
TRICKY BUSINESS
TRICKY QUESTION
TRIED FOR MURDER
TRIFLING AMOUNT
TRIFLING CHARGE
TRIFLING MATTER
TRIFLING REMARK
TRINITY COLLEGE
TRIPE AND ONIONS
TRIPLE ALLIANCE
TRISTRAM SHANDY
TRIUMPHAL CROWN
TRIVIAL PURSUIT
TROOP MOVEMENTS
TROOP THE COLOUR
TROPIC OF CANCER
TROUBLE BREWING
TROUBLED WATERS
TROUBLE IN STORE
TROUPE OF ACTORS
TROUSERS POCKET
TRUE CONFESSION
TRUMPED-UP STORY
TRUNDLE THEM OUT
TRY AND TRY AGAIN
TRY ONE'S FORTUNE

TRY ONE'S HARDEST
TUESDAY EVENING
TUESDAY MORNING
TUMBLER OF WATER
TUNBRIDGE WELLS
TURF ACCOUNTANT
TURKISH DELIGHT
TURKISH TOBACCO
TURN AT THE WHEEL
TURN DOWN THE BED
TURN DOWN THE GAS
TURN EVERY STONE
TURN OFF THE HEAT
TURN OF THE SCREW
TURN OF THE WHEEL
TURN ON ONE'S HEEL
TURN ON THE LIGHT
TURN OUT TO GRASS
TURN RIGHT ROUND
TURN TOPSYTURVY
TURN TO THE RIGHT
TURN UP ONE'S NOSE
TURN UPSIDE DOWN
TWELFTH CENTURY
TWELFTH OF APRIL
TWELFTH OF MARCH
TWELVE AND A HALF
TWELVE APOSTLES
TWELVE THOUSAND
TWENTIETH OF MAY
TWENTY THOUSAND
TWICE THE WEIGHT
TWIST OF TOBACCO
TWISTS AND TURNS
TWITTER OF BIRDS
TWO AND A QUARTER
TWO-HANDED SWORD
TWO-HEADED EAGLE
TWO WICKETS DOWN
TYPICAL EXAMPLE

U – 14

ULTERIOR MOTIVE
ULTERIOR OBJECT
ULTIMATE RESULT
ULTRA-VIOLET RAY
UNABLE TO CHOOSE
UNACCOUNTED FOR
UNBALANCED MIND
UNBOSOM ONSELF
UNBROKEN SPIRIT
UNCIVILIZED MAN
UNCLE TOM'S CABIN
UNDER A HANDICAP
UNDER AN EMBARGO

UNDER CROSS-FIRE
UNDER DETENTION
UNDERGO REPAIRS
UNDER GUARANTEE
UNDER ONE'S THUMB
UNDER RESTRAINT
UNDER SUSPICION
UNDER THE BONNET
UNDER THE CARPET
UNDER THE DOCTOR
UNDER THE GROUND
UNDER THE HAMMER
UNDER THE HARROW
UNDER TREATMENT
UNDER TWENTY-ONE
UNDRESS UNIFORM
UNDUE INFLUENCE
UNEARNED INCOME
UNEASY PROGRESS
UNFAMILIAR WORD
UNIFORM PATTERN
UNINVITED GUEST
UNIQUE OCCASION
UNITED SERVICES
UNIVERSAL AGENT
UNIVERSAL AUNTS
UNIVERSAL JOINT
UNIVERSAL PEACE
UNIVERSITY TERM
UNIVERSITY TOWN
UNIVERSITY VOTE
UNKNOWN COUNTRY
UNKNOWN ELEMENT
UNKNOWN SOLDIER
UNKNOWN WARRIOR
UNLIMITED SCOPE
UNLIMITED SPACE
UNMARRIED WOMAN
UNOCCUPIED FLAT
UNPLEASANT DUTY
UNPLOUGHED LAND
UNREQUITED LOVE
UNSALTED BUTTER
UNSETTLING NEWS
UNSUITABLE TIME
UNTER DEN LINDEN
UPWARDLY MOBILE
UNWELCOME GUEST
UPHILL STRUGGLE
UPON REFLECTION
UPRIGHT POSTURE
USUAL SIGNATURE
USURP THE THRONE

V – 14

VACATE ONE'S SEAT
VAGRANCY CHARGE
VAGUE SUSPICION
VAIN AS A PEACOCK
VALET DE CHAMBRE
VALID OBJECTION
VALSE DES FLEURS
VANILLA FLAVOUR
VANISHING CREAM
VANISHING POINT
VANISHING TRICK
VARIABLE TEMPER
VARIETY THEATRE
VARIOUS COLOURS
VARIOUS REASONS
VARNISH REMOVER
VARYING SUCCESS
VAST DIFFERENCE
VAST EXPERIENCE
VATICAN COUNCIL
VAUDEVILLE SHOW
VEER TO THE RIGHT
VEGETABLE CURRY
VEGETABLE FIBRE
VEGETABLE SALAD
VEGETABLE WORLD
VEGETARIAN DIET
VEGETARIAN DISH
VEGETARIAN MEAL
VENDING MACHINE
VENERABLE BEARD
VENERABLE RUINS
VENETIAN CARPET
VENETIAN SCHOOL
VENETIAN WINDOW
VENUS AND ADONIS
VERBAL ARGUMENT
VERBAL CONTRACT
VERBAL EVIDENCE
VERBATIM REPORT
VERIFY THE FACTS
VERSATILE ACTOR
VERTICAL FLIGHT
VESTED INTEREST
VETERAN SERVICE
VICTIM OF CHANGE
VICTORIA PALACE
VICTORIA REGINA
VIEW WITH FAVOUR
VIOLENT QUARREL
VIOLENT TEMPEST
VIOLETS ARE BLUE
VIOLIN CONCERTO
VISIBLE EXPORTS

VISIBLE HORIZON
VITAL PRINCIPLE
VOICE AN OPINION
VOLATILE LIQUID
VOLUNTEER CORPS
VOTING STRENGTH
VULGAR FRACTION
VULGAR LANGUAGE
VULGAR PARLANCE
VULNERABLE SPOT

W – 14

WAG A FOREFINGER
WAGGING TONGUES
WAIFS AND STRAYS
WAIT TILL THE END
WAKE WITH A START
WALKING HOLIDAY
WALKING LIBRARY
WALK INTO A PUNCH
WALK INTO DANGER
WALLOW IN LUXURY
WALLS OF JERICHO
WALPURGIS NIGHT
WALTER DE LA MARE
WALTZ COTILLION
WANTED BY THE LAW
WANT FOR NOTHING
WANT OF ALACRITY
WANT OF PRACTICE
WANT OF SYMMETRY
WARD IN CHANCERY
WARD OF THE COURT
WARDROBE DEALER
WARM FRIENDSHIP
WARM TO ONE'S WORK
WARNER BROTHERS
WARNING EXAMPLE
WAR OF ATTRITION
WAR OF EXPANSION
WARRANT OFFICER
WARREN HASTINGS
WARSAW CONCERTO
WARS OF THE ROSES
WARWICK DEEPING
WASH AND BRUSH-UP
WASH DIRTY LINEN
WASHING MACHINE
WASHINGTON POST
WASTE ONE'S WORDS
WATCH CAREFULLY
WATCH COMMITTEE
WATCH THE BIRDIE
WATERLOO BRIDGE
WATER ON THE KNEE

WATER THE GARDEN
WATER THE HORSES
WATER THE WICKET
WAVE OF VIOLENCE
WAVERLEY NOVELS
WEAK AT THE KNEES
WE ARE NOT AMUSED
WEARING APPAREL
WEATHER BALLOON
WEATHER OUTLOOK
WEATHER PROPHET
WEATHER STATION
WEDDING MORNING
WEDDING PRESENT
WEDDING SERVICE
WEDNESDAY NIGHT
WEEK-END VISITOR
WEEKLY MAGAZINE
WEEK'S GOOD CAUSE
WEIGH ONE'S WORDS
WEIGHTY PROBLEM
WELFARE OFFICER
WELL ACQUAINTED
WELL-CHOSEN WORD
WELL-EARNED REST
WELLINGTON BOOT
WELL-READ PERSON
WELL-WORN PHRASE
WELL WORTH WHILE
WELSH MOUNTAINS
WEMBLEY STADIUM
WENT WITH A SWING
WESTERN GERMANY
WEST HARTLEPOOL
WET ONE'S WHISTLE
WHAT DO YOU THINK?
WHAT IN THE WORLD?
WHAT OF THE CLOCK?
WHAT OF THE NIGHT?
WHAT'S THE DAMAGE?
WHAT'S THE MATTER?
WHAT THE DICKENS!
WHEELED TRAFFIC
WHEEL OF FORTUNE
WHICH WAY TO TURN
WHIGS AND TORIES
WHITE CHRISTMAS
WHITE CORPUSCLE
WHITE IN THE FACE
WHITE MAN'S GRAVE
WHITER THAN SNOW
WHITSUN HOLIDAY
WHOLE-MEAL BREAD
WHOLESALE PRICE
WIDDICOMBE FAIR
WIDELY BELIEVED

WIDEN THE BREACH
WIDE OF THE TRUTH
WIDE-OPEN SPACES
WIDE VOCABULARY
WIELD THE WILLOW
WIFE IN NAME ONLY
WILD ACCUSATION
WILD ENTHUSIASM
WILD EXCITEMENT
WILD-GOOSE CHASE
WILFRED PICKLES
WILLIAM AND MARY
WILLIAM HOGARTH
WILLING AND ABLE
WIN BY A KNOCK-OUT
WIND INSTRUMENT
WINDOW CURTAINS
WINDOW DRESSING
WINDOW ENVELOPE
WINDOW SHOPPING
WIND UP A COMPANY
WINE BY THE GLASS
WINNER TAKES ALL
WIN SECOND PRIZE
WINTER CLOTHING
WINTER PLANTING
WINTER QUARTERS
WINTER WOOLLIES
WISE AS A SERPENT
WITH A GOOD GRACE
WITH ALL MY HEART
WITH A VENGEANCE
WITHHOLD ASSENT
WITHOUT BLEMISH
WITHOUT CEASING
WITHOUT CONTEXT
WITHOUT MEASURE
WITHOUT PURPOSE
WITHOUT REMORSE
WITHOUT RESERVE
WITHOUT RESPECT
WITHOUT STRINGS
WITHOUT WARNING
WITH PERMISSION
WITH THE COLOURS
WITH THE CURRENT
WOMAN OF FASHION
WOMEN'S LAND ARMY
WOMEN'S QUARTERS
WOMEN'S SUFFRAGE
WONDERFUL SIGHT
WONDERFUL WORLD
WOOLLEN SWEATER
WOOLLY THINKING
WORCESTER SAUCE
WORKING CAPITAL

WORKING CLOTHES
WORKING FOREMAN
WORKING HOLIDAY
WORK IN PROGRESS
WORK LIKE A CHARM
WORK LIKE A HORSE
WORK LIKE A NAVVY
WORK LIKE BLAZES
WORK ONE'S TICKET
WORK TO SCHEDULE
WORDLY AFFAIRS
WORLD OF FASHION
WORLD OF MEANING
WORLD OF ONE'S OWN
WORLD OF REALITY
WORLD SITUATION
WORMWOOD SCRUBS
WORN TO A FRAZZLE
WORTH A BOB OR TWO
WORTH IMITATING
WORTH ONE'S WHILE
WORTHY CHAMPION
WORTHY OF ESTEEM
WORTHY OF PRAISE
WORTHY OF REMARK
WRAPPED IN GLOOM
WRATH OF THE GODS
WREAK VENGEANCE
WRESTLING MATCH
WRIGHT BROTHERS
WRING ONE'S HANDS
WRITTEN APOLOGY
WRITTEN CONSENT
WRITTEN IN VERSE
WRITTEN MESSAGE
WRONG DIRECTION
WRONGFUL ARREST

Y – 14

YACHTING CENTRE
YELLOWISH BROWN
YELLOW JAUNDICE
YELLOW SAPPHIRE
YORKSHIRE DALES
YORKSHIRE MOORS
YOUNG AND TENDER
YOUNGER BROTHER
YOUNGEST SISTER
YOUNG LOCHINVAR
YOUNG MAN'S FANCY
YOUNG PRETENDER
YOUNG SHOULDERS
YOU'RE TELLING ME!
YOUR EXCELLENCY
YOURS SINCERELY

YOU SHOULD WORRY!

A – 15

ABANDON ONE'S POST
ABERDEEN TERRIER
ABLAZE WITH LIGHT
ABODE OF WARRIORS
ABOVE EVERYTHING
ABOVE THE AVERAGE
ABOVE THE SURFACE
ABOVE THE WEATHER
ABRIDGED VERSION
ABRUPT DEPARTURE
ABSOLUTE MINIMUM
ABSOLUTE MONARCH
ABSTRACT PAINTER
ABSTRACT SCIENCE
ABUNDANCE OF FOOD
ABUSE OF LANGUAGES
ACADEMIC CIRCLES
ACCEPT A PROPOSAL
ACCEPTED MEANING
ACCEPTED VERSION
ACCIDENTAL DEATH
ACCIDENT OF BIRTH
ACCORDING TO PLAN
ACCOUNT RENDERED
ACCREDITED AGENT
A CHRISTMAS CAROL
ACQUISITIVE MIND
ACROSS THE STREET
ACTIVE SUPPORTER
ACT OF AGGRESSION
ACT OF DEDICATION
ACT OF FRIENDSHIP
ACT OF PARLIAMENT
ACT OF PROVIDENCE
ACT OF SETTLEMENT
ACT THE GIDDY GOAT
ADDED ATTRACTION
ADDISON'S DISEASE
ADD TO ONE'S INCHES
ADHESIVE PLASTER
ADJUTANT GENERAL
ADMIT EVERYTHING
ADOPTION SOCIETY
A DROP IN THE OCEAN
ADVANCED BOOKING
ADVANCED IN YEARS
ADVANCED STUDENT
ADVANCED STUDIES
ADVANCED THINKER
ADVERTISING SITE
AEROPLANE TRIALS
AFFLUENT SOCIETY

AFRAID OF COMPANY
AFER MY OWN HEART
AFTERNOON SIESTA
AGAINST ONE'S WILL
AGAINST THE CLOCK
AGAINST THE GRAIN
AGAINST THE RULES
AGE OF AUTOMATION
AGE OF DISCRETION
AGING POPULATION
AGREE BEFOREHAND
AGREE ON A VERDICT
AGREE TO DISAGREE
AHEAD OF SCHEDULE
AIDER AND ABETTER
AIMLESS ACTIVITY
AIR CHIEF MARSHAL
AIR CONDITIONING
AIRCRAFT CARRIER
AIREDALE TERRIER
AIR FORCE OFFICER
AIR FORCE RESERVE
AIR MINISTRY ROOF
AIR OF DETACHMENT
ALBERT CHEVALIER
ALDERSHOT TATTOO
ALEXANDRA PALACE
ALFRED HITCHCOCK
ALIMENTARY CANAL
A LITTLE LEARNING
ALIVE AND KICKING
ALL ALONG THE LINE
ALL FOUR QUARTERS
ALL MANNER OF WAYS
ALL-NIGHT SESSION
ALL-NIGHT SITTING
ALLOTMENT HOLDER
ALL OVER THE PLACE
ALL PASSION SPENT
ALL PULL TOGETHER
ALL-ROUND ABILITY
ALL-ROUND ATHLETE
ALL THE TRIMMINGS
ALL THE WORLD OVER
ALL THE YEAR ROUND
ALONE IN THE WORLD
ALTERNATIVE PLAN
ALTERNATIVE VOTE
AMATEUR CHAMPION
AMATEUR FOOTBALL
AMBIGUOUS SAYING
AMBITIOUS SCHEME
AMBULANCE DRIVER
AMERICAN EMBASSY
AMERICAN IN PARIS
AMMUNITION BOOTS

AMUSEMENT ARCADE
ANCIENT LANGUAGE
ANCIENT MONUMENT
ANCIENT PEDIGREE
ANDERSON SHELTER
AND SO SAY ALL OF US
ANGULAR VELOCITY
ANIMAL MAGNETISM
ANIMATED CARTOON
ANIMATED GESTURE
ANNIE GET YOUR GUN
ANNIVERSARY DATE
ANNOUNCE ONESELF
ANONYMOUS LETTER
ANOTHER CUP OF TEA
ANTARCTIC CIRCLE
ANTE-NATAL CLINIC
ANTE POST BETTING
ANTHONY TROLLOPE
ANTI-AIRCRAFT GUN
ANTIQUE MERCHANT
ANXIETY NEUROSIS
ANXIOUS TO PLEASE
ANY PORT IN A STORM
APPEALING GLANCE
APPEALING MANNER
APPLICATION FORM
APPLIED RESEARCH
APPLY THE CLOSURE
APPROACH MANHOOD
APPROXIMATE COST
APRIL THE SEVENTH
APRIL THE TWELFTH
ARMED NEUTRALITY
ARMED TO THE TEETH
AROUND THE CORNER
ARRIVAL PLATFORM
ARTICLE FOR SALE
ARTICLES OF FAITH
ARTIFICIAL FIBRE
ARTIFICIAL LIGHT
ARTIFICIAL SMILE
ARTIFICIAL STONE
ARTIFICIAL TEETH
ART OF MANAGEMENT
AS A MATTER OF FACT
AS AN ALTERNATIVE
ASCEND THE THRONE
ASCENSION ISLAND
AS FAR AS POSSIBLE
AS FAR AS YOU CAN GO
AS FRESH AS A DAISY
AS GENTLE AS A LAMB
AS GOOD AS ONE GETS
AS HARD AS GRANITE
ASHMOLEAN MUSEUM

AS KEEN AS MUSTARD
ASK FOR ONE'S CARDS
AS LIKE AS TWO PEAS
AS LONG AS YOU LIKE
AS NEAT AS A NEW PIN
AS OLD AS THE HILLS
AS QUIET AS A MOUSE
AS RICH AS CROESUS
ASSISTANT MASTER
ASSISTED PASSAGE
ASSOCIATED IDEAS
ASSORTED TOFFEES
AS STIFF AS A POKER
ASSUME A DISGUISE
AS THE SAYING GOES
ASTRAL INFLUENCE
ASTRONOMER ROYAL
A STUDY IN SCARLET
AS WHITE AS A SHEET
AT A DISADVANTAGE
AT A LOSS FOR WORDS
AT CLOSE QUARTERS
AT CROSS PURPOSES
ATLANTIC CHARTER
ATOMIC SUMARINE
ATTEMPTED MURDER
AT THE CROSS-ROADS
AT THE DROP OF A HAT
ATTORNEY GENERAL
AT TRINITY CHURCH
AUGUST THE EIGHTH
AUGUST THE FOURTH
AUGUST THE SECOND
AUSTERITY BUDGET
AUTOGRAPH HUNTER
AUTOMATIC CHANGE
AUTOMATIC PISTOL
AUTUMNAL EQUINOX
AUXILIARY FORCES
AUXILIARY TROOPS
AVERAGE SPECIMEN
AWKWARD CUSTOMER
AWKWARD POSITION
AWKWARD QUESTION

B – 15

BABY-FACED NELSON
BACHELOR OF MUSIC
BACHELOR'S BUTTON
BACKGROUND MUSIC
BACK OF THE BEYOND
BACKSTAGE NERVES
BACKWARD PEOPLES
BALACLAVA HELMET
BALANCE THE BOOKS

BALLROOM DANCING
BANKRUPTCY COURT
BANKS OF THE CLYDE
BANNER HEADLINES
BANNS OF MARRIAGE
BARBARA STANWYCK
BARBER OF SEVILLE
BARE POSSIBILITY
BARE SUBSISTENCE
BARGAIN BASEMENT
BARNUM AND BAILEY
BARON MUNCHAUSEN
BARRISTER'S CLERK
BARROW IN FURNESS
BARTHOLOMEW FAIR
BASIC INGREDIENT
BATCH OF RECRUITS
BATS IN THE BELFRY
BATTERSEA BRIDGE
BATTLE OF BRITAIN
BATTLE OF FLOWERS
BATTLE OF JUTLAND
BATTLE OF THE NILE
BAYONET PRACTICE
BEAST OF THE FIELD
BEATEN ON THE POST
BEAUTIFUL FIGURE
BEAUTY TREATMENT
BEAUTY UNADORNED
BECOME ENAMOURED
BECOME INVISIBLE
BED AND BREAKFAST
BEE IN ONE'S BONNET
BEER AND SKITTLES
BEFORE BREAKFAST
BEFORE THE FINISH
BEGINNERS, PLEASE
BEGINNING AND END
BEGIN THE BEGUINE
BEHAVE NATURALLY
BEHIND THE SCENES
BEHIND THE STUMPS
BELLOW LIKE A BULL
BELONG TO THE PAST
BELOW THE AVERAGE
BELOW THE HORIZON
BELOW THE SURFACE
BENEATH CONTEMPT
BENEFIT OF CLERGY
BENITO MUSSOLINI
BENJAMIN BRITTEN
BERNE CONVENTION
BERNESE OBERLAND
BERTRAND RUSSELL
BESSEMER PROCESS
BEST FOOT FORWARD

BEST OF ALL WORLDS
BET ON A CERTAINTY
BETRAY THE SECRET
BETTER AND BETTER
BETTER RELATIONS
BETWEEN THE LINES
BETWEEN TWO FIRES
BETWEEN YOU AND ME
BEVERIDGE REPORT
BEVERLEY NICHOLS
BEVERLEY SISTERS
BEWARE OF THE BULL
BEYOND ALL BOUNDS
BEYOND CRITICISM
BEYOND ONE'S DEPTH
BEYOND ONE'S GRASP
BEYOND ONE'S MEANS
BEYOND ONE'S PRIME
BEYOND ONE'S REACH
BEYOND THE FRINGE
BIGGER AND BETTER
BIGGER AND BIGGER
BILLIARDS PLAYER
BINDING CONTRACT
BIRDS OF A FEATHER
BIRTHDAY HONOURS
BIRTHDAY PRESENT
BIRTH OF THE BLUES
BITE ONE'S HEAD OFF
BLACK AS MIDNIGHT
BLACK AS THE DEVIL
BLACKBURN ROVERS
BLACK-COAT WORKER
BLACKMAIL LETTER
BLACKWALL TUNNEL
BLACKWATER FEVER
BLEACHING POWDER
BLISSFULLY HAPPY
BLOOD AND THUNDER
BLOOMSBURY GROUP
BLOW HOT; BLOW COLD
BLOW TO ONE'S PRIDE
BLUES IN THE NIGHT
BLUNT INSTRUMENT
BLUSHING HONOURS
BOARD AND LODGING
BOARDING OFFICER
BODLEIAN LIBRARY
BODY-LINE BOWLING
BODY OF KNOWLEDGE
BODY TEMPERATURE
BOLD IMAGINATION
BOLTED AND BARRED
BOLT FROM THE BLUE
BONDED WAREHOUSE
BOOKMAKER'S CLERK

BOOK OF REFERENCE
BORN IN THE PURPLE
BORROWING POWERS
BOTANICAL GARDEN
BOTTLE OF PERFUME
BOTTLE OF VINEGAR
BOTTOMLESS PURSE
BOTTOM OF THE FORM
BOTTOM OF THE HILL
BOTTOM OF THE POLL
BOTTOM THE WEAVER
BOWL AT THE STUMPS
BOWLED BY A YORKER
BOWLING ANALYSIS
BOW-STREET RUNNER
BOX OF CHOCOLATES
BRASS INSTRUMENT
BRAVE ALL HAZARDS
BREACH OF PROMISE
BREAD OF IDLENESS
BREAKFAST CEREAL
BREAKING OF BREAD
BREAK ON THE WHEEL
BREAK THE BAD NEWS
BREAK THE SILENCE
BREAST OF CHICKEN
BREATHE ONE'S LAST
BREATHLESS HURRY
BREATH OF SCANDAL
BRICKS AND MORTAR
BRIDES IN THE BATH
BRIDGE OF THE NOSE
BRIGADE OF GUARDS
BRIGADIER GERARD
BRIGHT AND BREEZY
BRIGHT AS A BUTTON
BRIGHT S A NEW PIN
BRIGHTON AND HOVE
BRIGHT PROSPECTS
BRIGHT YOUNGSTER
BRILLIANT SUNSET
BRING IN A VERDICT
BRING IN NEW BLOOD
BRING TO FRUITION
BRISTLE WITH RAGE
BRITISH COLUMBIA
BRITISH HONDURAS
BRITISH PASSPORT
BRITISH RAILWAYS
BROAD-BRIMMED HAT
BROADEN ONE'S MIND
BROADLY SPEAKING
BRONZE MEDALLIST
BROTHER JONATHAN
BROTHER OFFICERS
BROWN AS MAHOGANY

BRUSSELS SPROUTS
BUBBLE AND SQUEAK
BUDDING CHAMPION
BUDGET ESTIMATES
BUILDING SOCIETY
BULLDOG DRUMMOND
BULLET-PROOF VEST
BULL'S-EYE LANTERN
BUMP OF KNOWLEDGE
BURIAL OF THE DEAD
BURLINGTON HOUSE
BURNHAM ON CROUCH
BURNING QUESTION
BURN ONE'S BRIDGES
BURN ONE'S FINGERS
BURNT AT THE STAKE
BURNT TO A FRAZZLE
BURST AT THE SEAMS
BURST INTO FLAMES
BURST INTO FLOWER
BURST OF APPLAUSE
BURST OF LAUGHTER
BUSINESS ADDRESS
BUSINESS AFFAIRS
BUSINESS AS USUAL
BUSINESS CIRCLES
BUSINESS COLLEGE
BUSINESS CONTACT
BUSINESS FOOTING
BUSINESS MANAGER
BUSINESS MEETING
BUSINESS METHODS
BUSINESS ROUTINE
BUSINESS VENTURE
BUTTERFLY COLLAR
BUTTERFLY STROKE
BUTTON MUSHROOMS
BY FITS AND STARTS
BY HOOK OR BY CROOK
BY THE SHORT HAIRS
BYZANTINE EMPIRE
BYZANTINE SCHOOL

C – 15

CABINET MINISTER
CABLE TELEVISION
CALCIUM CHLORIDE
CALCULATING MIND
CALEDONIAN CANAL
CALL AN AMBULANCE
CALL ATTENTION TO
CALL IN THE DOCTOR
CALL IN THE POLICE
CALL NO MAN MASTER
CALL TO SURRENDER

CALM AS A MILL-POND
CAMBERWELL GREEN
CAMBRIDGE CIRCUS
CAMEMBERT CHEESE
CAME TO THE THRONE
CANADIAN PACIFIC
CANDLEWICK COVER
CANTERBURY BELLS
CANTERBURY TALES
CAPABILITY BROWN
CAPITAL GAINS TAX
CAPITAL OF FRANCE
CAPITAL OF NORWAY
CAPITAL OF SWEDEN
CAPITAL SENTENCE
CARDIFF ARMS PARK
CARDINAL NUMBERS
CARDINAL VIRTUES
CARDS ON THE TABLE
CARELESS DRIVING
CARELESS RAPTURE
CARES OF THE WORLD
CARPENTER'S BENCH
CARRIAGE AND PAIR
CARRIAGE FORWARD
CARRY CONVICTION
CARRY OUT ONE'S BAT
CARRY THE CAN BACK
CASH IN ONE'S CHIPS
CASH TRANSACTION
CASTING DIRECTOR
CASTLES IN THE AIR
CASTOR AND POLLUX
CASUAL REFERENCE
CASUALTY STATION
CAT AND THE FIDDLE
CATCH AS CATCH CAN
CATCH BY THE HEELS
CATCH ONE NAPPING
CATCH ONE'S BREATH
CATERING OFFICER
CATHEDRAL SQUARE
CAUGHT AMIDSHIPS
CAUGHT AND BOWLED
CAUGHT RED-HANDED
CAUSE A SENSATION
CAVALRY REGIMENT
CEASELESS ENERGY
CEDARS OF LEBANON
CELESTIAL SPHERE
CELLULOID COLLAR
CELLULOID EMPIRE
CENTRAL POSITION
CENTRE OF GRAVITY
CERTAIN EVIDENCE
CERTAIN QUANTITY

CERTIFIED INSANE
CHAMPAGNE BOTTLE
CHAMPAGNE SUPPER
CHANCE DISCOVERY
CHANCE ENCOUNTER
CHANCE OF SUCCESS
CHANGE DIRECTION
CHANGE OF ADDRESS
CHANGE OF CLIMATE
CHANGE OF CLOTHES
CHANGE OF COSTUME
CHANGE OF FORTUNE
CHANGE OF OPINION
CHANGE OF PURPOSE
CHANGE OF SCENERY
CHANGE OF TACTICS
CHANGE ONE'S IDEAS
CHANNEL CROSSING
CHANTREY BEQUEST
CHAPTER AND VERSE
CHARACTER SKETCH
CHARCOAL DRAWING
CHARGE TOO LITTLE
CHARITABLE CAUSE
CHARLES KINGSLEY
CHARLES LAUGHTON
CHARLES THE FIRST
CHARLOTTE BRONTÉ
CHATSWORTH HOUSE
CHEAP AT THE PRICE
CHEAP RESTAURANT
CHEAT THE GALLOWS
CHECK ONE'S COURSE
CHECK THE RECORDS
CHEERFUL CONSENT
CHEERFUL OLD SOUL
CHELSEA ARTS BALL
CHELSEA BARRACKS
CHEMICAL FORMULA
CHEMICAL PROCESS
CHEMICAL WARFARE
CHEQUERED CAREER
CHERCHEZ LA FEMME
CHESS TOURNAMENT
CHICKEN MARYLAND
CHICKEN SANDWICH
CHIEF MAGISTRATE
CHILDHOOD FRIEND
CHILDISH ATTEMPT
CHILD PSYCHOLOGY
CHILDREN'S ANNUAL
CHILDREN'S CORNER
CHILLED WITH FEAR
CHILLY RECEPTION
CHIPPED POTATOES
CHOCOLATE ÉCLAIR

CHOCOLATE FINGER	COACHING STATION
CHOCOLATE SUNDAE	COCKPIT OF EUROPE
CHOICE OF COLOURS	COCKTAIL CABINET
CHOICE OF WEAPONS	CODE OF BEHAVIOUR
CHOOSE ONE'S WORDS	COLD AS CHRISTMAS
CHRISTMAS ANNUAL	COLD COMFORT FARM
CHRISTMAS DINNER	COLDSTREAM GUARD
CHRISTMAS ISLAND	COLERIDGE TAYLOR
CHRISTMAS SEASON	COLLAPSIBLE BOAT
CHRISTMAS SPIRIT	COLLECT EVIDENCE
CHRISTOPHER WREN	COLLECTING POINT
CHRIST'S HOSPITAL	COLLECTION PLATE
CHURCH OF ENGLAND	COLLECT MATERIAL
CIGARETTE COUPON	COLLECT ONE'S WITS
CIGARETTE HOLDER	COLLECTOR'S PIECE
CINDERELLA DANCE	COLLIERY MANAGER
CIRCLE OF FRIENDS	COLLISION COURSE
CITY AND SUBURBAN	COLORADO SPRINGS
CITY CORPORATION	COLOUR BLINDNESS
CIVILIAN CLOTHES	COLOURFUL BORDER
CLAIMS OF SOCIETY	COLOURING MATTER
CLAIM THE VICTORY	COLOURLESS FLUID
CLAPHAM JUNCTION	COLOUR PREJUDICE
CLASHING COLOURS	COMBINATION LOCK
CLASH OF OPINIONS	COME DOWN TO EARTH
CLASSICAL BALLET	COME HOME TO ROOST
CLASSICAL WRITER	COME IN LIKE A LION
CLASSIC FEATURES	COME INTO CONTACT
CLASSICS SCHOLAR	COME INTO ONE'S OWN
CLEAN AS A WHISTLE	COME INTO THE OPEN
CLEANING UTENSIL	COME OUT ON STRIKE
CLEAN THE WINDOWS	COME TO A DEAD STOP
CLEAR AS DAYLIGHT	COME TO A DECISION
CLEAR CONSCIENCE	COME TO A FULL STOP
CLEAR IN ONE'S MIND	COME TO ATTENTION
CLEAR ONE'S THROAT	COME TO THE RESCUE
CLEAR REFLECTION	COME TO THINK OF IT
CLENCH ONE'S FISTS	COME UP TO SCRATCH
CLENCH ONE'S TEETH	COMFORTABLE SEAT
CLERK OF THE COURT	COMFORTING WORDS
CLERK OF THE HOUSE	COMMANDING VOICE
CLERK OF THE WORKS	COMMERCIAL HOTEL
CLEVER DECEPTION	COMMERCIAL VALUE
CLIFF MICHELMORE	COMMISSION AGENT
CLING LIKE IVY	COMMIT AN OFFENCE
CLINICAL LECTURE	COMMIT TO WRITING
CLINICAL SURGERY	COMMON AGREEMENT
CLOAK-ROOM TICKET	COMMON COMPLAINT
CLOSE AS AN OYSTER	COMMON KNOWLEDGE
CLOSE COMPANIONS	COMMON OWNERSHIP
CLOSE FRIENDSHIP	COMMUNAL FEEDING
CLOSER AND CLOSER	COMMUNAL KITCHEN
CLOSE TO THE SHORE	COMMUNITY CENTRE
CLOSING-DOWN SALE	COMPANION IN ARMS
CLOTHING COUPONS	COMPANION LADDER
CLOUD-CUCKOO LAND	COMPANION VOLUME

COMPANY DIRECTOR
COMPANY PROMOTER
COMPLETE ABANDON
COMPLETE CONTROL
COMPLETE DEBACLE
COMPLETE EDITION
COMPLETE FAILURE
COMPLETE SWINDLE
COMPLETE VICTORY
COMPLETE WASH-OUT
COMPLEX SENTENCE
COMPOUND A FELONY
COMPULSORY GAMES
CONCERTED ACTION
CONCERTED EFFORT
CONCERT PLATFORM
CONCLUSIVE PROOF
CONDITIONAL MOOD
CONDITION POWDER
CONFERENCE TABLE
CONFESS THE TRUTH
CONFIDENCE TRICK
CONFUSE THE ISSUE
CONGENITAL IDIOT
CONSCIENCE MONEY
CONSCIOUS HUMOUR
CONSENTING PARTY
CONSIDERABLE SUM
CONSIGNMENT NOTE
CONSOLATION RACE
CONSTANT ANXIETY
CONSTANT CHATTER
CONSULAR SERVICE
CONSUMMATE SKILL
CONTEMPT OF COURT
CONTINENTAL TIME
CONTROLLED PRICE
CONVENIENT PLACE
CONVERSION TABLE
CONVERTIBLE BOND
CONVIVIAL PERSON
COOKING UTENSILS
COOK THE ACCOUNTS
COOL AS A CUCUMBER
CORDIAL GREETING
CORNER THE MARKET
CORONATION COACH
CORONATION ROBES
CORONATION STONE
CORONER'S INQUEST
CORONER'S VERDICT
CORRECTED PROOFS
CORRECT ESTIMATE
CORRUGATED PAPER
COTTAGE BY THE SEA
COTTAGE HOSPITAL

COTTAGE INDUSTRY
COUNCIL OF ELDERS
COUNCIL OF EUROPE
COUNSEL'S OPINION
COUNTERFEIT COIN
COUNTER IRRITANT
COUNT FOR NOTHING
COUNT ONE'S CHANGE
COUNTRY OF ORIGIN
COUNT THE MINUTES
COUNT THE TAKINGS
COUNTY CRICKETER
COURT DRESSMAKER
COURT OF JUDGMENT
COVER MUCH GROUND
COVER ONE'S TRACKS
CRADLE OF THE DEEP
CRAMPED QUARTERS
CRAZY MIXED-UP KID
CREAMED POTATOES
CREASE RESISTANT
CREATE AN OPENING
CREATE A NUISANCE
CREATE A STOPPAGE
CREATIVE WRITING
CREATURE COMFORT
CREATURE OF HABIT
CREDULOUS PERSON
CREEPING BARRAGE
CREMORNE GARDENS
CRICKET PAVILION
CRIMINAL AT LARGE
CRIMINAL CLASSES
CRIMINAL LUNATIC
CRIMINAL NEGLECT
CRIMINAL OFFENCE
CRIPPLED FOR LIFE
CRITICAL OPINION
CROOKED SIXPENCE
CROSS-COUNTRY RUN
CROSSING THE LINE
CROSS THE CHANNEL
CROSS THE RUBICON
CROSSWORD PUZZLE
CROWD PSYCHOLOGY
CRUCIAL QUESTION
CRUSADING SPIRIT
CRUSHING VICTORY
CRUX OF THE MATTER
CUCKOO IN THE NEST
CUDGEL ONE'S BRAIN
CULTIVATE A HABIT
CULTIVATED PEARL
CULTIVATED TASTE
CUP OF BITTERNESS
CURRENT EXPENSES

CURSE OF SCOTLAND
CURTAIN MATERIAL
CUSTOMS OFFICIAL
CUT AND COME AGAIN
CUT A SORRY FIGURE
CUT DOWN EXPENSES
CUT ONESELF LOOSE

D – 15

DAILY OCCURRENCE
DAME LAURA KNIGHT
DAME NELLIE MELBA
DAMNING EVIDENCE
DAMON AND PYTHIAS
DAMPENED SPIRITS
DANCE ATTENDANCE
DANCE OF THE HOURS
DANCING MISTRESS
DANGEROUS CORNER
DANGEROUS PERSON
DANGEROUS VOYAGE
DANGEROUS WEAPON
DASH TO THE GROUND
DAVID AND GOLIATH
DAVY JONES' LOCKER
DAYLIGHT ROBBERY
DAY OF ABSTINENCE
DAY OF LIBERATION
DEAD AS A DOORNAIL
DEAD ON THE TARGET
DEAFENING CHEERS
DEAF TO ALL ADVICE
DEAL DESTRUCTION
DEAR LITTLE THING
DEATH BY DROWNING
DEATH ON THE ROADS
DEBT OF GRATITUDE
DECEIVED HUSBAND
DECIMAL FRACTION
DECISIVE VICTORY
DECLARED MISSING
DECLARE ONE'S LOVE
DECREE OF NULLITY
DEFECTIVE MEMORY
DEFECTIVE VISION
DEFENCE MINISTER
DEFENSIVE BATTLE
DEFENSIVE WEAPON
DEFERRED PAYMENT
DEFINITE ARTICLE
DELAYED REACTION
DELAYING TACTICS
DELICATE BALANCE
DELIRIUM TREMENS
DELIVERED BY HAND

DELIVER JUDGMENT
DELIVER THE GOODS
DEMAND AND SUPPLY
DEMAND ATTENTION
DEMENTIA PRAECOX
DEMOCRATIC PARTY
DEMOLITION SQUAD
DENIAL OF JUSTICE
DENTAL TREATMENT
DEPARTMENT STORE
DEPARTURE LOUNGE
DEPTHS OF DESPAIR
DESCENDING ORDER
DESCRIBE A CIRCLE
DESERTED VILLAGE
DESIGN FOR LIVING
DESIGNING FEMALE
DESIRABLE OBJECT
DESOLATE COUNTRY
DESPERATE PLIGHT
DESPERATE REMEDY
DETACHED OPINION
DETAILED ACCOUNT
DETENTION CENTRE
DETERRENT EFFECT
DEVALUE THE POUND
DEVELOPMENT AREA
DEVILLED KIDNEYS
DEVIL'S COMPANION
DEVIL'S PUNCH BOWL
DEVONSHIRE CREAM
DEVONSHIRE HOUSE
DIAMOND MERCHANT
DIAMOND NECKLACE
DIAMOND SMUGGLER
DICKIE HENDERSON
DICKIE VALENTINE
DICK WHITTINGTON
DIE IN THE ATTEMPT
DIE WITH LAUGHTER
DIFFERENT TASTES
DIFFICULT CHOICE
DIFFICULT MATTER
DIFFICULT PERSON
DIFFIDENT MANNER
DIG ONE'S OWN GRAVE
DINING-ROOM TABLE
DIPLOMATIC AGENT
DIPLOMATIC CORPS
DIPLOMATIC STAFF
DIRECT INFLUENCE
DIRECTION FINDER
DIRECTOR GENERAL
DIRT-TRACK RACING
DISAPPEARING ACT
DISARMAMENT PLAN

DISCARDED CUSTOM
DISCHARGE PAPERS
DISGUISE ONESELF
DISLOCATED ELBOW
DISORDERED BRAIN
DISORDERLY HOUSE
DISPENSE CHARITY
DISPENSE JUSTICE
DISPLACED PERSON
DISPOSABLE GOODS
DISPUTE THE FACTS
DISTANT LIKENESS
DISTANT PROSPECT
DISTANT RELATIVE
DISTINCTIVE NOTE
DISTORT THE TRUTH
DISTRESSING NEWS
DISTRESS WARRANT
DISTRICT OFFICER
DISTRICT RAILWAY
DISTRICT VISITOR
DISTURB THE PEACE
DIVIDEND WARRANT
DIVINE MESSENGER
DIVINITY STUDENT
DO A ROARING TRADE
DO AS THE ROMANS DO
DOCTOR OF SCIENCE
DOCUMENTARY FILM
DOG WITH TWO TAILS
DO-IT-YOURSELF FAN
DO-IT-YOURSELF KIT
DOLLAR RESOURCES
DOLLARS AND CENTS
DOMESTIC AFFAIRS
DOMESTIC ECONOMY
DOMESTIC OFFICES
DOMESTIC PROBLEM
DOMESTIC SCIENCE
DOMESTIC SERVANT
DOMESTIC SERVICE
DONE IN COLD BLOOD
DO ONE'S LEVEL BEST
DORA COPPERFIELD
DORCHESTER HOTEL
DORMITORY SUBURB
DO THE CHARLESTON
DO THE CIVIL THING
DO THE IMPOSSIBLE
DO THE RIGHT THING
DO THE WRONG THING
DO THINGS IN STYLE
DOUBLE ADVANTAGE
DOUBLE INDEMNITY
DOUBLE OR NOTHING
DOUBLE-QUICK TIME

DOUBLE SEVENTEEN
DOUBLE THE STAKES
DOUBLE WHITE LINE
DOUBLE YOUR MONEY
DOUBTFUL STARTER
DOWN IN THE DEPTHS
DOWN IN THE VALLEY
DOWN THE MOUNTAIN
DOWN THE STRAIGHT
DOWN TO THE GROUND
DOZENS AND DOZENS
DRAIN TO THE DREGS
DRAMATIC GESTURE
DRAMATIC SETTING
DRAMATIC SOCIETY
DRASTIC MEASURES
DRAW A COMPARISON
DRAW A DEEP BREATH
DRAW AN INFERENCE
DRAW A RED HERRING
DRAW CONCLUSIONS
DRAW IN ONE'S HORNS
DRAW INSPIRATION
DRAW ONE'S PENSION
DRAW THE CURTAINS
DREAMER OF DREAMS
DRESSING STATION
DRILLING MACHINE
DRILL INSTRUCTOR
DRINK ONE'S HEALTH
DRINK ON THE HOUSE
DRIVEN TO THE WALL
DRIVE RECKLESSLY
DROOPING SPIRITS
DROP IN THE BUCKET
DROP OF GOOD STUFF
DROP OVER THE SIDE
DRUG ON THE MARKET
DRUM AND FIFE BAND
DRUMHEAD SERVICE
DUAL CARRIAGE-WAY
DUAL PERSONALITY
DUBIOUS BLESSING
DUBLIN BAY PRAWNS
DUCHY OF CORNWALL
DUELLING PISTOLS
DUKE OF EDINBURGH
DUKE OF LANCASTER

E – 15

EAGER FOR THE FRAY
EARLY-CLOSING DAY
EARLY-MORNING TEA
EARNING CAPACITY
EARTHLY PARADISE

EASTERN COUNTIES
EASTERN QUESTION
EASY-PACED WICKET
EAT ONE'S HEART OUT
EBENEZER SCROOGE
ECLIPSE OF THE SUN
ECONOMIC WARFARE
EDINBURGH CASTLE
EDITORIAL COLUMN
EDITOR'S DECISION
EDMUND HOCKRIDGE
EDWARD THE FOURTH
EDWARD THE SECOND
EGG-AND-SPOON RACE
EIGHTEEN HUNDRED
EIGHTEEN PER CENT
EIGHTEENTH GREEN
EIGHTEENTH OF MAY
EIGHTH OF JANUARY
EIGHTH OF OCTOBER
EIGHT O'CLOCK NEWS
EIGHT OF DIAMONDS
ELABORATE DESIGN
ELABORATE DETAIL
ELECTION ADDRESS
ELECTION RESULTS
ELECTORAL DEFEAT
ELECTORAL SYSTEM
ELECTRICAL FAULT
ELECTRIC BATTERY
ELECTRIC BLANKET
ELECTRIC CIRCUIT
ELECTRIC CURRENT
ELECTRIC FURNACE
ELECTRICITY BILL
ELECTRIC MACHINE
ELECTRIC RAILWAY
ELECTRIC TOASTER
ELECTRONIC BRAIN
ELEVATED RAILWAY
ELEVENTH CENTURY
ELEVENTH OF APRIL
ELEVENTH OF MARCH
ELIZABETH TAYLOR
ELOCUTION LESSON
EMANUEL SHINWELL
EMERALD BRACELET
EMERALD NECKLACE
EMERGENCY POWERS
EMERGENCY RATION
EMOTIONAL RELIEF
ENCASED IN ARMOUR
ENDEAVOUR TO HELP
ENDLESS ARGUMENT
ENDLESS ATTEMPTS
END OF ONE'S TETHER

END OF THE CENTURY
END OF THE CHAPTER
END OF THE JOURNEY
ENDOWMENT POLICY
ENEMY OF PROGRESS
ENERGETIC PERSON
ENGAGEMENT DIARY
ENGINEER A STRIKE
ENGLAND AND WALES
ENGLISH LANGUAGE
ENGLISHMAN'S HOME
ENJOY GOOD HEALTH
ENJOY POOR HEALTH
ENTENTE CORDIALE
ENTER PARLIAMENT
EPICUREAN TASTES
EPSOM RACECOURSE
EQUESTRIAN SKILL
ERNEST HEMINGWAY
ERRONEOUS BELIEF
ERROR OF JUDGMENT
ERROR OF OMISSION
ESCAPED PRISONER
ESCAPE MECHANISM
ESPOUSE THE CAUSE
ESSENTIAL CLAUSE
ESTABLISH A CLAIM
ETERNAL TRIANGLE
ETON BOATING-SONG
EVENING STANDARD
EVEN MONEY CHANCE
EVERLASTING FAME
EVERY MOTHER'S SON
EVERY NOW AND THEN
EVERYONE'S FRIEND
EVIDENCE IN COURT
EXAGGERATED IDEA
EXALTED POSITION
EXAMINATION HALL
EXCELLENT CHANCE
EXCELLENT REASON
EXCELLENT RESULT
EXCEPTIONAL WORD
EXCESSIVE CHARGE
EXCESSIVE WEIGHT
EXCHANGE AND MART
EXCHANGE CONTROL
EXCHANGE GLANCES
EXCHANGE LETTERS
EXCHANGE OF VIEWS
EXCHANGE SIGNALS
EXCLAMATION MARK
EXCLUSIVE REPORT
EXCLUSIVE RIGHTS
EXCURSION TICKET
EXERCISE CONTROL

EXERCISE THE MIND
EXERCISE THE VETO
EXHAUSTION POINT
EXORBITANT PRICE
EXPANDING BULLET
EXPECT OTHERWISE
EXPENSE NO OBJECT
EXPENSIVE TASTES
EXPERT KNOWLEDGE
EXPLODE WITH RAGE
EXPLOSIVE CHARGE
EXPLOSIVE DEVICE
EXPORT AND IMPORT
EXPOSED POSITION
EXPOSED TO DANGER
EXPRESS CONTEMPT
EXPRESS DELIVERY
EXPRESSIVE SMILE
EXQUISITE CHOICE
EXTENSION OF TIME
EXTORTIONATE FEE
EXTREME KINDNESS
EXTREME MEASURES
EXTREME PATIENCE
EYEBROW TWEEZERS

F – 15

FACE LIKE A FIDDLE
FACE THE OTHER WAY
FACE THE PROSPECT
FACT OF THE MATTER
FACTS AND FIGURES
FADED REPUTATION
FAIR MAID OF PERTH
FAIR MEANS OR FOUL
FAIR WEAR AND TEAR
FAITHFUL ACCOUNT
FAITHFUL PROMISE
FAITHFUL SERVANT
FALKLAND ISLANDS
FALL ON HARD TIMES
FALL TO THE GROUND
FALSE ACCUSATION
FALSE APPEARANCE
FALSE CONCEPTION
FALSE IMPRESSION
FALSE REPUTATION
FAMILY ALLOWANCE
FAMILY GATHERING
FAMILY LOYALTIES
FAMILY SOLICITOR
FAMOUS LAST WORDS
FANCY-DRESS DANCE
FANNY BY GASLIGHT
FAN-TAILED PIGEON
FAREWELL ADDRESS

FAR FROM THE TRUTH
FARMING ACCOUNTS
FARTHING DAMAGES
FASHIONABLE AREA
FASTER THAN SOUND
FATAL ATTRACTION
FATHER AND MOTHER
FATHER CHRISTMAS
FATHER CONFESSOR
FATHERLESS CHILD
FAVOURABLE ISSUE
FAVOURABLE REPLY
FAVOURABLE START
FAVOURABLE TERMS
FEAR FOR ONE'S LIFE
FEAST FOR THE GODS
FEATHERED FRIEND
FEATHER ONE'S NEST
FEDERAL REPUBLIC
FEEBLE IMITATION
FEEL COMFORTABLE
FEEL IN ONE'S BONES
FEET ON THE GROUND
FELLOWSHIP HOUSE
FELLOW TRAVELLER
FEMININE PRONOUN
FENCED ENCLOSURE
FENCHURCH STREET
FESTIVAL GARDENS
FESTIVE OCCASION
FIELD OF ACTIVITY
FIELD PUNISHMENT
FIFTEEN AND A HALF
FIFTEENTH LETTER
FIFTEENTH OF JULY
FIFTEENTH OF JUNE
FIFTEEN THOUSAND
FIFTH OF DECEMBER
FIFTH OF FEBRUARY
FIFTH OF NOVEMBER
FIFTY-PENCE PIECE
FIGHT FOR FREEDOM
FIGHT LIKE DEVILS
FIGHT TO THE DEATH
FIGURATIVE SENSE
FILL IN THE CRACKS
FILTH AND SQUALOR
FINANCE MINISTER
FINANCIAL CRISIS
FINANCIAL WIZARD
FINDING'S KEEPING
FINE OPPORTUNITY
FINISHED PRODUCT
FINISHING SCHOOL
FINISHING STROKE
FIREWORK DISPLAY

FIRST-AID STATION
FIRST APPEARANCE
FIRST BEGININGS
FIRST-CLASS HOTEL
FIRST-CLASS MATCH
FIRST-CLASS STAMP
FIRST-FLOOR FRONT
FIRST IMPORTANCE
FIRST IMPRESSION
FIRST INSTALMENT
FIRST INTENTIONS
FIRST IN THE FIELD
FIRST IN THE QUEUE
FIRST LIEUTENANT
FIRST OCCURRENCE
FIRST OF DECEMBER
FIRST·OF FEBRUARY
FIRST OF NOVEMBER
FIRST PORT OF CALL
FIRST PRINCIPLES
FIRST-RATE ACTING
FIRST WICKET DOWN
FISH AND CHIP SHOP
FISHING INDUSTRY
FISHMONGERS' HALL
FIT OF GENEROSITY
FIT OF THE VAPOURS
FIVE AND A QUARTER
FIVE WICKETS DOWN
FIXED IMPRESSION
FLAGGING SPIRITS
FLAMBOROUGH HEAD
FLAMING NUISANCE
FLANNEL TROUSERS
FLAWLESS DIAMOND
FLAWLESS MANNERS
FLEETING GLIMPSE
FLEET OPERATIONS
FLEMISH LANGUAGE
FLICK OF THE WRIST
FLING INTO PRISON
FLIRT WITH THE LAW
FLOATING CAPITAL
FLOOR OF THE HOUSE
FLOURISHING TIME
FLOWER OF THE ARMY
FLY INTO A PASSION
FLY OFF THE HANDLE
FOLLOW PRECEDENT
FOLLOW THE HOUNDS
FOLLOW THE PLOUGH
FOND OF THE BOTTLE
FOOL OF THE FAMILY
FOOTBALL RESULTS
FOOT OF THE LADDER
FOR ALL ONE'S WORTH

FOR A YEAR AND A DAY
FORBIDDEN GROUND
FORCE AN ENTRANCE
FORCE THE BIDDING
FORCIBLE FEEDING
FOREIGN CURRENCY
FOREIGN EXCHANGE
FOREIGN LANGUAGE
FOREIGN MINISTER
FORENSIC CHEMIST
FORFEIT ONE'S BAIL
FORGED SIGNATURE
FORGET ONE'S PIECE
FORGIVING NATURE
FOR GOODNESS' SAKE!
FORGOTTEN CUSTOM
FORKED LIGHTNING
FORM A GOVERNMENT
FORMAL AGREEMENT
FORMAL COMPLAINT
FORMAL STATEMENT
FOR MANY A LONG DAY
FOR OLD TIMES' SAKE
FOR THE FIRST TIME
FOR THE THIRD TIME
FOR THE TIME BEING
FORTY-EIGHT HOURS
FORTY-NINTH STATE
FORWARDING AGENT
FORWARD MOVEMENT
FOR WHAT IT'S WORTH
FOSTER AN OPINION
FOUNDATION CREAM
FOUNDATION STONE
FOUNTAIN OF YOUTH
FOUR AND A QUARTER
FOURTEEN PER CENT
FOURTEENTH GREEN
FOURTEENTH OF MAY
FOURTH DIMENSION
FOURTH OF JANUARY
FOURTH OF OCTOBER
FOUR WICKETS DOWN
FRAGRANT PERFUME
FRANCIS OF ASSISI
FRANCO-GERMAN WAR
FRANKLY SPEAKING
FREDERICK DELIUS
FREE ASSOCIATION
FREEDOM FROM FEAR
FREEDOM FROM WANT
FREEDOM OF ACCESS
FREEDOM OF ACTION
FREEDOM OF CHOICE
FREEDOM OF SPEECH
FREEDOM OF THE AIR

FREE FROM SLAVERY
FREEHAND DRAWING
FREELANCE WRITER
FREE OF INCOME TAX
FREE TRANSLATION
FREEZE ONE'S BLOOD
FREEZING MIXTURE
FRENCH BREAKFAST
FRENCH DICTATION
FRENCH GRAND PRIX
FRENCH PEASANTRY
FRENCH SUBTITLES
FRENZIED EFFORTS
FREQUENT VISITOR
FRESH COMPLEXION
FRICASSEE OF VEAL
FRICTIONAL FORCE
FRIDAY AFTERNOON
FRIENDLY FEELING
FRIENDLY FOOTING
FRIENDLY GESTURE
FRIENDLY ISLANDS
FRIENDLY RIVALRY
FRIENDLY SOCIETY
FRIGHTENED CHILD
FROG IN THE THROAT
FROM ALL QUARTERS
FROM FIRST TO LAST
FROM HAND TO MOUTH
FROM LEFT TO RIGHT
FROM OBSERVATION
FROM STEM TO STERN
FROM THE ROOF-TOPS
FROM TOP TO BOTTOM
FRONT-LINE TROOPS
FROTH AT THE MOUTH
FRUITFUL SESSION
FRUITLESS SEARCH
FRUITS OF VICTORY
FUEL TO THE FLAMES
FULL-BOTTOMED WIG
FULL-DRESS DEBATE
FULL EXPLANATION
FULL OF INCIDENTS
FULL OF SURPRISES
FULL SPEED ASTERN
FULLY GUARANTEED
FUND OF KNOWLEDGE
FUNERAL CEREMONY
FUNERAL DIRECTOR
FURNISH EVIDENCE
FURNITURE POLISH
FUTURE EXISTENCE
FUTURE REFERENCE

G – 15

GAIN A REPUTATION
GAIN INFORMATION
GAIN ONE'S FREEDOM
GALA PERFORMANCE
GALL AND WORMWOOD
GAME FOR ANYTHING
GAME, SET AND MATCH
GARDEN OF ENGLAND
GARGANTUAN FEAST
GATE-LEGGED TABLE
GATHERING CLOUDS
GATHERING STICKS
GENERAL ASSEMBLY
GENERAL DE GAULLE
GENERAL DELIVERY
GENERAL ELECTION
GENERAL FACTOTUM
GENERAL HOSPITAL
GENERAL INTEREST
GENERAL LAUGHTER
GENERAL OVERHAUL
GENERAL PRACTICE
GENERATING PLANT
GENEROUS HELPING
GENEROUS MEASURE
GENETIC ENGINEER
GENTLEMAN FARMER
GEOFFREY CHAUCER
GEOGRAPHY LESSON
GEORGE THE FOURTH
GET CONFIDENTIAL
GET DOWN TO THE JOB
GET INTO HOT WATER
GET INTO MISCHIEF
GET ONE'S MONKEY UP
GET ON ONE'S NERVES
GET ON SWIMMINGLY
GET ON WITH THE JOB
GET OUT OF THE ROAD
GET OUT OF TROUBLE
GET THE ADVANTAGE
GET THE UPPER HAND
GET THE WORST OF IT
GET UP TO MISCHIEF
GET YOUR SKATES ON
GHOSTS OF THE PAST
GIFT FROM THE GODS
GIN AND ANGOSTURA
GIRD UP ONE'S LOINS
GIRLISH LAUGHTER
GIST OF THE MATTER
GIVE A LEATHERING
GIVE FULL DETAILS
GIVE IN THE MIDDLE

GIVE ONE A BAD TIME
GIVE ONE'S CONSENT
GIVE ONESELF AIRS
GIVE ONESELF AWAY
GIVE ONE THE WORKS
GIVE PARTICULARS
GIVE THE ALL-CLEAR
GIVE THE GAME AWAY
GIVE THE PASSWORD
GIVE THE SHOW AWAY
GIVE UP THE SPONGE
GLITTERING PRIZE
GLOBE ARTICHOKES
GLOOMY COMPANION
GLORIOUS HOLIDAY
GLORIOUSLY DRUNK
GLORIOUS TWELFTH
GLORIOUS VICTORY
GLUT ON THE MARKET
GO A LONG WAY ROUND
GO BY UNDERGROUND
GODDESS OF WISDOM
GOD-FORSAKEN HOLE
GOD SAVE THE QUEEN
GO IN FOR LUXURIES
GO INTO ECSTASIES
GOLDEN HANDSHAKE
GOLDEN RETRIEVER
GOLDEN SOVEREIGN
GONE WITH THE WIND
GOOD CIRCULATION
GOOD CITIZENSHIP
GOOD CONNECTIONS
GOOD DAY'S JOURNEY
GOOD ENOUGH TO EAT
GOOD HANDWRITING
GOOD HOUSEKEEPER
GOODNESS OF HEART
GOOD RESOLUTIONS
GOOD VENTILATION
GO OFF AT A TANGENT
GO OFF THE DEEP END
GO OUT OF BUSINESS
GO OVER THE GROUND
GORGEOUS WEATHER
GO THE LONGEST WAY
GO THROUGH WITH IT
GO TO MUCH TROUBLE
GO TO THE SCAFFOLD
GOVERNMENT GRANT
GOVERNMENT HOUSE
GOVERNOR GENERAL
GO WITHOUT SAYING
GO WITH THE STREAM
GRACE BEFORE MEAT
GRACEFUL GESTURE

GRADUAL PROGRESS
GRAMOPHONE MUSIC
GRAND INQUISITOR
GRANDIOSE MANNER
GRAND UNION CANAL
GRANT ABSOLUTION
GRANULATED SUGAR
GRAPEFRUIT JUICE
GRAVE MISGIVINGS
GREASE THE WHEELS
GREAT ASSISTANCE
GREATEST RESPECT
GREAT EXCITEMENT
GREAT EXHIBITION
GREAT IMPORTANCE
GREATLY ESTEEMED
GREATLY INDEBTED
GREATLY SUPERIOR
GREAT MISFORTUNE
GREAT POPULARITY
GREEK MEETS GREEK
GREEK RESTAURANT
GREEN CHARTREUSE
GREENHOUSE PLANT
GRENADIER GUARDS
GREYHOUND RACING
GRIEVOUS MISTAKE
GRILLED SAUSAGES
GRILLED TOMATOES
GRIST FOR THE MILL
GROCERY BUSINESS
GROSS NEGLIGENCE
GROSVENOR SQUARE
GROUND-FLOOR FLAT
GROUND-NUT SCHEME
GROW INDIFFERENT
GUARDED LANGUAGE
GUESS ONE'S WEIGHT
GUEST APPEARANCE
GUILTY BEHAVIOUR
GUILTY BUT INSANE
GUNNER'S DAUGHTER
GUNNERY PRACTICE
GUY DE MAUPASSANT

H – 15

HACKNEY CARRIAGE
HACKNEYED PHRASE
HACKNEYED SAYING
HAGUE CONVENTION
HAIL AND FAREWELL
HAILING DISTANCE
HALF AS MUCH AGAIN
HALF-TERM HOLIDAY
HALF THE DISTANCE

HALIBUT-LIVER OIL	HEAVEN BE PRAISED
HAMMER AND SICKLE	HEAVY CASUALTIES
HANDFUL OF SILVER	HEAVY PUNISHMENT
HANDSOME APOLOGY	HEIGHT OF FASHION
HANDSOME FORTUNE	HEIR PRESUMPTIVE
HANDSOME PRESENT	HEIR TO THE THRONE
HAND-TO-HAND FIGHT	HENRY THE SEVENTH
HANGED BY THE NECK	HERBACEOUS PLANT
HANGING ORNAMENT	HERBERT MORRISON
HANG OUT THE FLAGS	HEREDITARY TITLE
HANG UP A STOCKING	HEREWARD THE WAKE
HANSEL AND GRETEL	HERMIONE GINGOLD
HAPPY AS A SANDBOY	HEROIC QUALITIES
HAPPY IN ONE'S WORK	HERRING INDUSTRY
HARBOUR FEELINGS	HESITATION WALTZ
HARBOUR OF REFUGE	HIDE UNDERGROUND
HARD AND FAST RULE	HIGHER AND HIGHER
HARDEN ONE'S HEART	HIGHER CRITICISM
HARDNESS OF HEART	HIGHER EDUCATION
HARE AND TORTOISE	HIGHLAND COSTUME
HARMLESS LUNATIC	HIGHLY COMMENDED
HAROLD MACMILLAN	HIGHLY CONNECTED
HARP ON ONE STRING	HIGHLY DANGEROUS
HARROW ON THE HILL	HIGHLY DELIGHTED
HARVEST FESTIVAL	HIGHLY EFFICIENT
HAUL DOWN THE FLAG	HIGHLY QUALIFIED
HAUNCH OF VENISON	HIGH TEMPERATURE
HAUNTING REFRAIN	HINGE AND BRACKET
HAVE A BONE TO PICK	HIPPOCRATIC OATH
HAVE AN INTERVIEW	HIS MASTER'S VOICE
HAVE A SWEET TOOTH	HISTORICAL NOVEL
HAVE ONE'S REVENGE	HISTORIC PRESENT
HAVE THE BEST OF IT	HIT BELOW THE BELT
HAVE THE LAST WORD	HIT THE HEADLINES
HAVE THE PLEASURE	HIT THE HIGH SPOTS
HAVE THE WHIP-HAND	HOLD ONE TO RANSOM
HAVE WHAT IT TAKES	HOLD OUT ONE'S HAND
HAZARD AN OPINION	HOLD THE BEST HAND
HEAD IN THE CLOUDS	HOLD UP YOUR HANDS
HEAD OF THE FAMILY	HOLE IN THE CORNER
HEAD OF THE SCHOOL	HOLE IN THE GROUND
HEAD-ON COLLISION	HOLES AND CORNERS
HEALING OINTMENT	HOLIDAY BY THE SEA
HEALTH AND WEALTH	HOLY ROMAN EMPIRE
HEALTH INSURANCE	HOME CONSUMPTION
HEALTHY APPETITE	HOMERIC LAUGHTER
HEALTHY EXERCISE	HOMEWARD JOURNEY
HEAP COALS OF FIRE	HOME WITH THE MILK
HEARSAY EVIDENCE	HOMICIDAL MANIAC
HEARTBREAK HOUSE	HONEYMOON COUPLE
HEARTLESS MANNER	HONEYSUCKLE ROSE '
HEARTS ARE TRUMPS	HONOURS OF BATTLE
HEARTY BREAKFAST	HOPE AGAINST HOPE
HEARTY GREETINGS	HOPELESS FAILURE
HEATHROW AIRPORT	HORIZONTAL PLANE
HEAT OF THE MOMENT	HORNS OF A DILEMMA

HORRIBLE WEATHER
HORSE-SHOE MAGNET
HOSPITAL ALMONER
HOSPITAL GROUNDS
HOSPITAL SURGEON
HOSTILE EVIDENCE
HOTEL PROPRIETOR
HOT FROM THE PRESS
HOURS OF BUSINESS
HOURS OF IDLENESS
HOUSEHOLD CHORES
HOUSEHOLD DRUDGE
HOUSEHOLD TROOPS
HOUSING MINISTER
HOUSING SHORTAGE
HOVER ON THE BRINK
HOW GOES THE ENEMY?
HUCKLEBERRY FINN
HUDDLED TOGETHER
HUMAN EXPERIENCE
HUMANLY POSSIBLE
HUMANLY SPEAKING
HUMID ATMOSPHERE
HUNDRED THOUSAND
HUNDRED YEARS WAR
HUNGER AND THIRST
HUNGRY AS A HUNTER
HUSH-HUSH SUBJECT

I – 15

ICE-CREAM PARLOUR
ICE-CREAM SELLERS
ICE HOCKEY PLAYER
IDEAL SUGGESTION
IDLEWILD AIRPORT
ILLUSTRATED WORK
ILLUSTRIOUS PAST
IMITATION PEARLS
IMMACULATE STYLE
IMMEDIATE ACTION
IMMERSED IN STUDY
IMMERSION HEATER
IMMORTAL DREAMER
IMMOVABLE OBJECT
IMPENDING DANGER
IMPERIAL COLLEGE
IMPERIAL MEASURE
IMPLORING GLANCE
IMPORTANT MATTER
IMPORTANT PERSON
IMPOSSIBLE STORY
IMPRESSIVE SCENE
IMPROBABLE STORY
IMPROVED VERSION
IMPROVE IN HEALTH

IMPROVE ON NATURE
IMPULSIVE NATURE
IN A LESSER DEGREE
IN ALL CONSCIENCE
IN ALL DIRECTIONS
IN ALL LIKELIHOOD
INANIMATE MATTER
IN APPLE-PIE ORDER
IN A STRAIGHT LINE
INAUGURAL SPEECH
IN BLACK AND WHITE
INCIDENTAL MUSIC
INCLINE ONE'S HEAD
INCLUSIVE CHARGE
INCOME-TAX DEMAND
INCOME-TAX REBATE
INCOME-TAX RELIEF
INCOME-TAX RETURN
IN CONSIDERATION
INCREASED DEMAND
INDELIBLE PENCIL
INDEPENDENCE DAY
INDIAN ROPE-TRICK
INDIA-RUBBER BALL
INDIA-RUBBER BAND
INDIRECT CURRENT
INDIVIDUAL STYLE
INDOOR FIREWORKS
INDULGENT PARENT
INDUSTRIAL PLANT
IN EXTREME DANGER
INFAMOUS CONDUCT
INFANT MORTALITY
INFANTRY SOLDIER
INFERIOR ARTICLE
INFERIOR NUMBERS
INFERIOR QUALITY
INFERIOR VERSION
INFERNAL MACHINE
INFERNAL REGIONS
INFIRM OF PURPOSE
INFORMATION DESK
INFORMATION ROOM
INFORMED OPINION
IN FULL AGREEMENT
INGENIOUS DEVICE
INGENIOUS EXCUSE
INIQUITOUS PRICE
INITIAL EXPENSES
INJURED INNOCENT
IN JUXTAPOSITION
INNINGS DECLARED
INNOCENTS ABROAD
IN ONE'S RIGHT MIND
INORDINATE PRIDE
INORGANIC MATTER

IN SEARCH OF TRUTH
INSECURE FOOTING
IN SHARP CONTRAST
INSPECTOR FRENCH
INSTANT RESPONSE
INSTRUMENT BOARD
INSTRUMENT PANEL
INSUPARABLE ODDS
INSURANCE BROKER
INSURANCE OFFICE
INSURANCE POLICY
INTELLIGENT FOLK
INTELLIGENT TALK
INTERESTED PARTY
INTERIM DIVIDEND
INTERNAL AFFAIRS
IN THE ACCUSATIVE
IN THE ALTOGETHER
IN THE BACKGROUND
IN THE FIRST PLACE
IN THE FOREGROUND
IN THE LABORATORY
IN THE LAST RESORT
IN THE LIGHT OF DAY
IN THE LION'S MOUTH
IN THE MANNER BORN
IN THE MELTING-POT
IN THE MIDDLE EAST
IN THE NEAR FUTURE
IN THE NICK OF TIME
IN THE RIGHT PLACE
IN THE SAME BREATH
IN THE SHOP-WINDOW
IN THE SMALL HOURS
IN THE VERNACULAR
IN THE WILDERNESS
IN THE WITNESS-BOX
IN THE WRONG PLACE
INVALID CARRIAGE
INVENTIVE GENIUS
INVESTMENT TRUST
INVEST WITH POWER
INVISIBLE EXPORT
INVISIBLE IMPORT
INVITATION WALTZ
INVITED AUDIENCE
IRISH SWEEPSTAKE
IRREGULAR TROOPS
IRREPARABLE HARM
IRREPARABLE LOSS
ISLAND CONTINENT
ISSUE A CHALLENGE
ITALIAN VERMOUTH
IT'S THAT MAN AGAIN
IVAN THE TERRIBLE

J – 15

JACK OF ALL TRADES
JANUARY THE FIFTH
JANUARY THE FIRST
JANUARY THE NINTH
JANUARY THE SIXTH
JANUARY THE TENTH
JANUARY THE THIRD
JERRY-BUILT HOUSE
JEWEL AND WARRISS
JOBBING GARDENER
JOCKEY FOR PLACES
JOIN IN THE CHORUS
JOINT GOVERNMENT
JOIN THE MAJORITY
JOINT OPERATIONS
JOINT POSSESSION
JOLLY GOOD FELLOW
JUDGE FOR ONESELF
JUDGMENT OF PARIS
JUDGMENT SUMMONS
JUICE OF THE GRAPE
JULY THE ELEVENTH
JUMPING-OFF PLACE
JUNE THE ELEVENTH
JUNIOR BARRISTER
JUPITER SYMPHONY
JUST ABOUT ENOUGH

K – 15

KATHLEEN FERRIER
KEEN COMPETITION
KEENLY CONTESTED
KEEP AT A DISTANCE
KEEPER OF THE KEYS
KEEP IN CAPTIVITY
KEEP IN IGNORANCE
KEEP NOTHING BACK
KEEP OFF THE GRASS
KEEP ONE GUESSING
KEEP ONE'S BALANCE
KEEP ONE'S COUNSEL
KEEP ONE'S PROMISE
KEEP ONE'S SHIRT ON
KEEP ON THE COURSE
KEEP OUT OF THE WAY
KEEP THE DOOR OPEN
KEEP THINGS GOING
KEEP TO THE MIDDLE
KEEP UNDER ARREST
KENNETH McKELLAR
KERB-SIDE PARKING
KEY TO THE MYSTERY
KICK UP ONE'S HEELS

KID-GLOVE METHODS
KIDNEYS AND BACON
KINDLE OF KITTENS
KINDNESS OF HEART
KINGDOM OF HEAVEN
KING OF THE BEASTS
KING OF THE CASTLE
KING OF THE FOREST
KING OF THE JUNGLE
KITTEN ON THE KEYS
KNAVE OF DIAMONDS
KNIGHT COMMANDER
KNIGHT OF THE BATH
KNIGHT OF THE ROAD
KNIGHTS TEMPLARS
KNITTING MACHINE
KNITTING PATTERN
KNOW A THING OR TWO
KNOW ONE'S OWN MIND

L – 15

LABOUR CANDIDATE
LABOUR RELATIONS
LABOUR SUPPORTER
LACK OF EDUCATION
LACK OF KNOWLEDGE
LACK OF WILL POWER
LADDER OF SUCCESS
LADIES' COMPANION
LADIES IN WAITING
LAND OF MY FATHERS
LAND OF THE LIVING
LANDSCAPE ARTIST
LANGUAGE BARRIER
LANGUAGE PROBLEM
LANGUAGE TEACHER
LARGE PERCENTAGE
LARGE POPULATION
LAST BUT NOT LEAST
LASTING MOMUMENT
LAST PERFORMANCE
LATEST INVENTION
LATEST QUOTATION
LAUGH AND GROW FAT
LAUGHING JACKASS
LAUGH LIKE A DRAIN
LAUGH LIKE A HYENA
LAUGH OUT OF COURT
LAUGHTER IN COURT
LAURENCE OLIVIER
LAVENDER HILL MOB
LAY DOWN ONE'S ARMS
LAY DOWN ONE'S LIFE
LEAD A DOUBLE LIFE
LEAD A MERRY DANCE

LEADER OF FASHION
LEADER OF SOCIETY
LEADER OF THE BAND
LEADING BUSINESS
LEADING NOVELIST
LEADING QUESTION
LEADING THE FIELD
LEAGUE OF NATIONS
LEAP OVER THE MOON
LEARN ONE'S LESSON
LEATHER INDUSTRY
LEAVE FOOTPRINTS
LEAVE IN SUSPENSE
LEAVE IN THE LURCH
LEAVE IT TO CHANCE
LEAVE NOTHING OUT
LEAVE THE COUNTRY
LEAVE UNFINISHED
LEGAL DEPARTMENT
LEGAL PROFESSION
LEGAL SEPARATION
LEGAL SETTLEMENT
LEG BEFORE WICKET
LEGISLATIVE BODY
LEGITIMATE CLAIM
LEGITIMATE DRAMA
LEGITIMATE STAGE
LEGUMINOUS PLANT
LEICESTER SQUARE
LEIGHTON BUZZARD
LEISURED CLASSES
LEMON CHEESE-CAKE
LENGTH OF SERVICE
LENGTHY ARGUMENT
LENGTHY BUSINESS
LENIENT SENTENCE
LEONARDO DA VINCI
LESSEN THE STRAIN
LESS THAN THE DUST
LET DOWN ONE'S HAIR
LET ONE'S HAIR DOWN
LETTER OF REQUEST
LET THERE BE LIGHT!
LETTRES DE CACHET
LIBERAL MAJORITY
LIBERAL MINORITY
LICENCE ENDORSED
LICK AND A PROMISE
LICK ONE'S FINGERS
LIE IN ONE'S THROAT
LIE LIKE A TROOPER
LIFE-BOAT STATION
LIFT THE RECEIVER
LIFT UP ONE'S VOICE
LIFT UP YOUR HEART
LIGHT AS A FEATHER

LIGHT LITERATURE
LIGHT MACHINE-GUN
LIGHTNING SKETCH
LIGHTNING STRIKE
LIGHT OF THE WORLD
LIGHT PUNISHMENT
LIKE A DROWNED RAT
LIKE A DUTCH UNCLE
LIKE A HOUSE AFIRE
LIKE QUICKSILVER
LILY OF THE VALLEY
LINCOLN HANDICAP
LINCOLN MEMORIAL
LINE OF DIRECTION
LINE ONE'S POCKETS
LINK WITH THE PAST
LIQUID RESOURCES
LIST TO STARBOARD
LITERARY CIRCLES
LITERARY FORGERY
LITERARY OUTLINE
LITERARY SUBJECT
LITTLE ENGLANDER
LITTLE GENTLEMAN
LITTLE KNOWLEDGE
LITTLE MISS FIX-IT
LITTLE OR NOTHING
LITTLE WOODEN HUT
LIVE DANGEROUSLY
LIVE IN A SMALL WAY
LIVE IN SECLUSION
LIVE LIKE A PAUPER
LIVERPOOL STREET
LIVING TESTIMONY
LOADED WITH MONEY
LOAD OFF ONE'S MIND
LOAVES AND FISHES
LOCAL GOVERNMENT
LOCAL INHABITANT
LOCH NESS MONSTER
LOCKED AND BOLTED
LODGE A COMPLAINT
LOGICAL ARGUMENT
LOGICAL SEQUENCE
LONDON ALLOWANCE
LONDON TRANSPORT
LONG ARM OF THE LAW
LONGEST WAY ROUND
LONG LIVE THE KING!
LONG-TERM SOLDIER
LONG-WINDED STORY
LOOK BACK IN ANGER
LOOK FOR A WELCOME
LOOK FOR SYMPATHY
LOOK THE OTHER WAY
LOOK TO THE FUTURE

LORD CHAMBERLAIN
LORD HIGH ADMIRAL
LORD HIGH STEWARD
LORD MAYOR'S COACH
LORDS AND COMMONS
LORDS OF CREATION
LOSE COUNTENANCE
LOSE ONE'S BALANCE
LOSE ONE'S FOOTING
LOSE ONE'S HUSBAND
LOSE ONE'S STRIPES
LOSE ON THE SWINGS
LOSE THE ELECTION
LOST OPPORTUNITY
LOVE ME, LOVE MY DOG
LOVE OF ADVENTURE
LOVER AND HIS LASS
LOWER ONE'S SIGHTS
LOW SUBSCRIPTION
LUKEWARM SUPPORT
LUMP IN THE THROAT
LUNCHEON SAUSAGE
LUNCHEON VOUCHER
LUTON GIRLS' CHOIR
LUXURIANT GROWTH

M – 15

MAD AS A MARCH HARE
MAGAZINE ARTICLE
MAGAZINE SECTION
MAGIC INSTRUMENT
MAGNETIC COMPASS
MAGNIFYING GLASS
MAGNIFYING POWER
MAIN CLAIM TO FAME
MAIN LINE STATION
MAJESTY OF THE LAW
MAJORITY VERDICT
MAKE A COLLECTION
MAKE A CONFESSION
MAKE A FRESH START
MAKE ALTERATIONS
MAKE AN ASSERTION
MAKE AN EXCEPTION
MAKE APPLICATION
MAKE A PREDICTION
MAKE A RESOLUTION
MAKE A SUGGESTION
MAKE COMPARISONS
MAKE CONCESSIONS
MAKE CORRECTIONS
MAKE ONE'S FORTUNE
MAKE REPARATIONS
MAKE RESTITUTION
MAKE SHORT WORK OF

MAKE THE BEST OF IT	MEMBER OF SOCIETY
MAKE THE MOST OF IT	MEMBER OF THE CAST
MAKE THINGS CLEAR	MEMORIAL SERVICE
MAKE THINGS WORSE	MENTAL AGITATION
MALE SUPERIORITY	MENTAL BREAKDOWN
MALIGNANT GROWTH	MENTAL DEFECTIVE
MALIGN INFLUENCE	MENTAL FACULTIES
MALVERN FESTIVAL	MENTAL TELEPATHY
MANIC DEPRESSION	MENTAL TREATMENT
MANILLA ENVELOPE	MERCENARY TROOPS
MAN IN POSSESSION	MERCHANT SERVICE
MANNEQUIN PARADE	MERE COINCIDENCE
MAN OF EXPERIENCE	MERRY AS A CRICKET
MANY-HEADED BEAST	MERRY MONTH OF MAY
MARCH OF PROGRESS	MESSAGE RECEIVED
MARCH THE SEVENTH	METHOD OF WORKING
MARCH THE TWELFTH	MEXICAN HAIRLESS
MARGINAL COMMENT	MICHAEL FLANDERS
MARIE ANTOINETTE	MICHAEL HOLLIDAY
MARINE INSURANCE	MICHAELMAS DAISY
MARINER'S COMPASS	MICHAELMAS GOOSE
MARK OF AUTHORITY	MICHAEL REDGRAVE
MARK THE OCCASION	MIDDLE-AGE SPREAD
MARLENE DIETRICH	MIDDLE OF THE ROAD
MARRIAGEABLE AGE	MIDDLE OF THE ROOM
MARRIAGE ADVISER	MIDLAND COUNTIES
MARRIAGE BY PROXY	MIDNIGHT MATINEE
MARRIAGE LICENCE	MILITARY ACADEMY
MARRIAGE PARTNER	MILITARY BEARING
MARRIAGE PORTION	MILITARY COLLEGE
MARRIAGE SERVICE	MILITARY COLOURS
MARRIED QUARTERS	MILITARY FUNERAL
MARSHALLING YARD	MILITARY HISTORY
MARY'S LITTLE LAMB	MILITARY HONOURS
MASCULINE GENDER	MILITARY MISSION
MASQUERADE DRESS	MILITARY SERVICE
MASS INFORMATION	MILITARY STATION
MASS OBSERVATION	MILITARY TACTICS
MASTER CARPENTER	MILITARY TRIBUNE
MASTER CRAFTSMAN	MILITARY TWO-STEP
MASTER OF SCIENCE	MILITATE AGAINST
MATERIAL BENEFIT	MILLICENT MARTIN
MATERIAL SUCCESS	MILLIONAIRE'S ROW
MATERIAL WITNESS	MIND ONE'S MANNERS
MATERNAL FEELING	MIND THE WET PAINT
MATTER OF OPINION	MINIATURE POODLE
MAXIMUM PRESSURE	MINISTER OF POWER
MAY THE FIFTEENTH	MINISTER OF STATE
MAY THE SIXTEENTH	MINISTER OF WORKS
MAY THE THIRTIETH	MINISTRY OF POWER
MAY THE TWENTIETH	MINISTRY OF STATE
MEANS OF APPROACH	MINISTRY OF WORKS
MEAN WHAT ONE SAYS	MIRROR OF FASHION
MEASURE OF LENGTH	MISERABLE SINNER
MECHANICAL MEANS	MISS ONE'S FOOTING
MECHANICAL POWER	MISTRESS QUICKLY

MIXTURE AS BEFORE
MODEL OF INDUSTRY
MODE OF BEHAVIOUR
MODERATE DEMANDS
MODERATE DRINKER
MODERATE SUCCESS
MODEST BEHAVIOUR
MOLOTOV COCKTAIL
MOMENT OF MADNESS
MONASTERY GARDEN
MONDAY AFTERNOON
MONEY FOR NOTHING
MONEY FOR OLD ROPE
MONEY MAKES MONEY
MONTE CARLO RALLY
MONTH AFTER MONTH
MONTHLY MAGAZINE
MONTHLY PAYMENTS
MONTHS AND MONTHS
MONTHS OF THE YEAR
MONUMENTAL MASON
MOON AND SIXPENCE
MOONLIGHT SONATA
MORAL INJUNCTION
MORAL OBLIGATION
MORAL PHILOSOPHY
MORAL REARMAMENT
MORAL STANDPOINT
MORBID CURIOSITY
MORE THAN WELCOME
MORRISON SHELTER
MOST INTERESTING
MOST RESPECTABLE
MOTHER AND FATHER
MOTHERING SUNDAY
MOTHERLESS CHILD
MOTIVATING FORCE
MOTLEY GATHERING
MOTORING OFFENCE
MOUNTAIN OF FLESH
MOUNTAINOUS AREA
MOUNTAIN RAILWAY
MOUNTAIN TORRENT
MOUTH OF THE RIVER
MOVING SPECTACLE
MOVING STAIRCASE
MUCH OF A MUCHNESS
MUCH SOUGHT AFTER
MULBERRY HARBOUR
MULTIPLY BY EIGHT
MULTIPLY BY SEVEN
MULTIPLY BY THREE
MUNICH AGREEMENT
MURAL DECORATION
MURDEROUS WEAPON
MUSICAL DIRECTOR

MUSICAL FESTIVAL
MUSICAL INTERVAL
MUSIC-HALL ARTIST
MUSIC HATH CHARMS
MUSTARD AND CRESS
MUSTER UP COURAGE
MUTUAL AFFECTION
MUTUAL AGREEMENT
MUTUAL HOSTILITY
MUTUAL INSURANCE
MUTUAL SUSPICION
MY LEARNED FRIEND
MYTHOLOGICAL AGE

N – 15

NATIONAL COLOURS
NATIONAL COSTUME
NATIONAL DEFENCE
NATIONAL GALLERY
NATIONAL HOLIDAY
NATIONAL LIBERAL
NATIONAL LIBRARY
NATIONAL LOTTERY
NATIONAL SAVINGS
NATIONAL SERVICE
NATIONAL SOCIETY
NATIONAL THEATRE
NATURAL APTITUDE
NATURAL CAPACITY
NATURAL INSTINCT
NAUGHTY NINETIES
NAVAL ENGAGEMENT
NAVAL OPERATIONS
NAVAL TOURNAMENT
NAVIGATION LIGHT
NEARER AND NEARER
NEAREST RELATIVE
NEAT AS NINEPENCE
NEAT BUT NOT GAUDY
NEAT HANDWRITING
NEAT PIECE OF WORK
NECK-AND-NECK RACE
NECTAR OF THE GODS
NEEDLE AND COTTON
NEEDLE AND THREAD
NEGATIVE REQUEST
NEGLECT ONE'S DUTY
NEGOTIABLE BONDS
NERVOUS DISORDER
NEVER A CROSS WORD
NEVER-ENDING TASK
NEW ACQUAINTANCE
NEWCASTLE ON TYNE
NEWCASTLE UNITED
NEW ENGLISH BIBLE

NEWFOUNDLAND DOG
NEWGATE CALENDAR
NEWS COMMENTATOR
NEW SCOTLAND YARD
NEWS FROM NOWHERE
NEWSPAPER REPORT
NEWSPAPER SELLER
NIBBLE AT THE BAIT
NICE DISTINCTION
NICE LITTLE THING
NIGHT AFTER NIGHT
NIGHT ON THE TILES
NIGHT STARVATION
NINE AND A QUARTER
NINE AND SIXPENCE
NINE AND TENPENCE
NINE AND TWOPENCE
NINETEEN AND FIVE
NINETEEN AND FOUR
NINETEEN AND NINE
NINETEEN PER CENT
NINETEENTH OF MAY
NINE WICKETS DOWN
NINTH OF DECEMBER
NINTH OF FEBRUARY
NINTH OF NOVEMBER
NOBEL PEACE PRIZE
NOBLE SENTIMENTS
NOBODY'S BUSINESS
NO CONCERN OF MINE
NO DISTANCE AT ALL
NOISY NEIGHBOURS
NOMINATION PAPER
NON COMPOS MENTIS
NONE BUT THE BRAVE
NO PRESERVATIVES
NORFOLK DUMPLING
NORMAL BEHAVIOUR
NORMAL PROCEDURE
NORTHERN IRELAND
NORTH OF THE RIVER
NORTH OF THE TWEED
NO STONE UNTURNED
NOT A LIVING THING
NOTHING IN COMMON
NOT IN THE RUNNING
NOT OUT OF THE WOOD
NOT STRONG ENOUGH
NOTTING HILL GATE
NOVEL EXPERIENCE
NUCLEAR DISARMER
NUCLEAR REACTION
NUFFIELD COLLEGE
NUREMBERG TRIALS
NURSE A GRIEVANCE
NURSE AN AMBITION

NURSERY HANDICAP
NUTCRACKER SUITE

O – 15

OBEDIENT SERVANT
OBEY REGULATIONS
OBJECT OF CHARITY
OBJECT OF DISLIKE
OBJECT OF WORSHIP
OBLIQUE QUESTION
OBSERVATION POST
OCCASIONAL TABLE
OCCUPYING TENANT
OCTOBER THE FIFTH
OCTOBER THE FIRST
OCTOBER THE NINTH
OCTOBER THE SIXTH
OCTOBER THE TENTH
OCTOBER THE THIRD
ODDS-ON FAVOURITE
ODOUR OF SANCTITY
OFFENSIVE MANNER
OFFENSIVE REMARK
OFFENSIVE WEAPON
OFFER IN EXCHANGE
OFFICER IN CHARGE
OFFICER MATERIAL
OFFICER OF THE DAY
OFFICIAL INQUIRY
OFFICIAL JOURNAL
OFFICIOUS PERSON
OFF TO A FINE START
OFF TO A GOOD START
OF THE FIRST WATER
OLD ACQUAINTANCE
OLD-AGE PENSIONER
OLD AS METHUSELAH
OLD CONTEMPTIBLE
OLDER GENERATION
OLD FATHER THAMES
OLIVER GOLDSMITH
OMNIA VINCIT AMOR
ON ACTIVE SERVICE
ONCE IN A BLUE MOON
ONCE IN A LIFETIME
ON-COURSE BETTING
ONE AFTER ANOTHER
ONE MAN WENT TO MOW
ONE OF THE COMPANY
ONE OVER THE EIGHT
ONE STAGE AT A TIME
ONE THING AT A TIME
ONE WAY OR ANOTHER
ON HANDS AND KNEES
ON ONE'S HIGH HORSE
ON SPEAKING TERMS

ON THE BORDERLINE
ON THE BRADEN BEAT
ON THE BRIGHT SIDE
ON THE CREDIT SIDE
ON THE DOTTED LINE
ON THE RIGHT LINES
ON THE RIGHT SCENT
ON THE RIGHT TRACK
ON THE ROAD TO RUIN
ON THE WATER-WAGON
ON THE WRONG LINES
ON THE WRONG SCENT
ON THE WRONG TRACK
ON TOP OF THE WORLD
ON VISITING TERMS
ON WITH THE MOTLEY
OPEN-AND-SHUT CASE
OPEN COMPETITION
OPEN HOSTILITIES
OPENING CEREMONY
OPENING SENTENCE
OPEN SCHOLARSHIP
OPEN THE QUESTION
OPEN THE THROTTLE
OPEN TO CRITICISM
OPEN TO OBJECTION
OPEN TO SUSPICION
OPEN TO THE PUBLIC
OPPORTUNE MOMENT
OPPORTUNE REMARK
OPPOSING COUNSEL
OPPOSITE EXTREME
OPPOSITE MEANING
OPPOSITE PARTIES
OPPOSITION BENCH
OPPOSITION PARTY
OPTICAL ILLUSION
ORAL EXAMINATION
ORANGE FREE STATE
ORANGE MARMALADE
ORCHESTRAL MUSIC
ORCHESTRA STALLS
ORDERLY CORPORAL
ORDERLY SERGEANT
ORDNANCE OFFICER
ORGANISED LABOUR
ORIENTAL SCHOLAR
ORIGINAL MEANING
ORIGIN OF SPECIES
ORNAMENTAL PLANT
OUNCE OF PRACTICE
OUR MUTUAL FRIEND
OUTDOOR CLOTHING
OUTDOOR EXERCISE
OUT OF COMMISSION
OUT OF EMPLOYMENT

OUT OF HIS ELEMENT
OUT OF ONE'S SENSES
OUT OF PROPORTION
OUT OF THE COUNTRY
OUT OF THE PICTURE
OUT OF THE RUNNING
OUT-OF-THE-WAY SPOT
OUTRIGHT SCANDAL
OUTSIDE INTEREST
OUTSTANDING DEBT
OVER AND DONE WITH
OVERCOME BY GRIEF
OVERFLOW MEETING
OVERHEAD CHARGES
OVERHEAD RAILWAY
OVERSTEP THE MARK
OVER THE BASE-LINE

P – 15

PADDINGTON GREEN
PAINT THE TOWN RED
PAIR OF CALLIPERS
PAIR OF COMPASSES
PAIR OF DUMB-BELLS
PAIR OF STOCKINGS
PALACE OF SOVIETS
PALAEOLITHIC AGE
PARACHUTE TROOPS
PARAGON OF VIRTUE
PARENTAL CONSENT
PARENTAL CONTROL
PARKHURST PRISON
PARTIAL LIKENESS
PARTNERS IN CRIME
PARTY CONFERENCE
PASS ALONG PLEASE
PASS A RESOLUTION
PASS AWAY THE TIME
PASSIVE INTEREST
PASSIVE RESISTER
PASS ROUND THE HAT
PASS THE HAT ROUND
PASS WITH HONOURS
PASTEURIZED MILK
PATCH UP A QUARREL
PATENTLY OBVIOUS
PATERNAL FEELING
PATRICK CAMPBELL
PATRON OF THE ARTS
PATTERN OF VIRTUE
PAUSE FOR A MOMENT
PAWNBROKER'S SIGN
PAYABLE ON DEMAND
PAY COMPENSATION
PAY OFF OLD SCORES

PAY ONE'S RESPECTS	PIECE OF EVIDENCE
PEACE AT ANY PRICE	PIECE OF GOOD NEWS
PEACE CONFERENCE	PIECE OF NONSENSE
PEACE WITH HONOUR	PIECE OF ONE'S MIND
PEACHES AND CREAM	PILLAR OF SOCIETY
PECULIAR FLAVOUR	PINCHED WITH COLD
PENAL SETTLEMENT	PINK OF CONDITION
PENCIL SHARPENER	PIOUS SENTIMENTS
PENNY IN THE POUND	PIPPED AT THE POST
PEOPLE IN GENERAL	PIT OF THE STOMACH
PEOPLE OF FASHION	PLACE OF BUSINESS
PEOPLE OF QUALITY	PLAGUE OF LOCUSTS
PER ARDUA AD ASTRA	PLAIN-CLOTHES MAN
PERCENTAGE BASIS	PLANETARY SYSTEM
PEREGRINE FALCON	PLANNING OFFICER
PERFECT CREATURE	PLAY A DOUBLE GAME
PERFECT INTERVAL	PLAY A LOSING GAME
PERFECT LIKENESS	PLAY CAT AND MOUSE
PERFECTLY HONEST	PLAYERS' ENTRANCE
PERFECT NONSENSE	PLAY FIRST FIDDLE
PERFECT NUISANCE	PLAY HIDE-AND-SEEK
PERFECT STRANGER	PLAY ONE'S OWN HAND
PERFECT TREASURE	PLAY THE BAGPIPES
PERFORMING FLEAS	PLAY THE INFORMER
PERILOUS VENTURE	PLAY THE PARASITE
PERIOD FURNITURE	PLAYTHING OF FATE
PERISHABLE GOODS	PLAY TIDDLYWINKS
PERMANENT RECORD	PLEASANT EVENING
PERPETUAL MOTION	PLEASANT FLAVOUR
PERSONAL ACCOUNT	PLEASURE GARDENS
PERSONAL AFFRONT	PLEASURE GROUNDS
PERSONAL BENEFIT	PLEASURE STEAMER
PERSONAL EFFECTS	PLIGHT ONE'S TROTH
PERSONALITY CULT	PLOUGH THE FIELDS
PERSONAL OPINION	PLUM IN ONE'S MOUTH
PERSONAL PRONOUN	PLYMOUTH BROTHER
PERSONAL REASONS	PLYMOUTH HARBOUR
PERSONAL SERVICE	POCKET ONE'S PRIDE
PERSONA NON GRATA	POETICAL JUSTICE
PERTINENT REMARK	POINT-BLANK RANGE
PESTLE AND MORTAR	POINTED REMINDER
PETER AND THE WOLF	POINTLESS REMARK
PETER THE PAINTER	POINT OF NO RETURN
PETITION OF RIGHT	POLAR EXPEDITION
PETRIFIED FOREST	POLICE CONSTABLE
PETROL RATIONING	POLICE INSPECTOR
PHOTOGRAPH ALBUM	POLISHED MANNERS
PHYSICAL CRAVING	POLITICAL ASYLUM
PHYSICAL CULTURE	POLITICAL CAREER
PHYSICAL FATIGUE	POLITICAL EVENTS
PHYSICAL SCIENCE	POLITICAL OFFICE
PICK UP THE PIECES	POLITICAL RIGHTS
PICK UP THE THREAD	POLITICAL SPEECH
PICTURE OF HEALTH	POLITICAL THEORY
PICTURE OF MISERY	POLITICAL WEAPON
PICTURE POSTCARD	POLITICAL WRITER

POMP AND CEREMONY
POOR CIRCULATION
POOR CONSOLATION
POOR VENTILATION
POPEYE THE SAILOR
POPULAR LANGUAGE
PORTMANTEAU WORD
PORTRAIT GALLERY
PORTRAIT OF A LADY
PORTRAIT PAINTER
POSITION OF POWER
POSITION OF TRUST
POSITIVE ELEMENT
POST-DATED CHEQUE
POST-OFFICE GUIDE
POTENTIAL DANGER
POTENTIAL ENERGY
POWER OF ATTORNEY
POWER OF JUDGMENT
POWER OF RECOVERY
POWER OF THE PRESS
PRACTICAL RESULT
PRACTISE SORCERY
PRAIRIE SCHOONER
PRAYER FOR THE DAY
PREACH THE GOSPEL
PREACH TO THE WISE
PRECARIOUS STATE
PREFECT OF POLICE
PREFERENCE SHARE
PREFERRED SHARES
PRELIMINARY HEAT
PRELIMINARY STEP
PREMEDITATED ACT
PRE-PAID TELEGRAM
PREPARED TO FIGHT
PRESERVED GINGER
PRESERVING SUGAR
PRESIDENT MARCOS
PRESIDENT REAGAN
PRESS CONFERENCE
PRESSED FOR FUNDS
PRESSED FOR MONEY
PRESSED FOR SPACE
PRESS FOR PAYMENT
PRESS THE TRIGGER
PRESTON NORTH END
PRETTY MUCH ALIKE
PREVAILING TASTE
PREVAILING WINDS
PREVIOUS OFFENCE
PRICE ON ONE'S HEAD
PRICE REGULATION
PRICK ONE'S EARS UP
PRICK UP ONE'S EARS
PRIMARY ELECTION

PRIMITIVE COLOUR
PRINCE OF DENMARK
PRINCESS OF WALES
PRINCIPAL CLAUSE
PRINCIPAL PERSON
PRIOR CONDITIONS
PRIOR ENGAGEMENT
PRISONER OF STATE
PRISONER OF ZENDA
PRISONER'S FRIEND
PRIVATE CARRIAGE
PRIVATE CHANNELS
PRIVATE DEVOTION
PRIVATE HOSPITAL
PRIVATE LANGUAGE
PRIVATE PRACTICE
PRIVATE PROPERTY
PRIVATE QUARTERS
PRIVATE TEACHING
PRIVILEGED CLASS
PRIVY COUNCILLOR
PROBABLE STARTER
PROCESSED CHEESE
PRODIGAL'S RETURN
PROFESSED BELIEF
PROFESSIONAL AIR
PROFESSIONAL FEE
PROFESSIONAL MAN
PROFOUND THINKER
PROFOUND THOUGHT
PROGRAMME PARADE
PROGRAMME SELLER
PROHIBITION DAYS
PROHIBITION ZONE
PROLONG THE AGONY
PRONOUNCE GUILTY
PROOF OF PURCHASE
PROPERLY DRESSED
PROPER TREATMENT
PROPOSE MARRIAGE
PROSPECTIVE WIFE
PROUD AS A PEACOCK
PROVE ACCEPTABLE
PROVIDE THE MEANS
PROVINCIAL PAPER
PRUNES AND PRISMS
PUBLIC CHARACTER
PUBLIC DECEPTION
PUBLIC EDUCATION
PUBLIC ENCLOSURE
PUBLIC EXECUTION
PUBLIC KNOWLEDGE
PUBLIC MANIFESTO
PUBLIC OWNERSHIP
PUBLIC RELATIONS
PUBLIC-SCHOOL BOY

PUBLIC TRANSPORT
PUBLISH THE BANNS
PULL FOR THE SHORE
PULL ONE'S PUNCHES
PULL OUT THE STOPS
PULL-UP FOR CARMEN
PULL UP ONE'S SOCKS
PUNCTUATION MARK
PURCHASING POWER
PURE COINCIDENCE
PURELY AND SIMPLY
PURE MATHEMATICS
PURR WITH CONTENT
PURSUE AN INQUIRY
PURSUE THE MATTER
PUSS IN THE CORNER
PUT AN END TO IT ALL
PUT BACK THE CLOCK
PUT IN A WORD OR TWO
PUT IN POSSESSION
PUT IN QUARANTINE
PUT IN THE PICTURE
PUT INTO PRACTICE
PUT IT ANOTHER WAY
PUT IT ON THE SHELF
PUT ONE'S FOOT DOWN
PUT ONE'S FOOT IN IT
PUT ONE'S NAME DOWN
PUT ON ONE'S ARMOUR
PUT THE CLOCK BACK
PUTTING IT MILDLY
PUT UP A GOOD FIGHT
PUT UP FOR AUCTION

Q – 15

QUALIFIED PERSON
QUARTERLY REVIEW
QUARTER OF AN HOUR
QUARTER OF A POUND
QUARTER PAST FIVE
QUARTER PAST FOUR
QUARTER PAST NINE
QUARTER SESSIONS
QUARTER TO ELEVEN
QUARTER TO TWELVE
QUEEN OF DIAMONDS
QUEEN OF THE SOUTH
QUEEN'S MESSENGER
QUICKEN THE PULSE
QUICK OFF THE MARK
QUICK SUCCESSION
QUIET AS THE GRAVE
QUIET RESENTMENT
QUITE A CHARACTER
QUITE DELIGHTFUL

QUITE THE REVERSE
QUOTE FROM MEMORY

R – 15

RACE AGAINST TIME
RACIAL TOLERANCE
RACING CERTAINTY
RACKING HEADACHE
RADIO-ACTIVE ZONE
RADIO ASTRONOMER
RADIO JOURNALISM
RAILWAY ACCIDENT
RAILWAY CARRIAGE
RAILWAY JUNCTION
RAILWAY TERMINUS
RAIN CATS AND DOGS
RAIN STOPPED PLAY
RAISE A HUE AND CRY
RAISE OBJECTIONS
RAISE ONE'S SIGHTS
RAISE THE CURTAIN
RAISE THE SUBJECT
RAISE VEGETABLES
RALPH RICHARDSON
RAMSAY MACDONALD
RAPID SUCCESSION
RATTLING SUCCESS
RAZE TO THE GROUND
REACH FOR THE MOON
REACH PERFECTION
REACH ROCK-BOTTOM
READY AND WILLING
READY-BUILT HOUSE
READY FOR THE FRAY
READY-MADE EXCUSE
REARGUARD ACTION
REASONABLE DOUBT
REASONABLE OFFER
REASONABLE TERMS
RECENT DISCOVERY
RECEPTION CENTRE
RECKLESS EXPENSE
RECKLESS SPENDER
RECORDING STUDIO
RECOVER LOST TIME
RECOVER ONE'S MIND
RECOVER THE ASHES
RECRUITING DRIVE
RED-CURRANT JELLY
REDUCE TO NOTHING
REDUCE TO POVERTY
REDUCE TO SILENCE
RED, WHITE AND BLUE
REFILL ONE'S GLASS
REFLECTED VISION

REFRESHER COURSE
REFRESHMENT ROOM
REFRESHMENT TENT
REFUSE COLLECTOR
REGIMENTAL BADGE
REGIMENTAL MARCH
REGIMENTAL STAFF
REGIMENT OF WOMEN
REGISTRATION FEE
REGULAR CUSTOMER
REGULAR EXERCISE
REGULAR FEATURES
REGULAR PRACTICE
REGULATION DRESS
REGULATION SPEED
REIGNING MONARCH
RELATIVE DENSITY
RELATIVELY QUIET
RELATIVE PRONOUN
RELAXING CLIMATE
RELEASE ONE'S HOLD
RELIABLE QUALITY
RELIABLE SERVICE
RELIGIOUS BELIEF
RELIGIOUS MANIAC
REMARKABLE CHILD
REMARKABLE SIGHT
REMARKABLE VOICE
REMARKABLE WOMAN
REMEMBER NOTHING
REMOVE ALL TRACES
REMOVE MOUNTAINS
REMOVE THE TRACES
RENDER AN ACCOUNT
RENDER NECESSARY
RENT RESTRICTION
RE-OPEN OLD WOUNDS
REPAIRING CLAUSE
REPAIR THE DAMAGE
REPENT AT LEISURE
REPUBLICAN PARTY
REPULSE AN ATTACK
RESEARCH CHEMIST
RESERVE OF ENERGY
RESERVE STRENGTH
RESIDENTIAL AREA
RESIDENT SURGEON
RESTORATION FUND
RESTORATION PLAY
RESTORE TO HEALTH
RESTORE TO REASON
RESTORE TO SANITY
RESTRAINING HAND
RESTRICT IMPORTS
RESURRECTION DAY
RETORT COURTEOUS

RETURN IN TRIUMPH
RETURN TO SERVICE
RETURN TO THE PAST
REVERSION TO TYPE
RICHARD DIMBLEBY
RICHARD THE THIRD
RICHLY FURNISHED
RIDE A BROOMSTICK
RIDE A HOBBY-HORSE
RIDE OUT THE STORM
RIGHT DOWN THE CAR
RIGHT HONOURABLE
RIGHT OFF THE REEL
RIGHT OF PURCHASE
RIGHTS AND WRONGS
RIGHT TO THE POINT
RIGHT WAVELENGTH
RIGID DISCIPLINE
RINGING APPLAUSE
RIOTOUS ASSEMBLY
RIPE FOR MISCHIEF
RISE FROM THE DEAD
RISE WITH THE LARK
RITUAL FIRE-DANCE
ROARING TWENTIES
ROARS OF LAUGHTER
ROBBED OF FREEDOM
ROBIN GOODFELLOW
ROB WITH VIOLENCE
ROCK-BOTTOM PRICE
ROCK OF GIBRALTAR
ROGER DE COVERLEY
ROGET'S THESAURUS
ROLL OF WALLPAPER
ROLY-POLY PUDDING
ROMULUS AND REMUS
ROOM TEMPERATURE
ROOM TO SWING A CAT
ROOTED OBJECTION
ROOTED TO THE SPOT
ROOT OF THE MATTER
ROSS AND CROMARTY
ROTATION OF CROPS
ROTTEN AT THE CORE
ROTTEN TO THE CORE
ROUGHLY SPEAKING
ROUNDABOUT ROUTE
ROUND OF APPLAUSE
ROUND OF PLEASURE
ROYAL ALBERT HALL
ROYAL AND ANCIENT
ROYAL COMMISSION
ROYAL OPERA HOUSE
ROYAL TOURNAMENT
RUBBER TRUNCHEON
RUDDY COMPLEXION

RUDE FOREFATHERS
RUFFLED FEATHERS
RUFFLED FEELINGS
RUIN ONE'S CHANCES
RULES OF FOOTBALL
RUN A TEMPERATURE
RUN-AWAY MARRIAGE
RUN FOR ONE'S MONEY
RUN FOR PRESIDENT
RUN LIKE WILD-FIRE
RURAL POPULATION
RUSSIAN LANGUAGE
RUSSIAN ROULETTE

S – 15

SAFETY IN NUMBERS
SAIL INTO THE WIND
SAIL NEAR THE WIND
SAILOR'S HORNPIPE
SAINT GÉORGE'S DAY
SAINT MARLYLEBONE
SALES RESISTANCE
SALLY IN OUR ALLEY
SALMON AND SHRIMP
SAMSON AGONISTES
SANDWICH ISLANDS
SARATOGA SPRINGS
SARDINE SANDWICH
SARDINES ON TOAST
SATURATION POINT
SATURDAY EVENING
SATURDAY MORNING
SAUSAGE AND CHIPS
SAUSAGES AND MASH
SAVAGE CRITICISM
SAVE APPEARANCES
SAVINGS MOVEMENT
SAVOURY OMELETTE
SAY THE MAGIC WORD
SAY WITH EMPHASIS
SCALENE TRIANGLE
SCALES OF JUSTICE
SCALE THE HEIGHTS
SCENE OF THE CRIME
SCHEDULED FLIGHT
SCHNEIDER TROPHY
SCHOLASTIC AGENT
SCHOOLBOY HOWLER
SCHOOL INSPECTOR
SCHOOL OF DANCING
SCHOOL OF THOUGHT
SCIENTIFIC BOXER
SCIENTIFIC WORLD
SCOTTISH TERRIER
SCOTTISH THISTLE

SCRAPE THE BARREL
SCRATCH OF THE PEN
SCRATCHING ONE'S HEAD
SCRIBBLING BLOCK
SCRIMP AND SCRAPE
SCRIPTURE LESSON
SCRUFF OF THE NECK
SEA ISLAND COTTON
SEARCHING GLANCE
SEARCH ONE'S HEART
SEASIDE LANDLADY
SEATING CAPACITY
SEAWORTHY VESSEL
SECONDARY COLOUR
SECONDARY MATTER
SECONDARY MODERN
SECONDARY SCHOOL
SECOND-BEST THING
SECOND CHILDHOOD
SECOND FAVOURITE
SECOND-HAND GOODS
SECOND IN COMMAND
SECOND INTENTION
SECOND OF JANUARY
SECOND OF OCTOBER
SECOND-RATE HOTEL
SECOND TIME ROUND
SECRET ANIMOSITY
SECRET COURTSHIP
SECRET INFLUENCE
SECRET STAIRCASE
SECURITY COUNCIL
SECURITY MEASURE
SECURITY OFFICER
SEEDS OF MISTRUST
SEEK A COMPROMISE
SEEK INFORMATION
SEEK ONE'S FORTUNE
SEE NAPLES AND DIE
SEE ONE'S WAY CLEAR
SEE THE FUNNY SIDE
SEE WHAT YOU CAN DO
SELECT COMMITTEE
SELF-EDUCATED MAN
SELF-IMPOSED TASK
SELF-SERVICE SHOP
SELL INTO SLAVERY
SELL ONE'S COUNTRY
SEMOLINA PUDDING
SEND AN ULTIMATUM
SEND ROUND THE HAT
SEND THE CAP ROUND
SEND TO THE BOTTOM
SENIOR BARRISTER
SENIORES PRIORES
SENSATIONAL NEWS

SENSATION MONGER
SENSE OF DISTANCE
SENSE OF PLEASURE
SENSE OF SECURITY
SENSITIVE MARKET
SENSITIVE NATURE
SENSUAL PLEASURE
SENTENCE OF DEATH
SENTENCE TO DEATH
SENTIMENTAL GIRL
SEPARATION ORDER
SERIOUS ACCIDENT
SERIOUS LANGUAGE
SERIOUS QUESTION
SERMONS IN STONES
SERVANT QUESTION
SERVED WITH A WRIT
SERVE TWO MASTERS
SERVICE INCLUDED
SERVICE REVOLVER
SESAME AND LILIES
SET A GOOD EXAMPLE
SET A LOW STANDARD
SET OF FALSE TEETH
SET OF QUADRILLES
SETTLE AN ACCOUNT
SETTLE OLD SCORES
SETTLE THE MATTER
SET UP IN BUSINESS
SEVEN DEADLY SINS
SEVEN OF DIAMONDS
SEVENPENNY STAMP
SEVENTEEN AND SIX
SEVENTEEN AND TWO
SEVENTEENTH HOLE
SEVENTH OF AUGUST
SEVENTH SYMPHONY
SEVEN TIMES SEVEN
SEVENTY THOUSAND
SEVERE THRASHING
SHABBY GENTILITY
SHABBY TREATMENT
SHADY REPUTATION
SHAKE LIKE A JELLY
SHAKEN TO THE CORE
SHALLOW ARGUMENT
SHARPEN ONE'S WITS
SHARP IMPRESSION
SHEATHE THE SWORD
SHEEPSKIN JACKET
SHEER PERFECTION
SHEFFIELD UNITED
SHETLAND ISLANDS
SHIFT FOR ONESELF
SHIFT ONE'S GROUND
SHIP OF THE DESERT

SHIPPING COMPANY
SHIPPING MAGNATE
SHIP'S COMPLEMENT
SHIVER ME TIMBERS
SHOCKING SCANDAL
SHOCKING WEATHER
SHOOTING GALLERY
SHORTHAND TYPIST
SHORTHAND WRITER
SHORT OF PRACTICE
SHORT SHARP SHOCK
SHORT-TERM POLICY
SHOTGUN MARRIAGE
SHOT IN THE LOCKER
SHOUT OF LAUGHTER
SHOW DISCOURTESY
SHOW FAVOURITISM
SHOW INGRATITUDE
SHOW ONE'S COLOURS
SHOW TO ADVANTAGE
SHRED OF EVIDENCE
SHRINKING VIOLET
SHUFFLE THE CARDS
SICKNESS BENEFIT
SIEGE OF MAFEKING
SIGHT FOR THE GODS
SIGHT-SEEING TOUR
SIGN OF THE ZODIAC
SIGN THE REGISTER
SILENCE IS GOLDEN
SILENT AS THE TOMB
SILVER MEDALLIST
SIMPLE PLEASURES
SIMPLY AND SOLELY
SINCE THE YEAR DOT
SING ANOTHER SONG
SING ANOTHER TUNE
SINK ONE'S CAPITAL
SINK TO ONE'S KNEES
SINK TO THE BOTTOM
SIN OF COMMISSION
SIR EDWARD GERMAN
SIR FRANCIS DRAKE
SIR JOHN FALSTAFF
SISTER-OF CHARITY
SITUATION VACANT
SITUATION WANTED
SIXTEEN AND A HALF
SIXTEENTH LETTER
SIXTEENTH OF JULY
SIXTEENTH OF JUNE
SIXTEEN THOUSAND
SIXTH OF DECEMBER
SIXTH OF FEBRUARY
SIXTH OF NOVEMBER
SKELETON SERVICE

SKIM THE ROOF-TOPS
SKIN OF ONE'S TEETH
SKIP OUT OF THE WAY
SLAB OF CHOCOLATE
SLACKEN ONE'S PACE
SLAKE ONE'S THIRST
SLANG EXPRESSION
SLAPSTICK COMEDY
SLEEPING DRAUGHT
SLEEPING PARTNER
SLEEVELESS DRESS
SLIGHT VARIATION
SLINGS AND ARROWS
SLIP OF THE TONGUE
SLIPPERY AS AN EEL
SLIPPERY SURFACE
SLOUGH OF DESPOND
SLOW BOAT TO CHINA
SLOW IN THE UPTAKE
SLOWLY AND SURELY
SLOWLY BUT SURELY
SMALL PERCENTAGE
SMELTING FURNACE
SMOKE A CIGARETTE
SMOKY ATMOSPHERE
SNAKE IN THE GRASS
SNAP ONE'S FINGERS
SNAP ONE'S NOSE OFF
SOAKED TO THE SKIN
SOARING AMBITION
SOARING THOUGHTS
SOBERING THOUGHT
SOB ONE'S HEART OUT
SOCIAL DEMOCRATS
SOCIAL GATHERING
SOCIAL INSURANCE
SOCIAL OSTRACISM
SODA-WATER SYPHON
SODIUM CARBONATE
SOFT-NOSED BULLET
SOFT-SHOE SHUFFLE
SOLD INTO SLAVERY
SOLICITOR'S CLERK
SOLID FOUNDATION
SOLO PERFORMANCE
SOMEBODY OR OTHER
SOME CONSOLATION
SOMERSET MAUGHAM
SOMETHING IN HAND
SOMETHING ROTTEN
SOMETHING TO COME
SOMETHING TO GO ON
SOME TIME OR OTHER
SOMEWHERE AROUND
SO MUCH THE BETTER
SORRY FOR ONESELF

SOUND EXPRESSION
SOUND INVESTMENT
SOUND OF BOW BELLS
SOUND THE KEYNOTE
SOUND THE RETREAT
SOURCE OF TROUBLE
SOUTH AFRICAN WAR
SOUTHERN RAILWAY
SOUTH KENSINGTON
SOUTH OF THE RIVER
SOUTH OF THE TWEED
SOUTH SEA ISLANDS
SOVEREIGN REMEDY
SOW ONE'S WILD OATS
SPADES ARE TRUMPS
SPANISH BURGUNDY
SPANISH CHESTNUT
SPANISH LANGUAGE
SPARRING PARTNER
SPEAK FOR ONESELF
SPEAK IN A WHISPER
SPEAK OF THE DEVIL
SPECIAL DELIVERY
SPECIAL OCCASION
SPECIAL PLEADING
SPECIFIC GRAVITY
SPEED-BOAT RACING
SPEEDY VENGEANCE
SPELLING MISTAKE
SPINAL COMPLAINT
SPIRAL STAIRCASE
SPIRITED DISPLAY
SPLASH ONE'S MONEY
SPLENDID VICTORY
SPLENDID WEATHER
SPLIT INFINITIVE
SPOIL EVERYTHING
SPOIL ONE'S RECORD
SPOILS OF VICTORY
SPORTING CONDUCT
SPORTING FIXTURE
SPORTING GESTURE
SPORTS ANNOUNCER
SPORTS EQUIPMENT
SPOT ADVERTISING
SPOTLESSLY CLEAN
SPRAY OF DIAMONDS
SPREAD ONE'S WINGS
SPREAD THE GOSPEL
SPRING A SURPRISE
SPRINGER SPANIEL
SPUR OF THE MOMENT
SQUARE THE CIRCLE
SQUATTER'S RIGHTS
SQUATTING RIGHTS
SQUEEZED TO DEATH

STABLE COMPANION
STAGE DIRECTIONS
STAGE-DOOR JOHNNY
STAKE EVERYTHING
STAMP COLLECTING
STAMP COLLECTION
STAMP OF APPROVAL
STAND AND DELIVER
STANDARD EDITION
STANDARD ENGLISH
STANDARD PRODUCT
STAND BARE-HEADED
STAND IN FULL VIEW
STANDING OVATION
STAND IN THE LIGHT
STAND IN THE QUEUE
STAND NO NONSENSE
STAND ON CEREMONY
STAND ONE'S GROUND
STAND ON ONE'S HEAD
STAND ON ONE'S TOES
STAND STOCK-STILL
STANLEY HOLLOWAY
STANLEY MATTHEWS
STARK, STARING MAD
STAR OF BETHLEHEM
STARS AND STRIPES
START AN ARGUMENT
STARVED WITH COLD
STATE APARTMENTS
STATE ASSISTANCE
STATE DEPARTMENT
STATE ENTERPRISE
STATELESS PERSON
STATEMENT OF FACT
STATEMENT ON OATH
STATE OF COLLAPSE
STATE OF CONFLICT
STATE OF DISORDER
STATE OF EQUALITY
STATE OF SOBRIETY
STATION APPROACH
STATUE OF LIBERTY
STAY OF EXECUTION
STAY UNDERGROUND
STAY WHERE YOU ARE
STEALER OF HEARTS
STEAL THE THUNDER
STENTORIAN VOICE
STICKING PLASTER
STICK LIKE A LEECH
STICK OF DYNAMITE
STICKS AND STONES
STICK THE SPURS IN
STICK TO ONE'S GUNS
STICK TO ONE'S LAST

STICK TO THE FACTS
STICK TO THE POINT
STICK TO THE RULES
STICK TO THE TRUTH
STICKY SITUATION
STILL AS THE GRAVE
STILL OF THE NIGHT
STILL, SMALL VOICE
STIR THE PORRIDGE
STIR UP THE EMBERS
ST MARTIN'S SUMMER
ST MICHAEL'S MOUNT
STOCKS AND SHARES
STOCKTAKING SALE
STOMACH DISORDER
STOOD UP STRAIGHT
STOP ME AND BUY ONE!
STOPPED THE FIGHT
STOP THE BLEEDING
STOP WHERE YOU ARE
STORM OF APPLAUSE
STRAIGHT ACTRESS
STRAIGHT BOURBON
STRAIGHT DEALING
STRAIGHT IN FRONT
STRAIGHT STRETCH
STRAIN ONE'S LUNGS
STRAIN THE NERVES
STRANGE GOINGS-ON
STRANGE TO RELATE
STRAPPING FELLOW
STRATFORD ON AVON
STRAWS IN THE WIND
STREAM OF THOUGHT
STREAM OF TRAFFIC
STREET DIRECTORY
STRENUOUS EFFORT
STRESS AND STRAIN
STRETCHER BEARER
STRETCH ONE'S LEGS
STRICKEN IN YEARS
STRICTLY NEUTRAL
STRICTLY PRIVATE
STRIKE A BAD PATCH
STRIKE AN AVERAGE
STRIKE A RICH VEIN
STRIKE UP THE BAND
STRIKING SUCCESS
STRING ORCHESTRA
STRINGS ATTACHED
STRIVE FOR EFFECT
STROLLING PLAYER
STRONG INFLUENCE
STRONG OBJECTION
STRONG, SILENT MAN
STRONG SITUATION

STRONG WILL-POWER
STRUGGLE FOR LIFE
STRUGGLE THROUGH
STUBBORN AS A MULE
STUNT ONE'S GROWTH
ST VALENTINE'S DAY
STYGIAN DARKNESS
SUBJUNCTIVE MOOD
SUBMARINE CHASER
SUBMIT A QUESTION
SUBSTANTIAL MEAL
SUBURBAN STATION
SUCCESS ALL ROUND
SUCH SWEET SORROW
SUDDEN DEPARTURE
SUFFER IN SILENCE
SUGAR PLANTATION
SUITABLE PARTNER
SUITED TO THE PART
SUIT THE OCCASION
SUM AND SUBSTANCE
SUMMER LIGHTNING
SUMMER RESIDENCE
SUMMON UP COURAGE
SUNDAY AFTERNOON
SUNDAY NEWSPAPER
SUNDAY TELEGRAPH
SUN, MOON AND STARS
SUPERIOR NUMBERS
SUPERIOR OFFICER
SUPERIOR QUALITY
SUPERSONIC SPEED
SUPPLY AND DEMAND
SUPREME CONTEMPT
SURE OF ONE'S FACTS
SURPRISE IN STORE
SURPRISE VISITOR
SURPRISING THING
SURROGATE MOTHER
SUSPECTED PERSON
SUSPECT FOUL PLAY
SUSPEND SENTENCE
SUSPENSE ACCOUNT
SUSTAINED ACTION
SUSTAINED EFFORT
SUSTAIN INJURIES
SWALLOW AN INSULT
SWALLOW-TAIL COAT
SWEAR ALLEGIANCE
SWEAR ON THE BIBLE
SWEAT OF ONE'S BROW
SWEEPING CHANGES
SWEEPING REFORMS
SWEEPING SUCCESS
SWEEPING VICTORY
SWEEP THE CHIMNEY

SWEET FANNY ADAMS
SWEET SIMPLICITY
SWEET TO THE TASTE
SWIM FOR THE SHORE
SWIMMING COSTUME
SWIM WITH THE TIDE
SWORD OF DAMOCLES
SYDNEY WOODERSON
SYLVIA PANKHURST
SYMBOL OF JUSTICE
SYMPHONY CONCERT
SYNTHETIC RUBBER
SYSTEMATIC STUDY

T – 15

TABLEAUX VIVANTS
TABLE DECORATION
TABLE OF CONTENTS
TABLES AND CHAIRS
TAILOR AND CUTTER
TAKE A COLLECTION
TAKE A DEEP BREATH
TAKE A FLYING LEAP
TAKE A PHOTOGRAPH
TAKE A RESOLUTION
TAKE A SECOND LOOK
TAKE A STRONG LINE
TAKE FRENCH LEAVE
TAKE INTO ACCOUNT
TAKE INTO CUSTODY
TAKE IT LYING DOWN
TAKE IT ON THE CHIN
TAKE IT OR LEAVE IT
TAKEN AT THE FLOOD
TAKE ONE'S COAT OFF
TAKE ONE'S MEASURE
TAKE PRECAUTIONS
TAKE THE BLOOM OFF
TAKE THE CHILL OFF
TAKE THE LONG VIEW
TAKE THE SEA ROUTE
TAKE THE SHILLING
TAKE TO ONE'S HEELS
TAKE TO THE BOTTLE
TAKE UP THE THREAD
TALE OF TWO CITIES
TALES OF HOFFMANN
TANGERINE ORANGE
TANKARD OF BITTER
TAPERED TROUSERS
TASTE OF THE STRAP
TATTENHAM CORNER
TATTERED AND TORN
TEAR ONE'S CLOTHES

TEAR ONESELF AWAY	THE HOUSE OF USHER
TEARS OF LAUGHTER	THE INVISIBLE MAN
TECHNICAL SCHOOL	THE KING'S ENGLISH
TELEGRAPH OFFICE	THE LAP OF THE GODS
TELEPHONE NUMBER	THE LAST MINSTREL
TELEPHONE SYSTEM	THE LATE-LAMENTED
TELESCOPIC SIGHT	THE LONDON SEASON
TELEVISION TABLE	THE LONG VACATION
TELL IT NOT IN GATH	THE LOW COUNTRIES
TELL ONE'S FORTUNE	THE MAN IN THE MOON
TEMPERANCE HOTEL	THE MARSEILLAISE
TEMPORARY RELIEF	THE MERRY MONARCH
TEMPT PROVIDENCE	THE MORNING AFTER
TENACIOUS MEMORY	THE NAME'S THE SAME
TEN COMMANDMENTS	THE OLD PRETENDER
TENSE ATMOSPHERE	THE PLOT THICKENS
TENTH OF DECEMBER	THE POTTER'S WHEEL
TENTH OF FEBRUARY	THE POWERS THAT BE
TENTH OF NOVEMBER	THE PRETTY THINGS
TERENCE RATTIGAN	THE PRIMROSE PATH
TERM OF REFERENCE	THE PRIVY COUNCIL
TERRIBLE TRAGEDY	THE PROMISED LAND
TERRIBLE WEATHER	THE QUEEN OF SHEBA
TERRIFIC SERVICE	THE ROYAL SOCIETY
TERRITORIAL ARMY	THE SHOW MUST GO ON
TEST OF ENDURANCE	THE SKY'S THE LIMIT
THANKSGIVING DAY	THE SOUND OF MUSIC
THATCHED COTTAGE	THE SUBCONSCIOUS
THE AMOROUS PRAWN	THE SUN NEVER SETS
THE ANCIENT WORLD	THE SUPERNATURAL
THE ARTFUL DODGER	THE THANKSGIVING
THE BACK OF BEYOND	THE THREE ESTATES
THE BARON KNIGHTS	THE TIME WILL COME
THE BEGGAR'S OPERA	THE UNTOUCHABLES
THE BLACK COUNTRY	THE VERY REVEREND
THE BOHEMIAN GIRL	THE WOMAN IN WHITE
THE CAT AND FIDDLE	THE WORLD AT LARGE
THE COAST IS CLEAR	THE WORSE FOR WEAR
THE COMMON MARKET	THIEF IN THE NIGHT
THE COMMON PEOPLE	THINK BETTER OF IT
THE COMMONWEALTH	THINK THINGS OVER
THE COST OF LIVING	THINLY SCATTERED
THE DANCING YEARS	THIN ON THE GROUND
THE DEMON ALCOHOL	THIRD OF DECEMBER
THE DESCENT OF MAN	THIRD OF FEBRUARY
THE DEVIL YOU KNOW	THIRD OF NOVEMBER
THE ELEVENTH HOUR	THIRTEEN AT TABLE
THE EMPEROR JONES	THIRTEEN MINUTES
THE END OF THE ROAD	THIRTEEN OF A SUIT
THE FIRST SWALLOW	THIRTEEN PER CENT
THE FOUR FEATHERS	THIRTEENTH GREEN
THE FOURTH ESTATE	THIRTEENTH OF MAY
THE FOURTH OF JULY	THIRTIETH OF JULY
THE GARDEN OF EDEN	THIRTIETH OF JUNE
THE GOLDEN FLEECE	THIRTY-NINE STEPS
THE HAPPY WARRIOR	THIS YEAR OF GRACE

THORN IN ONE'S SIDE	TOO CLEVER BY HALF
THORN IN THE FLESH	TOO FULL FOR WORDS
THOUSAND GUINEAS	TOO GOOD TO BE TRUE
THREATENING LOOK	TOOK THE LONG VIEW
THREE BRASS BALLS	TOOLS OF THE TRADE
THREE-LEGGED RACE	TOOTHSOME MORSEL
THREE-LETTER WORD	TOPICAL ALLUSION
THREE LITTLE PIGS	TOPICAL INTEREST
THREE-MASTED SHIP	TOP-LEVEL MEETING
THREE MEN IN A BOAT	TOP OF THE MORNING
THREE MUSKETEERS	TOSSING THE CABER
THREE OF DIAMONDS	TOTAL ABSTINENCE
THREEPENNY OPERA	TOTAL CASUALTIES
THREE-PIECE SUITE	TO THE FULL EXTENT
THREE-TIERED CAKE	TO THE MANNER BORN
THREE TIMES THREE	TOUCH ROCK-BOTTOM
THRILLED WITH JOY	TOUGH ASSIGNMENT
THRILLING CLIMAX	TOUGH NUT TO CRACK
THROUGH CARRIAGE	TOURIST INDUSTRY
THROUGH THE NIGHT	TOWERING PASSION
THROUGH THE YEARS	TOWER OF STRENGTH
THROW IN ONE'S HAND	TRADE COMMISSION
THROW IN THE TOWEL	TRADE DELEGATION
THROW OFF THE YOKE	TRADE SUPPLEMENT
THROW OUT A FEELER	TRADITIONAL FARE
THROW TO THE WINDS	TRADITIONAL JAZZ
THUMBNAIL SKETCH	TRAFALGAR SQUARE
THURSDAY EVENING	TRAFFIC MOVEMENT
THURSDAY MORNING	TRAIN CONNECTION
TICKET COLLECTOR	TRAINING COLLEGE
TICKET INSPECTOR	TRAIN OF THOUGHT
TICKLE ONE'S FANCY	TRANSFER A PLAYER
TICKLE THE PALATE	TRANSPORT SYSTEM
TICKLISH PROBLEM	TRAVEL INCOGNITO
TIED HAND AND FOOT	TRAVEL IN COMFORT
TIES OF AFFECTION	TRAVELLER'S TALES
TIGHTEN ONE'S BELT	TRAVELLING CLOCK
TIGHTEN ONE'S GRIP	TRAVELLING CRANE
TIGHT-ROPE WALKER	TREASURED MEMORY
TILLER OF THE SOIL	TREATED LIKE DIRT
TILL WE MEET AGAIN	TREATY OF LOCARNO
TIME OF DEPARTURE	TRREE OF KNOWLEDGE
TIME ON ONE'S HANDS	TREMBLE WITH FEAR
TIP OF ONE'S TONGUE	TREMBLING POPLAR
TIPPED CIGARETTE	TREND OF THE TIMES
TITANIC STRENGTH	TRESPASS AGAINST
TITUS ANDRONICUS	TRIAL OF STRENGTH
TO A LESSER DEGREE	TRICK OF THE TRADE
TO HAVE AND TO HOLD	TRICKY SITUATION
TO LITTLE PURPOSE	TRIUMPHANT SMILE
TOMATOES ON TOAST	TROOP OF SOLDIERS
TOM, DICK AND HARRY	TROUBLE-FREE MIND
TOMORROW EVENING	TRUE TO THE LETTER
TOMORROW MORNING	TRUMPED-UP CHARGE
TOM, THE PIPER'S SON	TRY ANYTHING ONCE
TONSORIAL ARTIST	TRY ONE'S PATIENCE

WITCHES' CAULDRON
WITH A DIFFERENCE
WITH A LITTLE LUCK
WITH COMPLIMENTS
WITHERING GLANCE
WITHHOLD PAYMENT
WITHIN EASY REACH
WITHIN ONE'S GRASP
WITHOUT AN EFFORT
WITHOUT A PURPOSE
WITHOUT A SCRATCH
WITHOUT CEREMONY
WITHOUT INCIDENT
WITHOUT INTEREST
WITHOUT PARALLEL
WITHOUT THINKING
WOMAN OF FEW WORDS
WOMAN OF THE WORLD
WOMAN'S INTUITION
WOMAN'S PRIVILEGE
WOMEN'S INSTITUTE
WOODCUTTERS' BALL
WOODEN PARTITION
WOODY WOODPECKER
WOOLLEN INDUSTRY
WOOLWICH ARSENAL
WORK AGAINST TIME
WORKERS' PLAYTIME
WORKING MAJORITY
WORKING-MAN'S CLUB
WORK LIKE A NIGGER
WORK LIKE A TROJAN
WORK OF REFERENCE
WORK ONE'S PASSAGE
WORK UNDERGROUND
WORLD GOVERNMENT
WORLD OF COMMERCE

WORLD OF LEARNING
WORLD WITHOUT END
WORTHY ADVERSARY
WOUNDED FEELINGS
WRESTLING SCHOOL
WRETCHED WEATHER
WRINKLED WITH AGE
WRITING MATERIAL
WRITTEN CONTRACT
WRITTEN EVIDENCE
WRITTEN LANGUAGE
WRONG ASSUMPTION
WRONG IMPRESSION
WRONG WAVE-LENGTH
WROUGHT-IRON GATE

X – 15

XMAS DECORATIONS

Y – 15

YELLOWSTONE PARK
YELL WITH DELIGHT
YEOMEN OF ENGLAND
YESTERDAY'S PAPER
YIELD GRACEFULLY
YIELD TO PRESSURE
YORKSHIRE RELISH
YOU NEVER CAN TELL
YOUNG AND HEALTHY
YOUNGER DAUGHTER
YOUNGEST BROTHER
YOURS FAITHFULLY
YOURS OBEDIENTLY
YOUTH-CLUB LEADER

WORDS

A – 3

ABC
ACE
ACT
ADA
ADD
ADO
AFT
AGA
AGE
AGO
AHA
AID
AIL
AIM
AIN
AIR
AIT
ALB
ALE
ALL
ALP
ALT
AMP
ANA
AND
ANN
ANT
ANY
APE
APT
ARC
ARE
ARK
ARM
ART
ASH
ASK
ASP
ASS
ATE
AUK
AVA
AVE
AWA
AWE
AWL
AWN

AXE
AYE

B – 3

BAA
BAD
BAG
BAH
BAN
BAR
BAT
BAY
BBC
BED
BEE
BEG
BEN
BET
BEY
BIB
BID
BIG
BIN
BIS
BIT
BOA
BOB
BOG
BOO
BOW
BOX
BOY
BOZ
BUD
BUG
BUM
BUN
BUS
BUT
BUY
BYE

C – 3

CAB
CAD
CAM
CAN
CAP

CAR
CAT
CAW
CHA
CID
COB
COD
COG
COL
CON
COO
COP
COS
COT
COW
COX
COY
CRY
CUB
CUD
CUE
CUP
CUR
CUT
CWT

D – 3

DAB
DAD
DAM
DAN
DAW
DAY
DEB
DEE
DEN
DEW
DIB
DID
DIE
DIG
DIM
DIN
DIP
DOE
DOG
DOH
DON

DOT
DRY
DUB
DUD
DUE
DUG
DUN
DUO
DYE

E – 3

EAR
EAT
EAU
EBB
EEL
E'EN
E'ER
EFT
EGG
EGO
EKE
ELF
ELI
ELK
ELL
ELM
ELY
EMU
END
EON
ERA
ERE
ERG
ERR
ESS
ETC
EVE
EWE
EYE

F – 3

FAD
FAG
FAN
FAR
FAT

FAY
FEB
FED
FEE
FEN
FEW
FEY
FEZ
FIB
FIE
FIG
FIN
FIR
FIT
FIX
FLU
FLY
FOB
FOE
FOG
FOP
FOR
FOX
FRO
FRY
FUG
FUN
FUR

G – 3

GAB
GAD
GAG
GAL
GAP
GAR
GAS
GAT
GAY
GEE
GEM
GEN
GET
GIB
GIE
GIG
GIN
GNU

GOB	INK	LED	NAP	**P – 3**
GOD	INN	LEE	NAY	
GOG	ION	LEG	NCO	PAD
GOT	I.O.U.	LEI	NEB	PAH
GUM	IRE	LEO	NÉE	PAL
GUN	IRK	LET	NEO	PAM
GUT	ISM	LEW	NET	PAN
GUY	ITS	LEX	NEW	PAP
GYM	IVY	LIB	NIB	PAR
GYP		LID	NIL	PAS
		LIE	NIP	PAT
	J – 3	LIP	NIT	PAW
H – 3		LIT	NIX	PAX
	JAB	LOB	NOB	PAY
HAD	JAG	LOG	NOD	PEA
HAG	JAM	LOO	NOG	PEG
HAH	JAP	LOP	NOR	PEN
HAM	JAR	LOT	NOT	PEP
HAP	JAW	LOW	NOW	PER
HAS	JAY	LSD	NUB	PET
HAT	JET	LUD	NUN	PEW
HAW	JEW	LUG	NUT	PIE
HAY	JIB	LYE	NYE	PIG
HEM	JIG			PIN
HEN	JOB			PIP
HEP	JOE	**M – 3**	**O – 3**	PIT
HER	JOG			PLY
HEW	JOT	MAB	OAF	POD
HEY	JOY	MAC	OAK	POE
HID	JUG	MAD	OAR	POM
HIE	JUT	MAN	OAT	POP
HIM		MAP	OBI	POT
HIP		MAR	OCH	POW
HIS	**K – 3**	MAT	ODD	PRO
HIT		MAW	ODE	PRY
HOB	KAY	MAX	O'ER	PUB
HOD	KEG	MAY	OFF	PUG
HOE	KEN	MEN	OFT	PUN
HOG	KEY	MET	OHM	PUP
HOP	KID	MEW	OHO	PUS
HOT	KIM	MID	OIL	PUT
HOW	KIN	MIX	OLD	PYX
HUB	KIP	MOA	ONE	
HUE	KIT	MOB	OOF	
HUG		MOO	OPE	**R – 3**
HUM	**L – 3**	MOP	OPT	
HUN		MOT	ORB	RAG
HUT	LAC	MOW	ORC	RAJ
	LAD	MRS	ORE	RAM
	LAG	MUD	ORT	RAN
I – 3	LAM	MUG	OUR	RAP
	LAP	MUM	OUT	RAS
IAN	LAR		OVA	RAT
ICE	LAW		OWE	RAW
ICY	LAX	**N – 3**	OWL	RAY
ILK	LAY		OWN	RED
ILL	LBW	NAB		REF
IMP	LEA	NAG		

REP	SKY	TOR	WIT	AIRY
RET	SLY	TOT	WOE	AJAR
REV	SOB	TOW	WON	AKIN
REX	SOD	TOY	WOO	ALAR
RIB	SOL	TRY	WOT	ALAS
RID	SON	TUB	WOW	ALEE
RIG	SOP	TUG	WRY	ALGA
RIM	SOS	TUN	WYE	ALLY
RIO	SOT	TUP		ALMA
RIP	SOU	TUT		ALMS
ROB	SOW	TWA	**Y – 3**	ALOE
ROC	SOX	TWO		ALPS
ROD	SOY		YAH	ALSO
ROE	SPA		YAK	ALTO
ROM	SPY	**U – 3**	YAM	ALUM
RON	STY	UGH	YAP	AMBO
ROT	SUB	ULT	YAW	AMEN
ROW	SUE	UNA	YEA	AMID
ROY	SUM	UNO	YEN	AMMO
RUB	SUN	URE	YEP	AMOK
RUE	SUP	URN	YES	AMYL
RUG		USE	YET	ANEW
RUM		UVA	YEW	ANIL
RUN	**T – 3**		YON	ANNA
RUT	TAB		YOU	ANON
RYE	TAG	**V – 3**		ANTE
	TAJ	V.A.D.	**Z – 3**	APED
	TAN	VAN	ZAP	APEX
S – 3	TAP	VAT	ZED	APSE
	TAR	VET	ZIP	AQUA
SAC	TAT	VEX	ZOO	ARAB
SAD	TAU	VIA		ARCH
SAG	TAW	VIE		AREA
SAL	TAX	VIM	**A – 4**	ARIA
SAM	TEA	VIZ	ABBE	ARID
SAP	TEC	VOW	ABED	ARIL
SAT	TED		ABET	ARMS
SAW	TEE		ABLE	ARMY
SAX	TEG	**W – 3**	ABUT	ARTS
SAY	TEN	WAD	ACER	ARTY
SEA	THE	WAG	ACHE	ARUM
SEC	THO'	WAN	ACID	ASHY
SEE	THY	WAR	ACME	ASIA
SEN	TIC	WAS	ACNE	ASTI
SET	TIE	WAT	ACRE	ATOM
SEW	TIN	WAX	ADAM	ATOP
SEX	TIP	WAY	ADIT	AUNT
SHE	TIS	WEB	ADZE	AURA
SHY	TIT	WED	AFAR	AUTO
SIC	TOD	WEE	AGED	AVER
SIN	TOE	WEN	AGOG	AVID
SIP	TOG	WET	AGUE	AVON
SIR	TOM	WHO	AHEM	AVOW
SIS	TON	WHY	AHOY	AWAY
SIT	TOO	WIG	AIDA	AWED
SIX	TOP	WIN	AIDE	AWRY
SKI				

AXED	BEER	BORN	CALL	COAT
AXIL	BEET	BOSH	CALM	COAX
AXIS	BELL	BOSS	CAME	COCA
AXLE	BELT	BOTH	CAMP	COCK
AYAH	BEND	BOUT	CANE	COCO
	BENT	BOWL	CANT	CODA
	BERG	BOWS	CAPE	CODE
B – 4	BEST	BRAD	CARD	COIF
	BETA	BRAE	CARE	COIL
BAAL	BEVY	BRAG	CARL	COIN
BAAS	BIAS	BRAN	CARP	COIR
BABA	BIDE	BRAT	CART	COKE
BABE	BIER	BRAW	CASE	COLD
BABU	BIFF	BRAY	CASH	COLE
BABY	BIKE	BRED	CASK	COLT
BACK	BILE	BREN	CAST	COMA
BADE	BILK	BRER	CAVE	COMB
BAIL	BILL	BREW	CAVY	COME
BAIT	BIND	BRIE	CEDE	CONE
BAKE	BINE	BRIG	CELL	CONK
BALD	BING	BRIM	CELT	CONS
BALE	BIRD	BRIO	CENT	COOK
BALL	BITE	BROW	CERE	COOL
BALM	BLAB	BUCK	CERT	COON
BAND	BLED	BUDE	CHAP	COOP
BANE	BLEW	BUFF	CHAR	COOT
BANG	BLOB	BUHL	CHAT	COPE
BANK	BLOC	BULB	CHEF	COPT
BANT	BLOT	BULK	CHEW	COPY
BARB	BLOW	BULL	CHIC	CORD
BARD	BLUB	BUMP	CHIN	CORE
BARE	BLUE	BUNG	CHIP	CORK
BARK	BLUR	BUNK	CHIT	CORM
BARM	BOAR	BUOY	CHOP	CORN
BARN	BOAT	BURN	CHOW	COSH
BART	BODE	BURR	CHUB	COST
BASE	BODY	BURY	CHUG	COSY
BASH	BOER	BUSH	CHUM	COTE
BASK	BOGY	BUSS	CITE	COUP
BASS	BOIL	BUST	CITY	COVE
BAST	BOKO	BUSY	CLAD	COWL
BATH	BOLD	BUTT	CLAM	CRAB
BAUD	BOLE	BUZZ	CLAN	CRAG
BAWD	BOLL	BYRE	CLAP	CRAM
BAWL	BOLT	BYTE	CLAW	CRAN
BAYS	BOMB		CLAY	CRAW
BEAD	BOND		CLEF	CREW
BEAK	BONE	C – 4	CLIO	CRIB
BEAM	BONY		CLIP	CROP
BEAN	BOOB	CADE	CLOD	CROW
BEAR	BOOK	CADI	CLOG	CRUX
BEAT	BOOM	CAFÉ	CLOT	CUBE
BEAU	BOON	CAGE	CLOY	CUFF
BECK	BOOR	CAIN	CLUB	CULL
BEDE	BOOT	CAKE	CLUE	CULM
BEEF	BORE	CAKY	COAL	CULT
BEEN		CALF		

CURB	DEWY	DREW	ELIA	FEAT
CURD	DHOW	DRIP	ELMO	FEED
CURE	DIAL	DROP	ELSE	FEEL
CURL	DICE	DRUB	ELUL	FEET
CURT	DICK	DRUG	EMIR	FELL
CUSP	DIDO	DRUM	EMIT	FELT
CUTE	DIED	DUAL	ENOW	FEND
CYST	DIET	DUCE	ENSA	FERN
CZAR	DIGS	DUCK	ENVY	FETE
	DIKE	DUCT	EPEE	FEUD
D – 4	DILL	DUDE	EPIC	FIAT
	DIME	DUDS	ERGO	FIFE
DACE	DINE	DUEL	ERIC	FILE
DADO	DING	DUET	ERIN	FILL
DAFT	DINT	DUFF	ERNE	FILM
DAGO	DIRE	DUKE	EROS	FIND
DAIL	DIRK	DUKW	ERSE	FINE
DAIS	DIRT	DULL	ERST	FINN
DALE	DISC	DULY	ESPY	FIRE
DALI	DISH	DUMA	ETCH	FIRM
DAME	DISK	DUMB	ETNA	FISH
DAMN	DISS	DUMP	ETON	FIST
DAMP	DIVA	DUNE	ETUI	FIVE
DANE	DIVE	DUNG	EVEN	FIZZ
DANK	DOCK	DUNK	EVER	FLAG
DARE	DODO	DUPE	EVIL	FLAK
DARK	DOER	DUSE	EWER	FLAM
DARN	DOFF	DUSK	EXAM	FLAN
DART	DOGE	DUST	EXIT	FLAP
DASH	DOLE	DUTY	EXON	FLAT
DATA	DOLL	DYAK	EYED	FLAW
DATE	DOLT	DYED	EYOT	FLAX
DAUB	DOME	DYER	EYRE	FLAY
DAVY	DONE	DYKE	EYRY	FLEA
DAWN	DOOM			FLED
DAZE	DOOR			FLEE
D-DAY	DOPE	E – 4	F – 4	FLEW
DEAD	DORA			FLEX
DEAF	DORY	EACH	FACE	FLIP
DEAL	DOSE	EARL	FACT	FLIT
DEAN	DOSS	EARN	FADE	FLOE
DEAR	DOTE	EASE	FAIL	FLOG
DEBT	DOTH	EAST	FAIN	FLOP
DECK	DOUR	EASY	FAIR	FLOW
DEED	DOVE	EBON	FAKE	FLUE
DEEM	DOWN	ECHO	FALL	FLUX
DEEP	DOZE	ECRU	FAME	FOAL
DEER	DOZY	EDAM	FANG	FOAM
DEFT	DRAB	EDDA	FARE	FOIL
DEFY	DRAG	EDDY	FARM	FOLD
DELL	DRAM	EDEN	FARO	FOLK
DEMY	DRAT	EDGE	FASH	FOND
DENE	DRAW	EDGY	FAST	FONT
DENT	DRAY	EDIT	FATE	FOOD
DENY	DREE	EGAD	FAUN	FOOL
DESK	DREY	EIRE	FAWN	FOOT
		ELAN	FEAR	

FORD	GIFT	GUSH	HERS	HYMN
FORE	GILD	GUST	HEWN	HYPO
FORK	GILL	GYVE	HICK	
FORM	GILT		HIDE	
FORT	GIMP	**H – 4**	HIED	**I – 4**
FOUL	GIRD		HIGH	
FOUR	GIRL	HACK	HIKE	IBEX
FOWL	GIRT	HAFT	HILL	IBIS
FOXY	GIST	HA-HA	HILT	ICED
FRAU	GIVE	HAIL	HIND	ICON
FRAY	GLAD	HAIR	HINT	IDEA
FREE	GLEE	HAKE	HIRE	IDES
FRET	GLEN	HALE	HISS	IDLE
FROG	GLIB	HALF	HIST	IDLY
FROM	GLIM	HALL	HIVE	IDOL
FUEL	GLOW	HALO	HOAR	IMAM
FULL	GLUE	HALT	HOAX	IMPI
FUME	GLUM	HAME	HOBO	INCA
FUMY	GLUT	HAND	HOCK	INCH
FUND	G-MAN	HANG	HOED	INKY
FUNK	GNAT	HANK	HOLD	INTO
FURL	GNAW	HARD	HOLE	IOTA
FURY	GOAD	HARE	HOLM	IRAN
FUSE	GOAL	HARK	HOLT	IRIS
FUSS	GOAT	HARM	HOLY	IRON
FUZZ	GOBI	HARP	HOME	ISIS
	GODS	HART	HOMY	ISLE
	GOLD	HASH	HONE	ITCH
G – 4	GOLF	HASP	HONK	ITEM
	GONE	HATE	HOOD	
GAEL	GONG	HATH	HOOF	**J – 4**
GAFF	GOOD	HAUL	HOOK	
GAGE	GOOF	HAVE	HOOP	JACK
GAIN	GORE	HAWK	HOOT	JADE
GAIT	GORY	HAZE	HOPE	JAIL
GALA	GOSH	HAZY	HOPS	JAMB
GALE	GOTH	HEAD	HORN	JANE
GALL	GOUT	HEAL	HOSE	JAPE
GAME	GOWN	HEAP	HOST	JAZZ
GAMP	GRAB	HEAR	HOUR	JEAN
GANG	GRAF	HEAT	HOVE	JEEP
GAOL	GRAM	HEBE	HOWL	JEER
GAPE	GRAY	HEED	HUED	JEHU
GARB	GREW	HEEL	HUFF	JERK
GASH	GREY	HEIR	HUGE	JEST
GASP	GRID	HELD	HULA	JIFF
GATE	GRIM	HELL	HULK	JILL
GAUD	GRIN	HELM	HULL	JILT
GAUL	GRIP	HELP	HUMP	JINX
GAVE	GRIT	HEMP	HUNG	JOCK
GAWK	GROG	HERB	HUNK	JOEY
GAZE	GROW	HERD	HUNT	JOHN
GEAR	GRUB	HERE	HURL	JOKE
GENT	GULF	HERN	HURT	JOLT
GERM	GULL	HERO	HUSH	JOSS
GEUM	GULP	HERR	HUSK	JOVE
GIBE				JOWL

JUDO	LAIC	LIEU	LUDO	MERE
JUDY	LAID	LIFE	LUFF	MESH
JU-JU	LAIN	LIFT	LUGE	MESS
JUMP	LAIR	LIKE	LULL	METE
JUNE	LAKE	LILT	LUMP	MEWS
JUNK	LAMA	LILY	LUNG	MICA
JUNO	LAMB	LIMB	LURE	MICE
JURY	LAME	LIME	LURK	MIEN
JUST	LAMP	LIMN	LUSH	MIKE
	LANA	LIMP	LUST	MILD
	LAND	LIMY	LUTE	MILE
K – 4	LANE	LINE	LYNX	MILK
	LANK	LING	LYON	MILL
KALE	LAPP	LINK	LYRE	MIME
KEEL	LARD	LINO		MIND
KEEN	LARK	LINT		MINE
KEEP	LASH	LION	M – 4	MING
KELP	LASS	LIRA		MINI
KEMP	LAST	LIRE	MACE	MINK
KENT	LATE	LISP	MADE	MINT
KEPI	LATH	LIST	MAGI	MINX
KEPT	LAUD	LIVE	MAID	MIRE
KERB	LAVA	LOAD	MAIL	MIRY
KHAN	LAVE	LOAF	MAIM	MISS
KICK	LAWN	LOAM	MAIN	MIST
KILL	LAZE	LOAN	MAKE	MITE
KILN	LAZY	LOBE	MALE	MITT
KILO	LEAD	LOCH	MALL	MOAN
KILT	LEAF	LOCK	MALT	MOAT
KIND	LEAK	LODE	MAMA	MOCK
KINE	LEAL	LOFT	MANE	MODE
KING	LEAN	LOGO	MANX	MODS
KINK	LEAP	LOIN	MANY	MOKE
KIRK	LEAR	LOLL	MARE	MOLE
KISS	LEDA	LONE	MARK	MOLL
KITE	LEEK	LONG	MARL	MONK
KITH	LEER	LOOK	MARS	MOOD
KIWI	LEES	LOOM	MART	MOON
KNAP	LEET	LOON	MASH	MOOR
KNEE	LEFT	LOOP	MASK	MOOT
KNEW	LEND	LOOS	MASS	MOPE
KNIT	LENO	LOOT	MAST	MOPS
KNOB	LENS	LOPE	MATE	MORE
KNOT	LENT	LORD	MAUD	MORN
KNOW	LESS	LORE	MAUL	MOSS
KNUR	LEST	LORN	MAZE	MOST
KRIS	LETT	LORY	MEAD	MOTE
KUDU	LEVY	LOSE	MEAL	MOTH
KURD	LEWD	LOSS	MEAN	MOUE
KYLE	LIAR	LOST	MEAT	MOVE
	LICE	LOTH	MEED	MOWN
L – 4	LICK	LOUD	MEEK	MUCH
	LIDO	LOUR	MEET	MUCK
LACE	LIED	LOUT	MELT	MUFF
LACK	LIEF	LOVE	MEMO	MULE
LADE	LIEN	LUCK	MEND	MULL
LADY			MENU	

MURK	NULL	PAIL	PILE	PROX
MUSE	NUMB	PAIN	PILL	PUCE
MUSH		PAIR	PINE	PUCK
MUSK		PALE	PING	PUFF
MUST	**O – 4**	PALI	PINK	PULL
MUTE		PALL	PINT	PULP
MUTT	OAKS	PALM	PIPE	PUMA
MYTH	OAST	PANE	PISH	PUMP
	OATH	PANG	PITH	PUNK
	OBEY	PANT	PITY	PUNT
N – 4	OBIT	PAPA	PLAN	PUNY
	OBOE	PARA	PLAY	PUPA
NAIL	ODDS	PARD	PLEA	PURE
NAME	ODIN	PARE	PLOD	PURL
NAPE	OGEE	PARK	PLOP	PURR
NARD	OGLE	PARR	PLOT	PUSH
NARK	OGPU	PART	PLOY	PUSS
NAVE	OGRE	PASS	PLUG	PUTT
NAVY	OILY	PAST	PLUM	PYRE
NAZE	OKAY	PATE	PLUS	
NAZI	OLIO	PATH	POEM	
NEAP	OMAR	PAUL	POET	**Q – 4**
NEAR	OMEN	PAVE	POKE	
NEAT	OMIT	PAWL	POKY	QUAD
NECK	ONCE	PAWN	POLE	QUAY
NEED	ONER	PAYE	POLL	QUID
NEEP	ONLY	PEAK	POLO	QUIN
NE'ER	ONUS	PEAL	POMP	QUIP
NEON	ONYX	PEAR	POND	QUIT
NERO	OOZE	PEAT	PONY	QUIZ
NESS	OPAL	PECK	POOH	QUOD
NEST	OPEN	PEEK	POOL	
NETT	OPUS	PEEL	POOP	
NEWS	ORAL	PEEP	POOR	**R – 4**
NEWT	ORFE	PEER	POPE	
NEXT	ORGY	PEKE	PORE	RACE
NIBS	OTIC	PELF	PORK	RACK
NICE	OUCH	PELT	PORT	RACY
NICK	OURS	PENT	POSE	RAFT
NIGH	OUSE	PEON	POSH	RAGE
NINE	OUST	PERI	POST	RAID
NISI	OVAL	PERK	POSY	RAIL
NODE	OVEN	PERM	POUR	RAIN
NOEL	OVER	PERT	POUT	RAKE
NOLL	OVUM	PESO	PRAM	RALE
NONE	OWED	PEST	PRAY	RAMP
NOOK	OXEN	PHEW	PREP	RAND
NOON	OYES	PHIZ	PREY	RANI
NORM	OYEZ	PHUT	PRIG	RANK
NOSE		PICA	PRIM	RANT
NOSY		PICE	PROA	RAPE
NOTE	**P – 4**	PICK	PROD	RAPT
NOUN		PICT	PROM	RARE
NOUS	PACE	PIED	PROP	RASH
NOVA	PACK	PIER	PROS	RASP
NOWT	PACT	PIKE	PROW	RATE
NUDE	PAGE			RAVE
	PAID			RAZE

READ	ROSS	SCAB	SILO	SOFT
REAL	ROSY	SCAN	SILT	SOHO
REAM	ROTA	SCAR	SINE	SOIL
REAP	ROTE	SCOT	SING	SOKE
REAR	ROUE	SCOW	SINK	SOLA
REDE	ROUP	SCUD	SIRE	SOLD
REED	ROUT	SCUM	SITE	SOLE
REEF	ROVE	SCUT	SIZE	SOLO
REEK	RUBY	SEAL	SKEP	SOME
REEL	RUCK	SEAM	SKEW	SONG
REIN	RUDD	SEAN	SKID	SOON
REIS	RUDE	SEAR	SKIM	SOOT
RELY	RUED	SEAT	SKIN	SORE
REND	RUFF	SECT	SKIP	SORT
RENT	RUIN	SEED	SKIT	SO-SO
REST	RULE	SEEK	SKUA	SOUL
RHEA	RUMP	SEEM	SKYE	SOUP
RICE	RUNE	SEEN	SLAB	SOUR
RICH	RUNG	SEEP	SLAG	SOWN
RICK	RUNT	SEER	SLAM	SOYA
RIDE	RUSE	SELF	SLAP	SPAM
RIFE	RUSH	SELL	SLAT	SPAN
RIFF	RUSK	SEMI	SLAV	SPAR
RIFT	RUSS	SEND	SLAY	SPAT
RIGA	RUST	SENT	SLED	SPEC
RILE	RUTH	SEPT	SLEW	SPED
RILL	RYOT	SERB	SLID	SPIN
RIME		SERE	SLIM	SPIT
RIND		SERF	SLIP	SPIV
RING	S – 4	SETT	SLIT	SPOT.
RINK		SEWN	SLOE	SPRY
RIOT	SACK	SHAD	SLOG	SPUD
RIPE	SAFE	SHAG	SLOP	SPUN
RISE	SAGA	SHAH	SLOT	SPUR
RISK	SAGE	SHAW	SLOW	STAB
RITE	SAGO	SHED	SLUG	STAG
RIVE	SAID	SHEW	SLUM	STAR
ROAD	SAIL	SHIM	SLUR	STAY
ROAM	SAKE	SHIN	SLUT	STEM
ROAN	SAKI	SHIP	SMEE	STEN
ROAR	SALE	SHOD	SMEW	STEP
ROBE	SALT	SHOE	SMUG	STET
ROCK	SAME	SHOO	SMUT	STEW
RODE	SAND	SHOP	SNAG	STIR
ROLE	SANE	SHOT	SNAP	STOP
ROLL	SANG	SHOW	SNIP	STOW
ROME	SANK	SHUN	SNOB	STUB
ROMP	SANS	SHUT	SNOW	STUD
ROOD	SARD	SICK	SNUB	STUN
ROOF	SARI	SIDE	SNUG	STYE
ROOK	SARK	SIFT	SOAK	STYX
ROOM	SASH	SIGH	SOAP	SUCH
ROOT	SATE	SIGN	SOAR	SUCK
ROPE	SAUL	SIKH	SOCK	SUDS
ROPY	SAVE	SILK	SODA	SUED
ROSE	SAWN	SILL	SOFA	SUET
	SAXE			

SUEZ	TEEM	TOOT	UNIT	WAKE
SUIT	TELL	TOPE	UNTO	WALE
SULK	TEND	TORE	UPAS	WALK
SUMP	TENT	TORN	UPON	WALL
SUNG	TERM	TORT	URDU	WALT
SUNK	TERN	TORY	URGE	WAND
SURE	TEST	TOSH	URSA	WANE
SURF	THAI	TOSS	USED	WANT
SWAB	THAN	TOTE	USER	WARD
SWAG	THAT	TOUR		WARE
SWAM	THAW	TOUT		WARM
SWAN	THEE	TOWN	**V – 4**	WARN
SWAP	THEM	TRAM		WARP
SWAT	THEN	TRAP	VAIN	WART
SWAY	THEY	TRAY	VALE	WARY
SWIG	THIN	TREE	VAMP	WASH
SWIM	THIS	TREK	VANE	WASP
SWOP	THOR	TRET	VARY	WATT
SWOT	THOU	TREY	VASE	WAVE
SWUM	THRO	TRIM	VAST	WAVY
SYCE	THUD	TRIO	VEAL	WAXY
	THUG	TRIP	VEER	WEAK
	THUS	TROD	VEIL	WEAL
T – 4	TICK	TROT	VEIN	WEAN
	TIDE	TROY	VEND	WEAR
TACK	TIDY	TRUE	VENT	WEED
TACT	TIED	TRUG	VERB	WEEK
TAEL	TIER	TSAR	VERT	WEEP
TAFT	TIFF	TUBA	VERY	WEFT
TAIL	TIKE	TUBE	VEST	WEIR
TAKE	TILE	TUCK	VETO	WELD
TALC	TILL	TUFT	VICE	WELL
TALE	TILT	TUNA	VIDE	WELT
TALK	TIME	TUNE	VIED	WEND
TALL	TINE	TURF	VIEW	WENT
TAME	TING	TURK	VILE	WEPT
TAMP	TINT	TURN	VINE	WERE
TANG	TINY	TUSH	VIOL	WERT
TANK	TIRE	TUSK	VISA	WEST
TAPE	TOAD	TUTU	VIVA	WHAT
TARA	TOBY	'TWAS	VIVE	WHEN
TARE	TO-DO	TWIG	VOCE	WHET
TARN	TOED	TWIN	VOID	WHEW
TARO	TOFF	TWIT	VOLE	WHEY
TART	TOFU	TYKE	VOLT	WHIG
TASK	TOGA	TYNE	VOTE	WHIM
TASS	TOGS	TYPE		WHIN
TA-TA	TOIL	TYRE	**W – 4**	WHIP
TATE	TOLD	TYRO		WHIT
TAUT	TOLL		WADE	WHOA
TAXI	TOMB		WADI	WHOM
TEAK	TOME	**U – 4**	WAFT	WICK
TEAL	TONE		WAGE	WIDE
TEAM	TONY	UGLY	WAIF	WIFE
TEAR	TOOK	ULNA	WAIL	WILD
TEAT	TOOL	UNCO	WAIN	WILE
TEED		UNDO	WAIT	

WILL	YORE	ADDLE	ALLOW	ARGON
WILT	YOUR	ADEPT	ALLOY	ARGOT
WILY	YOWL	ADIEU	ALOFT	ARGUE
WIND	YO-YO	ADMIT	ALONE	ARGUS
WINE	YULE	ADMIX	ALONG	ARIEL
WING		ADOBE	ALOOF	ARIES
WINK		ADOPT	ALOUD	ARISE
WIPE	Z – 4	ADORE	ALPHA	ARMED
WIRE		ADORN	ALTAR	AROMA
WIRY	ZANY	ADSUM	ALTER	AROSE
WISE	ZEAL	ADULT	AMASS	ARRAS
WISH	ZEBU	AEGIS	AMAZE	ARRAY
WISP	ZERO	AERIE	AMBER	ARROW
WITH	ZEST	AESOP	AMBIT	ARSON
WOAD	ZETA	AFFIX	AMBLE	ARYAN
WOLD	ZEUS	AFIRE	AMEER	ASCOT
WOLF	ZINC	AFOOT	AMEND	ASDIC
WOMB	ZING	AFTER	AMISS	ASHEN
WONT	ZION	AGAIN	AMITY	ASHES
WOOD	ZONE	AGAPE	AMONG	ASHET
WOOF	ZOOM	AGATE	AMOUR	ASIAN
WOOL	ZULU	AGAVE	AMPLE	ASIDE
WORD		AGENT	AMPLY	ASKED
WORE	A – 5	AGILE	AMUCK	ASKEW
WORK		AGLEY	AMUSE	ASPEN
WORM	ABACK	AGLOW	ANENT	ASPIC
WORN	ABAFT	AGONE	ANGEL	ASSAY
WORT	ABASE	AGONY	ANGER	ASSES
WOVE	ABASH	AGREE	ANGLE	ASSET
WRAP	ABATE	AHEAD	ANGRY	ASTER
WREN	ABBEY	AHEAP	ANISE	ASTIR
WRIT	ABBOT	AIDED	ANKLE	ASTON
	ABEAM	AILED	ANNEX	ATILT
X – 4	ABELE	AIMED	ANNOY	ATLAS
	ABEND	AIRED	ANNUL	ATOLL
XMAS	ABHOR	AISLE	ANODE	ATONE
X-RAY	ABIDE	AITCH	ANONA	ATTAR
	ABIES	AKELE	ANTIC	ATTIC
	ABLER	ALACK	ANVIL	AUDIO
Y – 4	ABODE	ALARM	ANZAC	AUDIT
YANK	ABOIL	ALBUM	AORTA	AUGER
YARD	ABORT	ALDER	APACE	AUGHT
YARN	ABOUT	ALERT	APART	AUGUR
YAWL	ABOVE	ALGAE	APHIS	AUNTY
YAWN	ABUSE	ALGOL	APING	AURAL
YAWS	ABYSS	ALIAS	APISH	AVAIL
YEAH	ACHED	ALIBI	APORT	AVAST
YEAR	ACRID	ALIEN	APPAL	AVENS
YELL	ACTED	ALIGN	APPLE	AVERT
YELP	ACTON	ALIKE	APPLY	AVIAN
YETI	ACTOR	ALIVE	APRIL	AVION
YOGA	ACUTE	ALLAH	APRON	AVOID
YOGI	ADAGE	ALLAY	APTLY	AWAIT
YO-HO	ADAPT	ALLEY	ARABY	AWAKE
YOKE	ADDED	ALL-IN	ARECA	AWARD
YOLK	ADDER	ALLOT	ARENA	AWARE

AWASH	BEANO	BLANK	BORER	BROSE
AWFUL	BEARD	BARE	BORNE	BROTH
AWING	BEAST	BLASE	BORON	BROWN
AWOKE	BEDEW	BLAST	BOSOM	BRUIN
AXIAL	BEECH	BLAZE	BOSSY	BRUNT
AXIOM	BEEFY	BLEAK	BOSUN	BRUSH
AZTEC	BEERY	BLEAR	BOTCH	BRUTE
AZURE	BEFIT	BLEAT	BOUGH	BUDDY
	BEFOG	BLEED	BOULE	BUDGE
	BEGAD	BLEND	BOUND	BUFFS
B – 5	BEGAN	BLESS	BOWED	BUGGY
	BEGAT	BLEST	BOWEL	BUGLE
BABEL	BEGET	BLIMP	BOWER	BUILD
BACCY	BEGIN	BLIND	BOWIE	BUILT
BACON	BEGOT	BLINK	BOWLS	BULGE
BADGE	BEGUM	BLISS	BOXED	BULGY
BADLY	BEGUN	BLOCK	BOXER	BULKY
BAGGY	BEIGE	BLOKE	BOYER	BULLY
BAIRN	BEING	BLOND	BRACE	BUMPY
BAIZE	BELAY	BLOOD	BRACT	BUNCE
BAKED	BELCH	BLOOM	BRAID	BUNCH
BAKER	BELIE	BLOWN	BRAIN	BUNNY
BALED	BELLE	BLOWY	BRAKE	BUNTY
BALER	BELOW	BLUED	BRAND	BURGH
BALMY	BENCH	BLUER	BRASH	BURKE
BALSA	BERET	BLUES	BRASS	BURLY
BAMBI	BERRY	BLUEY	BRAVE	BURNT
BANAL	BERTH	BLUFF	BRAVO	BURRO
BANDY	BERYL	BLUNT	BRAWL	BURST
BANJO	BESET	BLURB	BRAWN	BUSBY
BANNS	BESOM	BLURT	BRAZE	BUSES
BANTU	BESOT	BLUSH	BREAD	BUSHY
BARED	BETEL	BOARD	BREAK	BUTTS
BARGE	BETTY	BOAST	BREAM	BUTTY
BARMY	BEVEL	BOBBY	BREED	BUXOM
BARON	BHANG	BOCHE	BREVE	BUYER
BARRY	BIBLE	BODED	BRIAR	BWANA
BASAL	BIDDY	BODGE	BRIBE	BY-LAW
BASED	BIDET	BOGEY	BRICK	BYWAY
BASIC	BIGHT	BOGGY	BRIDE	
BASIL	BIGOT	BOGIE	BRIEF	
BASIN	BIJOU	BOGUS	BRIER	C – 5
BASIS	BILGE	BOHEA	BRILL	
BASSO	BILLY	BOLAS	BRINE	CABAL
BASTE	BINGE	BONED	BRING	CABBY
BATCH	BINGO	BONES	BRINK	CABER
BATED	BIPED	BONNE	BRINY	CABIN
BATHE	BIRCH	BONUS	BRISK	CABLE
BATON	BIRTH	BOOBY	BROAD	CACAO
BATTY	BISON	BOOED	BROCK	CACHE
BAULK	BITCH	BOOST	BROIL	CADDY
BAWDY	BITER	BOOTH	BROKE	CADET
BAYED	BLACK	BOOTS	BRONX	CADGE
BEACH	BLADE	BOOTY	BROOD	CADRE
BEADS	BLAME	BORAX	BROOK	CAGED
BEADY	BLAND	BORED	BROOM	CAGEY
BE-ALL				CAIRN

CAKED	CHEEP	CLERK	COUNT	CRUDE
CAMEL	CHEER	CLICK	COUPE	CRUEL
CAMEO	CHESS	CLIFF	COURT	CRUET
CANAL	CHEST	CLIMB	COVER	CRUMB
CANDY	CHICK	CLIME	COVET	CRUMP
CANED	CHIDE	CLING	COVEY	CRUSE
CANNA	CHIEF	CLINK	COWED	CRUSH
CANNY	CHILD	CLOAK	COWER	CRUST
CANOE	CHILI	CLOCK	COYLY	CRYPT
CANON	CHILL	CLOSE	COZEN	CUBAN
CANTO	CHIME	CLOTH	CRACK	CUBED
CAPER	CHINA	CLOUD	CRAFT	CUBIC
CAPON	CHINE	CLOUT	CRAIG	CUBIT
CARAT	CHINK	CLOVE	CRAKE	CUPID
CARED	CHIPS	CLOWN	CRAMP	CURED
CARET	CHIRP	CLUCK	CRANE	CURER
CARGO	CHIVE	CLUMP	CRANK	CURIE
CARIB	CHOCK	CLUNG	CRASH	CURIO
CAROB	CHOIR	CLUNK	CRASS	CURLY
CAROL	CHOKE	CLUNY	CRATE	CURRY
CARRY	CHOPS	COACH	CRAVE	CURSE
CARTE	CHORD	COAST	CRAWL	CURVE
CARVE	CHORE	COATI	CRAZE	CUSHY
CASED	CHOSE	COBRA	CRAZY	CUTER
CASTE	CHUCK	COCKY	CREAK	CUTTY
CATCH	CHUMP	COCOA	CREAM	CYCLE
CATER	CHUNK	CODED	CREDO	CYDER
CATTY	CHURL	CODEX	CREED	CYNIC
CAULK	CHURN	COLIC	CREEK	CZECH
CAUSE	CHUTE	COLIN	CREEL	
CAVIL	CIDER	COLON	CREEP	
CAWED	CIGAR	COMET	CREPE	D – 5
CEASE	CINCH	COMIC	CREPT	
CEDAR	CIRCA	COMMA	CRESS	DADDY
CEDED	CIRCE	COMPO	CREST	DAILY
CELLO	CISSY	CONCH	CREWE	DAIRY
CERES	CITED	CONEY	CRICK	DAISY
CHAFE	CIVET	CONGA	CRIED	DALAI
CHAFF	CIVIC	CONGE	CRIER	DALLY
CHAIN	CIVIL	CONGO	CRIES	DAMON
CHAIR	CIVVY	CONIC	CRIME	DANCE
CHALK	CLACK	COOED	CRIMP	DANDY
CHAMP	CLAIM	COOMB	CRISP	DARBY
CHANT	CLAMP	CO-OPT	CROAK	DARED
CHAOS	CLAMS	COPAL	CROCK	DATED
CHAPS	CLANG	COPED	CROFT	DATUM
CHARD	CLANK	COPER	CRONE	DAUNT
CHARM	CLARE	COPRA	CRONY	DAVIT
CHART	CLASH	COPSE	CROOK	DAZED
CHARY	CLASP	CORAL	CROON	DEALT
CHASE	CLASS	CORGI	CRORE	DEATH
CHASM	CLEAN	CORNY	CROSS	DEBAR
CHEAP	CLEAR	CORPS	CROUP	DEBIT
CHEAT	CLEAT	COSTS	CROWD	DEBUG
CHECK	CLEEK	COUGH	CROWN	DEBUT
CHEEK	CLEFT	COULD	CROWN	DECAY

DECOR	DOILY	DROVE	ELDER	EVENS
DECOY	DOING	DROWN	ELECT	EVENT
DECRY	DOLCE	DRUID	ELEGY	EVERT
DEFER	DOLED	DRUNK	ELEMI	EVERY
DEIFY	DOLLY	DRUPE	ELEVE	EVICT
DEIGN	DOMED	DRYAD	ELFIN	EVOKE
DEITY	DONAH	DRYER	ELGIN	EXACT
DEKKO	DOÑAT	DRYLY	ELIDE	EXALT
DELAY	DONNA	DUCAL	ELITE	EXCEL
DELFT	DONOR	DUCAT	ELOPE	EXEAT
DELTA	DOPED	DUCHY	ELUDE	EXERT
DELVE	DORIC	DULLY	ELVER	EXILE
DEMOB	DORMY	DUMMY	EMBED	EXIST
DEMON	DOSED	DUMPS	EMBER	EXPEL
DEMUR	DOTED	DUMPY	EMEER	EXTOL
DENIM	DOTTY	DUNCE	EMEND	EXTRA
DENSE	DOUBT	DUPED	EMERY	EXUDE
DEPOT	DOUGH	DUSKY	EMMET	EXULT
DEPTH	DOUSE	DUSTY	EMPTY	EYING
DERBY	DOVER	DUTCH	ENACT	EYRE
DETER	DOWDY	DUVET	ENDED	
DEUCE	DOWEL	DWARF	END-ON	
DEVIL	DOWER	DWELL	ENDOR	F – 5
DHOBI	DOWNY	DWELT	ENDOW	FABLE
DHOTI	DOWRY	DYING	ENEMY	FACED
DIANA	DOYEN		ENJOY	FACET
DIARY	DOZED		ENNUI	FADDY
DIBIT	DOZEN	E – 5	ENROL	FAGIN
DICED	DRAFT		ENSUE	FAINT
DICKY	DRAIN	EAGER	ENTER	FAIRY
DICTA	DRAKE	EAGLE	ENTRY	FAITH
DIGIT	DRAMA	EAGRE	ENVOI	FAKED
DIMLY	DRANK	EARED	ENVOY	FAKIR
DINAR	DRAPE	EARLY	EPHOD	FALSE
DINED	DRAWL	EARTH	EPOCH	FAMED
DINER	DRAWN	EASED	EPOXY	FANCY
DINGO	DREAD	EASEL	EPSOM	FARAD
DINGY	DREAM	EATEN	EQUAL	FARED
DINKY	DREAR	EAVES	EQUIP	FARCE
DIODE	DREGS	EBBED	ERASE	FATAL
DIRGE	DRESS	EBONY	ERATO	FATED
DIRTY	DRIED	ECLAT	ERECT	FATES
DITCH	DRIER	EDGED	ERICA	FATLY
DITTO	DRIFT	EDICT	ERODE	FATTY
DITTY	DRILL	EDIFY	ERRED	FAULT
DIVAN	DRILY	EDUCE	ERROR	FAUNA
DIVED	DRINK	EERIE	ERUPT	FAUST
DIVER	DRIVE	EGGED	ESSAY	FEAST
DIVES	DROIT	EGRET	ESTER	FED-UP
DIVOT	DROLL	EIDER	ESTOP	FEIGN
DIXIE	DROME	EIGHT	ETHER	FEINT
DODGE	DRONE	EJECT	ETHIC	FELIX
DODGY	DROOL	EKING	ETHOS	FELON
DOGGO	DROOP	ELAND	ETHYL	FEMUR
DOGGY	DROPS	ELATE	ETUDE	FENCE
DOGMA	DROSS	ELBOW	EVADE	FERNY

FERRY	FLOOR	FROTH	GIANT	GRASS
FETCH	FLORA	FROWN	GIBED	GRATE
FETED	FLOSS	FROZE	GIBUS	GRAVE
FEVER	FLOUR	FRUIT	GIDDY	GRAVY
FEWER	FLOUT	FRUMP	GIGOT	GRAZE
FIBRE	FLOWN	FRYER	GIPSY	GREAT
FICHU	FLUFF	FUDGE	GIRTH	GREBE
FIELD	FLUID	FUGUE	GIVEN	GREED
FIEND	FLUKE	FULLY	GIVER	GREEK
FIERY	FLUKY	FUNGI	GIVES	GREEN
FIFTH	FLUNG	FUNKY	GLACÉ	GREET
FIFTY	FLUSH	FUNNY	GLADE	GREYS
FIGHT	FLUTE	FURRY	GLAND	GRIEF
FILCH	FLYER	FURZE	GLARE	GRILL
FILED	FOAMY	FUSED	GLASS	GRIME
FILLY	FOCAL	FUSEE	GLAZE	GRIMY
FILMY	FOCUS	FUSIL	GLEAM	GRIND
FILTH	FOGEY	FUSSY	GLEAN	GRIPE
FINAL	FOGGY	FUSTY	GLEBE	GRIST
FINCH	FOIST	FUTON	GLIDE	GRITS
FINED	FOLIO	FUZZY	GLINT	GROWN
FINER	FOLLY		GLOAT	GROAT
FINIS	FORAY		GLOBE	GROCK
FIORD	FORBY	**G – 5**	GLOOM	GROIN
FIRED	FORCE	GABLE	GLORY	GROOM
FIRST	FORGE	GAFFE	GLOSS	GROPE
FIRTH	FORGO	GAILY	GLOVE	GROSS
FISHY	FORME	GALOP	GLUED	GROUP
FITCH	FORTE	GAMED	GLUEY	GROUT
FITLY	FORTH	GAMIN	GNARL	GROVE
FIVER	FORTY	GAMMA	GNASH	GROWL
FIVES	FORUM	GAMUT	GNOME	GROWN
FIXED	FOSSE	GAPED	GODLY	GRUEL
FJORD	FOUND	GARTH	GOING	GRUFF
FLAIL	FOUNT	GASSY	GOLLY	GRUNT
FLAIR	FOXED	GATED	GONER	GUANO
FLAKE	FOYER	GAUDY	GOODS	GUARD
FLAKY	FRAIL	GAUGE	GOODY	GUAVA
FLAME	FRAME	GAUNT	GOOSE	GUESS
FLANK	FRANCE	GAUZE	GORED	GUEST
FLARE	FRANK	GAUZY	GORGE	GUIDE
FLASH	FRAUD	GAVEL	GORSE	GUILD
FLASK	FREAK	GAWKY	GOUDA	GUILE
FLECK	FREED	GAYER	GOUGE	GUISE
FLEET	FREER	GAZED	GOURD	GULCH
FLESH	FRESH	GECKO	GOUTY	GULES
FLICK	FRIAR	GEESE	GRACE	GULLY
FLIER	FRIED	GELID	GRADE	GUNNY
FLIES	FRILL	GENET	GRAFT	GUSTO
FLING	FRISK	GENIE	GRAIL	GUSTY
FLINT	FRITZ	GENOA	GRAIN	GUTTA
FLIRT	FRIZZ	GENRE	GRAND	GUTTY
FLOAT	FROCK	GENUS	GRANT	GUYED
FLOCK	FROND	GET-UP	GRAPE	GYPSY
FLONG	FRONT	GHOST	GRAPH	GYVES
FLOOD	FROST	GHOUL	GRASP	

H – 5	HIRED	ICING	JAMES	KNEEL
	HIRER	IDEAL	JAMMY	KNELL
HABIT	HITCH	IDIOM	JAPAN	KNELT
HADES	HIVED	IDIOT	JAUNT	KNIFE
HADJI	HIVES	IDLED	JAWED	KNOCK
HAIRY	HOARD	IDLER	JEANS	KNOLL
HALLO	HOARY	IDRIS	JELLY	KNOUT
HALMA	HOBBY	IDYLL	JEMMY	KNOWN
HALVE	HOCUS	IGLOO	JENNY	KNURL
HANDY	HODGE	ILIAD	JERKY	KOALA
HANKY	HOIST	ILIUM	JERRY	KOPIE
HAPLY	HOLLY	IMAGE	JETTY	KORAN
HAPPY	HOMER	IMAGO	JEWEL	KRAAL
HARDY	HONED	IMBUE	JEWRY	KRAIT
HARED	HONEY	IMPEL	JIBED	KRONE
HAREM	HOOCH	IMPLY	JIFFY	KUDOS
HARRY	HOOEY	INANE	JIMMY	KUKRI
HARSH	HOPED	INAPT	JINGO	KULAK
HASTE	HOPPY	INCOG	JINKS	KVASS
HASTY	HORDE	INCUR	JOINT	
HATCH	HORNY	INDEX	JOIST	
HATED	HORSE	INEPT	JOKED	L – 5
HAULM	HORSY	INERT	JOKER	
HAUNT	HOTEL	INFER	JOLLY	LABEL
HAVEN	HOTLY	INFIX	JONAH	LACED
HAVER	HOUND	INGLE	JOUST	LADEN
HAVOC	HOURI	INGOT	JUDAS	LADLE
HAWSE	HOUSE	INKED	JUDGE	LAGER
HAZEL	HOVEL	IN-LAW	JUICE	LAIRD
HEADS	HOVER	INLAY	JUICY	LAITY
HEADY	HOWDY	INLET	JULEP	LAKER
HEARD	HUBBY	INNER	JUMBO	LAMED
HEART	HUFFY	INPUT	JUMPY	LANCE
HEATH	HULLO	INSET	JUNTA	LANKY
HEDGE	HUMAN	INTER	JUROR	LAPEL
HEFTY	HUMID	INURE		LAPSE
HEIGH	HUMPH	IONIC		LARCH
HELIX	HUMUS	IRAQI	K – 5	LARDY
HELLO	HUNCH	IRATE		LARGE
HELOT	HUNKS	IRENE	KAPOK	LARGO
HE-MAN	HURRY	IRISH	KAYAK	LARRY
HENCE	HUSKY	IRKED	KEDGE	LARVA
HENNA	HUSSY	IRONS	KEEPS	LASSO
HENRY	HUTCH	IRONY	KETCH	LATCH
HEROD	HYDRA	ISLAM	KEYED	LATER
HERON	HYDRO	ISLET	KHAKI	LATEX
HEWED	HYENA	ISSUE	KIDDY	LATHE
HEWER	HYRAX	ITCHY	KINGS	LATIN
HIKED	HYTHE	IVIED	KINKY	LAUGH
HIKER		IVORY	KIOSK	LAURA
HILLY		IXION	KITTY	LAVED
HINDI	I – 5		KLOOF	LAXLY
HINDU			KNACK	LAY-BY
HINGE	ICENI	J – 5	KNARL	LAYER
HINNY	ICHOR		KNAVE	LAZED
HIPPO	ICIER	JABOT	KNEAD	LEACH
	ICILY	JADED	KNEED	LEAFY

LEANT	LODGE	MAIZE	MERRY	MORAY
LEARN	LOFTY	MAJOR	MESSY	MORON
LEASE	LOGAN	MAKER	METAL	MORSE
LEASH	LOGIC	MALAY	METED	MOSES
LEAST	LOLLY	MALTY	METER	MOSSY
LEAVE	LOOFA	MAMBA	METRE	MOTET
LEDGE	LOONY	MAMMA	MEWED	MOTIF
LEECH	LOOPY	MAMMY	MEZZO	MOTOR
LEERY	LOOSE	MANED	MIAOW	MOTTO
LEGAL	LOPED	MANET	MICKY	MOULD
LEGER	LORDS	MANGE	MIDAS	MOULT
LEGGY	LORIS	MANGO	MIDDY	MOUND
LEMON	LORRY	MANGY	MIDGE	MOUNT
LEMUR	LOSER	MANIA	MID-ON	MOURN
LENTO	LOTTO	MANLY	MIDST	MOUSE
LEPER	LOTUS	MANNA	MIGHT	MOUSY
LETHE	LOUGH	MANOR	MILCH	MOUTH
LET-UP	LOUIS	MANSE	MILER	MOVED
LEVEE	LOUSE	MAORI	MILKY	MOVER
LEVEL	LOUSY	MAPLE	MIMED	MOVIE
LEVER	LOVAT	MARCH	MIMIC	MOWED
LEWIS	LOVED	MARGE	MINCE	MOWER
LIANA	LOVER	MARRY	MINED	MUCKY
LIBEL	LOWER	MARSH	MINER	MUCUS
LIBRA	LOWLY	MASAI	MINIM	MUDDY
LICIT	LOYAL	MASER	MINOR	MUFTI
LIEGE	LUCID	MASHY	MINUS	MUGGY
LIFER	LUCKY	MASON	MIRTH	MULCH
LIGHT	LUCRE	MASSA	MISER	MULCT
LIKED	LUGER	MASSE	MISSY	MUMMY
LIKEN	LUMPY	MATCH	MISTY	MUMPS
LILAC	LUNAR	MATED	MITRE	MUNCH
LIMBO	LUNCH	MATER	MIXED	MURAL
LIMIT	LUNGE	MATEY	MIXER	MURKY
LINED	LUPIN	MATIN	MIX-UP	MUSED
LINEN	LURCH	MAUVE	MOCHA	MUSHY
LINER	LURED	MAVIS	MODEL	MUSIC
LINGO	LURID	MAWKY	MODEM	MUSTY
LINKS	LUSTY	MAXIM	MODUS	MUTED
LISLE	LYCEE	MAYBE	MOGUL	MUZZY
LISTS	LYING	MAYOR	MOIRE	MYNAH
LITHE	LYMPH	MEALY	MOIST	MYOPE
LITHO	LYNCH	MEANS	MOLAR	MYRRH
LITRE	LYRIC	MEANT	MOLLY	
LIVED		MEATH	MOLTO	
LIVEN		MEATY	MONDE	N – 5
LIVER	M – 5	MECCA	MONEY	NABOB
LIVID		MEDAL	MONTE	NACRE
LLAMA	MACAW	MEDIA	MONTH	NADIR
LLANO	MACON	MEDOC	MOOCH	NAIAD
LOACH	MADAM	MELEE	MOODY	NAIVE
LOAMY	MADGE	MELON	MOOED	NAKED
LOATH	MADLY	MERCY	MOONY	NAMED
LOBBY	MAFIA	MERGE	MOOSE	NANNY
LOCAL	MAGIC	MERIT	MOPED	NAPOO
LOCUM	MAGOG	MERLE	MORAL	NAPPY
	MAHDI			

NASAL	NOYAU	ORLON	PARTS	PILED
NASTY	NUDGE	ORLOP	PARTY	PILOT
NATAL	NURSE	ORMER	PASHA	PINED
NATTY	NUTTY	ORRIS	PASSE	PINKY
NAVAL	NYLON	OSIER	PASTE	PINNY
NAVEL		OTHER	PASTY	PIN-UP
NAVVY		OTTER	PATCH	PIOUS
NAWAB	O – 5	OUGHT	PATEN	PIPED
NAZIS	OAKEN	OUIJA	PATER	PIPER
NEDDY	OAKUM	OUNCE	PATIO	PIPIT
NEEDS	OARED	OUSEL	PATLY	PIQUE
NEEDY	OASIS	OUTDO	PATTY	PITCH
NEGRO	OATEN	OUTER	PAUSE	PITHY
NEGUS	OBEAH	OUTRE	PAVAN	PIVOT
NEIGH	OBESE	OVATE	PAVED	PIXEL
NERVE	OCCUR	OVERT	PAWED	PIXIE
NERVY	OCEAN	OVINE	PAWKY	PLACE
NEVER	OCHRE	OVOID	PAYEE	PLAID
NEWEL	OCTET	OVULE	PAYER	PLAIN
NEWLY	ODDLY	OWING	PEACE	PLAIT
NEWSY	ODEON	OWLET	PEACH	PLANE
NEXUS	ODIUM	OWNED	PEAKY	PLANK
NICER	ODOUR	OWNER	PEARL	PLANT
NICHE	OFFAL	OX-EYE	PEASE	PLATE
NIECE	OFFER	OXIDE	PEATY	PLATO
NIFTY	OFLAG	OXLIP	PECAN	PLAZA
NIGHT	OFTEN	OZONE	PEDAL	PLEAD
NIHIL	OGIVE		PEGGY	PLEAT
NINNY	OGLED		PEKOE	PLEBS
NINON	OILED	P – 5	PENAL	PLIED
NINTH	OKAPI	PACED	PENCE	PLUCK
NIOBE	OLDEN	PACER	PENNY	PLUMB
NIPPY	OLDER	PADDY	PEONY	PLUME
NITRE	OLEIC	PADRE	PERCH	PLUMP
NIZAM	OLIVE	PAEAN	PERDU	PLUSH
NOBBY	OMAHA	PAGAN	PERIL	POACH
NOBEL	OMBRE	PAGED	PERKY	PODGE
NOBLE	OMEGA	PAINT	PERRY	PODGY
NOBLY	ONION	PALED	PESKY	POESY
NODAL	ONSET	PALMY	PETAL	POILU
NODDY	OOMPH	PALSY	PETER	POINT
NOHOW	OOZED	PANDA	PETIT	POISE
NOISE	OPERA	PANED	PEWIT	POKED
NOISY	OPINE	PANEL	PHASE	POKER
NOMAD	OPIUM	PANIC	PHIAL	POLAR
NONCE	OPTED	PANSY	PHLOX	POLIO
NONET	OPTIC	PANTS	PHONE	POLKA
NOOSE	ORANG	PAPAL	PHOTO	POLLY
NORMA	ORATE	PAPAW	PIANO	POPPY
NORSE	ORBED	PAPER	PICEL	PORCH
NORTH	ORBIT	PAPPY	PICOT	PORED
NOSED	ORDER	PARCH	PIECE	PORKY
NOSEY	OREAD	PARED	PIETY	POSED
NOTCH	ORGAN	PARKY	PIGMY	POSER
NOTED	ORIEL	PARRY	PILAU	POSSE
NOVEL	ORION	PARSE	PILAW	POTTO

POTTY	PYGMY	RANEE	RESIN	ROWAN
POUCH	PYLON	RANGE	RESOW	ROWDY
POULT	PYRUS	RANGY	RETCH	ROWED
POUND		RAPID	RETRY	ROWEL
POWER		RARER	REVEL	ROWER
PRANG	Q – 5	RASED	REVUE	ROYAL
PRANK	QUACK	RATED	RHEUM	RUCHE
PRATE	QUADS	RATEL	RHINE	RUDDY
PRAWN	QUAFF	RATIO	RHINO	RUDER
PREEN	QUAIL	RATTY	RHOMB	RUGBY
PRESS	QUAKE	RAVED	RHYME	RUING
PRICE	QUAKY	RAVEL	RIANT	RULED
PRICK	QUALM	RAVEN	RIBES	RULER
PRIDE	QUANT	RAWLY	RIDER	RUMBA
PRIED	QUART	RAYON	RIDGE	RUMMY
PRIMA	QUASH	RAZED	RIFLE	RUNIC
PRIME	QUASI	RAZOR	RIGHT	RUN-IN
PRIMO	QUEEN	REACH	RIGID	RUNNY
PRINK	QUEER	REACT	RIGOR	RUPEE
PRINT	QUELL	READY	RILED	RURAL
PRIOR	QUERY	REALM	RIMED	RUSTY
PRISE	QUEST	RE-ARM	RINSE	RUTTY
PRISM	QUEUE	REBEL	RIPEN	
PRIVY	QUICK	REBID	RIPER	
PRIZE	QUIET	REBUS	RIPON	S – 5
PROBE	QUIFF	REBUT	RISEN	SABLE
PROEM	QUILL	RECCE	RISER	SABOT
PRONE	QUILT	RECTO	RISKY	SABRE
PRONG	QUINS	RECUR	RIVAL	SADLY
PROOF	QUIRE	REDAN	RIVEN	SAFER
PROPS	QUIRK	REDLY	RIVER	SAGAN
PROSE	QUIET	RE-DYE	RIVET	SAHIB
PROSY	QUITS	REEDY	ROACH	SAINT
PROUD	QUOIN	REEVE	ROAST	SAITH
PROVE	QUOIT	REFER	ROBED	SALAD
PROWL	QUOTA	REFIT	ROBIN	SALIC
PROXY	QUOTE	REFIX	ROBOT	SALIX
PRUDE	QUOTH	REGAL	ROCKY	SALLY
PRUNE		REICH	RODEO	SALMI
PSALM		REIGN	ROGER	SALON
PUFFY	R – 5	REINS	ROGUE	SALTS
PUKKA	RABBI	RELAX	ROMAN	SALTY
PULED	RABID	RELAY	ROMEO	SALVE
PULPY	RACED	RELET	RONDO	SALVO
PULSE	RACER	RELIC	ROOMY	SAMBA
PUNCH	RADAR	RELIT	ROOST	SAMMY
PUNIC	RADII	REMIT	ROPED	SANDY
PUPIL	RADIO	RENAL	ROSIN	SANER
PUPPY	RADIX	RENEW	ROTOR	SAPID
PUREE	RAGED	RENTE	ROUGE	SAPOR
PURER	RAINY	REPAY	ROUGH	SAPPY
PURGE	RAISE	REPEL	ROUND	SATAN
PURSE	RAJAH	REPLY	ROUSE	SATED
PUSSY	RAKED	REPOT	ROUTE	SATIN
PUTTY	RALLY	RERUN	ROVED	SATYR
PUT-UP	RANCH	RESET	ROVER	SAUCE

SAUCY	SEPAL	SHORN	SLATY	SNOUT
SAUNA	SEPIA	SHORT	SLAVE	SNOWY
SAUTÉ	SEPOY	SHOUT	SLEEK	SNUFF
SAVED	SERAI	SHOVE	SLEEP	SOAPY
SAVER	SERGE	SHOWN	SLEET	SOBER
SAVOY	SERIF	SHOWY	SLEPT	SOGGY
SAVVY	SERUM	SHRED	SLICE	SOLAR
SAWED	SERVE	SHREW	SLICK	SOLDO
SAXON	SETAE	SHRUB	SLIDE	SOLED
SAY-SO	SET-TO	SHRUG	SLIME	SOL-FA
SCALA	SET-UP	SHUCK	SLIMY	SOLID
SCALD	SEVEN	SHUNT	SLING	SOLUS
SCALE	SEVER	SHYLY	SLINK	SOLVE
SCALP	SEWER	SIBYL	SLOOP	SONIC
SCALY	SHACK	SIDED	SLOPE	SONNY
SCAMP	SHADE	SIDLE	SLOSH	SOOTH
SCANT	SHADY	SIEGE	SLOTH	SOOTY
SCARE	SHAFT	SIEVE	SLUMP	SOPPY
SCARF	SHAKE	SIGHT	SLUNG	SORBO
SCARP	SHAKO	SIGMA	SLUNK	SORER
SCENA	SHAKY	SILKY	SLUSH	SORRY
SCENE	SHALE	SILLY	SLYLY	SOUGH
SCENT	SHALL	SINCE	SMACK	SOUND
SCION	SHALT	SINEW	SMALL	SOUPY
SCOFF	SHAME	SINGE	SMART	SOUSE
SCOLD	SHANK	SINUS	SMASH	SOUTH
SCONE	SHAPE	SIOUX	SMEAR	SOWAR
SCOOP	SHARD	SIRED	SMELL	SOWED
SCOOT	SHARE	SIREN	SMELT	SOWER
SCOPE	SHARK	SISAL	SMILE	SPACE
SCORE	SHARP	SISSY	SMIRK	SPADE
SCORN	SHAVE	SIXTH	SMITE	SPAHI
SCOTS	SHAWL	SIXTY	SMITH	SPAKE
SCOUR	SHEAF	SIZED	SMOCK	SPANK
SCOUT	SHEAR	SKATE	SMOKE	SPARE
SCOWL	SHEEN	SKEAN	SMOKY	SPARK
SCRAG	SHEEP	SKEIN	SMOTE	SPASM
SCRAM	SHEER	SKIED	SNACK	SPATE
SCRAP	SHEET	SKIER	SNAIL	SPAWN
SCREE	SHEIK	SKIFF	SNAKE	SPEAK
SCREW	SHELF	SKILL	SNAKY	SPEAR
SCRIM	SHELL	SKIMP	SNARE	SPECK
SCRIP	SHEWN	SKINK	SNARL	SPECS
SCRUB	SHIED	SKIRL	SNATH	SPEED
SCRUM	SHIFT	SKIRT	SNEAD	SPELL
SCUFF	SHINE	SKULK	SNEAK	SPELT
SCULL	SHINY	SKULL	SNEER	SPEND
SCURF	SHIRE	SKUNK	SNICK	SPERM
SEAMY	SHIRK	SLACK	SNIDE	SPICE
SEDAN	SHIRT	SLADE	SNIFF	SPICK
SEDGE	SHOAL	SLAIN	SNIPE	SPICY
SEEDY	SHOCK	SLAKE	SNOEK	SPIED
SEINE	SHONE	SLANG	SNOOD	SPIKE
SEIZE	SHOOK	SLANT	SNOOP	SPIKY
SENNA	SHOOT	SLASH	SNORE	SPILL
SENSE	SHORE	SLATE	SNORT	SPILT

SPINE	STEEP	SUITE	TALLY	THINK
SPINY	STEER	SULKS	TALON	THIRD
SPIRE	STEIN	SULKY	TAMED	THOLE
SPITE	STERN	SULLY	TAMER	THONG
SPLAY	STICK	SUNNY	TAMIL	THORN
SPLIT	STIFF	SUN-UP	TAMMY	THOSE
SPODE	STILE	SUPER	TANGO	THREE
SPOIL	STILL	SURER	TANGY	THREW
SPOKE	STILT	SURGE	TANSY	THROB
SPOOF	STING	SURLY	TAPED	THROE
SPOOK	STINK	SWAIN	TAPER	THROW
SPOOL	STINT	SWALE	TAPIR	THUMB
SPOON	STOAT	SWAMP	TARDY	THUMP
SPOOR	STOCK	SWANK	TAROT	THYME
SPORE	STOEP	SWARD	TARRY	TIARA
SPORT	STOIC	SWARF	TASTE	TIBET
SPOUT	STOKE	SWARM	TATTY	TIBIA
SPRAT	STOLE	SWATS	TAUNT	TIDAL
SPRAY	STOMA	SWEAR	TAWNY	TIDED
SPREE	STONE	SWEAT	TAXED	TIGER
SPRIG	STONY	SWEDE	TEACH	TIGHT
SPRIT	STOOD	SWEEP	TEASE	TILED
SPUME	STOOK	SWEET	TEDDY	TILER
SPURN	STOOL	SWELL	TEENS	TILTH
SPURT	STOOP	SWEPT	TEENY	TIMED
SQUAB	STORE	SWIFT	TEETH	TIMID
SQUAD	STORK	SWILL	TEHEE	TIMON
SQUAT	STORM	SWINE	TEMPO	TINED
SQUAW	STORY	SWING	TEMPT	TINGE
SQUIB	STOUP	SWIPE	TENCH	TINNY
SQUID	STOUR	SWIRL	TENET	TIPSY
STACK	STOUT	SWISH	TENON	TIRED
STAFF	STOVE	SWISS	TENOR	TITAN
STAGE	STRAD	SWOON	TENSE	TITHE
STAGY	STRAP	SWOOP	TENTH	TITLE
STAID	STRAW	SWORD	TEPEE	TIZZY
STAIN	STRAY	SWORE	TEPID	TOADY
STAIR	STREW	SWORN	TEPOR	TOAST
STAKE	STRIP	SWUNG	TERRA	TODAY
STALE	STROP	SYLPH	TERRY	TODDY
STALK	STRUM	SYNOD	TERSE	TOKAY
STALL	STRUT	SYRUP	TESTY	TOKEN
STAMP	STUCK		THANE	TOMMY
STAND	STUDY		THANK	TONAL
STANK	STUFF	T – 5	THEFT	TONED
STARE	STUMP		THEIR	TONGA
STARK	STUNG	TABBY	THEME	TONIC
START	STUNK	TABLE	THERE	TOOTH
STATE	STUNT	TABOO	THERM	TOPAZ
STAVE	STYLE	TACIT	THESE	TOPEE
STEAD	STYLO	TACKY	THETA	TOPER
STEAK	SUAVE	TAFFY	THICK	TOPIC
STEAL	SUEDE	TAILS	THIEF	TOQUE
STEAM	SUETY	TAINT	THIGH	TORCH
STEED	SUGAR	TAKEN	THINE	TORSO
STEEL	SUING	TAKER	THING	TOTAL
		TALES		

TOTEM	TULIP	UNLET	VILLA	WEEDY
TOTED	TULLE	UNMAN	VIOLA	WEEPY
TOUCH	TUNED	UNPEG	VIPER	WEIGH
TOUGH	TUNER	UNPEN	VIRGO	WEIRD
TOWED	TUNIS	UNPIN	VIRTU	WELSH
TOWEL	TUNNY	UNSET	VIRUS	WENCH
TOWER	TURFY	UNTIE	VISIT	WHACK
TOWNY	TURPS	UNTIL	VISOR	WHALE
TOXIC	TUTOR	UNWED	VISTA	WHANG
TOXIN	TUTTI	UP-END	VITAL	WHARF
TOYED	TWAIN	UPPER	VIVAT	WHEAT
TRACE	TWANG	UPSET	VIVID	WHEEL
TRACK	TWEAK	URBAN	VIZOR	WHELK
TRACT	TWEED	URGED	VOCAL	WHELP
TRADE	TWEEN	URIAL	VODKA	WHERE
TRAIL	TWERP	USAGE	VOGUE	WHICH
TRAIN	TWICE	USHER	VOICE	WHIFF
TRAMP	TWILL	USING	VOILE	WHILE
TRASH	TWINE	USUAL	VOMIT	WHINE
TRAWL	TWINS	USURP	VOTED	WHIRL
TREAD	TWIRL	USURY	VOTER	WHISK
TREAT	TWIST	UTTER	VOUCH	WHIST
TREED	TWITE	UVULA	VOWED	WHITE
TREND	TWIXT		VOWEL	WHIZZ
TRESS	TYING		VYING	WHOLE
TREWS	TYPED	**V – 5**		WHOOP
TRIAL				WHORL
TRIBE		VAGUE		WHOSE
TRICE	**U – 5**	VALET	**W – 5**	WHOSO
TRICK		VALID		WIDEN
TRIED	U-BOAT	VALSE	WADED	WIDER
TRIER	UDDER	VALUE	WADER	WIDOW
TRILL	UHLAN	VALVE	WAFER	WIDTH
TRIPE	UKASE	VANED	WAGED	WIELD
TRITE	ULCER	VAPID	WAGER	WIGHT
TROLL	ULNAR	VASTY	WAGES	WILLY
TRONC	ULTRA	VAULT	WAGON	WINCE
TROOP	UMBEL	VAUNT	WAIST	WINCH
TROTH	UMBER	VELDT	WAITS	WINDY
TROUT	UMBRA	VENAL	WAIVE	WINED
TROVE	UNAPT	VENOM	WAKEN	WIPED
TRUCE	UNARM	VENUE	WALTZ	WIPER
TRUCK	UNBAR	VENUS	WANED	WIRED
TRUER	UNBID	VERGE	WANLY	WISER
TRULY	UNCLE	VERSE	WARES	WISPY
TRUMP	UNCUT	VERSO	WASHY	WITCH
TRUNK	UNDER	VERST	WASTE	WITHY
TRUSS	UNDID	VERVE	WATCH	WITTY
TRUST	UNDUE	VESPA	WATER	WIVES
TRUTH	UNFED	VESTA	WAVED	WODEN
TRY-ON	UNFIT	VETCH	WAVER	WOMAN
TRYST	UNFIX	VEXED	WAXED	WOMEN
TUBBY	UNIFY	VIAND	WAXEN	WOODY
TUBED	UNION	VICAR	WEALD	WOOED
TUBER	UNITE	VIDEO	WEARY	WOOER
TUDOR	UNITY	VIGIL	WEAVE	WORDY
	UNLED	VILER	WEDGE	
			WEEDS	

WORLD	WRATH	WRYLY	YAHOO	YOUTH
WORMY	WREAK		YAWED	YUCCA
WORRY	WRECK		YEARN	
WORSE	WREST	**X – 5**	YEAST	
WORST	WRING		YIELD	**Z – 5**
WORTH	WRIST	XEBEC	YODEL	
WOULD	WRITE	X-RAYS	YOKED	ZEBRA
WOUND	WRONG		YOKEL	ZEBUS
WOVEN	WROTE	**Y – 5**	YOUNG	ZINCO
WRACK	WRUNG	YACHT	YOURS	ZONAL
				ZONED

A – 6	ADVENT	ALPINI	ARCTIC
	ADVERT	ALUMNA	ARDENT
ABACUS	ADVICE	ALUMNI	ARDOUR
ABASED	ADVISE	ALWAYS	ARGALI
ABATED	AENEID	AMAZED	ARGENT
ABBESS	AERATE	AMAZON	ARGOSY
ABDUCT	AERIAL	AMBLED	ARGUED
ABIDED	AFFAIR	AMBLER	ARIGHT
ABJECT	AFFECT	AMBUSH	ARISEN
ABJURE	AFFIRM	AMOEBA	ARMADA
ABLAZE	AFFORD	AMORAL	ARMIES
ABLEST	AFFRAY	AMOUNT	ARMING
ABLOOM	AFGHAN	AMPERE	ARMLET
ABOARD	AFLAME	AMPLER	ARMOUR
ABOUND	AFLOAT	AMULET	ARMPIT
ABRADE	AFRAID	AMUSED	ARNICA
ABROAD	AFRESH	ANCHOR	AROUND
ABRUPT	AGARIC	ANCONA	AROUSE
ABSENT	AGEING	ANGINA	ARRACK
ABSORB	AGENCY	ANGLED	ARRANT
ABSURD ·	AGENDA	ANGLER	ARREAR
ABUSED	AGHAST	ANGOLA	ARREST
ACACIA	AGNATE	ANGORA	ARRIVE
ACCEDE	AGOING	ANIMAL	ARTERY
ACCENT	AGOUTI	ANIMUS	ARTFUL
ACCEPT	AGREED	ANKLET	ARTIST
ACCESS	AIDING	ANNALS	ASCEND
ACCORD	AILING	ANNEAL	ASCENT
ACCOST	AIMING	ANNEXE	ASHAKE
ACCRUE	AIR-BED	ANNUAL	ASHLAR
ACETIC	AIRBUS	ANOINT	ASHORE
ACHING	AIR-GUN	ANONYM	ASH-PAN
ACIDIC	AIRILY	ANSWER	ASH-PIT
ACK-ACK	AIRING	ANTHEM	ASKANT
ACQUIT	AIRMAN	ANTHER	ASKARI
ACROSS	AIR-SAC	ANTLER	ASKING
ACTING	AIRWAY	ANYHOW	ASLANT
ACTION	AKIMBO	ANYWAY	ASLEEP
ACTIVE	ALARUM	APACHE	ASPECT
ACTUAL	ALBEIT	APATHY	ASPIRE
ACUITY	ALBERT	APIARY	ASSAIL
ACUMEN	ALBINO	APIECE	ASSENT
ADAGIO	ALBION	APLOMB	ASSERT
ADDICT	ALCOVE	APPEAL	ASSESS
ADDING	ALIGHT	APPEAR	ASSIGN
ADDLED	ALKALI	APPEND	ASSIST
ADDUCE	ALLEGE	ARABIC	ASSIZE
ADHERE	ALLIED	ARABIS	ASSORT
ADJOIN	ALLIES	ARABLE	ASSUME
ADJURE	ALL-OUT	ARBOUR	ASSURE
ADJUST	ALLUDE	ARCADE	ASTERN
ADMIRE	· ALLURE	ARCADY	ASTHMA
ADONIS	ALMOND	ARCHED	ASTRAL
ADORED	ALMOST	ARCHER	ASTRAY
ADRIFT	ALPACA	ARCHLY	ASTUTE
ADROIT	ALPINE	ARCING	ASYLUM

ATHENE	BAILIE	BARTON	BEGGAR
AT-HOME	BAITED	BASALT	BEGGED
ATKINS	BAKERY	BASELY	BEGONE
ATOMIC	BAKING	BASHED	BEHALF
ATONED	BALAAM	BASING	BEHAVE
ATTACH	BALDER	BASKED	BEHEAD
ATTACK	BALDLY	BASKET	BEHELD
ATTAIN	BALEEN	BASQUE	BEHEST
ATTEND	BALING	BASSET	BEHIND
ATTEST	BALKAN	BASTED	BEHOLD
ATTIRE	BALKED	BATEAU	BELDAM
ATTUNE	BALLÁD	BATHED	BELFRY
AUBURN	BALLET	BATHER	BELIAL
AUGURY	BALLOT	BATHOS	BELIED
AUGUST	BALSAM	BATMAN	BELIEF
AUNTIE	BALTIC	BATTED	BELLOW
AURIST	BAMBOO	BATTEN	BELONG
AURORA	BANANA	BATTER	BELTED
AUSSIE	BANDED	BATTLE	BEMOAN
AUSTER	BANDIT	BAUBLE	BEMUSE
AUSTIN	BANGED	BAWBEE	BENDER
AUTHOR	BANGLE	BAWLED	BENGAL
AUTUMN	BANISH	BAWLEY	BENIGN
AVAUNT	BANKED	BAXTER	BENNET
AVENGE	BANKER	BAYARD	BENUMB
AVENUE	BANNED	BAYEUX	BENZOL
AVERSE	BANNER	BAYING	BERATE
AVIARY	BANTAM	BAZAAR	BERBER
AVIDLY	BANTER	BEACHY	BEREFT
AVOCET	BANYAN	BEACON	BERLIN
AVOWAL	BANZAI	BEADED	BERTHA
AVOWED	BAOBAB	BEADLE	BESIDE
AWAKEN	BARBED	BEAGLE	BESTED
AWEIGH	BARBEL	BEAKER	BESTIR
AWHEEL	BARBER	BEAMED	BESTOW
AWHILE	BARDIC	BEARER	BETAKE
AWNING	BARELY	BEATEN	BETHEL
AYE-AYE	BAREST	BEATER	BETIDE
AZALEA	BARGED	BEAUNE	BETONY
	BARGEE	BEAUTY	BETRAY
	BARING	BEAVER	BETTED
B – 6	BARIUM	BECALM	BETTER
	BARKED	BECAME	BETTOR
BAAING	BARKER	BECKET	BEWAIL
BABBLE	BARKIS	BECKON	BEWARE
BABOON	BARLEY	BECOME	BEYOND
BACKED	BARMAN	BEDAUB	BIASED
BACKER	BARNEY	BED-BUG	BIBBER
BACKUP	BARONY	BEDDED	BICEPS
BADGER	BARQUE	BEDDER	BICKER
BAFFLE	BARRED	BEDECK	BIDDER
BAGFUL	BARREL	BEDLAM	BIDDING
BAGGED	BARREN	BEETLE	BIFFED
BAGMAN	BARROW	BEFALL	BIGAMY
BAGNIO	BARSAC	BEFORE	BIG-END
BAILED	BARTER	BEFOUL	BIGGER

BIG-WIG	BOLDLY	BRASSY	BUMPED
BIKING	BOLERO	BRAVED	BUMPER
BILKED	BOLTED	BRAVER	BUNDLE
BILKER	BOMBED	BRAWNY	BUNGED
BILLED	BON-BON	BRAZED	BUNGLE
BILLET	BONDED	BRAZEN	BUNION
BILLIE	BONING	BREACH	BUNKED
BILLOW	BONNET	BREAST	BUNKER
BINARY	BONNIE	BREATH	BUNKUM
BINDER	BOODLE	BREECH	BUNSEN
BIONIC	BOOHOO	BREEKS	BUNTER
BIRDIE	BOOING	BREEZE	BUOYED
BISECT	BOOKED	BREEZY	BURBLE
BISHOP	BOOKIE	BRETON	BURDEN
BISLEY	BOOMED	BREVET	BUREAU
BISTRO	BOOTED	BREWED	BURGEE
BITING	BOOTEE	BREWER	BURGLE
BITTEN	BO-PEEP	BRIBED	BURIAL
BITTER	BORAGE	BRIDAL	BURIED
BLAMED	BORDER	BRIDGE	BURMAN
BLANCH	BOREAS	BRIDLE	BURNED
BLARED	BORING	BRIGHT	BURNER
BLAZED	BORROW	BRITON	BURNET
BLAZER	BORZOI	BROACH	BURRED
BLEACH	BOSCHE	BROADS	BURROW
BLEARY	BOSSED	BROGAN	BURSAR
BLENNY	BOSTON	BROGUE	BURTON
BLIGHT	BOTANY	BROKEN	BUSHEL
BLITHE	BOTHER	BROKER	BUSIED
BLONDE	BOTHIE	BROLLY	BUSILY
BLOODY	BOTTLE	BRONCO	BUSKER
BLOTCH	BOTTOM	BRONZE	BUSMEN
BLOTTO	BOUFFE	BROOCH	BUSTED
BLOUSE	BOUGHT	BROODY	BUSTER
BLOWED	BOUNCE	BROUGH	BUSTLE
BLOWER	BOUNTY	BROWSE	BUTANE
BLOWZY	BOURSE	BRUISE	BUTLER
BLUEST	BOVINE	BRUTAL	BUTTED
BLUING	BOWERY	BRUTUS	BUTTER
BLUISH	BOWING	BRYONY	BUTTON
BOATER	BOWLED	BUBBLE	BUYING
BOBBED	BOWLER	BUBBLY	BUZZED
BOBBIN	BOWMAN	BUCKED	BUZZER
BOBBLE	BOW-SAW	BUCKET	BYE-BYE
BODEGA	BOW-TIE	BUCKLE	BYGONE
BODGER	BOW-WOW	BUDDED	BYPASS
BODICE	BOXING	BUDDHA	BY-PLAY
BODILY	BOYISH	BUDGET	BY-ROAD
BODING	BRACED	BUFFED	BYWORD
BODKIN	BRACER	BUFFER	
BOFFIN	BRAHMA	BUFFET	C – 6
BOGGLE	BRAINY	BUGLER	
BOG-OAK	BRAISE	BULGAR	CABLED
BOILED	BRAKED	BULGED	CABMAN
BOILER	BRANCH	BULKED	CACHED
BOLDER	BRANDY	BULLET	CACHET

CACHOU	CARDED	CENSOR	CHUKKA
CACKLE	CAREEN	CENSUS	CHUMMY
CACTUS	CAREER	CENTRE	CHURCH
CADDIE	CARESS	CEREAL	CICADA
CADDIS	CARFAX	CERISE	CICELY
CADGED	CARIES	CHAFED	CICERO
CADGER	CARMAN	CHAFER	CINDER
CAESAR	CARMEN	CHAISE	CINEMA
CAGING	CARNAL	CHALET	CINQUE
CAHOOT	CARNET	CHALKY	CIPHER
CAIMAN	CARPED	CHANCE	CIRCLE
CAIQUE	CARPEL	CHANCY	CIRCUS
CAJOLE	CARPET	CHANGE	CIRRUS
CAKING	CARROT	CHANTY	CITING
CALICO	CARTED	CHAPEL	CITRIC
CALIPH	CARTEL	CHAPPY	CITRON
CALLER	CARTER	CHARGE	CITRUS
CALLOW	CARTON	CHARON	CIVICS
CALMED	CARVED	CHASED	CLAMMY
CALMLY	CASHED	CHASER	CLARET
CALVED	CASHEW	CHASSE	CLASSY
CAMBER	CASING	CHASTE	CLAUSE
CAMERA	CASINO	CHATTY	CLAWED
CAMLET	CASKET	CHEEKY	CLAYEY
CAMPED	CASSIA	CHEERY	CLEAVE
CAMPER	CASTLE	CHEESE	CLENCH
CAMPUS	CASTOR	CHEESY	CLERGY
CANAPE	CASUAL	CHEQUE	CLERIC
CANARD	CATCHY	CHERRY	CLEVER
CANARY	CATGUT	CHERUB	CLEVIS
CANCAN	CATHAY	CHESTY	CLICHE
CANCEL	CATKIN	CHEVAL	CLIENT
CANCER	CATNIP	CHEWED	CLIMAX
CANDID	CATSUP	CHILDE	CLINCH
CANDLE	CATTLE	CHILLI	CLINIC
CANINE	CAUCUS	CHILLY	CLIQUE
CANING	CAUDAL	CHIMED	CLOCHE
CANKER	CAUGHT	CHINTZ	CLOSED
CANNED	CAUSED	CHIPPY	CLOSER
CANNON	CAVEAT	CHIRPY	CLOSET
CANNOT	CAVERN	CHISEL	CLOTHE
CANOPY	CAVIAR	CHITTY	CLOUDY
CANTAB	CAVIES	CHOICE	CLOVEN
CANTED	CAVING	CHOKED	CLOVER
CANTER	CAVITY	CHOKER	CLOYED
CANTON	CAVORT	CHOLER	CLUMSY
CANTOR	CAXTON	CHOOSE	CLUTCH
CANUCK	CAYMAN	CHOOSY	COARSE
CANVAS	CAYUSE	CHOPIN	COATED
CANYON	CEASED	CHOPPY	COATEE
CAPFUL	CEDING	CHORAL	COAXED
CAPPED	CELERY	CHORUS	COAXER
CAPTOR	CELLAR	CHOSEN	COBALT
CARAFE	CELTIC	CHOUGH	COBBLE
CARBON	CEMENT	CHROME	COBNUT
CARBOY	CENSER	CHUBBY	COBURG

COBWEB	CONVOY	COWLED	CURACY
COCKED	COOEED	COW-MAN	CURARE
COCKER	COOING	COWRIE	CURATE
COCKLE	COOKED	COYOTE	CURBED
COCOON	COOKER	CRABBY	CURDLE
CODDED	COOKIE	CRADLE	CURFEW
CODGER	COOLED	CRAFTY	CURING
CODIFY	COOLER	CRAGGY	CURLED
CODING	COOLIE	CRAMBO	CURLER
CODLIN	COOLLY	CRANED	CURLEW
COERCE	COOPED	CRANKY	CURSED
COEVAL	COOPER	CRANNY	CURSOR
COFFEE	COPECK	CRATED	CURTLY
COFFER	COPIED	CRATER	CURTSY
COFFIN	COPIER	CRAVAT	CURVED
COGENT	COPING	CRAVED	CUSTOM
COGNAC	COPPED	CRAVEN	CUTEST
CO-HEIR	COPPER	CRAYON	CUTLER
COHERE	COPTIC	CRAZED	CUTLET
COHORT	COQUET	CREAMY	CUT-OFF
COILED	CORBEL	CREASE	CUT-OUT
COINED	CORDED	CREATE	CUTTER
COINER	CORDON	CRECHE	CUTTLE
COKING	CORKED	CREDIT	CYBORG
COLDER	CORKER	CREEPY	CYCLED
COLDLY	CORNEA	CREOLE	CYGNET
COLLIE	CORNED	CRESTA	CYMBAL
COLLOP	CORNER	CRETIN	CYMRIC
COLONY	CORNET	CREWEL	CYPHER
COLOUR	CORONA	CRIKEY	CYPRUS
COLUMN	CORPSE	CRINGE	
COMBAT	CORPUS	CRISES	
COMBED	CORRAL	CRISIS	**D – 6**
COMBER	CORSET	CRISPY	
COMEDY	CORTES	CRITIC	DABBED
COMELY	COSHED	CROCUS	DABBLE
COMFIT	COSIER	CROTCH	DACOIT
COMING	COSILY	CROUCH	DAFTLY
COMMIT	COSINE	CROWED	DAGGER
COMMON	COSMIC	CRUDER	DAHLIA
COMPEL	COSMOS	CRUISE	DAINTY
COMPLY	COSSET	CRUMBY	DAMAGE
CONCHY	COSTER	CRUNCH	DAMASK
CONCUR	COSTLY	CRUSTY	DAMMED
CONNED	COTTAR	CRUTCH	DAMNED
CONDOR	COTTER	CRYING	DAMPED
CONFAB	COTTON	CUBISM	DAMPEN
CONFER	COUGAR	CUBIST	DAMPER
CONGEE	COUPLE	CUCKOO	DAMPLY
CONGER	COUPON	CUDDLE	DAMSEL
CONKED	COURSE	CUDGEL	DAMSON
CONKER	COUSIN	CULLED	DANCED
CONSUL	COVERT	CUPFUL	DANCER
CONTRA	COWARD	CUPOLA	DANDER
CONVEX	COWBOY	CUPPED	DANDLE
CONVEY	COWING	CUP-TIE	DANGER
			DANGLE

DANIEL	DEFAME	DETOUR	DISTIL
DANISH	DEFEAT	DETUNE	DISUSE
DAPHNE	DEFECT	DEUCED	DITHER
DAPPER	DEFEND	DEVICE	DIVERS
DAPPLE	DEFIED	DEVISE	DIVERT
DARING	DEFILE	DEVOID	DIVEST
DARKEN	DEFINE	DEVOTE	DIVIDE
DARKER	DEFORM	DEVOUR	DIVINE
DARKLY	DEFRAY	DEVOUT	DIVING
DARNED	DEFTLY	DEWLAP	DOBBIN
DARNEL	DEFUSE	DEXTER	DOCILE
DARNER	DEGREE	DIADEM	DOCKED
DARTED	DE-ICER	DIAPER	DOCKER
DASHED	DEJECT	DIATOM	DOCKET
DATING	DELETE	DIBBED	DOCTOR
DATIVE	DELUDE	DIBBER	DODDER
DAUBED	DELUGE	DIBBLE	DODGED
DAVITS	DEMAND	DICING	DODGER
DAWDLE	DEMEAN	DICKER	DOFFED
DAWNED	DEMISE	DICKEY	DOG-FOX
DAY-BED	DEMODE	DICTUM	DOGGED
DAY-FLY	DEMOTE	DIDDLE	DOINGS
DAZING	DEMURE	DIESEL	DOLING
DAZZLE	DENIAL	DIETED	DOLLAR
DEACON	DENIED	DIFFER	DOLLED
DEADEN	DENIER	DIGEST	DOLLOP
DEADLY	DENOTE	DIGGER	DOLMEN
DEAFEN	DENSER	DIK-DIK	DOLOUR
DEAFLY	DENTAL	DIKING	DOMAIN
DEALER	DENUDE	DILATE	DOMINO
DEARER	DEODAR	DILUTE	DONATE
DEARIE	DEPART	DIMITY	DONGLE
DEARLY	DEPEND	DIMMED	DONJON
DEARTH	DEPICT	DIMMER	DONKEY
DEBASE	DEPLOY	DIMPLE	DOODLE
DEBATE	DEPORT	DIMPLY	DOOMED
DEBRIS	DEPOSE	DINGHY	DOPING
DEBTOR	DEPUTE	DINGLE	DORCAS
DEBUNK	DEPUTY	DINING	DORIAN
DECADE	DERAIL	DINKUM	DORMER
DECAMP	DERATE	DINNED	DORSAL
DECANT	DERIDE	DINNER	DOSAGE
DECEIT	DERIVE	DIPOLE	DOTAGE
DECENT	DERMAL	DIPPED	DOTARD
DECIDE	DERMIS	DIPPER	DOTING
DECKED	DESCRY	DIRECT	DOTTED
DECKLE	DESERT	DIREST	DOTTLE
DECODE	DESIGN	DISARM	DOUANE
DECREE	DESIRE	DISBAR	DOUBLE
DEDUCE	DESIST	DISBUD	DOUCHE
DEDUCT	DESPOT	DISCUS	DOUGHY
DEEMED	DETACH	DISHED	DOURLY
DEEPEN	DETAIL	DISMAL	DOUSED
DEEPER	DETAIN	DISMAY	DOWNED
DEEPLY	DETECT	DISOWN	DOWSED
DEFACE	DETEST	DISPEL	DOWSER

DOYLEY	E – 6	EMBODY	EREBUS
DOZING		EMBOSS	ERENOW
DRACHM	EAGLET	EMBRYO	ERMINE
DRAGON	EAR-CAP	EMERGE	ERODED
DRAPED	EARFUL	EMETIC	EROTIC
DRAPER	EARNED	EMIGRE	ERRAND
DRAWER	EARTHY	EMPIRE	ERRANT
DREAMT	EARWIG	EMPLOY	ERRATA
DREAMY	EASIER	ENABLE	ERRING
DREARY	EASILY	ENAMEL	ERSATZ
DREDGE	EASING	ENCAGE	ESCAPE
DRENCH	EASTER	ENCAMP	ESCHEW
DRESSY	EATING	ENCASE	ESCORT
DRIEST	EBBING	ENCASH	ESCUDO
DRIVEL	ECARTE	ENCORE	ESKIMO
DRIVEN	ECHOED	END-ALL	ESPIAL
DRIVER	ECLAIR	ENDEAR	ESPIED
DRONED	ECZEMA	ENDING	ESPRIT
DROPSY	EDDIED	ENDIVE	ESSENE
DROVER	EDGING	ENDURE	ESTATE
DROWSY	EDIBLE	ENERGY	ESTEEM
DRUDGE	EDITED	ENFOLD	ETCHED
DRY-BOB	EDITOR	ENGAGE	ETCHER
DRY-FLY	EDUCED	ENGINE	ETHICS
DRYING	EERILY	ENGULF	ETHNIC
DRYISH	EFFACE	ENIGMA	EUCHRE
DRY-ROT	EFFECT	ENJOIN	EUCLID
DUBBED	EFFETE	ENLACE	EULOGY
DUBBIN	EFFIGY	ENLIST	EUNUCH
DUCKED	EFFLUX	ENMESH	EUREKA
DUENNA	EFFORT	ENMITY	EUSTON
DUFFEL	EGG-CUP	ENNEAD	EVADED
DUFFER	EGGING	ENOUGH	EVENER
DUFFLE	EGG-NOG	ENRAGE	EVENLY
DUGONG	EGOISM	ENRICH	EVILLY
DUGOUT	EGOIST	ENROBE	EVINCE
DUIKER	EGRESS	ENSIGN	EVOLVE
DULCET	EIFFEL	ENSUED	EXCEED
DULLED	EIGHTH	ENSURE	EXCEPT
DULLER	EIGHTY	ENTAIL	EXCESS
DUMBLY	EITHER	ENTICE	EXCISE
DUMDUM	ELAINE	ENTIRE	EXCITE
DUMPED	ELAPSE	ENTITY	EXCUSE
DUNLIN	ELATED	ENTOMB	EXEMPT
DUNNED	ELDEST	ENTRAP	EXEUNT
DUPING	ELEVEN	ENTREE	EXHALE
DURBAR	ELFISH	ENVIED	EXHORT
DURESS	ELICIT	ENWRAP	EXHUME
DURHAM	ELIXIR	ENZYME	EXILED
DURING	ELOPED	EOCENE	EXODUS
DUSTER	ELUDED	EOLITH	EXOTIC
DUYKER	ELVISH	EQUATE	EXPAND
DYEING	ELYSEE	EQUINE	EXPECT
DYNAMO	EMBALM	EQUITY	EXPEND
DYNAST	EMBARK	ERASED	EXPERT
	EMBLEM	ERASER	EXPIRE

EXPIRY	FATTED	FILLET	FLIGHT
EXPORT	FATTEN	FILLIP	FLIMSY
EXPOSE	FATTER	FILMED	FLINCH
EXTANT	FAUCET	FILTER	FLINTY
EXTEND	FAULTY	FILTHY	FLITCH
EXTENT	FAVOUR	FINALE	FLOPPY
EXTORT	FAWNED	FINDER	FLORAL
EXUDED	FEALTY	FINELY	FLORET
EYEFUL	FEARED	FINERY	FLORID
EYEING	FEDORA	FINEST	FLORIN
EYELET	FEEBLE	FINGER	FLOSSY
EYELID	FEEBLY	FINIAL	FLOURY
	FEEDER	FINING	FLOWER
	FEELER	FINISH	FLUENT
F – 6	FELINE	FINITE	FLUFFY
	FELLAH	FINNAN	FLUKED
FABIAN	FELLED	FINNED	FLUNKY
FABLED	FELLER	FIRING	FLURRY
FABRIC	FELLOE	FIRKIN	FLUTED
FACADE	FELLOW	FIRMED	FLUXED
FACIAL	FELONY	FIRMLY	FLYING
FACILE	FELTED	FISCAL	FLY-NET
FACING	FEMALE	FISHED	FOALED
FACTOR	FENCED	FISHER	FOAMED
FADING	FENCER	FISHES	FOBBED
FAERIE	FENDED	FISTED	FO'C'SLE
FAG-END	FENDER	FISTIC	FODDER
FAGGED	FENIAN	FITFUL	FOEMAN
FAGGOT	FENNEL	FITTED	FOETID
FAILED	FERRER	FITTER	FOGGED
FAIRER	FERRET	FIXING	FOIBLE
FAIRLY	FERVID	FIXITY	FOILED
FAKING	FESCUE	FIZZED	FOKKER
FALCON	FESTAL	FIZZER	FOLDED
FALLAL	FESTER	FIZZLE	FOLDER
FALLEN	FETISH	FLABBY	FOLLOW
FALLOW	FETTER	FLAGON	FOMENT
FALSER	FETTLE	FLAKED	FONDER
FALTER	FEUDAL	FLAMED	FONDLE
FAMILY	FEWEST	FLANGE	FONDLY
FAMINE	FIACRE	FLANKS	FOOLED
FAMISH	FIANCÉ	FLARED	FOOTED
FAMOUS	FIASCO	FLASHY	FOOTER
FANGED	FIBBED	FLATLY	FOOTLE
FANNED	FIBBER	FLATTY	FOOZLE
FAN-TAN	FIBULA	FLAUNT	FORAGE
FARINA	FICKLE	FLAVIN	FORBID
FARING	FIDDLE	FLAXEN	FORBYE
FARMED	FIDGET	FLAYED	FORCED
FARMER	FIERCE	FLEDGE	FORDED
FARROW	FIGARO	FLEECE	FOREGO
FASCIA	FIGURE	FLEECY	FOREST
FASTED	FILIAL	FLESHY	FORGED
FASTEN	FILING	FLEXED	FORGER
FASTER	FILLED	FLEXOR	FORGET
FATHER	FILLER	FLICKS	FORGOT
FATHOM			

FORKED	FURROW	GAS-BAG	GIVING
FORMAL	FUSING	GASCON	GLADLY
FORMAT	FUSION	GASHED	GLANCE
FORMED	FUSSED	GASKET	GLARED
FORMER	FUTILE	GAS-MAN	GLASSY
FORMIC	FUTURE	GASPED	GLAZED
FOSSIL		GASPER	GLAZER
FOSTER		GASSED	GLIBLY
FOUGHT	**G – 6**	GATEAU	GLIDED
FOULED	GABBLE	GATHER	GLIDER
FOULLY	GABLED	GATING	GLITCH
FOURTH	GADDED	GAUCHE	GLOBAL
FOWLER	GADFLY	GAUCHO	GLOOMY
FOXILY	GADGET	GAUGED	GLORIA
FOXING	GAELIC	GAYEST	GLOSSY
FRACAS	GAFFED	GAZEBO	GLOVED
FRAMED	GAFFER	GAZING	GLOVER
FRAPPÉ	GAGGED	GEARED	GLOWED
FRAYED	GAGGLE	GEEZER	GLOWER
FREELY	GAIETY	GEIGER	GLUING
FREEZE	GAINED	GEISHA	GLUMLY
FRENCH	GAITER	GEMINI	GLYTCH
FRENZY	GALAXY	GENDER	GNAWED
FRESCO	GALLEY	GENERA	GNOMON
FRIARY	GALLIC	GENEVA	GOADED
FRIDAY	GALLON	GENIAL	GOATEE
FRIDGE	GALLOP	GENIUS	GO-BANG
FRIEND	GALLUP	GENTLE	GOBBET
FRIEZE	GALOOT	GENTLY	GOBBLE
FRIGHT	GALORE	GENTRY	GOBLET
FRIGID	GALOSH	GEORGE	GOBLIN
FRINGE	GAMBIT	GERMAN	GO-CART
FRISKY	GAMBLE	GERUND	GO-DOWN
FROGGY	GAMBOL	GEW-GAW	GODSON
FROLIC	GAMELY	GEYSER	GODWIT
FROSTY	GAMING	GHARRY	GOFFER
FROTHY	GAMMER	GHETTO	GOGGLE
FROWSY	GAMMON	GIBBER	GOITRE
FROZEN	GANDER	GIBBET	GOLDEN
FRUGAL	GANGER	GIBBON	GOLFER
FRUITY	GANNET	GIBING	GONGED
FRUMPY	GANTRY	GIBLET	GOODLY
FUDDLE	GAOLED	GIFTED	GOOGLY
FUDGED	GAOLER	GIGGLE	GOPHER
FULFIL	GAPING	GIGOLO	GORGED
FULHAM	GARAGE	GILDED	GORGET
FULLER	GARBLE	GILDER	GORGIO
FULMAR	GARCON	GILLIE	GORGON
FUMBLE	GARDEN	GILPIN	GORING
FUNDED	GARGLE	GIMBAL	GOSHEN
FUNGUS	GARISH	GIMLET	GOSPEL
FUNKED	GARLIC	GINGER	GOSSIP
FUNNEL	GARNER	GIRDED	GOTHIC
FURIES	GARNET	GIRDER	GOUGED
FURLED	GARRET	GIRDLE	GOVERN
FURORE	GARTER	GITANA	GOWNED

GRACED	GULLET	HARKEN	HERALD
GRACES	GULLEY	HARLOT	HERBAL
GRADED	GULPED	HARMED	HERDED
GRAINS	GUMMED	HARPED	HEREAT
GRAMME	GUN-MAN	HARRIS	HEREBY
GRANGE	GUN-MEN	HARROW	HEREIN
GRANNY	GUNNEL	HASTEN	HEREOF
GRASSY	GUNNER	HAT-BOX	HEREON
GRATER	GUN-SHY	HATING	HERESY
GRATIS	GURGLE	HAT-PEG	HERETO
GRAVEL	GURKHA	HAT-PIN	HERMES
GRAVEN	GURNET	HATRED	HERMIT
GRAVER	GUSHED	HATTED	HERNIA
GRAVES	GUSHER	HATTER	HEROIC
GRAZED	GUSSET	HAULED	HEROIN
GREASE	GUTTED	HAUNCH	HERPES
GREASY	GUTTER	HAVANA	HERREN
GREATS	GUZZLE	HAVING	HETMAN
GREECE	GYBING	HAWHAW	HEWING
GREEDY	GYPSUM	HAWKED	HEYDAY
GREENS	GYRATE	HAWKER	HIATUS
GRETNA		HAWSER	HICCUP
GRIEVE		HAYBOX	HIDDEN
GRILLE	**H – 6**	HAZARD	HIDING
GRILSE		HAZILY	HIEING
GRIMED	HACKED	HEADED	HIGHER
GRIMLY	HACKER	HEADER	HIGHLY
GRINGO	HACKLE	HEALED	HIKING
GRIPED	HAGGIS	HEALER	HILARY
GRIPPE	HAGGLE	HEALTH	HINDER
GRISLY	HAILED	HEAPED	HINDOO
GRITTY	HALLOA	HEARER	HINGED
GROATS	HALLOW	HEARSE	HINTED
GROCER	HALOED	HEARTH	HIPPED
GROGGY	HALTED	HEARTY	HIRING
GROOVE	HALTER	HEATED	HISSED
GROPED	HALVED	HEATER	HITHER
GROTTO	HAMLET	HEAVED	HITTER
GROUND	HAMMAM	HEAVEN	HOARSE
GROUSE	HAMMER	HEBREW	HOAXED
GROVEL	HAMPER	HECATE	HOAXER
GROWER	HANDED	HECKLE	HOBBLE
GROWTH	HANDLE	HECTIC	HOBNOB
GROYNE	HANGAR	HECTOR	HOCKEY
GRUBBY	HANGED	HEDGED	HOEING
GRUDGE	HANGER	HEEDED	HOGGET
GRUMPY	HANKER	HEE-HAW	HOLDER
GRUNDY	HANSEL	HEELED	HOLD-UP
GUFFAW	HANSOM	HEIFER	HOLIER
GUIDED	HAPPEN	HEIGHT	HOLILY
GUIDER	HARASS	HELIUM	HOLLOW
GUIDON	HARDEN	HELMET	HOMAGE
GUILTY	HARDER	HELPED	HOMELY
GUINEA	HARDLY	HELPER	HOMILY
GUITAR	HARD-UP	HEMMED	HOMING
GULLED	HARING	HEMPEN	HONEST
	HARKED		

HONING	HUSKED	INDIAN	INVOKE
HONKED	HUSSAR	INDICT	INWARD
HONOUR	HUSSIF	INDIGO	IODINE
HOODED	HUSTLE	INDITE	IONIAN
HOODIE	HUTTED	INDOOR	IRITIS
HOODOO	HYBRID	INDUCE	IRKING
HOOFED	HYMNAL	INDUCT	IRONED
HOOKAH	HYPHEN	INFAMY	IRONER
HOOKED	HYSSOP	INFANT	IRONIC
HOOKER		INFECT	ISABEL
HOOPED		INFEST	ISLAND
HOOPER	I – 6	INFIRM	ISOBAR
HOOP-LA		INFLOW	ISRAEL
HOOPOE	IAMBIC	INFLUX	ISSUED
HOOTED	IBERIA	INFORM	ISSUER
HOOTER	IBIDEM	INFUSE	ITALIC
HOPING	ICARUS	INHALE	ITCHED
HOPPED	ICE-AGE	INHERE	ITSELF
HOPPER	ICE-AXE	INJECT	
HORNED	ICE-CAP	INJURE	
HORNER	ICE-MAN	INJURY	J – 6
HORNET	ICE-SAW	INK-BAG	
HORRID	ICICLE	INKING	JABBED
HORROR	ICIEST	INK-POT	JABBER
HOSIER	IDIOCY	INK-SAC	JACKAL
HOSTEL	IDLING	INLAID	JACKED
HOTBED	IGNITE	INLAND	JACKET
HOT-DOG	IGNORE	INMATE	JAGGED
HOT-POT	IGUANA	INMOST	JAGUAR
HOTTER	ILLUDE	INNATE	JAILED
HOURLY	ILLUME	INROAD	JAILER
HOUSED	IMBIBE	INRUSH	JAMMED
HOWDAH	IMBUED	INSANE	JANGLE
HOWLED	IMMUNE	INSECT	JARGON
HOWLER	IMMURE	INSERT	JARRED
HOYDEN	IMPACT	INSIDE	JASPER
HUBBUB	IMPAIR	INSIST	JAUNTY
HUDDLE	IMPALA	INSOLE	JAWING
HUFFED	IMPALE	INSPAN	JAZZED
HUGELY	IMPART	INSTAL	JEERED
HUMANE	IMPEDE	INSTEP	JENNET
HUMBLE	IMPEND	INSTIL	JERBOA
HUMBLY	IMPISH	INSULT	JERKED
HUMBUG	IMPORT	INSURE	JERKIN
HUMMED	IMPOSE	INTACT	JERSEY
HUMOUR	IMPOST	INTAKE	JESTED
HUMPED	IMPUGN	INTEND	JESTER
HUNGER	IMPURE	INTENT	JESUIT
HUNGRY	IMPUTE	INTERN	JETSAM
HUNTED	INBORN	INTONE	JEWESS
HUNTER	INBRED	INURED	JEWISH
HURDLE	INCHED	INVADE	JIBBED
HURLED	INCISE	INVENT	JIGGED
HURRAH	INCITE	INVERT	JIGGLE
HURTLE	INCOME	INVEST	JIG-SAW
HUSHED	INDEED	INVITE	JILTED
	INDENT		JINGLE

JITTER	KEYPAD	LAID-UP	LEAFED
JOBBER	KIBOSH	LAMBED	LEAGUE
JOB-LOT	KICKED	LAMELY	LEAKED
JOCKEY	KICKER	LAMENT	LEANED
JOCOSE	KIDDED	LAMINA	LEANER
JOCUND	KIDDER	LAMING	LEAN-TO
JOGGED	KIDNAP	LAMMAS	LEAPED
JOHNNY	KIDNEY	LAMMED	LEASED
JOINED	KILLED	LANCED	LEAVEN
JOINER	KILLER	LANCER	LEAVER
JOKING	KILTED	LANCET	LEDGER
JOLTED	KILTIE	LANDAU	LEERED
JORDAN	KIMONO	LANDED	LEEWAY
JOSEPH	KINDER	LAPDOG	LEGACY
JOSSER	KINDLE	LAPFUL	LEGATE
JOSTLE	KINDLY	LAPPED	LEGATO
JOTTED	KINEMA	LAPSED	LEG-BYE
JOVIAL	KINGLY	LARDED	LEGEND
JOYFUL	KINKED	LARDER	LEGGED
JOYOUS	KIPPER	LARGER	LEGION
JUDAIC	KIRSCH	LARIAT	LEGIST
JUDGED	KIRTLE	LARRUP	LEGUME
JUGFUL	KISMET	LARVAE	LENDER
JUGGED	KISSED	LARVAL	LENGTH
JUGGLE	KISSER	LARYNX	LENTEN
JUJUBE	KITBAG	LASCAR	LENTIL
JULIAN	KITSCH	LASHED	LESION
JUMBLE	KITTEN	LASSIE	LESSEE
JUMPED	KLAXON	LASTED	LESSEN
JUMPER	KLUDGE	LASTLY	LESSER
JUNGLE	KNIFED	LATEEN	LESSON
JUNIOR	KNIGHT	LATELY	LESSOR
JUNIUS	KNOBBY	LATENT	LETHAL
JUNKER	KNOTTY	LATEST	LET-OFF
JUNKET	KOODOO	LATHER	LETTER
JURIST	KOREAN	LATTER	LEVANT
JUSTER	KOSHER	LAUDED	LEVITE
JUSTLY	KOWTOW	LAUDER	LEVITY
JUTTED	KULTUR	LAUNCH	LEWDLY
	KUMMEL	LAUREL	LEYDEN
		LAVING	LIABLE
K – 6		LAVISH	LIAISE
	L – 6	LAWFUL	LIBYAN
KAFFIR		LAWYER	LICHEN
KAISER	LAAGER	LAXITY	LICKED
KANAKA	LABIAL	LAYING	LIDDED
KAOLIN	LABOUR	LAYMAN	LIEDER
KEELED	LACING	LAY-OUT	LIFTED
KEENED	LACKED	LAZIER	LIFTER
KEENER	LACKEY	LAZILY	LIGNUM
KEENLY	LACTIC	LAZING	LIKELY
KEEPER	LADDER	LAZULI	LIKING
KENNEL	LADDIE	LEADED	LIMBED
KERNEL	LADING	LEADEN	LIMBER
KERSEY	LADLED	LEADER	LIMING
KETTLE	LAGGED	LEAD-IN	LIMPED
KEY-MEN	LAGOON		

LIMPET	LOLLOP	MAGNET	MARSHY
LIMPID	LONELY	MAGNUM	MARTEN
LINAGE	LONGER	MAGPIE	MARTIN
LINDEN	LOOFAH	MAGYAR	MARTYR
LINEAL	LOOKED	MAHOUT	MARVEL
LINEAR	LOOKER	MAIDEN	MASCOT
LINE-UP	LOOMED	MAIGRE	MASHED
LINGER	LOOPED	MAILED	MASHER
LINING	LOOPER	MAIMED	MASHIE
LINKED	LOOSEN	MAINLY	MASKED
LINNET	LOOTED	MAKE-UP	MASKER
LINTEL	LOOTER	MAKING	MASQUE
LIONEL	LOPING	MALADY	MASSED
LIPPED	LOPPED	MALAGA	MASSIF
LIQUID	LORDED	MALICE	MASTED
LIQUOR	LORDLY	MALIGN	MASTER
LISBON	LOSING	MALLET	MASTIC
LISPED	LOTION	MALLOW	MATING
LISSOM	LOUDER	MALTED	MATINS
LISTED	LOUDLY	MAMMAL	MATRIX
LISTEN	LOUNGE	MAMMON	MATRON
LISTER	LOUVRE	MANAGE	MATTED
LITANY	LOVELY	MANANA	MATTER
LITCHI	LOVING	MANCHU	MATURE
LITMUS	LOWEST	MANEGE	MAULED
LITTER	LOWING	MANFUL	MAUNDY
LITTLE	LUBBER	MANGER	MAUSER
LIVELY	LUFFED	MANGLE	MAY-BUG
LIVERY	LUGGED	MANIAC	MAYDAY
LIVING	LUGGER	MANIOC	MAYFLY
LIZARD	LULLED	MANNED	MAYHAP
LLOYD'S	LUMBAR	MANNER	MAYHEM
LOADED	LUMBER	MANTEL	MEADOW
LOADER	LUMPED	MANTIS	MEAGRE
LOAFED	LUNACY	MANTLE	MEALIE
LOAFER	LUNATE	MANTUA	MEANLY
LOANED	LUNGED	MANUAL	MEASLY
LOATHE	LUPINE	MANURE	MEDDLE
LOBATE	LURING	MAOIST	MEDIAL
LOBBED	LURKED	MAPPED	MEDIAN
LOCALE	LUSTED	MAQUIS	MEDICO
LOCATE	LUSTRE	MARAUD	MEDIUM
LOCKED	LUTINE	MARBLE	MEDLAR
LOCKER	LUXURY	MARCEL	MEDLEY
LOCKET	LYCEUM	MARGIN	MEDUSA
LOCK-UP		MARIAN	MEEKER
LOCUST		MARINE	MEEKLY
LODGED	**M – 6**	MARKED	MEETLY
LODGER		MARKER	MEGILP
LOFTED	MACRON	MARKET	MEGOHM
LOGGED	MADCAP	MARMOT	MEGRIM
LOGGIA	MADDEN	MAROON	MELLOW
LOG-HUT	MADDER	MARQUE	MELODY
LOGMAN	MADMAN	MARRED	MELTED
LOITER	MADRAS	MARRON	MELTER
LOLLED	MAENAD	MARROW	MELTON
	MAGGOT		

MEMBER	MINCED	MONDAY	MUMBLE
MEMOIR	MINCER	MONGOL	MUMMER
MEMORY	MINDED	MONIES	MURDER
MENACE	MINDER	MONIED	MURMUR
MENAGE	MINGLE	MONKEY	MURPHY
MENDED	MINIFY	MONODY	MUSCAT
MENDER	MINING	MOOING	MUSCLE
MENIAL	MINION	MOONED	MUSEUM
MENTAL	MINNIE	MOONER	MUSING
MENTOR	MINNOW	MOOTED	MUSKET
MERCER	MINOAN	MOOTER	MUSLIM
MERELY	MINTED	MOPING	MUSLIN
MERGED	MINUET	MOPISH	MUSSED
MERGER	MINUTE	MOPPED	MUSSEL
MERINO	MIRAGE	MOPPET	MUSTER
MERLIN	MIRING	MORALE	MUTATE
MERMAN	MIRROR	MORASS	MUTELY
MESHED	MISCUE	MORBID	MUTING
MESSED	MISERE	MORGUE	MUTINY
METEOR	MISERY	MORMON	MUTISM
METHOD	MISFIT	MOROSE	MUTTER
METHYL	MISHAP	MORRIS	MUTTON
METIER	MISLAY	MORROW	MUTUAL
METING	MISLED	MORSEL	MUZZLE
METRIC	MISSAL	MORTAL	MYOPIA
METTLE	MISSED	MORTAR	MYOPIC
MEWING	MISSEL	MOSAIC	MYRIAD
MIASMA	MISSIS	MOSLEM	MYRTLE
MICKLE	MISTER	MOSQUE	MYSELF
MICRON	MISUSE	MOSTLY	MYSTIC
MID-AIR	MITRAL	MOTHER	
MIDDAY	MITRED	MOTION	
MIDDEN	MITTEN	MOTIVE	N – 6
MIDDLE	MIXING	MOTLEY	
MIDGET	MIZZEN	MOTTLE	NAGGED
MID-OFF	MOANED	MOULDY	NAGGER
MID-RIB	MOATED	MOUNTY	NAILED
MIDWAY	MOBBED	MOUSER	NAILER
MIGHTY	MOBCAP	MOUSSE	NAMELY
MIGNON	MOBILE	MOUTHY	NAMING
MIKADO	MOB-LAW	MOVIES	NAPERY
MILADY	MOCKED	MOVING	NAPKIN
MILDEN	MOCKER	MOWING	NAPPED
MILDER	MODENA	MUCKED	NARROW
MILDEW	MODERN	MUCKER	NATANT
MILDLY	MODEST	MUCKLE	NATION
MILIEU	MODIFY	MUCOUS	NATIVE
MILKED	MODISH	MUDDLE	NATTER
MILKEN	MODULE	MUD-PIE	NATURE
MILKER	MOHAIR	MUFFED	NAUGHT
MILLED	MOHAWK	MUFFIN	NAUSEA
MILLER	MOIETY	MUFFLE	NEAPED
MILLET	MOLOCH	MUGGED	NEARBY
MILORD	MOLEST	MULISH	NEARER
MIMING	MOLTEN	MULLED	NEARLY
MIMOSA	MOMENT	MULLET	NEATLY
			NEBULA

NECKED	NOOSED	OBSESS	OPTIME
NECTAR	NORDIC	OBTAIN	OPTING
NEED-BE	NORMAL	OBTUSE	OPTION
NEEDED	NORMAN	OBVERT	ORACLE
NEEDER	NORROY	OCCULT	ORALLY
NEEDLE	NO-SIDE	OCCUPY	ORANGE
NEEDLY	NOSING	OCELOT	ORATED
NEGATE	NOTARY	O'CLOCK	ORATOR
NEPHEW	NOTICE	OCTANE	ORCHID
NEREID	NOTIFY	OCTANT	ORDAIN
NERVED	NOTING	OCTAVE	ORDEAL
NESTED	NOTION	OCTAVO	ORDURE
NESTLE	NOUGAT	OCULAR	ORGASM
NESTOR	NOUGHT	ODDITY	ORGIES
NETHER	NOVENA	ODIOUS	ORIENT
NETTED	NOVICE	OEDEMA	ORIGAN
NETTLE	NOWAYS	OFFEND	ORIGIN
NEUTER	NOWISE	OFFICE	ORIOLE
NEWISH	NOZZLE	OFFING	ORISON
NIBBED	NUANCE	OFFISH	ORMULU
NIBBLE	NUBIAN	OFFSET	ORNATE
NICELY	NUBILE	OGLING	ORPHAN
NICENE	NUCLEI	OGRESS	ORPHIC
NICEST	NUDELY	OILCAN	OSIRIS
NICETY	NUDGED	OIL-GAS	OSMIUM
NICHED	NUDISM	OILING	OSPREY
NICKED	NUDIST	OILMAN	OSSIFY
NICKEL	NUDITY	OIL-NUT	OSTEND
NICKER	NUGGET	OLDEST	OSTLER
NIGGER	NUMBED	OLDISH	OTIOSE
NIGGLE	NUMBER	OLIVER	OUSTED
NIMBLE	NUNCIO	OLIVET	OUTBID
NIMBLY	NURSED	OMELET	OUTCRY
NIMBUS	NURSER	OMENED	OUTDID
NIMROD	NUTANT	OMNIUM	OUTFIT
NINETY	NUTMEG	ONAGER	OUTFLY
NIPPED	NUT-OIL	ONCOST	OUTING
NIPPER	NUTRIA	ONE-MAN	OUTLAW
NIPPLE	NUZZLE	ONE-WAY	OUTLAY
NITRIC	NYBBLE	ONFLOW	OUTLET
NITWIT		ONIONY	OUTPUT
NO-BALL		ON-LINE	OUTRUN
NOBBLE	O – 6	ONRUSH	OUTSET
NOBLER		ONWARD	OUTWIT
NOBODY	OAFISH	OODLES	OVALLY
NODDED	OARAGE	OOLITE	OVERDO
NODDER	OARING	OOZING	OWLERY
NODDLE	OBELUS	OPAQUE	OWLISH
NODOSE	OBERON	OPENED	OWNING
NODULE	OBEYED	OPENER	OXALIC
NOGGIN	OBEYER	OPENLY	OX-EYED
NONAGE	OBITER	OPIATE	OXFORD
NONARY	OBJECT	OPINED	OXLIKE
NON-COM	OBLATE	OPPOSE	OXTAIL
NON-EGO	OBLIGE	OPPUGN	OXYGEN
NOODLE	OBLONG	OPTICS	OYSTER
	OBOIST		

P – 6	PARISH	PEARLY	PHAROS
	PARITY	PEBBLE	PHENOL
PACIFY	PARKED	PEBBLY	PHLEGM
PACING	PARKER	PECKED	PHOBIA
PACKED	PARKIN	PECKER	PHOEBE
PACKER	PARLEY	PECTEN	PHONED
PACKET	PARODY	PECTIC	PHONEY
PADDED	PAROLE	PECTIN	PHONIC
PADDER	PARROT	PEDANT	PHRASE
PADDLE	PARSED	PEDATE	PHYSIC
PADUAN	PARSEE	PEDDLE	PIAZZA
PAGING	PARSON	PEDLAR	PICKED
PAGODA	PARTED	PEELED	PICKER
PAINED	PARTER	PEELER	PICKET
PAIRED	PARTLY	PEEPED	PICKLE
PALACE	PASSED	PEEPER	PICKUP
PALATE	PASSEE	PEERER	PICNIC
PALELY	PASSER	PEEVED	PICRIC
PALING	PASSIM	PEEWIT	PIDGIN
PALISH	PASTED	PEGGED	PIECED
PALLAS	PASTEL	PEG-LEG	PIECER
PALLED	PASTIL	PEGTOP	PIEDOG
PALLET	PASTOR	PELLET	PIEMAN
PALLID	PASTRY	PELMET	PIERCE
PALLOR	PATCHY	PELOTA	PIFFLE
PALMAR	PATENT	PELVIC	PIGEON
PALMED	PATHIC	PELVIS	PIGNUT
PALMER	PATHOS	PENCIL	PIG-STY
PALTER	PATINA	PENMAN	PILAFF
PALTRY	PATOIS	PENNED	PILFER
PAMPAS	PATROL	PENNON	PILING
PAMPER	PATRON	PENTAD	PILLAR
PANADA	PATTED	PENT-UP	PILLAU
PANAMA	PATTEN	PENULT	PILLED
PANDER	PATTER	PENURY	PILLOW
PANDIT	PAUNCH	PEOPLE	PILULE
PANFUL	PAUPER	PEPPER	PIMPLE
PANNED	PAUSED	PEPSIN	PIMPLY
PANTED	PAUSER	PEPTIC	PINCER
PANTER	PAVAGE	PERIOD	PINDAR
PANTRY	PAVANE	PERISH	PINEAL
PANZER	PAVING	PERKED	PINGED
PAPACY	PAWING	PERMIT	PINING
PAPERY	PAWNED	PERSON	PINION
PAPISH	PAWNEE	PERTLY	PINKED
PAPISM	PAWNER	PERUKE	PINNED
PAPIST	PAWPAW	PERUSE	PIPING
PAPUAN	PAY-DAY	PESETA	PIPKIN
PARADE	PAYING	PESTER	PIPPED
PARCEL	PAY-OFF	PESTLE	PIPPIN
PARDON	PEACHY	PETARD	PIQUED
PAREIL	PEAHEN	PETITE	PIQUET
PARENT	PEAKED	PETREL	PIRACY
PARGET	PEALED	PETROL	PIRATE
PARIAH	PEANUT	PETTED	PISCES
PARING	PEA-POD	PEWTER	PISTIL

PISTOL	POETRY	POTION	PROTON
PISTON	POGROM	POT-LID	PROVED
PITCHY	POISED	POTMAN	PROVEN
PITIED	POISER	POTTED	PROVER
PITIER	POISON	POTTER	PRUNED
PITMAN	POKING	POUDRE	PRYING
PITSAW	POLICE	POUFFE	PSEUDO
PITTED	POLICY	POUNCE	PSYCHE
PLACED	POLING	POURED	PUBLIC
PLACER	POLISH	POURER	PUCKER
PLACET	POLITE	POUTED	PUDDLE
PLACID	POLITY	POUTER	PUFFED
PLAGUE	POLLED	POWDER	PUFFIN
PLAGUY	POLLEN	POW-WOW	PUG-DOG
PLAICE	POLLUX	PRAISE	PUISNE
PLAINT	POLONY	PRANCE	PUKKHA
PLANED	POMACE	PRATED	PULING
PLANER	POMADE	PRATER	PULLED
PLANET	POMMEL	PRAYED	PULLER
PLAQUE	POMONA	PRAYER	PULLET
PLASHY	POM-POM	PREACH	PULLEY
PLASMA	POMPON	PRECIS	PULPED
PLATAN	PONDER	PREFAB	PULPIT
PLATED	POODLE	PREFER	PULQUE
PLATEN	POOLED	PREFIX	PULSED
PLATER	POOPED	PREPAY	PUMICE
PLAYED	POORER	PRESET	PUMMEL
PLAYER	POORLY	PRESTO	PUMPED
PLEACH	POPERY	PRETOR	PUMPER
PLEASE	POPGUN	PRETTY	PUNCHY
PLEDGE	POPISH	PRE-WAR	PUNDIT
PLEIAD	POPLAR	PREYED	PUNIER
PLENTY	POPLIN	PREYER	PUNISH
PLENUM	POPPED	PRICED	PUNNET
PLEURA	POPPER	PRIDED	PUNTED
PLEXUS	POPPET	PRIEST	PUNTER
PLIANT	PORING	PRIMAL	PUPPED
PLIERS	PORKER	PRIMER	PUPPET
PLIGHT	PORKET	PRIMLY	PURDAH
PLINTH	POROUS	PRIMUS	PURELY
PLOUGH	PORTAL	PRINCE	PUREST
PLOVER	PORTER	PRIORY	PURGED
PLUCKY	PORTLY	PRISED	PURGER
PLUG-IN	POSEUR	PRISMY	PURIFY
PLUMED	POSING	PRISON	PURISM
PLUMPY	POSSET	PRIVET	PURIST
PLUNGE	POSSUM	PRIZED	PURITY
PLURAL	POSTAL	PROFIT	PURLED
PLUSHY	POSTED	PROLIX	PURLER
PLYERS	POSTER	PROMPT	PURPLE
PLYING	POTASH	PRONTO	PURRED
POCKED	POTATO	PROPEL	PURSED
POCKET	POTBOY	PROPER	PURSER
PODDED	POTEEN	PROSED	PURSUE
PODIUM	POTENT	PROSER	PURVEY
POETIC	POTHER	PROSIT	PUSHED

PUSHER	RADIUM	RASTER	REDDEN
PUTRID	RADIUS	RASURE	REDEEM
PUTSCH	RAFFIA	RATHER	RED-EYE
PUTTED	RAFFLE	RATIFY	RED-GUM
PUTTEE	RAFTER	RATING	RED-HOT
PUTTER	RAGGED	RATION	RED-OAK
PUZZLE	RAGING	RATTAN	REDRAW
PYEDOG	RAGLAN	RAT-TAT	REDUCE
PYEMIA	RAGMAN	RATTED	REDUIT
PYEMIC	RAGOUT	RATTER	RE-DYED
PYOSIS	RAG-TAG	RATTLE	RE-ECHO
PYRENE	RAIDED	RAVAGE	REEDED
PYRITE	RAIDER	RAVINE	REEFED
PYTHON	RAILED	RAVING	REEFER
	RAILER	RAVISH	REEKED
Q – 6	RAINED	RAWISH	REELED
	RAISED	RAZING	REELER
QUAGGA	RAISER	READER	REFILL
QUAGGY	RAISIN	REALLY	REFINE
QUAINT	RAJPUT	REALTY	REFLEX
QUAKED	RAKERY	REAMED	REFLOW
QUAKER	RAKING	REAMER	REFLUX
QUANGO	RAKISH	REAPED	REFOLD
QUARRY	RAMBLE	REAPER	REFOOT
QUARTO	RAMIFY	REARED	REFORM
QUARTZ	RAMMED	REARER	REFUEL
QUAVER	RAMMER	REASON	REFUGE
QUAYED	RAMPED	REAVOW	REFUND
QUEASY	RAMROD	REBATE	REFUSE
QUENCH	RANCHO	REBECK	REFUTE
QUEUED	RANCID	REBIND	REGAIN
QUINCE	RANDOM	REBOIL	REGALE
QUINSY	RANGED	REBORN	REGARD
QUINZE	RANGER	REBUFF	REGENT
QUIRED	RANKER	REBUKE	REGILD
QUIRKY	RANKLE	REBURY	REGIME
QUIVER	RANKLY	RECALL	REGINA
QUORUM	RANSOM	RECANT	REGION
QUOTED	RANTED	RECAST	REGIUS
	RANTER	RECEDE	REGIVE
	RAPHIA	RECENT	REGLOW
R – 6	RAPIER	RECESS	REGNAL
	RAPINE	RECIPE	REGNUM
RABBIN	RAPING	RECITE	REGRET
RABBIT	RAPPED	RECKED	REHANG
RABBLE	RAPPER	RECKON	REHASH
RABIES	RAREFY	RECOAL	REHEAR
RACIAL	RARELY	RECOCT	REHEAT
RACILY	RAREST	RECOIL	REINED
RACING	RARITY	RECOIN	REJECT
RACKED	RASCAL	RECORD	REJOIN
RACKER	RASHER	RECOUP	RELAID
RACKET	RASHLY	RECTOR	RELATE
RACOON	RASING	RECUSE	RELENT
RADIAL	RASPED	REDACT	RELICT
RADIAN	RASPER	REDCAP	RELIED
RADISH			

RELIEF	RESOLD	RIGGER	ROOMED
RELIER	RESORB	RIGOUR	ROOMER
RELISH	RESORT	RIG-OUT	ROOTED
RELIVE	RESOWN	RILING	ROOTER
RELOAD	RESTED	RILLED	ROOTLE
RELUME	RESULT	RILLET	ROPERY
REMADE	RESUME	RIMMED	ROPING
REMAIN	RETAIL	RIMMED	ROSARY
REMAKE	RETAIN	RINDED	ROSERY
REMAND	RETAKE	RINGER	ROSIED
REMARK	RETARD	RINSED	ROSIER
REMAST	RETINA	RINSER	ROSILY
REMEDY	RETIRE	RIOTED	ROSINY
REMIND	RETOLD	RIOTER	ROSTER
REMISE	RETOOK	RIPELY	ROTARY
REMISS	RETORT	RIPEST	ROTATE
REMOTE	RETRIM	RIPPED	ROT-GUT
REMOVE	RETYRE	RIPPER	ROTTED
RENAME	REUTER	RIPPLE	ROTTEN
RENDER	REVAMP	RIPPLY	ROTTER
RENNET	REVEAL	RIPSAW	ROTUND
RENOWN	REVERE	RISING	ROUBLE
RENTAL	REVERS	RISKED	ROUGED
RENTED	REVERT	RISKER	ROUMAN
RENTER	REVIEW	RISQUE	ROUSED
RENTES	REVILE	RITUAL	ROUSER
RE-OPEN	REVIVE	RIVAGE	ROUTED
REPACK	REVOKE	RIVING	ROUTER
REPAID	REVOLT	ROAMED	ROVING
REPAIR	REVVED	ROAMER	ROWING
REPASS	REWARD	ROARED	RUBATO
REPAST	REWOOD	ROARER	RUBBED
REPEAL	REWORD	ROBBED	RUBBER
REPEAT	RHESUS	ROBBER	RUBBLE
REPENT	RHEUMY	ROBING	RUBBLY
REPINE	RHYMED	ROBUST	RUBIED
REPLAY	RHYMER	ROCKED	RUBRIC
REPORT	RHYTHM	ROCKER	RUCKLE
REPOSE	RIALTO	ROCKET	RUDDER
REPPED	RIBALD	ROCOCO	RUDELY
REPUGN	RIBAND	RODENT	RUDEST
REPUTE	RIBBED	ROILED	RUEFUL
REREAD	RIBBON	ROLAND	RUFFED
RESAIL	RICHER	ROLLED	RUFFLE
RESALE	RICHES	ROLLER	RUFOUS
RESCUE	RICHLY	ROMAIC	RUGATE
RESEAT	RICKED	ROMANY	RUGGED
RESECT	RIDDEN	ROMIST	RUGGER
RESELL	RIDDLE	ROMPED	RUGOSE
RESEND	RIDGED	ROMPER	RUINED
RESENT	RIDING	RONDEL	RUINER
RESHIP	RIFFLE	ROOFED	RULING
RESIDE	RIFLED	ROOFER	RUMBLE
RESIGN	RIFLER	ROOKED	RUMOUR
RESINY	RIFTED	ROOKER	RUMPLE
RESIST	RIGGED	ROOKIE	RUMPUS

RUNLET	SAMPLE	SCRAWL	SEISIN
RUNNEL	SANDAL	SCREAM	SEIZED
RUNNER	SANDED	SCREED	SEIZIN
RUNWAY	SANELY	SCREEN	SIEZOR
RUSHED	SANEST	SCREWY	SELDOM
RUSHER	SANIFY	SCRIBE	SELECT
RUSSET	SANITY	SCRIMP	SELENE
RUSSIA	SAPPED	SCRIPT	SELLER
RUSTED	SAPPER	SCROLL	SELVES
RUSTIC	SAPPHO	SCRUFF	SENATE
RUSTLE	SARONG	SCULPT	SENDER
RUTTED	SASHES	SCUMMY	SENILE
	SATEEN	SCURFY	SENIOR
S – 6	SATING	SCURRY	SENORA
	SATINY	SCURVY	SENSED
SABLED	SATIRE	SCUTUM	SENSOR
SACHET	SATRAP	SCYLLA	SENTRY
SACKED	SATURN	SCYTHE	SEPSIS
SACKER	SAUCED	SEA-COB	SEPTET
SACRED	SAUCER	SEA-COW	SEPTIC
SADDEN	SAVAGE	SEA-DOG	SEPTUM
SADDLE	SAVANT	SEA-FOX	SEQUEL
SADISM	SAVING	SEA-GOD	SEQUIN
SAFARI	SAVORY	SEA-HOG	SERAPH
SAFELY	SAVOUR	SEALED	SEREIN
SAFEST	SAVVEY	SEALER	SERENE
SAFETY	SAW-FLY	SEAMAN	SERIAL
SAGELY	SAWING	SEAMED	SERIES
SAGEST	SAW-PIT	SEAMER	SERMON
SAGGED	SAW-SET	SEA-MEW	SEROUS
SAHARA	SAWYER	SEANCE	SERVED
SAILED	SAXONY	SEARCH	SERVER
SAILER	SAYING	SEARED	SESAME
SAILOR	SCABBY	SEASON	SESTET
SALAAM	SCALED	SEATED	SET-OFF
SALAME	SCALER	SEA-WAY	SETOSE
SALARY	SCALES	SECANT	SET-OUT
SALINE	SCAMPI	SECEDE	SETTEE
SALIVA	SCANTY	SECOND	SETTER
SALLOW	SCARAB	SECRET	SETTLE
SALMON	SCARCE	SECTOR	SEVERE
SALOON	SCARED	SECUND	SÈVRES
SALTED	SCATHE	SECURE	SEWAGE
SALTER	SCATTY	SEDATE	SEWING
SALTLY	SCENIC	SEDUCE	SEXTAN
SALUKI	SCHEME	SEEDED	SEXTET
SALUTE	SCHISM	SEEDER	SEXTON
SALVED	SCHOOL	SEEING	SEXUAL
SALVER	SCILLA	SEEKER	SHABBY
SALVIA	SCONCE	SEEMED	SHADED
SAMELY	SCORCH	SEEMER	SHADOW
SAMIAN	SCORED	SEEMLY	SHAGGY
SAMITE	SCORER	SEEPED	SHAKEN
SAMLET	SCOTCH	SEE-SAW	SHAKER
SAMOAN	SCOTIA	SEETHE	SHAMED
SAMPAN	SCRAPE	SEISED	SHANTY

SHAPED	SIENNA	SKIMPY	SMITER
SHAPER	SIERRA	SKINNY	SMITHY
SHARED	SIESTA	SKYISH	SMOKED
SHARER	SIFTED	SLABBY	SMOKER
SHAVED	SIFTER	SLAKED	SMOOTH
SHAVER	SIGHED	SLANGY	SMOUCH
SHEARS	SIGHER	SLAP-UP	SMUDGE
SHEATH	SIGNAL	SLATED	SMUDGY
SHEIKH	SIGNED	SLATER	SMUGLY
SHEKEL	SIGNER	SLAVED	SMUTCH
SHELLY	SIGNET	SLAVER	SMUTTY
SHELVE	SIGNOR	SLAVEY	SNAGGY
SHELVY	SILAGE	SLAVIC	SNAKED
SHERRY	SILENT	SLAYER	SNAPPY
SHIELD	SILICA	SLEAZY	SNARED
SHIFTY	SILKEN	SLEDGE	SNARER
SHIMMY	SILLER	SLEEPY	SNATCH
SHINDY	SILTED	SLEETY	SNEEZE
SHINER	SILVAN	SLEEVE	SNIFFY
SHINTO	SILVER	SLEIGH	SNIPER
SHIRES	SIMIAL	SLEUTH	SNIPPY
SHIRTY	SIMIAN	SLEWED	SNITCH
SHIVER	SIMILE	SLICED	SNIVEL
SHOALY	SIMMER	SLICER	SNOBBY
SHODDY	SIMNEL	SLIDER	SNOOZE
SHOOED	SIMONY	SLIGHT	SNORED
SHOPPY	SIMPER	SLINKY	SNORER
SHORED	SIMPLE	SLIPPY	SNOTTY
SHORER	SIMPLY	SLITHY	SNOUTY
SHORTS	SINEWY	SLIVER	SNOWED
SHOULD	SINFUL	SLOGAN	SNUBBY
SHOVED	SINGED	SLOPED	SNUDGE
SHOVEL	SINGER	SLOPPY	SNUFFY
SHOVER	SINGLE	SLOUCH	SNUGLY
SHOWER	SINGLY	SLOUGH	SOAKED
SHRANK	SINKER	SLOVAK	SOAKER
SHREWD	SINNER	SLOVEN	SOAPED
SHRIEK	SIPHON	SLOWER	SOARED
SHRIFT	SIPPED	SLOWLY	SOBBED
SHRIKE	SIPPER	SLUDGE	SOCAGE
SHRILL	SIPPET	SLUDGY	SOCCER
SHRIMP	SIRDAR	SLUICE	SOCIAL
SHRINE	SIRING	SLUING	SOCKED
SHRINK	SIRIUS	SLUMPY	SOCKET
SHRIVE	SIRRAH	SLURRY	SODDEN
SHROUD	SISKIN	SLUSHY	SODIUM
SHROVE	SISTER	SLYEST	SO-EVER
SHRUNK	SITTER	SMALLS	SOFISM
SHUCKS	SIZING	SMARMY	SOFTEN
SHYING	SIZZLE	SMARTY	SOFTER
SICKER	SKATED	SMEARY	SOFTLY
SICKEN	SKATER	SMELLY	SOILED
SICKLE	SKERRY	SMILAX	SOIREE
SICKLY	SKETCH	SMILED	SOLACE
SIDING	SKEWER	SMILER	SOLDER
SIDLED	SKILLY	SMIRCH	SOLELY

SOLEMN	SPIRED	STARCH	STREAK
SO-LONG	SPIRIT	STARED	STREAM
SOLVED	SPITED	STARER	STREET
SOLVER	SPLASH	STARRY	STRESS
SOMBRE	SPLEEN	STARVE	STREWN
SONANT	SPLICE	STATED	STRIAE
SONATA	SPLINE	STATER	STRICT
SONNET	SPOKEN	STATIC	STRIDE
SOONER	SPONGE	STATUE	STRIFE
SOOTHE	SPONGY	STATUS	STRIKE
SOPPED	SPOOKY	STAVED	STRING
SOPPER	SPOONY	STAVES	STRIPE
SORBET	SPOTTY	STAYED	STRIVE
SORDID	SPOUSE	STAYER	STROBE
SORELY	SPRAIN	STAY-IN	STRODE
SOREST	SPRANG	STEADY	STROKE
SORREL	SPRAWL	STEAMY	STROLL
SORROW	SPREAD	STEELY	STRONG
SORTED	SPRENT	STENCH	STROVE
SORTER	SPRING	STEPPE	STRUCK
SORTIE	SPRINT	STEREO	STRUNG
SOUGHT	SPRITE	STEWED	STUBBY
SOURCE	SPROUT	STICKY	STUCCO
SOURER	SPRUCE	STIFLE	STUDIO
SOURLY	SPRUNG	STIGMA	STUFFY
SOUSED	SPRYER	STILLY	STUMER
SOVIET	SPUNKY	STINGO	STUMPS
SOWING	SPURGE	STINGY	STUMPY
SOZZLE	SPURRY	STITCH	STUPID
SPACED	SPYING	STOCKY	STUPOR
SPACER	SPYISM	STODGE	STURDY
SPADED	SQUALL	STODGY	STYLAR
SPADIX	SQUARE	STOKED	STYLED
SPARED	SQUASH	STOKER	STYLET
SPARER	SQUAWK	STOLEN	STYLUS
SPARES	SQUEAK	STOLID	STYMIE
SPARKS	SQUEAL	STONED	STYRAX
SPARRY	SQUILL	STONER	SUABLE
SPARSE	SQUINT	STOOGE	SUBDUE
SPAVIN	SQUIRE	STORED	SUBITO
SPECIE	SQUIRM	STORER	SUBLET
SPECKY	SQUIRT	STORES	SUBMIT
SPEECH	STABLE	STOREY	SUBORN
SPEEDY	STABLY	STORMY	SUBTIL
SPENCE	STAGED	STOVED	SUBTLE
SPHERE	STAGER	STOVER	SUBTLY
SPHINX	STAGEY	STOWED	SUBURB
SPICED	STAKED	STOWER	SUBWAY
SPIDER	STALAG	STRAFE	SUCKED
SPIGOT	STALER	STRAIN	SUCKER
SPIKED	STALKY	STRAIT	SUCKLE
SPINAL	STAMEN	STRAKE	SUDDEN
SPINED	STANCE	STRAND	SUEING
SPINET	STANCH	STRASS	SUFFER
SPINNY	STANZA	STRATA	SUFFIX
SPIRAL	STAPLE	STRAWY	SUGARY

SUITED	SYLVAN	TAOIST	TENDON
SUITOR	SYMBOL	TAPING	TENNER
SUIVEZ	SYNDIC	TAPPED	TENNIS
SULKED	SYNTAX	TAPPER	TENSER
SULLEN	SYPHON	TAPPET	TENSED
SULTAN	SYRIAC	TARGET	TENTED
SULTRY	SYRIAN	TARIFF	TENTER
SUMMED	SYRINX	TARMAC	TENURE
SUMMER	SYRUPY	TARPON	TENUTO
SUMMIT	SYSTEM	TARSAL	TEPEFY
SUMMON		TARSIA	TERCET
SUNBOW		TARSUS	TERMED
SUNDAE	T – 6	TARTAN	TERMLY
SUNDAY		TARTAR	TERROR
SUNDER	TABARD	TARTLY	TESTED
SUNDEW	TABBED	TASKED	TESTER
SUN-DOG	TABLED	TASKER	TETCHY
SUNDRY	TABLET	TASSEL	TETHER
SUN-GOD	TABOUR	TASTED	TETRAD
SUN-HAT	TACKED	TASTER	TEUTON
SUNKEN	TACKER	TATLER	THALER
SUNLIT	TACKLE	TATTED	THALIA
SUNNED	TACTIC	TATTER	THANKS
SUNSET	TAGGED	TATTLE	THATCH
SUN-TAN	TAGGER	TATTOO	THAWED
SUPERB	TAG-RAG	TAUGHT	THEBAN
SUPINE	TAILED	TAURUS	THEIRS
SUPPED	TAILOR	TAUTEN	THEISM
SUPPER	TAKE-IN	TAUTER	THEIST
SUPPLE	TAKING	TAVERN	THENAR
SUPPLY	TALBOT	TAWDRY	THENCE
SURELY	TALCKY	TAWING	THEORY
SUREST	TALENT	TAXIED	THESIS
SURETY	TALKED	TAXING	THETIS
SURGED	TALKER	TCHICK	THEWED
SURREY	TALLER	TEA-CUP	THIEVE
SURTAX	TALLOW	TEAMED	THINLY
SURVEY	TALMUD	TEA-POT	THIRST
SUTLER	TAMELY	TEARER	THIRTY
SUTTEE	TAMEST	TEASED	THORNY
SUTURE	TAMPED	TEASEL	THORPE
SVELTE	TAMPER	TEASER	THOUGH
SWAMPY	TAMPON	TEA-SET	THRALL
SWANKY	TAM-TAM	TEA-URN	THRASH
SWARDY	TANDEM	TEDIUM	THREAD
SWARMY	TANGED	TEEING	THREAT
SWATCH	TANGLE	TEEMED	THRESH
SWATHE	TANGLY	TEETER	THRICE
SWAYED	TANKED	TEETHE	THRIFT
SWEATY	TANKER	TELLER	THRILL
SWERVE	TANNED	TEMPER	THRIVE
SWINGE	TANNER	TEMPLE	THROAT
SWIPED	TANNIC	TENACE	THRONE
SWIPES	TANNIN	TENANT	THRONG
SWITCH	TANNOY	TENDED	THROVE
SWIVEL	TAOISM	TENDER	THROWN

THRUSH	TISANE	TOURED	TROUPE
THRUST	TISSUE	TOUSLE	TROWEL
THWACK	TITBIT	TOUTED	TRUANT
THWART	TITHED	TOUTER	TRUDGE
THYMOL	TITLED	TOWAGE	TRUEST
THYMUS	TITTER	TOWARD	TRUISM
TIBIAL	TITTUP	TOWERY	TRUSTY
TICKED	TOCSIN	TOWING	TRYING
TICKER	TODDLE	TOWSER	TRY-OUT
TICKET	TOE-CAP	TOY-BOX	TSETSE
TICKLE	TOEING	TOYING	TUBAGE
TICKLY	TOFFEE	TOYISH	TUBBED
TIC-TAC	TOGGED	TOY-MAN	TUBING
TIDIED	TOGGLE	TRACED	TUCKED
TIDIER	TOILED	TRACER	TUCKER
TIDILY	TOILER	TRADED	TUFFET
TIEING	TOILET	TRADER	TUFTED
TIE-PIN	TOLEDO	TRAGIC	TUGGED
TIERCE	TOLLED	TRANCE	TUGGER
TIE-WIG	TOLLER	TRAPES	TUMBLE
TIFFIN	TOMATO	TRAPPY	TUMOUR
TIGHTS	TOMBED	TRASHY	TUMULI
TILERY	TOMBOY	TRAUMA	TUMULT
TILING	TOM-CAT	TRAVEL	TUNDRA
TILLED	TOMTIT	TREATY	TUNE-IN
TILLER	TOMTOM	TREBLE	TUNING
TILTED	TONGUE	TREMOR	TUNNED
TILTER	TONING	TRENCH	TUNNEL
TIMBAL	TONISH	TRENDY	TUPPED
TIMBER	TONSIL	TREPAN	TURBAN
TIMBRE	TOOLED	TREPID	TURBID
TIMELY	TOOTED	TRIBAL	TURBOT
TIMING	TOOTER	TRICAR	TUREEN
TIMIST	TOOTHY	TRICKY	TURFED
TINDER	TOOTLE	TRICOT	TURGID
TINGED	TOO-TOO	TRIFID	TURKEY
TINGLE	TOP-DOG	TRIFLE	TURNED
TINIER	TOP-HAT	TRILBY	TURNER
TINKER	TOPMAN	TRIMLY	TURNIP
TINKLE	TOPPED	TRINAL	TURN-UP
TINMAN	TOPPER	TRIODE	TURRET
TINNED	TOPPLE	TRIPLE	TURTLE
TINNER	TORERO	TRIPLY	TUSCAN
TIN-POT	TORPID	TRIPOD	TUSKED
TINSEL	TORPOR	TRIPOS	TUSKER
TINTED	TORQUE	TRISTE	TUSSLE
TINTER	TORRID	TRITON	TU-WHIT
TIP-CAT	TOSSED	TRIUNE	TU-WHOO
TIP-OFF	TOSSER	TRIVET	TUXEDO
TIPPED	TOSS-UP	TROIKA	TWEENY
TIPPET	TOTING	TROJAN	TWELVE
TIPPLE	TOTTED	TROLLY	TWENTY
TIPTOE	TOTTER	TROPHY	TWIGGY
TIPTOP	TOUCAN	TROPIC	TWINED
TIRADE	TOUCHY	TROPPO	TWINER
TIRING	TOUPEE	TROUGH	TWINGE

TWITCH	UNFOLD	UNSEAL	UPTAKE
TWO-PLY	UNFREE	UNSEAM	UPTURN
TWOULD	UNFURL	UNSEAT	UPWARD
TWO-WAY	UNGEAR	UNSEEN	URAEUS
TYBURN	UNGILD	UNSENT	URANIA
TYCOON	UNGILT	UNSEWN	URANIC
TYPHUS	UNGIRD	UNSHED	URANUS
TYPIFY	UNGIRT	UNSHOD	URBANE
TYPING	UNGLUE	UNSHOT	URCHIN
TYPIST	UNGOWN	UNSHUT	URGENT
TYRANT	UNGUAL	UNSOLD	URGING
TYRIAN	UNHAND	UNSOWN	URSINE
	UNHANG	UNSPIN	USABLE
U – 6	UNHASP	UNSTOP	USANCE
	UNHEWN	UNSUNG	USEFUL
UBIETY	UNHOLY	UNSURE	USURER
UGLIER	UNHOOK	UNTACK	UTERUS
UGLIFY	UNHUNG	UNTAME	UTMOST
UGLILY	UNHURT	UNTIDY	UTOPIA
ULLAGE	UNIPED	UNTIED	UVULAR
ULSTER	UNIQUE	UNTOLD	
ULTIMO	UNISON	UNTORN	
UMBRAL	UNITED	UNTROD	**V – 6**
UMLAUT	UNITER	UNTRUE	
UMPIRE	UNJUST	UNTUCK	VACANT
UNABLE	UNKEPT	UNTUNE	VACATE
UNAWED	UNKIND	UNUSED	VACUUM
UNBEND	UNKNOT	UNVEIL	VAGARY
UNBENT	UNLACE	UNWARY	VAGUER
UNBIND	UNLAID	UNWELL	VAINER
UNBOLT	UNLASH	UNWEPT	VAINLY
UNBORN	UNLENT	UNWIND	VALISE
UNBRED	UNLESS	UNWIRE	VALLEY
UNCAGE	UNLIKE	UNWISE	VALLUM
UNCASE	UNLOAD	UNWORN	VALOUR
UNCATE	UNLOCK	UNWRAP	VALUED
UNCIAL	UNMADE	UNYOKE	VALUER
UNCLAD	UNMAKE	UPBEAR	VALVED
UNCLOG	UNMASK	UPCAST	VAMPED
UNCOIL	UNOWED	UPDATE	VAMPER
UNCORD	UNPACK	UPHILL	VANDAL
UNCORK	UNPAID	UPHOLD	VANISH
UNCURL	UNPICK	UPKEEP	VANITY
UNDATE	UNPROP	UPLAND	VAN-MAN
UNDIES	UNREAD	UPLEAN	VAPOUR
UNDINE	UNREAL	UPLIFT	VARIED
UNDOCK	UNREST	UP-LINE	VARIER
UNDOER	UNRIPE	UPMOST	VARLET
UNDONE	UNROBE	UPPING	VASSAL
UNDULY	UNROLL	UPPISH	VASTER
UNEASE	UNROOF	UPRISE	VASTLY
UNEASY	UNROOT	UPROAR	VAULTY
UNEVEN	UNROPE	UPROOT	VECTOR
UNFAIR	UNRULY	UPRUSH	VEERED
UNFEED	UNSAFE	UPSHOT	VEILED
UNFELT	UNSAID	UPSIDE	VEINED
			VELLUM

VELOCE	VIRTUE	WALRUS	WELDER
VELOUR	VISAGE	WAMBLE	WELKIN
VELVET	VISCID	WAMPUM	WELLED
VENDED	VISHNU	WANDER	WELTED
VENDEE	VIZIER	WANGLE	WELTER
VENDER	VISION	WANING	WENDED
VENDOR	VISUAL	WANTED	WET-BOB
VENDUE	VITALS	WANTER	WETHER
VENEER	VIVACE	WANTON	WETTER
VENERY	VIVIFY	WARBLE	WHALER
VENIAL	VIZARD	WAR-CRY	WHEEZE
VENITE	VOICED	WARDED	WHEEZY
VENTED	VOIDED	WARDEN	WHENCE
VERBAL	VOIDER	WARDER	WHERRY
VERGED	VOLANT	WARIER	WHILED
VERGER	VOLLEY	WARILY	WHILES
VERIFY	VOLUME	WARMER	WHILOM
VERILY	VOODOO	WARMLY	WHILST
VERITY	VORTEX	WARMTH	WHIMSY
VERMIN	VOTARY	WARNED	WHINED
VERNAL	VOTING	WARPED	WHINER
VERSED	VOTIVE	WARREN	WHINNY
VERSER	VOWING	WASHED	WHIPPY
VERSUS	VOYAGE	WASHER	WHISKY
VERTEX	VULCAN	WASH-UP	WHITEN
VERVET	VULGAR	WASTED	WHITER
VESPER		WASTER	WHITES
VESSEL		WATERY	WHOLLY
VESTAL	**W – 6**	WATTLE	WHOMSO
VESTED	WADDED	WAVING	WICKED
VESTRY	WADDLE	WAX-END	WICKER
VETOED	WADING	WAXIER	WICKET
VETTED	WAFERY	WAXING	WIDELY
VEXING	WAFFLE	WAYLAY	WIDEST
VIABLE	WAFTED	WEAKEN	WIELDY
VIANDS	WAFTER	WEAKER	WIFELY
VICTIM	WAGGED	WEAKLY	WIGEON
VICTOR	WAGGLE	WEALTH	WIGGED
VICUNA	WAGGON	WEANED	WIGGLE
VIEWED	WAGING	WEAPON	WIGWAM
VIEWER	WAILED	WEARER	WILDER
VIGOUR	WAILER	WEASEL	WILDLY
VIKING	WAITED	WEAVER	WILFUL
VILELY	WAITER	WEAZEN	WILIER
VILEST	WAIVED	WEBBED	WILILY
VILIFY	WAIVER	WEB-EYE	WILLED
VINERY	WAKING	WEDDED	WILLER
VINOUS	WALKED	WEDGED	WILLOW
VINTED	WALKER	WEEDED	WILTED
VINTRY	WALLAH	WEEDER	WIMPLE
VIOLET	WALLED	WEEKLY	WINCED
VIOLIN	WALLER	WEEPER	WINCER
VIRAGO	WALLET	WEEVER	WINCEY
VIRGIN	WALLOP	WEEVIL	WINDED
VIRILE	WALLOW	WEIGHT	WINDER
VIROUS	WALNUT	WELDED	WINDLE

WINDOW	Y – 6	ABIGAIL	ADELPHI
WIND-UP		ABILITY	ADENOID
WINGED	YAMMER	ABJURED	ADHERED
WINGER	YANKED	ABJURER	ADHERER
WINKED	YANKEE	ABOLISH	ADIPOSE
WINKER	YAPPED	ABRADED	ADJOURN
WINKLE	YAPPER	ABREAST	ADJUDGE
WINNER	YARNED	ABRIDGE	ADJUNCT
WINNOW	YARROW	ABROACH	ADJURED
WINTRY	YAWING	ABSCESS	ADJURER
WIPING	YAWLED	ABSCOND	ADMIRAL
WIRING	YAWNED	ABSENCE	ADMIRED
WIZARD	YCLEPT	ABSINTH	ADMIRER
WISDOM	YEANED	ABSOLVE	ADONAIS
WISELY	YEARLY	ABSTAIN	ADOPTED
WISEST	YEASTY	ABUSING	ADORING
WISHED	YELLED	ABUSIVE	ADORNED
WISHER	YELLOW	ABUTTAL	ADRENAL
WISTLY	YELPED	ABUTTED	ADULATE
WITHAL	YELPER	ABYSMAL	ADVANCE
WITHER	YEOMAN	ABYSSAL	ADVERSE
WITHIN	YES-MAN	ACADEMY	ADVISED
WITTED	YESTER	ACCEDED	ADVISOR
WOBBLE	YOGISM	ACCLAIM	AEOLIAN
WOBBLY	YOICKS	ACCOUNT	AERATED
WOEFUL	YOKING	ACCRETE	AERATOR
WOLVES	YOLKED	ACCRUED	AEROBUS
WOMBAT	YONDER	ACCUSED	AFFABLE
WONDER	YORKER	ACCUSER	AFFABLY
WONTED	YOWLED	ACETATE	AFFINED
WOODED		ACETIFY	AFFIXED
WOODEN		ACETONE	AFFLICT
WOOFER	Z – 6	ACHATES	AFFRONT
WOOING		ACHERON	AFRICAN
WOOLLY	ZEALOT	ACHIEVE	AGAINST
WORDED	ZENANA	ACIDIFY	AGELESS
WORKED	ZENITH	ACIDITY	AGELONG
WORKER	ZEPHYR	ACK-EMMA	AGENDUM
WORMED	ZIG-ZAG	ACOLYTE	AGGRESS
WORSEN	ZILLAH	ACONITE	AGILELY
WORTHY	ZINNIA	ACQUIRE	AGILITY
WOUNDY	ZIPPED	ACREAGE	AGITATE
WRAITH	ZIRCON	ACROBAT	AGITATO
WREATH	ZITHER	ACTABLE	AGNOMEN
WRENCH	ZODIAC	ACTRESS	AGONIZE
WRETCH	ZONATE	ACTUARY	AGROUND
WRIGHT		ACTUATE	AIDLESS
WRITER	A – 7	ACUSHLA	AILERON
WRITHE		ACUTELY	AILMENT
WYVERN	ABANDON	ADAMANT	AIMLESS
	ABASHED	ADAPTED	AIR-BASE
	ABASING	ADAPTER	AIR-BATH
X – 6	ABATING	ADDENDA	AIR-CELL
	ABDOMEN	ADDRESS	AIR-HOLE
XANADU	ABETTED	ADDUCED	AIRLESS
XERXES	ABETTER	ADDUCER	AIRLIFT
X-RAYED	ABIDING		

AIRLINE	AMBLING	ANNOYED	ARCANUM
AIRLOCK	AMENDED	ANNUITY	ARCHAIC
AIR-MAIL	AMENITY	ANNULAR	ARCHERY
AIRPORT	AMERCED	ANNULET	ARCHING
AIR-PUMP	AMIABLE	ANODYNE	ARCHIVE
AIR-RAID	AMIABLY	ANOMALY	ARCHWAY
AIR SHIP	AMMETER	ANOSMIA	ARC-LAMP
AIR-TRAP	AMMONAL	ANOTHER	ARDENCY
AIRWAYS	AMMONIA	ANTACID	ARDUOUS
ALADDIN	AMNESIA	ANT-BEAR	ARENOSE
A-LA-MODE	AMNESTY	ANTENNA	ARIDITY
A-LA-MORT	AMONGST	ANT-HILL	ARIGHTS
ALARMED	AMORIST	ANTHONY	ARIPPLE
ALASKAN	AMOROUS	ANTHRAX	ARISING
ALBUMEN	AMPHORA	ANTIQUE	ARMHOLE
ALCALDE	AMPLEST	ANTI-RED	ARMIGER
ALCHEMY	AMPLIFY	ANTI-LIKE	ARMLESS
ALCOHOL	AMPOULE	ANT-LION	ARMOIRE
ALEMBIC	AMPULLA	ANTONYM	ARMOURY
ALENGTH	AMUSING	ANXIETY	AROUSAL
ALERTLY	AMUSIVE	ANXIOUS	AROUSED
ALFALFA	AMYLOID	ANYBODY	ARRAIGN
ALGEBRA	ANAEMIA	ANYWISE	ARRANGE
ALIDADE	ANAEMIC	APANAGE	ARRAYED
ALIGNED	ANAGRAM	APELIKE	ARRIVAL
ALIMENT	ANALOGY	APHASIA	ARSENAL
ALIMONY	ANALYSE	APHONIA	ARSENIC
ALIQUOT	ANALYST	APISHLY	ARTICLE
ALLAYED	ANARCHY	APOCOPE	ARTISAN
ALLEGED	ANATOMY	APOGEAN	ARTISTE
ALLEGRO	ANCHOVY	APOLOGY	ARTLESS
ALLERGY	ANCIENT	APOSTLE	ASCETIC
ALLOWED	ANDANTE	APPAREL	ASCRIBE
ALLOYED	ANDIRON	APPEASE	ASEPSIS
ALLUDED	ANDROID	APPLAUD	ASEPTIC
ALLURED	ANEMONE	APPLIED	ASEXUAL
ALLUVIA	ANEROID	APPOINT	ASHAMED
ALLYING	ANEURIN	APPRISE	ASHIVER
ALMANAC	ANGELIC	APPRIZE	ASHTRAY
ALMONER	ANGELUS	APPROVE	ASIATIC
ALMONRY	ANGERED	APRICOT	ASININE
ALMSMAN	ANGEVIN	APRONED	ASKANCE
ALREADY	ANGLICE	APROPOS	ASPERSE
ALSATIA	ANGLING	APSIDAL	ASPHALT
ALTERED	ANGRILY	APTNESS	ASPIRED
ALTHAEA	ANGUINE	AQUARIA	ASPIRIN
ALUMNUS	ANGUISH	AQUATIC	ASPRAWL
ALYSSUM	ANGULAR	AQUEOUS	ASPROUT
AMALGAM	ANILINE	ARABIAN	ASQUINT
AMASSED	ANILITY	ARABIST	ASSAGAI
AMATEUR	ANIMATE	ARACHIS	ASSAULT
AMATIVE	ANIMISM	ARAMAIC	ASSAYED
AMATORY	ANIMIST	ARBITER	ASSAYER
AMAZING	ANISEED	ARBUTUS	ASSEGAI
AMBAGES	ANNATES	ARCADED	ASSUAGE
AMBIENT	ANNEXED	ARCADIA	ASSUMED

ASSURED	AWAKING	BANGING	BEAR-PIT
ASSURER	AWARDED	BANKING	BEASTLY
ASTATIC	AWESOME	BANNING	BEATIFY
ASTOUND	AWFULLY	BANNOCK	BEATING
ASTRIDE	AWKWARD	BANQUET	BECAUSE
ASUNDER	AWNLESS	BANSHEE	BECLOUD
ATAVISM	AXIALLY	BANTING	BEDDING
ATELIER	AXLE-BOX	BAPTISM	BEDEVIL
ATHEISM	AXLE-PIN	BAPTIST	BEDEWED
ATHEIST	AXOLOTL	BAPTIZE	BED-GOWN
ATHIRST		BARBARY	BED-MATE
ATHLETE		BARBATE	BEDOUIN
ATHWART	**B – 7**	BARDISM	BEDPOST
ATOMIST		BARGAIN	BED-REST
ATOMIZE	BABBLED	BARGING	BEDROCK
ATONING	BABBLER	BARKING	BEDROOM
ATROPHY	BABYISH	BARMAID	BEDSIDE
ATTABOY	BABYISM	BARMIER	BEDSORE
ATTACHE	BABYLON	BARNABY	BED-TICK
ATTEMPT	BACCHIC	BARNOWL	BEDTIME
ATTIRED	BACCHUS	BARONET	BEDWARF
ATTRACT	BACILLI	BAROQUE	BEEF-TEA
ATTUNED	BACKEND	BARRACK	BEEHIVE
AUBERGE	BACKING	BARRAGE	BEE-LINE
AUCTION	BACKLOG	BARRIER	BEE-MOTH
AUDIBLE	BADNESS	BARRING	BEESWAX
AUDIBLY	BAFFLED	BASENJI	BEETLED
AUDITED	BAFFLER	BASHFUL	BEGGARY
AUDITOR	BAGGAGE	BASHING	BEGGING
AUGMENT	BAGGING	BASILIC	BEGLOOM
AUGURED	BAGPIPE	BASKING	BEGONIA
AURALLY	BAILAGE	BASSOON	BEGORED
AUREATE	BAILIFF	BASTARD	BEGRIME
AUREOLA	BAILING	BASTING	BEGUILE
AUREOLE	BAITING	BASTION	BEGUINE
AURICLE	BALANCE	BATH-BUN	BEHAVED
AUROCHS	BALCONY	BATHING	BEHOVED
AUSTERE	BALDEST	BATSMAN	BEJEWEL
AUSTRAL	BALDISH	BATTELS	BEKNOWN
AUTOBUS	BALDRIC	BATTERY	BELACED
AUTOCAR	BALEFUL	BATTING	BELATED
AUTONYM	BALKING	BATTLED	BELAYED
AUTOPSY	BALLAST	BATTLER	BELCHED
AVAILED	BALLBOY	BAULKED	BELCHER
AVARICE	BALLOON	BAUXITE	BELGIAN
AVENGED	BALMILY	BAWDILY	BELIEVE
AVENGER	BALMING	BAWLING	BELLHOP
AVERAGE	BAMBINO	BAYONET	BELLIED
AVERRED	BANBURY	BAY-TREE	BELLING
AVERTED	BANDAGE	BAYWOOD	BELLMAN
AVIATOR	BANDANA	BEACHED	BELLOWS
AVIDITY	BANDBOX	BEADING	BELOVED
AVOCADO	BANDEAU	BEAMING	BELTING
AVOIDED	BANDIED	BEARDED	BELYING
AVOWING	BANDING	BEARING	BEMAZED
AWAITED	BAND-SAW	BEARISH	BEMIRED
	BANEFUL		

BEMUSED	BILIOUS	BLOATER	BOMBARD
BENCHER	BILKING	BLOCKED	BOMBAST
BENDING	BILLING	BLONDIN	BOMBING
BENEATH	BILLION	BLOODED	BONANZA
BENEFIT	BILLOWY	BLOOMED	BONDAGE
BENGALI	BILTONG	BLOOMER	BONDING
BENISON	BINDING	BLOSSOM	BONDMAN
BENZENE	BIOCHIP	BLOTCHY	BONFIRE
BENZOIN	BIOLOGY	BLOTTED	BONNILY
BEPAINT	BIOTICS	BLOTTER	BOOKING
BEQUEST	BIPEDAL	BLOWFLY	BOOKISH
BERATED	BIPLANE	BLOW-GUN	BOOKLET
BEREAVE	BIRCHED	BLOWING	BOOKMAN
BERHYME	BIRDMAN	BLOW-OUT	BOOMING
BERRIED	BIRETTA	BLOWZED	BOORISH
BERSERK	BISCUIT	BLUBBER	BOOSTED
BERTHED	BISMUTH	BLUCHER	BOOSTER
BESEECH	BITTERN	BLUE-CAP	BOOT-LEG
BESHAME	BITUMEN	BLUEING	BOOZING
BESHONE	BIVALVE	BLUFFED	BORACIC
BESHREW	BIVOUAC	BLUFFER	BOREDOM
BESIDES	BIZARRE	BLUFFLY	BOROUGH
BESIEGE	BLABBED	BLUNDER	BORSTAL
BESMEAR	BLABBER	BLUNGER	BOSOMED
BESMOKE	BLACKED	BLUNTED	BOSSING
BESPEAK	BLACKEN	BLUNTER	BOSWELL
BESPOKE	BLACKER	BLUNTLY	BOTANIC
BESTIAL	BLACKLY	BLURRED	BOTCHED
BESTILL	BLADDER	BLURTED	BOTCHER
BESTING	BLAMING	BLUSHED	BOTTLED
BEST-MAN	BLANDLY	BLUSTER	BOTTLER
BESTREW	BLANKET	BOARDED	BOUDOIR
BETAKEN	BLANKLY	BOARDER	BOULDER
BETHINK	BLARING	BOARISH	BOULTER
BETHUMB	BLARNEY	BOASTED	BOUNCED
BETHUMP	BLASTED	BOASTER	BOUNCER
BETIDED	BLASTER	BOAT-CAR	BOUNDED
BETIMES	BLATANT	BOAT-FLY	BOUNDEN
BETITLE	BLATHER	BOATFUL	BOUNDER
BETOKEN	BLATTER	BOATING	BOUQUET
BETROTH	BLAZING	BOATMAN	BOURBON
BETTING	BLEAKER	BOBADIL	BOWLESS
BETWEEN	BLEAKLY	BOBBING	BOWLINE
BETWIXT	BLEATED	BOBBISH	BOWLING
BEWITCH	BLEMISH	BOB-SLED	BOWSHOT
BEZIQUE	BLENDED	BOB-STAY	BOX-CALF
BIASING	BLENDER	BOBTAIL	BOX-COAT
BIAXIAL	BLESSED	BODEFUL	BOX-IRON
BICYCLE	BLETHER	BOGGLED	BOX-KITE
BIDDING	BLIGHTY	BOILING	BOX-WOOD
BIFOCAL	BLINDED	BOLDEST	BOYCOTT
BIGGEST	BLINDER	BOLLARD	BOYHOOD
BIGGISH	BLINDLY	BOLLING	BRACING
BIGOTED	BLINKED	BOLOGNA	BRACKEN
BIGOTRY	BLISTER	BOLSTER	BRACKET
BILGING	BLOATED	BOLTING	BRAGGED

BRAIDED	BROCADE	BUMPKIN	CABBAGE
BRAILLE	BROILED	BUNCHED	CABBALA
BRAINED	BROILER	BUNDLED	CAB-FARE
BRAISED	BROKAGE	BUNGLED	CABINED
BRAKING	BROKING	BUNGLER	CABINET
BRAMBLE	BROMIDE	BUNKING	CABLING
BRAMBLY	BRONZED	BUNTING	CABOOSE
BRANCHY	BROODED	BUOYAGE	CAB-RANK
BRANDED	BROOKED	BUOYANT	CA'CANNY
BRASSIE	BROTHER	BUOYING	CACKLED
BRAVADO	BROUGHT	BURDOCK	CACKLER
BRAVELY	BROWNED	BURETTE	CADDISH
BRAVERY	BROWNER	BURGEON	CADENCE
BRAVEST	BROWNIE	BURGESS	CADENCY
BRAVING	BROWSED	BURGHAL	CADENZA
BRAVURA	BRUISED	BURGHER	CADGING
BRAWLED	BRUISER	BURGLAR	CAESURA
BRAWLER	BRUMOUS	BURGLED	CAFFEIN
BRAYING	BRUSHED	BURLIER	CAITIFF
BRAZIER	BRUSQUE	BURLING	CAJOLED
BRAZING	BRUTIFY	BURMESE	CAJOLER
BREADTH	BRUTISH	BURNING	CALCIFY
BREAKER	BRUTISM	BURNISH	CALCINE
BREATHE	BUBBLED	BURNOUS	CALCIUM
BREEDER	BUBONIC	BURRING	CALDRON
BREVITY	BUCKING	BURSARY	CALENDS
BREWERY	BUCKISH	BURTHEN	CALIBAN
BREWING	BUCKISM	BURYING	CALIBRE
BRIBERY	BUCKLED	BUSH-CAT	CALIPER
BRIBING	BUCKLER	BUSHIDO	CALKING
BRICKED	BUCKRAM	BUSHMAN	CALL-BOY
BRIDGED	BUCKSAW	BUSKING	CALLING
BRIDLED	BUCOLIC	BUS-STOP	CALLOUS
BRIDLER	BUDDING	BUSTARD	CALMING
BRIEFED	BUDGING	BUSTLED	CALOMEL
BRIEFER	BUDLESS	BUSTLER	CALORIC
BRIEFLY	BUFFALO	BUSYING	CALORIE
BRIGADE	BUFFING	BUTCHER	CALTROP
BRIGAND	BUFFOON	BUTLERY	CALUMET
BRIMFUL	BUGBEAR	BUTMENT	CALUMNY
BRIMMED	BUILT-UP	BUTT-END	CALVARY
BRIMMER	BULBOUS	BUTTERY	CALVING
BRINDLE	BULGING	BUTTING	CALYPSO
BRINISH	BULKIER	BUTTOCK	CAMBIUM
BRIOCHE	BULKING	BUTTONS	CAMBRIC
BRISKER	BULLACE	BUXOMLY	CAMELOT
BRISKET	BULL-DOG	BUYABLE	CAMORRA
BRISKLY	BULLIED	BUZZARD	CAMPHOR
BRISTLE	BULLING	BUZZING	CAMPING
BRISTLY	BULLION	BUZZ-SAW	CAMPION
BRISTOL	BULLOCK	BY-AND-BY	CANDIED
BRITISH	BULL-PUP	BYRONIC	CANDOUR
BRITTLE	BULRUSH		CANASTA
BROADEN	BULWARK		CANNERY
BROADER	BUMMALO	C – 7	CANNING
BROADLY	BUMPING	CABARET	CANTATA

CANTEEN	CASEMAN	CHAFING	CHEETAH
CANTING	CASHIER	CHAGRIN	CHELSEA
CANVASS	CASHING	CHAINED	CHEMISE
CAPABLE	CASSAVA	CHAIRED	CHEMIST
CAPABLY	CASSOCK	CHALDEE	CHEQUER
CAP-A-PIE	CASTING	CHALICE	CHERISH
CAPELIN	CASTLED	CHALLIS	CHEROOT
CAPERED	CAST-OFF	CHAMBER	CHERVIL
CAPERER	CASUIST	CHAMOIS	CHESTED
CAPITAL	CATALAN	CHAMPED	CHEVIOT
CAPITAN	CATARRH	CHANCED	CHEVRON
CAPITOL	CATCALL	CHANCEL	CHEWING
CAPORAL	CATCHER	CHANGED	CHIANTI
CAPPING	CATCHUP	CHANGER	CHICANE
CAPRICE	CATERAN	CHANNEL	CHICKEN
CAPRINE	CATERED	CHANTED	CHICORY
CAPROIC	CATERER	CHANTER	CHIDING
CAPSIZE	CAT-EYED	CHANTRY	CHIEFLY
CAPSTAN	CATFISH	CHAOTIC	CHIFFON
CAPSULE	CATHEAD	CHAPLET	CHIGNON
CAPTAIN	CATHODE	CHAPMAN	CHILEAN
CAPTION	CAT-LIKE	CHAPPED	CHILIAD
CAPTIVE	CATMINT	CHAPTER	CHILLED
CAPTURE	CAT'S-EYE	CHARADE	CHILLER
CAPULET	CAT'S-PAW	CHARGED	CHIMNEY
CARAMEL	CATTISH	CHARGER	CHINDIT
CARAVAN	CAUDATE	CHARILY	CHINESE
CARAVEL	CAULKED	CHARING	CHINKED
CARAWAY	CAUSING	CHARIOT	CHIP-HAT
CARBIDE	CAUSTIC	CHARITY	CHIPPED
CARBINE	CAUTION	CHARLEY	CHIPPER
CARCASE	CAVALRY	CHARMED	CHIRPED
CARDIAC	CAVE-MAN	CHARMER	CHIRPER
CARDING	CAVIARE	CHARNEL	CHIRRED
CARDOON	CAYENNE	CHARRED	CHIRRUP
CAREFUL	CEASING	CHARTED	CHITTER
CARIBOU	CEDARED	CHARTER	CHLORAL
CARIOUS	CEDILLA	CHASING	CHLORIC
CARKING	CEILING	CHASSIS	CHOIRED
CARLINE	CELLIST	CHASTEN	CHOKING
CARMINE	CENSING	CHATEAU	CHOLERA
CARNAGE	CENSURE	CHATTED	CHOOSER
CAROTID	CENTAUR	CHATTEL	CHOPPED
CAROUSE	CENTAVO	CHATTER	CHOPPER
CARPING	CENTIME	CHEAPEN	CHORALE
CARRIED	CENTRAL	CHEAPER	CHORTLE
CARRIER	CENTRED	CHEAPLY	CHOWDER
CARRION	CENTURY	CHEATED	CHRONIC
CARROTY	CERAMIC	CHEATER	CHUCKED
CARTAGE	CERTAIN	CHECKED	CHUCKLE
CARTING	CERTIFY	CHECKER	CHUMMED
CARTOON	CESSION	CHEDDAR	CHURCHY
CARVING	CESSPIT	CHEEKED	CHURNED
CASCADE	CHABLIS	CHEEPED	CHURRED
CASCARA	CHAFFED	CHEERED	CINDERY
CASE-LAW	CHAFFER	CHEERIO	CIRCEAN

CIRCLED	CLIPPED	COCKNEY	COMPETE
CIRCLET	CLIPPER	COCKPIT	COMPILE
CIRCUIT	CLIPPIE	COCONUT	COMPLEX
CISTERN	CLOAKED	COCOTTE	COMPORT
CITABLE	CLOBBER	CODDING	COMPOSE
CITADEL	CLOCKED	CODDLED	COMPOST
CITIZEN	CLOCKER	CODEINE	COMPOTE
CITRATE	CLOGGED	CODFISH	COMPUTE
CITRINE	CLOGGER	CODICIL	COMRADE
CIVILLY	CLOSELY	CODLING	CONCAVE
CIVVIES	CLOSEST	COERCED	CONCEAL
CLACKED	CLOSE-UP	COEXIST	CONCEDE
CLAIMED	CLOSING	COGENCY	CONCEIT
CLAIMER	CLOSURE	COGNATE	CONCEPT
CLAMANT	CLOTHED	COHABIT	CONCERN
CLAMBER	CLOTTED	COHERED	CONCERT
CLAMMED	CLOUDED	COHERER	CONCISE
CLAMOUR	CLOUTED	COIFFED	CONCOCT
CLAMPED	CLOWNED	COILING	CONCORD
CLAMPER	CLUBBED	COINAGE	CONCUSS
CLANGED	CLUBBER	COINING	CONDEMN
CLANKED	CLUB-LAW	COJUROR	CONDIGN
CLAP-NET	CLUB-MAN	COLDEST	CONDOLE
CLAPPED	CLUCKED	COLDISH	CONDONE
CLAPPER	CLUMBER	COLICKY	CONDUCE
CLARIFY	CLUMPED	COLITIS	CONDUCT
CLARION	CLUSTER	COLLATE	CONDUIT
CLARITY	CLUTTER	COLLECT	CONFECT
CLASHED	COACHED	COLLEEN	CONFESS
CLASPED	COACTED	COLLEGE	CONFEST
CLASPER	COAGENT	COLLIDE	CONFIDE
CLASSED	COAL-BED	COLLIER	CONFINE
CLASSIC	COAL-BOX	COLLOID	CONFIRM
CLATTER	COAL-GAS	COLLUDE	CONFLUX
CLAVIER	COALING	COLONEL	CONFORM
CLAWING	COALMAN	COLOURS	CONFUSE
CLAYING	COAL-PIT	COLTISH	CONFUTE
CLAYISH	COAL-TAR	COMBINE	CONGEAL
CLAY-PIT	COAL-TIT	COMBING	CONGEST
CLEANED	COARSEN	COMFORT	CONICAL
CLEANER	COARSER	COMICAL	CONIFER
CLEANLY	COASTAL	COMMAND	CONJOIN
CLEANSE	COASTED	COMMEND	CONJURE
CLEAN-UP	COASTER	COMMENT	CONJURY
CLEARED	COATING	COMMERE	CONNATE
CLEARER	COAXIAL	COMMODE	CONNECT
CLEARLY	COAXING	COMMONS	CONNING
CLEAVED	COBBING	COMMUNE	CONNIVE
CLEAVER	COBBLED	COMMUTE	CONNOTE
CLEMENT	COBBLER	COMPACT	CONQUER
CLEMMED	COCAINE	COMPANY	CONSENT
CLICKED	COCKADE	COMPARE	CONSIGN
CLIMATE	COCKEYE	COMPART	CONSIST
CLIMBED	COCKING	COMPASS	CONSOLE
CLIMBER	COCKLED	COMPEER	CONSOLS
CLINKED	COCKLER	COMPERE	CONSORT

CONSULT	CORSAIR	CRAKING	CROOKED
CONSUME	CORSLET	CRAMMED	CROONED
CONTACT	CORTEGE	CRAMMER	CROONER
CONTAIN	CORVINE	CRAMPED	CROPFUL
CONTEMN	COSHING	CRAMPON	CROPPED
CONTEND	COSIEST	CRANAGE	CROPPER
CONTENT	COSSACK	CRANIAL	CROQUET
CONTEST	COSTARD	CRANING	CROSSED
CONTEXT	COSTING	CRANIUM	CROSSLY
CONTORT	COSTIVE	CRANKED	CROWBAR
CONTOUR	COSTUME	CRANKLE	CROWDED
CONTRAS	COTERIE	CRASHED	CROWING
CONTROL	COTTAGE	CRASHER	CROWNED
CONTUSE	COTTONY	CRATING	CRUCIAL
CONVENE	COUCHED	CRAUNCH	CRUCIFY
CONVENT	COUGHED	CRAVING	CRUDELY
CONVERT	COULDST	CRAWLED	CRUDEST
CONVICT	COUNCIL	CRAWLER	CRUDITY
CONVOKE	COUNSEL	CRAZIER	CRUELTY
COOKERY	COUNTED	CRAZILY	CRUISED
COOKING	COUNTER	CRAZING	CRUISER
COOLEST	COUNTRY	CREAKED	CRUMBED
COOLING	COUPLED	CREAMED	CRUMBLE
COOLISH	COUPLER	CREASED	CRUMBLY
COOPING	COUPLET	CREATED	CRUMPED
CO-OPTED	COURAGE	CREATOR	CRUMPET
CO-PILOT	COURANT	CREEPER	CRUMPLE
COPIOUS	COURIER	CREMATE	CRUPPER
COPPERY	COURSED	CREMONA	CRUSADE
COPPICE	COURSER	CRENATE	CRUSADO
COPPING	COURTED	CREOSOL	CRUSHED
COPYING	COURTER	CRESSET	CRUSHER
COPYIST	COURTLY	CRESTED	CRUSTED
CORACLE	COUTEAU	CREVICE	CRY-BABY
CORBEAU	COUVADE	CRIBBED	CRYPTIC
CORBEIL	COVERED	CRICKED	CRYSTAL
CORDAGE	COVETED	CRICKET	CUBBING
CORDATE	COWBANE	CRIMPED	CUBBISH
CORDIAL	COW-CALF	CRIMSON	CUBICAL
CORDING	COWERED	CRINGED	CUBICLE
CORDITE	COWHERD	CRINGER	CUBITAL
CORINTH	COWHIDE	CRINKLE	CUBITED
CORKAGE	COWLICK	CRINOID	CUCKOLD
CORKING	COWLIKE	CRIPPLE	CUDDLED
CORK-LEG	COWLING	CRISPED	CUE-BALL
CORN-COB	COWSLIP	CRISPER	CUFFING
CORNEAL	COXCOMB	CRISPIN	CUIRASS
CORNICE	COYNESS	CRISPLY	CUISINE
CORNISH	COZENED	CROAKED	CULLING
COROLLA	COZENER	CROAKER	CULPRIT
CORONER	CRABBED	CROCHET	CULTURE
CORONET	CRACKED	CROCKED	CULVERT
CORRECT	CRACKER	CROCKET	CUMULUS
CORRODE	CRACKLE	CROESUS	CUNEATE
CORRUPT	CRADLED	CROFTER	CUNNING
CORSAGE	CRAGGED	CROODLE	CUPPING

CUPRITE	DALLIED	DECANAL	DELETED
CURABLE	DALLIER	DECAPOD	DELIGHT
CURACAO	DAMAGED	DECAYED	DELILAH
CURATOR	DAMMING	DECAYER	DELIMIT
CURBING	DAMNIFY	DECEASE	DELIVER
CURDING	DAMNING	DECEIVE	DELOUSE
CURDLED	DAMOSEL	DECENCY	DELPHIC
CURE-ALL	DAMPING	DECIBEL	DELTAIC
CURETTE	DAMPISH	DECIDED	DELUDED
CURIOUS	DANCING	DECIDER	DELUDER
CURLING	DANDIFY	DECIMAL	DELUGED
CURRANT	DANDLED	DECKING	DELVING
CURRENT	DANELAW	DECKLED	DEMERIT
CURRIED	DANGLED	DECLAIM	DEMESNE
CURRIER	DANGLER	DECLARE	DEMIGOD
CURRISH	DANKISH	DECLINE	DEMISED
CURSING	DANTEAN	DECODED	DEMODED
CURSIVE	DAPPLED	DECODER	DEMONIC
CURSORY	DARKEST	DECORUM	DEMONRY
CURTAIL	DARKISH	DECOYED	DENIZEN
CURTAIN	DARLING	DECREED	DENOTED
CURTANA	DARNING	DECRIAL	DENSELY
CURTEST	DARTING	DECRIED	DENSEST
CURTSEY	DASHING	DECRIER	DENSITY
CURVATE	DASHPOT	DECROWN	DENTING
CURVING	DASTARD	DEDUCED	DENTIST
CUSHION	DATABLE	DEEDING	DENTOID
CUSSING	DAUBING	DEEMING	DENTURE
CUSTARD	DAUNTED	DEEPEST	DENUDED
CUSTODY	DAUPHIN	DEEP-SEA	DENYING
CUSTOMS	DAWDLED	DEFACED	DEPLETE
CUT-AWAY	DAWDLER	DEFACER	DEPLORE
CUTICLE	DAWNING	DEFAMED	DEPLUME
CUTLASS	DAY-BOOK	DEFAMER	DEPOSAL
CUTLERY	DAY-STAR	DEFAULT	DEPOSED
CUTTING	DAYTIME	DEFENCE	DEPOSIT
CUT-WORM	DAYWORK	DEFIANT	DEPRAVE
CYCLING	DAZZLED	DEFICIT	DEPRESS
CYCLIST	DEAD-END	DEFILED	DEPRIVE
CYCLONE	DEAD-EYE	DEFILER	DEPUTED
CYCLOPS	DEADISH	DEFINED	DERANGE
CYNICAL	DEAD-SET	DEFINER	DERATED
CYPRESS	DEALING	DEFLATE	DERIDED
CYPRIAN	DEANERY	DEFLECT	DERIDER
CYPRIOT	DEAREST	DEFRAUD	DERIVED
CZARISM	DEATHLY	DEFUNCT	DERRICK
	DEBACLE	DEFYING	DERVISH
	DEBASED	DEGLAZE	DESCENT
D – 7	DEBASER	DEGRADE	DESCEND
	DEBATED	DE-ICING	DESCANT
DABBING	DEBATER	DEIFIED	DESERVE
DABBLED	DEBAUCH	DEIFORM	DESIRED
DABBLER	DEBITED	DEIGNED	DESIRER
DABSTER	DEBOUCH	DEISTIC	DESPAIR
DAFTEST	DECADAL	DELAYED	DESPISE
DAGGLED	DECAGON	DELAYER	DESPITE
DAISIED			

DESPOIL	DIMETER	DISTURB	DOUBTER
DESPOND	DIMMING	DISUSED	DOUCEUR
DESSERT	DIMMISH	DITCHED	DOUCHED
DESTINE	DIMNESS	DITCHER	DOUGHTY
DESTINY	DIMPLED	DITHERY	DOUREST
DESTROY	DINGING	DIURNAL	DOUSING
DETERGE	DINNING	DIVERGE	DOUTING
DETINUE	DIOCESE	DIVERSE	DOVECOT
DETRACT	DIORAMA	DIVIDED	DOWABLE
DETRAIN	DIOXIDE	DIVIDER	DOWAGER
DETRUDE	DIPLOMA	DIVINER	DOWDILY
DEVALUE	DIPOLAR	DIVISOR	DOWERED
DEVELOP	DIPPING	DIVORCE	DOWNING
DEVIATE	DIPTERA	DIVULGE	DOWSING
DEVILRY	DIREFUL	DIZZIED	DRABBER
DEVIOUS	DIRTIED	DIZZIER	DRACHMA
DEVISED	DIRTIER	DIZZILY	DRACULA
DEVISEE	DIRTILY	DOCKAGE	DRAFTED
DEVISER	DISABLE	DOCKING	DRAGGED
DEVISOR	DISAVOW	DODGERY	DRAGGLE
DEVOLVE	DISBAND	DODGING	DRAG-MAN
DEVOTED	DISCARD	DOESKIN	DRAG-NET
DEVOTEE	DISCERN	DOFFING	DRAGOON
DEW-DROP	DISCOID	DOG-BANE	DRAINED
DEW-FALL	DISCORD	DOGCART	DRAINER
DEWLESS	DISCOUS	DOG-DAYS	DRAPERY
DEXTRAL	DISCUSS	DOGFISH	DRAPING
DIABOLO	DISDAIN	DOGGING	DRAPPIE
DIAGRAM	DISEASE	DOGGISH	DRASTIC
DIALECT	DISEUSE	DOGHEAD	DRATTED
DIALLED	DISGUST	DOG-HOLE	DRAUGHT
DIAMOND	DISHFUL	DOGLIKE	DRAWBAR
DIARCHY	DISHING	DOG-NAIL	DRAWING
DIARIST	DISJOIN	DOGROSE	DRAWLED
DIBBLED	DISLIKE	DOG'S-EAR	DRAWLER
DICE-BOX	DISMAST	DOG-STAR	DRAW-NET
DICKENS	DISMISS	DOLEFUL	DRAYAGE
DICTATE	DISOBEY	DOLLIED	DRAYMAN
DICTION	DISPARK	DOLPHIN	DREADED
DIDDLED	DISPART	DOLTISH	DREAMED
DIDDLER	DISPLAY	DOMINIE	DREAMER
DIE-HARD	DISPONE	DONATOR	DREDGED
DIETARY	DISPORT	DONNING	DREDGER
DIETING	DISPOSE	DONNISH	DRESDEN
DIFFUSE	DISPUTE	DONSHIP	DRESSED
DIGGING	DISRATE	DOOMING	DRESSER
DIGITAL	DISROBE	DOORMAT	DRIBBLE
DIGNIFY	DISROOT	DOORWAY	DRIBLET
DIGNITY	DISRUPT	DORMANT	DRIFTED
DIGRESS	DISSECT	DORMICE	DRIFTER
DILATED	DISSENT	DOSSIER	DRILLED
DILATER	DISTAFF	DOTTIER	DRINKER
DILEMMA	DISTANT	DOTTING	DRIPPED
DILUENT	DISTEND	DOUBLED	DRIVING
DILUTED	DISTICH	DOUBLET	DRIZZLE
DILUTER	DISTORT	DOUBTED	DRIZZLY

DROLLED	DUNNISH	ECOLOGY	EMBOXED
DRONING	DUNNOCK	ECONOMY	EMBRACE
DRONISH	DUPABLE	ECSTASY	EMBROIL
DROOLED	DURABLE	EDDYING	EMBROWN
DROOPED	DURABLY	EDENTAL	EMENDED
DROPLET	DURANCE	EDIFICE	EMERALD
DROP-NET	DUSKIER	EDIFIED	EMERGED
DROPPED	DUSKILY	EDIFIER	EMINENT
DROPPER	DUSKISH	EDITING	EMITTED
DROUGHT	DUSTBIN	EDITION	EMOTION
DROWNED	DUSTIER	EDUCATE	EMOTIVE
DROWNER	DUSTING	EDUCING	EMPALED
DROWSED	DUSTMAN	EFFACED	EMPANEL
DRUBBED	DUSTPAN	EFFECTS	EMPEROR
DRUBBER	DUTEOUS	EFFENDI	EMPIRIC
DRUDGED	DUTIFUL	EGALITY	EMPLANE
DRUDGER	DWARFED	EGG-COSY	EMPOWER
DRUGGED	DWELLED	EGG-FLIP	EMPRESS
DRUGGER	DWELLER	EGOTISE	EMPTIED
DRUGGET	DWINDLE	EGOTISM	EMPTIER
DRUIDIC	DYNAMIC	EGOTIST	EMULATE
DRUMMED	DYNASTY	EJECTED	EMULOUS
DRUMMER		EJECTOR	ENABLED
DRUNKEN		ELAPSED	ENACTED
DRYDOCK	E – 7	ELASTIC	ENCAGED
DRY-EYED	EAGERLY	ELATING	ENCASED
DRY-FOOT	EANLING	ELATION	ENCAVED
DRYNESS	EARACHE	ELBOWED	ENCHAIN
DRY-SHOD	EAR-DROP	ELDERLY	ENCHANT
DUALISM	EAR-DRUM	ELECTED	ENCLASP
DUALIST	EAR-HOLE	ELECTOR	ENCLAVE
DUALITY	EARLDOM	ELECTRO	ENCLOSE
DUBBING	EARLESS	ELEGANT	ENCLOUD
DUBIETY	EARLIER	ELEGIAC	ENCODER
DUBIOUS	EARMARK	ELEGISE	ENCORED
DUCALLY	EARNEST	ELEGIST	ENCRUST
DUCHESS	EARNING	ELEMENT	ENDEMIC
DUCKING	EARRING	ELEVATE	ENDIRON
DUCTILE	EARSHOT	ELEVENS	ENDLESS
DUDGEON	EARTHED	ELF-LOCK	ENDLONG
DUELLED	EARTHEN	ELIDING	ENDMOST
DUELLER	EARTHLY	ELISION	ENDORSE
DUENESS	EASEFUL	ELLIPSE	ENDOWED
DUFFING	EASIEST	ELOPING	ENDOWER
DUKEDOM	EAST-END	ELUDING	ENDUING
DULCIFY	EASTERN	ELUSION	ENDURED
DULLARD	EASTING	ELUSIVE	ENDURER
DULLEST	EATABLE	ELUSORY	ENDWAYS
DULLING	EBB-TIDE	ELYSIAN	ENDWISE
DULLISH	EBONISE	ELYSIUM	ENERGIC
DUMPING	EBONITE	EMANATE	ENFORCE
DUMPISH	EBRIOUS	EMBARGO	ENFRAME
DUNCIAD	ECHELON	EMBASSY	ENGAGED
DUNGEON	ECHOING	EMBLAZE	ENGAGER
DUNNAGE	ECLIPSE	EMBOSOM	ENGINED
DUNNING	ECLOGUE	EMBOWER	ENGLISH

ENGORGE	EQUALLY	EXACTOR	FACTUAL
ENGRAFT	EQUATED	EXALTED	FACULTY
ENGRAIN	EQUATOR	EXAMINE	FADDISH
ENGRAVE	EQUERRY	EXAMPLE	FADDIST
ENGROSS	EQUINOX	EXCERPT	FADE-OUT
ENGUARD	ERASING	EXCISED	FAGGING
ENHANCE	ERASURE	EXCITED	FAIENCE
ENJOYED	ERECTED	EXCITER	FAILING
ENLACED	ERECTER	EXCLAIM	FAILURE
ENLARGE	ERECTLY	EXCLUDE	FAINTED
ENLIVEN	ERELONG	EXCUSED	FAINTER
ENNOBLE	EREMITE	EXECUTE	FAINTLY
ENOUNCE	ERMINED	EXEMPLA	FAIREST
ENQUIRE	ERODENT	EXERTED	FAIRING
ENQUIRY	ERODING	EXHALED	FAIRISH
ENRAGED	EROSION	EXHAUST	FAIRWAY
ENROBED	EROSIVE	EXHIBIT	FALLACY
ENSLAVE	ERRATIC	EXHUMED	FALLING
ENSNARE	ERRATUM	EXIGENT	FALSELY
ENSTAMP	ERUDITE	EXILING	FALSEST
ENSUING	ERUPTED	EXISTED	FALSIFY
ENSURED	ESCAPED	EXPANSE	FALSITY
ENTAMED	ESCAPER	EX-PARTE	FANATIC
ENTENTE	ESCHEAT	EXPENSE	FANCIED
ENTERED	ESPARTO	EXPIATE	FANFARE
ENTERIC	ESPOUSE	EXPIRED	FAN-MAIL
ENTHRAL	ESPYING	EXPLAIN	FANNING
ENTHUSE	ESQUIRE	EXPLODE	FANTAIL
ENTICED	ESSAYED	EXPLOIT	FANTAST
ENTICER	ESSENCE	EXPLORE	FANTASY
ENTITLE	ESTUARY	EXPOSED	FAR-AWAY
ENTRAIN	ETCHING	EXPOSER	FARCEUR
ENTRANT	ETERNAL	EXPOUND	FARCING
ENTREAT	ETHICAL	EXPRESS	FARMERY
ENTRUST	ETONIAN	EXPUNGE	FARMING
ENTWINE	EUGENIC	EXTINCT	FARMOST
ENTWIST	EUPHONY	EXTRACT	FARRAGO
ENURING	EUTERPE	EXTREME	FARRIER
ENVELOP	EVACUEE	EXTRUDE	FARTHER
ENVENOM	EVADING	EXUDING	FASCISM
ENVIOUS	EVANGEL	EXULTED	FASCIST
ENVIRON	EVASION	EYEBALL	FASHING
ENVYING	EVASIVE	EYE-BOLT	FASHION
EPAULET	EVENING	EYEBROW	FAST-DAY
EPERGNE	EVERTED	EYEHOLE	FASTEST
EPICARP	EVICTED	EYELASH	FASTING
EPICURE	EVICTOR	EYELESS	FATALLY
EPIGRAM	EVIDENT	EYESHOT	FATEFUL
EPISODE	EVIL-EYE	EYESORE	FAT-HEAD
EPISTLE	EVINCED	EYEWASH	FATIGUE
EPITAPH	EVOKING		FATNESS
EPITHET	EVOLVED		FATTEST
EPITOME	EWE-LAMB	**F – 7**	FATTISH
EPOCHAL	EXACTED		FATUITY
EQUABLE	EXACTER	FACETED	FATUOUS
EQUABLY	EXACTLY	FACTION	FAULTED
		FACTORY	

FAWNING	FIFTHLY	FLANNEL	FLOWERY
FEARFUL	FIGHTER	FLAPPED	FLOWING
FEARING	FIG-LEAF	FLAPPER	FLUENCY
FEASTED	FIGMENT	FLARING	FLUFFED
FEASTER	FIG-TREE	FLASHED	FLUKILY
FEATHER	FIGURAL	FLASHER	FLUKING
FEATURE	FIGURED	FLATLET	FLUMMOX
FEBRILE	FIGWORT	FLATTEN	FLUNKEY
FEDERAL	FILBERT	FLATTER	FLUSHED
FEEDING	FILCHED	FLAVOUR	FLUSTER
FEELING	FILCHER	FLAWING	FLUTING
FEE-TAIL	FILINGS	FLAYING	FLUTIST
FEIGNED	FILLING	FLECKED	FLUTTER
FEINTED	FILM-FAN	FLECKER	FLUVIAL
FELLING	FILMING	FLEDGED	FLY-AWAY
FELONRY	FINABLE	FLEECED	FLY-BOOK
FELSPAR	FINALLY	FLEECER	FLY-FLAP
FELTING	FINANCE	FLEEING	FLY-HALF
FELUCCA	FINDING	FLEETED	FLYLEAF
FEMORAL	FINESSE	FLEETER	FLYOVER
FENCING	FINICAL	FLEETLY	FLY-PAST
FENDING	FINICKY	FLEMING	FLY-TRAP
FEOFFEE	FINLESS	FLEMISH	FOALING
FERMENT	FINNISH	FLESHED	FOAMING
FERNERY	FIREARM	FLESHER	FOBBING
FERN-OWL	FIREBAR	FLESHLY	FOCUSED
FERRATE	FIRE-BOX	FLEURET	FOE-LIKE
FERRIED	FIREDOG	FLEXILE	FOG-BANK
FERROUS	FIREFLY	FLEXING	FOGGIER
FERRULE	FIREMAN	FLEXION	FOGGILY
FERTILE	FIREPAN	FLEXURE	FOGGING
FERVENT	FIRSTLY	FLICKED	FOG-HORN
FERVOUR	FISHERY	FLICKER	FOILING
FESTIVE	FISHILY	FLIGHTY	FOISTED
FESTOON	FISHING	FLIPPED	FOLDING
FETCHED	FISH-OIL	FLIPPER	FOLIAGE
FETLOCK	FISSILE	FLIRTED	FOLIATE
FEVERED	FISSION	FLITTED	FOLLIES
FEWNESS	FISSURE	FLITTER	FONDANT
FIANCEE	FITMENT	FLIVVER	FONDEST
FIBBING	FITNESS	FLOATED	FONDLED
FIBROID	FITTING	FLOATER	FONDLER
FIBROUS	FIXABLE	FLOCKED	FOOLERY
FIBSTER	FIXEDLY	FLOGGED	FOOLING
FIBULAR	FIXTURE	FLOODED	FOOLISH
FICTILE	FIZZING	FLOORED	FOOTBOY
FICTION	FIZZLED	FLOORER	FOOTING
FICTIVE	FLACCID	FLOPPED	FOOTLED
FIDDLED	FLAG-DAY	FLORIST	FOOTMAN
FIDDLER	FLAGGED	FLOTAGE	FOOTPAD
FIDGETY	FLAKING	FLOTANT	FOOT-ROT
FIELDED	FLAMING	FLOTSAM	FOOTWAY
FIELDER	FLANEUR	FLOUNCE	FOPPERY
FIERCER	FLANGED	FLOURED	FOPPISH
FIERILY	FLANKED	FLOUTED	FORAGED
FIFTEEN	FLANKER	FLOUTER	FORAGER

FORAYED	FRAZZLE	FUNGOID	GANGLIA
FORBADE	FREAKED	FUNGOUS	GANGWAY
FORBEAR	FRECKLE	FUNKING	GAPPING
FORBORE	FRECKLY	FUNNILY	GARAGED
FORCEPS	FREEDOM	FUNNING	GARBAGE
FORCING	FREEING	FURBISH	GARBLED
FORDING	FREEMAN	FURCATE	GARFISH
FORDONE	FREESIA	FURIOSO	GARGLED
FOREARM	FREEZER	FURIOUS	GARLAND
FOREIGN	FREIGHT	FURLING	GARMENT
FORELEG	FRESHEN	FURLONG	GARNISH
FOREMAN	FRESHER	FURNACE	GAROTTE
FORERAN	FRESHET	FURNISH	GARPIKE
FORERUN	FRESHLY	FURRIER	GAS-BUOY
FORESAW	FRETFUL	FURRING	GAS-COAL
FORESEE	FRETSAW	FURTHER	GAS-COKE
FORETOP	FRETTED	FURTIVE	GASEITY
FOREVER	FRIABLE	FUSIBLE	GASEOUS
FORFEIT	FRIEZED	FUSSIER	GAS-FIRE
FORFEND	FRIGATE	FUSSILY	GASHING
FORGAVE	FRILLED	FUSSING	GAS-LIME
FORGERY	FRINGED	FUSS-POT	GAS-MAIN
FORGING	FRISIAN	FUSTIAN	GAS-MASK
FORGIVE	FRISKED	FUSTIER	GAS-OVEN
FORGONE	FRISKER	FUZZIER	GASPING
FORKING	FRITTED	FUZZLED	GAS-PIPE
FORLORN	FRITTER		GAS-RING
FORMATE	FRIZZED		GASSING
FORMING	FRIZZLE	G – 7	GASTRIC
FORMULA	FROCKED		GATEMAN
FORSAKE	FROGGED	GABBING	GATEWAY
FORSOOK	FROGMAN	GABBLED	GATLING
FORTIFY	FRONDED	GABBLER	GAUDERY
FORTUNE	FRONTAL	GADDING	GAUDILY
FORWARD	FRONTED	GADDISH	GAUGING
FORWENT	FROSTED	GAEKWAR	GAULISH
FOULARD	FROTHED	GAFFING	GAUNTLY
FOULING	FROWARD	GAGGING	GAUNTRY
FOUNDED	FROWNED	GAINFUL	GAVOTTE
FOUNDER	FRUITED	GAINING	GAYNESS
FOUNDRY	FRUITER	GAINSAY	GAYSOME
FOWLING	FUCHSIA	GALATEA	GAZELLE
FOX-HUNT	FUDDLED	GALILEE	GAZETTE
FOXLIKE	FUDDLER	GALILEO	GEARING
FOXTAIL	FUDGING	GALLANT	GELDING
FOXTROT	FUEHRER	GALLEON	GELIDLY
FRAGILE	FUELLED	GALLERY	GEMMING
FRAILLY	FULCRUM	GALLING	GENERAL
FRAILTY	FULGENT	GALLOWS	GENERIC
FRAME-UP	FULLEST	GALUMPH	GENESIS
FRAMING	FULL-PAY	GAMBIST	GENETIC
FRANKED	FULSOME	GAMBLED	GENITAL
FRANKLY	FUMBLED	GAMBLER	GENOESE
FRANTIC	FUMBLER	GAMBOGE	GENTEEL
FRAUGHT	FUNDING	GAMEFUL	GENTIAN
FRAYING	FUNERAL	GAME-LEG	GENTILE
		GANGING	

GENTLER	GLOBING	GOSLING	GRECISM
GENUINE	GLOBOID	GOSSIPY	GRECIZE
GEOLOGY	GLOBOSE	GOUACHE	GREENER
GEORDIE	GLOBULE	GOUGING	GREENLY
GERMANE	GLOOMED	GOULASH	GREETED
GESTAPO	GLORIED	GOURMET	GREMLIN
GESTURE	GLORIFY	GOUTILY	GRENADE
GETABLE	GLOSSED	GRABBED	GREY-HEN
GET-AWAY	GLOSSER	GRABBER	GREYISH
GETTING	GLOTTIC	GRABBLE	GREYLAG
GHASTLY	GLOTTIS	GRACING	GRIDDED
GHERKIN	GLOWING	GRADATE	GRIDDLE
GHILLIE	GLUCOSE	GRADELY	GRIEVED
GHOSTLY	GLUE-POT	GRADING	GRIFFIN
GIBLETS	GLUMMER	GRADUAL	GRIFFON
GIDDILY	GLUTTED	GRAFTED	GRILLED
GIFTING	GLUTTON	GRAFTER	GRIMACE
GIGGLED	GNARLED	GRAINED	GRIMING
GIGGLER	GNARRED	GRAINER	GRIMMER
GILDING	GNASHED	GRAMMAR	GRINDER
GIMBALS	GNAWING	GRAMPUS	GRINNED
GIN-FIZZ	GNOSTIC	GRANARY	GRIPING
GINGERY	GOADING	GRANDAD	GRIPPED
GINGHAM	GO-AHEAD	GRANDAM	GRIPPER
GIN-SHOP	GOATISH	GRANDEE	GRISTLE
GIRAFFE	GOBBLED	GRANDER	GRISTLY
GIRDING	GOBBLER	GRANDLY	GRITTED
GIRDLED	GOBELIN	GRANDMA	GRIZZLE
GIRDLER	GODDESS	GRANGER	GRIZZLY
GIRLISH	GODETIA	GRANITE	GROANED
GIRTHED	GODHEAD	GRANTED	GROCERY
GIZZARD	GODHOOD	GRANTEE	GROMMET
GLACIAL	GODLESS	GRANTER	GROOMED
GLACIER	GODLIER	GRANTOR	GROOVED
GLADDEN	GODLIKE	GRANULE	GROPING
GLADDER	GODLILY	GRAPERY	GROSSER
GLAD-EYE	GODSEND	GRAPHIC	GROSSLY
GLAMOUR	GODSHIP	GRAPNEL	GROUNDS
GLANCED	GODWARD	GRAPPLE	GROUPED
GLARING	GOGGLED	GRASPED	GROUPER
GLASSES	GOGGLES	GRASPER	GROUSED
GLAZIER	GOITRED	GRASSED	GROUSER
GLAZING	GOLFING	GRATIFY	GROUTED
GLEAMED	GOLIATH	GRATING	GROWING
GLEANED	GONDOLA	GRAVELY	GROWLED
GLEANER	GONGING	GRAVEST	GROWLER
GLEEFUL	GOOD-BYE	GRAVIED	GROWN-UP
GLIDING	GOOD-DAY	GRAVITY	GRUBBED
GLIMMER	GOODISH	GRAVURE	GRUBBER
GLIMPSE	GOODMAN	GRAZIER	GRUDGED
GLINTED	GOOSERY	GRAZING	GRUDGER
GLISTEN	GORDIAN	GREASED	GRUFFER
GLISTER	GORGING	GREASER	GRUFFLY
GLITTER	GORILLA	GREATER	GRUMBLE
GLOATED	GORMAND	GREATLY	GRUNTED
GLOBATE	GORSEDD	GRECIAN	GRUNTER

GRUYERE	HAILING	HARSHER	HECKLER
GUARDED	HAIRCUT	HARSHLY	HECTARE
GUDGEON	HAIR-OIL	HARVEST	HEDGING
GUELDER	HAIRPIN	HASHING	HEDONIC
GUERDON	HALBERD	HASHISH	HEEDFUL
GUESSED	HALCYON	HASSOCK	HEEDING
GUESSER	HALF-PAY	HASTIER	HEELING
GUICHET	HALFWAY	HASTILY	HEELTAP
GUIDAGE	HALF-WIT	HASTING	HEFTIER
GUIDING	HALIBUT	HATABLE	HEFTILY
GUILDER	HALOGEN	HATCHER	HEIGH-HO
GUILDRY	HALTING	HATCHET	HEINOUS
GUIPURE	HALVING	HATEFUL	HEIRDOM
GULLERY	HALYARD	HATLESS	HEIRESS
GULLIED	HAMBURG	HAT-RACK	HELICAL
GULLING	HAMMOCK	HAUBERK	HELICON
GUMBOIL	HAMSTER	HAUGHTY	HELL-CAT
GUMBOOT	HAMULAR	HAULAGE	HELLENE
GUMDROP	HANDBAG	HAULIER	HELLISH
GUMMING	HANDFUL	HAULING	HELPFUL
GUM-TREE	HANDIER	HAUNTED	HELPING
GUNBOAT	HANDILY	HAUNTER	HEMLOCK
GUN-DECK	HANDING	HAUTBOY	HEMMING
GUN-FIRE	HANDLED	HAUTEUR	HENBANE
GUNNERY	HANDLER	HAWKBIT	HEN-COOP
GUNNING	HANDSAW	HAWKING	HENNAED
GUNROOM	HANGDOG	HAWK-OWL	HENNERY
GUNSHOT	HANGING	HAY-BAND	HENPECK
GUN-SITE	HANGMAN	HAYCOCK	HENWIFE
GUNWALE	HANG-NET	HAYFORK	HEPATIC
GURGLED	HANSARD	HAY-LOFT	HERBAGE
GURNARD	HAPLESS	HAYRICK	HERBARY
GUSHING	HAP'ORTH	HAYSEED	HERBIST
GUSTILY	HAPPIER	HAYWARD	HERBOUS
GUTTING	HAPPILY	HAYWIRE	HERDING
GUZZLED	HARBOUR	HAZIEST	HERETIC
GUZZLER	HARDEST	HEADILY	HERITOR
GYMNAST	HARDIER	HEADING	HEROINE
GYRATED	HARDILY	HEADMAN	HEROISM
	HARDISH	HEADWAY	HEROIZE
	HARD-PAN	HEALING	HERONRY
H – 7	HARDSET	HEALTHY	HERRING
	HARD-WON	HEAPING	HERSELF
HABITAT	HAREING	HEARING	HESSIAN
HABITED	HARELIP	HEARKEN	HEXAGON
HABITUE	HARICOT	HEARSAY	HEXAPOD
HACKBUT	HARKING	HEARTED	HICKORY
HACKING	HARMFUL	HEARTEN	HIDALGO
HACKLED	HARMING	HEATHEN	HIDEOUS
HACKNEY	HARMONY	HEATING	HIDE-OUT
HACK-SAW	HARNESS	HEAVE-TO	HIGGLED
HADDOCK	HARPING	HEAVIER	HIGGLER
HAFTING	HARPIST	HEAVILY	HIGHDAY
HAGGARD	HARPOON	HEAVING	HIGHEST
HAGGISH	HARRIED	HEBRAIC	HIGH-HAT
HAGGLED	HARRIER	HECKLED	HIGHWAY

HILLIER	HORN-OWL	HUSTLER	IMPINGE
HILLMAN	HORRIFY	HUTMENT	IMPIOUS
HILLOCK	HOSANNA	HYDRANT	IMPLANT
HILLTOP	HOSIERY	HYDRATE	IMPLIED
HIMSELF	HOSPICE	HYGIENE	IMPLORE
HINNIED	HOSTAGE	HYMNIST	IMPOSED
HINTING	HOSTESS	HYMNODY	IMPOSER
HIPPING	HOSTILE		IMPOUND
HIRABLE	HOSTLER		IMPRESS
HIRCINE	HOTFOOT	I – 7	IMPREST
HIRSUTE	HOTNESS		IMPRINT
HISSING	HOTSPUR	IBERIAN	IMPROVE
HISTORY	HOTTEST	ICEBERG	IMPULSE
HITCHED	HOT-WALL	ICEBOAT	IMPUTED
HITTING	HOUNDED	ICE-FLOE	IMPUTER
HITTITE	HOUSAGE	ICEPACK	INANELY
HOARDED	HOUSING	ICE-RINK	INANITY
HOARDER	HOVERED	ICHABOD	INAPTLY
HOAXING	HOVERER	ICINESS	INBEING
HOBBLED	HOWBEIT	IDEALLY	INBOARD
HOBNAIL	HOWDY-DO	IDIOTIC	INBOUND
HOGGING	HOWEVER	IDOLISE	INBREAK
HOGGISH	HOWLING	IDYLLIC	INBREED
HOGWASH	HUDDLED	IGNEOUS	INCENSE
HOGSWEED	HUDDLER	IGNITED	INCHING
HOISTED	HUELESS	IGNITER	INCISED
HOISTER	HUFFILY	IGNOBLE	INCISOR
HOLDALL	HUFFING	IGNOBLY	INCITED
HOLDING	HUFFISH	IGNORED	INCLINE
HOLIDAY	HUGGING	ILL-BRED	INCLUDE
HOLIEST	HULKING	ILLEGAL	INCOMER
HOLLAND	HULLING	ILL-FAME	INCUBUS
HOLM-OAK	HUMANLY	ILLICIT	INCURVE
HOLSTER	HUMBLED	ILLNESS	INDEXED
HOMERIC	HUMBLER	ILL-TIME	INDITED
HONESTY	HUMDRUM	ILLUMED	INDOORS
HONEYED	HUMERUS	ILL-USED	INDRAWN
HONITON	HUMIDLY	IMAGERY	INDUCED
HONKING	HUMMING	IMAGINE	INDULGE
HOODING	HUMMOCK	IMAGING	INEPTLY
HOODLUM	HUMULUS	IMBIBED	INERTIA
HOOFING	HUNCHED	IMBIBER	INERTLY
HOOKING	HUNDRED	IMBRUED	INEXACT
HOOPING	HUNTING	IMBUING	INFANCY
HOOTING	HURDLED	IMITATE	INFANTA
HOPEFUL	HURDLER	IMMENSE	INFANTE
HOPKILN	HURLING	IMMERSE	INFERNO
HOPLITE	HURRIED	IMMORAL	INFIDEL
HOPPING	HURRIER	IMMURED	INFIELD
HOP-POLE	HURTFUL	IMPALED	INFIXED
HOP-VINE	HURTLED	IMPASSE	INFLAME
HORIZON	HUSBAND	IMPEACH	INFLATE
HORMONE	HUSHABY	IMPEDED	INFLECT
HORNBAR	HUSHING	IMPERIL	INFLICT
HORNING	HUSKING	IMPETUS	INFUSED
HORNISH	HUSTLED	IMPIETY	INFUSER

INGENUE	INWARDS	JETTING	JUNKMAN
INGOING	INWOVEN	JEZEBEL	JUPITER
INGRATE	IODISED	JIBBING	JURY-BOX
INGRESS	IONISED	JIB-BOOM	JURYMAN
INHABIT	IRACUND	JIGGING	JUSSIVE
INHALED	IRANIAN	JIGGLED	JUSTICE
INHALER	IRIDIUM	JILTING	JUSTIFY
INHERED	IRKSOME	JIM-CROW	JUTTING
INHERIT	IRONING	JINGLED	JUVENAL
INHIBIT	ISHMAEL	JITTERS	
INHUMAN	ISLAMIC	JITTERY	
INITIAL	ISOLATE	JOBBERY	K – 7
INJURED	ISOTOPE	JOBBING	
INJURER	ISSUING	JOBLESS	KAMERAD
INKHORN	ISTHMUS	JOCULAR	KATYDID
INKLING	ITALIAN	JOGGING	KEENEST
INKWELL	ITALICS	JOGGLED	KEENING
INLACED	ITCHING	JOGTROT	KEEPING
INLAYER	ITEMISE	JOINDER	KENTISH
INNINGS	ITERATE	JOINERY	KESTREL
INQUEST	IVORIED	JOINING	KETCHUP
INQUIRE	IVY-BUSH	JOINTED	KEYBOLT
INQUIRY		JOINTER	KEYED-UP
INSHORE		JOINTLY	KEYHOLE
INSIDER	J – 7	JOISTED	KEYNOTE
INSIGHT		JOLLIER	KEY-RING
INSIPID	JABBING	JOLLIFY	KEYWORD
INSPECT	JACINTH	JOLLILY	KHAMSIN
INSPIRE	JACKASS	JOLLITY	KHEDIVE
INSTALL	JACKDAW	JOLTING	KICKING
INSTANT	JACKING	JONQUIL	KICK-OFF
INSTEAD	JACKPOT	JOSTLED	KIDDING
INSULAR	JACK-TAR	JOTTING	KILLING
INSULIN	JACOBIN	JOUNCED	KILLJOY
INSURED	JACUZZI	JOURNAL	KILN-DRY
INSURER	JADEDLY	JOURNEY	KILOBIT
INTEGER	JAGGING	JOUSTED	KINDEST
INTENSE	JAILING	JOYLESS	KINDLED
INTERIM	JAMMING	JOY-RIDE	KINDRED
INTONED	JANGLED	JUBILEE	KINETIC
INTRUDE	JANITOR	JUDAISM	KINGCUP
INTRUST	JANUARY	JUDAIST	KINGDOM
INTWINE	JARRING	JUDAISE	KINGPIN
INURING	JASMINE	JUDGING	KINKING
INVADED	JAVELIN	JUGGING	KINLESS
INVADER	JAWBONE	JUGGINS	KINSHIP
INVALID	JAZZING	JUGGLED	KINSMAN
INVEIGH	JEALOUS	JUGGLER	KIRTLED
INVERSE	JEERING	JUGULAR	KISSING
INVIOUS	JEHOVAH	JUICIER	KITCHEN
INVITED	JELLIED	JU-JITSU	KNACKER
INVITER	JELLIFY	JUKE-BOX	KNAPPED
INVOICE	JERICHO	JUMBLED	KNAPPER
INVOKED	JERKING	JUMBLER	KNARLED
INVOKER	JESTFUL	JUMPING	KNAVERY
INVOLVE	JESTING	JUNIPER	KNAVISH
	JETTIED		KNEADED

KNEECAP	LAPWING	LEEMOST	LIKABLE
KNEE-PAN	LARCENY	LEERILY	LIKENED
KNIFING	LARDING	LEERING	LILY-PAD
KNITTED	LARGELY	LEE-SIDE	LIMBATE
KNITTER	LARGEST	LEE-TIDE	LIMBING
KNOBBED	LARGISH	LEEWARD	LIME-PIT
KNOBBLY	LARKING	LEGALLY	LIMINAL
KNOCKED	LASHING	LEGATEE	LIMITED
KNOCKER	LASHKAR	LEGGING	LIMITER
KNOCK-ON	LASSOED	LEGIBLE	LIMNING
KNOTTED	LASTING	LEGIBLY	LIMPING
KNOUTED	LATAKIA	LEG-IRON	LINCTUS
KNOW-ALL	LATCHED	LEGLESS	LINEAGE
KNOWING	LATCHET	LEG-PULL	LINEATE
KNUCKLE	LATENCY	LEISURE	LINEMAN
KNURLED	LATERAL	LEMMING	LINGUAL
KOUMISS	LATERAN	LENDING	LINKAGE
KREMLIN	LATHING	LENGTHY	LINKBOY
KRISHNA	LATTICE	LENIENT	LINKING
KURSAAL	LATVIAN	LENTOID	LINSEED
	LAUDING	LEONINE	LION-CUB
	LAUGHED	LEOPARD	LIONESS
L – 7	LAUNDER	LEOTARD	LIONISM
	LAUNDRY	LEPROSY	LIONISE
LABIATE	LAW-BOOK	LEPROUS	LIPPING
LACKING	LAWLESS	LESBIAN	LIQUATE
LACONIC	LAW-LORD	LET-DOWN	LIQUEFY
LACQUER	LAW-SUIT	LETTING	LIQUEUR
LACTATE	LAXNESS	LETTISH	LISPING
LACTOSE	LAYERED	LETTUCE	LISSOME
LADLING	LAYETTE	LEUCOMA	LISTING
LADY-DAY	LAYLAND	LEVELLY	LITERAL
LAGGARD	LAZIEST	LEVERED	LITHELY
LAGGING	LAZY-BED	LEVERET	LITHIUM
LAKELET	LEACHED	LEVYING	LITHOID
LAMBENT	LEADING	LEXICAL	LITOTES
LAMBING	LEAFAGE	LEXICON	LITURGY
LAMBKIN	LEAFING	LIAISON	LIVABLE
LAMINAR	LEAFLET	LIBERAL	LIVENED
LAMMING	LEAGUED	LIBERTY	LIVE-OAK
LAMP-LIT	LEAGUER	LIBRARY	LIVERED
LAMPOON	LEAKAGE	LICENCE	LOADING
LAMPREY	LEAKING	LICENSE	LOAFING
LANCERS	LEANDER	LICITLY	LOAMING
LANCING	LEANEST	LICKING	LOANING
LANDING	LEANING	LIDLESS	LOATHED
LANDTAG	LEAPING	LIE-ABED	LOATHER
LAND-TAX	LEARNED	LIFTING	LOATHLY
LANGUID	LEARNER	LIGATED	LOBBIED
LANGUOR	LEASHED	LIGHTED	LOBBING
LANKIER	LEASING	LIGHTEN	LOBELIA
LANOLIN	LEATHER	LIGHTER	LOBSTER
LANTERN	LEAVING	LIGHTLY	LOBULAR
LANYARD	LECTERN	LIGNIFY	LOCALLY
LAPPING	LECTION	LIGNITE	LOCATED
LAPPISH	LECTURE	LIGNOSE	LOCKAGE
LAPSING			

LOCKING	LOW-TIDE	MAGGOTY	MANTLED
LOCKJAW	LOYALLY	MAGICAL	MANTLET
LOCK-OUT	LOYALTY	MAGINOT	MANTRAP
LODGING	LOZENGE	MAGNATE	MANURED
LOFTIER	LUCENCY	MAGNETO	MANX-CAT
LOFTILY	LUCERNE	MAGNIFY	MAPPING
LOFTING	LUCIDLY	MAHATMA	MAPPIST
LOG-BOOK	LUCIFER	MAHJONG	MARABOU
LOGGING	LUCKIER	MAIL-BAG	MARBLED
LOGICAL	LUCKILY	MAILING	MARCHED
LOGLINE	LUFFING	MAIL-VAN	MARCHER
LOG-REEL	LUGGAGE	MAIMING	MARINER
LOG-ROLL	LUGGING	MAINOUR	MARITAL
LOG-SHIP	LUGMARK	MAINTOP	MARKING
LOGWOOD	LUGSAIL	MAJESTY	MARLINE
LOLLARD	LUGWORM	MALACCA	MARLING
LOLLING	LULLABY	MALAISE	MARLPIT
LOMBARD	LULLING	MALARIA	MARQUEE
LONG-AGO	LUMBAGO	MALAYAN	MARQUIS
LONGBOW	LUMINAL	MALISON	MARRIED
LONGEST	LUMPIER	MALLARD	MARRING
LONG-HOP	LUMPING	MALLING	MARROWY
LONGING	LUMPISH	MALMSEY	MARSALA
LONGISH	LUNATIC	MALTESE	MARSHAL
LONG-LEG	LUNCHED	MALTING	MARTIAL
LONG-RUN	LUNETTE	MALTMAN	MARTIAN
LOOKING	LUNGING	MAMMARY	MARTINI
LOOKOUT	LURCHED	MAMMOTH	MARTLET
LOOMING	LURCHER	MANACLE	MARXIAN
LOOPING	LURKING	MANAGED	MARXISM
LOOSELY	LUSHING	MANAGER	MARXIST
LOOSING	LUSTFUL	MANAKIN	MASHING
LOOTING	LUSTIER	MANATEE	MASH-TUB
LOPPING	LUSTILY	MANCHET	MASKING
LORDING	LUSTING	MANDATE	MASONIC
LORELEI	LYCHNIS	MANDREL	MASONRY
LORINER	LYDDITE	MANDRIL	MASSAGE
LOSABLE	LYING-IN	MANGLED	MASSEUR
LOTTERY	LYINGLY	MANGLER	MASSING
LOTTING	LYNCHED	MANGOLD	MASSIVE
LOUDEST	LYRICAL	MANHOLE	MASTERY
LOUNGED		MANHOOD	MASTIFF
LOUNGER	**M – 7**	MAN-HOUR	MASTING
LOURING		MAN-HUNT	MASTOID
LOUSILY	MACABRE	MANIKIN	MATADOR
LOUTISH	MACADAM	MANILLA	MATCHED
LOVABLE	MACAQUE	MANITOU	MATCHET
LOW-BORN	MACHETE	MANKIND	METALOT
LOW-BRED	MACHINE	MANLESS	MATINEE
LOWDOWN	MADDEST	MANLIKE	MATTING
LOWERED	MADDING	MAN-MADE	MATTOCK
LOW-GEAR	MADEIRA	MANNING	MATURED
LOWLAND	MADNESS	MANNISH	MAUDLIN
LOW-LIFE	MADONNA	MAN-ROPE	MAULING
LOWLILY	MAESTRO	MANSARD	MAUNDER
LOWNESS	MAGENTA	MANSION	MAWKISH

MAXIMAL	MIAULED	MISERLY	MOLLIFY
MAXIMUM	MICROBE	MISFALL	MOLLUSC
MAYFAIR	MICROHM	MISFIRE	MONARCH
MAY-LILY	MIDLAND	MISFORM	MONEYED
MAY-MORN	MID-LIFE	MISGAVE	MONGREL
MAYORAL	MIDMOST	MISGIVE	MONIKER
MAYPOLE	MIDRIFF	MISHEAR	MONITOR
MAY-TIME	MIDWIFE	MISJOIN	MONKISH
MAY-WEED	MIGRANT	MISLAID	MONOCLE
MAZURKA	MIGRATE	MISLEAD	MONSOON
MEADOWY	MIDLEST	MISLIKE	MONSTER
MEANDER	MILDEWY	MISNAME	MONTHLY
MEANEST	MILEAGE	MISRATE	MOOCHED
MEANING	MILFOIL	MISREAD	MOODILY
MEASLED	MILIARY	MISRULE	MOONING
MEASLES	MILITIA	MISSAID	MOONISH
MEASURE	MILKILY	MISSEEM	MOONLIT
MEAT-TEA	MILKING	MISSEND	MOORAGE
MECHLING	MILKMAN	MISSENT	MOOR-HEN
MEDDLED	MILKSOP	MISSILE	MOORING
MEDDLER	MILL-DAM	MISSING	MOORISH
MEDIATE	MILLIER	MISSION	MOOTING
MEDICAL	MILLING	MISSIVE	MOPPING
MEETING	MILLION	MISTAKE	MORALLY
MEGABIT	MIMESIS	MISTRELL	MORDANT
MEISSEN	MIMETIC	MISTERM	MORELLO
MELANGE	MIMICAL	MISTFUL	MORNING
MELODIC	MIMICRY	MISTILY	MOROCCO
MELTING	MINARET	MISTIME	MORPHIA
MEMENTO	MINCING	MISTRAL	MORTISE
MENACED	MINDFUL	MISTUNE	MORTIFY
MENACER	MINDING	MISUSED	MOSELLE
MENDING	MINERAL	MITHRAS	MOTORED
MENFOLK	MINERVA	MIXABLE	MOTTLED
MENTHOL	MINGLED	MIXEDLY	MOULDED
MENTION	MINGLER	MIXTURE	MOULDER
MERCERY	MINIBUS	MIZZLED	MOULTED
MERCURY	MINIKIN	MOANFUL	MOUNDED
MERGING	MINIMAL	MOANING	MOUNTED
MERITED	MINIMUM	MOBBING	MOUNTER
MERLING	MINIMUS	MOBBISH	MOURNED
MERMAID	MINSTER	MOBSMAN	MOURNER
MERRIER	MINTING	MOCKERY	MOUSING
MERRILY	MINUTED	MOCKING	MOUTHED
MESEEMS	MIOCENE	MOCK-SUN	MOUTHER
MESHING	MIRACLE	MODALLY	MOVABLE
MESSAGE	MISCALL	MODESTY	MOVABLY
MESSIAH	MISCAST	MODICUM	MUCKING
MESSING	MISCITE	MODISTE	MUD-BATH
METHANE	MISCUED	MODULAR	MUD-CART
METONIC	MISDATE	MODULUS	MUDDIED
METTLED	MISDEAL	MOHICAN	MUDDIER
MEWLING	MISDEED	MOIDORE	MUDDILY
MEXICAN	MISDEEM	MOILING	MUDDING
MAISMAL	MISDOER	MOISTEN	MUDDLED
MIAUING	MISDONE	MOLE-RAT	MUDFISH

MUD-FLAT	NAKEDLY	NEUTRON	NOTABLE
MUD-HOLE	NAMABLE	NEW-BORN	NOTABLY
MUDLARK	NANKEEN	NEWGATE	NOTANDA
MUEZZIN	NAPHTHA	NEW-MADE	NOTCHED
MUFFING	NAPLESS	NEWNESS	NOTEDLY
MUFFLED	NAPPING	NEWSBOY	NOTHING
MUFFLER	NARRATE	NEWSMAN	NOTICED
MUGGING	NARWHAL	NIAGARA	NOURISH
MUGGINS	NASALLY	NIBBLED	NOVELTY
MUGGISH	NASCENT	NIBBLER	NOWHERE
MUGWUMP	NASTIER	NIBLICK	NOXIOUS
MULATTO	NASTILY	NICKING	NUCLEAR
MULCHED	NATTIER	NIGELLA	NUCLEUS
MULCTED	NATTILY	NIGGARD	NUDGING
MULLING	NATURAL	NIGGLED	NULLIFY
MULLION	NATURED	NIGGLER	NULLITY
MUMBLED	NAUGHTY	NIGHTIE	NUMBERS
MUMBLER	NAZIISM	NIGHTLY	NUMBING
MUMMERY	NEAREST	NIMBLER	NUMERAL
MUMMIED	NEATEST	NINE-PIN	NUNNERY
MUMMIFY	NEBULAE	NINTHLY	NUNNISH
MUMMING	NEBULAR	NIPPERS	NUPTIAL
MUMPING	NECKING	NIPPIER	NURSERY
MUMPISH	NECKLET	NIPPIES	NURSING
MUNCHED	NECKTIE	NIPPING	NURTURE
MUNCHER	NEEDFUL	NIRVANA	NUTTING
MUNDANE	NEEDIER	NITRATE	NUT-TREE
MURKIER	NEEDILY	NITROUS	NUZZLED
MURKILY	NEEDING	NOBBLED	
MURRAIN	NEEDLED	NOBBLER	
MUSCLED	NEGATED	NOBLEST	**O – 7**
MUSETTE	NEGLECT	NO-CLAIM	OAFLIKE
MUSHING	NEGLIGE	NODATED	OAK-LEAF
MUSICAL	NEGRESS	NODDING	OAKLING
MUSK-RAT	NEGROID	NODULAR	OARFISH
MUSTANG	NEIGHED	NODULED	OARLOCK
MUSTARD	NEITHER	NOGGING	OARSMAN
MUSTILY	NEMESIS	NOISILY	OATCAKE
MUTABLE	NEOLOGY	NOISING	OATMEAL
MUTABLY	NEPOTIC	NOISOME	OBELISK
MUTANDA	NEPTUNE	NOMADIC	OBESITY
MUTTONY	NERVING	NOMINAL	OBEYING
MUZZILY	NERVOUS	NOMINEE	OBLIGED
MUZZLED	NEST-EGG	NON-ACID	OBLIGEE
MYNHEER	NESTING	NONAGON	OBLIGER
MYSTERY	NESTLED	NONPLUS	OBLIGOR
MYSTIFY	NESTLER	NONSTOP	OBLIQUE
	NETBALL	NONSUCH	OBLOQUY
	NET-CORD	NON-SUIT	OBSCENE
N – 7	NETTING	NOONDAY	OBSCURE
	NETTLED	NORFOLK	OBSERVE
NABBING	NETTLER	NORWICH	OBTRUDE
NAGGING	NETWORK	NOSEBAG	OBVERSE
NAILERY	NEURINE	NOSEGAY	OBVIATE
NAILING	NEUROSE	NOSTRIL	OBVIOUS
NAIVELY	NEUTRAL	NOSTRUM	OCARINA
NAIVETE			

OCCIPUT	OPINION	OUTMOVE	OXONIAN
OCCLUDE	OPOSSUM	OUTPLACE	
OCEANIA	OPPIDAN	OUTPLAY	P – 7
OCEANIC	OPPOSED	OUTPOST	PACIFIC
OCTAGON	OPPOSER	OUTPOUR	PACKAGE
OCTAVUS	OPPRESS	OUTRAGE	PACK-ICE
OCTETTE	OPTICAL	OUTRIDE	PACKING
OCTOBER	OPTIMUM	OUTRODE	PACKMAN
OCTOPOD	OPULENT	OUTSAIL	PADDING
OCTOPUS	ORATING	OUTSELL	PADDLED
OCTUPLE	ORATION	OUTSIDE	PADDLER
OCULIST	ORATORY	OUTSIZE	PADDOCK
ODDMENT	ORBITAL	OUTSOLD	PADLOCK
ODDNESS	ORCHARD	OUTSPAN	PADRONE
ODORANT	ORDERED	OUTSTAY	PAGEANT
ODOROUS	ORDERER	OUTTALK	PAILFUL
ODYSSEY	ORDERLY	OUTVOTE	PAINFUL
OEDIPUS	ORDINAL	OUTWALK	PAINING
OFFENCE	ORDINEE	OUTWARD	PAINTED
OFFERED	OREADES	OUTWEAR	PAINTER
OFFERER	ORGANIC	OUTWORK	PAIRING
OFFHAND	ORIFICE	OUTWORN	PALADIN
OFFICER	ORIGAMI	OVARIAN	PALATAL
OFF-LINE	OROLOGY	OVATION	PALAVER
OFFSIDE	ORPHEAN	OVERACT	PALETOT
OGREISH	ORPHEUS	OVERALL	PALETTE
OILCAKE	ORTOLAN	OVERATE	PALFREY
OILSHOP	OSCULAR	OVERAWE	PALLING
OILSKIN	OSMANLI	OVERBID	PALMARY
OIL-WELL	OSTEOID	OVERBUY	PALMATE
OLDNESS	OSTRICH	OVERDID	PALMERY
OLDSTER	OTTOMAN	OVERDUE	PALMING
OLD-TIME	OUTSELF	OVEREAT	PALMIST
OLYMPIA	OUSTING	OVERFAR	PALM-OIL
OLYMPIC	OUTBACK	OVERJOY	PALPATE
OLYMPUS	OUTBRAG	OVERLAP	PALSIED
OMINOUS	OUTCAST	OVERLAY	PANACEA
OMITTED	OUTCOME	OVERLIE	PANACHE
OMNIBUS	OUTCROP	OVERMAN	PANCAKE
OMNIFIC	OUTDARE	OVERPAY	PANDEAN
ONE-EYED	OUTDONE	OVERPLY	PANDORA
ONEFOLD	OUTDOOR	OVERRAN	PANICKY
ONENESS	OUTFACE	OVERRUN	PANNAGE
ONERARY	OUTFALL	OVERSEA	PANNIER
ONEROUS	OUTFLOW	OVERSEE	PANNING
ONESELF	OUTGOER	OVERSET	PANOPLY
ONE-STEP	OUTGROW	OVERSEW	PAN-PIPE
ONGOING	OUTHAUL	OVERTAX	PANSIED
ONWARDS	OUTLAND	OVERTLY	PANTHER
OPACITY	OUTLAST	OVERTOP	PANTIES
OPALINE	OUTLEAP	OVIDIAN	PANTILE
OPALISE	OUTLIER	OVOIDAL	PANTING
OPEN-AIR	OUTLINE	OVOLOGY	PAPALLY
OPENING	OUTLIVE	OWL-LIKE	PAPERED
OPERATE	OUTLOOK	OXIDATE	PAPERER
OPINING	OUTMOST	OXIDISE	PAPILLA

PAPOOSE	PAY-BOOK	PEPPERY	PHINEAS
PAPRIKA	PAY-DIRT	PEPSINE	PHOEBUS
PAPULAR	PAY-LIST	PEPTICS	PHOENIX
PAPYRUS	PAYLOAD	PEPTONE	PHONATE
PARABLE	PAYMENT	PERCEPT	PHONICS
PARADED	PAY-ROLL	PERCHED	PHOTISM
PARADOX	PEACHED	PERCHER	PHRASED
PARAGON	PEACHER	PERCUSS	PHRENIC
PARAPET	PEACOCK	PERDURE	PHYSICS
PARASOL	PEAFOWL	PERFECT	PIANIST
PARBOIL	PEAKING	PERFIDY	PIANOLA
PARCHED	PEAKISH	PERFORM	PIASTRE
PARESIS	PEALING	PERFUME	PIBROCH
PARETIC	PEARLED	PERFUSE	PICADOR
PARKING	PEASANT	PERGOLA	PICCOLO
PARLOUR	PEA-SOUP	PERHAPS	PICKAXE
PARLOUS	PEATBOG	PERIAPT	PICKING
PARODIC	PEAT-HAG	PERIDOT	PICKLED
PARQUET	PEBBLED	PERIQUE	PICQUET
PARRIED	PECCANT	PERIWIG	PICTISH
PARSING	PECCAVI	PERJURE	PICTURE
PARSLEY	PECKING	PERJURY	PIEBALD
PARSNIP	PECKISH	PERKIER	PIECING
PARTAKE	PECTATE	PERKILY	PIERAGE
PARTIAL	PECTINE	PERKING	PIERCED
PARTING	PEDDLED	PERMUTE	PIERCER
PARTNER	PEDDLER	PERPLEX	PIERROT
PARVENU	PEDICEL	PERRIER	PIFFLED
PASCHAL	PEDICLE	PERSEUS	PIG-EYED
PASSAGE	PEELING	PERSIAN	PIGGERY
PASSING	PEEPING	PERSIST	PIGGING
PASSION	PEERAGE	PERSONA	PIGGISH
PASSIVE	PEERESS	PERSPEX	PIG-IRON
PASSKEY	PEERING	PERTAIN	PIG-LEAD
PASSMAN	PEEVISH	PERTURB	PIGMENT
PASTERN	PEGASUS	PERUSAL	PIGSKIN
PASTIME	PEGGING	PERUSED	PIGTAIL
PASTING	PELAGIC	PERUSER	PIGWASH
PASTURE	PELICAN	PERVADE	PIKELET
PATBALL	PELISSE	PERVERT	PIKEMAN
PATCHED	PELTING	PESTLED	PILEATE
PATCHER	PENALLY	PETERED	PILGRIM
PATELLA	PENALTY	PETRIFY	PILLAGE
PATHWAY	PENANCE	PETROUS	PILLBOX
PATIENT	PENATES	PETTILY	PILLING
PATNESS	PENDANT	PETTING	PILLION
PATRIOT	PENDENT	PETTISH	PILLORY
PATTERN	PENGUIN	PETUNIA	PILLOWY
PATTING	PEN-NAME	PEW-RENT	PILOTED
PAUCITY	PENNANT	PFENNIG	PIMENTO
PAULINE	PENNIED	PHAETON	PIMPLED
PAUNCHY	PENNING	PHALANX	PINCERS
PAUSING	PENSION	PHANTOM	PINCHED
PAWNING	PENSIVE	PHARAOH	PINCHER
PAYABLE	PENTODE	PHARYNX	PINFOLD
PAY-BILL	PEOPLED	PHILTRE	PINGING

PINGUID	PLASHED	POACHER	POSTING
PINGUIN	PLASTER	POETESS	POSTMAN
PINHOLE	PLASTIC	POINTED	POSTURE
PINK-EYE	PLATEAU	POINTER	POST-WAR
PINKING	PLATING	POISING	POTABLE
PINKISH	PLATOON	POLE-AXE	POTENCY
PINNACE	PLATTED	POLECAT	POT-HERB
PINNATE	PLATTER	POLEMIC	POT-HOLE
PINNING	PLAUDIT	POLENTA	POT-HOOK
PINT-POT	PLAY-BOX	POLICED	POT-LUCK
PIONEER	PLAYBOY	POLITER	POT-SHOT
PIOUSLY	PLAY-DAY	POLITIC	POTTAGE
PIP-EMMA	PLAYFUL	POLLACK	POTTERY
PIPERIC	PLAYING	POLLARD	POTTING
PIPETTE	PLEADED	POLL-AXE	POUCHED
PIPLESS	PLEADER	POLLING	POULARD
PIPPING	PLEASED	POLL-MAN	POULTRY
PIQUANT	PLEASER	POLL-TAX	POUNCED
PIQUING	PLEATED	POLLUTE	POUNDED
PIRATED	PLEDGED	POLYGON	POUNDER
PIROGUE	PLEDGEE	POLYPUS	POURING
PISCARY	PLEDGER	POMFRET	POUTING
PITAPAT	PLENARY	POMMARD	POVERTY
PITCHED	PLENISH	POMPOUS	POWDERY
PITCHER	PLENIST	PONIARD	POWERED
PITCOAL	PLEROMA	PONTIFF	PRAETOR
PITEOUS	PLEURAL	PONTOON	PRAIRIE
PITFALL	PLEXURE	POOH-BAH	PRAISED
PIT-HEAD	PLIABLE	POOLING	PRAISER
PITHILY	PLIABLY	POOPING	PRALINE
PITIFUL	PLIANCY	POOREST	PRANCED
PITTING	PLIMSOL	POOR-LAW	PRANGED
PITYING	PLODDED	POPCORN	PRANKED
PIVOTAL	PLODDER	POPEDOM	PRATIES
PIVOTED	PLOPPED	POP-EYED	PRATING
PLACARD	PLOTTED	POPPIED	PRATTLE
PLACATE	PLOTTER	POPPING	PRAYING
PLACEBO	PLUCKED	POPPLED	PREACHY
PLACING	PLUCKER	POP-SHOP	PREBEND
PLACKET	PLUGGER	POPULAR	PRECEDE
PLAFOND	PLUGGED	PORCINE	PRECEPT
PLAGUED	PLUMAGE	PORK-PIE	PRECISE
PLAGUER	PLUMBED	PORT-BAR	PREDATE
PLAINER	PLUMBER	PORTEND	PREDICT
PLAINLY	PLUMING	PORTENT	PREDOOM
PLAITED	PLUMMET	PORTICO	PREEMPT
PLAITER	PLUMPED	PORTIFY	PREENED
PLANARY	PLUMPER	PORTING	PREFACE
PLANING	PLUMPLY	PORTION	PREFECT
PLANISH	PLUNDER	PORTRAY	PRELACY
PLANKED	PLUNGED	POSSESS	PRELATE
PLANNED	PLUNGER	POSTAGE	PRELECT
PLANNER	PLUVIAL	POST-BAG	PRELUDE
PLANTAR	PLUVIUS	POST-BOY	PREMIER
PLANTED	PLYWOOD	POST-DAY	PREMISE
PLANTER	POACHED	POSTERN	PREMISS

PREMIUM
PREPAID
PREPARE
PRESAGE
PRESENT
PRESIDE
PRESSED
PRESSER
PRESUME
PRETEND
PRETEXT
PRETZEL
PREVAIL
PREVENT
PREVIEW
PREYING
PRICING
PRICKED
PRICKER
PRICKLE
PRICKLY
PRIDIAN
PRIDING
PRIMACY
PRIMAGE
PRIMARY
PRIMATE
PRIMELY
PRIMING
PRIMULA
PRINKED
PRINTED
PRINTER
PRISING
PRITHEE
PRIVACY
PRIVATE
PRIVILY
PRIVITY
PRIZING
PROBANG
PROBATE
PROBING
PROBITY
PROBLEM
PROCEED
PROCESS
PROCTOR
PROCURE
PRODDED
PRODDER
PRODIGY
PRODUCE
PRODUCT
PROFANE
PROFESS

PROFFER
PROFILE
PROFUSE
PROGENY
PROGRAM
PROJECT
PROLATE
PROLONG
PROMISE
PROMOTE
PRONELY
PRONGED
PRONOUN
PROOFED
PROPHET
PROPOSE
PROPPED
PROSAIC
PROSIFY
PROSILY
PROSING
PROSODY
PROSPER
PROTEAN
PROTECT
PROTEGE
PROTEIN
PROTEST
PROTEUS
PROUDER
PROUDLY
PROVERB
PROVIDE
PROVINE
PROVING
PROVISO
PROVOKE
PROVOST
PROWESS
PROWLED
PROWLER
PROXIMO
PRUDENT
PRUDERY
PRUDISH
PRUNING
PRUSSIC
PRYTHEE
PSALTER
PSYCHIC
PUBERTY
PUBLISH
PUCKISH
PUDDING
PUDDLED
PUDDLER

PUDDOCK
PUERILE
PUFFING
PUFFIER
PUFFILY
PUGMILL
PUG-NOSE
PULLING
PULLMAN
PULL-OUT
PULPING
PULPOUS
PULSATE
PULSING
PUMPAGE
PUMPING
PUMPKIN
PUNCHED
PUNCHER
PUNCTUM
PUNGENT
PUNNING
PUNSTER
PUNTING
PURGING
PURITAN
PURLIEU
PURLING
PURLOIN
PURPLED
PURPORT
PURPOSE
PURRING
PURSING
PURSUED
PURSUER
PURSUIT
PURVIEW
PUSHFUL
PUSHING
PUSTULE
PUTREFY
PUTTIED
PUTTING
PUZZLED
PUZZLER
PYGMEAN
PYJAMAS
PYRAMID
PYRETIC
PYREXIA
PYRITES
PYRITIC
PYROSIS
PYROTIC
PYRRHIC

PYTHIAD
PYTHIAN

Q – 7

QUACKED
QUAFFED
QUAFFER
QUAILED
QUAKING
QUALIFY
QUALITY
QUANTIC
QUANTUM
QUARREL
QUARTAN
QUARTER
QUARTET
QUASHED
QUASSIA
QUAVERY
QUEENED
QUEENLY
QUEERER
QUEERLY
QUELLED
QUELLER
QUEROUS
QUERIED
QUERIST
QUESTED
QUESTER
QUESTOR
QUIBBLE
QUICKEN
QUICKER
QUICKIE
QUICKLY
QUIESCE
QUIETED
QUIETEN
QUIETER
QUIETLY
QUIETUS
QUILLED
QUILTED
QUILTER
QUINARY
QUINATE
QUININE
QUINTET
QUIPPED
QUITTAL
QUITTED
QUITTER
QUI-VIVE
QUIXOTE

QUIZZED	RANSACK	REBORED	REEVING
QUIZZER	RANTING	REBOUND	REFEREE
QUONDAM	RAPHAEL	REBUILD	REFINED
QUOTING	RAPIDLY	REBUILT	REFINER
	RAPPING	REBUKED	REFLECT
R – 7	RAPPORT	REBUKER	REFLOAT
RABIDLY	RAPTURE	RECEDED	REFORGE
RACCOON	RAREBIT	RECEIPT	RE-FOUND
RACKETY	RASHEST	RECEIVE	REFRACT
RACKING	RASPING	RECHEAT	REFRAIN
RACQUET	RATABLE	RECITAL	REFRAME
RADDLED	RATAFIA	RECITED	REFRESH
RADIANT	RATATAT	RECITER	REFUGEE
RADIATE	RATCHED	RECKING	REFUSAL
RADICAL	RATCHET	RECLAIM	REFUSED
RADICLE	RATTING	RECLAME	REFUSER
RADIOED	RATTLED	RECLASP	REFUTED
RAFFISH	RATTLER	RECLINE	REFUTER
RAFFLED	RAT-TRAP	RECLOSE	REGALED
RAFFLER	RAUCOUS	RECLUSE	REGALIA
RAGEFUL	RAVAGED	RECOUNT	REGALLY
RAG-FAIR	RAVINED	RECOVER	REGATTA
RAGGING	RAWHIDE	RECROSS	REGENCY
RAGTIME	RAWNESS	RECRUIT	REGIMEN
RAGWEED	RAYLESS	RECTIFY	REGNANT
RAGWORT	REACHED	RECTORY	REGORGE
RAIDING	REACHER	RECURVE	REGREET
RAIL-CAR	REACTED	REDCOAT	REGRESS
RAILING	REACTOR	REDDEST	REGULAR
RAILWAY	READIED	REDDISH	REGULUS
RAIMENT	READIER	RED-EYED	REHOUSE
RAINBOW	READILY	RED-FISH	REIGNED
RAINING	READING	REDHEAD	REINING
RAISING	READMIT	REDNESS	REINTER
RAKE-OFF	READOPT	REDOUBT	REISSUE
RALLIED	READORN	REDOUND	REJOICE
RAMADAN	READOUT	REDPOLL	REJOINT
RAMBLED	REAGENT	REDRAFT	REJUDGE
RAMBLER	REALISE	REDRAWN	RELABEL
RAMEKIN	REALISM	REDRESS	RELAPSE
RAMEOUS	REALIST	REDSKIN	RELATED
RAMLINE	REALITY	RED-TAPE	RELATER
RAMMING	REALLOT	REDUCED	RELATOR
RAMPAGE	REALTOR	REDUCER	RELAXED
RAMPANT	RE-ANNEX	REDWING	RELAYED
RAMPART	REAPING	REDWOOD	RELEASE
RAMPING	REAPPLY	REEKING	RELIANT
RAMPION	REARGUE	RE-ELECT	RELIEVE
RANCHED	REARING	REELING	RELIGHT
RANCHER	REARISE	RE-ENACT	RELIVED
RANCOUR	REARMED	RE-ENDOW	RELUMED
RANGERS	RE-AROSE	RE-ENJOY	RELYING
RANGING	REAWAKE	RE-ENTER	REMAINS
RANKEST	REBATED	RE-ENTRY	REMARRY
RANKING	REBIRTH	RE-EQUIP	REMBLAI
RANKLED	REBLOOM	RE-ERECT	REMNANT

REMODEL	RESOUND	REWROTE	ROASTER
REMORSE	RESPECT	REYNARD	ROBBERY
REMOTER	RE-SPELL	RHEMISH	ROBBING
REMOULD	RE-SPELT	RHENISH	ROCKERY
REMOUNT	RESPIRE	RHODIAN	ROCKIER
REMOVAL	RESPITE	RHOMBUS	ROCKILY
REMOVED	RESPLIT	RHUBARB	ROCKING
REMOVER	RE-SPOKE	RHYMING	RODLIKE
RENAMED	RESPOND	RHYMIST	ROEBUCK
RENDING	RESTAMP	RIBBING	ROGUERY
RENEWAL	RESTATE	RIBLESS	ROGUISH
RENEWED	REST-DAY	RIBSTON	ROILING
RENT-DAY	RESTFUL	RICHEST	ROISTER
RENTIER	RESTING	RICKETS	ROLLICK
RENTING	RESTIVE	RICKETY	ROLLING
REORDER	RESTOCK	RIDDING	ROMANCE
REPAINT	RESTORE	RIDDLED	ROMANIC
REPAPER	RESUMED	RIDDLER	ROMAUNT
REPINED	RESURGE	RIFLING	ROMPERS
REPINER	RETAKEN	RIFTING	ROMPING
REPLACE	RETINUE	RIGGING	ROMPISH
REPLANT	RETIRAL	RIGHTED	RONDEAU
REPLETE	RETIRED	RIGHTEN	ROOFING
REPLEVY	RETOUCH	RIGHTER	ROOKERY
REPLICA	RETRACE	RIGHTLY	ROOKING
REPLIED	RETRACT	RIGIDLY	ROOMAGE
REPLIER	RETREAD	RIMLESS	ROOMFUL
REPOINT	RETREAT	RIMMING	ROOMIER
REPOSAL	RETRIAL	RINDING	ROOMILY
REPOSED	RETRIED	RINGING	ROOMING
REPOSER	RETYPED	RINGLET	ROOSTED
REPRESS	REUNIFY	RINSING	ROOSTER
REPRINT	REUNION	RIOTING	ROOTING
REPRISE	REUNITE	RIOTOUS	ROPEWAY
REPROOF	REURGED	RIPCORD	ROSEATE
REPROVE	REVALUE	RIPOSTE	ROSE-BAY
REPRUNE	REVELRY	RIPPING	ROSE-BOX
REPTILE	REVENGE	RIPPLED	ROSE-BUD
REPULSE	REVENUE	RISIBLE	ROSETTE
REPUTED	REVERED	RISIBLY	ROSIEST
REQUEST	REVERIE	RISKIER	ROSTRUM
REQUIEM	REVERSE	RISKING	ROTATED
REQUIRE	REVERSI	RISOTTO	ROTATOR
REQUITE	REVILED	RISSOLE	ROTTING
REREDOS	REVILER	RIVALRY	ROTUNDA
RESCIND	REVISAL	RIVETED	ROUGHED
RE-SCORE	REVISED	RIVETER	ROUGHEN
RESCUED	REVISER	RIVIERA	ROUGHER
RESCUER	REVISIT	RIVULET	ROUGHLY
RESEIZE	REVIVAL	ROAD-HOG	ROULADE
RESERVE	REVIVED	ROADMAN	ROULEAU
RESHAPE	REVIVER	ROAD-MAP	ROUNDED
RESIDED	REVOKED	ROADWAY	ROUNDEL
RESIDER	REVOLVE	ROAMING	ROUNDER
RESIDUE	REVVING	ROARING	ROUNDLY
RESOLVE	REWRITE	ROASTED	ROUND-UP

ROUSING	SADNESS	SAVAGED	SCOOPER
ROUTING	SAFFRON	SAVANNA	SCOOTED
ROUTINE	SAGGING	SAVE-ALL	SCOOTER
ROWDIER	SAILING	SAVELOY	SCORIFY
ROWDILY	SAINTED	SAVINGS	SCORING
ROWLOCK	SAINTLY	SAVIOUR	SCORNED
ROYALLY	SALIENT	SAVOURY	SCORNER
ROYALTY	SALLIED	SAWDUST	SCORPIO
RUB-A-DUB	SALLOWY	SAWFISH	SCOURED
RUBBING	SALSIFY	SAWMILL	SCOURER
RUBBISH	SALT-BOX	SAW-WORT	SCOURGE
RUB-DOWN	SALTIER	SAXHORN	SCOWLED
RUBICON	SALTING	SCABIES	SCRAGGY
RUCHING	SALTIRE	SCABRID	SCRAPED
RUCKING	SALTISH	SCALDED	SCRAPER
RUCKLED	SALT-PAN	SCALENE	SCRAPPY
RUCTION	SALT-PIT	SCALING	SCRATCH
RUDDIER	SALUTED	SCALLOP	SCRAWLY
RUDDILY	SALVAGE	SCALPED	SCRAWNY
RUFFIAN	SALVING	SCALPEL	SCREECH
RUFFING	SAMOVAR	SCALPER	SCREEVE
RUFFLED	SAMOYED	SCAMPED	SCREWED
RUNNING	SAMPLED	SCAMPER	SCREWER
RUINOUS	SAMPLER	SCANDAL	SCRIBAL
RUMBLED	SAMURAI	SCANNED	SCRIBED
RUMBLER	SANCTUM	SCANNER	SCRIBER
RUMMAGE	SANCTUS	SCANTLE	SCROOGE
RUMNESS	SANDBAG	SCANTLY	SCRUBBY
RUMPLED	SAND-BOX	SCAPULA	SCRUFFY
RUNAWAY	SANDBOY	SCARCER	SCRUMPY
RUNNING	SAND-EEL	SCARFED	SCRUNCH
RUNTIME	SAND-FLY	SCARIFY	SCRUPLE
RUPTURE	SAND-PIT	SCARING	SCUDDED
RURALLY	SAPHEAD	SCARLET	SCUFFLE
RUSHING	SAPIENT	SCARPED	SCULLED
RUSH-MAT	SAPLESS	SCARRED	SCULLER
RUSSETY	SAPLING	SCATHED	SCUPPER
RUSSIAN	SAPPHIC	SCATTER	SCUTATE
RUSTIER	SAPPING	SCAUPER	SCUTTLE
RUSTILY	SAPWOOD	SCENERY	SCYTHED
RUSTING	SARACEN	SCENTED	SEA-BANK
RUSTLED	SARCASM	SCEPTIC	SEA-BEAR
RUSTLER	SARCOMA	SCEPTRE	SEA-BEET
	SATANIC	SCHEMED	SEA-BIRD
S – 7	SATCHEL	SCHEMER	SEA-BOAT
SABBATH	SATIATE	SCHERZO	SEA-CALF
SACKAGE	SATIETY	SCHOLAR	SEA-CARD
SACKBUT	SATINET	SCHOLIA	SEA-COAL
SACKFUL	SATIRIC	SCIATIC	SEA-COCK
SACKING	SATISFY	SCIENCE	SEA-COOK
SACRIST	SAUCIER	SCISSOR	SEA-CROW
SADDEST	SAUCILY	SCOFFED	SEA-DACE
SADDLED	SAUCING	SCOFFER	SEA-FIRE
SADDLER	SAUNTER	SCOLDED	SEA-FISH
SAD-EYED	SAURIAN	SCOLLOP	SEA-FOAM
SADIRON	SAUSAGE	SCOOPED	SEA-FOLK

SEAFOOD	SEED-OIL	SEXTAIN	SHIPPED
SEA-FOWL	SEEKING	SEXTANT	SHIPPER
SEA-GATE	SEEMING	SEXTILE	SHIP-WAY
SEA-GIRT	SEEPAGE	SHACKLE	SHIRKED
SEA-GULL	SEETHED	SHADIER	SHIRKER
SEA-HARE	SEGMENT	SHADILY	SHIRRED
SEA-HAWK	SEIZING	SHADING	SHIVERY
SEA-KALE	SEIZURE	SHADOWY	SHOALED
SEA-KING	SELF-FED	SHAFTED	SHOCKED
SEA-LARK	SELFISH	SHAGGED	SHOCKER
SEA-LEGS	SELLING	SHAKILY	SHOEING
SEALERY	SELTZER	SHAKING	SHOE-TIE
SEA-LILY	SELVAGE	SHALLOP	SHOOING
SEA-LINE	SEMATIC	SHALLOT	SHOOTER
SEALING	SEMI-GOD	SHALLOW	SHOP-BOY
SEA-LION	SEMINAL	SHAMBLE	SHOPMAN
SEA-MARK	SEMITIC	SHAMING	SHOPPED
SEA-MILE	SEMIPED	SHAMMED	SHOPPER
SEAMING	SEMITIC	SHAMMER	SHORING
SEA-MOSS	SENATOR	SHAMPOO	SHORTED
SEA-PIKE	SENDING	SHAPELY	SHORTEN
SEA-PORT	SEND-OFF	SHAPING	SHORTER
SEARING	SENEGAL	SHARING	SHOTGUN
SEA-RISK	SENSING	SHARPEN	SHOTTED
SEA-ROOM	SENSORY	SHARPER	SHOUTED
SEA-SALT	SENSUAL	SHARPLY	SHOUTER
SEASICK	SEPTATE	SHATTER	SHOVING
SEASIDE	SEQUENT	SHAVIAN	SHOW-BOX
SEA-SLUG	SEQUOIA	SHAVING	SHOWERY
SEATING	SERBIAN	SHEAFED	SHOWILY
SEA-VIEW	SERENER	SHEARER	SHOWING
SEA-WALL	SERFAGE	SHEATHE	SHOWMAN
SEAWARD	SERFDOM	SHEAVED	SHREDDY
SEAWEED	SERIATE	SHEBEEN	SHRILLY
SEA-WIFE	SERINGA	SHEDDER	SHRINED
SEA-WING	SERIOUS	SHEERED	SHRIVEL
SEA-WOLF	SERPENT	SHEETED	SHRIVEN
SEA-WORM	SERRATE	SHELLAC	SHROUDS
SECEDED	SERRIED	SHELLED	SHRUBBY
SECEDER	SERVANT	SHELLER	SHUDDER
SECLUDE	SERVIAN	SHELTER	SHUFFLE
SECONDO	SERVICE	SHELTIE	SHUNNED
SECRECY	SERVILE	SHELVED	SHUNNER
SECRETE	SERVING	SHERBET	SHUNTED
SECTILE	SESSION	SHERIFF	SHUNTER
SECTION	SET-BACK	SHEWING	SHUT-EYE
SECULAR	SET-DOWN	SHIFTED	SHUTTER
SECURED	SETTING	SHIFTER	SHUTTLE
SECURER	SETTLED	SHIKARI	SHYLOCK
SEDUCED	SETTLER	SHIMMER	SHYNESS
SEDUCER	SEVENTH	SHINGLE	SHYSTER
SEEABLE	SEVENTY	SHINGLY	SIAMESE
SEEDBED	SEVERAL	SHINING	SIBLING
SEEDILY	SEVERED	SHIP-BOY	SICK-BAY
SEEDING	SEVERER	SHIPFUL	SICK-BED
SEED-LAC	SEXLESS	SHIP-MAN	SICKEST

SICKISH	SKIFFLE	SLICKER	SMUDGED
SIDEARM	SKILFUL	SLIDDER	SMUDGER
SIDECAR	SKILLED	SLIDING	SMUGGLE
SIDLING	SKILLET	SLIMILY	SNAFFLE
SIFFLED	SKIMMED	SLIMMER	SNAGGED
SIFTING	SKIMMER	SLINGER	SNAGGER
SIGHING	SKIMPED	SLIPPED	SNAKING
SIGHTED	SKINFUL	SLIPPER	SNAKISH
SIGHTER	SKINNED	SLIPWAY	SNAPPED
SIGHTLY	SKINNER	SLITHER	SNAPPER
SIGNIFY	SKIPPED	SLITTED	SNARING
SIGNING	SKIPPER	SLITTER	SNARLED
SIGNORA	SKIPPET	SLOBBER	SNATCHY
SIGNORY	SKIRLED	SLOE-GIN	SNEAKED
SILENCE	SKIRTED	SLOGGED	SNEAKER
SILENUS	SKIRTER	SLOGGER	SNEERED
SILICIC	SKITTER	SLOPING	SNEERER
SILICON	SKITTLE	SLOPPED	SNEEZED
SILK-HAT	SKIVING	SLOTTED	SNICKED
SILKIER	SKULKED	SLOUCHY	SNICKER
SILKILY	SKY-BLUE	SLOWEST	SNIFFED
SILK-MAN	SKY-HIGH	SLOWING	SNIFFLE
SILLIER	SKYLARK	SLUBBER	SNIFTED
SILLILY	SKYLINE	SLUDGER	SNIFTER
SILTING	SKYSAIL	SLUGGED	SNIGGER
SILVERN	SKYWARD	SLUICED	SNIGGLE
SILVERY	SLABBED	SLUMBER	SNIPING
SIMILAR	SLABBER	SLUMMER	SNIPPED
SIMPLER	SLACKED	SLUMPED	SNIPPER
SINCERE	SLACKEN	SLURRED	SNIPPET
SINEWED	SLACKER	SLYNESS	SNOOKER
SINGING	SLACKLY	SMACKED	SNOOPED
SINGLED	SLAKING	SMACKER	SNOOPER
SINGLET	SLAMMED	SMARTED	SNOOZED
SINKING	SLANDER	SMARTEN	SNOOZER
SINLESS	SLANGED	SMARTER	SNORING
SINNING	SLANTED	SMARTLY	SNORTED
SINUATE	SLANTLY	SMASHED	SNORTER
SINUOUS	SLAPPED	SMASHER	SNOUTED
SIPPING	SLASHED	SMASH-UP	SNOW-ICE
SIRGANG	SLASHER	SMATTER	SNOWILY
SIRLOIN	SLATING	SMEARED	SNOWMAN
SIROCCO	SLAVERY	SMELLED	SNUBBED
SISTINE	SLAVING	SMELLER	SNUBBER
SITTING	SLAVISH	SMELTED	SNUFFED
SITUATE	SLAYING	SMELTER	SNUFFER
SIXFOLD	SLEDDED	SMICKER	SNUFFLE
SIXTEEN	SLEDGED	SMILING	SNUGGLE
SIXTHLY	SLEEKED	SMIRKED	SOAKAGE
SIZABLE	SLEEKER	SMITING	SOAKING
SIZZLED	SLEEKLY	SMITTEN	SO-AND-SO
SKATING	SLEEPER	SMOKIER	SOAPBOX
SKEPFUL	SLEETED	SMOKILY	SOAPING
SKEPTIC	SLEIGHT	SMOKING	SOARING
SKETCHY	SLENDER	SMOOTHE	SOBBING
SKIDDED	SLICING	SMOTHER	SOBERED

SOBERLY	SPANGLY	SPIRING	SQUALOR
SOCIETY	SPANIEL	SPIRTED	SQUARED
SOCKEYE	SPANISH	SPITING	SQUASHY
SOCKING	SPANKED	SPITTED	SQUATTY
SOFTEST	SPANKER	SPITTER	SQUEEZE
SOFTISH	SPANNED	SPITTLE	SQUELCH
SOIGNEE	SPANNER	SPLASHY	SQUIFFY
SOILING	SPARELY	SPLAYED	SQUIRED
SOJOURN	SPARING	SPLEENY	STABBED
SOLACED	SPARKED	SPLENIC	STABBER
SOLDIER	SPARKLE	SPLICED	STABLED
SOLICIT	SPARRED	SPLODGE	STACKED
SOLIDLY	SPARROW	SPLODGY	STACKER
SOLIDUS	SPARTAN	SPLOTCH	STADIUM
SOLOIST	SPASTIC	SPOILED	STAFFED
SOLOMON	SPATIAL	SPOILER	STAGERY
SOLUBLE	SPATTER	SPONDEE	STAGGER
SOLVENT	SPATULA	SPONGED	STAGING
SOLVING	SPAWNED	SPONGER	STAIDLY
SOMATIC	SPAWNER	SPONSAL	STAINED
SOMEHOW	SPEAKER	SPONSON	STAINER
SOMEONE	SPEARED	SPONSOR	STAITHE
SONGFUL	SPEARER	SPOOFED	STAKING
SONSHIP	SPECIAL	SPOOLED	STATELY
SOOTHED	SPECIES	SPOONED	STALEST
SOOTHER	SPECIFY	SPORRAN	STALKED
SOOTING	SPECKED	SPORTED	STALKER
SOPHISM	SPECKLE	SPORTER	STALLED
SOPHIST	SPECTRA	SPOTTED	STAMINA
SOPPING	SPECTRE	SPOTTER	STAMMER
SOPRANO	SPEEDED	SPOUSAL	STAMPED
SORCERY	SPEEDER	SPOUTED	STAMPER
SORDINE	SPEED-UP	SPOUTER	STAND-BY
SORITES	SPELLED	SPRAYED	STANDER
SORORAL	SPELLER	SPRAYEY	STAND-TO
SOROSIS	SPELTER	SPRIGGY	STAND-UP
SORRILY	SPENCER	SPRIGHT	STAPLED
SORTING	SPENDER	SPRINGE	STAPLER
SOTTISH	SPEWING	SPRINGY	STARCHY
SOUFFLÉ	SPHERAL	SPRUCED	STARDOM
SOULFUL	SPHERED	SPUMING	STARING
SOUNDLY	SPHERIC	SPUN-OUT	STARKLY
SOUNDED	SPICERY	SPURNED	STARLIT
SOUNDER	SPICILY	SPURNER	STARRED
SOUPÇON	SPICING	SPURRED	STARTED
SOUREST	SPIDERY	SPURREY	STARTER
SOURING	SPIKING	SPURTED	STARTLE
SOURISH	SPILLED	SPURTLE	STARVED
SOUSING	SPILLER	SPUR-WAY	STATANT
SOUTANE	SPINACH	SPUTNIK	STATELY
SOUTHER	SPINATE	SPUTTER	STATICS
SOU'WEST	SPINDLE	SPY-BOAT	STATING
SOZZLED	SPINDLY	SPYHOLE	STATION
SPACIAL	SPINNER	SQUABBY	STATIST
SPACING	SPINNEY	SQUALID	STATUED
SPANGLE	SPIRANT	SQUALLY	STATURE

STATUTE	STOCKED	STUTTER	SUICIDE
STAUNCH	STOICAL	STYGIAN	SUITING
STAVING	STOKING	STYLING	SULKIER
STAYING	STOMACH	STYLISE	SULKILY
STEALER	STONILY	STYLISH	SULKING
STEALTH	STONING	STYLIST	SULLAGE
STEAMED	STOOGED	STYLITE	SULLENS
STEAMER	STOOKED	STYLOID	SULLIED
STEELED	STOOPED	STYMIED	SULPHUR
STEEPED	STOOPER	SUASION	SULTANA
STEEPEN	STOPGAP	SUASIVE	SUMLESS
STEEPER	STOPPED	SUASORY	SUMMARY
STEEPLE	STOPPER	SUAVELY	SUMMERY
STEEPLY	STORAGE	SUAVITY	SUMMING
STEERED	STORIED	SUBACID	SUMMONS
STEERER	STORING	SUBBING	SUMPTER
STELLAR	STORMED	SUBDEAN	SUN-BATH
STEMLET	STORMER	SUBDUAL	SUNBEAM
STEMMED	STOUTER	SUBDUCT	SUN-BEAT
STENCIL	STOUTLY	SUBDUED	SUN-BIRD
STENTOR	STOWAGE	SUBDUER	SUNBURN
STEPNEY	STOWING	SUBEDIT	SUN-DIAL
STEPPED·	STRANGE	SUBFUSC	SUNDOWN
STEPPER	STRATUM	SUB-HEAD	SUNFISH
STEPSON	STRATUS	SUBJECT	SUNLESS
STERILE	STRAYED	SUBJOIN	SUNNING
STERNAL	STRAYER	SUBLATE	SUNRISE
STERNER	STREAKY	SUBLIME	SUNSPOT
STERNLY	STREAMY	SUBRENT	SUNWARD
STERNUM	STRETCH	SUBSALT	SUNWISE
STETSON	STREWED	SUBSIDE	SUPPING
STEWARD	STRIATE	SUBSIDY	SUPPLED
STEWING	STRIKER	SUBSIGN	SUPPORT
STEWPAN	STRINGY	SUBSIST	SUPPOSE
STEWPOT	STRIPED	SUBSOIL	SUPREME
STICKER	STRIVEN	SUBSUME	SURCOAT
STICKLE	STRIVER	SUBTEND	SURDITY
STICK-UP	STROKED	SUBTILE	SURFACE
STIFFEN	STROKER	SUBTLER	SURFEIT
STIFFER	STROPHE	SUBTYPE	SURGENT
STIFFLY	STUBBED	SUBURBS	SURGEON
STIFLED	STUBBLE	SUBVENE	SURGERY
STILLED	STUBBLY	SUBVERT	SURGING
STILLER	STUCK-UP	SUCCEED	SURLIER
STILTED	STUDDED	SUCCESS	SURLILY
STILTON	STUDENT	SUCCOUR	SURLOIN
STIMULI	STUDIED	SUCCUMB	SURMISE
STINGER	STUFFED	SUCKING	SURNAME
STINKER	STUFFER	SUCKLED	SURPASS
STINTED	STUMBLE	SUCKLER	SURPLUS
STINTER	STUMPED	SUCROSE	SURTOUT
STIPEND	STUMPER	SUCTION	SURVIVE
STIPPLE	STUNNED	SUFFICE	SUSPECT
STIRRED	STUNNER	SUFFUSE	SUSPEND
STIRRER	STUNTED	SUGARED	SUSPIRE
STIRRUP	STUPEFY	SUGGEST	SUSTAIN

SUTURAL	SYLPHID	TANNERY	TEMPLED
SUTURED	SYMPTOM	TANNING	TEMPLET
SWABBED	SYNAXIS	TANTRUM	TEMPTED
SWABBER	SYNCOPE	TAPERED	TEMPTER
SWADDLE	SYNESIS	TAPIOCA	TENABLE
SWAGGER	SYNODAL	TAPPING	TENANCY
SWAGMAN	SYNONYM	TAPROOM	TENDING
SWAHILI	SYRINGE	TAPROOT	TENDRIL
SWALING		TAPSTER	TENFOLD
SWALLOW		TARDIER	TENSELY
SWAMPED	T – 7	TARDILY	TENSEST
SWANKED		TARNISH	TENSILE
SWAPPED	TABASCO	TARRIED	TENSION
SWARDED	TABINET	TARRIER	TENSITY
SWARMED	TABLEAU	TARRING	TENTHLY
SWARTHY	TABLING	TARTISH	TENT-PEG
SWASHED	TABLOID	TARTLET	TENUITY
SWASHER	TABOOED	TASKING	TENUOUS
SWATTED	TABULAR	TASTIER	TERMING
SWATTER	TACITLY	TASTILY	TERMINI
SWAYING	TACKING	TASTING	TERMITE
SWEALED	TACKLED	TATTERY	TERNARY
SWEARER	TACTFUL	TATTING	TERNATE
SWEATED	TACTICS	TATTLED	TERRACE
SWEATER	TACTILE	TATTLER	TERRAIN
SWEDISH	TACTION	TAUNTED	TERRENE
SWEEPER	TACTUAL	TAUNTER	TERRIER
SWEETEN	TADPOLE	TAURINE	TERRIFY
SWEETER	TAFFETA	TAUTEST	TERRINE
SWEETLY	TAGGING	TAXABLE	TERSELY
SWELLED	TAIL-END	TAX-FREE	TERTIAN
SWELTER	TAILING	TAXI-CAB	TESTACY
SWELTRY	TAINTED	TAXYING	TESTATE
SWERVED	TAKE-OFF	TEACAKE	TESTIER
SWERVER	TAKINGS	TEACHER	TESTIFY
SWIFTER	TALIPED	TEA-COSY	TESTILY
SWIFTLY	TALIPES	TEA-GOWN	TESTING
SWIGGED	TALKIES	TEA-LEAF	TETANUS
SWILLED	TALKING	TEAMING	TEXTILE
SWILLER	TALLBOY	TEARFUL	TEXTUAL
SWIMMER	TALLEST	TEARING	TEXTURE
SWINDLE	TALLIED	TEA-ROSE	THALIAN
SWINERY	TALLIER	TEASING	THANAGE
SWINGED	TALLISH	TEA-TIME	THANKED
SWINGER	TALLOWY	TEA-TREE	THAWING
SWINISH	TALLY-HO	TECHNIC	THEATRE
SWIPING	TALONED	TEDDING	THEOREM
SWIRLED	TAMABLE	TEDIOUS	THERAPY
SWISHED	TAMBOUR	TEEMFUL	THEREAT
SWISHER	TANGLED	TEEMING	THEREBY
SWIZZLE	TANGENT	TEENAGE	THEREIN
SWOLLEN	TANGLED	TELERGY	THEREOF
SWOONED	TANGOED	TELLING	THEREON
SWOOPED	TANKAGE	TEMPERA	THERETO
SWOPPED	TANKARD	TEMPEST	THERMAL
SWOTTED	TANNAGE	TEMPLAR	THERMOS
	TANNATE		

THESEUS	TIMIDLY	TONNEAU	TRACERY
THICKEN	TIMOTHY	TONSURE	TRACHEA
THICKER	TIMPANI	TONTINE	TRACING
THICKET	TIMPANO	TOOLING	TRACKED
THICKLY	TINDERY	TOOTHED	TRACKER
THIEVED	TINFOIL	TOOTING	TRACTOR
THIMBLE	TINGING	TOOTLED	TRADING
THINKER	TINGLED	TOPARCH	TRADUCE
THINNED	TINIEST	TOP-BOOT	TRAFFIC
THINNER	TINKING	TOPCOAT	TRAGEDY
THIRDLY	TINKLED	TOP-HOLE	TRAILED
THIRSTY	TINKLER	TOPIARY	TRAILER
THISTLE	TIN-MINE	TOPICAL	TRAINED
THISTLY	TINNING	TOPKNOT	TRAINEE
THITHER	TIN-TACK	TOPLESS	TRAINER
THOLING	TINTAGE	TOPMAST	TRAIPSE
THOUGHT	TINTING	TOPMOST	TRAITOR
THREADY	TINTYPE	TOPPING	TRAJECT
THRIFTY	TINWARE	TOPPLED	TRAMCAR
THRIVED	TIP-CART	TOPSAIL	TRAMMEL
THRIVEN	TIPPING	TOPSIDE	TRAMPED
THRIVER	TIPPLED	TOPSMAN	TRAMPER
THROATY	TIPPLER	TOPSOIL	TRAMPLE
THRONAL	TIPSILY	TORCHON	TRAMWAY
THRONED	TIPSTER	TORMENT	TRANCED
THROUGH	TIPTOED	TORNADO	TRANSIT
THROWER	TISSUED	TORPEDO	TRANSOM
THUMBED	TITANIA	TORRENT	TRANTER
THUMPED	TITANIC	TORSION	TRAPEZE
THUMPER	TITHING	TORTURE	TRAPPED
THUNDER	TITLARK	TORYISM	TRAPPER
THYROID	TITLING	TOSSILY	TRASHED
THYSELF	TITMICE	TOSSING	TRAVAIL
TIARAED	TITULAR	TOSSPOT	TRAWLED
TIBETAN	TOADIED	TOTALLY	TRAWLER
TICKING	TOASTED	TOTTERY	TREACLE
TICKLED	TOASTER	TOUCHED	TREACLY
TICKLER	TOBACCO	TOUCHER	TREADER
TIDDLER	TOBYMAN	TOUGHEN	TREADLE
TIDE-WAY	TOCCATA	TOUGHLY	TREASON
TIDIEST	TODDLED	TOURING	TREATED
TIDINGS	TODDLER	TOURISM	TREATER
TIE-BEAM	TOE-NAIL	TOURIST	TREBLED
TIERCEL	TOGGERY	TOURNEY	TREEING
TIGHTEN	TOILFUL	TOUSING	TREFOIL
TIGHTER	TOILING	TOUSLED	TREKKED
TIGHTLY	TOLLAGE	TOUTING	TREKKER
TIGRESS	TOLL-BAR	TOWARDS	TRELLIS
TIGRISH	TOLLING	TOWBOAT	TREMBLE
TILBURY	TOLLMAN	TOWERED	TREMBLY
TILLAGE	TOMBOLA	TOWLINE	TREMOLO
TILLING	TOMFOOL	TOWNISH	TRESTLE
TILTING	TOMPION	TOW-PATH	TRIABLE
TIMBREL	TONGUED	TOW-ROPE	TRIBUNE
TIME-LAG	TONIGHT	TOYSHOP	TRIBUTE
TIMEOUS	TONNAGE	TOYSOME	TRICEPS

TRICKED	TRUNDLE	TWIDDLE	UNCARED
TRICKER	TRUSSED	TWIGGED	UNCASED
TRICKLE	TRUSTED	TWINGED	UNCEDED
TRICKLY	TRUSTEE	TWINING	UNCHAIN
TRICKSY	TRUSTER	TWINKLE	UNCHARY
TRICORN	TRY-SAIL	TWINNED	UNCINAL
TRIDENT	TRYSTED	TWIRLED	UNCIVIL
TRIFLED	TSARINA	TWIRLER	UNCLASP
TRIFLER	TSARIST	TWISTED	UNCLEAN
TRIFORM	T-SQUARE	TWISTER	UNCLEAR
TRIGAMY	TUBBING	TWITTED	UNCLOAK
TRIGGER	TUBBISH	TWITTER	UNCLOSE
TRILLED	TUBULAR	TWOFOLD	UNCLOUD
TRILOGY	TUCKING	TWONESS	UNCOUTH
TRIMMED	TUCK-OUT	TWOSOME	UNCOVER
TRIMMER	TUESDAY	TWO-STEP	UNCROSS
TRINARY	TUFTING	TYNWALD	UNCROWN
TRINGLE	TUGBOAT	TYPHOID	UNCTION
TRINITY	TUGGING	TYPHOON	UNDATED
TRINKET	TUITION	TYPHOUS	UNDEIFY
TRINKLE	TUMBLED	TYPICAL	UNDERDO
TRIOLET	TUMBLER	TYRANNY	UNDERGO
TRIPLED	TUMBREL	TZARINA	UNDOING
TRIPLET	TUMIDLY		UNDRAPE
TRIPOLI	TUMULAR		UNDRAWN
TRIPPED	TUMULUS	**U – 7**	UNDRESS
TRIPPER	TUNABLE		UNDRIED
TRIREME	TUNABLY	UKULELE	UNDYING
TRISECT	TUNEFUL	ULULATE	UNEARTH
TRITELY	TUNNAGE	ULYSSES	UNEATEN
TRIUMPH	TUNNERY	UMBERED	UNEQUAL
TRIVIAL	TURBINE	UMBRAGE	UNEXACT
TROCHEE	TURFING	UMBROSE	UNFADED
TRODDEN	TURGENT	UMPIRED	UNFAITH
TROLLED	TURGITE	UMPTEEN	UNFILED
TROLLER	TURKISH	UNACTED	UNFITLY
TROLLEY	TURMOIL	UNAGING	UNFIXED
TROLLOP	TURNCAP	UNAIDED	UNFOUND
TROOPED	TURNERY	UNAIRED	UNFROCK
TROOPER	TURNING	UNAPTLY	UNFUSED
TROPICS	TURNKEY	UNARMED	UNGIVEN
TROTTED	TURN-OUT	UNASKED	UNGLUED
TROTTER	TUSSLED	UNAWARE	UNGODLY
TROUBLE	TUSSOCK	UNBAKED	UNGUENT
TROUNCE	TUSSORE	UNBEGUN	UNHANDY
TROUPER	TUTELAR	UNBLIND	UNHAPPY
TROWING	TUTORED	UNBLOCK	UNHARDY
TRUANCY	TWADDLE	UNBLOWN	UNHASTY
TRUCKED	TWANGED	UNBOSOM	UNHEARD
TRUCKER	TWANGLE	UNBOUND	UNHEEDY
TRUCKLE	TWANKED	UNBOWED	UNHINGE
TRUDGED	TWEAKED	UNBRACE	UNHIRED
TRUFFLE	TWEEDLE	UNBRAID	UNHITCH
TRUMPED	TWEENIE	UNBUILT	UNHIVED
TRUMPET	TWEETER	UNBURNT	UNHOPED
TRUNCAL	TWELFTH	UNCAGED	UNHORSE
		UNCANNY	

UNHOUSE	UNSLING	UPRISEN	VARIETY
UNICITY	UNSLUNG	UPSTAGE	VARIOUS
UNICORN	UNSOLID	UPSTART	VARMINT
UNIDEAL	UNSOUND	UPSURGE	VARNISH
UNIFIED	UNSPELL	UPSWEEP	VARSITY
UNIFIER	UNSPENT	UP-TRAIN	VARYING
UNIFORM	UNSPIED	UPWARDS	VASTEST
UNITARY	UNSPIKE	URALITE	VATICAN
UNITING	UNSPILT	URANITE	VAULTED
UNJOINT	UNSPLIT	URANIUM	VAULTER
UNKEMPT	UNSPOIL	URGENCY	VAUNTED
UNKNOWN	UNSTACK	USELESS	VEERING
UNLACED	UNSTAID	USHERED	VEHICLE
UNLADEN	UNSTEEL	USUALLY	VEILING
UNLATCH	UNSTICK	USURPED	VEINING
UNLEARN	UNSTUCK	USURPER	VEINOUS
UNLEASH	UNSWEET	UTENSIL	VELLUMY
UNLIMED	UNSWEPT	UTILISE	VELOURS
UNLINED	UNSWORN	UTILITY	VELVETY
UNLIVED	UNTAKEN	UTOPIAN	VENALLY
UNLOOSE	UNTAMED	UTTERED	VENDING
UNLOVED	UNTAXED	UTTERER	VENISON
UNLUCKY	UNTHINK	UTTERLY	VENOMED
UNMANLY	UNTILED	UXORIAL	VENTAGE
UNMARRY	UNTIRED		VENTAIL
UNMEANT	UNTRIED	V – 7	VENTING
UNMEWED	UNTRULY	VACANCY	VENT-PEG
UNMIXED	UNTRUSS	VACATED	VENTRAL
UNMOIST	UNTRUTH	VACATOR	VENTURE
UNMORAL	UNTUNED	VACCINE	VERANDA
UNMOULD	UNTWINE	VACUITY	VERBENA
UNMOVED	UNTWIST	VACUOLE	VERBOSE
UNNAMED	UNTYING	VACUOUS	VERDANT
UNNERVE	UNURGED	VAGRANT	VERDICT
UNNOTED	UNUSUAL	VAGUELY	VERDURE
UNOILED	UNVEXED	VAGUEST	VERGING
UNOWNED	UNVOWED	VAINEST	VERIEST
UNPAVED	UNWAGED	VALANCE	VERONAL
UNPERCH	UNWEARY	VALIANT	VERSIFY
UNPLAIT	UNWEAVE	VALIDLY	VERSING
UNPLUMB	UNWIRED	VALUING	VERSION
UNQUIET	UNWOOED	VALVATE	VERTIGO
UNRAKED	UNWOUND	VAMOOSE	VERVAIN
UNRAVEL	UNWOVEN	VAMPING	VESICLE
UNREADY	UNWRUNG	VAMPIRE	VESTIGE
UNREEVE	UNYOKED	VANDYKE	VESTING
UNRIVET	UNZONED	VANESSA	VESTRAL
UNROBED	UPBORNE	VANILLA	VETERAN
UNROYAL	UPBRAID	VANNING	VETOING
UNRULED	UPDATED	VANTAGE	VIADUCT
UNSATED	UPENDED	VANWARD	VIBRANT
UNSCREW	UPGRADE	VAPIDLY	VIBRATE
UNSEXED	UPHEAVE	VAPOURS	VIBRATO
UNSHORN	UPLYING	VAPOURY	VICEROY
UNSHOWN	UPRAISE	VARIANT	VICIOUS
UNSIZED	UPRIGHT	VARIATE	VICTORY

VICTUAL	WAGERED	WASTREL	WELL-MET
VIEWING	WAGGERY	WATCHED	WELL-OFF
VILLAGE	WAGGING	WATCHER	WELL-SET
VILLAIN	WAGGISH	WATCHET	WELL-WON
VILLEIN	WAGGLED	WATERED	WELSHED
VINEGAR	WAGONER	WATERER	WELSHER
VINTAGE	WAGTAIL	WATTLED	WELTING
VINTNER	WAILING	WAVELET	WENDING
VIOLATE	WAISTED	WAVERED	WESTERN
VIOLENT	WAITING	WAVERER	WESTING
VIOLIST	WAIVING	WAXBILL	WETDOCK
VIRGATE	WAKEFUL	WAXDOLL	WETNESS
VIRTUAL	WAKENED	WAX-MOTH	WETTEST
VISAGED	WAKENER	WAX-PALM	WETTING
VIS-A-VIS	WALKING	WAX-TREE	WETTISH
VISCOUS	WALLABY	WAXWING	WHACKED
VISIBLE	WALL-EYE	WAXWORK	WHACKER
VISIBLY	WALLING	WAY-BILL	WHALING
VISITED	WALLOON	WAYMARK	WHARFED
VISITOR	WALTZED	WAYSIDE	WHARVES
VISORED	WALTZER	WAYWARD	WHATNOT
VITALLY	WANGLED	WAYWISE	WHEATEN
VITAMIN	WANNESS	WAYWORN	WHEEDLE
VITIATE	WANNISH	WEAKEST	WHEELED
VITRIFY	WANTAGE	WEALDEN	WHEELER
VITRINE	WARBLED	WEALTHY	WHEEZED
VITRIOL	WARBLER	WEANING	WHELPED
VIVIDLY	WARDING	WEARIED	WHEREAS
VIXENLY	WAREFUL	WEARIER	WHEREAT
VOCABLE	WARFARE	WEARILY	WHEREBY
VOCALLY	WARHOOP	WEARING	WHEREIN
VOICING	WARIEST	WEARISH	WHEREOF
VOIDING	WARLIKE	WEATHER	WHEREON
VOLCANO	WARLOCK	WEAVING	WHERESO
VOLTAGE	WAR-LORD	WEBBING	WHERETO
VOLTAIC	WARMEST	WEB-FOOT	WHETHER
VOLUBLE	WARMING	WEBSTER	WHETTED
VOLUBLY	WARNING	WEB-TOED	WHETTER
VOLUTED	WARPATH	WEDDING	WHIFFED
VOTABLE	WARPING	WEDGING	WHIFFLE
VOUCHED	WARRANT	WEDLOCK	WHILING
VOUCHEE	WARRING	WEEDING	WHIMPER
VOUCHER	WARRIOR	WEEKDAY	WHIMSEY
VOYAGED	WARSHIP	WEEK-END	WHINING
VOYAGER	WAR-SONG	WEENING	WHIPPED
VULGATE	WART-HOG	WEEPING	WHIPPER
VULPINE	WAR-WORN	WEFTAGE	WHIPPET
VULTURE	WASHING	WEIGHED	WHIP-SAW
	WASH-OUT	WEIGHER	WHIP-TOP
W – 7	WASH-POT	WEIGHTY	WHIRLED
	WASH-TUB	WEIRDER	WHIRRED
WADDING	WASP-FLY	WEIRDLY	WHIRLER
WADDLED	WASPISH	WELCOME	WHISKER
WADDLER	WASSAIL	WELDING	WHISKEY
WAFERED	WASTAGE	WELFARE	WHISPER
WAFTING	WASTING	WELLING	WHISTLE

WHITELY	WITCHED	WRESTLE	ZONULAR
WHITEST	WITHERS	WRICKED	ZOOIDAL
WHITHER	WITHOUT	WRIGGLE	ZOOLITE
WHITING	WITLESS	WRIGGLY	ZOOLOGY
WHITISH	WITLING	WRINGER	ZOOMING
WHITLOW	WITNESS	WRINKLE	
WHITSUN	WITTIER	WRINKLY	
WHITTLE	WITTILY	WRITHED	**A – 8**
WHIZZED	WIZENED	WRITING	ABASHING
WHIZZER	WOBBLED	WRITTEN	ABATABLE
WHOEVER	WOBBLER	WRONGED	ABATTOIR
WHOOPEE	WOESOME	WRONGER	ABDICANT
WHOOPED	WOLF-CUB	WRONGLY	ABDICATE
WHOOPER	WOLF-DOG	WROUGHT	ABDUCTED
WHOPPED	WOLFISH	WRYNECK	ABDUCTOR
WHOPPER	WOLF-NET	WRYNESS	ABERDEEN
WHORLED	WOLFRAM	WYCH-ELM	ABERRANT
WIDENED	WOMANLY		ABERRATE
WIDENER	WOOD-ANT	**X – 7**	ABETMENT
WIDGEON	WOODCUT		ABETTING
WIDOWED	WOODMAN	X-RAYING	ABEYANCE
WIDOWER	WOOLLEN		ABHORRED
WIELDED	WOOLMAN	**Y – 7**	ABHORRER
WIELDER	WOOMERA	YANKING	ABJECTLY
WIGGERY	WORDILY	YAPPING	ABJURING
WIGGING	WORDING	YARDAGE	ABLATION
WIGGLED	WORDISH	YARD-ARM	ABLATIVE
WIGGLER	WORK-BAG	YARDING	ABLENESS
WIGLESS	WORK-BOX	YARD-MAN	ABLUTION
WILDCAT	WORKDAY	YARNING	ABNEGATE
WILDEST	WORKING	YASHMAK	ABNORMAL
WILDING	WORKMAN	YAWNING	ABORTING
WILDISH	WORK-SHY	YEARNED	ABORTION
WILIEST	WORLDLY	YELLING	ABORTIVE
WILLING	WORMING	YELLOWY	ABRADING
WILLOWY	WORN-OUT	YELPING	ABRASION
WILTING	WORRIED	YEW-TREE	ABRASIVE
WIMPLED	WORRIER	YIDDISH	ABRIDGED
WINCHED	WORSHIP	YIELDED	ABROGATE
WINDAGE	WORSTED	YORKIST	ABSENTED
WINDBAG	WOTTING	YOUNGER	ABSENTEE
WINDIER	WOULD-BE	YOWLING	ABSENTLY
WINDILY	WOULDST	YULE-LOG	ABSINTHE
WINDING	WOUNDED		ABSOLUTE
WINDROW	WOUNDER	**Z – 7**	ABSOLVED
WINDSOR	WRANGLE	ZANYISM	ABSOLVER
WINE-BAG	WRAPPED	ZEALFUL	ABSONANT
WINGING	WRAPPER	ZEALOUS	ABSORBED
WINGLET	WREAKED	ZEOLITE	ABSTRACT
WINKING	WREAKER	ZESTFUL	ABSTRUSE
WINNING	WREATHE	ZESTING	ABSURDLY
WINSOME	WREATHY	ZINCOID	ABUNDANT
WIREMAN	WRECKED	ZIONISM	ABUSABLE
WIRE-WAY	WRECKER	ZIONIST	ABUTMENT
WISHFUL	WRESTED	ZIPPING	ABUTTING
WISTFUL	WRESTER	ZONALLY	ACADEMIC

ACANTHUS	ADJOINED	AGRIMONY	ALLOYING
ACCEDING	ADJUDGED	AGRONOMY	ALLSPICE
ACCENTED	ADJURING	AIRGRETTE	ALLUDING
ACCEPTED	ADJUSTER	AIRBORNE	ALLURING
ACCEPTER	ADJUTANT	AIR-BRAKE	ALLUSION
ACCEPTOR	ADMIRING	AIR-BRICK	ALLUSIVE
ACCIDENT	ADMITTED	AIRCRAFT	ALLUSORY
ACCOLADE	ADMIXING	AIREDALE	ALLUVIAL
ACCORDED	ADMONISH	AIRFIELD	ALLUVION
ACCOSTED	ADOPTING	AIR-GRAPH	ALLUVIUM
ACCOUTRE	ADOPTION	AIRINESS	ALMIGHTY
ACCREDIT	ADOPTIVE	AIR-LINER	ALPHABET
ACCRUING	ADORABLE	AIR-PILOT	ALPINIST
ACCURACY	ADORABLY	AIRPLANE	ALSATIAN
ACCURATE	ADORNING	AIR-POWER	ALTERING
ACCURSED	ADROITLY	AIRSCREW	ALTHOUGH
ACCUSANT	ADSCRIPT	AIR-SHAFT	ALTITUDE
ACCUSING	ADULATED	AIR-SPACE	ALTRUISM
ACCUSTOM	ADULATOR	AIRSTRIP	ALTRUIST
ACERBATE	ADVANCED	AIRTIGHT	AMARANTH
ACERBITY	ADVERTED	ALACRITY	AMASSING
ACESCENT	ADVISING	ALARM-GUN	AMAZEDLY
ACHIEVED	ADVISORY	ALARMING	AMBITION
ACIDNESS	ADVOCACY	ALARMIST	AMBROSIA
ACIDOSIS	ADVOCATE	ALBACORE	AMBULANT
ACONITIC	ADVOWSON	ALBANIAN	AMBULATE
ACORN–CUP	AERATING	ALBINISM	AMBUSHED
ACOUSTIC	AERATION	ALDEHYDE	AMENABLE
ACQUAINT	AERIALLY	ALDERMAN	AMENABLY
ACQUIRED	AERIFIED	ALEATORY	AMENDING
ACRIDITY	AERIFORM	ALEHOUSE	AMERICAN
ACRIMONY	AERONAUT	ALFRESCO	AMETHYST
ACROSTIC	AEROSTAT	ALGERIAN	AMICABLE
ACTINISM	AESTHETE	ALGORISM	AMICABLY
ACTIVATE	AFFECTED	ALHAMBRA	AMMONIAC
ACTIVELY	AFFIANCE	ALICANTE	AMMONITE
ACTIVITY	AFFINITY	ALIENATE	AMORTISE
ACTUALLY	AFFIRMED	ALIENISM	AMOUNTED
ACTUATED	AFFIRMER	ALIENIST	AMPHIBIA
ACTUATOR	AFFIXING	ALIGHTED	AMPUTATE
ADAPTING	AFFLATUS	ALIGNING	AMUSABLE
ADAPTIVE	AFFLUENT	ALKALINE	ANABASIS
ADDENDUM	AFFORDED	ALKALOID	ANACONDA
ADDICTED	AFFOREST	ALLAYING	ANAGLYPH
ADDITION	AFFRIGHT	ALL-CLEAR	ANALOGUE
ADDUCING	AGAR-AGAR	ALLEGING	ANALYSED
ADDUCTOR	AGEDNESS	ALLEGORY	ANALYSER
ADENOIDS	AGGRIEVE	ALLELUIA	ANALYSIS
ADEPTION	AGITATED	ALLERGIC	ANALYTIC
ADEQUACY	AGITATOR	ALLEYWAY	ANARCHIC
ADEQUATE	AGLIMMER	ALL-FIRED	ANATHEMA
ADHERENT	AGNATION	ALL-FOURS	ANATOMIC
ADHERING	AGNOSTIC	ALLIANCE	ANCESTOR
ADHESION	AGONISED	ALLOCATE	ANCESTRY
ADHESIVE	AGRARIAN	ALLOTTED	ANCHORED
ADJACENT	AGREEING	ALLOWING	ANCHORET

ANDERSON	APOPLEXY	ARPEGGIO	ATHLETIC
ANECDOTE	APOSTASY	ARQUEBUS	ATLANTIC
ANEURISM	APOSTATE	ARRANGED	ATLANTIS
ANGELICA	APPALLED	ARRANTLY	ATOMISED
ANGERING	APPARENT	ARRAYING	ATOMISER
ANGLICAN	APPEALED	ARRESTED	ATONABLE
ANGRIEST	APPEARED	ARRIVING	ATREMBLE
ANGSTROM	APPEASED	ARROGANT	ATROCITY
ANIMATED	APPEASER	ARROGATE	ATROPINE
ANIMATOR	APPENDED	ARSONIST	ATTACHED
ANISETTE	APPENDIX	ARTERIAL	ATTACKED
ANNALIST	APPETITE	ARTESIAN	ATTACKER
ANNAMITE	APPLAUSE	ARTFULLY	ATTAINED
ANNEALED	APPLE-PIE	ARTICLED	ATTENDED
ANNELIDA	APPLIQUE	ARTIFICE	ATTESTED
ANNEXING	APPLYING	ARTISTIC	ATTICISIM
ANNOTATE	APPOSITE	ARTISTRY	ATTIRING
ANNOUNCE	APPRAISE	ASBESTOS	ATTITUDE
ANNOYING	APPRISED	ASCENDED	ATTORNEY
ANNUALLY	APPRIZED	ASCIDIUM	ATTUNING
ANNULATE	APPROACH	ASCORBIC	AUDACITY
ANNULLED	APPROVAL	ASCRIBED	AUDIENCE
ANODISED	APPROVED	ASH-STAND	AUDITING
ANOINTED	APPROVER	ASPERITY	AUDITION
ANSERINE	APTEROUS	ASPERSED	AUDITORY
ANSWERED	APTITUDE	ASPHODEL	AUGURING
ANT-EATER	AQUARIUM	ASPHYXIA	AUGUSTAN
ANTECEDE	AQUARIUS	APSIRANT	AUGUSTLY
ANTEDATE	AQUATINT	ASPIRATE	AURICULA
ANTELOPE	AQUEDUCT	ASPIRING	AURIFORM
ANTENNAE	AQUIFORM	ASSAILED	AUSTRIAN
ANTENNAL	AQUILINE	ASSASSIN	AUTARCHY
ANTERIOR	ARACHNID	ASSAYING	AUTOCRAT
ANTEROOM	ARBITRAL	ASSEMBLE	AUTO-DA-FE
ANTIBODY	ARBOREAL	ASSENTED	AUTO-DYNE
ANTIDOTE	ARBOURED	ASSERTED	AUTOGYRO
ANTIMONY	ARCADIAN	ASSESSED	AUTOMATA
ANTI-NAZI	ARCHAISM	ASSESSOR	AUTONOMY
ANTIPHON	ARCHDUKE	ASSIGNED	AUTUMNAL
ANTIPOLE	ARCHIVES	ASSIGNEE	AVAILING
ANTIPOPE	ARCHNESS	ASSIGNOR	AVENGING
ANTI-TANK	ARCTURUS	ASSISTED	AVERAGED
ANTITYPE	ARDENTLY	ASSONANT	AVERRING
ANTLERED	ARGONAUT	ASSORTED	AVERSELY
ANYTHING	ARGUABLE	ASSUAGED	AVERSION
ANYWHERE	ARGUFIED	ASSUMING	AVIATION
APERIENT	ARGUMENT	ASSURING	AVIFAUNA
APERITIF	ARIDNESS	ASSYRIAN	AVIONICS
APERTURE	ARMAMENT	ASTERISK	AVOIDING
APHIDIAN	ARMATURE	ASTEROID	AVOWABLE
APHORISM	ARMCHAIR	ASTONISH	AVOWABLY
APHORIST	ARMORIAL	ASTRAGAL	AVOWEDLY
APIARIST	ARMOURED	ASTUTELY	AWAITING
APICALLY	ARMOURER	ATABRINE	AWAKENED
APOLLYON	AROMATIC	ATHELING	AWARDING
APOLOGIA	AROUSING	ATHENIAN	AXLE-TREE

B – 8	BANNERET	BAVARIAN	BEHOLDER
	BANNEROL	BEACHING	BEHOVING
BABBLING	BANTERED	BEAD-WORK	BELABOUR
BABY-FACE	BANTERER	BEAMLESS	BELAYING
BABY-FARM	BANTLING	BEARABLE	BELCHING
BABYHOOD	BAPTISED	BEARABLY	BELIEVED
BACCARAT	BARATHEA	BEARDING	BELIEVER
BACCHANT	BARBARIC	BEARINGS	BELITTLE
BACHELOR	BARBECUE	BEARLIKE	BELLBIND
BACKBITE	BARBERRY	BEARSKIN	BELL-BIRD
BACKBONE	BARBETTE	BEATIFIC	BELL-BUOY
BACKCHAT	BARBICAN	BEAUTIFY	BELLOWED
BACK-DOOR	BARDLING	BEAVERED	BELL-PULL
BACKDROP	BAREBACK	BECALMED	BELL-ROPE
BACKFIRE	BAREFOOT	BECHAMEL	BELL-TENT
BACKHAND	BARGEMAN	BECHANCE	BELLWORT
BACKLASH	BARITONE	BECKONED	BELLYFUL
BACK-ROOM	BARNABAS	BECOMING	BELLYING
BACKSIDE	BARNACLE	BEDAUBED	BELONGED
BACK-STEP	BARN-DOOR	BED-CHAIR	BEMOANED
BACKWARD	BARNYARD	BEDECKED	BENCHING
BACKWASH	BAROLOGY	BEDEWING	BENDABLE
BACONIAN	BARONAGE	BEDIMMED	BENEDICK
BACTERIA	BARONESS	BED-LINEN	BENEDICT
BACTRIAN	BARONIAL	BEDMAKER	BENEFICE
BADGERED	BAROUCHE	BEDPLATE	BENIGNLY
BADINAGE	BARRACKS	BED-QUILT	BENJAMIN
BAFFLING	BARRATOR	BED-STAFF	BENUMBED
BAGUETTE	BARRATRY	BEDSTEAD	BEQUEATH
BAKELITE	BARRENLY	BEDSTRAW	BERATING
BALANCED	BARTERED	BEDTABLE	BERBERRY
BALANCER	BARTERER	BEE-BREAD	BEREAVED
BALDNESS	BARYTONE	BEE-EATER	BERGAMOT
BALLCOCK	BASALTIC	BEEFIEST	BERI-BERI
BALLISTA	BASEBALL	BEER-PUMP	BERRYING
BALLOTED	BASELESS	BEERSHOP	BESIEGED
BALLROOM	BASELINE	BEESWING	BESIEGER
BALLYHOO	BASEMENT	BEETLING	BESMIRCH
BALLYRAG	BASENESS	BEETROOT	BESOTTED
BALMORAL	BASILICA	BEFITTED	BESOUGHT
BALUSTER	BASILISK	BEFLOWER	BESPOKEN
BANALITY	BASKETRY	BEFOGGED	BESSEMER
BANDAGED	BASS-DRUM	BEFOOLED	BESTIARY
BANDANNA	BASS-HORN	BEFOULED	BESTOWAL
BANDEAUX	BASSINET	BEFRIEND	BESTOWED
BANDITTI	BASS-TUBA	BEGGARED	BESTREWN
BANDSMAN	BASS-VIOL	BEGGARLY	BESTRIDE
BANDYING	BASTARDY	BEGINNER	BESTRODE
BANISHED	BASTILLE	BEGOTTEN	BETAKING
BANISTER	BATAVIAN	BEGRIMED	BETA-RAYS
BANJOIST	BATHROOM	BEGRUDGE	BETEL-NUT
BANK-BILL	BATSWING	BEGUILED	BETIDING
BANK-BOOK	BATTENED	BEHAVING	BETRAYAL
BANKNOTE	BATTERED	BEHEADED	BETRAYED
BANK-RATE	BATTLING	BEHEMOTH	BETRAYER
BANKRUPT	BAULKING	BEHOLDEN	BETTERED

BEVELLED	BLACKLEG	BLUEBIRD	BOOK-POST
BEVERAGE	BLACKOUT	BLUEBOOK	BOOKSHOP
BEWAILED	BLAMABLE	BLUECOAT	BOOKWORM
BEWARING	BLAMABLY	BLUE-EYED	BOOSTING
BEWIGGED	BLAMEFUL	BLUEFISH	BOOT-HOOK
BEWILDER	BLANCHED	BLUENESS	BOOTJACK
BIBLICAL	BLANDEST	BLUENOSE	BOOTLACE
BIBULOUS	BLANDISH	BLUFFEST	BOOT-LAST
BICAUDAL	BLANKEST	BLUFFING	BOOTLESS
BICKERED	BLANKING	BLUISHLY	BOOT-TREE
BICOLOUR	BLASTING	BLUNTING	BORDEAUX
BICYCLED	BLATANCY	BLUNTISH	BORDERED
BIDDABLE	BLAZONED	BLURRING	BORDERER
BIENNIAL	BLEACHED	BLURTING	BORECOLE
BIGAMIST	BLEAKEST	BLUSHFUL	BORROWED
BIGAMOUS	BLEAKISH	BLUSHING	BORROWER
BIG-BONED	BLEATING	BLUSTERY	BOTANIST
BIGNONIA	BLEEDING	BOARDING	BOTCHERY
BILBERRY	BLENCHED	BOASTFUL	BOTCHING
BILL-BOOK	BLENDING	BOASTING	BOTHERED
BILLETED	BLENHEIM	BOAT-HOOK	BOTTLING
BILLHEAD	BLESSING	BOATRACE	BOTTOMED
BILLHOOK	BLIGHTED	BOBBINET	BOTTOMRY
BILLIARD	BLIGHTER	BOBOLINK	BOTULISM
BILLY-BOY	BLIMPERY	BODLEIAN	BOUFFANT
BILLY-CAN	BLINDAGE	BODYLINE	BOUILLON
BINDWEED	BLINDEST	BOG-BERRY	BOUNCING
BINNACLE	BLINDING	BOG-EARTH	BOUNDARY
BINOMIAL	BLINDMAN	BOGEYISM	BOUNDING
BIOGRAPH	BLINKERS	BOGEYMAN	BOWINGLY
BIOMETRY	BLINKING	BOGGLING	BOWSPRIT
BIOSCOPE	BLISSFUL	BOG-WHORT	BOX-PLEAT
BIRCHING	BLISTERY	BOHEMIAN	BOYISHLY
BIRDBATH	BLITHELY	BOLDNESS	BRACELET
BIRDCAGE	BLITHEST	BOLTHOLE	BRACKISH
BIRDCALL	BLITZING	BOLT-ROPE	BRADBURY
BIRDLIKE	BLIZZARD	BOMB-FREE	BRADSHAW
BIRD-LIME	BLOATING	BONA-FIDE	BRAGGART
BIRDSEED	BLOCKADE	BONDMAID	BRAGGING
BIRD'S-EYE	BLOCKING	BONDSMAN	BRAIDING
BIRD-SONG	BLOOD-HOT	BONE-IDLE	BRAIN-FAG
BIRTHDAY	BLOODIED	BONELESS	BRAINING
BIRTHDOM	BLOODILY	BONHOMIE	BRAIN-PAN
BISECTED	BLOODING	BONIFACE	BRAISING
BISECTOR	BLOOD-RED	BONNETED	BRAKEMAN
BISEXUAL	BLOOMERS	BONSPIEL	BRAKE-VAN
BISTABLE	BLOOMING	BOOBYISH	BRAMBLED
BITINGLY	BLOSSOMY	BOOBYISM	BRANCHED
BITTERLY	BLOTCHED	BOOHOOED	BRANDIED
BI-WEEKLY	BLOTTING	BOOKCASE	BRANDING
BLABBING	BLOWBALL	BOOK-CLUB	BRANDISH
BLACKCAP	BLOW-HOLE	BOOK-DEBT	BRAND-NEW
BLACKFLY	BLOW-PIPE	BOOKLAND	BRASSARD
BLACK-GUM	BLUDGEON	BOOKLESS	BRASS-HAT
BLACKING	BLUE-BACK	BOOKMARK	BRASSICA
BLACKISH	BLUEBELL	BOOK-NAME	BRAWLING

BRAZENED	BUCKBEAN	**C – 8**	CANOODLE
BRAZENLY	BUCKETED		CANOPIED
BREACHED	BUCKHORN	CABIN-BOY	CANTERED
BREAKAGE	BUCKJUMP	CABOODLE	CANTICLE
BREAKING	BUCKLING	CABOTAGE	CAPACITY
BREASTED	BUCKSHEE	CABRIOLE	CAPERING
BREATHED	BUCK-SHOT	CABSTAND	CAPITANO
BREATHER	BUCKSKIN	CACHALOT	CAPITATE
BREECHED	BUDDHISM	CACKLING	CAPRIOLE
BREECHES	BUDDHIST	CADENCED	CAPSICUM
BREEDING	BUDGETED	CADILLAC	CAPSULAR
BRETHREN	BUFFETED	CAERLEON	CAPTIOUS
BREVIARY	BUILDING	CAFFEINE	CAPTURED
BREWSTER	BULKHEAD	CAJOLERY	CAPUCHIN
BRIBABLE	BULKIEST	CAJOLING	CAPYBARA
BRICKBAT	BULL-CALF	CAKESHOP	CARAPACE
BRICKING	BULLDOZE	CAKEWALK	CARBOLIC
BRICK-RED	BULLETIN	CALABASH	CARBONIC
BRICK-TEA	BULLFROG	CALAMINE	CARBURET
BRIDGING	BULLHEAD	CALAMITY	CARDAMOM
BRIDLING	BULLRING	CALCINED	CARD-CASE
BRIEFING	BULL'S-EYE	CALCULUS	CARDIGAN
BRIGHTEN	BULLYING	CALENDAR	CARDINAL
BRIGHTLY	BULLYRAG	CALENDER	CAREENED
BRIMLESS	BUMMAREE	CALF-LOVE	CAREERED
BRIMMING	BUNCHING	CALFSKIN	CAREFREE
BRINDLED	BUNDLING	CALIBRED	CARELESS
BRINE-PAN	BUNGALOW	CALIPASH	CARESSED
BRINE-PIT	BUNG-HOLE	CALIPERS	CAREWORN
BRINGING	BUNGLING	CALL-BIRD	CARILLON
BRISLING	BUNKERED	CALLIOPE	CARINATE
BRISTLED	BUOYANCY	CALL-NOTE	CARNIVAL
BROACHED	BURBERRY	CALL-OVER	CAROLINE
BROADEST	BURDENED	CALMNESS	CAROLLED
BROADISH	BURGLARY	CAMBERED	CAROUSAL
BROCADED	BURGLING	CAMBRIAN	CAROUSED
BROCCOLI	BURGUNDY	CAMELLIA	CARPETED
BROCHURE	BURROWED	CAMISOLE	CARRIAGE
BROILING	BURSTING	CAMOMILE	CARRIOLE
BROKENLY	BUSH-BABY	CAMPAIGN	CARRYING
BROODING	BUSHBUCK	CAMP-FIRE	CART-LOAD
BROOKING	BUSHVELD	CAMSHAFT	CARYATID
BROOKLET	BUSINESS	CAM-WHEEL	CASCADED
BROUGHAM	BUSYBODY	CANADIAN	CASE-BOOK
BROWBEAT	BUSYNESS	CANAILLE	CASEMATE
BROWLESS	BUTCHERY	CANALISE	CASEMENT
BROWNING	BUTTERED	CANASTER	CASE-SHOT
BROWNISH	BUTTONED	CANDIDLY	CASHMERE
BROWNOUT	BUTTRESS	CANDYING	CASKETED
BROWSING	BUZZWORD	CANE-MILL	CASSETTE
BRUISING	BYPASSED	CANISTER	CASTANET
BRUNETTE	BYRONISM	CANKERED	CASTAWAY
BRUSHING	BY-STREET	CANNIBAL	CAST-IRON
BRUSSELS		CANNONED	CASTLING
BRYOLOGY		CANOEIST	CASTRATE
BUBBLING		CANONISE	CASUALLY

CASUALTY	CHAFFING	CHIASMUS	CIVILIAN
CATACOMB	CHAINING	CHICANED	CIVILITY
CATALYST	CHAIR-BED	CHICK-PEA	CIVILISE
CATAPULT	CHAIRING	CHILDBED	CLACKING
CATARACT	CHAIRMAN	CHILDISH	CLAIMANT
CATCHFLY	CHALDRON	CHILDREN	CLAIMING
CATCHING	CHALICED	CHILIASM	CLAMBAKE
CATEGORY	CHALKING	CHILIAST	CLAMPING
CATERING	CHALK-PIT	CHILLIER	CLANGING
CATHEDRA	CHAMPING	CHILLING	CLANGOUR
CATHOLIC	CHAMPION	CHILTERN	CLANKING
CATILINE	CHANCERY	CHIMAERA	CLANNISH
CATONIAN	CHANCING	CHIMERIC	CLANSHIP
CAT'S-FOOT	CHANDLER	CHINAMAN	CLANSMAN
CAT'S-MEAT	CHANGING	CHIN-CHIN	CLAPPING
CAT'S-TAIL	CHANTING	CHINKING	CLAPTRAP
CAULDRON	CHAPBOOK	CHIPMUNK	CLARENCE
CAULKING	CHAPELRY	CHIPPERY	CLARINET
CAUSALLY	CHAPERON	CHIPPING	CLASHING
CAUSERIE	CHAPITER	CHIRPING	CLASPING
CAUSEUSE	CHAPLAIN	CHIRRING	CLASSIER
CAUSEWAY	CHAPPING	CHIT-CHAT	CLASSIFY
CAUTIOUS	CHARCOAL	CHIVALRY	CLASSING
CAVALIER	CHARGING	CHLORATE	CLASSMAN
CAVATINA	CHARLOCK	CHLORIDE	CLASS-WAR
CAVE-BEAR	CHARMING	CHLORINE	CLAVICLE
CAVERNED	CHARRING	CHLOROUS	CLAYMORE
CAVILLED	CHARTING	CHOICELY	CLEANING
CAVORTED	CHARTISM	CHOIRBOY	CLEANSED
CELERIAC	CHARTIST	CHOLERIC	CLEANSER
CELERITY	CHASSEUR	CHOOSING	CLEAR-CUT
CELIBACY	CHASTELY	CHOPPING	CLEAREST
CELIBATE	CHASTISE	CHOP-SUEY	CLEARING
CELLARER	CHASTITY	CHORALLY	CLEAVAGE
CELLARET	CHASUBLE	CHORTLED	CLEAVING
CELLULAR	CHATTLES	CHORUSED	CLEMATIS
CEMENTED	CHATTING	CHOW-CHOW	CLEMENCY
CEMETERY	CHAUFFER	CHRISTEN	CLENCHED
CENOTAPH	CHEATING	CHROMIUM	CLERICAL
CENSORED	CHECKERS	CHUCKING	CLEVERER
CENSURED	CHECKING	CHUCKLED	CLEVERLY
CENTAURY	CHECK-OUT	CHUMP-END	CLICKING
CENTRING	CHEEKING	CHURLISH	CLIMATIC
CEPHALIC	CHEEPING	CHURNING	CLIMBING
CERAMICS	CHEERFUL	CICATRIX	CLINCHED
CERASTES	CHEERILY	CICERONE	CLINGING
CERBERUS	CHEERING	CIDER-CUP	CLINICAL
CEREBRAL	CHEMICAL	CINCHONA	CLINKING
CEREBRUM	CHENILLE	CINNABAR	CLIPPERS
CEREMENT	CHERUBIC	CINNAMON	CLIPPING
CEREMONY	CHERUBIM	CIPHERED	CLIQUISH
CERULEAN	CHESHIRE	CIRCLING	CLOAKING
CERVICAL	CHESSMAN	CIRCULAR	CLOCKING
CESAREAN	CHESTING	CITATION	CLODDISH
CESSPOOL	CHESTNUT	CITY-BRED	CLOGGING
CETACEAN	CHEVYING	CIVET-CAT	CLOISTER

CLOSE-CUT	COERCION	COMPLAIN	CONTRARY
CLOSETED	COERCIVE	COMPLETE	CONTRAST
CLOTHIER	COFFERED	COMPLIED	CONTRITE
CLOTHING	COFFINED	COMPOSED	CONTRIVE
CLOTTING	COGENTLY	COMPOSER	CONTUSED
CLOUDILY	COGITATE	COMPOUND	CONVENED
CLOUDING	COGNOMEN	COMPRESS	CONVENER
CLOUDLET	COG-WHEEL	COMPRISE	CONVERGE
CLOUTING	COHERENT	COMPUTED	CONVERSE
CLOWNERY	COHERING	COMPUTER	CONVEXLY
CLOWNING	COHESION	CONCEDED	CONVEYED
CLOWNISH	COHESIVE	CONCEIVE	CONVEYOR
CLUBBING	COIFFEUR	CONCERTO	CONVINCE
CLUBBISH	COIFFING	CONCLAVE	CONVOKED
CLUB-FOOT	COIFFURE	CONCLUDE	CONVOYED
CLUBLAND	COINCIDE	CONCOURS	CONVULSE
CLUB-MOSS	COINLESS	CONCRETE	COOEEING
CLUB-ROOM	COLANDER	CONDENSE	COOK-SHOP
CLUB-ROOT	COLDNESS	CONDOLED	COOLNESS
CLUB-RUSH	COLE-SLAW	CONDONED	COOPERED
CLUCKING	COLEWORT	CONDUCED	CO-OPTING
CLUELESS	COLISEUM	CONFETTI	CO-OPTION
CLUMPING	COLLAPSE	CONFIDED	COPPERED
CLUMSIER	COLLARED	CONFINED	COPULATE
CLUMSILY	COLLARET	CONFLICT	COPY-BOOK
CLUTCHED	COLLATED	CONFOUND	COPYHOLD
CLUTCHED	COLLATOR	CONFRERE	COQUETRY
COACH-BOX	COLLEGER	CONFRONT	COQUETTE
COACHDOG	COLLIDED	CONFUSED	CORDUROY
COACHFUL	COLLIERY	CONFUTED	CORDWAIN
COACHING	COLLOQUY	CONGRESS	CORN-BEEF
COACHMAN	COLLUDED	CONGREVE	CORNEOUS
COACTIVE	COLONIAL	CONJOINT	CORNERED
CO-AGENCY	COLONISE	CONJUGAL	CORPORAL
COALESCE	COLONIST	CONJUNCT	CORRIDOR
COAL-HOLE	COLLOSSAL	CONJURED	CORRODED
COAL-MINE	COLOSSUS	CONJURER	CORSELET
COAL-SHIP	COLOURED	CONJUROR	CORSICAN
COARSELY	COLUMNAR	CONNIVED	CORUNDUM
COARSEST	COLUMNED	CONNOTED	CORVETTE
COASTING	COMATOSE	CONQUEST	COSINESS
COBBLING	COMBINED	CONSERVE	COSMETIC
COBWEBBY	COME-BACK	CONSIDER	COSSETED
COCKADED	COMEDIAN	CONSOLED	COSTLIER
COCKATOO	COMMANDO	CONSOMME	COST-PLUS
COCK-CROW	COMMENCE	CONSPIRE	COSTUMED
COCKEREL	COMMERCE	CONSTANT	CO-TENANT
COCK-EYED	COMMONER	CONSTRUE	COTSWOLD
COCKLING	COMMONLY	CONSULAR	COTTAGER
COCKSPUR	COMMUNAL	CONSUMED	COTTONED
COCKSURE	COMMUNED	CONSUMER	COUCHANT
COCKTAIL	COMMUTED	CONTANGO	COUCHING
CODDLING	COMPARED	CONTEMPT	COUGHING
CODIFIED	COMPETED	CONTENTS	COUNTESS
CO-EDITOR	COMPILED	CONTINUE	COUNTING
COERCING	COMPILER	CONTRACT	COUPLING

COURSING	CRESTING	CURATORY	DATALESS
COURTESY	CRETONNE	CURBLESS	DATE-LINE
COURTIER	CREVASSE	CURDLING	DATE-PALM
COURTING	CRIBBAGE	CURELESS	DATE-PLUM
COUSINLY	CRIBBING	CURRENCY	DAUGHTER
COVENANT	CRIMINAL	CURRICLE	DAUNTING
COVENTRY	CRIMPING	CURRYING	DAUPHINE
COVERAGE	CRINGING	CURSEDLY	DAWDLING
COVERING	CRINKLED	CURTNESS	DAYBREAK
COVERLET	CRIPPLED	CURTSIED	DAYDREAM
COVERTLY	CRITERIA	CUSPIDOR	DAYLIGHT
COVETING	CRITICAL	CUSTOMER	DAY-TO-DAY
COVETOUS	CRITIQUE	CUT-GLASS	DAZZLING
COWARDLY	CROAKING	CUTHBERT	DEAD-BEAT
COWERING	CROCKERY	CUTPURSE	DEADENED
COWHOUSE	CROCKING	CUT-WATER	DEAD-HEAD
CO-WORKER	CROMLECH	CYCLAMEN	DEAD HEAT
COXSWAIN	CROOKING	CYCLE-CAR	DEADLIER
CRABBING	CROONING	CYCLICAL	DEADLINE
CRACKING	CROPPING	CYCLONIC	DEADLOCK
CRACK-JAW	CROSSBAR	CYLINDER	DEADNESS
CRACKLED	CROSSBOW	CYNICISM	DEAD WOOD
CRACKNEL	CROSSCUT	CYNOSURE	DEAFENED
CRACKPOT	CROSSING	CZARITZA	DEAFNESS
CRADLING	CROTCHED		DEANSHIP
CRAFTIER	CROTCHET	**D – 8**	DEARNESS
CRAFTILY	CROUCHED	DABBLING	DEATH-BED
CRAMMING	CROUPIER	DABCHICK	DEBARRED
CRAMPING	CROWDING	DAEDALUS	DEBASING
CRANE-FLY	CROWFOOT	DAFFODIL	DEBATING
CRANKING	CROWNING	DAFTNESS	DEBILITY
CRANNIED	CRUCIBLE	DAINTILY	DEBITING
CRASHING	CRUCIFIX	DAIRYING	DEBONAIR
CRAVENLY	CRUISING	DAIRYMAN	DEBUNKED
CRAWFISH	CRUMBLED	DALESMAN	DEBUTANT
CRAWLING	CRUMPLED	DALLYING	DECADENT
CRAYFISH	CRUNCHED	DALMATIA	DECAMPED
CRAYONED	CRUSADED	DAMAGING	DECANTED
CRAZIEST	CRUSADER	DAMNABLE	DECANTER
CREAKING	CRUSHING	DAMOCLES	DECAYING
CREAMERY	CRUSTILY	DAMPENED	DECEASED
CREAMING	CRUTCHED	DAMPNESS	DECEIVED
CREASING	CUBIFORM	DANDIEST	DECEIVER
CREATING	CUCUMBER	DANDLING	DECEMBER
CREATION	CUDDLING	DANDRUFF	DECENTLY
CREATIVE	CUL-DE-SAC	DANDYISH	DECIDING
CREATURE	CULINARY	DANDYISM	DECIMATE
CREDENCE	CULPABLE	DANGLING	DECIPHER
CREDIBLE	CULPABLY	DANSEUSE	DECISION
CREDIBLY	CULTURED	DAPPLING	DECISIVE
CREDITED	CUVERIN	DARINGLY	DECK-HAND
CREDITOR	CUMBRIAN	DARKENED	DECLARED
CREEPING	CUPBOARD	DARKLING	DECLASSE
CREMATED	CUPIDITY	DARKNESS	DECLINED
CREOSOTE	CUPREOUS	DARK-ROOM	DECODING
CRESCENT	CURATIVE	DATA-BANK	DECORATE

DECOROUS	DEMERARA	DESTINED	DIHEDRAL
DECOYING	DEMIJOHN	DETACHED	DILATING
DECREASE	DEMISING	DETAILED	DILATION
DECREPIT	DEMOBBED	DETAINED	DILATORY
DECRYING	DEMOCRAT	DETECTED	DILIGENT
DEDICATE	DEMOLISH	DETECTOR	DILUTING
DEDUCING	DEMONIAC	DETERRED	DILUTION
DEDUCTED	DEMONISM	DETESTED	DILUVIAL
DEEDPOLL	DEMPSTER	DETHRONE	DIMINISH
DEEMSTER	DEMURELY	DETONATE	DIMPLING
DEEPENED	DEMURRED	DETRITUS	DINER-OUT
DEEP-LAID	DENARIUS	DEUCEDLY	DING-DONG
DEERSKIN	DENATURE	DEVALUED	DINGIEST
DEFACING	DENIABLE	DEVIATED	DINORNIS
DEFAMING	DENOTING	DEVILISH	DINOSAUR
DEFEATED	DENOUNCE	DEVILISM	DIOCESAN
DEFENDED	DENUDING	DEVILLED	DIORAMIC
DEFENDER	DEPARTED	DEVISING	DIPLOMAT
DEFERRED	DEPENDED	DEVOLVED	DIRECTED
DEFIANCE	DEPICTED	DEVONIAN	DIRECTLY
DEFILING	DEPILATE	DEVOTING	DIRECTOR
DEFINING	DEPLETED	DEVOTION	DIRTIEST
DEFINITE	DEPLORED	DEVOURED	DIRTYING
DEFLATED	DEPLOYED	DEVOUTLY	DISABLED
DEFOREST	DEPONENT	DEWBERRY	DISABUSE
DEFORMED	DEPORTED	DEWINESS	DISAGREE
DEFRAYAL	DEPORTEE	DEXTROSE	DISALLOW
DEFRAYED	DEPOSING	DEXTROUS	DISARMED
DEFTNESS	DEPRAVED	DIABETES	DISARRAY
DEGRADED	DEPRIVED	DIABETIC	DISASTER
DEIFYING	DEPUTING	DIABOLIC	DISBURSE
DEIGNING	DEPUTISE	DIAGNOSE	DISCIPLE
DEJECTED	DERAILED	DIAGONAL	DISCLAIM
DEJEUNER	DERANGED	DIALLING	DISCLOSE
DELAYING	DERATING	DIALOGUE	DISCOUNT
DELECTUS	DERELICT	DIAMETER	DISCOVER
DELEGACY	DERIDING	DIANTHUS	DISCREET
DELEGATE	DERISION	DIAPASON	DISEASED
DELETING	DERISIVE	DIASTASE	DISGORGE
DELETION	DERISORY	DIASTOLE	DISGRACE
DELICACY	DERIVING	DIATOMIC	DISGUISE
DELICATE	DEROGATE	DIATONIC	DISHEVEL
DELIRIUM	DESCRIBE	DIATRIBE	DISINTER
DELIVERY	DESCRIED	DIBBLING	DISJOINT
DELOUSED	DESERTED	DICKERED	DISLIKED
DELPHIAN	DESERTER	DICTATED	DISLODGE
DELUDING	DESERVED	DICTATOR	DISLOYAL
DELUGING	DESIGNED	DIDACTIC	DISMALLY
DELUSION	DESIGNER	DIDDLING	DISMAYED
DELUSIVE	DESIRING	DIETETIC	DISMOUNT
DEMAGOGY	DESIROUS	DIFFERED	DISORDER
DEMANDED	DESISTED	DIFFRACT	DISOWNED
DEMARCHE	DESOLATE	DIFFUSED	DISPATCH
DEMEANED	DESPATCH	DIGESTED	DISPENSE
DEMENTED	DESPISED	DIGGINGS	DISPERSE
DEMENTIA	DESPOTIC	DIGITATE	DISPIRIT

DISPLACE	DOG'S-MEAT	DOWNHILL	DROWSILY
DISPOSAL	DOG'S-NOSE	DOWNLAND	DROWSING
DISPOSED	DOG-TIRED	DOWN-LINE	DRUBBING
DISPROOF	DOG-TOOTH	DOWNLINK	DRUDGERY
DISPROVE	DOG-WATCH	DOWNPOUR	DRUDGING
DISPUTED	DOLDRUMS	DOWNWARD	DRUGGING
DISQUIET	DOLLED-UP	DOXOLOGY	DRUGGIST
DISROBED	DOLOMITE	DOZINESS	DRUIDISM
DISSOLVE	DOLOROSO	DRAFTING	DRUMFIRE
DISSUADE	DOLORUS	DRAGGING	DRUMFISH
DISTANCE	DOMELIKE	DRAGGLED	DRUMHEAD
DISTASTE	DOMESDAY	DRAG-HOOK	DRUMMING
DISTINCT	DOMESTIC	DRAG-HUNT	DRUNKARD
DISTRACT	DOMICILE	DRAGOMAN	DRY-CLEAN
DISTRAIN	DOMINANT	DRAINAGE	DRY-GOODS
DISTRAIT	DOMINATE	DRAINING	DRY-NURSE
DISTRESS	DOMINEER	DRAMATIC	DRY-PLATE
DISTRICT	DOMINION	DRAM-SHOP	DRY-POINT
DISTRUST	DOMINOES	DRAUGHTS	DRYSTONE
DISUNION	DONATING	DRAUGHTY	DUCHESSE
DISUNITE	DONATION	DRAWABLE	DUCKBILL
DISUNITY	DOOMSDAY	DRAWBACK	DUCK-HAWK
DITCHING	DOORBELL	DRAWBOLT	DUCKLING
DITHERED	DOORKNOB	DRAW-GEAR	DUCK-MOLE
DITTY-BAG	DOORLESS	DRAWLING	DUCK'S-EGG
DITTY-BOX	DOORNAIL	DRAW-LINK	DUCK-SHOT
DIVE-BOMB	DOORPOST	DRAW-WELL	DUCKWEED
DIVERGED	DOORSTEP	DREADFUL	DUELLING
DIVERTED	DORMANCY	DREADING	DUELLIST
DIVESTED	DORMOUSE	DREAMFUL	DUETTING
DIVIDEND	DORSALLY	DREAMILY	DUETTIST
DIVIDING	DOTARDLY	DREAMING	DUKELING
DIVINELY	DOTINGLY	DREARILY	DUKERIES
DIVINITY	DOTTEREL	DREDGING	DUKESHIP
DIVISION	DOUBLETS	DRENCHED	DULCIMER
DIVORCED	DOUBLING	DRESSING	DULL-EYED
DIVORCEE	DOUBLOON	DRIBBLED	DULLNESS
DIVULGED	DOUBTFUL	DRIBBLET	DUMB-BELL
DIZZYING	DOUBTING	DRIFT-ICE	DUMBNESS
DOCILITY	DOUCHING	DRIFTING	DUMB-SHOW
DOCKYARD	DOUGHBOY	DRIFT-NET	DUMPLING
DOCTORED	DOUGHNUT	DRIFT-WAY	DUNGAREE
DOCTRINE	DOUM-PALM	DRILLING	DUNG-CART
DOCUMENT	DOURNESS	DRINKING	DUNG-FORK
DODDERED	DOVECOTE	DRIPPING	DUNGHILL
DODDERER	DOVE-EYED	DRIVABLE	DUODENAL
DOGBERRY	DOVELIKE	DRIZZLED	DUODENUM
DOG-EARED	DOVETAIL	DROLLERY	DUOLOGUE
DOGESHIP	DOWDYISH	DROOLING	DURATION
DOG-FACED	DOWDYISM	DROOPING	DUST-CART
DOGGEDLY	DOWELLED	DROP-GOAL	DUST-COAT
DOGGEREL	DOWEL-PIN	DROPPING	DUST-HOLE
DOGHOUSE	DOWERING	DROPSIED	DUTCHMAN
DOG-LATIN	DOWNCAST	DROPWORT	DUTIABLE
DOGMATIC	DOWNCOME	DROUGHTY	DUTY-FREE
DOG'S-BODY	DOWNFALL	DROWNING	DUTY-PAID

DWARFING	EGGSHELL	EMBUSSED	ENGENDER
DWARFISH	EGG-SLICE	EMENDING	ENGINEER
DWELLING	EGG-SPOON	EMERGENT	ENGRAVED
DWINDLED	EGG-TOOTH	EMERGING	ENGRAVER
DYE-HOUSE	EGG-WHISK	EMERITUS	ENGULFED
DYESTUFF	EGOISTIC	EMERSION	ENHANCED
DYNAMICS	EGYPTIAN	EMIGRANT	ENJOINED
DYNAMISM	EIGHTEEN	EMIGRATE	ENJOYING
DYNAMIST	EIGHTHLY	EMINENCE	ENLACING
DYNAMITE	EJECTING	EMISSARY	ENLARGED
DYNASTIC	EJECTION	EMISSION	ENLARGER
	EJECTIVE	EMISSIVE	ENLISTED
	ELAPSING	EMITTING	ENMESHED
E – 8	ELATEDLY	EMPHASIS	ENNOBLED
EAGLE-OWL	ELBOWING	EMPHATIC	ENORMITY
EARPHONE	ELDORADO	EMPLANED	ENORMOUS
EARPIECE	ELDRITCH	EMPLOYED	ENOUNCED
EARTHING	ELECTING	EMPLOYEE	ENQUIRED
EARTH-NUT	ELECTION	EMPLOYER	ENQUIRER
EASEMENT	ELECTIVE	EMPORIUM	ENRAGING
EASINESS	ELECTRIC	EMPTYING	ENRICHED
EASTERLY	ELECTRON	EMPURPLE	ENROLLED
EASTWARD	ELEGANCE	EMPYREAN	ENSCONCE
EAU-DE-VIE	ELEGANCY	EMULATED	ENSHRINE
EBENEZER	ELEGIAST	EMULATOR	ENSHROUD
EBONISED	ELEGISED	EMULSIFY	ENSLAVED
ECLECTIC	ELEPHANT	EMULSINE	ENSNARED
ECLIPSED	ELEVATED	EMULSION	ENSURING
ECLIPTIC	ELEVATOR	EMULSIVE	ENTAILED
ECONOMIC	ELEVENTH	ENABLING	ENTANGLE
ECSTATIC	ELF-CHILD	ENACTING	ENTERING
EDENTATA	ELICITED	ENACTION	ENTHRONE
EDENTATE	ELIGIBLE	ENACTIVE	ENTHUSED
EDGE-TOOL	ELIGIBLY	ENCAMPED	ENTICING
EDGEWAYS	ELLIPSIS	ENCASHED	ENTIRELY
EDGEWISE	ELLIPTIC	ENCASING	ENTIRETY
EDGINESS	ELONGATE	ENCIRCLE	ENTITLED
EDIFYING	ELOQUENT	ENCLOSED	ENTOMBED
EDITRESS	ELSEWISE	ENCOMIUM	ENTR'ACTE
EDUCABLE	ELVISHLY	ENCORING	ENTRAILS
EDUCATED	EMACIATE	ENCROACH	ENTRANCE
EDUCATOR	EMANATED	ENCUMBER	ENTREATY
EDUCIBLE	EMBALMED	ENCYCLIC	ENTRENCH
EDUCTION	EMBALMER	ENDANGER	ENTWINED
EEL-GRASS	EMBANKED	ENDEARED	ENVELOPE
EEL-SPEAR	EMBARKED	ENDORSED	ENVIABLE
EERINESS	EMBATTLE	ENDOWING	ENVIABLY
EFFACING	EMBEDDED	ENDURING	ENVIRONS
EFFECTED	EMBEZZLE	ENERGISE	ENVISAGE
EFFICACY	EMBITTER	ENERVATE	EOLITHIC
EFFLUENT	EMBLAZON	ENFACING	EPHEMERA
EFFLUVIA	EMBODIED	ENFEEBLE	EPICERIE
EFFUSING	EMBOLDEN	ENFILADE	EPICYCLE
EFFUSION	EMBOLISM	ENFOLDED	EPIDEMIC
EFFUSIVE	EMBOSSED	ENFORCED	EPIGRAPH
EGG-PLANT	EMBRACED	ENGAGING	EPILEPSY

EPILOGUE
EPIPHANY
EPISODIC
EQUALISE
EQUALITY
EQUALLED
EQUATING
EQUATION
EQUIPAGE
EQUIPPED
ERASABLE
ERECTING
ERECTION
EREWHILE
ERUPTING
ERUPTION
ERUPTIVE
ESCALADE
ESCALLOP
ESCAPADE
ESCAPING
ESCAPISM
ESCAPIST
ESCHEWED
ESCORTED
ESCULENT
ESOTERIC
ESPALIER
ESPECIAL
ESPOUSAL
ESPOUSED
ESSAYING
ESSAYISH
ESSAYIST
ESTEEMED
ESTIMATE
ESTRANGE
ESURIENT
ETCETERA
ETERNITY
ETHEREAL
ETHNICAL
ETRUSCAN
EUGENICS
EULOGISE
EULOGIST
EUPHONIC
EURASIAN
EUROPEAN
EVACUATE
EVADABLE
EVENNESS
EVENSONG
EVENTFUL
EVENTIDE
EVENTUAL

EVERMORE
EVERSION
EVERTING
EVERYDAY
EVERYONE
EVICTING
EVICTION
EVIDENCE
EVILDOER
EVINCING
EVOLVING
EXACTING
EXACTION
EXALTING
EXAMINED
EXAMINEE
EXAMINER
EXCAVATE
EXCEEDED
EXCEPTED
EXCHANGE
EXCISING
EXCISION
EXCITING
EXCLUDED
EXCUSING
EXECRATE
EXECUTED
EXECUTOR
EXEMPLAR
EXEMPTED
EXEQUIES
EXERCISE
EXERTING
EXERTION
EXHALING
EXHORTED
EXHUMING
EXIGENCY
EXISTENT
EX-LIBRIS
EXORCISE
EXORCISM
EXPANDED
EXPECTED
EXPEDITE
EXPENDED
EXPERTLY
EXPIATED
EXPIRING
EXPLICIT
EXPLODED
EXPLORED
EXPLORER
EXPONENT
EXPORTED

EXPORTER
EXPOSING
EXPOSURE
EXPUNGED
EXTENDED
EXTENSOR
EXTERIOR
EXTERNAL
EXTOLLED
EXTORTED
EXTRUDED
EXULTANT
EXULTING
EYEGLASS
EYE-PIECE
EYE-TEETH
EYE-TOOTH
EYE-WATER

F – 8

FABULOUS
FACE-ACHE
FACELESS
FACE-LIFT
FACIALLY
FACILELY
FACILITY
FACTIOUS
FACTOTUM
FADELESS
FADINGLY
FAILSAFE
FAINTEST
FAINTING
FAINTISH
FAIRNESS
FAITHFUL
FALCONER
FALCONET
FALCONRY
FALDERAL
FALLIBLE
FALLOWED
FALSETTO
FALTERED
FAMILIAR
FAMISHED
FAMOUSLY
FANCIFUL
FANCYING
FANDANGO
FANGLESS
FANLIGHT
FANTASIA
FARCICAL

FAREWELL
FAR-FLUNG
FARINOSE
FARMYARD
FARRIERY
FARROWED
FARTHEST
FARTHING
FASCISTA
FASCIST!
FASTENED
FASTNESS
FATALISM
FATALIST
FATALITY
FATHERED
FATHERLY
FATHOMED
FATIGUED
FATTENED
FAUBOURG
FAULTILY
FAULTING
FAUTEUIL
FAVOURED
FEARLESS
FEARSOME
FEASIBLE
FEASIBLY
FEASTING
FEATHERY
FEATURED
FEBRUARY
FECKLESS
FEDERATE
FEEBLISH
FEEDBACK
FEED-PIPE
FEIGNING
FEINTING
FELICITY
FELLSIDE
FELO-DE-SE
FEMININE
FEMINISE
FEMINISM
FEMINIST
FENCIBLE
FEROCITY
FERRETED
FERRYING
FERRYMAN
FERVENCY
FERVIDLY
FESTALLY
FESTERED

FESTIVAL	FIRMNESS	FLIMSIES	FOLK-TALE
FETCHING	FIRMWARE	FLIMSILY	FOLLICLE
FETTERED	FISHABLE	FLINCHED	FOLLOWED
FEUDALLY	FISH-BALL	FLINGING	FOLLOWER
FEVERFEW	FISH-CAKE	FLIP-FLAP	FOMENTED
FEVERING	FISH-GLUE	FLIP-FLOP	FONDLING
FEVERISH	FISH-HAWK	FLIPPANT	FONDNESS
FEVEROUS	FISH-HOOK	FLIPPING	FOODLESS
FIBROSIS	FISH-MEAL	FLIRTING	FOOLSCAP
FIDDLING	FISH-POND	FLITTING	FOOTBALL
FIDELITY	FISH-SKIN	FLOATING	FOOT-BATH
FIDGETED	FISH-TAIL	FLOCK-BED	FOOTFALL
FIELD-DAY	FISHWIFE	FLOCKING	FOOTGEAR
FIELD-GUN	FISSURED	FLOGGING	FOOTHILL
FIELDING	FITFULLY	FLOODING	FOOTHOLD
FIENDISH	FIVEFOLD	FLOODLIT	FOOTLESS
FIERCELY	FIXATION	FLOORING	FOOTLING
FIERCEST	FIXATIVE	FLOPPILY	FOOTMARK
FIFTIETH	FIZZLING	FLOPPING	FOOTNOTE
FIGHTING	FLABBILY	FLORALLY	FOOTPATH
FIGURANT	FLAGGING	FLORENCE	FOOT-RACE
FIGURINE	FLAGRANT	FLORIDLY	FOOT-ROPE
FIGURING	FLAG-SHIP	FLOTILLA	FOOTRULE
FILAMENT	FLAMBEAU	FLOUNCED	FOOTSLOG
FILCHING	FLAMINGO	FLOUNDER	FOOTSORE
FILIALLY	FLANKING	FLOURING	FOOTSTEP
FILIGREE	FLAP-JACK	FLOURING	FOOTWEAR
FILLETED	FLAPPING	FLOURISH	FOOTWORN
FILMGOER	FLASHILY	FLOUTING	FOOZLING
FILM-STAR	FLASHING	FLOWERED	FORAGING
FILTERED	FLATFISH	FLOWERET	FORAYING
FILTHIER	FLATFOOT	FLUENTLY	FORBORNE
FILTHILY	FLAT-IRON	FLUFFING	FORCEDLY
FILTRATE	FLATNESS	FLUIDITY	FORCEFUL
FINALIST	FLAT-RACE	FLUMMERY	FORCIBLY
FINALITY	FLATTERY	FLUORIDE	FORDABLE
FINANCED	FLATTEST	FLUORINE	FOREBEAR
FINDABLE	FLATTISH	FLURRIED	FOREBODE
FINENESS	FLATWORM	FLUSHING	FORECAST
FINE-SPUN	FLAUNTED	FLUSTERY	FOREDECK
FINESSED	FLAUTIST	FLYBLOWN	FOREDONE
FINGERED	FLAWLESS	FLY-MAKER	FOREDOOM
FINISHED	FLAX-LILY	FLY-PAPER	FOREFOOT
FINISHER	FLAX-SEED	FLYSHEET	FOREGONE
FIREBACK	FLEABANE	FLYWHEEL	FOREHAND
FIRE-BALL	FLEA-BITE	FOAMLESS	FOREHEAD
FIRE-BOMB	FLECKING	FOCUSING	FORELAND
FIRECLAY	FLEECING	FOG-BOUND	FORELOCK
FIREDAMP	FLEETEST	FOGGIEST	FOREMAST
FIRE-HOSE	FLEETING	FOLDEROL	FOREMOST
FIRELOCK	FLETCHER	FOLDLESS	FORENAME
FIRE-PLUG	FLEXIBLE	FOLIAGED	FORENOON
FIRESHIP	FLEXIBLY	FOLIATED	FORENSIC
FIRESIDE	FLICKING	FOLKLAND	FOREPART
FIRE-STEP	FLIGHTED	FOLKLORE	FOREPEAK
FIREWOOD	FLIMFLAM	FOLK-SONG	FORESAID

FORESAIL	FREE-LOVE	FUNK-HOLE	GASOLINE
FORESEEN	FREENESS	FURBELOW	GAS-STOVE
FORESHIP	FREE-PORT	FURLOUGH	GAS-TIGHT
FORESHOW	FREE-SHOT	FURROWED	GATELESS
FORESTAY	FREE-WILL	FURTHEST	GATEPOST
FORESTER	FREEZING	FUSELAGE	GATHERED
FORESTRY	FRENZIED	FUSILIER	GAUNTLET
FORETELL	FREQUENT	FUTILELY	GAZETTED
FORETOLD	FRETTING	FUTILITY	GEARCASE
FOREWARN	FRETWORK	FUTURISM	GELATINE
FOREWORD	FREUDIAN	FUTURIST	GENDARME
FORGIVEN	FRICTION	FUTURITY	GENERATE
FORGOING	FRIENDLY		GENEROUS
FORMALIN	FRIESIAN		GENETICS
FORMALLY	FRIGHTEN	G – 8	GENIALLY
FORMERLY	FRIGIDLY		GENITIVE
FORMLESS	FRILLING	GABBLING	GENOCIDE
FORMULAE	FRINGING	GABLE-END	GEOMETRY
FORSAKEN	FRIPPERY	GADABOUT	GEORGIAN
FORSOOTH	FRISKILY	GADZOOKS	GERANIUM
FORSWEAR	FRISKING	GAINSAID	GERMANIC
FORSWORE	FRIZZLED	GAITERED	GESTURED
FORSWORN	FROCKING	GALACTIC	GHOSTING
FORTIETH	FRONTAGE	GALILEAN	GHOULISH
FORTRESS	FRONTIER	GALLIPOT	GIANTESS
FORTUITY	FRONTING	GALLOPED	GIBBERED
FORWARDS	FROSTILY	GALLOWAY	GIBINGLY
FOSTERED	FROSTING	GALVANIC	GIDDIEST
FOUGASSE	FROTHILY	GAMBLING	GIGANTIC
FOULNESS	FROTHING	GAMECOCK	GIGGLING
FOUL PLAY	FROU-FROU	GAME-LAWS	GIG-LAMPS
FOUNDING	FROWNING	GAMENESS	GILT-EDGE
FOUNTAIN	FRUCTIFY	GAMESTER	GIMCRACK
FOURFOLD	FRUGALLY	GANGLION	GINGERLY
FOURSOME	FRUIT-BUD	GANGRENE	GIN-SLING
FOURTEEN	FRUIT-FLY	GANGSTER	GIRDLING
FOURTHLY	FRUITFUL	GANYMEDE	GIRLHOOD
FOXGLOVE	FRUITING	GAOLBIRD	GIVE-AWAY
FOXHOUND	FRUITION	GAPINGLY	GLADDEST
FOXINESS	FRUITLET	GARBLING	GLADIOLI
FRACTION	FRUMPISH	GARDENED	GLADNESS
FRACTURE	FUDDLING	GARDENER	GLADSOME
FRAGMENT	FUELLING	GARDENIA	GLANCING
FRAGRANT	FUGITIVE	GAREFOWL	GLASNOST
FRAILISH	FULL-BACK	GARGANEY	GLASSFUL
FRAME-SAW	FULL-FACE	GARGLING	GLASSILY
FRANKING	FULLNESS	GARGOYLE	GLAUCOMA
FRANKISH	FULL-STOP	GARISHLY	GLAUCOUS
FRANKLIN	FUMBLING	GARNERED	GLEAMING
FRAULEIN	FUMELESS	GARRETED	GLEANING
FREAKISH	FUMIGANT	GARRISON	GLIBNESS
FRECKLED	FUMIGATE	GARROTTE	GLIMPSED
FREEBORN	FUNCTION	GARTERED	GLINTING
FREED-MAN	FUNDABLE	GASIFIED	GLISSADE
FREEHAND	FUNDLESS	GASLIGHT	GLOAMING
FREEHOLD	FUNEREAL	GAS-METER	GLOATING
		GAS-MOTOR	

GLOBULAR	GRACIOUS	GROUTING	HALL-MARK
GLOBULIN	GRADATED	GROWABLE	HALLOOED
GLOOMILY	GRADIENT	GROWLING	HALLOWED
GLORIOUS	GRADUATE	GRUBBIER	HALTERED
GLORYING	GRAFTING	GRUBBING	HAMMERED
GLOSSARY	GRAINING	GRUDGING	HAMPERED
GLOSSILY	GRANDDAD	GRUESOME	HANDBALL
GLOSSING	GRANDEST	GRUMBLED	HANDBELL
GLOWERED	GRANDEUR	GRUMBLER	HANDBILL
GLOW-WORM	GRANDSON	GUARDIAN	HANDBOOK
GLOXINIA	GRANTING	GUARDING	HANDCART
GLUMMEST	GRANULAR	GUERNSEY	HANDCUFF
GLUMNESS	GRAPHICS	GUIDABLE	HANDGRIP
GLUTTING	GRAPHITE	GUIDANCE	HANDHOLD
GLUTTONY	GRAPPLED	GUILEFUL	HANDICAP
GNASHING	GRASPING	GUILTILY	HANDLINE
GOAL-LINE	GRASSING	GULF-WEED	HANDLING
GOATHERD	GRATEFUL	GULLIBLE	HANDLOOM
GOAT-MOTH	GRATUITY	GULLIVER	HANDMADE
GOATSKIN	GRAVAMEN	GUMPTION	HANDMAID
GOAT'S-RUE	GRAVELLY	GUM-RESIN	HANDMILL
GOBBLING	GRAYLING	GUN-LAYER	HAND-PICK
GODCHILD	GREASILY	GUNMETAL	HANDPOST
GODSPEED	GREASING	GUNSMITH	HANDRAIL
GOFFERED	GREATEST	GUNSTOCK	HANDSOME
GOGGLING	GREEDILY	GURGLING	HAND-WORK
GOINGS-ON	GREENERY	GUTTERED	HANDYMAN
GOLD-DUST	GREEN-FLY	GUTTURAL	HANGER-ON
GOLDENLY	GREENING	GUZZLING	HANGNAIL
GOLDFISH	GREENISH	GYMKHANA	HANDOVER
GOLD-FOIL	GREEN-TEA	GYRATING	HANKERED
GOLD-LACE	GREETING	GYRATION	HAPPENED
GOLD-LEAF	GREYNESS	GYRATORY	HAPPIEST
GOLDLESS	GRID-BIAS		HARA-KIRI
GOLD-MINE	GRIDIRON		HARANGUE
GOLD-SIZE	GRIEVOUS	**H – 8**	HARASSED
GOLF-BALL	GRILLING		HARDBAKE
GOLF-CLUB	GRIMACED	HABITUAL	HARDENED
GOLGOTHA	GRIMALDI	HACIENDA	HARDIEST
GOLLIWOG	GRIMMEST	HAGGLING	HARDNESS
GONENESS	GRIMNESS	HAIRLESS	HARDSHIP
GOODLIER	GRINDING	HAIRLINE	HARDTACK
GOODNESS	GRINNING	HALF-BACK	HARDWARE
GOODWIFE	GRIPPING	HALF-BOOT	HARDWOOD
GOODWILL	GRISELDA	HALF-BRED	HAREBELL
GOOGLIES	GRITTING	HALF-COCK	HARMLESS
GOOSE-EGG	GRIZZLED	HALF-DEAD	HARMONIC
GORGEOUS	GROANING	HALF-DONE	HARRIDAN
GOSSAMER	GROG-SHOP	HALF-FACE	HARROWED
GOSSIPED	GROOMING	HALF-MAST	HARRYING
GOURMAND	GROOVING	HALF-MOON	HASTENED
GOVERNED	GROSBEAK	HALF-NOTE	HASTINGS
GOVERNOR	GROUNDED	HALF-PAST	HATBRUSH
GOWNSMAN	GROUNDER	HALF-SEAS	HATCHERY
GRABBING	GROUPING	HALF-TIME	HATCHING
GRACEFUL	GROUSING	HALF-TINT	HATCHWAY
		HALF-TONE	

HATSTAND	HELPMEET	HOCKTIDE	HOTHOUSE
HAT-TRICK	HELVETIA	HOGMANAY	HOT-PLATE
HAUNTING	HEMP-SEED	HOGSHEAD	HOT-PRESS
HAUSFRAU	HENCHMAN	HOISTING	HOUNDING
HAWAIIAN	HEN-HOUSE	HOLDFAST	HOUR-HAND
HAWFINCH	HEN-ROOST	HOLINESS	HOUSEBOY
HAWK-EYED	HEPTAGON	HOLLANDS	HOUSE-DOG
HAWK-MOTH	HEPTARCH	HOLLOWED	HOUSE-FLY
HAWTHORN	HERALDED	HOLLOWLY	HOUSE-TAX
HAY-FEVER	HERALDIC	HOLOGRAM	HOVERING
HAYFIELD	HERALDRY	HOLYROOD	HOWITZER
HAYMAKER	HERCULES	HOMEBORN	HUCKSTER
HAYSTACK	HERD-BOOK	HOMEBRED	HUDDLING
HAZARDED	HERDSMAN	HOME-FARM	HUDIBRAS
HAZEL-NUT	HEREDITY	HOMELAND	HUGENESS
HAZINESS	HEREUNTO	HOMELESS	HUGUENOT
HEADACHE	HEREUPON	HOMELIKE	HUMANELY
HEADACHY	HEREWITH	HOME-MADE	HUMANISE
HEADBAND	HERITAGE	HOMESICK	HUMANISM
HEAD-BOOM	HERMETIC	HOMESPUN	HUMANIST
HEADGEAR	HESITANT	HOMEWARD	HUMANITY
HEADIEST	HESITATE	HOMICIDE	HUMBLING
HEADLAND	HESPERUS	HONESTLY	HUMIDIFY
HEADLESS	HIAWATHA	HONEY-BEE	HUMIDITY
HEADLINE	HIBERNIA	HONEYDEW	HUMILITY
HEADLONG	HIBISCUS	HONEY-POT	HUMMOCKY
HEAD-REST	HICCOUGH	HONORARY	HUMORIST
HEADSHIP	HICCUPED	HONOURED	HUMOROUS
HEAD-WIND	HIGHBALL	HOODWINK	HUMOURED
HEAD-WORK	HIGHBORN	HOOFLESS	HUMPBACK
HEARABLE	HIGHBRED	HOOF-MARK	HUNGERED
HEARTILY	HIGHBROW	HOOKWORM	HUNGRILY
HEATHERY	HIGHLAND	HOOLIGAN	HUNTRESS
HEATHROW	HIGH-LIFE	HOOP-IRON	HUNTSMAN
HEAT-SPOT	HIGHNESS	HOPELESS	HURDLING
HEAT-WAVE	HIGH-ROAD	HOPINGLY	HURRYING
HEAVENLY	HIGH-SPOT	HORNBEAM	HURTLING
HEAVIEST	HIGH-TIDE	HORNBILL	HUSHED-UP
HECKLING	HI-JACKED	HORNLESS	HUSH-HUSH
HECTORED	HI-JACKER	HORNPIPE	HUSKIEST
HEDGEHOG	HILARITY	HOROLOGY	HUSTINGS
HEDGE-HOP	HILL-FOLK	HORRIBLE	HUSTLING
HEDGEROW	HILL-FORT	HORRIBLY	HYACINTH
HEEDLESS	HILLOCKY	HORRIDLY	HYDRATED
HEELBALL	HILLSIDE	HORRIFIC	HYDROGEN
HEFTIEST	HINDERED	HORSE-BOX	HYGIENIC
HEIGHTEN	HINDMOST	HORSE-BOY	HYMN-BOOK
HEIRLESS	HINDUISM	HORSE-CAR	HYPERION
HEIRLOOM	HIP-JOINT	HORSE-FLY	HYPHENED
HELLENIC	HIRELING	HORSEMAN	HYPHENED
HELL-FIRE	HISTORIC	HOSE-PIPE	HYPNOSIS
HELMETED	HITCHING	HOSE-REEL	HYPNOTIC
HELMLESS	HITHERTO	HOSPITAL	HYSTERIA
HELMSMAN	HOARDING	HOSTELRY	
HELPLESS	HOARSELY	HOTCHPOT	I – 8
HELPMATE	HOBBLING	HOTELIER	ICE-BOUND

ICE-CREAM	IMPENDED	INDUCTED	INSOMNIA
ICE-FIELD	IMPERIAL	INDULGED	INSOMUCH
ICE-HOUSE	IMPETIGO	INDUSTRY	INSPIRED
ICE-PLANT	IMPINGED	INEDIBLE	INSPIRER
ICE-WATER	IMPISHLY	INEQUITY	INSPIRIT
ICE-YACHT	IMPLICIT	INEXPERT	INSTANCE
IDEALISE	IMPLORED	INFAMOUS	INSTINCT
IDEALISM	IMPLYING	INFANTRY	INSTRUCT
IDEALIST	IMPOLITE	INFECTED	INSULATE
IDEALITY	IMPORTED	INFERIOR	INSULTED
IDENTIFY	IMPORTER	INFERNAL	INSURING
IDENTITY	IMPOSING	INFERRED	INTAGLIO
IDEOLOGY	IMPOSTOR	INFESTED	INTEGRAL
IDLENESS	IMPOTENT	INFINITE	INTENDED
IDOLATER	IMPRISON	INFINITY	INTENTLY
IDOLATRY	IMPROPER	INFIRMLY	INTERACT
IDOLISED	IMPROVED	INFLAMED	INTER-COM
IGNITING	IMPROVER	INFLATED	INTEREST
IGNITION	IMPUDENT	INFLATOR	INTERIOR
IGNOMINY	IMPUGNED	INFORMAL	INTERLAY
IGNORANT	IMPUNITY	INFORMED	INTERMIX
IGNORING	IMPURELY	INFORMER	INTERNAL
ILL-BLOOD	IMPURITY	INFRA-RED	INTERNED
ILL-FATED	IMPUTING	INFRINGE	INTERNEE
ILL-TIMED	INACTION	INFUSING	INTERPOL
ILL-TREAT	INACTIVE	INFUSION	INTERRED
ILLUDING	INASMUCH	INFUSIVE	INTERVAL
ILLUMINE	INCENSED	INHALANT	INTIMACY
ILLUSION	INCEPTOR	INHALING	INTIMATE
ILLUSIVE	INCHOATE	INHERENT	INTONING
ILLUSORY	INCIDENT	INHERING	INTREPID
IMAGINED	INCISELY	INHESION	INTRIGUE
IMBECILE	INCISING	INIMICAL	INTRUDER
IMBIBING	INCISION	INIQUITY	INUNDATE
IMITABLE	INCISIVE	INITIATE	INVADING
IMITATED	INCISORY	INJECTED	INVASION
IMITATOR	INCITING	INJECTOR	INVASIVE
IMMANENT	INCLINED	INJURING	INVEIGLE
IMMATURE	INCLUDED	INKINESS	INVENTED
IMMERSED	INCOMING	INK-MAKER	INVENTOR
IMMINENT	INCREASE	INKSTAND	INVERTER
IMMINGLE	INCUBATE	INLAYING	INVESTED
IMMOBILE	INCURRED	INNATELY	INVESTOR
IMMODEST	INCURVED	INNOCENT	INVITING
IMMOLATE	INDEBTED	INNOVATE	INVOICED
IMMORTAL	INDECENT	INNUENDO	INVOKING
IMMUNISE	INDENTED	INQUIRED	INVOLVED
IMMUNITY	INDEXING	INQUIRER	INWARDLY
IMPACTED	INDIAMAN	INSANELY	IODISING
IMPAIRED	INDICATE	INSANITY	IOLANTHE
IMPALING	INDICTED	INSCRIBE	IREFULLY
IMPARITY	INDIGENT	INSECURE	IRISHISM
IMPARTED	INDIRECT	INSERTED	IRONBARK
IMPEDING	INDITING	INSIGNIA	IRONCLAD
IMPELLED	INDOLENT	INSISTED	IRON-GREY
IMPELLER	INDUCING	INSOLENT	IRONICAL

IRONSIDE	JEW'S-HARP	KILOWATT	LAMBSKIN
IRONWARE	JIGGERED	KINDLIER	LAMENESS
IRONWOOD	JIGGLING	KINDLING	LAMENTED
IRONWORK	JIGMAKER	KINDNESS	LAMINATE
IRRIGATE	JINGLING	KING-CRAB	LAMPLESS
IRRITANT	JINGOISM	KINGLIKE	LAMPPOST
IRRITATE	JOCKEYED	KINGPOST	LAND-CRAB
ISABELLE	JOCOSELY	KINGSHIP	LANDFALL
ISLAMISM	JOCOSITY	KINKAJOU	LAND-GIRL
ISLAMITE	JOCUNDLY	KINSFOLK	LANDLADY
ISLANDED	JODHPURS	KIPPERED	LANDLESS
ISLANDER	JOGGLING	KISS-CURL	LANDLORD
ISOBARIC	JOHANNES	KNAPPING	LANDMARK
ISOLATED	JOINTING	KNAPSACK	LANDRAIL
ISOLATOR	JOINTURE	KNAPWEED	LANDSLIP
ISOTHERM	JOKINGLY	KNEADING	LANDSMAN
ISSUABLE	JOLLIEST	KNEE-DEEP	LANDWARD
ISTHMIAN	JONATHAN	KNEE-HIGH	LANDWEHR
ITERATED	JONGLEUR	KNEELING	LAND-WIND
	JOSTLING	KNICKERS	LANGUAGE
	JOUNCING	KNIGHTED	LANGUISH
J – 8	JOUSTING	KNIGHTLY	LANKIEST
	JOVIALLY	KNITTING	LAPELLED
JABBERED	JOYFULLY	KNITWEAR	LAPIDARY
JACKAROO	JOYOUSLY	KNOCKING	LAP-JOINT
JACKETED	JOYSTICK	KNOCK-OUT	LARBOARD
JACOBEAN	JUBILANT	KNOTLESS	LARGESSE
JACOBITE	JUDGMENT	KNOTTIER	LARKSPUR
JACQUARD	JUDICIAL	KNOTTING	LARRIKIN
JAGGEDLY	JUGGLERY	KNOUTING	LARRUPED
JAILBIRD	JUGGLING	KNOWABLE	LASSOING
JAMBOREE	JUGOSLAV	KNUCKLED	LATCHKEY
JANGLING	JULIENNE	KOHINOOR	LATENESS
JAPANESE	JUMBLING	KOHLRABI	LATENTLY
JAPANNED	JUNCTION	KOTOWING	LATHERED
JAPONICA	JUNCTURE		LATHWORK
JAUNDICE	JUNKETED		LATINISE
JAUNTIER	JUSTNESS	**L – 8**	LATINISM
JAUNTILY	JUVENILE		LATINIST
JAUNTING		LABELLED	LATINITY
JAVANESE		LABOURED	LATITUDE
JEALOUSY	**K – 8**	LABOURER	LATTERLY
JEANETTE		LABURNUM	LATTICED
JEJUNELY	KANGAROO	LACERATE	LAUDABLE
JELLYBAG	KEDGEREE	LACEWING	LAUDABLY
JEOPARDY	KEEL-HAUL	LACK-A-DAY	LAUDANUM
JEREMIAD	KEENNESS	LACKEYED	LAUGHING
JEREMIAH	KEEPSAKE	LACROSSE	LAUGHTER
JEROBOAM	KERCHIEF	LADDERED	LAUNCHED
JERRICAN	KEROSENE	LADLEFUL	LAUREATE
JEST-BOOK	KEYBOARD	LADYBIRD	LAVA-LIKE
JET-BLACK	KEY-MONEY	LADYLIKE	LAVATORY
JETPLANE	KEYSTONE	LADY-LOVE	LAVENDER
JETTISON	KICKABLE	LADYSHIP	LAVISHED
JEWELLED	KICKSHAW	LAKELAND	LAVISHLY
JEWELLER	KID-GLOVE	LAMBENCY	LAWFULLY
JEWISHLY	KILOGRAM	LAMB-LIKE	

LAWGIVER	LIFEBELT	LITTORAL	LOUDNESS
LAWMAKER	LIFEBOAT	LIVE-AXLE	LOUNGING
LAWYERLY	LIFEBUOY	LIVE-BAIT	LOVEBIRD
LAXATIVE	LIFELESS	LIVELONG	LOVE-KNOT
LAYERING	LIFELIKE	LIVENING	LOVELACE
LAZINESS	LIFELINE	LIVE-RAIL	LOVELESS
LEACHING	LIFELONG	LIVERIED	LOVE-LIFE
LEADSMAN	LIFE-PEER	LIVERISH	LOVELILY
LEAFLESS	LIFE-RAFT	LIVEWIRE	LOVELOCK
LEANNESS	LIFE-SIZE	LOADLINE	LOVELORN
LEAP-FROG	LIFETIME	LOANABLE	LOVE-NEST
LEAP-YEAR	LIFE-WORK	LOATHING	LOVESICK
LEARNING	LIFTABLE	LOBBYING	LOVESOME
LEASABLE	LIGAMENT	LOBBYIST	LOVINGLY
LEASHING	LIGATURE	LOCALISE	LOWERING
LEATHERY	LIGHTING	LOCALISM	LOYALIST
LEAVENED	LIGHTISH	LOCALITY	LUBBERLY
LEAVINGS	LIGHT-PEN	LOCATING	LUCIDITY
LEBANESE	LIKEABLE	LOCATION	LUCKIEST
LECTURED	LIKENESS	LOCK-GATE	LUCKLESS
LECTURER	LIKENING	LOCKSMAN	LUCKY-DIP
LEE-BOARD	LIKEWISE	LOCUTION	LUKEWARM
LEE-SHORE	LILLIPUT	LODESTAR	LUMBERED
LEFTHAND	LIME-FREE	LODGINGS	LUMINARY
LEFTWARD	LIME-KILN	LODGMENT	LUMINOUS
LEFT-WING	LIMERICK	LOG-CABIN	LUMPFISH
LEGALISE	LIME-TREE	LOG-CANOE	LUNCHEON
LEGALISM	LIME-WASH	LOITERED	LUNCHING
LEGALIST	LIMITING	LOITERER	LUNG-FISH
LEGALITY	LINCHPIN	LOLLIPOP	LURCHING
LEGATION	LINEALLY	LOLLOPED	LUSCIOUS
LEG-BREAK	LINEARLY	LONDONER	LUSTIEST
LEMONADE	LINESMAN	LONESOME	LUSTROUS
LENGTHEN	LINGERED	LONGBOAT	LUTHERAN
LENIENCE	LINGERIE	LONGHAND	LYCH-GATE
LENIENCY	LINGUIST	LONG-LEGS	LYNCHING
LENT-LILY	LINIMENT	LONG-SHIP	LYNCH-LAW
LESSENED	LINNAEUS	LONG-SLIP	LYNX-EYED
LETHARGY	LINOLEUM	LONGSTOP	LYRE-BIRD
LETTERED	LINOTYPE	LONG-TERM	LYRICISM
LEVELLED	LIONISED	LONGWAYS	
LEVELLER	LIP-STICK	LONGWISE	
LEVERAGE	LIQUIDLY	LONICERA	M – 8
LEVERING	LIQUORED	LOOKER-ON	
LEVIABLE	LISTENED	LOOPHOLE	MACARONI
LEVITATE	LISTENER	LOOP-LINE	MACAROON
LEWDNESS	LISTEN-IN	LOOSE-BOX	MACERATE
LEWISITE	LISTLESS	LOOSENED	MACHINED
LIBATION	LITERACY	LOPSIDED	MACKEREL
LIBELLED	LITERARY	LORD-LIKE	MADDENED
LIBERATE	LITERATE	LORDLING	MADELINE
LIBERIAN	LITERATI	LORD'S-DAY	MADHOUSE
LIBRETTO	LITIGANT	LORDSHIP	MADRIGAL
LICENSED	LITIGATE	LORIKEET	MAGAZINE
LICENSEE	LITTERED	LOSINGLY	MAGICIAN
LIEGEMAN	LITTLE-GO	LOTHARIO	MAGNESIA
			MAGNETIC

MAGNOLIA	MARATHON	MEANTIME	MILDNESS
MAHARAJA	MARAUDER	MEASURED	MILE-POST
MAHOGANY	MARBLING	MEAT-SAFE	MILITANT
MAIDENLY	MARCHING	MECHANIC	MILITARY
MAIL-BOAT	MARGINAL	MEDDLING	MILKMAID
MAIL-CART	MARGRAVE	MEDIATED	MILKWEED
MAIL-CLAD	MARIGOLD	MEDIATOR	MILL-HAND
MAIN-DECK	MARINADE	MEDICATE	MILLIARD
MAINLAND	MARINATE	MEDICINE	MILLIBAR
MAINMAST	MARITIME	MEDIEVAL	MILLINER
MAINSAIL	MARJORAM	MEDIOCRE	MILLPOND
MAINSTAY	MARKEDLY	MEDITATE	MILLRACE
MAINTAIN	MARKETED	MEEKNESS	MILTONIC
MAINYARD	MARKSMAN	MEETNESS	MIMICKED
MAJESTIC	MARMOSET	MEGABYTE	MINATORY
MAJOLICA	MAROCAIN	MEGALITH	MINCE-PIE
MAJORITY	MAROONED	MELLOWED	MINDLESS
MALAPROP	MARQUESS	MELLOWLY	MINGLING
MALARIAL	MARQUISE	MELODEON	MINIMISE
MAL-DE-MER	MARRIAGE	MELODISE	MINISTER
MALIGNED	MARRYING	MELODIST	MINISTRY
MALINGER	MARSH-GAS	MEMBERED	MINORITY
MALODOUR	MARSH-HEN	MEMBRANE	MINOTAUR
MALT-KILN	MARSH-TIT	MEMORIAL	MINSTREL
MALT-MILL	MARTELLO	MEMORISE	MINUTELY
MALTREAT	MARTINET	MEM-SAHIB	MINUTEST
MALTSTER	MARTYRED	MENACING	MINUTIAE
MALT-WORM	MARZIPAN	MENDABLE	MINUTING
MANACLED	MASSACRE	MENTALLY	MIRRORED
MAN-CHILD	MASSAGED	MERCHANT	MIRTHFUL
MAN-EATER	MASSEUSE	MERCIFUL	MISAPPLY
MAN-HATER	MASTERED	MERICARP	MISCARRY
MAN-HOURS	MASTERLY	MERIDIAN	MISCHIEF
MAN-OF-WAR	MAST-HEAD	MERINGUE	MISCOUNT
MANPOWER	MASTLESS	MERITING	MISCUING
MANDAMUS	MASTODON	MERRIEST	MISDATED
MANDARIN	MATCHBOX	MESSMATE	MISDEALT
MANDATOR	MATCHING	MESS-ROOM	MISDOING
MANDIBLE	MATERIAL	MESSUAGE	MISDRAWN
MANDOLIN	MATERIEL	METALLED	MISERERE
MANDRAKE	MATERNAL	METALLIC	MISFIRED
MANDRILL	MATHILDA	METAPHOR	MISGUIDE
MANELESS	MATRONLY	METEORIC	MISHEARD
MANFULLY	MATTERED	METERAGE	MISHMASH
MANGLING	MATTRESS	METHINKS	MISJUDGE
MANGROVE	MATURELY	METHODIC	MISNAMED
MANIACAL	MATURING	METRICAL	MISNOMER
MANICURE	MATURITY	MIDDLING	MISOGAMY
MANIFEST	MAVERICK	MIDNIGHT	MISOGYNY
MANIFOLD	MAY-QUEEN	MIDSHIPS	MISPLACE
MANNERLY	MAYORESS	MIGHTILY	MISPRINT
MANORIAL	MAZINESS	MIGRAINE	MISQUOTE
MANTILLA	MEAGRELY	MIGRATED	MISRULED
MANTLING	MEALTIME	MIGRATOR	MISSHAPE
MANUALLY	MEAL-WORM	MILANESE	MISSPELL
MANURING	MEANNESS	MILDEWED	MISSPELT

MISSPEND	MONOTONY	MOURNING	MYOSOTIS
MISSPENT	MONOTYPE	MOUSE-EAR	MYRMIDON
MISSTATE	MONOXIDE	MOUTHFUL	MYSTICAL
MISTAKEN	MONSIEUR	MOUTHING	MYTHICAL
MISTEACH	MONUMENT	MOVELESS	
MISTIMED	MOOCHING	MOVEMENT	
MISTITLE	MOONBEAM	MOVINGLY	N – 8
MISTRESS	MOONCALF	MUCHNESS	NACREOUS
MISTRIAL	MOONFACE	MUCILAGE	NAIL-FILE
MISTRUST	MOONFISH	MUCK-HEAP	NAINSOOK
MISTUNED	MOONLESS	MUCK-RAKE	NAMELESS
MISUSAGE	MOORCOCK	MUDDLING	NAMESAKE
MISUSING	MOORFOWL	MUDDYING	NAPOLEON
MITIGATE	MOORLAND	MUDGUARD	NARCISSI
MITTENED	MOOT-HALL	MUFFLING	NARCOSIS
MIZZLING	MOOTABLE	MULBERRY	NARCOTIC
MNEMONIC	MOQUETTE	MULCHING	NARGHILE
MOBILITY	MORALIST	MULCTING	NARRATED
MOBILIZE	MORALITY	MULE-DEER	NARRATOR
MOCCASIN	MORALIZE	MULETEER	NARROWED
MOCKABLE	MORATORY	MULISHLY	NARROWER
MODELLED	MORAVIAN	MULTIPLE	NARROWLY
MODELLER	MORBIDLY	MULTIPLY	NATATION
MODERATE	MOREOVER	MUMBLING	NATATORY
MODERATO	MORIBUND	MUNCHING	NATIONAL
MODESTLY	MOROCCAN	MUNIMENT	NATIVELY
MODIFIED	MOROSELY	MUNITION	NATIVITY
MODIFIER	MORPHEAN	MURALLED	NATTERED
MODISHLY	MORPHEUS	MURDERED	NATTIEST
MODULATE	MORPHINE	MURDERER	NATURISM
MOISTURE	MORTALLY	MURIATED	NATURIST
MOLASSES	MORTARED	MURMURED	NAUSEATE
MOLE-CAST	MORTGAGE	MUSCATEL	NAUSEOUS
MOLEHILL	MORTISED	MUSCULAR	NAUTICAL
MOLESKIN	MORTUARY	MUSHROOM	NAUTILUS
MOLECULE	MOSQUITO	MUSICIAN	NAVIGATE
MOLESTED	MOSS-CLAD	MUSINGLY	NAVY BLUE
MOLLUSCA	MOSS-ROSE	MUSK-BALL	NAZARENE
MOMENTUM	MOTHERED	MUSK-DEER	NAZARITE
MONARCHY	MOTHERLY	MUSK-PEAR	NAZIFIED
MONASTIC	MOTIONED	MUSK-PLUM	NEARNESS
MONDAINE	MOTIVATE	MUSK-ROSE	NEATHERD
MONETARY	MOTOR-BUS	MUSKETRY	NEATNESS
MONEYBOX	MOTOR-CAR	MUSQUASH	NEBULOUS
MONGOOSE	MOTORING	MUSTERED	NECKBAND
MONITORY	MOTORIST	MUTATION	NECKBEEF
MONKEYED	MOTORMAN	MUTENESS	NECKLACE
MONKFISH	MOTTLING	MUTILATE	NEEDLESS
MONKHOOD	MOUFFLON	MUTINEER	NEEDLING
MONOCLED	MOULDING	MUTINIED	NEGATING
MONOGAMY	MOULTING	MUTINOUS	NEGATION
MONOGRAM	MOUNDING	MUTTERED	NEGATIVE
MONOLITH	MOUNTAIN	MUTUALLY	NEGLIGEE
MONOPOLY	MOUNTIES	MUZZLING	NEGROISM
MONORAIL	MOUNTING	MYCELIUM	NEIGHING
MONOTONE	MOURNFUL	MYCOLOGY	NEO-LATIN

NEOPHYTE	NOSERING	OBSTRUCT	ONE-HORSE
NEPALESE	NOSEBAND	OBTAINED	ONE-SIDED
NEPOTISM	NOSELESS	OBTRUDED	ONLOOKER
NESTLING	NOTANDUM	OBTUSELY	OOLOGIST
NETTLING	NOTATION	OBVIATED	OPEN-EYED
NEURITIS	.NOTCHING	OCCASION	OPEN-WORK
NEUROSIS	NOTEBOOK	OCCIDENT	OPENCAST
NEUROTIC	NOTELESS·	OCCLUDED	OPENNESS
NEWCOMER	NOTICING	OCCULTLY	OPERA-HAT
NEWSHAWK	NOTIFIED	OCCUPANT	OPERATED
NEWS-REEL	NOTIONAL	OCCUPIED	OPERATIC
NEWS-ROOM	NOVELIST	OCCUPIER	OPERATOR
NIBBLING	NOVEMBER	OCCURRED	OPERETTA
NIBELUNG	NOWADAYS	OCHREOUS	OPIUM-DEN
NICENESS	NUDENESS	OCTOROON	OPPONENT
NICKNAME	NUGATORY	OCTUPLET	OPPOSING
NICOTINE	NUISANCE	OCULARLY	OPPOSITE
NIGGLING	NUMBERED	ODIOUSLY	OPTICIAN
NIGHTCAP	NUMBNESS	ODOMETER	OPTIMISM
NIGHTJAR	NUMERARY	OERLIKON	OPTIMIST
NIGHTMAN	NUMERATE	OFF-BREAK	OPTIONAL
NIGHT-OWL	NUMEROUS	OFFPRINT	OPULENCE
NIHILISM	NUMSKULL	OFFSHOOT	ORACULAR
NIHILIST	NUPTIALS	OFF-SHORE	ORANGERY
NIHILITY	NURSLING	OFF-STAGE	ORATORIO
NINEFOLD	NURTURED	OFFENDED	ORCADIAN
NINEPINS	NUT-BROWN	OFFENDER	ORDAINED
NINETEEN	NUTHATCH	OFFERING	ORDERING
NITRATED	NUTMEGGY	OFFICIAL	ORDINARY
NITROGEN	NUTRIENT	OFTTIMES	ORDNANCE
NOBBLING	NUTSHELL	OHMMETER	ORGANDIE
NOBILITY	NUZZLING	OILCLOTH	ORGANISM
NOBLEMAN		OILFIELD	ORGANIST
NOBLESSE		OIL-GLAND	ORGANISE
NOCTURNE	O – 8	OIL-PAPER	ORIENTAL
NOISETTE		OIL-PRESS	ORIENTED
NOMADISM	OAK-APPLE	OILSKINS	ORIGINAL
NOMINATE	OBDURACY	OILINESS	ORNAMENT
NON-CLAIM	OBDURATE	OILSTONE	ORNATELY
NON-ELECT	OBEDIENT	OINTMENT	ORPHANED
NONJUROR	OBEISANT	OLD-TIMER	ORTHODOX
NON-MORAL	OBITUARY	OLD-WORLD	OSCULANT
NON-PARTY	OBJECTED	OLEANDER	OSCULATE
NON-RIGID	OBJECTOR	OLEASTER	OSSIFIED
NON-TOXIC	OBLATION	OLIPHANT	OTOSCOPE
NON-UNION	OBLATORY	OLIVE-OIL	OUTBOARD
NONESUCH	OBLIGANT	OLYMPIAD	OUTBOUND
NONSENSE	OBLIGATE	OLYMPIAN	OUTBREAK
NOONTIDE	OBLIGATO	OLYMPICS	OUTBURST
NORMALCY	OBLIGING	OMELETTE	OUTCLASS
NORMALLY	OBLIVION ·	OMISSION	OUTDOING
NORSEMAN	OBSCURED	OMISSIVE	OUTDOORS
NORTHERN	OBSERVED	OMITTING	OUTFACED
NORTHING	OBSERVER	OMPHALOS	OUTFIELD
NORTHMAN	OBSESSED	ONCE-OVER	OUTFLANK
NOSEDIVE	OBSOLETE	ONCOMING	OUTFLASH
	OBSTACLE		

OUTFLING	OVERDRAW	OVERTONE	PARAFFIN
OUTFLOWN	OVERDREW	OVERTURE	PARAKEET
OUTFLUSH	OVERFAST	OVERTURN	PARALLAX
OUTGOING	OVERFEED	OVERWASH	PARALLEL
OUTGROWN	OVERFILL	OVERWEAR	PARALYSE
OUTHOUSE	OVERFISH	OVERWIND	PARAMOUR
OUTLAWED	OVERFLOW	OVERWORK	PARNAOIA
OUTLAWRY	OVERFOLD	OVERWORN	PARASITE
OUTLEAPT	OVERFOND	OXIDIZED	PARAVANE
OUTLEARN	OVERFULL	OX-PECKER	PARCHING
OUTLINED	OVERGIVE	OX-TONGUED	PARDONED
OUTLIVED	OVERGROW		PARENTAL
OUTLYING	OVERHAND	**P – 8**	PARGETED
OUTMARCH	OVERHANG		PARGETER
OUTPACED	OVERHAUL	PACIFIED	PARISIAN
OUTPOWER	OVERHEAD	PACIFIER	PARLANCE
OUTRAGED	OVERHEAR	PACIFISM	PARLEYED
OUTRANGE	OVERHEAT	PACIFIST	PARMESAN
OUTREACH	OVERJUMP	PACK-LOAD	PARODIED
OUTRIDER	OVERKIND	PACK-MULE	PARODIST
OUTRIGHT	OVERLAID	PACKETED	PAROXYSM
OUTSHINE	OVERLAIN	PADDLING	PARRYING
OUTSHONE	OVERLAND	PAGANISE	PARTAKEN
OUTSIDER	OVERLEAF	PAGANISH	PARTERRE
OUTSLEEP	OVERLEAP	PAGANISM	PARTHIAN
OUTSLEPT	OVERLOAD	PAGINATE	PARTICLE
OUTSLIDE	OVERLOCK	PAINLESS	PARTISAN
OUTSMART	OVERLONG	PAINTING	PART-SONG
OUTSPEAK	OVERLOOK	PAKISTAN	PASSABLE
OUTSPENT	OVERLORD	PALATIAL	PASSABLY
OUTSPOKE	OVERMUCH	PALATINE	PASSBOOK
OUTSTAND	OVERNEAT	PALE-EYED	PASSER-BY
OUTSTARE	OVERNICE	PALE-FACE	PASSOVER
OUTSTOOD	OVERPAID	PALENESS	PASSPORT
OUTSTRIP	OVERPASS	PALISADE	PASSWORD
OUTSWEAR	OVERRAKE	PALL-MALL	PASTICHE
OUTVALUE	OVERRATE	PALLIATE	PASTILLE
OUTVENOM	OVERRIDE	PALLIDLY	PASTORAL
OUTVOTED	OVERRIPE	PALM-TREE	PASTURED
OUTWARDS	OVERRULE	PALPABLE	PATCHING
OUTWEIGH	OVERSEAS	PALPABLY	PATENTED
OVEN-BIRD	OVERSEEN	PAMPERED	PATENTEE
OVERALLS	OVERSEER	PAMPHLET	PATENTOR
OVERARCH	OVERSELL	PANCAKED	PATERNAL
OVERAWED	OVERSEWN	PANCREAS	PATHETIC
OVERBEAR	OVERSHOE	PANDERED	PATHLESS
OVERBOIL	OVERSHOT	PANELLED	PATIENCE
OVERBOLD	OVERSIDE	PANGOLIN	PATTERED
OVERBUSY	OVERSIZE	PANICKED	PATTYPAN
OVERCAME	OVERSLIP	PANORAMA	PAVEMENT
OVERCAST	OVERSOLD	PANTHEON	PAVILION
OVERCOAT	OVERSTAY	PAPERING	PAWNSHOP
OVERCOLD	OVERSTEP	PARABOLA	PAY-CLERK
OVERCOME	OVERTAKE	PARABOLE	PAY-SHEET
OVERDONE	OVERTASK	PARADING	PEACEFUL
OVERDOSE	OVERTIME	PARADISE	PEACHING

PEA-GREEN	PERSUADE	PINE-WOOD	PLAYTIME
PEARMAIN	PERTNESS	PING-PONG	PLEACHED
PEASECOD	PERUSING	PININGLY	PLEADING
PEAT-MOOR	PERUVIAN	PINIONED	PLEASANT
PEATMOSS	PERVADED	PINK-EYED	PLEASING
PECTORAL	PERVERSE	PIN-MAKER	PLEASURE
PECULIAR	PESTERED	PIN-MONEY	PLEATING
PEDAGOGY	PESTLING	PINNACLE	PLEBEIAN
PEDALLED	PETERING	PINPOINT	PLECTRUM
PEDANTIC	PETERMAN	PIPE-CASE	PLEDGING
PEDANTRY	PETITION	PIPECLAY	PLEIADES
PEDDLERY	PETRONEL	PIPE-FISH	PLETHORA
PEDDLING	PETULANT	PIPE-LINE	PLEURISY
PEDESTAL	PHALANGE	PIPE-RACK	PLIANTLY
PEDICURE	PHANTASM	PIPE-WORK	PLIGHTED
PEDIGREE	PHANTASY	PIQUANCY	PLIOCENE
PEDIMENT	PHARISEE	PIRATING	PLODDING
PEEP-HOLE	PHARMACY	PISCATOR	PLOPPING
PEEP-SHOW	PHEASANT	PISTOLET	PLOTTING
PEERLESS	PHILOMEL	PITCHING	PLOUGHED
PEIGNOIR	PHONE-BOX	PITIABLE	PLUCKILY
PEKINESE	PHONETIC	PITIABLY	PLUCKING
PELLAGRA	PHOSGENE	PITILESS	PLUGGING
PELL-MELL	PHOSPHOR	PITTANCE	PLUG-UGLY
PELLUCID	PHRASING	PIVOT-MAN	PLUMBAGO
PEMMICAN	PHRYGIAN	PIVOTING	PLUMB-BOB
PENALISE	PHTHISIS	PIXY-RING	PLUMBING
PENCHANT	PHYSICAL	PLACATED	PLUM-CAKE
PENDULUM	PHYSIQUE	PLACEMAN	PLUM-DUFF
PENELOPE	PIANETTE	PLACIDLY	PLUMELET
PENITENT	PICAROON	PLAGIARY	PLUMPEST
PENKNIFE	PICKETED	PLAGUILY	PLUMPING
PENN'ORTH	PICKLING	PLAGUING	PLUNGING
PENOLOGY	PICKLOCK	PLAITING	PLURALLY
PENT-ROOF	PICK-ME-UP	PLANGENT	PLUTARCH
PENTAGON	PICKWICK	PLANKING	PLUTONIC
PENWIPER	PICTURED	PLANKTON	PLUVIOUS
PENWOMAN	PIERCING	PLANLESS	POACHING
PEOPLING	PIFFLING	PLANNING	POCHETTE
PEPPERED	PIG-FACED	PLANTAIN	POCKETED
PERCEIVE	PIKEHEAD	PLANTING	POCKMARK
PERCHING	PILASTER	PLANTLET	POETICAL
PERFORCE	PILCHARD	PLASHING	POETIZED
PERFUMED	PILFERED	PLATEFUL	POIGNANT
PERIANTH	PILLAGED	PLATFORM	POIGNARD
PERICARP	PILLARED	PLATINIC	POINTING
PERILOUS	PILLOWED	PLATINUM	POISONED
PERIODIC	PILOTAGE	PLATONIC	POISONER
PERISHED	PILOTING	PLATTING	POLARITY
PERJURED	PIN-WHEEL	PLATYPUS	POLARIZE
PERMEATE	PINAFORE	PLAYABLE	POLE-JUMP
PERMUTED	PINCE-NEZ	PLAYBILL	POLE-STAR
PERORATE	PINCHERS	PLAYBOOK	POLEMICS
PEROXIDE	PINCHING	PLAYGOER	POLICING
PERSONAL	PINE-CLAD	PLAYMATE	POLISHED
PERSPIRE	PINE-CONE	PLAYSOME	POLITELY

POLITICS	POT-PLANT	PRETTIFY	PROPOSER
POLLUTED	POTSHERD	PRETTILY	PROPOUND
POLONIUM	POT-STICK	PREVIOUS	PROPPING
POLTROON	POT-STILL	PRICKING	PROROGUE
POLYGAMY	POTTERED	PRICKLED	PROSEMAN
POLYGLOT	POUCHING	PRIDEFUL	PROSPECT
POLYGRAM	POULTICE	PRIESTLY	PROTEGEE
POMANDER	POUNCING	PRIGGERY	PROTOCOL
POMPEIAN	POUNDAGE	PRIGGISH	PROTOZOA
PONDERED	POUNDING	PRIMATES	PROTRACT
POND-LILY	POWDERED	PRIMEVAL	PROTRUDE
POND-WEED	POWERFUL	PRIMNESS	PROVABLE
PONTIFEX	POWWOWED	PRIMROSE	PROVABLY
PONTIFIC	PRACTICE	PRINCELY	PROVIDED
PONY-SKIN	PRACTISE	PRINCEPS	PROVINCE
POOH-POOH	PRAISING	PRINCESS	PROVOKED
POOLROOM	PRANCING	PRINTING	PROWLING
POOR-LAWS	PRANDIAL	PRINTOUT	PRUDENCE
POORNESS	PRANGING	PRIORESS	PRUNELLA
POOR-RATE	PRATTLED	PRIORITY	PRUSSIAN
POPELING	PREACHED	PRISONER	PRYINGLY
POPINJAY	PREACHER	PRISTINE	PSALMIST
POPISHLY	PREAMBLE	PRIZEMAN	PSALMODY
POPULACE	PRECEDED	PROBABLE	PSALTERY
POPULATE	PRECINCT	PROBABLY	PTOMAINE
POPULOUS	PRECIOUS	PROCEEDS	PUBLICAN
POROSITY	PRECLUDE	PROCLAIM	PUBLICLY
PORPHYRY	PREDATED	PROCURED	PUCKERED
PORPOISE	PRE-ELECT	PRODDING	PUDDLING
PORRIDGE	PREENING	PRODIGAL	PUFF-BALL
PORTABLE	PRE-ENTRY	PRODUCED	PUFF-PUFF
PORTHOLE	PRE-EXIST	PRODUCER	PUG-FACED
PORTIERE	PREFACED	PROFANED	PUGILISM
PORTLAND	PREFIXED	PROFILED	PUGILIST
PORTRAIT	PREGNANT	PROFITED	PUISSANT
POSEIDON	PREJUDGE	PROFOUND	PULINGLY
POSINGLY	PRELUDED	PROGRESS	PULLOVER
POSITION	PREMIERE	PROHIBIT	PULSATOR
POSITIVE	PREMISED	PROLAPSE	PUMP-ROOM
POSSIBLE	PREMISES	PROLIFIC	PUNCHEON
POSSIBLY	PRENATAL	PROLIXLY	PUNCHING
POSTABLE	PRENTICE	PROLOGUE	PUNCTUAL
POSTCARD	PREPARED	PROMISED	PUNCTURE
POST-DATE	PRESAGED	PROMOTED	PUNGENCY
POST-FREE	PRESCIND	PROMOTER	PUNINESS
POST-HORN	PRESENCE	PROMPTED	PUNISHED
POSTICHE	PRESERVE	PROMPTER	PUNITIVE
POSTMARK	PRESIDED	PROMPTLY	PUNITORY
POST-PAID	PRESS-BOX	PRONG-HOE	PUPATION
POSTPONE	PRESSING	PROOFING	PUPPETRY
POST-TIME	PRESSMAN	PROPERLY	PUPPYISH
POSTURED	PRESSURE	PROPERTY	PUPPYISM
POTATION	PRESTIGE	PROPHECY	PURBLIND
POTENTLY	PRE-STUDY	PROPHESY	PURCHASE
POTHERED	PRESUMED	PROPOSAL	PURENESS
POT-HOUSE	PRETENCE	PROPOSED	PURIFIED

PURPLING	QUESTION	RAKISHLY	RE-ASCENT
PURPLISH	QUEUEING	RALLYING	REASONED
PURPOSED	QUIBBLED	RAMADHAN	RE-ASSERT
PURSEFUL	QUICKEST	RAMBLING	RE-ASSESS
PURSE-NET	QUICKSET	RAMIFIED	RE-ASSIGN
PURSLANE	QUIDNUNC	RAMPAGED	REASSURE
PURSUANT	QUIETEST	RAMPANCY	RE-ATTACH
PURSUING	QUIETUDE	RAM'S-HORN	RE-ATTAIN
PURVEYED	QUILLING	RANCHERO	REBATING
PURVEYOR	QUILL-PEN	RANCHING	REBELLED
PUSHBALL	QUILTING	RANCHMAN	RE-BOILED
PUSHBIKE	QUIPPING	RANCIDLY	REBUFFED
PUSS-MOTH	QUIRKING	RANDOMLY	REBUKING
PUSS-TAIL	QUISLING	RANKLING	REBURIED
PUSSY-CAT	QUITRENT	RANKNESS	REBUTTAL
PUTTYING	QUITTING	RANSOMED	REBUTTED
PUZZLING	QUIXOTIC	RAPACITY	RECALLED
PYRIFORM	QUIXOTRY	RAPE-SEED	RECANTED
PYROXENE	QUIZZERY	RAPIDITY	RECEDING
	QUIZZING	RAREFIED	RECEIVED
	QUOTABLE	RARENESS	RECEIVER
Q – 8	QUOTIENT	RASCALLY	RECENTLY
		RASHNESS	RECESSED
QUACKERY		RATAPLAN	RECHARGE
QUACKING	R – 8	RATEABLE	RECISION
QUACKISH		RATE-BOOK	RECITING
QUADRANT	RABBETED	RATIFIED	RECKLESS
QUADRATE	RABELAIS	RATIONAL	RECKONED
QUADRIGA	RABIDITY	RATIONED	RECLINED
QUADROON	RACECARD	RATS-BANE	RECLOSED
QUAFFING	RACEGOER	RAT'S-TAIL	RECLOTHE
QUAGMIRE	RACINESS	RATTLING	RECOILED
QUAILING	RACK-RENT	RAVAGING	RECOINED
QUAINTER	RACKETED	RAVELLED	RE-COLOUR
QUAINTLY	RADIALLY	RAVENING	RE-COMMIT
QUAKERLY	RADIANCE	RAVENOUS	RE-CONVEY
QUANDARY	RADIATED	RAVINGLY	RECORDED
QUANTITY	RADIATOR	RAVISHED	RECORDER
QUARRIED	RADIOING	RAW-BONED	RECOUPED
QUARTERN	RAFFLING	RE-ABSORB	RECOURSE
QUARTERS	RAFTERED	RE-ACCUSE	RECOVERY
QUASHING	RAFTSMAN	REACHING	RECREANT
QUATORZE	RAG-PAPER	REACTION	RECREATE
QUATRAIN	RAG-WHEEL	REACTIVE	RECURRED
QUAVERED	RAGGEDLY	READABLE	RECURVED
QUEASILY	RAGINGLY	READABLY	RED-FACED
QUEEN-BEE	RAGSTONE	RE-ADJUST	RED-SHIRT
QUEENING	RAILHEAD	RE-AFFIRM	REDDENED
QUEEREST	RAILLERY	REALIZED	REDEEMED
QUEERING	RAILROAD	REALNESS	REDEEMER
QUEERISH	RAINBAND	RE-APPEAR	REDIRECT
QUELLING	RAINBIRD	REAR-RANK	RE-DIVIDE
QUENCHED	RAINCOAT	RE-ARMING	RED-NOSED
QUENCHER	RAINDROP	REARMOST	REDOLENT
QUERYING	RAINFALL	REARWARD	REDOUBLE
QUESTFUL	RAINLESS	RE-ASCEND	REDSHANK
QUESTING	RAKEHELL		

REDUCING	REISSUED	REPAIRED	RESPIRED
RE-DYEING	REJECTED	REPAIRER	RESPONSE
RE-ECHOED	REJOICED	REPARTEE	RE-STATED
REED-MACE	REJOINER	REPASSED	REST-CURE
REED-STOP	RE-JUDGED	REPAYING	RESTLESS
REEF-KNOT	REKINDLE	REPEALED	RESTORED
REELABLE	RELANDED	REPEATED	RESTORER
RE-EMBARK	RELAPSED	REPEATER	RESTRAIN
RE-EMBODY	RELATING	REPELLED	RESTRICT
RE-EMERGE	RELATION	REPENTED	RE-STRIKE
RE-ENLIST	RELAXING	REPINING	RESULTED
RE-EXPORT	RELAYING	REPLACED	RESUMING
REFASTEN	RELEASED	RE-PLEDGE	RE-SUMMON
REFERRED	RELEGATE	REPLYING	RETAILED
REFILLED	RELEVANT	RE-POLISH	RETAILER
REFINERY	RELIABLE	REPORTED	RETAINED
REFINING	RELIABLY	REPORTER	RETAINER
REFITTED	RELIANCE	REPOSING	RETAKING
REFLEXED	RELIEVED	RE-POTTED	RETARDED
REFORGED	RELIGION	REPRIEVE	RETICENT
REFORMED	RELISHED	REPRISAL	RETICULE
REFORMER	RE-LIVING	REPROACH	RETIRING
REFRAMED	RE-LOADED	REPROVAL	RETORTED
REFUNDED	REMAINED	REPROVED	RE-TOSSED
REFUSING	REMAKING	RE-PRUNED	RETRACED
REFUTING	REMANENT	REPTILIA	RETRENCH
REGAINED	RE-MANNED	REPUBLIC	RETRIEVE
REGALING	REMARKED	REPUGNED	RETROACT
REGALITY	REMARQUE	REPULSED	RE-TRYING
REGARDED	REMEDIAL	RE-PURIFY	RETURNED
RE-GATHER	REMEDIED	REPUTING	RE-UNITED
REGICIDE	REMEMBER	REQUIRED	REVALUED
REGILDED	REMINDED	REQUITAL	RE-VAMPED
REGIMENT	REMINDER	REQUITED	REVEALED
REGIONAL	REMISSLY	RE-ROOFED	REVEILLE
REGISTER	REMITTAL	RE-SCORED	REVELLED
REGISTRY	REMITTED	RESCRIPT	REVELLER
REGNANCY	RE-MODIFY	RESCUING	REVENGED
RE-GROUND	REMOTELY	RESEARCH	REVEREND
REGROWTH	REMOVING	RESEATED	REVERENT
REGULATE	RENAMING	RESEMBLE	REVERING
RE-HANDLE	RENDERED	RESENTED	REVERSAL
REHASHED	RENEGADE	RESERVED	REVERSED
REHEARSE	RENEWING	RESETTLE	RE-VETTED
RE-HEATED	RENOUNCE	RESIDENT	REVIEWED
RE-HOUSED	RENOVATE	RESIDUAL	REVIEWER
REIGNING	RENOWNED	RESIDUUM	REVILING
RE-IGNITE	RENTABLE	RESIGNED	REVISING
RE-IMPORT	RENT-FREE	RESISTED	REVISION
REIMPOSE	RENT-ROLL	RE-SOLDER	REVIVIFY
REINDEER	RE-NUMBER	RESOLUTE	REVIVING
RE-INFECT	RE-OBTAIN	RESOLVED	REVOKING
RE-INFUSE	RE-OCCUPY	RESONANT	REVOLTED
RE-INSERT	RE-OPENED	RE-SORTED	REVOLVED
RE-INSURE	RE-OPPOSE	RESOURCE	REVOLVER
RE-INVEST	RE-ORDAIN	RESOWING	REWARDED

RE-WORDED	ROLY-POLY	ROUTEING	SAGO-PALM
RHAPSODY	ROMANCED	ROVINGLY	SAILABLE
RHEOSTAT	ROMANCER	ROWDYISH	SAIL-BOAT
RHETORIC	ROMANISE	ROWDYISM	SAILLESS
RHOMBOID	ROMANISH	ROWELLED	SAIL-LOFT
RHYTHMIC	ROMANIST	ROYALISM	SAIL-PLAN
RIBALDRY	ROMANTIC	ROYALIST	SAIL-ROOM
RIBBONED	ROOD-BEAM	RUBBISHY	SAIL-YARD
RICHNESS	ROOD-LOFT	RUBICUND	SAINFOIN
RICKSHAW	ROOD-TREE	RUCKSACK	SALACITY
RICOCHET	ROOFLESS	RUDENESS	SALAD-OIL
RIDDANCE	ROOF-TREE	RUDIMENT	SALADING
RIDDLING	ROOSTING	RUEFULLY	SALARIED
RIDEABLE	ROOT-BEER	RUFFLING	SALEABLE
RIDICULE	ROOT-CROP	RUGGEDLY	SALEABLY
RIFENESS	ROOT-HAIR	RUINABLE	SALE-ROOM
RIFF-RAFF	ROOTLESS	RUINATED	SALESMAN
RIFLEMAN	ROPE-WALK	RULELESS	SALE-WORK
RIGADOON	ROPE-YARN	RULINGLY	SALIENCE
RIGHTFUL	ROPINESS	RUMANIAN	SALIFIED
RIGHTING	ROSARIAN	RUMBLING	SALINITY
RIGIDITY	ROSARIUM	RUMINANT	SALLYING
RIGOROUS	ROSE-BUSH	RUMINATE	SALMONET
RING-BARK	ROSE-GALL	RUMMAGED	SALOPIAN
RING-BOLT	ROSE-HUED	RUMOURED	SALT-BUSH
RINGBONE	ROSE-KNOT	RUMPLING	SALTLESS
RING-DOVE	ROSEMARY	RUNABOUT	SALT-LICK
RINGWORM	ROSE-PINK	RUNAGATE	SALT-MINE
RIPARIAN	ROSE-ROOT	RUNNER-UP	SALTNESS
RIPENESS	ROSE-TREE	RURALISE	SALT-WELL
RIPPLING	ROSETTED	RURALISM	SALT-WORT
RISKIEST	ROSEWOOD	RURALIST	SALUTARY
RITUALLY	ROSE-WORM	RURALITY	SALUTING
RIVALLED	ROSINESS	RUSHLIKE	SALVABLE
RIVER-BED	ROSINING	RUSTLESS	SALVAGED
RIVER-GOD	ROSIN-OIL	RUSTLING	SAMENESS
RIVER-HOG	ROTARIAN	RUTHLESS	SAMPHIRE
RIVER-MAN	ROTATING	RYE-GRASS	SAMPLING
RIVÉTING	ROTATION		SANCTIFY
ROAD-BLOCK	ROTATIVE		SANCTION
ROADLESS	ROTATORY	**S – 8**	SANCTITY
ROADSIDE	ROT-GRASS		SANDBANK
ROADSTER	ROTIFERA	SABOTAGE	SANDBATH
ROASTING	ROTTENLY	SABOTEUR	SAND-BIRD
ROBOTICS	ROUGHAGE	SACKLESS	SAND-CRAB
ROBUSTLY	ROUGH-DRY	SACK-RACE	SAND-DUNE
ROCK-ALUM	ROUGH-HEW	SACREDLY	SAND-FISH
ROCK-CAKE	ROUGHING	SACRISTY	SAND-FLEA
ROCK-DOVE	ROUGHISH	SADDENED	SAND-HILL
ROCKETED	ROULETTE	SADDLERY	SAND-IRON
ROCKLESS	ROUND-ARM	SADDLING	SAND-REED
ROCK-ROSE	ROUNDERS	SADDUCEE	SAND-REEL
ROCK-SALT	ROUNDING	SADFACED	SAND-ROLL
ROCK-WORK	ROUNDISH	SAGACITY	SAND-SHOT
ROGATION	ROUNDLET	SAGAMORE	SAND-STAR
ROLL-CALL	ROUND-TOP	SAGENESS	SAND-TRAP

SAND-WASP	SCAPULAR	SCRIBING	SEASCAPE
SANDWICH	SCARCELY	SCRIMPED	SEA-SHELL
SANDWORM	SCARCITY	SCRIMPLY	SEA-SHORE
SANDWORT	SCARFING	SCROFULA	SEA-SHRUB
SANENESS	SCARF-PIN	SCROUNGE	SEA-SNAIL
SANGUINE	SCARLESS	SCRUB-OAK	SEA-SNAKE
SANITARY	SCARRING	SCRUBBED	SEASONED
SANSKRIT	SCATHING	SCRUBBER	SEA-TROUT
SAPIDITY	SCAVENGE	SCRUPLED	SEA-WATER
SAPIENCE	SCENARIO	SCRUTINY	SEA-WOMAN
SAPPHIRE	SCENE-MAN	SCUDDING	SEA-WRACK
SARABAND	SCENT-BAG	SCUFFLED	SECATEUR
SARATOGA	SCENT-BOX	SCULLERY	SECEDING
SARDONIC	SCEPTRED	SCULLING	SECLUDED
SARDONYX	SCHEDULE	SCULLION	SECONDED
SARGASSO	SCHEMING	SCULPTOR	SECONDLY
SARSENET	SCHILLER	SCUMBLED	SECRETED
SASH-CORD	SCHNAPPS	SCURRIED	SECRETLY
SATANISM	SCHOOLED	SCURRIES	SECURELY
SATANITY	SCHOONER	SCURVILY	SECURING
SATIABLE	SCIATICA	SCUTTLED	SECURITY
SATIATED	SCIMITAR	SCYTHIAN	SEDATELY
SATIRIST	SCISSORS	SEA-ACORN	SEDATIVE
SATIRIZE	SCOFFING	SEA-ADDER	SEDIMENT
SATURATE	SCOLDING	SEA-BEAST	SEDITION
SATURDAY	SCOOP-NET	SEABOARD	SEDUCING
SAUCEBOX	SCOOPING	SEABORNE	SEDULITY
SAUCEPAN	SCOOTING	SEA-BREAM	SEDULOUS
SAUTERNE	SCORCHED	SEACOAST	SEED-CAKE
SAVAGELY	SCORCHER	SEA-CRAFT	SEED-COAT
SAVAGERY	SCORNFUL	SEA-DEVIL	SEED-CORN
SAVAGING	SCORNING	SEA-EAGLE	SEED-GALL
SAVANNAH	SCORPION	SEAFARER	SEED-LEAF
SAVEABLE	SCOTCHED	SEA-FIGHT	SEEDLESS
SAVINGLY	SCOT-FREE	SEA-FRONT	SEEDLING
SAVOURED	SCOTSMAN	SEA-FROTH	SEED-PLOT
SAVOYARD	SCOTTISH	SEAGOING	SEEDSMAN
SAWBONES	SCOURGED	SEA-GREEN	SEEDTIME
SAW-FRAME	SCOURING	SEA-HEATH	SEESAWED
SAW-GRASS	SCOUTING	SEA-HOLLY	SEETHING
SAW-HORSE	SCOWLING	SEA-HORSE	SIEDLITZ
SAW-TABLE	SCRABBLE	SEA-HOUND	SEIGNEUR
SCABBARD	SCRAGGED	SEA-LEVEL	SEIGNIOR
SCABIOSA	SCRAGGLY	SEALSKIN	SEIZABLE
SCABIOUS	SCRAMBLE	SEAMANLY	SELECTED
SCABROUS	SCRAPING	SEAMIEST	SELECTOR
SCAFFOLD	SCRAPPED	SEAMLESS	SELF-HEAL
SCALABLE	SCRATCHY	SEAMSTER	SELF-HELP
SCALDING	SCRAWLED	SEA-NYMPH	SELFLESS
SCALPING	SCREAMED	SEA-PERCH	SELF-LIKE
SCAMPING	SCREAMER	SEAPLANE	SELF-LOVE
SCAMPISH	SCREECHY	SEA-PLANT	SELF-MADE
SCANNING	SCREENED	SEA-PURSE	SELF-PITY
SCANSION	SCREEVER	SEARCHED	SELFSAME
SCANTIES	SCREWING	SEARCHER	SELF-WILL
SCANTILY	SCRIBBLE	SEA-ROVER	SELLABLE

SELVEDGE	SHAGREEN	SHOPPING	SIDESMAN
SEMANTIC	SHAMBLES	SHOPWORN	SIDE-STEP
SEMESTER	SHAMEFUL	SHORTAGE	SIDE-VIEW
SEMI-NUDE	SHAMMING	SHORT-CUT	SIDEWALK
SEMINARY	SHAMROCK	SHORT-LEG	SIDEWAYS
SEMINOLE	SHANGHAI	SHORT-RIB	SIFFLEUR
SEMITISM	SHANKING	SHOT-HOLE	SIFFLING
SEMITONE	SHARP-CUT	SHOT-SILK	SIGHTING
SEMOLINA	SHARPING	SHOULDER	SIGNABLE
SEMPSTER	SHARP-SET	SHOUTING	SIGNALLY
SENILITY	SHEARING	SHOW-BILL	SIGNIEUR
SENNIGHT	SHEATHED	SHOW-CARD	SIGNLESS
SENORITA	SHEAVING	SHOW-CASE	SIGNPOST
SENSEFUL	SHEDDING	SHOW-DOWN	SILENCED
SENSIBLE	SHEEP-DIP	SHOWERED	SILENCER
SENSIBLY	SHEEPDOG	SHOW-ROOM	SILENTLY
SENSUOUS	SHEEPFLY	SHOW-YARD	SILICATE
SENTENCE	SHEEPISH	SHRAPNEL	SILKWORM
SENTIENT	SHEEP-PEN	SHREDDED	SILLABUB
SENTINEL	SHEEP-RUN	SHREWDLY	SILURIAN
SENTRY-GO	SHEERING	SHREWISH	SILVANUS
SEPARATE	SHEER-LEG	SHRIEKED	SIMMERED
SEPTUPLE	SHEETING	SHRILLED	SIMPERED
SEQUENCE	SHELDUCK	SHRIMPED	SIMPLIFY
SERAGLIO	SHELLING	SHRIMPER	SIMULANT
SERAPHIC	SHELVING	SHRINKER	SIMULATE
SERAPHIM	SHEPHERD	SHROUDED	SINCIPUT
SERENADE	SHERATON	SHRUGGED	SINECURE
SERENATA	SHIELDED	SHUCKING	SINFULLY
SERENELY	SHIFTILY	SHUFFLED	SINGABLE
SERENEST	SHIFTING	SHUNNING	SINGEING
SERENITY	SHILLING	SHUNTING	SINGLING
SERGEANT	SHIMMING	SHUT-DOWN	SING-SING
SERIALLY	SHIN-BONE	SHUTTING	SINGSONG
SERIATIM	SHINGLED	SIBERIAN	SINGULAR
SERJEANT	SHINGLES	SIBILANT	SINISTER
SERRATED	SHINNING	SIBILATE	SINK-HOLE
SERVITOR	SHIPLESS	SICILIAN	SIPHONAL
SET-PIECE	SHIPLOAD	SICKENED	SIPHONIC
SETTLING	SHIPMATE	SICKLILY	SIPHONED
SEVERELY	SHIPMENT	SICK-LIST	SISTERLY
SEVERING	SHIPPING	SICKNESS	SISYPHUS
SEVERITY	SHIP-WORM	SICK-ROOM	SITUATED
SEWERAGE	SHIPYARD	SIDE-ARMS	SIXPENCE
SEWER-GAS	SHIREMAN	SIDE-BEAM	SIXTIETH
SEXTUPLE	SHIRKING	SIDE-COMB	SIZEABLE
SEXUALLY	SHIRTING	SIDE-DISH	SIZINESS
SFORZATO	SHIVERED	SIDE-DRUM	SIZZLING
SHABBIER	SHOCKING	SIDELINE	SKEAN-DHU
SHABBILY	SHOEBILL	SIDELING	SKELETAL
SHACKING	SHOEHORN	SIDE-LOCK	SKELETON
SHACKLED	SHOELACE	SIDELONG	SKETCHED
SHADDOCK	SHOELESS	SIDE-NOTE	SKEWBALD
SHADIEST	SHOOTING	SIDEREAL	SKEWERED
SHADOWED	SHOP-BELL	SIDE-SHOW	SKIDDING
SHAFTING	SHOP-GIRL	SIDE-SLIP	SKIM-MILK

SKIMMING	SLOUCHED	SNIVELLY	SOLECISE
SKIMPING	SLOUGHED	SNOBBERY	SOLECISM
SKIN-DEEP	SLOVENLY	SNOBBISH	SOLECIST
SKINLESS	SLOWNESS	SNOOPING	SOLEMNLY
SKINNING	SLOW-WORM	SNOOZING	SOLENESS
SKIPJACK	SLUGGARD	SNORTING	SOLENOID
SKIPPING	SLUGGING	SNOWBALL	SOLIDIFY
SKIRLING	SLUGGISH	SNOWBIRD	SOLIDITY
SKIRMISH	SLUICING	SNOWBOOT	SOLITARY
SKIRTING	SLUMMING	SNOWDROP	SOLITUDE
SKITTISH	SLUMPING	SNOWFALL	SOLSTICE
SKITTLES	SLURRING	SNOWLESS	SOLUTION
SKULKING	SLUTTISH	SNOWLIKE	SOLVABLE
SKULL-CAP	SLYBOOTS	SNOWLINE	SOLVENCY
SKUNKISH	SMACKING	SNOW-SLED	SOMBRERO
SKYLIGHT	SMALL-ALE	SNOWSHOE	SOMEBODY
SKY-PILOT	SMALLEST	SNUBBING	SOMERSET
SKYSCAPE	SMALLISH	SNUBBISH	SOMESUCH
SLABBING	SMALLPOX	SNUB-NOSE	SOMETIME
SLACKING	SMARTING	SNUFFBOX	SOMEWHAT
SLAMMING	SMASHING	SNUFFERS	SOMNIFIC
SLANGILY	SMEARING	SNUFFLED	SONATINA
SLANGING	SMELLING	SNUGGERY	SONG-BIRD
SLANTING	SMELTING	SNUGGING	SONG-BOOK
SLAP-BANG	SMIRCHED	SNUGGLED	SONGLESS
SLAPDASH	SMIRKING	SNUGNESS	SONGSTER
SLAPJACK	SMOCKING	SOAPBALL	SON-IN-LAW
SLAPPING	SMOKABLE	SOAPSUDS	SONORITY
SLASHING	SMOKE-BOX	SOAP-TEST	SONOROUS
SLATE-AXE	SMOKE-DRY	SOAP-TREE	SOOTHING
SLATTERN	SMOOTHED	SOAPWORT	SORBONNE
SLAVERED	SMOOTHLY	SOB-STUFF	SORCERER
SLAVONIC	SMORZATO	SOBRANJE	SORDIDLY
SLEDGING	SMOTHERY	SOBRIETY	SOREHEAD
SLEEPILY	SMOULDER	SO-CALLED	SORENESS
SLEEPING	SMUDGING	SOCIABLE	SORORITY
SLEETING	SMUGGLED	SOCIABLY	SORROWED
SLIDABLE	SMUGGLER	SOCIALLY	SORTABLE
SLIGHTLY	SMUGNESS	SOCKETED	SOUCHONG
SLIMMING	SNACK-BAR	SOCKLESS	SOUGHING
SLIMNESS	SNAFFLED	SOCRATES	SOULLESS
SLINGING	SNAGGING	SODDENED	SOUNDING
SLINKING	SNAPPING	SOFTENED	SOUR-EYED
SLIP-KNOT	SNAPPISH	SOFT-EYED	SOURNESS
SLIPPERY	SNAPSHOT	SOFTLING	SOURPUSS
SLIPPING	SNARLING	SOFTNESS	SOUTHERN
SLIPSHOD	SNATCHED	SOFT-SOAP	SOUTHPAW
SLITHERY	SNATCHER	SOFTWARE	SOUVENIR
SLITTING	SNEAKING	SOFT-WOOD	SOZZLING
SLIVERED	SNEERING	SOILLESS	SPACELAB
SLOGGING	SNEEZING	SOIL-PIPE	SPACIOUS
SLOP-BOWL	SNICKING	SOLACING	SPADILLE
SLOP-PAIL	SNIFFING	SOLARIUM	SPALPEEN
SLOPPING	SNIPPETY	SOLATIUM	SPANDREL
SLOTHFUL	SNIPPING	SOLDERED	SPANGLED
SLOTTING	SNIP-SNAP	SOLDIERY	SPANKING

SPANLESS	SPLOTCHY	SQUEEGEE	STEADIED
SPANNING	SPLUTTER	SQUEEZED	STEADILY
SPAN-ROOF	SPOILING	SQUEEZER	STEADING
SPARERIB	SPOLIATE	SQUIBBED	STEALING
SPARKING	SPONGING	SQUIGGLE	STEALTHY
SPARKLER	SPOOFING	SQUINTED	STEAMING
SPARKLET	SPOOKISH	SQUIREEN	STEAM-TUG
SPARRING	SPOONFUL	SQUIRING	STEELING
SPARSELY	SPOONILY	SQUIRMED	'STEEL-PEN
SPAVINED	SPOONING	SQUIRREL	STEEPING
SPAWNING	SPORADIC	SQUIRTED	STEEPLED
SPEAKING	SPORTFUL	STABBING	STEERAGE
SPEARING	SPORTING	STABLING	STEERING
SPEARMAN	SPORTIVE	STACCATO	STEINBOK
SPECIFIC	SPOTLESS	STACKING	STELLATE
SPECIMEN	SPOTTING	STAFFING	STEMLESS
SPECIOUS	SPOUTING	STAGGERS	STEMMING
SPECKING	SPRAGGED	STAGHORN	STEPPING
SPECKLED	SPRAINED	STAGNANT	STERLING
SPECTRAL	SPRAWLED	STAGNATE	STERNWAY
SPECTRUM	SPRAYING	STAINING	STICKING
SPEEDIER	SPREADER	STAIR-ROD	STICKLER
SPEEDILY	SPRIGGED	STAIRWAY	STIFFISH
SPEEDING	SPRINGER	STALKING	STIFLING
SPEEDWAY	SPRINKLE	STALL-FED	STIGMATA
SPELLING	SPRINTED	STALLING	STILETTO
SPEND-ALL	SPRINTER	STALLION	STILLING
SPENDING	SPROCKET	STALWART	STIMULUS
SPERM-OIL	SPRUCELY	STAMENED	STINGILY
SPHAGNUM	SPRUCIFY	STAMPEDE	STINGING
SPHERICS	SPRUCING	STAMPING	STING-RAY
SPHEROID	SPUN-YARN	STANDARD	STINKPOT
SPHERULE	SPUR-GALL	STANDING	STINTING
SPICCATO	SPUR-GEAR	STANDISH	STIPPLED
SPICE-BOX	SPURIOUS	STAND-OFF	STIRRING
SPIFFING	SPURLESS	STAND-PAT	STITCHED
SPIKELET	SPURNING	STANHOPE	STOCKADE
SPILLING	SPURRING	STAPLING	STOCKIER
SPILLWAY	SPURTING	STARCHED	STOCKILY
SPINDLED	SPYGLASS	STARDUST	STOCKING
SPINNING	SPY-MONEY	STARFISH	STOCKIST
SPINSTER	SQUABBLE	STARGAZE	STOCKMAN
SPIRACLE	SQUADRON	STARLESS	STOCKPOT
SPIRALLY	SQUALLED	STAR-LIKE	STOICISM
SPIRITED	SQUANDER	STARLING	STOLIDLY
SPITEFUL	SQUARELY	STARRING	STONE-PIT
SPITFIRE	SQUARING	STARTING	STOOKING
SPITTING	SQUARISH	STARTLED	STOOPING
SPITTOON	SQUASHED	STARVING	STOPCOCK
SPLASHED	SQUATTED	STARWEED	STOPPAGE
SPLATTER	SQUATTER	STARWORT	STOPPING
SPLAYING	SQUAWKED	STATUARY	STORABLE
SPLENDID	SQUAWMAN	STATURED	STORMING
SPLICING	SQUEAKED	STAY-BOLT	STOWAWAY
SPLINTER	SQUEAKER	STAY-LACE	STRADDLE
SPLITTER	SQUEALED	STAYSAIL	STRAGGLE

STRAIGHT	STURGEON	SUPERTAX	SWINDLER
STRAINED	SUBAGENT	SUPINELY	SWINGING
STRAINER	SUBDUING	SUPPLANT	SWIRLING
STRAITEN	SUBGENUS	SUPPLIED	SWISHING
STRANDED	SUBGRADE	SUPPLIER	SWITCHED
STRANGER	SUBGROUP	SUPPOSED	SWOONING
STRANGLE	SUBHUMAN	SUPPRESS	SWOOPING
STRAPPED	SUB-LEASE	SURCEASE	SWOPPING
STRATEGY	SUBMERGE·	SURENESS	SWORD-ARM
STRATIFY	SUBORDER	SURETIES	SWORD-CUT
STRAYING	SUBORNED	SURF-BOAT	SWOTTING
STREAKED	SUBPOENA	SURFACED	SYBARITE
STREAMED	SUB-POLAR	SURGICAL	SYCAMORE
STREAMER	SUBSERVE	SURMISED	SYLLABIC
STRENGTH	SUBSIDED	SURMOUNT	SYLLABLE
STRESSED	SUBTITLE	SURNAMED	SYLLABUS
STRETCHY	SUBTLETY	SURPLICE	SYMBOLIC
STREWING	SUBTRACT	SURPRISE	SYMMETRY
STRICKEN	SUBURBAN	SURROUND	SYMPATHY
STRICTLY	SUBURBIA	SURVEYED	SYMPHONY
STRIDENT	SUCCINCT	SURVEYOR	SYNDROME
STRIDING	SUCHLIKE	SURVIVAL	SYNOPSIS
STRIKING	SUCKLING	SURVIVED	SYSTEMIC
STRINGED	SUDDENLY	SURVIVOR	
STRIPING	SUFFERED	SUSPENSE	
STRIPPED	SUFFERER	SWABBING	**T – 8**
STRIPPER	SUFFICED	SWADDLED	
STROKING	SUFFIXED	SWAMPING	TABBY-CAT
STROLLED	SUFFRAGE	SWAMP-OAK	TABLEAUX
STROLLER	SUFFUSED	SWAN-LIKE	TABLEFUL
STRONGLY	SUGARING	SWAN-NECK	TABOOING
STROPPED	SUICIDAL	SWANNERY	TABULATE
STRUGGLE	SUITABLE	SWANKING	TACITURN
STRUMMED	SUITABLY	SWAPPING	TACKLING
STRUMPET	SUITCASE	SWARMING	TACTICAL
STRUTTED	SULLENLY	SWASTIKA	TACTLESS
STRUTTER	SULLYING	SWATHING	TAFFRAIL
STUBBING	SULPHATE	SWATTING	TAIL-BOOM
STUBBLED	SULPHIDE	SWEARING	TAILLESS
STUBBORN	SULPHITE	SWEATILY	TAILORED
STUCCOED	SULPHURY	SWEATING	TAIL-RACE
STUD-BOLT	SUMMONED	SWEEPING	TAIL-ROPE
STUD-BOOK	SUNBURNT	SWEEP-NET	TAINTING
STUDDING	SUNBURST	SWEET-BAY	TAKINGLY
STUD-FARM	SUNDERED	SWEETING	TALENTED
STUDIOUS	SUN-DRIED	SWEETISH	TALISMAN
STUDWORK	SUNDRIES	SWEET-OIL	TALKABLE
STUDYING	SUNLIGHT	SWEET-PEA	TALLNESS
STUFFING	SUN-PROOF	SWEET-SOP	TALLYING
STULTIFY	SUNSHADE	SWELLING	TALLYMAN
STUMBLED	SUNSHINE	SWERVING	TAMARIND
STUMPING	SUNSHINY	SWIFTEST	TAMARISK
STUNNING	SUPERBLY	SWIGGING	TAMEABLE
STUNTING	SUPERHET	SWILLING	TAMELESS
STUPIDLY	SUPERIOR	SWIMMING	TAMENESS
STURDILY	SUPERMAN	SWINDLED	TAMPERED

TANGIBLE	TENDENCY	THREADED	TINPLATE
TANGIBLY	TENDERED	THREATEN	TINSELLY
TANGLING	TENDERLY	THREE-PLY	TINSMITH
TANNABLE	TENEMENT	THRESHED	TINSTONE
TANTALUS	TENON-SAW	THRESHER	TINTLESS
TAPERING	TENTACLE	THRILLED	TIPPLING
TAPESTRY	TERMINAL	THRILLER	TIPSTAFF
TAPEWORM	TERMINUS	THRIVING	TIRELESS
TARBOOSH	TERMLESS	THROBBED	TIRESOME
TARRAGON	TERRACED	THRONGED	TITANIUM
TARRYING	TERRAPIN	THROSTLE	TITIVATE
TARTARIC	TERRIBLE	THROTTLE	TITMOUSE
TARTNESS	TERRIBLY	THROWING	TITTERED
TASTABLE	TERRIFIC	THRUMMED	TITULARY
TASTE-BUD	TERTIARY	THUDDING	TOADFLAX
TASTEFUL	TESTABLE	THUGGERY	TOADYING
TATTERED	TESTATOR	THUMBING	TOADYISH
TATTLING	TEST-CASE	THUMB-POT	TOADYISM
TATTOOED	TEST-TUBE	THUMPING	TOBOGGAN
TAUNTING	TETCHILY	THUNDERY	TODDLING
TAUTENED	TETHERED	THURSDAY	TOGETHER
TAUTNESS	TETRAGON	THWACKED	TOILSOME
TAVERNER	TETRARCH	THWARTED	TOILWORN
TAWDRILY	TEUTONIC	TICK-BEAN	TOLBOOTH
TAXATION	TEXTBOOK	TICKETED	TOLERANT
TEA-CADDY	THAILAND	TICKLING	TOLERATE
TEA-CHEST	THALLIUM	TICKLISH	TOLL-GATE
TEACHING	THANKFUL	TICK-TICK	TOM-NODDY
TEA-CLOTH	THANKING	TICK-TOCK	TOMAHAWK
TEA-HOUSE	THATCHED	TIDEGATE	TOMBLESS
TEAMSTER	THATCHER	TIDELESS	TOMMY-BAR
TEAMWORK	THEMATIC	TIDE-LOCK	TOMMY-GUN
TEA-PARTY	THEOLOGY	TIDEMARK	TOMMY-ROT
TEA-PLANT	THEORISE	TIDEMILL	TOMORROW
TEASPOON	THEORIST	TIDES-MAN	TONALITY
TEA-TABLE	THESPIAN	TIDINESS	TONELESS
TEARDROP	THICKEST	TIGER-CAT	TONSURED
TEAR-DUCT	THICKISH	TIGERISH	TOOTHFUL
TEARLESS	THICKSET	TIGHTWAD	TOOTLING
TEENAGER	THIEVERY	TILLABLE	TOP-DRESS
TEETHING	THIEVING	TILT-YARD	TOP-HEAVY
TEETOTAL	THIEVISH	TIMBERED	TOP-NOTCH
TEETOTUM	THINGAMY	TIME-BALL	TOPPLING
TEHEEING	THINKING	TIME-BILL	TOREADOR
TELEGRAM	THINNESS	TIME-BOOK	TORPIDLY
TELETEXT	THINNING	TIME-CARD	TORTILLA
TELEVISE	THINNISH	TIME-FUSE	TORTOISE
TELLTALE	THINNEST	TIMELESS	TORTUOUS
TEMERITY	THIRSTED	TIME-WORK	TORTURED
TEMPERED	THIRTEEN	TIMEWORN	TORTURER
TEMPLATE	THOLE-PIN	TIMIDITY	TOTALISE
TEMPORAL	THORACIC	TIMOROUS	TOTALITY
TEMPTING	THOROUGH	TINCTURE	TOTTERED
TENACITY	THOUSAND	TINGLING	TOUCHILY
TENANTED	THRALDOM	TINKERED	TOUCHING
TENANTRY	THRASHED	TINKLING	TOUGHEST

TOUGHISH	TRECENTO	TRUE-LOVE	TWITTING
TOUSLING	TREE-CRAB	TRUENESS	TWO-EDGED
TOWERING	TREE-DOVE	TRUMPERY	TWO-FACED
TOWN HALL	TREE-FERN	TRUMPING	TWOPENCE
TOWNLESS	TREE-FROG	TRUNCATE	TWOPENNY
TOWNSHIP	TREELESS	TRUNDLED	TWO-SIDED
TOWNSMAN	TREENAIL	TRUNKFUL	TWO-SPEED
TOWN-TALK	TREKKING	TRUNNION	TYMPANIC
TOXAEMIA	TREMBLED	TRUSSING	TYPANUM
TOXICANT	TREMBLER	TRUSTFUL	TYPE-HIGH
TOXICITY	TRENCHED	TRUSTILY	TYPIFIED
TOYISHLY	TRENCHER	TRUSTING	TYROLEAN
TRACHEAL	TRENDING	TRUTHFUL	TYROLESE
TRACHEAN	TRESPASS	TRYSTING	TYRRANIC
TRACKAGE	TRIALITY	TSARITSA	
TRACKING	TRIANGLE	TUBERCLE	
TRACKMAN	TRIARCHY	TUBEROSE	U – 8
TRACKWAY	TRIASSIC	TUBEROUS	UBIQUITY
TRACTILE	TRIAXIAL	TUCKSHOP	UDOMETER
TRACTION	TRIBUNAL	TUG-OF-WAR	UGLINESS
TRACTIVE	TRICKERY	TUMBLING	ULTERIOR
TRACTORY	TRICKILY	TUNELESS	ULTIMATA
TRADUCED	TRICKING	TUNGSTEN	ULTIMATE
TRAGICAL	TRICKLED	TUNING-IN	ULULATED
TRAILING	TRICYCLE	TURBANED	UMBRELLA
TRAIL-NET	TRIFLING	TURBIDLY	UNABASED
TRAINING	TRILLING	TURF-CLAD	UNABATED
TRAIN-OIL	TRILLION	TURGIDLY	UNAFRAID
TRAIPSED	TRIMMING	TURKOMAN	UNAMAZED
TRAMPING	TRIMNESS	TURMERIC	UNAMUSED
TRAMPLED	TRIPLANE	TURNCOAT	UNATONED
TRAMROAD	TRIPLETS	TURNCOCK	UNAVOWED
TRANCING	TRIPLING	TURNDOWN	UNAWARES
TRANQUIL	TRIPPING	TURNOVER	UNBACKED
TRANSACT	TRIPTYCH	TURNPIKE	UNBARBED
TRANSEPT	TRIUMVIR	TURNSPIT	UNBARRED
TRANSFER	TRIVALVE	TURRETED	UNBATHED
TRANSFIX	TROLLING	TUSSOCKY	UNBEATEN
TRANSHIP	TROLLOPY	TUTELAGE	UNBELIEF
TRANSMIT	TROMBONE	TUTELARY	UNBIASED
TRAPBALL	TROOPING	TUTORAGE	UNBIDDEN
TRAPDOOR	TROPHIES	TUTORIAL	UNBLAMED
TRAPPING	TROPICAL	TUTORING	UNBLOODY
TRAPPIST	TROTTING	TWANGING	UNBOILED
TRASHILY	TROUBLED	TWEAKING	UNBOLTED
TRAVERSE	TROUNCED	TWEEZERS	UNBOOTED
TRAVESTY	TROUSERS	TWIDDLED	UNBOUGHT
TRAWLING	TROUTLET	TWIDDLER	UNBRACED
TREACLED	TRUANTLY	TWIGGING	UNBRIDLE
TREADING	TRUCKAGE	TWILIGHT	UNBROKEN
TREADLED	TRUCKING	TWILLING	UNBUCKLE
TREASURE	TRUDGEON	TWIN-BORN	UNBUDDED
TREASURY	TRUDGING	TWINKLED	UNBUOYED
TREATING	TRUE-BLUE	TWIRLING	UNBURDEN
TREATISE	TRUE-BORN	TWISTING	UNBURIED
TREBLING	TRUE-BRED	TWITCHED	UNBURNED

UNBUTTON	UNENDING	UNJUDGED	UNSEATED
UNCAGING	UNERRING	UNJUSTLY	UNSEEDED
UNCALLED	UNEVENLY	UNKINDLY	UNSEEING
UNCAPPED	UNFADING	UNKINGLY	UNSEEMLY
UNCASING	UNFAIRLY	UNLACING	UNSETTLE
UNCAUGHT	UNFASTEN	UNLARDED	UNSHADED
UNCHASTE	UNFENCED	UNLASHED	UNSHAKEN
UNCHEWED	UNFILLED	UNLAWFUL	UNSHAVED
UNCLENCH	UNFIXING	UNLEARNT	UNSHAVEN
UNCLOSED	UNFOLDED	UNLIKELY	UNSLAKED
UNCLOTHE	UNFORCED	UNLOADED	UNSMOKED
UNCLOUDY	UNFORMED	UNLOCKED	UNSOCIAL
UNCOATED	UNFOUGHT	UNLOOSED	UNSOILED
UNCOCKED	UNFRAMED	UNLOVELY	UNSOLDER
UNCOILED	UNFROZEN	UNLOVING	UNSOLVED
UNCOINED	UNFURLED	UNMAKING	UNSORTED
UNCOMBED	UNGAINLY	UNMANNED	UNSOUGHT
UNCOMELY	UNGENTLE	UNMAPPED	UNSPARED
UNCOMMON	UNGENTLY	UNMARKED	UNSPEEDY
UNCOOKED	UNGIFTED	UNMARRED	UNSPIKED
UNCORKED	UNGILDED	UNMASKED	UNSPOILT
UNCOSTLY	UNGIRDED	UNMELTED	UNSPOKEN
UNCOUPLE	UNGIVING	UNMILKED	UNSTABLE
UNCTUOUS	UNGLAZED	UNMILLED	UNSTATED
UNCURBED	UNGLOVED	UNMOCKED	UNSTEADY
UNCURLED	UNGLUING	UNMODISH	UNSTITCH
UNDAMPED	UNGROUND	UNMOORED	UNSTRUNG
UNDEFIED	UNGUIDED	UNMOVING	UNSUITED
UNDENTED	UNGULATA	UNNERVED	UNSURELY
UNDERACT	UNGULATE	UNOPENED	UNSWAYED
UNDERAGE	UNGUMMED	UNPACKED	UNTACKED
UNDERARM	UNHANDED	UNPAIRED	UNTANGLE
UNDERBID	UNHANGED	UNPEELED	UNTANNED
UNDERCUT	UNHARMED	UNPEGGED	UNTAPPED
UNDER-DOG	UNHASPED	UNPENNED	UNTASTED
UNDERFED	UNHEATED	UNPICKED	UNTAUGHT
UNDERLAY	UNHEDGED	UNPINNED	UNTENDED
UNDERLET	UNHEEDED	UNPLACED	UNTESTED
UNDERLIE	UNHEROIC	UNPOISED	UNTETHER
UNDER-LIP	UNHINGED	UNPOSTED	UNTHAWED
UNDERPAY	UNHOOKED	UNPRETTY	UNTHREAD
UNDERPIN	UNHORSED	UNPRICED	UNTHROWN
UNDERTOW	UNHOUSED	UNPROVED	UNTIDILY
UNDEVOUT	UNICYCLE	UNPRUNED	UNTILLED
UNDIMMED	UNIFYING	UNRAISED	UNTIMELY
UNDIPPED	UNIMBUED	UNREASON	UNTINGED
UNDIVINE	UNIONISM	UNREELED	UNTIRING
UNDOCKED	UNIONIST	UNROBING	UNTOWARD
UNDOUBLE	UNIQUELY	UNROLLED	UNTRACED
UNDRAPED	UNITEDLY	UNROOFED	UNTUCKED
UNDREAMT	UNIVALVE	UNROUTED	UNTURFED
UNDULANT	UNIVERSE	UNRUFFLE	UNTURNED
UNDULATE	UNIVOCAL	UNSADDLE	UNTWINED
UNDULOUS	UNJOINED	UNSAFELY	UNVALUED
UNEARNED	UNJOYFUL	UNSALTED	UNVARIED
UNEASILY	UNJOYOUS	UNSEALED	UNVEILED

UNVENTED	VANADIUM	VIEWDATA	VOYAGEUR
UNVERSED	VANGUARD	VIEWLESS	VULGARLY
UNVOICED	VANISHED	VIGILANT	
UNWANTED	VANQUISH	VIGNETTE	**W – 8**
UNWARILY	VAPIDITY	VIGOROSO	
UNWARMED	VAPORIZE	VIGOROUS	WADDLING
UNWARNED	VAPOROUS	VILENESS	WAFERING
UNWASHED	VARIABLE	VILIFIED	WAGELESS
UNWEDDED	VARIABLY	VILLAGER	WAGERING
UNWEEDED	VARIANCE	VILLAINY	WAGGLING
UNWIELDY	VARICOSE	VINE-CLAD	WAGGONER
UNWISELY	VASCULAR	VINE-GALL	WAGONFUL
UNWONTED	VASELINE	VINEGARY	WAGON-LIT
UNWORTHY	VASTNESS	VINEYARD	WAINSCOT
UNYOKING	VAULTING	VIOLABLE	WAITRESS
UPHEAVAL	VAUNTING	VIOLATOR	WAKENING
UPLIFTED	VEGETATE	VIOLENCE	WALKABLE
UPRAISED	VEHEMENT	VIPERINE	WALK-OVER
UPRISING	VELOCITY	VIPERISH	WALLAROO
UPROOTED	VENALITY	VIPEROUS	WALL-EYED
UPSTAIRS	VENDETTA	VIRGINAL	WALLOPED
UPSTREAM	VENDIBLE	VIRGINIA	WALLOWED
UPSTROKE	VENDIBLY	VIRILITY	WALTZING
UPTHRUST	VENEERED	VIRTUOSO	WANDERER
UPTURNED	VENERATE	VIRTUOUS	WANGLING
UPWARDLY	VENETIAN	VIRULENT	WANTONLY
URBANITY	VENGEFUL	VISCERAL	WARBLING
URBANISE	VENOMOUS	VISCOUNT	WAR-DANCE
URGENTLY	VENT-HOLE	VISIGOTH	WARDMOTE
URSIFORM	VENT-PLUG	VISITANT	WARDRESS
URSULINE	VENTURED	VISITING	WARDROBE
USEFULLY	VERACITY	VITALITY	WARDROOM
USHERING	VERANDAH	VITALISE	WARDSHIP
USURIOUS	VERBALLY	VITIATED	WAR-HORSE
USURPING	VERBATIM	VITREOUS	WARINESS
UTILIZED	VERBIAGE	VIVACITY	WARMNESS
UTTERING	VERDANCY	VIVARIUM	WARPAINT
UXORIOUS	VERDERER	VIVA-VOCE	WAR-PLANE
	VERIFIED	VIVIFIED	WARRANTY
	VERMOUTH	VIVISECT	WAR-WEARY
V – 8	VERONESE	VIXENISH	WAR-WHOOP
	VERONICA	VOCALIST	WASHABLE
VACATING	VERTEBRA	VOCALITY	WASHAWAY
VACATION	VERTICAL	VOCALIZE	WASHBALL
VAGABOND	VESTMENT	VOCATION	WASHBOWL
VAGRANCY	VESUVIAN	VOCATIVE	WASP-BITE
VAINNESS	VEXATION	VOIDABLE	WASTEFUL
VALANCED	VEXINGLY	VOLATILE	WATCHDOG
VALENCIA	VIBRATED	VOLCANIC	WATCHFUL
VALERIAN	VIBRATOR	VOLITION	WATCHING
VALETING	VIBURNUM	VOLLEYED	WATCH-KEY
VALHALLA	VICARAGE	VOLPLANE	WATCHMAN
VALIDATE	VICINITY	VOMITING	WATERCAN
VALIDITY	VICTORIA	VORACITY	WATER-HEN
VALOROUS	VICTUALS	VOTARESS	WATER-ICE
VALUABLE	VIEWABLE	VOUCHING	WATERING
VAMOOSED			

WATERMAN	WHATEVER	WINESKIN	WORSENED
WATER-RAM	WHEATEAR	WING-CASE	WORSTING
WATER-RAT	WHEEDLED	WINGLESS	WORTHILY
WATER-TAP	WHEELING	WINNOWED	WOUNDING
WATERWAY	WHEEZILY	WINTERED	WRACKING
WATT-HOUR	WHEEZING	WINTERLY	WRANGLED
WATTLING	WHELPING	WIRELESS	WRANGLER
WAVEBAND	WHENEVER	WIRE-WORM	WRAPPING
WAVELESS	WHEREVER	WIRINESS	WRATHFUL
WAVELIKE	WHETTING	WISEACRE	WREAKING
WAVERING	WHIMBREL	WISHBONE	WREATHED
WAVINESS	WHINCHAT	WISTARIA	WRECKAGE
WAXCLOTH	WHINNIED	WITHDRAW	WRECKING
WAXLIGHT	WHIPCORD	WITHDREW	WRENCHED
WAX-PAPER	WHIPHAND	WITHERED	WRESTING
WAXWORKS	WHIPLASH	WITHHELD	WRESTLED
WAYFARER	WHIPPING	WITHHOLD	WRESTLER
WAYGOOSE	WHIRLING	WIZARDLY	WRETCHED
WAYLEAVE	WHIRRING	WIZARDRY	WRIGGLED
WEAKENED	WHISKING	WOEFULLY	WRINGING
WEAK-EYED	WHISTLED	WOLF-FISH	WRINKLED
WEAKLING	WHITE-HOT	WOLF-SKIN	WRISTLET
WEAKNESS	WHITENED	WOMANISH	WRITHING
WEARABLE	WHITTLED	WONDERED	WRONGFUL
WEARYING	WHIZZING	WONDROUS	WRONGING
WEED-HOOK	WHODUNIT	WODD-ACID	
WEEDLESS	WHOOPING	WOODBINE	
WEIGHING	WHOPPING	WOODCOCK	X – 8
WEIGHTED	WICKEDLY	WODDLAND	XYLONITE
WELCOMED	WIDE-EYED	WOODLARK	
WELDABLE	WIDENESS	WOODLESS	Y – 8
WELL-BORN	WIDENING	WOOD-LICE	
WELL-BRED	WIDOWING	WOODMOTE	YACHTING
WELLDOER	WIELDING	WOOD-PULP	YEAR-BOOK
WELL-HEAD	WIFEHOOD	WOOD-SHED	YEARLING
WELL-HOLE	WIFELESS	WOODSMAN	YEARNING
WELL-KNIT	WIFELIKE	WOOD-VINE	YELLOWED
WELLNIGH	WIGGLING	WOODWORK	YEOMANLY
WELL-READ	WIGMAKER	WOODWORM	YEOMANRY
WELLSIAN	WILDFIRE	WOOD-WREN	YIELDING
WELL-TO-DO	WILDFOWL	WOOINGLY	YODELLED
WELL-WORN	WILDNESS	WOOLSACK	YOKELESS
WELSHING	WILFULLY	WOOLWORK	YOUNGEST
WELSHMAN	WILINESS	WORDBOOK	YOUNGISH
WEREWOLF	WILLOWED	WORDLESS	YOURSELF
WESLEYAN	WINCHMAN	WORKABLE	YOUTHFUL
WESTERLY	WINDFALL	WORKADAY	YUGO-SLAV
WESTWARD	WINDLASS	WORKGIRL	YULETIDE
WET-NURSE	WINDLESS	WORKROOM	
WHACKING	WINDMILL	WORKSHOP	
WHALEMAN	WINDOWED	WORMCAST	Z – 8
WHALE-OIL	WINDPIPE	WORMGEAR	ZEPPELIN
WHANGHEE	WIND-PUMP	WORM-HOLE	
WHANGING	WINDWARD	WORMLIKE	A – 9
WHARFAGE	WINE-CASK	WORMWOOD	
WHARFING	WINELESS	WORRYING	ABANDONED

ABASEMENT	ACTUATION	AESTHETIC	ALGEBRAIC
ABASHMENT	ACUTENESS	AESTIVATE	ALGORITHM
ABATEMENT	ADAPTABLE	AETIOLOGY	ALIENABLE
ABDICATED	ADDICTING	AFFECTING	ALIENATED
ABDOMINAL	ADDICTION	AFFECTION	ALIGHTING
ABDUCTING	ADDRESSED	AFFECTIVE	ALIGNMENT
ABDUCTION	ADDRESSEE	AFFIANCED	ALIMENTAL
ABHORRENT	ADDUCIBLE	AFFIDAVIT	ALIMENTED
ABHORRING	ADDUCTION	AFFILIATE	ALINEMENT
ABIDINGLY	ADDUCTIVE	AFFIRMING	ALKALISED
ABJECTION	ADENOIDAL	AFFLATION	ALLAYMENT
ABNEGATED	ADENOTOMY	AFFLICTED	ALLELUIAH
ABOLITION	ADHERENCE	AFFLUENCE	ALLEMANDE
ABOMINATE	ADJACENCY	AFFORDING	ALLEVIATE
ABOUNDING	ADJECTIVE	AFFRONTED	ALLIGATED
ABRIDGING	ADJOINING	AFOREHAND	ALLIGATOR
ABROGATED	ADJOURNED	AFORESAID	ALLITERAL
ABSCINDED	ADJUDGING	AFORETIME	ALLOCATED
ABSCONDED	ADJUNCTLY	AFRICAANS	ALLOTTING
ABSENTING	ADJUSTING	AFTER-CARE	ALLOWABLE
ABSOLVING	ADMIRABLE	AFTERGLOW	ALLOWABLY
ABSORBENT	ADMIRABLY	AFTERLIFE	ALLOWANCE
ABSORBING	ADMIRALTY	AFTERMATH	ALLOWEDLY
ABSTAINER	ADMISSION	AFTERNOON	ALMOND-OIL
ABSTINENT	ADMISSIVE	AFTER-PART	ALMSHOUSE
ABSURDITY	ADMISSORY	AFTERWARD	ALOES-WOOD
ABUNDANCE	ADMITTING	AGGRAVATE	ALONGSIDE
ABUSIVELY	ADMIXTURE	AGGREGATE	ALOOFNESS
ACCENTING	ADOPTABLE	AGGRESSOR	ALPENHORN
ACCEPTING	ADOPTEDLY	AGGRIEVED	ALTAR-TOMB
ACCESSION	ADORATION	AGITATION	ALTERABLE
ACCESSORY	ADORNMENT	AGONISING	ALTERABLY
ACCLIVITY	ADRENALIN	AGONISTIC	ALTERCATE
ACCOMPANY	ADULATING	AGREEABLE	ALTERNATE
ACCORDING	ADULATION	AGREEABLY	ALTIMETER
ACCORDION	ADULATORY	AGREEMENT	ALTO-VIOLA
ACCOUNTED	ADULTERER	AGRONOMIC	ALUMINIUM
ACCRETION	ADULTNESS	AIMLESSLY	AMARYLLIS
ACCRETIVE	ADUMBRATE	AIR-ENGINE	AMASSABLE
ACCUSABLE	ADVANCING	AIR-FILTER	AMAZEMENT
ACETYLENE	ADVANTAGE	AIR-FUNNEL	AMAZINGLY
ACHIEVING	ADVENTIST	AIR-INTAKE	AMAZONIAN
ACIDIFIED	ADVENTURE	AIR-JACKET	AMBERGRIS
ACIDIFIER	ADVERBIAL	AIR-POCKET	AMBIGUITY
ACIDULATE	ADVERSARY	AIR-VESSEL	AMBIGUOUS
ACIDULOUS	ADVERSELY	AIRWORTHY	AMBITIOUS
ACOUSTICS	ADVERSITY	AITCHBONE	AMBLINGLY
ACQUIESCE	ADVERTENT	ALABASTER	AMBROSIAL
ACQUIRING	ADVERTING	ALARM-BELL	AMBROSIAN
ACQUITTAL	ADVERTISE	ALARM-POST	AMBULANCE
ACQUITTED	ADVISABLE	ALBATROSS	AMBUSCADE
ACRIDNESS	ADVISABLY	ALCHEMIST	AMBUSHING
ACROBATIC	ADVOCATED	ALCOHOLIC	AMENDABLE
ACROPOLIS	AERODROME	ALECONNER	AMENDMENT
ACTUALITY	AEROMOTOR	ALERTNESS	AMIDSHIPS
ACTUARIAL	AEROPLANE	ALETASTER	AMOROUSLY

AMORPHISM	ANOINTING	APPREHEND	ASSAULTED
AMORPHOUS	ANOMALISM	APPRISING	ASSAYABLE
AMORTIZED	ANOMALOUS	APPROBATE	ASSEMBLED
AMOUNTING	ANONYMOUS	APPROVING	ASSENTING
AMPERSAND	ANOPHELES	AQUILEGIA	ASSERTING
AMPHIBIAN	ANSWERING	ARABESQUE	ASSERTION
AMPHIBOLE	ANTARCTIC	ARACHNOID	ASSERTIVE
AMPLENESS	ANTECEDED	ARBITRARY	ASSESSING
AMPLIFIED	ANTEDATED	ARBITRATE	ASSIDUITY
AMPLIFIER	ANTENATAL	ARBORETUM	ASSIDUOUS
AMPLITUDE ·	ANTHELION	ARCHANGEL	ASSIGNING
AMPUTATED	ANTHOLOGY	ARCH-DRUID	ASSISTANT
AMPUTATOR	ANTIPATHY	ARCHDUCAL	ASSISTING
AMUSEMENT	ANTIPHONY	ARCHDUCHY	ASSOCIATE
AMUSINGLY	ANTIPODAL	ARCH-ENEMY	ASSOILING
ANALGESIA	ANTIPODES	ARCHETYPE	ASSONANCE
ANALOGISE	ANTIQUARY	ARCH-FIEND	ASSORTING
ANALOGIST	ANTIQUATE	ARCHITECT	ASSUAGING
ANALOGOUS	ANTIQUELY	ARCHIVIST	ASSUETUDE
ANALYSING	ANTIQUITY	ARDUOUSLY	ASSURABLE
ANARCHISM	ANTITOXIC	ARGENTINE	ASSURANCE
ANARCHIST	ANTITOXIN	ARGUFYING	ASSUREDLY
ANATOMISE	ANXIOUSLY	ARMADILLO	ASTHMATIC
ANATOMIST	APARTHEID	ARMISTICE	ASTOUNDED
ANCESTRAL	APARTMENT	ARM'S-REACH	ASTRADDLE
ANCHORAGE	APARTNESS	ARRAIGNED	ASTRAKHAN
ANCHORING	APATHETIC	ARRANGING	ASTROLABE
ANCHORITE	APERITIVE	ARRESTING	ASTROLOGY
ANCHOR-MAN	APHORISED	ARROGANCE	ASTRONOMY
ANCIENTLY	APISHNESS	ARROWHEAD	ASYMMETRY
ANCILLARY	APOCRYPHA	ARROWROOT	ATAVISTIC
ANECDOTAL	APOLOGISE	ARSENICAL	ATHANASIA
ANGEL-FISH	APOLOGIST	ARSENIOUS	ATHEISTIC
ANGELICAL	APOSTOLIC	ARTEMISIA	ATHENAEUM
ANGLICISE	APPALLING	ARTHRITIC	ATHLETICS
ANGLICISM	APPARATUS	ARTHRITIS	ATLANTEAN
ANGLIFIED	APPEALING	ARTICHOKE	ATOMISING
ANGOSTURA	APPEARING	ARTICULAR	ATONEMENT
ANGUISHED	APPEASING	ARTIFICER	ATROCIOUS
ANGULARLY	APPELLANT	ARTILLERY	ATROPHIED
ANGULATED	APPELLATE	ARTLESSLY	ATTACHING
ANIMALISE	APPENDAGE	ASCENDANT	ATTACKING
ANIMALISM	APPENDANT	ASCENDENT	ATTAINDER
ANIMATING	APPENDING	ASCENDING	ATTAINING
ANIMATION	APPERTAIN	ASCENSION	ATTAINTED
ANIMOSITY	APPETISER	ASCERTAIN	ATTEMPTED
ANNEALING	APPLAUDED	ASCRIBING	ATTENDANT
ANNOTATED	APPLE-JACK	ASHAMEDLY	ATTENDING
ANNOTATOR	APPLE-JOHN	ASPARAGUS	ATTENTION
ANNOUNCER	APPLIANCE	ASPERATED	ATTENTIVE
ANNOYANCE	APPLICANT	ASPERSING	ATTENUATE
ANNUITANT	APPLICATE	ASPERSION	ATTESTING
ANNULARLY	APPOINTED	ASPHALTIC	ATTICISED
ANNULATED	APPORTION	ASPIRATED	ATTRACTED
ANNULLING	APPRAISAL	ASSAILANT	ATTRIBUTE
ANNULMENT	APPRAISED	ASSAILING	ATTRITION

AUBERGINE	BAKESTONE	BATTENING	BELVEDERE
AUDACIOUS	BAKSHEESH	BATTERING	BEMOANING
AUGMENTED	BALALAIKA	BATTLEAXE	BENEFITED
AUSTERELY	BALANCING	BATTLE-CRY	BENGALESE
AUSTERITY	BALCONIED	BAWDINESS	BENIGHTED
AUSTRALIA	BALD-PATED	BAYONETED	BENIGNANT
AUTHENTIC	BALEFULLY	BAY-WINDOW	BENIGNITY
AUTHORESS	BALKINGLY	BEANFEAST	BENZOLINE
AUTHORISE	BALLASTED	BEANSTALK	BEREAVING
AUTHORITY	BALLERINA	BEARDLESS	BERYLLIUM
AUTOCRACY	BALLISTIC	BEATIFIED	BESEECHED
AUTOGRAPH	BALLOT-BOX	BEATITUDE	BESETTING
AUTOMATIC	BALLOTING	BEAU-IDEAL	BESIEGING
AUTOMATON	BALL-POINT	BEAU-MONDE	BESMEARED
AUTONOMIC	BAMBOOZLE	BEAUTEOUS	BESOTTING
AUXILIARY	BANDAGING	BEAUTIFUL	BESPATTER
AVAILABLE	BANDEROLE	BECALMING	BESTIALLY
AVAILABLY	BANDICOOT	BECKONING	BESTIRRED
AVALANCHE	BANDOLIER	BEDAZZLED	BESTOWING
AVERAGELY	BANDWIDTH	BEDECKING	BETHOUGHT
AVERAGING	BANEFULLY	BEDFELLOW	BETHUMBED
AVERTEDLY	BANISHING	BEDLAMITE	BETOKENED
AVOCATION	BANQUETED	BEDRAGGLE	BETRAYING
AVOCATIVE	BANQUETTE	BEDRIDDEN	BETROTHAL
AVOIDABLE	BAPTISING	BEDSPREAD	BETROTHED
AVOIDANCE	BAPTISMAL	BEECHMAST	BETTERING
AVUNCULAR	BARBARIAN	BEEFEATER	BEVELLING
AWAKENING	BARBARISM	BEEFLOWER	BEWAILING
AWARDABLE	BARBARITY	BEEFSTEAK	BEWITCHED
AWESTRUCK	BARBAROUS	BEELZEBUB	BICKERING
AWFULNESS	BARBECUED	BEER-MONEY	BICYCLING
AWKWARDLY	BARBERING	BEFALLING	BICYCLIST
AXIOMATIC	BAREBONED	BEFITTING	BIFURCATE
	BAREFACED	BEFOGGING	BIGOTEDLY
	BARGAINED	BEFOOLING	BILATERAL
B – 9	BARLEY-MOW	BEFOULING	BILINGUAL
	BARMECIDE	BEGETTING	BILLABONG
BABYLONIC	BAROGRAPH	BEGGARING	BILLETING
BACCHANAL	BAROMETER	BEGINNING	BILLIARDS
BACCHANTE	BARONETCY	BEGRIMING	BILLOWING
BACILLARY	BARRELLED	BEGRUDGED	BILLYCOCK
BACKBOARD	BARRICADE	BEGUILING	BILLY-GOAT
BACKPIECE	BARRISTER	BEHAVIOUR	BIMONTHLY
BACKSIGHT	BARTENDER	BEHEADING	BINDINGLY
BACK-SLANG	BARTERING	BEHOLDING	BINOCULAR
BACKSLIDE	BASHFULLY	BELEAGUER	BINOMINAL
BACKSPACE	BASILICAN	BELIEVING	BIOGRAPHY
BACKSTAFF	BASILICON	BELITTLED	BIOLOGIST
BACKWARDS	BASKETFUL	BELL-GLASS	BIONOMICS
BACKWATER	BAS-RELIEF	BELLICOSE	BIPARTITE
BACKWOODS	BASTINADO	BELL-METAL	BIRTHMARK
BADGERING	BASTIONED	BELLOWING	BIRTHRATE
BADMINTON	BATH-BRICK	BELL-PUNCH	BISECTING
BAGATELLE	BATH-CHAIR	BELLYBAND	BISECTION
BAILIWICK	BATH-METAL	BELLY-ROLL	BISHOPRIC
BAKEHOUSE	BATTALION	BELONGING	BLABBERED

BLACKBALL	BOARHOUND	BRACTLESS	BROADWAYS
BLACKBIRD	BOAR-SPEAR	BRAINLESS	BROADWISE
BLACKCOCK	BOASTLESS	BRAINWAVE	BROCADING
BLACKENED	BOAT-HOUSE	BRAKELESS	BROKERAGE
BLACKHEAD	BOATSWAIN	BRAKESMAN	BRONCHIAL
BLACKJACK	BOB-SLEIGH	BRAMBLING	BROOD-MARE
BLACKLEAD	BOBTAILED	BRANCHING	BROOKWEED
BLACK-LIST	BODYGUARD	BRANCHLET	BROTHERLY
BLACKMAIL	BOG-MYRTLE	BRASS-BAND	BROWNNESS
BLACKNESS	BOLD-FACED	BRASSERIE	BRUMMAGEM
BLADEBONE	BOLOGNESE	BRASSIERE	BRUSHWOOD
BLAEBERRY	BOLSHEVIK	BRAZENING	BRUTALISE
BLAMELESS	BOLSTERED	BRAZILIAN	BRUTALITY
BLANCHING	BOMB-AIMER	BRAZIL-NUT	BRUTISHLY
BLANDNESS	BOMBARDED	BREACHING	BRYTHONIC
BLANKETED	BOMBARDON	BREADLESS	BUCCANEER
BLANKNESS	BOMBASTIC	BREAD-ROOM	BUCKBOARD
BLASPHEME	BOMBAZINE	BREAKABLE	BUCKETFUL
BLASPHEMY	BOMB-PROOF	BREAKDOWN	BUCKETING
BLATHERED	BOMBSHELL	BREAKFAST	BUCKHOUND
BLAZONING	BOMBSIGHT	BREAKNECK	BUCK'S-HORN
BLEACHING	BONDSLAVE	BREASTPIN	BUCKTHORN
BLEAR-EYED	BONDWOMAN	BREATHING	BUCKTOOTH
BLEMISHED	BONNETING	BREECHING	BUCKWAGON
BLENCHING	BONNINESS	BREWHOUSE	BUCKWHEAT
BLESSEDLY	BON-VIVANT	BRIAR-ROOT	BUDGETING
BLETHERED	BOOBY-TRAP	BRAC-A-BRAC	BUFFETING
BLIGHTING	BOOKISHLY	BRICK-CLAY	BUGLE-CALL
BLINDFOLD	BOOKMAKER	BRICKDUST	BULGARIAN
BLINDNESS	BOOK-PLATE	BRICK-KILN	BULGINESS
BLINDWORM	BOOKSTALL	BRICKWORK	BULKINESS
BLISTERED	BOOKSTAND	BRICKYARD	BULLFIGHT
BLOCKADED	BOOKSTORE	BRIDECAKE	BULLFINCH
BLOCKHEAD	BOOMERANG	BRIDELESS	BULLY-BEEF
BLOOD-BATH	BOORISHLY	BRIDESMAN	BULWARKED
BLOOD-HEAT	BOOTSTRAP	BRIDEWELL	BUMBLE-BEE
BLOODLESS	BORDERING	BRIDLE-WAY	BUMBLEDOM
BLOODSHED	BORROWING	BRIEFLESS	BUMPINESS
BLOODSHOT	BOSPHORUS	BRIEFNESS	BUMPTIOUS
BLOODWORM	BOTANICAL	BRIGADIER	BUOYANTLY
BLOODYING	BOTHERING	BRILLIANT	BURDENING
BLOSSOMED	BOTTOMING	BRIMSTONE	BURGEONED
BLOTCHING	BOULEVARD	BRIQUETTE	BURLESQUE
BLUBBERED	BOUNDLESS	BRISKNESS	BURLINESS
BLUEBEARD	BOUNTEOUS	BRISTLING	BURNISHED
BLUE-BERRY	BOUNTIFUL	BRITANNIC	BURROWING
BLUE-BLACK	BOURGEOIS	BRITTLELY	BUSHINESS
BLUE-BLOOD	BOWER-BIRD	BRITTLING	BUTCHERED
BLUESTONE	BOW-LEGGED	BROACHING	BUTTERCUP
BLUFFNESS	BOWSTRING	BROADBEAN	BUTTERFLY
BLUNDERED	BOWSTRUNG	BROADBILL	BUTTERING
BLUNTNESS	BOW-WINDOW	BROADBRIM	BUTTONING
BLUSTERED	BOXING-DAY	BROADCAST	BUXOMNESS
BLUSTERER	BOX-OFFICE	BROADENED	BUZZINGLY
BOANERGES	BOYCOTTED	BROADNESS	BY-PASSAGE
BOARDABLE	BRACKETED	BROADSIDE	BY-PRODUCT

BYSTANDER	CANTINGLY	CATALYSIS	CESSATION
BYZANTINE	CANVASSED	CATALYTIC	CETACEOUS
	CANVASSER	CATAMARAN	CHAFFERED
C – 9	CAPACIOUS	CATAMOUNT	CHAFFINCH
	CAPACITOR	CATARRHAL	CHAFFLESS
CABALLERO	CAPARISON	CATCHABLE	CHAGRINED
CABLEGRAM	CAPILLARY	CATCH-CROP	CHAIN-GANG
CABRIOLET	CAPITALLY	CATCHMENT	CHAINLESS
CACOPHONY	CAPITULAR	CATCHPOLE	CHAIN-MAIL
CADDIS-FLY	CAPRICCIO	CATCHWEED	CHAINWORK
CADETSHIP	CAPRICORN	CATCHWORD	CHALLENGE
CAESARIAN	CAPSIZING	CATECHISE	CHAMELEON
CAFETERIA	CAPTAINCY	CATECHISM	CHAMFERED
CAIRNGORM	CAPTIVATE	CATECHIST	CHAMPAGNE
CALABOOSE	CAPTIVITY	CATERWAUL	CHANDLERY
CALCIFIED	CAPTURING	CATHEADED	CHANGEFUL
CALCINING	CARBONATE	CATHEDRAL	CHAPTERED
CALCULATE	CARBONISE	CAUCASIAN	CHAR-A-BANC
CALENDULA	CARBUNCLE	CAUSALITY	CHARACTER
CALIBRATE	CARDBOARD	CAUSATION	CHARINESS
CALIPHATE	CAREENING	CAUSATIVE	CHARIVARI
CALLA-LILY	CAREERING	CAUSELESS	CHARLATAN
CALLIPERS	CAREFULLY	CAUTERISE	CHARLOTTE
CALLOSITY	CARESSING	CAUTIONED	CHARTERED
CALLOUSLY	CARMELITE	CAVALCADE	CHARTLESS
CALORIFIC	CARNALITY	CAVENDISH	CHASEABLE
CALVINISM	CARNATION	CAVERNOUS	CHASTENED
CALVINIST	CARNIVORA	CAVILLING	CHASTISED
CAMBERING	CAROLLING	CAVORTING	CHATTERED
CAMPANILE	CAROUSING	CEASELESS	CHAUFFEUR
CAMPANULA	CARPENTER	CEILINGED	CHEAPENED
CAMP-FEVER	CARPENTRY	CELANDINE	CHEAPNESS
CAMPSTOOL	CARPETING	CELEBRANT	CHEATABLE
CANALISED	CARPINGLY	CELEBRATE	CHECKMATE
CANCELLED	CARRIABLE	CELEBRITY	CHECK-REIN
CANCEROUS	CARTESIAN	CELESTIAL	CHEEK-BONE
CANDIDACY	CARTHORSE	CELESTINE	CHEERLESS
CANDIDATE	CARTILAGE	CELLARAGE	CHEESEFLY
CANDIFIED	CARTOUCHE	CELLARMAN	CHEESEVAT
CANDLEMAS	CARTRIDGE	CELLULOID	CHEMISTRY
CANDYTUFT	CARTWHEEL	CELLULOSE	CHEQUERED
CANE-CHAIR	CASHEWNUT	CEMENTING	CHERISHED
CANE-SUGAR	CASHIERED	CENSORIAL	CHEVALIER
CANKER-FLY	CASSEROLE	CENSORING	CHICANERY
CANKERING	CASSOWARY	CENSURING	CHICANING
CANKEROUS	CASTIGATE	CENTENARY	CHICKADEE
CANNON-BIT	CASTILIAN	CENTIGRAM	CHICKLING
CANNONADE	CASTOR-OIL	CENTIPEDE	CHICKWEED
CANNONING	CASTRATED	CENTRALLY	CHIDINGLY
CANONICAL	CAST-STEEL	CENTRE-BIT	CHIEFLESS
CANONISED	CASUISTIC	CENTURION	CHIEFTAIN
CANOODLED	CASUISTRY	CEREBRATE	CHILBLAIN
CANOPYING	CATACLYSM	CERTAINLY	CHILDHOOD
CANTABILE	CATALEPSY	CERTAINTY	CHILDLESS
CANTALOUP	CATALOGUE	CERTIFIED	CHILDLIKE
CANTERING	CATALYSER	CERTITUDE	CHILLNESS

CHINA-CLAY	CLERK-LIKE	COEQUALLY	COMFORTER
CHINA-ROSE	CLERKSHIP	COERCIBLE	COMICALLY
CHINASHOP	CLIENTELE	COETERNAL	COMINFORM
CHINATOWN	CLIMACTIC	COEXISTED	COMINTERN
CHINAWARE	CLIMBABLE	COFFEE-BUG	COMMANDED
CHIROPODY	CLINCHING	COFFEE-CUP	COMMANDER
CHISELLED	CLOAKROOM	COFFEE-POT	COMMENCED
CHITTERED	CLOCK-GOLF	COFFERDAM	COMMENDED
CHOCK-FULL	CLOCKWISE	COGITABLE	COMMENSAL
CHOCOLATE	CLOCKWORK	COGITATED	COMMENTED
CHOP-HOUSE	CLOG-DANCE	COGNATION	COMMINGLE
CHORISTER	CLOISONNÉ	COGNISANT	COMMISSAR
CHORTLING	CLOISTERS	COGNITION	COMMITTAL
CHORUSING	CLOSENESS	COGNITIVE	COMMITTED
CHRISTIAN	CLOSETING	COHABITED	COMMITTEE
CHRISTMAS	CLOTH-HALL	COHEIRESS	COMMODITY
CHROMATIC	CLOTHYARD	COHERENCE	COMMONAGE
CHROMATIN	CLOUDLESS	COHERENCY	COMMOTION
CHRYSALIS	CLOUDLINE	COHERITOR	COMMOVING
CHUCKLING	CLOUT-NAIL	COINCIDED	COMMUNING
CHURCHILL	CLOVE-PINK	COLCHICUM	COMMUNION
CHURCHING	CLUBBABLE	COLD-CREAM	COMMUNISE
CHURCHMAN	CLUBHOUSE	COLLAPSED	COMMUNISM
CICATRICE	CLUSTERED	COLLARING	COMMUNIST
CICATRISE	CLUTCHING	COLLATING	COMMUNITY
CIGARETTE	CLUTTERED	COLLATION	COMMUTING
CINERARIA	COACHWORK	COLLEAGUE	COMPACTED
CINGALESE	COAGULANT	COLLECTED	COMPACTLY
CIPHERING	COAGULATE	COLLECTOR	COMPANION
CIPHER-KEY	COAL-BLACK	COLLEGIAN	COMPARING
CIRCUITED	COALESCED	COLLIDING	COMPASSED
CIRCULATE	COALFIELD	COLLIMATE	COMPASSES
CIRRHOSIS	COAL-HOUSE	COLLISION	COMPELLED
CIVILISED	COALITION	COLLOCATE	COMPELLING
CLAIMABLE	COAL-MINER	COLLODION	COMPETENT
CLAMBERED	COARSENED	COLLOIDAL	COMPETING
CLAMOROUS	COASTLINE	COLLOTYPE	COMPLIANT
CLAMOURED	COASTWISE	COLLUSION	COMPLETED
CLAPBOARD	COATFROCK	COLLUSIVE	COMPLEXLY
CLARENDON	COAXINGLY	COLLUSORY	COMPLAINT
CLARET-CUP	COBDENISM	COLONELCY	COMPLYING
CLARIFIED	COBDENITE	COLONISED	COMPONENT
CLARIONET	COBWEBBED	COLONNADE	COMPORTED
CLASSIBLE	COCHINEAL	COLORIFIC	COMPOSING
CLASSICAL	COCK-A-HOOP	COLOSSEUM	COMPOSITE
CLATTERED	COCKFIGHT	COLOUR-BOX	COMPOSTED
CLEANLILY	COCKHORSE	COLOURING	COMPOSURE
CLEANNESS	COCKINESS	COLOURIST	COMPRISED
CLEANSING	COCKROACH	COLOURMAN	COMPUTING
CLEARANCE	COCKSCOMB	COLTSFOOT	CONCAVELY
CLEAR-EYED	COCKSFOOT	COLUMBIAN	CONCAVITY
CLEARNESS	COCK'S-HEAD	COLUMBINE	CONCEALED
CLEAVABLE	COCOA-BEAN	COMBATANT	CONCEDING
CLEMENTLY	COCOA-PLUM	COMBATIVE	CONCEITED
CLENCHING	COCO-DE-MER	COMBINING	CONCEIVED
CLERGYMAN	CODIFYING	COMFORTED	CONCERNED

CONCERTED	CONQUEROR	COOPERAGE	COTTER-PIN
CONCIERGE	CONSCIOUS	CO-OPERATE	COTTON-GIN
CONCISELY	CONSCRIBE	COOPERING	COTTONING
CONCLUDED	CONSCRIPT	COPARTNER	COTYLEDON
CONCOCTED	CONSENSUS	CO-PATRIOT	COUNTABLE
CONCORDAT	CONSENTED	COPESTONE	COUNTERED
CONCOURSE	CONSERVED	COPIOUSLY	COUNTLESS
CONCRETED	CONSIGNED	COPPERING	COUNTRIFY
CONCUBINE	CONSIGNEE	COPPERISH	COURT-CARD
CONCURRED	CONSIGNOR	COPSEWOOD	COURTEOUS
CONCUSSED	CONSISTED	COPYRIGHT	COURTESAN
CONDEMNED	CONSOLING	COQUETTED	COURTLIKE
CONDENSED	CONSONANT	CORALLINE	COURTSHIP
CONDENSER	CONSORTED	CORALLITE	COURTYARD
CONDIGNLY	CONSPIRED	CORALLOID	COVERTURE
CONDIMENT	CONSTABLE	CORAL-REEF	COWARDICE
CONDITION	CONSTANCY	CORBELLED	COXCOMBRY
CONDOLING	CONSTRAIN	CORDELIER	CRAB-APPLE
CONDONING	CONSTRICT	CORDIALLY	CRABBEDLY
CONDUCING	CONSTRUCT	COREOPSIS	CRACKLING
CONDUCIVE	CONSTRUED	CORIANDER	CRAFTSMAN
CONDUCTED	CONSULATE	CORKSCREW	CRAMP-IRON
CONDUCTOR	CONSULTED	CORMORANT	CRANBERRY
CONFERRED	CONSUMING	CORN-BREAD	CRANKCASE
CONFESSED	CONTAGION	CORNCRAKE	CRAPULENT
CONFESSOR	CONTAINED	CORNELIAN	CRAPULOUS
CONFIDANT	CONTAINER	CORNERING	CRASSNESS
CONFIDENT	CONTENTED	CORNFLOUR	CRAYONING
CONFIDING	CONTESTED	CORN-POPPY	CRAZINESS
CONFIGURE	CONTINENT	CORN-SALAD	CREAM-LIKE
CONFINING	CONTINUAL	CORNSTALK	CREAM-LAID
CONFIRMED	CONTINUED	COROLLARY	CREAM-WOVE
CONFLUENT	CONTINUUM	CORONETED	CREDITING
CONFORMED	CONTORTED	CORPORATE	CREDULITY
CONFUCIAN	CONTOURED	CORPOREAL	CREDULOUS
CONFUSING	CONTRALTO	CORPOSANT	CREMATING
CONFUSION	CONTRIVED	CORPULENT	CREMATION
CONFUTING	CONTUMACY	CORPUSCLE	CRENATURE
CONGEALED	CONTUMELY	CORRECTED	CREPITANT
CONGENIAL	CONTUSING	CORRECTLY	CREPITATE
CONGESTED	CONTUSION	CORRECTOR	CRESCENDO
CONGRUENT	CONUNDRUM	CORRELATE	CRETINISM
CONGRUITY	CONVENING	CORRODING	CREVICING
CONGRUOUS	CONVERGED	CORROSION	CRIMELESS
CONICALLY	CONVERSED	CORROSIVE	CRIMSONED
CONJOINED	CONVERTED	CORRUGATE	CRINKLING
CONJUGATE	CONVEXITY	CORRUPTED	CRINOLINE
CONJURING	CONVEYING	CORTICATE	CRIPPLING
CONNECTED	CONVICTED	CORTISONE	CRISPNESS
CONNECTOR	CONVINCED	CORUSCATE	CRITERION
CONNEXION	CONVIVIAL	COSMOGONY	CRITICISE
CONNIVING	CONVOKING	COSMOLOGY	CRITICISM
CONNOTING	CONVOLUTE	COSSETING	CROCHETED
CONNUBIAL	CONVOYING	COSTUMIER	CROCODILE
CO-NOMINEE	CONVULSED	COTANGENT	CROOKBACK
CONQUERED	COOK-HOUSE	COTILLION	CROOKEDLY

CROQUETTE	CUSTODIAN	DEBAUCHED	DEFEATING
CROSSBEAM	CUSTOMARY	DEBENTURE	DEFEATISM
CROSSBILL	CUTANEOUS	DEBOUCHED	DEFECTION
CROSS-EYED	CUTICULAR	DEBUTANTE	DEFECTIVE
CROSS-FIRE	CUTTER-BAR	DECADENCE	DEFENDANT
CROSS-HEAD	CUTTHROAT	DECAGONAL	DEFENDING
CROSSNESS	CUTTINGLY	DECALCIFY	DEFENSIVE
CROSSROAD	CYCLOPEAN	DECALITRE	DEFERENCE
CROSSTALK	CYCLORAMA	DECALOGUE	DEFERRING
CROSS-WIND	CYNICALLY	DECAMERON	DEFIANTLY
CROSSWISE	CYTOPLASM	DECAMETRE	DEFICIENT
CROSSWORD		DECAMPING	DEFINABLE
CROTCHETY	**D – 9**	DECANTING	DEFINABLY
CROUCHING	DACHSUND	DECEITFUL	DEFLATING
CROWBERRY	DAEDALIAN	DECEIVING	DEFLATION
CROW'S-FEET	DAIRY-FARM	DECENNIAL	DEFLECTED
CROW'S-FOOT	DAIRYMAID	DECENNIUM	DEFLECTOR
CROW'S-NEST	DAISY-BUSH	DECEPTION	DEFLEXION
CROW-STONE	DALLIANCE	DECEPTIVE	DEFOLIATE
CRUCIFIED	DALMATIAN	DECIDABLE	DEFORMING
CRUCIFORM	DAMASCENE	DECIDEDLY	DEFORMITY
CRUMBLING	DAMOCLEAN	DECIDUOUS	DEFRAUDED
CRUMPLING	DAMPENING	DECILLION	DEFRAYING
CRUNCHING	DAMPISHLY	DECIMALLY	DEISTICAL
CRUSADING	DANDELION	DECIMATED	DEJECTING
CRUSTACEA	DANDIFIED	DECIMETRE	DEJECTION
CRYPTOGRAM	DANGEROUS	DECK-CHAIR	DELEGATED
CUBICALLY	DANNEBROG	DECK-HOUSE	DELICIOUS
CUCKOLDED	DANTESQUE	DECLAIMED	DELIGHTED
CUDGELLED	DAREDEVIL	DECLARANT	DELIMITED
CULMINATE	DARKENING	DECLARING	DELINEATE
CULTIVATE	DARTINGLY	DECLINING	DELIRIOUS
CULTURING	DARWINIAN	DECLIVITY	DELIVERED
CULTURIST	DARWINISM	DECOCTION	DELIVERER
CUMBERING	DASHBOARD	DECOLLETE	DEMAGOGIC
CUNEIFORM	DASTARDLY	DECOMPLEX	DEMAGOGUE
CUNNINGLY	DATUM-LINE	DECOMPOSE	DEMANDANT
CUPBEARER	DAUNTLESS	DECONTROL	DEMANDING
CUPRESSUS	DAVENPORT	DECORATED	DEMARCATE
CURBSTONE	DAY-LABOUR	DECORATOR	DEMEANING
CURIOSITY	DAY-SCHOOL	DECOY-DUCK	DEMEANOUR
CURIOUSLY	DAY-SPRING	DECREASED	DEMI-MONDE
CURLINESS	DEACONESS	DECREEING	DEMISSION
CURLINGLY	DEAD-ALIVE	DECREMENT	DEMITTING
CURRENTLY	DEADENING	DECUMBENT	DEMOCRACY
CURRISHLY	DEAFENING	DECUSSATE	DEMULCENT
CURRYCOMB	DEATH-BLOW	DEDICATED	DEMURRAGE
CURSORIAL	DEATHLESS	DEDUCIBLE	DEMURRANT
CURSORILY	DEATHLIKE	DEDUCTING	DEMURRING
CURTAILED	DEATH-MASK	DEDUCTION	DENIGRATE
CURTAINED	DEATH-RATE	DEDUCTIVE	DENOUNCED
CURTILAGE	DEATH-ROLL	DEEPENING	DENSENESS
CURTSYING	DEATH-TRAP	DEEP-TONED	DENTATION
CURVATURE	DEATH-WARD	DEFALCATE	DENTISTRY
CURVETTED	DEBARRING	DEFAULTED	DENTITION
CUSHIONED	DEBATABLE	DEFAULTER	DEODORANT

DEODORISE	DESPONDED	DICHOTOMY	DISBANDED
DEPARTING	DESPOTISM	DICHROMIC	DISBARRED
DEPARTURE	DESTINING	DICKERING	DISBELIEF
DEPASTURE	DESTITUTE	DICTATING	DISBRANCH
DEPENDANT	DESTROYED	DICTATION	DISBUDDED
DEPENDENT	DESTROYER	DICTATORY	DISBURDEN
DEPENDING	DESUETUDE	DIDACTICS	DISBURSED
DEPICTING	DESULTORY	DIESINKER	DISCARDED
DEPILATED	DETACHING	DIETETICS	DISCERNED
DEPLENISH	DETAILING	DIETITIAN	DISCHARGE
DEPLETING	DETAINING	DIFFERENT	DISCLOSED
DEPLETION	DETECTING	DIFFERING	DISCOLOUR
DEPLETIVE	DETECTION	DIFFICILE	DISCOMFIT
DEPLETORY	DETECTIVE	DIFFICULT	DISCOURSE
DEPLORING	DETENTION	DIFFIDENT	DISCOVERY
DEPLOYING	DETERRING	DIFFLUENT	DISCREDIT
DEPLUMING	DETERGENT	DIFFUSING	DISCUSSED
DEPORTING	DETERMINE	DIFFUSION	DISDAINED
DEPOSITED	DETERRENT	DIFFUSELY	DISEMBARK
DEPOSITOR	DETERRING	DIFFUSIVE	DISEMBODY
DEPRAVING	DETESTING	DIGESTING	DISENGAGE
DEPRAVITY	DETHRONED	DIGESTION	DISENTAIL
DEPRECATE	DETONATED	DIGESTIVE	DISENTOMB
DEPRESSED	DETONATOR	DIGITALIN	DISFAVOUR
DEPRIVING	DETRACTED	DIGITALIS	DISFIGURE
DEPTHLESS	DETRACTOR	DIGNIFIED	DISGORGED
DEPUTISED	DETRAINED	DIGNITARY	DISGRACED
DERAILING	DETRIMENT	DIGRESSED	DISGUISED
DERANGING	DETRITION	DILATABLE	DISGUSTED
DERIVABLE	DEVASTATE	DILIGENCE	DISHCLOTH
DERIVABLY	DEVELOPED	DILUTEDLY	DISH-CLOUT
DERMATOID	DEVELOPER	DIMENSION	DISH-COVER
DEROGATED	DEVIATION	DIMORPHIC	DISHONEST
DERRING-DO	DEVIL-FISH	DINGINESS	DISHONOUR
DERRINGER	DEVILLING	DINING-CAR	DISHWATER
DESCANTED	DEVILMENT	DIPHTHONG	DISINFECT
DESCENDED	DEVIOUSLY	DIPLOMACY	DISJOINED
DESCRIBED	DEVISABLE	DIPTEROUS	DISLIKING
DESCRYING	DEVITRIFY	DIRECTING	DISLOCATE
DESECRATE	DEVOLUTED	DIRECTION	DISLODGED
DESERTING	DEVOLVING	DIRECTIVE	DISMANTLE
DESERTION	DEVONPORT	DIRECTORY	DISMASTED
DESERVING	DEVOURING	DIREFULLY	DISMAYING
DESICCANT	DEWLAPPED	DIRIGIBLE	DISMEMBER
DESICCATE	DEXTERITY	DIRTINESS	DISMISSAL
DESIGNATE	DEXTEROUS	DIRT-TRACK	DISMISSED
DESIGNING	DIABOLISM	DISABLING	DISOBEYED
DESIRABLE	DIAERESIS	DISABUSED	DISOBLIGE
DESIRABLY	DIAGNOSED	DISACCORD	DISOWNING
DESISTING	DIAGNOSIS	DISAFFECT	DISPARAGE
DESOLATED	DIALECTAL	DISAFFIRM	DISPARATE
DESPAIRED	DIALECTIC	DISAGREED	DISPARITY
DESPERADO	DIAL-PLATE	DISAPPEAR	DISPELLED
DESPERATE	DIAPERING	DISARMING	DISPENSED
DESPISING	DIAPHRAGM	DISAVOWAL	DISPENSER
DESPOILED	DIARRHOEA	DISAVOWED	DISPERSAL

DISPERSED	DIZZINESS	DROMEDARY	EDUCATION
DISPLACED	DOCK-CRESS	DROP-SCENE	EFFECTING
DISPLAYED	DOCTORATE	DROPSICAL	EFFECTIVE
DISPLEASE	DOCTORING	DRUM-MAJOR	EFFECTUAL
DISPORTED	DOCTRINAL	DRUMSTICK	EFFICIENT
DISPOSING	DODDERING	DRUNKENLY	EFFLUENCE
DISPRAISE	DODECAGON	DRYSALTER	EFFLUVIUM
DISPROVED	DOGGINESS	DUALISTIC	EFFLUXION
DISPUTANT	DOGMATISE	DUBIOUSLY	EFFULGENT
DISPUTING	DOGMATISM	DUBITABLE	EGLANTINE
DISRATING	DOGMATIST	DUBITABLY	EGREGIOUS
DISREGARD	DOG'S-TOOTH	DUCK-BOARD	EGRESSION
DISRELISH	DOG-VIOLET	DUCK'S-FOOT	EIDER-DOWN
DISREPAIR	DOLEFULLY	DUCTILELY	EIDOGRAPH
DISREPUTE	DOLTISHLY	DUCTILITY	EIGHTFOLD
DISROBING	DOMICILED	DUMB-BELLS	EIGHTIETH
DISROOTED	DOMINANCE	DUMBFOUND	EIGHTSOME
DISRUPTED	DOMINICAL	DUMPINESS	EIRENICON
DISSECTED	DO-NOTHING	DUMPISHLY	EJACULATE
DISSEMBLE	DOOR-PLATE	DUNGEONED	EJECTMENT
DISSENTED	DOOR-STONE	DUODECIMO	ELABORATE
DISSENTER	DORMITORY	DUODENARY	ELBOW-ROOM
DISSERVED	DOSS-HOUSE	DUPLICATE	ELDERSHIP
DISSIPATE	DOUBTLESS	DWINDLING	ELDER-WINE
DISSOLUTE	DOUGHTILY	DYNAMICAL	ELECTORAL
DISSOLVED	DOVE'S-FOOT	DYNAMITED	ELECTRESS
DISSONANT	DOWDINESS	DYSENTERY	ELECTRIFY
DISSUADED	DOWELLING	DYSPEPSIA	ELECTRODE
DISTANCED	DOWERLESS	DYSPEPTIC	ELEGANTLY
DISTANTLY	DOWNGRADE	DYSTROPHY	ELEMENTAL
DISTEMPER	DOWNINESS		ELEVATING
DISTENDED	DOWNRIGHT	E – 9	ELEVATION
DISTILLED	DOWNWARDS	EAGERNESS	ELEVATORY
DISTILLER	DRABBLING	EAGLE-EYED	ELICITING
DISTORTED	DRACONIAN	EARLINESS	ELIMINATE
DISTRAINT	DRAFTSMAN	EARMARKED	ELLIPSOID
DISTURBED	DRAGGLING	EARNESTLY	ELOCUTION
DISUNITED	DRAGON-FLY	EARTHWARD	ELONGATED
DITHERING	DRAINABLE	EARTHWORK	ELOPEMENT
DITHYRAMB	DRAINPIPE	EARTHWORM	ELOQUENCE
DIURNALLY	DRAMATISE	EASEFULLY	ELSEWHERE
DIVAGATED	DRAMATIST	EAST-ENDER	ELUCIDATE
DIVERGENT	DRAWN-WORK	EASY-CHAIR	EMACIATED
DIVERGING	DRAY-HORSE	EASY-GOING	EMANATING
DIVERSELY	DREAM-LAND	EAVESDROP	EMANATION
DIVERSIFY	DREAMLESS	EBONISING	EMBALMING
DIVERSION	DREAMLIKE	EBULLIENT	EMBANKING
DIVERSITY	DRENCHING	ECCENTRIC	EMBARGOED
DIVERTING	DRIBBLING	ECLIPSING	EMBARKING
DIVESTING	DRIFT-LESS	ECONOMICS	EMBARRASS
DIVIDABLE	DRIFTWOOD	ECONOMISE	EMBATTLED
DIVIDEDLY	DRINKABLE	ECONOMIST	EMBEDDING
DIVISIBLE	DRINKLESS	ECTOPLASM	EMBELLISH
DIVISIBLY	DRIPSTONE	EDELWEISS	EMBEZZLED
DIVORCING	DRIVELLED	EDITORIAL	EMBEZZLER
DIVULGING	DRIZZLING	EDUCATING	EMBODYING

EMBOSSING	ENGRAVING	EPILEPTIC	EVAPORATE
EMBOWERED	ENGROSSED	EPISCOPAL	EVASIVELY
EMBRACING	ENGULFING	EPISTOLIC	EVENTUATE
EMBRASURE	ENHANCING	EPITOMISE	EVERGLADE
EMBROIDER	ENIGMATIC	EQUALISED	EVERGREEN
EMBROILED	ENJOINING	EQUALISER	EVERYBODY
EMBRYONIC	ENJOYABLE	EQUALLING	EVIDENTLY
EMENDATOR	ENJOYABLY	EQUIPMENT	EVOCATION
EMERGENCE	ENJOYMENT	EQUIPOISE	EVOLUTION
EMERGENCY	ENLARGING	EQUIPPING	EXACTABLE
EMINENTLY	ENLIGHTEN	EQUITABLE	EXACTNESS
EMOLLIENT	ENLISTING	EQUIVOCAL	EXAMINING
EMOLUMENT	ENLIVENED	ERADICATE	EXCALIBUR
EMOTIONAL	ENMESHING	ERECTNESS	EXCAVATED
EMPHASISE	ENOUNCING	ERRAND-BOY	EXCAVATOR
EMPIRICAL	ENQUIRING	ERRONEOUS	EXCEEDING
EMPLOYING	ENRAPTURE	ERSTWHILE	EXCELLENT
EMPOWERED	ENRICHING	ERUDITELY	EXCELSIOR
EMPTINESS	ENROLLING	ERUDITION	EXCEPTING
EMULATING	ENROLMENT	ESCALADED	EXCEPTION
EMULATION	ENSCONCED	ESCALATOR	EXCEPTIVE
EMULATIVE	ENSHRINED	ESCHEATED	EXCESSING
ENACTMENT	ENSLAVING	ESCORTING	EXCESSIVE
ENAMELLED	ENSNARING	ESPERANTO	EXCHANGED
ENAMOURED	ENTAILING	ESPIONAGE	EXCHANGER
ENCASHING	ENTANGLED	ESPLANADE	EXCHEQUER
ENCAUSTIC	ENTERTAIN	ESPOUSING	EXCISABLE
ENCHANTED	ENTHRONED	ESQUIRING	EXCISEMAN
ENCIRCLED	ENTHUSING	ESSENTIAL	EXCITABLE
ENCLASPED	ENTITLING	ESTABLISH	EXCLAIMED
ENCLOSING	ENTOURAGE	ESTAMINET	EXCLUDING
ENCLOSURE	EN-TOUT-CAS	ESTEEMING	EXCLUSION
ENCOMPASS	ENTRANCED	ESTIMABLE	EXCLUSIVE
ENCOUNTER	ENTREATED	ESTIMABLY	EXCORIATE
ENCOURAGE	ENTRECHAT	ESTIMATOR	EXCREMENT
ENCRUSTED	ENTREMETS	ESTOPPING	EXCRETION
ENDEARING	ENTRUSTED	ESTRANGED	EXCRETIVE
ENDEAVOUR	ENTWINING	ESTREATED	EXCRETORY
ENDLESSLY	ENUMERATE	ESTUARINE	EXCULPATE
ENDOCRINE	ENUNCIATE	ETERNALLY	EXCURSION
ENDORSING	ENVELOPED	ETHICALLY	EXCURSIVE
ENDOSPERM	ENVENOMED	ETHIOPIAN	EXCUSABLE
ENDOWMENT	ENVIOUSLY	ETHNOLOGY	EXCUSABLY
ENDURABLE	ENVISAGED	ETIOLATED	EXECRABLE
ENDURABLY	ENVOYSHIP	ETIQUETTE	EXECRABLY
ENDURANCE	ENWRAPPED	ETYMOLOGY	EXECRATED
ENERGETIC	EPAULETTE	EUCHARIST	EXECUTANT
ENERGISER	EPHEMERAL	EUCLIDEAN	EXECUTING
ENERVATED	EPICENTRE	EULOGIZED	EXECUTION
ENFEEBLED	EPICUREAN	EUPHEMISE	EXECUTIVE
ENFILADED	EPICURISM	EUPHEMISM	EXECUTORY
ENFOLDING	EPICYCLIC	EUPHONIUM	EXECUTRIX
ENFORCING	EPIDERMAL	EVACUATED	EXEMPLARY
ENGINE-MAN	EPIDERMIC	EVALUATED	EXEMPLIFY
ENGIRDING	EPIDERMIS	EVANESCED	EXEMPTION
ENGIRDLED	EPIGRAPHY	EVANGELIC	EXEMPTIVE

EXERCISED	EXTREMISM	FATTINESS	FILTRATED
EXFOLIATE	EXTREMIST	FAULTLESS	FINANCIAL
EXHALABLE	EXTREMITY	FAVOURING	FINANCIER
EXHAUSTED	EXTRICATE	FAVOURITE	FINANCING
EXHIBITED	EXTRINSIC	FAWNINGLY	FINEDRAWN
EXHIBITOR	EXTRUDING	FEARFULLY	FINESSING
EXHORTING	EXTRUSION	FEATHERED	FINGERING
EXISTENCE	EXUBERANT	FEATURING	FINICALLY
EX-OFFICIO	EXUBERATE	FEBRIFUGE	FINICKING
EXOGAMOUS	EXUDATION	FECUNDITY	FINISHING
EXOGENOUS	EXULTANCY	FEDERATED	FIRE-ALARM
EXONERATE	EYEBRIGHT	FEELINGLY	FIREBRAND
EXORCISED	EYE-OPENER	FEE-SIMPLE	FIREBRICK
EXPANDING		FEIGNEDLY	FIRECREST
EXPANSILE		FELONIOUS	FIRE-EATER
EXPANSION	F – 9	FEMINISED	FIRE-GUARD
EXPANSIVE		FENCELESS	FIRE-IRONS
EXPATIATE	FABRICATE	FENESTRAL	FIRELIGHT
EXPECTANT	FACE-CLOTH	FENLANDER	FIREPLACE
EXPECTING	FACE-GUARD	FERMENTED	FIREPROOF
EXPEDIENT	FACSIMILE	FEROCIOUS	FIREWATER
EXPEDITED	FACTITIVE	FERRETING	FIRMAMENT
EXPENDING	FACTORIAL	FERROTYPE	FIRSTBORN
EXPENSIVE	FACTORISE	FERRYBOAT	FIRST-FOOT
EXPIATING	FADDINESS	FERTILELY	FIRSTHAND
EXPIATION	FAGGOTING	FERTILISE	FIRST-RATE
EXPIATORY	FAILINGLY	FERTILITY	FISH-CURER
EXPLAINED	FAINTNESS	FERVENTLY	FISHERMAN
EXPLETIVE	FAIRY-LAMP	FESTERING	FISHINESS
EXPLICATE	FAIRYLAND	FESTIVELY	FISH-KNIFE
EXPLOITED	FAIRY-LIKE	FESTIVITY	FISH-SPEAR
EXPLORING	FAIRY-TALE	FESTOONED	FISSILITY
EXPLOSION	FALDSTOOL	FETIDNESS	FISTULOUS
EXPLOSIVE	FALERNIAN	FETISHISM	FITTINGLY
EXPORTING	FALLOPIAN	FETTERING	FITTING-UP
EXPOUNDED	FALLOWING	FEUDALISE	FIXEDNESS
EXPRESSED	FALSEHOOD	FEUDALISM	FLACCIDLY
EXPRESSLY	FALSENESS	FEUDALITY	FLAGELLUM
EXPULSION	FALSIFIED	FEUDATORY	FLAGEOLET
EXPULSIVE	FALTERING	FIBRELESS	FLAGRANCY
EXPUNGING	FAMISHING	FIBRIFORM	FLAGSTAFF
EXPURGATE	FANATICAL	FICTIONAL	FLAGSTONE
EXQUISITE	FANCY-FREE	FIDDLE-BOW	FLAMBEAUX
EXTEMPORE	FANTAILED	FIDGETING	FLAMELESS
EXTENDING	FANTASTIC	FIDUCIARY	FLAMINGLY
EXTENSILE	FARMHOUSE	FIELDFARE	FLANNELLY
EXTENSION	FARMSTEAD	FIELDSMAN	FLARINGLY
EXTENSIVE	FARROWING	FIERINESS	FLATTENED
EXTENUATE	FASCIATED	FIFE-MAJOR	FLATTERED
EXTOLLING	FASCINATE	FIFTEENTH	FLATTERER
EXTORTING	FASHIONED	FILIATION	FLAUNTING
EXTORTION	FASTENING	FILIGREED	FLAVOROUS
EXTRACTED	FATEFULLY	FILLETING	FLAVOURED
EXTRACTOR	FATHERING	FILLIPING	FLEETNESS
EXTRADITE	FATHOMING	FILMINESS	FLESHLESS
EXTREMELY	FATIGUING	FILTERING	FLICKERED
	FATTENING		

FLIGHTILY	FORCE-PUMP	FOXTAILED	FULFILLED
FLINCHING	FOREARMED	FRACTIOUS	FULGURITE
FLINTLOCK	FOREBODED	FRACTURED	FULL-BLOWN
FLIPPANCY	FORE-CABIN	FRAGILELY	FULL-DRESS
FLITTERED	FORECLOSE	FRAGILITY	FULL-FACED
FLOATABLE	FORECOURT	FRAGRANCE	FULL-GROWN
FLOODGATE	FOREDATED	FRAGRANCY	FULL-PITCH
FLOOD-MARK	FOREFRONT	FRAILNESS	FULL-SWING
FLOOD-TIDE	FOREGOING	FRAMEWORK	FULMINANT
FLOORLESS	FOREIGNER	FRANCHISE	FULMINATE
FLORIDITY	FORE-JUDGE	FRANCISCA	FULSOMELY
FLOTATION	FORESHEET	FRANGIBLE	FUMIGATED
FLOUNCING	FORESHORE	FRANKNESS	FUNGICIDE
FLOWCHART	FORESHOWN	FRATERNAL	FUNICULAR
FLOWERING	FORE-SIGHT	FRAUDLESS	FUNNELLED
FLOWERPOT	FORESTALL	FRECKLING	FUNNINESS
FLOWINGLY	FORETASTE	FREEBOARD	FURBISHED
FLUCTUATE	FORETOKEN	FREELIVER	FURIOUSLY
FLUIDNESS	FOREWOMAN	FREEMASON	FURNISHED
FLUKINESS	FORFEITED	FREESTONE	FURNISHER
FLUMMOXED	FORGATHER	FREE-WHEEL	FURNITURE
FLUORSPAR	FORGETFUL	FREIGHTED	FURROWING
FLURRYING	FORGIVING	FREIGHTER	FURTHERED
FLUSHNESS	FORLORNLY	FRENCHIFY	FURTHERER
FLUSTERED	FORMALISE	FRENCHMAN	FURTIVELY
FLUTE-LIKE	FORMALISM	FREQUENCY	FUSILLADE
FLUTTERED	FORMALIST	FRESHENED	FUSSINESS
FLUXIONAL	FORMALITY	FRESHNESS	FUSTIGATE
FLY-BITTEN	FORMATION	FRETFULLY	FUSTINESS
FLYING-FOX	FORMATIVE	FRIBBLING	
FLYING-JIB	FORMULARY	FRICASSEE	
FLY-POWDER	FORMULATE	FRICATIVE	G – 9
FOAMINGLY	FORMULISM	FRIGHTFUL	GABARDINE
FODDERING	FORMULIST	FRIGIDITY	GABERDINE
FOGGINESS	FORSAKING	FRITTERED	GADDINGLY
FOG-SIGNAL	FORTHWITH	FRIVOLITY	GAINFULLY
FOLIATION	FORTIFIED	FRIVOLOUS	GAINSAYER
FOLK-DANCE	FORTITUDE	FRIZZLING	GAITERING
FOLLOWING	FORTNIGHT	FROCK-COAT	GALACTOSE
FOMENTING	FORTUNATE	FROG-MARCH	GALANTINE
FOOLHARDY	FORTY-FIVE	FROGMOUTH	GALINGALE
FOOLISHLY	FORWARDED	FROG-SPAWN	GALLANTRY
FOOLPROOF	FORWARDLY	FROLICKED	GALLERIED
FOOTBOARD	FOSSILISE	FRONTAGER	GALLICISE
FOOT-FAULT	FOSSORIAL	FRONTWARD	GALLICISM
FOOTPLATE	FOSTERAGE	FROSTBITE	GALLINULE
FOOT-POUND	FOSTERING	FROSTLESS	GALLIVANT
FOOTPRINT	FOSTER-SON	FROWARDLY	GALLOPING
FOOTSTALK	FOUNDERED	FRUCTUOUS	GALLOPADE
FOOTSTOOL	FOUNDLING	FRUGALITY	GALLSTONE
FOPPISHLY	FOUNDRESS	FRUIT-CAKE	GALVANISE
FORAGE-CAP	FOUR-HORSE	FRUIT-TREE	GALVANISM
FORASMUCH	FOURPENCE	FRUSTRATE	GALVANIST
FORBIDDEN	FOURPENNY	FRUTICOSE	GAMBOLLED
FORCELESS	FOUR-SCORE	FRYING-PAN	GAMMA-RAYS
FORCEMEAT	FOXHUNTER	FUGACIOUS	GAMMONING

GANGBOARD	GEOMETRIC	GLOWERING	GRAPESHOT
GANGRENED	GERFALCON	GLOWINGLY	GRAPEVINE
GARDENING	GERMANDER	GLUCOSIDE	GRAPPLING
GARIBALDI	GERMANISM	GLUEYNESS	GRASPABLE
GARLANDED	GERMANIUM	GLUTINOUS	GRASSLAND
GARNERING	GERMICIDE	GLYCERIDE	GRASSLESS
GARNISHED	GERMINANT	GLYCERINE	GRASS-PLOT
GARNISHEE	GERMINATE	GNAWINGLY	GRATIFIED
GARNISHER	GERUNDIAL	GOATISHLY	GRATINGLY
GARNITURE	GERUNDIVE	GO-BETWEEN	GRATITUDE
GARRETEER	GESTATION	GODFATHER	GRAVELESS
GARROTTED	GESTATORY	GODLESSLY	GRAVELLED
GARROTTER	GESTURING	GODLINESS	GRAVEL-PIT
GARRULITY	GET-AT-ABLE	GODMOTHER	GRAVENESS
GARRULOUS	GHOSTLIKE	GODPARENT	GRAVEYARD
GARTERING	GHOST-MOTH	GOFFERING	GRAVITATE
GAS-BURNER	GIANTLIKE	GOLDCLOTH	GREATCOAT
GAS-CARBON	GIBBERING	GOLDCREST	GREATNESS
GASCONADE	GIBBERISH	GOLDEN-ROD	GREENBACK
GAS-COOKER	GIDDINESS	GOLDFINCH	GREEN-EYED
GAS-ENGINE	GIFT-HORSE	GOLDSMITH	GREENGAGE
GASEOUSLY	GILL-COVER	GOLF-LINKS	GREENHORN
GAS-FITTER	GILT-EDGED	GONDOLIER	GREENNESS
GASHOLDER	GIMLETING	GOODNIGHT	GREENROOM
GASIFYING	GIN-PALACE	GOOSANDER	GREENSAND
GAS-MANTLE	GINGERADE	GOOSEFOOT	GREENWICH
GASOMETER	GINGER-ALE	GOOSENECK	GREENWOOD
GASPINGLY	GINGER-POP	GOOSE-STEP	GREGORIAN
GAS-RETORT	GINGLYMUS	GOOSEWING	GRENADIER
GASTRITIS	GIRANDOLE	GORGONIAN	GRENADINE
GASTROPOD	GIRL-GUIDE	GOSPELLER	GREYBEARD
GATEHOUSE	GIRLISHLY	GOSSAMERY	GREYHOUND
GATE-MONEY	GIRONDIST	GOSSIPING	GREYSTONE
GATHERING	GLACIATED	GOTHAMITE	GRIEVANCE
GAUCHERIE	GLADDENED	GOUTINESS	GRILL-ROOM
GAUDINESS	GLADIATOR	GOVERNESS	GRIMACING
GAUNTNESS	GLADIOLUS	GOVERNING	GRIMALKIN
GAVELKIND	GLADSTONE	GRABBLING	GRIMINESS
GAZETTEER	GLAIREOUS	GRACE-NOTE	GRIPINGLY
GAZETTING	GLAMOURED	GRACILITY	GRISAILLE
GEARWHEEL	GLANDULAR	GRADATING	GRIST-MILL
GELIGNITE	GLARINGLY	GRADATION	GRITSTONE
GEMMATION	GLASSLIKE	GRADATORY	GRIZZLING
GENEALOGY	GLASSWARE	GRADGRIND	GROOMSMAN
GENERALLY	GLASS-WORK	GRADUALLY	GROPINGLY
GENERATED	GLASSWORT	GRADUATED	GROSSNESS
GENERATOR	GLENGARRY	GRADUATOR	GROTESQUE
GENIALITY	GLIDINGLY	GRANDAUNT	GROUNDAGE
GENTEELLY	GLIMMERED	GRAND-DUKE	GROUND-ASH
GENTILITY	GLIMPSING	GRANDIOSE	GROUNDING
GENTLEMAN	GLISSADED	GRAND-JURY	GROUND-IVY
GENUFLECT	GLISTENED	GRANDNESS	GROUNDNUT
GENUINELY	GLITTERED	GRANDSIRE	GROUND-OAK
GEOGRAPHY	GLOBE-FISH	GRAND-SLAM	GROUNDSEL
GEOLOGISE	GLOBOSITY	GRANULATE	GROVELLED
GEOLOGIST	GLORIFIED	GRANULOUS	GRUELLING

GRUFFNESS	HALF-CASTE	HAWK-EAGLE	HERBARIUM
GRUMBLING	HALFCROWN	HAWK-NOSED	HERBIVORE
GRUNDYISM	HALFPENNY	HAWKSBILL	HERCULEAN
GUARANTEE	HALF-PRICE	HAWSE-HOLE	HEREABOUT
GUARANTOR	HALF-ROUND	HAYMAKING	HEREAFTER
GUARD-BOAT	HALF-SHAFT	HAZARDING	HERETICAL
GUARDEDLY	HALF-TIMER	HAZARDOUS	HERITABLE
GUARDLESS	HALLOWEEN	HEAD-DRESS	HERITABLY
GUARDROOM	HALTERING	HEADFRAME	HERMITAGE
GUARDSHIP	HALTINGLY	HEADLINES	HERONSHAW
GUARDSMAN	HAMADRYAD	HEADLIGHT	HESITANCY
GUERRILLA	HAMPERING	HEADMONEY	HESITATED
GUESSABLE	HAMSTRING	HEADPHONE	HETERODOX
GUESSWORK	HAMSTRUNG	HEADPIECE	HEXACHORD
GUEST-WISE	HANDBRACE	HEADSTALL	HEXAGONAL
GUIDE-BOOK	HANDCUFFS	HEADSTOCK	HEXAMETER
GUIDELESS	HANDGLASS	HEADSTONE	HEXASTYLE
GUIDE-POST	HANDINESS	HEALINGLY	HEXATEUCH
GUIDE-RAIL	HANDIWORK	HEALTHFUL	HIBERNATE
GUIDE-ROPE	HANDPRESS	HEALTHILY	HIBERNIAN
GUILDHALL	HANDSCREW	HEARKENED	HIDEBOUND
GUILELESS	HANDSPIKE	HEARTACHE	HIDEOUSLY
GUILLEMOT	HANKERING	HEARTBURN	HIERARCHY
GUILLOCHE	HANSEATIC	HEARTENED	HIGH BLOWN
GUILTLESS	HAPHAZARD	HEARTFELT	HIGH-FLIER
GUINEA-PIG	HAPPENING	HEARTHRUG	HIGHFLOWN
GUMMINESS	HAPPINESS	HEARTLESS	HIGH-FLYER
GUN-BARREL	HARANGUED	HEARTSICK	HIGH-TONED
GUNCOTTON	HARBINGER	HEARTWOOD	HIGH-WATER
GUNPOWDER	HARBOURED	HEATH-CLAD	HILARIOUS
GUNRUNNER	HARDBOARD	HEATH-COCK	HILLINESS
GUSHINGLY	HARD-BOUND	HEAVINESS	HINDERING
GUSTATORY	HARDENING	HEBRIDEAN	HINDRANCE
GUTTERING	HARDFACED	HECTOGRAM	HINDSIGHT
GYMNASIUM	HARDIHOOD	HECTORING	HINTINGLY
GYROSCOPE	HARDINESS	HEDGELESS	HIPPOCRAS
	HARDSHELL	HEEDFULLY	HISSINGLY
	HARLEQUIN	HEEL-PIECE	HISTOLOGY
H – 9	HARMFULLY	HEFTINESS	HISTORIAN
	HARMONICA	HEINOUSLY	HOAR-FROST
HABITABLE	HARMONICS	HEIR-AT-LAW	HOARINESS
HABITABLY	HARMONISE	HELIOGRAM	HOARSTONE
HABITUATE	HARMONIST	HELLEBORE	HOBGOBLIN
HACKNEYED	HARMONIUM	HELLENIAN	HOBNOBBED
HAGGARDLY	HARNESSED	HELLENISE	HOCUSSING
HAGGISHLY	HARROVIAN	HELLENISM	HODOMETER
HAGIOLOGY	HARROWING	HELLENIST	HOGBACKED
HAGRIDDEN	HARSHNESS	HELLBOUND	HOGGISHLY
HAILSTONE	HARTSHORN	HELLISHLY	HOLLANDER
HAILSTORM	HARVESTED	HEMICYCLE	HOLLOWING
HAIRBROOM	HARVESTER	HEMSTITCH	HOLLYHOCK
HAIRBRUSH	HASTINESS	HENPECKED	HOLOCAUST
HAIRCLOTH	HATCHMENT	HEPATITIS	HOLOGRAPH
HAIRINESS	HATEFULLY	HEPTARCHY	HOLSTERED
HALF-BLOOD	HAUGHTILY	HERALDING	HOLYSTONE
HALF-BOUND	HAVERSACK	HERBALIST	HOMEBOUND
HALF-BREED			

HOMESTEAD	HUMANNESS	ILL-HUMOUR	IMPOLITIC
HOMICIDAL	HUMBLE-BEE	ILLIBERAL	IMPORTANT
HOMOLOGUE	HUMBLE-PIE	ILLICITLY	IMPORTING
HOMONYMIC	HUMBUGGED	ILL-JUDGED	IMPORTUNE
HOMOPHONE	HUMILIATE	ILL-NATURE	IMPOSABLE
HOMOPHONY	HUMMOCKED	ILLOGICAL	IMPOSTURE
HOMOPTERA	HUMOURING	ILL-TIMING	IMPOTENCE
HONEY-BEAR	HUNCHBACK	ILLUMINED	IMPOTENCY
HONEYCOMB	HUNDREDTH	IMAGELESS	IMPOUNDED
HONEYLESS	HUNGARIAN	IMAGINARY	IMPRECATE
HONEYMOON·	HUNGERING	IMAGINING	IMPRESSED
HONEYWORT	HURRICANE	IMBROGLIO	IMPRINTED
HONORIFIC	HURRIEDLY	IMITATING	IMPROMPTU
HONOURING	HURTFULLY	IMITATION	IMPROVING
HOOKNOSED	HUSBANDED	IMITATIVE	IMPROVISE
HOPEFULLY	HUSBANDRY	IMMANENCE	IMPRUDENT
HOPGARDEN	HUSHMONEY	IMMEDIACY	IMPUDENCE
HOP-PICKER	HUSKINESS	IMMEDIATE	IMPUGNING
HOP-PILLOW	HYBRIDISE	IMMENSELY	IMPULSION
HOP-POCKET	HYBRIDISM	IMMENSITY	IMPULSIVE
HOPSCOTCH	HYBRIDITY	IMMERSING	IMPUTABLE
HOREHOUND	HYDRANGEA	IMMERSION	INABILITY
HOROSCOPE	HYDRAULIC	IMMIGRANT	INAMORATO
HOROSCOPY	HYDROLOGY	IMMIGRATE	INANIMATE
HORRIFIED	HYDROSTAT	IMMINENCE	INANITION
HORSEBACK	HYDROXIDE	IMMODESTY	INAPTNESS
HORSE-BEAN	HYMNOLOGY	IMMORALLY	INARCHING
HORSEHAIR	HYPERBOLA	IMMOVABLE	INAUDIBLE
HORSELESS	HYPERBOLE	IMMOVABLY	INAUDIBLY
HORSEMEAT	HYPERICUM	IMMUNISED	INAUGURAL
HORSEPLAY	HYPHENING	IMMUTABLE	INAURATED
HORSEPOND	HYPNOLOGY	IMMUTABLY	INCAPABLE
HORSERACE	HYPNOTISM	IMPACTING	INCAPABLY
HORSESHOE	HYPNOTIST	IMPACTION	INCARNATE
HORSETAIL	HYPOCAUST	IMPAIRING	INCENSING
HORSEWHIP	HYPOCRISY	IMPARTIAL	INCENSORY
HOSTELLER	HYPOCRITE	IMPARTING	INCENTIVE
HOSTILELY	HYSTERICS	IMPASSION	INCEPTION
HOSTILITY		IMPASSIVE	INCEPTIVE
HOT-HEADED		IMPATIENS	INCESSANT
HOTTENTOT	I – 9	IMPATIENT	INCIDENCE
HOUR-GLASS	ICELANDER	IMPEACHED	INCIPIENT
HOUSEBOAT	ICELANDIC	IMPELLENT	INCLEMENT
HOUSEHOLD	ICHNEUMON	IMPELLING	INCLINING
HOUSELEEK	ICHTHYOID	IMPENDENT	INCLUDING
HOUSELESS	ICONOLOGY	IMPENDING	INCLUSION
HOUSEMAID	IDEALISED	IMPERFECT	INCLUSIVE
HOUSEROOM	IDENTICAL	IMPERIOUS	INCOGNITO
HOUSEWIFE	IDEOGRAPH	IMPETUOUS	INCOMMODE
HOUSEWORK	IDIOMATIC	IMPINGING	INCORRECT
HOWSOEVER	IGNORAMUS	IMPIOUSLY	INCORRUPT
HUCKABACK	IGNORANCE	IMPLANTED	INCREASED
HUFFINESS	IGUANODON	IMPLEMENT	INCREMENT
HUFFISHLY	ILLEGALLY	IMPLICATE	INCUBATED
HUMANISED	ILLEGIBLE	IMPLORING	INCUBATOR
HUMANKIND	ILLEGIBLY	IMPLOSION	INCULCATE

INCULPATE	INFIRMITY	INSIDIOUS	INTERNODE
INCUMBENT	INFLAMING	INSINCERE	INTERPLAY
INCURABLE	INFLATING	INSINUATE	INTERPOSE
INCURABLY	INFLATION	INSIPIDLY	INTERPRET
INCURIOUS	INFLECTED	INSISTENT	INTERRING
INCURRING	INFLEXION	INSISTING	INTERRUPT
INCURSION	INFLICTED	INSOLENCE	INTERSECT
INCURSIVE	INFLOWING	INSOLUBLE	INTERVENE
INCURVING	INFLUENCE	INSOLVENT	INTERVIEW
INDECENCY	INFLUENZA	INSPANNED	INTERWOVE
INDECORUM	INFOLDING	INSPECTED	INTESTACY
INDELIBLE	INFORMANT	INSPECTOR	INTESTATE
INDELIBLY	INFORMING	INSPIRING	INTESTINE
INDEMNIFY	INFRINGED	INSTALLED	INTIMATED
INDEMNITY	INFURIATE	INSTANCED	INTONATED
INDENTING	INFUSIBLE	INSTANTLY	INTRICACY
INDENTION	INFUSORIA	INSTIGATE	INTRICATE
INDENTURE	INGENIOUS	INSTILLED	INTRIGUED
INDICATED	INGENUITY	INSTITUTE	INTRINSIC
INDICATOR	INGENUOUS	INSULARLY	INTRODUCE
INDICTING	INGESTION	INSULATED	INTROVERT
INDIGENCE	INGLENOOK	INSULATOR	INTRUDING
INDIGNANT	INGRAINED	INSULTING	INTRUSION
INDIGNITY	INGROWING	INSURABLE	INTRUSIVE
INDISPOSE	INHABITED	INSURANCE	INTUITION
INDOLENCE	INHERENCE	INSURGENT	INTUITIVE
INDRAUGHT	INHERITED	INTEGRANT	INUNCTION
INDUCTING	INHERITOR	INTEGRATE	INUNDATED
INDUCTION	INHIBITED	INTEGRITY	INUREMENT
INDUCTIVE	INHUMANLY	INTELLECT	INUTILITY
INDULGING	INITIALLY	INTENDANT	INVALIDED
INDULGENT	INITIATED	INTENSELY	INVECTIVE
INDURATED	INJECTING	INTENSIFY	INVEIGHED
INDWELLED	INJECTION	INTENSION	INVEIGLED
INEBRIATE	INJURIOUS	INTENSITY	INVENTING
INEBRIETY	INJUSTICE	INTENSIVE	INVENTION
INEFFABLE	INKBOTTLE	INTENTION	INVENTIVE
INEFFABLY	INKHOLDER	INTERBRED	INVENTORY
INELASTIC	INNERMOST	INTERCEDE	INVERSELY
INELEGANT	INNERVATE	INTERCEPT	INVERSION
INEPTNESS	INNKEEPER	INTERDICT	INVERTING
INERRABLE	INNOCENCE	INTERFACE	INVESTING
INERRABLY	INNOCUOUS	INTERFERE	INVIDIOUS
INERRANCY	INNOVATED	INTERFOLD	INVIOLATE
INERTNESS	INNOVATOR	INTERFUSE	INVISIBLE
INFANTILE	INOCULATE	INTERJECT	INVISIBLY
INFANTINE	INODORATE	INTERLACE	INVOICING
INFATUATE	INODOROUS	INTERLAID	INVOLUCRE
INFECTING	INORGANIC	INTERLARD	INVOLVING
INFECTION	INQUIRING	INTERLEAF	INWROUGHT
INFECTIVE	INSATIATE	INTERLINE	IRASCIBLE
INFERENCE	INSCRIBED	INTERLOCK	IRASCIBLY
INFERRING	INSENSATE	INTERLOPE	IRKSOMELY
INFERTILE	INSERTING	INTERLUDE	IRONBOUND
INFESTING	INSERTION	INTERMENT	IRONMOULD
INFIRMARY	INSETTING	INTERNING	IRONSMITH

IRONSTONE	JOSS-HOUSE	**L – 9**	LAZARETTO
IRRADIANT	JOSS-STICK		LEADINGLY
IRRADIATE	JOURNEYED	LABELLING	LEAFINESS
IRREGULAR	JOVIALITY	LABORIOUS	LEAF-METAL
IRRIGATED	JOYLESSLY	LABOURING	LEAF-MOULD
IRRITABLE	JOCUNDITY	LABYRINTH	LEAFSTALK
IRRITABLY	JUDAS-TREE	LACE-CORAL	LEAKINESS
IRRITANCY	JUDGEMENT	LACE-FRAME	LEAN-FACED
IRRITATED	JUDGESHIP	LACERATED	LEAPINGLY
IRRUPTION	JUDICIARY	LACHRYMAL	LEARNABLE
ISINGLASS	JUDICIOUS	LACTATION	LEARNEDLY
ISLAMITIC	JUICELESS	LAGGINGLY	LEASEHOLD
ISOLATING	JUICINESS	LAIRDSHIP	LEASTWAYS
ISOLATION	JUMPINESS	LAMB'S-WOOL	LEASTWISE
ISOMETRIC	JUNIORITY	LAMELLATE	LEAVENING
ISOSCELES	JURIDICIAL	LAMENTING	LECHERING
ISRAELITE	JUSTICIAR	LAMINATED	LECHEROUS
ITALICISE	JUSTIFIED	LAMPBLACK	LECTURING
ITERATING	JUTTINGLY	LAMPLIGHT	LEERINGLY
ITERATION	JUVENILIA	LAMPOONED	LEGALISED
ITERATIVE	JUXTAPOSE	LANCEWOOD	LEGENDARY
ITINERANT		LAND-AGENT	LEGER-LINE
ITINERARY		LANDAULET	LEGIONARY
ITINERATE	**K – 9**	LAND-FORCE	LEGISLATE
	KENNELLED	LANDGRAVE	LEISURELY
	KENTLEDGE	LANDOWNER	LEITMOTIF
J – 9	KERBSTONE	LANDSCAPE	LENGTHILY
	KERNELLED	LAND-SHARK	LENIENTLY
JACARANDA	KIDNAPPED	LANDSLIDE	LEPROUSLY
JACK-KNIFE	KIDNAPPER	LANGUIDLY	LESSENING
JACK-PLANE	KILDERKIN	LANKINESS	LETHARGIC
JACK-SNIPE	KILN-DRIED	LANTHANUM	LETTER-BOX
JACKSTRAW	KILOLITRE	LAODICEAN	LETTERING
JACK-TOWEL	KILOMETRE	LARCENOUS	LEUCOCYTE
JACQUERIE	KINGCRAFT	LARGENESS	LEVANTINE
JANISSARY	KINSWOMAN	LARGHETTO	LEVANTING
JANSENISM	KIPPERING	LASSITUDE	LEVELLING
JANSENIST	KITCHENER	LASTINGLY	LEVELNESS
JARRINGLY	KITTENISH	LATERALLY	LEVIATHAN
JAY-WALKER	KITTIWAKE	LATHERING	LEVITICUS
JEALOUSLY	KNAVISHLY	LATTICING	LIABILITY
JEERINGLY	KNEADABLE	LAUDATION	LIBELLING
JELLYFISH	KNEE-PIECE	LAUDATORY	LIBELLOUS
JENNETING	KNIFE-EDGE	LAUGHABLE	LIBERALLY
JESSAMINE	KNIFE-REST	LAUGHABLY	LIBERATED
JESTINGLY	KNIGHTAGE	LAUNCHING	LIBERATOR
JEWELLERY	KNIGHTING	LAUNDERER	LIBERTINE
JEWEL-LIKE	KNITTABLE	LAUNDRESS	LIBRARIAN
JITTERBUG	KNOCKDOWN	LAURELLED	LIBRATION
JOBMASTER	KNOTGRASS	LAVISHING	LICENSING
JOCULARLY	KNOWINGLY	LAWGIVING	LICHENOUS
JOINTEDLY	KNOWLEDGE	LAWLESSLY	LIFEBLOOD
JOINT-HEIR	KNUCKLING	LAWMAKING	LIFEGUARD
JOINTRESS	KYMOGRAPH	LAWMONGER	LIGHTABLE
JOLLINESS		LAWNMOWER	LIGHTENED
JOLLYBOAT		LAY-FIGURE	LIGHTLESS
JOLTINGLY			

LIGHTNESS	LOGARITHM	MACHINING	MANOEUVRE
LIGHTNING	LOGICALLY	MACHINIST	MANOMETER
LIGHTSHIP	LOGISTICS	MACROCOSM	MANY-SIDED .
LIGHT-YEAR	LOGOGRIPH	MADDENING	MARAUDING
LILACEOUS	LOGOMACHY	MADREPORE	MARCASITE
LIME-JUICE	LOINCLOTH	MAELSTROM	MARCHPANE
LIMELIGHT	LOITERING	MAFFICKED	MARESCHAL
LIMESTONE	LOLLOPING	MAGICALLY	MARGARINE
LIME-WATER	LONGCLOTH	MAGNESIAN	MARGINING
LIMITABLE	LONG-DOZEN	MAGNESIUM	MARINATED
LIMITEDLY	LONGEVITY	MAGNETISE	MARITALLY
LIMITLESS	LONG-FIELD	MAGNETISM	MARKET-DAY
LIMNOLOGY	LONGINGLY	MAGNETITE	MARKETING
LIMOUSINE	LONGITUDE	MAGNIFICO	MARMALADE
LIMPIDITY	LOOSENESS	MAGNIFIED	MARMOREAL
LIMPINGLY	LOQUACITY	MAGNITUDE	MAROONING
LINCRUSTA	LORGNETTE	MAHARANEE	MARQUETRY
LINEALITY	LOUSINESS	MAHOMEDAN	MARROWFAT
LINEAMENT	LOUTISHLY	MAILCOACH	MARROWISH
LINEATION	LOVE-APPLE	MAIL-GUARD	MARSHLAND
LINGERING	LOVE-CHILD	MAIL-TRAIN	MARSUPIAL
LION-HEART	LOVE-FEAST	MAIN-BRACE	MARTIALLY
LIONISING	LOWERMOST	MAINFRAME	MARTINMAS
LIQUATING	LOWLANDER	MAINSHEET	MARTYRING
LIQUATION	LOWLINESS	MAJORDOMO	MARTYRDOM
LIQUEFIED	LOW-MINDED	MAJORSHIP	MARVELLED
LIQUIDATE	LOW-NECKED	MAKE-PEACE	MASCULINE
LIQUIDITY	LUBRICANT	MAKESHIFT	MASSACRED
LIQUORICE	LUBRICATE	MALACHITE	MASSAGING
LIQUORISH	LUBRICITY	MALADROIT	MASSIVELY
LISPINGLY	LUBRICOUS	MALARIOUS	MASTERDOM
LISTENING	LUCIDNESS	MALFORMED	MASTERFUL
LITERALLY	LUCK-PENNY	MALICIOUS	MASTERING
LITERATIM	LUCRATIVE	MALIGNING	MASTICATE
LITHENESS	LUCUBRATE	MALIGNANT	MATCHLESS
LITHESOME	LUCULLIAN	MALIGNITY	MATCHLOCK
LITHOLOGY	LUDICROUS	MALLEABLE	MATCHWOOD
LITHOTINT	LUMBERMAN	MALLEOLUS	MATERNITY
LITHOTYPE	LUMBRICAL	MALMAISON	MATRIARCH
LITIGABLE	LUMPISHLY	MAMMALIAN	MATRICIDE
LITIGATED	LUNISOLAR	MAMMALOGY	MATRIMONY
LITIGIOUS	LUSTFULLY	MANNIFORM	MATRONAGE
LITTERING	LUSTINESS	MANACLING	MATTERING
LITURGIST	LUXURIANT	MAN-AT-ARMS	MAULSTICK
LIVERWORT	LUXURIATE	MANCUNIAN	MAUNDERED
LIVERYMAN	LUXURIOUS	MANDATORY	MAUSOLEUM
LIVIDNESS	LYMPHATIC	MANDOLINE	MAWKISHLY
LOADSTONE		MANDUCATE	MAXILLARY
LOAF-SUGAR	**M – 9**	MANGANESE	MAXIMISED
LOATHSOME		MANGINESS	MAYFLOWER
LOBSCOUSE	MACCABEAN	MANHANDLE	MAYORALTY
LOCKSMITH	MACCABEES	MANIFESTO	MEADOW-RUE
LOCOMOTOR	MACEDOINE	MANLINESS	MEALINESS
LODESTONE	MACERATED	MANNEQUIN	MEANDERED
LODGEABLE	MACHINATE	MANNERISM	MEANINGLY
LOFTINESS	MACHINERY	MANNISHLY	MEANWHILE

MEASURING	METALLOID	MINIATURE	MOCKINGLY
MEATINESS	METAMERIC	MINIMISED	MODELLING
MECHANICS	METAPLASM	MINT-JULEP	MODERATED
MECHANISE	METEROID	MINT-SAUCE	MODERATOR
MECHANIST	METHODISM	MINUTE-GUN	MODERNISE
MEDALLION	METHODIST	MIRRORING	MODERNISM
MEDALLIST	METHOUGHT	MIRTHLESS	MODERNIST
MEDIAEVAL	METHYLATE	MISALLIED	MODERNITY
MEDIATING	METHYLENE	MISATTEND	MODIFYING
MEDIATION	METROLOGY	MISBECAME	MODULATED
MEDIATORY	METRONOME	MISBECOME	MODULATOR
MEDICABLE	MEZZANINE	MISBEHAVE	MOISTENED
MEDICALLY	MEZZOTINT	MISBELIEF	MOISTNESS
MEDICATED	MICACEOUS	MISCALLED	MOLECULAR
MEDICINAL	MICROBIAL	MISCHANCE	MOLE-SHREW
MEDULLARY	MICROCHIP	MISCREANT	MOLESTING
MEGAPHONE	MICROCOSM	MISDATING	MOLETRACK
MEGASCOPE	MICROFILM	MISDIRECT	MOLLIFIED
MELANOSIS	MICROTOME	MISEMPLOY	MOLLUSCAN
MELIORISM	MICROVOLT	MISERABLE	MOMENTARY
MELLOWING	MICROWAVE	MISERABLY	MOMENTOUS
MELODIOUS	MIDDLEMAN	MISFORMED	MONARCHAL
MELODRAMA	MIDDLINGS	MISGIVING	MONARCHIC
MELPOMENE	MIDINETTE	MISGOTTEN	MONASTERY
MELTINGLY	MID-STREAM	MISGOVERN	MONDAYISH
MEMORABLE	MID-SUMMER	MISGUIDED	MONETISED
MEMORABLY	MIDWIFERY	MISHANDLE	MONEYLESS
MEMORANDA	MIDWINTER	MISINFORM	MONEYWORT
MEMORISED	MIGRATING	MISJOINED	MONGERING
MENAGERIE	MIGRATION	MISJUDGED	MONGOLIAN
MENDACITY	MIGRATORY	MISLAYING	MONKEYING
MENDELIAN	MILDEWING	MISMANAGE	MONKEY-NUT
MENDELISM	MILESTONE	MISMARKED	MONKSHOOD
MENDICANT	MILITANCY	MISNAMING	MONOBASIC
MENDICITY	MILITATED	MISPLACED	MONOCHORD
MENNONITE	MILK-FEVER	MISQUOTED	MONOCOQUE
MENSHEVIK	MILK-FLOAT	MISRATING	MONOCULAR
MENTALITY	MILKINESS	MISREPORT	MONODRAMA
MENTIONED	MILK-PUNCH	MISRULING	MONOGRAPH
MERCENARY	MILK-TOOTH	MISSHAPED	MONOLOGUE
MERCILESS	MILK-VETCH	MISSHAPEN	MONOMANIA
MERCURIAL	MILLBOARD	MISSIONER	MONOMETER
MERCUROUS	MILLENARY	MISSTATED	MONOPLANE
MERCY-SEAT	MILLENIAL	MISTAKING	MONOTONIC
MERGANSER	MILLEPEDE	MISTAUGHT	MONOTREME
MERRIMENT	MILLIGRAM	MISTIMING	MONSIGNOR
MERRINESS	MILLINERY	MISTINESS	MONSTROUS
MESMERISE	MILLIONTH	MISTITLED	MOODINESS
MESMERISM	MILLIPEDE	MISTLETOE	MOON-DAISY
MESSENGER	MILLSTONE	MISTUNING	MOONLIGHT
MESSIANIC	MILL-WHEEL	MITHRAISM	MOONRAKER
MESSINESS	MIMICKING	MITIGATED	MOONSHINE
METABOLIC	MINCEMEAT	MNEMONICS	MOONSHINY
METALLING	MINCINGLY	MNEMOSYNE	MOONSTONE
METALLISE	MINEFIELD	MOANFULLY	MORALISED
METALLIST	MINELAYER	MOBILISED	MORBIDITY

MORDACITY	MUSK-SHREW	NERVOUSLY	NOXIOUSLY
MORDANTLY	MUSSULMAN	NEURALGIA	NULLIFIED
MORMONISM	MUSTACHIO	NEURALGIC	NUMBERING
MORTALITY	MUSTERING	NEURATION	NUMERABLE
MORTGAGED	MUSTINESS	NEUROLOGY	NUMERALLY
MORTGAGEE	MUTILATED	NEUROPATH	NUMERATED
MORTGAGOR	MUTINYING	NEUROTOMY	NUMERATOR
MORTIFIED	MUTUALITY	NEUTRALLY	NUMERICAL
MORTISING	MUZZINESS	NEVERMORE	NURSEMAID
MOSCHATEL	MYSTICISM	NEWSPAPER	NURTURING
MOSS-GROWN	MYSTIFIED	NEWTONIAN	NUTRIMENT
MOSSINESS	MYTHICISE	NICKNAMED	NUTRITION
MOTHERING	MYTHOLOGY	NICTITATE	NUTRITIVE
MOTIONING		NIGGARDLY	NUTTINESS
MOTOR-BOAT		NIGHT-CLUB	NYSTAGMUS
MOULDABLE	**N – 9**	NIGHTFALL	
MOULDERED		NIGHT-GOWN	**O – 9**
MOULD-LOFT	NAILBRUSH	NIGHT-HAWK	
MOULD-WARP	NAKEDNESS	NIGHT-LESS	OAST-HOUSE
MOUND-BIRD	NAMEPLATE	NIGHT-LINE	OBBLIGATO
MOUNTABLE	NARCISSUS	NIGHTMARE	OBEDIENCE
MOUSE-HOLE	NARRATING	NIGHT-SOIL	OBEISANCE
MOUSE-HUNT	NARRATION	NINETIETH	OBESENESS
MOUSE-TAIL	NARRATIVE	NIPPINGLY	OBEYINGLY
MOUSETRAP	NARROWING	NITRIFIED	OBFUSCATE
MOUSTACHE	NASALISED	NOBLENESS	OBJECTIFY
MOUTHLESS	NASEBERRY	NOCTURNAL	OBJECTION
MUCKINESS	NASTINESS	NOISELESS	OBJECTIVE
MUCKSWEAT	NATURALLY	NOISINESS	OBJURGATE
MUDDINESS	NAUGHTILY	NOISOMELY	OBLIGATED
MULLIONED	NAUSEATED	NOMINALLY	OBLIQUELY
MULTIFORM	NAVELWORT	NOMINATED	OBLIQUITY
MULTITUDE	NAVICULAR	NOMINATOR	OBLIVIOUS
MUMCHANCE	NAVIGABLE	NONENTITY	OBLONGISH
MUMMIFIED	NAVIGATED	NONILLION	OBNOXIOUS
MUMMIFORM	NAVIGATOR	NONPAREIL	OBSCENELY
MUNDANELY	NECESSARY	NON-SEXUAL	OBSCENITY
MUNICIPAL	NECESSITY	NONSUIITED	OBSCURANT
MUNITIONS	NECKCLOTH	NORMALISE	OBSCURELY
MURDERING	NECKLACED	NORMALITY	OBSCURING
MURDERESS	NECK-PIECE	NORTH-EAST	OBSCURITY
MURDEROUS	NECTARINE	NORTHERLY	OBSEQUIAL
MURKINESS	NEEDFULLY	NORTHWARD	OBSERVANT
MURMURING	NEEDINESS	NORTH-WEST	OBSERVING
MURMUROUS	NEEDLEFUL	NORWEGIAN	OBSESSION
MUSCADINE	NEEDLE-GUN	NOSEPIECE	OBSTETRIC
MUSCOVITE	NEFARIOUS	NOSTALGIA	OBSTINACY
MUSEFULLY	NEGATIVED	NOSTALGIC	OBSTINATE
MUSHINESS	NEGLECTED	NOTEPAPER	OBTAINING
MUSICALLY	NEGLIGENT	NOTIFYING	OBTRUDING
MUSIC-BOOK	NEGOTIATE	NOTORIETY	OBTRUSION
MUSIC-HALL	NEGROHEAD	NOTORIOUS	OBTRUSIVE
MUSK-APPLE	NEIGHBOUR	NOURISHED	OBVERSION
MUSKETEER	NEOLITHIC	NOVELETTE	OBVERSELY
MUSKINESS	NEPENTHES	NOVICIATE	OBVERTING
MUSK-MELON	NEPTUNIAN	NOVITIATE	OBVIATING
	NERVELESS		

OBVIOUSLY	ORANGEADE	OUTWORKED	PALANQUIN
OCCIPITAL	ORANGEMAN	OVERACTED	PALATABLE
OCCLUDING	ORANGE-PIP	OVERAWING	PALAVERED
OCCLUSION	ORATORIAL	OVERBLOWN	PALE-FACED
OCCULTISM	ORBICULAR	OVERBOARD	PALISADED
OCCUPANCY	ORCHESTRA	OVERBUILD	PALLADIAN
OCCUPYING	ORCHIDIST	OVERCLOUD	PALLADIUM
OCCURRING	ORDAINING	OVERCROWD	PALLIASSE
OCTAGONAL	ORDINANCE	OVERDOING	PALLIATED
OCTENNIAL	ORGANZINE	OVERDOSED	PALM-HOUSE
OCTILLION	ORGIASTIC	OVERDRAFT	PALMISTRY
ODALISQUE	ORIENTATE	OVERDRAWN	PALPITATE
ODDFELLOW	ORIFLAMME	OVERDRIVE	PAMPERING
ODOROUSLY	ORIGINATE	OVERHASTY	PANCAKING
ODOURLESS	ORPHANAGE	OVERJOYED	PANDERING
OENOTHERA	ORTHODOXY	OVERLADEN	PANEGYRIC
OFFENSIVE	OSCILLATE	OVERLEAPT	PANELLING
OFFERABLE	OSCULATED	OVERLYING	PANHANDLE
OFFERTORY	OSSIFYING	OVERNIGHT	PANOPLIED
OFFHANDED	OSTEOLOGY	OVERPOWER	PANORAMIC
OFFICERED	OSTEOPATH	OVERPROOF	PANSLAVIC
OFFICIANT	OSTRACISE	OVERRATED	PANTALOON
OFFICIATE	OTHERNESS	OVERREACH	PANTHEISM
OFFICINAL	OTHERWISE	OVERRULED	PANTHEIST
OFFICIOUS	OUT-AND-OUT	OVERSHOOT	PANTINGLY
OFFSPRING	OUTBRAVED	OVERSIGHT	PANTOMIME
OFTENNESS	OUTERMOST	OVERSLEEP	PAPER-MILL
OIL-COLOUR	OUTFACING	OVERSPEND	PAPILLARY
OIL-ENGINE	OUTGROWTH	OVERSTATE	PARABOLIC
OLEOGRAPH	OUT-JOCKEY	OVERSTOCK	PARACHUTE
OLEOMETER	OUTLANDER	OVERTAKEN	PARACLETE
OLEORESIN	OUTLASTED	OVERTHROW	PARAGRAPH
OLFACTORY	OUTLAWING	OVERTRUMP	PARALYSED
OLIGARCHY	OUTLEAPED	OVERVALUE	PARALYSIS
OLIGOCENE	OUTLINING	OVERWHELM	PARALYTIC
OLIVE-YARD	OUTLIVING	OVERWOUND	PARAMOUNT
OMBUDSMAN	OUTMANNED	OVIPAROUS	PARASITIC
OMINOUSLY	OUTNUMBER	OWNERSHIP	PARATAXIS
OMISSIBLE	OUT-OF-DOOR	OXIDATION	PARBOILED
ON-LICENCE	OUTPACING	OXIDISING	PARBUCKLE
ONSETTING	OUTPLAYED	OXYGENATE	PARCELLED
ONSLAUGHT	OUTRAGING	OXYGENIZE	PARCHMENT
OPALESCED	OUTRANGED	OXYGENOUS	PARDONING
OPALISING	OUTRIDDEN	OYSTER-BED	PAREGORIC
OPERATING	OUTRIDING		PARENTAGE
OPERATION	OUTRIGGED		PARGETING
OPERATISE	OUTRIGGER	**P – 9**	PARHELION
OPERATIVE	OUTSAILED		PARLEYING
OPPORTUNE	OUTSPOKEN	PACEMAKER	PARLEYVOO
OPPOSABLE	OUTSPREAD	PACHYDERM	PAROCHIAL
OPPRESSED	OUTSTARED	PACIFYING	PARODYING
OPPRESSOR	OUT-TALKED	PACKETING	PAROTITIS
OPTOMETER	OUTVALUED	PACKHORSE	PARQUETRY
OPTOPHONE	OUTVOTING	PADLOCKED	PARRICIDE
OPULENTLY	OUTWARDLY	PAGANISED	PARSIMONY
OPUSCULUM	OUTWITTED	PAGEANTRY	PARSONAGE
		PAINFULLY	

PARTAKING	PENHOLDER	PERSPIRED	PILFERING
PARTHENON	PENINSULA	PERSUADED	PILLAR-BOX
PARTIALLY	PENITENCE	PERTAINED	PILLORIED
PARTITION	PENNIFORM	PERTINENT	PILLOWING
PARTITIVE	PENNILESS	PERTURBED	PILOT-BOAT
PARTNERED	PENNYWISE	PERVADING	PILOTFISH
PARTRIDGE	PENNYWORT	PERVASION	PIMPERNEL
PASSENGER	PENSIONED	PERVASIVE	PINCHBECK
PASSERINE	PENSIONER	PERVERTED	PINEAPPLE
PASSIVELY	PENSIVELY	PESSIMISM	PINIONING
PASSIVITY	PENTAGRAM	PESSIMIST	PINNACLED
PASTORALE	PENTECOST	PESTERING	PIONEERED
PASTURAGE	PENTHOUSE	PESTILENT	PIPESTONE
PASTURING	PENURIOUS	PESTOLOGY	PIPISTREL
PATCHOULI	PEPPERBOX	PETERSHAM	PIQUANTLY
PATCHWORK	PEPPERING	PETRIFIED	PIRATICAL
PATENTING	PERCEIVED	PETROLEUM	PIROUETTE
PATERNITY	PERCHANCE	PETTICOAT	PISCATORY
PATHOLOGY	PERCHERON	PETTINESS	PISCIFORM
PATIENTLY	PERCOLATE	PETTISHLY	PISTACHIO
PATRIARCH	PERCUSSED	PETULANCE	PITCHFORK
PATRICIAN	PERDITION	PHAGOCYTE	PITCH-PINE
PATRICIDE	PEREGRINE	PHALANGER	PITCHPIPE
PATRIMONY	PERENNIAL	PHALAROPE	PITEOUSLY
PATRIOTIC	PERFECTED	PHARISAIC	PITHECOID
PATRISTIC	PERFECTLY	PHENOMENA	PITHINESS
PATROLLED	PERFERVID	PHILANDER	PITIFULLY
PATRONAGE	PERFORATE	PHILATELY	PITUITARY
PATRONESS	PERFORMED	PHILIPPIC	PITYINGLY
PATRONISE	PERFORMER	PHILOLOGY	PIZZICATO
PATTERING	PERFUMERY	PHLEBITIS	PLACARDED
PATTERNED	PERFUMING	PHONETICS	PLACATING
PAUPERISE	PERIMETER	PHONOGRAM	PLACE-KICK
PAUSINGLY	PERIPHERY	PHONOLOGY	PLACIDITY
PAYMASTER	PERISCOPE	PHOSPHATE	PLAINNESS
PEACEABLE	PERISHING	PHOSPHINE	PLAINSONG
PEACEABLY	PERISTYLE	PHOSPHITE	PLAINTIFF
PEA-JACKET	PERJURING	PHOTOCELL	PLAINTIVE
PEARLWORT	PERMANENT	PHOTO-PLAY	PLANE-IRON
PEASANTRY	PERMEABLE	PHOTOSTAT	PLANETARY
PECULATED	PERMEABLY	PHRENETIC	PLANETOID
PECUNIARY	PERMEATED	PHYSICIAN	PLANTABLE
PEDAGOGIC	PERMITTED	PHYSICIST	PLASTERED
PEDAGOGUE	PERMUTING	PHYSICKED	PLASTERER
PEDALLING	PERORATED	PICKABACK	PLATEMARK
PEDICULAR	PERPENDED	PICKETING	PLATE-RACK
PEDOMETER	PERPETUAL	PICTORIAL	PLATINISE
PEEVISHLY	PERPLEXED	PICTURING	PLATITUDE
PEKINGESE	PERSECUTE	PIECEMEAL	PLATONISE
PELLITORY	PERSEVERE	PIECE-WORK	PLATONISM
PENALISED	PERSIMMON	PIER-GLASS	PLATONIST
PEN-AND-INK	PERSISTED	PIETISTIC	PLAUSIBLE
PENCILLED	PERSONAGE	PIGHEADED	PLAUSIBLY
PENDRAGON	PERSONATE	PIGMENTAL	PLAY-ACTOR
PENDULOUS	PERSONIFY	PIGNORATE	PLAYFULLY
PENETRATE	PERSONNEL	PIKESTAFF	PLAYGOING

PLAYHOUSE	PONDEROUS	PRECEDING	PRETENDER
PLAYTHING	POOR-HOUSE	PRECENTOR	PRETERITE
PLEACHING	POPPYCOCK	PRECEPTOR	PRETTYISH
PLEASANCE	POPULARLY	PRECIPICE	PREVAILED
PLENARILY	POPULATED	PRECISELY	PREVALENT
PLENITUDE	PORBEAGLE	PRECISIAN	PREVENTED
PLENTEOUS	PORCELAIN	PRECISION	PREVISION
PLENTIFUL	PORCUPINE	PRECLUDED	PRICELESS
PLEURITIC	PORRINGER	PRECOCITY	PRICKLING
PLIGHTING	PORTATIVE	PRECURSOR	PRIDELESS
PLINTHITE	PORTENDED	PREDATING	PRIESTESS
PLOUGHBOY	PORTERAGE	PREDATORY	PRIMARILY
PLOUGHING	PORTERESS	PREDESIGN	PRIMATIAL
PLOUGHMAN	PORTFOLIO	PREDICANT	PRIMITIVE
PLUMBLINE	PORTRAYAL	PREDICATE	PRINCEDOM
PLUMB-RULE	PORTRAYED	PREDICTED	PRINCIPAL
PLUMELESS	POSSESSED	PREDOOMED	PRINCIPIA
PLUMPNESS	POSSESSOR	PRE-ENGAGE	PRINCIPLE
PLUNDERED	POST-DATED	PREFACING	PRINTLESS
PLURALISE	POST-ENTRY	PREFATORY	PRINTSHOP
PLURALISM	POSTERIOR	PREFERRED	PRISMATIC
PLURALIST	POSTERITY	PREFIGURE	PRIVATEER
PLURALITY	POST-HASTE	PREFIXING	PRIVATELY
PLUS-FOURS	POST-NATAL	PREFORMED	PRIVATION
PLUTOCRAT	POSTPONED	PREGNANCY	PRIVILEGE
PLUTONIUM	POSTULANT	PREJUDGED	PROBATION
PNEUMATIC	POSTULATE	PREJUDICE	PROBATIVE
PNEUMONIA	POSTURING	PRELATURE	PROBOSCIS
PNEUMONIC	POTASSIUM	PRELUDING	PROCEDURE
POCKETING	POTBOILER	PRELUSIVE	PROCEEDED
POETASTER	POTENTATE	PREMATURE	PROCESSED
POIGNANCY	POTENTIAL	PREMISING	PROCLITIC
POINTEDLY	POT-POURRI	PREMOTION	PRO-CONSUL
POINTLESS	POTTERING	PREOCCUPY	PROCREANT
POINTSMAN	POULTERER	PREOPTION	PROCREATE
POISONOUS	POULTICED	PREORDIAN	PROCURING
POKERWORK	POUNCE-BOX	PREPACKED	PRODUCING
POLARIZED	POURBOIRE	PREPARING	PROFANELY
POLEMICAL	POURPOINT	PREPAYING	PROFANING
POLE-VAULT	POWDER-BOX	PRESAGING	PROFANITY
POLICEMAN	POWDERING	PRESBYTER	PROFESSED
POLISHING	POWERLESS	PRESCIENT	PROFESSOR
POLITESSE	POWER-LOOM	PRESCRIBE	PROFFERED
POLITICAL	POWWOWING	PRESCRIPT	PROFILING
POLLINATE	PRACTICAL	PRESENTED	PROFITEER
POLLUTING	PRACTISED	PRESENTLY	PROFITING
POLLUTION	PRAGMATIC	PRESERVED	PROFUSELY
POLONAISE	PRATINGLY	PRESERVER	PROFUSION
POLYANDRY	PRATTLING	PRESIDENT	PROGNOSIS
POLYGONAL	PRAYERFUL	PRESIDING	PROGRAMME
POLYSTYLE	PRAYINGLY	PRESSGANG	PROJECTED
POMMELLED	PREACHIFY	PRESSMARK	PROJECTOR
POMPADOUR	PREACHING	PRESS-ROOM	PROLIXITY
POMPOSITY	PREAMBLED	PRESSWORK	PROLOGUED
POMPOUSLY	PREBENDAL	PRESUMING	PROLONGED
PONDERING	PRECEDENT	PRETENDED	PROMENADE

PROMINENT	PUBLISHER	PYROMETER	RABBITING
PROMISING	PUCKERING	PYROXYLIC	RABIDNESS
PROMOTING	PUERILELY	PYROXYLIN	RACEHORSE
PROMOTION	PUERILITY		RACIALISM
PROMPTING	PUERPERAL		RACKETEER
PRONENESS	PUFF-ADDER	Q – 9	RACKETING
PRONOUNCE	PUFFINESS	QUADRATIC	RACONTEUR
PROOFLESS	PUFFINGLY	QUADRATED	RADIALITY
PROPAGATE	PUGNACITY	QUADRILLE	RADIANTLY
PROPELLED	PUISSANCE	QUADRUPED	RADIATING
PROPELLER	PULLULATE	QUADRUPLE	RADIATION
PROPHETIC	PULMONARY	QUAKERISH	RADIATIVE
PROPONENT	PULMONATE	QUAKERISM	RADICALLY
PROPOSING	PULPINESS	QUAKINGLY	RADIOGRAM
PROPRIETY	PULSATING	QUALIFIED	RADIOLOGY
PROROGUED	PULSATILE	QUARRYING	RAFTERING
PROSCRIBE	PULSATION	QUARRYMAN	RAG-PICKER
PROSECUTE	PULSATIVE	QUARTERED	RAIL-FENCE
PROSELYTE	PULSATORY	QUARTERLY	RAILINGLY
PROSINESS	PULSELESS	QUARTETTE	RAIN-GAUGE
PROSODIST	PULVERISE	QUARTZITE	RAININESS
PROSPERED	PUNCHBOWL	QUASIMODO	RAINPROOF
PROSTRATE	PUNCTILIO	QUAVERING	RAIN-WATER
PROTECTED	PUNCTUATE	QUEEN-POST	RAMIFYING
PROTECTOR	PUNCTURED	QUEERNESS	RAMPAGING
PROTESTED	PUNGENTLY	QUENCHING	RAMPANTLY
PROTHESIS	PUNISHING	QUERULOUS	RAMPARTED
PROTOTYPE	PUPILLARY	QUIBBLING	RANCIDITY
PROTOZOAN	PUPPYHOOD	QUICKENED	RANCOROUS
PROTOZOIC	PURCHASED	QUICKLIME	RANSACKED
PROTRUDED	PURCHASER	QUICKNESS	RANSOMING
PROUDNESS	PURGATION	QUICKSAND	RANTINGLY
PROVENDER	PURGATIVE	QUICKSTEP	RAPACIOUS
PROVIDENT	PURGATORY	QUICK-TIME	RAPIDNESS
PROVIDING	PURIFYING	QUIESCENT	RAPTORIAL
PROVISION	PURITANIC	QUIESCING	RAPTUROUS
PROVISORY	PURLOINED	QUIETENED	RAREE-SHOW
PROVOKING	PURPORTED	QUIETNESS	RAREFYING
PROXIMATE	PURPOSELY	QUINQUINA	RASCALITY
PROXIMITY	PURPOSING	QUINTETTE	RASPATORY
PRUDENTLY	PURPOSIVE	QUINTUPLE	RASPBERRY
PRUDISHLY	PURSUANCE	QUITCLAIM	RATEPAYER
PRURIENCE	PURULENCE	QUITTABLE	RATIONALE
PRURIENCY	PURVEYING	QUITTANCE	RATIONING
PSALMODIC	PUSHINGLY	QUIVERING	RAVELLING
PSEUDONYM	PUSTULATE	QUIXOTISM	RAVISHING
PSORIASIS	PUTREFIED	QUIZZICAL	RAZORBACK
PSYCHICAL	PUTRIDITY	QUOTATION	RAZORBILL
PSYCHOSIS	PUZZLEDOM	QUOTELESS	RAZOREDGE
PTARMIGAN	PYORRHOEA		RAZORFISH
PTOLEMAIC	PYRACANTH		REACHABLE
PUBESCENT	PYRAMIDAL	R – 9	REACTANCE
PUBLICISE	PYROGENIC	RABBETING	READDRESS
PUBLICIST	PYROLATRY	RABBINATE	READINESS
PUBLICITY	PYROMANCY	RABBINISM	READJOURN
PUBLISHED	PYROMANIA	RABBINIST	READOPTED

READORNED	RECONDITE	REFERRING	REISSUING
READY-MADE	RECONFIRM	REFILLING	REITERATE
REALISING	RECONQUER	REFINEDLY	REJECTING
REALISTIC	RECONVENE	REFITMENT	REJECTION
REALLEGED	RECONVERT	REFITTING	REJECTIVE
REANIMATE	RECORDING	REFLECTED	REJOICING
REANNEXED	RECOUNTED	REFLOATED	REJOINDER
REAPPLIED	RECOUPING	REFLOWING	REJOINING
REAPPOINT	RECOVERED	REFOLDING	REJOINTED
REARGUARD	RECREANCY	REFORGING	REJUDGING
REARRANGE	RECREATED	REFORMING	REKINDLED
REASONING	RECREMENT	REFORMIST	RELANDING
REASSURED	RECROSSED	REFORTIFY	RELAPSING
REAVOWING	RECRUITED	RE-FOUNDED	RELAXABLE
REBAPTISE	RECTANGLE	REFRACTED	RELEASING
REBELLING	RECTIFIED	REFRACTOR	RELEGATED
REBELLION	RECTIFIER	REFRAINED	RELENTING
REBINDING	RECTITUDE	REFRAMING	RELETTING
REBLOOMED	RECTORATE	REFRESHED	RELEVANCE
REBOILING	RECTORIAL	REFRESHER	RELEVANCY
REBOUNDED	RECUMBENT	REFULGENT	RELIEVING
REBUFFING	RECURRENT	REFUNDING	RELIGIOUS
REBURYING	RECURRING	REFURBISH	RELIQUARY
REBUTTING	RECURVATE	REFURNISH	RELISHING
RECALLING	RECURVING	REFUSABLE	RELOADING
RECANTING	REDACTING	REFUTABLE	RELUCTANT
RECAPTURE	REDACTION	REGAINING	REMAINDER
RECASTING	REDBREAST	REGARDANT	REMAINING
RECEIPTED	REDDENING	REGARDFUL	REMANDING
RECEIVING	REDEEMING	REGARDING	REMANNING
RECENSION	REDELIVER	REGICIDAL	REMARKING
RECEPTION	RED-HANDED	REGILDING	REMARRIED
RECEPTIVE	REDINGOTE	REGISTRAR	REMEDYING
RECESSING	RED-LETTER	REGORGING	REMINDFUL
RECESSION	REDOLENCE	REGRANTED	REMINDING
RECESSIVE	REDOUBLED	REGRADING	REMISSION
RECHARGED	REDOUBTED	REGRETFUL	REMISSIVE
RECHERCHE	REDOUNDED	REGRETTED	REMITTING
RECIPIENT	REDRAFTED	REGULARLY	REMOULDED
RECKONING	REDRAWING	REGULATED	REMOUNTED
RECLAIMED	REDRESSED	REGULATOR	REMOVABLE
RECLINATE	REDUCIBLE	REHANDLED	RENASCENT
RECLINING	REDUCTION	REHANGING	RENDERING
RECLOSING	REDUNDANT	REHASHING	RENDITION
RECLOTHED	RE-ECHOING	REHEARING	RENEWABLE
RECOALING	RE-ELECTED	REHEARSAL	RENOVATED
RECOASTED	RE-EMERGED	REHEARSED	RENOVATOR
RECOGNISE	RE-ENACTED	RE-HEATING	REOPENING
RECOILING	RE-ENFORCE	REHOUSING	REORDERED
RECOINING	RE-ENTERED	REICHSTAG	REPACKING
RECOLLECT	RE-ENTRANT	RE-IGNITED	REPAINTED
RECOMBINE	RE-EXAMINE	REIMBURSE	REPAIRING
RECOMMEND	REFASHION	REINFORCE	REPARABLE
RECOMPILE	REFECTION	REINSTALL	REPARABLY
RECOMPOSE	REFECTORY	REINSTATE	REPASSING
RECONCILE	REFERENCE	REINSURED	REPASTING

REPAYABLE	RESERVIST	RETRACTOR	RING-STAND
REPAYMENT	RESETTING	RETREATED	RIOTOUSLY
REPEALING	RESETTLED	RETRIEVED	RITUALISM
REPEATING	RESHIPPED	RETRIEVER	RITUALIST
REPELLENT	RESIDENCE	RETRIMMED	RIVALLING
REPELLING	RESIDENCY	RETROCEDE	RIVERSIDE
REPENTANT	RESIDUARY	RETRODDEN	ROAD-HOUSE
REPENTING	RESIGNING	RETROFLEX	ROADSTEAD
REPERTORY	RESILIENT	RETROUSSE	ROARINGLY
REPLACING	RESISTANT	RETROVERT	ROCK-BASIN
REPLAITED	RESISTING	RETURNING	ROCK-BOUND
REPLANTED	RESOLUBLE	REUNIFIED	ROCK-CRESS
REPLEDGED	RESOLVENT	REUNITING	ROCKETING
REPLENISH	RESOLVING	REVALUING	ROCKINESS
REPLETION	RESONANCE	REVAMPING	ROGUISHLY
REPLY-PAID	RESONATED	REVEALING	ROISTERED
REPOINTED	RESONATOR	REVELLING	ROISTERER
REPORTAGE	RESORBENT	REVENGING	ROLLICKED
REPORTING	RESORBING	REVERENCE	ROMANCING
REPOSEFUL	RESORTING	REVERSELY	ROMANISED
REPOSSESS	RESOUNDED	REVERSING	ROMPISHLY
REPOTTING	RESPECTED	REVERSION	ROOMINESS
REPREHEND	RESPECTER	REVERTING	ROOTSTOCK
REPRESENT	RE-SPELLED	REVETMENT	ROPEMAKER
REPRESSED	RESPIRING	REVETTING	ROQUEFORT
REPRIEVED	RESPONDED	REVICTUAL	ROSACEOUS
REPRIMAND	RESTAMPED	REVIEWING	ROSE-APPLE
REPRINTED	RESTATING	REVISITED	ROSE-NOBLE
REPROBATE	RESTEMMED	REVIVABLE	ROSE-WATER
REPRODUCE	RESTFULLY	REVOCABLE	ROSINANTE
REPROVING	REST-HOUSE	REVOCABLY	ROTOGRAPH
REPRUNING	RESTIVELY	REVOLTING	ROTUNDITY
REPTILIAN	RESTOCKED	REVOLVING	ROUGHCAST
REPUBLISH	RESTORING	REVULSION	ROUGHENED
REPUDIATE	RESTRAINT	REVULSIVE	ROUGH-HEWN
REPUGNANT	RESULTANT	REWARDING	ROUGHNESS
REPULSING	RESULTING	REWORDING	ROUGHSHOD
REPULSION	RESURGENT	REWRITING	ROUNDED-UP
REPULSIVE	RESURRECT	REWRITTEN	ROUNDELAY
REPUTABLE	RETAILING	RHAPSODIC	ROUNDHEAD
REPUTABLY	RETAINING	RHEUMATIC	ROUNDNESS
REPUTEDLY	RETALIATE	RHINOLOGY	ROUNDSMAN
REQUESTED	RETARDING	RHUMB-LINE	ROUSINGLY
REQUIRING	RETENTION	RHYMELESS	ROWDINESS
REQUISITE	RETENTIVE	RHYMESTER	ROWELLING
REQUITING	RETEXTURE	RICE-PAPER	RUDDINESS
RE-READING	RETICENCE	RIDERLESS	RUFFIANLY
RESCINDED	RETICULAR	RIDGE-POLE	RUINATION
RE-SCORING	RETICULUM	RIDICULED	RUINOUSLY
RESEATING	RETORTING	RIGHTEOUS	RUMINATED
RESECTION	RETORTION	RIGHT-HAND	RUMMAGING
RESELLING	RETORTIVE	RIGHTNESS	RUMOURING
RESEMBLED	RETOSSING	RIGMAROLE	RUPTURING
RESENDING	RETOUCHED	RING-FENCE	RUSSOPHIL
RESENTFUL	RETRACING	RINGLETED	RUSTICATE
RESERVING	RETRACTED	RING-OUZEL	RUSTICITY

RUSTINESS	SAPIDNESS	SCORCHING	SECLUSION
RUTHENIUM	SAPIENTLY	SCORIFIED	SECLUSIVE
	SAPPINESS	SCOTCHING	SECONDARY
S – 9	SARCASTIC	SCOTCHMAN	SECONDING
	SARTORIAL	SCOUNDREL	SECRETARY
SACCHARIC	SASSAFRAS	SCRAGGILY	SECRETING
SACCHARIN	SASSENACH	SCRAGGING	SECRETION
SACKCLOTH	SATELLITE	SCRAMBLED	SECRETIVE
SACRAMENT	SATIATING	SCRAMBLER	SECRETORY
SACRARIUM	SATIATION	SCRAPPING	SECTARIAL
SACRIFICE	SATINWOOD	SCRAPBOOK	SECTARIAN
SACRILEGE	SATIRICAL	SCRAP-HEAP	SECTIONAL
SACRISTAN	SATIRISED	SCRATCHED	SECULARLY
SADDENING	SATISFIED	SCRAWLING	SEDENTARY
SADDLE-BAG	SATURATED	SCREAMING	SEDITIOUS
SADDLEBOW	SATURNIAN	SCREECHED	SEDUCTION
SAFEGUARD	SATURNINE	SCREENING	SEDUCTIVE
SAFETY-PIN	SAUCEBOAT	SCREWBALL	SEED-GRAIN
SAFFLOWER	SAUCINESS	SCRIBBLED	SEEDINESS
SAFFRONED	SAUNTERER	SCRIBBLER	SEED-PEARL
SAGACIOUS	SAVOURING	SCRIMMAGE	SEEMINGLY
SAGE-BRUSH	SAVOURILY	SCRIMPING	SEE-SAWING
SAGITTATE	SAXIFRAGE	SCRIMSHAW	SEGMENTAL
SAILCLOTH	SAXOPHONE	SCRIPTURE	SEGMENTED
SAILMAKER	SCALELESS	SCRIVENER	SEGREGATE
SAILPLANE	SCALINESS	SCROLLING	SEIGNIORY
SAINT-LIKE	SCALLOPED	SCROUNGED	SELECTING
SALACIOUS	SCALLYWAG	SCROUNGER	SELECTION
SALE-PRICE	SCANTLING	SCRUBBING	SELECTIVE
SALICYLIC	SCANTNESS	SCRUM-HALF	SELFISHLY
SALIENTLY	SCAPEGOAT	SCRUMMAGE	SELVEDGED
SALIFYING	SCAPEMENT	SCRUPLING	SEMANTICS
SALIVATED	SCAPULARY	SCRUTATOR	SEMAPHORE
SALLOWISH	SCARECROW	SCUFFLING	SEMBLANCE
SALLYPORT	SCARFRING	SCULPTURE	SEMIBREVE
SALTATION	SCARIFIER	SCUMBLING	SEMICOLON
SALTATORY	SCATTERED	SCURRYING	SEMIFLUID
SALTISHLY	SCAVENGER	SCUTCHEON	SEMILUNAR
SALT-MARSH	SCENTLESS	SCUTTLING	SEMINATED
SALTPETRE	SCEPTICAL	SEA-ANCHOR	SEMIVOCAL
SALT-WATER	SCHEDULED	SEA-BREACH	SEMIVOWEL
SALUBRITY	SCHEMATIC	SEA-BREEZE	SENESCENT
SALVARSAN	SCHILLING	SEAFARING	SENESCHAL
SALVATION	SCHNORKEL	SEA-LAWYER	SENIORITY
SAMARITAN	SCHOLARLY	SEA-LETTER	SENSATION
SANCTUARY	SCHOLIAST	SEA-NETTLE	SENSELESS
SANDALLED	SCHOOLBOY	SEARCHING	SENSITISE
SAND-BLAST	SCHOOLING	SEA-ROBBER	SENSITIVE
SAND-BLIND	SCHOOLMAN	SEA-ROCKET	SENSORIAL
SANDGLASS	SCIENTIAL	SEASONING	SENSORIUM
SANDINESS	SCIENTIST	SEA-SQUIRT	SENSUALLY
SANDPAPER	SCINTILLA	SEA-URCHIN	SENTENCED
SANDPIPER	SCISSORED	SEAWORTHY	SENTIMENT
SANDSTONE	SCLEROSIS	SEBACEOUS	SENTRY-BOX
SANGFROID	SCLEROTIC	SECESSION	SEPARABLE
SANHEDRIN	SCORBUTIC	SECLUDING	SEPARABLY

SEPARATED	SHIPMONEY	SIGNALIZE	SLIGHTING
SEPARATOR	SHIPOWNER	SIGNALLED	SLIMINESS
SEPTEMBER	SHIPSHAPE	SIGNALMAN	SLIP-COACH
SEPTENARY	SHIPWRECK	SIGNATORY	SLIPPERED
SEPULCHRE	SHIRTLESS	SIGNATURE	SLITHERED
SEQUACITY	SHIVERING	SIGNBOARD	SLIVERING
SEQUESTER	SHOEBLACK	SIGNIFIED	SLOBBERED
SERENADED	SHOEBRUSH	SIGNORINA	SLOP-BASIN
SERMONISE	SHOEMAKER	SILENCING	SLOPINGLY
SERRATION	SHOPWOMAN	SILICATED	SLOUCH-HAT
SERVIETTE	SHORELESS	SILICEOUS	SLOUCHING
SERVILELY	SHOREWARD	SILKINESS	SLOUGHING
SERVILITY	SHORTCAKE	SILLINESS	SLOWCOACH
SERVITUDE	SHORTENED	SILVER-FOX	SLOW-MATCH
SESSIONAL	SHORTFALL	SILVERING	SLUMBERED
SETACEOUS	SHORTHAND	SIMILARLY	SMALL-ARMS
SET-SQUARE	SHORT-HOSE	SIMMERING	SMALL-BEER
SEVENFOLD	SHORTNESS	SIMPLETON	SMALLNESS
SEVENTEEN	SHORT-SLIP	SIMULATED	SMARTENED
SEVENTHLY	SHOTPROOF	SINCERELY	SMARTNESS
SEVERABLE	SHOULDERS	SINCERITY	SMILELESS
SEVERALLY	SHOVELLED	SINGINGLY	SMILINGLY
SEVERALTY	SHOVELFUL	SINGLETON	SMIRCHING
SEVERANCE	SHOVEL-HAT	SINISTRAL	SMOCKLESS
SEXENNIAL	SHOVELLER	SINLESSLY	SMOKE-BOMB
SEXUALITY	SHOWBREAD	SINUOSITY	SMOKELESS
SFORZANDO	SHOWERING	SINUOUSLY	SMOKINESS
SHACKLING	SHOWINESS	SIPHONAGE	SMOOTHING
SHADINESS	SHOW-PLACE	SIPHONING	SMOTHERED
SHADOWING	SHREW-MOLE	SISYPHEAN	SMUG-FACED
SHAFTLESS	SHRIEKING	SITUATION	SMUGGLING
SHAKEDOWN	SHRILLING	SIXFOOTER	SMUTCHING
SHAKINESS	SHRIMPING	SIXTEENTH	SNAFFLING
SHALLOWLY	SHRIMP-NET	SKEDADDLE	SNAIL-LIKE
SHAMBLING	SHRINKAGE	SKETCHILY	SNAKE-BIRD
SHAMELESS	SHRINKING	SKETCHING	SNAKE-ROOT
SHAMPOOED	SHROUDING	SKEW-WHIFF	SNAKEWEED
SHAPELESS	SHRUBBERY	SKILFULLY	SNAKE-WOOD
SHARPENED	SHRUBLESS	SKINFLINT	SNATCHING
SHARPNESS	SHRUGGING	SKYROCKET	SNICKERED
SHATTERED	SHUDDERED	SLABSTONE	SNIFFLING
SHEAR-LEGS	SHUFFLING	SLACKENED	SNIGGERED
SHEATHING	SIBILANCE	SLACKNESS	SNIVELLED
SHEEPCOTE	SIBYLLINE	SLANDERED	SNOWBERRY
SHEEPFOLD	SICCATIVE	SLANTWISE	SNOWBLIND
SHEEP-HOOK	SICKENING	SLAPSTICK	SNOW-BOUND
SHEEPSKIN	SIDEBOARD	SLATINESS	SNOWDRIFT
SHEEPWALK	SIDEBURNS	SLAUGHTER	SNOWFIELD
SHEER-HULK	SIDELIGHT	SLAVE-LIKE	SNOWFLAKE
SHELDRAKE	SIDE-TABLE	SLAVERING	SNOW-GOOSE
SHELLBACK	SIDETRACK	SLAVISHLY	SNOWSTORM
SHELLFISH	SIGHINGLY	SLAVONIAN	SNUB-NOSED
SHIELDING	SIGHTLESS	SLEEPLESS	SNUFFLING
SHIFTLESS	SIGHTSEER	SLEIGHING	SNUGGLING
SHINGLING	SIGNAL-BOX	SLENDERLY	SOAPINESS
SHINTOISM	SIGNAL-GUN	SLIDE-RULE	SOAPSTONE

SOARINGLY	SPARKLING	SPRIGGING	STARINGLY
SOBERNESS	SPASMODIC	SPRIGHTLY	STARLIGHT
SOBRIQUET	SPATTERED	SPRINGING	STAR-SHELL
SOCIALISE	SPATULATE	SPRINGBOK	STARTLING
SOCIALISM	SPEAKABLE	SPRING-GUN	STATELESS
SOCIALIST	SPEAK-EASY	SPRINKLED	STATEMENT
SOCIALITE	SPEARHEAD	SPRINKLER	STATEROOM
SOCIALITY	SPEARMINT	SPRINTING	STATESMAN
SOCIOLOGY	SPECIALLY	SPROUTING	STATIONED
SODA-WATER	SPECIALTY	SPUR-ROYAL	STATIONER
SOFTENING	SPECIFIED	SPUR-WHEEL	STATISTIC
SOJOURNED	SPECKLESS	SPUTTERED	STATUETTE
SOLARISED	SPECKLING	SQUABBLED	STATUTORY
SOLDERING	SPECTACLE	SQUALIDLY	STAUNCHED
SOLDIERLY	SPECTATOR	SQUALLING	STAYMAKER
SOLEMNISE	SPECULATE	SQUASHING	STEADFAST
SOLEMNITY	SPEECH-DAY	SQUATTING	STEADYING
SOLICITED	SPEECHFUL	SQUAWKING	STEAMBOAT
SOLICITOR	SPEECHIFY	SQUEAKING	STEAMPIPE
SOLIDNESS	SPELLABLE	SQUEALING	STEAMSHIP
SOLILOQUY	SPERMATIC	SQUEAMISH	STEEL-CLAD
SOLITAIRE	SPHERICAL	SQUEEZING	STEELYARD
SOMETHING	SPHINCTER	SQUELCHED	STEEPENED
SOMETIMES	SPICINESS	SQUIGGLED	STEEPNESS
SOMEWHERE	SPIKENARD	SQUINTING	STEERABLE
SOMNOLENT	SPILLIKIN	SQUIRMING	STEERSMAN
SONNETEER	SPINDLING	SQUIRTING	STELLATED
SOOTINESS	SPINDRIFT	STABILISE	STERILISE
SOPHISTRY	SPINELESS	STABILITY	STERILITY
SOPHOMORE	SPINNAKER	STABLEBOY	STERNMOST
SOPORIFIC	SPINNERET	STABLEMAN	STERNNESS
SORCERESS	SPIRALITY	STACKYARD	STERNPOST
SORRINESS	SPIRITING	STAGE-PLAY	STEVEDORE
SORROWFUL	SPIRITUAL	STAGGERED	STEWARDLY
SORROWING	SPLASHING	STAGHOUND	STEWARTRY
SORTILEGE	SPLAY-FOOT	STAGINESS	STIFFENED
SOSTENUTO	SPLENDOUR	STAGNANCY	STIFFENER
SOTTISHLY	SPLENETIC	STAGNATED	STIFFNESS
SOTTO-VOCE	SPLINTERY	STAIDNESS	STIGMATIC
SOUBRETTE	SPLINTING	STAINLESS	STILLBORN
SOULFULLY	SPLIT-RING	STAIRCASE	STILL-LIFE
SOUNDLESS	SPOKESMAN	STAIRHEAD	STILLNESS
SOUNDNESS	SPOLIATED	STAKE-BOAT	STILL-ROOM
SOUP-PLATE	SPONSORED	STALACTIC	STIMULANT
SOUTHDOWN	SPOON-BAIT	STALEMATE	STIMULATE
SOUTH-EAST	SPOONBILL	STALENESS	STINGLESS
SOUTHERLY	SPOON-FEED	STALKLESS	STINKBOMB
SOUTHWARD	SPORE-CASE	STAMMERED	STIPPLING
SOUTH-WEST	SPORTLESS	STAMMERER	STIPULATE
SOU'-WESTER	SPORTSMAN	STAMP-DUTY	STIRABOUT
SOVEREIGN	SPOUT-HOLE	STAMPEDED	STITCHERY
SPADEWORK	SPOUTLESS	STANCHING	STITCHING
SPAGHETTI	SPRAGGING	STANCHION	STOCKADED
SPANGLING	SPRAINING	STARBOARD	STOCKDOVE
SPARENESS	SPRAWLING	STARCHING	STOCKFISH
SPARINGLY	SPREADING	STARGAZER	STOCKINET

STOCKINGS	STRIPLING	SUCCOURED	SURROGATE
STOCKLESS	STRIPPING	SUCCULENT	SURVEYING
STOCKWHIP	STROLLING	SUCCUMBED	SURVIVING
STOCKYARD	STROMATIC	SUCKERING	SUSPECTED
STOICALLY	STRONG-BOX	SUDORIFIC	SUSPENDED
STOKEHOLD	STRONTIUM	SUFFERING	SUSPENDER
STOLIDITY	STROPPING	SUFFICING	SUSPICION
STOMACHAL	STRUCTIVE	SUFFIXING	SUSTAINED
STOMACHER	STRUGGLED	SUFFOCATE	SWADDLING
STOMACHIC	STRUMMING	SUFFRAGAN	SWAGGERED
STONECHAT	STRUTTING	SUFFUSING	SWALLOWED
STONE-COLD	STRYCHNIC	SUFFUSION	SWANSDOWN
STONECROP	STUCCOING	SUGAR-BEET	SWARTHILY
STONE-DEAD	STUD-GROOM	SUGAR-CANE	SWEET-CORN
STONE-DEAF	STUD-HORSE	SUGARLESS	SWEETENED
STONELESS	STUDIEDLY	SUGAR-LOAF	SWEETMEAT
STONE-PINE	STUMBLING	SUGAR-MILL	SWEETNESS
STONEWALL	STUPEFIED	SUGAR-MITE	SWEET-SHOP
STONINESS	STUPIDITY	SUGAR-PINE	SWELTERED
STOOL-BALL	STUTTERER	SUGARPLUM	SWIFTNESS
STOPPERED	STYLISHLY	SUGGESTED	SWIMMERET
STOP-PRESS	STYLOBATE	SULKINESS	SWINDLING
STOP-WATCH	SUBAGENCY	SULPHURIC	SWINEHERD
STOREROOM	SUBALTERN	SUMMARILY	SWING-BOAT
STORESHIP	SUBCOSTAL	SUMMARISE	SWING-DOOR
STORMCOCK	SUBDEACON	SUMMATION	SWINGEING
STORM-CONE	SUBDIVIDE	SUMMING-UP	SWINGLING
STORMSAIL	SUB-EDITOR	SUMMONING	SWINISHLY
STORTHING	SUBFAMILY	SUMPTUARY	SWITCHING
STORYBOOK	SUBJACENT	SUMPTUOUS	SWITCHMAN
STOUTNESS	SUBJECTED	SUNBONNET	SWIVEL-EYE
STOVEPIPE	SUBJOINED	SUNFLOWER	SWIVELLED
STRADDLED	SUBJUGATE	SUNSTROKE	SWORDBELT
STRAGGLED	SUBLIMATE	SUPERFINE	SWORDBILL
STRAGGLER	SUBLIMELY	SUPERHEAT	SWORD-CANE
STRAINING	SUBLIMITY	SUPERPOSE	SWORDFISH
STRANDING	SUBLUNARY	SUPERSEDE	SWORDHILT
STRANGELY	SUBMARINE	SUPERVENE	SWORD-LILY
STRANGLED	SUBMERGED	SUPERVISE	SWORDSMAN
STRANGLER	SUBMITTED	SUPPLIANT	SYBARITIC
STRAPPADO	SUBNORMAL	SUPPLYING	SYCOPHANT
STRAPPING	SUBORNING	SUPPORTED	SYLLABARY
STRAPWORK	SUBSCRIBE	SUPPORTER	SYLLABIFY
STRATAGEM	SUBSCRIPT	SUPPOSING	SYLLABLED
STRATEGIC	SUBSERVED	SUPPURATE	SYLLEPSIS
STREAKING	SUBSIDING	SUPREMACY	SYLLOGISE
STREAMING	SUBSIDISE	SUPREMELY	SYLLOGISM
STREAMLET	SUBSISTED	SURCHARGE	SYLPH-LIKE
STRENUOUS	SUBSTANCE	SURCINGLE	SYMBIOSIS
STRESSING	SUBTENANT	SURFACING	SYMBIOTIC
STRETCHED	SUBTENDED	SURLINESS	SYMBOLISE
STRETCHER	SUBVERTED	SURMISING	SYMBOLISM
STRIATION	SUCCEEDED	SURNAMING	SYMBOLIST
STRICTURE	SUCCENTOR	SURPASSED	SYMMETRIC
STRINGENT	SUCCESSOR	SURPRISED	SYMPHONIC
STRINGING	SUCCOTASH	SURRENDER	SYMPHYSIS

SYMPOSIUM	TELEMETER	THEREUPON	TINSELLED
SYNAGOGUE	TELEMETRY	THEREWITH	TIPSINESS
SYNCOPATE	TELEOLOGY	THERMIDOR	TIPSY-CAKE
SYNDICATE	TELEPATHY	THESAURUS	TIREDNESS
SYNODICAL	TELEPHONE	THICKENED	TITILLATE
SYNONYMIC	·TELEPHONY	THICKNESS	TITIVATED
SYNOPTIST	TELEPHOTO	THICK-KNEE	TITRATION
SYNOVITIS	TELEPRINT	THICK-SKIN	TITTERING
SYNTHESIS	TELESCOPE	THIGH-BONE	TITTLEBAT
SYNTHETIC	TELLINGLY	THINKABLE	TITULARLY
SYRINGING	TELLURIUM	THIRSTILY	TOADEATER
SYSTEMISE	TELLUROUS	THIRSTING	TOADSTONE
	TEMPERATE	THIRTIETH	TOADSTOOL
T – 9	TEMPERING	THORNBACK	TOAST-RACK
	TEMPORARY	THORNBUSH	TOLERABLE
TABLATURE	TEMPORISE	THORNLESS	TOLERABLY
TABLELAND	TEMPTRESS	THRASHING	TOLERANCE
TABLE-TALK	TENACIOUS	THREADING	TOLERATED
TABULARLY	TENACULUM	THREEFOLD	TOLL-BOOTH
TABULATED	TENANTING	THRESHING	TOMBSTONE
TACTICIAN	TENDERING	THRESHOLD	TONSORIAL
TACTILITY	TENSENESS	THRIFTILY	TOOTHACHE
TAILBOARD	TENTATIVE	THRILLING	TOOTHLESS
TAILORESS	TEPEFYING	THROBBING	TOOTHPICK
TAILORING	TEPIDNESS	THRONGING	TOOTHSOME
TAILPIECE	TEREBINTH	THROTTLED	TOPICALLY
TALBOTYPE	TERMAGANT	THROWSTER	TORMENTED
TALKATIVE	TERMINATE	THRUMMING	TORMENTIL
TALLOWING	TERRACING	THRUSTING	TORMENTOR
TALLY-CARD	TERRIFIED	THUMB-MARK	TORPEDOED
TALLYSHOP	TERRITORY	THUMB-NAIL	TORPIDITY
TALMUDIST	TERRORISE	THUMB-RACK	TORPIFIED
TAMPERING	TERRORISM	THUNDERED	TORREFIED
TANGERINE	TERRORIST	THUNDERER	TORSIONAL
TANTALIZE	TERSENESS	THWACKING	TORTURING
TAP-DANCER	TESTAMENT	THWARTING	TORTUROUS
TARANTULA	TESTATRIX	THYRISTOR	TOTTERING
TARDINESS	TESTIFIED	TICKETING	TOUCHABLE
TARNISHED	TESTIMONY	TIDEGAUGE	TOUCH-HOLE
TARPAULIN	TESTINESS	TIDE-TABLE	TOUCHWOOD
TARTAREAN	TETHERING	TIDE-WATER	TOUGHENED
TASSELLED	TETRALOGY	TIGER-LILY	TOUGHNESS
TASTELESS	TETRARCHY	TIGER-MOTH	TOWELLING
TATTERING	TEXTUALLY	TIGER-WOOD	TOWN-CLERK
TATTOOING	THANKLESS	TIGHTENED	TOWN-CRIER
TAUTENING	THATCHING	TIGHTNESS	TOWN-HOUSE
TAUTOLOGY	THEOCRACY	TIGHTROPE	TOWN-MAJOR
TAWNINESS	THEOCRASY	TIMBERMAN	TOWNSFOLK
TAXIDERMY	THEOMACHY	TIMEPIECE	TRACEABLE
TAXIMETER	THEOMANCY	TIME-SHARE	TRACKLESS
TEACHABLE	THEORISED	TIMETABLE	TRACTABLE
TEASELLED	THEOSOPHY	TIMIDNESS	TRACTABLY
TECHNICAL	THEREFORE	TIMOCRACY	TRADEMARK
TECHNIQUE	THEREFROM	TINCTURED	TRADESMAN
TEDIOUSLY	THEREINTO	TINDERBOX	TRADE-WIND
TELEGRAPH	THEREUNTO	TINKERING	TRADITION

TRADUCING	TRIVIALLY	UNABASHED	UNDAMAGED
TRAGEDIAN	TRI-WEEKLY	UNACCUSED	UNDAUNTED
TRAINABLE	TROOPSHIP	UNACTABLE	UNDECEIVE
TRAINBAND	TROUBLING	UNADAPTED	UNDECIDED
TRAIN-MILE	TROUBLOUS	UNADOPTED	UNDEFILED
TRAIPSING	TROUNCING	UNADORNED	UNDEFINED
TRAITRESS	TROUSERED	UNADVISED	UNDERDONE
TRAMPLING	TROUSSEAU	UNALLOYED	UNDERFEED
TRANSCEND	TROWELLED	UNALTERED	UNDERFOOT
TRANSFORM	TRUCKLING	UNAMENDED	UNDERGONE
TRANSFUSE	TRUCULENT	UNAMIABLE	UNDERHAND
TRANSIENT	TRUMPETER	UNAMUSING	UNDERHUNG
TRANSLATE	TRUNCATED	UNANIMITY	UNDERLAID
TRANSMUTE	TRUNDLING	UNANIMOUS	UNDERLAIN
TRANSPIRE	TRUNK-HOSE	UNASHAMED	UNDERLINE
TRANSPORT	TUGGINGLY	UNASSURED	UNDERLING
TRANSPOSE	TUMESCENT	UNBARRING	UNDERMINE
TRAPEZIUM	TUNEFULLY	UNBEKNOWN	UNDERMOST
TRAPEZOID	TUNNELLED	UNBENDING	UNDERPAID
TRATTORIA	TURBINATE	UNBINDING	UNDERPART
TRAUMATIC	TURBULENT	UNBLOCKED	UNDERPLOT
TRAVELLER	TURFINESS	UNBLUNTED	UNDERRATE
TRAVERSED	TURF-SPADE	UNBOLTING	UNDERSELL
TREACHERY	TURGIDITY	UNBOSOMED	UNDERSHOT
TREADMILL	TURNIP-FLY	UNBOUNDED	UNDERSIGN
TREASURED	TURNSTONE	UNBRACING	UNDERSOLD
TREASURER	TURNTABLE	UNBRIDLED	UNDERTAKE
TREATMENT	TURPITUDE	UNBRUISED	UNDERTONE
TREE-PIPIT	TURQUOISE	UNBUCKLED	UNDERTOOK
TRELLISED	TUTORSHIP	UNBUCKLES	UNDERVEST
TREMBLING	TWADDLING	UNCANNILY	UNDERWEAR
TREMULOUS	TWENTIETH	UNCAPPING	UNDERWENT
TRENCHANT	TWIDDLING	UNCEASING	UNDERWOOD
TRENCHING	TWINKLING	UNCERTAIN	UNDERWORK
TREPANNED	TWISTABLE	UNCHANGED	UNDESIRED
TRIATOMIC	TWITCHING	UNCHARGED	UNDILUTED
TRIBALISM	TWITTERED	UNCHARTED	UNDIVIDED
TRIBESMAN	TWO-HANDED	UNCHECKED	UNDOUBTED
TRIBUNATE	TWO-MASTED	UNCLAIMED	UNDRAINED
TRIBUTARY	TYMPANIST	UNCLEARED	UNDREAMED
TRICKLING	TYPEMETAL	UNCLIPPED	UNDRESSED
TRICKSTER	TYPICALLY	UNCLOGGED	UNDULATED
TRICUSPID	TYPIFYING	UNCLOSING	UNDUTIFUL
TRIENNIAL	TYRANNISE	UNCLOTHED	UNEARTHED
TRIGAMIST	TYRANNOUS	UNCLOUDED	UNEARTHLY
TRIHEDRAL		UNCOILING	UNEATABLE
TRIHEDRON		UNCONCERN	UNELECTED
TRILINEAR	U – 9	UNCORKING	UNENGAGED
TRILITHON	UGLIFYING	UNCOUNTED	UN-ENGLISH
TRILOBATE	ULCERATED	UNCOUTHLY	UNENVIOUS
TRILOBITE	ULTIMATUM	UNCOVERED	UNEQUABLE
TRINOMIAL	ULULATING	UNCROPPED	UNEQUALLY
TRISECTED	ULULATION	UNCROSSED	UNEXCITED
TRITENESS	UMBELLATE	UNCROWDED	UNEXERTED
TRIUMPHAL	UMBILICAL	UNCROWNED	UNEXPIRED
TRIUMPHED	UMBILICUS	UNCURLING	UNEXPOSED

UNFAILING	UNLOOSING	UNRESCUED	UNTRAINED
UNFEELING	UNLOVABLE	UNRESTFUL	UNTRIMMED
UNFEIGNED	UNLUCKILY	UNRESTING	UNTRODDEN
UNFITNESS	UNMANNING	UNREVISED	UNTUCKING
UNFITTING	UNMANURED	UNREVIVED	UNTUTORED
UNFLEDGED	UNMARRIED	UNREVOKED	UNTWINING
UNFOLDING	UNMASKING	UNRIDDLED	UNTWISTED
UNFOUNDED	UNMATCHED	UNRIGGING	UNUSUALLY
UNFROCKED	UNMERITED	UNRIPENED	UNVACATED
UNFURLING	UNMINDFUL	UNRIPPING	UNVARYING
UNGALLANT	UNMOORING	UNROLLING	UNVEILING
UNGIRDING	UNMOULDED	UNROASTED	UNVISITED
UNGRANTED	UNMOUNTED	UNROUNDED	UNWAKENED
UNGRUDGED	UNMOURNED	UNRUFFLED	UNWARLIKE
UNGUARDED	UNMUFFLED	UNRUMPLED	UNWATCHED
UNGUMMING	UNMUSICAL	UNSADDLED	UNWATERED
UNHANDILY	UNMUZZLED	UNSALABLE	UNWEARIED
UNHANDLED	UNNAMABLE	UNSAVOURY	UNWEAVING
UNHAPPILY	UNNATURAL	UNSCANNED	UNWEIGHED
UNHARMFUL	UNNERVING	UNSCATHED	UNWELCOME
UNHATCHED	UNNOTICED	UNSCOURED	UNWILLING
UNHEALTHY	UNOBVIOUS	UNSCREWED	UNWINDING
UNHEEDFUL	UNOFFERED	UNSEALING	UNWINKING
UNHEEDING	UNOPPOSED	UNSEATING	UNWITTILY
UNHELPFUL	UNORDERED	UNSELFISH	UNWOMANLY
UNHINGING	UNORDERLY	UNSETTLED	UNWORLDLY
UNHITCHED	UNPACKING	UNSEVERED	UNWORRIED
UNHOOKING	UNPAINFUL	UNSHACKLE	UNWOUNDED
UNHOPEFUL	UNPAINTED	UNSHAPELY	UNWRAPPED
UNHORSING	UNPEGGING	UNSHEATHE	UNWREATHE
UNHURTFUL	UNPENNING	UNSHIPPED	UNWRECKED
UNIFORMLY	UNPERUSED	UNSHRIVEN	UNWRITTEN
UNIMPEDED	UNPICKING	UNSIGHTLY	UNWROUGHT
UNIMPLIED	UNPIERCED	UNSINKING	UPANISHAD
UNINDUCED	UNPINNING	UNSKILFUL	UPBRAIDED
UNINJURED	UNPITYING	UNSKILLED	UPHEAVING
UNINSURED	UNPLAITED	UNSOUNDLY	UPHOLDING
UNINVITED	UNPLANTED	UNSPARING	UPHOLSTER
UNINVOKED	UNPLEADED	UNSPOILED	UPLIFTING
UNIPAROUS	UNPLEASED	UNSPOTTED	UPPER-HAND
UNISEXUAL	UNPLEDGED	UNSTAINED	UPPERMOST
UNITARIAN	UNPLUGGED	UNSTAMPED	UPRIGHTLY
UNIVALENT	UNPLUMBED	UNSTINTED	UPROOTING
UNIVERSAL	UNPOINTED	UNSTOPPED	UPSETTING
UNJOINTED	UNPOPULAR	UNSTRIPED	UPTURNING
UNKNOTTED	UNPOTABLE	UNSTUDIED	USELESSLY
UNKNOWING	UNPRAISED	UNSULLIED	USHERETTE
UNLASHING	UNPRESSED	UNTACKING	USUALNESS
UNLATCHED	UNPRINTED	UNTAINTED	UTILISING
UNLEARNED	UNQUIETLY	UNTAMABLE	UTTERANCE
UNLEASHED	UNREALITY	UNTANGLED	UTTERMOST
UNLIGHTED	UNREBUKED	UNTEMPTED	
UNLIMITED	UNREFINED	UNTENABLE	
UNLOADING	UNREFUTED	UNTHANKED	V – 9
UNLOCATED	UNRELATED	UNTIRABLE	VACCINATE
UNLOCKING	UNRENEWED	UNTOUCHED	VACILLATE

VADE-MECUM	VERSIFORM	VOLUNTARY	WATERBIRD
VAGUENESS	VERTEBRAL	VOLUNTEER	WATERBUCK
VAINGLORY	VESICULAR	VOODOOISM	WATERBUTT
VALANCING	VESTIBULE	VORACIOUS	WATERCART
VALENTINE	VESTIGIAL	VOUCHSAFE	WATERFALL
VALIANTLY	VESTRYMAN	VULCANISE	WATER-FERN
VALIDATED	VEXATIOUS	VULCANISM	WATER-FLAG
VALUATION	VIABILITY	VULCANITE	WATERFLEA
VALUELESS	VIBRATING	VULGARIAN	WATERFOWL
VAMOOSING	VIBRATION	VULGARISE	WATER-GALL
VAMPIRISM	VICARIATE	VULGARISM	WATER-HOLE
VANDALISM	VICARIOUS	VULGARITY	WATERLESS
VANISHING	VICENNIAL	VULNERARY	WATERLINE
VAPORISED	VICEREGAL	VULTURINE	WATERMARK
VAPOURING	VICIOUSLY	VULTURISH	WATERMILL
VARIATION	VICTIMISE	VULTURISM	WATER-POLO
VARIEGATE	VICTORIAN	VULTUROUS	WATER-RAIL
VARIOUSLY	VICTORINE		WATER-RATE
VARNISHED	VIDEOTAPE		WATERSHED
VASSALAGE	VIEWPOINT	**W – 9**	WATERSIDE
VEERINGLY	VIGILANCE		WATER-TANK
VEGETABLE	VIGILANTE	WAGGISHLY	WATER-VOLE
VEHEMENCE	VINACEOUS	WAGNERIAN	WATERWEED
VEHICULAR	VINDICATE	WAGONETTE	WATERWORN
VELVETEEN	VINOMETER	WAILINGLY	WATTMETER
VENEERING	VIOLATING	WAISTBAND	WAVEMETER
VENERABLE	VIOLATION	WAISTBELT	WAXWORKER
VENERABLY	VIOLENTLY	WAISTCOAT	WAYFARING
VENERATED	VIOLINIST	WAIST-DEEP	WAYWARDLY
VENGEANCE	VIRGILIAN	WAITINGLY	WAYZGOOSE
VENIALITY	VIRGINIAN	WAKEFULLY	WEAKENING
VENTILATE	VIRGINITY	WAKE-ROBIN	WEAK-KNEED
VENTRALLY	VIRTUALLY	WALL-FRUIT	WEALTHILY
VENTRICLE	VIRULENCE	WALLOPING	WEARILESS
VENTURING	VISCIDITY	WALLOWING	WEARINESS
VERACIOUS	VISCOSITY	WALLPAPER	WEARISOME
VERBALISE	VISCOUNTY	WALL-PLATE	WEATHERED
VERBASCUM	VISIONARY	WALL-SIDED	WEATHERLY
VERBOSELY	VISITABLE	WALPURGIS	WEB-FOOTED
VERBOSITY	VISUALIZE	WANDERING	WEDGEWISE
VERDANTLY	VITALISED	WAREHOUSE	WEDNESDAY
VERDIGRIS	VITIATING	WARNINGLY	WEED-GROWN
VERDUROUS	VITIATION	WARRANTED	WEEPINGLY
VERIDICAL	VITRIFIED	WARRANTEE	WEEVILLED
VERIFYING	VITRIOLIC	WARRANTOR	WEIGHABLE
VERITABLE	VIVACIOUS	WASHBOARD	WEIGHTILY
VERITABLY	VIVIDNESS	WASHERMAN	WEIGHTING
VERMICIDE	VIVIFYING	WASH-HOUSE	WEIRDNESS
VERMICULE	VIZIERATE	WASHINESS	WELCOMING
VERMIFORM	VOCALISED	WASHSTAND	WELCOMELY
VERMIFUGE	VOICELESS	WASPISHLY	WELLBEING
VERMILION	VOL-AU-VENT	WASSAILED	WELL-HOUSE
VERMINOUS	VOLLEYING	WASTELESS	WELL-TIMED
VERRUCOSE	VOLPLANED	WASTE-PIPE	WELL-WATER
VERSATILE	VOLTE-FACE	WATCHCASE	WESTERING
VERSIFIER	VOLTMETER	WATCHFIRE	WESTERNER
		WATCHWORD	

WESTWARDS
WHALEBOAT
WHALEBONE
WHATSOE'ER
WHEEDLING
WHEELBASE
WHEREFORE
WHEREINTO
WHEREUNTO
WHEREUPON
WHEREWITH
WHETSTONE
WHICHEVER
WHIFFLING
WHIMPERED
WHIMSICAL
WHININGLY
WHINNYING
WHINSTONE
WHIPGRAFT
WHIPPER-IN
WHIPSNAKE
WHIPSTOCK
WHIRLIGIG
WHIRLPOOL
WHIRLWIND
WHISKERED
WHISPERED
WHISPERER
WHISTLING
WHITEBAIT
WHITEBEAM
WHITEFISH
WHITEHEAD
WHITE-HEAT
WHITE-IRON
WHITENESS
WHITENING
WHITETAIL

WHITEWASH
WHITEWING
WHITEWOOD
WHITTLING
WHIZZBANG
WHOLENESS
WHOLESALE
WHOLESOME
WHOSOEVER
WIDEAWAKE
WIDOWHOOD
WIELDABLE
WILLINGLY
WILLOWISH
WILSONITE
WINDHOVER
WINDINESS
WINDINGLY
WINDOW-BOX
WINEGLASS
WINEPRESS
WINE-STONE
WINKINGLY
WINNINGLY
WINNOWING
WINSOMELY
WINTERING
WIREDRAWN
WIREGUAZE
WISTFULLY
WITCH-HUNT
WITHDRAWN
WITHERING
WITHSTAND
WITHSTOOD
WITLESSLY
WITNESSED
WITTICISM

WITTINESS
WITTINGLY
WOEBEGONE
WOLFISHLY
WOLFHOUND
WOLFSBANE
WOLF'S-CLAW
WOLVERINE
WOMANHOOD
WOMANKIND
WOMAN-LIKE
WOMENFOLK
WOMENKIND
WONDERING
WONDERFUL
WOOD-ASHES
WOODBLOCK
WOODCHUCK
WOODCRAFT
WOOD-HOUSE
WOODINESS
WOODLAYER
WOODLOUSE
WOOD-NYMPH
WORDINESS
WORKHOUSE
WORKMANLY
WORK-TABLE
WORKWOMAN
WORLDLING
WORLDWIDE
WORMEATEN
WORM-WHEEL
WORRIMENT
WORSENING
WORTHLESS
WOUNDLESS
WOUNDWORT

WRANGLING
WREATHING
WRENCHING
WRESTLING
WRIGGLING
WRINKLING
WRISTBAND
WRONGDOER
WRYNECKED
WYCH-HAZEL

X – 9

XANTHIPPE
XYLOPHONE

Y – 9

YACHTSMAN
YANKEEISM
YARDSTICK
YAWNINGLY
YELLOWING
YELLOWISH
YESTERDAY
YGGDRASIL
YORKSHIRE
YOUNGLING
YOUNGSTER

Z – 9

ZEALOUSLY
ZIGZAGGED
ZIRCONIUM
ZOOGRAPHY
ZOOLOGIST
ZOOPHYTIC